American Casebook Series
Hornbook Series and Basic Legal Texts
Nutshell Series

of

WEST PUBLISHING COMPANY
P.O. Box 64526
St. Paul, Minnesota 55164–0526

ACCOUNTING

Faris' Accounting and Law in a Nutshell, 377 pages, 1984 (Text)

Fiflis, Kripke and Foster's Teaching Materials on Accounting for Business Lawyers, 3rd Ed., 838 pages, 1984 (Casebook)

Siegel and Siegel's Accounting and Financial Disclosure: A Guide to Basic Concepts, 259 pages, 1983 (Text)

ADMINISTRATIVE LAW

Davis' Cases, Text and Problems on Administrative Law, 6th Ed., 683 pages, 1977 (Casebook)

Davis' Basic Text on Administrative Law, 3rd Ed., 617 pages, 1972 (Text)

Gellhorn and Boyer's Administrative Law and Process in a Nutshell, 2nd Ed., 445 pages, 1981 (Text)

Mashaw and Merrill's Cases and Materials on Administrative Law–The American Public Law System, 2nd Ed., 976 pages, 1985 (Casebook)

Robinson, Gellhorn and Bruff's The Administrative Process, 3rd Ed., approximately 950 pages, 1986 (Casebook)

ADMIRALTY

Healy and Sharpe's Cases and Materials on Admiralty, 2nd Ed., approximately 900 pages, 1986 (Casebook)

Maraist's Admiralty in a Nutshell, 390 pages, 1983 (Text)

Sohn and Gustafson's Law of the Sea in a Nutshell, 264 pages, 1984 (Text)

AGENCY—PARTNERSHIP

Fessler's Alternatives to Incorporation for Persons in Quest of Profit, 2nd Ed., approximately 300 pages, 1986 (Casebook)

AGENCY—PARTNERSHIP—Continued

Henn's Cases and Materials on Agency, Partnership and Other Unincorporated Business Enterprises, 2nd Ed., 733 pages, 1985 (Casebook)

Reuschlein and Gregory's Hornbook on the Law of Agency and Partnership, 625 pages, 1979, with 1981 pocket part (Text)

Seavey, Reuschlein and Hall's Cases on Agency and Partnership, 599 pages, 1962 (Casebook)

Selected Corporation and Partnership Statutes and Forms, 555 pages, 1985

Steffen and Kerr's Cases and Materials on Agency-Partnership, 4th Ed., 859 pages, 1980 (Casebook)

Steffen's Agency-Partnership in a Nutshell, 364 pages, 1977 (Text)

AGRICULTURAL LAW

Meyer, Pedersen, Thorson and Davidson's Agricultural Law: Cases and Materials, 931 pages, 1985 (Casebook)

ALTERNATIVE DISPUTE RESOLUTION

Kanowitz' Cases and Materials on Alternative Dispute Resolution, 1024 pages, 1986 (Casebook)

AMERICAN INDIAN LAW

Canby's American Indian Law in a Nutshell, 288 pages, 1981 (Text)

Getches and Wilkinson's Cases on Federal Indian Law, 2nd Ed., approximately 750 pages, 1986 (Casebook)

ANTITRUST LAW

Gellhorn's Antitrust Law and Economics in a Nutshell, 2nd Ed., 425 pages, 1981 (Text)

Gifford and Raskind's Cases and Materials on Antitrust, 694 pages, 1983 with 1985 Supplement (Casebook)

List current as of January, 1986

ANTITRUST LAW—Continued

Hovenkamp's Economics and Federal Antitrust Law, Student Ed., 414 pages, 1985 (Text)

Oppenheim, Weston and McCarthy's Cases and Comments on Federal Antitrust Laws, 4th Ed., 1168 pages, 1981 with 1985 Supplement (Casebook)

Posner and Easterbrook's Cases and Economic Notes on Antitrust, 2nd Ed., 1077 pages, 1981, with 1984–85 Supplement (Casebook)

Sullivan's Hornbook of the Law of Antitrust, 886 pages, 1977 (Text)

See also Regulated Industries, Trade Regulation

ART LAW

DuBoff's Art Law in a Nutshell, 335 pages, 1984 (Text)

BANKING LAW

Lovett's Banking and Financial Institutions in a Nutshell, 409 pages, 1984 (Text)

Symons and White's Teaching Materials on Banking Law, 2nd Ed., 993 pages, 1984 (Casebook)

BUSINESS PLANNING

Epstein and Scheinfeld's Teaching Materials on Business Reorganization Under the Bankruptcy Code, 216 pages, 1980 (Casebook)

Painter's Problems and Materials in Business Planning, 2nd Ed., 1008 pages, 1984 (Casebook)

Selected Securities and Business Planning Statutes, Rules and Forms, 470 pages, 1985

CIVIL PROCEDURE

Casad's Res Judicata in a Nutshell, 310 pages, 1976 (text)

Cound, Friedenthal, Miller and Sexton's Cases and Materials on Civil Procedure, 4th Ed., 1202 pages, 1985 with 1985 Supplement (Casebook)

Ehrenzweig, Louisell and Hazard's Jurisdiction in a Nutshell, 4th Ed., 232 pages, 1980 (Text)

Federal Rules of Civil-Appellate-Criminal Procedure—West Law School Edition, 852 pages, 1985

Friedenthal, Kane and Miller's Hornbook on Civil Procedure, 876 pages, 1985 (Text)

Kane's Civil Procedure in a Nutshell, 2nd Ed., 306 pages, 1986 (Text)

Karlen, Meisenholder, Stevens and Vestal's Cases on Civil Procedure, 923 pages, 1975 (Casebook)

Koffler and Reppy's Hornbook on Common Law Pleading, 663 pages, 1969 (Text)

CIVIL PROCEDURE—Continued

Marcus and Sherman's Complex Litigation–Cases and Materials on Advanced Civil Procedure, 846 pages, 1985 (Casebook)

Park's Computer-Aided Exercises on Civil Procedure, 2nd Ed., 167 pages, 1983 (Coursebook)

Siegel's Hornbook on New York Practice, 1011 pages, 1978 with 1985 Pocket Part (Text)

See also Federal Jurisdiction and Procedure

CIVIL RIGHTS

Abernathy's Cases and Materials on Civil Rights, 660 pages, 1980 (Casebook)

Cohen's Cases on the Law of Deprivation of Liberty: A Study in Social Control, 755 pages, 1980 (Casebook)

Lockhart, Kamisar and Choper's Cases on Constitutional Rights and Liberties, 5th Ed., 1298 pages plus Appendix, 1981, with 1985 Supplement (Casebook)—reprint from Lockhart, et al. Cases on Constitutional Law, 5th Ed., 1980

Vieira's Civil Rights in a Nutshell, 279 pages, 1978 (Text)

COMMERCIAL LAW

Bailey's Secured Transactions in a Nutshell, 2nd Ed., 391 pages, 1981 (Text)

Epstein and Martin's Basic Uniform Commercial Code Teaching Materials, 2nd Ed., 667 pages, 1983 (Casebook)

Henson's Hornbook on Secured Transactions Under the U.C.C., 2nd Ed., 504 pages, 1979 with 1979 P.P. (Text)

Murray's Commercial Law, Problems and Materials, 366 pages, 1975 (Coursebook)

Nordstrom and Clovis' Problems and Materials on Commercial Paper, 458 pages, 1972 (Casebook)

Nordstrom and Lattin's Problems and Materials on Sales and Secured Transactions, 809 pages, 1968 (Casebook)

Nordstrom, Murray and Clovis' Problems and Materials on Sales, 515 pages, 1982 (Casebook)

Selected Commercial Statutes, 1389 pages, 1985

Speidel, Summers and White's Teaching Materials on Commercial and Consumer Law, 3rd Ed., 1490 pages, 1981 (Casebook)

Stockton's Sales in a Nutshell, 2nd Ed., 370 pages, 1981 (Text)

Stone's Uniform Commercial Code in a Nutshell, 2nd Ed., 516 pages, 1984 (Text)

Uniform Commercial Code, Official Text with Comments, 994 pages, 1978

UCC Article 9, Reprint from 1962 Code, 128 pages, 1976

UCC Article 9, 1972 Amendments, 304 pages, 1978

COMMERCIAL LAW—Continued

Weber and Speidel's Commercial Paper in a Nutshell, 3rd Ed., 404 pages, 1982 (Text)
White and Summers' Hornbook on the Uniform Commercial Code, 2nd Ed., 1250 pages, 1980 (Text)

COMMUNITY PROPERTY

Mennell's Community Property in a Nutshell, 447 pages, 1982 (Text)
Verrall and Bird's Cases and Materials on California Community Property, 4th Ed., 549 pages, 1983 (Casebook)

COMPARATIVE LAW

Barton, Gibbs, Li and Merryman's Law in Radically Different Cultures, 960 pages, 1983 (Casebook)
Glendon, Gordon and Osakive's Comparative Legal Traditions: Text, Materials and Cases on the Civil Law, Common Law, and Socialist Law Traditions, 1091 pages, 1985 (Casebook)
Glendon, Gordon, and Osakwe's Comparative Legal Traditions in a Nutshell, 402 pages, 1982 (Text)
Langbein's Comparative Criminal Procedure: Germany, 172 pages, 1977 (Casebook)

COMPUTERS AND LAW

Mason's An Introduction to the Use of Computers in Law, 223 pages, 1984 (Text)

CONFLICT OF LAWS

Cramton, Currie and Kay's Cases-Comments-Questions on Conflict of Laws, 3rd Ed., 1026 pages, 1981 (Casebook)
Scoles and Hay's Hornbook on Conflict of Laws, Student Ed., 1085 pages, 1982 (Text)
Scoles and Weintraub's Cases and Materials on Conflict of Laws, 2nd Ed., 966 pages, 1972, with 1978 Supplement (Casebook)
Siegel's Conflicts in a Nutshell, 469 pages, 1982 (Text)

CONSTITUTIONAL LAW

Engdahl's Constitutional Power in a Nutshell: Federal and State, 411 pages, 1974 (Text)
Lockhart, Kamisar, Choper and Shiffrin's Cases-Comments-Questions on Constitutional Law, 6th Ed., approximately 1590 pages, 1986 (Casebook)
Lockhart, Kamisar and Choper's Cases-Comments-Questions on the American Constitution, 5th Ed., 1185 pages plus Appendix, 1981, with 1985 Supplement (Casebook)—abridgment of Lockhart, et al. Cases on Constitutional Law, 5th Ed., 1980

CONSTITUTIONAL LAW—Continued

Manning's The Law of Church-State Relations in a Nutshell, 305 pages, 1981 (Text)
Miller's Presidential Power in a Nutshell, 328 pages, 1977 (Text)
Nowak, Rotunda and Young's Hornbook on Constitutional Law, 3rd Ed., Student Ed., approximately 1100 pages, 1986 (Text)
Rotunda's Modern Constitutional Law: Cases and Notes, 2nd Ed., 1004 pages, 1985, with 1985 Supplement (Casebook)
Williams' Constitutional Analysis in a Nutshell, 388 pages, 1979 (Text)
See also Civil Rights

CONSUMER LAW

Epstein and Nickles' Consumer Law in a Nutshell, 2nd Ed., 418 pages, 1981 (Text)
McCall's Consumer Protection, Cases, Notes and Materials, 594 pages, 1977, with 1977 Statutory Supplement (Casebook)
Selected Commercial Statutes, 1389 pages, 1985
Spanogle and Rohner's Cases and Materials on Consumer Law, 693 pages, 1979, with 1982 Supplement (Casebook)
See also Commercial Law

CONTRACTS

Calamari & Perillo's Cases and Problems on Contracts, 1061 pages, 1978 (Casebook)
Calamari and Perillo's Hornbook on Contracts, 2nd Ed., 878 pages, 1977 (Text)
Corbin's Text on Contracts, One Volume Student Edition, 1224 pages, 1952 (Text)
Fessler and Loiseaux's Cases and Materials on Contracts, 837 pages, 1982 (Casebook)
Freedman's Cases and Materials on Contracts, 658 pages, 1973 (Casebook)
Friedman's Contract Remedies in a Nutshell, 323 pages, 1981 (Text)
Fuller and Eisenberg's Cases on Basic Contract Law, 4th Ed., 1203 pages, 1981 (Casebook)
Hamilton, Rau and Weintraub's Cases and Materials on Contracts, 830 pages, 1984 (Casebook)
Jackson and Bollinger's Cases on Contract Law in Modern Society, 2nd Ed., 1329 pages, 1980 (Casebook)
Keyes' Government Contracts in a Nutshell, 423 pages, 1979 (Text)
Reitz's Cases on Contracts as Basic Commercial Law, 763 pages, 1975 (Casebook)
Schaber and Rohwer's Contracts in a Nutshell, 2nd Ed., 425 pages, 1984 (Text)

COPYRIGHT

See Patent and Copyright Law

CORPORATIONS

Hamilton's Cases on Corporations—Including Partnerships and Limited Partnerships, 3rd Ed., approximately 1223 pages, 1986 with 1986 Statutory Supplement (Casebook)

Hamilton's Law of Corporations in a Nutshell, 379 pages, 1980 (Text)

Henn's Cases on Corporations, 1279 pages, 1974, with 1980 Supplement (Casebook)

Henn and Alexander's Hornbook on Corporations, 3rd Ed., Student Ed., 1371 pages, 1983 (Text)

Jennings and Buxbaum's Cases and Materials on Corporations, 5th Ed., 1180 pages, 1979 (Casebook)

Selected Corporation and Partnership Statutes, Regulations and Forms, 555 pages, 1985

Solomon, Stevenson and Schwartz' Materials and Problems on Corporations: Law and Policy, 1172 pages, 1982 with 1984 Supplement (Casebook)

CORPORATE FINANCE

Hamilton's Cases and Materials on Corporate Finance, 895 pages, 1984 (Casebook)

CORRECTIONS

Krantz's Cases and Materials on the Law of Corrections and Prisoners' Rights, 3rd Ed., approximately 760 pages, 1986 (Casebook)

Krantz's Law of Corrections and Prisoners' Rights in a Nutshell, 2nd Ed., 384 pages, 1983 (Text)

Popper's Post-Conviction Remedies in a Nutshell, 360 pages, 1978 (Text)

Robbins' Cases and Materials on Post Conviction Remedies, 506 pages, 1982 (Casebook)

CREDITOR'S RIGHTS

Bankruptcy Code, Rules and Forms, Law School and C.L.E. Ed., 602 pages, 1984

Epstein's Debtor-Creditor Law in a Nutshell, 3rd Ed., 383 pages, 1986 (Text)

Epstein and Landers' Debtors and Creditors: Cases and Materials, 2nd Ed., 689 pages, 1982 (Casebook)

Epstein and Sheinfeld's Teaching Materials on Business Reorganization Under the Bankruptcy Code, 216 pages, 1980 (Casebook)

LoPucki's Player's Manual for the Debtor-Creditor Game, 123 pages, 1985 (Coursebook)

Riesenfeld's Cases and Materials on Creditors' Remedies and Debtors' Protection, 3rd Ed., 810 pages, 1979 with 1979 Statutory Supplement and 1981 Case Supplement (Casebook)

CREDITOR'S RIGHTS—Continued

White's Bankruptcy and Creditor's Rights: Cases and Materials, 812 pages, 1985 (Casebook)

CRIMINAL LAW AND CRIMINAL PROCEDURE

Abrams', Federal Criminal Law and its Enforcement, approximately 978 pages, 1986 (Casebook)

Cohen and Gobert's Problems in Criminal Law, 297 pages, 1976 (Problem book)

Dix and Sharlot's Cases and Materials on Criminal Law, 2nd Ed., 771 pages, 1979 (Casebook)

Federal Rules of Civil-Appellate-Criminal Procedure—West Law School Edition, 852 pages, 1985

Grano's Problems in Criminal Procedure, 2nd Ed., 176 pages, 1981 (Problem book)

Israel and LaFave's Criminal Procedure in a Nutshell, 3rd Ed., 438 pages, 1980 (Text)

Johnson's Cases, Materials and Text on Criminal Law, 3rd Ed., 783 pages, 1985 (Casebook)

Kamisar, LaFave and Israel's Cases, Comments and Questions on Modern Criminal Procedure, 5th ed., 1635 pages plus Appendix, 1980 with 1985 Supplement (Casebook)

Kamisar, LaFave and Israel's Cases, Comments and Questions on Basic Criminal Procedure, 5th Ed., 869 pages, 1980 with 1985 Supplement (Casebook)—reprint from Kamisar, et al. Modern Criminal Procedure, 5th ed., 1980

LaFave's Modern Criminal Law: Cases, Comments and Questions, 789 pages, 1978 (Casebook)

LaFave and Israel's Hornbook on Criminal Procedure, Student Ed., 1142 pages, 1985 with 1985 P.P. (Text)

LaFave and Scott's Hornbook on Criminal Law, 2nd Ed., approximately 800 pages, 1986 (Text)

Langbein's Comparative Criminal Procedure: Germany, 172 pages, 1977 (Casebook)

Loewy's Criminal Law in a Nutshell, 302 pages, 1975 (Text)

Saltzburg's American Criminal Procedure, Cases and Commentary, 2nd Ed., 1193 pages, 1985 with 1985 Supplement (Casebook)

Uviller's The Processes of Criminal Justice: Investigation and Adjudication, 2nd Ed., 1384 pages, 1979 with 1979 Statutory Supplement and 1983 Update (Casebook)

CRIMINAL LAW AND CRIMINAL PROCEDURE—Continued

Uviller's The Processes of Criminal Justice: Adjudication, 2nd Ed., 730 pages, 1979. Soft-cover reprint from Uviller's The Processes of Criminal Justice: Investigation and Adjudication, 2nd Ed. (Casebook)

Uviller's The Processes of Criminal Justice: Investigation, 2nd Ed., 655 pages, 1979. Soft-cover reprint from Uviller's The Processes of Criminal Justice: Investigation and Adjudication, 2nd Ed. (Casebook)

Vorenberg's Cases on Criminal Law and Procedure, 2nd Ed., 1088 pages, 1981 with 1985 Supplement (Casebook)

See also Corrections, Juvenile Justice

DECEDENTS ESTATES

See Trusts and Estates

DOMESTIC RELATIONS

Clark's Cases and Problems on Domestic Relations, 3rd Ed., 1153 pages, 1980 (Casebook)

Clark's Hornbook on Domestic Relations, 754 pages, 1968 (Text)

Krause's Cases and Materials on Family Law, 2nd Ed., 1221 pages, 1983 with 1986 Supplement (Casebook)

Krause's Family Law in a Nutshell, 2nd Ed., approximately 420 pages, 1986 (Text)

Krauskopf's Cases on Property Division at Marriage Dissolution, 250 pages, 1984 (Casebook)

ECONOMICS, LAW AND

Goetz' Cases and Materials on Law and Economics, 547 pages, 1984 (Casebook)

See also Antitrust, Regulated Industries

EDUCATION LAW

Alexander and Alexander's The Law of Schools, Students and Teachers in a Nutshell, 409 pages, 1984 (Text)

Morris' The Constitution and American Education, 2nd Ed., 992 pages, 1980 (Casebook)

EMPLOYMENT DISCRIMINATION

Player's Cases and Materials on Employment Discrimination Law, 2nd Ed., 782 pages, 1984 (Casebook)

Player's Federal Law of Employment Discrimination in a Nutshell, 2nd Ed., 402 pages, 1981 (Text)

See also Women and the Law

ENERGY AND NATURAL RESOURCES LAW

Laitos' Cases and Materials on Natural Resources Law, 938 pages, 1985 (Casebook)

ENERGY AND NATURAL RESOURCES LAW—Continued

Rodgers' Cases and Materials on Energy and Natural Resources Law, 2nd Ed., 877 pages, 1983 (Casebook)

Selected Environmental Law Statutes, 786 pages, 1985

Tomain's Energy Law in a Nutshell, 338 pages, 1981 (Text)

See also Environmental Law, Oil and Gas, Water Law

ENVIRONMENTAL LAW

Bonine and McGarity's Cases and Materials on the Law of Environment and Pollution, 1076 pages, 1984 (Casebook)

Findley and Farber's Cases and Materials on Environmental Law, 2nd Ed., 813 pages, 1985 (Casebook)

Findley and Farber's Environmental Law in a Nutshell, 343 pages, 1983 (Text)

Rodgers' Hornbook on Environmental Law, 956 pages, 1977 with 1984 pocket part (Text)

Selected Environmental Law Statutes, 786 pages, 1985

See also Energy Law, Natural Resources Law, Water Law

EQUITY

See Remedies

ESTATES

See Trusts and Estates

ESTATE PLANNING

Kurtz' Cases, Materials and Problems on Family Estate Planning, 853 pages, 1983 (Casebook)

Lynn's Introduction to Estate Planning, in a Nutshell, 3rd Ed., 370 pages, 1983 (Text)

See also Taxation

EVIDENCE

Broun and Meisenholder's Problems in Evidence, 2nd Ed., 304 pages, 1981 (Problem book)

Cleary and Strong's Cases, Materials and Problems on Evidence, 3rd Ed., 1143 pages, 1981 (Casebook)

Federal Rules of Evidence for United States Courts and Magistrates, 337 pages, 1984

Graham's Federal Rules of Evidence in a Nutshell, 429 pages, 1981 (Text)

Kimball's Programmed Materials on Problems in Evidence, 380 pages, 1978 (Problem book)

Lempert and Saltzburg's A Modern Approach to Evidence: Text, Problems, Transcripts and Cases, 2nd Ed., 1296 pages, 1983 (Casebook)

Lilly's Introduction to the Law of Evidence, 486 pages, 1978 (Text)

EVIDENCE—Continued

McCormick, Elliott and Sutton's Cases and Materials on Evidence, 5th Ed., 1212 pages, 1981 (Casebook)

McCormick's Hornbook on Evidence, 3rd Ed., Student Ed., 1155 pages, 1984 (Text)

Rothstein's Evidence, State and Federal Rules in a Nutshell, 2nd Ed., 514 pages, 1981 (Text)

Saltzburg's Evidence Supplement: Rules, Statutes, Commentary, 245 pages, 1980 (Casebook Supplement)

FEDERAL JURISDICTION AND PROCEDURE

Currie's Cases and Materials on Federal Courts, 3rd Ed., 1042 pages, 1982 with 1985 Supplement (Casebook)

Currie's Federal Jurisdiction in a Nutshell, 2nd Ed., 258 pages, 1981 (Text)

Federal Rules of Civil-Appellate-Criminal Procedure—West Law School Edition, 852 pages, 1985

Forrester and Moye's Cases and Materials on Federal Jurisdiction and Procedure, 3rd Ed., 917 pages, 1977 with 1985 Supplement (Casebook)

Redish's Cases, Comments and Questions on Federal Courts, 878 pages, 1983 with 1986 Supplement (Casebook)

Vetri and Merrill's Federal Courts, Problems and Materials, 2nd Ed., 232 pages, 1984 (Problem Book)

Wright's Hornbook on Federal Courts, 4th Ed., Student Ed., 870 pages, 1983 (Text)

FUTURE INTERESTS

See Trusts and Estates

IMMIGRATION LAW

Aleinikoff and Martin's Immigration Process and Policy, 1042 pages, 1985 (Casebook)

Weissbrodt's Immigration Law and Procedure in a Nutshell, 345 pages, 1984 (Text)

INDIAN LAW

See American Indian Law

INSURANCE

Dobbyn's Insurance Law in a Nutshell, 281 pages, 1981 (Text)

Keeton's Cases on Basic Insurance Law, 2nd Ed., 1086 pages, 1977

Keeton's Basic Text on Insurance Law, 712 pages, 1971 (Text)

Keeton's Case Supplement to Keeton's Basic Text on Insurance Law, 334 pages, 1978 (Casebook)

Keeton's Programmed Problems in Insurance Law, 243 pages, 1972 (Text Supplement)

INSURANCE—Continued

York and Whelan's Cases, Materials and Problems on Insurance Law, 715 pages, 1982, with 1985 Supplement (Casebook)

INTERNATIONAL LAW

Buergenthal and Maier's Public International Law in a Nutshell, 262 pages, 1985 (Text)

Folsom, Gordon and Spanogle's International Business Transactions – a Problem-Oriented Coursebook, 1160 pages, 1986 (Casebook)

Henkin, Pugh, Schachter and Smit's Cases and Materials on International Law, 2nd Ed., 1152 pages, 1980, with Documents Supplement (Casebook)

Jackson's Legal Problems of International Economic Relations, 1097 pages, 1977, with Documents Supplement (Casebook)

Kirgis' International Organizations in Their Legal Setting, 1016 pages, 1977, with 1981 Supplement (Casebook)

Weston, Falk and D'Amato's International Law and World Order—A Problem Oriented Coursebook, 1195 pages, 1980, with Documents Supplement (Casebook)

Wilson's International Business Transactions in a Nutshell, 2nd Ed., 476 pages, 1984 (Text)

INTERVIEWING AND COUNSELING

Binder and Price's Interviewing and Counseling, 232 pages, 1977 (Text)

Shaffer's Interviewing and Counseling in a Nutshell, 353 pages, 1976 (Text)

INTRODUCTION TO LAW STUDY

Dobbyn's So You Want to go to Law School, Revised First Edition, 206 pages, 1976 (Text)

Hegland's Introduction to the Study and Practice of Law in a Nutshell, 418 pages, 1983 (Text)

Kinyon's Introduction to Law Study and Law Examinations in a Nutshell, 389 pages, 1971 (Text)

See also Legal Method and Legal System

JUDICIAL ADMINISTRATION

Nelson's Cases and Materials on Judicial Administration and the Administration of Justice, 1032 pages, 1974 (Casebook)

JURISPRUDENCE

Christie's Text and Readings on Jurisprudence—The Philosophy of Law, 1056 pages, 1973 (Casebook)

JUVENILE JUSTICE

Fox's Cases and Materials on Modern Juvenile Justice, 2nd Ed., 960 pages, 1981 (Casebook)

LAW SCHOOL PUBLICATIONS—Continued

JUVENILE JUSTICE—Continued

Fox's Juvenile Courts in a Nutshell, 3rd Ed., 291 pages, 1984 (Text)

LABOR LAW

Gorman's Basic Text on Labor Law—Unionization and Collective Bargaining, 914 pages, 1976 (Text)

Leslie's Labor Law in a Nutshell, 2nd Ed., 397 pages, 1986 (Text)

Nolan's Labor Arbitration Law and Practice in a Nutshell, 358 pages, 1979 (Text)

Oberer, Hanslowe and Andersen's Cases and Materials on Labor Law—Collective Bargaining in a Free Society, 2nd Ed., 1168 pages, 1979, with 1979 Statutory Supplement and 1982 Case Supplement (Casebook)

See also Employment Discrimination, Social Legislation

LAND FINANCE

See Real Estate Transactions

LAND USE

Callies and Freilich's Cases and Materials on Land Use, approximately 1250 pages, 1986 (Casebook)

Hagman's Cases on Public Planning and Control of Urban and Land Development, 2nd Ed., 1301 pages, 1980 (Casebook)

Hagman and Juergensmeyer's Hornbook on Urban Planning and Land Development Control Law, 2nd Ed., Student Edition, approximately 580 pages, 1986 (Text)

Wright and Gitelman's Cases and Materials on Land Use, 3rd Ed., 1300 pages, 1982 (Casebook)

Wright and Wright's Land Use in a Nutshell, 2nd Ed., 356 pages (Text)

LEGAL HISTORY

Presser and Zainaldin's Cases on Law and American History, 855 pages, 1980 (Casebook)

See also Legal Method and Legal System

LEGAL METHOD AND LEGAL SYSTEM

Aldisert's Readings, Materials and Cases in the Judicial Process, 948 pages, 1976 (Casebook)

Berch and Berch's Introduction to Legal Method and Process, 550 pages, 1985 (Casebook)

Bodenheimer, Oakley and Love's Readings and Cases on an Introduction to the Anglo-American Legal System, 161 pages, 1980 (Casebook)

Davies and Lawry's Institutions and Methods of the Law—Introductory Teaching Materials, 547 pages, 1982 (Casebook)

LEGAL METHOD AND LEGAL SYSTEM—Continued

Dvorkin, Himmelstein and Lesnick's Becoming a Lawyer: A Humanistic Perspective on Legal Education and Professionalism, 211 pages, 1981 (Text)

Fryer and Orentlicher's Cases and Materials on Legal Method and Legal System, 1043 pages, 1967 (Casebook)

Greenberg's Judicial Process and Social Change, 666 pages, 1977 (Casebook)

Kelso and Kelso's Studying Law: An Introduction, 587 pages, 1984 (Coursebook)

Kempin's Historical Introduction to Anglo-American Law in a Nutshell, 2nd Ed., 280 pages, 1973 (Text)

Kimball's Historical Introduction to the Legal System, 610 pages, 1966 (Casebook)

Murphy's Cases and Materials on Introduction to Law—Legal Process and Procedure, 772 pages, 1977 (Casebook)

Reynolds' Judicial Process in a Nutshell, 292 pages, 1980 (Text)

See also Legal Research and Writing

LEGAL PROFESSION

Aronson, Devine and Fisch's Problems, Cases and Materials on Professional Responsibility, 745 pages, 1985 (Casebook)

Aronson and Weckstein's Professional Responsibility in a Nutshell, 399 pages, 1980 (Text)

Mellinkoff's The Conscience of a Lawyer, 304 pages, 1973 (Text)

Mellinkoff's Lawyers and the System of Justice, 983 pages, 1976 (Casebook)

Pirsig and Kirwin's Cases and Materials on Professional Responsibility, 4th Ed., 603 pages, 1984 (Casebook)

Schwartz and Wydick's Problems in Legal Ethics, 285 pages, 1983 (Casebook)

Selected Statutes, Rules and Standards on the Legal Profession, 276 pages, Revised 1984

Smith's Preventing Legal Malpractice, 142 pages, 1981 (Text)

Wolfram's Hornbook on Modern Legal Ethics, Student Edition, approximately 950 pages, 1986 (Text)

LEGAL RESEARCH AND WRITING

Cohen's Legal Research in a Nutshell, 4th Ed., 450 pages, 1985 (Text)

Cohen and Berring's How to Find the Law, 8th Ed., 790 pages, 1983. Problem book by Foster and Kelly available (Casebook)

Cohen and Berring's Finding the Law, 8th Ed., Abridged Ed., 556 pages, 1984 (Casebook)

Dickerson's Materials on Legal Drafting, 425 pages, 1981 (Casebook)

Felsenfeld and Siegel's Writing Contracts in Plain English, 290 pages, 1981 (Text)

LEGAL RESEARCH AND WRITING—Continued

Gopen's Writing From a Legal Perspective, 225 pages, 1981 (Text)

Mellinkoff's Legal Writing—Sense and Nonsense, 242 pages, 1982 (Text)

Rombauer's Legal Problem Solving—Analysis, Research and Writing, 4th Ed., 424 pages, 1983 (Coursebook)

Squires and Rombauer's Legal Writing in a Nutshell, 294 pages, 1982 (Text)

Statsky's Legal Research, Writing and Analysis, 2nd Ed., 167 pages, 1982 (Coursebook)

Statsky and Wernet's Case Analysis and Fundamentals of Legal Writing, 2nd Ed., 441 pages, 1984 (Text)

Teply's Programmed Materials on Legal Research and Citation, 334 pages, 1982. Student Library Exercises available (Coursebook)

Weihofen's Legal Writing Style, 2nd Ed., 332 pages, 1980 (Text)

LEGISLATION

Davies' Legislative Law and Process in a Nutshell, 2nd Ed., approximately 300 pages, 1986 (Text)

Nutting and Dickerson's Cases and Materials on Legislation, 5th Ed., 744 pages, 1978 (Casebook)

Statsky's Legislative Analysis: How to Use Statutes and Regulations, 2nd Ed., 217 pages, 1984 (Text)

LOCAL GOVERNMENT

McCarthy's Local Government Law in a Nutshell, 2nd Ed., 404 pages, 1983 (Text)

Michelman and Sandalow's Cases-Comments-Questions on Government in Urban Areas, 1216 pages, 1970, with 1972 Supplement (Casebook)

Reynolds' Hornbook on Local Government Law, 860 pages, 1982 (Text)

Valente's Cases and Materials on Local Government Law, 2nd Ed., 980 pages, 1980 with 1982 Supplement (Casebook)

MASS COMMUNICATION LAW

Gillmor and Barron's Cases and Comment on Mass Communication Law, 4th Ed., 1076 pages, 1984 (Casebook)

Ginsburg's Regulation of Broadcasting: Law and Policy Towards Radio, Television and Cable Communications, 741 pages, 1979, with 1983 Supplement (Casebook)

Zuckman and Gayne's Mass Communications Law in a Nutshell, 2nd Ed., 473 pages, 1983 (Text)

MEDICINE, LAW AND

King's The Law of Medical Malpractice in a Nutshell, 340 pages, 1977 (Text)

MEDICINE, LAW AND—Continued

Shapiro and Spece's Problems, Cases and Materials on Bioethics and Law, 892 pages, 1981 (Casebook)

Sharpe, Fiscina and Head's Cases on Law and Medicine, 882 pages, 1978 (Casebook)

MILITARY LAW

Shanor and Terrell's Military Law in a Nutshell, 378 pages, 1980 (Text)

MORTGAGES

See Real Estate Transactions

NATURAL RESOURCES LAW

See Energy and Natural Resources Law

NEGOTIATION

Edwards and White's Problems, Readings and Materials on the Lawyer as a Negotiator, 484 pages, 1977 (Casebook)

Williams' Legal Negotiation and Settlement, 207 pages, 1983 (Coursebook)

OFFICE PRACTICE

Hegland's Trial and Practice Skills in a Nutshell, 346 pages, 1978 (Text)

Strong and Clark's Law Office Management, 424 pages, 1974 (Casebook)

See also Computers and Law, Interviewing and Counseling, Negotiation

OIL AND GAS

Hemingway's Hornbook on Oil and Gas, 2nd Ed., Student Ed., 543 pages, 1983 (Text)

Huie, Woodward and Smith's Cases and Materials on Oil and Gas, 2nd Ed., 955 pages, 1972 (Casebook)

Kuntz, Lowe, Anderson and Smith's Cases and Materials on Oil and Gas Law, approximately 805 pages, 1986 (Casebook)

Lowe's Oil and Gas Law in a Nutshell, 443 pages, 1983 (Text)

See also Energy and Natural Resources Law

PARTNERSHIP

See Agency—Partnership

PATENT AND COPYRIGHT LAW

Choate and Francis' Cases and Materials on Patent Law, 2nd Ed., 1110 pages, 1981 (Casebook)

Miller and Davis' Intellectual Property—Patents, Trademarks and Copyright in a Nutshell, 428 pages, 1983 (Text)

Nimmer's Cases on Copyright and Other Aspects of Entertainment Litigation, 3rd Ed., 1025 pages, 1985 (Casebook)

LAW SCHOOL PUBLICATIONS—Continued

POVERTY LAW

Brudno's Poverty, Inequality, and the Law: Cases-Commentary-Analysis, 934 pages, 1976 (Casebook)

LaFrance, Schroeder, Bennett and Boyd's Hornbook on Law of the Poor, 558 pages, 1973 (Text)

See also Social Legislation

PRODUCTS LIABILITY

Noel and Phillips' Cases on Products Liability, 2nd Ed., 821 pages, 1982 (Casebook)

Noel and Phillips' Products Liability in a Nutshell, 2nd Ed., 341 pages, 1981 (Text)

PROPERTY

Aigler, Smith and Tefft's Cases on Property, 2 volumes, 1339 pages, 1960 (Casebook)

Bernhardt's Real Property in a Nutshell, 2nd Ed., 448 pages, 1981 (Text)

Boyer's Survey of the Law of Property, 766 pages, 1981 (Text)

Browder, Cunningham and Smith's Cases on Basic Property Law, 4th Ed., 1431 pages, 1984 (Casebook)

Bruce, Ely and Bostick's Cases and Materials on Modern Property Law, 1004 pages, 1984 (Casebook)

Burby's Hornbook on Real Property, 3rd Ed., 490 pages, 1965 (Text)

Burke's Personal Property in a Nutshell, 322 pages, 1983 (Text)

Chused's A Modern Approach to Property: Cases-Notes-Materials, 1069 pages, 1978 with 1980 Supplement (Casebook)

Cohen's Materials for a Basic Course in Property, 526 pages, 1978 (Casebook)

Cunningham, Stoebuck and Whitman's Hornbook on the Law of Property, Student Ed., 916 pages, 1984 (Text)

Donahue, Kauper and Martin's Cases on Property, 2nd Ed., 1362 pages, 1983 (Casebook)

Hill's Landlord and Tenant Law in a Nutshell, 2nd Ed., approximately 353 pages, 1986 (Text)

Moynihan's Introduction to Real Property, 254 pages, 1962 (Text)

Uniform Land Transactions Act, Uniform Simplification of Land Transfers Act, Uniform Condominium Act, 1977 Official Text with Comments, 462 pages, 1978

See also Real Estate Transactions, Land Use

PSYCHIATRY, LAW AND

Reisner's Law and the Mental Health System, Civil and Criminal Aspects, 696 pages, 1985 (Casebooks)

REAL ESTATE TRANSACTIONS

Bruce's Real Estate Finance in a Nutshell, 2nd Ed., 262 pages, 1985 (Text)

REAL ESTATE TRANSACTIONS—Continued

Maxwell, Riesenfeld, Hetland and Warren's Cases on California Security Transactions in Land, 3rd Ed., 728 pages, 1984 (Casebook)

Nelson and Whitman's Cases on Real Estate Transfer, Finance and Development, 2nd Ed., 1114 pages, 1981, with 1986 Supplement (Casebook)

Nelson and Whitman's Hornbook on Real Estate Finance Law, 2nd Ed., Student Ed., 941 pages, 1985 (Text)

Osborne's Cases and Materials on Secured Transactions, 559 pages, 1967 (Casebook)

REGULATED INDUSTRIES

Gellhorn and Pierce's Regulated Industries in a Nutshell, 394 pages, 1982 (Text)

Morgan, Harrison and Verkuil's Cases and Materials on Economic Regulation of Business, 2nd Ed., 666 pages, 1985 (Casebook)

Pozen's Financial Institutions: Cases, Materials and Problems on Investment Management, 844 pages, 1978 (Casebook)

See also Mass Communication Law, Banking Law

REMEDIES

Dobbs' Hornbook on Remedies, 1067 pages, 1973 (Text)

Dobbs' Problems in Remedies, 137 pages, 1974 (Problem book)

Dobbyn's Injunctions in a Nutshell, 264 pages, 1974 (Text)

Friedman's Contract Remedies in a Nutshell, 323 pages, 1981 (Text)

Leavell, Love and Nelson's Cases and Materials on Equitable Remedies and Restitution, 4th Ed., approximately 900 pages, 1986 (Casebook)

McCormick's Hornbook on Damages, 811 pages, 1935 (Text)

O'Connell's Remedies in a Nutshell, 2nd Ed., 325 pages, 1985 (Text)

York, Bauman and Rendleman's Cases and Materials on Remedies, 4th Ed., 1029 pages, 1985 (Casebook)

REVIEW MATERIALS

Ballantine's Problems

Black Letter Series

Smith's Review Series

West's Review Covering Multistate Subjects

SECURITIES REGULATION

Hazen's Hornbook on The Law of Securities Regulation, Student Ed., 739 pages, 1985 (Text)

Ratner's Securities Regulation: Materials for a Basic Course, 3rd Ed., 1000 pages, 1986 (Casebook)

SECURITIES REGULATION—Continued

Ratner's Securities Regulation in a Nutshell, 2nd Ed., 322 pages, 1982 (Text)

Selected Securities and Business Planning Statutes, Rules and Forms, 470 pages, 1985

SOCIAL LEGISLATION

Hood and Hardy's Workers' Compensation and Employee Protection Laws in a Nutshell, 274 pages, 1984 (Text)

LaFrance's Welfare Law: Structure and Entitlement in a Nutshell, 455 pages, 1979 (Text)

Malone, Plant and Little's Cases on Workers' Compensation and Employment Rights, 2nd Ed., 951 pages, 1980 (Casebook)

See also Poverty Law

SPORTS LAW

Schubert, Smith and Trentadue's Sports Law, approximately 400 pages, 1986 (Text)

TAXATION

Dodge's Cases and Materials on Federal Income Taxation, 820 pages, 1985 (Casebook)

Dodge's Federal Taxation of Estates, Trusts and Gifts: Principles and Planning, 771 pages, 1981 with 1982 Supplement (Casebook)

Garbis and Struntz' Cases and Materials on Tax Procedure and Tax Fraud, 829 pages, 1982 with 1984 Supplement (Casebook)

Gelfand and Salsich's State and Local Taxation and Finance in a Nutshell, 309 pages, 1986 (Text)

Gunn's Cases and Materials on Federal Income Taxation of Individuals, 785 pages, 1981 with 1985 Supplement (Casebook)

Hellerstein and Hellerstein's Cases on State and Local Taxation, 4th Ed., 1041 pages, 1978 with 1982 Supplement (Casebook)

Kahn and Gann's Corporate Taxation and Taxation of Partnerships and Partners, 2nd Ed., 1204 pages, 1985 (Casebook)

Kragen and McNulty's Cases and Materials on Federal Income Taxation: Individuals, Corporations, Partnerships, 4th Ed., 1287 pages, 1985 (Casebook)

McNulty's Federal Estate and Gift Taxation in a Nutshell, 3rd Ed., 509 pages, 1983 (Text)

McNulty's Federal Income Taxation of Individuals in a Nutshell, 3rd Ed., 487 pages, 1983 (Text)

Posin's Hornbook on Federal Income Taxation of Individuals, Student Ed., 491 pages, 1983 with 1985 pocket part (Text)

Rose and Raskind's Advanced Federal Income Taxation: Corporate Transactions—Cases, Materials and Problems, 955 pages, 1978 (Casebook)

TAXATION—Continued

Selected Federal Taxation Statutes and Regulations, 1402 pages, 1985

Sobeloff and Weidenbruch's Federal Income Taxation of Corporations and Stockholders in a Nutshell, 362 pages, 1981 (Text)

TORTS

Christie's Cases and Materials on the Law of Torts, 1264 pages, 1983 (Casebook)

Dobbs' Torts and Compensation—Personal Accountability and Social Responsibility for Injury, 955 pages, 1985 (Casebook)

Green, Pedrick, Rahl, Thode, Hawkins, Smith and Treece's Cases and Materials on Torts, 2nd Ed., 1360 pages, 1977 (Casebook)

Green, Pedrick, Rahl, Thode, Hawkins, Smith, and Treece's Advanced Torts: Injuries to Business, Political and Family Interests, 2nd Ed., 544 pages, 1977 (Casebook)—reprint from Green, et al. Cases and Materials on Torts, 2nd Ed., 1977

Keeton, Keeton, Sargentich and Steiner's Cases and Materials on Torts, and Accident Law, 1360 pages, 1983 (Casebook)

Kionka's Torts in a Nutshell: Injuries to Persons and Property, 434 pages, 1977 (Text)

Malone's Torts in a Nutshell: Injuries to Family, Social and Trade Relations, 358 pages, 1979 (Text)

Prosser and Keeton's Hornbook on Torts, 5th Ed., Student Ed., 1286 pages, 1984 (Text)

Shapo's Cases on Tort and Compensation Law, 1244 pages, 1976 (Casebook)

See also Products Liability

TRADE REGULATION

McManis' Unfair Trade Practices in a Nutshell, 444 pages, 1982 (Text)

Oppenheim, Weston, Maggs and Schechter's Cases and Materials on Unfair Trade Practices and Consumer Protection, 4th Ed., 1038 pages, 1983 with 1986 Supplement (Casebook)

See also Antitrust, Regulated Industries

TRIAL AND APPELLATE ADVOCACY

Appellate Advocacy, Handbook of, 2nd Ed., approximately 250 pages, 1986 (Text)

Bergman's Trial Advocacy in a Nutshell, 402 pages, 1979 (Text)

Binder and Bergman's Fact Investigation: From Hypothesis to Proof, 354 pages, 1984 (Coursebook)

Goldberg's The First Trial (Where Do I Sit?, What Do I Say?) in a Nutshell, 396 pages, 1982 (Text)

Haydock, Herr and Stempel's, Fundamentals of Pre-Trial Litigation, 768 pages, 1985 (Casebook)

Hegland's Trial and Practice Skills in a Nutshell, 346 pages, 1978 (Text)

TRIAL AND APPELLATE ADVOCACY—Continued

Hornstein's Appellate Advocacy in a Nutshell, 325 pages, 1984 (Text)
Jeans' Handbook on Trial Advocacy, Student Ed., 473 pages, 1975 (Text)
McElhaney's Effective Litigation, 457 pages, 1974 (Casebook)
Nolan's Cases and Materials on Trial Practice, 518 pages, 1981 (Casebook)
Parnell and Shellhaas' Cases, Exercises and Problems for Trial Advocacy, 171 pages, 1982 (Coursebook)
Sonsteng, Haydock and Boyd's The Trialbook: A Total System for Preparation and Presentation of a Case, Student Ed., 404 pages, 1984 (Coursebook)

TRUSTS AND ESTATES

Atkinson's Hornbook on Wills, 2nd Ed., 975 pages, 1953 (Text)
Averill's Uniform Probate Code in a Nutshell, 425 pages, 1978 (Text)
Bogert's Hornbook on Trusts, 5th Ed., 726 pages, 1973 (Text)
Clark, Lusky and Murphy's Cases and Materials on Gratuitous Transfers, 3rd Ed., 970 pages, 1985 (Casebook)
Gulliver's Cases and Materials on Future Interests, 624 pages, 1959 (Casebook)
Gulliver's Introduction to the Law of Future Interests, 87 pages, 1959 (Casebook)—reprint from Gulliver's Cases and Materials on Future Interests, 1959
McGovern's Cases and Materials on Wills, Trusts and Future Interests: An Introduction to Estate Planning, 750 pages, 1983 (Casebook)
Mennell's Cases and Materials on California Decedent's Estates, 566 pages, 1973 (Casebook)
Mennell's Wills and Trusts in a Nutshell, 392 pages, 1979 (Text)
Powell's The Law of Future Interests in California, 91 pages, 1980 (Text)

TRUSTS AND ESTATES—Continued

Simes' Hornbook on Future Interests, 2nd Ed., 355 pages, 1966 (Text)
Turano and Radigan's Hornbook on New York Estate Administration, approximately 575 pages, 1986 (Text)
Uniform Probate Code, 5th Ed., Official Text With Comments, 384 pages, 1977
Waggoner's Future Interests in a Nutshell, 361 pages, 1981 (Text)
Waterbury's Materials on Trusts and Estates, approximately 1100 pages, 1986 (Casebook)

WATER LAW

Getches' Water Law in a Nutshell, 439 pages, 1984 (Text)
Sax and Abram's Cases and Materials on Legal Control of Water Resources in the United States, 941 pages, 1986 (Casebook)
Trelease and Gould's Cases and Materials on Water Law, 4th Ed., approximately 758 pages, 1986 (Casebook)
See also Energy and Natural Resources Law, Environmental Law

WILLS

See Trusts and Estates

WOMEN AND THE LAW

Kay's Text, Cases and Materials on Sex-Based Discrimination, 2nd Ed., 1045 pages, 1981, with 1986 Supplement (Casebook)
Thomas' Sex Discrimination in a Nutshell, 399 pages, 1982 (Text)
See also Employment Discrimination

WORKERS' COMPENSATION

See Social Legislation

CASES AND MATERIALS ON

WATER LAW

Fourth Edition

By

Frank J. Trelease
Professor of Law, University of the Pacific
McGeorge School of Law
Dean Emeritus, University of Wyoming
College of Law

George A. Gould
Professor of Law, University of the Pacific
McGeorge School of Law

AMERICAN CASEBOOK SERIES

WEST PUBLISHING CO.
ST. PAUL, MINN., 1986

50 West Kellogg Boulevard
P.O. Box 64526
St. Paul, Minnesota 55164–0526

Printed in the United States of America

Library of Congress Cataloging in Publication Data

Trelease, Frank J., 1913–
Cases and materials on water law.

(American casebook series)
Includes index.
1. Water-rights—United States—Cases. I. Gould, George, 1942– . II. Title. III. Series.
KF646.A7T7 1986 346.7304'691 86–4105
347.3064691

ISBN 0–314–98400–3

T. & G. Water Law 4th Ed. ACB

Preface

The senior editor of *Cases on Water Law* welcomes aboard Professor George A. Gould, former student and present colleague, long-time editor of the *Water Law Newsletter,* published by the Rocky Mountain Mineral Law Foundation. The new co-editor brings to the Fourth Edition a fresh look at many facets of the fast-moving subject of water law.

The new book retains the basic structure and teachable arrangement of Dean Trelease's earlier editions, but both the veteran natural resources teacher and the professor new to the field will find here the most modern update of the concepts of property law, public rights, state administration, environmental controls and federal powers that make this subject so challenging.

Man uses water to satisfy his needs, and water law started with the legal means for acquiring and perfecting rights to supply his demands on this vital resource. The course begins with prior appropriation, to give the student a look at the most structured form of property right to water, the basic concept that must be shaped and modified to accommodate the rights of others, to protect the environment, and to advance the public interest. In the western states, where from the beginning scarcity was seen as a limit on use, water law developed into statutory codes which were largely directed toward irrigation and must now be adapted to protection of scenic and ecological values and accommodating the growth of population and industry.

For the eastern states, riparian law is placed in its modern setting, since today squabbles between neighboring farmers and mill owners over little brooks are not the major problems of eastern water law. Municipal water supply, large scale irrigation, manufacturing and energy production are making new demands on eastern waters that were unprecedented in the formative era of riparian rights, while at the same time environmental concerns and recreational uses are exerting counter-pressures against use. This is the modern field of action, and eastern statutory regulation is emphasized. East and west, groundwater pumping has increased tremendously, and the trend toward groundwater management and conjunctive use is given full treatment.

Public rights have assumed an importance that calls for a separate chapter. Special emphasis is given the revival of the public trust concept and its expansion into the new field of environmental protection, culminating in California's *Mono Lake* decision that engrafts public trust limitations on appropriative rights. Large portions of environmental law, including NEPA's impact, are presented as limits on private uses and public projects. Pollution control is considered both in the relation of water quality to water quantity in the establishment of water rights, and in the restraints placed on private rights and state laws by the Clean Water Act's discharge permits, land use plans and dredge and fill permits.

Federal water law has seen the greatest growth since publication of the third edition. The Supreme Court has dealt with interstate commerce in water, equitable apportionment, interstate compacts, and put the final touches on *Arizona v. California.* Changes in federal substantive law affect the navigation servitude, small hydroelectric projects and the reclamation laws. Indian water rights have seen the most action. From the district courts to the Supreme Court, ongoing litigation is finally clarifying some of the troublesome uncertainties that have created strained relations between western neighbors.

The major debt the editors acknowledge is that owed to Dean Gordon Schaber and McGeorge School of Law, University of the Pacific, for the support that made this new edition possible. Peter E. Glick, a senior student at McGeorge and Assistant Editor of the Pacific Law Journal, has been a most diligent and thorough research assistant. Special thanks are due to Annemarie Pierce, who did the major part of the typing and word processing, and to Gloria Durr, who picked up the extra burden imposed on the secretarial staff.

FRANK J. TRELEASE
GEORGE A. GOULD

Sacramento, California
March 1986

Summary of Contents

Table of Contents

Table of Cases

The principal cases are in italic type. Cases cited or discussed are in roman type. References are to Pages.

CASES AND MATERIALS ON
WATER LAW
Fourth Edition

*

Chapter 1

INTRODUCTION TO WATER LAW

WATER POLICIES FOR THE FUTURE

Report of the National Water Commission, 1–6, 17 (1973).

The United States is blessed with a bountiful supply of water, although it is not always in the right place at the right time nor of the right quality. Because of the general abundance of water, national water policy has evolved over most of the past century as if water had no cost and there were no limits to its availability. But as demands come close to and in some regions even exceed supplies of water, it becomes necessary to seek ways to increase efficiency in the use of water. At the same time, there is a great and proper national concern that water be used in ways compatible with its vital role in sustaining a healthful and esthetically pleasing natural environment. * * *

A persistent tendency of water resources planning has been the issuance of single valued projections of water use into the future under a continuation of present policies, leading to astronomical estimates of future water requirements.

The amount of water that is actually used in the future will depend in large measure on public policies that are adopted. The National Water Commission is convinced that there are few water "requirements," except for relatively small amounts for drinking, cleaning, fire fighting in municipalities, and similar other essential social and environmental purposes. But there are "demands" for water and water-related services that are affected by a whole host of other factors and policy decisions, some in fields far removed from what is generally considered to be water policy. For example, the invention of the kitchen garbage disposal unit greatly increased the load on municipal sewage treatment plants, and the decision to support the price of cotton led to vast increases in irrigated acreage on the High Plains of Texas.

It is impractical, and in fact undesirable, to attempt to forecast precise levels of future water use on the basis of past water use. How much water will be used, where, and for what purposes will depend on the policies that are adopted. * * *

In formulating a national water policy, two measurements of water must be considered, quantity and quality. The latter, of course, is a relative term depending on the use which is to be made of the water.

The source of all water available to the Nation is precipitation. Precipitation for the 48 contiguous States averages about 30 inches a year, enough for most purposes, but it is neither evenly nor regularly distributed. Annual precipitation varies from over 100 inches in coastal regions of the Pacific Northwest to less than 4 inches in parts of the Southwest. In Alaska, the normal annual precipitation ranges from about 5 inches in the extreme north to more than 200 inches at places along the southern panhandle. In Hawaii and Puerto Rico also there is great variability in precipitation from place to place.

Only a portion of the precipitation flows from the watershed into streams or ground water basins. The runoff from a watershed is more variable than precipitation because consumptive use in the watershed is satisfied before runoff occurs. Runoff also varies greatly within a given year and between years. Within a normal year, the ratio of maximum flow to minimum flow may be 500 to 1. Average annual runoff varies from near zero in the Great Salt Lake desert to more than 50 inches in the Olympic Peninsula. It exceeds 10 inches in the third of the country in which the climate is considered to be humid, and it is less than 1 inch in the third of the country considered to be arid.

In general, the lowest flow deviates least from the mean and therefore is most dependable in the Northwest, the Northeast, and the Southeast. The areas of greatest flow variability are the arid regions of the Southwest and North Central parts of the contiguous United States. But even in the humid areas a series of dry years may result in serious drought conditions such as occurred in the Northeast during the period 1961 to 1966.

Quality determines the usability of water in any particular location. Over time, water quality in many of the Nation's streams and estuaries has deteriorated through the cumulative effects of two separate but often concurrent actions. The first, of great concern in most of the Western United States, is the concentration of dissolved solids in the streamflow. This concentration occurs because part of the water withdrawn for such uses as irrigation returns to the stream bearing dissolved material. When water is evaporated from reservoirs the salts remain and their concentration is increased. Finally, any diversion of flow leaves less water to dilute high salt concentrations due to natural causes, such as salt springs. * * *

The second type of water quality deterioration is caused by the generation and disposal of residuals by both producers and consumers. Marketable goods are produced and residuals, the material and energy byproducts that are not incorporated into the product, are frequently disposed of in water. Consumer use of goods results in wastes such as old automobile bodies, disposable bottles and cans, sewage, carbon monoxide, newspapers, and heat, all of which may end up in and pollute water. Many of these wastes are misplaced resources that can and should be put to use. Broadly speaking, all raw material and energy inputs to any system ultimately become residuals to be disposed of in a gaseous, liquid, or solid state, or as energy. When these residuals are disposed of in the Nation's streams they degrade water quality and may make the streamflow unsuitable for other purposes, or make treatment necessary before it can be used again. Water quality of streams in the vicinity of many of the Nation's largest metropolitan areas is diminished in this way. * * *

Water use consists of (1) intake uses, (2) onsite uses, and (3) instream or flow uses. Intake uses include water for domestic, agricultural, and industrial purposes—uses that actually remove water from its source. Onsite uses consist mainly of water consumed by swamps, wetlands, evaporation from the surface of water bodies, natural vegetation, unirrigated crops, and wildlife. Flow uses include water for estuaries, navigation, waste dilution, hydroelectric power and also some fish and wildlife and recreational uses.

Water uses are measured in two ways, by amount withdrawn and by amount consumed. Water withdrawn is water diverted from its natural course for use, and may be returned later for further use. Water consumed is water that is incorporated into a product or lost to the atmosphere through evaporation and transpiration, and cannot be reused. Water consumption is the more important indicator, since some part of withdrawn water can usually be reused, although not always near the point where the first withdrawal takes place. Under certain circumstances, therefore, large water withdrawals over a short time period may become critical, adversely affecting onsite and instream uses. * * *

Water use is responsive to many variables in policy and technology as well as to rates of growth in the population and the economy which cannot be forecast with any assurance. Thus, any projection of the future need for water based only on past trends is quite likely to be wrong. What must be done is to study a variety of alternative futures in which the factors affecting water use are explicitly considered. The alternative futures discussed in this chapter indicate the wide ranges of policy choices, tradeoffs, and flexibility in water use that are available. The Commission believes that all policy planning activities should give consideration to a wide range of possible choices so that there is assurance that the selected course of action will, regardless of any future which can reasonably develop, be a sound decision for the Nation. In the words of René Dubos, "trend is not destiny."

Notes

1. The National Water Commission was largely concerned with national policy, government expenditures, technology, economics, and institutional arrangements. Nevertheless it recognized the importance of water law to a greater extent than any other governmental study that preceded

it, and its subsidiary legal studies are some of the most important writings on modern water law.

2. Water is our most precious resource! "Thy necessity is yet greater than mine" said the dying Sir Phillip Sidney as he offered the last drops in his flask to a wounded soldier at the Battle of Zutphen in 1586. But all the water in the world is not contained in Sir Phillip's little cup.

Arizona is another place where water is precious. The retail price of treated water in Tempe, Arizona is roughly $180 per acre-foot. An acre-foot of water weighs 1,358 tons. Thus, the price of treated water is about 13 cents per ton. Farmers using untreated water pay as little as one-half cent per ton. The price of dirt in Tempe varies from $5.00 to $15.00 per ton, depending on its quality. Therefore, if water were "dirt cheap," in Tempe it would cost from forty to one thousand times as much as it currently does.[1] What, then, does "precious" mean?

TRELEASE, FEDERAL–STATE RELATIONS IN WATER LAW

National Water Commission, Legal Study No. 5, pp. 2–8 (1971).

Man uses water in many ways. For some he leaves the water in its natural setting. A boy swims in a neighbor's pond. A trout fisherman casts his fly into the riffles of a mountain stream. A vacationer tows his girl on water skis behind a power boat. The owner of a summer home merely sits and enjoys the view of a lake or brook. The tugs and barges of a navigation company ply a great river. A city discharges the wastes of its people and industries into the river.

Most of man's uses of water require that its physical occurrence be altered. A power company's dam builds up the pressure that enables it to turn turbines and generators. A farmer diverts the water from a stream to irrigate his fields and orchards. A manufacturer withdraws it from an underground source to use as a raw material or to wash and treat other materials. A city pumps large quantities through its mains for use in homes and commercial establishments. Any of these users may store water for future use, or a government agency may build a great multipurpose reservoir project to supply them all.

Man has slowly come to realize that there is not enough water anywhere on this globe to permit every user to do with it as he pleases. Not even the vast oceans can be mistreated without repercussions. Although the hydrologic cycle endlessly replenishes the fresh water of the earth there is not enough for all to use at will. Water is to this extent a scarce commodity and law is needed to allocate its use among men. Water law has arisen, as other laws arise, to order the activities of man in relation to water so as to allow and encourage desirable activities and to prevent or restrict undesirable conduct. Like other laws governing scarce things, the institutional framework of American

1. This example was provided by Professor John D. Leshy, Arizona State University College of Law.

water law is a combination of interacting property rights, economic forces and public regulation.

All of the water uses described in the opening paragraphs are desired by and have utility and value to the users. Not all will be protected by law and given the property status of a "water right." The boy's desire to swim is outweighed by the neighboring landowner's right to full possession of his land. The trout fisherman and motorboater similarly may have no private rights if the stream or lake is on private land but they may have "public rights" and be entitled to protection if the water is open to the public under the governing law. The tugboat also operates under a public right of navigation, but if the captain finds his highway blocked by a dam constructed by the sovereign government he will have no recourse. The owner of the summer home, who receives not only pleasure but also increased land value from the lake or brook, may have a protected interest in the water in some states but not in others. The city which saves money by discharging raw sewage into a stream, spoiling it for others or imposing costs of treatment on them, has no property right to continue its use.

The hydroelectric power company needs legal protection for its substantial investment in dam and power plant. In most jurisdictions it has a perpetual water right, in others a right for a term of years sufficiently long to allow it to amortize its sunk costs. The farmer provides the best illustration of the way in which the law may be varied to reflect the desirability of an activity. In a western state where irrigation reclaimed the desert and is much favored, he has a water right as permanent as the title to his land. In an eastern state where irrigation is still somewhat new and strange, he may have no right at all if his land does not border on the stream, and if it does, his use is theoretically subject to displacement by some other more reasonable use of the water. Under some modern eastern water statutes he has a right that lasts for a term of years, or one that may be cancelled "in the public interest." The manufacturer withdrawing ground water receives different protection in different states, but in one way or another he is assured of a supply. The city supplying the domestic needs of its people has the firmest of water rights, preferred over all others, though it may have to pay damages if it injures other existing rights. Its customers may not have property rights in a strict sense, but they are protected by municipal or public utility law that guarantees them service at reasonable rates. The government has seen to it that its dam has a water right, but the consumers of the water stored behind it may have almost any sort of right ranging from a temporary use until the water is needed for another purpose, through a contract right that may be subject to an infinite number of agreed-upon terms, to a property right in the works.

The allocation of property rights in water resources follows the pattern set for other resources like minerals or like land itself. Since water is a renewable resource producing a flow of benefits, what is allocated is its use, the right to take and use it over a period of time. Water uses may add substantially to the value of land, and most require a substantial investment in facilities for withdrawing and using it. The use of water is usually the basis of an enterprise which has a value as a going concern. The purpose behind much of water law is to insure that water users will receive a future water supply that will enable them to continue their uses, plan for the future and realize their expectations. While the law gives absolute and unqualified certainty to few property interests and may ascribe different degrees of security to different interests in or uses of a resource, it generally follows a strong policy of encouraging enterprise and development with a system of property rights that will give some assurance that the activity will not be subjected to premature termination without compensation.

Another essential of water law is that it should follow and implement a wise policy of resource allocation, one that will insure the use of the resource to produce the maximum benefits for man and for society as a whole. This is generally accomplished by allocating the use of water to individuals who put it to use, so that private initiative is employed to increase the general as well as individual welfare. By giving security to water rights and protection to water uses, investments in water resources development and in enterprises dependent upon water use are encouraged. By permitting the grant and transfer of water rights, the use of water can be changed to higher and more beneficial uses through the economic process of purchase by persons and entities who can pay the price because of the greater value or productivity of the water in the new use. By regulations restricting water uses to those which are reasonable and beneficial, harmful uses and other undesirable effects are minimized. By other regulations restricting water uses that interfere with public uses and are contrary to the public interests, the public good is promoted and protected.

When a water user is given a property right in water, that right is relational and takes on meaning only when the interests of the owner interact or clash with the interests of others. The function of any rule of property is to mark out boundaries, to define what the owner can do and what others may not do. The owner of a water right has a "right" to do certain things. This means that he is privileged to do those things without liability to others and that other persons have a duty not to interfere with his use. If a non-riparian farmer starts the irrigation of a field and diverts water away from the intake of a riparian water user who has the water right, the latter may sue for the violation of his right. But if an upstream riparian exercises his right by making a use of water that keeps it from reaching the ditch of a downstream non-riparian, there is no liability.

None of this is to say that all water rights are fixed, certain and secure. The legal tenure of the owner may be a perpetual right subject only to loss by condemnation, a defeasible right which will end with the happening of an event, a right which lasts for a specified period or a right which may be terminated at any time by another person or a government. Some that are legally subject to loss of water by the exercise of the rights of others are secure enough for practical purposes because the abundance of water in the particular locale gives a physical security that replaces certainty of legal tenure. On the other hand some that are legally secure and definite may be almost worthless because there is not enough water to supply them. Some defeasible water rights may be secure enough for their owners because the likelihood of their loss is known and they can make plans based on probabilities. Some water rights have uncertain boundaries and do not clearly describe the acts which may be performed under them. Some are matters of record, some have been adjudicated, some are established by historical evidence and some may be clearly determined only after litigation. Even among the firmer rights litigation occurs, just as does litigation over land titles and boundaries. On the whole, although there have been some major legal battles over water rights, there are surprisingly few lawsuits. Most water rights are known, respected and accepted. There is peace among the water users in most valleys.

TRELEASE, NEW WATER LEGISLATION: DRAFTING FOR DEVELOPMENT, EFFICIENT ALLOCATION AND ENVIRONMENTAL PROTECTION

XII Land and Water L.Rev. 385 (1977).

[W]hat if there is not enough to satisfy all rights? What physical security does the law provide, what guarantees that the holder of a right will get water? When there is a shortage of water, which water uses get it? These questions go to the heart of the law, indeed, shortages are what the law of water rights is all about. There is little need for water rights if there is plenty of water for all.

The word "shortage" needs to be defined. It is meaningless unless demand is considered as well as supply. On a variable stream there may be an annual shortage if the normal or average low flows cannot support existing uses, although much high water flows to the sea. There may be shortages induced by drought if a usually sufficient supply fails in some years. There may be a shortage although the stream is running full, if the full flow is needed for fisheries, navigation, or environmental concerns. There may be no shortage even though every drop is used if the stream is so controlled that annual and perennial flows are equated by storage and the smoothed-out supply is fully but not over allocated. Such a firm right to a firm supply puts the water user in the best of all worlds.

In all cases, however, the physically available supply limits the water that can be withdrawn and the state, if it is to avoid chaos, must limit the claims to it. Inevitably, this limit will have an element of temporal priority to it. When claims equal supply, no more can be granted. New demands for better uses must then be accommodated by some mechanism for flexibility, as discussed above. Such a limit can be easily fixed if the supply is fixed. When the source fluctuates and sometimes can fill all needs but sometimes cannot, some method of allocating or distributing the immediately available water must be devised.

There are at least five ways of doing this. One is to enforce strict temporal priority, as exemplified by American prior appropriation. Another is to apply equal sharing enforced by proportionate reduction, as among some riparian irrigators. A third is to follow a statutory list of preferences, giving priority according to a fixed ranking of the values of different uses. A fourth is to distribute the water as determined by administrative discretion based on various economic and social factors. A fifth is to put up the water for sale or auction, as practiced in some Moslem communities.

Notes

1. Many other variations can be made in the details of a water right. The method of acquisition can be *ministerio legis* if the law allows certain persons to initiate their right by their own actions, it can be acquired with ownership of land, it can be granted by the legislature or by an administrative agency. Its duration may be perpetual, contingent on continued use, for a term of years, terminable upon a contingency or terminable at will by a state agency. It may be personal to the holder, tied inseverably to land, or transferable at will. The water may be free or paid for by an initial lump sum or by a unit price.

2. Obviously water law includes much more than the rights of individuals to abstract water from its source. Nevertheless, such rights form the basis of most water use and the impact of other laws and uses upon private rights is a convenient viewpoint from which to study those other laws.

3. Some uses of water are made not as an exercise of private rights but by virtue of governmental powers. The United States, for instance, has no "water rights" for Hoover Dam on the Colorado River, but the Constitution and federal statutes authorize the Bureau of Reclamation to construct and operate it.

4. "Public rights" empower members of the public to make certain uses in place of certain waters, for example, the public has rights of navigation and fishing in navigable waters.

5. Many problems of "water law" are better framed as questions of whether certain conduct is tortious rather than whether it is the exercise of a property right.

6. Much water is abstracted or stored by organizations that act as middlemen who distribute the water to its ultimate consumers. Much institutional law relating to business organizations, cooperatives, public utilities, municipal corporations, and myriad forms of public districts may be "water law," especially insofar as it governs the rights of consumers

between themselves, against the distributor, or against the holders of other water rights.

TRELEASE, THE MODEL WATER CODE, THE WISE ADMINISTRATOR AND THE GODDAM BUREAUCRAT

14 Nat. Resources J. 207 (1974).

The Code is designed for an easterner seeking a new water law for his state. He should clearly understand this choice. To help him, I offer an analogy to another resource with which he is quite familiar, and which like water must be wisely used, protected, sometimes preserved from use, and which must be shifted from old uses to new and more desirable uses as times and needs change. *Think land.* Land is just as valuable and indispensable a resource as water. Our lives and our wealth depend upon it. The government, the ultimate source of title, wishes to see that the resource is put to its highest and best use. It could do this administratively. A "land bureaucrat" could allow its temporary use for particular regulated purposes at will or for a term of years, but when a new or better use is seen, reallocate it by moving off the present tenant and installing a new one. Instead, the government allocates the land in discrete and identifiable parcels, as private property. The land laws make these property rights very firm and secure. Land is then available for use by individuals to produce wealth. Since each person will try to make the best use of it that he can, the total of individual wealth will approach the production of maximum national wealth. Yet new and more productive uses by a different person may come to be seen desirable. Since the land is a valuable asset, if it were to be transferred to another person without compensation, the first holder would be impoverished and the later enriched. Therefore, the laws provide that the property rights are not only secure but are also voluntarily transferable. The land can be bought by the new user for the new purpose by paying the owner a price. In most cases the government is willing to let the change occur because it knows the new use is better than the old, since otherwise the buyer could not afford to pay the seller the capitalized value of the seller's use plus a profit. If private land uses and transfers are likely to have harmful effects on others, however, zoning laws, land use planning laws and other regulatory devices may be used to prevent the harm. If the government comes to need the land for a public purpose that outweighs its value for private purposes, it has power to condemn it. In this fashion, social plans for schools, roads, parks, green belts and housing projects are implemented. If such needs are known before the government has disposed of the land, it may reserve it and prevent the acquisition of private rights: no homesteads in Yellowstone Park.

How is the situation different if we say "water" instead of "land" in the above paragraph?

DUNNING, REFLECTIONS ON THE TRANSFER OF WATER RIGHTS

4 J.Contemp.L. 109 (1977).

The commodity school of thought regarding water rights transfers has become an increasingly significant one among water resources economists and lawyers in recent years. The commodity school is that which suggests in general that water should be treated as a commodity like any other and points to the advantages of enhanced transferability of the water right.

In its simplest form, the commodity approach to water resources embraces three principal points: First, the economically most productive uses of water resources are the best uses, provided adequate accounting is made for direct third party impacts. Second, the market, preferably as free a market as possible, will bring about the economically most productive uses, because the price mechanism will direct water resources to those uses most highly valued by various users. Third, certainty in the definition of property rights in water resources and a minimum of legal and institutional barriers to the transferability of those rights are necessary if this market is to be developed.

* * *

The notion that the economically most productive uses of water resources are necessarily the best ones is a difficult one to accept. Unfortunately, many discussions of the transferability of water rights simply take this point as an accepted premise without ever attempting to justify it. Yet the heart of the problem is whether economic theory alone should dictate the use of water resources or whether economic theory should be but one factor, among others, which determines how these resources are utilized. It is inadequate to say that a particular resource should be put to a higher valued use rather than to a lower valued use if value means dollar value in the marketplace, and if we know that many benefits from a given pattern of resource utilization are so diffused that they will not be represented in the public bidding.

* * *

Nonetheless, those with a pro-transfer bent use highly developed markets for other resources as an example. Professor Frank Trelease recently advised his audience to "think land." * * *

* * *

Land, like air and water, seems a fundamental resource. But if the purpose of thinking land is to move toward a free market in well-defined property rights, then the analogy is perhaps unfortunate. Zoning and planning laws increasingly have modified the security and value of land rights. Furthermore, although land rights have been viewed primarily from a commodity perspective in past centuries, examples of Aldo Leopold's "land ethic"[2] are now creeping into the land law. Dramatic evidence of changing notions of property rights in land can be seen, for example, in judicial treatment of swamp and marsh land. Another straw in the wind, and a rather startling one, came recently in an opinion written by Chief Justice Breitel for an unanimous Court of Appeals in the State of New York.[3] In a case regarding the landmark preservation provisions of the City of New York, Justice Breitel suggested that for constitutional purposes a property owner is not absolutely entitled to receive a return on so much of the property value as was created by social investment. According to Justice Breitel, the return may constitutionally be limited to that part of the property's value which was created by the efforts of the property owner, not the accumulated indirect social and direct governmental investment in the physical property, its functions, and its surroundings. In view of these developments in land law, which amount to a considerable erosion in the security and value of the traditional fee simple absolute, perhaps instead of the water lawyers thinking land, the land lawyers should think water.

Notes

1. John Dewey stated the general goal of all law as " * * * a plan for organizing otherwise independent and potentially conflicting energies into a scheme which avoids waste, a scheme allowing a maximum utilization of energy." Human Nature and Conduct (1921). Roscoe Pound expressed the same thought in much the same way: "What we are seeking to do and must do in a civilized society is to adjust relations and order conduct in a world in which the goods of existence, the scope of free activity and the objects on which to exert free activity are limited, and the demands on those goods and those objects are infinite. To order the activities of men in their endeavor to satisfy their demands so as to enable satisfaction of as much of the whole scheme of demands with the least friction and waste has * * * been what law makers and tribunals and jurists have been striving for." My Philosophy of Law (1941).

2. "A good water law should be based on a proper value system; it should have an underlying bias that elicits general support. Some water laws are focused on the resource, they seem almost to enshrine the water: it is treated as our most precious resource, it is to be protected, preserved, conserved. Other laws seem dominated by the notion that the purpose of law is to serve the public or the government: the water must produce the optimum development, the maximum economic benefit, and at the same time protect the public, the state, from undesirable activities of water users. My bias is in a third direction—toward people. People benefit from water use or nonuse. A statute may encourage people to act along desirable lines or deter them from harmful conduct, but its major function should be to provide people with the tools they need to accomplish their

2. A. Leopold, A Sand County Almanac (1949).

3. Penn Central Transportation Co. v. City of New York, 42 N.Y.2d 324, 366 N.E.2d 1271, 397 N.Y.S.2d 914 (1977).

goals and satisfy their wants. Law is man's creation; law should serve man, not things or governments. If the law is to be comprehensive it must, of course, protect the resource and promote the public good, but it is *people* who want to preserve the natural features of lakes and streams; it is *people* whose farms and factories contribute not only profit to them but prosperity to the state, and it is *people* who make up the population of cities." Trelease, A Water Management Law for Arkansas, 6 Univ.Ark.L.Rev. 369, 371–72 (1983).

3. "There are two general solutions available to an industry needing new water supplies: it can develop new sources of water or it can transfer water from an existing use. While transfers have occurred for years, the more typical response in the past was to develop new sources. * * * The cheaply developed water was taken first. The water which remains consists largely of snowmelt run-off and flood water which require the construction of expensive storage facilities if a dependable supply is to be available. * * * [Water] reallocation should begin to occur before all water is allocated; reallocation is costly privately and socially. * * *

"Thus, in developing the appropriation doctrine, western courts viewed a water right as an independent property interest which might be changed or transferred freely, subject only to the limitation that no injury to other appropriators could result from the change. This view undoubtedly resulted from the nature of an appropriation right. Unlike the riparian doctrine which treats water rights as an incident of land ownership—one of the sticks of the bundle, so to speak—the appropriation doctrine treats a water right as an independent property interest which arises as a result of, and only as a result of, the application of water to beneficial use. Since an appropriative right arises independently, it is a separate and independently transferable property interest." Gould, Conversion of Agricultural Water Rights to Industrial Use, 27B Rocky Mtn.Min.L.Inst. 1791 (1982).

4. Not all economists regard property-style water rights as the ultimate in water law. One sees water as a natural monopoly that requires large public investment in storage and transportation facilities, and advocates an institutional solution: putting water in the hands of large public utilities which sell the capacity of their facilities at fixed periodic prices. Gaffney, Economic Aspects of Water Resources Policy, 28 Am.J.Econ. and Sociology 131 (1969). Another sees the state as a monopolist, selling water at demand-generated prices determined so that the quantity and quality demanded at that price just equal the available supply. Johnson, An Optimal State Water Law: Fixed Water Rights and Flexible Market Prices, 57 Va.L.Rev. 345 (1971).

WATER RIGHTS IN THE UNITED STATES

Types of Water Rights. Rights to abstract and use the water of streams in the United States are based on two quite different doctrines, the law of riparian rights and the law of prior appropriation. Each type of right is a property interest created by or obtained under state law, but they have very different characteristics. Most states recognize only one or the other, although in several states both kinds of rights can exist.

Riparian rights are governed by the common law. The modern form of riparian law gives each owner of land bordering on the stream a right to make a reasonable use of the water and imposes liability on the upper riparian owner who unreasonably interferes with that use. The right exists whether or not the water is actually used, and a use may be initiated at any time. The use must usually be made on the riparian land and within the watershed of the stream. A non-riparian who uses water is liable to any riparian he injures and conversely a riparian who initiates a use which interferes with a prior non-riparian use is subject to no liability. Some states do not give effect to attempts of riparian proprietors to grant their water rights to non-riparians.

Appropriative rights are governed primarily by statute. An appropriation may be described as a state administrative grant that allows the use of a specific quantity of water for a specific beneficial purpose if water is available in the source free from the claims of others with earlier appropriations. The right is initiated by an application for a permit. The place of use is not restricted to riparian land or even to the watershed. The right may be sold and its use or place of use changed, and it may cease to exist if it is not used.

Riparian law, developed in the green countrysides of England and Eastern America, seems to be based on the unspoken premise that if rights to the use of water are restricted to those persons who have access to it through the ownership of the banks and if those persons will restrict their demands on the water to reasonable uses, there will be enough for all. Appropriation law, developed in the arid West, is usually thought of as a system for water-short areas. Where there is not enough for everyone, the rule of priority insures that those who obtain rights will not have their water taken by others who start later. The theory is that as demands arise water rights to supply them will be given out until the water is exhausted, after which those with new demands must purchase rights. Because western streams fluctuate greatly, appropriation law places much emphasis on distribution of scarce water to the persons entitled to it. This is an ongoing process, while riparian law is more sporadic. While in some western states riparian law has been used to distribute shares of scarce water among riparian irrigators, regardless of when they initiated their uses, much of the thrust of riparian law is to adjust uses so that all riparians can be accommodated. The late professor Jacob Beuscher of Wisconsin once said that eastern riparian law is not so much a system of water allocation as a fire fighting device used to settle the few disputes that arose between users of the generally abundant supplies.

The territorial extent of these doctrines is not easy to map. Nine states have Simon-pure appropriation law, the "Colorado Doctrine" which has existed from their beginnings. These are Alaska, Arizona, Colorado, Idaho, Montana, Nevada, New Mexico, Utah, and Wyoming.

Ten have the "California Doctrine" which recognizes both riparian rights and appropriations, but all of these are substantially "appropriation states" in that that law is the most important today. Only in California and to a limited extent in Nebraska are there possibilities of initiating new uses by exercising riparian rights. In the others, Kansas, Mississippi, North Dakota, Oklahoma, Oregon, South Dakota, Texas and Washington, riparian rights are the historical basis of some uses but all new uses are appropriative.

It would be misleading to say that the water law of the other thirty-one states is common law riparianism. Eleven control the initiation of substantially all new uses by administrative permits—Delaware, Florida, Georgia, Iowa, Kentucky, Maryland, Minnesota, New Jersey, North Carolina, South Carolina and Wisconsin (agriculture and mining). Some of these statutes regulate only riparian uses, but several permit nonriparian uses as well. The remaining mainland states may have the doctrine of riparian rights as their common law, but it has been heavily overlaid with statutes which control dams on navigable streams, hydro-electric dams or all dams, statutes which authorize nonriparian use of water stored in dams, statutes which authorize and control the abstraction of water by cities, districts and state agencies, and quite recently, with statutes controlling private uses for the protection of minimum flows and environmental values. In most "riparian states" these statutes rather than the common law are the important features of modern water law.

Louisiana belongs in this class although her riparian rights stem from the Civil Code rather than the common law. Hawaii has a unique blend of ancient customary rights, prescriptive rights, and a limited application of riparian rights.

The law of underground water forms a somewhat different pattern. Ground water, usable water under the surface of the earth, is found in aquifers, porous earth formations such as gravel, sandstone or fractured limestone, which hold a substantial amount of water and permit it to move through the formation. Aquifers are usually fed by seepage from the surface, and often discharge water into springs and streams. Some narrowly confined aquifers have been treated as "underground streams" and the law of surface streams is applied to them. Most ground water in aquifers, however, is so physically different from water in streams that historically it was treated differently. The first rules were of ownership: the land owner was regarded as owning the water underneath his land and was permitted to take whatever quantity he could capture. A number of state courts then imposed requirements that the owner's use of ground water must be reasonable and connected with use of the overlying land. Some have applied a rule of correlative rights similar to riparian doctrines of reasonable sharing. Many have superimposed substantial statutory regulation on the exercise of these common law doctrines. A number of western states now have statutes adapting rules of prior appropriation to ground water.

The ownership rule is in force in Connecticut, Maine, Massachusetts, Mississippi, Rhode Island, Texas and Vermont; the reasonable use rule in Alabama, Arizona, Illinois, Indiana, Iowa, Kentucky, Maryland, Michigan, Missouri, New Hampshire, New York, North Carolina, Ohio, Pennsylvania, Tennessee, Virginia, West Virginia, and Wisconsin, although in some of these states the decisions are not clear or the classification is based on dicta. Louisiana has a similar rule of capture based on the Civil Code. Correlative rights are the rule in Arkansas, California, Nebraska and New Jersey. Common law rules seem completely superseded by permit systems in Delaware, Florida, Georgia, Hawaii, Minnesota, and South Carolina, and permits are required for many uses or in some parts of the state in Nebraska, New Jersey, New York, North Carolina, Virginia and Wisconsin. Fourteen states apply the law of prior appropriation; in Alaska, Kansas, Montana, North Dakota and Utah the same law applicable to surface streams, in Colorado, Idaho, Nevada, New Mexico, Oklahoma, Oregon, South Dakota, Washington and Wyoming, a separate groundwater code. In addition groundwater districts which exercise many controls on withdrawals exist in California, Colorado, Florida, Nebraska, New Mexico and Texas.

WATER MEASUREMENT

In determining the rate of flow of a stream or ditch, the unit of measurement in common use today is the cubic foot per second, commonly abbreviated to "second foot", "c.f.s.", or "cu. ft. p. s. t." (per second of time). This unit is made the official standard of measurement by statute in most of the western states. To determine the flow in cubic feet per second the area of the cross-section of the ditch or stream in square feet is multiplied by the velocity of the water in feet per second. The average velocity of the full stream must be computed, since near the sides and bottom and at the surface the water will be slowed by friction and will flow at a lesser rate than at the center of the stream. A wide variety of weirs, flumes, meters and registers are used to measure the flow of water.

The "miner's inch" or "inch of water" is a unit that formerly was widely used for the measurement of small flows, although it has been to a large extent superseded today. It is the quantity of water that will be discharged through a one-inch square orifice under a certain pressure. As usually measured, a box or dam containing the orifice is set in the stream or main ditch so that the water stands at a certain height above the orifice and the water is discharged through it into the ditch, or from the main ditch into a lateral. The vertical dimension of the orifice remains constant at one inch, and as the horizontal dimension is increased the number of miner's inches of water is increased, so that if it measures one inch by ten inches, it will deliver ten miner's inches of water. The head of water above the orifice varied from 4 to 6 inches, according to the custom of the locality, and since the greater the head, the higher the pressure and the greater the discharge, the flow described by "one miner's inch" can be translated into cubic feet per second only if the exact conditions of the measurement are known. In an effort to standardize it, many states have adopted legislative definitions. As measured in Colorado, a second foot is equal to 38.4 miner's inches, but in Arizona, California, Montana, Nevada and Oregon it takes 40 inches, and in Idaho, Nebraska, New Mexico, North Dakota, South Dakota and Utah 50 inches to make a cubic foot per second.

When the total volume of water is to be measured, the common unit is the "acre foot", the amount of water that will cover one acre to a depth of one foot. This is 43,560 cubic feet, or 325,851 gallons (1 cubic foot = 7.48 gallons). It can be readily seen that if gallons were always the measure for stored water, the capacity of some of our larger reservoirs would run into astronomical figures. A typical surburban family of five consumes approximately one acre-foot of water per year. The relation of flow to quantity is that one second foot running for 24 hours will deliver 1.98 acre feet. The flow of streams is usually expressed in "acre feet per year" and the total quantity delivered on land is given as "acre feet per acre".

Occasionally other measurements of water are used. In referring to pumped water, especially from underground sources, "gallons per minute" is the customary measure of flow. 448.8 g.p.m. equal one cubic foot per second. Municipal uses are often calculated in millions of gallons per day. One million gallons is 3.07 acre feet, and one m.g.d. is approximately 1.55 cubic feet per second.

Chapter 2

PRIOR APPROPRIATION

SECTION 1. ORIGIN

IRWIN v. PHILLIPS

Supreme Court of California, 1855.
5 Cal. 140.

HEYDENFELDT, J., delivered the opinion of the Court. MURRAY, C.J., concurred.

The several assignments of error will not be separately considered, because the whole merits of the case depend really on a single question, and upon that question the case must be decided. The proposition to be settled is whether the owner of a canal in the mineral region of this State, constructed for the purpose of supplying water to miners, has the right to divert the water of a stream from its natural channel, as against the claims of those who, subsequent to the diversion, take up lands along the banks of the stream, for the purpose of mining. It must be premised that it is admitted on all sides that the mining claims in controversy, and the lands through which the stream runs and through which the canal passes, are a part of the public domain, to which there is no claim of private proprietorship; and that the miners have the right to dig for gold on the public lands was settled by this Court in the case of Hicks et al. v. Bell et al., 3 Cal. 219.

It is insisted by the appellants that in this case the common law doctrine must be invoked, which prescribes that a water course must be allowed to flow in its natural channel. But upon an examination of the authorities which support that doctrine, it will be found to rest upon the fact of the individual rights of landed proprietors upon the stream, the principle being both at the civil and common law that the owner of lands on the banks of a water course owns to the middle of the stream, and has the right in virtue of his proprietorship to the use of the water in its pure and natural condition. In this case the lands are the property either of the State or of the United States, and it is not necessary to decide to which they belong for the purposes of this case.

It is certain that at the common law the diversion of water courses could only be complained of by riparian owners, who were deprived of the use, or those claiming directly under them. Can the appellants assert their present claim as tenants at will? To solve this question it must be kept in mind that their tenancy is of their own creation, their tenements of their own selection, and subsequent, in point of time, to the diversion of the stream. They had the right to mine where they pleased throughout an extensive region, and they selected the bank of a stream from which the water had been already turned, for the purpose of supplying the mines at another point.

Courts are bound to take notice of the political and social condition of the country which they judicially rule. In this State the larger part of the territory consists of mineral lands, nearly the whole of which are the property of the public. No right or intent of disposition of these lands has been shown either by the United States or the State governments, and with the exception of certain State regulations, very limited in their character, a system has been permitted to grow up by the voluntary action and assent of the population, whose free and unrestrained occupation of the mineral region has been tacitly assented to by the one government, and heartily encouraged by the expressed legislative policy of the other. If there are, as must be admitted, many things connected with this system, which are crude and undigested, and subject to fluctuation and dispute, there are still some which a universal sense of necessity and propriety have so firmly fixed as that they have come to be looked upon as having the force and effect of *res judicata.* Among these the most important are the rights of miners to be protected in the possession of their selected localities, and the rights of those who, by prior appropriation, have taken the waters from their natural beds, and by costly artificial works have conducted them for miles over mountains and ravines, to supply the necessities of gold diggers, and without which the most important interests of the mineral region would remain without development. So fully recognized have become these rights, that without any specific legislation conferring or confirming them, they are alluded to and spoken of in various acts of the Legislature in the same manner as if they were rights which had been vested by the most distinct expression of the will of the law makers; as for instance, in the Revenue Act "canals and water races" are declared to be property subject to taxation, and this when there was none other in the State than such as were devoted to the use of mining. Section 2 of Article IX. of the same Act, providing for the assessment of the property of companies and associations, among others mentions "dam or dams, canal or canals, or other works for mining purposes." This simply goes to prove what is the purpose of the argument, that however much the policy of the State, as indicated by her legislation, has conferred the privilege to work the mines, it has equally conferred the right to divert the streams from their natural channels, and as these two rights stand upon an equal footing, when they conflict, they must be decided by the fact of priority, upon the maxim of equity, *qui prior est in tempore, potior est in jure.* The miner who selects a piece of ground to work, must take it as he finds it, subject to prior rights, which have an equal equity, on account of an equal recognition from the sovereign power.

If it is upon a stream, the waters of which have not been taken from their bed, they cannot be taken to his prejudice; but if they have been already diverted, and for as high and legitimate a purpose as the one he seeks to accomplish, he has no right to complain, no right to interfere with the prior occupation of his neighbor, and must abide the disadvantages of his own selection.

It follows from this opinion that the judgment of the Court below was substantially correct, upon the merits of the case presented by the evidence, and it is therefore affirmed.

Notes

1. "While the squatters were busy establishing claim clubs in the Mississippi Valley and Great Plains region, another group of hardy Americans was busy pioneering the rugged Sierra Nevada Mountains of California. Like the pioneers of the midwest, these people were also trespassers upon the public lands. They were venturing into an almost unknown wilderness, a land that the United States had scarcely obtained title to, and over which it had not as yet established any real governmental authority. The Mexican jurisdiction over the territory had been brought to an end and the state government had not yet been established. * * *

"In January of 1848, two Americans, John A. Sutter and James T. Marshall, while building a sawmill on the American River in the mountain regions of California discovered gold in the mill race. * * * Within a period of two or three years the population of California increased from two or three thousand people to two or three hundred thousand people.

* * *

"A vast and intricate field of mining law was to develop from these few simple rules as adopted in the early California mining districts. For a quarter of a century and more, mining law was the most significant field of law in the West. But the mining districts are of current significance not only because of the law of mining but also because of the law of water which owes its origin to them. A good many of the mines in California were placer mines. Water is essential to the operation of a placer mine. But a great many of these placer mines were situated a considerable distance from the stream and frequently entirely beyond the drainage of the stream. Just as there were not enough mines for all the people, there was not enough water for all the mines. Now the Anglo-American doctrine of riparian water rights was established on the premise that water belonged to the owner of the land adjacent to the stream and that while each land owner had a right to use the water still he was obligated to return it to the stream undiminished in quality and quantity for his neighboring riparian owner immediately below him on the stream. Such a law was of course worked out to meet the economic needs of a group of eastern factory owners and mill operators. It was a law made in a damp moist country, and simply did not fit the needs of the western miners. Hence, they were again thrown upon their own resources to work out a system wherein the greatest amount of good could be obtained from the limited amount of water.

"The miners met this problem just as they met the problem of adjusting the right to use a limited number of mines among a multitude of people. They applied the doctrine of prior appropriation to the water just as they did to the mining claims, and they limited the amount of water each person could use to the amount that he originally appropriated from the stream to operate his mine. The size of the ditch was used to determine the quantity of water originally taken. They also decreed that a failure to use the water for a given time worked an abandonment of the right to take the water just as a failure to work the mine worked an abandonment of the mine.

"It was soon discovered by those who went to farm that the water law as worked out by the miners was much more appropriate to their needs in such an arid country than the riparian rights which their ancestors had worked out in the humid East. Hence, the law of water, as originally worked out in the mining districts of California, was soon to become the water law of the entire arid west." McGowen, The Development of Political Institutions on the Public Domain, 11 Wyo.L.J. 1, 8–14 (1956).

2. Eddy v. Simpson, 3 Cal. 249 (1853), dealt obliquely with prior appropriation and is sometimes cited as the first case stating the doctrine.

3. A Spanish or Mexican origin for prior appropriation was suggested in Hagerman Irrigation Co. v. McMurry, 16 N.M. 172, 113 P. 823 (1911), and Maricopa County Municipal Water Conservation District v. Southwest Cotton Co., 39 Ariz. 65, 4 P.2d 369 (1931). These courts traced the doctrine back to the power of the sovereign, under civil law, to dispose of public waters by grant. But in Lux v. Haggin, 69 Cal. 255, 10 P. 674 (1886), the court held that the Spanish and Mexican law applicable to territory ceded from Mexico was superseded by statutes adopting the common law. A confusing note was added by Motl v. Boyd, 116 Texas 86, 286 S.W. 458 (1926), in which a dictum equated the Mexican law with riparian rights. However, some excellent scholarly research led the Texas courts to repudiate this dictum in State v. Valmont Plantations, 346 S.W.2d 853 (Tex.Civ. App.1961), affirmed 163 Tex. 381, 355 S.W.2d 502 (1962). After an exhaustive study of historical and legal materials, it was concluded that a Spanish or Mexican grant of land riparian to the Rio Grande did not carry with it an appurtenant irrigation right, and that the Spanish and Mexican irrigation system was not a system of riparian law, but required a specific grant of the water.

4. Sir William Blackstone, apparently misinterpreting early cases basing the particular litigated water rights on prescription from ancient custom, stated: "If a stream be unoccupied, I may erect a mill thereon, and detain the water; yet not so as to injure my neighbor's prior mill, or his meadow: for he hath by the first occupancy acquired a property in the current." 2 Bl.Comm. *403 (1765). From this, it has been argued that prior appropriation was the common law of England, before the importation of "French" riparian principles in the early nineteenth century. Wiel, Waters: American Law and French Authority, 33 Harvard L.Rev. 133 (1919). A quite conclusive argument exposing the fallacies of Blackstone and Wiel and showing the riparian nature of the early English law of water

courses is found in Maass and Zobel, Anglo-American Water Law: Who Appropriated the Riparian Doctrine? 10 Public Policy 109 (1960).

5. The Massachusetts mill acts, dating back to colonial times, gave the riparian owner of a mill dam a superior right over others who might later erect dams that interfered with the first by unreasonably withholding the water above it or backing up water upon it from below. See Smith v. Agawam Canal Co., 84 Mass. (2 Allen) 355 (1861).

6. Trelease, New Water Legislation: Drafting for Development, Efficient Allocation and Environmental Protection, XII Land and Water L.Rev. 385 (1977):

"I think one of those notions is that when a person has taken, used, become accustomed to, and made a livelihood from water, it becomes 'his water,' and that one who takes it from him has 'stolen his water.' I used to think that prior appropriation was an American invention, but now I am convinced it was simply the verbal identification of a very widespread human trait.

"Teclaff, in his survey of 57 countries, tells us that seniority in use is the most common of all bases for distributing water among users.[1] In its most explicit form, prior appropriation exists not only in 19 American states, but also in the four western provinces of Canada, in Taiwan (China), Iran, Rhodesia, Zambia and the Philippines. There are strong elements of it in several South American countries. The 1963 British Water Resources Act creates a 'protected right' indistinguishable from an appropriation, though enforced in an unusual roundabout manner.

"Protection based on temporal priority is to some degree implicit in many other laws. Before state controls came into being, customary water rights, held from time immemorial or for prescriptive periods, were everywhere protected. When state authority to use water was instituted, the notion that a state should not make successive grants of the same water to different people appeared in most such laws. Permits, licenses or concessions, whatever they may be called, are not to be issued to the detriment of existing uses in most of the Spanish American countries, in several of the eastern United States, in Tanzania, and in Italy. Practically every new water code has given some sort of group preference to uses in existence when the code was adopted.

"Some evidence indicates a subliminal recognition of priority even where the law is specifically to the contrary. * * * Even under modern statutes that subject the allocation and distribution of water to administrative discretion, the administrators in Great Britain, Kenya and Mexico have eased their burden by issuing permits that authorize the withdrawal of water only when there is a surplus over the needs of existing users."

7. As the preceding materials indicate, most legal authorities conclude that the American form of the appropriation doctrine originated in the mining camps of California. However, irrigation, not mining, has been and continues to be the principal use of water in the west. As a result, the

1. Abstraction and Use of Water: A Comparison of Legal Regimes—U.N./ST/ECA/154 (1972).

needs and problems of irrigated agriculture have been a major influence in the development of the appropriation doctrine. To a significant degree, the appropriation doctrine is irrigation law.

The influence of irrigation is illustrated by the title *Irrigation Institutions* which Elwood Mead gave to his 1903 book on western water law. Similarly, Wells A. Hutchins, writing in 1942, began his discussion of the appropriation doctrine with the following sentence: "It is undeniable that in the arid portions of the Western States irrigation is essential to agriculture." Hutchins, Selected Problems In The Law Of Water Rights In The West 64 (1942).

The foregoing is intended to provide the student with a perspective in understanding the law of prior appropriation. It is not meant to suggest that the appropriation doctrine is an anachronism, suited only to the needs of an agricultural society. The doctrine has demonstrated a capacity to meet the needs of a dynamic society in the past, and there is every reason to expect it will continue to do so in the future.

8. Despite the application of the appropriation doctrine in Irwin v. Phillips, in a series of subsequent cases, the most famous of which is Lux v. Haggin, 69 Cal. 255, 10 P. 674 (1866), the California Supreme Court held that a patent to riparian land carried with it riparian rights. Thus, California came to recognize both appropriative and riparian rights in a system which came to be known as the "California doctrine." At one time at least nine other states—those on the west coast and the great plains—applied the California doctrine, but all except California and perhaps Nebraska now apply the appropriation doctrine exclusively.

The California doctrine integrates appropriative and riparian rights essentially as follows. Riparian rights associated with a particular tract of riparian lands are subordinate to all appropriative rights [rights for the use of water on non-riparian lands] which were created before the particular tract of riparian lands was patented. These riparian rights are superior to all appropriative rights created after the riparian lands were patented, regardless of the time at which the riparian rights are actually exercised. Lux v. Haggin and the California doctrine are explored more fully in chapter 3, section 6.

9. Private water rights are almost exclusively a matter of state law, not federal law. An extensive legal and scholarly debate has raged over the theoretical basis for state jurisdiction over water rights in the west. This debate primarily results from the original ownership of western lands by the federal government and from the reasoning that, because of this, the federal government also must have "owned" all waters in the west. Such reasoning was responsible for the California doctrine discussed in the preceding note. However, the debate has had little practical significance where jurisdiction over private water rights is concerned. Whatever it might have done, the federal government has left the creation, definition, and control of private water rights to the states. The debate has only had practical significance when the federal government has asserted rights on its own behalf or in connection with a federal program, project, or activity. Consequently, the debate is left to chapter 8, section 1, in which federal powers and federal-state conflicts are developed in depth.

SECTION 2. ATTRIBUTES

STATE OF IDAHO, DEPARTMENT OF PARKS v. IDAHO DEPARTMENT OF WATER ADMINISTRATION

Supreme Court of Idaho, 1974.
96 Idaho 440, 530 P.2d 924.

SHEPARD, CHIEF JUSTICE.

This is an appeal and a cross-appeal from a judgment of the district court in an action wherein the Idaho Department of Parks, pursuant to statute, sought to appropriate in trust for the people of Idaho certain unappropriated waters of the Malad Canyon. * * *

In 1971 the Idaho Legislature enacted I.C. § 67–4307. In essence the statute directs the Department of Parks of the State of Idaho to appropriate in trust for the people of Idaho certain unappropriated natural waters of the Malad Canyon in Gooding County, Idaho. Additionally, it declares (1) that the preservation of the waters for scenic beauty and recreation uses is a beneficial use of water; (2) that the public use of those waters is of greater priority than any other use save domestic consumption, and (3) that the unappropriated state land located between the highwater marks on either bank of these waters is to be used and preserved in its present condition as a recreational site for the people of Idaho.

Pursuant to the statute the Idaho Department of Parks filed an application for a permit to appropriate the water specified by the statute. The waters in question arise in part at least from springs in the canyon and are natural waters. There appears no argument but that there is unappropriated water available for appropriation.

That application was protested by the Idaho Water Users Association, Twin Falls Canal Company, and the North Side Canal Company under the provisions of I.C. § 42–203. Those parties are cross-appellants herein and are hereafter designated "Water Users." * * *

We now reach the issue as to whether there must be an actual physical diversion of the water in order to support an appropriation. This issue was raised upon appeal by both the Department of Water Administration and the Water Users, both of whom assert error in the trial court's determination that such physical diversion was not necessary.

The precise language of article 15, section 3, does not bear on this question but merely declares "[t]he right to divert and appropriate the unappropriated waters of any natural stream to beneficial use, shall never be denied * * *." Certain language in the late case of Glenn Dale Ranches, Inc. v. Shaub, 94 Idaho 585, 494 P.2d 1029 (1972) and the earlier cases of Sandpoint Water and Light Company v. Panhandle Development Company, 11 Idaho 405, 83 P. 347 (1905), and Hutchinson

v. Watson Slough Ditch Co., 16 Idaho 484, 101 P. 1059 (1909) can be read as suggesting that our constitution requires an actual physical diversion of water in order to claim an appropriative right. However, a close reading of those cases indicates that the actual holdings of the cases insofar as they relate to the necessity of an actual physical diversion are based on statutory requirements.

We hold that our Constitution does not require actual physical diversion. We deem it clear that until the time of the enactment of the statute in question herein Idaho's statutory scheme regulating the appropriation of water has contemplated an actual physical diversion. See I.C. §§ 42–101, 42–201, 42–202. See however Comment, The Prerequisite of a Man-Made Diversion in the Appropriation of Water Rights—State ex rel. Reynolds v. Miranda, 83 N.M. 443, 493 P.2d 409 (1972); 13 Natural Resources J. 170 (1973).

We note that the Colorado constitution is similar to Idaho's article 15, section 3, and provides:

> "Diverting unappropriated water * * *—The right to divert the unappropriated waters of any natural stream to beneficial uses shall never be denied * * *" Article XVI, sec. 6, Constitution of Colorado.

In Genoa v. Westfall, 141 Colo. 533, 349 P.2d 370 (1960) the Colorado court held that an actual physical diversion was not necessary to a water appropriation so long as the appropriator intends to apply the waters to a beneficial use and actually applies them to that use. The rationale of *Genoa* became suspect after the decision of the Colorado court in Lamont v. Riverside Irrigation District, 498 P.2d 1150 (Colo. 1972), but the matter appears to have been now laid at rest following the 1973 Colorado legislation wherein its statutory law of appropriation was amended so as to permit appropriation without actual diversion. 2 Colorado Session Laws, 1973, ch. 442. Further it does not appear that Colorado courts have relied upon their constitution to establish an actual physical diversion requirement.

An examination of the statutory law of Idaho however reveals a different problem. As a general proposition one must set forth the location and description of a proposed physical diversion of water in an application for a permit to appropriate water. I.C. § 42–202. The Idaho legislature in 1971 made compliance with the statutory permit procedure mandatory. Idaho Session Laws, Ch. 177 (1971); See I.C. § 42–103, 42–201.

In the statute before us, I.C. § 67–4307, the Idaho legislature has clearly stated a policy at odds with its previous general statutory scheme of water appropriation. I.C. § 67–4307 directs parks "to appropriate [not 'divert and appropriate'] the unappropriated natural spring flow" of the Malad Canyon and declares the "preservation of water in the area described for its scenic beauty and recreational purposes" is a beneficial use. Furthermore, the statute states that "license shall issue at any time upon proof of beneficial use to which said waters are now dedicated." We deem it clear that the legislature intended no physical diversion of water be required in the appropriation of the subject waters.

It is axiomatic that where a general statute and a specific statute deal with the same subject matter and are in conflict, the provisions of the specific statute must control. State v. Roderick, 85 Idaho 80, 375 P.2d 1005 (1962); State ex rel. Taylor v. Taylor, 58 Idaho 656, 78 P.2d 125 (1938). It is also clear that where two statutes conflict the latest expression of the legislative will must prevail. Employment Security Agency v. Joint Class "A" School District No. 151, 88 Idaho 384, 400 P.2d 377 (1965).

We deem it to be the intent of the Idaho Legislature to dispense with any physical diversion requirement in the case of the appropriation directed in I.C. § 67–4307. Any other construction would nullify the obvious purpose of I.C. § 67–4307. Courts should if possible in construing a statute give it an interpretation which does not in effect nullify the statute. DeRousse v. Higginson, 95 Idaho 173, 505 P.2d 321 (1973).

The judgment of the district court is affirmed and the case is remanded to the Department of Water Administration for further proceedings consistent with the views contained herein. Costs to respondent.

DONALDSON, J., concurs.

BAKES, JUSTICE (concurring specially):

* * *

The common law doctrine of water rights was based upon the riparian system which limited the use of water to the stream, or to lands adjacent to the stream bed and required the water to be returned to the stream's natural drainage, thus preventing any use which effectively diminished or removed the water from the stream channel on a permanent basis. While the riparian system of water use had some support in the early history of the west, it was soon apparent that the most productive use of water in these arid areas could not be accomplished by limiting the use of water to lands adjoining the stream and in the stream's drainage, and requiring return of the water to the stream from which it was taken at a point on the riparian land upon which it was used, and thus a different system of water rights was necessary. * * *

As I view Article 15, § 3, of the Constitution, which guarantees "[t]he right to divert and appropriate the unappropriated waters of any natural stream to beneficial use * * *" the use of the word "divert" in that section by the Constitutional Convention in 1890 was a constitutional recognition of the supremacy of the prior appropriation doctrine with its concomitant right to remove waters from the stream bed and not return them, over the riparian system which would in effect require water to remain in the stream. In my view the use of the word "divert" was not used with the intention by the framers of the Constitution that no appropriate water right could be obtained without a diversion, but was inserted to guarantee the right of an appropriator to remove the water from the stream and consume it in a beneficial use and not return it. In summary, the word "divert" in Article 15, § 3, was used to mandate the supremacy of the prior appropriation doctrine over the riparian system and not to constitutionally limit the manner in which a prior appropriator could obtain his water right.

Where an appropriative water right does not require a diversion to make it effective and beneficial, in the absence of a statute requiring a diversion there appears to be no practical reason why a diversion should be required. * * *

DONALDSON, J., concurs.

MCQUADE, JUSTICE (dissenting).

I join in the dissent of Justice McFadden, but feel compelled to address myself to an issue which was not passed upon in his dissent. I do not agree with the majority's position that there may be created a valid appropriative water right in the absence of an actual physical diversion of the water from its natural locus or condition.

A diversion is generally required in order to perfect water rights by appropriation. Hutchins in his treatise on water rights in the western states quotes with approval the following language from a California case,

> "To constitute a valid appropriation of water, three elements must always exist: (1) An intent to apply it to some existing or contemplated beneficial use; (2) an *actual diversion from the natural channel by some mode sufficient for the purpose;* and (3) an application of the water within a reasonable time to some beneficial use. * * *" [Emphasis added]

This, Hutchins concludes, expresses the consensus of the western judiciary, not only when the opinion was written but currently. * * *

Article 15, sec. 3 of the Idaho Constitution reads in pertinent part, "The right to divert *and* appropriate the unappropriated waters of any natural stream to beneficial uses, shall never be denied, except that the state may regulate and limit the use thereof for power purposes." [Emphasis added]

It is significant that the conjunctive was used when the Constitution was written, i.e., divert *and* appropriate rather than the disjunctive, i.e., divert *or* appropriate. In the absence of any contrary evidence, we should presume that the framers of the Idaho Constitution chose the conjunctive deliberately and that they intended it be accorded its ordinary meaning. * * *

MCFADDEN, JUSTICE (dissenting).

In water law, the verb "appropriate" means to acquire a right to use "public water." * * * An appropriation may be made for "private" beneficial use or for "public" beneficial use. * * * However, if the state in its sovereign capacity already has the right to use "public water" for a certain beneficial use, it obviously cannot "acquire" that right—in other words, the state cannot "appropriate" water in such a case, because it cannot "acquire" a right that it already has. * * * In my view, the in-stream use of a natural stream for recreational purposes and for scenic beauty is a public beneficial use which inheres in the state's sovereign ownership of such water. Therefore, since the state already has the right to so use the water, it cannot acquire the right to "appropriate" the water for these purposes. * * *

To allow the state to in effect reserve water from appropriation in furtherance of non-proprietary, non-power purposes—when the framers of the Constitution contemplated that private beneficial users could appropriate water being held by the state in its sovereign capacity—amounts to nothing less than a denial of the constitutional right to appropriate the "unappropriated waters" of any natural stream. * * *

In conclusion, although I believe that recreation and scenic beauty can and should be taken into consideration on a case by case basis, they cannot be used as an excuse to deny all future appropriation of water for other purposes, at least until the Constitution is amended.

Notes

1. Many courts have stated definitions of an appropriation, usually in terms of the physical acts involved in a typical appropriation. A composite of these might be that an appropriation requires an intent to appropriate, notice of the appropriation, compliance with state laws, a diversion of the water from a natural stream, and its application, with reasonable diligence and within a reasonable time, to a beneficial use. Many of these elements will be dealt with in detail later in this book.

2. What constitutes a diversion? A dam alone, which caused overflow of a meadow without the aid of ditches, was held sufficient in Thomas v. Guiraud, 6 Colo. 530 (1883). In Wyoming, when erosion washed out the outlet of a small prairie lake, a local chapter of the Isaak Walton League obtained a permit to erect a small dam that served only to maintain the natural level of the water.

3. Whether an actual diversion is essential to an appropriation was of some importance in the early days of the West when pioneers took advantage of natural conditions. Utah and Nevada held that reaping the benefits of natural overflow and percolation irrigation was not an appropriation of the water, Hardy v. Beaver County Irrigation Co., 65 Utah 28, 234 P. 524 (1924), Walsh v. Wallace, 26 Nev. 299, 67 P. 914 (1902), but Oregon held that a water right was so acquired, In re Silvies River, 115 Or. 27, 237 P. 322 (1925). The Oregon court suggested that as time passed the necessities of economy might require the appropriator to install a controlled system of diversion. Colorado codified this rule in its "meadow right" statute, see Broad Run Investment Co. v. Deuel & Snyder Improvement Co., 47 Colo. 573, 108 P. 755 (1910).

Where horses, cattle, and sheep do their own diverting, stockmen who regularly and repeatedly pastured the animals on land on which a spring arises or through which a stream flows were said to have appropriated enough water to supply the herds. Steptoe Livestock Co. v. Gulley, 53 Nev. 163, 295 P. 772 (1931). In Utah the animals may drink but the owner obtains no protectable right. Adams v. Portage Irrigation Reservoir & Power Co., 95 Utah 1, 72 P.2d 648 (1937).

In recent years there has been a flurry of cases on the point. Stockwater appropriations have been upheld in Hunter v. U.S., 398 F.2d 148 (9th Cir.1967); Stevenson v. Steele, 93 Idaho 4, 453 P.2d 819 (1969); and England v. Ally Ong Hing, 105 Ariz. 65, 459 P.2d 498 (1969). On the other hand, lack of diversion prevented an appropriation of water seeping from a reservoir, although benefits from subirrigation resulted, Lamont v. Riverside Irrigation District, 179 Colo. 134, 498 P.2d 1150 (1972), and grazing stock on and cutting hay from the bottom of a wash was held insufficient to create an appropriation in State ex rel. Reynolds v. Miranda, 83 N.M. 443, 493 P.2d 409 (1972).

4. Stockwatering and natural irrigation involve offstream uses, and water actually leaves the stream bed. In the State of Washington an administrative agency allowed an appropriation for instream use, as reported in Rocky Mountain Mineral Law Newsletter (Water Law issue) Vol. V, No. 8 (1972):

"On June 6, 1972, the Pollution Control Hearings Board of Washington reversed a refusal by the Department of Ecology to permit Dr. Donald E. Bevan to appropriate water of non-navigable Cherry Creek, where it crosses Dr. Bevan's property, for the purposes of scientific research in raising fish. The Department had taken the position that an appropriation of water in Washington requires either a diversion or some impedance to the flow. Dr. Bevan, who is an internationally known member of the faculty of the College of Fisheries at the University of Washington, had presented uncontradicted testimony that any diversion or impedance of the flow would tend to defeat the purposes of his research, which involved introducing valuable fish not native to Cherry Creek for spawning purposes. In addition, damming or diversion would disturb the natural ecology. In the Matter of Donald E. Bevan v. State of Washington, Department of Ecology, PCHB No. 48.

"The substance of the Board's decision is epitomized by the following addendum to the Board's Findings of Fact, Conclusions and order:

" 'This case may be sui generis by reason of the unusual nature of the use for which the water is required. We decide only the issue squarely presented to us; i.e., an appropriation of water for a beneficial use cannot be denied because no diversion or impedance is required.

" 'Nor do we regard this application as in any sense the establishment of a minimum flow by private action from June 1 to October 31 of each year. The State is entitled to take such action as it may desire in establishing a minimum flow. Dr. Bevan's use being nonconsumptive; the only limitation that we see on the Department of Ecology is to restrict any diversion from upstream sources that would reduce the amount available to Dr. Bevan during the designated period below 5.0 cubic feet per second.' "

5. The instream appropriation involved in the principal case is one of a variety of approaches which states have utilized to protect "instream values." A more complete discussion of the protection of instream values and methods to achieve this purpose is found at page 54.

6. Colorado River Water Conservation District v. Colorado Water Conservation Bd., 197 Colo. 469, 594 P.2d 570 (1979) is in accord with the principal case on both constitutional and statutory grounds. The Board applied for appropriations in three segments of the Crystal River, pursuant to Colo.Rev.Stat.1973 §§ 37–92–102 and 103, which authorized it to acquire minimum flows on natural streams and lakes "as may be required to preserve the natural environment to a reasonable degree."

Two California Courts of Appeal ruled that without a diversion of the stream no appropriation of instream flows could be made for fishery purposes by the State Director of Fish and Game or a nonprofit sportsmen's organization. Fullerton v. State Water Resources Control Bd., 90 Cal.App. 3d 590, 153 Cal.Rptr. 518 (1979); California Trout, Ltd. v. State Water Resources Control Bd., 90 Cal.App.3d 816, 153 Cal.Rptr. 672 (1979). The California Supreme Court denied review in both cases.

7. The requirement of intent has little vitality today, since water rights in most states are initiated by filing an application for a permit accompanied by substantial engineering work. Perhaps clear proof that the application was filed only with intent to establish a paper claim could lead to its denial. Cf. the early case of Power v. Switzer, 21 Mont. 523, 55 P. 32 (1898), where the turning of Uncle George's Creek out of its banks for no apparent purpose was held not to constitute an appropriation. In Colorado, which has no permit law, the requirement of intent is still important. See City and County of Denver v. Colorado River Water Conservation District, 696 P.2d 730 (Colo.1985).

8. The application for a permit also supplies the requirement of notice in most states. Again, it still has importance in Colorado. Notice need not take the form of filing a claim; any overt act sufficient to constitute notice to interested persons of the proposed demand upon the water supply is sufficient. This usually takes the form of a survey of the land. However, in City of Aspen v. Colorado River Water Conservation District, 696 P.2d 758 (Colo.1985) the court held that acts "on the land" were not required, reversing its earlier position on this point.

EMPIRE WATER & POWER CO. v. CASCADE TOWN CO.

Circuit Court of Appeals of the United States, Eighth Circuit, 1913.
205 F. 123.

This is an appeal from a decree in favor of the Cascade Town Company perpetually enjoining the Empire Water & Power Company and its officers from interfering with the normal flow of the waters of a stream in Cascade Canyon, near Colorado Springs, Colo. The facts appear from the statement of the trial court, as follows:

"Complainant, the Cascade Town Company, owns several hundred acres of land up Ute Pass, about 11 miles from Colorado Springs.

Fountain creek flows through Ute Pass in an easterly direction, and as it passes the lands of the complainant company its waters are augmented by those of Cascade creek, short in length of flow, but precipitous, which come down from the watershed of the northerly slope of Pike's Peak to the westerly. The said complainant company and its predecessors in title have owned these lands for many years, and began improving them as a summer resort more than 20 years ago, and have maintained them as such ever since, and have not sought to utilize them otherwise. For that purpose they have constructed hotels there and built cottages, roads, and trails on its land extending up through Cascade Canon, through which the stream of the same name flows, and on beyond into the mountains, laid out, dedicated to the public, and improved a small park in said canon, made a lake and fountain, built a pavilion or auditorium for conventions, and otherwise improved its grounds, thereby adding to the attractions of the place as left by nature. The complainant company and its predecessors are not, and were not, municipal corporations, but business ventures created for the purpose of maintaining their property as a resort for tourists during the summer season. The place is known as Cascade. * * * It has a permanent population of 50 or 60 people. Among other attractions held out in its advertisements are Cascade Canon and the falls of Cascade creek through the canon. The canon and falls are rare in beauty and constitute the chief attraction. Without them the place would not be much unlike any other part of Ute Pass. The canon is about three-quarters of a mile long and very deep; its floor and sides are covered with an exceptionally luxuriant growth of trees, shrubbery, and flowers. This exceptional vegetation is produced by the flow of Cascade creek through the canon and the mist and spray from its falls. * * *

"The defendant was incorporated for the purpose, among other things, of generating electricity by water power, and to dispose of the same as a commodity; and to execute that purpose it sent its agents on to the watershed of Pike's Peak, above the head of Cascade Canon, and located a reservoir site and did some acts, at small expense, looking to the execution of that purpose, whereby it intended and expected to impound the waters in such reservoir and later conduct it in pipes down the mountain to and beyond the property of the complainant company. And thereupon these complainants filed their several bills asking that the defendant be enjoined from so doing, as a threatened injury to their vested rights.

"It is found as a fact that if the defendant does impound the waters of Cascade creek above the falls and conduct it therefrom in pipes, as aforesaid, the falls in the canon and the vegetation on its floor and sides will be largely, if not wholly, destroyed, and the canon hence become a dry gulch, and that all the waters flowing in said stream are needed by complainant company, and are necessary for the aforesaid purposes to which they have been applied by said complainant."

HOOK, CIRCUIT JUDGE. * * * The waters of natural streams in Colorado are subject to state regulation, and may be appropriated to beneficial uses for domestic, agricultural, and manufacturing purposes. * * * The defendants, who were enjoined, contemplated a use for manufacturing. In this branch of the case the controversy was over the character of complainant's use, its relation to that proposed by defendants, and the extent of complainant's appropriation and application of the water. It is urged that a use for a summer resort is not a beneficial use for either domestic or agricultural purposes. Counsel say that the views and standards of the early settlers were reflected in the state Constitution, and that it should be construed accordingly; that they did not plan for rest and recreation, and that to them "domestic" had to do with sustenance for man and beast, and cleanliness; and that "agricultural" related to the raising of crops. We think such a view is too narrow. If the commerce clause of the federal Constitution had been construed in that way, much of the growth of this country would have been arrested. In framing Constitutions wisdom frequently requires the use of general terms, which should be held as progressively adaptable to natural development and as open to embrace new instances as they arise and come clearly within the spirit of the provisions. Thus, in Lamborn v. Bell, 18 Colo. 346, 32 P. 989, 20 L.R.A. 241, the term "milling purposes" in the provision of the state Constitution authorizing the appropriation of private property was held broadly to include manufacturing purposes and specifically that of an electric power plant, though the milling of ore and grain was doubtless uppermost in mind when the Constitution was adopted. Places such as that described here, favored by climatic conditions, improved by the work of man, and designed to promote health by affording rest and relaxation are assuredly beneficial. They are relatively as important as sanitariums or hospitals, and should not be dismissed by calling them mere resorts for idleness. They are a recognized feature of the times, are important in their influence upon health, and multitudes of people avail themselves of them from necessity. Cascade is well described as a place of this kind. With its railroad station, hotels, cottages, waterworks, park, roads, and trails and its 12,000 or 15,000 annual visitors, it is a summer city. That it is not an incorporated municipality, but is largely a private venture, is, we think, unimportant. Nor need the purpose to which the waters of the stream are devoted be a single one of those named in the classification in the Constitution. It need not be exclusively domestic nor exclusively agricultural. It may be and is both, like that of the ordinary city with its homes, business places, parks, and public grounds.

It is clear that complainant intended to appropriate the waters of the stream to its purpose. The intent was openly manifested by the extensive improvement of its property by buildings, roads, etc., in reliance, not only on the use of the water in the ditches that were constructed, but also on the continued natural falls and flow of the stream. At this point, however, we experience the most difficulty with complainant's case. The laws of Colorado are designed to prevent waste of a most valuable but limited natural resource, and to confine the use to needs. By rejecting the common-law rule they deny the right of the landowner to have the stream run in its natural way without diminution. He cannot hold to all the water for the scant vegetation which lines the banks but must make the most efficient use by applying it to his land. See Schodde v. Water Co., 224 U.S. 107, 32 S.Ct. 470, 56 L.Ed. 686, a case from Idaho, where a landowner claimed the whole current of a stream to raise part of the water to his land. The case before us is exceptional, but we think complainant is not entitled to a continuance of the falls solely for their scenic beauty. The state laws proceed upon more material lines. Complainant also relies upon the distribution by the falls of moisture for the trees and other vegetable growth on its lands, which it has extensively improved. As we have said, its intent to appropriate the waters has been shown by its expenditures and improvements beyond what is served by its ditches. Has there been that actual application which the law requires? Undoubtedly a landowner may rely upon an efficient application by nature, and need do no more than affirmatively to avail himself of it (Thomas v. Guiraud, 6 Colo. 530; Larimer, etc., Co. v. People, 8 Colo. 614, 9 P. 794); but the use in that way should not be unnecessarily or wastefully excessive. If all the water flowing over the falls, directly applied to the lands in the usual way of irrigation, would be required to produce the effect of the distributed mist and spray as now utilized, we think defendants would have no right to divert it for a manufacturing purpose. If nature accomplishes a result which is recognized and utilized, a change of process by man would seem unnecessary. But the trial court based its decision of this branch of the case largely upon the artistic value of the falls, and made no inquiry into the effectiveness of the use of the water in the way adopted as compared with the customary methods of irrigation. In all other respects the conclusions of the court were in accord with the views we have expressed. It may be that if the attention of the lawmakers had been directed to such natural objects of great beauty they would have sought to preserve them, but we think the dominant idea was utility, liberally and not narrowly regarded, and we are constrained to follow it. * * *

The decree of the trial court is reversed and remanded for further proceedings in conformity with this opinion.

Notes

1. "Beneficial use shall be the basis, measure and limit to the use of water." Ariz.Rev.Stat. § 45–131. Virtually identical pronouncements are made in the statutes of a number of other states. See Nev.Rev.Stat. 533.035 (1984), N.Mex. Const.Art. 16, § 3; N.Mex.Stat.Ann.1978, § 72–1–2; No.Dak.Cent.Code 61–04–01.2; So.Dak. Codified Laws 46–1–8; Wyo.Stat. 1977 § 41–3–101.

2. "Up to this point this paper has dealt with whether a particular type of use, as such, has received court or legislative approval as a 'reasonable use' or 'beneficial use,' and has attempted to point out the

limits of the legal definition of such use. This may seem a sterile approach to an economist, to consider each use in the abstract and to tag it as reasonable or unreasonable, beneficial or not beneficial, yet by and large that has been the method of the courts and legislatures until quite recently. This seemingly one sided approach has resulted in this list of uses characterized as reasonable or beneficial in general, and seemingly the courts have merely approved of a particular use that has come in question if it falls within one of these categories. But actually there are few absolutes on this list. * * * "

"But as competition for the supply grew fiercer, and as the realization grew upon the courts and legislatures that the allocation of water involved a problem in the conservation of natural resources, new concepts evolved, that each use must not only be beneficial in the abstract sense, but must also be a reasonable and economic use in the light of other demands for the little water remaining to be allocated." Trelease, The Concept of Reasonable Beneficial Use in the Law of Surface Streams, 12 Wyo.L.J. 1, 14–15 (1957).

" 'Beneficial use' is the use of that amount of water that is reasonable and appropriate under reasonably efficient practices to accomplish without waste the purpose for which the appropriation is lawfully made. * * * " Colo.Rev.Stat.1973 § 37–92–103(4).

"The right to water or to the use or flow of water in or from any natural stream or water course in this State is and shall be limited to such water as shall be reasonably required for the beneficial use to be served and such right does not and shall not extend to the waste or unreasonable method of use or unreasonable method of diversion of water. * * * " West's Ann.Calif. Const. Art. 10, § 2.

"It has become elementary doctrine in the arid region that no one is entitled to a greater quantity of water for any particular use or purpose than is reasonably necessary to supply the needs of the claimant for the specified purpose. This is true, regardless of the quantity that has been used for such purposes and the length of time it may have been used. * * * " Big Cottonwood Tanner Ditch Co. v. Shurtliff, 49 Utah 569, 164 P. 856 (Utah 1916).

3. State of Colorado, Huston, et al. v. Southwestern Colorado Water Conservation District et al., 671 P.2d 1294 (Colo.1983), involved a large number of claims related to energy development in Colorado:

"The class VII claimants, asserting rights to withdraw both tributary and nontributary ground water, challenge the ruling of the special water judge concerning their applications that neither dust control nor land reclamation is a beneficial use. The judge based his conclusion on the fact that no Colorado cases have involved an appropriation of water for these purposes and that, therefore, such beneficial uses have never been approved. We disagree with the judge's conclusion that dust control and land reclamation are not beneficial uses as a matter of law and reverse this aspect of the trial court's decision.

"With respect to the applicant's claims for tributary water, the cases and statutes implementing the constitutional right to appropriate such water supply the framework for determining which uses are 'beneficial.' The Colorado Constitution specifically recognizes three types of beneficial uses that will support an appropriation of tributary water: domestic, agricultural and manufacturing. Colo. Const. Art. XVI, § 6. However, our cases have held that appropriations of tributary water are not limited to those examples given in the constitution. In City and County of Denver v. Sheriff, 105 Colo. 193, 96 P.2d 836 (1939), we stated:

> 'The term "beneficial use" is not defined in the Constitution. What is beneficial use, after all, is a question of fact and depends upon the circumstances in each case.'

105 Colo. at 204, 96 P.2d at 842. Thus, we have recognized municipal use, which includes a variety of uses incident to governmental activities, as a beneficial use. City of Westminster v. Church, 167 Colo. 1, 445 P.2d 52 (1968). Consistent with this flexible approach taken in the case law, section 37–92–103(4) of the 1969 Act provides the following expansive definition of beneficial use for implementation of the constitutional right to appropriate waters of the state:

" 'Beneficial use' is the use of that amount of water that is reasonable and appropriate under reasonably efficient practices to accomplish without waste the purpose for which the appropriation is lawfully made and, without limiting the generality of the foregoing, includes the impoundment of water for recreational purposes, including fishery or wildlife. For the benefit and enjoyment of present and future generations, 'beneficial use' shall also include the appropriation by the state of Colorado in the manner prescribed by law of such minimum flows between specific points or levels for and on natural streams and lakes as are required to preserve the natural environment to a reasonable degree.

"In addition, the general assembly has recognized the beneficial nature of both land reclamation and dust control in other statutory enactments. Those engaged in mining are required by various statutes to reclaim land adversely affected by such activity. * * * Similarly, the prevention of air pollution by dust (or 'particulate matter') has been provided for in the Colorado Air Quality Control Act, * * * Moreover, section 34–29–107, C.R.S.1973 requires a coal mine owner to utilize 'water, water with a wetting agent added to it, or some other effective method' to allay excessive coal dust, as a safety measure. * * * In light of the flexible approach taken in the case law toward application of the 'beneficial use' concept, and given the legislative expressions of concern for reclamation of mined land and abatement of dust pollution, we believe that land reclamation and dust control are beneficial uses."

4. Like Colorado, a number of other states have enacted statutory definitions of "beneficial use" in recent years. Consider whether the following definitions are helpful in determining if a particular use is beneficial:

" 'Beneficial use', unless otherwise provided, means: (a) a use of water for the benefit of the appropriator, other persons, or the public, including, but not limited to agricultural (including stock water), domestic, fish and wildlife, industrial, irrigation, mining, municipal, power, and recreational uses; * * *" Rev.Code Mont.1983 § 85–2–102(2).

" 'Beneficial use' means a use of water for a purpose consistent with the best interests of the people of the state." No.Dak.Cent.Code 61–04–01.1 1.

" 'Beneficial use,' any use of water within or outside the state, that is reasonable and useful and beneficial to the appropriator, and at the same time is consistent with the interests of the public of this state in the best utilization of water supplies; " So.Dak. Codified Laws 46–1–6(6).

"Uses of water for domestic, stock watering, industrial, commercial, agricultural, irrigation, hydroelectric power production, mining, fish and wildlife maintenance and enhancement, recreational, and thermal power production purposes, and preservation of environmental and aesthetic values, and all other uses compatible with the enjoyment of the public waters of the state, are declared to be beneficial." West's Rev.Code Wash.Ann. 90.54.020(1).

5. The enhancement of recreational opportunities by appropriating water for the purpose offers some possibilities but is subject to many limitations. While appropriations are private rights, they may further social purposes if owned by the developer of a resort, as in the instant case, and they may be owned by a public entity such as a governmental park department and thus be made available to the public. It is obvious, however, that many values ascribed to water, especially some held by the public, cannot be preserved by appropriating the water. While in *Cascade* the owner was able to protect the water directly used for its grounds and lakes, the court's insistence on an efficient application meant that it could not preserve in its natural state the waterfall that was a major attraction of the resort.

In 1973 Colorado broadened its statutory definition of the term "beneficial use" to include appropriations by the state of such minimum flows between specific points on natural streams and lakes "as are required to preserve the natural environment to a reasonable degree." Colo.Rev.Stat. 1973, § 37–92–103(4). The law is implemented by granting the Colorado Conservation Board the power to appropriate the minimum flow. The Board must request recommendations from the Division of Wildlife and the Division of Parks and Outdoor Recreation. The state has no preferential right, but may appropriate the water only in the same manner as a nongovernmental water user. Under this law, could the Board preserve a similar waterfall?

Could a sportsmen's organization appropriate a minimum flow to preserve fish habitat under the Colorado statutes? Should it be permitted to do so? Consider the following views:

"[I]nstream uses differ from water rights applied to the more traditional beneficial uses in that the public is the real beneficiary of the dedication. * * * Because the benefits of instream uses inevitably redound to the public generally rather than the claimant, only public rather than private bodies should be permitted to claim water for instream uses." Tarlock, The Recognition of Instream Flow Rights: "New" Public Western Water Rights, 25 Rocky Mountain Mineral Law Institute 24–1, 24–3 (1979). A contrary view, arguing for the "privitization" of instream rights, was expressed in Huffman, Instream Water Use, Public and Private Alternatives, ch. 8,

Water Rights: Scarce Resource Allocation, Bureaucracy, and the Environment (Anderson ed. 1983).

West's Ann.Cal.Water Code § 1243 states, "The use of water for recreation and preservation and enhancement of fish and wildlife resources is a beneficial use of water." Does this authorize the instream appropriation of water? See note 6, supra page 29.

6. The various opinions in State of Idaho, Department of Parks v. Idaho Department of Water Administration, supra p. 23, give a variety of views on the subject. For the majority:

"The Water Users also assert error in the trial court's determination that the preservation of aesthetic values and recreational opportunities for the citizens of this state is a beneficial use in the sense that they will support an appropriative water right under the Idaho Constitution.

"The foundation of the Water Users' argument is that the five uses specified in article 15, section 3 of the Constitution, i.e., domestic, agriculture, mining, manufacturing and power are exclusive and thus are the only uses that are cognizable beneficial uses under our Constitution. We reject that argument. * * * We note that numerous other western states have recognized through legislation that utilization of water for scenic or recreational purposes is a beneficial use. 1 W.A. Hutchins, Water Rights Laws in the Nineteen Western States, ch. 8, p. 542 (1971). Such legislation in other states carries no binding effect on this court but, in the absence of persuasive case law to the contrary, it would appear to indicate that the use of water for providing recreational and aesthetic pleasure represents an emerging recognition in this and other states of social values and benefits from the use of water."

Concurring:

"Our research does not disclose any case in which any court has attempted to define the term "beneficial use." Comment, Water Appropriation for Recreation, I Land and Water Law Review 209, 210 (1966). * * * I think we should look to very practical considerations in attempting to construe it. Prior to the time that the Constitution was adopted there were a number of common uses of water which were neither domestic, mining, agricultural nor manufacturing. A community would store water in a tank for use in fighting fires. The operator of a livery stable or a stockyard would water the stock kept there. Logging operations used water both to transport logs and for storage in mill ponds. Communities would use water wagons to settle dust on their dirt streets. The railroad used water for its steam engines and other uses related to the operation of the railroad. All of these uses were undoubtedly considered beneficial, but none of them were domestic, mining, agricultural or manufacturing. I do not believe that by adopting Article 15, § 3, of the Idaho Constitution that it was intended that uses such as these could no longer be considered beneficial uses. On the contrary, the universal expectation must have been that such uses could continue and could be the subject of an appropriation. Many of those uses still continue today, and the changing needs of our society are generating new uses for water which are neither domestic, agricultural, mining nor manufacturing. As an example, many privately owned public swimming pools or health facilities have applied for and received licenses to drill their own wells to supply their water needs. Natural hot water springs have been extensively developed into health resorts, e.g., Lava Hot Springs, upon the assumption that they have obtained a valid right to the use of the water in their facilities. Such uses could not be considered as domestic, mining, agricultural or manufacturing as used in Article 15, § 3, without unduly broadening the definitions of the terms, yet such uses are no doubt beneficial from a societal point of view in that they contribute to the general welfare of the citizenry; and unless a valid water right could be obtained for such a use, not only would society suffer by the loss of such uses, but a great deal of capital which has been invested in reliance upon the validity of a right to such a use for water would be in jeopardy. * * *

"With the exception of those uses elevated to beneficial status by Article 15, § 3, of the Constitution, the concept of what is or is not a beneficial use must necessarily change with changing conditions. For example, if we were now presented with a question of whether or not using water to operate a public swimming pool, a fountain, or to flood a tract to provide ice for a skating rink were beneficial uses, a good argument could be presented that such uses, although not domestic, mining, agricultural or manufacturing uses, were nevertheless beneficial. But we cannot say that such uses will always be beneficial because conditions might so change that these uses would be an unjustifiable use of water needed for other purposes. The notion of beneficiality of use must include a requirement of reasonableness."

Dissenting:

"I note, however, that the effect of a proposed appropriation upon scenic beauty and recreation can and should be considered in determining whether the use contemplated is "beneficial" within the meaning of the Constitution. Comment, Water Appropriation for Recreation, 1 Land & Water L.Rev. 209, 221 (1966). In other words, where the benefits of a proposed use are outweighed by the attendant detriment to scenic beauty and recreation, the use is not a "beneficial use," and the application for a permit to appropriate public waters for that use should be denied. As always, the question of beneficial use must be determined on a case by case basis, since the benefits of a particular proposed appropriation may outweigh the detriment to recreation and scenic beauty."

7. A recent episode in Montana illustrates the effect of changing societal attitudes on the concept of beneficial use. In 1974, when massive coal development seemed imminent, the Montana legislature enacted a provision which stated that "the use of water for slurry to export coal from Montana is not a beneficial use." 1974 Mont.L., ch. 192. Concern about possible commerce clause problems caused the legislature to drop the export language in 1979, resulting in a complete ban on the use of water for coal slurry transportation. 1979 Mont.L., ch. 552 In 1985, after the coal boom had collapsed, the legislature repealed the ban entirely. H.B. 680, § 24, 49th Legislature (1985).

8. At what point in time is the determination made that a particular use is beneficial? If the purpose of a long standing appropriation is found

to be no longer beneficial, does the right cease? Consider Fairfield Irrigation Co. v. White, 18 Utah 2d 93, 416 P.2d 641 (1966):

"We are quite in accord with the idea that the running of water on fields in the non-growing winter season may be wasteful; and that even though the right to such a use may have been established, in situations where there is scarcity of water for more important needs it may be considered as secondary. In this arid region water and its uses are so vital to the public welfare that it has been characterized as its very life blood. Accordingly, it is essential that putting water to the highest and best beneficial use should not only be encouraged but carefully safeguarded. Consistent with this necessity, and due to the nature of water, whether in streams or basins above or underground, it is not subject to absolute ownership in the same way other property is. It belongs to the public and the rights to use it are appropriable by private individuals only under conditions prescribed by law. Where the right to such a secondary use as the winter flooding of lands is shown to exist, in situations where there is a scarcity of water for more critical needs, for example, for drinking water and for culinary and domestic purposes, the right to use water for winter flooding of lands should be considered and adjudged in relation to those more critical and primary needs.

"The questions as to whether there is a beneficial use and, when the problem becomes pertinent, which use should have preference, can best be determined by the trier of the facts. Under the circumstances shown here, where it appears that the parties had so used the water for a long period of time; that the agricultural use of their lands depended upon it; where they had prepared it with ditches, furrows and dams to make efficient use of the water; and the order specifies that it must be used only when the land is not frozen to assure absorption, we cannot say that the order made is unsupported by the evidence nor that it is unreasonable under the circumstances. Therefore it should not be disturbed."

To what extent does the fact that a water right is a vested property interest limit the ability of the state to terminate it because the purpose of use is no longer considered beneficial? Could the Montana statute quoted in the preceding note have been used to terminate the use of water in a slurry pipeline which existed prior to the enactment of the statute? See Enterprise Irrigation District v. Willis, infra page 57.

9. The student may be interested to learn that Cascade Falls still flow. On remand the trial court decreed that the town company had first appropriated all the water of Cascade Creek except for one-half second foot, the defendant was enjoined from interfering with the remaining natural flow and its filing for the larger water right was set aside as a cloud on the plaintiff's title. Decree, Case No. 413, In Equity, District Court of the United States for the District of Colorado, October 15, 1915, (brought to the editor's attention by Michael D. White, Esquire, of Denver, Colorado). By what magic were the falls preserved, in view of the mandate of the Circuit Court of Appeals? The decree recites that it was entered "by consent of the parties hereto."

WATER: THE YEARBOOK OF AGRICULTURE

United States Department of Agriculture, 1955.
pp. 42, 43.

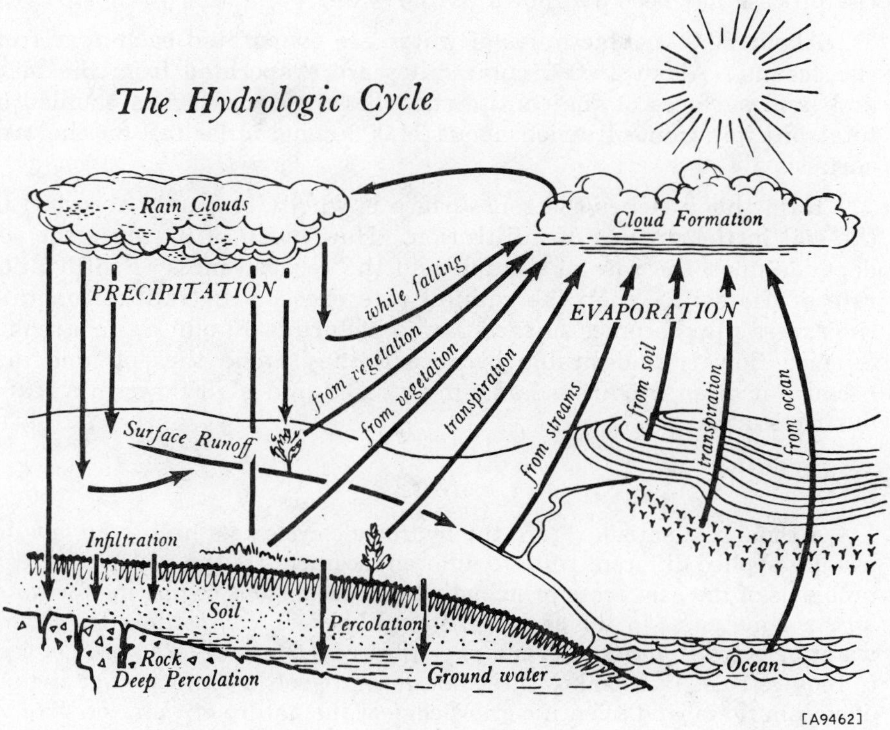

The unending circulation of the earth's moisture and water is called the water cycle. It is a gigantic system operating in and on the land and oceans of the earth and in the atmosphere that surrounds the earth.

The cycle has no beginning or ending, but because our discussion must start someplace, we can think of it as beginning with the waters of the oceans, which cover about three-fourths of the earth's surface.

Water from the surface of the oceans is evaporated into the atmosphere.

That moisture in turn is lifted and is eventually condensed and falls back to the earth's surface as precipitation.

The part of the precipitation that falls as rain, hail, dew, snow, or sleet on the land is of particular concern to man and agriculture.

Some of the precipitation, after wetting the foliage and ground, runs off over the surface to the streams. It is the water that sometimes causes erosion and is the main contributor to floods. Of the precipitation that soaks into the ground, some is available for growing plants and for evaporation. Some reaches the deeper zones and slowly percolates through springs and seeps to maintain the streams during dry periods. The streams in turn eventually lead back to the oceans, where the water originated. It is because of this never-ending circulation that the process has become known as the water cycle, or hydrologic cycle.

About 80,000 cubic miles of water are evaporated each year from the oceans. About 15,000 cubic miles are evaporated from the lakes and land surfaces of the continents. Total evaporation is equaled by total precipitation, of which about 24,000 cubic miles fall on the land surfaces. * * *

Rain that reaches the soil surface is wholly or partly absorbed by the soil in the process of infiltration. How much of it enters the soil depends upon the rate of rainfall and the receptiveness or infiltration rate of the soil. When the rainfall rate exceeds the infiltration rate, the excess rain becomes surface flow, which runs off quickly to streams. Surface flow is undesirable because it may erode the soil and also because it often produces damagingly rapid and high flows in streams during storms.

Note

Although scientists regard the hydrologic cycle as a unity, the law has usually applied different rules to different segments of the cycle. The legal problems of the past arose principally between persons competing for water at the same point in the cycle. Disputes between competitors for ground water or between users or drainers of diffused surface waters were not seen to require rules identical to those developed to settle conflicts over the use of stream flows, and scientific knowledge of the nature of water occurrence and the interrelationship of different classes of water was lacking. Thus each type of case was handled separately, and different bodies of law grew up concerned with different types of water occurrence. It is therefore important to determine the legal classification of an occurrence of water in order to discover the rules which the courts will apply to it.

See Oklahoma Water Resources Bd. v. Lawton, 580 P.2d 510 (Okl.1978). The water in controversy was a spring which for a million years had flowed more than a million gallons per day (approximately 1.5 cubic feet per second). This flowed over the ground in a diffused manner for a short distance before forming a definite stream that flowed into a lake forming a part of the city's water supply. Under the Oklahoma Groundwater Law an overlying landowner who can put the water to a beneficial use is entitled to an allocation of the maximum annual yield of the basin based on his proportion of the acreage overlying the basin. 82 Okl.Stat.Ann. §§ 1020.1–1020.22. Under Oklahoma's modernized version of the Field Code, "The owner of the land owns water standing thereon, or flowing over or under its surface but not forming a definite stream. The use of groundwater shall be governed by the Oklahoma Groundwater Law. Water running in a definite stream, formed by nature over or under the surface, may be used by him for domestic purposes * * * as long as it remains there, but he may not prevent the natural flow of the stream, or of the natural spring from which it commences its definite course, nor pursue nor pollute the same, as such water then becomes public water and is subject to appropriation for the benefit and welfare of the people of the State, as provided by law." 60 Okl. Stat.Ann. § 60. Under Oklahoma's stream water law an appropriation can be made only if, "The proposed use does not interfere with domestic or existing appropriative uses." 82 Okl.Stat.Ann. § 105.12(3). The landowner, desiring to encase the spring and tap its source before the water reached the surface, sought a groundwater permit, which the board granted. The court reversed: "The test is not how immediately spring water forms a definite stream, but rather, whether the spring water forms a definite stream. If it forms a definite stream, it is public water from its inception, and may not be diverted for private use unless appropriated as stream water. We hold that when natural spring water forms a definite stream, the water in the stream and the spring itself, from its inception, is to be classified as stream water and appropriated as such."

STATE v. HIBER

Supreme Court of Wyoming, 1935.
48 Wyo. 172, 44 P.2d 1005.

[Adamson received a permit from the state to construct a reservoir on a "natural stream" known as Adamson Draw. The draw, described by several witnesses as a "swale", drained about 300 acres, mostly on the lands of Hiber, above Adamson's lands. The dam was partially constructed when Hiber built on his land, without a permit, a dam across the draw 200 feet long and 13 feet high. The state brought this action to abate Hiber's dam as an illegal structure and to enjoin him from interfering with the natural flow of the draw. The lower court found for the defendant. Other facts are stated in the opinion.]

BLUME, JUSTICE. * * * Under section 1, article 8 of the Constitution of the State, "the waters of all natural streams, springs, lakes or other collections of still water, within the boundaries of the state are hereby declared to be the property of the state." * * * The controlling question, accordingly, is as to whether or not the assertion that the draw is a natural stream is correct. Counsel for the state contend that in an arid region the term "natural stream" should be construed liberally. So much we may, for the purposes of this case, concede. But it is further contended that "the proper test of distinction, according to the rule laid down * * * as to what constitutes a natural stream or water course is whether or not the water is in such shape as to make it susceptible to application for beneficial use." The test proposed does not seem to be justified by any authorities, even by Popham v. Holloron, 84 Mont. 442, 275 P. 1099, which was decided under a statute not at all like ours, and which in its facts differs materially from those in the case at bar. * * *

If, then, the water in question here was surface water, or what comes to the same thing, if it was not the water of a natural stream, the court was right in finding for the defendant, as to his right to impound it. As to whether it is the one or the other in a specific case is not always easy to determine, and is generally, or often, a question of fact. * * * "Surface water," it has been said, is that which is diffused over the surface of the ground, derived from falling rains and melting snows, and continues to be such, and may be impounded by the owner of the land, until it reaches some well-defined channel in which it is accustomed to, and does, flow with other waters; or until it reaches some permanent lake or pond, and it then ceases to be surface water and becomes the water of the water course, or a lake or a pond, as the case may be. * * * This, accordingly, brings us directly to the point as to whether or not the waters in controversy reached such definite channel—in other words, whether Adamson Draw was a natural stream or water course. * * *

It is said by Kinney, supra, § 303, that "according to the great weight of authority, the essential characteristics of a water course are: A channel, consisting of a well-defined bed and banks, and a current of water." Some exceptions have been made, the definition has not been applied in all cases, and it may be difficult to give one that is universally applicable. United States v. Ide (C.C.A.) 277 F. 373. Too much stress ought not, perhaps, be placed upon any one of the elements mentioned, and all should be given due consideration. Farnham, supra, § 455. However, the definition given has been approved in recent cases. * * * In Hutchinson v. Watson Slough Ditch Co., 16 Idaho 484, 101 P. 1059, 1060, 133 Am.St.Rep. 125, which involved appropriation of water, the court held that: "a water course is a stream of water flowing in a definite channel, having a bed and sides or banks, and discharging itself into some other stream or body of water. The flow of water need not be constant, but must be more than mere surface drainage occasioned by extraordinary causes; there must be substantial indications of the existence of a stream, which is ordinarily a moving body of water." In Simmons v. Winters, 21 Or. 35, 27 P. 7, 9, 28 Am.St. Rep. 727, also involving appropriation of water, the Oregon court, after citing and quoting from a number of decisions, finally stated: "The conclusion to be deduced from these decisions is that a water-course is a stream of water usually flowing in a particular direction, with well-defined banks and channels, but that the water need not flow continuously,—the channel may sometimes be dry; that the term 'water-course' does not include water descending from the hills, down the hollows and ravines, without any definite channel, only in times of rain and melting snow; but that where water, owing to the hilly or mountainous configuration of the country, accumulates in large quantities from rain and melting snow, and at regular seasons descends through long deep gullies or ravines upon the lands below, and in its onward flow carves out a distinct and well-defined channel, which even to the casual glance bears the unmistakable impress of the frequent action of running water, and through which it has flowed from time immemorial, such a stream is to be considered a water-course, and to be governed by the same rules."

Courts of other western states have taken the same view; that of Arizona in Maricopa County, etc., v. Southwest Cotton Co., supra; that of Montana in Le Munyon v. Gallatin Valley Ry. Co., supra; that of California in Lux v. Haggin, 69 Cal. 255, 4 P. 919, 10 P. 674, 769; that of Washington in Tierney v. Yakima County, 136 Wash. 481, 239 P. 248. Kinney, supra, § 302, says that: "A water course does not include surface water conveyed from higher to lower levels for limited periods, during the melting of snow, or during or soon after a heavy fall of rain, through hollows or ravines, which at all other portions of the year are entirely dry. These occasional bursts of water, which in times of freshets, or of melting ice or snow, descend from the hills and inundate the country, have none of the characteristics of a water course." The water, as already indicated, need not run through the entire year. 67 C.J. 681. On that subject Kinney, supra, says in section 307 that: "Those who are acquainted with the streams and water courses of the arid Rocky Mountain region of this country, draining as they do steep, mountain areas with their swift currents, running over gravelly and rocky bottoms, know that often in a dry summer month many of them are entirely dry, at least upon the surface. All of them, nevertheless, have well defined beds, channels, banks and currents of water, at least the greater portion of the year." Again, it is said that a water course does not include the water flowing in the hollows or ravines in land, which is mere surface water from rain or melting snow (i.e., snow lying and melting on the land) and is discharged through them from a higher to a lower level, but which at other times are destitute of water; that such hollows or ravines are not, in legal contemplation, water courses. * * * Kinney, supra, § 312. And it has been stated that "it is almost the unanimous doctrine that swales are not, in their strict legal sense, water courses." Kinney, supra, § 314. Farnham, supra, § 457, maintains that the source of water which flows in a channel claimed to be a water course is a more satisfactory test than is the presence or absence of a channel. But even he holds that there must be more than surface water, unless it comes from a large area of country, and is so continuous in its flow that it takes upon itself the character of a water course. So it is said in 27 R.C.L. 1064 that a "water course is the condition created by a stream of water having a well defined and substantial existence, and that if this substantial existence is present the fact that the stream is not strong enough to create for itself bed and banks is not sufficient to defeat its character as a water course." Hinkle v. Avery, 88 Iowa 47, 55 N.W. 77, 78, 45 Am.St.Rep. 224, and Miller & Lux v. Madera Canal, etc., Co., 155 Cal. 59, 99 P. 502, 22 L.R.A.,N.S., 391, are cited. In the Iowa case the water in question came from a spring, running continuously, at times in a well-defined channel with banks, at times spreading out several rods, later again coming together again in a narrow, well-defined, and single channel, with the current visible along the entire course. Here the substantial existence of the stream could not be questioned, and the case presents a feature altogether absent in the case at bar. In the California case it was held that where a stream flows in a continuous current, the fact that the water thereof, on account of the level character of the lands, spreads over a large area, without apparent banks, does not affect its character as a water course; the overflow caused by ordinary rainfall is but a part thereof. Other cases, cited in note to 1 L.R.A.,N.S., 757, are of a similar character, and have no application in the case at bar. See in this connection Miller v. Eastern Ry. & Lumber Co., 84 Wash. 31, 146 P. 171. So while too strict adherence to the definition that, to constitute a water course, there must be a stream flowing in a bed with banks, has at times given trouble, that definition is, ordinarily, correct and sufficient. Note 1 L.R.A.,N.S., 757. * * *

Testing the facts in this case by these rules of law, we think we must hold that there was ample testimony to sustain the finding and judgment of the trial court, and that the state has failed, at least by a preponderance of the evidence, to show that Adamson Draw is a natural stream. According to most, if not all, of the evidence, it is dry nearly all the time; the main exception being in the spring. It is covered with grass; it has no banks; it is easily crossed by a vehicle almost everywhere; its main course is confined to the lands of the defendant. Its commencement is but a short distance beyond the north boundary thereof, and it has not been shown that it extends southward to a great length; at least, so far as the evidence shows it has no natural outlet. The run of the water therein is confined to a short period in the spring time when the snows melt; or heavy rains at other times may cause it to run for a short period of time. It is even doubtful, by reason of the porous soil, that any water would in any event reach the defendant's reservoir. Judging from the testimony, no one would instantaneously perceive that it is a water course. It is, of course, marked on the ground, as all draws are, but that it has been worn out by the water, in view of its grassy condition and the absence of banks, is not very likely, even though the testimony of the witness Morrow might, in answer to a double and leading question put to him, be understood to the contrary. The watershed is small; at least half of it, if not more, is confined to the lands of the defendant, and it would seem that the case may be said to resolve itself into the question as to whether or not the defendant has the right to impound water coming from melting snows and heavy rains, which fall onto his lands and on a small adjoining area, and which drain into a depression on defendant's lands. We think he has that right under the circumstances disclosed herein, or, at least, the trial court had the right to so find. * * *

The judgment of the trial court should, accordingly, be affirmed, and it is so ordered.

Notes

1. In addition to the exceptions to the definition of a water course discussed in the principal case, consider the Fresno slough, which flows sometimes northward and sometimes southward, held part of a water

course in Turner v. James Canal Co., 155 Cal. 82, 99 P. 520 (1909), and consider also Medano Creek, which disappears into sand dunes. See Medano Ditch Co. v. Adams, 29 Colo. 317, 68 P. 431 (1902).

Compare, with the descriptive definition in the principal case, the functional treatment in Hoefs v. Short, 114 Tex. 501, 273 S.W. 785, 40 A.L.R. 833 (1925). Barilla Creek runs for one or two days after rains fall on its 350 square mile watershed, from one to twenty-two times a year. The court said, "When it is said that a stream in order to be a natural water course to which water rights attach must have bed, banks, a current of water, and a permanent source of water supply, we have only described in detail such physiographic and meteorological characteristics as make the use of the stream for irrigation practicable. When it is once shown that the waters of a stream are so confined and persistent in their course, and flow with such frequency and volume that it is both practicable and valuable to irrigate therefrom, it is a stream to which such water rights attach. With reference to the phrase 'definite and permanent source of supply of water', frequently used by the courts as describing a necessary requisite of an irrigable stream, all that is meant is that there must be sufficient water carried by the stream at such intervals as may make it practicable to irrigate from or use the stream."

In Oklahoma Water Resources Board v. Central Oklahoma Master Conservancy District, 464 P.2d 748 (Okl.1969), a city owned the entire watershed of a small creek, and, claiming "the right to capture water falling on its property for private use," dammed the stream. Held, an illegal appropriation of the stream. "Diffused surface waters lose their original character when they reach some well-defined channel in which they are accustomed to, and do, flow with other waters, or when they reach some permanent lake or pond. They then become 'a constituent part' of the stream, lake or pond, as the case may be. Diffused surface water may be appropriated by the owner of land over which it flows and become his property *when captured by him before it enters a definite stream.* Thereafter it is no longer subject to appropriation by the landowner."

2. The constitutions or statutes of several western states define water that is subject to appropriation so as to conform to the water course concept, e.g., Colo.Const. art. 16, § 5, "natural streams"; N.Mex.Const. art. 16, § 2 "perennial or torrential". In several statutes waters are defined so as to exclude diffused surface water. See No.Dak.Cent.Code 61–01–01; Ariz.Rev.Stat. § 45–131A. On the other hand, the laws of some states refer to "all sources of water supply" or "all waters". Nev.Rev.Stat. 533.025; Or. Rev.Stat. 537.110; Utah Code Ann.1953, 73–1–1. No cases seem to have construed these terms in the context of a dispute between an appropriator from a stream and the owner of land claiming diffused surface waters tributary to the stream.

3. Compare and contrast the following:

Thomas, Hydrology v. Water Allocation in the Eastern United States, In The Law of Water Allocation in the Eastern United States (Haber & Bergen eds. 1958) 165, 173: "Of all the various 'diffused surface waters,' those that would be most likely to affect streamflow are the waters gathered on or flowing over the surface after precipitation. Such waters contribute materially to storm runoff, and especially to floods. Land owners within any drainage basin, therefore, by holding these 'diffused' waters on their land could reduce the streamflow materially; and if all overland flow could be prevented, the water in watercourses would consist largely of the discharge from ground-water reservoirs. Thus if the landowners have absolute ownership of both the ground water and diffused surface water on their lands, a surface-water appropriator cannot be assured of a secure water right. * * * [I]t is reported that soil-conservation practices have reduced the flow of many streams in west Texas. At a water conference last September at Texas A & M College it was conceded that, with continuing reduction of base flow and reduction of storm runoff from minor storms, some surface-water appropriators would eventually have rights to nothing but the runoff during major floods."

West's Ann.Calif.Water Code, § 1252.1: "An appropriation of water of any stream or other source of water under this part does not confer authority upon the appropriator to prevent or interfere with soil conservation practices above the point of diversion in the watershed in which such stream or other source originates, which practices do not themselves constitute an appropriation for which a permit is required by this part."

Belle Fourche River Compact, Art. 5, 58 Stat. 94 (1944): "Wyoming and South Dakota agree that the unappropriated waters of the Bell Fourche River as of the date of this compact shall be allocated to each state as follows: 90% to South Dakota, 10% to Wyoming; provided that allocations to Wyoming shall be exclusive of the use of these waters for domestic and stock use, and Wyoming shall be allowed unrestricted use for these purposes, except that no reservoir for such use shall exceed 20 acre-feet in capacity."

4. Springs which form a water course are usually held to be a part of the water course, and their use is governed by the law, riparian or appropriative, applicable to water courses. In Arizona, "springs on the surface" are appropriable by statute, even though they do not flow beyond the boundary of the land on which they arise. Ariz.Rev.Stat. § 45–131A; Parker v. McIntyre, 47 Ariz. 484, 56 P.2d 1337 (1936).

In Melville v. Salt Lake County, 570 P.2d 687 (Utah 1977), the court said, "No one owns or can own water in this state, regardless of whether that water is found in the form of a spring, stream, lake, pond or under the ground. One can only acquire the right to use the water. One's right to use the water is measured by the amount he puts to beneficial use without interfering with another person's right to the use of the water.

Lakes and ponds are mentioned as sources of appropriable water in several state constitutions and statutes, and are generally treated as a part of the water course which feeds them or originates from them. A lake may be appropriable though it is not an integral part of a stream, and has neither a visible source of supply nor an outlet. Proctor v. Sim, 134 Wash. 606, 236 P. 114 (1925).

5. "Groundwater"—water under the surface of the earth capable of being brought to the surface in usable quantities—is subject to appropriation in most of the western states. Most of this chapter is applicable to appropriations of groundwater, but discussion of special problems which

arise because of the nature of its physical occurrence is postponed to Chapter 4.

R.J.A., INC. v. WATER USERS ASSOCIATION OF DISTRICT NO. 6

Supreme Court of Colorado, 1984.
690 P.2d 823.

LOHR, JUSTICE.

R.J.A., Inc. (applicant) appeals from a judgment of the water judge for water division 1 denying its application for a developed water right. The applicant based its claim on a project that will reduce water loss from a marshy mountain meadow by removing the underlying peat moss, thereby eliminating a saturated, seepy condition. This will decrease evaporation from the soil and surface and reduce evapotranspiration from grassy vegetation. We affirm the judgment.

R.J.A., Inc. operates a summer resort business on property located south of Estes Park, Colorado, in a mountain valley approximately 9000 feet above sea level. The property is situated at the headwaters of Tahosa Creek, which flows into St. Vrain Creek, a tributary of the South Platte River. This land originally included a 27-acre peat moss marsh which was approximately 3000 years old and, thus, was in existence long before any water rights were established on the South Platte River system. Historically, water entered this marsh from several surface streams and springs, and the area was much wetter than the surrounding lands. According to the applicant, loss of water to the atmosphere was higher from this peat moss marsh than from a well-drained mountain meadow of equivalent size. This is because the soil was saturated at or near surface level, resulting in relatively high rates of evaporation from the soil and standing water on the surface and evapotranspiration from the grassy vegetation growing throughout the marsh. While substantial amounts of water were lost to the atmosphere in this manner, the remaining water eventually moved through or around the marsh to become the headwaters of Tahosa Creek.

In the early 1970s, the applicant undertook a project to remove the extensive deposits of peat moss underlying the marsh, drain the land, and convert the marsh to a well-drained meadow more suitable for use in the applicant's resort business. At the time of the water court hearing in 1982, R.J.A., Inc. had completed about three quarters of the planned work.

In 1979, R.J.A., Inc. filed an application for a developed water right in the district court for water division 1, seeking a decree for 22.5 acre feet absolute and 20.8 acre feet conditional to be used for augmentation and other specified beneficial uses. See section 37–92–302(1)(a), 15 C.R.S. (1973). The applicant claimed that the drainage of the marsh and elimination of the saturated, seepy condition would reduce the rates of evaporation and evapo-transpiration, and thereby would decrease consumptive use of water by 43.3 acre feet per year. Because this would represent a net gain to the stream, the applicant asserted that its water right should not be subject to administration under the priority system.

* * *

The applicant contends that a developed water right for tributary water, free from the priority system, may be recognized where a claimant increases the natural flow of a stream by reducing consumptive uses that existed before the first appropriations were made on the stream. In support of this position, the applicant relies upon a line of cases in which we have recognized rights to developed water based upon addition of water to an existing supply. We hold that reduction of consumptive use of tributary water cannot provide the basis for a water right that is independent of the system of priorities on the stream.

As the trial court found, the water involved in the application before us is tributary to Tahosa Creek. The Water Right Determination and Administration Act of 1969, Article 92 of Chapter 37, 15 C.R.S. (1973) (the 1969 Act), provides a comprehensive scheme for adjudication of rights to tributary water and for administration of the distribution of such water. That act provides for adjudication and administration under a system of priorities, implementing the constitutionally based right of prior appropriation in waters of natural streams. * * * Nowhere in the entire scheme of the 1969 Act is there a suggestion that rights to tributary water independent of the priority system can be obtained.

The applicant urges, however, that we have previously recognized that developed water rights, independent of the priority system, may be established as to tributary water in appropriate circumstances. We have stated on several occasions that one who increases the flow of a natural stream by adding water that otherwise would not reach the stream is entitled to the use of the water to the extent of the increase. * * *

* * *

Review of our cases relating to developed water brings us to the same conclusion that we reached in *Shelton Farms* that under prior case law "[no] person has been granted a water right free from the call of the river for water which has always been tributary to a stream." 187 Colo. at 187, 529 P.2d at 1325. Thus, the developed water cases provide no support for the applicant's position.

In *Shelton Farms* we considered an application with many similarities to the one now before us. There, we reversed judgments of the water court awarding water rights free from the call of senior decreed water rights on the Arkansas River. The trial court had decreed these rights based upon the reduction of evaporation and evapotranspiration effected by clearing phreatophytes from the land and filling in a marshy area. We concluded that, since the water in question had always been tributary to the stream and was not water new to the river system, the developed water cases were inapposite. We rejected the argument that demonstration of lack of injury to vested rights could serve as a basis for recognition of a water right outside the priority system, 187 Colo. at 188–90, 529 P.2d at 1325–27, and concluded:

> [Present section 37–92–306, 15 C.R.S. (1973) prescribing the ranking of water rights by priorities] cannot be ignored * * *. There is nothing in the plain language of the statute to except appellees' plans [for award of water rights independent of the priority system] from the priority date system. Thus, we hold that all water decrees of any kind are bound to the call of the river, subject to any specific exceptions found within the law. To hold any other way would be to weaken the priority system, and create a superclass of water rights never before in existence.[a]

187 Colo. at 190, 529 P.2d at 1326.

In *Shelton Farms* we recognized the importance of maximizing beneficial use of Colorado's water. See Fellhauer v. People, 167 Colo. 320, 447 P.2d 986 (1968). We noted, however, that subsequent to *Fellhauer's* strong emphasis on the importance of maximum utilization of this scarce resource, the General Assembly had not authorized the creation of a water right outside the priority system through elimination of a prior consumptive use, as sought by the applicant here. *Shelton Farms,* 187 Colo. at 188–89, 529 P.2d at 1325–26.

The applicant argues that *Shelton Farms* is not controlling because the phreatophytes in that case grew after the early water rights had been established on the river. Therefore, the plants were aptly characterized as "water thieves," and we visualized the generation of a new industry of "planting and harvesting trees to create water rights superior to the oldest decrees on the Arkansas * * *." 187 Colo. at 191, 529 P.2d at 1327. In the present case, however, the peat bog existed long before initiation of the earliest water right on the South Platte system. The water lost from the river system by evaporation and evapotranspiration from the seepy bog was never available for utilization by holders of senior rights. While this difference is real, we do not consider it controlling.

A separate strand of analysis supported our decision in *Shelton Farms.* We expressed concern over adoption of a rule of law that would encourage widespread destruction of plant life, with attendant likeli-

a. We distinguished between "developed" and "salvaged" water. The former is new water not previously part of the river system, i.e., it is imported or nontributary water. The latter is tributary water made available for beneficial use through elimination of waste. Only developed water can be made the basis of a right independent of the priority system. *Shelton Farms,* 187 Colo. at 187, 529 P.2d at 1324–25; see Sweetwater Development Corp. v. Schubert Ranches, Inc., 188 Colo. 379, 383, 535 P.2d 215, 218 (1975). One example of a developed water right described in *Shelton Farms* clearly involves tributary water—the capture, storage and utilization of flood waters. 187 Colo. at 187, 529 P.2d at 1324. There are valid reasons consistent with the priority system for entering a decree in favor of the person capturing such waters. Despite our dicta in *Shelton Farms,* such a decree does not involve a right to developed water independent of the priority system.

hood of irreparable erosion and the creation of a barren wasteland. We said, "the waters of Colorado belong to the people, but so does the land. There must be a balancing effect, and the elements of water and land must be used in harmony to the maximum feasible use of both." 187 Colo. at 191, 529 P.2d at 1327. *Cf. In Re Rules and Regulations,* 674 P.2d 914 (Colo.1984) (environmental concerns are properly to be taken into account in rules and regulations promulgated by the state engineer to govern administration of diversions of tributary water).

The water rights sought here are based upon alterations of long existing physical characteristics of the land. Alteration of natural conditions and vegetation in order to save water carries with it the potential for adverse effects on soil and bank stabilization, soil productivity, wildlife habitat, fisheries production, water quality, watershed protection and the hydrologic cycle. See Harrison and Sandstrom, The Groundwater-Surface Water Conflict and Recent Colorado Water Legislation, 43 U.Colo.L.Rev. 1, 2 (1971); F. Trelease, Water Law: Resource Use and Environmental Protection 59 (2d ed. 1974). Whether to recognize such rights, and thus to encourage innovative ways of reducing historical consumptive uses by modifying conditions found in nature, is a question fraught with important public policy considerations. As such, the question is especially suited for resolution through the legislative process.

In the 1969 Act, the General Assembly has used priority of appropriation as the sole criterion for ranking rights to tributary water. As we recognized in *Shelton Farms,* the general legislative policy of maximizing beneficial and integrated use of surface and subsurface water must be implemented with a sensitivity to the effect on other resources. The General Assembly has addressed the accommodation of the policy of maximum utilization of water and the policy of preservation of natural resources, but only in a limited way. It has expressed its concern that maximum utilization of water be balanced by preservation of the natural environment "to a reasonable degree" by authorizing appropriations on behalf of the people of the state of Colorado for that latter purpose. §§ 37–92–102(3) and 103(4), 15 C.R.S. (1973), the relevant portions of which were adopted in 1973 in Ch. 442, secs. 1 and 2, §§ 37–92–102(3) and 37–92–103(4), 1973 Colo.Sess.Laws 1521, 1521–22.

Then, in 1975, shortly after the *Shelton Farms* case was decided, the General Assembly revised the definition of "plan for augmentation" to affirm that neither the salvage of tributary waters by eradicating phreatophytes nor the increase of runoff by making land surfaces impermeable provides an increased supply of water that may be utilized to support a plan for augmentation. § 37–92–103(9), 15 C.R.S. (1983 Supp.). These partial approaches to the problem reflect a cautious step-by-step legislative approach in addressing the issues. It is noteworthy, however, that in neither of these statutes has the legislature deviated from the basic priority system for tributary water when engrafting refinements upon the system.

The phreatophytes in *Shelton Farms* may have presented a factually more compelling case for rejection of recognition of a developed water right through their eradication than is present here. The larger consideration of achieving maximum feasible use of both land and water, however, is also present here, with the result that we find what we said in *Shelton Farms* equally applicable in this case:

> No one on any river would be adverse to a schematic and integrated system of developing this kind of water supply with control and balancing considerations. But to create such a scheme is the work of the legislature, through creation of appropriate district authorities with right of condemnation on a selective basis, not for the courts. Until such time as the legislature responds, action such as appellees' should not be given court sanction.

187 Colo. at 192, 529 P.2d at 1327.

We affirm the judgment of the water court.

Notes

1. Phreatophytes (a Greek word meaning "well-plants") grow in stream bottoms and literally pump water through their structure and transpire it from their foliage.

"Along many of the river valleys of the West, saltcedars and other generally worthless vegetation (willows, cottonwoods, mesquite, greasewood, and certain reeds and weeds) have crowded onto river bottom land to such an extent that they now cover nearly 16 million acres and discharge into the atmosphere an estimated 20 to 25 million acre-feet of water annually. These plants, having their roots in the ground water, have first call on available water supplies, leaving for man only that which they cannot use. Losses are particularly acute in the water shortage States of Arizona and New Mexico, where the warmer climate leads to greater consumption of water, particularly by the saltcedars. Elimination of the consumptive waste from these plants provides an excellent opportunity for increasing the usefulness of available water supplies.

"* * * Federal and State agencies are * * * carrying on experiments and studies to determine ways and means whereby water lost through evaporation and transpiration can be salvaged for beneficial use. Estimates of possible savings in water through eradication and control range as high as 25 percent of present loss, or 6 million acre-feet annually, but additional research into the most economical methods for eradication and control is needed." Senate Select Committee on National Water Resources, Report of the Committee Pursuant to S.Res. 48, Senate Report No. 29, 86th Congress, 1st Session 108–109 (1961)."

Not everyone is enthusiastic about proposals for saving water by phreatophyte removal:

"A case in point is Arizona, where Federal agencies are studying or proposing the removal of phreatophytes—deep rooted vegetation—from the banks of many rivers in the state. The main purpose of the removal is to conserve water in that arid state. * * *

"Bitterly opposing the phreatophyte removal projects, some of which are already under way, are conservationists and wildlife proponents who say that the riverbank vegetation is the only major wildlife habitat in the arid state. Remove it, they say, and the adverse effects on wildlife will be devastating and sometimes irreversible. Some also mention indications, somewhat less supported by scientific evidence, that the effects on fisheries may be equally detrimental. * * *

"The dove, quail, grey hawk and black-bellied tree duck are some of the birds affected, according to Arizona Game and Fish Department. Other types of wildlife are also affected, of course, including deer and javelina. Although waterfowl do not use the plant cover directly, it forms sanctuaries for ducks and geese using the Pacific Flyway. * * *" Gilluly, Wildlife versus Irrigation, 99 Science News 184 (1971).

2. In contrast to the principal case, the California Water Resources Control Board has required the eradication of phreatophytes as a condition for receiving a permit to appropriate water. See People v. Shirokow, 26 Cal.3d 301, 162 Cal.Rptr. 30, 605 P.2d 859 (1980).

3. In the Matter of the General Determination of the Rights to the Use of Surface and Ground Waters of the Payette River Drainage Basin, 107 Idaho 221, 687 P.2d 1348 (1984) involved a dispute over water emanating from a mine portal which would not have existed had there been no mine. The owners of the mine argued that the water was "developed water" and thus was not subject to appropriation by others. The court ruled otherwise, holding that it was public groundwater subject to appropriation.

4. What of artificially induced precipitation? The state of the art of weather modification was described in National Water Commission, Water Policies for the Future, 348 (1973):

"The most significant advance in recent technology has been the development of mathematical models which explain the effects of seeding and which can be used, in a limited number of cases, to predict likely precipitation changes with some degree of confidence. This prediction capability varies with the three types of cloud systems, described below as orographic, convective, and cyclonic.

"The most promising precipitation augmentation results have been obtained from 'orographic' cloud systems, where mountain ranges force moisture-laden air upward to form clouds. Orographic precipitation is the predominant form in the Western United States, where most precipitation accumulates during the winter season at higher elevations as snow. In the Colorado River Basin, for example, orographic cloud systems provide a very high percentage of the annual precipitation. The conditions necessary to increase precipitation from such clouds have been reasonably well established. The resulting average annual increases in precipitation, under existing techniques, may range from zero up to about 20 percent.

"The Bureau of Reclamation estimates that a cloud seeding program for a 14,300-square mile area of the Colorado River Basin could increase precipitation about 15 percent, which would yield approximately 1,870,000 acre-feet of increased net annual runoff. This estimate was based on some generalized assumptions that certain losses normally experienced after precipitation but before runoff, as well as some losses due to resulting increased vegetation, would occur. The estimate is useful for the purpose for which it was intended—as a preproject estimate for pilot investigations. However, it has not yet been proven by actual experience.

"Precipitation augmentation is more complex for 'convective' type clouds, which frequently are associated with thunderstorms and cover relatively small areas. These clouds are formed by the lifting of air resulting from heating at the earth's surface. Although these cloud systems occur throughout the Nation, they provide the primary summertime precipitation for the extensive agricultural areas of the Midwest, as well as for the high plains east of the Rocky Mountains. Experiments have demonstrated that seeding convective clouds may increase precipitation. The magnitude of increases, however, cannot yet be predicted with assurance.

"Relatively few modification experiments have been conducted on 'cyclonic' storms, in which the lifting action stems from the interaction of cold and warm air masses. These storm systems occur over large areas of the United States and provide major precipitation to all areas, especially to areas east of the Rocky Mountains. The documented results of the few precipitation augmentation tests conducted on cyclonic cloud systems have been inconclusive.

"Increases in average precipitation do not necessarily produce proportional increases in usable water supply, for several reasons. First, there is not a linear relationship between precipitation and runoff. That is to say, 1 inch of additional precipitation in a given season does not yield the same incremental additions to usable water supply as an earlier or a later inch of precipitation, depending on, among other things, the amount of precipitation which has already occurred in that season.

"Secondly, although research data are limited, most investigators conclude that opportunities to increase precipitation in drought periods, when increases in water supply are disproportionately valuable, are less frequent than in wet periods, when water supply increases carry less utility. This disproportion between the effects in wet and dry periods can result in making some of the increased supply during wet periods unusable unless there is sufficient storage capacity available to hold water from wet to dry periods. For streams with a high degree of storage regulation, such as the Colorado River, any augmentation of flows is likely to be usable.

"Vegetal cover of marginal value may expand as a result of increased precipitation. Unless such increases are controlled through land management techniques, such expanded vegetation can reduce the usable water yield from precipitation augmentation."

Things had not much improved by 1977. Neyman, in "A Statistician's View of Weather Modification Technology (A Review)," 74 Proceedings National Academy of Sciences 4714 (1977), summarized his review of the scientific literature as follows:

"*Question i.* Is the present cloud seeding technology reliably confirmed as a means of alleviating drought? *Answer:* No.

"*Question ii.* Is there evidence that cloud seeding affects precipitation and if so, what are the indicated effects? *Answer:* It appears established that cloud seeding does affect precipitation and does so over areas far in excess of the intended targets, occasionally up to distances on the order of hundreds of kilometers. In some cases the effects are large increases and in some others large decreases in precipitation. The several hypothetical mechanisms advanced to explain these effects and to predict them vary in their empirical support and convincingness. In particular, much of the existing literature, some of it stemming from official sources, is slanted and unreliable."

Most of the litigation has involved unsuccessful attempts to collect damages for the harms allegedly caused by artificial precipitation; most of the legislation is concerned with regulatory and institutional controls of the activity. See Johnson, Federal Organization for the Control of Water Modification, 10 Natural Resources J. 222 (1970); Davis, Weather Modification Law Developments, 27 Okl.L.Rev. 409 (1974); McKenzie, Weather Modification: A Review of the Science and Law, 6 Environmental L.Rev. 387 (1975).

From the "water law" standpoint, the best article is Pierce, Legal Aspects of Weather Modification—Snowpack Augmentation in Wyoming, 2 Land & Water L.Rev. 273 (1967), speculating on the rights of the "rain maker" to capture, store, use and sell the water he adds to the natural stream flow. See also Fischer, Weather Modification and the Right of Capture, 8 Nat.Res.Lawyer 639 (1976).

WITHDRAWAL OF WATERS FROM APPROPRIATION: THE PROTECTION OF INSTREAM USES

The terms "instream values" or "instream uses" are used to describe values or uses associated with water in a stream, such as recreation, aesthetics, fish and wildlife maintenance, and general environmental preservation. In recent years there has been a growing recognition of instream uses, and most western states have adopted one or more of the techniques described below to provide for such uses.

Efforts to preserve instream values go back over half a century. In 1915, the Oregon lawmakers took the first step: "The following streams and water thereof forming waterfalls in view of, or near, the Columbia River Highway, from Sandy River to Hood River, are herewith withdrawn from appropriation or condemnation, and shall not be diverted or interrupted for any purpose whatsoever * * * [naming 23 streams and the falls they formed]." Or.Rev.Stat. 538.200.

In 1929, the Oregon legislature preserved a fishing stream: "Subject to such water rights as are existing at the time of the taking effect of this act, the waters flowing in the main channel of the Rogue River from * * * to its confluence with the Pacific Ocean, are hereby withdrawn from appropriation; provided, that this act shall not prevent the appropriation and use of such water for domestic, stock, irrigation and municipal purposes; and provided further, that it shall not prevent the appropriation, diversion and use of the water of any tributary streams" See Or.Rev.Stat. 538.270. While it looks like the proviso swallowed the provision, a second section made it clear that the statute was intended to prevent the construction of dams in this famous stretch of salmon and steelhead water. The present Chapter 538 contains a much enlarged list, amendments and additions having been made in 1931, 1935, 1953, 1959, 1963, and 1971. In 1955 the Oregon legislature added an administrative approach, authorizing the Oregon Water Resources Board to withdraw streams from appropriation. Or. Rev.Stat. 536.410.

Rev.Wash.Code Ann. 90.22 and 90.54 illustrate a related method for the withdrawal of waters from appropriation: the reservation of minimum flows. These statutes provide for the establishment and protection of "minimum flows" and "base flows" by the Department of Ecology. A minimum flow reservation does not withdraw a stream from appropriation; rather it prevents subsequent appropriators from depleting the stream below the minimum flows reserved. The reservation of minimum flows is closely related to the instream flow appropriation, discussed below.

The Montana legislature has created an interesting variation of the minimum flow reservation. The 1973 Water Use Act, Rev.Code Mont. 1983 § 85–2–316, enables the state, the United States, and any political subdivision or agency of either to apply to the Board of Natural Resources and Conservation "to reserve waters for existing or future beneficial uses, or to maintain a minimum flow, level, or quality or water throughout the year * * *." No specified grounds or purposes are required for reservation, and the only limitation was that the reservation be in the public interest. Reservations are subject to periodic review, at least once every 10 years for purposes of extension, revocation or modification.

State of Idaho, Department of Parks v. Idaho Department of Water Administration, supra, p. 23 illustrates a further technique to protect instream uses: the appropriation of water by a state agency to preserve instream flows. This technique was used as early as 1925 in Idaho. Essential developments in the utilization of this technique were the elimination of a diversion as a requirement for an appropriation and the recognition that the protection of instream values is a beneficial use of water. Both of these developments were discussed previously in this chapter.

An example of another technique is found in the Oklahoma Scenic Rivers Act, 82 Okl.Stat.Ann. §§ 1451–1458:

> "**§ 1452.** (a) The Oklahoma Legislature finds that some of the free-flowing streams and rivers of Oklahoma possess such unique natural scenic beauty, water conservation, fish, wildlife and outdoor recreational values of present and future benefit to the people of the state that it is the policy of the Legislature to preserve these areas for the benefit of the people of Oklahoma. For this purpose there are hereby designated certain 'scenic river areas' to be preserved as a part

of Oklahoma's diminishing resource of free-flowing rivers and streams."

* * *

"**§ 1453.** Once an area is designated as a 'scenic river area' it is an expression of legislative intent that the stream or river in the area designated be preserved in its free-flowing condition and that the stream or river shall not be impounded by any large dam or structure except as specifically authorized by the Legislature. No agency or official of state government shall authorize or concur in plans of local, state or federal agencies for the construction, operation, or maintenance of any dam or related project in any 'scenic river area', without legislative consent, except as needed by the municipalities located in the counties or the immediate vicinity of the 'scenic river area' for their own municipal or domestic water supply and where such structures will not significantly interfere with the preservation of the stream as a scenic free-flowing stream."

* * *

The California "free-flowing rivers" statute provides: "It is the policy of the State of California that certain rivers which possess extraordinary scenic, recreational, fishery or wildlife values shall be preserved in their free-flowing state * * *. 'Free-flowing' means existing or flowing without artificial impoundment, diversion or other modification. * * * The following rivers and segments thereof are designated as components of the system * * * Klamath River * * * Trinity River * * * Smith River * * * Eel River * * * American River." West's Ann.Cal.Pub.Res.Code §§ 5093.50 to 5093.69. Certain possibilities remain for flood control work and the use of water for domestic supply.

Other techniques and developments include the denial or conditioning of appropriations to protect instream flows and the expansion of the public trust doctrine. These developments are discussed elsewhere in the book.

Note

Various approaches and developments in the protection of instream values are discussed and evaluated in Tarlock, The Recognition of Instream Flow Rights: "New" Public Western Water Rights, 25 Rocky Mountain Mineral Law Institute 24–1 (1979) and Tarlock, Appropriation for Instream Flow Maintenance: A Progress Report on "New" Public Western Water Rights, 1978 Utah Law Rev. 211 (1978). In addition, the Western Energy and Land Use Team, Office of Biological Services, Fish and Wildlife Service, U.S. Department of Interior in Fort Collins, Colorado has produced and assembled an extensive amount of technical and legal literature relating to the protection of instream values.

ENTERPRISE IRRIGATION DISTRICT v. WILLIS

Supreme Court of Nebraska, 1939.
135 Neb. 827, 284 N.W. 326.

CARTER, JUSTICE. This is a suit for an injunction brought by the Enterprise Irrigation District against Robert H. Willis, chief of the bureau of irrigation, water power and drainage, and A. C. Tilley, state engineer. At the time the suit was commenced the defendants were threatening to close the headgates of plaintiff's irrigation canal for the alleged reason that plaintiff had received all the water to which it was entitled during the irrigation season in question. In its petition the plaintiff asked that the defendants be enjoined from preventing it from diverting all the water that could be put to a beneficial use in the growing of crops. The trial court denied an injunction and plaintiff appeals.

The record discloses that in the year 1889 the Enterprise Ditch Company made an appropriation of water from the North Platte river, in accordance with the law of appropriation then in existence, in an amount in excess of 138.90 second-feet, subject only to the common-law rule that no more water could be diverted and appropriated than could be applied to a beneficial use. Thereafter the Enterprise Ditch Company sold its irrigation works and water appropriation to the plaintiff. Subsequent to the enactment of the irrigation law of 1895, chapter 69, providing for the creation of a state board of irrigation and for filing of claims and adjudication of water rights, a claim for such appropriation was filed with the state board of irrigation claiming an appropriation of 138.90 second-feet of water with a priority date of March 28, 1889. On January 7, 1897, the state board of irrigation entered its order, finding, adjudging and adjudicating that said appropriation was a valid appropriation for 138.90 second-feet of water with a priority of March 28, 1889, limited only by the rule that the amount so diverted should not be in excess of the amount that could be applied to a beneficial use. No appeal was taken from this order.

The irrigation laws of 1877 and 1889, the only ones on the subject at the time of plaintiff's appropriation, place no limitations upon the quantity of water that could be appropriated, save and except that the appropriation must be for some useful or beneficial purpose and within the limits of the capacity of the diversion works. See Laws 1877, p. 168; Laws 1889, c. 68. The irrigation law of 1895 limited for the first time the quantity of water that could be appropriated to a specific amount, the statute stating "that no allotment for irrigation shall exceed one cubic foot per second for each 70 acres of land, for which said appropriation shall be made." Laws 1895, c. 69, § 20. The same act also provided: "Nothing in this act contained shall be so construed as to interfere with or impair the rights to water appropriated and acquired prior to the passage of this act." Laws 1895, c. 69, § 49. In 1911, the legislature placed a further limitation upon the quantity of water that could be appropriated, the statute providing, "that no allotment for irrigation shall exceed one cubic foot per second of time for each seventy acres of land nor *three acre-feet in the aggregate during one calendar year for each acre of land for which such appropriation shall be made.*" Laws 1911, c. 153, § 19. (Italics ours). These same limitations appear in the irrigation law contained in the civil administrative code law of 1919. Laws 1919, c. 190, p. 837. The 1919 law also provided: "Nothing in this article contained shall be so construed as to interfere with or impair the rights to water appropriated and acquired prior to the fourth day of April, 1895." Laws 1919, p. 832. The last two cited sections of the civil administrative code of 1919 remain in force and are designated as sections 81–6311 and 46–506, respectively, Comp.St.1929. It is the contention of the defendants that the limitation of three acre-feet in the aggregate during one calendar year for each acre of land for which the appropriation shall have been made, as contained in section 81–6311, Comp.St.1929, applies to plaintiff's appropriation and, that amount having been exceeded at the time this suit was commenced, the plaintiff was not entitled to any more water and defendants should not be enjoined from closing the headgates of plaintiff's canal. Plaintiff contends that its appropriation is a right vested as of March 28, 1889, and that the statute in question has no retroactive force and, if such retroactive construction be placed upon it, it is violative of the due process clauses of the Constitution of Nebraska (article 1, § 3) and the Fourteenth Amendment to the Constitution of the United States, U.S.C.A. Defendants contend that the statute is a proper exercise of the police power of the state and is not inhibited by either the state or federal Constitutions. * * *

That an appropriator of public water, who has complied with existing statutory requirements, obtains a vested property right has been announced by this court on many occasions. * * * This brings us to the question, whether the subsequent condition imposed, limiting appropriations for irrigable lands to three acre-feet per acre for each calendar year, applies retroactively to appropriations obtained prior thereto, and, if so, is it inimical to the due process provisions of the state and federal Constitutions?

The record discloses that plaintiff had used 3.50 acre-feet of water for every acre of irrigable land in the district when the order was issued to close the headgate. * * *

Many persons engaged in farming within the plaintiff district testified that the water used by them had been used in the usual and ordinary way to produce crops, that there had been no waste or misapplication of the irrigation water, and that, at the time the closing of the headgate was threatened, their crops were in need of water. They also testified that a failure to obtain water would have resulted in a material decrease in the crop returns from their lands.

The defendants produced the evidence of two experts who testified that they had made many experiments as to the amount of water required to grow certain kinds of crops on various kinds of lands, including the types of land found in the plaintiff district. The conclusions of these witnesses were that three acre-feet of water was sufficient to grow the kind of crops raised on the lands within the Enterprise Irrigation district. The experiments testified to were made under conditions very dissimilar from those under which the farmers of the plaintiff district were forced to operate. * * *

It must be borne in mind that the quantity of water that can be diverted under a vested water right for irrigation purposes is an element of importance equal to that of its priority in determining its value. While such a right may be regulated and supervised by the state and its administrative officers for the purpose of protecting all adjudicated rights of appropriators having an interest in the waters of the stream, yet a law of this character cannot operate to divest rights already vested at the time it was enacted. While vested water rights may be interfered with within reasonable limits under the police power of the state to secure a proper regulation and supervision of them for the public good, any interference that limits the quantity of water or changes the date of its priority to the material injury of its holder is more than regulation and supervision and extends into the field generally referred to as a deprivation of a vested right. * * *

The various irrigation acts of this state show an intent on the part of the legislature not to interfere with or impair appropriation rights which vested prior to the enactment of the 1895 irrigation law. Construing these acts in connection with the provision in section 81–6311, Comp.St.1929, limiting the amount of water that could be used in a calendar year to three acre-feet for each irrigable acre, we reach the conclusion that this statutory provision was never intended to have any retroactive effect upon plaintiff's appropriation right which vested in 1889. To place any other construction upon the provision would make it inimical to applicable provisions in the state and federal constitutions. * * *

We conclude that, under the facts presented to the trial court, an injunction should have been granted.

Reversed.

Notes

1. Accord: Quinn v. John Whitaker Ranch Co., 54 Wyo. 367, 92 P.2d 568 (1939). The Wyoming statute allowing one c.f.s. for 70 acres, Wyo.Stat. 1977, § 41–4–317, has been modified, first in 1945 and again in 1985, apparently to protect existing practices of heavy flooding of hay lands. Under the 1945 surplus water act, Wyo.Stat.1977, §§ 41–4–318 to 41–4–324, water flowing in excess of the total amount required by all appropriations existing on March 1, 1945 is surplus water. Each appropriator of the direct flow of the stream having a priority with a date prior to March 2, 1945 is entitled to divert an additional one c.f.s. for each 70 acres if he can apply it to beneficial use. In other words, each appropriation is doubled if the

appropriator can use it, but the surplus water appropriation relates back only to March 1, 1945, not to the original date of appropriation. If there is not enough surplus water to supply all of the surplus rights, all claimants share it.

The 1985 excess water rights act, Wyo.Stat.1985 Supp., §§ 41–4–329 to 41–4–331, applies a similar procedure to direct flow rights having priorities between March 1, 1945 and March 1, 1985. That is, these appropriations are also doubled if there is "excess" water available. Excess water is water not required by rights existing on March 1, 1985, including the 1945 surplus water rights. Excess water rights have a March 1, 1985 priority. Rights granted after March 1, 1985 are subject to both surplus and excess water rights and receive only one c.f.s. for every 70 acres.

2. See Shupe, Waste in Western Water Law: A Blueprint for Change, 61 Ore.L.Rev. 483 (1982) for the view that the constitutional limitations expressed in the principal case are outmoded and can be avoided by the concept of waste ("nonbeneficial use") and the application of forfeiture statutes.

3. A number of other states have statutes which place a definite limit upon the quantity of water which an appropriator can receive for irrigation. So.Dak.Codified Laws 46–5–6, 1 c.f. for 70 acres, or 3 acre feet; Idaho Code § 42–202, 1 c.f.c. for 50 acres. See also West's Ann.Cal.Water Code, § 1004, 2½ acre feet per acre year for the irrigation of uncultivated areas not devoted to cultivated crops.

Nevada and New Mexico have repealed their former fixed statutory limitations. Nev.Rev.Stat. 533.070, N.Mex.1953 Comp.Laws § 72–5–18. The New Mexico law now reads: "In the issuance of permits to appropriate water for irrigation or in the adjudication of rights to the use for such purposes the amount allowed shall be based upon beneficial use and in accordance with good agricultural practices and the amount allowed shall not exceed such amount. The State Engineer shall permit the amount allowed to be diverted at a rate consistent with good agricultural practices and which will result in the most effective use of available water in order to prevent waste." In Reynolds v. Niccum, 102 N.M. 330, 695 P.2d 480 (1985), Niccum questioned the propriety of the procedure used by the State Engineer under this statute. In upholding the State Engineer, the court described the procedure as follows:

"The State Engineer, to determine the correct water duty, prepared a hydrographic survey which grouped users according to the source of their water rights. Using a nationally recognized and proven formula, the State Engineer allotted water duty along each stream. The formula was developed to determine 'consumptive use' water by irrigated crops. See Determining Water Requirements For Settling Water Disputes, 4 N.R.J. 29 (1964). The formula uses a procedure to estimate water requirements and may be used to:

> transpose observed consumptive use data from one area to other areas for which only climatological data are available. The amount of water supplied from natural sources is subtracted from the computed total consumptive use, giving the net consumptive irrigation water requirement that must be met for optimum crop production. This net

requirement, divided by the irrigation efficiency, gives the irrigation water requirement of the crop.

Id. at 31. The numbers used in the formula were based on the average needs of the group of users along each stream, not on the needs of one particular stream user.

"After reviewing the formula, the methodology used, and after receiving evidence concerning climate and soil variations, both special masters found that the averaging of water duties of users along a particular source stream was an appropriate and reasonable procedure for determining Niccum's water duty."

In Kansas, which straddles the boundary between arid and humid zones, the administrative allowance is 2 acre feet per year in the western section, 1½ in the central part, and 1 near the eastern boundary. Smrha, Problems of Water Administration in Kansas, 5 Kans.L.Rev. 649, 655 (1957).

4. "Although the expression 'Duty of Water', in the opinions of some present-day scholarly hydrologists and technical engineers, may be outmoded, provincial, unscientific, and otherwise objectionable, nevertheless it is a term well understood and accepted by every rancher and farmer who has had practical experience in the artificial irrigation of land for the production of crops. It is that measure of water, which, by careful management and use, without wastage, is reasonably required to be applied to any given tract of land for such period of time as may be adequate to produce therefrom a maximum amount of such crops as ordinarily are grown thereon. It is not a hard and fast unit of measurement, but is variable according to conditions. In their briefs, counsel for respondents refer to the case of Trinchera Ranch Co. v. Trinchera Irrigation Dist., 83 Colo. 451, 459, 460, 266 P. 204, asserting that we therein set up standards of evidence in such type of cases. These were not intended as essential elements of proof, but only as suggestions of matters properly to be considered in determining the duty of water. Land characteristics at the place of use are important; location; slope; depth of soil; whether it is loose or close; if underlain with gravel or impervious material; its composition and general adaptability for the growing of irrigated crops; all are taken into consideration. Climate is a feature not to be overlooked, as also are the kinds of crops ordinarily grown thereon and the proportion of the area devoted to each type of crop and the rotation thereof. In fact, every element that concerns or affects the consumption of water in the particular case before the court is to be considered." Farmers Highline Canal & Reservoir Co. v. City of Golden, 129 Colo. 575, 272 P.2d 629, 634 (1954).

5. Reservoirs require special rules. Since the purpose of constructing large reservoirs is to balance out the lean and the fat years, the courts have been liberal in allowing "carryover storage." Federal Land Bank v. Morris, 112 Mont. 445, 116 P.2d 1007 (1941), East Side Canal and Irrigation Co. v. U.S., 76 F.Supp. 836 (Ct.Cl.1948). In Idaho storage rights for irrigation are limited to 5 acre feet per year. Idaho Code § 42–202. In most states the quantity allowed is governed by the capacity of the reservoir, what it will hold as a result of a single filling, not what it can be made to hold by successive fillings and emptyings. Windsor Reservoir and Canal Co. v.

Lake Supply Ditch Co., 44 Colo. 214, 98 P. 729 (1908). The one-filling rule is usually applied so that if at the beginning of a particular "water year" a reservoir is partly full with carryover storage, only the balance needed to fill it can be taken during that year. This works fairly well where spring runoff is stored for use during a short irrigation season, but the rule can require unnecessary construction of excess storage capacity if the demand for water from the reservoir is constant throughout the year, as for a city or industry, since it prevents the use of a small regulating facility that can be filled, partially drained and refilled to take full advantage of predictable river fluctuations. Compare Wheatland Irrigation District v. Pioneer Canal Co., 464 P.2d 533 (Wyo.1970). The rule has also played a part in preventing efficient use of a single reservoir by not permitting the capacity that is left unfilled under one priority to be used to hold water available under another priority or from another source. Orchard City Irrigation District v. Whitten, 146 Colo. 127, 361 P.2d 130 (1961). Compare Denver v. Northern Colorado Water Conservancy District, 130 Colo. 375, 276 P.2d 992 (1954), where the one-filling rule, added to the pioneer rule that the capacity of the ditch is the top measure of a water right, was used to block an imaginative feat of modern engineering. Denver filed a map and statement showing a diversion of 1600 cubic feet of water per second through a tunnel under the Continental Divide. This quantity of water was available only during short periods of spring run-off. Later it was planned to save a major portion of construction costs by building a smaller tunnel that would carry only 788 second feet, and to accumulate the water in a reservoir at the rate of 1600 second feet when there was that quantity flowing in the river and then run it through the smaller tunnel as fast as the latter would carry it off. The reservoir was the Dillon Dam which had a late storage priority for its full capacity. "One cannot add water to a full cup, and may not have a second decree for water from the same source to be held at the same time in the same reservoir to which a decree has already been ordered to its full capacity. Further, the rule is elementary that the first essential of an appropriation is the actual diversion of the water with intent to apply to a beneficial use. * * * Water can be actually diverted only by taking it from the stream. The amount so diverted is necessarily limited to the capacity of the ditch or tunnel through which diversion is made. * * * Where water is stored in a channel reservoir, a ditch headed in such reservoir has no right by virtue of direct use decree to deplete such storage. * * *"

Three dissenting judges pointed out that with its late priority the reservoir, as a practical matter, would never be full when the proposed diversion of 1600 second feet was being made. "Thus the illustration of the 'full cup' fails to hold water. * * * Unquestionably the city of Denver would have the right to appropriate the 1600 cubic feet per second of water by the construction of a tunnel of that capacity. This objective could be obtained with no grounds for opposition by the expenditure of an additional $10,000,000 of the peoples' money. If the same result can be obtained by the substitution of a mechanical operational equivalent to the larger tunnel I am at a loss to understand why the increased burden on the taxpayers should be required. * * * In all normal operations the Dillon Dam would serve two functions: (1) as a headworks for diverting Denver's direct appropriation through the tunnel; and (2) for catching an occasional flood in the late summer. * * * There is no reason why the Dillon Dam cannot fulfill in succession both the diverting and the storage functions."

6. Trelease, Preferences to The Use of Water, 27 Rocky Mountain Law Review, 133, 138–140 (1955):

"Obviously a water supply for a city must keep a step ahead of the needs of its inhabitants; a city cannot obtain water from day to day as demand increases. A city without some excess water or promise of water cannot grow, and typically municipal supplies are procured in large amounts that exceed present needs and permit expansion. This fact is recognized in the statutes of several states that allow municipalities to apply for permits to appropriate water for future requirements, and the courts in other states have permitted such appropriations to satisfy the needs resulting from population increases. The Colorado court has suggested limits on this doctrine that are probably implicit in all these statutes and cases: the appropriation should take care of a normal increase within a reasonable period of time.

"In most of these states there is no express requirement that the water be put to immediate beneficial use, and such appropriations may be regarded as exceptions to the rule of beneficial use or as extensions of the doctrine of 'relation back,' which gives the appropriator a reasonable time within which to put the water to use without loss of priority. To this extent such appropriations reserve the water for the use of the community, and its eventual application to beneficial use constitutes the exercise of a preference over intervening appropriators who have been using the water in the meantime. On the other hand, California and Colorado do not permit such a bare claim and require that the water be put to beneficial use during the time when no municipal use is being made of it. Colorado statutes allow the water to be leased to irrigators in the interim; in California the water may be given to irrigators under temporary permits or to the municipality to dispose of as a public utility. Of course both of these states allow a reasonable time to complete such an appropriation. In a Colorado adjudication proceeding, a city in the process of constructing works may be given a conditional decree by which it receives an inchoate right to water beyond its immediate needs; the exact measure of the appropriation can be definitely adjudicated when the water is finally applied beneficially. The same result is reached in California by the issuance of a permit to make an appropriation that will ripen into a license to divert water to the extent of the actual beneficial use made within the time allowed for completion of the work.

7. There is some evidence that the attitude of the Colorado Supreme Court toward the appropriation of water to meet the future needs of municipalities is becoming less generous. In City and County of Denver v. Colorado River Water Conservation District, 696 P.2d 730 (Colo.1985), the record disclosed only that Denver was seeking water rights on the assumption that the growing population on the eastern slope of the Rockies would produce a general need for more water in the future. The court held that Denver could not have formed the necessary intent to appropriate any particular amount of water until it had plans to use that water within its

own boundaries, firm contractual commitments to supply that water to users outside its boundaries, or agency relationships with such users. The court remanded the case to the lower court to take evidence on these matters. The court relied on an earlier decision, Colorado River Water Conservation District v. Vidler Tunnel Water Co., 197 Colo. 413, 594 P.2d 566 (1979). In that case, the court denied a conditional decree to a private corporation which sought to divert water from the western slope to the eastern slope of the Rockies for sale to municipalities because the corporation had no contract or agency relationship with municipalities "justifying its claim to represent those whose future needs are asserted."

SALT RIVER VALLEY USERS' ASSOCIATION v. KOVACOVICH

Arizona Court of Appeals, 1966.
3 Ariz.App. 28, 411 P.2d 201.

EDWIN THURSTON, SUPERIOR COURT JUDGE. These actions, consolidated for purpose of appeal, were brought by appellant in the Yavapai County Superior Court seeking a permanent injunction against appellees to enjoin the use of waters of the Verde River upon certain land situate in Yavapai County, and asking for determination with respect to whether or not valid and existing water rights were legally existing appurtenant to such land. In the basic actions, each of the parties filed motions for summary judgment and each motion submitted to the lower court upon an agreed statement of facts together with supporting memoranda and exhibits. The statement of facts agreed to by the parties is as follows:

1. That the defendants and their predecessors in interest have made valid appropriations of water from the Verde River for irrigation purposes upon a portion of the lands owned by them;

2. That prior to 1933 in the Kovacovich action and prior to 1950 in the Ward action, certain additional lands owned by the respective defendants were not used for farming purposes nor was irrigation water applied thereon;

3. That neither the defendants nor their predecessors in interest ever made application under the Arizona Water Code to appropriate water for these additional lands;

4. That during and after 1933 in the Kovacovich action and during 1950 in the Ward action, the defendants, respectively, undertook in addition the cultivation of approximately thirty-five (35) acres and forty (40) acres of land adjacent to the land upon which the parties already had a valid water appropriation by irrigating said lands with water from the Verde River; and

5. That because of water-saving practices, no more water was thus used by the defendants to irrigate all of their lands here involved than was formerly used upon only their lands with a valid water appropriation.

The lower Court denied injunctive relief in each action and confirmed the right of appellees to beneficially use, as presently used, that quantity of water used by the appellee Kovacovich during or prior to 1933 and by the appellee Ward during or prior to 1950. * * *

In essence this case involves the narrow issue of whether or not an owner of land having a valid appurtenant water right may through water-saving practices apply the water thus saved to immediately adjacent lands owned by that person, without need to apply for the right to use such additional waters under the State Water Code. The further issue is that since the application of such waters would not result in less quantity of water flowing to the use of the appellants herein as owners of lower and subordinate water rights than would have previously occurred, have appellants been damaged whereby they are entitled to injunctive relief?

It was argued that decision of this issue in favor of appellants would result in penalizing persons who, through their industry, effort and expenses, engage in water-saving practices. The water-saving practices here referred to include improvement of ditches and concrete lining of ditches. This Court is of the opinion that the water-saving practices entered into by appellees not only result in conservation of water but also other benefits to appellees such as weed and vegetation growth control along such irrigation ditches and reduction of time and cost of maintenance of such ditches. Certainly any effort by users of water in Arizona tending toward conservation and more economical use of water is to be highly commended. However, commendable practices do not in themself create legal rights.

Historically, the development of water rights in Arizona created confusion by attempts to apply some of the strict concepts of common law riparian rights to the peculiar circumstances of not only the use of water but the need for its economical use prevalent in Arizona. The confusion concomitant with early attempts to apply the law with respect to use of water in Arizona progressed through several stages, including that where the right to use water appeared to be vested in the owner of land whereby same could be traded, leased or sold in much the same manner as other property. In an effort to achieve some degree of order out of the chaos then existing, our Courts through a series of decisions developed and applied what we today refer to as the "Doctrine of Beneficial Use." This doctrine is clearly enunciated in Gillespie Land & Irrigation Co. v. Buckeye Irr. Co. et al., 75 Ariz. 377, 384, 257 P.2d 393, 397, 398 (1953).

"Slosser v. Salt River Valley Canal Co. [7 Ariz. 376, 65 P. 332], supra; Gould v. Maricopa Canal Co., 8 Ariz. 429, 76 P. 598; Brockman v. Grand Canal Co., 8 Ariz. 451, 76 P. 602; Tattersfield v. Putnam, 45 Ariz. 156, 41 P.2d 228; Olsen v. Union Canal & Irr. Co., 58 Ariz. 306, 119 P.2d 569. The holding in all of these cases is to the effect that a water right is attached to the land on which it is beneficially used and becomes appurtenant thereto, and that the right is not in any individual or owner of the land. It is in no sense a floating right, nor can the right, once having attached to a particular piece of land, be made to do duty to any other land, with certain exceptions, e.g., where the land is washed away."

This doctrine was further implemented by enactment of a series of statutes, today referred to as the State Water Code, wherein matters pertaining to application of waters to new lands or changes in use of waters previously appropriated was placed under the jurisdiction of the Arizona State Land Department. In addition these statutes prescribe certain standards to be followed by the State Land Department with respect to applications for acquisition of change in the use of water. Title 45, Chapter 1, Articles 1–6, Arizona Revised Statutes.

This Court is of the opinion that the Doctrine of Beneficial Use precludes the application of waters gained by water conservation practices to lands other than those to which the water was originally appurtenant. * * * Under the doctrine of beneficial use, the appellees are not entitled under all circumstances to appropriate a given number of acre feet of water per year. Beneficial use is the measure and limit to the use of water. A.R.S. § 45–201, subsec. B. The appellees may only appropriate the amount of water from the Verde River as may be beneficially used in any given year upon the land to which the water is appurtenant even though this amount may be less than the maximum amount of their appropriation. They may not take a quantity of water in excess of their appropriation even though they could beneficially use the same upon water right land. If in a given year, this should constitute an appropriation and use of all the water available at that particular point on the Verde River, subordinate owners of water rights have no cause to complain. However, in those years when water in excess of that which appellees may beneficially use upon the appurtenant land to which their water right attaches, all water which may flow to lower and subordinate owners of water rights is no longer of concern to appellees. Any practice, whether through water-saving procedures or otherwise, whereby appellees may in fact reduce the quantity of water actually taken inures to the benefit of other water users and neither creates a right to use the waters saved as a marketable commodity nor the right to apply same to adjacent property having no appurtenant water rights. It is believed that any other decision would result in commencement of return to the very area of confusion and chaos which gave rise to the development and application of the concept of beneficial use.

The judgment of the lower Court is reversed with instructions to the lower Court to issue an injunction on behalf of appellant as against appellees as prayed for in appellant's complaints.

Notes

1. What is the nature of the "water right" in *Kovacovich?* A right to divert a quantity of water or a right to irrigate land?

2. Not all states follow *Kovacovich.* Colorado and Utah permit an appropriator to enlarge the lands under irrigation if it can be shown that the expanded use will not result in injury to other appropriators. In both states the statutory change in use procedures (transfer procedures), examined in section 5 of this chapter, are used for this purpose. See, Danielson v. Kerbs, 646 P.2d 363 (Colo.1982); East Bench Irrigation Co. v. Deseret Irrigation Co., 2 Utah 2d 170, 271 P.2d 449 (1954). California codified this approach in 1982 in an effort to promote conservation. See West's Ann.Cal.Water Code §§ 1010, 1011.

3. If the irrigator's ditch is long or dug through porous soil, a considerable amount of water may be lost by evaporation and seepage between the point where it is diverted and the place of use. At which point should the right of the appropriator be measured? A California court, in a controversy between irrigators, stated, "Respondents, as a matter of law, have the right to divert by means of earthen ditches. They cannot be compelled to construct impervious conduits in order that seepage water may be made available to appellant. An appropriator is not compelled either to irrigate in the most scientific manner known or to divert in the most scientific manner known." Tulare Irrigation District v. Lindsay-Strathmore Irrigation District, 3 Cal.2d 489, 45 P.2d 972, 1009 (1935). An Idaho case holds the opposite: "Appellant contends that he cannot apply the full 70 inches to his crops because nearly half is lost as it is conducted from the stream or canal to the place of use. As a result, he is required to draw some 40 more inches from the stream in order to deliver adequate water to the crops. However, the public policy against wasting water prohibits additional diversions to compensate for unreasonable loss. This Court has held that the appropriator must construct flumes, pipes, or other lining if necessary to prevent such unreasonable loss. Accordingly, waters appropriated will be measured for their sufficiency from the point of diversion, not from the place of use." Glenn Dale Ranches, Inc. v. Shaub, 94 Idaho 585, 494 P.2d 1029 (1972).

Is the Idaho court correct in saying that the use of "carriage water" is wasteful? Unless the irrigator can afford to line his ditch, he will not be able to irrigate all of his land. Would that be a waste of land? If he can use carriage water instead of concrete to get the full amount needed on his land, would it be a waste of concrete to line the ditch?

Implicit in *Kovacovich* is the rule that the duty of water is measured at the place of use. *Kovacovich* gives no incentive to the appropriator to save the water. Does this mean that the carriage water in other Arizona ditches will go to waste even though, as in *Kovacovich,* it is worth saving?

4. What is waste of water? See National Water Commission, Water Policies for the Future 304–305, 1973: "Substantial savings can be made through improved efficiency in the use of water for irrigation. * * * For example, a statement submitted to the Commission by the Utah-Idaho Sugar Company at its public conference in Spokane indicates that that Company achieved substantial reduction in water use when it switched in the early 1960's from gravity-flow irrigation to sprinkler irrigation on its Osgood Project in Southeastern Idaho. The U–I Osgood Project consists of approximately 6,000 acres of irrigated land and is not a federal reclamation

project. Prior to the change to sprinkler irrigation, the Commission was told, the project had been 'water hungry.' After the change, which included squaring up fields and other modernizations, an additional 1,000 acres of land could be put under irrigation and the useage of water per acre for irrigation crops was cut in half."

A rancher in a high altitude, northern Idaho valley grows one crop of "wild hay" per year to supply winter feed for his cattle, drawing over 2 acre feet per acre in the short irrigating season, using "wild flood" irrigation methods. An equipment salesman tells him that with pumps and sprinklers he could grow the same or a slightly better crop with one-half the water. He does not buy the pumps and sprinklers. Is he wasting water?

On the plains downstream from the rancher, the U–I Company could grow sugar beets of higher cash value than the hay grown by the rancher. Because of his early priority, however, the rancher gets the water. Is this waste?

5. In Colorado v. New Mexico, 459 U.S. 176, 103 S.Ct. 539, 74 L.Ed.2d 348 (1982), the State of Colorado sought a declaration that some water in the small Vermejo River was available for appropriation in that state, even though essentially all of the water in the stream was diverted and consumed downstream in New Mexico. O'Connor and Powell, JJ., concurring in a judgment sending the case back for further findings, stated:

"In this case, the Special Master has cast an accusatory finger at the Vermejo Conservancy District, concluding that '[t]he system of canals used to transport the water to the fields is inefficient.'

"Undoubtedly, there is evidence in the record indicating that large losses of water occur through seepage and evaporation in transporting waters of the Vermejo through open ditches for irrigation and stock watering. It is a leap, however, from observing that large losses occur to concluding, as Colorado would have the Court do, that the practices of the Conservancy District are wasteful or unreasonable. As the Court observes, the extent of the duty to conserve that may be placed upon the user is limited to measures that are 'financially and physically feasible,' Wyoming v. Colorado, 259 U.S. 419, 484, 42 S.Ct. 552, 564, 66 L.Ed. 999 (1922), and 'within practicable limits.' Ibid.[2] Nevertheless, in concluding that the Conservancy District's distribution system is 'inefficient,' the Special Master made no factual finding that improved economy in that system is within the practicable means available to the District."

6. Water Policies for the Future, supra, p. 1, at p. 305: "It must not be assumed, however, that all irrigation water in excess of consumptive use is lost to the system. In many cases, perhaps most cases, the water is returned to the stream as stream flow or serves to recharge ground water. Some excess water is needed in almost all irrigated areas to leach salts from the soil."

2. It is significant to note that in Wyoming v. Colorado, 259 U.S. 419, 42 S.Ct. 552, 66 L.Ed. 999 (1922), upon which the Court relies for the proposition that an affirmative duty to conserve may be imposed on the States, ante, at 546, the Wyoming appropriators *already* had storage facilities in place for equalizing the river's natural flow.

7. California State Water Resources Control Board, Permit Term No. 12:

"**Title:** Continuing Authority—Water Rights

"**When Used:** All permits

"**Term:** Pursuant to California Water Code Section 100, all rights and privileges under this permit and under any license issued pursuant thereto, including method of diversion, method of use, and quantity of water diverted, are subject to the continuing authority of the State Water Resources Control Board in accordance with law and in the interest of the public welfare to prevent waste, unreasonable use, unreasonable method of use, or unreasonable method of diversion of said water.

"This continuing authority of the Board may be exercised by imposing specific requirements over and above those contained in this permit with a view to minimizing waste of water and to meeting the reasonable water requirements of permittee without unreasonable draft on the source. Permittee may be required to implement such programs as (1) reusing or reclaiming the water allocated; (2) restricting diversions so as to eliminate agricultural tailwater or to reduce return flow; (3) suppressing evaporation losses from water surfaces; (4) controlling phreatophytic growth; and (5) installing, maintaining, and operating efficient water measuring devices to assure compliance with the quantity limitations of this permit and to determine accurately water use as against reasonable water requirements for the authorized project. No action will be taken pursuant to this paragraph unless the Board determines, after notice to affected parties and opportunity for hearing, that such specific requirements are physically and financially feasible and are appropriate to the particular situation."

In Environmental Defense Fund, Inc. v. East Bay Municipal Utility District, 26 Cal.3d 183, 161 Cal.Rptr. 466, 605 P.2d 1 (1980), the California court held that the State constitutional prohibitions against waste, unreasonable use and unreasonable method of use (West's Ann.Cal. Const. Art. 10, § 2) gave persons other than appropriators the right to complain against unreasonable and wasteful diversions. Private persons and organizations with an interest in preserving instream values of recreational opportunities, scenic beauty, stream fishing, wild river enjoyment and whitewater rafting sued to require that a large diversion from a river much used for recreation be moved downstream where these activities would be undisturbed. Although the project had received a permit to appropriate the water, the Water Resources Control Board had retained jurisdiction under a permit condition similar to the above. The court held that a complaint alleging that this constitutes an unreasonable method of diversion stated a cause of action, and that the courts had concurrent jurisdiction with the Board to enforce the constitutional prohibition.

8. Is the elimination of "waste" by government fiat a good policy? Reconsider the materials on page 9 to 12. Consider also the following views:

"With careful planning, none of the problems associated with reducing wasteful water rights is insurmountable. Legislatures can formulate measures, if required, to make resource tradeoff decisions and to distribute the cost of modernization through all sectors of the economy. There are indeed prices to be paid, but they must not be allowed to overshadow the need for proper water management. As growth continues in the arid West, the quality of life in the region will depend on maintaining a reliable water supply and natural streamflows. Without a commitment to efficient water use, not only will segments of the agricultural industry be threatened by increased problems of erosion and salinity, but all sectors of the economy could be undermined by the resulting water constraints. Consequently, the time has come for state governments to implement the move to water conservation." Shupe, Waste in Western Water Law: A Blueprint for Change, 61 Ore.L.Rev. 483, 521 (1982).

"Many writers seem to view the statutory and judicial prohibition of 'waste' with approval and argue that water should be put to 'beneficial' use. It is somewhat difficult to understand this position. The logic of the situation is the same as in the case of statutory preferences or the loss of water rights through non-use. It is not clear why a person should not be free to use his own property as he sees fit, providing losses are not imposed upon others. If water rights are salable, and if protection is provided to third parties, it is difficult to see how the problem of waste would become important. To deny rationality in the use of one's own water right is to question the basis of private decisions in the use of all resources. The problem here is to define water rights in such a way that they do become real property and susceptible to market allocation by the forces of supply and demand.

"The California case of *Chow v. Santa Barbara* [3] can be used to illustrate judicial judgments on waste of water. Chow, as a riparian water user, had used for many years the flood waters of a stream for leaching purposes on his riparian lands. In 1933 the California Supreme Court declared this use of water to be unreasonable and also wasteful:

> [I]t is the established law of this state that as between riparian proprietors the right of each as against the other is confined and restricted to the amount of water reasonably necessary for useful and beneficial riparian purposes.
>
> The duty not to commit waste is enjoined on all users of water.

As a result the city of Santa Barbara was allowed to appropriate the 'waste' waters formerly used by Chow *without* any compensation.

"There is probably little doubt that the economic worth of the water to the city exceeded the value of the water for leaching purposes. What is important here is that (1) the court took the responsibility of saying that the well-established practice of leaching was wasteful and unreasonable, and that (2) Chow was deprived of his use of water without compensation. If Chow's property right had been clearly defined, the city of Santa Barbara could have purchased that right in the ordinary manner of transfer of property. This case invites reflection upon the application of riparian law and upon the efficacy of judicial decision-making." Milliman, Water Law and Private Decisionmaking: A Critique, 2 J. Law & Econ. 41, 50–51, copyright 1959 by the University of Chicago.

3. Chow v. City of Santa Barbara, 217 Cal. 673, 22 P.2d 5 (1933).

LEMMON v. HARDY

Supreme Court of Idaho, 1974.
95 Idaho 778, 519 P.2d 1168.

McQuade, Justice.

This action arises out of a dispute over the priority to the use of certain waters of Box Canyon Creek in Gooding County, Idaho. On June 19, 1969, the appellants, George Lemmon and Norman Standal, filed an application for water permit no. 36–7066 to divert 400 cubic feet of water from Box and Blind Canyon Creek. The application stated that the purpose of the diversion was for fish propagation, and that the water would be applied to land leased from the Idaho Power Company and/or Magic Springs, Inc. Notice of the application was published and the respondent Richard M. Kaster filed a protest.

On October 8, 1969, the respondents, Earl M. Hardy and Richard Kaster, were declared the successful bidders on the same Idaho Power Company property which the appellants had claimed as a leasehold in their application for a water permit. The respondents filed an application for water permit no. 36–7091 on October 27, 1969, for the diversion of 300 cubic feet of water from Box Canyon Creek for fish propagation. The application stated that the water was to be applied to the land purchased from the Idaho Power Company. Protests to the application were filed by the appellants.

On November 26, 1969, the appellants filed an "amended application" for permit no. 36–7066 for a total of 400 cubic feet of water from Box and Blind Canyon Creeks. * * * The amended application changed the point of diversion and place of use of the water. Protests against the amended application were filed by the respondents.

The Department of Water Administration (hereinafter referred to as the Department) consolidated all the above protests and a hearing was held before the Director of the Department (hereinafter referred to as the Director) on October 19, 1970. Findings of fact, conclusions of law and an order were issued by the Director on April 28, 1971, which found that there was insufficient water available to satisfy both applications. The Director ordered that both applications be approved and water permits issued, but that the appellants' priority date to the use of the water be postdated from the date of their original application of June 19, 1969, to the date of their amended application of November 26, 1969. The respondents' priority date remained October 27, 1969.

* * * The respondents' protests were filed on the basis that the appellants' application for a water permit was not filed in good faith but for speculative purposes.

* * * The Director quotes extensively from *Kinney* on irrigation and water rights in reaching the conclusion that it is not speculation to file an application for a water permit without possessing any legal right to the use of the property designated as the point of diversion and place

of use. The quotations include the statement that "Even trespassers upon the lands owned by others may make valid appropriations of water * * *." [a] The Director concluded that trespassers may make valid appropriations of water in Idaho and he cited the cases of Mahoney v. Neiswanger; [b] Sarret v. Hunter [c] and First Security Bank v. State of Idaho [d] to support his conclusion. All three cases are limited on their facts to appropriations that were made on unsurveyed federally owned land. *Kinney* states that a "* * * settler upon the unsurveyed lands of the United States has never been regarded as a trespasser * * *." The cases clearly do not support the broad proposition that all trespassers may establish valid water rights.

Furthermore in the case of Bassett v. Swenson [e] it was held that,

> "It is quite generally held that a water right initiated by trespass is void. That is to say, one who diverts water and puts it to a beneficial use by aid of a trespass does not, pursuant to such trespass, acquire a water right. Any claim of right thus initiated is void."

The *Bassett* case involved a trespass upon land privately owned. The rule as to trespass and water rights in Idaho appears to be that a water right initiated on the unsurveyed public domain is valid, but a water right initiated by trespass on private property is invalid.

In the case at bar the land designated as the point of diversion and place of use in appellants' original application was private property not owned by the appellants and therefore no valid water right could be developed on it. Since no valid water right was possible, it can be concluded that the application was filed for speculative purposes, not for development of a water right.

The Director also relied on the cases of Marshall v. Niagara Springs Orchard Co.[f] and Bassett v. Swenson in holding that it was not speculation to file an application for the use of water on designated land without a possessory interest in the land. Both cases involved power companies that filed applications for the use of water before obtaining the land for the point of diversion and power facilities by condemnation. It was held that filing an application without land ownership did not invalidate the application as long as the description of the diversion works was not obtained through trespass. The *Marshall* and *Bassett* cases are distinguishable from this action. The power companies possessed the power of condemnation which permitted them to acquire the necessary land. They were not seeking land upon which to beneficially use the water, but solely for the power site generation purposes. The appellants in this action had shown no means of acquiring the land stated in their original application.

a. 2 C. Kinney, The Law of Irrigation and Water Rights § 688 at 1190 (1912).

b. 6 Idaho 750, 59 P. 561 (1899).

c. 32 Idaho 536, 185 P. 1072 (1919).

d. 49 Idaho 740, 291 P. 1064 (1930).

e. 51 Idaho 256, 5 P.2d 722 (1931).

f. 22 Idaho 144, 125 P. 208 (1912).

The appellants' filing an application for a water permit with no possessory right in the land designated as the place of use amounted to speculation in and of itself. It is required by I.C. § 42–202 that an application for a water permit set forth,

> "4. The location and description of the proposed ditch, channel or other work and the amount of water to be diverted and used.
>
> * * *
>
> "The application shall be accompanied by a plan and map in duplicate of the proposed works for the diversion and application of the water to a beneficial use, showing the character, location and dimensions of the proposed reservoirs, dams, canals, ditches, pipe lines and all other works proposed to be used by them in the diversion of the water, and the area and location of the lands proposed to be irrigated." (Amended 1973).

Lack of a possessory interest in the property designated as the place of use is speculation. Persons may not file an application for a water right and then seek a place for use thereof.

The Director's order that the appellants' priority date be post-dated to the date of their amended application of November 26, 1969, is correct and the order is affirmed.

Notes

1. The first appropriations in the west were made by persons who were on the public domain of the United States without authority. As to whether such persons were trespassers, see Basey v. Gallagher, 87 U.S. (20 Wall.) 670, 22 L.Ed. 452 (1875). Trespassers on private lands have been held to have made valid appropriations in Seaweard v. Pacific Live Stock Co., 49 Or. 157, 88 P. 963 (1907), where the trespasser later acquired a lease on the lands, and in Smith v. Logan, 18 Nev. 149, 1 P. 678 (1883), where the trespasser was permitted to transfer the water right acquired to other lands, when dispossessed. Ownership of the soil, or possession plus the intent and ability to acquire title, was required in Avery v. Johnson, 59 Wash. 332, 109 P. 1028 (1910), holding that an appropriation could not be dated back to the time the ditches were dug by a squatter on public lands not then open to entry. This rule was applied in Tattersfield v. Putnam, 45 Ariz. 156, 41 P.2d 228 (1935), to hold that public land inadvertently included under and irrigated by the ditch of a neighboring landowner had no appurtenant water right, so a subsequent homesteader of the land acquired no water right to continue the irrigation.

Montana at one time had a statutory requirement limiting appropriations for irrigation to persons owning or in possession of land, but this was omitted in the Code of 1895. See Bailey v. Tintinger, 45 Mont. 154, 122 P. 575 (1912). In Scherck v. Nichols, 55 Wyo. 4, 95 P.2d 74 (1939), one Hill applied for and received permits to appropriate water for use on lands owned by Ryan, his brother-in-law, and Dickinson. He had no interest in any of these lands. He quitclaimed his rights to Ryan, to whom certificates of appropriation were issued for all the lands. Held, Hill was a volunteer acting on behalf of Ryan and Dickinson, and Ryan a volunteer acting as benefactor of Dickinson, and by ratification of the landowners the rights attached to the lands.

2. A full discussion of the capacity of various persons and entities to appropriate water is found in 1 Hutchins, Water Rights Laws in the Nineteen Western States 238–269 (1971).

3. "The general rule, in any event, is that one at least rightfully in possession of land, even though not the owner, may make a valid appropriation in connection with such land, which water right remains his property and does not become the property of the landowner. * * * A lessee, then, can make an appropriation in his own behalf, which is his property unless he is acting as agent for the lessor; and his right to transfer the appropriation to other land on the conclusion of his lease will then depend upon the State rule governing transfers of place of use and perhaps point of diversion, and upon the physical feasibility of making the change." Hutchins, Selected Problems in the Law of Water Rights, (1942) p. 311.

In Department of State Lands v. Pettibone, ___ Mont. ___, 702 P.2d 948, (1985) the Montana Supreme Court held that, because of the special fiduciary duties of the state toward school lands, title to an appropriation made by a lessee of school lands was vested in the state and could not be alienated by the state without receiving full compensation. In dicta, the court also announced a more general rule that appropriations made by a lessee stay with the leasehold lands when the lessee departs unless there are express provisions to the contrary.

4. It was early decided that an alien might appropriate water on the public domain although he was not eligible to acquire the land by homestead. Santa Paula Water Works v. Peralta, 113 Cal. 38, 45 P. 168 (1896). However, "alien land laws" may, if constitutional, prevent Japanese and other oriental aliens from acquiring appropriations. See McGovney, The Anti-Japanese Land Laws of California and Ten Other States, 35 Cal.L.Rev. 7 (1947), Note, 1 Wyo.L.J. 127 (1947).

5. A related question concerns the appropriator who goes without permission onto the land of another in order to dig a ditch from the stream to his lands. In some jurisdictions such a trespass may void the appropriation or be grounds for denial of a permit. Minton v. Coast Property Corp., 151 Or. 208, 46 P.2d 1029 (1935), certiorari denied 297 U.S. 704, 56 S.Ct. 442, 80 L.Ed. 992, rehearing denied 297 U.S. 727, 56 S.Ct. 573, 80 L.Ed. 1010; Idaho Power Co. v. Buhl, 62 Idaho 351, 111 P.2d 1088 (1941). In Scherck v. Nichols, supra Note 1, it was held that a person contesting the Ryan and Dickinson appropriations could not complain that the rights were initiated by trespass since the trespass would render the water rights voidable only as against the owner of the land. In Oregon, a person may enter another's land for the purpose of locating a point of diversion and surveying the line of ditches and sites for reservoirs. Or.Rev.Stat. 537.320. See also Utah Code Ann.1953, § 73–3–19, and compare Kaiser Steel Corp. v. W.S. Ranch Co., infra p. 114.

6. Could the Izaak Walton League appropriate water for a reservoir to be stocked with fish and opened for public fishing? See Lake Shore Duck Club v. Lake View Duck Club, 50 Utah 76, 166 P. 309, 310, 311 (1917):

"The vital question, then, to be determined is, Can an appropriation of water be made under the laws of this state for the irrigation of unsurveyed, uninclosed, unoccupied public domain of the United States for the sole production of food for wild water fowl, which, when propagated and raised, must, of necessity, be as accessible to capture, destruction, and appropriation to use, by any other person who may see fit to hunt upon the land, as to the person who went through the form of making an appropriation? * * *

"We have searched in vain for any authority in support of appellant's claim of a valid appropriation of the water in controversy. The beneficial use stated in the application is not in question. We are not disposed to hold that any use of water tending to supply man or domestic animals with food is not beneficial. But for the purpose of effecting a valid appropriation of water under the statutes of this state we are decidedly of the opinion that the beneficial use contemplated in making the appropriation must be one that inures to the exclusive benefit of the appropriator and subject to his complete dominion and control."

No other state seems to have placed a similar limitation on appropriations. In Scherck v. Nichols, supra note 1, the Wyoming court (in a different context) stated: " * * * it is not contrary to the policy of this state that a man may apply for the diversion of water for the ultimate use of it by another. * * * A man cannot apply for water, or divert it, for idle purposes. He must claim it, if he wants to separate it from the unappropriated body of water. But the claim need not, we think, be personal in the sense that no one else can reap the benefit thereof." Is the Utah rule of exclusive benefit consistent with *Empire,* supra p. 29. With the appropriation of water by a district or distributing company for use by its consumers?

COFFIN v. LEFT HAND DITCH CO.

Supreme Court of Colorado, 1882.
6 Colo. 443.

HELM, J. Appellee, who was plaintiff below, claimed to be the owner of certain water by virtue of an appropriation thereof from the south fork of the St. Vrain creek. It appears that such water, after its diversion, is carried by means of a ditch to the James creek, and thence along the bed of the same to Left Hand creek, where it is again diverted by lateral ditches and used to irrigate lands adjacent to the last named stream. Appellants are the owners of lands lying on the margin and in the neighborhood of the St. Vrain below the mouth of said south fork thereof, and naturally irrigated therefrom.

In 1879 there was not a sufficient quantity of water in the St. Vrain to supply the ditch of appellee and also irrigate the said lands of appellant. A portion of appellee's dam was torn out, and its diversion of water thereby seriously interfered with by appellants. The action is brought for damages arising from the trespass, and for injunctive relief to prevent repetitions thereof in the future.

The answer of appellants, who were defendants below, is separated into six divisions.

First. A specific denial of all the material allegations of the complaint. * * *

Third, fourth, fifth and sixth are separate answers by individual defendants, setting up a right to the water diverted, by virtue of ownership of lands along the St. Vrain, and in some instances also by appropriations of water therefrom. But it nowhere appears by sufficient averment that such appropriations of defendants making the same were actually made prior to the diversion of water through appellee's ditch.

Demurrers were sustained to all of the above defenses or answers except the first, and exceptions to the rulings duly preserved; trial was had before a jury upon the issues made by the complaint and answer as it then remained, and verdict and judgment given for appellee. * * *

It is contended by counsel for appellants that the common law principles of riparian proprietorship prevailed in Colorado until 1876, and that the doctrine of priority of right to water by priority of appropriation thereof was first recognized and adopted in the constitution. But we think the latter doctrine has existed from the date of the earliest appropriations of water within the boundaries of the state. The climate is dry, and the soil, when moistened only by the usual rainfall, is arid and unproductive; except in a few favored sections, artificial irrigation for agriculture is an absolute necessity. Water in the various streams thus acquires a value unknown in moister climates. Instead of being a mere incident to the soil, it rises, when appropriated, to the dignity of a distinct usufructuary estate, or right of property. It has always been the policy of the national, as well as the territorial and state governments, to encourage the diversion and use of water in this country for agriculture; and vast expenditures of time and money have been made in reclaiming and fertilizing by irrigation portions of our unproductive territory. Houses have been built, and permanent improvements made; the soil has been cultivated, and thousands of acres have been rendered immensely valuable, with the understanding that appropriations of water would be protected. Deny the doctrine of priority or superiority of right by priority of appropriation, and a great part of the value of all this property is at once destroyed.

The right to water in this country, by priority of appropriation thereof, we think it is, and has always been, the duty of the national and state governments to protect. The right itself, and the obligation to protect it, existed prior to legislation on the subject of irrigation. It is entitled to protection as well after patent to a third party of the land over which the natural stream flows, as when such land is a part of the public domain; and it is immaterial whether or not it be mentioned in the patent and expressly excluded from the grant.

The act of congress protecting in patents such right in water appropriated, when recognized by local customs and laws, "was rather a voluntary recognition of a pre-existing right of possession, constituting a valid claim to its continued use, than the establishment of a new one." Broder v. Notoma W. & M. Co., 11 Otto, 274.

We conclude, then, that the common law doctrine giving the riparian owner a right to the flow of water in its natural channel upon and over his lands, even though he makes no beneficial use thereof, is inapplicable to Colorado. Imperative necessity, unknown to the countries which gave it birth, compels the recognition of another doctrine in conflict therewith. And we hold that, in the absence of express statutes to the contrary, the first appropriator of water from a natural stream for a beneficial purpose has, with the qualifications contained in the constitution, a prior right thereto, to the extent of such appropriation. See Shilling v. Rominger, 4 Col. 103. * * *

It is urged, however, that even if the doctrine of priority or superiority of right by priority of appropriation be conceded, appellee in this case is not benefitted thereby. Appellants claim that they have a better right to the water because their lands lie along the margin and in the neighborhood of the St. Vrain. They assert that, as against them, appellee's diversion of said water to irrigate lands adjacent to Left Hand creek, though prior in time, is unlawful.

In the absence of legislation to the contrary, we think that the right to water acquired by priority of appropriation thereof is not in any way dependent upon the *locus* of its application to the beneficial use designed. And the disastrous consequences of our adoption of the rule contended for, forbid our giving such a construction to the statutes as will concede the same, if they will properly bear a more reasonable and equitable one.

The doctrine of priority of right by priority of appropriation for agriculture is evoked, as we have seen, by the imperative necessity for artificial irrigation of the soil. And it would be an ungenerous and inequitable rule that would deprive one of its benefit simply because he has, by large expenditure of time and money, carried the water from one stream over an intervening watershed and cultivated land in the valley of another. It might be utterly impossible, owing to the topography of the country, to get water upon his farm from the adjacent stream; or if possible, it might be impracticable on account of the distance from the point where the diversion must take place and the attendant expense; or the quantity of water in such stream might be entirely insufficient to supply his wants. It sometimes happens that the most fertile soil is found along the margin or in the neighborhood of the small rivulet, and sandy and barren land beside the larger stream. To apply the rule contended for would prevent the useful and profitable cultivation of the productive soil, and sanction the waste of water upon the more sterile lands. It would have enabled a party to locate upon a stream in 1875, and destroy the value of thousands of acres, and the improvements thereon, in adjoining valleys, possessed and cultivated for the preceding decade. Under the principle contended for, a party owning land ten miles from the stream, but in the valley thereof, might deprive a prior appropriator of the water diverted therefrom whose lands are within a thousand yards, but just beyond an intervening divide. * * *

The judgment of the court below will be affirmed.

Notes

1. Prior appropriation began with a rejection of the riparian watershed limitation, see Irwin v. Phillips, supra p. 17. Yet in some states a strong sectionalism has developed along the lines of basin divides, and local politics have produced inroads on the freedom to transfer water from water-rich areas to water-short areas. Consider the following provisions of the California Water Code, relating to state "appropriations" of water and their assignment or release to actual appropriators and to authorization of the Central Valley Project and the California Water Plan:

"Section 10505. No priority under this part shall be released nor assignment made of any application that will, in the judgment of the commission, deprive the county in which the water covered by the application originates of any such water necessary for the development of the county.

"Section 11460. In the construction and operation by the department of any project under the provisions of this part a watershed or area wherein water originates, or an area immediately adjacent thereto which can conveniently be supplied with water therefrom, shall not be deprived by the department directly or indirectly of the prior right to all of the water reasonably required to adequately supply the beneficial needs of the watershed, area, or any of the inhabitants or property owners therein.

"Section 11461. In no other way than by purchase or otherwise as provided in this part shall water rights of a watershed, area, or the inhabitants be impaired or curtailed by the department, but the provisions of this article shall be strictly limited to the acts and proceedings of the department, as such, and shall not apply to any persons or state agencies.

"Section 11462. The provisions of this article shall not be so construed as to create any new property rights other than against the department as provided in this part or to require the department to furnish to any person without adequate compensation therefor any water made available by the construction of any works by the department.

"Section 11463. In the construction and operation by the department of any project under the provisions of this part, no exchange of the water of any watershed or area for the water of any other watershed or area may be made by the department unless the water requirements of the watershed or area in which the exchange is made are first and at all times met and satisfied to the extent that the requirements would have been met were the exchange not made, and no right to the use of water shall be gained or lost by reason of any such exchange."

The California statutes are treated historically and analytically in Johnson, Major Interbasin Transfers—Legal Aspects, National Water Commission Legal Study No. 7, 74–81 (1971).

2. See also the limitation placed on the powers of Colorado water conservancy districts:

" * * * However, any works or facilities planned and designed for the exportation of water from the natural basin of the Colorado river and its tributaries in Colorado, by any district created under this article, * * * shall be designed, constructed and operated in such a manner that the present appropriations of water and in addition thereto prospective uses of water for irrigation and other beneficial consumptive use purposes, including consumptive uses for domestic, mining and industrial purposes, within the natural basin of the Colorado river in the state of Colorado, from which water is exported, will not be impaired nor increased in cost at the expense of the water users within the natural basin. The facilities and other means for the accomplishment of said purpose shall be incorporated in, and made a part of any project plans for the exportation of water from said natural basin in Colorado." Colo.Rev.Stat.1973 § 37–45–118(1)(b)(iv).

This statute translates into a requirement for "compensatory storage," a reservoir which the exporting district must construct on the western slope of the continental divide to replace with stored water the direct flow taken to the eastern slope, even though the water is not needed for present western slope uses. The City of Denver, although a major exporter of Colorado River water, is not bound by this law. Metropolitan Suburban Water Users Association v. Colorado River Water Conservation District, 148 Colo. 173, 365 P.2d 273 (1961). The Colorado constitutional guarantee that the right to appropriate water "shall never be denied" was held not to proscribe this limitation on the powers of an instrumentality of the state in Central Colorado Water Conservancy Dist. v. Colorado River Water Conservation Dist., 186 Colo. 193, 526 P.2d 302 (1974).

3. In Nebraska, an 1895 statute required that unused irrigation water be returned to the river of origin or the Missouri River. Neb.Rev.Stat. § 46–265. In 1936 this was held to prevent interbasin surface water diversions, since it would be impracticable to transport irrigation return flow back across the divide to the river of origin. The decision was perhaps influenced by the drought conditions of the 1930's and a fear that a large irrigation project planned for use of the Platte River in the Blue and Republican river basins might dry up the Platte River valley. Osterman v. Central Nebraska Public Power and Irrigation District, 131 Neb. 356, 268 N.W. 334 (1936). *Osterman* was overruled in Little Blue Natural Resources District v. Lower North Platte Resources District, 206 Neb. 535, 294 N.W.2d 598 (1980). The Court noted that all of Nebraska is ultimately drained by the Missouri River, and ruled that cross-divide divisions are governed by the general statute permitting appropriations wherever there is unappropriated water and the appropriation would not be otherwise detrimental to the public welfare.

4. Texas and Oklahoma have statutes requiring the consideration of in-basin needs before granting permits for out-of-basin diversions. See 82

Okl.Stat.Ann. § 105.12, par. 4; San Antonio v. Texas Water Commission, 407 S.W.2d 752 (Tex.1966).

5. In the absence of statute an appropriation may be made by diverting water with a ditch that taps the stream in one state and carries the water across a state line to a place of use in another state. The courts of the state where the diversion is made will protect the appropriation. Willey v. Decker, 11 Wyo. 496, 73 P. 210 (1903). Most of the western states, however, enacted statutes designed to see that the benefits of water use remained within the state of origin. Limitations on exports of water took a number of forms: absolute embargoes, requirements of specific legislative approval, requirements for a discretionary permit, and (alone or in conjunction with permission for export) a requirement that the receiving state grant reciprocal privileges. Some statutes applied to all sources, others only to streams or to groundwater. See Hutchins, Ellis and DeBraal, Water Right Laws in the Nineteen Western States, 389–396 (1971); Clyde, State Prohibitions on the Interstate Exportation of Scarce Water Resources, 53 U.Colo.L.Rev. 529 (1982). In 1982 this pattern was considerably altered when Sporhase v. Nebraska, 458 U.S. 941, 102 S.Ct. 3456, 73 L.Ed. 2d 1254 (1982) held that the Commerce Clause of the United States Constitution invalidated a Nebraska statute that would have prevented the owner of a farm lying partly in Nebraska and partly in Colorado from piping water from a well on the Nebraska side across the state line to irrigate the Colorado field. The Nebraska statute required an exporter to obtain a permit, issued if the State Department of Water Resources found that the withdrawal would be reasonable, not contrary to the conservation and use of the source and not detrimental to the public welfare, and that the receiving state granted reciprocal rights to use its water within Nebraska. Mr. Sporhase had a common law right to use a share of groundwater on his overlying Nebraska land. Colorado's law forbade all exports of water, and when Sporhase started to irrigate his Colorado land without a permit, the Nebraska Attorney General procured an injunction. On appeal to the United States Supreme Court, the Court ruled that groundwater is an "article of commerce" subject to the potential, though unexercised, regulatory power of Congress, and held that Nebraska could not build into the water right restrictions that unreasonably burden interstate commerce. The Court did indicate a number of factors that might permit some preference for in-state uses. Several states have since amended their laws to give as much protection to local needs as is permissible under the *Sporhase* guidelines. The case, those laws, and other federal limitations on state water law and water rights are considered infra in Chapter 8, at section 1.

CITY AND COUNTY OF DENVER v. NORTHERN COLORADO WATER CONSERVANCY DISTRICT

Supreme Court of Colorado, 1954.
130 Colo. 375, 276 P.2d 992.

[Proceedings for the adjudication of water rights to the Blue River. The Blue, Williams Fork and Fraser rivers are tributaries of the Colorado River, having their headwaters on the western slope of the continental divide. Denver is on the eastern slope. As early as 1914, Denver had made a reconnaissance of the western slope as a possible source of future water. In 1921 it employed a consulting engineer, who began surveys for diversions from the Fraser and Williams Fork. In 1922 he made preliminary surveys in the basin of the Blue, and filed with the State Engineer a map and statement for a transmountain diversion of 1200 c.f.s. through a tunnel headed on a tributary of the Blue. In 1926 another survey showed that a lower tunnel from the Blue itself could capture the water of several more tributaries through collection ditches, and in 1927 another filing was made for a 1600 c.f.s. tunnel at the new site. Several years of geological investigations disclosed unfavorable conditions along the line of the second proposed tunnel and plans were drawn for a third tunnel at about the same site but with a different direction. In 1941 further engineering work showed that a dam and reservoir at Dillon on the Blue River would eliminate the need for collection ditches, and a new filing was made showing the reservoir and a new location for the tunnel, 20 feet lower in elevation and 3500 feet farther down stream. Later, the plan of operation was revised to call for storage of water in the reservoir at the rate of 1600 c.f.s., and releases at a slower rate through a smaller tunnel with a capacity of 788 c.f.s. Work was begun on this tunnel in 1946.

In the meantime, Denver had proceeded to construct diversion works and tunnels for the waters of the Fraser and Williams Fork rivers, and reservoirs and works on the eastern slope to hold and distribute the western slope waters. In other proceedings, it was decreed rights to appropriate waters of the Fraser and Williams Fork.

In this proceeding, Denver claimed 1200 c.f.s. with a priority of 1921 and 400 c.f.s. with a priority of 1927. The Conservancy District resisted this claim and filed a claim for its large storage reservoir farther down on the Blue, with a priority of 1937. The district court allowed this claim, and decreed to Denver a right to 788 c.f.s. with a priority of 1946. Denver appeals.]

STONE, CHIEF JUSTICE. * * * [S]erious questions are raised by Denver's challenge to the priority date awarded the Blue River project in the decree. The basic law is not disputed, to wit: (1) that priority of appropriation shall give the better right as between those using the water for the same purpose; (2) that as to the rights here involved a municipal corporation has no different status from that of an individual or any other party to the proceeding; (3) that although an appropriation is not complete until actual diversion and use, still the right may relate back to the time when the first open step was taken giving notice of intent to secure it; * * * (4) that right to relate back is conditional that construction thereafter was prosecuted with reasonable diligence, and conditional further that there was then "a fixed and definite purpose to take it up and carry it through," State of Wyoming v. Colorado, 259 U.S. 419, 42 S.Ct. 552, 567, 66 L.Ed. 999; * * * and (5), that the questions of reasonable diligence and of fixed and definite purpose are questions of fact to be determined by the trial court from the evidence. * * *

There is no evidence that any work even of survey, on the Blue River project was begun on July 4, 1921, or at any time prior to the summer of 1922. The claim for the 1921 date is based solely on the fact that survey was started on that date on Denver's Williams Fork and Fraser River projects and the contention that those two projects and the Blue River project constitute in fact a single irrigation project, and consequently that in the determination of the date when the first step was taken, and also in the determination of reasonable diligence since such date, the three projects should be considered as a single project.

In determining the date "when the first step was taken," a survey made on the Fraser River or on the Williams Fork would of itself be no evidence of intent to appropriate water from the Blue River. Certainly such a survey in a far distant basin supplying water to another stream would constitute no notice to another appropriator of such intent. The filing of a plat of method of diversion from the Fraser or Williams Fork would be no evidence of intent to appropriate water from the Blue or notice of such intent. Therefore, there is nothing to support the contention that the priority should be dated as of July 4, 1921. At most, the priority for the Blue River project could date back only to the time when the first step was taken in construction of a project on the Blue River.

In determining reasonable diligence, also, we find no ground for holding, as urged by Denver, that the Blue River project, the Williams Fork project and Fraser River project are each units of a single project so that the construction work on those projects and the expenses incurred thereon can be considered as part of the construction of the Blue River project. Denver's claim for its Blue River project was made by survey, plat and filing entirely separate from those of its Fraser and Williams Fork projects. It seeks priority to water from an entirely separate stream, not even confluent with the Fraser River or Williams Fork except to the extent that each is ultimately a tributary of the Colorado River. It seeks water to be diverted from an entirely separate drainage basin. It was surveyed and planned after those projects. It directly affects other claimants who are protestants here but not directly affected by those projects. It is to be carried through an entirely separate conduit,—the Fraser River being diverted through the Moffat Tunnel and the Williams Fork through the Jones Pass Tunnel, and the Blue, as now planned, to be carried in the Montezuma tunnel to be bored through the Continental Divide many miles to the south of the others. Its water rights are here sought to be adjudicated as entirely separate from the rights of those projects. It has even less relation to the Fraser River and Williams Fork projects than to Denver's South Platte water system with which it will share the same river channel and reservoirs. In fact, the only relation between the Blue River project and these other projects is that their several waters may ultimately rest in common filtration and concentration plants, and that by means of exchange they may be used cooperatively for supplying prior rights or filling storage reservoirs such as would be probable in the case of any other independent water right. The priority of appropriation which gives the better right under our Constitution is priority on a stream rather than on a project, and any diligence in construction to permit dating back of priority on the Blue River must be diligence relating to and promoting the Blue River appropriation. No such relation here appears. Therefore, diligence in the prosecution of the Fraser and Williams Fork projects cannot be imputed to the Blue River project. However, the fact that the City of Denver was engaged in the construction of these or other enterprises may properly be considered together with all other evidence as to existing facilities and ability of the city in determination of the issue of reasonable diligence. * * *

During the entire period from 1927 to 1946, substantially all the work done and all the money spent by Denver in connection with its Blue River project was for investigation and exploratory work or work in connection with Eastern Slope reservoirs which were not dependent on any one plan for diversion or even on Blue River water. This and similar evidence before the trial court presented substantial support to the contention of protestants that Denver had no fixed and definite plan and no definite point of diversion prior to * * * 1946, and supported the decree of the trial court consistent therewith.

As to the second question, that of diligence:

In summary, the evidence showed that the * * * plan of 1923 has been abandoned without any construction whatever; that following the filing of the * * * plan in 1927, no evidence of actual excavation work in connection with its proposed tunnel appeared until 1942, some fifteen years later, when a cut was made and a small exploratory tunnel was driven about 400 feet at a place then intended to be the west portal to ascertain the condition of the ground. The proposed location of the portal has since been changed and a part of the excavation has caved in. No other work was performed on the ground until July 1946 when work at the east portal of the tunnel was started. Denver's Chief Engineer testified that "That was the first actual construction work." * * *

It appears that throughout the period from 1936 to 1941 efforts were made by the City to induce the United States Bureau of Reclamation to build the project, but without success. There was no evidence of any effort by Denver to finance the project itself prior to the year 1946, but only of efforts to induce the United States to do so.

To support its contention that this work was sufficient to satisfy the requirements of reasonable diligence, Denver cites Tausig v. Moffat Tunnel Co., 106 Colo. 384, 106 P.2d 363, wherein it was held that surveys, preparation of maps, acquiring of rights of way and options and obtaining a contract for the carriage of water through the Moffat

Tunnel, drilling of test holes, clearing of timber along proposed ditch lines and other similar work was sufficient to satisfy the requirement of reasonable diligence in construction of a ditch leading to the Moffat Tunnel. However, there the party seeking diversion of the water was a private company of apparently limited resources. The dating back was apparently for a period of less than five years, and the decision of this court affirmed the finding of the trial court, holding that there was due diligence; while here, we are asked to hold such that expenditures on the part of a great city, without shown limitation upon its financial capacity, spread out over a period of nearly twenty years would require us to reverse the decision of the trial court and say that such expenditures were evidence of reasonable diligence as a matter of law.

Kinney, in his great work on irrigation, says: "Probably the best definition of the word diligence was given by Lewis, C.J., in rendering the opinion in an early Nevada case, Ophir Silver Min. Co. v. Carpenter, 4 Nev. 534. It is there defined as 'the steady application to business of any kind, constant effort to accomplish any undertaking.' 'It is the doing of an act or series of acts with all possible expedition, with no delay except such as may be incident to the work itself.'" Kinney on Irrigation and Water Rights, Vol. 2, § 735. * * *

It is undisputed that during a period of about twenty years, Denver had not even begun the actual construction of its project and had made no effort whatever as appears from the record towards financing it, but only a laudible but fruitless attempt after nine years of inaction to induce the United States Reclamation Service to finance it for the joint use of Denver and the South Platte Water Users Association. Meanwhile others have worked diligently and long to put a part of this water to actual use. The record before us does not show such conclusive evidence of "steady application" to the business of constructing the project or of such "constant effort to accomplish" it as to require us to hold that the trial court erred in refusal to date back Denver's appropriation, to the loss of such prior users. On the contrary, in order to sustain Denver's claim, we should have to establish as a law of Colorado that a great city or a great corporation, by the filing of a plat of a water diversion plan and the fitful continuance of surveys and exploratory operations, could paralyze all development in a river basin for a period of nineteen years without excavating a single shovel full of dirt in actual construction and without taking any step towards bond issue or other financing plan of its own for carrying out its purpose; that for nineteen years no farmer could build a ditch to develop his farm and no other city or industry could construct a project for use of water in that area without facing loss of their water when and if the city or corporation which filed the plat should actually construct its project. This we cannot do. * * *

[Affirmed.]

MOORE, JUSTICE (dissenting). * * * *To what extent can a claimant of water change his plan of development without that change amounting to a relinquishment of his claim?*

As will be seen from the quotation in De Haas v. Benesch, supra, there are some changes which can be made in the plan of a water development which will not constitute a relinquishment of the project. One criterion for determination of this problem was used by the United States Supreme Court in the case of State of Wyoming v. Colorado, 259 U.S. 419, 42 S.Ct. 552, 66 L.Ed. 999, where the changes planned had to do with the determination of "whether" the would-be appropriator would proceed at all with the diversion project. Such changes are to be distinguished from those which go rather to selection of the most economical or effective means to be employed for the accomplishment of a diversion and use of water, concerning which there already is a fixed and definite intention to take. Once the decision has been made to proceed with the project, continuing investigations and changes are simply evidence of diligence and endeavor to accomplish the greatest good at a minimum of cost to the public, not abandonment of the project. * * * Changes undertaken with the apparent intent to improve or make more efficient or less costly the whole work to be undertaken, should be regarded as the natural diligence of a prudent man rather than the want of constancy in the prosecution of the undertaking. * * *

May a claimant of water offer evidence to show that the water claimed is part of an interrelated system involving other water rights, and, if so, is work on various parts of such interrelated system to be considered in determining the diligence with which each of the component water rights in the system is being developed?

This question must be answered in the affirmative. With respect to the development of a water right to irrigate a single piece of land through a single ditch to which water is diverted through one headgate, it would be obvious that diligence could be shown by reference to work on any, or all, of the three component parts: diversion dam, carrying ditch, or distribution laterals.

As the works become more complex, including, several sources of supply, wider spread uses, and a variety of purposes, a project may cross county lines, irrigation district or irrigation division lines, and different jurisdictional lines for adjudicating the water rights involved. It does not appear that there is any point at which a water system becomes so large that its parts no longer relate to each other in such a way that work on one part may not constitute diligence with respect to completion of the whole including its other parts. It may well be that a single entity may have holdings so extensive that many of them are unrelated to others. In such a case, work on one holding would not constitute work on an unrelated holding.

It appears, therefore, that the test of the extent to which work on one part of a water system may properly relate to another for the purpose of determining due diligence, is whether the parts of the work relate to a single integrated purpose intimately enough that progress on one part has a direct bearing upon another part. What we are really considering is whether or not the work done is within the limits of what is reasonably to be considered as customary to an enterprise unified under single management and in which impairment of any part tends to directly impair the remaining parts, or in which construction of one part directly contributes to the whole which is comprised of other parts.

Much of the evidence which was admitted, and that which was erroneously excluded, established the fact that the city of Denver has one interrelated water system which should have been considered as a whole in so far as the question of reasonable diligence of the city in going forward with the Blue River diversion is concerned. Even without the full delineation of fact which might have been presented had the trial court not restricted evidence to the Blue River unit alone, the only evidence in the record concerning Denver's efforts shows a continuing good faith endeavor to accomplish the appropriation for which she now seeks a conditional decree. * * * The majority opinion comments that: "There was no evidence of any effort by Denver to finance the project itself prior to the year 1946, but only of efforts to induce the United States to do so." Unmentioned is the fact, which every citizen then living well knows, that in 1929 the whole nation trembled and lay prostrate in depression; that the public treasuries were empty; that for years thereafter any attempt to finance such a large undertaking upon the local level would have been sheer folly; and that the only hope for resources sufficient to warrant a start at construction was to seek the financial backing of the United States. In those years all business, both public and private, looked only to Washington for rescue from total collapse.

At about the time when another approach to the financial problem might reasonably have been expected to succeed, World War II broke out and thereafter for several years the productive energies of all the people were concentrated on the war effort. Men and materials were not to be had for any development of this kind, which could possibly wait. Just as soon as the conflict ended and war demands relaxed, construction of the tunnel began, and, despite inadequate financing and disappointments, the city has gone forward with the work.

For the foregoing reasons I am of the opinion that the City and County of Denver is entitled to a conditional decree for 1600 cubic feet per second, with a priority date as of October 19, 1927.

HOLLAND and KNAUSS, JJ., concur in this dissent.

Notes

1. Compare Colorado River Water Conservation District v. Twin Lakes Reservoir and Canal Company, 181 Colo. 53, 506 P.2d 1226 (1973):

"It appears from the record that delays in completion of the enlargement after the 1930 survey were attributable to the size and complexity of the total project; to land acquisition problems; and to financial difficulties. Appellee's project involves an immense collection system of tunnels, ditches, reservoirs, and irrigation canals. In addition, lengthy litigation held up land purchases and certain construction for several years. And finally, all of this was financed with obvious difficulties through a depression and two wars by a relatively small group of private farmers. Under these circumstances, the project as a whole proceeded slowly but not without a showing of reasonable diligence. As long as a water system as a whole is being completed with due diligence, the fact that a small part of it is slow to progress is inconsequential. The priority applies to the total project."

See also Four Counties Water Users Association v. Colorado River Water Conservation District, 159 Colo. 499, 414 P.2d 469 (1966), where the court sustained substantial changes in plans and allowed an early priority based on the original plans, quoting the dissenting, not the majority, opinion in the principal case.

Two more recent cases may indicate a shift to stricter application of the rule of diligence. In Colorado River Water Conservation District v. Denver, 640 P.2d 1139 (Colo.1982) the appropriator produced evidence of litigation, political activities and other efforts to protect conditional water rights and promote its projects, but no on-site work or other activities specifically related to individual projects had been performed. This was held insufficient to establish reasonable diligence. A finding of diligence, said the Court, requires proof of "an intention to use the water, coupled with concrete action amounting to diligent efforts to finalize the intended appropriation. * * * A record which shows only a hope some day to use the water, with prior years of inaction, will not support the claim." In the second case, also entitled Colorado River Water Conservation District v. Denver, 642 P.2d 510 (Colo.1982), the court held that litigation by the holder of a conditional right, opposing the application of others for water rights which would compete for the same water, was not sufficient to show diligence in the completion of its own right.

2. Where a permit is required for an appropriation, the priority date of the appropriation is the date of the filing of the application for permit. Since an application for a permit must be accompanied by detailed maps and statements of information, much planning and surveying must be completed before the application can be filed. A small project, inconsistent with a larger and more complex one, could be initiated and the application filed after much preliminary work was done on the larger but before a filing could be made for it. In New Mexico a notice of intention may be filed, which will fix the date of priority if a formal application for a permit is made within a reasonable time. N.Mex.1953 Comp.Laws § 72–5–1. But the filing date itself may not be the controlling factor. See Young & Norton v. Hinderlider, infra p. 135.

3. Colorado, which has no fixed statutory rule, has had a number of difficult cases in which the "first act" to initiate an appropriation has been disputed. See Four Counties Water Users Association v. Colorado River Water Conservation District, 161 Colo. 416, 425 P.2d 259 (1967) and the cases discussed in notes 7 and 8 p. 29, supra.

4. In a number of states following the permit system, the requirement of due diligence has been crystalized by statutes setting forth a specific time within which the work must be commenced, (6 mos., Reissue Neb.Rev. Stat.1943, § 46–238, (Reissue of 1974) 2 years, Ariz.Rev.Stat. § 45–150) the

physical works must be completed, (five years, N.Mex.Stat.Ann.1978 Laws § 72–5–1, Wyo.Stat.1977, § 41–4–506) and the water applied to beneficial use (five years, Idaho Code, § 42–204). These are often coupled with intermediate standards for testing diligence, such as that one-fifth of the work must be completed within one-half the time allowed. (So.Dak. Codified Laws 46–5–25, see Neb.Rev.Stat.1943, § 46–238 (Reissue of 1984), one-tenth within one year.) Extensions of these periods may be granted by the state water officials upon a showing of "good cause," which usually amounts to much the same as "due diligence." Associated Enterprises, Inc. v. Toltec Watershed Improvement Dist., 578 P.2d 1359 (Wyo.1978). For an extreme case, see Carbon Canal Co. v. Sanpete Water Users Association, 10 Utah 2d 376, 353 P.2d 916 (1960), where the court upheld extensions totaling 36 years, and Carbon Canal Co. v. Sanpete Water Users Association, 19 Utah 2d 6, 425 P.2d 405 (1967), where it finally lost its patience and terminated the permit. In some states, progress reports must be filed with water officials. Nev.Rev.Stat. 533.390.

Although Colorado does not utilize a permit system, it has taken steps to assure that showings of diligence are made on a regular basis. The Colorado statutes require the recipient of a conditional decree, which is functionally similar to an appropriation permit, to obtain a finding of diligence from the water court every fourth year after receiving the conditional right. Colo.Rev.Stat.1973, 37–92–301(4). In Bar 70 Enterprises v. Highland Ditch Ass'n, 694 P.2d 1253 (Colo.1985) the Colorado Supreme Court applied the statute strictly, terminating a conditional right where an application for a finding of diligence was filed only four days late.

5. In determining reasonable diligence, how far can lack of physical progress be excused by financial troubles? (In re Hood River, 114 Or. 112, 227 P. 1065 (1924); Maricopa County Municipal Water Conservation Dist. No. 1 v. Southwest Cotton Co., 39 Ariz. 65, 4 P.2d 369 (1931)). Pioneer difficulties and slowness of settlement? (In re Hood River, supra, Campbell v. Wyoming Development Co., 55 Wyo. 347, 100 P.2d 124 (1940)). Litigation? (Metropolitan Suburban Water Users Association v. Colorado River Water Conservation Dist., 148 Colo. 173, 365 P.2d 273 (1961); Associated Enterprises v. Toltec Watershed Improvement District, supra Note 4). See, generally, 1 Hutchins, Water Rights Laws in the Nineteen Western States 373–389 (1971).

STATE EX REL. CARY v. COCHRAN

Supreme Court of Nebraska, 1940.
138 Neb. 163, 292 N.W. 239.

CARTER, JUSTICE. This is an action of mandamus brought by a number of irrigators under the Kearney canal, on behalf of themselves and others similarly situated, and by the Central Power Company, which, with the exception of one small user of water, is the owner of the oldest water appropriation on the Platte river and its tributaries. The respondents are the governor, the state engineer, and the chief of the bureau of irrigation and his subordinates. The petition prays for the issuance of a writ of mandamus compelling the proper administration and enforcement of the irrigation laws of the state for the purpose of protecting the irrigation and power rights of the relators from alleged unlawful diversions of water above relators' canal by junior appropriators. The trial court denied the writ and dismissed the petition of the relators. Relators thereupon perfected an appeal to this court.

It is not disputed that the waters of the Platte river and its tributaries are subject to appropriation for irrigation and power purposes upon the principle that priority of time bestows priority of right, and that pursuant to such principle the Central Power Company, through its predecessors in interest, was adjudicated and given a priority upon the Platte river, as of September 10, 1882, of 140 cubic feet per second of flow of water for power purposes, and a further appropriation, as of February 12, 1920, of 485 cubic feet per second for the same purposes. It is also admitted by the pleadings that 22 second-feet of water have been adjudicated to certain lands in Buffalo county for irrigation purposes with a priority dating of September 10, 1882, and which, for the purposes of this suit, will be treated as the property of certain of the relators claiming to be the owners thereof in this litigation. The foregoing appropriations of water, bearing the priority dating of September 10, 1882, are prior in time to all appropriations on the Platte river and its tributaries in Nebraska, except an appropriation to the Nelson Radcliffe canal in Morrill county with a priority dating of June 1, 1882, for 2.77 cubic feet of water per second of time. * * *

The respondents, as officers, agents and employees of the bureau of irrigation, are charged by law with the duty of the administration and enforcement of the irrigation laws of the state and the distribution of the waters of the Platte river and its tributaries within the state in accordance with adjudicated priorities. It is the contention of relators that respondents, in administering and enforcing the irrigation laws of the state and in the distribution of water for irrigation, have continuously permitted and allowed junior appropriators, situated above the headgate of the Central Power Company, to take and use water for irrigation, storage, and other purposes, without regard to priority and to the prejudice and damage of the relators. * * *

Losses from evaporation and transpiration are heavy, due to the wide and shallow character of the river. Changes of temperature and varying types of wind add to the uncertainty of the losses resulting from these changing conditions. Losses from percolation vary along the various sectors of the river. * * * Experts with experience on the river estimate that the loss in delivering water from North Platte to the headgate of the Kearney canal with a wet river bed amounts to three times the amount of delivery, and with a dry river bed that it is almost impossible to get water through without a flood or a large sustained flow. In other words, it requires approximately 700 second-feet of water at North Platte to deliver 162 second-feet at the headgate of the Kearney canal when the river bed is wet. The underlying sand and gravel beds thicken as the river moves east. With the bed of the river on the surface of these sand and gravel deposits, it requires a huge amount of water to recharge the river channel and surrounding water table after the river bed once becomes dry. Until the water table is built up to the surface of the river bed, the river channel will not support a continuous flow. * * *

Appropriations of water are made throughout the length of the river. The priority dates of these appropriations have no relation whatever to their location on the stream. Hence, very early appropriations may be found at the upper and lower ends of the stream, while very late appropriations are likewise found at both ends. In times of water shortage, the later appropriators are the first to be deprived of water. The closing of canals in accordance with the inverse order of their priority dates necessarily requires certain canals to close their headgates all along the stream at the same time. Water moves down the stream at approximately 25 miles per day with the result that it requires approximately ten days to deliver water from the state line to the Kearney headgate under normal conditions. The resulting lag therefore becomes an important factor to be considered. * * *

The real question to be decided, however, is the determination of the duty imposed upon the officers of the state in administering the waters of the stream when the available supply of water at the headgate of the Kearney canal is reduced to an amount less than the 162 second-feet to which the relators are entitled. The rights of relators to the use of this water as against all appropriators subsequent to September 10, 1882, cannot be questioned. It is the duty of the administrative officers of the state to recognize this right and to give force to relators' priority. This requires that junior appropriators be restrained from taking water from the stream so long as such water can be delivered in usable quantities at the headgate of the Kearney canal. If it appear that all the available water in the stream would be lost before its arrival at the headgate of the Kearney canal, it would, of course, be an unjustified waste of water to attempt delivery. Whether a definite quantity of water passing a given point on the stream would, if not diverted or interrupted in its course, reach the headgate of the Kearney canal in a usable quantity creates a very complicated question of fact. It therefore is the duty of the administrative officers of the state to determine from all available means, including the factors hereinbefore discussed, whether or not a usable quantity of water can be delivered at the headgate of the Kearney canal. It necessarily follows that this finding of fact must be determined in the first instance by the officers charged with the administration of the stream. The finding of fact thus made is final unless it appears that it was unreasonable or arbitrarily made. The determination of the facts is an administrative function, and an order or course of conduct based thereon raises only the question whether the administrator was supported in his finding by evidence indicating his action was not unreasonable or arbitrary.

After determination that a given quantity of water passing a certain point on the river would not, even if uninterrupted, reach the headgate of the Kearney canal in usable quantities, the administrative officers of the state may lawfully permit junior appropriators to divert it for irrigation purposes. This results ofttimes in having junior appropriators receiving a head of water at a time when an appropriator farther downstream is getting none, though he is prior in time. Such situations are not therefore conclusive evidence of unlawful diversions.

Amici curiae urges that the doctrine of reasonable use is in force in this state and that it should be applied to the case at bar. We recognize the principle that the public has an interest in the public waters of the state and it is the use thereof only that may be appropriated. Even though an adjudicated appropriation may be vested, it may be subjected to regulation and control by the state by virtue of its police power. It may likewise be circumscribed to the extent that a limited diversion for a specified purpose will not permit of an undue interference with the rights of other appropriators on the stream. But we cannot agree that the doctrine of reasonable use can be applied in a case where delivery of a usable quantity of water can be made, although the losses suffered in so doing are great. To permit the officers of the state the right to say whether prospective losses would or would not justify the delivery of usable quantities of water would clothe such officers with a discretion incompatible with the vested interests of the relators, and destroy the very purpose of the doctrine of appropriation existent in this state. When upstream appropriators applied for and received adjudicated priorities, they did so with the knowledge that there was an earlier appropriator at the lower end of the stream whose rights had to be recognized. When the relators applied for and received their adjudications, they are likewise presumed to have known that other appropriators would obtain inferior rights above them that would have to be recognized. Each is required to respect the vested rights of the others, even though some hardships may be thereby imposed. We therefore hold that the doctrine of reasonable use does not extend so far as to authorize the administrator of the waters of the stream to refrain from delivering a usable quantity of water to a senior appropriator because it might appear to him that excessive losses would result. The duty of the administrator, in administering the waters of the stream by virtue of the police power of the state, is to enforce existing priorities, not to determine, change or amend them. But in regulating the distribution of water it may become incidentally necessary for him to ascertain for that purpose only whether a prior appropriator is injured by a diversion above him. This finding of fact must be made, not to change existing priorities, but in order to determine whether or not a distribution of water may be made to a junior appropriator in accordance with existing priorities. * * *

The administration of the waters of the stream must be in accordance with the law announced in this opinion. The administrator testifies to his willingness to so administer the stream and, in fact, contends that he has so administered it. We doubt not that he will endeavor to so administer it in the future. * * * After a consideration of the pleadings, the evidence, and all the circumstances, surrounding the case, we think the trial court was justified in the exercise of such discretion in denying the writ prayed for. We likewise believe that the action will accomplish the desired end without the issuance of the writ at the time and in the form in which it was asked. We therefore hold that the district court did not err in denying the writ.

Affirmed.

Notes

1. The rule of this case has been criticized as an example of waste built into the appropriation doctrine. See Fischer, Western Experience and Eastern Appropriation Proposals, in The Law of Water Allocation in the Eastern United States (Haber and Bergen eds.) 75 (1958); and Maloney, Ausness and Morris, a Model Water Code iv, 77, 158 (1972). But see Trelease, The Model Water Code, the Wise Administrator and the Goddam Bureaucrat, 14 Nat.Res.J. 207 (1974):

"The 'waste' caused by the downstream senior on the dwindling stream should concern the easterner not at all. His streams gain water throughout their length, they do not lose it to desert soils. That such waste exists, even in the west, is doubtful. * * * A waste of 538 c.f.s.? The richer lands are at Kearney, and perhaps more can be produced there, at least the North Platte irrigators have never seen fit to buy out the Kearney irrigators. A better explanation is that the 538 c.f.s. feed the alluvial aquifer underlying a vast sea of corn and alfalfa that stretches along the valley, irrigated by thousands of wells. At any rate, the fault is not that of prior appropriation law but of historical accident." [4]

2. Trelease, Climate Change and Water Law, in Climate, Climatic Change and Water Supply (Wallis, Ed., National Research Council, National Academy of Sciences, 1977):

"The rule of priority operates even in a normal year, not only in time of shortage. On an unregulated stream (one without storage dams) from which many irrigators draw water, all may open their ditches in the spring as the mountain snowpacks melt and the stream is high. As the flow decreases during the dry summer, the diversion works are shut off in inverse order of priority. The last ditch is first closed; the first need never be. The entire burden of the lessened flow falls on the junior appropriator. He loses all his water; the senior, none. Some have called this a harsh rule, but it should be remembered that the low flow is insufficient for all, and that equal shares for everybody would be sufficient for none. The rule of priority does guarantee a firm supply to all for whom the source is

4. Nebraska was settled from east to west as the homesteaders encroached on Indian territory, so the early priorities are in the downstream east. In Colorado, however, the lands at the foot of the Rockies were settled first so the senior rights are there, and the downstream lands were settled later as the junior appropriators pushed eastward against the Cheyennes of the Smoky Hills.

sufficient, and the senior irrigators can build a stable agriculture unmatched in humid climes. The junior appropriator is not unlike the farmer in a semihumid area who must take his chances on rain. If he can only count on spring flood water, he will grow one crop of wild hay and will not plant a late maturing crop like sugar beets. The senior may grow an orchard or a vineyard, the junior will plant corn, since he may gamble on the loss of an annual crop but not of a permanent investment.

"Since the low flow will accommodate so few users, storage is desirable to detain the spring flood for release in the late summer. The rule of priority also determines who will pay for the dam—it is the junior appropriator who will get the benefit from it. In return for his investment, he will often have a better right than many seniors, since his stored water will carry him late into the year when the base flow becomes insufficient for all but a few. For this reason, seniors will often join in a dam project in order to receive supplemental water to firm up their late season supply. * * *

"Applying the rule of priority to the physical results of drought or climatic change may have some unexpected effects. It is not correct to think that drought will simply fall upon the most junior appropriators and wipe them out. In the long run, of course, the juniors will be those squeezed out, but many holders of senior and intermediate priorities may be affected. It will depend in part on the nature of the change, whether it takes the form of an extraordinarily 'subnormal' water year, an 'unexpectedly long' series of low water years, or a 'permanent' change in climate that reduces the long-term yield to some new norm. In most subnormal years, the high water begins to drop at an earlier date than usual, and as the flow subsides each junior appropriator will 'go out of priority' and must close his intake some indeterminate number of days earlier than he would have if the year had been within the 'normal' range. On an unregulated stream, the odds will be changed on all the bets. The original marginal junior rights become untenable and forfeit, the moderately secure rights are now risky, and the relatively certain are smaller in number. If the subnormality consists of unusually low base flows, the seniors who depend on late summer flows may get hurt the worst. If the drought flattens out the peaks and there is less high water than expected, then junior storage projects bear the brunt. Where large-scale storage has been built to equate the supply, the planners had in mind some combination of bad years to be hurdled. If that 'design drought' were never exceeded, every right would be as good as any other; but if the dams are finally run dry, a substantial block of shares—all of those that depend on the junior project—will fail together.

"Variations in the pattern of multiyear drought will also change the incidence of hardship. The North Platte River, to take an example, is a fully regulated stream on which the annual and perennial fluctuations have been ironed out by two large projects with different priorities. The earliest, Pathfinder Dam, has low storage in proportion to the land it serves, while the more recent project, Seminoe Dam, has large storage but a late priority. A short-term drought with several years of very low flows would dry up Pathfinder but might be well within the carryover capacity of

Seminoe, while a long sequence of mediocre years would hardly affect Pathfinder but would ruin the Seminoe project."

3. In Colorado a senior appropriator's complaint to the water commissioner that upstream juniors are taking his water and should be regulated is known as "calling the river." When shutting down the junior does not improve the senior's water supply, a "futile call" has occurred. The Water Right Determination and Administration Act of 1969 deals with the matter both substantively and procedurally: "No reduction of any lawful diversion because of the operation of the priority system shall be permitted unless such reduction would increase the amount of water available to and required by water rights having senior priorities." Colo.Rev.Stat.1973, 37–92–102(2)(d).

"Each division engineer shall order the total or partial discontinuance of any diversion in his division to the extent the water being diverted is not necessary for application to a beneficial use; and he shall also order the total or partial discontinuance of any diversion in his division to the extent the water being diverted is required by persons entitled to use water under water rights having senior priorities, but no such discontinuance shall be ordered unless the diversion is causing or will cause material injury to such water rights having senior priorities. In making his decision as to the discontinuance of a diversion to satisfy senior priorities the division engineer shall be governed by the following: The materiality of injury depends on all factors which will determine in each case the amount of water such discontinuance will make available to such senior priorities at the time and place of their need. Such factors include the current and prospective volumes of water in and tributary to the stream from which the diversion is being made; distance and type of stream bed between the diversion points; the various velocities of this water, both surface and underground; the probable duration of the available flow; and the predictable return flow to the affected stream. Each diversion shall be evaluated and administered on the basis of the circumstances relating to it and in accordance with provisions of this article and the court decrees adjudicating and confirming water rights. In the event a discontinuance has been ordered pursuant to the foregoing, and nevertheless such does not cause water to become available to such senior priorities at the time and place of their need, then such discontinuance order shall be rescinded." Colo.Rev.Stat.1973, 37–92–502(2).

4. Diversions from tributaries may be regulated in favor of senior appropriators from the main stream below the junction, Strickler v. City of Colorado Springs, 16 Colo. 61 (1891), but not infrequently practical considerations lead to separate administration of intermittent tributaries. For example, in Nebraska v. Wyoming, 325 U.S. 589, 65 S.Ct. 1332, 89 L.Ed. 1815 (1945), the Court entered a decree protecting prior Nebraska appropriators of the North Platte River from violations of priority by Wyoming irrigators from the main stream, but said regarding the tributaries: "Below Pathfinder and above Geurnsey the Special Master dealt only with diversions from the main river. He concluded that the run-off of the tributaries becomes so far exhausted before any shortage of water occurs in the main river that any regulation of the tributary diversions would be of no

material benefit. The tributary inflow is greater than the depletion of the river. There is some out-of-priority diversions as we have noted. But * * * practical difficulties of applying restrictions which would reduce the amount of water used by the hundreds of small irrigators would seem to outweigh any slight benefit which senior appropriators might obtain."

5. Seasonal priorities exist in some states. They entitle the appropriator to take water only during certain periods or seasons, so that other persons who initiated their rights at later dates may have a better claim to water during other times of the year. Some courts have rigidly frozen the pioneer pattern of use, restricting the use of the lands to the original crop irrigated, or even incorporating the personal habits of the original appropriator into the water right. Oliver v. Skinner, 190 Or. 423, 226 P.2d 507 (1951) (an appropriation for irrigating hay lands, never used after July 1st, cannot be used for crops requiring water later in the year); Santa Paula Water Works v. Peralta, 113 Cal. 38, 45 P. 168 (1896) (24 hours per week beginning Saturday noon); Thorne v. McKinley Bros., 5 Cal.2d 704, 56 P.2d 204 (1936) (never at night).

The more modern rule is that unless the claim, permit or decree upon which the right is founded imposes time limits on its use, the appropriator can take the water at any time he can put it to the beneficial use for which it was appropriated. See Harkey v. Smith, 31 N.M. 521, 247 P. 550 (1926): "In this connection it is to be observed that the doctrine of seasonal appropriation is not well adapted to general agriculture, such as that in which the parties are here engaged. The right, to be effective, must authorize the rotation of crops and variation of times or methods of the irrigation thereof, from year to year, as experience may dictate, or conditions of the lands, or markets for agricultural products, might seem to render advisable. * * * The farmer must have the water whenever, in pursuance of any reasonable plan, he requires it for his crops, or the preparation of his lands for planting; otherwise his right will be too precarious to be of any practical value."

6. Usually there is no division of the year into an irrigation season and a storage season, so as to give later direct users a seasonal preference over earlier reservoirs or vice versa. People ex rel. Park Reservoir Co. v. Hinderlider, 98 Colo. 505, 57 P.2d 894 (1936). However, a Nebraska statute forbids the impounding of water during the time it is required in ditches for direct irrigation. Neb.Rev.Stat.1943, § 46–241. (Reissue of 1984).

CACHE LaPOUDRE WATER USERS ASS'N v. GLACIER VIEW MEADOWS

Supreme Court of Colorado, 1976.
550 P.2d 288.

GROVES, JUSTICE.

The applicant Glacier View Meadows, a limited partnership, is a developer of residential lots in the mountains northwest of Fort Collins, Colorado. It filed with the water court two applications for approval of a plan of augmentation. The plans would provide future owners of presently unimproved lots with domestic water from wells to be drilled in the future. * * * The court granted approval of the plan for augmentation in the first two applications. We affirm with some modifications. * * *

The objector, Cache LaPoudre Water Users Association, is a non-profit protective association, whose members own substantial reservoir and direct flow decrees on the Cache LaPoudre River. * * *

The applicant owns 75 "preferred shares" of the Mountain and Plains Irrigation Company, which entitle applicant to both reservoir and direct flow water. Applicant acquired these 75 shares from Ideal Cement Company, Dreher Pickle Company and City of Fort Collins, which historically had made year-around use of their water. Under the plan some of applicant's reservoir rights will be used to replace consumptively used water from proposed wells. The water from the wells will be exclusively devoted to in-house, residential domestic use. Under the two applications which are the subject of the court's decree, there will be a maximum of 1892 single-family residential units. In some cases, one well will furnish water for more than one unit.

The reservoirs containing replacement water and the points of discharge of water therefrom into the stream, as well as all of the residential units and the points of return flow therefrom into the stream, lie above the points of diversion of any water of the objectors.

Of the 1892 units, at ultimate development 105 units are expected to use an evapotranspiration system of sewage disposal. The consumptive use for these 105 units will be 100% of the water diverted from wells. This 100% will be replaced entirely by reservoir water plus enough to account for evaporative losses during transportation in the stream.

The remaining 1787 units, when ultimately developed, will have septic-soil absorption sewage systems. From these latter diversions there will be a consumptive use of not more than 10% and at least 90% will constitute return flow to the stream. Replacement water for the 10%, plus an amount sufficient to embrace transportation losses, will be replenished by the aforementioned releases from the reservoirs.

The rate of flow permitted and claimed for each well will be four gallons per minute for each dwelling unit to be served by any well. The plan is predicated upon the assumption that each dwelling unit will be occupied by 3.5 persons 365 days a year, and that each person will require 80 gallons of well water per day. The entire consumptive use of well water (including those units having 100% consumptive use) will not exceed 89 acre feet per year. 55 of applicant's 75 shares will be devoted to replacement of this consumptively used water. 55 shares represent an amount of 94.71 acre feet per year. After deducting 5% for transportation losses, 89.97 feet remain for replacement. * * *

As mentioned earlier, the applicant acquired the 75 shares from Ideal Cement Company, Dreher Pickle Company and the City of Fort Collins. Historically, only 25% of the water used by these three returned to the stream. The plan allocates the water from 20 of the 75 shares of stock for use in the stream in lieu of the 25% return flow which no longer exists.

It is contemplated by the plan that, so long as its provisions are followed, there will be no injury to the holders of prior rights. However, if there is a call by a right superior to the association's priority rights, that call must be met. The water court concluded that the only thing that will upset the plan will be an extended period of drought. If such a drought causes insufficient water to be available for replacement, the well water users will be obliged to acquire additional water by lease or otherwise, or else to reduce their consumptive use, to the end that water consumptively used under the plan will not exceed that available for replacement. * * *

The principal argument of the objectors is that, except during flood stages, the Cache LaPoudre River is over-appropriated. With this we agree. Hall v. Kuiper, 181 Colo. 130, 510 P.2d 329 (1973). The argument continues that, unless there is 100% replacement of the water taken from the wells, senior water rights will be injured and there will be a violation of the Water Right Determination and Administration Act of 1969 (section 37–92–101 et seq., C.R.S.1973, hereinafter called the "Act"), and the rules and regulations of the State Engineer's office. * * *

First, we look to the Act, and here quote some of the legislative declaration underlying it and the definition of "plan for augmentation":

> "(1) It is hereby declared to be the policy of the state of Colorado that all waters originating in or flowing into this state, whether found on the surface or underground, have always been and are hereby declared to be the property of the public, dedicated to the use of the people of the state, subject to appropriation and use in accordance with law. As incident thereto, it is the policy of this state to integrate the appropriation, use, and administration of underground water tributary to a stream with the use of surface water in such a way as to maximize the beneficial use of all of the waters of this state.
>
> " 'Plan for argumentation' means a detailed program to increase the supply of water available for beneficial use in a division or portion thereof by the development of new or alternate means or points of diversion, by a pooling of water resources, by water exchange projects, by providing substitute supplies of water, by the development of new sources of water, or by any other appropriate means." Section 37–92–103(9), C.R.S.1973.

We find that the plan of augmentation has been formulated and approved consonant with, and in furtherance of, the purpose and intent of our recent statutes; and that the plan is valid.

We hold here * * * that under the plans for augmentation involved water is available for appropriation when the diversion thereof does not injure holders of vested rights.

Objectors cite Southeastern Colorado Water Conservancy District v. Shelton Farms, 187 Colo. 181, 529 P.2d 1321 (1974), in which this court ruled that one, who cuts down water-consuming vegetation (phreatophytes) along the Arkansas River, does not have a right to a decree for an equivalent amount of water to that consumed by the vegetation, free of the call of the river. In the opinion it was stated, "Appellees would substitute the priority doctrine with a lack of injury doctrine." The judgment was reversed and the cause remanded to the trial court with directions to vacate the decree. The indication from the foregoing that *Shelton Farms* stands for the proposition that lack of injury does not cause water to be available for appropriation must be analyzed. *Shelton Farms* involved a factual situation which makes it distinguishable from this. * * *

There, the senior rights had adjusted to the loss of the water caused by the growth of phreatophytes; and, once returned to the river, the water would still belong to the senior users in satisfaction of their decrees. In the instant case, the water to be used in replacement never was that of the senior users. Here, there is not displacement "*from the time and place of* their need." Under the findings here, the stream will be the same, irrespective of the well diversions.

Under the circumstances of this case, there is no significant difference between the prior appropriation doctrine, and the lack of injury doctrine. Here, where senior users can show no injury by the diversion of water, they cannot preclude the beneficial use of water by another. Fellhauer v. People, 167 Colo. 320, 447 P.2d 986 (1968), was cited as authority in *Shelton Farms.* It is likewise authority here. As was there said, "As administration of water approaches its second century the curtain is opening upon the new drama of *maximum utilization* and how constitutionally that doctrine can be integrated into the law of *vested rights.*"

We rule that, in a matter such as this one, water is available for appropriation if the taking thereof does not cause injury. Therefore, the argument of the objectors, to the effect that water withdrawn from the wells must be replaced 100%, falls.

Notes

1. The rights of the junior appropriator begin at the limits of the rights of the senior. For other examples of the rights of the junior appropriator to change natural conditions, see Clausen v. Armington, 123 Mont. 1, 212 P.2d 440 (1949); Knutson v. Huggins, 62 Idaho 662, 115 P.2d 421 (1941).

2. One of the most common situations in which a junior asserts his rights against the senior occurs when some change in point of diversion, place of use or manner of use is made in the senior right, to the alleged detriment of the junior appropriator. The prior appropriator has no right, as against the junior appropriator, to waste water, to increase the amount or extend the time of his diversion so as to put it to double use by irrigation

of other lands, nor to lend, rent or sell to others the excess water. Enlarged Southside Irrigation Ditch Co. v. John's Flood Ditch Co., 116 Colo. 580, 183 P.2d 552 (1947). In Colorado, this rule is often phrased in terms of a vested right of the junior appropriator to the continuation of stream conditions as they existed at the time of his appropriation. See Farmers Highline Canal & Reservoir Co. v. Golden, infra p. 197. This is an over-simplification that is subject to many exceptions, since the second user of water is not protected against its loss in every case of change in the manner and form of the first use. See Metropolitan Denver Sewage Disposal District No. 1 v. Farmer's Reservoir and Irrigation Co., 179 Colo. 36, 499 P.2d 1190 (1972). For thirty years Denver had deposited the effluent from its municipal sewage treatment plant into the South Platte River above the headgate of the irrigation company. When the plant became inadequate the sewage was transported to a large new metropolitan plant whose outfall was downstream from the plaintiff's point of diversion. Held, in an action for a declaratory judgment, downstream appropriators have no vested right of control over the works of the upstream appropriator, and a change in the point of return to the stream is not subject to the no-harm rule. See also Cleaver v. Judd, infra p. 227, where return flows the junior had used were recaptured in the course of more efficient use by the senior. In Colorado's "dirty water case," A–B Cattle Co. v. United States, 196 Colo. 539, 589 P.2d 57 (1978), complaint was made by irrigators from the Bessemer Ditch that the muddy water of the Arkansas River, which had sealed the ditch with silt, had been replaced by the Bureau of Reclamation with clear, clean reservoir water, which leaked out of the ditch so that less water arrived at the place of use. In a 4–3 decision, the court decided, in effect, that plaintiffs had a water right, not a silt right, and no claim to compensation.

3. Not infrequently senior appropriators may claim all the summer flow in the downstream reaches of a stream, while a reservoir site lies above them and undeveloped lands above that. Junior appropriators may build the reservoir, appropriate the senior's natural flow for the upstream land and substitute the stored water on the downstream land. Reno v. Richards, 32 Idaho 1, 178 P. 81 (1918). Where senior appropriators claim all the natural flow within a valley, a junior may import water from a different watershed, use the natural flow himself and deliver the imported water to the senior. Wilder Irrigation Dist. v. Jorgenson, 64 Idaho 538, 136 P.2d 461 (1943).

4. True rotation does not violate the doctrine of priority, but is a variation in its administration. Where there is water enough for each of several small appropriations, each appropriator in turn may take the total share of all for a short interval, in order to give each an "irrigating head" of a manageable quantity of water and to cut down on seepage and evaporation. Most of the western states have statutes permitting and regulating the practice of rotation by agreement, e.g., Wyo.Stat.1977, § 41–3–612. Sometimes courts have imposed rotation upon appropriators by decree, where more efficient utilization of small flows will result. McCoy v. Huntley, 60 Or. 372, 119 P. 481 (1911); Big Cottonwood Tanner Ditch Co. v. Shurtliff, 49 Utah 569, 164 P. 856 (1917). Compare Harris v. Harrison, infra p. 307 (rotation among riparians).

Where water users draw from a community ditch or have shares entitling them to participate in the water right of a mutual ditch company or an irrigation district, so that all rights are of equal dignity, it is usual to rotate the water to them and allow each a specified number of "water days", rather than to distribute the water to all at once and allow small quantities to dribble into many laterals simultaneously.

5. Rotation sometimes can provide a physical solution to the problem of State ex rel. Cary v. Cochran, supra p. 97. See Albion-Idaho Land Co. v. Naf Irrigation Co., 97 F.2d 439 (10th Cir.1938), where downstream prior appropriators sought to enjoin upstream junior diversions on a mountain stream that annually fluctuated from 180 to 0 second feet. The lower court made a 4-year study the basis of its decree: "When the volume of the flow in the stream is sufficient to reach the diversion points in the lower division and afford the users in that division a practical head for irrigation purposes, the decree awards the users in that division a priority to the extent of 560 acre feet. * * * Thereafter the decree divides the water on the basis of acreage in the two divisions until 750 acre feet additional have been diverted and thereafter so long as the diversions exceed 37.2 second feet. When the flow falls below 36.2 second feet and still continues in sufficient volume to reach the diversion point in the lower division and there afford a practical head for irrigation, the decree gives 12 day's flow to the lower division. After such additional 12 day's flow has been received by the lower division the decree again divides the water on the basis of acreage. * * * We are of the opinion that the trial court is entitled to commendation for the thorough and painstaking manner in which it inquired into and ascertained the relevant facts and for working out a very practical plan for a division of the waters of the stream whereby the priorities of the several users are fully recognized, waste is eliminated, and the greatest possible utilization of the waters of the stream is effected."

PHILLIPS v. GARDNER

Court of Appeals of Oregon, 1970.
2 Or.App. 423, 469 P.2d 42.

SCHWAB, CHIEF JUDGE. The defendant watermaster, who is charged with the duty of distributing water in Yamhill County in accordance with the rights of each user, threatened to cut off plaintiffs' domestic water supply and to empty plaintiffs' impoundment for that purpose to give water to a downstream user who holds the water right for irrigation prior in time to plaintiffs' domestic right. Plaintiffs brought suit to enjoin the defendant watermaster from so doing, claiming a statutory priority for domestic use under ORS 540.140. The trial judge granted the injunction and the defendant watermaster appeals, contending that ORS 540.140 has no application to the facts of this case. The plaintiffs' water certificate has a priority date of June 7, 1947; the downstream property owner's water certificate has a priority date of August 26, 1919.

During the months of August and September 1967, there was not sufficient water to serve both appropriators. The watermaster threatened to cut off plaintiffs' water supply and this gave rise to the suit in question. This controversy relates to surface water only, not to ground water available through wells.

ORS 540.140 was enacted in 1893. It reads:

> "When the waters of any natural stream are not sufficient for the service of all those desiring the use of the same, those using the water for domestic purposes shall, subject to such limitations as may be prescribed by law, have the preference over those claiming such water for any other purpose, and those using the water for agricultural purposes shall have the preference over those using the same for manufacturing purposes."

The statute has never been cited or discussed in any of the numerous opinions of the Oregon Supreme Court dealing with the application of Oregon water laws.

Oregon first adopted a comprehensive water code in 1909. Since then this code has been subject to major amendments. The reasons for the extensive body of statutory law and court rulings relating to the use and conservation of water in Oregon are succinctly set out in the Preface to United States Dep't of Agriculture, Selected Problems in the Law of Water Rights in the West, Misc.Pub. No. 418 (Wells A. Hutchins 1942):

> "By and large, water is plentiful east of the tier of States from North Dakota to Texas. Within those six States and their western neighbors, however, water is scarce and provides a limiting factor on the productivity of the soil. It is understandable, therefore, that the water law of these Western States presents a complexity of pattern and a fullness of development not to be found in the law relating to waters in the East * * *."

The 1909 Act established a system for the filing of applications for the appropriation of water with the state engineer in § 47 (ORS 537.130(1)), and provided in § 46 (ORS 537.140), that applications contain, among other information, the nature and amount of proposed use. Section 46 discloses that the legislature had in mind that there were varying uses of water for among the uses to which it there refers are those for agriculture, power, municipal water supply and mining. Section 54 (ORS 537.250(3)) provides "The right acquired by an appropriation shall date from the filing of the application in the office of the State Engineer."

The Act, § 73, provides "All laws and parts of laws so far as in conflict or inconsistent with the provisions of this act are hereby repealed."

The plaintiffs argue that despite the provisions of the 1909 Water Act the holder of a certificate for domestic water use has a preference by virtue of ORS 540.140 over a prior recorded water right for other purposes. * * *

Although the 1909 Act did not directly state that thereafter priorities should be based on priority in time and not on nature of use, the whole thrust of the Act clearly indicates such a purpose. The insufficiency of water in parts of Oregon is what gave rise to Oregon's comprehensive water code commencing with the 1909 Act. Priorities are meaningful only in times of shortage. If we were to apply ORS 540.140 as plaintiffs would have us do, in times of shortage—the only time when there is any reason for priorities—water would be allocated based upon the nature of the various uses involved, not on the basis of the effective date of appropriation. The result would be that the priorities established by the 1909 Act and subsequent additions to it would be effective only as to appropriators within similar categories of use. It is hard for us to conceive that the 1909 and subsequent legislatures could have intended such a result without one word in the statutes to indicate their desire to adopt such a complicated scheme. It may be that ORS 540.140 still has viability as to rights which were perfected prior to 1909 or as to rights bearing the same effective date. Since neither situation is involved in the case at bar, we need not consider those possibilities here.

Appealing as plaintiffs' humanistic arguments may be, if viewed from a single point of view, it is our opinion that the statutory interpretation they seek is in conflict with what we perceive as clear legislative intent—the substitution of priority based on time of appropriation for the pre-1909 statutory preference (ORS 540.140) based on the nature of the use.

Reversed and remanded for the entry of a decree in accordance with this opinion.

Notes

1. Does this decision mean that Gardner goes thirsty? See City of Thornton v. The Farmers Reservoir and Irrigation Co., infra at p. 214.

2. "Preference" can refer to one of several quite different things: (1) In time of shortage, the water is devoted to the preferred use instead of to a non-preferred purpose although the latter has the prior right. (2) Where applicants compete for permits to appropriate a supply of unappropriated water insufficient for all proposed uses, the preferred user gets the water right, regardless of the relative priority of filing the applications. (3) Where a change is needed in the use of appropriated water, the preferred user may condemn and pay for a prior right for a non-preferred use. The principal case involves a supposed preference of the first type. Preferences of the second type are discussed infra at p. 165, of the third at p. 214. Other doctrines sometimes result in one or another type of preference existing under certain circumstances. See Trelease, Preferences to the Use of Water, 27 Rocky Mtn. Law Rev. 133 (1955).

3. So.Dak. Codified Laws 46–1–5: "It is the established policy of this state: (1) That the use of water for domestic purposes is the highest use of water and takes precedence over all appropriative rights, if it is exercised in a manner consistent with public interest as provided in § 46–1–2;"

Utah Code Ann.1953, 73–3–21: "Appropriators shall have priority among themselves according to the dates of their respective appropriations, so that each appropriator shall be entitled to receive his whole supply before any subsequent appropriator shall have any right; provided, in times of scarcity, while priority of appropriation shall give the better right as between those using water for the same purpose, the use for domestic purposes, without unnecessary waste, shall have preference over use for all other purposes, and use for agricultural purposes shall have preference over use for any other purpose except domestic use."

STATE EX REL. CROWLEY v. DISTRICT COURT

Supreme Court of Montana, 1939.
108 Mont. 89, 88 P.2d 23.

JOHNSON, CHIEF JUSTICE. * * * The suit in question is for damages for alleged interference with plaintiff's use of irrigation water from the Madison River in 1935, 1936 and 1937. There are nine causes of action, which are grouped as to years. The first three relate to 1935, the next three to 1936, and the last three to 1937. Thus there are three causes of action with reference to each of the three years. * * *

The second group, comprising causes 2, 5 and 8, is based upon the allegations that the defendants impounded by their dams the entire natural flow of the river so that the water level at plaintiff's point of diversion was so low that he could not divert water into his ditches by his diversion dam, although the latter was suitable and efficient for the purpose and was a reasonably adequate means of diversion, and reasonably constructed and maintained to divert water from the river to plaintiff's land in spite of the fluctuations in flow incidental to the reasonable and lawful use of water by all persons lawfully entitled to use the same. The exact allegations relative to these points will be set forth below. The demurrers to these causes of action numbered 2, 5 and 8 were sustained. * * *

The allegations of the causes are those usual to actions of this kind. Defendants' contentions are that plaintiff has no cause of action merely because their acts so reduced the flow that he could not divert his appropriated water by his reasonably efficient diversion system; that he should have alleged that not enough was left to permit his diversion without leaving any water in the stream. In other words, they contend that plaintiff has no cause of action if there are 200 inches of water at his point of diversion, even though he cannot get the water into his ditches without a pump; that an appropriator's vested interest is only in the use of the quantum of water appropriated by him without reference to his means or manner of diversion, however reasonably efficient; that not reasonable efficiency but absolute efficiency is required. To this theory we cannot assent without doing violence to the entire principle of water rights by appropriation. If it is to be followed, there are few, if any, irrigation water rights in the state of Montana, however long established, which could not in effect be destroyed entirely by subsequent appropriations. One hundred per cent efficiency can be furnished by no system of diversion, and certainly by none financially available to the average water user. The law does not defeat its own end by requiring the impossible. The marginal character of many farming enterprises, and especially of the smaller ones, is well known, and if defendants' argument is followed, vested interests will be seriously affected and rights limited by the necessity of installing diversion systems by which the last drop may be taken from the stream.

There is no question that waste of our water resources must be minimized in the general interest, but it is equally manifest that there is a vanishing point at which the possible waste of water would be more than overcome by the waste incidental to the abandonment of reasonably efficient diversion systems and the establishment of diversion systems whose expense is neither warranted nor permitted by the benefit to be derived from the water.

It is well established that subsequent appropriators take with notice of the conditions existing at the time of their appropriations. In making their appropriation of storage or other water and their expenditures in connection therewith, defendants and their predecessors were chargeable with knowledge of the existing conditions, with reference not only to the amount of prior appropriations, but also to the existing diversion systems of prior appropriators. They cannot now argue that they are limited by the amount but not the means of prior appropriations, however reasonably efficient under the circumstances, or that so long as they leave the exact amount of plaintiff's appropriation in the river at his point of diversion, they have no further duty and that it is his worry and not theirs how or whether he can divert it upon his land. His right is to divert and use the water, not merely to have it left in the streambed; that is the essential difference between riparian and appropriation rights. * * *

Defendants contend that the case of Schodde v. Twin Falls Land & Water Co., 224 U.S. 107, 32 S.Ct. 470, 56 L.Ed. 686, affirming 9 Cir., 161 F. 43, 88 C.C.A. 207, sustains their contention that a prior appropriator has no vested interest in his means of diversion. It cannot be so construed. In that case plaintiff had appropriated 1250 inches of water from Snake River in Idaho, for use on his ranch of 429 acres, and diverted it by means of large waterwheels operated by the stream flow. The defendant thereafter constructed a dam nine miles below to supply water to about 5,000 settlers for the irrigation of approximately 300,000 acres of land. The dam backed the water up beyond plaintiff's waterwheels so that the current was no longer available to operate them. Plaintiff sued for damages in the federal court of Idaho, and defendant's demurrer was sustained. On appeal the Ninth Circuit Court of Appeals affirmed the trial court's action on the ground that there was no attempted appropriation of water to run the wheels, and that there could be none under the laws of Idaho without an actual diversion for the purpose, and upon the further ground that the statute expressly authorizing the use of rams and other machines to lift appropriated water from streams gave a mere license, and not an appurtenance to the water right appropriated. In other words, the right to the flow of the river constituted neither an appropriation of the flow nor an appurtenance to the irrigation water actually appropriated. It also held that where the method of diversion was obviously unreasonable and inefficient it could not be used where it interfered with the reasonable use of water by others. Obviously, of course, under the circumstances of that case, it was unreasonable to prevent the irrigation of 300,000 acres by an unusual and inefficient method of diverting water for 429 acres. The complaint there was not that the defendant had taken water out of the stream so as to interfere with the waterwheels; as a matter of fact, the defendant had confined more water there. What it had deprived plaintiff of was not the water, but the force of the water, which was no part of his appropriation. This can be made clear by an analogy. If, instead of building waterwheels to utilize the force of the stream, he had constructed windmills to employ the force of the wind, it would have been entirely clear that his complaint was not of water right interference, but of something entirely different. If the conditions were such that he could have recovered for an obstruction to the flow of the wind to his windmills, it would still have been something entirely apart from and not appurtenant to his water right. This is clear from the opinion of the Circuit Court of Appeals in 161 F. at page 45, as follows: "It is contended on the part of the plaintiff that the current of the river is necessarily appurtenant to the water location and that the means of utilizing that current is attached as an appurtenance to the appropriation. We have not been referred to any case—and we know of none—where either of these propositions has been upheld. The claim that the right to the current of the river is appurtenant to the water location is contrary to well-established principles of the common law governing such a relation. The water location was an appropriation and diversion of a certain quantity of the flowing water of the stream. The current of the river is part of the stream. There can be no right to the current of a stream as appurtenant to a diversion of the flowing waters of the stream. The two rights in such case would be equal and of the same character and quality, and one such right cannot be appurtenant to the other." The court then went on to show that there had been no diversion or appropriation of water for power purposes, so that plaintiff's asserted right against defendant's interference was not a water right, and concluded by quoting the decision of this court in Fitzpatrick v. Montgomery, 20 Mont. 181, 50 P. 416, 63 Am.St.Rep. 622, to the effect that the tendency and spirit of legislation in the northwest had been to prevent a monopoly of water.

On certiorari the United States Supreme Court, speaking through Mr. Chief Justice White, said: "The trial court recognized fully the right of the plaintiff to the volume of water actually appropriated for a beneficial purpose. It nevertheless dismissed the complaint on the ground that there was no right under the Constitution and laws of the state of Idaho to appropriate the current of the river so as to render it impossible for others to apply the otherwise unappropriated waters of the river to beneficial uses. The court did not find it necessary to deny that power might be one of the beneficial purposes for which appropriations of water might be made, but in substance held that to uphold as an appropriation the use of the current of the river to the extent required to work the defendant's wheels would amount to saying that a limited taking of water from the river by appropriation for a limited beneficial use justified the appropriation of all the water in the river as incident to the limited benefit resulting from the use of the water actually appropriated. The court said: 'It is conceded and is beyond question, that the statute law as well as judicial authority directly protects plaintiff in all water he has actually appropriated, diverted, and used; but there is no statute, nor so far as known, any judicial rulings, protecting him in the establishment and in the use of his water wheels, as he claims to, and must, use them for the diversion of water to his land.' * * * It is unquestioned that what he has actually diverted and used upon his land, he has appropriated; but can it be said that all the water he uses or needs to operate his wheels is an appropriation? As before suggested, there is neither statutory nor judicial authority that such a use is an appropriation. Such use also lacks one of the essential attributes of an appropriation,—it is not reasonable.' " * * *

The rule in this connection is well stated as follows in Long on Irrigation, 2nd ed., 202, 203, sec. 116: "The irrigator may employ any means best suited to the existing physical conditions, and all the circumstances of the case, though undoubtedly he will be required to employ reasonably economical means, so as to prevent unnecessary waste. * * * As already stated, the means of diversion employed must not be unnecessarily wasteful (Doherty v. Pratt, 34 Nev. 343, 124 P. 574), but when ditches and flumes are the usual and ordinary means of diverting water, parties who have made their appropriations by such means cannot be compelled to substitute iron pipes, though they will be required to prevent unnecessary waste by keeping their ditches and flumes in good repair (Barrows v. Fox, 9 Cal. 63, 32 P. 811)." * * *

Plaintiff alleges that he has diverted the water by means of a wing dam of brush, rocks and dirt, and proceeds to allege that the means of diversion was at the time in question "suitable and efficient for the diversion of water," and "a reasonably adequate means of diversion and reasonably constructed and maintained" for the purpose, notwithstanding the fluctuations incidental to the reasonable and lawful use of water by all those entitled, including defendants. These are statements of ultimate facts, and causes numbered 2, 5 and 8 sufficiently state causes of action. It follows that the demurrers should have been overruled. * * *

[Reversed.]

Notes

1. In *Schodde,* distinguished in the principal case, both the Court of Appeals and the Supreme Court used the following illustration: "Suppose from a stream of 1000 inches a party diverts and uses 100, and in some way uses the other 900 to divert his 100, could it be said that he had made such a reasonable use of the 900 as to constitute an appropriation of it? Or, suppose that when the entire 1000 inches are running, they so fill the channel that by a ditch he can draw off to his land his 100 inches, can he then object to those above him appropriating and using the other 900 inches, because it will so lower the stream that his ditch becomes useless? This would be such an unreasonable use of the 900 inches as will not be tolerated under the law of appropriation."

2. What is "the time in question" at which the reasonableness of the means of diversion is to be determined? As of what time was the determination made in *Crowley?* Compare In re Willow Creek, 74 Or. 592, 144 P. 505 (1914), in which the court said that a crude and wasteful manner of irrigation was sufficient to establish a right for an amount of water necessary to irrigate the land in a proper manner, though it must be replaced by modern economical methods. Similarly, In re Silvies River, 115 Or. 27, 237 P. 322 (1925), granted an appropriation to a person who took advantage of natural irrigation by harvesting or utilizing the crops grown on the land, but stated that within a reasonable time, as circumstances permit and necessities require, the building of an artificial irrigation system would be required in order to effect an economical use of the water and prevent waste.

3. No.Dak.Cent.Code 61–04–06.3: "Priority of appropriation does not include the right to prevent changes in condition of water occurrence, such as the increase or decrease of stream flow, or the lowering of a water table, artesian pressure, or water level, by later appropriators, if the prior appropriator can reasonably acquire his water under the changed conditions."

WARNER VALLEY STOCK CO. v. LYNCH

Supreme Court of Oregon, 1959.
215 Or. 523, 336 P.2d 884.

O'CONNELL, JUSTICE. This is an appeal from a decree of the Circuit Court for Lake County ordering the State Engineer to issue to the applicant-respondent, Warner Valley Stock Company, permits for the construction of two storage reservoirs for the impoundment of certain waters in Warner Valley and to issue permits for the appropriation of the waters so impounded.

The objectors-appellants are landowners in Warner Valley who attack the decree principally upon the ground that the issuance of such permits would be in violation of their vested rights in the flow of the waters proposed to be stored and appropriated by the applicant. * * *

The principal objections presented at the hearing and urged on this appeal are predicated upon claimed rights to the water as determined in a decree of the Circuit Court for Lake County, dated September 30, 1929 which, with minor modifications, affirmed the findings and order of determination of the State Engineer in the proceedings for adjudication of the relative rights to the use of the waters of Warner Lakes and their tributaries.

More specifically, the objections are as follows. It is claimed that the impoundment of the waters in the proposed reservoirs will reduce the flow of waters to Hart Lake from Twentymile Creek and Deep Creek. Those objectors who rely upon the overflow of Hart Lake to irrigate their lands contend that the retention of the water by the applicant would interfere with this overflow and would constitute an impairment of their vested right to such waters. It is claimed that the right to this method of irrigation by natural overflow and drainage was acquired by use, and affirmed by the 1929 adjudication of the water rights in Warner Valley. One of the questions before us is whether such a right exists. Stated differently, the question raised by this protest is: Do these objectors have the right to insist that Hart Lake be fed with waters none of which, below the point of overflow, will be used for application upon the land in Warner Valley, but will serve only to raise the surface of the lake to the point of overflow? * * *

We must, therefore, construe the findings and order of determination upon which the decree of 1929 was based. * * * In passing upon this claim in the proceedings which culminated in the 1929 decree, the State Engineer stated in his findings and order:

> "It is generally conceded that the present method of irrigation by natural overflow is an extremely wasteful one. * * * Hart Lake is a shallow body of water, and in its former natural state overflowed through three or more main channels or sloughs. These channels extended down the valley, but were well defined only for short distances, soon widening out into mere depressions. In the high water seasons the water overflowed from the sloughs and spread over a wide area of the valley, continuing northward through a series of lakes for a distance of twenty miles or more. It appears that after the valley became somewhat settled, in order to cause the water to reach higher areas, the flow of the water from the lake was retarded by placing dams in its outlets, thereby raising the lake surface until it overflowed the lands more uniformly. This control of the lake overflow has apparently been exercised by the more or less common consent of all the land owners affected. * * *
>
> " 'Nature has been very generous' to Contestants in this case. Thousands of acres have been irrigated for them, practically without expense or effort on their part. But the system is wasteful, and more economical methods must be employed to keep pace with modern developments. It would be a step backwards to permit them to maintain a large body of water in Hart Lake at a certain level merely for the purpose of continuing the 'natural flooding' system of irriga-

tion. * * * The ease with which Contestants have been able to divert their water has been merely their own good fortune. It was not a right, but merely a privilege, to be enjoyed only until rendered impracticable by a fuller development and use of the unappropriated waters."

This finding was adopted by the circuit court in the decree rendered in 1929. In the decree of October 15, 1954, from which the present appeal was taken, the circuit court held "That the methods of use and diversion by Objectors of the waters of Hart Lake by permitting the same to overflow the banks of said Lake are hereby declared to be wasteful and have been only a privilege and not a right * * *."

The conclusion that the objectors had acquired a privilege only to divert the waters by means of overflow and not a right to do so was based upon the lower court's interpretation of the 1929 decree. The overflow method of diversion described as a privilege both in the decree of 1929 and 1954 is wasteful in two respects, (1) because after the water leaves the lake it is permitted to spread out as a consequence of which there is considerable loss of water through evaporation and seepage, and (2) because such a method, if recognized as a vested right, would render the water in the lake unappropriable until the objectors had received three acre feet per acre for 6,532.15 acres. The finding and order upon which the 1929 decree was based described as wasteful both of these consequences of recognizing the overflow method of diversion and considered each of the reasons stated above as sufficient to render the interest of the overflow claimants a mere privilege. We think that this analysis of the objectors' interest is correct. * * *

The 1929 decree (by adopting the language of the State Engineer) made it quite clear that the method of diversion described was "not a right, but merely a privilege to be enjoyed only until rendered impracticable by a fuller development and use of the unappropriated waters." That time has come. We hold that the method of diversion by way of natural overflow is a privilege only and cannot be insisted upon by the objectors if it interferes with the appropriation by others of the waters for a beneficial use. This is consistent with the principle announced in Hough v. Porter, supra, and In re Water Rights of Silvies River, supra. See also, In re Willow Creek, 1915, 74 Or. 592, 144 P. 505, 146 P. 475.

The objectors rely upon several cases in support of their contention that their method of diversion of water by natural overflow could not be impaired by a subsequent appropriation. Oliver v. Jordan Valley Land & Cattle Co., 1933, 143 Or. 249, 16 P.2d 17, 22 P.2d 206; Oliver v. Skinner and Lodge, 1951, 190 Or. 423, 226 P.2d 507; Salt Lake City v. Gardner, 1911, 39 Utah 30, 114 P. 147; State ex rel. Crowley v. District Court, 1939, 108 Mont. 89, 88 P.2d 23, 121 A.L.R. 1031; United States v. Gerlach Live Stock Co., 339 U.S. 725, 70 S.Ct. 955, 94 L.Ed. 1231, 20 A.L.R.2d 633. In each of these cases, the interest in the waters which the court protected was a vested right. In the *Oliver* cases, the appropriator established that he had an adjudicated right to a certain quantity of water stored in a lake and, in addition, an adjudicated right as well as the State Engineer's permit to divert the water by pumping and by gravity flow through a ditch. In the instant case, the right acquired by the objectors to the waters overflowing the lake did not include the *right* to divert those waters by natural overflow; the *privilege* to so divert the water recognized in the 1929 decree was subject to subsequent rights to use the water more economically. The evidence conclusively shows that the water which would otherwise have to lie idle in Hart Lake in order to cause it to overflow is now needed for a beneficial use.

It should be emphasized that the objectors whose lands are irrigated by the waters from Hart Lake have acquired a vested right in waters of Warner Valley. By their original application of water to a beneficial use, subsequently recognized by the adjudication of 1929, the objectors acquired a right to irrigate 6,532.15 acres. These rights they still have. The fact that they no longer have the privilege of a natural overflow *method* of diversion does not mean that their right to the waters in Warner Valley exists only if the water in fact overflows Hart Lake. We interpret the 1929 decree as vesting in them a right to a certain quantity of water, viz., three acre feet per acre for 6,532.15 acres. * * *

The objectors contend that they will be put to great expense in the construction of a pumping distribution system if they are deprived of the natural overflow method of diversion. However, the decree protects the objectors by the following provision:

> "(d) That in addition to the quantity of water necessary to satisfy the above rights, additional water from the seasonal flow of Warner Lakes and their tributaries shall be delivered into Hart Lake at said Stone Bridge to compensate for seepage and evaporation in Hart Lake and to maintain a water level in Hart Lake so that water can be delivered to the pumps without construction of ditches of excessive lengths and for efficient operation of the pumps."

The objectors rely upon cases holding that if a subsequent appropriator desires to change stream conditions for his own benefit he must bear the cost which the change imposes upon a prior appropriator. Oliver v. Jordan Valley Land & Cattle Co., supra; Oliver v. Skinner, supra; Dry Gulch Ditch Co. v. Hutton, 1943, 170 Or. 656, 133 P.2d 601; Salt Lake City v. Gardner, 1911, 39 Utah 30, 114 P. 147; Big Cottonwood Tanner Ditch Co. v. Shurtliff, 1919, 56 Utah 196, 189 P. 587. In these cases the prior appropriator had a right to continue the method of diversion which was affected. The objectors have no adjudicated right to diversion by overflow and in this respect the cited cases are not applicable. But the objectors' pumping rights for 6,006.85 acres are vested rights and if the withdrawal of water by the applicant unreasonably interferes with those rights the objectors are entitled to relief. * * *

[Affirmed.]

Notes

1. Coase, The Problem of Social Cost, 3 J.Law and Econ. 1 (1960):

"This paper is concerned with those actions of business firms which have harmful effects on others. The standard example is that of a factory the smoke from which has harmful effects on those occupying neighbouring properties. The economic analysis of such a situation has usually proceeded in terms of a divergence between the private and social product of the factory, in which economists have largely followed the treatment of Pigou in *The Economics of Welfare.* The conclusions to which this kind of analysis seems to have led most economists is that it would be desirable to make the owner of the factory liable for the damage caused to those injured by the smoke, or alternatively, to place a tax on the factory owner varying with the amount of smoke produced an equivalent in money terms to the damage it would cause, or finally, to exclude the factory from residential districts (and presumably from other areas in which the emission of smoke would have harmful effects on others). It is my contention that the suggested courses of action are inappropriate, in that they lead to results which are not necessarily, or even usually, desirable.

"The traditional approach has tended to obscure the nature of the choice that has to be made. The question is commonly thought of as one in which A inflicts harm on B and what has to be decided is: how should we restrain A? But this is wrong. We are dealing with a problem of a reciprocal nature. To avoid the harm to B would inflict harm on A. The real question that has to be decided is: should A be allowed to harm B or should B be allowed to harm A? The problem is to avoid the more serious harm. I instanced in my previous article the case of a confectioner the noise and vibrations from whose machinery disturbed a doctor in his work. To avoid harming the doctor would inflict harm on the confectioner. The problem posed by this case was essentially whether it was worth while, as a result of restricting the methods of production which could be used by the confectioner, to secure more doctoring at the cost of a reduced supply of confectionary products. * * *

"The court's decision established that the doctor had the right to prevent the confectioner from using his machinery. But, of course, it would have been possible to modify the arrangements envisaged in the legal ruling by means of a bargain between the parties. The doctor would have been willing to waive his right and allow the machinery to continue in operation if the confectioner would have paid him a sum of money which was greater than the loss of income which he would suffer from having to move to a more costly or less convenient location or from having to curtail his activities at this location or, as was suggested as a possibility, from having to build a separate wall which would deaden the noise and vibration. The confectioner would have been willing to do this if the amount he would have to pay the doctor was less than the fall in income he would suffer if he had to change his mode of operation at this location, abandon his operation or move his confectionery business to some other location. The solution of the problem depends essentially on whether the continued use of the machinery adds more to the confectioner's income than it subtracts from the doctor's. But now consider the situation if the confectioner had won the case. The confectioner would then have had the right to continue operating his noise and vibration-generating machinery without having to pay anything to the doctor. The boot would have been on the other foot: the doctor would have had to pay the confectioner to induce him to stop using the machinery. If the doctor's income would have fallen more through continuance of the use of this machinery than it added to the income of the confectioner, there would clearly be room for a bargain whereby the doctor paid the confectioner to stop using the machinery. That is to say, the circumstances in which it would not pay the confectioner to continue to use the machinery and to compensate the doctor for the losses that this would bring (if the doctor had the right to prevent the confectioner's using his machinery) would be those in which it would be in the interest of the doctor to make a payment to the confectioner which would induce him to discontinue the use of the machinery (if the confectioner had the right to operate the machinery). * * * With costless market transactions, the decision of the courts concerning liability for damage would be without effect on the allocation of resources. * * *

"Judges have to decide on legal liability but this should not confuse economists about the nature of the economic problem involved. * * * The doctor's work would not have been disturbed if the confectioner had not worked his machinery; but the machinery would have disturbed no one if the doctor had not set up his consulting room in that particular place. * * * If we are to discuss the problem in terms of causation, both parties caused the damage. If we are to attain an optimum allocation of resources, it is therefore desirable that both parties should take the harmful effect (the nuisance) into account in deciding on their course of action. It is one of the beauties of a smoothly operating pricing system that, as has already been explained, the fall in the value of production due to the harmful effect would be a cost for both parties. * * *

"Of course, if market transactions were costless, all that matters (questions of equity apart) is that the rights of the various parties should be well-defined and the results of legal actions easy to forecast. But as we have seen, the situation is quite different when market transactions are so costly as to make it difficult to change the arrangement of rights established by the law. In such cases, the courts directly influence economic activity. It would therefore seem desirable that the courts should understand the economic consequences of their decisions and should, insofar as this is possible without creating too much uncertainty about the legal position itself, take these consequences into account when making their decisions. Even when it is possible to change the legal delimitation of rights through market transactions, it is obviously desirable to reduce the need for such transactions and thus reduce the employment of resources in carrying them out. * * *

"The problem which we face in dealing with actions which have harmful effects is not simply one of restraining those responsible for them. What has to be decided is whether the gain from preventing the harm is greater than the loss which would be suffered elsewhere as a result of stopping the action which produces the harm. In a world in which there are costs of rearranging the rights established by the legal system, the courts, in cases relating to nuisance, are, in effect, making a decision on the economic problem and determining how resources are to be employed. It was argued that the courts are conscious of this and that they often make, although not always in a very explicit fashion, a comparison between what would be gained and what lost by preventing actions which have harmful effects. But the delimitation of rights is also the result of statutory enactments. Here we also find evidence of an appreciation of the reciprocal nature of the problem. While statutory enactments add to the list of nuisances, action is also taken to legalize what would otherwise be nuisances under the common law. The kind of situation which economists are prone to consider as requiring corrective Government action is, in fact, often the result of Government action. Such action is not necessarily unwise. But there is a real danger that extensive Government intervention in the economic system may lead to the protection of those responsible for harmful effects being carried too far. * * *

"It would clearly be desirable if the only actions performed were those in which what was gained was worth more than what was lost. But in choosing between social arrangements within the context of which individual decisions are made, we have to bear in mind that a change in the existing system which will lead to an improvement in some decisions may well lead to a worsening of others. Furthermore we have to take into account the costs involved in operating the various social arrangements (whether it be the working of a market or of a government department), as well as the costs involved in moving to a new system. In devising and choosing between social arrangements we should have regard for the total effect. This, above all, is the change in approach which I am advocating."

2. Note that Professor Coase puts "problems of equity" aside in concluding that it makes no difference in resource allocation whether or not, to translate into our terms, the priority of the first right includes the right to maintain an inefficient means of diversion. If in the *Crowley* situation the loss to Crowley's crops is less than the benefit the power company obtains when the extra water required by the inefficient wing dam is held back, the water will be stored in the company's reservoir, whether the company has to pay Crowley or not. If the benefit to the company is less than the crop loss the water will be released, either because if the company is liable it will be cheaper to release it than to pay damages, or if not liable the company will make a profit by accepting Crowley's offer to buy the water at a price somewhere between the company's benefit and his loss. Whether an improved dam will be built is similarly independent of the rule of liability. If the water is stored in the reservoir and if the cost of building an improved diversion dam is less than the crop loss, the dam will be built. If Crowley has no claim against the company, he will build it to eliminate his crop loss. If the company is liable, it will build it or pay Crowley to build it rather than continuing to pay the greater damages. If the water is released from the reservoir because it has less value to the company than to Crowley, the new dam will not be built. The "inefficient" wing dam then remains as the most efficient method of utilizing the resource.

What "problems of equity" remain? Although maximum efficiency in resource allocation is obtainable under either rule, *ought* the cost of constructing the improved dam be placed on the power company or on the irrigator? Does it make any difference if all the water users are irrigators, as in *Warner Valley?*

If the prior appropriator's means of diversion is protected, does the relief given by the court make any difference? Crowley asked for damages. If he had sought and obtained an injunction, would the Coasian analysis of the situation change? Suppose there are a number of persons situated similarly to Crowley, all of whose diversion works need to be improved to get the desirable combination of irrigation and power. If each is given the right to an injunction, is the Coasian optimum more or less likely to be reached?

KAISER STEEL CORPORATION v. W.S. RANCH COMPANY

Supreme Court of New Mexico, 1970.
81 N.M. 414, 467 P.2d 986.

MOISE, CHIEF JUSTICE. In this case, involving a simple but interesting fact situation we are called upon to answer two legal problems of first impression in this jurisdiction. These are: (1) Is § 75–1–3, N.M. S.A.1953, constitutional as applied to the parties and facts in this case? (2) Is inverse condemnation the exclusive remedy available to defendant-appellant, hereinafter referred to as "Ranch"?

Plaintiff-appellee, hereinafter referred to as "Kaiser," owns a tract of land located some distance from the Vermejo River in Colfax County, New Mexico, which tract is completely surrounded by lands owned by Ranch. Kaiser also owns certain water rights in the river, which it is entitled to use for industrial purposes. See W.S. Ranch Company v. Kaiser Steel Corporation, 79 N.M. 65, 439 P.2d 714 (1968), where certain of the rights of the parties to the water were litigated.

In order for Kaiser to use the water in a coal mine being developed by it, the water had to be made available on its land. This was accomplished in 1966 by the simple expedient of Kaiser sending its employees onto the lands of Ranch, drilling some holes or wells in the stream bed, and laying a pipeline from the river source across the lands of Ranch to the coal property of Kaiser, all without seeking permission of Ranch, or undertaking to condemn under § 75–1–3, supra * * * [Kaiser then filed an action for declaratory judgment.]

After issue was joined * * *, Ranch filed a motion for judgment on the pleadings and Kaiser asked for summary judgment. The trial court granted summary judgment to Kaiser, and made the following determinations:

> "2. The Court hereby declares that Kaiser Steel Corporation, a corporation, has, under § 75–1–3, New Mexico Statutes Annotated, 1953 Compilation, which statute is constitutional under the Constitution of the State of New Mexico, the power of eminent domain for the

purpose of entry upon, and use of, the lands more particularly described in the Amended Complaint on file herein for the purpose of diversion and transportation of its recognized water rights to its York Canyon Mine and processing facilities; and

"3. That the exclusive remedy of the Defendant, W.S. Ranch Company, for the existing entry upon and use of said lands described in the Amended Complaint for the said water distribution purpose is that of 'inverse condemnation' as set forth under Section 22–9–22, New Mexico Statutes Annotated, 1953 Compilation, as Amended."

We here consider whether the court ruled correctly on these two issues.

We restate the first question which we are called on to determine as follows: Does the New Mexico Constitution permit a taking of private property by a person, firm or corporation, for the conveyance of water for use in an industrial endeavor, specifically coal mining? Refining the issue further, it becomes one of whether the question of public use turns on the ultimate purpose for which the property was taken, or on the nature of the product (water) involved.

Section 75–1–3, supra, reads as follows:

"The United States, the state of New Mexico, or any person, firm, association or corporation, may exercise the right of eminent domain, to take and acquire land right of way for the construction, maintenance and operation of reservoirs, canals, ditches, flumes, aqueducts, pipelines or other works for the storage or conveyance of water for beneficial uses, including the right to enlarge existing structures, and to use the same in common with the former owner; any such right of way for canal, ditch, pipeline, or other means for the conveyance of water shall in all cases be so located as to do the least damage to private or public property consistent with proper use and economical construction. Such land and right of way shall be acquired in the manner provided by law for the condemnation and taking of private property in the state of New Mexico for railroad, telegraph, telephone and other public uses and purposes. The engineers and surveyors of the United States, the state and of any person, firm or corporation shall have the right to enter upon the lands and waters of the state and of private persons and of private and public corporations, for the purpose of making hydrographic surveys and examinations and surveys necessary for selecting and locating suitable sites and routes for reservoirs, canals, pipelines and other waterworks, subject to responsibility for any damage done to such property, in making such surveys."

The statute clearly provides a right in "any person, firm, association or corporation" to condemn land right of way for "construction, maintenance and operation" of "canals, ditches, * * * pipelines or other works for the storage or conveyance of water for beneficial uses, * * *."

It is the position of Ranch that if § 75–1–3, supra, is read to permit a taking for any "beneficial use" it necessarily conflicts with the New Mexico Constitution, Art. II, § 20, which reads in its entirety, "Private property shall not be taken or damaged for public use without just compensation."

At the outset, there can be no question under our Constitution that the taking or damaging of private property through eminent domain is permitted for none other than a public use. Threlkeld v. Third Judicial District Court, 36 N.M. 350, 15 P.2d 671, 86 A.L.R. 547 (1932). * * *

Consideration of this issue requires us to look to our constitutional provisions relating specifically to water. We note Art. XVI, §§ 1, 2 and 3, which we quote:

> "Section 1. All existing rights to the use of any waters in this state for any useful or beneficial purpose are hereby recognized and confirmed.
>
> "Section 2. The unappropriated water of every natural stream, perennial or torrential, within the state of New Mexico, is hereby declared to belong to the public and to be subject to appropriation for beneficial use, in accordance with the laws of the state. Priority of appropriation shall give the better right.
>
> "Section 3. Beneficial use shall be the basis, the measure and the limit of the right to the use of water."

We perceive in these provisions that water was placed in a unique category in our Constitution—something that cannot be said of lumbering, coal mining, or any other element or industry. The reason for this is of course too apparent to require elaboration. Our entire state has only enough water to supply its most urgent needs. Water conservation and preservation is of utmost importance. Its utilization for maximum benefits is a requirement second to none, not only for progress, but for survival. Recognition of these facts, as well as a conviction that the doctrine of prior appropriation was better suited to accomplishing the desired ends than was the common law riparian doctrine must have been the principal reason for the adoption in this state of the prior appropriation doctrine as the law applicable to water. See Yeo v. Tweedy, 34 N.M. 611, 615, 286 P. 970 (1929).

Admittedly, the use of water for irrigation was held by our Territorial Supreme Court to be a public use, making legal the provision of our law permitting a taking of the land of another, by an individual, to convey water to the place where the use was to be made. The Albuquerque Land and Irrigation Company v. Gutierrez, 10 N.M. 177, 61 P. 357 (1900), aff'd 188 U.S. 545, 23 S.Ct. 338, 47 L.Ed. 588 (1903). This case was held controlling in the later cases of City of Albuquerque v. Garcia, supra; and Young v. Dugger, 23 N.M. 613, 170 P. 61 (1918). See also Pueblo of Isleta v. Tondre, 18 N.M. 388, 137 P. 86 (1913). That water holds a unique position in our public policy was recognized in Threlkeld v. Third Judicial District Court, supra, where we said:

> " * * * [W]e already had a policy, also time-honored, as to waters. We had nationalized them. Not as a source of public revenue, as minerals are retained for royalties; but as an elemental necessity, like air, which must not be allowed to fall under private control. *Only*

> *by invoking the power of eminent domain can the state distribute its own waters as its public policy requires. A right of way taken for that purpose is in a large sense devoted to public use.* This policy finds general and express recognition in the Constitution. It is impossible to suppose that any interpretation of 'public use' was intended to upset it." (Emphasis added.)

We now approach the crucial question of whether the "ultimate use," i.e., irrigation, mining, lumbering, etc., is controlling, and determinative of the question of "public use," or, is the answer controlled by the fact that the condemnation at issue is for a right of way to carry water?

* * * We would first note that each of our cases wherein a public use has been found in situations involving transportation of water (and consequently condemnation by private parties for rights of way was held permissible) has been a case involving irrigation. However, it should be noted that in no circumstance have we stated or suggested that right of way to convey water for industrial or other "beneficial" uses would not be for "public use." That we did not indulge in that hazardous pastime of incorporating dicta covering issues not present is to our credit. Only now when we are at last directly faced with the problem involving right of way for conveying water for industrial use is the time for us to speak on it.

We recognize that coal mining in New Mexico is not a public endeavor and that because of the lack of the element of "public use" the right of eminent domain would not exist in private parties for a roadway over which to transport coal. Gallup American Coal Co. v. Gallup Southwestern Coal Co., supra. However, that fact does not foreclose the possibility of a "public use" for the beneficial utilization of water for a purpose other than irrigation. As a matter of fact, we find ourselves unable to rationalize use of water by a private citizen for irrigation as a public use, and at the same time the use of the same water by the same person for mining coal not to be. We do not suppose for a moment that it is the use for growing crops or producing food that has moved this Court to hold as it has concerning irrigation as a public use. Rather, it must have been the fact of beneficial use of water which unquestionably is of the greatest importance to the state, that dictated the result. Appropriation is not complete until the water has been put to beneficial use. State ex rel. State Engineer v. Crider, 78 N.M. 312, 431 P.2d 45 (1967). *It is beneficial use that is of primary importance,* not the particular purpose (ultimate use) to which the water is put. Such beneficial uses would be impossible to accomplish without the means to transport or convey the water from its source to the place of utilization. Thus, out of necessity, in 1907, the right of eminent domain was provided for the "storage and conveyance of water for beneficial uses,"—not for irrigation or domestic purposes alone, *but for all beneficial uses.* (Ch. 49, § 3, N.M.S.L.1907). The particular ultimate use is not important, so long as the water is applied beneficially in accomplishing it. * * *

We conclude that the act permitting condemnation for rights of way to convey water is not vulnerable to the attack here levied against it, since it is in the public interest that distribution of water be provided so long as the use to which the water is to be put is beneficial, and accordingly such distribution is a public use as well.

Having determined that Kaiser could legally and constitutionally acquire the right of way to convey its water across the property of Ranch by condemnation, we must still consider if Ranch could recover in an action in trespass because Kaiser entered the property without first instituting legal proceedings seeking to condemn. Otherwise stated, is inverse condemnation the only legal remedy open to Ranch for Kaiser's entering and utilizing the land of Ranch, or may Ranch sue in trespass? No question of the right to the equitable remedy of injunction is here presented. * * *

Ranch would have us restrict the area for exclusive resort to inverse condemnation to the situations where there has been an incidental injury or damage with no direct taking, or where there has been an unintentional taking. While admittedly damages without a direct taking give rise to an inverse condemnation action, see Springer Transfer Co. v. Board of Com'rs of Bernalillo County, 43 N.M. 444, 94 P.2d 977 (1939), we do not see anything in the language of the statute to justify the limitation urged upon us. Neither do we see any reason to hold our statutory inverse condemnation to be the exclusive remedy where the action is against the sovereign, but not when it is against a private condemnor. Section 22–9–22, supra, here applicable, makes not only the "state of New Mexico or any agency or political subdivision thereof" liable to the owner of property under the circumstances therein set forth, but also makes "[a]ny person, firm or corporation authorized by the Constitution or laws of this state to exercise the right of eminent domain" equally subject to suit. This section is clear that suit is permitted by the landowner, when there has been not only a damaging of private property but a taking as well, if just compensation has not been paid, or a proper condemnation action either has not been instituted or prosecuted to final judgment. We see in the plain language of the statute a complete method for obtaining compensation in the exact circumstances of this case. Therefore, it follows, and we so hold, that the objective sought to be accomplished by the inverse condemnation statute is not so limited as urged above. * * *

We would add a word to the effect that we fully appreciate the dilemma faced by both parties at the outset of the dispute that gave rise to this litigation. There had been no clear pronouncement by this Court that a party in Kaiser's position could exercise eminent domain for a right of way to convey water to a coal mine. Kaiser had the choice of attempting to obtain an answer to the question either by commencing condemnation which would have involved protracted litigation on the question of whether a public use was present, and their right to condemn, or they could have sought declaratory relief in the first instance as they belatedly have done in this proceeding. On the other hand, they could take a calculated risk and proceed on the theory they had the right to condemn, and if they did not commence an action, that in the end Ranch would receive the same damages through inverse condemnation as it would have through condemnation.

Of course, if Kaiser miscalculated and it was determined that they were mistaken in their belief that they had the right to condemn, [a] trespass action undertaken by Ranch would have been proper, and substantial damages would have been adjudged against Kaiser as a trespasser.

While we certainly do not recommend proceeding as Kaiser did in the instant case, and would again emphasize the risks of damages of major consequences, we must nevertheless conclude that in this instance no one has suffered. Kaiser had the right under the facts of this case to condemn the right of way they occupied for the purpose for which it was taken, and may be held liable for damages to the owner only in an inverse condemnation action. It follows that the judgment appealed from should be affirmed.

Notes

1. The validity of a similar statute under the Fourteenth Amendment to the United States Constitution was upheld in Clark v. Nash, 198 U.S. 361, 25 S.Ct. 676, 49 L.Ed. 1085 (1905):

"In some states, probably in most of them, the proposition contended for by the plaintiffs in error would be sound. But whether a statute of a state permitting condemnation by an individual for the purpose of obtaining water for his land or for mining should be held to be a condemnation for a public use, and, therefore, a valid enactment, may depend upon a number of considerations relating to the situation of the state and its possibilities for land cultivation, or the successful prosecution of its mining or other industries. * * * The rights of a riparian owner in and to the use of the water flowing by his land are not the same in the arid and mountainous states of the West that they are in the states of the East. These rights have been altered by many of the Western states by their constitutions and laws, because of the totally different circumstances in which their inhabitants are placed, from those that exist in the states of the East, and such alterations have been made for the very purpose of thereby contributing to the growth and prosperity of those states, arising from mining and the cultivation of an otherwise valueless soil, by means of irrigation. This court must recognize the difference of climate and soil, which render necessary these different laws in the states so situated.

"We are of opinion, having reference to the above peculiarities which exist in the state of Utah, that the statute permitting the defendant in error, upon the facts appearing in this record, to enlarge the ditch, and obtain water for his own land, was within the legislative power of the state."

2. A "ditch right" is a separate property interest from a water right. The acquisition of a water right does not automatically result in the acquisition of a right to transport the water across the lands of others. Often the two are linked, and, carrying out the intention of the parties, it has been held that a conveyance of a ditch may carry with it the water right as an appurtenance, Williams v. Harter, 121 Cal. 47, 53 P. 405 (1898), or that the ditch may be regarded as an appurtenance of the water right and pass with a deed to the latter, Jacob v. Lorenz, 98 Cal. 332, 33 P. 119 (1893). Often they are sufficiently separate that one can be sold independently of the other, or that abandonment of the water right does not bring the existence of the ditch right-of-way to an end. Ada County Farmers' Irrigation Co. v. Farmers' Canal Co., Ltd., 5 Idaho 793, 51 P. 990 (1898). This case also points out that the ditch itself is more than a hole in the ground, that it is a valuable structure, an asset subject to sale.

3. Rights of way for ditches can be acquired by purchase, or obtained by prescription where their existence and use has been adverse to the servient estate for the period of the statute of limitations. Where oral permission has been given by the owner of the servient estate so that the use is not adverse, the water user may still have a permanent ditch right in the form of an "executed parol license" or a "license by estoppel." See Gustin v. Harting, 21 Wyo. 1, 121 P. 522 (1912).

The owner of an easement for a ditch has a secondary easement to enter and to inspect, repair, maintain or otherwise use the easement. O'Connor v. Brodie, 153 Mont. 129, 454 P.2d 920 (1969).

4. Rights of way for canals and ditches over the federal public domain were first authorized in 1866. The first statutes gave the water user general permission to use the land, but later laws required the filing of applications and specific approval, normally in the form of a "use permit." These have been repealed and replaced by the Federal Land Policy and Management Act of 1976 (the "B.L.M. Organic Act"):

"The Secretary of the Interior, with respect to public lands, and the Secretary of Agriculture with respect to lands within the National Forest system (except wilderness areas) are authorized to grant, issue or renew rights of way under or through such lands for reservoirs, canals, ditches, flumes, laterals, pipes, pipelines, tunnels and other facilities and systems for the impoundment, storage, transportation or distribution of water." Rather elaborate procedures are required. Rights of way are limited to a reasonable term and are subject to an annual rental and elaborate conditions and regulations. P.L. 94–579, §§ 501–511, 706; 43 U.S.C.A. §§ 1751–1771.

5. As western cities expand over former farmlands, irrigation ditches following the contour of the country present problems to subdivision developers. The general rule is that the location of an easement cannot be changed by either the servient or the dominant owner without the other's consent. This rule was followed in Stamatis v. Johnson, 71 Ariz. 134, 224 P.2d 201 (1950), but on rehearing the landowner was allowed to install a covered tile pipe on the original right-of-way of the ditch it replaced. 72 Ariz. 158, 231 P.2d 956 (1951). The Colorado court allowed a landowner to fill in another's ditch across his land and substitute a ditch of equal

efficiency along the sides of the land. Brown v. Bradbury, 110 Colo. 537, 135 P.2d 1013 (1943). This practice is permitted in Idaho by statute. Idaho Code § 42–1207. In Boz-Lew Builders v. Smith, 174 Mont. 448, 571 P.2d 389 (1977), a land developer filled in a ditch that had apparently been used since 1866, and built a fourplex apartment over it. The developer was ordered to find a way of getting the water around or through his property, to pay damages, and to pay attorneys' fees.

SECTION 3. REGULATION

WYOMING HEREFORD RANCH v. HAMMOND PACKING CO.

Supreme Court of Wyoming, 1925.
33 Wyo. 14, 236 P. 764.

KIMBALL, J. This action involves rights to the use of the waters of Crow creek, a stream rising west of the city of Cheyenne, and flowing in a general easterly direction through that city and through lands owned by the Hammond Packing Company and the Wyoming Hereford Ranch. The plaintiff, the Wyoming Hereford Ranch, and the defendant the Hammond Packing Company are appropriators of the waters of said creek for the purpose of irrigation. * * *

In addition to its rights under the decree of 1888, the plaintiff claimed an appropriation through the Bolln ditch for the irrigation of about 200 acres. The decree of the district court upheld this claim and established the right as prior and superior to the rights of the defendant under its permits of 1909 and 1911, hereinbefore mentioned. It is conceded that whatever right the plaintiff has to divert and use water through the Bolln ditch was acquired since the adoption of the Constitution and the enactment of the state water law of 1890. Article 8 of the Constitution contains the following provisions:

> "Section 1. The waters of all natural streams, springs, lakes or other collections of still water, within the boundaries of the state, are hereby declared to be the property of the state.
>
> "Sec. 2. There shall be constituted a board of control, to be composed of the state engineer and superintendents of the water divisions; which shall, under such regulations as may be prescribed by law, have the supervision of the waters of the state and of their appropriation, distribution and diversion, and of the various officers connected therewith. Its decisions to be subject to review by the courts of the state.
>
> "Sec. 3. Priority of appropriation for beneficial uses shall give the better right. No appropriation shall be denied except when such denial is demanded by the public interest. * * *
>
> "Sec. 5. There shall be a state engineer who shall be appointed by the governor of the state and confirmed by the senate; he shall hold his office for the term of six (6) years, or until his successor shall have been appointed and shall have qualified. He shall be president of the

board of control, and shall have general supervision of the waters of the state and of the officers connected with its distribution. No person shall be appointed to this position who has not such theoretical knowledge and such practical experience and skill as shall fit him for the position."

At the first session of the state Legislature, there was enacted a law approved December 22, 1890, "providing for the supervision and use of the waters of the state." Chapter 8, Laws of Wyoming 1890–91. Section 34 of that act provided, among other things, that any one thereafter intending to appropriate any of the public waters of the state should, before commencing construction, enlargement, or extension of any distributing works, or performing any work in connection with said appropriation, make an application to the president of the board of control for a permit to make such appropriation. It requires that the application for a permit shall, among other things, state the source from which the appropriation is to be made, the amount of the appropriation, the location and character of the proposed works, and the time at which the application of water to beneficial purposes shall be made, which time is limited to the time required for the completion of the work when prosecuted with due diligence. If it is intended that the water should be used for irrigation, the application should describe the lands to be irrigated. It is further provided that the application shall state additional facts required by the board of control. On receipt of the application, it is filed and recorded in the office of the state engineer, and if on investigation it is found that there is unappropriated water in the source of supply named in the application, and if the appropriation is not otherwise detrimental to the public welfare, the engineer shall approve the application. The application indorsed with such approval is then returned to the applicant, "who shall, on receipt thereof, be authorized to proceed with such work, and to take such measures as may be necessary to perfect such appropriation." It is further provided that—

"If there is no unappropriated water in the source of supply, or if, in the judgment of the state engineer, such appropriation is detrimental to public interests, the state engineer shall refuse such appropriation, and the party making such application shall not prosecute such work, so long as such refusal shall continue in force."

There is provision for appeal from the action of the state engineer to the board of control and from the board to the courts. These provisions of section 34 of the Act of 1890 have continued in force to the present day without any amendments material to our present inquiry. Sections 835 to 842, Wyo.C.S.1920.

It is conceded as to the Bolln ditch that the plaintiff has never conformed to the provisions of this law, and we are required to decide whether, under the Constitution and the legislation of 1890, a lawful appropriation of waters can be made without a permit, and without an application therefor. The question is one of considerable importance and of some difficulty. Its solution requires a careful consideration of the foregoing provisions of the Constitution and statutes.

Directing our attention first to statute law of 1890, there would seem to be little need for construction or interpretation. When it is provided that before commencing the construction or enlargement of any distributing works, there must be an application for a permit, and that, if approval of the permit is refused, the party applying therefor shall not prosecute such work, it would seem quite clear, so far as the statute is concerned, that the permit is a condition precedent to the right to divert and appropriate water. If an applicant for a permit has no right to divert waters until the application is approved, it surely was not intended that a person who has never made such application could legally divert and use the waters of the state. Similar statutes seem to have been given their obvious meaning in Nebraska. Castle Rock Irrigation, etc., Co. v. Jurisch, 67 Neb. 377, 93 N.W. 690. It is argued, however, that section 3 of article 8 of the state Constitution, supra, requires a different construction, and that though a permit is necessary in order that the appropriator may have priority as of the date of filing the permit, an "appropriation" can still be made as under previous laws by diversion and use without a permit, with the only difference that such an appropriation will have priority only from the time of the application of the water to the beneficial use. The effect of the contention is that the statutes requiring a permit, if construed as preventing a diversion and use of the waters of the state without a permit, are unconstitutional.

The declaration of section 3, article 8, of the Constitution, that "priority of appropriation for beneficial uses shall give the better right," must be construed in connection with section 1 of the same article, declaring that the waters of all natural streams, etc., are the property of the state; section 2 providing that the board of control shall, under such regulations as may be prescribed by law, have the supervision of such waters and of their appropriation, distribution, and diversion, and the last sentence of section 3, that no appropriation shall be denied except when such denial is demanded by the public interest. In the first place, it is to be noted that the framers of the Constitution deliberately refrained from including in that instrument any definition of the word "appropriation." Debates of Wyoming Constitutional Convention, pp. 498, 500, 504. This was after the attention of the members of the convention had been called to the fact that some courts had construed an appropriation as being the commencement of work which was diligently pursued until the water was applied to the beneficial use, and other courts had held that it was the actual application of the water to the beneficial use. It is clear, from the reports of the proceedings of the constitutional convention that the precise method and system subsequently embodied in the law of 1890 was within the purpose of the convention. Farm Inv. Co. v. Carpenter, supra, at page 144. A member of the committee of the convention on agriculture, irrigation, and water rights, in reply to an inquiry concerning the meaning of section 3, supra, described in rather forceful language the old and the proposed new system of obtaining water rights, as follows (Debates, pp. 504, 505):

> "Mr. Burritt: I will explain to Mr. Hay. The present system, as the gentleman well knows, is for a man to rush out to the creek, as has been done in the gentleman's own county, and without consulting anybody, finding out anything about whether there is any water there or not, he rushes in and begins a ditch, and rushes into court and begins a lawsuit. Now this system proposes to revise the order of things, and instead of rushing all over the country, and beginning a ditch and taking the chances about getting any water, we propose to have them get permission to construct ditches from the board of control. In other words, all the information necessary to enable a man to do the wise thing in this matter will be with the board of control. This provision is to revise this system from what we have it now, and instead of allowing ditches to be taken out without any system at all, to have a man find out from the board of control just what he can do."

The contemporaneous construction of these provisions of the Constitution by the administrative officers is shown in the report of Mr. Elwood Mead, who was territorial engineer at the time of the adoption of the Constitution, and state engineer upon the admission of the state into the Union. This report, evidently prepared after the adoption of the Constitution, but before the admission of the state, contains the following (2 Ann.Rep.Terr.Eng.Wyo. p. 97):

> "If state ownership is to be anything but a delusion, if it is to be more than nominal, there must be the same authority and control over streams and over diversion of water as is now exercised by the general government over the occupation and settlement of public lands. No diversion or appropriation should be permitted, therefore, until the sanction of the territory, through its constituted authorities, has been obtained, and the beneficial character of the proposed use established. Such oversight and precaution is necessary for the proper protection of public interests (public water supply being of greater agricultural value than public lands) and in order that controversies growing out of extravagant and injurious claims may be avoided.
>
> "Instead of the present absence of supervision over either the nature of the diversion and use or the amount of the claim, I would recommend that each and every intending appropriator be required to make application to the irrigation authorities for a permit to divert and use the public waters and that approval of such authorities must be had before work is begun. For convenience in recording, and as a matter of economy, I would recommend that all such applications be made to the territorial engineer." * * *

In determining the meaning of a written law, it is proper to consider the evils sought to be remedied. The laws of the territory had permitted the diversion of water without any state supervision of the works and without any adequate notice and record of the amount, purpose, and date of the appropriation. Defective and badly located diversion works often made the use of water wasteful. No right became definite until it was adjudicated in court, and adjudications were often long delayed and then made on inaccurate testimony and without any disinterested measurements of the ditches or of the lands irrigated. Until such an adjudication, no subsequent appropriation could be made with safety, for no one could tell the amount of unappropriated water in the stream. The evils attendant on such a system, and the importance of providing a different system that would give the state the unquestioned right of control, had become well recognized at the time the Constitution was framed. See 2 Annual Rep. Terr.Eng.Wyo. (1889) pp. 3, 12, 16, 37, 41, 58, 69, and 98. To correct these defects in the old system, it was provided by the Constitution not only that the waters of the state are the property of the state but also that those waters, and their appropriation, distribution, and diversion, shall be under the supervision of a state board of control. This supervision, it was hoped, would cure many of the evils of the old system, and we think that hope has been justified by the later events. The constitutional declaration that priority of appropriation for beneficial uses shall give the better right was not intended to prevent the Legislature from prescribing reasonable conditions that must be complied with before a lawful appropriation could be made. Their power in this respect is both recognized and limited by the further provision of the Constitution, carried into the statutes, that "no appropriation shall be denied except when such denial is demanded by the public interests." In interpreting this language, we must give consideration to the contemporaneous recognition not only of the importance of state supervision of the diversion of waters, but also of the fact that such supervision could not be effective, nor intelligently exercised, without accurate and complete information of proposed appropriations. The Legislature has decided that the public interests demand that such information shall be given to the state board by an application for a permit, and that until such an application is approved, no appropriation can be lawfully made. We believe these requirements are reasonable in so far at least as they are questioned in this case. * * *

A different decision would leave prevalent many of the acknowledged evils of the territorial system intended to be superseded by the system of state control contemplated by the Constitution and carried into effect by the law of 1890. The plaintiff is willing in this case to concede that its right under the Bolln ditch would take priority only from the date of the application of the water to the land. Another claimant of a similar right might not be willing to make that concession. If a right may be lawfully acquired by diversion and use since 1890 without compliance with the state laws, it might be impossible to find a sufficient reason for holding that the right would not have priority as of the date of commencement of the work. If that condition should prevail, there would seem to be no advantage to be gained by proceeding under a permit, and we would be thrown back to the confusion incident to the haphazard methods of the old system. * * *

It follows that the part of the decree which gives the plaintiff a priority for use of water through the Bolln ditch cannot be upheld.

Notes

1. In the early history of appropriation law, the word "appropriation" was used in its crudest sense, of a taking of possession, and a legal right flowed from the physical acts of constructing a ditch, diverting the water and applying it to use. Nevertheless, a need was felt by the appropriators for improving their legal position, and following the common procedure of staking a mining claim, the custom arose of posting a notice of claim upon the bank of the stream near the point of diversion. The courts recognized such a notice as evidence of the possessory right to the water. Thompson v. Lee, 8 Cal. 276 (1857). Later these procedures were codified in a number of states by statutes which required the posting of a more elaborate notice and its recordation in the county where posted. These systems were optional. A failure to comply did not affect the validity of the rights acquired by diversion and application to beneficial use, though it did affect the date of priority. If an appropriator did not post and file a notice, his priority dated from the time of completion of the appropriation, but if he did, his priority related back to the start of work. Once the application to beneficial use was made, an unfiled appropriation was a complete and vested right, and took precedence over any subsequently initiated appropriations.

The defects in this system are obvious. "Claims are filed in the different counties, and as Montana rivers are long, the water-right records of a single stream are often found in several counties. Musselshell River forms a part of the boundary between Fergus and Meagher, Yellowstone, Dawson, and Custer counties. Ditches on one side of the stream are recorded in one county, and ditches on the other side of the river in another county. It would require a journey of several hundred miles and an examination of five sets of county records to ascertain the extent of the claims to this stream." Mead, Irrigation Institutions 301 (1903).

2. The permit system of initiating appropriations is now found in all of the states recognizing the appropriation doctrine except Colorado. It is the exclusive method in each state. Although Idaho has long had permits, until 1971 it had a dual system. A "statutory water right" was obtained under permit, but a "constitutional right" could be acquired by diversion and use without any formalities. The principal incentive to go the permit route was that the statutory right had a priority relating back to the date of the application for permit while the constitutional right dated from its completion. The new statute is explicit that the right to use water can be acquired only by permit and not otherwise. Idaho Code §§ 42–103, 42–201. See Barber, Statutory Water Rights and Permits, 9 Idaho L.Rev. 1 (1972).

Until 1973 Montana appropriations on "unadjudicated streams" could be obtained by diversion and use, but their priority would date from completion, not commencement, unless an 1885 statute requiring posting and filing of notice was followed. On "adjudicated streams" a 1921 statute set up what might be called a judicial permit system. An intending appropriator had to file a petition in the court which had entered the decree, all affected appropriators were named as defendants and a final or conditional decree added the new appropriation to the list of water right holders. For some of the difficulties inherent in this procedure, see Stone, Are There Any Adjudicated Streams in Montana?, 19 Mont.L.Rev. 19 (1956); Stone, the Long Count on Dempsey: No Final Decision in Water Right Adjudication, 31 Mont.L.Rev. 1 (1969).

The 1973 permit procedure (Mont.Code Ann.1979 §§ 85–2–301 to 85–2–401) was enacted pursuant to a new state constitution adopted in 1972, which provided, "The legislature shall provide for the administration, control and regulation of water rights * * *" Mont. Const. art. 9, § 3(4).

Some statutes contain express exceptions to the requirement of a permit for certain classes of small appropriations or appropriations from some sources. See Vernon's Tex.Codes Ann.Water §§ 11.142, 11.143; So. Dak.Comp.Laws 46–5–8.

3. The procedures for obtaining a permit to appropriate are not identical in all states where a permit is required. Although the statutes have a common origin and many basic similarities, they contain many variations, and a person seeking a permit must carefully check and follow the practice of the particular state. Most of the states provide for publication of notice of the filing of the application to any person who may be affected by the proposed appropriation. In others the practice was to issue permits *ex parte,* but modern administrative procedure acts supply the requirements of notice and hearing.

4. Several states have a dual permit system for stored irrigation waters. The person intending to impound the waters must make application for a "primary permit" to construct the reservoir; the person intending to use the water on particular land must apply for a "secondary permit" to appropriate the stored water to the land. See Ariz.Rev.Stat. § 45–151; Or.Rev.Stat. 537.300; Wash.Rev.Code Ann. 90.03.370; Wyo.Stat. 1977, § 41–3–301. These dual permits are discussed in Cookingham v. Lewis, 58 Or. 484, 114 P. 88 (1911); Condict v. Ryan, 79 Wyo. 211, 333 P.2d 684 (1958); and Nebraska v. Wyoming, 325 U.S. 589, 65 S.Ct. 1332, 89 L.Ed. 1815 (1945).

5. Not until 1980 did California settle this point. Many early water cases involved claims that persons who took water to irrigate nonriparian land or stored it for future use were violating the riparian rights of downstream landowners (see Chapter 3, infra). The upstream nonriparian uses were validated, however, if they had been exercised for the period of the statute of limitations and the user had obtained prescriptive rights. In these cases the terms "prescriptive rights" and "appropriations" were sometimes used interchangeably and sometimes independently. The 1914 Water Commission Act established a permit system (West's Ann.Cal. Water Code §§ 1201 et seq.), and in 1923 an amendment declared that compliance with this procedure was the exclusive method of acquiring the right to appropriate or use water subject to appropriation (§ 1225). For years lawyers debated whether or not one who acquired an appropriative right by prescription must comply with the Board's permit procedure. People v.

Shirokow, 26 Cal.3d 301, 162 Cal.Rptr. 30, 605 P.2d 859 (1980), decided that he must. Shirokow's predecessor had constructed a small dam for a stockwater and fishing pond on an intermittent stream. After Shirokow acquired the land in 1960, he applied for a permit to store the water. Apparently the Water Resources Control Board thought there was no unappropriated water available; it informed him that it would grant the permit only if he would institute a brush control program to salvage the needed water (cf. *R.J.A., Inc.,* supra p. 47). Shirokow abandoned his application when he found this would cost $8,500, but nevertheless continued to impound the water, relying on his "prescriptive right." In 1976 the state brought this action, and Shirokow was enjoined from further unauthorized diversions of the water:

"Even if arguendo we were to hold defendant was not required to comply with the statutory appropriation procedures, his claim of a prescriptive right would fail for two reasons.

"First, public rights cannot be lost by prescription. Defendant alleged and the trial court agreed that as against the state he had perfected a prescriptive right. Both were mistaken. What is being challenged is the state's governmental interest in regulating the use of public waters rather than any proprietary interest in the water claimed by defendant. The stipulated facts do not reveal that the state was using the water; indeed, defendant admits the state, if successful in obtaining the injunction, will not make use of the water. Thus it is undisputed that the state's interest here at stake in nonproprietary.

"More than a century ago, in Hoadley v. San Francisco (1875) 50 Cal. 265, 274–276, we articulated the rule that property held by the state in trust for the people cannot be lost through adverse possession. * * *

"The second reason defendant cannot prevail in his claim of a prescriptive right is that the stipulated facts do not provide the necessary elements. Defendant has not shown his diversion was hostile to the interests of any downstream user; we are told only that there was general community knowledge that the dam and reservoir existed and water was impounded. Since it is axiomatic that common law prescriptive rights are based on adverse use, such rights could not have been obtained by defendant by a taking of excess water which did not invade the interests of another. * * * Not only did defendant fail to identify any downstream users having actual knowledge of his diversion (see Pabst v. Finmand (1922) 190 Cal. 124, 129–130, 211 P. 11), no downstream users were parties to this action. Accordingly, the court lacked jurisdiction to adjudicate their rights vis-a-vis those of defendant."

COLORADO APPROPRIATION PROCEDURES

Since the Colorado Constitution declares, "The right to divert the unappropriated waters of any natural stream to beneficial uses shall never be denied" (Art. XVI, Sec. 6), it has generally been assumed that a permit system is unavailable in that state. Colorado was the first state to create the office of State Engineer, but his duties are confined to regulating the works of appropriators and distributing water according to decrees entered by courts in proceedings to adjudicate all rights to a stream or segment of a stream. Colorado had an early precursor of a permit system in her "map and statement law", which provided that any person constructing works for an appropriation shall, "within sixty days after the commencement of such construction * * * make a filing in the office of the State Engineer," consisting of an accurate map of the project and detailed information on the works, including the time of commencement of the works or the survey for it. This early attempt to at least record the initiation of rights was emasculated by holdings that the map and statement were evidentiary only and were not required for the validity of an appropriation. An appropriation could be made without compliance with the statute and if a map and statement were filed, the completed appropriation need not conform to them. See DeHaas v. Benesch, 116 Colo. 344, 181 P.2d 453 (1947).

When an adjudication proceeding was initiated all appropriators had to file their claims in court or lose their priority. If a person had commenced an appropriation but had not applied the water to beneficial use, he received a "conditional decree" fixing his priority. If subsequent supplemental adjudications were initiated by others, he had to establish that he was continuing to proceed with reasonable diligence to complete his appropriation or prove he had completed it. See Taussig v. Moffat Tunnel Water and Development Co., 106 Colo. 384, 106 P.2d 363 (1940).

The Water Right Determination and Adjudication Act of 1969 introduced a complete new procedure. The Act carves the state into seven water divisions, each covering a major river basin. Colo.Rev. Stat.1973, § 37–92–201. One district judge in the division is designated a "water judge." He is assisted by a "water clerk" who is in charge of all records of water matters and by such "water referees" as may be necessary §§ 37–92–203 and 37–92–204. Since amended in several procedural details, the Act in effect makes each water court an administrative agency with complete records of and supervision over newly initiated and incomplete water rights.

"Any person who desires a determination of a water right or a conditional water right and the amount and priority thereof, including a determination that a conditional water right has become a water right by reason of the completion of the appropriation, * * * [or] quadrennial finding of reasonable diligence shall file with the water clerk * * * a verified application setting forth facts supporting the ruling sought * * *." § 37–92–302(1)(a). The application must contain a detailed description of the right sought. Elaborate provisions for notice, protests of applications and investigations and rulings by the referee are set out. Twice a year the water judge holds hearings on protests to referees' rulings and orders referred to him by the referee, and enters a judgment and decree embodying his rulings on all cases before him. §§ 37–92–303 and 37–92–304.

While theoretically an appropriation can be made without compliance with the statute, it can never receive an enforceable priority unless these procedures are followed. Although the relative priorities of all water rights or conditional water rights applied for during a calendar year are determined, all of them must be decreed to be junior to all water rights applied for in previous years. § 37–92–306. An applicant whose appropriation is not complete receives a decree for a conditional water right, and in every fourth calendar year thereafter he must obtain a finding by the referee that reasonable diligence has been used in the development of the proposed appropriation. § 37–92–301(4).

LOWER COLORADO RIVER AUTHORITY v. TEXAS DEPARTMENT OF WATER RESOURCES

Supreme Court of Texas, 1984.
689 S.W.2d 873.

KILGARLIN, JUSTICE.

We reverse the judgments of the courts below because those courts have misconstrued and misapplied Tex.Water Code Ann. § 11.134. We hold that the term "unappropriated water" means the amount of water remaining after taking into account all existing uncancelled permits and filings valued at their recorded levels.

The Water District applied for a permit to impound over 500,000 acre-feet of water from the Colorado River at the Stacy Dam site southeast of Ballinger, Texas. * * *

* * * The right to impound water had to be obtained by the Water District, through a Department permit. Tex.Water Code Ann. § 11.121. To acquire a permit, the Water District had to satisfy the statutory grounds of Tex.Water Code Ann. § 11.134(b)(2) & (3):

Action on Application

* * *

(b) The commission shall grant the application only if:

* * *

(2) unappropriated water is available in the source of supply; and

(3) the proposed appropriation:

* * *

(B) does not impair existing water rights or vested riparian rights; and

(C) is not detrimental to the public welfare.

The Colorado River waters are presently charged with four types of outstanding water rights. There are vested riparian rights, certified filings, permits to appropriate water, and certificates of adjudication. The Colorado is an inconstant stream. There is insufficient water to satisfy the existing rights during drought, but the water supply is capable of supplying additional users during times of abundant rain.

The Department developed a sophisticated computerized model of the seasonally varying inflow to the Colorado at various points along the river. One goal of the computer model was to allow the staff to obtain a reasonably accurate scientific estimate whether there was "unappropriated water" at points along the river, at least during some seasons or months.

The computer model assumed that all existing recorded water rights in the Colorado River basin would be exercised in the maximum amounts authorized, or to the extent of water available from the inflows. The staff study concluded that "very little water would be available for appropriation at the proposed reservoir site. * * * The estimated firm yield of the reservoir for these quantities of appropriable water is 3,120 acre-feet per year * * *." The study also concluded that the proposed reservoir would adversely affect two existing downstream lakes—Lake Travis and Lake Buchanan—by reducing the firm yield of each by approximately fifteen percent.

The Water District rebutted the staff conclusion by expert studies and testimony. The studies used the hydrologic data from the staff report but discounted the recorded filings in a number of ways. As to certified filings, the experts presented historical use data to demonstrate that the maximum amount claimed under the filings had never in fact been used, and that some claims necessarily had not been "perfected." As to riparian rights, many of the riparian claims were invalid because they were based on Spanish and Mexican land grants that did not include riparian rights. Finally, experts testified that demographic projections and historical use data indicated that the full amounts authorized under uncancelled permits would not be used. By subtracing the estimated amounts that would not be used from the recorded filings, the Water District's expert witnesses concluded there was sufficient water available for the proposed Stacy Reservoir. Similarly, they concluded that downstream rights would not be impaired if occasional flow-throughs were allowed.

The Commission made finding 15 that there was "unappropriated water" within the meaning of section 11.134(b)(2).

> After recognizing downstream existing appropriations and claims below Stacy Dam, the Commission finds that there are unappropriated flows in the Colorado River at the dam site sufficient to permit the impoundment of 554,340 acre-feet of water at elevations 1151.5 feet above mean sea level and the diversion and consumptive use of not to exceed 113,000 acre-feet of water per annum without impairing existing water rights, provided releases of water from the reservoir are made from time to time in such quantities as may be necessary to provide water to which all superior and senior water rights are entitled.

The undisputed evidence in this record is that existing uncancelled permits and filings, valued at their recorded levels, leave an insufficient supply of "unappropriated water for Stacy Dam." Sections 11.134(b)(2)

& (3) are unambiguous in their statements that the Commission shall grant applications for new water rights only if there is available unappropriated water and the new appropriation does not impair existing water rights or vested riparian rights. Additionally, granting additional permits cannot be detrimental to public welfare. Basically, our decision is that the article prohibits "double permitting" or the stacking of appropriated waters on appropriated waters.

* * *

Section 11.134(b)(2) finds its source in section 19 of the 1913 Act and its reenactment in section 24 of the 1917 Act. Representative D.W. Glasscock, a principal author of the 1913 Act, stated that the purpose of the 1913 Act was to prevent overappropriation of rivers and thus to insure the stability necessary to attract development capital. An initial purpose of the permit system has been to insure as much as possible that the water granted in a permit would be available when the project was completed. Section 11.146(e), by providing that water granted under *any* permit is not again subject to a new permit to appropriate until the permit has been cancelled in whole or in part, is consistent with the overall legislative purpose.

* * *

The court of appeals rationalized that the statement in Motl v. Boyd, 116 Tex. 82, 286 S.W. 458 (1926), that the Board of Water Engineers would merely consult their records to determine the amount of existing appropriations, was not contrary to its holding in this case. "Records," to the court of appeals, included the required annual reports which showed how much water the permittee actually used. The court of appeals reasoned that in consulting its records, to determine whether there existed "unappropriated water," the Board would consider how much of the recorded appropriation was going unused. That rationalization is directly contrary to the legislature's purpose. According to the 1953 Act, even if the records under the existing permit indicated the appropriator had not used any water at all for the last 10 years, it was still necessary to cancel the unused permit before the water covered by it would again be subject to a new appropriation.

* * *

The majority of the court of appeals reasoned, through a series of rhetorical questions, that the term, "unappropriated water," included unused waters that were subject to existing permits. The court reasoned that any other construction would mean the Commission and its predecessor agencies had shirked their statutory duty by allowing Texas rivers to become overappropriated. There can be no doubt that the prevention of overappropriation was a principal goal of the legislative scheme. Nineteenth Biennial Report of the Board of Water Engineers 8 (1948–50); Cox, The Texas Board of Water Engineers, 7 Texas L.Rev. 86, 96 (1928). The fact that some rivers are overappropriated does not mean the state's water agencies have failed in their duty. Because of changing circumstances, the vagaries of nature or the possibility of erroneous assumptions about the inflow amounts to the rivers, overappropriation may exist. These circumstances may make any river overappropriated, particularly during a drought period, and thus there can be no substitute for enforcement. The Texas statutes protect senior water rights from actual impairment. No matter how many permits the Commission issues, the action is purely administrative, and it cannot divest or impair prior rights.

Conclusion

Under the law, the Department may not grant permits when its own records show that the supply must come from an existing downstream permittee's water that the Department speculates he will not actually need. Section 11.025 places a limit on the amount of water that can be used beneficially or the amount the senior holders can claim, even though the face amount of their permits may be more. Among other things, that limitation serves to distribute the water appropriately when there is a drought. It does not mean the Department may intentionally overappropriate. A contrary decision would return water rights to the state of chaos that the act is designed to avoid. For example, upstream junior permit holders whose grants depended upon an overappropriation of the stream would suffer the most from deprivation of water in times of drought. The water source they had come to rely upon would be denied them.

* * *

We reverse the judgments of the courts below and set aside the permit granted by the Texas Department of Water Resources to the Colorado River Municipal Water District.

* * *

Ray, Justice, concurring.

I agree with the court's conclusion that "unappropriated water" must not include water already granted under an existing, uncancelled permit. I do not agree with the court's disposition of setting aside the Commission's order. I would remand the case to the Commission for further proceedings in accordance with the opinion.

* * * The Commission's error was applying the wrong definition of "unappropriated water." This court had not previously expressly addressed the question. Had the water district presented its application under the proper standard, it could have simultaneously sought partial or total cancellations of unused water rights under existing certified filings and permits. Although the district can now file a new application using the proper definition, that action would not be a complete remedy. Both the priority of an appropriation and the claimant's right to use the water date from the filing of the *application* with the Department. Tex.Water Code Ann. § 11.141 (Supp.1984). Since the misconception of the law caused the Commission to commit error, I believe it is appropriate to preserve the district's priority by remanding to the Commission for proper proceedings under the correct legal standard.

OPINION ON MOTION FOR REHEARING

KILGARLIN, JUSTICE.

* * * Because an examination of authorities on the issue demonstrates that a remand is more appropriate than a reversal and rendition, we reverse the judgments of the courts below and remand the cause to the Texas Department of Water Resources pursuant to our power under the Administrative Procedure and Texas Register Act, Tex.Rev.Civ.Stat.Ann. art. 6252–13a, § 19(e)(4) (Vernon Supp.1984).
* * *

Notes

1. Statutes in a number of western states express criteria similar to those in Vernons Tex.Code Ann., Water Code § 11.134(b). See e.g. Mont. Code Ann. 1983, § 85–2–311; Reissue Neb.Rev.Stat.1943 § 46–235; Wyo. Stat.1977, § 41–4–503.

2. Because the rule of priority protects an existing appropriation from interference by a newly permitted appropriation, is there ever any need to deny an appropriation on the ground that there is no unappropriated water in the source or that it would conflict with or impair existing rights? See Little Cottonwood Water Co. v. Sandy City, 123 Utah 242, 258 P.2d 440 (1953), where an application for a ground water permit was protested by appropriators from a surface stream who contended that pumping from the adjacent aquifer would steal water from the stream. Held, the permit should be granted, since it merely has the effect of allowing the applicant to proceed with his plans to try to appropriate new water and does not adjudicate that there are unappropriated waters in the source. The permit gives the applicant no right to take and use the water until an adjudication has been made that an appropriation has been accomplished, and in those proceedings the actual availability of water may be determined. Accord, Ernst v. Superior Court, 82 Ariz. 17, 307 P.2d 911 (1957).

Both the supply of and the demand for western water are highly variable. A major portion of western stream flow comes from melting snow caps on the mountains and a particular stream may approach flood stage each spring and dwindle to a trickle in the late summer and fall. Winter snowfall and summer rains will vary, bringing lean years and fat years of stream flow. The appropriator with an early right may not use the water at all times, or during each year. Industries, cities and irrigators may desire water at different times of the year. Water rights may be abandoned or forfeited. The applicant may be willing to take his place at the foot of the priority list and accept what is colloquially called a "flood water right." For these reasons, most state officials regard the permit as little more than a hunting license.

3. The principal case deals with the demand side of the equation. What of the supply side? Should the Commission use flows available in a drought year to calculate whether unappropriated water is available. Flows available in an "average" year? Flows available in a high-flow year? The Commission staff concluded that the reservoir would only have a "firm

yield" of 3,120 acre-feet per year. What assumptions about supply did the staff use in reaching this conclusion?

One purpose for building a reservoir is to even out supply by permitting water to be captured in high-flow years for use in low-flow years. Does the principal case mean that a permit can no longer be granted for a reservoir for this purpose in Texas?

What policy is served by the principal case? Is the risk that an applicant may have miscalculated and that no water will be available to satisfy his right different from a number of other business risks which the applicant faces?

4. In Southeastern Colorado Water Conservancy Dist. v. City of Florence, 688 P.2d 715 (Colo.1984) the court concluded that it would be improper to deny a conditional water right on the basis that the right would cause injury to senior rights, reasoning that a conditional right cannot legally injure existing water rights. Nevertheless, a Colorado statute provides that a claimant of a conditional right must show that water "can be and will be diverted." Colo.Rev.Stat.1973, 37–92–305(9)(b). The court held a conditional right could not be granted where the evidence showed that there would only be water for one or two days once every 25 years.

YOUNG & NORTON v. HINDERLIDER

Supreme Court of New Mexico, 1910.
15 N.M. 666, 110 P. 1045.

On the 1st day of October, 1907, M.C. Hinderlider filed with the territorial engineer an application for a permit to appropriate 200 second feet of the flow of the La Plata river in San Juan county, N.M., and for the construction of a storage reservoir with a storage capacity of 12,406 acre feet for the purpose of reclaiming and irrigating about 14,000 acres of land in said county. On December 20, 1907, Messrs. Young & Norton for themselves and others filed with the territorial engineer an application for a permit to appropriate the waters of the same stream in the same county and territory, for the purpose of reclaiming and irrigating about 5,000 acres of land, being a part of the same land covered by the Hinderlider project. This last application included the construction of a storage reservoir with a storage capacity of 10,149 acre feet for the purpose of storing the flood waters of the said river and applying the same to the reclamation of the said 5,000 acres of land. After the publication of the notice required by law and on the 19th day of March, 1908, the said Young, Norton, and others filed with the territorial engineer a protest against the approval of the said Hinderlider application. That after a hearing before the territorial engineer and on July 20, 1908, he rendered an opinion sustaining said protest rejecting the Hinderlider application and approving the application of the protestants. * * *

[The Territorial Engineer found that Hinderlider's filing covered much public land as well as the private land owned by protestants, that his project would cost $40 per acre; that Young and Norton and others they represent are settled on about 5,500 acres of land, their project is for the irrigation of the settled land, and would cost about $20 per acre; that there was water available for about 5,000 to 6,000 acres, that either applicant could and would complete his appropriation, but that Young and Norton's project was more within the water supply. Hinderlider appealed to the Board of Water Commissioners, which ruled that the power of the Engineer to reject an application as contrary to the public interest is limited to cases in which the project would be a menace to the public health and safety, and ordered Hinderlider's application approved. The District Court affirmed, and Young and Norton appealed.]

ABBOTT, J. We think the decision of the district court was justified and probably required by the statement of facts on which it was heard; but we find that statement very incomplete and unsatisfactory as the basis of a decision in such a cause. If it were a matter of private interest alone, a question simply between two rival applicants for the right to use the waters in question, we should content ourselves with affirming the decision of the district court. But the question is much broader than that, and includes the public interest as well, by the terms of the statute under which the territorial engineer, the water commissioners, and the courts have jurisdiction of the subject-matter.

The view apparently adopted by the water commissioners in their decision that the power of the territorial engineer to reject an application, "if in his opinion the approval thereof would be contrary to the public interest" (section 28), is limited to cases in which the project would be a menace to the public health or safety is we think, not broad enough. There is no such limitation expressed in terms of the statute, and we think not by implication. The declaration in the first section of the statute that the waters therein described are "public waters," and the fact that the entire statute is designed to secure the greatest possible benefit from them for the public, should be borne in mind. It is, for instance, obviously for the public interest that investors should be protected against making worthless investments in New Mexico, and especially that they should not be led to make them through official approval of unsound enterprises. If there is available unappropriated water of the La Plata river for only 5,000 or 6,000 acres of land, it would be contrary to the public interest that a project for irrigating 14,000 acres with that water should receive an official approval which would, perhaps, enable the promoters of it to market their scheme, to sell stock reasonably sure to become worthless, and land which could not be irrigated, at the price of irrigated land. Such a proceeding would in the end result only in warning capital away from the territory. The failure of any irrigation project carries with it not only disastrous consequences to its owners and to the farmers who are depending on it, but besides tends to destroy faith in irrigation enterprises generally.

It may be said that the territorial engineer could have approved the Hinderlider project for the number of acres which could be irrigated from it. He makes it clear, however, from his report, that the cost of the works for that project would be much greater than for works fit to irrigate the land which could really be irrigated from the available water there. While that element is not conclusive on the question of public interest, we think it should be taken into account. It may be that, of the 5,000 or 6,000 acres there which it is claimed can be irrigated at an expense of $10 or $12 per acre under the Young-Norton project, a thousand acres could be irrigated at $5 per acre because of its being at a lower level or nearer the water than the other land. But that would not justify refusing the owners of the other 4,000 or 5,000 acres the privilege of irrigating their lands, under a plan which would increase the cost of irrigation to the owners of the thousand acres. And the same may be said of the Hinderlider project as compared with the Young-Norton project. The mere fact that irrigation under the former project would cost more per acre than under the latter is not conclusive that the former project should be rejected. But the attempt to cover too much land may have gone so far that the cost of irrigation under that project would be so excessive that the owners of land under the project could not pay the water rates and farm their lands at a profit. The statute provides that the charges for irrigation shall be "reasonable"; but what is reasonable in any case must depend largely on the cost of constructing and operating the irrigation works.

The agreed statement of facts on which the judgment of the district court is based may be held to include by reference the findings of the territorial engineer and those of the board of water commissioners, although it is not made clear that they are to be a part of the stipulated facts, as it should be if that was the intention of the parties. Even if they are to be considered, we are still without proper material for a conclusion. The territorial engineer finds that the Young-Norton project is "better within the available water supply." But that furnished no reason why he should not have approved the earlier project for the amount of land there is water for. He does not find that the cost of water under the Hinderlider project would be prohibitory or excessive, but only that it would be considerably greater per acre than under the Young-Norton project. The price which the owners of land can afford to pay for irrigation must depend in part on the use to which it can be put.

For ordinary farm crops $40 per acre for water might be prohibitory, while for fruit or garden truck in certain localities it might not be excessive. But neither the territorial engineer nor the water commissioners have touched on that point in their reports. The territorial engineer apparently bases his approval of the latter project as against the former on the fact that Young and Norton and their associates are actual settlers on the land, while Hinderlider is not a resident of the territory. We do not say this circumstance should have no weight in determining the question of the public interest, but we think it should not outweigh the other considerations to which we have referred.

On the other hand, the water commissioners find that there is available unappropriated flood water of the La Plata river, but do not find whether there is enough for 14,000 or any other number of acres, nor whether the cost of the Hinderlider project would be such as necessarily to make the irrigation charges under it prohibitory or excessive. * * *

The cause is therefore remanded to the district court to obtain facts through the water commissioners and territorial engineer, or by agreement of counsel, or otherwise, essential to a satisfactory decision of the cause. It is not meant to limit the district court to the precise points we have named, but to leave the matter open for the introduction of any facts bearing on the question of public interest. And the judgment of the district court is set aside in order that it may on further consideration render such decision as it shall deem proper.

Notes

1. Trelease, A Water Code for Alaska 14–17 (1962):

"A good law is one that will promote some fundamental and generally accepted public policy. The traditional American form of resource development is to permit private enterprise to operate, subject to regulation. By giving individuals rights to develop the resource in their own interests the economy of the state and of the nation is developed for the benefit of all. This is the pattern already chosen for Alaska's water resources law. The Constitution of the State, Article VIII, provides:

" 'Section 1. It is the policy of the State to encourage the settlement of its land and the development of its resources by making them available for maximum use consistent with the public interest.'

" 'Section 2. The legislature shall provide for the utilization, development, and conservation of all natural resources belonging to the State, including land and waters, for the maximum benefit of its people.'

"These two ideals, maximum use and the public interest, are therefore the goals which this law should help the people to achieve.

"We often say that we should develop and regulate our resources so as to get the maximum benefits from them. In practice, we can rarely be sure that the maximum goal has been reached. We are generally content with the knowledge that if we are better off with a particular resource use than without it, we have at least taken a step toward achieving the maximum. This water code should assist in the determination of whether we are better off, since it provides measures and procedures for the weighing of advantages against disadvantages of a proposed water use before action is taken. If we desire, we can use a very useful device given to us by the economists and apply the 'benefit-cost formula', which indicates that a project is desirable if the ratio of benefits to costs is favorable. If two people wish the same water for inconsistent purposes, the benefit-cost formula can be used to determine the one that promises the greater benefits and comes the closest to the maximization ideal, hence the one that should be granted the water use. Where only one user seeks the right to water, and the benefits exceed costs, the project can be considered a step toward maximum use. If time demonstrates that another use of the water would be better, flexibility can be achieved by providing for transferable water rights that will enable the use of the water to shift from the old less productive use to the new more productive one, and still another step toward maximum use will have been taken.

"The benefit-cost approach need not be concerned entirely with dollar values such as the cost of cement and the price of potatoes. Many intangibles can enter into the formula—the value of lives saved by a flood control project, the value of a strengthened state economy, the value of public health, the worth of public recreation. The last is a major factor to be considered in a law for Alaskan water use. The State desires to preserve the recreational opportunities which its citizens now have and to improve its reputation as a vacation land. A very large part of the outdoor recreation of both the Alaskan and the 'outsider' depends upon water. Today's problem is to find a middle ground between the famous engineer's dictum that every drop of water that runs to the sea without returning a cash value is wasted, and the conservationist who feels that conservation is the opposite of beneficial use, that we must lock up our water resources and save them from economic exploitation. The benefit-cost approach affords a meeting ground for these views and a method of reconciling them. Some economists have tried to make the process easier by developing methods that value recreational opportunities in terms of dollars, attempts which quite often produce startlingly large values. But even if this is impossible, and the 'beneficial uses' can be weighed against recreational values only in subjective terms of value judgments, the device gives a means of reaching informed decisions after considering all factors.

"Alaska's Constitution directs the legislature to seek not only maximum benefits but also the public interest. This term is often left undefined, but it is also capable of being given an economic interpretation. In seeking maximization, in figuring benefits and costs, we must not fail to consider adverse effects on other persons or on the public generally for which compensation is not paid. If there are no detrimental side effects on others and no social losses, and if benefits exceed costs, the project can be said to be in the public interest because it helps the State to achieve maximum use of the water resource. But even if the user's benefits exceed his cost, we must also count the costs he imposes on others. For instance, if some activity on an Alaskan stream muddies the water during spawning season so that millions of salmon eggs cannot hatch, the profits from such an operation are taken at least in part from the pockets of the salmon fishermen. Many times the persons who suffer such losses cannot be identified, and the losses are spread over a large number of people, but the losses are nevertheless real. On the other hand, we must be sure that the economic growth of the State is not retarded by overzealous blocking of important projects in order to preserve other resources of comparatively slight value.

"Furthermore, in determining the public interest, each proposed use must be weighed against other possible future uses that might be forestalled. 'Foregone benefits' of alternative uses of the water are 'induced adverse effects' of a project, to use the economist's language, and must be counted as costs. Here the planning provisions of the proposed Code are of paramount importance, because individual proposals should be measured against the ultimate maximum beneficial use as determined by plans, programs and policies developed after careful research, investigation, and consideration of alternatives. * * *

"Making decisions such as these will be very difficult. No law can make them, they must be made by people. No economic formula can solve these problems by push button techniques. Although Sections 211, [46.15.110] 403, 404 and 407 of the proposed Code incorporate the benefit-cost idea, (following the model of some of the Wisconsin Statutes, Sections 31.06(3) and 107.05(3)) the balancing of benefits against cost must be performed by the exercise of judgment. Mathematical equivalents could be used if desired, to insure that some factors are not vastly overweighed. Indeed, the Code could be amended to delete the formula, yet surely the administrators would consider these same factors in determining the public interest. It is believed that the real strength of the Code lies in its procedures, which will enable all viewpoints to be brought together and all factors considered, so that choices will be made, not by action of an appropriator or polluter, and not to further the policy of a single-purpose agency, but on an informed basis by officials responsible to the State for 'maximum use consistent with the public interest', for the 'maximum benefit of (all) its people.' "

2. Alaska Stat. 46.15.080. Criteria for Issuance of Permit.

"(a) The commissioner shall issue a permit if he finds that

(1) rights of a prior appropriator will not be unduly affected;

(2) the proposed means of diversion or construction are adequate;

(3) the proposed use of water is beneficial; and

(4) the proposed appropriation is in the public interest.

(b) In determining the public interest, the commissioner shall consider

(1) the benefit to the applicant resulting from the proposed appropriation;

(2) the effect of the economic activity resulting from the proposed appropriation;

(3) the effect on fish and game resources and on public recreational opportunities;

(4) the effect on public health;

(5) the effect of loss of alternate uses of water that might be made within a reasonable time if not precluded or hindered by the proposed appropriation;

(6) harm to other persons resulting from the proposed appropriation;

(7) the intent and ability of the applicant to complete the appropriation; and

(8) the effect upon access to navigable or public waters."

In 1973 the State of Washington added an express cost-benefit formula to her statutes: "Allocation of waters among potential uses and users shall be based generally on the securing of the maximum net benefits for the people of the State. Maximum net benefits shall constitute total benefits less costs including opportunities lost." Wash.Rev.Code Ann. 90.54.020(2).

3. In addition to the power to deny outright an application for a permit, the agency may grant it subject to public-interest conditions. See Kirk v. State Board of Irrigation, 90 Neb. 627, 134 N.W. 167 (1912): "We think there is no doubt of the power and duty of the state board of irrigation to determine such questions. 'If there is unappropriated water in the source of supply named in the application, and if such appropriation is not otherwise detrimental to the public welfare, the state board, through its secretary, shall approve the same.' Comp.St.1911, c. 93a, art. 2, § 28. Thus the state board of irrigation is made the guardian of the public welfare in the appropriation of the public waters of the state, and this necessarily devolves upon that board a large discretion in such matters. If the public welfare demands it, they may grant a qualified and limited right of appropriation and in the beneficial use of the water so appropriated."

4. The newest permit statute does not expressly provide for denial of a permit on general grounds of public interest. Mont.Code Ann.1983 § 85–2–311. Neither did the Idaho statute until the lack was supplied in part by a 1978 amendment to Idaho Code § 42–203 which permitted a refusal "* * * where the proposed use * * * will conflict with the local public interest, where the local public interest is defined as the affairs of the people in the area directly affected by the proposed use."

5. To what extent might the requirement of "beneficial use" substitute for a public interest standard? Is an appropriation which is not in the "public interest" a beneficial use of water? See the dissenting opinion of Justice McFadden in *State of Idaho,* supra p. 26.

TANNER v. BACON

Supreme Court of Utah, 1943.
103 Utah 494, 136 P.2d 957.

WADE, JUSTICE. This is an appeal by Caleb Tanner, plaintiff on the judgment roll from a judgment of the District Court, in an action to review the decision of the State Engineer rejecting the application of the plaintiff to appropriate waters in the Provo River for power purposes. The application was filed in the office of the State Engineer on February 28, 1925, for the appropriation of 100 c.f.s. of the waters of the Provo River, to be diverted into the Provo Bench Canal and conveyed therein about 10,300 feet to a power plant. * * *

Prior thereto, in 1921, the legislature created the Water Storage Commission. In 1922, that commission contracted with the United States Bureau of Reclamation for the planning and the investigation of the possibilities of storing the waters of the Weber, Duchesne and Provo river systems. Such investigations and plans were commenced immediately and have continued up to the time of the commencement of this action, and at the time that plaintiff's application was filed the State of Utah had spent more than $25,000 thereon. As a result thereof a reclamation project was formed for the purpose of bringing the unappropriated waters of the Weber and Duchesne rivers river systems into the Provo river system, and the construction thereon of a large storage reservoir to be known as the Deer Creek Project. It was planned that the waters so stored would be used to supplement the supply for domestic and culinary purposes for many cities and towns in Summit, Utah and Salt Lake Counties, and also supplement the supply for irrigation and industrial purposes in those counties. Pursuant to these plans, in 1924, the State of Utah filed numerous applications to appropriate the above mentioned waters. Later these applications were assigned to the United States. * * *

[T]here is only one application found by the court to have been filed, and upon which the United States and the Provo River Water Users' Association base their claims which was filed subsequent to plaintiff's application. Our problem in this case deals with that application alone. As found by the trial court the description of that application is in part as follows: "Application No. 12,144—dated April 3, 1936, covering an exchange of water between the Deer Creek division of the Provo River Project and the interest of Utah Lake, whereby Provo river water, up to 30,000 acre feet annually, may be stored in the Deer Creek Reservoir in lieu of certain seepage return flow and/or other waters belonging to the United States which will flow into and augment the water supply of Utah Lake as a result of the construction and operation of the Deer Creek Reservoir * * *."

By this application it is proposed to store annually in the Deer Creek Reservoir 30,000 acre feet of the flood waters of Provo river, which has been appropriated to a beneficial use after it reaches Utah Lake. It being anticipated that the construction and operation of the Deer Creek reservoir will cause sufficient water to reach Utah Lake by seepage and return flow, to satisfy the demands of the prior appropriators of such waters. The storing of these flood waters might interfere with the use which plaintiff proposes to make of the unappropriated waters of Provo river. This presents the proposition of whether the court erred in holding that the rights which plaintiff may acquire under his application are subject to the rights which the United States and the Provo River Water Users' Association may acquire under application 12,144 above described, which was filed subsequent to the plaintiff's application.

The District Court's decision is not contrary to the doctrine of priorities. Counsel argues that under that doctrine, every person who applies to appropriate unappropriated waters of this state has an unqualified right to have such application approved. This is not the law. Sec. 10, Chap. 67, Laws of Utah, 1919, which contains the law on that subject which was in effect at the time plaintiff's application was filed (now 100–3–21, Utah Code Anno.1943), applies only to vested rights, and not to the right to appropriate water in the future. The law which governed the right to make future appropriations when plaintiff filed his application is Sec. 48, Chap. 67, Laws of Utah for 1919, (as amended is now 100–3–8, U.C.A.1943) which provides: "Where there is no unappropriated water in the proposed source of supply, or where the proposed use will conflict with prior applications or existing rights, or where the approval of such application would in the opinion of the State Engineer *interfere with the more beneficial use for irrigation, domestic or culinary purposes, stock watering, power or mining development, manufacturing, or would prove detrimental to the public welfare,* it shall be the duty of the State Engineer to reject such application." (Italics added.) * * *

Sec. 1, Chap. 67, Laws of Utah 1919 (which as amended is now 100–1–1, U.C.A.1943), provides: "The water of all streams and other sources in this State, whether flowing above or under the ground, in known or defined channels, is hereby declared to be the property of the public, subject to all existing rights to the use thereof."

These statutes may not vest the state with the proprietary ownership of the water but they clearly do enjoin upon the state the duty to control the appropriation of the public waters in a manner that will be for the best interests of the public. The precise question involved in this case has never been passed on by this court but similar questions have been before the courts of other states, under statutes much like ours, where it has been invariably held that the state may reject or limit applications to appropriate its unappropriated waters.

* * *

Here the state had spent in excess of $25,000 merely in investigation and planning for this project, prior to the filing of plaintiff's application. The United States was interested and had indicated its willingness to construct the project if sufficient water could be obtained for storage purposes, and proper arrangements could be made with the holders of the power rights on the streams in question. The plans which were then in the formative stages contemplated the expenditure of large sums of money to bring the water from the Weber river and to tunnel through a mountain to the Duchesne river to obtain the necessary water for this project. By this project it is planned to supplement the supply of water for domestic and irrigation purposes to a larger portion of the population of this state. In the face of this, if plaintiff's application were approved without limitations, he would be entitled to have the flood waters of the Provo river run through his plant, and thereby prevent the storage thereof in the Deer Creek reservoir, regardless of how great the demand for water might be, and regardless of the fact that if it were stored it might be used for power purposes during the dry seasons and at the same time be used for domestic and irrigation purposes. Thus the facts found are sufficient to support the decree and the District Court did not act arbitrarily. * * *

The decision of the District Court is affirmed with costs to the respondents.

WOLFE, CHIEF JUSTICE (concurring). I concur. I assume that the State Engineer could not reject an application on the ground that if approved it would "prove detrimental to the public welfare" because in his mind he conceived some ultimate or remote public project which would need the water. A farsighted person with imagination and bold conceptions may visualize projects which in the future may be most beneficial to the state. Perhaps we should plan a campaign for the most effective use of all unappropriated waters of the state and work to that end, but until such plans are formulated, or at least the water is withdrawn from appropriation for such purposes, I do not conceive that ideal conceptions for future and better public use of water in the State Engineer's head can be the basis for refusing to approve an application. It is not now necessary to draw the line on the degree of concreteness to which plans or projects must have attained to form bases for legal rejections by the Engineer. Suffice it to say in this case that the Deer Creek project reached a point in conception and realization where it could definitely be said to be against public interest to affirm any application which would interfere with its fruition.

MOFFAT, JUSTICE (dissenting). The propositions decided by the principal opinion are based upon the findings and decree of the trial court. The opinion states that it recognizes the doctrine and law of priority in the appropriation of water. Notwithstanding the statement, it proceeds to give priority to an application filed subsequent to the Tanner application. * * *

Whether the principal opinion intended to endorse as the law the statement that "the district court's decision [here affirmed] is not contrary to the doctrine of priorities," the doctrine of the opinion is utterly destructive of the doctrine of priority in the appropriation and use of water in this State. I therefore dissent.

Notes

1. "Mention should be made of the fact that water projects often involve large capital investments in permanent or semi-permanent works. Decisions to undertake such works have a certain physical inflexibility and irrevocability which underlines the importance of careful, long-range planning, regardless of the system of water rights in effect and whether water resource development is public or private." Bagley, Some Economic Considerations in Water Use Policy, 5 Kan.L.R. 499, 510 (1957).

2. In addition to "opportunity costs," as the economist terms the benefits foregone when one alternative development is chosen rather than another, the law also recognizes "social costs" and "externalities" or "spillovers".

Big Horn Power Co. v. State, 23 Wyo. 271, 148 P. 1110 (1915), contains a recital of the State Engineer's action refusing, in the public interest, to issue a permit for a dam unless the applicant reduced its height so as not to interfere with the use of the canyon for a railroad bed. The canyon provided the only economical grade for railroad connections from the northwest part of the state to the rest of the state.

In re Martha Lake Water Co., 152 Wash. 53, 277 P. 382 (1929), involved an application to appropriate water for irrigation of nonriparian land. The application was opposed by a number of persons owning property bordering on the lake, purchased because of its access to the water for bathing, boating, fishing, and for summer homes. If the permit were granted the appropriator would lower the lake approximately twelve inches during the dry season, causing the water edge to recede from eight to fifty feet. "The question in the present case * * * involves * * * the right of a riparian proprietor to complain when the waters of that lake are sought to be lowered to his substantial and material damage. The [appropriator] has no right to thus damage the riparian proprietors upon the lake without first having acquired the right to do so by eminent domain."

BANK OF AMERICA NAT. TRUST AND SAV. ASS'N v. STATE WATER RESOURCES CONTROL BD.

California Court of Appeal, Third District, 1974.
42 Cal.App.3d 198, 116 Cal.Rptr. 770.

RICHARDSON, PRESIDING JUSTICE.

Bank of America (hereinafter "Bank") appeals following judgment dismissing its petition filed under Code of Civil Procedure section 1094.5, for writ of mandate against State Water Resources Control Board (hereinafter "Board"). The petition before us initially challenged the validity of two conditions which the Board attached to its decision granting Bank's application to appropriate water. The parties having resolved their disagreement as to one of the conditions, Bank, accordingly, has abandoned its attack as to it. The remaining condition, focal point of our inquiry, was designated as condition 11, and requires public access to certain reservoirs on the Bank's property. * * *

Bank is corporate co-trustee of the Pension Trust Fund for Operating Engineers, a fund established to provide pension benefits for employees represented by Operating Engineers Local Union No. 3. As such trustee, Bank owns approximately 3,500 acres of land in eastern Sacramento County on both sides of the Cosumnes River. This property, commonly known as Rancho Murieta, was purchased by the Fund for the purposes of investment. In furtherance of the investment purpose, a land use plan was prepared and approved by the County of Sacramento (hereinafter "County") for the development of Rancho Murieta. The general plan adopted by County envisions an eventual population of 25,000 in 18 to 22 years.

In the course of planning for the water supply of Rancho Murieta, Bank filed with the Board application No. 23416 for the appropriation from the Cosumnes River of six cubic feet of water per second (cfs), plus 3,900 acre-feet per annum (afa) of water, for irrigation, municipal, recreational and industrial purposes. The proposed appropriation constitutes Rancho Murieta's principal water source. * * * Under application 23416 it was proposed that water be diverted from the Cosumnes River and carried by gravity flow to two main holding reservoirs, Chesbro and Guadalupe, with a total storage capacity of 3,900 acre feet. From these reservoirs the water, after passing through a water treatment plant, it was contemplated would then be distributed throughout the project. * * *

In August 1971, the Board issued its decision approving the applications to appropriate water. The allowable period of diversion for irrigation, municipal, recreational and stock watering purposes was limited. The Board noted various protests had been filed by other water users from the Cosumnes River, industrial and governmental, who claimed riparian, appropriative and other landowner rights. The Board further noted that all protesters, including Fish & Game had withdrawn their protests. Fish & Game had reached a written agreement with Bank which assured a minimum flow in the Cosumnes to protect fish life, and provided that its terms would be included in any permits issued on the applications to appropriate water.

Pursuant to the findings, the Board ordered that the applicant's petitions be granted subject to several conditions, among them, central to our consideration, condition 11 which reads in full as follows: "*The reservoir(s) shall be kept open to the public for recreational use* subject to a reasonable charge for any services or facilities that are provided by permittee. * * *"

As we have noted, when the original applications were filed several protests resulted, among them that of Fish & Game. On October 2, 1970, Bank and Fish & Game signed a written agreement the preamble of which recited that the Cosumnes River supported fish of different species and that the parties had agreed on the terms and manner of diversion which would "assure the continued protection and maintenance of the fishery resources of the Cosumnes River." For the purposes of "the protection and preservation of fish life" the parties agreed upon six detailed conditions regulating the amount and periods of diversion. These conditions constituted a detailed formula for withdrawal of water that were keyed to seasonal dates, to maximum and minimum total flows in the river, and to the manner of measurements of the flows. The formula also provided for continuing jurisdiction in the Board to modify the minimum fisheries' flows requirements to conform to such subsequent determinations as, periodically, the Board might make to assure fish protection.

The oral testimony was offered by four witnesses. Three testified on behalf of the Bank, David U. Holmes, Dr. Joseph B. Franzini,

Stanford Professor and water consultant to the project, and Dr. Joel F. Gustafson, Ecology Professor at San Francisco State College. Robert Reavis, a fishery biologist employed by Fish & Game testified on its behalf. We have carefully reviewed their testimony. A substantial quantity of documentary evidence was introduced including maps, diagrams, reports, surveys, and the staff report of Mr. Reavis dated August 1970. This latter report dealt exclusively with the effect on salmon of the proposed diversions. In order to protect the salmon and warm water fish three conditions to the diversion were recommended: (1) There would be no diversion at all when the Cosumnes flow at the Michigan Bar measuring station is less than 70 cfs; (2) when the flow is 70 to 175 cfs, up to 6 cfs may be diverted but may not be reduced below 70 cfs; and (3) when the flow exceeds 175 cfs the maximum proposed diversion is allowed. The first two recommendations were incorporated in the Decision and the third, as modified, was also included. The record shows that the fishery demands of the Cosumnes were adequately met by the conditions imposed.

The terms of the formula were incorporated in the decision of the Board and Fish & Game withdrew its protest. * * *

Following the Bank's Petition for Partial Reconsideration, the Board clarified its reasons for imposing condition 11. Among other things it said: " * * * *It is difficult to evaluate the effect that this reduction of flow in the river may have on the fishery, but the 'trade-off' will be more nearly equal if the benefits of the diversion for recreation are made public.* * * * " (Emphasis added.)

It becomes clear that the Board's reason for condition 11 was that the approved diversion would reduce the flow of the river which, in turn, would have an uncertain effect on the "fishery." Further, the diversion would result in "diminished recreational value" of the Cosumnes because of its lower level downstream. These two factors—the undetermined effect on fish and lessened recreational prospects caused by lower water level—prompted the Board to require as a "trade-off" public access to the Rancho Murieta recreational reservoirs.

While Fish & Game's determination that the formula fixed in the agreement is adequate to support fish life is not binding on the Board, Fish & Game's judgment in this matter is entitled to great weight. Charged with a statutory obligation, Fish & Game is the guardian and custodian of the public's deep and continuing interest in the fish and game resources of this state. It has the collective experience and expertise to make the essential determinations in the technical areas of water flows and fish maintenance. The agreed formula was negotiated and approved by Fish & Game and we cannot presume that its conclusions were not carefully reached. Of greater significance is the fact that nowhere in the record does there appear before the Board any evidence that adoption of the formula would adversely affect, diminish, or impair the fishery. We accordingly, conclude that the first basis for imposition of the condition, preservation of the fish life in the

Cosumnes downstream from the diversion, has been otherwise adequately assured.

The remainder of our inquiry relates to whether substantial evidence in the record establishes a "diminished recreational value" of the Cosumnes warranting a "trade-off" or exchange for condition 11. Our review of the record discloses no such evidence. There are clear inferences from the record that the water level of the Cosumnes below the diversion during certain times of the year will be lower because of it, but there is no testimony as to its degree or, more importantly, as to its effect in terms of recreational use of the river, present or prospective. No testimony written or oral was presented which in any substantial manner pointed to the specifics of impairment of recreational activities.

We note that one of the exhibits, a report prepared by the U.S. Department of the Interior, on the Feasibility of Water Supply Development, Cosumnes River Diversion of the Central Valley Project, described general recreational activities around *reservoirs* as "boating, swimming, waterskiing, and fishing," and that shoreline activity includes "camping, picnicking, sightseeing, hiking and related activities." We envision that the boating and waterskiing activities in a stream like the Cosumnes because of its size and configuration would be very limited with or without the diversion, but the remaining recreational uses will be unimpaired insofar as disclosed by the Board record. No evidence, written or oral, was presented which indicated that the lower water level would change or affect the recreational utilization of the Cosumnes downstream from the diversion.

We have heretofore underscored the primacy of the "public interest" in the considerations before the Board and have emphasized the broad discretion vested in it. Nonetheless, we apply a measure of substantiality in reviewing the evidence supporting the Board's action. * * *

The record, in our view, is barren of evidence which is of "ponderable legal significance" in support of the conclusion that the diversion would result in a reduction in the recreational value of the Cosumnes. While fully accepting the rule giving primacy to the public interest, we may not leave to speculation the nature of its impairment. Condition 11 constitutes an onerous burden. The Board, in our view, has the jurisdiction and the right to impose a condition requiring public access but only for precise and specific reasons founded on tangible record evidence.

To summarize, we conclude that the record lacks substantial evidence supporting condition 11 and it must fail.

The judgment of dismissal is reversed.

Notes

1. See Robie, Some Reflections on Environmental Considerations in Water Rights Administration, 2 Ecology L.Q. 695 (1972).

2. Since 1965, West's Ann.Cal. Water Code § 1257 has required an application for a permit to appropriate water to set forth all data and information reasonably available to the applicant or that can be obtained from the Department of Fish and Game concerning the extent, if any, to which fish and wildlife would be affected by the appropriation, and a statement of any measures proposed to be taken for the protection of fish and wildlife in connection with the appropriation.

The Alaska Water Use Act requires that in the issuance of a permit one criterion for determining the public interest shall be "the effect on fish and game resources and on public recreational opportunities." Alaska Stat. 46.15.080.

The Oregon Water Resources Board "shall have due regard for conserving the highest use of the water for all purposes, including irrigation, domestic use, municipal water supply, power development, public recreation, protection of commercial and game fishing and wildlife, fire protection, mining, industrial purposes, navigation, scenic attraction or any other beneficial use to which the water may be applied for which it may have a special value to the public." Or.Rev.Stat. 537.170(3)(a).

Since 1971 the Utah State Engineer has been instructed to reject an application for an appropriation if he has reason to believe that it will "unreasonably affect the public recreation or the natural stream environment." Utah Code Ann.1953 Repl. 7C, § 73–3–8.

The Washington Water Resources Act of 1971 contains a "general declaration of fundamentals for utilization and management of water of the state," which include the following:

"(3) The quality of the natural environment shall be protected and, where possible, enhanced as follows:

"(a) Perennial rivers and streams of the state shall be retained with base flows necessary to provide for preservation of wildlife, fish, scenic, aesthetic and other environmental values, and navigational values. Lakes and ponds shall be retained substantially in their natural condition. Withdrawals of water which would conflict therewith shall be authorized only in those situations where it is clear that overriding considerations of the public interest will be served." Wash.Rev.Code Ann. 90.54.020.

In Little Blue Natural Resources District v. North Platte Natural Resources District, 210 Neb. 862, 317 N.W.2d 726 (1982), the Nebraska Supreme Court ruled that the director of the Department of Water Resources must consult with the Game and Parks Commission to determine whether proposed surface water appropriations would interfere with the existence of threatened or endangered wildlife species or their habitat.

3. How do you value environmental gains and losses? Economists would prefer a common denominator for all factors and have long struggled with the problem caused by the lack of a market in which prices are fixed for many experiences and opportunities. In the beginning the emphasis was on "recreation." How can recreational opportunities be fitted into the benefit-cost calculus? Can dollar values be assigned to the intangibles of pleasure? By valuing the facility as an asset, like a painting by an old master? By totaling gross expenditures by sportsmen? By capitalizing

"derived values" from admittance fees and user charges for comparable private recreational opportunities? See Trelease, Policies for Water Law: Property Rights, Economic Forces and Public Regulation, 5 Natural Resources J. 1, 18–23 (1965), and materials cited.

A valuable insight, that one measurement of an intangible is its opportunity costs, was offered by Milliman:

"Intangibles are those wants or values which cannot be directly measured by the common denominator of dollars and cents. Major gains and costs to society cannot be ignored just because they are incapable of dollar measurement, because they cannot be bought and sold, or because organized markets for them do not exist. Examples of alleged intangible values in the resources field stem from national defense considerations, the theme of balanced development, the family farm, the saving of human life and the preservation of historical or scenic sites. But market inadequacy for provision of intangibles does not mean that they should be exempt from rational consideration or from at least some economic analysis. No intangible has infinite value. All intangibles have costs. The least that can be done is to specify and to make very clear to all concerned the cost of obtaining the intangible. As a *minimum* the intangible must be worth as much as it costs in terms of alternatives sacrificed if it is to be approved. Second, it is often possible to place a *maximum* value on the intangible if it can be produced by alternative means. For example, the value of a particular facility for preserving human life can be worth no more than the cost of preserving human life in other ways. Such considerations may reduce the common tendency to consider intangibles as exceptions to economic calculus." Milliman, Can People Be Trusted with Natural Resources? 38 Land Economics 199, 216 (1962).

A modern technique of the economists is to "display" environmental factors in terms of physical or ecological criteria, adding qualitative measurements where possible. See Water Resources Council, Economic and Environmental Principles and Guidelines for Water and Land Resources Implementation Studies, (March 10, 1983). The National Water Commission commissioned two studies along these lines. The student interested in pursuing the economic aspect will find interesting Goldman, Environmental Quality and Water Development, National Technical Information Service, Nos. PB 207 17, PB 207 114. A more legally oriented study of institutional arrangements and procedures for balancing environmental and developmental values is Hillhouse and DeWeerdt, Legal Devices for Accommodating Water Resources Development and Environmental Values, National Technical Information Service, No. PB 208 835 (1971).

4. Does the authority to reject or condition appropriations because of effects on the environment eliminate the need for the withdrawal of water from appropriation to protect instream values? Consider the following:

"Some states (such as California) authorize retention of water in the source for purposes of fishery protection and recreation on a case-by-case basis when considering new applications to appropriate. This process is less desirable than that of the Model Water Code for two reasons. First, the Code's reservation device provides advance notice of a contemplated appropriation, while the case-by-case procedure does not allow a determination until a project has been fully planned and a specific applicant is before the appropriate administrative agency. Second, the extent of the reservation on a case-by-case basis will necessarily be determined by weighing the utility of the specific project against the value of the instream use instead of basing such reservation on general public policy. It is difficult for noneconomic uses based on such policy to be broadly considered." Robie, Modernizing State Water Rights Laws: Some Suggestions for New Directions, 1974 Utah L.Rev. 760, 770 (1974).

The California Department of Fish and Game has complained that the use of permit conditions provides little permanent protection to instream values. The department has noted that bypass flows required of one appropriator often become a target for subsequent appropriation downstream, forcing it to make its case for instream protection again and again, with the possibility that it may be successful in nine cases only to lose on the tenth. See Schneider, Legal Aspects of Instream Water Use in California, Governors Commission to Review California Water Rights Law, Staff Paper No. 6, pp. 44–45 (1975).

Does the following report suggest a means of overcoming the shortcomings described above?

"Nebraska Director of Water Resources John Neuberger has closed two streams in western Nebraska to appropriation. The moratorium was imposed after water right cancellation hearings, field investigations, and Department of Water Resources reports. After reviewing these materials, Director Neuberger determined that issuance of additional stream diversion permits would not be in the public interest, presumably because the water supply is inadequate to support additional uses. In addition, the moratoria will avoid 'additional and unjustifiable administrative costs.' The Department will, however, continue to consider applications to store water and use stored water from Lodgepole and Pumpkinseed Creeks." Rocky Mountain Mineral Law Foundation, Water Law Newsletter, Vol. XIII, No. 1, p. 5 (1980).

STEMPEL v. DEPARTMENT OF WATER RESOURCES

Supreme Court of Washington, 1973.
82 Wash.2d 109, 508 P.2d 166.

UTTER, JUSTICE. The Department of Water Resources of the State of Washington appeals from a superior court decree which remands for further investigation a department decision approving an application for water appropriation. This department is now replaced by the Department of Ecology as of July 1, 1970. RCW 43.21A. * * *

On April 10, 1967, an appropriation application, pursuant to RCW 90.03.250, was filed by Loon Lake Park Company, the intervenor-respondent. The application was for 0.7 cubic feet per second of water to be taken from Loon Lake which would be provided to 143 lots located in the vicinity of Loon Lake for domestic water use. Loon Lake is 28 miles north of Spokane, is 2.6 miles long, covers 1,118 acres, and has a maximum depth of 104 feet. About 20 of the lots owned by the company abut the lake. All the lots are presently able to secure water from three nearby wells, which Loon Lake Park Company alleges provide unsatisfactory water because of its high iron content.

When notice of the application was published, pursuant to RCW 90.03.280, objections were received by the department from 36 persons, including the respondents Stemple and Luiten. The protesters were concerned with numerous pollution and health problems they foresaw as imminent if further water was withdrawn from the lake. On February 15, 1968, a public meeting was held on the application. On April 30, 1968, an order, based on the meeting and the department's investigations (conducted pursuant to RCW 90.03.290), was entered approving the application. Soon thereafter, the respondent protesters appealed the order and requested a hearing on the matter. The water right permit to the Loon Lake Park Company was stayed and a hearing officer was appointed to hear the contested case. RCW 34.04. Hearings were held on July 30 and 31, 1968, and resulted in an affirmance of the department's actions. Respondents Stempel and Luiten then sought, on May 27, 1969, judicial review of the department's otherwise final order entered on May 2, 1969. RCW 34.04.130.

At the time of the initiation of the application in 1967, the requirements governing the department's rulings upon such applications were contained in RCW 90.03.290, which is part of the original 1917 water code, unamended since 1947. The statute requires the department to make essentially four determinations prior to the issuance of a water use permit: (1) what water, if any, is available; (2) to what beneficial uses the water is to be applied; (3) will the appropriation impair existing rights; and (4) will the appropriation detrimentally affect the public welfare. * * *

The record reveals evidence as to the amount of water in Loon Lake for each month from 1950 to the present, and the maximum amount of water necessary to satisfy the Loon Lake Park Company appropriation if granted (one-half inch of lake water). * * * The evidence amply establishes the availability of water.

Second, the use of water for domestic purposes is a beneficial use (RCW 43.27A.020 and RCW 90.54.020(1)) and the record reveals evidence of the department's determination it was for that beneficial purpose that the application was submitted.

Third, no evidence exists to contradict the department's determination that the lowering of Loon Lake by a maximum of one-half inch would not impair the existing rights of riparian owners on the lake. * * * The department's determinations as to the first three statutory criteria are valid.

The department contends that the statute's fourth requirement for determination—"detriment to the public welfare"—does not require examination of potential pollution resulting from the issuance of the appropriation permit and the appropriation. The department's reasoning is the 1917 water code's sole purpose was to provide a system for the distribution of state waters, and when the "public welfare" element is read in that context, the phrase relates to the withdrawal of water and not to pollution and health concerns. State v. Lawrence, 165 Wash. 508, 510, 6 P.2d 363 (1931). The department further asserts whatever pollution, sanitation, sewage or health difficulties may arise because of the water use permit issuance, there exist other departments with legislative authority to respond to the problems.

These contentions are no longer meritorious in light of the enactment of two significant and far-reaching statutes, the State Environmental Policy Act of 1971 (SEPA) (RCW 43.21C), and the Water Resources Act of 1971 (WRA) (RCW 90.54). These two statutes apply to this case and the department is obligated, under them, to consider the total environmental and ecological factors to the fullest in deciding major matters.

The mistreatment of the environment has long been a concern in many sectors of our society, but the enactments of SEPA and WRA, as well as their national counterparts, declare a legislative mandate of the ecological ethic. SEPA strongly declares our state environmental policy. RCW 43.21C.010, 43.21C.020. It is a policy recognizing the necessary harmony between humans and the environment in order to prevent and eliminate damage to the environment and biosphere, as well as to promote the welfare of humans and the understanding of our ecological systems. To ensure that these values of ecological health become part of the decision-making process in our rapid, highly commercial and industrial society, SEPA requires various governmental branches and agencies to submit environmental impact statements before pursuing specified actions. RCW 43.21C.030(c)(i). The environmental impact reports require a detailed statement by the responsible official on:

(i) the environmental impact of the proposed action;

(ii) any adverse environmental effects which cannot be avoided should the proposal be implemented;

(iii) alternatives to the proposed action;

(iv) the relationship between local short-term uses of man's environment and the maintenance and enhancement of long-term productivity; and

(v) any irreversible and irretrievable commitments of resources which would be involved in the proposed action should it be implemented.

Environmental protection has thus become a mandate to every state and local agency and department. Consideration of environmental values is advanced under SEPA. In the preparation of impact statements, SEPA requires consultation with other agencies, the studied development of appropriate alternatives to proposed projects, and recognition of "the world-wide and long-range character of environmental problems." See RCW 43.21C.030(d), (e) and (f). All of the foregoing shall "[u]tilize a systematic, interdisciplinary approach * * * in decision making which may have an impact on man's environment". RCW 43.21C.030(a).

We recognize SEPA does not demand any particular substantive result in governmental decision making, for it indicates "other considerations of state policy" (RCW 43.21C.030(2)(a–g)) continue to be the responsibility of the agencies. "Environmental amenities" will undoubtedly often conflict with "economic and technical considerations." In essence, what SEPA requires, is that the "presently unquantified environmental amenities and values will be given appropriate consideration in decision making along with economic and technical considerations." RCW 43.21C.030(2)(b). It is an attempt by the people to shape their future environment by deliberation, not default.

There being no argument that the issuance of the water use permit in this case does not amount to a major action significantly affecting the quality of the environment, (RCW 43.21C.030(2)(c)), the department is required to act in accordance with the provisions of SEPA in conducting its additional investigation under the remand decree.

The Water Resources Act of 1971 (WRA), though dealing with only one aspect of our environment, is as vigorous as SEPA in its policy declaration. The state water resource policy finds that the public health, preservation of natural resources and aesthetic values are deserving of promotion, in addition to the state's economic well-being. RCW 90.54.010.

RCW 90.54.020(3) requires that the quality of the natural environment "shall be protected" and, where possible, enhanced as follows:

> (a) * * * Lakes and ponds shall be retained substantially in their natural condition. *Withdrawals of water* which would conflict therewith shall be authorized only in those situations where it is clear that overriding considerations of the public interest will be served.
>
> (b) Waters of the state shall be of high quality. Regardless of the quality of the waters of the state, *all wastes and other materials and substances proposed for entry into said waters shall be provided with all known, available, and reasonable methods of treatment prior to entry.* * * * wastes and other materials and substances shall not be allowed to enter such waters which will reduce the existing quality thereof, except in those situations where it is clear that overriding considerations of the public interest will be served.

(Italics ours.) The department is therefore required, in accordance with the above cited and other relevant provisions of WRA, to evaluate the possible pollution reentry problems resulting from the domestic water use in the vicinity of the lake. * * *

The matter is remanded to the department for further action in accordance with this decision.

Notes

1. Since Friends of Mammoth v. Mono County, 8 Cal.3d 247, 104 Cal. Rptr. 761, 502 P.2d 1049 (1972) and the subsequent amendment of the California Environmental Quality Act, it is now clear that an environmental impact statement is required to be prepared by the California State Water Resources Control Board prior to the issuance of a permit for an appropriation of water that would have "a significant effect on the environment." See Robie, Some Reflections on Environmental Considerations in Water Rights Administration, 2 Ecology L.Q. 695 (1972). Cf. County of Inyo v. Yorty, 32 Cal.App.3d 795, 108 Cal.Rptr. 377 (1973); Environmental Defense Fund, Inc. v. Coastside County Water District, 27 Cal.App.3d 695, 104 Cal.Rptr. 197 (1972).

2. How does the environmental impact statement fit into the traditional requirement of "the public interest?"

SHOKAL v. DUNN

707 P.2d 441 (Idaho 1985).

[Dunn, the director of the Idaho Department of Water Resources, issued a permit to Trout Co. for an appropriation from Billingsley Creek for fish propogation and hydropower generation. Shokal and others who had protested the issuance of the permit appealed the decision to the district court. Judge Schroeder reversed and remanded Dunn's decision, finding the Department of Water Resources consideration of two issues inadequate: (1) The financial ability of the applicant to complete the project, and (2) the local public interest with respect to the project. On remand, Dunn again approved the permit, after substantial changes were made in the project to comply with water quality standards set by Dunn. An appeal was again taken to the district court, this time before Judge Smith. Judge Smith again reversed and remanded. Judge Smith's decision was appealed to the Idaho Supreme Court.]

BISTLINE, Justice.

* * *

While we affirm the decision of the district court to remand for a new hearing, we differ on the matters necessary for consideration at the new hearing. We hold that Water Resources used the proper standard for and has adequately dealt with the financing question. In addition, although we in general affirm the district court's order as it related to public interest matters, we modify in part the district court's guidelines.

* * *

After the second hearing, Water Resources issued findings of fact and conclusions of law including stringent requirements regarding effluent discharge. Trout Co. determined its first plan was unable to comply with the new water quality standards imposed by Water Resources. Trout Co. reworked the plans for the project and submitted a Contemplated Operational Criteria for the Trout Co. Fish Raising

Facility (Operational Criteria). Among other changes, this document called for a scaled down facility designed to comply with the water quality standards set by Water Resources. The Director then determined that compliance with the established conditions had been achieved and issued a final order granting the permit to Trout Co. This final order was issued without further hearing. Appellants, protestants below, contended it was a procedural error for Water Resources to fail to grant an additional hearing at which the appellants could object to and/or cross-examine the Operational Criteria; hence, they contended that the final order was made upon unlawful procedure. The district court agreed, and we agree with the district court.

* * *

In sum, the protestants, as concerned parties, were entitled to a hearing at which they could object to the Operational Criteria, cross-examine witnesses, and present their own evidence.

By denying the protestants these rights, the Director erred procedurally. But, as discussed below, we can define no substantive error to date on the part of Water Resources. Thus, while reversal of the agency is inappropriate, the amended application is properly remanded for a new hearing to correct the procedural error. * * * We affirm the district court's order remanding for additional proceedings, but in accordance with the remainder of this opinion. The following two parts discuss the matters for reconsideration.

FINANCING

* * *

THE LOCAL PUBLIC INTEREST

Since Water Resources's decisions on financing are reinstated, the only matters for the agency to consider on remand are those which relate generally to the local public interest. I.C. § 42–203A(5)(e). We turn first to the interpretation of this provision, a question of first impression before this Court.

A. Defining the Local Public Interest

Under I.C. § 42–203A(5)(e), if an applicant's appropriation of water "will conflict with the local public interest, where the local public interest is defined as the affairs of the people in the area directly affected by the proposed use," then the Director "may reject such application and refuse issuance of permit therefor, or may partially approve and grant a permit for a smaller quantity of water than applied for, or may grant a permit upon conditions."

* * *

B. Specific Considerations Raised Below

1. Finality of Design

In order to be able to assess a project's impact on the public interest, the project's design must be definite enough to reflect its impacts and implications. Judge Smith held that because the applicant has the burden of proof to show a project is worthy of issuance of a permit, "the design of the proposed facility should be final, detailed and not schematic." He elaborated on the finality issue by stating:

> The department should not have to issue a permit on conditions that the Department review the final plans. The final plans should be presented to the Department with the application for a permit. Thus, all interested parties could review the plans, cross-examine in regard thereto and offer suggestions that might be helpful in reducing any adverse impact. The issuance of the permit, therefore, would also constitute approval of the plan.
>
> Any application for a permit that is not substantially complete in its engineering so that it cannot be properly evaluated for a here-and-now financial commitment or for impact on the public, can be readily denied by the Director. If he cannot grant the permit without establishing substantial conditions, he should deny the permit with leave to amend the application if he so desires affording all interested parties an opportunity to be heard if and when the application is amended. Such process would hopefully preclude some accusations that a Director is acting arbitrarily, capriciously or unreasonably.

In our perception, Judge Smith's language requires an applicant to present "blueprint quality" plans at the outset of seeking a permit, much in the same vein as his "here and now" standard of financing required ready cash. We are not persuaded that blueprint quality plans of a facility are always necessary when applying for a permit to appropriate water. Rather, the design plan for a proposed facility depends on the nature of the facility, the complexity of the proposal, and the extent of the proposed appropriation's impact on the local area. In this particular case, the Department will determine at the hearing on the amended application whether blue print quality plans and drawings are a prerequisite to giving approval. In all cases the plans should be sufficient to generally apprise the public of the efficacy of the proposed use in the planned facility, and of its potential impact.

2. *Dewatering*

The dewatering of Billingsley Creek raises significant public interest and public trust concerns. In his discussion of the issue Judge Smith simply declared that "the rights of an appropriator prevail over riparian rights." Such a statement on its face fails to account for the state's policy of providing for minimum stream flows, and for the public's legitimate interests in the stream environment, wildlife, aesthetics, recreation, and alternative uses. However, after reviewing the record, we agree with Judge Smith that Water Resources has dealt properly with the dewatering issue. Therefore we affirm Judge Smith's holding that there is no "legal basis for reversing the Department decision on the grounds that a portion of Billingsley Creek would be dewatered from 125 CFS to a 25 CFS minimum for an approximate 700 ft. stretch of the creek."

3. Health Hazard

Judge Smith opined that the law will not allow Billingsley Creek to become a nuisance or a health hazard, adding also that "a permit cannot issue which would allow construction of a project contrary to the authority of the Board of Health in policing water for pollution." Hence, Judge Smith concluded that the Director had authority to consider whether the design of any particular facility will meet all environmental requirements.

We believe this to be a correct assessment of the law, but add a word of caution regarding the differing functions of Water Resources and the Department of Health and Welfare. Water Resources must oversee the water resources of the state, insuring that those who have permits and licenses to appropriate water use the water in accordance with the conditions of the permits and licenses and the limits of the law. It is not the primary job of Water Resources to protect the health and welfare of Idaho's citizens and visitors—that role is vested in the Department of Health and Welfare, including compliance with the water quality regulations and monitoring effluent discharge in our state's waterways. Nevertheless, although these agencies may have separate functions, Water Resources is precluded from issuing a permit for a water appropriation project which, when completed, would violate the water quality standards of the Department of Health and Welfare. It makes no sense whatsoever for Water Resources to blindly grant permit requests without regard to water quality regulations. Hence, Water Resources should condition the issuance of a permit on a showing by the applicant that a proposed facility will meet the mandatory water quality standards. Under this rule, Water Resources has the authority to withhold a permit application until it receives a proposed design which appears to be in compliance with the water quality standards. Once the conditional permit is granted, Water Resources has continuing jurisdiction over compliance with the conditions of the permit, including suspension or revocation of the permit for proven violations of the permit's conditions regarding water quality.

The Department of Health and Welfare continues to have the primary responsibility for policing water quality control in this state, and can exercise in personam jurisdiction over those who violate the state's water pollution laws. While it often may be both more feasible and more reasonable for Health and Welfare to take remedial steps against one violating the pollution laws, either by forcing compliance or shutting down a facility, than to resist an application for a permit in the first instance, Health and Welfare certainly has the right to be heard in proceedings before Water Resources. And, as appointed guardian of the quality of Idaho water, its views are entitled to consideration.

In sum, we agree with the district court, Judge Smith, that Water Resources cannot issue a permit which would allow construction of a project violative of the laws regulating water quality. However, later compliance with those laws after construction of a facility generally will be a proper concern of the Department of Health and Welfare.

Conclusion

The above elements of the public interest, together with other elements and factors which Water Resources deems relevant, will be considered at the hearing on the amended application. Water Resources should accept relevant testimony and other evidence providing additional information on the public interest.

The decision of the district court is reversed in part, affirmed in part, and remanded for further proceedings consonant herewith. No costs or attorney's fees allowed.

UNITED PLAINSMEN ASS'N v. NORTH DAKOTA STATE WATER CONSERVATION COMM.

Supreme Court of North Dakota, 1976.
247 N.W.2d 457.

PEDERSON, JUSTICE.

This is an appeal by the United Plainsmen Association, a North Dakota non-profit corporation, from a decision of the district court of Burleigh County dismissing the complaint for failure to state a claim upon which relief could be granted.

The complaint sought an injunction against the North Dakota State Water Conservation Commission and Vernon Fahy, State Engineer. Should this court find that the trial court erred, then United Plainsmen asks for a temporary restraining order against the Commission and the State Engineer pending trial on the merits. We hold that the district court did err in dismissing the complaint, we deny a temporary restraining order, and remand the case for further proceedings. * * *

The injunction sought by United Plainsmen would have prevented the State Engineer from issuing future water permits for coal-related power and energy production facilities until there is a comprehensive short- and long-term plan for the conservation and development of the State's natural resources, which, United Plainsmen contends, is required by § 61–01–26, NDCC, and the common law Public Trust Doctrine existing in this State. Section 61–01–26 reads as follows:

> "In view of legislative findings and determination of the ever-increasing demand and anticipated future need for water in North Dakota for every beneficial purpose and use, it is hereby declared to be the water resources policy of the state that:
>
> "1. The public health, safety and general welfare, including without limitation, enhancement of opportunities for social and economic

growth and expansion, of all of the people of the state, depend in large measure upon the optimum protection, management and wise utilization of all of the water and related land resources of the state;

"2. Well-being of all of the people of the state shall be the overriding determinant in considering the best use, or combination of uses, of water and related land resources;

"3. Storage of the maximum water supplies shall be provided wherever and whenever deemed feasible and practicable;

"4. Accruing benefits from these resources can best be achieved for the people of the state through the development, execution and periodic updating of comprehensive, coordinated and well-balanced short- and long-term plans and programs for the conservation and development of such resources by the departments and agencies of the state having responsibilities therefor;

"5. Adequate implementation of such plans and programs shall be provided by the state through cost-sharing and cooperative participation with the appropriate federal and state departments and agencies and political subdivisions within the limitation of budgetary requirements and administrative capabilities; * * *

"The provisions of this chapter shall not be construed to in any manner limit, impair or abrogate the rights, powers, duties or functions of any department or agency of the state having jurisdiction or responsibilities in the field of water and related land resources conservation, development or utilization."

United Plainsmen argues that the language of subsection 4 of that statute imposes mandatory planning responsibility upon the State Engineer, which constitutes a condition precedent to the issuance of temporary or permanent water permits in this State. We do not agree. In the light of the qualifying proviso at the end of § 61–01–26, we must conclude that subsection 4 thereof is "hortatory and precatory, but not mandatory." See Dathe v. Wildrose School District No. 91, 217 N.W.2d 781, 782 (N.D.1974).

Although it is not mandatory, § 61–01–26, entitled "Declaration of state water resources policy," is a significant advisory policy statement. The last sentence therein clearly indicates that it is not to be construed to limit, impair or abrogate the rights, powers, duties or functions of any department or agency of the State. This statute provides but little support for United Plainsmen's contention that the State Engineer must complete short- and long-term planning as a condition precedent to the issuance of water permits.

We note, also, that the Legislature has reserved to itself the task of research in the areas of natural resources use and the determination of governmental responsibility for the results or impacts from developments, and to assure that "there shall not be material detrimental deterioration of the environment or quality of life in North Dakota." See Section 4 of Chapter 4, Session Laws of 1975.

The foregoing, however, does not relieve the Commission and State Engineer of mandatory planning responsibilities with respect to the issuance of water permits, and we note that counsel for the Commission emphasized in his argument that the State Engineer and the Commission do have plans and do not reject the concept of prior planning. We agree with United Plainsmen that the discretionary authority of state officials to allocate vital state resources is not without limit but is circumscribed by what has been called the Public Trust Doctrine.

This doctrine was first clearly defined in Illinois Central Railroad v. Illinois, 146 U.S. 387, 13 S.Ct. 110, 36 L.Ed. 1018 (1892), a case in which the United States Supreme Court was called upon to decide the competency of the State of Illinois to convey, by legislative grant, a portion of Chicago's harbor on Lake Michigan to the Illinois Central Railroad.

> "That the State holds the title to the lands under the navigable waters of Lake Michigan, within its limits, in the same manner that the State holds title to soils under tide water, by the common law, we have already shown, and that title necessarily carries with it control over the waters above them whenever the lands are subjected to use. * * * It is a title held in trust for the people of the State that they may enjoy the navigation of the waters, carry on commerce over them, and have liberty of fishing therein freed from the obstruction or interference of private parties." 146 U.S. at 452, 13 S.Ct. at 118.

> "The State can no more abdicate its trust over property in which the whole people are interested, like navigable waters and soils under them, so as to leave them entirely under the use and control of private parties, except in the instance of parcels mentioned for the improvement of the navigation and use of the waters, or when parcels can be disposed of without impairment of the public interest in what remains, than it can abdicate its police powers in the administration of government and the preservation of the peace." 146 U.S. at 453, 13 S.Ct. at 118. * * *

The Commission, the State Engineer, and the lower court, while acknowledging the existence of this doctrine in North Dakota, interpret it in a narrow sense, limiting its applicability to conveyances of real property. We do not understand the doctrine to be so restricted. The State holds the navigable waters, as well as the lands beneath them, in trust for the public. North Dakota's Constitution, Article XVII, § 210, states:

> "All flowing streams and natural water courses shall forever remain the property of the state for mining, irrigating and manufacturing purposes."

Section 61-01-01, NDCC, further defines the public waters of this State:

> "All waters within the limits of the state from the following sources of water supply, namely: * * * belong to the public and are subject to appropriation for beneficial use and the right to the use of

these waters for such use, shall be acquired pursuant to the provisions of chapter 61–04."

These statutes provide a means by which those who seek use of public waters can petition the State Engineer for water permits. In the performance of this duty of resource allocation consistent with the public interest, the Public Trust Doctrine requires, at a minimum, a determination of the potential effect of the allocation of water on the present water supply and future water needs of this State. This necessarily involves planning responsibility. The development and implementation of some short- and long-term planning capability is essential to effective allocation of resources "without detriment to the public interest in the lands and waters remaining."

We believe that § 61–01–01, NDCC, expresses the Public Trust Doctrine. * * * Confined to traditional concepts, the Doctrine confirms the State's role as trustee of the public waters. It permits alienation and allocation of such precious state resources only after an analysis of present supply and future need.

The Legislature has indicated its desire to see such planning take place, although not in mandatory language. Until the Legislature speaks more forcefully, we think the Public Trust Doctrine requires, as a minimum, evidence of some planning by appropriate state agencies and officers in the allocation of public water resources, and that the Environmental Law Enforcement Act (Chapter 32–40, NDCC) requires more than a plenary dismissal of the action.

United Plainsmen has requested a temporary restraining order, enjoining the further issuance of water permits pending trial on the merits in the lower court. A temporary injunction or restraining order may be granted if it appears by the complaint that the plaintiffs are entitled to the relief requested, and that such relief consists of restraining acts which would, if continued, produce injury to the plaintiffs during the litigation. Section 32–06–02, NDCC. We are not convinced that a temporary restraining order is necessary or advisable in this instance.

During oral argument counsel for appellees stated that, of the total number of water permits considered each year, a very small percentage is in the industrial category relating to energy conversion. Of that small percentage of industrial water-use applications considered, only a few are actually granted and some that are granted will never be used because of other causes which prevent the intended development.

We express no opinion about the ultimate outcome of the trial on the merits, should that point be reached in this case. We acknowledge, however, that there is merit in the argument that the extent of planning is somewhat related to the sums appropriated therefor by the Legislature. It may be that the planning being done by the Commission, according to the oral argument made in this Court, is sufficient.

We hold that the dismissal was premature and improvident under the circumstances. The amended complaint charges a failure to devise any water conservation plan, as well as a failure to consider injury to the public. For the purpose of the motion to dismiss, the trial court and this Court must consider all allegations of the complaint to be true. We hold, accordingly, that the complaint does state a claim upon which relief could be granted, if proved, and, therefore, must be reinstated.

Reversed and remanded for further proceedings.

Notes

1. How specific and binding should the plan be? The California Water Plan is an example of an older type of plan—a list of 376 dams and related facilities on rivers and streams throughout the state, prepared by the Department of Water Resources in 1957 and approved by the legislature in 1959. Yet when one water district applied for a permit to construct one of the listed dams and another sought approval of an inconsistent project that would displace the listed dam but better use existing facilities, the latter was preferred by the State Water Rights Board and its choice was upheld in Johnson Rancho County Water Dist. v. State Water Rights Bd., 235 Cal.App.2d 863, 45 Cal.Rptr. 589 (1965). The court noted that the plan itself included a recommendation that more detailed studies of component features were necessary to determine their need, engineering feasibility and financial feasibility, and that further investigation might indicate alternative projects. The court also noted that the legislature had not made the plan binding but had merely directed the Board (now the Water Resources Control Board) to "give consideration to any general or coordinated plan * * * including the California Water Plan * * * and any modification thereto * * *."

2. The Wyoming statutes mandate a more flexible, ongoing process, Wyo.Stat.1977:

§ 41–2–107. Water resources plans; review; submission to commission.

"The commission shall formulate and from time to time review and revise water and related land resources plans for the state of Wyoming and for appropriate regions and river basins. The plans shall implement the policies stated in the Wyoming constitution and in statutes pertaining to the state's water and related land resources."

§ 41–2–108. Consultation; hearings; studies and plan coordination.

"(a) In the formulation of these plans the commission may:

(i) (Repealed);

(ii) Consult with and receive the views of persons, local groups and organizations representing water users, special interests, industries and the public interest, and acquire data and information relating to water, water use, water conservation, and water quality from government agencies, departments and other sources;

(iii) Coordinate the water resources plans with other government agencies and departments;

(iv) Undertake studies, investigations, surveys and research relevant to the formulation of the water resources plans and enter into contracts and arrangements for the same with any government agency, department, or any person, firm, university, institution, or state or national organization;

(v) Adopt, in whole or in part, studies and reports made by other governmental agencies, state or federal; and

(vi) Perform other related activities or functions as are relevant and appropriate to the formulation of water resources plans."

§ 41–2–109. Content of plans; identification; evaluation.

"(a) The water resources plans shall, to the extent deemed practical:

(i) Identify, describe and inventory the occurrence, amounts, availability and quality of water resources, current uses of water, activities that affect the quality of water, and activities that are dependent on, affected by, or relate to water and uses of water;

(ii) Identify and describe prospective needs and demands for water and opportunities for water development, control, withdrawal, storage, conservation, supply, distribution, drainage and disposal;

(iii) Identify and specify for each plan appropriate state, regional and local goals and objectives for management of water resources, including the obtaining of economic efficiency and a desirable distribution of income, the protection of the health, safety and welfare of the people, the protection and encouragement of particular industries and activities, the protection and enhancement of the environment and recreation; and

(iv) Evaluate and compare prospective and anticipated uses and projects, including combinations and coordinations thereof, uses of alternative sources of water and alternative uses of water, in terms of goals identified pursuant to paragraph (iii) of this subsection."

§ 41–2–110. Publication and recommendation of plans.

"(a) The commission shall:

(i) Publish the water resources plans as they are formulated and adopted and disseminate them to people, industries and government departments and agencies;

(ii) Give advice and assistance if requested to government departments and agencies, furnish to them the appropriate plans, and make available related subsidiary and additional data and information, or data and information related to plans in the process of preparation;

(iii) Recommend action or legislation needed to implement and carry out the plans.

(iv) (Repealed)."

3. Trelease, Recommendations for Water Resources Planning & Administration, A Report to the State of Alaska 16, 18 (1977):

"A plan cannot solve unforeseeable problems, but it can provide a procedure and analytical method which when applied to new and unforeseen situations will lead to correct solutions. This is what the Water Use Act attempts to do. The act is itself a planning statute. All law is a planning tool, in the sense that it authorizes or encourages acts deemed desirable and discourages or forbids actions deemed undesirable, but the Water Use Act is even more explicit: * * * [See Alaska Stat. 46.15.080, supra Note 2, page 148.]

"Thus, if a new water use is for a beneficial purpose, does not affect prior users and has sound engineering, if it creates wealth for the water user and indirectly for the state without deleterious side effects on other people, fish and game, recreation and public access, and if it does not foreclose other better uses of water, then it is a 'planned' use even though no one in government ever thought of it or studied the particular water resource or planned its disposition. * * *

"*Use of the Plan.* Many shortcuts to this type of analysis can be supplied by the State Water Plan. The plan can and should give the Department considerable assistance in the disposition of an individual case even though it was not specifically contemplated in the plan. The plan should provide standards for construction of works and performance of machinery, tests for waste and inefficient use, guidelines to indicate what is in the public interest. The planning process ought to produce a narrowing of the range of acceptable uses. Then, at the permitting stage, applications for permits for uses that employ unacceptable methods, that do not meet guidelines of efficiency, that belong to a class to be subordinated to more desirable uses, can be denied by reference to the plan instead of being investigated and adjudicated individually in repetitious and protracted proceedings. The plan's description of the resource, identification of possible uses and analyses of conflicts and problems may reveal the externalties of a particular project and identify the issues that need to be determined in processing a permit application. On the other hand the plan may not only identify issues but solve them, and the plan's yardsticks and guidelines may offer easy solutions to recurring and similar cases. Thus many cases can be 'routinized' with safety, with only the problem cases being sorted out for individual treatment. Criteria for identifying the routine case can be stated in terms of size (e.g., less than x c.f.s. or g.p.m. of diversion), purpose and size (y c.f.s. for offstream placer mining), or source and purpose (single dwelling domestic well from shallow groundwater)."

4. Preference statutes are a more static form of planning:

No.Dak.Cent.Code 61–04–06.1: "Preference in granting permits. When there are competing applications for water from the same source, and the source is insufficient to supply all applicants, the state engineer shall adhere to the following order of priority:

1. Domestic use.
2. Municipal use.
3. Livestock use.
4. Irrigation use.
5. Industrial use.
6. Fish, wildlife, and other outdoor recreation."

West's Ann.Cal.Water Code § 106: "It is hereby declared to be the established policy of this state that the use of water for domestic purposes is the highest use of water and that the next highest use is for use in irrigation."

In implementing this statute, the California authorities not only have chosen applications for preferred uses over presently competing applications, but have subordinated current non-preferred uses to future preferred uses, for example, by inserting into a permit for a hydroelectric power project the condition, "The right to store and use water for power purposes under this permit shall not interfere with future appropriation of said water for agricultural or municipal purposes." This procedure was upheld in East Bay Municipal Utility Dist. v. Department of Public Works, 1 Cal. 2d 476, 35 P.2d 1027 (1934).

FARM INVESTMENT CO. v. CARPENTER

Supreme Court of Wyoming, 1900.
9 Wyo. 110, 61 P. 258.

POTTER, C.J. This suit was instituted in the district court of Johnson county for the purpose of securing a decree quieting the title of plaintiff to the right to use water from French creek for the irrigation of certain lands, as against each and all of the defendants, who, it is alleged, are asserting prior and superior rights to the plaintiff. An appropriation by plaintiff's grantor in the year 1879, and the continued use and application of the water so appropriated, are set out, and in consequence thereof a right superior to the defendants is alleged to reside in the plaintiff. The answer of but one of the defendants is in the record. Admitting the original appropriation alleged in the petition, and the ownership of plaintiff to the water right acquired thereby, if any, the answer, as a separate defense, after disclosing the claim of the answering defendant to the use of certain of the waters of the stream for irrigation purposes by reason of an appropriation in 1883, sets up an adjudication by the state board of control of the rights of the various claimants to the use of the water of said stream on or about October, 1893, in accordance with the provisions of chapter 8 of the Laws of 1890–91; the same being an act entitled "An act providing for the supervision and use of the waters of the state." It is alleged that all the notices required by said act were duly given and published, and that the plaintiff had actual notice, and that the proceedings were conducted in accordance with the statutory provisions, and that neither the plaintiff nor his grantors appeared or submitted any proof of their alleged rights. It is also alleged that by the order of the said board in that proceeding the defendant was awarded a certain priority for a definite quantity of water, for which a certificate was issued to him, and that "no amount of water whatever was awarded or decreed to the plaintiff or to any other person for use upon the lands described in said plaintiff's petition." Wherefore it is averred that the plaintiff has abandoned its rights, and is now estopped from asserting the same. * * *

[Counsel for plaintiff contended that the statutory provisions for the adjudication were unconstitutional. The district court certified the constitutional questions directly to the supreme court for answer.]

The expressions of the constitution relating to irrigation and water rights are as follows: "Water being essential to industrial prosperity, of limited amount, and easy of diversion from its natural channels, its control must be in the state, which, in providing for its use, shall equally guard all the various interests involved." Article 1, § 31. "The waters of all natural streams, springs, lakes, or other collections of still water, within the boundaries of the state, are hereby declared to be the property of the state." Article 8, § 1. "There shall be constituted a board of control to be composed of the state engineer, and superintendents of the water divisions; which shall, under such regulations as may be prescribed by law, have the supervision of the waters of the state and of their appropriation, distribution and diversion, and of the various officers connected therewith. Its decisions to be subject to review by the courts of the state." Id. § 2. * * *

Pursuant to the constitutional requirements, the first state legislature, by an act entitled "An act providing for the supervision and use of the waters of the state," approved December 22, 1890, created the state board of control, divided the state into four water divisions, and provided for the appointment of a superintendent for each division. * * * By the act in question, also, a system of procedure to be inaugurated and conducted by the board is established, wherein and whereby the board is directed and empowered to ascertain, adjudicate, and determine the priorities of rights of the various claimants from the same stream, and the former legislation authorizing such adjudication by a special proceeding in the district court is repealed. * * *

Concerning the proceedings preliminary to an order of determination, it will sufficiently answer our purpose to state that notices are required to be published and sent by registered mail to each person having a recorded claim to waters of the stream or streams embraced in the adjudication proceedings, showing when the engineer will begin a measurement of the stream and the several diverting works, and the time and place when the superintendent will commence the taking of testimony. Accompanying the notice, there is required to be sent to the claimant a blank form, on which the claimant is required to present in writing, under oath, certain specified facts relating to his appropriation. Upon the completion of the testimony the same is to be opened to public inspection at a time and place mentioned in a notice thereof to be previously published and sent by mail to the several claimants. An opportunity is provided for any interested party to contest before the superintendent and the board the claim of any other persons who may have submitted their proof. Upon the completion of the evidence in the original hearing, and in all contests, the same is required to be transmitted to the board of control. In the meantime the engineer or his assistant is required to make an examination and measurement of the stream and the works diverting water therefrom, as well as of the irrigated lands, or lands susceptible of irrigation from the various ditches or canals taking water from the stream then under consideration, and to make a map or plat showing the course of the stream, the location of each ditch, and the lands irrigated or susceptible of irrigation therefrom. Sections 872 and 873 are as follows:

> "Sec. 872. At the first regular meeting of the board of control, after the completion of such measurement by the state engineer, and the return of said evidence by said division superintendent, it shall be the duty of the board of control to make, and cause to be entered of record in its office, an order determining and establishing the several priorities of right to the use of waters of said stream, and the amounts of appropriations of the several persons claiming water from such stream, and the character and kind of use for which said appropriation shall be found to have been made. Each appropriation shall be determined in its priority and amount, by the time by which it shall have been made and the amount of water which shall have been applied for beneficial purposes. * * *
>
> "Sec. 873. As soon as practicable after the determination of the priorities of appropriation of the use of waters of any stream, it shall be the duty of the secretary to issue to each person, association or corporation represented in such determination, a certificate to be signed by the state engineer, as president of the board of control, and attested under seal by the secretary of said board, setting forth the name and post-office address of the appropriator; the priority number of such appropriations; the amount of water appropriated; and if such appropriation be for irrigation a description of the legal subdivisions of land to which said water is to be applied. * * *"

Provision is made for an appeal, by any party feeling himself aggrieved, from the decision of the board to the district court, and from that court to the supreme court.

Counsel for the plaintiff contend that the act of December 22, 1890, is unconstitutional, in so far as it confers upon the board of control authority to determine the priorities of rights to the use of water. * * * The position maintained by counsel is that a determination of the priorities of rights to the use of water involves solely a judicial inquiry into rights to property as between private parties, and that the jurisdiction to undertake such an investigation and adjudicate therein can be constitutionally lodged only in some court which is by article 5 of the constitution vested with judicial power. The statute nowhere attempts to devest the courts of any jurisdiction granted to them by the constitution to redress grievances and afford relief at law or in equity under the ordinary and well-known rules of procedure. A purely statutory proceeding is created, to be set in motion by no act or complaint of any injured party, but which in each instance is to be inaugurated by order of the board,—a proceeding which is to result, not in a judgment for damages to a party for injuries sustained, nor the issuance of any writ or process known to the law for the purpose of preventing the unlawful invasion of a party's rights or privileges; but the finality of the proceeding is a settlement or adjustment of the priorities of appropriation of the public waters of the state, and is followed by the issuance of a certificate to each appropriator, showing his relative standing among other claimants, and the amount of water to which he is found to be entitled. * * *

The other fundamental principles expressed in the constitution are that control of the public waters must be in the state, which, in providing for their use, shall equally guard all the various interests involved. Such control shall consist in a supervision of the waters, their appropriation, distribution, and diversion, by a board of control, to be composed of certain designated officers, with an officer of technical and practical knowledge and experience at its head; and priority of appropriation shall give the better right. Let us inquire into the nature and subject of the supervisory power of the board. * * * It has already been suggested that the supervision of the board affects individual appropriations, and concerns the distribution of water to individual claimants. Any effort to supervise and control the waters of the state, their appropriation and distribution, in the absence of an effective ascertainment of the several priorities of rights, must result in practical failure in times when official intervention is most required. In fact, that had been demonstrated under our former system. In the development of the irrigation problem under the rule of prior appropriation, perplexing questions are continually arising, of a technical and practical character. As between an investigation in the courts and by the board, it would seem that an administrative board, with experience and peculiar knowledge along this particular line, can in the first instance, solve the questions involved, with due regard to private and public interests, conduct the requisite investigation, and make the ascertainment of individual rights, with greater facility, at less expense to interested parties, and with a larger degree of satisfaction to all concerned. In the opinion of an able law writer upon this subject, the powers of the board of control in this respect constitute one of the most praiseworthy features of our legislation. He says: "In the state of Wyoming, at least, there will no longer be the ludicrous spectacle of learned judges solemnly decreeing the right to from two to ten times the amount of water flowing in a stream, or, in fact, amounts so great that the channel of the stream could not possibly carry them; thus practically leaving the questions at stake as unsettled as before." Kin. Irr. § 493. * * *

The determination required to be made by the board is, in our opinion, primarily administrative rather than judicial in character. The proceeding is one in which a claimant does not obtain redress for an injury, but secures evidence of title to a valuable right,—a right to use a peculiar public commodity. That evidence of title comes properly from an administrative board, which, for the state in its sovereign capacity, represents the public, and is charged with the duty of conserving public as well as private interests. The board, it is true, acts judicially; but the power exercised is quasi judicial only, and such as, under proper circumstances, may appropriately be conferred upon executive officers or boards. The jurisdiction bears some resemblance to that of the land department of the government concerning the disposal of the public lands. * * *

We are not persuaded that the act is void, as conferring judicial power upon the board in violation of the constitution. That the board was expected to exercise quasi judicial functions is apparent from that provision of section 2 of article 8 of the constitution requiring its decisions to be subject to review by the courts. * * *

Notes

1. The western states were slow to recognize the necessity for determining titles to and priority of water rights and providing accurate records of them. Litigation between appropriators, in the form of suits for damages, injunctions, and to quiet title, sufficed for a time.

Two-party litigation had its limitations. In an equity suit between two appropriators, the trial court decreed that the plaintiff was the owner of the first right to divert the waters of the source and that the defendant was the owner of a large right, subject only to the prior right of the plaintiff. Other appropriators, claiming rights prior to both, sought a writ of prohibition to set aside the decree. Denied. "Although [the decrees are] general in form, and broad enough in language to include the whole world, they can have no such effect. They are binding on the parties to the action and their privies, but upon no one else. As to strangers claiming rights in the waters of the lake the decrees in no manner affect them. The decrees are not even evidence of adverse rights. Strangers may proceed as if the decrees had never been entered." State ex rel. McConihe v. Steiner, 58 Wash. 578, 109 P. 57 (1910). The rights of third persons likewise have no effect upon a judgment as to the relative rights of the litigants. "Neither do we think that the trial court was called upon, at the instance of the defendants, entire strangers in every aspect to other appropriators, to inquire into and pass upon the question whether appropriators of water below the mouth of the proposed canal of appellee would be injured by the construction of the canal. The rights of such persons will not, of course, be injuriously affected by the decree in this cause, and *non constat* but that they may yet intervene for their own protection, if they deem that the construction of the canal will be an invasion of their rights, or that they may be willing to forego objection to the construction of the canal." Gutierres v. Albuquerque Land & Irrigation Co., 188 U.S. 545, 23 S.Ct. 338, 47 L.Ed. 588 (1903).

Lasky, From Prior Appropriation to Economic Distribution of Water by the State, 1 Rocky Mt.L.Rev. 161, 189 (1929):

"As a means to settle rights, suits between A and B contesting had proved inadequate, from the outset, as we have seen. To obtain an adequate judicial procedure, Colorado early, 1879, turned to legislation. But, contemporaneously, legislation lacking, the courts in other states were forced to proceed on analogies to common-law or equitable remedies.

"The first requirement was to call into court a large number or all of the users on the stream and to bind all by one decree. The analogy everywhere hit upon, and still used in Montana in almost its bare form, was the old bill of peace. The principle of it is finely laid down by the Nebraska court:

"'* * * where a large number of persons is claiming the right to divert and use the water of a stream * * * we know of no sound reason why a suit in equity to determine and adjust such rights and enjoin interference with such rights by others may not be maintained. * * * In some states, they [such suits] have been provided by statute, but in the absence of statutes they have been upheld under general principles of equity jurisdiction. * * * This principle has been appealed to frequently over litigation of water rights, and has been held to permit of a single suit by a plaintiff against all of a large number of persons having or claiming rights in the water of the stream which infringed on the rights of such plaintiff. * * * The chief difficulty in such cases arises from the fact that the several defendants have several rights and interests, and are not so connected in interest that a determination as to one would include them all. * * * [However] the plaintiff might properly bring such an action * * * so far as it comes within the scope of a bill of peace, to avoid multiplicity of suits.' [Crawford Co. v. Hathaway, 67 Neb. 325, 369, 370, 93 N.W. 781, 796 (1903)].

"The inadequacies of the device were obvious. Even where the courts extended the idea of the bill of peace to allow the plaintiff to cite in all the users on the stream in order that the decree would bind all, the rights of users on tributaries relative to those in the suit were undetermined so that after all the decree might be a mere '*fulmum brutum,*' the expense to the plaintiff was prohibitive, the difficulty of serving notice on all the parties nigh insurmountable, the adjudication slow."

2. In 1881 Colorado broke away from lawsuit procedures but retained the judicial forum by the enactment of an adjudication procedure with a unique round robin feature. All claimants within a water district were joined, any claim could be contested by any party, and the validity, quantity and priority of each water right was settled in relation to all of the others. Since a district covered only a part of a stream system, coordination between districts was accomplished by allowing users in one district to join in the proceedings in another, or to contest within four years the priorities awarded in another. The decrees were brought up to date from time to time and new uses were added to the list in supplemental adjudications, but no priority could be awarded that was earlier than the latest right adjudicated under the prior decree. Rights not brought to completion were awarded a conditional decree which could ripen into an appropriation if the water was later applied to beneficial use in compliance with the requirements for reasonable diligence. The procedures were modified and recodified in 1943. For descriptions of these early procedures, see Lasky, From Prior Appropriation to Economic Distribution of Water by the State—Via Irrigation Administration, 1 Rocky Mtn.L.Rev. 1, 190–198 (1929); Chilson, Adjudication and Administration of Water Rights in the State of Colorado, Proceedings, Water Law Conference, University of Texas School of Law, 80, 87 (1956).

The Colorado procedure served as the inspiration, if not the model, for the administrative and administrative-judicial procedures described in the principal case and in Note 4 below. The Colorado Water Rights Determination and Administration Act of 1969, Colo.Rev.Stat.1973, §§ 37–92–101 to –602, will result in the consolidation of all decreed water rights into new "tabulations" as described infra, p. 177.

Montana clung to the classic lawsuit, only slightly modified, until 1973. For the troubles and problems of the embattled and litigious appropriators of Montana, see Stone, Are There Any Adjudicated Streams in Montana? 19 Mont.L.Rev. 19 (1957); Stone, ed., Improving Montana Water Law, 20 Mont.L.Rev. 60, 63 (1958); Stone, The Long Count on Dempsey; No Final Decision on Water Rights Adjudication, 31 Mont.L.Rev. 1 (1969); Stone, Montana Water Rights—A New Opportunity, 34 Mont.L.Rev. 57 (1973). Professor Stone's role changed from that of a voice crying in the wilderness to that of a major prophet with the enactment of the Montana Water Use Act of 1973, Mont.Code Ann.1979, §§ 85–2–101 to –123.

3. The Wyoming court's views on administrative and constitutional law were quite advanced for the period. See Lasky, supra Note 1, at pp. 203–216. Texas adopted the Wyoming system in 1917, but it was struck down in Board of Water Engineers v. McKnight, 111 Tex. 82, 229 S.W. 301 (1921), as unconstitutionally giving an administrative board judicial power over vested property rights. The constitutionality of subsequent legislation, the Texas Water Adjudication Act of 1967, Vernon's Tex.Code Ann. Water Code §§ 11.301–11.341 was upheld in In re Adjudication of the Water Rights of the Upper Guadalupe River, 642 S.W.2d 438 (Tex.1982). The court noted that prior to the act the water law of Texas had been in a "chaotic state," and ruled:

"A significant difference between the 1917 Irrigation Act and the procedure under the Water Rights Adjudication Act is that the agency does not make the final determination of rights. There is a two-step procedure. The Commission makes its determination which is followed by an automatic and mandatory judicial review. * * *

"By statute, the standard of review under the Adjudication Act is neither a substantial evidence review nor a de novo review. It is a review made independently of the Commission's adjudication, and a review exercised on those parts of the Commission's determination to which exceptions were timely leveled. In passing on the exceptions, the court may, as in the case now before us, hear additional evidence. Tex.Water Code Ann. § 11.321. The exceptions are the pleadings which the court acts upon with or without a jury trial. The burden of proof is upon the one who levels the exceptions. * * * We conclude that the act, unlike the statutes construed in *McKnight,* 111 Tex. 82, 229 S.W. 301, * * * provides a constitutional method for adjudication."

4. Most states have adopted one of several variations on the Wyoming theme, designed to combine in some degree the efficiency of the administrative action with the sanctity of a court decree. These systems are described and tabulated in Stone, Montana Water Rights—A New Opportunity, 34 Mont.L.Rev. 57, 70–71 (1973):

"The Wyoming system authorizes the Board of Control to select streams for adjudication, to publish notice of the investigation and hearing, and (after a hearing by the Division Superintendent) to make the determination of rights which is conclusive and binding upon all. An aggrieved person may appeal to the courts.

"The Oregon system starts out similarly to the Wyoming system, in that the State Engineer publishes and mails notice, conducts an investigation and hearing, and makes a determination of all rights. But then this administrative order of determination is filed in a circuit court, where interested parties may file exceptions, and from which emanates a final court decree of adjudication which is conclusive and binding upon all, subject to appeal to the Supreme Court of Oregon.

"The Bien Code system derives its name from Morris Bien of the U.S. Reclamation Service who drafted this system of stream adjudication in 1903. It provides for an administrator such as the State Engineer to prepare a hydrographic survey and transmit it to the state Attorney General, who then brings an action in court based upon the Engineer's findings and determinations. Some of the states which use the Bien Code provide for publication of notice and a conclusive decree.

"The following is a summary chart of the systems in effect in the Western states:

State	Type of System	Who Investigates & Hears?	Who's Word is Final?	Comment	Provide for Publication?	Conclusive?	How Court Becomes Engaged.
Alaska	Wyo.	Comm./Nat. Res.	Comm./ Nat. Res.		Yes	Impliedly	Appeal
Ariz.	Oreg.	St. Land Dept.	Court		Yes	Yes	Filed in Court
Calif.	Oreg.	Water Res. Bd.	Court		Yes	Yes	Filed in Court
Colo.		Referee under a Water Judge	Court	Prior adjuds. take priority.	Yes	Yes	Court proceeding
Hawaii		Court	Court	Private party or state may bring suit.	Yes	Yes, except persons out of state	Court proceeding
Ida.	Oreg.	St. Recl. Eng.	Court		Yes	Yes	Filed in Court
Kans.	Oreg.	Chief Eng'r.	Court	Determination does not settle rights inter-sese but an appeal would have that result.[43]	Yes	Yes if appealed to court	Appeal by anyone aggrieved.
Mont.[44]		1. Dept./Nat. Res.'	Court		No	No	Court proceeding
		2. Court	Court	Private suit.	No	No	Court proceeding
Nebr.	Wyo.	Dir/Water Res.	Dept./ Nat. Res.		Yes	Yes	Appeal
Nevada	Oreg.	St. Eng'r.	Court		Yes	Yes	Filed in Court
N. Mex.	Bien	St. Eng'r.	Court	St. Eng. delivs. hydr. survey to Atty. Gen. who sues. Court may use referees.	Yes	Yes	Court proceeding
N. Dak.	Bien	St. Eng'r.	Court	Same as N. Mex. Says all claimants shall be joined.	No	?[45]	Court proceeding
Okla.	1. Bien	Water Res. Bd.	Court	Board delivs. hydr. survey to Atty. Gen. who sues claimants[46]	No	No	Court proceeding
	2. Oreg.	Water Res. Bd.	Court	Same as Kansas[47]	Yes	Yes, if appealed to Court	Appeal by anyone aggrieved.
Oreg.	Oreg.	St. Eng'r.	Court		Yes	Yes	Filed in Court
S. Dak.	Bien	Water Res. Comm.	Court	Atty. Gen. sues, then W. Res.Comm. makes hydr. surv.	No	No	Court proceeding
Texas	Oreg.	Water Rights Comm.	Court		Yes	Yes	Filed in Court
Utah	Like Bien	St. Eng'r.	Court	St. Eng'r sues, makes hydr. surv. & recommends decree	Yes	Yes	Court proceeding
Wash.	Like Bien	Sup./Water Res.	Court	Sup./Water Res. files in Court, conducts investig. & hearing & reports to Court	Yes	Yes	Court proceeding
Wyo.	Wyo.	Div. Suptndt.	Bd./ Control		Yes	Yes	Appeal to Court

The 1973 Montana procedure adopted after this article was published would be classified as a Bien-like system. However, frustrated by the slow progress of adjudications under this procedure, the Montana legislature adopted a Colorado-like procedure in 1979. This legislation divided the state into four water divisions, created a water judge and water master for each division, and required all water users to file claims by January 1, 1982 (subsequently extended to April 30, 1982 by the Montana Supreme Court). Claims not filed by the deadline are conclusively presumed to be abandoned. This legislation provides for the water judge to issue a preliminary decree, for the filing of objections, for hearings by the judge, and ultimately for a final decree. See Mont.Code Ann.1983 §§ 85–2–211 to 85–2–243.

5. As to coordination of the priorities of parties to different adjudications of confluent streams, see Campbell v. Wyoming Development Co., 55 Wyo. 347, 100 P.2d 124 (1940) and Alamosa-LaJara Water Users Ass'n v. Gould, 674 P.2d 914 (Colo.1984).

6. Water administrative agencies have not been given exclusive jurisdiction over the adjudication of priorities, and unadjudicated priorities may be litigated in suits between their owners. Crawford Co. v. Hathaway, 67 Neb. 325, 93 N.W. 781 (1903); Territory of Hawaii v. Gay, 32 Hawaii 404 (1932). In Simmons v. Ramsbottom, 51 Wyo. 419, 68 P.2d 153 (1937), the Board of Control had given plaintiff's rights a general date of "1884", and defendant's rights a date of "February 1884". Held, the court might determine the relative priorities without first resubmitting the case to the Board of Control. Conceding the power of the legislature to make the administrative proceeding exclusive, the court found no intent to do so in the statute.

Although administrative water agencies do not have exclusive or primary jurisdiction, their decisions are final and binding on collateral attack. "The Board of Control was given complete and exclusive jurisdiction to make general adjudication of the waters of this state as to priority and amount to which the several appropriators are entitled. The jurisdiction of the courts is (aside from appeals) confined to determining the rights of the parties in individual cases to the extent that the Board has not acted." Campbell v. Wyoming Development Co., 55 Wyo. 347, 100 P.2d 124 (1940).

7. After a general adjudication proceeding has been held, new rights are added to the list of priorities by procedures for separately adjudicating rights acquired by permits. The permit ripens into a license or certificate of appropriation, upon proof of completion of the works and application of the water to beneficial use. See, e.g., Wyo.Stat.1977, § 41–4–511.

All Wyoming streams were adjudicated by 1922. When Federal water rights became subject to adjudication in state court proceedings (see infra p. 812), Wyoming adopted a "Bien-like" amendment to the declaratory judgment act providing for judicial general adjudications of all water rights and interests in state waters represented by unadjudicated permits or not represented by decrees, certificates or permits. Wyo.Stat.1977, § 1–37–106.

McINTIRE, THE DISPARITY BETWEEN STATE WATER RIGHTS RECORDS AND ACTUAL WATER USE PATTERNS

5 Land & Water L.Rev. 22, 26–30 (1970).

Most of the western states experience significant deviations between the actual practices of water users in the field and the information recorded in the office of the water administration officials. The extent of the problem, and the seriousness of the deviations in the other states is not known, but the magnitude of the problem in Wyoming is enormous and is apparently statewide. In 1955, the records of the State Engineer showed that the adjudicated, direct flow water rights from the Little Laramie River totaled 417,000 acres, but the acreage actually irrigated by direct flow from the Little Laramie was only 200,000 acres, which is only 48% of the adjudicated acreage. In the North Platte River Basin in central and eastern Wyoming direct flow surface water rights are adjudicated to 890,554 acres, but only 569,131 acres, 64% of the adjudicated acreage, were actually irrigated as of 1967. In one reach of a river in the water-rich highlands of west central Wyoming, direct flow surface water rights are adjudicated to 10,839 acres, but only 6,600 acres are actually irrigated, 61% of the acreage shown to be irrigated by the State Engineer's records.

Many factors have been mentioned as explaining the difference between the number of acres having adjudicated water rights and the substantially lesser number of acres actually being irrigated, but the two most plausible are (1) lack of water in the source sufficient to irrigate all of the lands adjudicated, and (2) the practice of concentrating the water diverted onto fewer acres than the water right shows.

The discrepancies existing in the North Platte River Basin result from both of these factors. * * *

To compound the problem, there is no indication in the records as to what extent the lands upon which water is applied correspond to the lands to which water rights are adjudicated. Incomplete, uncertain or inaccurate descriptions of land in old water right applications, the tendency of appropriators to overstate their water use, unscientific methods of irrigation rendering land unproductive, the difficulty of detecting changes in place of use, unauthorized changes in regulated headgates, and other factors preclude the assumption that all appropriators are necessarily applying their water to lands described in their water rights.

Another source of inaccuracy may arise from the description of the point of diversion of water. Wyoming statutes have long required an applicant for a surface water right to describe in his application the location and description of the proposed ditch and diversion works, among other things. But for an almost equal length of time, Wyoming courts have held that an appropriator has the right to change his place of diversion as a matter of right, provided only that no other appropriators on the stream are injured. It was not until 1965 that the legislature enacted a statute prohibiting changes in the point of diversion without the prior approval of and subject to conditions imposed by the State Engineer. Prior to 1965, unrecorded changes of an appropriator's point of diversion were not uncommon.

There may also be errors in the State Engineer's records regarding the nature of the use which is being made of the water, but because of the general terms by which the type of use is described in the water right (i.e., "municipal," "irrigation") it is not expected that such errors, if they exist, would be sufficiently widespread to create a serious problem.

Another aspect of the problem, potentially more detrimental to future development of state water resources than "paper rights," is the substantial number of permits for unconstructed projects remaining on the records affecting all areas of the state. In the North Platte River Basin, in which the acreage having adjudicated water rights already exceeds the actual irrigated acreage by over 220,000 acres, there are an additional 260,605 acres of land covered by such conditional permits still in good standing. On the Laramie River in southeastern Wyoming, as of 1955, there were ten outstanding permits for water rights for the Wheatland Irrigation Project alone, with priorities going back as far as 1904 * * *. The danger in this situation is that, when the diversion and conveyance work is finally completed and the water applied to beneficial use, the priority date of the water right so used relates back to the date of the original application so long as the permit remains in good standing. [Footnotes omitted.]

Notes

1. Similar problems exist in at least eight other western states, according to McIntire. Wyoming's streams were all adjudicated in the period from 1892 to 1922, and in some other states the records are as old. In still others a different problem exists because many streams have not been adjudicated. See also Dewsnup, Improvement of State Water Right Records, National Water Commission Legal Study No. 4A (1971).

2. Since McIntire wrote his article, several states have taken steps to improve their water rights records. Legislation enacted in 1969 in Washington required all persons whose rights were not evidenced by a permit or certificate to register their rights with a state agency by June 30, 1974. Rights not registered by that deadline are conclusively deemed to have been waived and relinquished. See West's Rev.Code Wash.Ann. 90.14.010 to 90.14.910. Idaho enacted water registration legislation patterned after the Washington act in 1978. See Idaho Code §§ 42–241 to 42–247. The Idaho legislation required the registration of all rights not based on a permit or license by June 30, 1983, and provided that failure to register would provide grounds for instituting an action for forfeiture of the right. In both states the legislation was enacted to provide a record of numerous rights which, for historical reasons, were not represented by a permit, certificate, or license. See Grant, Registration of Constitutional Method

Water Rights, 17 Idaho Law Rev. 7 (1980) for the view that the Idaho legislation, and inferentially the Washington legislation, will not cure all the record deficiencies which hamper water rights administration and planning.

In 1979, Montana, which did not have a permit requirement until 1973 and which had never had a comprehensive adjudication of water rights, began a state-wide effort to adjudicate all water rights. See Mont. Code Ann.1983 §§ 85–2–211 to 85–2–243 (1983).

The Colorado Water Rights Determination and Adjudication Act of 1969, Colo.Rev.Stat.1973 §§ 37–92–101 to 37–92–602, described partially on page 128, requires a continuous suit of adjudication in each of the state's seven water divisions. This procedure assures that incomplete appropriations (conditional rights) and newly completed appropriations are adjudicated and integrated into the water rights records on an ongoing basis. In addition, each division engineer is required to make periodic tabulations (quadrennially beginning in 1988) in order of seniority of all water rights within his division. These tabulations reflect judgments and decrees entered by the water court since the previous tabulation which determine, change, or otherwise affect water rights. Persons who wish to object to tabulations are permitted to do so, revisions deemed appropriate are made, and the tabulations are filed with the water court. The tabulations form the basis for the administration of water rights by the state engineer and divisions engineers. However, the tabulations are not adjudications and do not themselves alter water rights.

Each division engineer is also required to prepare a periodic abandonment list (decennially beginning in 1990), listing all rights which appear to have been partially or totally abandoned. After providing for an opportunity for protests and revision, these lists are filed with the water court. Once again, the statutes provide an opportunity for protests and a hearing. Thereafter, the water judge enters a decree which is conclusive as to rights determined to have been abandoned.

3. In most western states the actual distribution of water and regulation of headgates and storage works is performed by a state official known as a water commissioner, working under a central state water agency. The Colorado system is typical:

"Here is an entire state * * * divided into district covering every stream, creek, or runlet from which water is taken. And up and down these streams, creeks and runlets patrol in every irrigating season a small army of commissioners and deputies who have absolutely complete control of all the water. Not a drop may be diverted not only without their consent but without their actually setting the gates and superintending the diversion. All the districts are combined into divisions along drainage lines, and in each division there is an engineer, a captain over the privates; to him come frequent reports, perhaps daily, perhaps telegraphic, of the flow in every creek, of the rainfall in the headwaters and the mountains, from which he calculates the amount of water which will flow into each district on each day, and upon which, knowing from his records who is entitled to water, in what order, and how much, he 'marshals' the water of all the tributaries in the area and orders its distribution, perhaps from day to day, so that those who are entitled to water shall receive it, whether they be ditch or reservoir owners. At the top is the state engineer who commands the whole array. It is a most complete police system, controlling every phase of the distribution; and more." Lasky, From Prior Appropriation to Economic Distribution of Water by the State, 1 Rocky Mt. L.Rev. 161, 262 (1929).

The water commissioner's acts are ministerial, comparable to those of a sheriff or police officer, so that his regulation of a headgate requires no notice or hearing. Hamp v. State, 19 Wyo. 377, 118 P. 653 (1911). Disregard of his orders, or opening a headgate closed by him, is in most states a misdemeanor. Persons aggrieved by his acts may appeal to his supervisor and eventually to the central state water agency and to the courts. However, the administrative law doctrine of "exhaustion of administrative remedies" seems to have no application here. The failure to appeal from an adverse decision of the commissioner up through the administrative hierarchy does not make his action binding on the courts in a later proceeding between two appropriators. Ryan v. Tutty, 13 Wyo. 122, 78 P. 661 (1904). Nor does the doctrine of "prior resort" apply in Wyoming. An appropriator aggrieved by another's unlawful diversion may sue for damages or for an injunction without first calling upon the water commissioner to regulate the ditches. Van Buskirk v. Red Buttes Land & Livestock Co., 24 Wyo. 183, 156 P. 1122 (1916). Not so in New Mexico. A downstream senior on a regulated stream "must make his needs known," and cannot sue for damage to crops because upstream juniors took all the water, when he did not serve a demand on either the water master or the State Engineer. Worley v. United Borax & Chemical Corp., 78 N.M. 112, 428 P.2d 651 (1967).

4. For many years Idaho law allowed both "statutory" water rights obtained in compliance with the permit statute and "constitutional" water rights self-initiated by diverting water and putting it to beneficial use. § 42–607 Idaho Code directs watermasters distributing water in time of shortage to treat constitutional rights which have never been adjudicated as "subsequent to any adjudicated, decreed, permit or licensed right" regardless of alleged priority dates. In Nettleton v. Higginson, 98 Idaho 87, 558 P.2d 1048 (1977), a plaintiff claiming that his prior unadjudicated right had been subordinated to junior recorded rights challenged the constitutionality of the statute on three grounds: deprivation of property without due process, denial of equal protection, and taking of property without just compensation. The court found the statute constitutional in all respects.

5. Suits by an appropriator against water officials raise difficult procedural problems of party joinder and res judicata. In Mitchell Irrigation District v. Whiting, 59 Wyo. 52, 136 P.2d 502 (1943), a senior appropriator sued for a mandatory injunction requiring the water commissioner to close the headgates of junior ditches above the plaintiff's point of diversion. Held, the junior appropriators were indispensable parties and must be joined in the suit. In Merrill v. Bishop, 69 Wyo. 5, 237 P.2d 186 (1951), a senior sued for an injunction against the water commissioner closing his headgate for the benefit of downstream juniors. Held, the juniors are not indispensable parties. How can these be distinguished? See also McLean

v. Farmers Highline Canal & Reservoir Co., 44 Colo. 184, 98 P. 16 (1908). In an action by A against a water commissioner, judgment by default was entered enjoining defendant from closing A's headgate except in favor of prior appropriators named in a particular decree. In a later action by A against B, an appropriator claiming under another decree, it was held that the first suit was not res judicata as to B, even though B had notice of the first action and had been requested to defend it. Lower Latham Ditch Co. v. Louden Irrigating Canal Co., 27 Colo. 267, 60 P. 629 (1900). On the other hand, where the first action was between appropriators, it was said: "[T]he question cannot be relitigated between the same parties or their privies, and the defendants, water officials, are in privity with the Ft. Lyon Company. They have no interest of their own. They must obey the decree." On application for rehearing this was qualified as follows: "It is urged that the water officials are not privies to the Ft. Lyon Company. Perhaps not technically, but what we mean is that they must turn out the water according to the judgment of the court, and so are bound thereby as if they had been parties thereto." Reorganized Catlin Consolidated Canal Co. v. Hinderlider, State Engineer, 80 Colo. 522, 253 P. 389 (1927).

6. In Laramie Rivers Co. v. LeVasseur, 65 Wyo. 414, 202 P.2d 680 (1949), plaintiff began an action in the district court for a declaratory judgment as to the relative rights of the parties, appropriators from the same stream. Defendant had previously obtained a permit to construct a reservoir, and after the bringing of the action commenced proceedings before the Board of Control for the adjudication of its right. The Board decreed to defendant a right, by relation, prior to plaintiff's right. Plaintiff appealed to the district court, the appeal was consolidated with the action, and the court confirmed the adjudication of the Board and ruled against the plaintiff in the action. On appeal to the supreme court, plaintiff contended that since the district court first acquired jurisdiction of the subject matter, the Board was without jurisdiction.

The court said: "But a not dissimilar point arose in the case of Crawford Co. v. Hathaway, 67 Neb. 325, 93 N.W. 781, 60 L.R.A. 889. There is a board in Nebraska similar to the Board of Control in this state, and in the creation of which the legislature of Nebraska followed the Wyoming laws, as stated in the foregoing case. Weil on Water Rights, 3rd Ed., page 1106, refers the foregoing case, and states that while it was held that courts have the right to adjudicate water rights, it was also held 'that it is within the discretion of the court to remand the parties to their remedies by application to the board.' See 93 N.W. 793. There is good reason for that. Irrigation matters frequently involve many technicalities in connection with which courts cannot be expected to be experts, while the members of the Board of Control supposedly are. Now, if the trial court would have had the right to ask the parties to go and have the matters of priorities first determined by the Board of Control, there would be no reason to hold that the parties may not themselves initiate proceedings before it, at least in the absence of the court's objection, if, in the meantime, the action brought in court has not been finally determined, as is true in this case. In other words, we can find no good reason why the court may not avail itself of the aid which may be furnished by having a previous adjudication of the right made by the Board of Control, just as it might refer a case to a referee, and that is in substance the situation in this case."

The California court has repeatedly reminded the trial courts of their power to call upon the state's administrative agencies for expert assistance. In one such case the court said, "The facilities of the commission can, in this manner, be made available to the trial court and that court can thus secure independent and impartial expert advice not colored by personal interest. Incidentally, the procedure outlined in this section will secure representation of the state in such actions, thus insuring the protection of the rights of the public." Tulare Irrigation Dist. v. Lindsay-Strathmore Irrigation Dist., 3 Cal.2d 489, 45 P.2d 979 (1935). See also Kans.Stat.Ann. 82a–725.

What would prompt the reverse practice, of administrative use of the courts to enforce the water laws? See a 1973 Wyoming enactment:

"(a) Upon the request of the state engineer, the attorney general shall bring suit in the name of the state of Wyoming, in the proper district court, to enjoin the unlawful appropriation, diversion or use of the waters of the state, or the waste or loss thereof. A showing of injury in such suits shall not be required as a condition to the issuance of any temporary restraining order, preliminary or permanent injunction. If an appeal is taken from the judgment or decree entered by the district court in such suit, it shall be the duty of the supreme court, at the request of one of the parties, to advance the appeal to the head of its docket and give it precedence over all other civil causes in the hearing and determination thereof." Wyo.Stat.1977, § 41–2–111.

7. State regulatory statutes commonly give the state engineer or an equivalent agency control over engineering features affecting the safety of dams, the adequacy of works, etc. It is the responsibility of one who applies for and obtains a water right to provide at his own expense a proper control mechanism and measuring device. Vandehey v. Wheeler, 507 P.2d 831 (Or.App.1973).

SECTION 4. LOSS

CF & I STEEL CORPORATION v. PURGATOIRE RIVER WATER CONSERVANCY DISTRICT

Supreme Court of Colorado, 1973.
183 Colo. 135, 515 P.2d 456.

GROVES, JUSTICE. Plaintiff-appellant (CF & I) commenced proceedings to change the points of diversion of decreed water rights. At the conclusion of CF & I's testimony, the court dismissed the proceedings on the ground that the water rights had been abandoned. We affirm. * * *

The city of Trinidad timely filed a statement of opposition, alleging abandonment. About a year later and prior to any hearing the Purgatoire River Water Conservancy District (called the District) entered its appearance and alleged abandonment. The court held a hearing under CF & I's application for change of points of diversion approximately two months following the District's entry of appearance.

For many years prior to 1918 CF & I operated a number of small coal mines and had washeries at each mine. The water here involved was used at the Sopris Mine in the Purgatoire River Valley. In 1918 CF & I constructed a central washery at Pueblo and discontinued the small washeries. At that time it removed its pipeline and pumps used to convey the water at the Sopris Mine. CF & I has made no use of this water since that time.

In 1950 CF & I opened its Allen Mine and in 1959 made an economic feasibility study as to a washery at the Allen Mine. Nothing resulted from this. In 1972 it made a preliminary design study on the same subject. The present proceeding is to authorize points of diversion so that the water could be used in a washery at the Allen Mine. However, CF & I has not yet determined whether it will construct such a washery. In its brief CF & I states:

> "The economic (or cost) factors considered by CF & I are constantly changing and it *may* become economically feasible to construct the washery at the Allen Mine at any time." (Emphasis supplied).
>
> * * *

No citation of authority is required for the basic proposition that abandonment occurs when there is non-use coupled with an intention to abandon. Non-use for an unreasonable period creates a rebuttable presumption that there was an intention to abandon. Sieber v. Frink, 7 Colo. 148, 2 P. 901 (1883). Here, 54 years of non-use was an unreasonable period in the light of 20 years being so held in San Luis Valley Irrigation District v. Alamosa, 55 Colo. 386, 135 P. 769 (1913), and 40 years being so held in Sieber v. Frink, supra. The question thus becomes, Did the trial court err in finding that CF & I did not overcome the presumption of abandonment?

The CF & I position is contained in the following excerpts from its brief:

> "The uncontradicted facts established by CF & I establish a valid reason for the original and continued nonuse of this water. CF & I bowed to the economic facts of life in 1918 and, since that date, it has continually surveyed the constantly changing economic facts. Neither 'hopes' nor 'desires' have been involved in this process. The only reason for the nonuse of these water rights stems from those economic facts and, unfortunately, no person or company is immune from economics.
>
> * * *
>
> "We submit that the water court erred as a matter of law in that it applied a rather simplistic test to the undisputed facts of this case. Under Colorado law, the intent to abandon cannot be presumed or inferred unless there is an absence of proof of some fact or condition excusing the nonuse. In this case, there was no absence of such proof, but, rather, CF & I established by undisputed facts that there was

'some fact or condition excusing the nonuse.' Substantial economic and practical factors required that the use of these water rights be discontinued and those factors remained in force as compelling reasons for continued nonuse until such time as CF & I went to a single source of coking coal. At that point, the shifting factors of transportation costs, mining costs and washing costs, together with the high capital expenditure required for a new coal washery at the Allen Mine, have had an inhibiting effect, but, notwithstanding these practical and economic difficulties, CF & I has set aside the requisite land for this washery caused an economic feasibility study to be performed and secured a preliminary design study."

We approve, however, of the following statement by the trial judge further in the judgment:

> " 'To rebut the presumption of abandonment arising from such long period of nonuse, there must be established not merely expressions of desire or hope or intent, but some fact or condition excusing such long nonuse.' Knapp v. Water District, 131 Colo. 42, 279 P.2d 420. The claimed economic factors do not satisfactorily accomplish this."

We cannot accept the economics-justified-non-use argument. Considering the large demands for all of the appropriatable water in this state and the consequent high value of water, it might be said that nearly every abandoned water right could have its non-use justified by the economics that might prevail sometime in the future for use of this water at some other place. This gleam-in-the-eye philosophy is not consistent with the protection and preservation of existing water rights.

CF & I has cited Hallenbeck v. Granby Ditch & Res. Co., 160 Colo. 555, 420 P.2d 419 (1966), several times in its brief. It is true that it was there said that a "reasonable justification for non-use may very well exist where it can be shown that economic, financial or legal difficulties or natural calamities prevented the storing of all the water that was originally decreed." In *Hallenbeck* financial difficulties especially during the depression years, curtailed the reservoir owner's ability to keep the reservoir in peak operating condition. It appears that there were continuous expenditures and that as the owner's financial capability increased, the construction was performed which permitted full use of the decreed water rights. *Hallenbeck* presented a vastly different picture than we have here. CF & I made it impossible to divert water at its decreed points and did not use a drop of the water for 54 years.

In viewing the issue of abandonment, one must look to the water right as decreed and not to some possible hoped-for future use at some undetermined place. * * *

Judgment affirmed.

Notes

1. Where an appropriator sold his land with water right, and later repurchased the land and irrigated with water obtained by renting other

water rights, he abandoned his prior right. Brockman v. Grand Canal Co., 8 Ariz. 451, 76 P. 602 (1904). In Beaver Park Water, Inc. v. City of Victor, 649 P.2d 300 (Colo.1982), the court held that an appropriator which had mortgaged its rights, leased them to a city for a backup supply, and held protracted negotiations leading to their sale had negated the presumption of abandonment created by 20 years of nonuse. Turning water into another ditch, but not using it, was held a mere pretense not preventing abandonment in Parsons v. Ft. Morgan Reservoir & Irrigation Co., 56 Colo. 146, 136 P. 1024 (1913), but the yearly turning of water into a broken ditch, whence it shortly returned to the stream, was held to negative an intent to abandon in Featherman v. Hennessy, 42 Mont. 535, 113 P. 751 (1911). It was held that the owners of water rights might testify as to their intentions in Gassert v. Noyes, 18 Mont. 216, 44 P. 959 (1896).

2. Where an appropriator is decreed water far in excess of his needs, the failure to make any attempt to put such excess to use is held to constitute an abandonment. New Mercer Ditch Co. v. Armstrong, 21 Colo. 357, 40 P. 989 (1895).

3. The Colorado Water Right Determination and Administration Act of 1969 provides that a ten-year failure to apply available water to beneficial use will create a rebuttable presumption of abandonment. Colo.Rev. Stat.1973, 37–92–402(11).

STATE EX REL. REYNOLDS v. SOUTH SPRINGS CO.

Supreme Court of New Mexico, 1969.
80 N.M. 144, 452 P.2d 478.

TACKETT, JUSTICE. This suit was brought in the District Court of Chaves County seeking a declaratory judgment. The court, sitting without a jury, considered the stipulations and testimony and entered judgment for plaintiff, declaring the defendants had lost their water rights by abandonment, forfeiture or nonuse. * * *

The sole issue to be determined in this case is whether or not appellants' water rights have been forfeited or abandoned by nonuse under § 75–5–26, N.M.S.A., 1953 Comp., as the same existed prior to the 1965 amendment, which reads as follows:

> "When the party entitled to the use of water fails to beneficially use all or any part of the water claimed by him, for which a right of use has vested, for the purpose for which it was appropriated or adjudicated, except the waters for storage reservoirs, for a period of four [4] years, such unused water shall revert to the public and shall be regarded as unappropriated public water; Provided, however, that forfeiture shall not *necessarily* occur if circumstances beyond the control of the owner have caused nonuse, such that the water could not be placed to beneficial use by diligent efforts of the owner." (Emphasis added) * * *

Appellants contend that the water rights established by the Hope Decree were not abandoned, as there was no intent to abandon the rights, citing 2 Kinney on Irrigation and Water Rights, 2d Ed., 2012, § 1116 (1912), in part as follows:

> "As to whether or not a water right, the water itself, the ditch, canal, or other works have actually been abandoned or not, depends upon the facts and circumstances surrounding each particular case, tending to prove the essential elements of an abandonment, namely, the intent and the acts of the party charged with abandoning such a right. * * * Abandonment is most usually proved by evidence of the failure of the party charged to use the right, or the water, or to keep the works necessary for the utilization of the water in repair; and if such nonusage or neglect is continued for an unreasonable period, it may fairly create the presumption of the intention to abandon; * * *."

In this case, the water rights had not been utilized for some 32 years and the ditches and canals carrying the flow of water from the South Springs River had not been maintained; roads had been constructed across some of the ditches; and some of the ditches had been closed and houses built thereon, or in close proximity thereto. The failure to use a water right for an unreasonable time is evidence of the intention to abandon it and, in the instant case, no action was taken by appellants to utilize the water rights, if any existed, from 1958 until 1965. Our statute, § 75–5–26, supra, has a four-year period of limitation and, if nothing is done within that limitation, such unused water is reverted to the public and shall be regarded as unappropriated public water.

Further, Kinney, supra, at 2020–2021, § 1118, distinguishes abandonment from forfeiture:

> "Water rights, ditches, and canals, and other works, together with the easements over the lands of others for the same, may be lost by forfeiture. Although the terms 'abandonment' and 'forfeiture' are oftentimes used interchangeably, even by the courts, upon the subject of the loss of water rights, and other rights used in connection therewith, there is a decided distinction in their legal significance, and one which, in view of the forfeiture clauses enacted by recent legislation, should be observed. While, upon the one hand, abandonment is the relinquishment of the right by the owner with the intention to forsake and desert it, forfeiture, upon the other hand, is the involuntary or forced loss of the right, caused by the failure of the appropriator or owner to do or perform some act required by the statute. Forfeiture is a 'punishment annexed by law to some illegal act or negligence in the owner of lands, tenements, or hereditaments, whereby he loses all his interests therein.'
>
> "The element of intent, therefore, so necessary in the case of an abandonment, is not a necessary element in the case of forfeiture. In fact, a forfeiture may be worked directly against the intent of the owner of the right to continue in the possession and the use of the right. Therefore forfeiture as applied to water rights and other rights in this connection is the penalty fixed by statute for the failure to do,

or the unnecessary delay in doing, certain acts tending toward the consummation of a right within a specified time; or, after the consummation of the right, the failure to use the same for the period specified by the statute. * * * "

By the forfeiture of the rights which are claimed by appellants, but who failed to use them, the policy of our constitution (Art. VI, §§ 1, 2 and 3) and statutes (§ 75–11–2, N.M.S.A., 1953 Comp.) is fostered, and the waters made to do the greatest good to the greatest number. This is on the theory that the continuance of the title to a water right is based upon continuing beneficial use, and where the right is not exercised for a certain period of time (four years), the statute declares that the right to the unused portion is forfeited. See Comments, Water Rights, Failure to Use, Forfeiture, 6 Natural Resources J. 127 (1966).

We regret that forfeiture and abandonment have been used interchangeably, as the element of intention is required in the doctrine of abandonment. This is not so in forfeiture. Kinney, supra.

This court, in State ex rel. Erickson v. McLean, 62 N.M. 264, 308 P.2d 983 (1957), construed § 75–11–8, N.M.S.A., 1953 Comp., a similar statute dealing with underground water rights, as a strict forfeiture statute, and cited Kinney, supra, to the effect that such forfeiture is a "punishment annexed by law to some *illegal act*," as abandonment of a right is present only when intentional relinquishment occurs. In McLean it was concluded that an appropriative right is lost by a nonbeneficial user for a period of four years. In the case before us, if appellants obtained appropriative rights to the use of the water in question, any such rights have now become lost by continuous nonuse for more than four years, as shown by the evidence, and such rights (if any) are forfeited.

In Green Valley Ditch Co. v. Frantz, 54 Colo. 226, 129 P. 1006 at p. 1008 (1913), quoting with approval from North American Exploration Co. v. Adams, 104 F. 404 (8th Cir.1900), it is stated:

> " * * * 'The abandonment of the right to divert and use the waters of a stream is not different in its nature or character from the renunciation of any other right which is asserted and maintained by its use. It may be express or implied. It may be effected by a plain declaration of an intention to abandon it; and it may be inferred from acts or failures to act so inconsistent with an intention to retain it that the unprejudiced mind is convinced of the renunciation.' " * * *

In New Mexico, where the statute excuses forfeiture when "circumstances beyond the control of the owner have caused nonuse," the trier of fact must weigh the evidence in each case to determine whether a sufficient showing of excuse for nonuse has been made. The trial court, in the instant case, was trying both issues, forfeiture and abandonment, as nonuse alone is not sufficient to show intent to abandon.

In Utt v. Frey, 106 Cal. 392, 39 P. 807 (1895), and Seiber v. Frink, 7 Colo. 148, 2 P. 901 (1884), it was held that nonuse is competent evidence of intent to abandon.

After a long period of nonuse, the burden of proof shifts to the holder of the right to show the reasons for nonuse. Mountain Meadow Ditch & Irrigation Co. v. Park Ditch & Reservoir Co., 130 Colo. 537, 277 P.2d 527 (1954).

In other Colorado cases, the court held that periods of forty, thirty and eighteen years constituted "unreasonable periods of nonuse and raised a strong presumption of abandonment." Northern Colorado Irr. Co. v. Burlington Ditch, Reservoir & Land Co. et al., 74 Colo. 159, 219 P. 1071 (1923); South Boulder Canon Ditch Co. v. Davidson Ditch & Reservoir Co. et al., 87 Colo. 391, 288 P. 177 (1930). We are duly impressed with the reasoning of Commonwealth Irr. Co. v. Rio Grande Canal Water Users' Ass'n, 96 Colo. 478, 45 P.2d 622 (1935), wherein the relationship of nonuse and intent to abandon a water right is more clearly explained. The court, 45 P.2d at 623, said:

> " * * * But where by clear and convincing evidence it is shown that for an unreasonable time available water has not been used, an intention to abandon may be inferred in the absence of proof of some fact or condition excusing such nonuse. * * * "

The trial court's findings and conclusions are supported by substantial evidence. Finding no error, the judgment appealed from is affirmed.

Notes

1. The statutes vary considerably in their language and in the period of nonuse that will result in forfeiture. See Hutchins, Selected Problems in the Law of Water Rights in the West, 392–4 (1942). Neither the legislatures nor the courts have been careful to preserve the distinction between abandonment and forfeiture, or to use these words as words of art. For example, Reissue Neb.Rev.Stat.1943, §§ 46–229 to 46–229.05 speak in terms of forfeiture, but in State v. Oliver Bros., 119 Neb. 302, 228 N.W. 864 (1930), the court required an intent similar to the necessary element of common law abandonment. However, Ramsay v. Gottsche, 51 Wyo. 516, 69 P.2d 535 (1937) held that a forfeiture must be effected by a "voluntary act," and did not occur when the appropriator was prevented from using water from several years by floods that washed out his diversion dams and ditches. In 1973 the Wyoming legislature amended the forfeiture statute to provide that forfeiture will occur if the appropriator fails "either intentionally or unintentionally" to use water. Wyo.Stat.1977, § 41–3–401. Did this amendment overrule *Ramsay*?

2. California apparently keeps the theory of abandonment and adds forfeiture. Utt v. Frey, 106 Cal. 392, 39 P. 807 (1895) is the first foursquare application of the law of abandonment of water rights, although its existence had been previously acknowledged. The Civil Code of 1872 provided, "The appropriation must be for some useful or beneficial purpose, and when the appropriator or his successor in interest ceases to use it for such a purpose the right ceases." (Preserved today as West's Ann.Cal.Water Code § 1240.) In the same year as Utt v. Frey, the California court combined this section with another Civil Code section providing for extinguishment of

servitudes by disuse for five years, and "* * * by analogy, we hold that a continuous nonuser for five years will forfeit the right." Smith v. Hawkins, 120 Cal. 86, 52 P. 139 (1895). In 1917 the legislature added the following section to the 1913 Water Commission Act: "When the person entitled to the use of water fails to beneficially use all or any part of the water claimed by him, for which a right of use has vested, for the purpose for which it was appropriated or adjudicated, for a period of three years, such unused water reverts to the public and shall be regarded as unappropriated public water." West's Cal.Ann.Water Code § 1241. Until 1980 the five year period applied to stream water rights vested prior to the Water Commission Act and the three year statute to rights acquired by permit and license under the Water Commission Act and its successor the Water Code. Erickson v. Queen Valley Ranch Co., 22 Cal.App.3d 578, 99 Cal.Rptr. 446 (1971). In 1980, the legislature made the period uniform for all rights by amending § 1241 to require five years of nonuse.

3. In Horse Creek Conservation Dist. v. Lincoln Land Co., 54 Wyo. 320, 92 P.2d 572 (1939), the court required the complaining party to show that he would be appreciably benefitted by a declaration of forfeiture of the earlier rights, and held that a late-priority junior appropriator with a "flood water right," who would receive little water whether the questioned right were used or not, had no standing to initiate the proceedings. However, a 1985 amendment gives standing to all junior appropriators. See Wyo.Stat. 1985 Supp., § 41–3–401. In Affolter v. Rough and Ready Irrigating Ditch Co., 60 Colo. 519, 154 P. 738 (1916), the court held that a junior appropriator had the right to maintain an action to declare an abandonment whenever the effect of such judgment would be of special benefit to him.

4. In Louth v. Kaser, 364 P.2d 96 (Wyo.1961), the court held that the statutory procedure for declaration of forfeiture was not exclusive, and that the question of abandonment and forfeiture could be decided in private litigation. The issue can arise in many types of litigation in which the water right of either plaintiff or defendant is challenged. In Kearney Lake, Land and Reservoir Co. v. Lake DeSmet Reservoir Co., 487 P.2d 324 (Wyo.1971), the Wyoming Supreme Court came to regard this concurrent jurisdiction of administrative agencies and courts as not entirely satisfactory. Held, that primary jurisdiction should rest with the administrative agency, that when an issue of forfeiture or abandonment arises in a civil case the court should ordinarily certify the issue to the State Board of Control, and that the Board should make the initial determination and report its findings and conclusions back to the court. Finally, the Wyoming legislature gave the Board exclusive original jurisdiction over forfeiture proceedings in 1973. Wyo.Stat.1977, § 41–3–401.

BAUGH v. CRIDDLE

Supreme Court of Utah, 1967.
19 Utah 2d 361, 431 P.2d 790.

HENRIOD, JUSTICE: Appeal from a judgment in a quiet title action pertaining to water rights, based on priorities. Affirmed, without costs.

Baugh's predecessors in interest had an 1860 priority to use Logan River water nonconsumptively to run a mill wheel to produce power. By mesne conveyances of such right, it came to one Crowther. In 1946, the mill burned down. This prevented continued use of the water for such purpose, which necessitated statutory procedural requirements to perpetuate such rights. In 1950 an application was made to the State Engineer for an extension of time to resume the use for the purpose theretofore employed. This request was granted to January 1, 1955. On November 19, 1954, Crowther wrote an unverified letter to the Engineer saying he had purchased machinery and that "the whole job should be ready by the first of the year." On November 30th the Engineer replied that "unless evidence is supplied this office on or before January 1, 1955 that this water has actually been put to use again or that you file a new request for extension of time * * * this water right will revert to the public,"—enclosing an application form for such purpose. On December 29th, Crowther by unverified letter, replied that the machinery had been installed and that "this will be actually running on the 30th." On February 10, 1955, six weeks after the statutory deadline, Crowther filed the Engineer's form stating that the beneficial use had been resumed within the extension period. On February 17, 1955, the Engineer wrote Crowther stating that the water right had been terminated and had reverted to the public, for failure to prove up on the right in time,[a] and that if Crowther did not appeal within 60 days from the Engineer's decision, it probably would be final, and again on February 25, reminded Crowther of this fact. On March 2, Crowther, by letter, asked the Engineer to reconsider his decision. On March 7, the Engineer wrote Crowther again, saying he could not reconsider the decision and that the former would have to petition for a timely review,—which Crowther never did.

On March 16, Crowther made a new application for water rights on the same river, for the same purpose. The application was granted, and 71.5 acre feet were awarded him as against the 87 acre feet he had before he lapsed such right by failing to file properly and within time under the statute. Ten years later, Baugh, successor to Crowther, filed this suit against the State Engineer, asserting that 1) the State Engineer had no right to terminate the rights of Crowther, 2) that failure to appeal from the Engineer's decision does not prejudice plaintiff's rights here, and that 3) there was a resumption of use that occurred within the extension period.

All three contentions, it seems to us, may be answered by pointing out that the statute controlled here irrespective of the Engineer's written conclusions and judgment, and that Baugh's predecessor in interest, according to the clear evidence adduced, did not comply with the statutory interdiction re preservation and perpetuation of such rights. In Mosby Irrigation Co. v. Criddle,[b] a case similar to the case here anent complying with water legislation, we said:

a. Utah Code Ann.1953, 73–1–4.

b. 11 Utah 2d 41, 354 P.2d 848 (1960).

"The instant application lapsed by reason of * * * failure to submit proof of appropriation on the due date. It lapsed in accordance with the express mandate of the statute and not because of the action of any state officer." * * *

In this arid state, where water is the heartbeat of our economy, more and more it becomes quite obvious that development of water must require strict adherence to statutory sanctions, without delay or nonconformance thereto,—lest our whole economy lag to the detriment of our future. It must be a rare and highly equitable case that should justify a departure from this principle,—which we do not find in the case here.

Notes

1. Appropriation statutes are silent on the duration of water rights. The Supreme Court of the United States once said that an appropriation is a "vested right to take and divert from the same source, and to use and consume the same quantity of water annually forever." Arizona v. California, 283 U.S. 423, 459, 51 S.Ct. 522, 75 L.Ed. 1154 (1931). Is the tenure of the water right like that of land held in fee simple absolute? Does a forfeiture statute make it more like a fee simple determinable, or a fee simple subject to condition subsequent? At what time does an abandoned or a forfeited right cease to exist? If the holder of the right does not use the water for the statutory period, but commences to use it again before a declaration of forfeiture, is the right revived? In Sturgeon v. Brooks, 73 Wyo. 436, 281 P.2d 675 (1955), the court indicated that the right continued to exist until it was formally declared terminated, and that if reuse started before proceedings were brought, the right was reinstated. However, in Wheatland Irrigation Dist. v. Laramie Rivers Co., 659 P.2d 561 (Wyo.1983) the court rejected the argument that the commencement of repairs necessary for reuse prior to the institution of a forfeiture action was sufficient, holding that only actual use prior to the action would reinstate the right.

A different view was stated in Affolter v. Rough and Ready Irrigation Ditch Company, 60 Colo. 519, 154 P. 738 (1916): "We do not understand that this is of that class of cases which requires that an action be brought immediately after such an abandonment takes place, or that a subsequent appropriator need bring it until some one again seeks to make claim to it under the decree. Until this is done, the subsequent appropriator is in possession to the extent at least that he uses and enjoys its benefits, alleged in this case to have been for 29 years. After abandonment, when it actually takes place, he has no reason for believing that any one will ever make claim to it again by virtue of the decree under which it was awarded, and until this is done he cannot be said to be guilty of laches in failing to bring an action to have it declared abandoned."

Is the difference between Wyoming and Colorado explained by the fact that Colorado applies abandonment whereas Wyoming applies forfeiture?

Compare the Utah statute in the principal case, Utah Code Ann.1953, § 73–1–4, in which forfeiture is apparently automatic after five years of nonuse, with the New Mexico statute in *South Springs*, as amended,

N.Mex.1953 Comp.Laws § 75–5–28, which requires nonuse for one year after notice and a declaration of nonuse is given by the State Engineer.

2. The Director of the Washington Department of Ecology in June, 1976, promulgated Washington Administrative Code Sections 173–596–010, et seq., to limit future water rights to renewable permits of 50 years duration if the quantity appropriated is 40 cubic feet per second or more, or if the water is to be used to irrigate 2000 acres or more of "a total project or operating unit"—a term undefined in the regulation. Renewability of permit under the regulation may be decided any time prior to end of the 45th year, based on broadly stated criteria. Criteria particularly favor water for the "family farm unit," expressly defined as "not more than 2,000 acres," but "family" is undefined.

3. Prior appropriation law is sometimes criticized as conducive to waste or at least giving no incentive to save water. Cf. *Kovacovich* and notes, supra pages 64 to 70. In an effort to promote conservation and efficiency in the use of water, the 1982 California legislature provided that an appropriator may keep for his own benefit water saved by conservation efforts or as a result of using reclaimed or polluted water in lieu of appropriated water. The legislation also provides that cessation or reduction in the use of appropriated water as a result of these activities shall be deemed the equivalent of a reasonable beneficial use of the appropriated water and will not result in forfeiture of the water right. West's Ann.Calif. Water Code §§ 1010, 1011.

4. Where a statute or permit establishes a particular duty of water (e.g., 1cfs/70 acres), will forfeiture lie if an appropriator concentrates his right on only a part of the required acreage? Consider:

N.Mex.Stat.Ann.1978, § 72–5–28F: "The owner or holder of a valid water right or permit to appropriate waters for agricultural purposes appurtenant to designated or specified lands, may apply the full amount of water covered by or included in said water right or permit to any part of such designated or specified tract, without penalty or forfeiture."

Wyo.Stat.1977, § 41–3–401(f): "An appropriation for irrigation use is not subject to partial abandonment for failure of the appropriator to irrigate part of the lands described in his permit or certificate of appropriation during the successive five (5) year period if:

(i) Facilities to divert the water and to apply it to beneficial use upon the lands which were not irrigated existed in usable form during the period of nonuse; and

(ii) There was not a sufficient supply of water available, because of regulation for prior water rights or because shortage of supply resulted in insufficient water to satisfy the appropriation in full, to irrigate the lands for which abandonment is sought provided that a diligent effort was made to use the supply which was available."

5. To what extent can forfeiture and abandonment procedures be used to cure the problems of divergence between the water rights that appear formally on the records and the use of water in practice? In Nebraska, the Department of Water Resources is given the responsibility of making examinations of ditches "as often as necessary" and of initiating cancella-

tion proceedings on its own motion. Reissue Neb.Rev.Stat.1943, § 46–229.01. See Colo.Rev.Stat.1973, 37–92–402, Wyo.Stat.1979, § 41–3–402, Mont.Rev.Code 1979, § 85–2–405; Tex. Water Rights Commission v. Wright, 464 S.W.2d 642 (Tex.1971).

HAMMOND v. JOHNSON

Supreme Court of Utah, 1937.
94 Utah 20, 66 P.2d 894.

LARSON, JUSTICE. This is an appeal upon the judgment roll from a decree and judgment of the district court of Grand county. Plaintiff brought the action to quiet his title to the waters of Barber Spring and enjoin the defendants from asserting claim or right to any of the waters of the spring. Plaintiff predicates his right to all the waters of the spring upon adverse possession and user. Defendants deny plaintiff's adverse possession and user and allege that in 1898 and again in 1900 the district court of Grand county by decrees duly entered, had adjudicated the right to the waters of Pack creek, including Barber Spring, a tributary thereof, as between the predecessors in interest of the plaintiff on the one hand, and defendants and their predecessors in interest on the other, wherein defendants were awarded the waters of Barber Spring for seven consecutive days out of every ten, and the predecessors of plaintiff were allocated the waters of said spring for three consecutive days out of every ten days. The trial court entered its judgment against plaintiff and decreed that the rights of the parties are now as fixed in the decrees of 1898 and 1900, as set forth by defendants, and awarded defendants their costs. Plaintiff prosecutes this appeal upon the judgment roll, asserting that the conclusions of law and the judgment and decree are not supported by and are contrary to the findings of fact. * * * Two questions are presented for determination: First: Can water rights be acquired in this state by adverse user and possession? Second: If the first question be answered in the affirmative, do the findings of fact establish a title by adverse user and possession? If either of the questions be answered in the negative, the judgment of the trial court must stand. If both questions be answered in the affirmative, the judgment must be reversed. We shall consider them in their order.

First. "Water of all streams and other sources in this state, whether flowing above or under the ground in known or defined natural channels, is hereby declared to be the property of the public, subject to all existing rights to the use thereof." R.S.Utah 1933, 100–1–1. * * * But the right to the use of water, once established or obtained, is a valuable property right and upon its sale or transfer requires the same form and solemnity as a transfer of real estate. R.S. Utah 1933, 100–1–10. * * *

That title to real estate may be acquired by adverse possession is too elemental to require discussion or citation of authorities, but since respondent contends that the statutes of the state relative to appropriation and abandonment of water has modified the general rule and excepted water rights from the laws governing other real estate, we have set forth groundwork for a proper understanding of the question here presented and its solution. The statutes governing title by adverse possession of real estate are sections 104–2–7 to 104–2–12, inclusive, R.S.1933, and provide the elements of adverse possession and what must be shown to establish title. This court has, in a number of cases, approved and recognized the holding that title to water rights may be based upon adverse user and possession; outlined the matters that must be shown to maintain such title, and upheld title when such elements were proved. * * *

But respondents argue that all these cases, except the one last cited, were either tried or were based upon rights claimed to have been acquired prior to the enactment of the law of appropriation of water through the office of the state engineer, and (1) since the enactment of that statute, water rights can only be acquired by appropriation through the office of the state engineer and can only be lost by abandonment, and when abandoned it reverts to the state; and (2) if water can be acquired by adverse user and possession since the enactment of the appropriation laws, it cannot be so done after adjudication of the rights, and in defiance of the terms of the adjudication decree. The answer to the first proposition is found within the terms of the statute, relative to appropriation. Sections 100–3–1 and 100–3–2, R.S.1933, read:

> "Rights to the use of the *unappropriated public waters* in this state may be acquired by appropriation in the manner hereinafter provided, and not otherwise." Section 100–3–1.

> "Any person who is a citizen * * * in order hereafter to acquire the right to the use of any *unappropriated public water* in this state shall, before commencing the construction * * * make an application in writing to the state engineer." Section 100–3–2. (Italics added.)

It is clear from the language that the sections above quoted apply only to acquiring rights in the *unappropriated public water*, and have no reference to water rights which have passed to private ownership. * * * One may obtain rights to the use of public waters by appropriation or may obtain private rights to the use of water by purchase, lease, or grant in recognition of the owner's title, or in derogation and defiance of the owner's title by disseisin of the owner and use and possession of the right for the statutory time, commonly called "adverse possession." The adverse possessor does not rely upon any act or deed of the owner, but upon his own act or deed. He does not claim through his predecessor, but against him. He recognizes that his predecessor has some right, title, or color of title in the property, but refuses to honor or submit to it. He enters as a conquistador, bent upon acquiring that which another possessed, not necessarily vi et armis, by killing or physically ejecting the owner, but by the process of assuming and exercising the rights and prerogatives of the owner, without his consent and in defiance of the owner's will. He plants his flag, his standard, as it were, upon the property as notice to the owner and all the world that he has taken possession, and henceforth will govern and control it; that the property henceforth has a new owner and that he proposes to maintain that title and possession against all.

From Attila, the Hun, down through the colonial expansions of the Seventeenth and Eighteenth centuries to the present, the right of one with sufficient nerve and courage to extend his dominions by the simple process of taking possession has been recognized, subject only to growing and more definite and refined methods and requirements of manifesting the possession and the intention to take and hold. And so the statutes give force and effect to this old principle by providing that one may so dispossess another and obtain his rights and properties, by the simple expedient of taking possession thereof and evidencing the intention to claim and keep the property by acts that can leave no doubt that the intruder is not there as a mere trespasser. The conditions which, as a matter of law, satisfy this requirement are set forth in sections 104–2–9 to 104–2–12, inclusive, and are usually stated to be, "open, notorious, peaceable and exclusive occupation of the premises under claim of right, or color of title, for a period of seven years continuously, adversely and in hostility to all claims of superior rights in any other person, without interruption of possession by the owner or prior claimants, and the payment of all taxes lawfully levied against the property."

Coming then to the second question: Do the findings of fact show a title by adverse possession in appellant as against respondents? * * * It is * * * found that from about February 24, 1925, to the commencement of this action in October 1934 (almost ten years), plaintiff and his predecessor in title did use all the waters of Barber Springs for irrigation, culinary, domestic, and stock-raising purposes, exclusively, continuously, and without interruption, openly, notoriously, adversely, and hostile to defendants, under a claim of right and title, with the knowledge, but without the consent, and over the protests and objections of the defendants; that there were no interruptions of plaintiff's use, although defendants stated that plaintiff was stealing the water from them. * * *

The finding by the court that defendants uttered word protests only against plaintiff's use of the water only emphasizes the adverse nature of plaintiff's holding and use, and negatives the possibility that plaintiff's use may have been permissive. It is a specific finding that defendants knew that plaintiff had invaded their dominions, was taking and claiming the water, and put them upon notice to assert their rights and repossess the property within the statutory period or lose the right to the adverse claimant. Likewise the finding by the court that defendants said plaintiff was stealing their water negatives an abandonment of the water by defendants so it could not revert to the public and be again subject to appropriation. * * *

It follows that the conclusions of law and judgment and decree are not sustained by and are contrary to the findings of fact. The cause is remanded to the district court of Grand county with directions to set aside the conclusions of law and judgment and decree, and enter new conclusions and decree in harmony with this opinion. Costs to appellant. * * *

ON PETITION FOR REHEARING

94 Utah 35, 75 P.2d 164.

* * * A brief has been filed on behalf of the state engineer in support of the petition for a rehearing. He is not a party to the action, but filed a brief, urging that we reconsider our decision, because he thinks the opinion as rendered, 66 P.2d 894, 896, affects the right of the state and deprives it of rights in the waters. * * * The opinion does not bar, or affect, any rights which the state or any other person, not a party or claiming under a party, had or could assert in or to the waters in question. * * *

The petition for a rehearing is denied.

WOLFE, JUSTICE. I dissent. I think we should have a rehearing in order that we may determine whether title to a water right may be obtained against any one by adverse possessing. * * * Moreover, on principle, I have doubts whether a person can obtain adverse possession of a right as distinguished from lands. The right to use water is a right only to the use of water, and that water becomes the property of the appropriator only when it is reduced to possession. I may obtain title by adverse possession of land which I can adversely occupy and possess, but how can I adversely possess a right? If a life tenant, as against the remainderman, has a right to cut cordwood for fuel from the woodlands, can someone having no relation to the remainderman and no consent of the life tenant obtain the life tenant's right by taking the cordwood? Or, better still, is an illustration where one has a right to pasture his cows in the commons. May some outsider by pasturing his cattle there illegally obtain the right of the other to pasture by a so-called adverse user or possession? May one who is using water which another has the right to use from the common source of water, like from the common source of pasture, obtain adverse possession of the other's right to use water? Water, for purposes of recording and transfer, is considered as real estate, but does that mean it has all the attributes of real estate? Can anyone occupy or possess fugitive water? Certainly, the law cannot give the same physical properties to running water as real estate possesses. I am concerned about these conceptions. Can one by purporting to use something another has the right to use gain title by so-called adverse user rather than by adverse possession? If so, can this be done when the failure on the part of the one legally entitled to use the water, works an abandonment and a reversion to the common source of the water, when title to the water in the common source is in the public or feeds rights of subsequent appropriators? The law specifies no right may be obtained therein except by appropriation, which is obtained after the culmination of certain prescribed steps. * * *

Notes

1. In 1939 the Utah legislature amended its statutes by adding the following sentences to the sections relating to permits to appropriate and to abandonment: "No right to the use of water either appropriated or unappropriated can be acquired by adverse use or adverse possession." Utah Code Ann.1953, 73–3–1. "The provisions of this section are applicable whether such unused or abandoned water is permitted to run to waste or is used by others without right." Utah Code Ann.1953 73–1–4. An almost exactly parallel development took place in Nevada. Application of Filippini, 66 Nev. 17, 202 P.2d 535 (1949); Nevada Rev.Stat. 533.060. Kansas and Alaska have similar statutes. Kan.Stat.Ann. 82a–705; Alaska Stat. 46.15.040(a).

2. In Campbell v. Wyoming Development Co., 55 Wyo. 347, 100 P.2d 124, 102 P.2d 745 (1940) the court denied a claim of upstream appropriators to prescriptive rights to use more water than was decreed to them, as against a downstream junior appropriator. The decision was based upon no adverse user in fact, and after an elaborate review of the facts and the law, the court said, "We do not mean to intimate, or seem to concur in the view, that a prescriptive title to water may be acquired in this state, particularly since 1890, when the legislature enacted a law requiring the initiation of all water rights to be pursuant to a permit from the State Engineer. We do not need to enter into that question in this case. See the case of Wyoming Hereford Ranch v. Hammond Packing Co., 33 Wyo. 14, 236 P. 764." The court resolved the issue in 1985, holding that a water right may not be acquired by adverse possession. Lewis v. Board of Control, 699 P.2d 822 (Wyo.1985).

Compare Mountain Meadow Ditch & Irrigation Co. v. Park Ditch & Reservoir Co., 130 Colo. 537, 277 P.2d 527, 528 (1954): " * * * a water right does not represent actual ownership of any part of the stream, but only the right to claim the amount needed up to the volume of the priority at the headgate of the ditch, and the taking of water from the stream by junior claimants elsewhere or by virtue of other priorities is not hostile to the title of the senior priority but hostile to the stream, that is, to the public. The unappropriated water of every stream is the property of the public against which title by adverse user may not be acquired."

3. Suppose a squatter, claiming adversely to the owner of land, obtains title to the land by adverse possession. Does he become the owner of a water right which is appurtenant to the land, and which he used during the prescriptive period? See Cook v. Hudson, 110 Mont. 263, 103 P.2d 137 (1940).

4. Can a right by prescription be obtained by long continued use of water after it has been appropriated and diverted from the stream, and is stored in a reservoir or is running in a ditch? See Grandby Ditch &

Reservoir Co. v. Hallenbeck, 127 Colo. 236, 255 P.2d 965 (1953); Verwolf v. Low Line Irrigation Co., 70 Mont. 570, 227 P. 68 (1924).

5. Can the use of water by a junior appropriator adversely to a senior downstream right ever result in the junior right becoming superior to the senior? In Lewis v. Board of Control, 699 P.2d 822 (Wyo.1985), upstream juniors argued that downstream seniors had abandoned their right by permitting the juniors to divert water out of priority. In rejecting this argument the court said:

"Contestants' original claim before the State Board of Control was for an abandonment or partial abandonment. However, this claim is also premised on an adverse possession theory.

* * *

"The evidence is clear that the BQ appropriators utilized all the water that was available to them. In times when less than 16.5 c.f.s. were available, they consistently diverted the full amount that was available, and contacted a water official for administrative regulation. It is the duty of the officers charged with regulating water to make distribution in accordance with established priorities. Quinn v. John Whitaker Ranch Co., 54 Wyo. 367, 92 P.2d 568 (1939). The BQ appropriators had the right to rely on the water officials to do their jobs. If said officials were not effective in their regulation, that alone will not work to effect a water abandonment, considering the facts herein that (1) the BQ appropriators consistently called for regulation when the flow of water in Twin Creek fell below 16.5 c.f.s.; (2) such regulation was attempted; and (3) such regulation failed primarily due to the refusal of contestants to abide by the lawful orders of the water officials." Accord: Coryell v. Robinson, 118 Colo. 225, 194 P.2d 342 (1948).

On the other hand, in Idaho and Montana many such suits have been entertained. A search reveals no case in which the junior appropriator has met this burden and secured such a reversal of priorities. See Note, Prescriptive Rights to the Use of Water in Montana, 3 Mont.L.R. 135 (1942). Both states have recently moved to alleviate the problem. Mont. Rev.Code 1947, § 89–880: "A right to appropriate water may not be acquired by any other method, including by adverse use, adverse possession, prescription or estoppel; the method prescribed by this act is exclusive." Idaho Code § 42–607: "* * * so long as a duly elected water master is charged with the administration of the waters within a water district, no water user within such district can adversely possess the right of any other water user."

6. Is there something to be said for confirming and legalizing long-continued uses and practices that do not square with the paper titles to water rights? See Colo.Rev.Stat.1973, 37–92–4–1(b)(VI): "If, in the preparation of the tabulations provided for in this section, the application of the preceding principles [for determining priorities] would cause in any particular case a substantial change in the priority of a particular water right to the extent theretofore lawfully enjoyed for a period of not less than eighteen years, then the division engineer shall designate the priority for that water right in accordance with historic practice. * * *" For some of the difficulties involved in holding appropriators to their paper titles, see

Stone, Montana Water Rights—A New Opportunity, 34 Mont.L.Rev. 57, 59–68 (1973). For some of the difficulties involved either in strict enforcement of laws against those who have long ignored them or in "confirming" illegal uses, see McIntyre, The Disparity Between State Water Rights, Records and Actual Water Use Patterns, 5 Land & Water L.Rev. 22, 37–44 (1970).

At this point a professor may choose to take up the possible termination of water rights by the exercise of the navigation servitude and the public trust. In that case, the recommended assignments are to United States v. Rands, pages 650 - 656; Kaiser Aetna v. United States, pages 657 - 663; Diana Club v. Husting, pages 546 - 551; Illinois Central Railroad v. Illinois, pages 551 - 557; and National Audubon Society v. Superior Court, pages 557 - 570.

SECTION 5. TRANSFER

FARMERS HIGHLINE CANAL & RESERVOIR CO. v. CITY OF GOLDEN

Supreme Court of Colorado, 1954.
129 Colo. 575, 272 P.2d 629.

CLARK, JUSTICE. To review a judgment and decree favorable to defendant in error, City of Golden, in an action to change the point of diversion of certain water rights heretofore adjudicated to the Swadley ditch out of Clear Creek upstream a distance of some five miles to the headgate of the Church ditch, plaintiffs in error present the cause in our Court by writ of error. We will herein refer to the parties as they were aligned in the trial court where the City of Golden was petitioner and plaintiffs in error appeared as respondents.

Petitioner claimed ownership of said water rights by recent purchase and conveyance by deed, and sought to have changed, not only the point of diversion, but likewise, the manner of use, said rights having previously been employed under the Swadley ditch in the irrigation of farm lands, and petitioner is now seeking to devote the same to municipal uses by way of increase to the domestic supply of water for the City of Golden as well as for the irrigation of lawns, gardens and similar purposes within the city. The trial court granted the petition, and by its decree authorized the change of 0.844 cubic feet of water per second of time under priority number thirteen, dated May 14, 1861, and 0.92 cubic feet of water per second of time under priority number twenty-one under date June 1, 1862, for a total of 1.764 cubic feet of water per second of time. * * *

With respect to the facts, the parties hereto are in complete disagreement, and the evidence, limited and inadequate, as to us it seems to be, is in serious conflict. With respect to many legal issues, counsel for the respective parties are quite in accord. It is recognized that water is a property right, subject to sale and conveyance, and that under proper conditions not only may the point of diversion be changed, but likewise the manner of use. It further is recognized that such change may be permitted, by proper court decree, only in such instances as it is specifically shown that the rights of other users from the same source are not injuriously affected by such change, and that the burden of proof thereof rests upon petitioner. These principles have been enunciated by our Court time and again in many decisions. Here, there appears no disagreement as to the law but a wide divergence of theory in its applicability.

There is absolutely no question that a decreed water right is valuable property; that it may be used, its use changed, its point of diversion relocated; and that a municipal corporation is not precluded from purchasing water rights previously used for agricultural purposes and thereafter devoting them to municipal uses, provided that no adverse effect be suffered by other users from the same stream, particularly those holding junior priorities.

Equally well established, as we have repeatedly held, is the principle that junior appropriators have vested rights in the continuation of stream conditions as they existed at the time of their respective appropriations, and that subsequent to such appropriations they may successfully resist all proposed changes in points of diversion and use of water from that source which in any way materially injures or adversely affects their rights. * * *

[I]n Enlarged Southside Irrigation Ditch Co. v. John's Flood Ditch Co., 116 Colo. 580, 585, 183 P.2d 552, * * * Mr. Justice Stone declared the principle that the owner of a priority for irrigation has no right, as against a junior appropriator, to waste water, to increase the amount or extend the time of his diversion so as to put it to double use by irrigation of other lands; nor to lend, rent or sell to others the excess water. "The well-recognized right to change either the point of diversion of the water right or its place of use is always subject to the limitation that such change shall not injure the rights of subsequent appropriators." * * *

Under subhead (d) of its findings, the trial court stated that it was convinced that, under no tenable theory of the case would any injury be done if 1.2 cubic feet of water per second of time out of priorities thirteen and twenty-one were allowed to be transferred, as requested by Golden. Then, under subdivision (e), the trial court "determined to authorize the change of point of diversion of Golden's priorities numbered thirteen and twenty-one, but effectuate the relinquishment of its priority number forty-four." True, under subhead (d) of its findings, the trial court further stated that it was not persuaded that water rights of any users appearing as protestants would be injured by granting decree for the full amount of all three priorities, but it specifically found that no injury would result if the diversion point of 1.2 cubic feet of water per second of time were authorized to be changed, and then proceeded to change the whole of the two oldest priorities for 1.764 cubic feet of water per second of time. This inconsistency of itself would be sufficient to justify a remand of the cause to the trial court for correction, but there appears a far more urgent necessity for reversal. As we have hereinbefore stated, the evidence presented before the trial court is conflicting and from our standpoint not altogether satisfactory. The principal witness who testified in behalf of the petitioner was one Wheeler, an engineer; while the principal witness who testified for protestants was one Lowe, likewise an engineer. Their testimony primarily was based upon two conflicting statistical theories, Mr. Wheeler using the Lowry-Johnson method, and Mr. Lowe the Blaney-Criddle method. The testimony of Mr. Wheeler was considerably more favorable to petitioner than was that of respondents' engineer; nevertheless, Mr. Wheeler testified that in his opinion there might be permitted, without injury to the stream, a change of point of diversion for 1.2 cubic feet of water. An effort was made to have him enlarge upon that amount, but he would not so commit himself other than to say that if an amount were transferred in addition to 1.2 cubic feet of water per second of time the effect on the stream would be so infinitesimal that it could not be measured. Mr. Wheeler's testimony was the extreme of all testimony before the court, both as to acreage irrigated under these decrees from the Swadley ditch, and the amount thereof for which point of diversion might properly be changed without injury to junior appropriators.

Regardless of this, the trial court, with no evidence whatever to support him, presumed to enter a finding that no injurious effect would result if the entire amount of the two older priorities, aggregating 1.764 cubic feet of water per second of time, was transferred, and that if any injury did result therefrom, it would be a general injury and could not affect any of the respondents specifically. The fallacy of such presumption is readily apparent. When any injury is permitted under the assumption that it is general to the stream, it immediately becomes clear that such instances multiplied might become very serious. Where general injury would result to the stream by the transfer, the change could not be authorized without injury to junior appropriators because it is their rights, proportionate with senior rights, that consume the whole stream. * * *

Where it appears that the change sought to be made will result in depletion to the source of supply and result in injury to junior appropriators therefrom, the decree should contain such conditions as are proper to counteract the loss, and should be denied only in such instances as where it is impossible to impose reasonable conditions to effectuate this purpose. City of Colorado Springs v. Yust, 126 Colo. 289, 249 P.2d 151. * * * What condition and limitation should be imposed depends upon the facts and surrounding circumstances in each particular instance. In this case it would require a full accounting not only of the amount of water reasonably required for the irrigation of Swadley lands and the proper return flow to the creek therefrom, but also should be taken into account the actual consumptive use of the City of Golden and the probable return flow to Clear Creek from such uses. If the return flow from the City use be shown to be greater than the return flow from the irrigation of farm lands, naturally the period and extent of use might be increased by the petitioner and the conditions imposed would not have to be so severe as where it would appear that the return flow was equal. It is the purpose of the law, both statutory and by decision, to protect all appropriators and holders of water rights; to this end all elements of loss to the stream by virtue of the proposed change should be considered and accounted for; and thereupon such appropriate provisions of limitation inserted in the decree as the facts would seem to warrant. * * *

As it now stands, we regard the judgment unsupported by proper record evidence. In this instance it would be improper to order dismissal of this action; but it should be and is remanded with direction to the trial court to vacate the decree heretofore entered and for further proceedings in conformity with the rules and principles herein set forth.

Notes

1. Fox, Water: Supply, Demand and the Law, 32 Rocky Mt. Law Review 452, 456 (1960): "In the absence of new sources of low cost water, ways must be found for supporting more people with a given quantity of fresh water if the growth of the West we anticipate is to be accommodated. * * * [T]he pattern of water use in the West must change. In 1955 almost 90% of the withdrawals in the eleven western states were for irrigation purposes and less than 9% were for industrial uses. In the future it seems certain that these proportions will be altered significantly in view of the fact that an acre foot of water dedicated to industrial use—and possibly to recreation—will provide more income and employment and thus support more people than an acre foot dedicated to irrigation. * * * [T]he task of the policy maker is to provide an environment which will facilitate an orderly transition in water use where such a transition is desirable."

The pattern of use described by Fox remains essentially unchanged today. See U.S. Water Resources Council, The Nation's Water Resources 1975–2000, Vol. 1, pp. 29–41 (1978).

2. The principal difficulty in attempting to treat a water right as a salable property right is that many water uses are subject to a peculiar interdependency. Since the same water can be used and reused by several persons, all may have water rights that entitle them to receive the same molecules of water. If the sale and transfer of one person's water right will result in making those molecules unavailable to another who also has a right to them, the first user has sold the latter's water as well as his own.

"Return flow is a common phenomenon in Western irrigated regions and many water rights are predicated wholly or partly upon it. For example, on streams such as the Provo in Utah, downstream development occurred first, and return flow from junior upstream diversions not only satisfied the requirements of earlier downstream appropriators but actually benefited them by prolonging the seasonal supply. On the other hand, on the South Platte in Colorado, upstream development occurred first and the increasing return flow made progressive downstream development possible and eventually added materially to the value of the junior downstream rights." Hutchins, Selected Problems in the Law of Water Rights in the West 331 (1942).

A sale that results in the transfer out of the watershed of the total diversion made by a seller whose use produced return flow will reduce the quantity of water available to appropriators below the point of return. If they are senior to the transferred right, the rule of priority protects them; if they are juniors, they are nevertheless protected by the rule against transfers that cause them harm. This usually results in the rule of thumb that the person making the transfer can take only the amount consumed by the original use. Can a water right for a completely non-consumptive use such as for power or mining never be sold? Could an irrigator of land on one side of a stream sell his entire diversion to his neighbor who wishes to irrigate the land on the other side? Could an appropriator upstream from both new and old diversion points ever show an injury that would prevent or limit the change? See CF & I Steel Corp. v. Rooks, 178 Colo. 110, 495 P.2d 1134 (1972).

A city that purchases an irrigation water right for transfer out of the basin must pay for all the farmer's water but will receive only the fraction he consumed. When it brings the water into its watershed and uses it, return flows and sewer effluent will be added to the natural supply. Can the city recoup its "loss" by selling this water to others? See Denver v. Fulton Irrigating Ditch Co., 179 Colo. 47, 506 P.2d 144 (1972); National Water Commission, Water Policies for the Future 263–264 (1973).

Illustrations of the problems and difficulties encountered in in-basin transfers, upstream and downstream, are given in Ellis, Water Transfer Problems: Law, in Water Research (Kneese and Smith, eds.) 233 (1966).

3. The Colorado Court has since adopted the concept of "historic use" in Westminster v. Church, 167 Colo. 1, 445 P.2d 52 (1968):

"It was proper, therefore, for the district court to examine the state engineer's records introduced into evidence to determine the historical use of the Eggleston No. 2 and McKenzie Ditch water rights during the period 1938–59. The purpose and effect of this inquiry was not to readjudicate the issue of Jenkins' abandonment, but simply to ascertain the extent of actual historical usage by Jenkins and the Rodgers.

"Perhaps defendant's allegations of error—because of the trial court's examination into the state engineer's records—stems from the fact that the term 'historical use' is not very prevalent in the prior decisions of this court and the belief that we had not heretofore sanctioned any such yardstick. * * * Precedent for the trial court's limitation of the direct flow rights finds sanction in the apropos language of this court to be found in Enlarged Southside Irrigation Ditch Company v. John's Flood Ditch Company, 116 Colo. 580, 183 P.2d 552, as follows:

'* * * The owner of a priority for irrigation has no right, as against a junior appropriator, to waste it; neither has he the right to increase the amount or extend the time of his diversion to enable him to put it to double use by irrigation of other lands in addition to those for which it was appropriated * * *; nor to lend, rent or sell to others the excess water after irrigation of the land for which it was appropriated, to the detriment of junior appropriators, and such limitation of right of use cannot be circumvented by shifting the use to other lands. The well-recognized right to change either the point of diversion of the water right or its place of use is always subject to the limitation that such change shall not injure the rights of subsequent appropriators.' "

The impact of the "historic use" rule can be substantial. In *Basin Electric*, infra p. 204, the decreed diversion rate for the rights being transferred was 98.73 c.f.s. The rights were appurtenant to 7,388 acres of land. Finding that only 3,730 acres were actually under irrigation at the time of transfer, the diversion rate for the transferred appropriation was set by the Board of Control at 46.77 c.f.s. Similarly, consumptive use figures were based on the acreage under irrigation, producing a quantity much smaller than would have resulted from considering all of the lands.

What is the relationship between the practice of examining "historic use" in a transfer proceeding and an abandonment or forfeiture action? The Colorado Supreme Court has held a prior unsuccessful abandonment action does not bar an examination of the appropriator's historic practices in a change in use proceeding. City of Westminister v. Church, supra, note 3. See also Weibert v. Rothe Bros., Inc., 200 Colo. 310, 618 P.2d 1367 (1980).

4. The New Mexico Court insists that if the right has been adjudicated the description in the decree fixes the nature and extent of the right to be transferred. W.S. Ranch Co. v. Kaiser Steel Co., 79 N.M. 65, 439 P.2d 714 (1968). However, the Court noted the possibilities of finding a partial abandonment of the right and said,

"Allied to the above contention is the claim that the order permits Kaiser to make an extended use of the water right and amounts to a new appropriation. This argument is based upon the proposition that the Vermejo River is a "losing" stream and that there is more water available at the new place of diversion than at the old; that because of this, Kaiser is really obtaining a new appropriation for the additional water, but with the original priority date. This argument is at first blush plausible, because it was agreed by the expert witnesses that during most years there were times when there was insufficient water available to satisfy upstream rights which had a priority higher than those of the 163.4 acres. Nevertheless, the fallacy of the argument is apparent—Kaiser is only entitled to the amount of water that would be available at the old point of diversion as provided in the adjudication decree—it can take no more. Such is the position taken both by Kaiser and the state engineer, and in view of this concession by them, we see no reason to disagree. But as long as a decree remains in effect, Kaiser is entitled to take the amount of water adjudicated to this right, if, but only if, it can do so without detriment to the rights of other water users on the stream. In this connection we recognize that changing the place of diversion cannot enlarge or expand the water right at the expense of other appropriators or the state."

5. In most states the administrative agencies that regulate the appropriation and distribution of water have the power to approve or disapprove transfers and changes after proceedings at which all interested parties are represented. Ariz.Rev.Stat. § 45–172; West's Ann.Cal.Water Code §§ 1700–1706; Idaho Code § 42–222; Kan.Stat.Ann.1977, § 82a–708b; Mont.Code Ann.1983 §§ 85–2–402 and 85–2–403; N.Mex.Stat.Ann.1978, § 72–5–24; No.Dak.Cent.Code 61–04–15; Or.Rev.Stat. 540.510; Utah Code Ann.1953, 73–3–3; Wash.Rev.Code Ann. 90.03.380; and Wyo.Stat.1977, § 41–3–104. In Texas the same result was reached by a decision which required an amended permit when such a change was made, and gave the water officials power to approve the amended permit just as original permit is approved. Clark v. Briscoe Irrigation Co., 200 S.W.2d 674 (Tex.Civ.App. 1947).

In Colorado, the former "change in point of diversion" procedure illustrated in the principal case has been abolished and an application for a change is handled by the Water Judge under the Water Right Determination and Adjudication Act of 1969. Colo.Rev.Stat.1973, §§ 37–92–101 to 37–92–602. A contrast between judicial and administrative regulations is found in Seastone and Hartman, Alternative Institutions for Water Transfers: The Experience in Colorado and New Mexico, 39 Land Economics 31 (1963).

6. The battle of the experts in *Farmer's Highline*, supra, illustrates the difficulties of determining consumptive use. In CF & I Steel Corp. v. Rooks, supra Note 2, p. 201, the objecting parties offered no experts to dispute the testimony of the experts of those seeking the change—and lost the battle. In East Bench Irrigation Co. v. Deseret Irrigation Co., 2 Utah 2d 170, 271 P.2d 449 (1954) a massive program of modernization, changes and rearrangement of the water rights in a 42-mile stretch of the Sevier River was permitted on condition that the flow was not decreased at a check point above the lower appropriators' headgates.

"Plaintiffs' proposed changes will not create an impossible administrative problem. All the above ground flow of water from the south fork which reaches the lower users of the Sevier River flows past the Kingston measuring station. If the same flow in volume and quantity is maintained from day to day at that station in operating under the proposed changes as would have flowed past that station without the changes, defendants' vested rights will be fully protected. To compute and determine under the operation of the changes what the amount of such flow would have been without the changes presents a difficult problem, for it is impossible to verify the accuracy of such computation by actual test. However, there are records for many years past of the flow of water at the Kingston and Hatch measuring stations and other such stations on the sources of water which make up this river stream. There are also records of the water fall on this water shed, of the water content of the snow which has accumulated in past years on various snow courses thereon, of the temperature and water content of the atmosphere and of other conditions which would affect the flow at Kingston. The record contains much expert testimony to the effect that in future years with the system operated under the proposed changes, the amount of the water flow which would have passed Kingston from day to day under the old system can be determined with reasonable accuracy, and the trial court made findings to that effect."

On the other hand the return flow from a small diversion such as was involved in *Farmer's Highline* may be known to exist yet impossible to detect in a substantial stream. Typical stream measurement techniques usually have a margin of error of 2% or more.

Who has the burden of proof? The Colorado statute requires the applicant for a change to show the "absence of any injurious effect". Colo. Rev.Stat.1984 Supp., § 37–92–304(3). Colorado also allows a trial period: "Any decision of the water judge * * * dealing with a change of water right * * * shall include the condition that the approval of such change * * * shall be subject to reconsideration by the water judge on the question of injury to the vested rights of others for such period * * * as is necessary or desirable to preclude or remedy any such injury." Colo.Rev. Stat.1984 Supp., § 37–92–304(6).

7. In most of the western states a water right is appurtenant to the land upon which the water is used, and a conveyance of the land passes title to the water right to the grantee, though the conveyance makes no mention of the water right. Frank v. Hicks, 4 Wyo. 502, 35 P. 475 (1894). However, in Colorado the answer to the question of whether a deed to land conveys the water right depends upon the intention of the grantor. Bessemer Irrigating Ditch Co. v. Woolley, 32 Colo. 437, 76 P. 1053 (1904); cf. James v. Barker, 99 Colo. 551, 64 P.2d 598 (1937). If the land is divided, the amount appurtenant to each tract is that which was beneficially used on that part of the land prior to the sale, Stephens v. Burton, 546 P.2d 240 (Utah 1976), or is a proportionate share of the entire right. Crow v. Carlson, 107 Idaho 461, 690 P.2d 916 (1984).

BASIN ELECTRIC POWER COOPERATIVE v. STATE BD. OF CONTROL

Supreme Court of Wyoming, 1978.
578 P.2d 557.

ROSE, JUSTICE.

These consolidated appeals primarily concern the State Board of Control's decision not to grant the Basin Electric Power Cooperative the right to transfer certain historic closed-basin return flows, as requested in Basin's petition to change the use and point of diversion under certain acquired water appropriations. Basin's petition, filed pursuant to § 41–3–104, W.S.1977, was contested by the Upper Laramie Users, Inc., the Wheatland Irrigation District (an organization then denominated as the Laramie River Water Users), the Middle Laramie Water Users Association, and certain other interested parties. After hearings in May and July, 1975, the Board granted Basin's petition and entered findings of fact and conclusions of law on May 6, 1976. * * * On January 25, 1977, the district court entered its order affirming the decision of the Board of Control. Basin has appealed only from that portion of the order which concerns the above-mentioned closed-basin return flows. * * *

Basin's petition to the Board of Control requested that three water appropriations, which it has acquired, be changed from agricultural uses to a preferred use for industrial purposes so that it would have water to service its steam power generation requirements at its Laramie River Station near Wheatland, Wyoming. The appropriations in question are from the Laramie River, through the Boughton Ditch, and have historically been used for the irrigation of meadow lands located on the R.O. Corporation and Wallis Ranches, east of U.S. Highway No. 30 and north of State Highway No. 34, in Albany County. Basin's plan is to sever these water rights from the above lands and transport the water down the Laramie River for storage at the proposed Grayrocks Reservoir, there to be utilized at its power facility.

A unique factual situation is present in that a topographic divide separates the 3,730 acres historically irrigated under the Boughton Ditch. Of the total acreage actually irrigated, 794 acres lie above and 2,937 acres lie below the topographic divide.

Above the divide, irrigation return flows are able to find their way back to the Laramie River for use by other appropriators. Below the divide, however, the irrigation return flows enter the Long Lake Basin, a geological enclosure which precludes the return of any waters to the Laramie River for use by other appropriators. The record discloses that, as defined by the Board, there was a historic consumptive use above and below the divide equal to 3,117 acre-feet of water. * * * The amount of water consumptively used was found to be Basin's maximum seasonal entitlement. Basin claims that this amount (3,117 acre-feet) should be increased by the return flows below the topographic divide which enter the Long Lake closed basin—which it calculates would be an additional 2,215 acre-feet of water. Basin makes this claim on the two-pronged theory that this amount was a necessary part of the irrigation of lands in the Long Lake closed basin and was historically lost to the Laramie River system.

On the other hand, the Board concluded—*as a matter of fact*—that these closed-basin return flows had not been "beneficially consumptively used" below the topographic divide and could not be transferred, *regardless of whether or not they return to the Laramie River system.*

Section 41–3–104, provides that when a change in use, or change in place of use of water is applied for, certain factors must be considered by the Board. These considerations are:

(a) The amount of water historically diverted under the existing use.

(b) The historic rate of diversion under the existing use.

(c) The historic amount consumptively used under the existing use.

(d) The historic amount of return flow.

The statute thus provides that the quantity of water transferred shall not affect the quantities of water contemplated by these factors—

"nor in any manner injure other existing lawful appropriators." Basin's interpretation of the statute would lead to the conclusion that each of the above four limitations modify the general prohibition of injury to other appropriators. In other words—argues Basin—factors "a," "b," "c," and "d" above are irrelevant to a change-of-use application unless it can be shown that other appropriators are injured by the effect of one or more of them. According to this reasoning, it follows that since the closed-basin return flows do not return to the Laramie River, there is, therefore, no injury to other appropriators if more than the "historic amount" of water "consumptively used under the existing use" below the divide is transferred. (The quotes are from § 41–3–104.) Since this is so—says Basin—the statute is not offended by the seller-appropriator's transfer of the entire appropriation, regardless of what the facts show the historical-use factor to be.

On the other hand, other interested water users, together with the Board, contend that the statute imposes separate and independent restrictions on the amount of water which can be transferred—*regardless of the existence of injury to other appropriators.*

The Wyoming change-in-use statute, admittedly ambiguous, is unique to western water law, although its principles are not new or unfamiliar. The divergent contentions of the parties are themselves evidence of the ambiguity which characterizes § 41–3–104, supra. Since the statute is ambiguous, it falls to us to construe it, and in so doing we must view the language used by the framers in light of the purposes they intended to accomplish. * * *

While the legislative declaration of intent and purpose is not binding upon us, it is, nevertheless, worthy of consideration as an aid to construction. The title to § 41–3–104, supra, as originally enacted, provided:

> "AN ACT to create Section 41–4–1 of the statutes relating to procedure to change use or place of use of water right; *and providing only historic amount of water used or diverted under the right may be transferred.*" [Emphasis supplied] Session Laws of Wyoming, 1973, ch. 170.

The announced purpose, then of § 41–3–104 was to provide a procedure for those wishing to change a water right, *and* to place limitations on the amount of water which could be transferred. Basin argues with this, urging that the only purpose of the statute was to embrace what Basin interprets to be the basic premise laid down by this court in Johnston v. Little Horse Creek Irrigating Co., 13 Wyo. 208, 79 P. 22, 24, where it is stated:

> "* * * The *only* limitation upon the right of sale of a water right separate from the land to which it was first applied, and to which it has become appurtenant, laid down by any of the authorities, is that

it shall not injuriously affect the rights of other appropriators. * * " [Emphasis supplied]

However, Basin, utilizing its interpretation of the *Johnston* holding and in seeking to apply it to the facts of this case, would conclude that, since there was no injurious effect upon the rights of other appropriators, then there is no statutorily imposed limitation upon the right to transfer a water right. We cannot agree. The situation here is so different from that of *Johnston* that the narrow rule of that case, as urged by Basin, is of little value to these deliberations. Here we have a statutory direction not extant when *Johnston* was decided; and here the issue is beneficial, consumptive use, where—in *Johnston* —no such issue was present.

We readily acknowledge that the statute incorporates certain change-of-use concepts previously recognized by this court. See, Comment: "Changing Manner and Place of Use of Water Rights in Wyoming," Wyo.Land and Water L.Rev., Volume X, No. 2, 455, 466 (1975). We cannot, however, presume that the *only* purpose of a statute is to declare what has, prior to its enactment, been declared to be the law. There would be no reason for its enactment if that were so. United States v. Douglas-Willan Sartoris Co., 3 Wyo. 287, 22 P. 92. In ascertaining legislative intent, we must look to the mischief the statute was intended to cure, the historical setting surrounding its enactment, the public policy of the state, the conclusions of the law and all other prior and contemporaneous facts and circumstances. Carter v. Thompson Realty Co., 58 Wyo. 279, 131 P.2d 297.

While this court has for many years recognized that one of the fundamental principles applicable to any transfer of water rights for change in use is the avoidance of injury (Johnston v. Little Horse Creek Irrigation Co., supra), equally fundamental is the principle which holds that an appropriator obtains a transferable water right only to the extent that he has put his appropriation to a beneficial use. * * *

The key to understanding the application of beneficial-use concepts to a change-of-use proceeding is a recognition that the issues of nonuse and misuse are inextricably interwoven with the issues of change of use and change in the place of use. This is true even without the formal initiation of abandonment proceedings under the statutes. If an appropriator, either by misuse or failure to use, has effectively abandoned either all or part of his water right through noncompliance with the beneficial-use requirements imposed by law, he could not effect a change of use or place of use for that amount of his appropriation which had been abandoned. See Rocky Mountain Power Company v. White River Electric Association, 151 Colo. 45, 376 P.2d 158, 161, and Flasche v. Westcolo Co., 112 Colo. 387, 149 P.2d 817. * * *

Prior to the enactment of § 41–3–104, supra, the laws of Wyoming did not clearly recognize the role played by the concept of beneficial use in the context of a change-of-use proceeding. Emphasis was placed, in cases where such changes were allowed [a], on the avoidance of injury to other appropriators. * * *

Keeping these various principles and problems in mind, we turn to the language of § 41–3–104, supra, in our effort to construe the statute. We must give effect, if possible, to every word, clause and sentence of the statute. State ex rel. Benham v. Cheever, 71 Wyo. 303, 257 P.2d 337, 340–341; and Wheatland Irrigation District v. Short, 80 Wyo. 136, 339 P.2d 403, 409. Each of the clauses containing the restrictions on the quantity of water which may be imposed in the granting of a petition to change the use or place of use of a water right, is separated by the word "nor." The conjunction "nor" performs the same function in negative propositions as does the word "or" in positive propositions, i.e., marking distribution, an alternative, or apposition. Coxson v. Doland, N.Y., 2 Daly's 66, 67. The word "or" is usually used in the disjunctive sense, and when two clauses are expressed in the disjunctive, this generally indicates alternatives, requiring separate treatment. Matter of Adoption of Voss, Wyo., 550 P.2d 481, 485. Cf., Manning & Martin v. State Board of Equalization, 58 Wyo. 425, 133 P.2d 373, 374. In other words, the subject of each clause should be considered separately, without requiring that the subjects both be satisfied. Utilizing these concepts in construing § 4–3–108, W.S.1977 [§ 41–9.1, W.S.1957, 1975 Cum.Supp.], we are forced to the conclusion that the statute forecloses anyone desiring to effect a change of use from transferring more water than has been historically consumptively used, *regardless* of the injury or lack thereof to other appropriators. Such a conclusion is fortified by the consideration which takes into account the fact that the statute speaks of both consumptive use *and* return flows.

In the usual situation—where return flows feed the stream—an appropriator would be allowed to change only the amount of his consumptive use because other appropriators would otherwise be injured. In this respect, the consumptive-use and return-flow factors overlap. Where there are no return flows to the stream, as is the situation here with respect to application of water below the divide, the return-flow factor has no relevance. Nevertheless, the consumptive-use factor must still be applied to determine the amount of water which can be transferred. Any other construction would render the consumptive-use requirement of the statute meaningless. Although of less importance in the normal return-flow situation, the consumptive-use limitation becomes significant in cases like that presented here and in other cases where there is a disparity between actual usage and adjudicated rights.

To the extent, then, that the historic consumptive-use limitation in this statute goes beyond the purpose of avoiding injury to other appro-

a. For an excellent analysis of the history of transfers of water rights in Wyoming, see Trelease and Lee, "Priority and Progress—Case Studies in the Transfer of Water Rights," Vol. 1, No. 1, Wyo.Land & Water L.Rev. 1 (1966).

priators, the legislature must have intended to address the objective of assuring that water is beneficially used. * * *

Basin contends that the Board acted arbitrarily and not in conformity with the law by restricting Basin's right of transfer to the irrigation water consumed by crops in the Long Lake closed basin instead of all water allocated under the prior appropriation. In support of this proposition, Basin points out that it is impossible to avoid some runoff from an irrigation operation, citing 2 Kinney on Water Rights and Irrigation at page 1614, and thus the closed-basin return flows herein were a necessary part of the irrigation process and the beneficial use of these appropriated waters. Basin, therefore, is challenging two aspects of the Board's decision: (1) Conclusion of Law No. 6, supra, which defines consumptive use as essentially the amount of water consumed by the crop; and (2) Finding of Fact No. 34 (fn. 5, supra), which discloses a finding that return flows below the topographic divide were not consumptively used.

We find that the Board's response to the central question is amply supported by the evidence, when viewed in the light of the accepted definition of "consumptive use," and its importance within the context of acquired water rights. The evidence clearly discloses that only approximately 2,451 acre-feet of water had been historically beneficially, consumptively used below the topographic divide. The remaining 2,215 acre-feet of water that reached the closed basin was lost essentially to surface evaporation and subsurface recharge. Basin would have us embrace a position holding that this amount of water was beneficially, consumptively used merely because usually some excess water is incident to the irrigation process. This we cannot do. As pointed out in the Board's brief:

> "To allow Basin Electric the right to waters diverted in excess of that amount necessary for the production of the crops in question would be to grant it a windfall based upon application of the Boughton Ditch water in excess of that which was beneficially used. * * *" If the amount necessary in good faith for crop production below the divide was only 2,451 acre-feet of water, any water in excess of that amount—excluding carriage water not relevant here—served no useful purpose insofar as Basin's predecessors were concerned. See, 1 Clark, Waters and Water Rights, § 55.3, at p. 385.

Over-application amounting to waste must be understood in a relative sense. In the instant case, excess waters above the divide historically returned to the river for use by other appropriators. Basin admits it is not entitled to this amount of water, because, under § 41–3–104, supra, it is not entitled to decrease the amount of return flows. Were it not for the unique geographic situation present here, excess waters below the divide would also return to the river for use by other appropriators. Had this excess amount of water not been diverted from the river in the first instance, it would have been available for use by other appropriators. It is the diversion of more water than can be consumed in good faith in the irrigation process which creates the wasteful, non-beneficial use situation now before us. This is not to say that an appropriator must find a way to return such waters to their source—it is only to say that an appropriator does not acquire a water right in water which he historically has not beneficially used. Not having acquired a water right therein, he or his successor is not entitled to change the use of such waters.

Since the Board, in essence, found that excess waters below the divide had historically gone to waste, Basin could, therefore, acquire no right to the excess. See, Trelease, "The Concept of Reasonable Beneficial Use in the Law of Surface Streams," Vol. 12, No. 1, Wyo.L.J. 1, 14, 16. As a result, Basin's argument, that a denial of the right to transfer such waters is a taking without due process, is without merit.

We hold that the Board's action in limiting the amount which could be transferred to 3,117 acre-feet of water was reasonable and in conformity with the law.

McClintock, Justice, with whom Raper, Justice, joins, dissenting.

I do not disagree with many of the basic legal propositions stated by the majority. I accept their interpretation of the change-of-use statute as one intended to restrict the extent of a water right which can be transferred to a new use to that quantity of water which historically has been consumptively used under the right sought to be transferred. However, I deny that the legislature may constitutionally so limit a pre-1909 [b] right which, as I read the decision of this court in Johnston v. Little Horse Creek Irrigating Co., 13 Wyo. 208, 79 P. 22 (1904), constituted a property right to the full extent that the same had been actually and beneficially used, the only limitation upon the transfer being that it should "not injuriously affect the rights of other appropri-

b. Following *Johnston* the legislature enacted Ch. 97, S.L. of Wyoming 1905, which consistent with the language in that opinion declared invalid any transfer of water rights from the lands for which acquired "which shall be injurious to any prior or subsequent appropriator." The *Johnston* case came under attack from the then State Engineer as being based on an erroneous understanding of the facts and Elwood Mead, Wyoming's first State Engineer and considered the father of the irrigation law in Wyoming, went so far as to express the wish that the legislature "will overcome the mischievous tendencies of the Supreme Court decision in Johnston v. The Little Horse Creek Ditch Company * * *." (See Ninth Biennial Report of the State Engineer 1907–1908, pp. 73–74, 76). Ch. 68, § 1, S.L. of Wyoming 1909 provides in part that

> "* * * Water being always the property of the State, rights to its use shall attach to the land for irrigation, or to such other purpose or object for which acquired in accordance with the beneficial use made and for which the right receives public recognition, under the law and the administration provided thereby. *Water rights cannot be detached from the lands, place or purpose for which they are acquired, without loss of priority.*" (Emphasis added)

The history of the Wyoming law with respect to changes of use, limitations thereon, and exceptions to the limitations is well set forth in Priority and Progress—Case Studies in the Transfer of Water Rights, by Frank J. Trelease and Dellas W. Lee in 1 Land and Water Law Review 1 (1966). The matter is further explored in a comment, Changing Manner and Place of Use of Water Rights in Wyoming, 10 Land and Water Law Review 455 (1975) by Dan B. Riggs. It is clear that the year 1909 marks an important division point in water law in this respect.

ators." 13 Wyo. at 228, 79 P. at 24. While I would concede the right of the legislature to impose any restrictions it saw fit upon the transfer of water rights initiated after the enactment of the 1973 law and probably would agree that that restriction would be applicable to water rights which had their inception after enactment of Ch. 68, S.L. of Wyoming 1909, I believe that to apply the present change-of-use statute to rights which accrued before 1909, whether state or territorial, is an unwarranted and undue interference with and deprivation of property without due process of law, in violation both of the 14th Amendment to the Federal Constitution and § 6 of Art. I of the Wyoming Constitution. I would therefore hold this new restriction in change of use to be unconstitutional and void as to pre-1909 rights, which include the right here in question.

To the best of my knowledge, it has been a fact of irrigation practice from its very inception that all water applied to a given tract of land for the irrigation of crops or grass thereon is not totally consumed in the process and some of that water so applied, however careful the irrigator may be, will find its way back to the stream. Under the circumstances that have usually prevailed, the first appropriator took water for irrigation, others came along and made similar appropriations, and due to the fact that none of them would require the full amount of their nominal appropriations at all times and the further fact that a certain amount of the water used by them usually returns to the stream, the total nominal appropriations from the stream can substantially exceed the amount of water that is flowing in the stream at any one time and actually available for use. The junior appropriators are said to acquire a vested right in the continuance of conditions as of the time of their appropriations.

I readily concede that in the ordinary case, where the return flow is to the same stream from which the appropriation is made, my distinction between beneficial and consumptive use would not benefit the appropriator seeking to change or transfer his right, since he must leave in the stream that amount of water which represented the return flow. But this limitation is imposed because of injury to other appropriators whose rights have vested and is an inherent limitation upon the water right vested in the senior appropriator. In the case at bar, without the presence of injury to other appropriators and merely by declaring the two uses to be synonymous, this court effects an arbitrary reduction of the amount of water transferred.

The board of control has made no determination that more water was being used for the purpose of getting water to the roots of the plants than was necessary. Without such a finding the board's conclusion that "the waters leaving the irrigated lands as return flow below the Topographic Divide, and entering Long Lake, are not being beneficially, consumptively used for the purposes for which the subject rights were acquired" is without factual foundation and indicates confusion on the part of the board. The question is not whether the return flow to

Long Lake represents a beneficial use; the question is whether the water has been beneficially used in the irrigation of lands before commencing its flow into this lake. There is no prohibition in our law against diversion of water to another watershed, Moyer v. Preston, 6 Wyo. 308, 321, 44 P. 845, 848 (1896); Willey v. Decker, 11 Wyo. 496, 530, 73 P. 210, 220 (1903); State of Wyoming v. State of Colorado, 259 U.S. 419, 466, 42 S.Ct. 552, 66 L.Ed. 999 (1922), reh. den. 260 U.S. 1, 43 S.Ct. 2, 66 L.Ed. 1026. The use upon the lands draining into Long Lake was legal; it was beneficial. To me, there is no basis upon which the board could use the two terms in one connection.

Engineering experts for Basin in this case tried very hard and, I think, effectively, to take into consideration all reasonable limitations upon the extent of the irrigation right. They determined that a considerable portion of the water rights sought to be transferred had not been used at all and no attempt was made to transfer that water. Intensive and less intensive uses were distinguished and a formula for determining the amount of return flow from both these uses was made. Due account was given to the irrigation season. As to those water rights used on land where the return flow was to the Laramie River, a proper deduction was made for that loss of return flow; in other words, that amount of water was left in the stream to prevent injury to other appropriations. But for many years and throughout the history of the water right the water now in dispute has been removed from the Laramie River drainage so that historically and before the rights of other appropriators had attached, all of the appropriation had been lost to the Laramie and its appropriators. Basin made no deduction for return flow as to this water because it was not necessary to prevent injury. The board's denial of this transfer clearly gives a windfall to users on the Laramie and at the same time effects a substantial diminution of the transferrable water right. Such diminution can only operate to reduce the value of the right so that in my judgment the refusal to permit the change represents a material interference with the property right as defined in *Johnston.* This interference cannot be justified on the basis of some overriding state or public interest as original owner of the water or in the exercise of any police power, and upon the facts of this case it is improper and unjustified deprivation of interference with property which therefore is prohibited by both the federal and state constitutions.

Notes

1. The article cited by the court reviews Wyoming's long and interesting struggle with its "no-change statute", a much-criticized law that ran counter to economic sense. Enacted in 1909, it laid down the rule that water rights could not be detached from the land, place or purpose for which they were acquired, without loss of priority. Recognizing, however, that cities and an influential railroad could not take their place at the foot of the priority list on over-appropriated streams, the original statute allowed any water right to be condemned to supply water for preferred

domestic and transportation purposes. Thereafter the legislature made numerous other exceptions, each time yielding to practical needs and economic pressures. Since stored water was often used to supplement the supply for different lands in different years, in 1921 the basic statute was amended to apply only to "water rights for the direct use of the natural unstored flow," and to declare that reservoir water and rights might be sold, leased, transferred and used upon such land as desired. In 1945 the legislature permitted the amendment of land descriptions in permits to describe new lands "when it appears desirable or necessary," which was administratively determined to be only if the land became seeped or salted. To give a legal basis to a desirable Bureau of Reclamation project, a 1947 statute permitted the owners of appropriative rights to agree to arrangements which amounted to exchanges of water rights and their use on different lands. When Bureau of Reclamation dams flooded large areas of irrigated land, a 1951 statute, since amended in three legislatures, permitted the owners of the water rights to transfer them to other lands. When large developments of coal and iron were stymied for lack of water, the list of preferred uses to which water rights could be transferred was amended by adding steam power plants in 1955 and industrial purposes in 1957. Under the spur of the interstate highway program, in 1959 the State Highway Commission was permitted to acquire the temporary use of water for highway construction. In legislation dealing not with water rights but with the powers of organizations, the Fish and Game Commission was empowered to acquire water for fish hatcheries and public fishing areas, and irrigation districts, public irrigation districts, public irrigation and power districts, water conservancy districts, water and sewer districts and watershed improvement districts were all given powers to purchase water rights. A most important exception, declared by a federal court and confirmed by administrative practice, was that pre-1909 water rights could not constitutionally be restricted by the statute and were freely transferable. Hughes v. Lincoln Land Co., 27 F.Supp. 972 (D.Wyo.1939). All of these exceptions were detailed and examples of their exercise were documented in Trelease and Lee, Priority and Progress—Case Studies of the Transfer of Water Rights, 1 Land & Water L.Rev. 1 (1966); and Trelease, Transfer of Water Rights—Errata and Addenda—Sales for Recreational Purposes and to Districts, 2 Land & Water L.Rev. 321 (1967).

Did the court really look at "the evil to be remedied" in construing the 1973 statute?

2. Compare the Colorado court's use of "historic" factors as modifiers or illustrations of the general policy against injury to other appropriators, supra p. 201, Note 3. See also Twin Lakes Reservoir and Canal Co. v. Aspen, 193 Colo. 478, 568 P.2d 45 (1977), involving water taken through the continental divide: "In the consideration of change of points of diversion and of use, we are accustomed generally to situations in which the water remains in the same water shed. In such cases, two of the primary factors to be considered are any change in the consumptive use of the water and any change in return flow to the stream from irrigation. In contrast, once [this] water flows into the transmountain diversion tunnel, so far as Western Slope users are concerned, there is a 100% consumptive use."

3. In three states, restrictions on transfers of water rights have been adopted by substantially identical statutes providing that a water right shall remain appurtenant to the land on which it is used, but if for any reason it should at any time become impracticable to beneficially or economically use the water on the land to which it is appurtenant, the right may be severed from the land and transferred to other land without loss of priority, if such change has the approval of the state water authorities and can be made without detriment to existing rights. Nev.Rev.Stat. 533.040, 533.325; 82 Okl.Stat.1984–85 Supp., § 105.22; So.Dak. Codified Laws 46–5–34 to 46–5–36. In Nevada the statute applies to all water rights, in the other states, only to rights for irrigation, leaving other rights freely transferable upon compliance with procedures for obtaining approval. The South Dakota statute does not affect water rights vested prior to its enactment in 1907. Jewett v. Redwater Irrigating Ass'n, 88 S.D. 390, 220 N.W.2d 834 (1974). Arizona, Kansas and North Dakota at one time had statutes prohibiting or severely restricting transfers and changes of water rights. Ariz.Laws 1919, c. 64, § 48; Kans.Laws 1891, c. 133, Art. 2, § 5; N.D.Laws 1905, c. 34, § 51.

Nebraska water rights are generally thought to be nontransferrable apart from the land and incapable of being changed to a different place of use. Yeutter, A Legal-Economic Critique of Nebraska Watercourse Law, 44 Neb.L.Rev. 11, 35 (1965). But see 1 Hutchins, Water Right Laws in the Nineteen Western States 463–466 (1971) for an interesting analysis of the statutes and cases which indicates that all such changes are not definitely foreclosed.

4. A permit to appropriate water has been recognized as a property right, albeit inchoate, but the Wyoming court recently refused to allow an agricultural development company to transfer the unused part of its permit to a steam generation electric power plant, and to change the place of use, point of diversion and means of conveyance. Green River Development Co. v. FMC Corp., 660 P.2d 339 (Wyo.1983). The statute involved in Basin Electric (casebook page 213) was held to give no authority to approve such a change. Under the reasoning of that case, the permittee had never applied the water to beneficial use, hence it had no water right which qualified for transfer.

CITY OF THORNTON v. THE FARMERS RESERVOIR AND IRRIGATION CO.

Supreme Court of Colorado, 1978.
194 Colo. 526, 575 P.2d 382.

GROVES, JUSTICE.

The City of Thornton ("Thornton"), a home rule municipality, on November 14, 1973 brought a proceeding in eminent domain against The Farmers Reservoir and Irrigation Company ("Farmers"). The property sought to be condemned may be described generally as the water and water rights, ditches and ditch rights of the Standley Lake Division of Farmers. * * *

Farmers is a mutual ditch company, organized and acting under sections 7–42–101 et seq., C.R.S.1973. The Standley Lake Division is one of four divisions of Farmers' extensive water distribution system. The legal title of the property sought to be condemned is in Farmers. At the time the action was brought Farmers had 1105 shareholders, 271 of whom held shares allocated to the Standley Lake Division. * * *

On June 29, 1975 the Water Rights Condemnation Act was adopted, to become effective on July 1, 1975. Sections 38–6–201 through 216, C.R.S.1973 (1976 Supp.). This legislation is here referred to as the 1975 Act. With notable exceptions, the 1975 Act contains the same provisions as sections 38–6–101 through 118, C.R.S.1973 (Eminent Domain Proceedings by Cities and Towns).

We now consider some of these exceptions. The 1975 Act provides that, in its petition for condemnation filed in the district court, the municipality shall pray for the appointment of three commissioners "to determine the issue of the necessity of exercising eminent domain as proposed in the petition." The 1975 Act further states that no municipality shall be allowed to condemn water rights for any anticipated or future needs in excess of 15 years. The 1975 Act further specifies that the municipality shall prepare a "community growth development plan" and a detailed statement concerning the proposed condemnation of water rights and the effect of the taking of the same. The plan and statement are to be presented to the commissioners. * * *

The 1975 Act contains the following provisions relating to the commission:

> The municipality's petition for condemnation of a water right "shall pray for the appointment of three disinterested commissioners appointed by the court * * * to determine the issue of the necessity of exercising eminent domain as proposed in the petition and, if the condemnation is to be allowed, to appraise the award of damages." Section 38–6–202(1), C.R.S.1973 (1976 Supp.).
>
> Prior to any hearing of condemnation the municipality shall prepare and update a community growth development plan and a detailed statement describing: (1) the water rights to be required and their present uses; (2) the effects from the change of the use of the water to the proposed use, including economic and environmental effects; (3) unavoidable adverse and irreversible effects from the taking; and (4) alternative sources of water supply that might be acquired. These statements shall be presented to the commission. Section 203.
>
> It is the duty of the commissioners to "[e]xamine and assess the growth development plan and statement provided by the municipality * * * obtain necessary information pursuant to powers granted * * * and make a determination as to the necessity of exercising the power of eminent domain for the proposed purposes." The commissioner shall provide "one of the following

recommendations to the court, based upon their findings: (I) There exists no need and necessity for condemnation as proposed." Section 207(1).

The commissioners shall, after hearing, certify the proper compensation to be made to the owners of property to be taken but, if "the commissioners find there exists no need and necessity for the condemnation proposed, they shall make no finding as to the value of the condemned property." Section 207(3) and (4).

After filing of the report of the commissioners, written objections may be made thereto. "Any party interested in said proceeding may introduce such evidence as may tend to establish the right of the matter. The burden of proof to change any finding, award, or assessment of said commissioners shall be upon the person objecting thereto. * * * The court, for good cause shown, may modify, alter, change, annul, or confirm the report of the commissioners, or any part thereof, or may order a new appraisement and assessment as to any of the property affected in the proceeding by the same commissioners or by other commissioners appointed by the court." Section 210.

The provisions of the 1975 Act relating to the appointment, action and effect of a commission to determine the issue of necessity of exercising eminent domain are unconstitutional as applied to Thornton as a home rule municipality. These provisions are in conflict with the express grant of eminent domain powers to home rule cities by Colo. Const. Art. XX, Sec. 1.

The 1975 Act does not state specifically the effect of a finding by the commission that there exists no need or necessity for condemnation as proposed. It is to be implied from the Act, however, that such a finding of the commission prevents the proposed condemnation; or, with the burden of proof upon a person objecting thereto, such finding is subject to judicial review. * * *

We quote with approval this statement from the brief of the amicus curiae, Colorado Municipal League:

"The power of eminent domain is an inherent attribute of sovereignty limited only by applicable portions of the state and federal constitutions, and the exercise of the right of eminent domain is the exercise of the sovereign power. People of Colorado v. District Court, 207 F.2d 50 (10th Cir.1953). A portion of that sovereign power is granted directly by the people of the state of Colorado to the citizens of home rule municipalities through the adoption of Sections 1 and 6 of Article XX of the Colorado Constitution."

Colo. Const. Art. XX, Sec. 1 provides in part that a home rule municipality:

"*shall have the power, within or without its territorial limits, to* construct, *condemn and purchase,* purchase, acquire, lease, add to, maintain, conduct and operate, *water works,* light plants, power plants, transportation systems, heating plants, and any other public utilities or works or ways local in use and extent, in whole or in part, *and everything required therefore* * * * and * * * the same or any part thereof may be purchased by said city and county which may enforce such purchase by proceedings at law as in taking land for public use by right of eminent domain." (emphasis added.)

By the adoption of Article XX, and particularly the above quoted provisions thereof, the people of Colorado intended to, and in effect did, delegate to home rule municipalities full power to exercise the right of eminent domain in the effectuation of any lawful, public and municipal purpose, including particularly the acquisition of water rights. Toll v. Denver, 139 Colo. 462, 340 P.2d 862 (1959); and Fishel v. Denver, 106 Colo. 576, 108 P.2d 236 (1940).

The determination of necessity is an essential part of the power of eminent domain and, once necessity is determined by legislative act, no further finding or adjudication is required. Londoner v. Denver, 52 Colo. 15, 119 P. 156 (1911). The determination of necessity by Thornton was not reviewable by the judiciary absent a showing of fraud or bad faith. Colorado State Board of Land Commissioners v. District Court, 163 Colo. 338, 430 P.2d 617 (1967); Dallasta v. Department of Highways, 153 Colo. 519, 387 P.2d 25 (1963); Mack v. Highway Commission, 152 Colo. 300, 381 P.2d 987 (1963); Denver v. Board of Commissioners, 113 Colo. 150, 156 P.2d 101 (1945); and Lavelle v. Town of Julesburg, 49 Colo. 290, 112 P. 774 (1911).

Relying on cases such as Denver v. Sweet, 138 Colo. 41, 329 P.2d 441 (1958), the respondents argue that the determination of necessity is a matter of statewide concern and, as a result, a home rule municipality is subject to statutory limitations in this area. We fully recognize that, generally, the legislative powers of a home rule municipality are superior with respect to local and municipal matters; and that, in cases of conflict between a statute and the ordinance of a home rule city relating to a matter of statewide concern, the statute must govern. Here, however, there is involved a specific constitutional power granted to home rule municipalities and, even though the matter may be of statewide concern, the General Assembly has no power to enact any law that denies a right specifically granted by the Colorado Constitution. * * *

The judgment of the district court is reversed and the cause remanded with directions to vacate the order of dismissal and to proceed not inconsonant with the views herein expressed.

ERICKSON, JUSTICE, dissenting:

I respectfully dissent.

The majority opinion concludes that the City of Thornton is not subject to the provisions of the Water Rights Condemnation Act of 1975, section 38–6–201 through 216, C.R.S.1973 (1976 Supp.), because Thornton is a home rule city with the power of eminent domain, as provided in Article XX, Section 1 of the Colorado Constitution. The Colorado Constitution, however, grants a home rule municipality exclusive control only over matters of local and municipal concern. Matters of statewide concern remain subject to statewide regulation. Spears Free Clinic and Hospital For Poor Children v. State Board of Health, 122 Colo. 147, 220 P.2d 872 (1950); People v. McNichols, 91 Colo. 141, 13 P.2d 266 (1932).

A municipality's election to exercise eminent domain powers to condemn water rights is a matter of statewide concern, subject to statutory regulation by the General Assembly. Expanding water requirements of growing municipal populations are causing much of Colorado's scarce water, previously devoted to agricultural use, to be acquired for municipal use. Municipal condemnation of water rights necessarily has a tremendous impact upon the economies of agricultural areas and disrupts farm operations which are far distant from the condemning city. Therefore, I cannot accept the majority's conclusion that this area of statewide concern cannot be regulated on a statewide basis by the Water Rights Condemnation Act of 1975. * * *

I would, therefore, affirm the district court's dismissal.

CARRIGAN, J., has authorized me to say that he joins me in this dissent.

Notes

1. Gray and Nobe, Water Resource Economics, Externalities and Institutions in the United States, Proceedings, International Conference on Global Water Systems, Valencia, Spain (1975):

"[A] brief historical perspective is in order. Thornton had developed rapidly during the 1950s as a suburb of Denver, the major metropolitan center of the intermountain region of the nation. Since its incorporation in 1956, the City of Thornton has grown so that it now encompasses 17 square miles and has a population of 27,000 people. During its period of rapid growth, the City of Denver provided adequately for its municipal water requirements so no serious thought was given to whether or not it would continue to do so indefinitely. In recent years, however, proposed additional trans-mountain diversions for augmenting Denver's water supply have been opposed because of adverse environmental impacts. Faced with a potential future limit to its growth due to an upper limit on its source of Denver water, the City of Thornton set out to satisfy its needs from alternative sources. This decision led in turn to the condemnation proceedings filed against the irrigation water users in the vicinity.

"The fact that the City of Thornton has resorted to condemnation proceedings is a clear indication of the great difficulty and high cost of obtaining alternative, new water supplies in its region. Thus, it can be inferred that such an option also does not exist for the irrigators if they lose their existing water rights. What are the adverse implications of this situation? First of all, it must be recognized that farmers in the area would not necessarily be forced out of agriculture. They could revert to dryland farming and continue to grow most of the crops now being produced. But yields will decline drastically and so will net incomes per acre (in the order of magnitude of dropping from a long term average of $200/acre under irrigation to $40/acre under dryland farming). In the short run, yields will drop even lower because, under irrigation, plant nutrients are applied in excess of the levels plants can utilize under dryland conditions, and it will take several years to leach out the excess.

"In addition, indirect—but nonetheless significant—adverse effects of the transfer of water rights in these cases would result. These are as follows:

1. Since real estate taxes are unlikely to decline in response to lower income yields under dryland farming, there would be abandonment of some farm land (presumably to other uses).

2. There will certainly be a displacement or loss of sunk capital invested by farmers in their irrigation systems, land leveling, and in equipment utilized in irrigated farming in excess of that required in dryland farming.

3. There will be a broadbased reduction in secondary benefits that have been accruing from irrigated agriculture to others in the vicinity, including farm labor jobs, farm machinery and fertilizer sales, plus lower sales volume in the food processing sector.

4. The farms affected are primary grain producers; the Front Range area of Colorado is already grain deficient and subsequent reduction in production will particularly affect a large number of grain dependent industries, including breweries, beef cattle feedlots, feed mills, and elevators.

5. Finally, there will be loss of open space as some of the agricultural area is built up in residential and industrial uses which will adversely affect the quality of life of the area via increased pollution and congestion (and will trigger another round of increasing water demand)."

2. Although most states require administrative officials to consider the "public interest" or "public welfare" in processing a permit application (see section 3 of this chapter), most states do not impose similar requirements where transfer applications are concerned. Consequently, social costs other than the direct injury to the water right of another appropriator generally have not been recognized as the type of damage that will be considered in determining the allowability of a change in a water right. An Idaho transfer was opposed on the ground that the land from which the water was to be taken would decrease in taxable value so that taxes and assessments for local highway and school districts would be decreased and the burden on other taxpayers would be increased. The objection was overruled, In re Robinson, 61 Idaho 462, 103 P.2d 693 (1940). On the other hand, when a Colorado farmer who received his water from a mutual ditch sold his right to a city which did not use the ditch, the objection that there would be one less person to share the costs of operation and maintenance was met by requiring the city to continue to pay the farmer's share of the ditch's expenses. Brighton Ditch Co. v. Englewood, 124 Colo. 366, 237 P.2d 116 (1951).

There are exceptions, however. A Nevada statute provides that the state engineer is to approve a change in use if it does not impair existing rights and is not "detrimental to the public interest." Nev.Rev.Stat. 533.370(3). In Clark v. Briscoe, 200 S.W.2d 674 (Tex.Civ.App.1947) the court concluded that consideration of the public interest was required in a change in use proceeding, although not expressly required by the Texas statutes. The court reasoned that failure to require it in a change in use might result in defeat of circumvention of the statutory requirement to consider the public interest in the initial issuance of a permit. West's Ann. Calif.Water Code § 1735 directs the Board of control to approve trial transfers only when it concludes that "such a transfer would not unreasonably affect fish, wildlife, or other instream beneficial uses." A recently enacted New Mexico statute authorizes a change in use "if such changes * * * are not contrary to conservation of water within the state and not detrimental to the public welfare of the state * * *." 1985 Sess.L., ch. 201, codified at N.Mex.Comp.Laws § 72–5–23.

In 1975, when the Wyoming Legislature foresaw that the state's coal resources would require much water and could give rise to transfers of large quantities of water from agricultural land far distant from the coal fields, it added the following language to the statute that required a showing of no injury to other appropriators, "The Board of Control shall consider all facts it believes pertinent to the transfer which may include the following: (i) the economic loss to the community and the state if the use from which the right is transferred is discontinued; (ii) the extent to which such economic loss will be offset by the new use; (iii) whether other sources of water are available for the new use." Wyo.Stat.1977, § 41–3–104. See Note, Changing Manner and Place of Use in Wyoming, X Land & Water L.Rev. 455 (1975); Trelease, The Changing Water Market for Energy, 5 J.Contemp.L. 83 (1979).

3. A great deal of western water is supplied to irrigators by public irrigation districts which have constructed large dams and canals or have contracted for delivery of large quantities of water from U.S. Bureau of Reclamation projects. The ability of a water user to sell his share of the district supply may depend upon conceptual notions of who owns the water right or whether the water is appurtenant to land, rather than on questions of the desirability of the change and whether injury would befall anyone. In some states the district may have a veto over the change, it must give its approval to such a transfer. The power of the district to sell its water outside its service area may depend upon the same considerations, as well as on the terms of the statute under which it was formed or the documents of incorporation, and on whether the water is "surplus" or in use. The transferability of Bureau of Reclamation water varies from project to project and may depend on the legislation authorizing it, whether the project is paid out, and upon the residency of the parties. The entire matter is "extraordinarily murky" and is dealt with in some detail in Meyers and Posner, Toward an Improved Market in Water Resources (National Water Commission, Legal Study No. 4, 1971).

4. In each western state, cities and towns are given the power to condemn water rights for the purpose of obtaining a municipal supply, and

hence have a preferred right in this sense, although most of the statutes conferring the power are found in the laws relating to municipal governments and not in the water codes. Statutes granting a preference for domestic use are also construed as conferring the power of eminent domain. See Town of Sterling v. Pawnee Ditch Extension Co., 42 Colo. 421, 94 P. 339 (1908).

In Nebraska and Idaho the constitutions give an order of precedence between various uses when the waters of a stream are not sufficient for all, and each expressly provides for condemnation and compensation as the means of acquiring the water of the non-preferred user. Neb. Const. Art. 15, § 6; Idaho Const. Art. 15, § 3. Wyoming's statutory list of preferences is carried into execution by a combination of eminent domain and an administrative procedure authorizing the change of use. Wyo.Stat.1977, §§ 41–3–102, 41–3–103.

5. Some municipalities in the southwest claim "pueblo rights," rights for municipal purposes that are superior to those of agricultural appropriators and that permit a city to expand its uses and take without compensation water put to use long before the city's exercise of the right. The historical basis for such rights is dubious. They are generally said to be a remnant of the southwest's Spanish heritage, stemming from Spanish or Mexican grants to agricultural villages which have since grown up into American cities. A document which established the village of Pitic in Sonora, Mexico, is claimed to have granted the inhabitants unrestricted rights to water and provided that pueblos established thereafter were to have like privileges. In California it has been held that a modern city's pueblo right, which had lain dormant for over a century, was superior to the right of an irrigation company that had expended large sums in the development of a project. San Diego v. Cuyamaca Water Co., 209 Cal. 105, 287 P. 475 (1930). In Note, 18 Calif.L.R. 572 (1930), it is suggested that the modern pueblo rights enforced in California are considerably broader than the ancient rights originally granted. In New Mexico, the court originally doubted whether such a right could exist with the present state constitution and laws, New Mexico Products Co. v. New Mexico Power Co., 42 N.M. 311, 77 P.2d 634 (1937), but in Cartwright v. Public Service Co. of New Mexico, 66 N.M. 64, 343 P.2d 654 (1958) it confirmed the right of the town of Las Vegas, and the water company distributing water to its inhabitants, to take all of the waters of the river running through the town, expanding withdrawals as the water becomes necessary for the use of its inhabitants.

Modern research indicates that such rights never existed in Spanish or Mexican law. Although the existence and validity of the document known as the "Plan of Pitic" has been questioned, its authenticity seems established by the better evidence. Meyer, Water in the Hispanic Southwest, 33 (1984). More cogent is the argument that even though the plan was genuine and was intended as the model for the settlement of other towns, it did not give the pueblos the type of "prior and paramount" right that the California and New Mexico courts claim for it. Meyer says, "The water advantage that the corporate community enjoyed over the individual, on the basis of legal right, was by no means absolute. * * * As early as 1573, King Philip II * * * specified that grants of land and water should be made in such a way as to result in no prejudice to existing Indian towns, existing Spanish towns, 'nor to individual persons.' * * * Two hundred years after the ordinances of Philip II the Plan de Pitic reaffirmed exactly the same principle. Article 2 of the plan specifies that, when a new town is established, its boundaries should not result in injury to established Indian towns or to individuals. The principle of individual rights is stated even more forcefully in Article 19, which admonishes water judges not to 'give anyone in the town more than his fair share in order to protect the rights of individuals not residing in the town.' * * * The protection of individual rights vis-à-vis those of the corporate community did not change with Mexican independence." Meyer, 157, 158.

Nevertheless, the California Supreme Court reaffirmed the existence of pueblo rights in Los Angeles v. San Fernando, 14 Cal.3d 199, 123 Cal.Rptr. 1, 537 P.2d 1250 (1975), primarily on the basis that the City of Los Angeles had long relied on its claim to all water of the Los Angeles River and that San Fernando had never relied on the nonexistence of pueblo rights.

6. West's Ann.Cal.Water Code, §§ 1392, 1629 provide that a person accepting a permit or license to appropriate does so under the condition that no value in excess of the actual amount paid to the state therefor shall be claimed for the permit or license or for any right granted or acquired under the water code, in any valuation for purposes of sale to or condemnation by the state or any city, irrigation district or other political subdivision of the state. Section 1245 makes municipal corporations and water companies liable for all damage resulting from the taking of water. How can these be reconciled? See also Or.Rev.Stat. 537.280, 537.290.

TRELEASE, THE MODEL WATER CODE, THE WISE ADMINISTRATOR AND THE GODDAM BUREAUCRAT

14 Nat.Resources J. 207 (1974).

The easterner could improve on western law in several respects. If the thought of priority distribution in times of shortage raises fears that the most economical or desirable uses may be foreclosed, it is still possible to avoid calling in the Bureaucrat and to let the parties solve the problem. One defect in most western appropriation laws is the failure to provide for sales of water, as distinguished from sales of water rights. Yet some secondary western water rights, shares of stock in a reservoir or ditch company, are used in this fashion. For example, some water users in Wyoming grow hay for cattle, some grow sugar beets. Late in the season, a rancher may hold stock that entitles him to so many acre feet of reservoir water while a beet farmer's stream has run dry. Hay produces $25 to $40 an acre, sugar beets $60 to $75. What happens is that the farmer "rents" the rancher's water right at a price somewhere between the profit he will realize on the beets and the profit the rancher will lose on the hay. In New Mexico, a statute enacted in 1967 permits "leasing of the use of water" by an appropriator to any other person, with the approval of the State Engineer. Under this act, growers of beans who anticipate a high price buy water from potato growers who face a glutted market. Maximum efficiency is reached, since the high-value crop is produced, and both water users share the profits. The Code's Bureaucrat could not do as well. If he were charged with distributing Wyoming water on the basis of economic efficiency he would allocate the water to the beet grower, but the lucky farmer would get all his profits while the unfortunate rancher would suffer a severe loss. If he attempted to avoid this by a criterion of equity, and gave half the water to each, the highest and best use would not be served and maximum production would not be reached.

Another example of how temporary transfers of rights or sales of water would be of great utility is that of the city which gambled on a junior right and is faced with an unusual drought. If farmers hold the priority, I would assume that the Bureaucrat would say that the city has the better use and would cut off the farmers' supply. The city would get the water but the farmers would be bankrupted. This is a social cost which must be reckoned, and the best way to account for it is to have the city pay for the farmers' lost crops. An eastern statute could improve on the system by allowing only owners of permits to make purchases, and by limiting quantities to enough to make up the shortage in the permitted supply. This would avoid the use of water by unauthorized persons or in unauthorized quantities. Cities could be given the power of eminent domain to enable them to take temporary control of water rights at a fair compensation.

Notes

1. Gaffney, Economic Aspects of Water Resource Policy, 28 Am.J. Econ. and Sociology 131, 140 (1969) (a very critical review of all water law, treating prior appropriation only slightly less roughly than riparian rights):

"d. Rationing under scarcity. Under the 'first in time, first in right' doctrine, appropriators are senior and junior to one another along a scale from the first to the last. When water falls low, the juniors drop out first and lose everything before the next senior appropriator loses anything. In result, there is no pooling of risk whatever. The top senior has a 100 per cent firm supply; the last junior has a supply so uncertain it is unusable. Two basic economizing principles are denied. One is marginal productivity. The junior appropriator who loses all his water obviously loses marginal units of high productivity, while the senior retains marginal units of low productivity. The other is pooling of risk. The doctrine is conceived in terms of an assumed necessity for vertical integration: that is, there is no market for the raw material, water, but every user rather owns his own supply. His supply is a piece of the larger common supply, but his piece is defined in such a way as greatly to increase the aggregate variability of supply above that which nature imposes; to increase the uncertainty as well; and, finally, to distribute these risks unequally."

2. Temporary changes of water rights are allowed in Utah with the permission of the State Engineer, Utah Code Ann.1953, 73–3–3, and in Wyoming for "highway construction or repair, railroad roadbed construction or repair, or other temporary purposes," Wyo.Stat.1977, § 41–3–110.

3. Trelease, A Proposed Water Resources Act for Jamaica, Working Document No. 2, AGL:SF/JAM 12, Food and Agriculture Organization of the United Nations, 18 (1973):

"Section 18. *Arrangements for Temporary Use of Water*

"(1) If any licensee cannot obtain the full amount of water specified in his license under the provisions of section (17) of this Act, he may lease the right of another licensee for a sufficient time or purchase water from another licensee in a sufficient quantity to make up said full amount, if the Commissioner is notified of such transaction and determines that no other licensee or domestic user will be prejudiced thereby.

"(2) If the National Water Authority, the Kingston and St. Andrew Water Commission, any parish council or any other supplier of water to the public for domestic and municipal purposes, or any person whose continued use of water in time of shortage is determined by the Commissioner to be in the public interest, cannot obtain or probably will not be able to obtain in the near future the full amount of water specified in its or his license under the provisions of section (17) of this Act, it or he may apply to the Commissioner for an emergency order, and the Commissioner, if he determines that an emergency exists, may order the license of any person to be suspended or may order any person withdrawing water under a license to furnish water to the applicant. In such cases the Minister shall fix the amount of compensation to be paid for water so furnished or for damage or loss resulting from such suspension, and may suspend the order if the amount is not promptly paid."

4. See Angelides and Bardach, Water Banking, How to Stop Wasting Agricultural Water (Institute for Contemporary Studies, San Francisco, California, 1978) for examples of "water banking" in California water districts and proposals for facilitating and extending the practice. During the California drought of 1977 the Bureau of Reclamation and the State Department of Water Resources instituted emergency practices of buying water from some districts or farmers and selling it to others. Some sellers had alternate sources of supply (e.g., Metropolitan Water District of Southern California could use Colorado River water and sell its right to Northern California water imported by the Department of Water Resources) but some rice growers "deposited" water in the "bank" because the price received for water was more attractive than the prospective profit from the grain. Some groundwater is regularly "banked" (pooled) by Southern California groundwater management districts. The monograph urges legislation to eliminate obstacles and objections and to authorize the middleman function of districts and interdistrict transactions.

The Bureau of Reclamation's temporary water bank was set up by the Drought Emergency Act of 1977, P.L. 95–18, 43 U.S.C.A. § 502 note, which authorized the Secretary of the Interior to purchase water from willing sellers at a negotiated price that would not include undue benefit or profit compared to benefits of normal irrigation use of the water. The Secretary might assist willing buyers (irrigators on federal projects) to purchase water at prices fixed by the Secretary, financed where necessary by five year interest-free loans.

Why were the elaborate provisions for sales through an intermediary and control of prices thought necessary? Would a water brokerage or a water marketplace serve as well to get buyers and sellers together at negotiated prices?

5. Water rights are limited to the quantity needed for the beneficial use to be served. Many statutes authorize water districts to sell "surplus water" outside their usual service areas. Would such a sale be an admission that the district is claiming more water than it needs? In 1982 the California legislature, seeking to promote conservation measures, solved this dilemma in part by enacting West's Ann.Cal. Water Code § 1011(b): "Water, or the right to the use of water, the use of which has ceased or been reduced as the result of water conservation efforts as described in subdivision (a), may be sold, leased, exchanged or otherwise transferred pursuant to any provision of law relating to the transfer of water or water rights, including, but not limited to, provisions of law governing any change in point of diversion, place of use, and purpose of use due to the transfer." § 1010(b) gives the same privilege of selling water saved by the substitution of reclaimed or polluted water for the water appropriated.

TRELEASE, TRANSFER OF WATER RIGHTS—ERRATA AND ADDENDA

2 Land & Water L.Rev. 321 (1967).

A recent issue of the *Land and Water Law Review* carried an extensive study of the laws of Wyoming relating to the transfer of water rights.[5] The article detailed the history of Wyoming's "no change" statute ("Water rights * * * cannot be detached from the lands, place or purpose for which they are acquired * * * "), noted a number of exceptions to its application and set out case studies of the way in which the law and its exceptions had operated.

The senior author listed ten exceptions to the restraints imposed by the statute, nine of them statutory. In his conclusion he noted that these exceptions had not yet swallowed the rule and stated,

> The remnants of the no-change rule may interfere with future desirable transfers. * * * Two of today's (and tomorrow's) most important problems remain unprovided for. One is the use of water for recreation, to maintain minimum or sustained reservoir levels for fishing and boating, to maintain a minimum flow or to restore natural flow in streams for sport fishing. Some day, not too far away, the economic advantages of these activities may outweigh the value of present uses. Public and private entities may be willing to pay a proper price for the needed water, the owners of the water rights may be very desirous of receiving the money, but the law has no mechanism for consummating the transaction.

An eleventh exception has been brought to light, not by research but by chance. It makes most of this quotation erroneous. In 1939 the legislature created the Wyoming Game and Fish Commission, a strong department that was to become a model in many other states, endowed

5. Trelease & Lee, Priority and Progress—Case Studies of the Transfer of Water Rights, 1 Land & Water L.Rev. 1 (1966).

with broad powers over almost all aspects of fish and wildlife management. Among these appears the following: "To acquire * * * waters in the name of the state by purchase, lease, agreement, gift or devise suitable for the purposes herein enumerated and to develop, improve, operate and maintain the same for the following purposes: (1) Fish hatcheries, rearing ponds, * * * (2) Management of * * * fishes and the restoration, propagation or protection of the same. (3) Public * * * fishing * * * areas * * *." [6]

If this statute is to be given any meaning, it must operate as still another exception to the no-change rule, adding the Fish and Game Commission to the list of cities, railroads, steam power plants, industries and the highway department, as another privileged entity permitted to purchase water for its needs. If water may be purchased for fish hatcheries and the maintenance of public fishing areas, clearly the water rights must be detached from their original place and purpose.

Neither the records of the Fish and Game Department nor of the State Engineer's office disclose any example of the exercise of this power. However, the state has become the owner of water rights appurtenant to lands which the Fish and Game Commission purchased for public fishing areas. The water rights have been exercised only for minimal irrigation of the lands, to prevent their loss by abandonment or forfeiture. According to the statute, there is no reason why they may not be operated and maintained strictly for the suitable operation and maintenance of the public fishing areas—in other words, left in the stream, though protected by priority from upstream junior diverters. If the Commission had land for a public fishing area, but insufficient water, there would seem to be no reason why it could not purchase the right of an upstream appropriator and transfer it down to the public area, there to run in the stream for the restoration and protection of the fish. If no other damage to other appropriators would result, it might purchase a water right and change its place of diversion and use to a reservoir open to public fishing. It might purchase reservoir capacity for maintaining minimum levels and flows in a public area.

The statute goes on to give the Commission power "To sell or exchange * * * water * * * which is no longer of any practical use to the commission, and cover all funds received from such sales into the Wyoming game and fish fund." In some cases in which the Commission purchases irrigated land as a public fishing area, it could recoup part of its costs and still preserve the water for its purposes by selling the water right to a downstream user.

It can thus be seen that most of the "important problems" raised by the senior author of the article do not exist. "To that learned author, a thorough-going reprimand." [7]

6. Wyo.Stat.1957 § 23–15(b).

7. Prosser, Business Visitors and Invitees, 26 Minn.L.Rev. 573 n. 215 (1942), criticizing the author of Prosser, Torts (1941).

Note

Sacramento Union, July 5, 1978:

"**Group Donates Trout Stream.** Coeur D'Alene, Idaho. A San Francisco conservation group has donated a trout stream to the U.S. Forest Service, the agency has announced.

"The Trust for Public Land has donated 9.67 acres along the north fork of Grouse Creek near Lake Pend Oreille for Forest Service management. The stream is a 'prolific producer' of Kamloops trout, said James Cooper, fisheries biologist for the agency.

"Of nearly 5,000 miles of fish streams in the Idaho Panhandle National Forest, only 25 miles are Kamloops spawning waters, Cooper said.

"The land, valued at about $6,000, will be managed mainly to protect the creek and fish, said Ralph Kizer, forest supervisor."

SECTION 6. REUSE

CLEAVER v. JUDD

Supreme Court of Oregon, 1964.
238 Or. 266, 393 P.2d 193.

O'CONNELL, JUSTICE. Defendants appeal from a decree enjoining them from diverting the waters in an unnamed draw which are used by plaintiffs for irrigation purposes.

The suit may be described roughly as a contest between an irrigation district and two owners of farm land over the right to water in a draw extending through a part of the irrigation district. Defendants contend that aside from surface water runoff the water in the draw consists solely of waste and seepage water from its irrigation project and that they have a right to recapture these waters while still within the boundaries of the reclamation project. Plaintiffs contend that the waters are not solely waste and seepage waters but consist, in part at least, of water having a source other than the irrigation project.

The defendant Payette Oregon Slope Irrigation District was organized in 1912 to provide water for the irrigation of agricultural lands within its boundaries. In 1919 and 1922 plaintiffs predecessors obtained water right certificates for the limited use of water flowing along the draw. Defendants do not contest plaintiffs' claim to the water under these certificates. In 1937 the Owyhee Federal Reclamation Project was extended to the Owyhee District and the additional water used on the project began to create a drainage problem in the draw. A drain was constructed in 1938 to alleviate the problem. After the construction of the drain plaintiffs took water from that structure for irrigation purposes.

In early 1956 the project undertook construction of a ditch to recover for re-use in the district some of the waste water flowing in the draw. Later in 1956 plaintiffs filed application for and received permits from the Oregon State Engineer for the irrigation of lands in addition to those covered by the 1919 and 1922 certificates. After issuance of the permits the plaintiffs opened the diversion ditch to allow the water to flow to their land. Defendants rebuilt the ditch and plaintiffs brought suit to enjoin the diversion of the water.

* * * The question is, then, whether defendants' right to the waters flowing in the draw were subsequent or prior to the rights of plaintiffs. If, as contended by plaintiffs, the waste and seepage waters from defendants' irrigation project join with the waters of a natural stream flowing in the draw, then defendants would lose their right to recapture such waste and seepage waters. Under such circumstances all of the water in the stream would be subject to appropriation. * * * If, however, the waters in the draw have their source solely in the waste and seepage waters and the occasional surface water runoff, then defendants would be entitled to recapture the water before it left the lands of the district.

The evidence is conflicting as to whether the waters flowing in the draw had their source solely from waste, seepage and surface runoff or from other sources sufficient to characterize the watercourse as a stream. Examining the record de novo, as we must, we are of the opinion that the evidence supports defendants' contention that a natural stream has never existed in the unnamed draw in question.

The only question remaining is whether the facts bring the instant case within the principle that an owner may recapture waste and seepage water before it leaves his land.[a] An irrigation district, being a municipal corporate entity, is regarded as an owner for the purpose of applying this principle. Therefore, if the waste and seepage water is recaptured for re-use within the boundaries of the district, those who have previously used such waters have no cause of action for having been deprived of the water. This is made clear in Stevens v. Oakdale Irr. Dist., 13 Cal.2d 343, 90 P.2d 58 (1939). In that case the plaintiffs brought suit to restrain an irrigation district from recapturing waste and seepage water and preventing its escape down a natural channel to plaintiffs' land. It was held that one who diverts water from a stream is entitled to exclusive control of that water, including the wastage incident to irrigation so long as he uses it for beneficial purposes. It was further held that in the process of controlling appropriated water a natural channel may be used as a temporary conduit and the water subsequently recaptured so long as the recapture is effected before the water leaves the owner's land or that of the irrigation district. In reaching this conclusion the court reasoned that a property right in water once used ceases when possession of the corpus of the specific

a. It has been recognized in Oregon that an appropriator is justified in recapturing waste water remaining on his own land (see Barker et al. v. Sonner et al., 135 Or. 75, 79, 294 P. 1053 (1930)). When such water leaves the irrigation district land or the control of the owner of the land and returns to the stream it is recognized as free, unappropriated water and a part of the stream flow. (See Jones v. Warmsprings Irrigation District, 162 Or. 186, 198, 91 P.2d 542 (1939)).

water is lost or abandoned. But, it was pointed out, this loss or abandonment of the corpus of specific water does not constitute a loss or abandonment of the water right itself, and although other parties may properly use water which has been lost or abandoned, they are not entitled to compel a similar abandonment in the future.

In the case at bar the waste and seepage water was recaptured within the defendant irrigation district.[b] We regard it as immaterial that a part of the waste and seepage may have had its source in one of the other irrigation districts in the Owyhee Federal Reclamation Project. For the purpose of applying the principle that an owner may recapture waste and seepage water, the project may be treated as an entity.

The decree of the lower court is reversed.

Notes

1. How can the rule of this case be reconciled with Farmers Highline v. Golden, supra p. 197?

Comstock v. Ramsey, 155 Colo. 244, 133 P. 1107 (1913) is the leading case holding that return flow seeping from the lands of a prior appropriator cannot be intercepted and reused *on different lands* when the water is tributary to the stream and junior appropriators have relied on it to serve their ditches downstream from the point of reentry. The same rule relied on in *Farmers Highline,* that junior appropriators are entitled to have conditions on the stream maintained as they were when the junior appropriations were made, was relied on in *Comstock.*

2. What is the touchstone for determining the right of the original appropriator to recapture waste water and reuse it for the original purpose? In Binning v. Miller, 55 Wyo. 451, 102 P.2d 54 (1940), the right to recapture waste water still on the original land and to reuse it on that land was apparently regarded as existing indefinitely, without time limit. In Lasson v. Seely, 120 Utah 679, 238 P.2d 418 (1951), the test was a physical one, whether the waste water has reentered a natural stream so that the first appropriator has lost control of it or whether he intercepted it before its return. In Jones v. Warmsprings Irrigation Dist., 162 Or. 186, 91 P.2d 542 (1939), intent was stressed. It was held that the intent to recapture must exist at the time the water is appropriated, and that the water is abandoned to downstream users if that intent is not exercised within a reasonable time. In U.S. v. Haga, 276 F. 41 (D.Idaho, 1921), the principal requisite was that the first appropriator be able to identify the recaptured water as that added by his operations.

b. The respondents rely upon * * * Jones v. Warmsprings Irrigation District, 162 Or. 186, 91 P.2d 542 (1939). * * * In the Warmsprings case irrigation water was allowed to drain through the soil and return to the river without measurement. It was held that water which so returned to the stream flow was subject to appropriation by others. In the case at bar the waste and seepage water is recaptured before it reaches a stream.

FUSS v. FRANKS

Supreme Court of Wyoming, 1980.
610 P.2d 17.

ROSE, JUSTICE.

[Waste-water from the plaintiffs' lands collected in a drainage ditch built by the Goshen County Irrigation District (G.I.D.) in the borrow pit of a "ditch-rider" road, which ran along the lower end of the plaintiffs' lands. The water was carried by the drainage ditch to the borrow pit of a state highway where it flowed for some distance, eventually crossing the highway in an underground pipe constructed by G.I.D. After the water crossed the highway, one of the plaintiffs, Fuss, had for many years used it to irrigate a piece of land. Fuss held no appropriation to use the water on this piece of land. The defendant, Frank, received an appropriation permit to construct a dam in the highway borrow pit to intercept the water and use it as a supplemental supply for his lands.]

* * *

We will address these following issues, which we find to be dispositive of all material questions raised by the appellants:

* * *

Point 1: Was the water from the highway borrow pit lawfully appropriated by Franks?

Whether or not Franks' appropriation was lawful is resolved by answering whether or not the State Engineer had authority to approve the Franks permit in July of 1979.

In this case, there was testimony that the seepage water in contest here would, if uninterrupted, flow into a natural stream. This is a qualifying requirement for appropriation. Binning v. Miller, 55 Wyo. 451, 102 P.2d 54 (1940).

In *Binning* we said:

> "* * * And so it is held in a number of cases that seepage water which, if not intercepted, would naturally reach the stream, is just as much a part of the stream as the waters of any tributaries and must be permitted to return thereto, if the owner cannot make beneficial use thereof. Rock Creek Ditch Co. v. Miller, 93 Mont. 248, 17 P.2d 1074, and note thereto in 89 A.L.R. 218–227; 67 C.J. 1006, 1015. That would seem to be the more reasonable rule in irrigating states. * * *" 102 P.2d at 61.

This concept was reaffirmed in Bower v. Big Horn Canal Association, 77 Wyo. 80, 307 P.2d 593 (1957).

The permit having been issued to Franks, this constituted prima facie evidence of his right to take the water. Hunziker v. Knowlton, 78 Wyo. 241, 322 P.2d 141 (1958). This being so, it fell to appellants to allege facts sufficient to show that they had a right to the water superior to that of Franks, the permittee. *Binning,* supra.

Appellants say in their brief:

"* * * The appropriator who captures upon his land waters not fully used for irrigation, sometimes referred to as waste water, may recapture the water for beneficial *use upon his premises for which the water had been appropriated.* * * *" (Emphasis supplied.)

That is a correct statement of law. It cannot, however, inure to the favor of appellants under the facts of this case.

We commented upon *Binning,* supra, where the facts were uniquely similar to those to be found here, when, in *Bower,* supra, we said:

"* * * The real question in the case [*Binning*] was whether the prior appropriation of what was termed in the original application as 'waste and seepage water' was good as against the owner of the land *from which said water came.* The court held that the seepage water which formed a natural stream might be appropriated, subject to the right of the land owner to use the water for beneficial purposes *upon the land for which the water forming the seepage was originally appropriated.*" (Emphasis and bracketed matter supplied.) 307 P.2d at 600.

This language means that the owner of land upon which seepage or waste water rises has the right to use and reuse—capture and recapture—such waste waters for use only "upon the land for which the water forming the seepage was originally appropriated." When the water leaves the land for which it was appropriated and would, if left to flow uninterrupted, reach a natural stream, it becomes eligible to other and separate appropriation for other and different uses. It leaves the landowner upon which the seepage rose, and from which it has escaped, without any superior right to such water by reason of its having been utilized upon the land to which it was first appropriated.

We recognized this concept in *Bower,* supra, when we said:

"* * * Additionally, it is equitable, in accordance with the constitutional provisions of this State, and in line with our previous holdings, that we here decree seepage water arising on Bower's land to be subject *to appropriation* by him (subject to prescribed procedures) for lands *other than those upon which the seepage arises.* * * *" (Emphasis supplied.) 307 P.2d at 602.

The "prescribed procedures" referred to are the application requirements for a water permit under the statutes. The rationale for this rule finds its genesis in the doctrine long since established in this state to the effect that waters become appurtenant to the lands for which they are acquired and, unless the statutes are followed with respect to change of use, the waters cannot be detached and assigned to other land without the loss of priority. Scherck v. Nichols, 55 Wyo. 4, 95 P.2d 74 (1939).

The water which accumulates in the collection ditch separating the Franks land from Bremers, Fusses and Baumgartner in Section 5, and which thereafter runs into the highway right-of-way originates on the land of the last three mentioned owners and is adjudicated in the name of the individual landowners for use upon their particular land tracts. This fact statement is undisputed. Therefore, once the water escapes the aforementioned Bremers, Fusses and Baumgartner lands in Section 5 and finds its way to the collection ditch and thence to the highway right-of-way, it must be regarded as having escaped the land to which it is appropriated and, since it would, if undisturbed, have flowed to a natural stream, it, therefore, becomes eligible for other appropriation. *Binning,* supra; and *Bower,* supra.

Franks' permit was valid because the Fusses, Bremers and Baumgartner had no superior right to the water after it left their properties to accumulate in the collection ditch and from there flow to the highway right-of-way borrow pit.

* * *

Affirmed in part, reversed in part, and remanded.

Notes

1. A Californian found a method of compelling the continuance of the source of the water. What kind of a right did the servient owner have in Krieger v. Pacific Gas & Electric Co., 119 Cal.App.3d 137, 173 Cal.Rptr. 751 (1981)? The Utica Ditch originally crossed public land that was later patented to Krieger's predecessor. By federal statute the patented land was subject to a right of way for the ditch. When PG & E acquired the water right it began to "gunite" the ditch, line it with sprayed liquid concrete. Krieger sought an injunction. PG & E cross-complained against Krieger's siphoning water from the ditch with a hose. The court held that the original earthen ditch "fixed the extent of the servitude," and enjoined further guniting as an enlargement of the easement, not within the "secondary easement" to make repairs. The "riparian vegetation" subsisting on the leakage was a benefit enjoyed by the landowner, said the court, and its loss would be an increase in the burden of the easement. No waste was involved, in the court's mind, the seepage was said to be beneficial to the riparian vegetation. Although the injunction against the siphon was held appropriate, the final declaration of the rights of the parties was, "The water flowing in the ditch is the property of PG & E, and [Krieger] has no right to that water; however, water which percolates, leaks or seeps through the ditch to [Krieger's] property thereby becomes his property."

2. "Waste water" or "tail water," surface return flow from irrigation, is a common phenomenon in irrigated country. Common law or civil law rules of drainage of natural surface waters do not apply to waters artificially brought upon the land. The owner of the upper irrigated land must acquire from the owner of the lower land permission or an easement to drain the waste water across the land. Loosli v. Heseman, 66 Idaho 469, 162 P.2d 393 (1945). The upper owner may, however, discharge into a water course on the lower land such reasonable quantities of excess waters as can be carried away without injury to the lower lands. Provident Irrigation District v. Cecil, 126 Cal.App.2d 13, 271 P.2d 157 (1954). It has been said that every irrigation project eventually becomes a drainage

project. Ditches for the collection of waste water and its redistribution to other users, and for the drainage of what would otherwise become seeped and boggy lands, are commonly constructed as part of modern projects, or as additions to older projects, by drainage districts or by the irrigation district that distributes the water.

THAYER v. CITY OF RAWLINS

Supreme Court of Wyoming, 1979.
594 P.2d 951.

ROSE, JUSTICE.

This appeal concerns the rights of the defendant water users to effluent water discharge by the City of Rawlins. By virtue of water rights dating from 1900, the City of Rawlins has imported all of its municipal water supplies from the North Platte River and from Sage Creek, a tributary of the North Platte River. After using the water for municipal purposes, the City has historically discharged the resulting effluent into a channel, known as Sugar Creek, which connects with the North Platte River. In the past, the point of this discharge was above the points at which the defendants diverted the effluent for irrigation, stock water and other purposes. Defendants diverted the effluent pursuant to certificates of appropriations giving them priorities to the Sugar Creek effluent dating from 1914. To be in compliance with state and federal water-quality laws, the City must now meet certain minimum-quality standards before discharging water into Sugar Creek. To meet these standards, the City of Rawlins proposes to establish an aerated lagoon system at a location which will cause the purified water to reach Sugar Creek at a point below the defendants' point of diversion. In an effort to determine the legal effect of this proposal, the City sought and was granted a judgment declaring that the defendants were not entitled to compensation for the loss of this water. We will affirm the district court's judgment.

Certain aspects of this case justify a full and detailed explanation of the facts. According to an Agreed Statement of Facts, the City acquired water rights, in 1923, to water originating at the head waters of Sage Creek, a tributary of the North Platte River. Thereafter, water wells—previously providing the City with water—were abandoned, and the City became totally dependent on the Sage Creek-North Platte water. This water, which is piped some 32 miles to the City, was supplemented by additional water rights obtained in 1966. The remainder of the water supplied to the City is by virtue of a water right obtained by assignment from the Union Pacific Water Company in 1904. This water is transported some 16 miles from the North Platte River to the City through another pipeline.

It is agreed that Sugar Creek consists of a channel which heads some 16 miles west of Rawlins. The channel parallels the south side of the Union Pacific Railroad from a point west of the City to a point about 4 miles east of Rawlins, where it bends north across the railroad and meanders northeasterly, eventually emptying into the Platte River. Originally, the channel of Sugar Creek was used as an open sewer for parts of Rawlins. Subsequently, sanitary sewer mains were installed and the sewage was carried to a point east of Rawlins where it was again disgorged into the Sugar Creek channel. Since the City began disgorging its waste waters into Sugar Creek, the defendants perfected certificates of appropriations, claiming the right to use water out of Sugar Creek at points below where the City disgorges its sewage.

Evidence adduced at trial indicates that whatever flow of water occurred in Sugar Creek below the City was attributable to the City's discharge of sewage. From April to October of each year, this discharge would amount to a daily average of 2.76 cubic-feet-per-second of water. Above the City, a flow occurred in Sugar Creek only after a rainstorm or during snow-melt. The City's expert classified Sugar Creek above the City as an ephemeral stream, or one that runs only in direct response to rainfall and high snow-melt events and not as a result of ground-water flow. In the 1930's, a diversion dam was constructed—apparently without approval of State authorities—which directs this flow into an area known as Hogback Lake. At trial, the City stipulated that it would not object to actions taken to prevent this flow from entering Hogback Lake or to the restoration of the natural channel of Sugar Creek for this purpose.

Subject to the above-mentioned stipulations, the district court found that Sugar Creek was not a natural stream and, therefore, the defendants' appropriations were invalid and did not entitle them to compensation by reason of the City's proposed actions. The court found that the City had the power to recapture all of its future sewage for the purpose of disposing of it in any manner it deemed appropriate. Finally, the court found that the State Engineer had no jurisdiction over the Rawlins facilities or the water in question, and that his approval was not required for the planned changes.

Defendants state their position as follows:

> "I. The State Engineer and State Board of Control have jurisdiction over the proposed Rawlins facilities and waters of Sugar Creek which must be invoked before judicial determination is proper.
>
> "II. Defendants have vested property rights that are established in Wyoming water law and are entitled to compensation before those water rights are taken away."

Entitlement to Compensation

Defendants premise their claim to compensation on the belief that Sugar Creek below the City of Rawlins has, due to the passage of a long period of time, become a natural stream subject to appropriation, thus entitling the defendants to protections afforded to other holders of water rights in the state.

Defendants also assert that Sugar Creek *above* the City is a natural stream. Frankly, we fail to see the importance of classifying the portion of Sugar Creek that lies above Rawlins. The extent to which the defendants have a right or interest in this upper flow of water is not at issue in this case. To the extent that they have a right to such waters—a question we do not here decide—the City has agreed not to interfere with a restoration of the natural channel of this portion of Sugar Creek. The importance of classifying Sugar Creek above the City is further lessened when it is realized that the water, for which defendants seek compensation, is derived solely from discharges that have their source in the North Platte River and tributaries thereof. These waters are entirely distinct from those, if any, originating in the Sugar Creek drainage basin above the City of Rawlins.

While it is true that these defendants have acquired certificates of appropriations, indicating a right to waters contained in Sugar Creek, we find that the validity of these permits—for purposes of protection from the City's proposed actions, and compensation—turns on an analysis of the parties' relative rights to the use of these imported waters. If the City, insofar as these defendants are concerned, has the unrestricted right to change its use and the point of discharge of these imported waters, then it matters little that these defendants hold water permits or have relied on these waters in the past for irrigation and other purposes. The issue of whether Sugar Creek has become a natural stream loses its importance in this context. If the City has the unrestricted right referred to above, then—with the possible exception of its relationship to certain jurisdictional matters—the determination of whether Sugar Creek below the City is a natural stream would be a resolution of a nonissue.

More than fifty years ago, this court stated, in Wyoming Hereford Ranch v. Hammond Packing Co., 33 Wyo. 14, 236 P. 764, 772 (1925):

> "* * * Even in this state, where the conservation of water for irrigation is so important, we would not care to hold that in disposing of sewage the city could not adopt some means that would completely consume it. It might, we think, be diverted to waste places, or to any chosen place where it would not become a nuisance, without any consideration of the demands of water users who might be benefited by its disposition in some other manner. * * *"

While we may not rely on the Wyoming Hereford Ranch decision for a disposition of the present case—due to significant factual distinctions—it is somewhat prophetic with respect to the clash, between concepts of western water law and the directives of environmental-protection statutes, now before us. We will not, however, attempt to decide all of the potential questions that are bound to arise as the demands for cleaner environment begin to impinge on the availability of sufficient supplies of water. For example, we are not asked in this case to theorize with respect to the rights of water users on the North Platte River in the event that the City had gone ahead with its original plan to entirely consume, through treatment, the waters it imports from the North Platte and its tributaries. These questions and others related thereto are bound to arise, but it is important to understand that they are not now before the court. See, gen., Comment, "Water Law—Cessation of Return Flow as a Means of Complying With Pollution Control Laws," 12 Land & Water L.Rev. 431 (1977); and Muys, "Quality v. Quantity: The Federal Water Pollution Control Act's Quiet Revolution in Western Water Rights Administration," 23 Rocky Mt.Min.L.Inst. 1013 (1977). As a result, our discussion and disposition of this case will be narrowly drawn.

The fundamental question becomes: Do the defendants have a right to compensation for a loss occasioned by the City's change in the point of discharge of imported waters? It has been stated that generally junior appropriators have vested rights in a continuation of stream conditions existing at the time of their appropriations, thus entitling them to resist changes in points of diversion or use which materially affect their rights. See, Farmers Highline Canal & Reservoir Co. v. Golden, 129 Colo. 575, 272 P.2d 629 (1954); and § 4–3–104, W.S.1977. However, an importer of water—at least insofar as these defendants are concerned—has the right to reuse, successively use and make disposition of imported waters. See, City and County of Denver Bd. of Water Commissioners v. Fulton Irrigating Ditch Co., Colo., 179 Colo. 47, 506 P.2d 144 (1972). Even though, at the time of the Fulton Irrigation Ditch decision, there was a statute authorizing the conclusion reached, the Colorado Supreme Court opined that the rule would be the same without the statute, subject to contrary contractual obligations. 506 P.2d at 147.

The right of the City to use such imported waters finds its roots in the common law of property and the Puritan ethic: One who by his own effort adds to the supply of a stream, is entitled to the water even though a senior priority might be without water. A person should reap the benefit of his own efforts, and a priority relates only to the *natural* supply of the stream at the time of appropriation. Clark, "Background and Trends in Water Salvage Law," 15 Rocky Mt.Min.L.Inst. 421, 434–444 (1969).

These concepts are not new to Wyoming water law, since they have been applied to protect the right of a senior appropriator to recapture waste and seepage water. See, Binning v. Miller, 55 Wyo. 451, 102 P.2d 54 (1940); and Bower v. Big Horn Canal Ass'n, 77 Wyo. 80, 307 P.2d 593 (1957). See gen., Clark, supra, at 459–460; Burkart v. Meiberg, 37 Colo. 187, 86 P. 98 (1906); Green Valley Ditch Co. v. Schneider, 50 Colo. 606, 115 P. 705 (1911); and Tongue Creek Orchard Co. v. Town of Orchard City, 131 Colo. 177, 280 P.2d 426 (1955). The lower landowner using such water merely takes his chances as to future supplies, no matter how long he uses such water. Binning v. Miller, supra, 102 P.2d at 60.

Defendants seem to want this court to declare that the City has abandoned its right to make a change in the point of discharge of these imported waters. We indicated in Binning v. Miller, supra, that if the senior appropriator had allowed the lower landowner to use waste water for 35 years, but then legitimately began to use it himself, the lower landowner would have no right to complain—"The water is always different from year to year." 102 P.2d at 62. See, also, Stevens v. Oakdale Irrigation Dist., 13 Cal.2d 343, 90 P.2d 58 (1939). This question, in its broad sense, was raised but not answered in the Fulton Irrigation Ditch case, supra. See, gen., Williams, "Optimizing Water Uses: The Return Flow Issue," 44 U.Colo.L.Rev. 301, 318–321 (1973). We hold that in the imported-water context—which gives the importer the unrestricted right to reuse, successively use and make disposition—the importer's right to do these things is not subject to abandonment insofar as these defendants are concerned. It must be remembered that any other holding would be inconsistent with the fact that the defendants depend entirely on the City's sufferance—it is always free to terminate the importation. Under such circumstances, we are reluctant to declare an abandonment. * * *

JURISDICTION

Defendants assert that the State Engineer and the State Board of Control have authority to resolve their conflict with the City under Article 8, Wyoming Constitution, and three sets of statutory provisions: (1) Section 41–3–104, W.S.1977, dealing with changes of use or places of use; (2) section 41–3–305, W.S.1977, dealing with the storage of direct-flow water rights; and (3) section 41–3–615, W.S.1977, dealing with the construction of diversion dams. * * *

We turn, then, to the statutory provisions which purportedly vest the State Engineer or Board of Control with primary jurisdiction over the City's proposed actions. Defendants claim that the City's water-treatment proposal constitutes either a change or expansion in use—because the water will be used as a purifying agent, instead of only as a flushing agent—or a change in the place of use, because the sewage will be transported for treatment to a place outside the city limits. The City, on the other hand, contends that there will be no change in use since the use will still be for municipal purposes, and that the place of use will remain with the City of Rawlins. The only change, according to the City, is a change in the place of discharge.

The difficulty in attempting to classify the changes required by water-pollution-control laws has been noted. Comment, supra, 12 Land & Water L.Rev. 431, 448. The Colorado Supreme Court has indicated that changes in points of discharge of sewage are not governed by the same rules as changes in points of diversion. Metropolitan Denver Sewage Disposal Dist. No. 1 v. Farmers Reservoir and Irrigation Co., 179 Colo. 36, 38, 499 P.2d 1190, 1193 (1972). See, City of Boulder v. Boulder & Left Hand Ditch Co., 557 P.2d 1182, 1185–1186 (1976). This conclusion has, in turn, been severely criticized. Williams, supra, at 304–311. We find no need, however, to put a label on what the City of Rawlins proposes to do, in order to determine whether the City must file a petition under § 41–3–104, supra.

The purpose of § 41–3–104, supra, is to provide a procedure for those wishing to change a water right *and* to place limitations on the quantity of water that can be transferred. Basin Electric Power Cooperative v. State Bd. of Control, 578 P.2d 557, 561 (Wyo.1978). We must ask why the City's proposal should be subjected to these procedures. The manifest result of a § 41–3–104 proceeding is the entry of a Board of Control order limiting the amount of water transferred by a change in use or a change in the place of use. Insofar as these defendants are concerned, we have already held that the City has the *unrestricted* right to reuse, successively use and make disposition of these imported waters. If these rights are not subject to restriction, it would be anomolous to require the City to submit to a procedure that assumes that restrictions are permissible and, indeed, required. As a result, we hold that the State Engineer and Board of Control have no jurisdiction, by virtue of § 41–3–104, supra, over the controversy between these parties. * * *

Affirmed for the reasons stated herein.

ROONEY, JUSTICE, dissenting, with whom RAPER, CHIEF JUSTICE joins.

I dissent. I agree with the contention of the defendants that this matter is prematurely in the courts, and that the board of control should first apply its expertise in passing on the issues. * * *

The necessary expertise and experience in water matters are with the board of control and the office of the state engineer. They are conversant with the new problems occasioned by increased industrial and municipal needs for water; additional use of water for recreational purposes; transbasin diversions; interstate aspects of water availability and control; intrusion into underground acquifers; diversions of underground streams; development of chemical and physical methods for control of initial flow, for control of return flow and for control of storage of water; pollution; and waste. And they are conversant with the interplay of these new problems on customary and historical use of water. * * *

All of Art. 8, Wyoming Constitution, has to do with irrigation and water rights. Section 3 of Art. 8, Wyoming Constitution, provides that "[p]riority of appropriation for beneficial uses shall give the better right." Portions of § 2 of Art. 8, Wyoming Constitution, are emphasized as follows:

> "There shall be constituted a board of control, to be composed of the state engineer and superintendents of the water divisions; which shall, under such regulations as may be prescribed by law, have the supervision of the waters of the state and of their *appropriation, distribution and diversion,* and of the various officers connected therewith. Its decisions to be *subject to review by the courts* of the state." (Emphasis supplied.)

Supervision of "distribution and diversion" includes supervision of water which is not appropriated, and it includes supervision of appropriated water at times and places other than those involved at the initial distribution or diversion. It includes supervision of individual appropriations, of trans-basin appropriations, of trans-state deliveries, of underground water—in short, of all water. Sussex Land & Live Stock Co. v. Midwest Refining Co., 8th Cir.1923, 294 F. 597, 603, on appeal from U.S.D.C., Wyoming, has been said to stand for the proposition that, pursuant to §§ 1 and 3 of Art. 8 of the Wyoming Constitution, a priority of right in water includes the quality as well as the quantity. Quality is a proper concern of the board of control. In the Wyoming Environmental Quality Act, § 35–11–101 et seq., W.S.1977 the legislature was careful to preserve the preeminence of the jurisdiction of the state engineer and the board of control in water matters by providing:

> "Nothing in this act:
>
> * * *
>
> "(c) Limits or interferes with the jurisdiction, duties or authority of the state engineer, the state board of control, * * *." Sec. 35–11–1104, W.S.1977.

The majority opinion overlooks this primary jurisdiction and the extensive control of quantity and quality of water in the board of control for the purpose of securing beneficial use of it. The majority opinion lays its cornerstone on the proposition that an importer of water has the unobstructed right to reuse, successively use and make disposition of imported waters. The importer, then, would have supervision over the appropriation, distribution and diversion of such water. Imported water is no less precious than any other kind of water. The mere fact that it is transported from one basin to another does not make it more subject to waste, more subject to the whims of any private citizen, less subject to the requirement of beneficial use, or less subject to the constitutional supervision of the board of control. If there is case law to the contrary, I would reverse it. If there is statutory law to the contrary, I would hold such to be unconstitutional. * * *

The majority opinion has here invalidated certificates of appropriation issued by the board of control—and this is done in a proceeding which is collateral to the proceeding in which the appropriations were granted. * * *

This case had its origin in a very worthy direction to the City of Rawlins to clean up its discarded water. To do so will cost money. It would be incongruous, in view of the value of water in Wyoming, to not also direct the city to preserve the water as it cleans it—preserve it for additional beneficial use. This may cost more money. Cleaning water is no more worthy than preserving it. The board of control should determine the relation of beneficial use to other aspects of the project. The board may authorize the project as now planned. It may direct pumping to the original place of discharge. It may direct a different method of cleaning. It may require payment of just compensation to the damaged appropriators. It may require change in reservoir construction to provide for a deeper but less extensive body of water so as to reduce evaporation. It may reach the same conclusion as did the district court. * * *

I would reverse and remand with directions that the plaintiff be ordered to submit the plans for the project to the state engineer for review and approval.

Notes

1. Compare Pulaski Irrigating Ditch Co. v. Trinidad, 70 Colo. 565, 203 P. 681 (1922). The municipal supply for the City of Trinidad was taken from the Las Animas River. After use, the water was deposited as raw sewage into settling pits, from which it seeped back into the river. When the city built a treatment plant, it proposed to sell the purified water to the owners of the Model Ditch. Senior appropriators downstream protested.

"It is elementary that the waters of the public streams of this state belong to the people, and that appropriators acquire only a right of use. It is also settled law that an appropriator is limited in his use of water to his actual needs. He must not waste it, and if there is a surplus remaining after use it must be returned to the stream whence it came. * * *

"The use of water in cities by which it is contaminated is principally as a vehicle for carrying away noxious matter; and when that duty has been discharged and the city, under its obligations to prevent the sewage becoming obnoxious, has withdrawn the solid matter from the water, the water should be returned to the stream. It has performed the service required of it as truly as has water which has passed over a millwheel. * * *

"It is said, however, that the city might have disposed of the sewage by evaporating the water from it, from which it is argued that it had a right to destroy the water; hence it could not belong to the public.

"It would seem that, according to the established public policy of this state, this right to destroy the water by evaporation can exist only when there is no other practicable method of disposing of the sewage; that is to say, if all other methods were very expensive as compared with the cost of evaporation, public policy might, in the interest of the community producing sewage, permit its disposal by the evaporation of the water. That case, however, is not before us. We are dealing with water which the city is voluntarily purifying.

"To turn this water back into the river will not increase the river's flow above what it would have been had the water not been diverted, and it is not therefore developed water. Applying the principle heretofore laid down, it seems clear that the water here in question does not belong to the city, and that it has no right to sell it."

Another important point is that the stream in question was discovered in 1594 by a small detachment of Spanish explorers who were killed there by Indians. When their bodies were found on its banks by the main party, the river was named El Rio de Las Animas Perdidas, since they had died unshriven. Later, French trappers with a gentler theology decided their souls were not hopelessly lost and renamed the stream the Purgatoire. Still later the cowboys found this hard to get their tongues around and the river became the Picketwire. The Spanish, French and American versions can all be found in modern use. On the Western Slope of Colorado the reverse occurred, and a "Frenchified" spelling was given to the stream the cowboys had already named Piceance Creek.

2. "Land treatment" of sewage has assumed considerable modern importance in light of the "no discharge policy" which is now the national goal for preserving the purity of streams, Federal Water Pollution Control Amendments of 1972, 33 U.S.C.A. § 1251(a)(1). See Note—Cessation of Return Flow as a Means of Complying with Pollution Control Laws, XII Land & Water L.Rev. 431 (1977).

3. The City of Los Angeles brings water from the Owens River Valley to the San Fernando Valley where it spreads part of it in gravel pits and spreading grounds with the object of having it sink beneath the surface to join other water in the gravels of the valley floor. It sells other parts of it to farmers of the San Fernando Valley, 27½% of which also sinks beneath the surface. Both the induced recharge and the return flows join waters normally present in the valley and eventually become part of the surface flow of the Los Angeles River, from which the city takes its water. The cities of Glendale and Burbank pump water from wells in the valley. Held, the city of Los Angeles has a prior right to both the recharge and the return flow. Los Angeles v. Glendale, 23 Cal.2d 68, 142 P.2d 289 (1943). The court, per Traynor, J., stated:

"Plaintiff had a prior right to the use of the water brought to the San Fernando Valley. It did not abandon that right when it spread the water for the purpose of economical transportation and storage. It used a similar storage system at the source of this supply in the Owens River Valley. By availing itself of these natural reservoirs, it spared its citizens the cost of financing the construction of additional dams, if, indeed, appropriate sites were available at the lower end of the aqueduct. Early in the history of the state, this court recognized the advantage of permitting the use of natural surface facilities, stream beds, dry canyons and the like, for the transportation of water (Hoffman v. Stone, 7 Cal. 46; Butte Canal & Ditch Co. v. Vaughn, 11 Cal. 143, 70 Am.Dec. 769) for 'It would be a harsh rule * * * to require those engaged in these enterprises to construct an actual ditch along the whole route through which the waters were carried, and to refuse them the economy that nature occasionally afforded in the shape of a dry ravine, gulch, or cañon." Hoffman v. Stone, 7 Cal. at page 49. The rule of these cases was incorporated into section 1413 of the Civil Code. In codifying this rule, designed to encourage the use of natural facilities, the Legislature could hardly have intended to abrogate the right to use other natural facilities for similar purposes. Under these circumstances, the maxim expressio unius alterius exclusio est is inapplicable. * * * It would be as harsh to compel plaintiff to build reservoirs when natural ones were available as to compel the construction of an artificial ditch beside a stream bed. In making water available for irrigation, plaintiff sought not only to increase cultivation of the land, but to convey some of the water into the underground reservoir of the valley. Thus, in selling water to the farmers, as in spreading water, plaintiff was interested in its economical transportation and storage.

"The use by others of this water as it flowed to the subterranean basin does not cut off plaintiff's rights. * * *

"It is immaterial whether the farmers who use the imported water acquire their rights through a transfer of land that includes a water right (United States v. Ide, supra) or by some other means. See Stevens v. Oakdale Irr. Dist., supra. In any event the importer brings the water to the land of the farmer, and the farmer uses it. Nothing would be gained by requiring plaintiff to change the form of its contracts from a 'sale' of the water to a transfer of the right to its use. In making water available, plaintiff selected an area where it could recover as much water as possible from seepage, and it should not be deprived of the benefit of its foresight."

4. In Jensen v. Department of Ecology, 102 Wn.2d 109, 685 P.2d 1068 (1984), the court held that imported irrigation water which percolates into an aquifer is "artificially stored ground water." As such, the court held the water is not subject to appropriation by another as public ground water. The court rejected the argument that the importer, the Bureau of Reclamation, had abandoned or forfeited the water, finding that the Bureau intended to recapture it from the inception of the irrigation project and had, in fact, utilized natural and artificial systems to control and channel it. The court also rejected the argument that the water had lost its identity as artificially stored ground water by being commingled with natural ground water.

5. In Nebraska v. Wyoming, 325 U.S. 589, 65 S.Ct. 1332, 89 L.Ed. 1815 (1945), the State of Nebraska alleged that the Bureau of Reclamation's Kendrick Project, under construction on the North Platte River in Wyoming, would injure appropriators downstream in Nebraska. The project would be supplied almost entirely by water stored in Seminoe Dam and diverted at Alcova Dam to the project lands in Wyoming. Return flows from the project were estimated to be 96,000 acre feet, 46,000 during the irrigation season. The Bureau did not wish to use the water below the point where it returned to the river, but could use it to enlarge the project. It therefore proposed to divert an amount equivalent to this return flow through the canal at Alcova "in lieu of" recapturing the actual return flow. The following quotation from U.S. v. Haga, 276 F. 41 (D.1921), quoted with approval in Ide v. U.S., 263 U.S. 497, 44 S.Ct. 182, 68 L.Ed. 407 (1924), was urged as authority for so doing.

"One who by the expenditure of money and labor diverts appropriable water from a stream, and thus makes it available for fruitful purposes, is entitled to its exclusive control so long as he is able and willing to apply it to beneficial uses, and such right extends to what is commonly known as wastage from surface run off and deep percolation, necessarily incident to practical irrigation. Considerations of both public policy and natural justice strongly support such a rule. Nor is it essential to his control that the appropriator maintain continuous actual possession of such water. So long as he does not abandon it or forfeit it by failure to use, he may assert his rights. It is not necessary that he confine it upon his own land or convey it in an artificial conduit. It is requisite, of course, that he be able to identify it; but, subject to that limitation, he may conduct it through natural channels and may even commingle it or suffer it to commingle with other waters. In short, the rights of an appropriator in these respects are not affected by the fact that the water has once been used."

The Court refused to permit the diversion. "But we think the proposal is basically not in accord with the principle underlying the Ide case. That principle is that although the water rights belong to the landowners, the owner of the irrigation project has an interest in the appropriative rights to the extent of obtaining the fullest use of the water for the project. It may therefore, retain control over the water until abandonment. We think it goes too far to say that when the return flows are abandoned, they may nevertheless be exchanged for upstream diversions by the same amount. When the return flows are abandoned, they become subject to appropriation downstream. See 2 Kinney, Irrigation and Water Rights (2d Ed.1912) § 1114. They no longer remain subject to control for further use in the project. Any claim to them or their equivalent under the form of an 'in lieu of' diversion is lost."

6. Employment of the right to sell newly-produced return flows is urged as a partial solution to the problem faced by a purchaser who must buy all of a former user's diversion yet will acquire only his consumptive use. The discrepancy between what the former user sells and what the new user gets may be 50%. If the purchaser can in turn sell his return flows, he can recoup this loss in part. See Hartman and Seastone, Efficiency Criteria for Market Transfers of Water, 1 Water Resources Research 165 (1965). The National Water Commission has joined in the suggestion, Water Policies for the Future 269 (1973).

Chapter 3

RIPARIAN RIGHTS

SECTION 1. BASIS OF RIGHT

ANAHEIM UNION WATER CO. v. FULLER

Supreme Court of California, 1907.
150 Cal. 327, 88 P. 978.

SHAW, J. This is an action to enjoin the defendants from diverting water from the Santa Ana river. Judgment in favor of the plaintiffs as prayed for was given in the court below. The defendants appeal from the judgment, and from an order denying their motion for a new trial.

The plaintiffs own lands through which the Santa Ana river flows. They have been accustomed for many years to irrigate this land with waters from the river, and for that purpose there is required, during the irrigating season, a continuous flow of 400 miners' inches of water. The defendants, or some of them, own land on the river, situated above the land of the plaintiffs, and upon it they had built a dam in the river and were thereby diverting water from the stream, which, by means of a ditch, they were conducting to other lands owned by them and were there using it for irrigation. The plaintiffs claim, and the court found, that the land which the defendants were thus irrigating with water from the river was not riparian thereto. * * *

Some distance below the land of the plaintiffs a tributary, known as "Chino creek," enters the Santa Ana river. Chino creek also has a tributary, known as "Mill creek," which enters Chino creek 1½ miles above the confluence of the latter with the Santa Ana river. The defendants take the water from the river, above the land of the plaintiffs, in a ditch which extends across the low bottom to the high land or bluff, and then extends along the bluff, at a grade less than that of the river, gradually getting further above and away from the river until it reaches and crosses the divide, or summit of the elevated land, between the watershed of the river and that of Mill creek. The court found that the land irrigated with water from this ditch lies beyond this divide, and is wholly within the watershed of Mill creek, and that it does not abut upon the stream of the Santa Ana, and is not riparian thereto. Land which is not within the watershed of the river is not riparian thereto, and is not entitled as riparian land, to the use or benefit of the water from the river, although it may be part of an entire tract which does extend to the river. * * *

The defendants claim that these findings are contrary to the evidence, and that this rule does not apply to the land they seek to irrigate, because, while it is wholly within the Mill creek watershed, it is also within the general watershed of the Santa Ana river, considered as an entirety including the valley from its sources to its mouth. This fact does not affect the case, at least so far as the land of the plaintiffs is concerned. The principal reasons for the rule confining riparian rights to that part of lands bordering on the stream which are within the watershed are that, where the water is used on such land, it will, after such use, return to the stream, so far as it is not consumed, and that, as the rainfall on such land feeds the stream, the land is in consequence entitled, so to speak, to the use of its waters. Where two streams unite, we think the correct rule to be applied, in regard to the riparian rights therein, is that each is to be considered as a separate stream, with regard to lands abutting thereon above the junction, and that land lying within the watershed of one stream above that point is not to be considered as riparian to the other stream. The fact that the streams are of different size, or that both lie in one general watershed, or drainage basin, should not affect the rule, nor should it be changed by the additional fact that the two watersheds are separated merely by the summit or crown of a comparatively low table land, or "mesa," as it is called in the evidence, and not by a sharp or well-defined ridge, range of hills, or mountains. The reasons for the rule are the same in either case. In some cases it may be difficult to distinguish the line of separation. This seems to have been a case of that sort. Nevertheless, we think there is evidence sufficient to support the finding of the court that there is a dividing line between the two watersheds, and that the land irrigated by defendants lies upon the slope which descends into Mill creek. It is not necessary to discuss this evidence in detail.

The evidence also supports the finding that the land irrigated by the defendants does not abut upon, or extend to, the river. If the owner of a tract abutting on a stream conveys to another a part of the land not contiguous to the stream, he thereby cuts off the part so conveyed from all participation in the use of the stream and from riparian rights therein, unless the conveyance declares the contrary. Land thus conveyed and severed from the stream can never regain the riparian right, although it may thereafter be reconveyed to the person who owns the part abutting on the stream, so that the two tracts are again held in one ownership. * * * All the land belonging to the defendants, including the Smith tract, which was in part irrigated, was originally a part of the Jurupa rancho, which abutted upon the river. The original owner of that rancho subdivided it by arbitrary lines, corresponding to the government surveys, and sold and conveyed it in parcels according to that survey. Under the rule above stated the conveyance by him of a tract not contiguous to the stream would sever such tract from the riparian interest and deprive it of subsequent participation in the use of the water of the river, the right to which previously attached to the entire rancho. The tract which includes the irrigated land of the defendants is not at any point contiguous to the river. At the time the action was begun it was owned by the defendant Smith. He was not the owner of any adjoining land which lay contiguous to the river. After the action was begun he conveyed this land, to certain of the other defendants, some of whom owned adjoining lands extending from the Smith land to the river. This subsequent conveyance gave those defendants a continuous ownership of land extending from the river to and including the Smith land. This contiguous ownership, however, did not confer upon the Smith land the riparian rights of which it was deprived, when Smith, or his predecessors, obtained it by a conveyance which severed it from the portion of the Jurupa rancho abutting upon the river. * * *

It is further contended that the plaintiffs' land is in no wise damaged by the diversion complained of, and hence that the diversion cannot be enjoined. * * *

On this point the defendants cite several cases in which it is held that a lower riparian owner cannot enjoin a diversion by another riparian proprietor above, unless he can show that such diversion works damage to him, and that it is more than a just proportion of the water to which the upper owner is entitled. Such decisions are not applicable to this case. Riparian owners have correlative rights in the stream, and neither is a trespasser against the other until he diverts more than his share and injures and damages the other thereby. Here the defendants were not, with respect to the land irrigated, riparian owners, but were trespassers on plaintiffs' property rights from the beginning, and the continuance of the trespass for a sufficient time would divest the right of the plaintiffs with respect to the water diverted. * * *

The defendants urge that inasmuch as the plaintiffs need but 400 inches of water for their land, and there remained in the stream, after defendants' diversion, more than 2000 inches, which flows down to and beyond the plaintiffs' land, and which is more than they can possibly use thereon, that it therefore follows that no damage can ever ensue, even if the diversion is unlawful and should ripen into a prescriptive right by continuance; and hence that their diversion should not be enjoined. The theory of the law of riparian rights in this state is that the water of a stream belongs by a sort of common right to the several riparian owners along the stream; each being entitled to sever his share for use on his riparian land. The fact that a large quantity of water flows down the stream by and beyond the plaintiffs' land does not prove that it goes to waste, nor that the plaintiffs are entitled to take a part of it, as against other riparian owners or users below. Nor can it be said that plaintiffs, on account of the present abundance, could safely permit defendants to acquire, as against them, a right to a part of the water. The riparian right is not lost by disuse, and other riparian owners above may take or others below may be entitled to take, and may insist upon being allowed to take, all of the stream, excepting only sufficient for the plaintiffs' land. In either alternative, the taking of a part of the water by the defendants would not leave enough for the plaintiffs' use. There is nothing in this case to show how much water is required above and below by those having rights in the stream. In view of the well-known aridity of the climate, and the high state of cultivation in the vicinity, the court could almost take judicial notice that in years of ordinary rainfall there is no surplus of water in the stream over that used by the various owners under claim of right. But, however this may be, it is settled by the decisions above cited that a party, situated as the plaintiffs are, can enjoin an unlawful diversion, in order to protect and preserve his riparian right.

The findings support the judgment, and we are unable to perceive any substantial or material conflict in them. We find no error in the record.

The judgment and order are affirmed.

Notes

1. Accord, Yearsley v. Cater, 149 Wash. 285, 270 P. 804 (1928); Watkins Land Co. v. Clements, 98 Tex. 578, 86 S.W. 733 (1905). The "source of title" test of the extent of riparian lands was summarized in Boehmer v. Big Rock Creek Irrigation Dist., 117 Cal. 19, 48 P. 908 (1897), by saying that the riparian right extends only to the smallest tract held under one title in the chain of title leading to the present owner. Under this rule, the amount of riparian land is constantly diminishing.

2. In Crawford Co. v. Hathaway, 67 Neb. 325, 93 N.W. 781 (1903), the court suggested that since the government disposed of the public domain in 40 acre tracts, riparian rights should be limited to such subdivisions, but in computing damages for loss of riparian rights by condemnation, the court later decided that damage to entire sections (640 acres) should be considered. McGinley v. Platte Valley Public Power and Irrigation Dist., 132 Neb. 292, 271 N.W. 864 (1937).

3. A contrasting theory is that of "unity of title". In Jones v. Conn, 39 Or. 30, 64 P. 855 (1901), the court said, "It would seem, therefore, that any person owning land which abuts upon or through which a natural stream of water flows is a riparian proprietor, entitled to the rights of such, without regard to the extent of his land, or from whom or when he acquired his title. The fact that he may have procured the particular tract washed by the stream at one time, and subsequently purchased land adjoining it, will not make him any the less a riparian proprietor, nor should it alone be a valid objection to his using the water on the land last acquired. The only thing necessary to entitle him to the right of a riparian proprietor is to show that the body of land owned by him borders upon a

stream." This rule was approved in Clark v. Allaman, 71 Kan. 206, 80 P. 571 (1905), and is adopted by the American Law Institute in Restatement (Second) of Torts, § 843, Comment *c.* (1979).

4. It was once thought that land to be riparian had to include a part of the bed of the watercourse or border on public watercourse whose bed is in private ownership. Restatement, Torts, § 843 (1939). The Restatement (Second) of Torts § 843 (1979) now takes the position that ownership of the bed is immaterial.

Some powers and privileges relating to the stream and commonly denominated as riparian rights may require either ownership of the bed or public access to the water. These include the building of dams and probably the commercial cutting of ice. But cases prohibiting an adjacent land owner from performing these acts deal with trespasses on another's land and not directly with the rights of the contiguous owner to use the water if he can do so without trespass. The possibilities of such uses are many. A number of early California and Washington cases have held that there is a riparian right to the natural overflow of a stream which annually goes out of its banks. Lux v. Haggin, 69 Cal. 255, 10 P. 674 (1886); Still v. Palouse Irrigation & Power Co., 64 Wash. 606, 117 P. 466 (1911). There are many cases which hold that a riparian owner may go upstream on the land of another and with permission divert water to the riparian land. Rose v. Mesmer, 142 Cal. 332, 75 P. 905 (1904); Redwater Land & Canal Co. v. Reed, 27 S.D. 194, 130 N.W. 85 (1911). Where the bank is vertical it is possible for a contiguous owner who does not own the stream bed to cut a ditch in the bank and divert water without committing any trespass on the bed itself. A very recent case expressly holding that ownership of the bed is not a requisite is Bouris v. Sargent, 94 Ill.App.2d 251, 236 N.E.2d 15 (1968).

The rule requiring ownership of or public access to the bed was thought to be justified by several cases. One clearly supported the rule, Rockwell v. Baldwin, 53 Ill. 19 (1869). Several involved a trespass to the bed: Whittier v. Montpelier Ice Co., 90 Vt. 16, 96 A. 378 (1916); Jewell v. Gardner, 12 Mass. 310 (1815); Adams v. Barney, 25 Vt. 222 (1853); or the commercial cutting of ice, Allan v. Weber, 80 Wis. 531, 50 N.W. 514 (1891). One was based on the old rule that boating over another's land is a trespass. Kilgo v. Cook, 174 Ark. 432, 295 S.W. 355 (1927).

As to the status of the bed itself as riparian land, see the omitted portions of the opinion in *Anaheim* (bottom lands, apparently sometimes overflowed). A statute granting riparian owners bordering on tidal waters the sole right of planting and gathering oysters in front of their lands for 500 yards to seaward gives rights which are protected from private infringement, though subject to superior rights of the public and the state. Cleary v. State Highway Comm., 219 Miss. 284, 68 So.2d 468 (1953). There are no cases dealing directly with the status as riparian proprietors of persons who have rights to tidelands affected by river water, but who own no uplands. However, such a status may be inferred from Grant v. United States, 192 F.2d 482 (4th Cir.1951), which held that a person holding a lease from the state for cultivation of oysters on lands beneath tidal waters may complain of stream pollution which destroys the beds.

"The right of a riparian owner to the use of water bordering upon his land does not, as plaintiffs contend, arise from the fact that the water is flowing, and that any part thereof taken from the stream is immediately replaced by water from the current above it. It comes from the situation of the land with respect to the water, the opportunity afforded thereby to divert and use the water upon the land, the natural advantages and benefits resulting from the relative positions, and the presumption that the owner of the land acquired it with a view to the use and enjoyment of these opportunities, advantages, and benefits." Turner v. James Canal Co., 155 Cal. 82, 99 P. 520 (1909).

6. Riparian rights have been described as part and parcel of the land itself, corporeal hereditaments, incorporeal hereditaments, easements, appurtenances and as tenancies in common in the stream. What are the characteristics of these species of property? What is the value of approaching a problem concerning riparian rights in this manner? See Bennett, Some Uncertainties in the Law of Water Rights, 21 So.Cal.L.R. 344 (1948); Bennett, Some Fundamentals of Legal Interests in Water Supplies, 22 So. Cal.L.R. 1 (1948).

In Stewart v. Bridges, 249 Ga. 626, 292 S.E.2d 702 (1982), one lakeshore proprietor sued another to enjoin use of the water for irrigation. It was held error for the trial court to instruct the jury (1) that the parties had a tenancy in common in the water of the lake and the defendant irrigator therefore had no superior right to use the water to the exclusion of the plaintiff, and (2) that the plaintiff, as the owner of the part of the lake bed, was entitled to possession and control of the water vertically above his land, and hence to "lateral support" for that water.

7. Under the majority rule, a city lying on a river bank or fronting a lake is not regarded as a riparian proprietor with a riparian right to take water for public water supply, Emporia v. Soden, 25 Kan. 588 (1881), Town of Purcellville v. Potts, 179 Va. 514, 19 S.E.2d 700 (1942); contra, Canton v. Shock, 66 Ohio St. 19, 63 N.E. 600 (1902).

The water rights of cities, public utilities, and public agencies furnishing domestic and municipal water supply in "riparian rights states" that follow the majority rule are examined infra, pp. 332 to 342. In several cases cities have been treated, without discussion and perhaps inadvertently, as if they were riparian proprietors. See, for example, Sayles v. Mitchell, 60 S.D. 592, 245 N.W. 390 (1932).

THOMPSON v. ENZ

Supreme Court of Michigan, 1967.
379 Mich. 667, 154 N.W.2d 473.

KAVANAGH, JUSTICE. Plaintiffs filed a complaint in the Barry county circuit court against defendants claiming violation of their rights as riparian owners on Gun Lake and seeking a declaratory judgment to that effect. Both parties moved for summary judgment. Plaintiffs were granted the relief requested.

Defendants appealed to the Court of Appeals, which reversed the judgment of the trial court and directed that summary judgment be entered for defendants.

Leave to appeal to this Court was granted.

This case concerns certain property rights in and around Gun Lake, which is situated partly in Barry county and partly in Allegan county. The parties agree that this lake has approximately 2,680 acres of surface area and approximately 30 miles of shore line.

The defendant corporation is a contract purchaser of a riparian parcel of land having approximately 1,415 feet of frontage on said lake, and the individual defendants are the sole stockholders of the corporation.

Plaintiffs are riparian owners of other property abutting Gun Lake.

The State of Michigan sought and was granted permission in the trial court to file a brief amicus curiae. The State is a riparian owner of a large parcel of land abutting the lake.

Defendants are in the process of developing and subdividing their parcel of land into from 144 to 153 lots. Of these lots, approximately 16 will abut on the natural shore line of the lake. The remainder of the lots will front on canals. To give the back lot purchasers access to the lake the defendants' plan calls for excavating across riparian lots Nos 13 and 76. (See plat.) The defendants purport to grant to the purchasers of those lots fronting on the canals riparian rights to the lake and rights of access through the excavation to the lake. The back lots would have frontage on the canals of approximately 11,000 feet.

The following questions are raised on appeal:

1. May a right of access to Gun Lake be created by dredging an artificial canal from the lake through lots having frontage on Gun Lake to back lots having no frontage thereon, and may ownership of such lots carry with it riparian rights? * * *

"Riparian land" is defined as a parcel of land which includes therein a part of or is bounded by a natural watercourse. 4 Restatement, Torts, § 843, p. 326. * * *

Artificial watercourses are waterways that owe their origin to acts of man, such as canals, drainage and irrigation ditches, aqueducts, flumes, and the like. 4 Restatement, Torts, § 841, subd. h., p. 321.

Land abutting on an artificial watercourse has no riparian rights. * * *

We, therefore, conclude that parcels of land to be subdivided from the main tract of land bordering on Gun Lake have no riparian rights as: (1) they neither include therein a part of nor are they bounded by Gun Lake, and (2) the canal itself would be an artificial watercourse giving rise to no riparian rights.

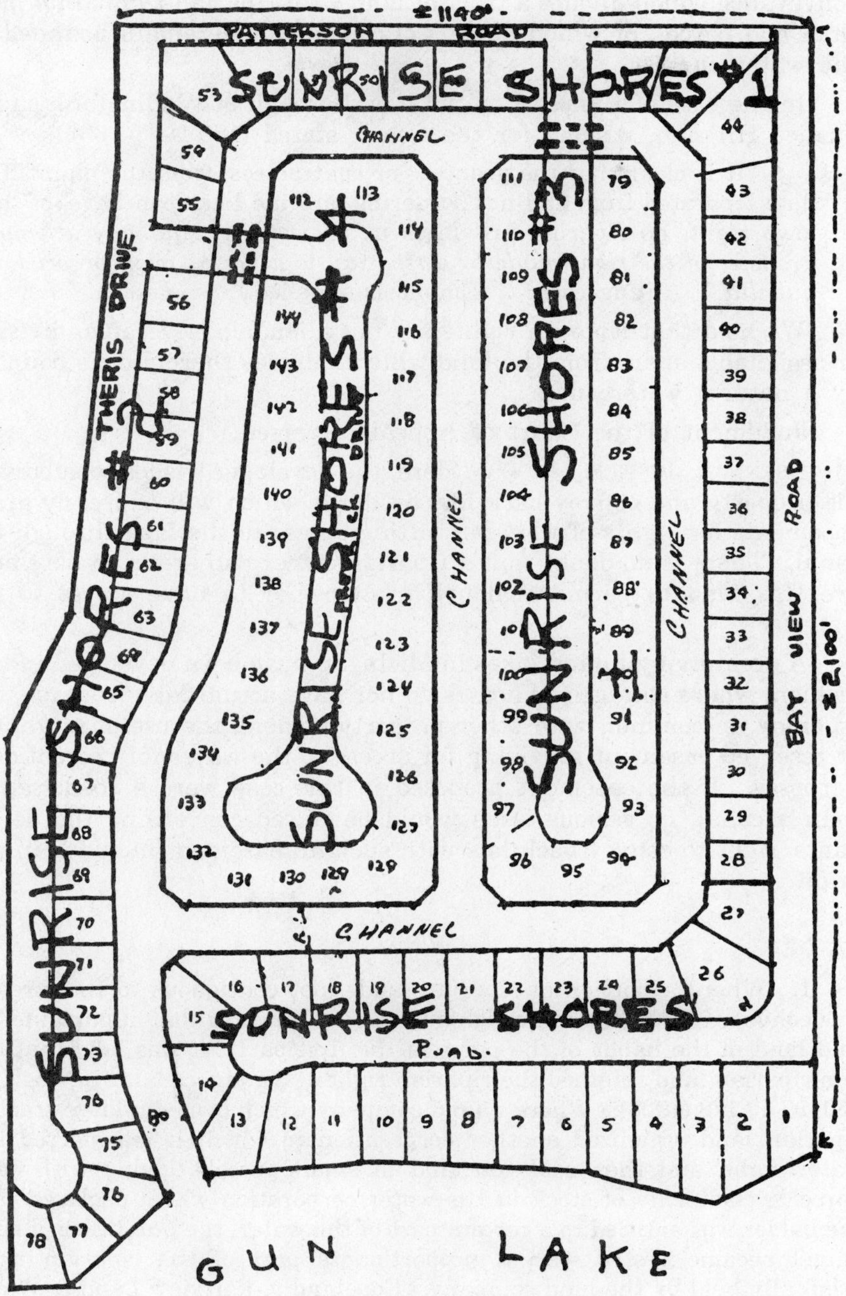

All Lots Front on the Channel or the Lake.

[A9464]

The remaining question for decision is whether or not riparian rights may be conveyed to a grantee or reserved by the grantor in a conveyance which divides a tract of land with riparian rights into more than one parcel, of which parcels only one would remain bounded by the watercourse.

In the case of Harvey Realty Co. v. Borough of Wallingford, supra, Justice Hinman, writing for the Court, stated (150 A. p. 63):

> "It is clear that the grantees or contractees, from the plaintiff, of lots separated from and not bordering on Pine Lake can have, of their own right, no riparian privileges in its waters. *And any attempted transfer of the right made by a riparian to a nonriparian proprietor is invalid.*" (Citing cases.) (Emphasis supplied.) * * *

We hold that riparian rights are not alienable, severable, divisible or assignable apart from the land which includes therein or is bounded by a natural watercourse.

Judgment of the Court of Appeals reversed.

BRENNAN, JUSTICE. * * * Here, the developer wishes to subdivide his property and convey back lots by deeds which will expressly grant easements for rights of way, permitting access to the lake through the canal. There is no doubt that a riparian owner can grant an easement over his land to permit a nonriparian owner to have access to the water.

A great many inland lakes in Michigan have been developed in this fashion, where cottages or homes do not have actual lake frontage, but do enjoy, in common with other property owners, the use of a granted or reserved easement providing for access to the water for recreational purposes. If the easement proposed in this case were a road, rather than a canal, no serious issue would be raised concerning the defendants' right to convey back lots with such an easement included in the grant. * * *

Notes

1. Where a portion of riparian lands, not contiguous to the stream, was conveyed with "the same rights to the use of water that appurtained to said land in the hands of the party of the first part", it was held that the non-riparian land retained the riparian rights. Strong v. Baldwin, 154 Cal. 150, 97 P. 178 (1908). Where a land company which owned a large tract of riparian land organized another corporation to which it transferred the water right, and then sold the land in small parcels, giving with each parcel a certificate of stock in the water corporation which declared that the holder was entitled to a certain part of the water, the purchaser of each parcel became vested with a proportionate part of the riparian right originally held by the land company. Copeland v. Fairview Land & Water Co., 165 Cal. 148, 131 P. 119 (1913). The partition of a riparian tract among tenants in common does not destroy the riparian character of the plots lying away from the stream. Rancho Santa Margarita v. Vail, 11 Cal. 2d 501, 81 P.2d 533 (1938).

Where plaintiff's land is situated below the junction of two branches of a stream, he cannot complain of the transportation, by a defendant who has riparian lands above the forks, of water out of one branch for irrigation use in the watershed of the other branch. Rancho Santa Margarita v. Vail, supra.

2. Questions of the extent of riparian lands have not often been litigated in the eastern states. A conveyance of an upland portion of a riparian tract was held not to carry with it a portion of the riparian right in Harvey Realty Company v. Wallingford, 111 Conn. 352, 150 A. 60 (1930). The watershed limitation clearly finds acceptance, see Farnham, The Permissible Extent of Riparian Land, 7 Land & Water L.Rev. 31 (1972). Farnham argues for the adoption of a "reasonable limit" rule that can be supported by an analysis of some cases. Neither the "smallest tract" rule of *Boehmer*, supra n. 1, p. 247, nor the "government subdivision" rule of *Crawford*, supra n. 2, p. 247, seem to have been adopted by eastern courts. A Wisconsin administrative agency which issues permits to riparian irrigators has construed the term riparian land to mean that land bordering on a lake or stream which has been in the same ownership in an uninterrupted chain of title from the original government patent. Ellis, Beuscher, Howard and DeBraal, Water-Use Law and Administration in Wisconsin 17 (1970).

As for the status and rights of landowners on man-made bodies of water, see Evans, Riparian Rights in Artificial Lakes and Streams, 16 Mo. L.Rev. 93 (1951).

3. Riparian rights relate to water courses, including springs and lakes, but not to every source in other phases of the hydrologic cycle. See *State v. Hiber*, supra, page 41, and Note 1 thereto for other materials on what constitutes a water course. Diffused surface water resulting from precipitation may be captured and used, or dammed and redirected, by the owner of the land on which the waters are found, even though the water would otherwise reach a stream and these activities diminish the flow of the stream with adverse effects on riparian proprietors below. *Broadbent v. Ramsbotham*, 11 Ex. 602, 156 Eng.Rep. 971 (Exch.1856).

4. Many controversies over surface water arise because the landowners are trying to get rid of it, rather than to capture and use it. In the law of drainage two rules have competed for acceptance by the courts, and a third has developed. Some courts follow the "common enemy" rule, under which the possessor of land may protect himself against surface water as best he can, building dikes to keep the water off his land or drains to cast it down onto lower lands.[1] Others apply the "civil law" rule, borrowed from European countries, which subjects each piece of land to a servitude for the natural flow of water across it, so that a landowner cannot prevent water from coming to his land, nor may he collect it so it flows from his land in unusual quantities, or change the direction of the natural drainage.[2]

Each of these rules has obvious disadvantages and both have been modified in some states by statute or decision. Thus some courts applying the civil law rule have held that the natural flow may be changed if damage is slight, or if the landowner is protecting himself from extraordi-

1. Young v. Moore, 236 S.W.2d 740 (Mo. App.1951); Stacy v. Walker, 222 Ark. 819, 262 S.W.2d 889 (1953).

2. Robinson v. Belanger, 332 Mich. 657, 52 N.W.2d 538 (1952); Gott v. Franklin, 307 Ky. 466, 211 S.W.2d 680 (1948).

nary flood water.[3] Some courts have imposed liability despite the common enemy rule where the upper owner has discharged unusually large flows on the lower.[4] A few courts have blended such modifications into a third rule that "reasonable" interference with surface water is permissible when the utility of the drainage outweighs the gravity of the harm.[5] Statutes requiring railroads to maintain ditches along and openings in road beds are common.[6]

The distinction between surface water and water in water courses is equally important here, for these rules do not permit an obstruction of a water course or its diversion into a new channel.

Most drainage is performed today by drainage districts, which are public bodies established to build common works to drain a large area of land. They are formed with the approval of a court or county board when the majority of the landowners in the area desire the improvement. They are financed by assessments on all improved lands, and these assessments can be levied and enforced regardless of whether a minority landowner desires to participate. The actions of such public districts are not limited by the laws of private drainage, and if damage is done to others the district may nevertheless proceed, making compensation payments where necessary and adding them to the costs of the project.

A comprehensive treatment of the law of a single state is found in a symposium, Illinois Drainage Law, 1960 U.Ill.L.Forum 189–300.

5. Drainage and filling of swamps and marshes to produce farmland and residential sites was once "reclamation," encouraged and subsidized by the United States Department of Agriculture's Soil Conservation Service and Agricultural Conservation Program. Now it is "destruction of wetlands" and of the wilderness and wildlife habitat they provide. Protection of the environmental and ecological features of wetlands is now a function of water quality control, and is regulated by discharge permits and "dredge and fill" permits under §§ 402 and 404 of the Federal Clean Water Act. See infra, Chapter 8 at pages 746 to 749 and 757 to 768.

STRATTON v. MT. HERMON BOYS' SCHOOL

Supreme Judicial Court of Massachusetts, 1913.
216 Mass. 83, 103 N.E. 87.

RUGG, C.J. The plaintiff, the owner of a mill upon a small stream, sues the defendant, an upper riparian proprietor upon the same stream, for wrongful diversion of water therefrom to his injury. The material facts are that the defendant owns a tract of land through which the stream flows and upon which also is a spring confluent to the stream. Upon this land it has been established pumping apparatus whereby it diverts about 60,000 gallons of water each day from the spring and stream to another estate belonging to it and not contiguous to its land adjacent to this stream, but located about a mile away in a different

3. Bolinger v. Murray, 18 La.App. 158, 137 So. 761 (1931); McManus v. Otis, 61 Cal.App.2d 432, 143 P.2d 380 (1943).

4. Clark v. Springfield, 241 S.W.2d 100 (Mo.App.1951).

5. Stouder v. Dashner, 242 Iowa 1340, 49 N.W.2d 859 (1951); Iven v. Roder, 431 P.2d 321 (Okl.1967).

6. Peterson v. Northern Pacific R. R. Co., 132 Minn. 265, 156 N.W. 121 (1916).

watershed, for the domestic and other uses of a boys' school with dormitories, gymnasium and other buildings and a farm. The number of students increased from 363 in 1908 to 525 in 1911, while the number of teachers, employés and other persons on the estate was over 100. During the latter year there were kept on the farm 103 cattle, 28 horses and 90 swine. There was a swimming pool, laundry, canning factory and electric power plant, for the needs of all of which water was supplied from this source. There was evidence tending to show that this diversion caused a substantial diminution in the volume of water which otherwise in the natural flow of the stream would have come to the plaintiff's land and in the power which otherwise might have been developed upon his wheel by the force of the current.

The defendant requested the court to rule in effect that diversion of water to another nonriparian estate owned by it was not conclusive evidence that the defendant was liable, but that the only question was whether it had taken an unreasonable quantity of water under all the circumstances. This request was denied and the instruction given that the defendant's right was confined to a reasonable use of the water for the benefit of its land adjoining the water course, and of persons properly using such land, and did not extend to taking it for use upon other premises, and that if there was such use the plaintiff was entitled to recover at least nominal damages even though he had sustained no actual loss. The exceptions raise the question as to the soundness of the request and of the instruction given. * * *

In the main, the use by a riparian owner by virtue of his right as such must be within the watershed of the stream, or at least that the current of the stream shall be returned to its original bed before leaving the land of the user. This is implied in the term "riparian." It arises from the natural incidents of running water. A brook or river, so far as concerns surface indication, is inseparably connected with its watershed and owes the volume of current to its area. A definite and fixed channel is a part of the conception of a water course. To divert a substantial portion of its flow is the creation of a new and different channel, which to that extent defeats the reasonable and natural expectations of the owners lower down on the old channel. Abstraction for use elsewhere not only diminishes the flow of the parent stream but also increases that which drains the watershed into which the diversion is made, and may injure thereby riparian rights upon it. Damage thus may be occasioned in a double aspect. The precise point whether riparian rights include diversion in reasonable quantities for a proper use on property outside the watershed has never been decided in this commonwealth. There are numerous decisions in other jurisdictions to the effect that the rights of a riparian proprietor do not extend to uses on land outside the watershed. These were made in cases where actual perceptible damages were wrought by the diversion. * * *

There are numerous expressions to the effect that the rights of riparian ownership extend only to use upon and in connection with an estate which adjoins the stream and cannot be stretched to include uses reasonable in themselves, but upon and in connection with nonriparian estates. * * * These principles, however, are subject to the modification that the diversion, if for a use reasonable in itself, must cause actual perceptible damage to the present or potential enjoyment of the property of the lower riparian proprietor before a cause of action arises in his favor. This was settled after an elaborate discussion by Chief Justice Shaw in Elliot v. Fitchburg R.R., 10 Cush. 191, 57 Am.Dec. 85. That case has been widely cited with approval by courts of many states. The soundness of its reasoning never has been questioned. That was a case where an upper riparian proprietor granted to the defendant railroad corporation a right to erect a dam across a stream and conduct water to its depot not on a riparian estate for use in furnishing their locomotive steam engines with water. The plaintiff, a lower riparian proprietor, was denied the right to recover nominal damages in the absence of proof of actual damages, although the principle was fully recognized that an action would lie for any encroachment upon the substantial rights of the lower owner though causing no present damage. The distinction is between a diversion which causes a present or potential injury to the lower estate for a valuable use and one which cannot produce such a result. There have been numerous decisions touching the question whether appropriation of water by an institution like the defendant to the extent here shown can be regarded as within the rights of a riparian proprietor. * * * But it is unnecessary to discuss or review them or to decide whether the true rule in such cases is not the one here established.

The governing principle of law in a case like the present is this: A proprietor may make any reasonable use of the water of the stream in connection with his riparian estate and for lawful purposes within the watershed, provided he leave the current diminished by no more than is reasonable, having regard for the like right to enjoy the common property by other riparian owners. If he diverts out of the watershed or upon a disconnected estate the only question is whether there is actual injury to the lower estate for any present or future reasonable use. The diversion alone without evidence of such damage does not warrant a recovery even of nominal damages. * * *

Exceptions overruled.

Notes

1. Perhaps no feature of riparian law has received more adverse and critical comment than the concept that the waters are reserved for the benefit of the lands along the stream, and that rights to the use of water are special privileges of the owners of such lands. See Zeigler, Water Use under Common Law Doctrines, in Water Resources and the Law, 49, 70–72 (1958):

"With the growth of population numbers and the ever-expanding industrial and irrigative developments, the demand for water has increased continually. These demands come from the nonriparian as well as the dweller along the stream; from the city dweller as well as the riparian farmer. * * *

"Apart from the problem of uncertainty and instability of a riparian's right to use water, there is the problem of supplying water to non-riparian land. It is impossible for all people to be riparians. The increasing population and industrial expansion require the utilization of lands which are not adjacent to surface water supplies. In most [riparian] states, use of stream or lake water on non-riparian land is prohibited. This is considered as unreasonable or as unlawful per se. The water of a stream or lake is for the riparians only. * * * The prohibition on non-riparian uses precludes the distribution of water from areas of plenty to areas of drought or great demand, and the water, where available, may be wasted. * * *

"The social and economic disadvantages presented by the riparian doctrine as applied to present day living conditions appear substantial and worthy of legislative attention."

Compare Cribbet, Illinois Water Rights Law, 28 (1958): "This does not appear to be a major problem. Practically, water can be most efficiently used close to its source and land with riparian rights can always be purchased just as one purchases oil land, gravel pits, etc. This is largely a matter of economics rather than a serious legal problem."

Which would be the preferable rule for determining the extent of riparian land, source of title or unity of title? Would it make a difference whether the land were located in California, where appropriators may make non-riparian uses, but new riparian uses are superior to them, or in a midwestern state where riparian rights are the only source of water titles?

2. Restatement (Second) of Torts 855 (1979), *Comment:* [7]

b. *Reasonableness of nonriparian uses by a riparian.* Although there is authority to the contrary, many courts have held that a nonriparian use by a riparian proprietor may be reasonable and entitled to protection against interference through an unreasonable use. This rule follows the policy that riparian law should be utilitarian and should encourage the maximum beneficial use of water, and it places no artificial and absolute restrictions on the riparian proprietor to whom the privilege of water use belongs. The best land for irrigation or the best location for a factory may not lie on the riverbank, and if that land is owned by the proprietor of riparian land it may be reasonable to allow him to make the best use of his right to the water by using it on the nonriparian land. For example, it may be reasonable for a riparian proprietor who owns a mine on nonriparian land to use water for processing ore at the mine mouth, rather than to transport the ore to a mill on the riverbank.

3. The rule stated in this Comment is supported by Elliott v. Fitchburg Ry. Co., 10 Cush. 191 (Mass.1852); Atchison, T. & S.F. Ry. v. Shriver, 101 Kan. 257, 166 P. 519 (1917); Harris v. Norfolk & Western Ry. Co., 153 N.C. 542, 69 S.E. 623 (1910); Lawrie v. Silsbey, 76 Vt. 240, 56 A. 1106 (1904); Gillis v. Chase, 67 N.H. 161, 31 A. 18 (1892); Texas Co. v. Burkett,

117 Tex. 16, 296 S.W. 273 (1927); Smith v. Stanolind Oil Co., 197 Okl. 499, 172 P.2d 1002 (1946).

The English and American "natural flow" jurisdictions are of course to the contrary. Ormerod v. Todmorden Mill Co., 11 Q.B. 155 (1883); Hendrix v. Roberts Marble Co., 175 Ga. 389, 165 S.E. 223 (1932). American cases following the "crystallized rule" that a nonriparian use is per se unreasonable are Stratton v. Mt. Hermon Boys School, 216 Mass. 83, 103 N.E. 87 (1913); Garwood v. New York Central Railroad, 83 N.Y. 400 (1881); Brown v. Chase, 125 Wash. 542, 217 P. 23 (1923); Boehmer v. Big Rock Creek Irr. Dist., 117 Cal. 19, 48 P. 908 (1897).

4. Suppose the plaintiff's mill had not been on the stream at the time the school initiated its use of water and that in 1920 the plaintiff wished to construct a mill but was told by his engineer that there was insufficient flow because of the defendant's diversion. Plaintiff then sues defendant for damages. Same result? Could plaintiff have sued for an injunction as the facts stood in 1911? In 1920, under the above supposition?

SECTION 2. REASONABLE USE

RESTATEMENT OF THE LAW, SECOND, TORTS (1979)

Chapter 41, Interference with the Use of Water ("Riparian Rights").[8]

Introductory Note on the Nature of Riparian Rights and Legal Theories for Determination of the Rights

Riparian rights—history. In the early English common law there was little litigation over the private use of water. Uses of water were limited mainly to withdrawals for domestic purposes and impoundments for running small grist mills. Many early cases were concerned with the effects of grants by landowners of privileges to operate mills, and many involved problems of prescription and ancient rights that had existed from time immemorial. Several cases contained language that could be construed as stating a rule of priority, that the first user had a better right than a later user, while some seemed to be based on the "golden rule," that one should not so use his property as to cause harm to others. Underlying all the cases, however, was the idea that there could be property rights to the use of running water that stemmed from the ownership of the land through which the stream flowed. Throughout the formative period there is evidence that the courts were searching for an appropriate legal standard that would permit the fullest beneficial use of the rivers and streams.

With the advent of the Industrial Revolution there came a marked increase in the use of water for powering machinery, and industrial wastes added a new dimension to pollution problems. In the resulting increase of litigation over water use the underlying principle was brought forth and clearly stated: each riparian proprietor has a right

8. Copyright 1979. Reprinted with the permission of the American Law Institute.

to use the stream as it passes his property, but no riparian proprietor has a right to use water to the injury of another. This developed into what has been called the natural flow theory, which required the stream to be left substantially unchanged except for minor effects of reasonable means of harnessing and using it as it passed.

As American industry grew it became obvious that many economically and socially desirable uses of water could not fit this pattern of leaving the streams substantially unchanged. A large mill required not merely a small dam to create a head of water but a reservoir for storage of water. The consumption of water increased as steam power freed the mills from the river banks, irrigation expanded and railroads and other industries multiplied. The idea of preserving the natural stream gave way to the need to alter it materially in order to enable the water to be put to these beneficial uses. The use, not the stream, came to be the thing protected by law, and injury to a reasonable use became the tort. In this fashion the common law of riparian rights split into two fundamentally different theories. One is the natural flow theory adopted by the English courts and still used to some extent in some American states. The other is the reasonable use theory more recently adopted by most American jurisdictions. An understanding of the cardinal features of each of these theories of riparian rights is essential to an understanding of the rules stated in this Topic.

The natural flow theory. Under this theory the primary or fundamental right of each riparian proprietor of a watercourse is to have the body of water flow as it was wont to flow in nature, qualified only by the privilege of each to make limited uses of the water. * * *

In the early days of the Industrial Revolution when many mills and factories were powered by water, the doctrine served a very utilitarian purpose as it passed the water down from one mill dam to the next. In today's economy it is not utilitarian and prohibits many beneficial uses of water although those uses may be causing no one any harm and although the water would run to waste if not so used.

The reasonable use theory. Under the reasonable use theory the primary or fundamental right of each riparian proprietor on a watercourse or lake is to be free from unreasonable uses that cause harm to his own reasonable use of the water. Emphasis is placed on a full and beneficial use of the advantages of the stream or lake, and each riparian proprietor has a privilege to make a reasonable use of water for any purpose, provided that his use does not cause harm to the reasonable uses of others. Each riparian must make his use in a manner that will accommodate as many other uses as possible. * * *

The major advantage of this theory is that it tends to promote the beneficial use of water resources.

The reasonable use theory has won an almost complete victory in the American courts, although a considerable amount of natural flow language can still be found. Some cases do not require a clear distinction, since the natural flow theory allows many reasonable accommodations between users and the reasonable use theory sometimes results in holdings that the maintenance of a stream or lake in its natural condition is reasonable under particular circumstances. Even when the reasonable use rule is applied in its strictest form, the natural flow preference for "natural wants" is preserved in the form of a preference for domestic uses. Some courts have applied the reasonable use theory in cases between riparians and the natural flow theory in cases between a riparian and a nonriparian. In some western states the streams were regarded merely as sources for irrigating the arid land and the courts applied the reasonable use theory to its ultimate extreme and permitted the streams to be dried up completely. In eastern states, however, where a stream is regarded as an amenity that may add value to land though it remains unused, courts that usually apply the reasonable use rule will sometimes use natural flow language to preserve a living stream, although what is preserved is the minimum flow required to protect its values, not the full natural flow.

Notes

1. An interesting theory that the riparian doctrine stems from the civil law, was imported into this country in the early nineteenth century and then found its way to England, was expounded in Weil, Waters, American Law and French Authority, 33 Harv.L.Rev. 133 (1919). More recent research has pretty well exploded it. Maas and Zobel, Anglo-American Water Law: Who Appropriated the Riparian Doctrine? 10 Public Policy 109 (1960).

2. "Most Eastern States originally embraced some version of the natural flow doctrine, and in some States the courts persist in using natural flow language, but as a matter of practical fact in every riparian State the present test of legality is whether the riparian owner is making a reasonable use of his water." National Water Commission, Summary-Digest of State Water Laws (Dewsnup, Jensen and Swenson, eds.) 33 (1973). Perhaps there is some remnant of the attitude that as against a nonriparian the riparian is entitled to the natural flow, similar to that expressed in Anaheim Union Water Co. v. Fuller, 150 Cal. 322, 88 P. 978 (1907), reprinted supra p. 241. The California rule was changed to reasonable use in all relationships by Cal. Const. Art. X, § 2 (adopted in 1928), which declared that " * * * Riparian rights in a stream or watercourse attach to, but no more than so much of the flow thereof as may be required or used * * * for the purposes for which such lands are, or may be made adaptable, in view of such reasonable and beneficial uses * * *."

In the other western states recognizing riparian rights, the reasonable use rule is clearly the modern law, though some early dicta stated the natural flow theory. Leading cases are Clark v. Allaman, 71 Kan. 206, 80 P. 571 (1905); Meng v. Coffey, 67 Neb. 500, 93 N.W. 713 (1903); McDonough v. Russell-Miller Milling Co., 38 N.D. 465, 165 N.W. 504 (1917); Smith v. Stanolind Oil & Gas Co., 197 Okl. 499, 172 P.2d 1002 (1946); Jones v. Conn, 39 Or. 30, 64 P. 855, 65 P. 1068 (1901); Lone Tree Ditch Co. v. Cyclone

Ditch Co., 15 S.D. 519, 91 N.W. 352 (1902); Watkins Land Co. v. Clements, 98 Tex. 578, 86 S.W. 733 (1905); Brown v. Chase, 125 Wash. 542, 217 P. 23 (1923).

COLLENS v. NEW CANAAN WATER COMPANY

Supreme Court of Connecticut, 1967.
155 Conn. 477, 234 A.2d 825.

COTTER, ASSOCIATE JUSTICE. The plaintiffs are owners of residential properties along the Noroton River in New Canaan. The defendant is a specially chartered public utility supplying water to a part of New Canaan and is also a riparian owner on the Noroton River. The property of the plaintiffs Beryl and Elizabeth Collens lies upstream from that of the defendant; the remaining plaintiffs are lower riparian proprietors. In substance, the plaintiffs in their complaint alleged that the defendant had intercepted and diverted waters of the Noroton River by means of wells and ditches, and thereby reduced and at times completely depleted the natural flow of the waters of the river to the plaintiffs' lands and ponds, and that this constituted an unlawful interference with the plaintiffs' rights as riparian owners. After a trial, the court rendered judgment for each of the plaintiffs as hereinafter more particularly set forth. The defendant appealed. * * *

Prior to trial, the plaintiffs were allowed to amend their complaint, which originally sought extensive equitable relief and punitive damages of $15,000, by adding claims for compensatory damages in the total amount of $112,500. Although the amendment introduced a claim for compensatory damages, and certain of the plaintiffs were awarded a total of $6900 pursuant to this portion of the case, this addition to the complaint and prayers for relief did not mean that the plaintiffs thereby pleaded a new cause of action as claimed by the defendant. Vickery v. New London N.R. Co., 87 Conn. 634, 640, 89 A. 277. * * *

Certain pertinent facts are uncontested and were properly found by the court. In 1957 the defendant purchased a parcel of property along the Noroton River, which runs in a southerly direction from a point in New Canaan for a total length of between four and five miles and empties into Long Island Sound. Beginning in 1959, the defendant made extensive changes in that property, including the digging of a lagoon, the removal of boulders from the river so as to leave a smooth bottom, and the widening of the river itself. The plaintiffs make no claim that the defendant dug on any property of any of the plaintiffs or on property which did not belong to the defendant. The lagoon was connected to the river by ditches and measured approximately 175 feet in length, ten feet below the level of the riverbed in depth, and thirty feet wide at its widest point. Another ditch, measuring 110 feet long, fifteen feet wide and six feet deep, was excavated by the defendant to the northwest of the lagoon and connected to it by means of a culvert. After the digging was completed, water from the river was allowed to flow into the lagoon.

The defendant also installed five wells in the general vicinity of the river and the lagoon, the closest being fifty feet from the river and the furthest 120 feet. These wells were so designed as to enable the defendant to pump subterranean waters into its main lines of distribution. Pumping operations were initiated on a limited basis in July of 1960. The amount of water contributed to the defendant's system from the wells at its Noroton River site increased substantially between 1960 and 1964, reaching a total of over 90 million gallons in the latter year. The period of greatest pumping has generally been during the summer months. In 1964 the defendant began deepening its lagoon, but the work was halted by town officials for reasons unconnected with this lawsuit.

The plaintiffs, as riparian owners, use the Noroton River for such recreational activities as swimming, boating and fishing. In addition, the flow of the river materially enhances the scenic value of the plaintiffs' properties. During the summer months of 1960, 1961 and 1962, the condition of the river, and the ponds through which it flows, was generally satisfactory. Beginning in the summer of 1963, however, and continuing through the summers of 1964 and 1965, the flow of the river in the vicinity of the plaintiffs' properties was substantially diminished. At various times the river flowed into the defendant's lagoon but ceased flowing altogether to the south (downstream) of the lagoon. On other occasions the riverbed became dry in the general vicinity below the Collens pond and upstream from the lagoon. At all times during the periods in question, however, the river flowed into the Collens pond, located approximately 600 feet upstream from the defendant's lagoon. On September 27, 1965, the river flowed past the defendant's lagoon, but the riverbed became dry at a point less than 200 feet downstream. On that day, the flow of the river at a dam on the Collens pond was measured at approximately 300,000 gallons per day, while the flow at a point immediately below the defendant's well site, 500 feet downstream from the dam, was 80,000 to 100,000 gallons per day. The drying up of the riverbed and ponds resulted in the presence of dead fish, created an offensive odor, and impaired the recreational and scenic advantages of the plaintiffs' properties. * * *

The plaintiffs, as riparian owners along the Noroton River, are entitled to the natural flow of the water of the running stream through or along their land, in its accustomed channel, undiminished in quantity or unimpaired in quality. Adams v. Greenwich Water Co., 138 Conn. 205, 217, 83 A.2d 177; see Hartford Rayon Corporation v. Cromwell Water Co., 126 Conn. 194, 198, 10 A.2d 587; 93 C.J.S. Waters § 9; 56 Am.Jur., Waters, § 13; see also Greenwich Water Co. v. Adams, 145 Conn. 535, 538, 144 A.2d 323. This is not a case of interference with percolating waters, as in cases such as Roath v. Driscoll, 20 Conn. 533, 541. Rather, this is a case of interference with the waters of an established and visible stream or river, although the interference occurs beneath the surface.

It is immaterial in what manner the diversion of the stream by the defendant is effected. Diversion or diminution of the natural flow of a surface stream to the detriment of the riparian owners by the defendant's pumping water from wells supplied by the underground waters which support the visible stream is an interference with the rights of the riparian owners which entitles them to injunctive relief and damages for the injury sustained. Smith v. City of Brooklyn, 160 N.Y. 357, 360, 54 N.E. 787, 45 L.R.A. 664; 93 C.J.S. Waters, § 61 a, p. 726. It has been recognized as a proposition of hydraulics that the flow of a stream may be diverted or diminished by the use of wells as was found to have occurred in the present case. Barton Land & Water Co. v. Crafton Water Co., 171 Cal. 89, 152 P. 48.

The amount of compensatory damages fixed by the court was not unreasonable. "In the nature of things such damages are not susceptible of exact pecuniary computation and must be left largely to the sound judgment of the trier." Nailor v. C.W. Blakeslee & Sons, Inc., 117 Conn. 241, 246, 167 A. 548, 550. * * *

As a special defense, it was alleged that severe drought conditions prevailed in the Noroton River area during the summers of 1963 and 1964 and that these conditions caused the drying of rivers and the elimination of surface streams. See 1 Am.Jur.2d 681, Act of God, § 5; 1 C.J.S. Act of God, p. 1427. The defendant claims error in the court's not finding proven this special defense and in the court's conclusion that the rain shortage was not a predominant and substantial factor in the drying up of the Noroton River. The burden was on the defendant to prove the allegations of its special defense of unusual drought, and that the drought, rather than the acts of the defendant, constituted the proximate cause of the plaintiffs' damages.

Although the court found that drought conditions had existed in the area, causing a general deficiency in the flow of natural water courses, and although the plaintiffs do not dispute that rain shortages diminish the volume of such courses, there is no finding that the drought was the predominant cause of the continuing damage suffered by the plaintiffs. In the light of the facts found by the court, including the fact that at all times during the periods in question the river flowed into the Collens pond, situated 900 feet upstream from the defendant's installations, it cannot be said that the court was in error in rejecting the defendant's claim with respect to drought as the proximate cause of the claimed damage. The defendant was adequately warned of the adverse effects which its operations were having on the plaintiffs' properties and took no substantial action to remedy the situation. Under the circumstances of this case, the defendant cannot take refuge in the fact that, in addition to the proven violation of the plaintiffs' riparian rights, the drought may have been a contributing factor in causing the injuries complained of. * * *

The court found that the defendant possessed other substantial supplies of water and prior to 1960 had no need of the supply in

question. The defendant had never availed itself of the condemnation power it possessed, and it may presently exercise this power to meet any demands which may be affected by the enforcement of this order. See Adams v. Greenwich Water Co., 138 Conn. 205, 83 A.2d 177; Harding v. Stamford Water Co., 41 Conn. 87, 95. At no time was a basis established by the defendant from which the court could find that the enjoining of the diversion of water into the lagoon or the restricting of the pumping in any way handicapped the defendant in meeting the demands of its customers. The decree also sets a norm or standard in definite terms and grants a reasonable opportunity to the defendant to inspect the rate of flow. On the facts established by the plaintiffs, and in the absence of circumstances such as those existing in Adams v. Greenwich Water Co., supra, 138 Conn. 214, 83 A.2d 177, it cannot be said that the form of the injunction was improper or unreasonable.
* * *

There is no error.

Notes

1. Restatement (Second) of Torts (1979): [9]

§ 850. Harm by One Riparian Proprietor to Another

A riparian proprietor is subject to liability for making an unreasonable use of the water of a watercourse or lake that causes harm to another riparian proprietor's reasonable use of water or his land.

Comment:

a. The principal factors involved in the determination of the reasonableness or unreasonableness of a use of water are stated in § 850A and discussed in the Comments to that Section.

b. Interests protected. The primary interest protected under the rule of this Section is the right of a riparian proprietor to make a reasonable use of the water of the adjacent stream or lake. Interference with that right is the most frequent type of harm resulting from another riparian's use of the water. A riparian right is an incident of the land, and a riparian proprietor's interest in the use and enjoyment of the water is given protection against invasion on much the same basis as are his interests in the use and enjoyment of the land itself. If the defendant's use reduces the quantity of water available for the plaintiff's use, the controversy has some aspects of a conflict between claimants to tangible property. If the defendant's use does not affect the quantity of water but instead interferes with the plaintiff's use and enjoyment of the water in place, the controversy has some aspects of a conflict between owners of concurrent or superimposed interests in land.

Other interests that may be affected by a use of water are the riparian proprietor's right to the possession of land, his right to its physical integrity and his interest in maintaining those qualities that give it value. * * *

9. Copyright 1979. Reprinted with the permission of the American Law Institute.

§ 850A. REASONABLENESS OF THE USE OF WATER

The determination of the reasonableness of a use of water depends upon a consideration of the interests of the riparian proprietor making the use, of any riparian proprietor harmed by it and of society as a whole. Factors that affect the determination include the following: (a) The purpose of the use, * * * (c) the economic value of the use, (d) the social value of the use, * * *.

Comment:

a. Determination of reasonable or unreasonable use. The reasonableness or unreasonableness of a use of water by a riparian proprietor must be determined by a court or jury from a number of points of view and upon the consideration of a number of factors. A conflict arising out of a claim of harm to one riparian proprietor caused by the water use of another proprietor involves an examination of the use or interest alleged to be harmed, the use causing the harm, the effect that the latter has upon the former and the effects upon society, the economy and the environment of making the uses and of resolving the conflict.

In a suit between two riparian users of water the reasonableness of both uses is in issue. The plaintiff, in order to show he has a right that has been violated, must establish that his use of the water is reasonable. (See § 850, Comment *c*).

2. In somewhat similar Connecticut cases, in which, however, the defendants left living streams flowing past plaintiffs' lands, injunctions were issued conditionally, to go into effect only upon the failure of defendants to pay for the plaintiffs' rights. Adams v. Greenwich Water Co., 138 Conn. 205, 83 A.2d 177 (1951); Dimmock v. New London, 157 Conn. 9, 245 A.2d 569 (1968).

"No case has been found of actual compensation to downstream riparian owners for losses in recreational uses or scenic values resulting from diminished flow. In the case of Adams v. Greenwich Water Company numerous riparian proprietors along the Mianus River brought action to enjoin diversion from the river. The court refused to enjoin the diversion but 'issued an injunction designed to force the defendant into either: (1) ceasing to withdraw water from the Mianus River; or (2) properly initiating an action to purchase the right to continue the diversion of water from the river by eminent domain.' The water company did initiate eminent domain proceedings, but there was no actual compensation. Some flow was maintained, and apparently the riparian owners were not interested in collecting nominal damages for losses in recreational and scenic values." Leonard, An Economic Evaluation of Connecticut Water Law, Report No. 11, Institute of Water Resources, Univ. of Conn. 21 (1970).

3. A "right to view" was recognized in Los Angeles v. Aitken, 10 Cal. App.2d 460, 52 P.2d 585 (1935). The city, condemning littoral rights to lands surrounding a lake to be drained for municipal supply, objected to substantial damages being awarded persons who withdrew no water from the lake.

"The lake has no outlet. It is situated in a volcanic mountainous region east of the Yosemite Valley. It has an elevation of 6,426 feet above the level of the sea. This elevation has remained substantially the same during all of the time of which we have knowledge. The lake is unique in its character, occupying a depression in the midst of lofty mountains and extinct volcanic cones. It is ten miles in width and fifteen miles in length with a maximum depth of 150 feet. In the middle of the lake are two small islands. The water of the lake is permeated with mineral salt and alkali to such an extent that it is unfit for domestic use or for irrigation.

"Mono Lake is situated on the now famous Tioga Highway connecting Los Angeles with Lake Tahoe. From Mono a frequently traveled thoroughfare extends through a timbered country to the Yosemite Valley. The picturesque beauty, the highly colored rocks and precipitous walls and the rare surroundings of Mono Lake attract an increasing number of tourists to its popular resorts. John Muir, the late famous exploring scientist, half a century ago said of this locality: 'This beauty * * * is of a still higher order, enticing us lovingly on through gentian meadows and groves of rustling aspen to Lake Mono, where, spirit-like, our happy stream vanishes. * * * Mountains, red, gray, and black, rise close at hand on the right, whitened around their bases with banks of enduring snow; on the left swells the huge red mass of Mount Gibbs, while in front the eye wanders down the shadowy canon, and out on the warm plain of Mono, where the lake is seen gleaming like a burnished metallic disk, with clusters of lofty volcanic cones to the south of it.'

"But this limitation of riparian rights of owners of land to a necessary use for beneficial purposes does not mean that the water must be actually used in irrigating the land or consumed for domestic purposes. It does not authorize the appropriation of littoral rights to land bordering on the margin of a lake without the payment of just compensation therefor, when the very value of the land depends on the maintenance of the lake in its natural condition. Irrigation and household uses of water are not the only reasonable or beneficial purposes for which it may be employed, even though the presence of mineral salts or alkali in the water renders it unfit for human consumption or domestic use.

"For the reason that the existence of Mono Lake in its natural condition, with all of its attractive surroundings, is the vital thing that furnishes to the respondents' marginal land almost its entire value, and that the draining of the lake will nearly destroy the value of their properties and the incident littoral rights thereto, it seems clear that the lake is not being used by the respondents for an unreasonable or nonbeneficial purpose, but, upon the contrary, that their use of the lake in its natural condition is reasonably beneficial to their land, and the littoral rights thereof may therefore not be appropriated, even for a higher or more beneficial use for public welfare, without just compensation therefor."

4. For a case in which the harm resulted to land itself, not to water rights, see Dunlap v. Carolina Power Co., 212 N.C. 814, 195 S.E. 43 (1938).

BOTTON v. STATE

Supreme Court of Washington, 1966.
69 Wash.2d 751, 420 P.2d 352.

HILL, JUDGE. The State of Washington, through its Department of Game, acquired by purchase a waterfront lot on Phantom Lake (non-navigable) which it has developed to be used as a public fishing access area. Its use or abuse, for that purpose, has resulted in the present action by other owners of waterfront property on the lake, asking that the state be enjoined from maintaining its public access area.

The trial court made very comprehensive findings of fact:

> Since the defendant, through its Game Department, put in the public access area, the plaintiffs have suffered the following as a result of it:
>
> 1. The fair market value of plaintiffs' property has been decreased.
>
> 2. Thievery on the lake has greatly increased, particularly the stealing of boats, oars, outdoor furniture, tools and miscellaneous items of personal property of all kinds. In many of the cases it was definitely ascertained that the thieves gained access to the lake from the public access area.
>
> 3. Persons relieving themselves in the lake as well as on the property and front yards of various of the plaintiffs, to the considerable embarrassment and annoyance of the plaintiffs, their families and guests.
>
> 4. Beer cans, worm cans, sandwich bags, pop bottles, rafts, and other assorted trash has been deposited in the lake and on the plaintiffs' beaches in considerable quantity.
>
> 5. Repeated and frequent trespasses on the plaintiffs' front yards, docks, beaches and property. In addition to the trespasses by persons coming in by the access area, numerous other trespassers have crossed the plaintiffs' yards, docks, beaches and property from other adjoining residential areas, and which trespassers, when confronted by the plaintiffs, have justified their actions by saying to the effect that, "Well, now, it's a public lake, isn't it."
>
> 6. Numerous of the plaintiffs, their children and grandchildren, have severely and frequently been cut by broken beer bottles left on the beaches.
>
> 7. Fishermen using plaintiffs' docks, and fishing immediately adjacent to their beaches and front yards, would refuse to leave when requested and would stare and make remarks when plaintiffs, their wives and daughters would try to use their beaches for sun bathing, swimming or the entertainment of guests. The plaintiffs, as a result of this, cut down very considerably in their use of their front yards and beaches.

8. Although hunting and shooting on the lake are illegal, hunters come in and hunt and shoot on the lake. Persons also come in and shoot at ducks with air rifles.

9. Speed boating on the lake has greatly increased. In some cases it has increased to the extent that it has become a danger to the plaintiffs' children.

10. The public use of the lake has interfered with the plaintiffs' use of the lake for boating, swimming, fishing and recreational purposes.

11. The noise on the lake has substantially increased.

From these findings, the trial court drew the legal conclusions that the state's opening up of the lake to public use through its access area, without resorting to eminent domain, constituted a taking and damaging of private property without compensation to the owners thereof; and that the state's opening up of the lake to public use constituted an unreasonable interference with the rights of the plaintiffs.

Based on these conclusions, the trial court entered an injunction enjoining the state

> from maintaining its public access area on Phantom Lake as a public access area and from admitting the public to Phantom Lake and across the access area until such time as it condemns the plaintiffs' property and property rights in the manner provided by law.

The state appeals, urging that as a riparian owner on a nonnavigable lake it can permit the public to enjoy the right to fish from boats over every portion of the lake so long as this does not constitute an unreasonable interference with the rights of the other riparian owners. This implies an obligation to police and control the use of the nonnavigable lake by the public to prevent such use becoming an unreasonable interference with the rights of the other riparian owners thereon.

The lake is small and shallow, covering 63.2 acres, and with depths running from extremely shallow to a maximum of 47 feet near the middle. The shore of the lake is partly surrounded with nice homes (most of the homeowners reside on the lake the year-round) and partly by as yet undeveloped properties. It lies between Lake Washington and Lake Sammamish (within only a few hundred feet of the latter), both of which are large, navigable lakes with many public access areas, parks, and beaches. There are no commercial establishments, resorts or public beaches on Phantom Lake. Nor were there any public streets, roads, or street ends which would give the public an access to the lake, until the state, acting through its Department of Game, acquired approximately a hundred feet of lake frontage, extending back some 800 feet to a public thoroughfare, and developed it to provide an access for fishermen and their boats.

There has been no serious attempt by the state to limit access to the lake to fishermen; and the trial court found that this access area had been open to any member of the public. We do not question the right of the state, as a riparian owner, to ignore the county's zoning regulations and to permit the public, as its licensees, access to the lake over its property. There is, however, a limitation, and that is that it cannot permit such use of its property as constitutes an unreasonable interference with the rights of the other riparian owners.

We have stated the law applicable in the present case quite succinctly in Snively v. Jaber, 48 Wash.2d 815, 821, 296 P.2d 1015, 1019, 57 A.L.R.2d 560 (1956):

> We hold that with respect to the boating, swimming, fishing, and other similar rights of riparian proprietors upon a nonnavigable lake, these rights or privileges are owned in common, and that any proprietor or his licensee may use the entire surface of a lake so long as he does not unreasonably interfere with the exercise of similar rights by the other owners. This rule does not have the effect of making the nonnavigable lake public, since a stranger has no right to enter upon the lake without the permission of an abutting owner. The rule we have announced affords equal protection to the interest of all riparian owners in the use of the water and seeks to promote the greatest beneficial use by each with a minimum of harm to other owners.

In that case, the defendant Jaber had a dance hall, picnic grounds, and a swimming area on Angle Lake (nonnavigable) and rented some 30 rowboats to the public. The conduct of the licensees in rented rowboats was such that the trial court found it necessary to enjoin that operation for a 2-year period, and this we affirmed.

The depredations and conduct of Jaber's licensees, which warranted an injunction in that case, could be characterized as a Sunday-school picnic as compared with the indecencies and obscenities to which the other riparian owners on Phantom Lake have been subjected. Added to this is the physical danger to other riparian owners, their children and grandchildren from broken beer bottles left on the beaches and from the operation of speed boats dangerously close to bathers and swimmers near the shore. While the trial court's injunction was justified at the time of trial, it was too extensive in time and was not properly conditioned as to termination.

The dedicated people who make up the great fishing fraternity in this state should not be deprived of the opportunity and pleasure of fishing for perch, crappie, and the like (the water is too warm for trout) because of the conduct of a relatively few hooligans.

The state, as a riparian owner, does not have to acquire by condemnation the rights of the other riparian owners before it permits fishermen in reasonable numbers access to the waters of Phantom Lake; but it does have the obligation, and counsel for the state so concede, to so regulate the number and conduct of its licensees as to prevent any undue interference with the rights of other riparian owners.

The injunction should be continued only until the state, through its Department of Game, presents a plan for the controlled operation of its property that satisfies the trial court that the rights of other riparian owners will be adequately safeguarded. The state is entitled to all the rights of a riparian owner, but it should also accept the responsibility of a riparian owner for the conduct of its licensees.

We are in accord with the trial court's conclusion, from the facts in this case, that there has been an unreasonable interference by the state's licensees with the rights of other riparian owners and that an injunction was properly granted, but it should be modified and limited as indicated herein; and the cause is remanded for that purpose.

Each party will bear his own costs on this appeal.

DONWORTH, WEAVER, and HAMILTON, JJ., concur.

FINLEY, JUDGE (concurring specially in the majority opinion).

We are confronted in this appeal with a complex natural resources problem certain to become more and more acute in this age of a geometrically increasing demand by more and more people for outdoor recreational and leisure time activities. The problem is one of insuring that the greatest possible number of Washingtonians, and others, are able to utilize reasonably the natural resources of our state for recreational activity. * * *

If the problem is approached strictly in the sense of the legal concept of "riparian rights," its solution will be a restricted and limited one, and probably inadequate, in terms of its recognition of either the rights of the public or the rights of the individual lakefront owners. The same kind of danger or limitation is apparent in approaching the problem solely in terms of the legal concept of state ownership of the waters of nonnavigable lakes. Again, in the best tradition of the common law, some gloss upon the legal concept of "riparian rights" and upon the legal concept of state ownership of the waters of the lake seems indicated and necessary for a juristic accommodation of the conflicting interests and rights of members of the public and the private owners of water front on Phantom Lake. Without employing or adverting to the foregoing nomenclature, or characterization, it seems to me the reasoning of the majority opinion by Judge Hill resolves the problem in a common-sense, practicable way—again, in the best tradition of the common law—and that the results reached constitute an adequate and highly desirable solution of the problem involved. * * *

OTT, JUDGE (concurring in part and dissenting in part).

Phantom Lake has been open for public fishing continuously since 1926. It is not a popular fishermen's lake because it is stocked only with spiny ray fish. On opening day in 1963, only 50 fishermen appeared, who caught a total of 9 fish. The evidence was undisputed that seldom were more than 6 boats on the lake at any one time. It is this limited use by the public that the riparian owners wish to exclude entirely.

The majority sustain the injunction until such time as the Department of Game "presents a plan for the controlled operation of its property that satisfies the trial court that the rights of other riparian owners will be adequately safeguarded."

With this holding, I do not agree for the following reasons:

(1) One who builds his home on the shore of public waters of this state is aware that the public will use those waters for recreational purposes, and that such use may be abused by relatively few members of the public and by other riparian owners. The debits of such living must be measured against the credits of the scenic beauty and the many recreational pleasures enjoyed by those who are the owners of waterfront property.

(2) The majority do not suggest what type of "plan" will be acceptable to this court. Are 50 boats on opening day and less than 6 boats a day thereafter too many on this 63-acre lake? I do not believe that this use is excessive or that regulations limiting the number of boats on Phantom Lake have been shown to be necessary.

Should the "plan" of the game department require that the Sheriff of King County station a deputy on Phantom Lake from daylight until dark to keep under surveillance the operators of the 6 boats in order to arrest the offenders if the general misdemeanors complained of are committed? I doubt whether the sheriff could find, much less afford, sufficient officers to police so intensively the myriad lakes in King County.

Should the "plan" require that the game department be authorized to police all of the lakes of this state, including Phantom Lake, to prevent violation of the general misdemeanor laws? Such a plan must be submitted to the legislature, not to the courts. The legislature has vested in the game protectors of this state limited authority to enforce only the game laws. RCW 77.12.070. A game protector has no more authority to arrest a person for general misdemeanors than has a riparian owner.

The legislature, in the exercise of its discretion, has vested solely in the local authorities power to enforce the general misdemeanor laws. The record before us establishes that the riparian owners on Phantom Lake never sought the aid of such officers when they observed these laws being violated.

Any "plan" which the game department might suggest would be advisory only to those authorities whose duty it is to enforce the general misdemeanor laws of this state.

For the reasons stated, the injunction should be dissolved and the action dismissed.

ROSELLINI, C.J., and HUNTER and HALE, JJ., concur with OTT, J.

Notes

1. Upon retrial and second appeal of *Thompson v. Enz,* supra, page 249, the Michigan supreme court ruled that the developer's canals that would give boat access to the lake from 128 back lots created by subdivision of the defendant's riparian tract (see *plat,* supra, page 251) would be unreasonable and a violation of the riparian rights of other lakefront property owners. The evidence showed, however, that several other large tracts had been similarly subdivided and canalized. The trial court had said, "Defendants contend that plaintiffs and others are contributing their share to the congestion. * * * The answer to this is that the others were there before the breaking point was reached." The supreme court approved the trial judge's finding but held that the injunction could not issue, the plaintiffs being estopped because, with notice of the dredging, they had stood by while nearly all the defendants' canals had been excavated before seeking preventive relief. The dissenting judge stated, "These defendants do not propose to exercise any rights or inaugurate any uses which are in the slightest fashion more detrimental to the lake than the existing uses of other lake owners. * * * The trial court would brand these defendants' use as the 'straw that broke the camel's back,' and in the name of preserving to these plaintiffs a quasi-monopoly to use a lake which belongs to the people of Michigan, our Court would approve the arbitrary, unlawful and unconstitutional confiscation of the defendants' property without payment of compensation therefor." Thompson v. Enz, 385 Mich. 103, 188 N.W.2d 579 (1971).

It is often said that all riparian proprietors have "equal rights." How equal are the rights of *Botton* and the state to use Phantom Lake? But for the estoppel, how equal would be the rights of plaintiff and defendants in *Thompson v. Enz?*

2. A number of cases have held that swimming or boating on the surface of the water above that portion of the bed owned by another are trespasses. Lembeck v. Nye, 47 Ohio St. 336, 24 N.E. 686 (1890); Decker v. Baylor, 133 Pa. 168, 19 A. 351 (1890); Shandelee Camp v. Rosenthal, 233 N.Y.S. 11 (1929); Sanders v. DeRose, 207 Ind. 90, 191 N.E. 331 (1934). Beginning with Beach v. Hayner, 207 Mich. 93, 173 N.W. 487 (1919), the common use rule adopted in *Botton* has taken hold in a number of states where water recreation is of special importance. Improved Realty Corp. v. Sowers, 195 Va. 317, 78 S.E.2d 588 (1953); Johnson v. Seifert, 257 Minn. 159, 100 N.W.2d 689 (1960); Duval v. Thomas, 114 So.2d 791 (Fla.1959).

3. In Bach v. Sarich, 74 Wash.2d 575, 445 P.2d 648 (1968), the parties were riparians surrounding Bitter Lake, a small 19-acre non-navigable lake in Seattle. The bed was privately owned, and a zoning ordinance designated the defendant's portion of the bed as open for apartment use. Defendant started construction on an apartment building that would extend 180 feet into the lake, built partly on lake fill and partly on piers. Plaintiffs, claiming a common right to use the surface, obtained an objection. The court said that the building could not be considered a reasonable use of the lake surface by the defendant since it was not a riparian use at all, it was

not "intimately associated with the water." See Johnson and Morry, Filling and Building on Small Lakes—Time for Judicial and Legislative Controls, 45 Wash.L.Rev. 27 (1970).

4. As is true of prior appropriation law, riparian law, although concerned with private rights, can serve to some degree the objectives of enhancing and producing recreational opportunities available to the public. In Snively v. Jaber, followed in the principal case, and in *Botton* itself, the Washington court permits riparian proprietors operating a commercial resort and a public park to invite the public to share in their riparian rights to recreational uses of water. In a famous eastern case, McCord v. Big Brothers Movement, 120 N.J.Eq. 446, 185 A. 480 (1936), the use of water for a swimming pool used by a large number of boys at a summer camp was enjoined. "Riparian rights can be claimed only by the owner thereof, and they include the use of the waters of a stream for ordinary and reasonable bathing privileges, which extend only to the owner, his family, and inmates and guests of his household. The transfer to a large number of invitees of the bathing use of transported waters exceeds the reasonable use to which the riparian owner is entitled."

The rules of riparian law that preserve living streams, restrict the extent of riparian land and restrict non-riparian uses offer a form of blunt-instrument protection of some environmental values.

5. Restatement (Second) of Torts (1979) § 850A, *Comment f:* [10]

On the other hand, even if a use is beneficial from the standpoint of the user, it may have adverse effects on others or on public interests. These effects may outweigh its economic benefits and produce a net deficit in terms of social value. In many cases, adversely affected persons may vindicate their interests through remedies for violation of private and public rights (see §§ 847A, 856(4)), but even when the undesirable features of a water use do not rise to the level of public or private nuisance or a violation of a private or public right they should be counted as social costs and weighed against the economic values produced.

Illustration:

3. A has an ornamental fish pond on a small stream. Above his land lies the woodland of B, who makes no use of the water. For several miles a highway gives motorists a beautiful view of the stream in the wooded valley. C, a riparian proprietor above B, diverts sufficient water from the stream to cause harm to A and to spoil the beauty of the stream. In A's suit against C, the loss of the public view may be considered in determining the reasonableness or unreasonableness of C's use.

Contra: Boomer v. Atlantic Cement Co., 26 N.Y.2d 219, 309 N.Y.S.2d 312, 257 N.E.2d 870 (1970).

6. The *Botton* and *Thompson* cases may illustrate another facet of the Restatement (Second) of Torts (1979):

10. Copyright 1979. Reprinted with the permission of the American Law Institute.

§ 850A. Reasonableness of the Use of Water [11]

The determination of the reasonableness of a use of water depends upon a consideration of the interests of the riparian proprietor making the use, of any riparian proprietor harmed by it and of society as a whole. Factors that affect the determination include the following: * * *, (b) the suitability of the use to the watercourse or lake, * * *.

d. Suitability of use. Watercourses and lakes vary in size and character and in the amount of water they provide for use. Not all are susceptible of the same types of use. On smaller streams and lakes there is always some conflict of interest when a number of proprietors use water, but the conflict may be magnified unnecessarily if ill-planned uses require more water than the stream normally delivers or are otherwise incompatible with the normal use of the source.

Suitability may relate to other factors, including the social values and social costs of a use. A use of water may affect other persons beside the immediate parties to the lawsuit. A use that has some economic value to the user may cause considerable harm to recreational and environmental values in downstream reaches of the stream. In determining the reasonableness of the use the presence of these social harms may render the use unsuitable for the particular watercourse although it might be perfectly suitable for others.

Another aspect of suitability relates to the state of development of the waters by other riparian proprietors and the usual and customary methods of carrying out development and obtaining the benefits of water use. The use must fit into the pattern of other uses so as to cause as little disruption as possible.

See also as to suitability of use, *Botton,* supra p. 267, and Timm v. Bear, 29 Wis. 254 (1871). Compare Mason v. Hoyle, 56 Conn. 255, 14 A. 786 (1888): "In the next place, a reasonable use is one adopted to the character and capacity of the stream, * * * The other fact found, that five days' detention of the water has enabled the defendant to run [his mill] only five hours shows still more forceably the enormous disproportion of his machinery to the capacity of the stream during the dry season." The court also emphasized that prior to the time the defendant enlarged his mill the custom had been to use run-of-the-river power, using the dams only to provide a head of water. This long established mode of running the mills was considered as an element in determining that the intermittent use by the enlarged dam was unreasonable. See also Dunlap v. Carolina Power & Light Co., 212 N.C. 814, 195 S.E. 43 (1938); Apfelbacher v. State, 167 Wis. 233, 167 N.W. 244 (1918).

7. Beuscher, Appropriation Water Law Elements in Riparian Doctrine States, 10 Buffalo L.Rev. 448, 453 (1961):

"Mill dam acts gave a private eminent domain power to entrepreneurs who chose to construct dams on streams flowing through riparian lands, a power to build the dam, flow the lands of an upstream riparian and be free of any obligation except to pay the value of the flowage right if the damaged landowner sued in time. More striking, for our purposes, however, is the express guarantee of appropriative status given to the riparian who first constructed a dam. No subsequent dam could be erected to the injury of any mill lawfully existing.[12] As a matter of fact, independent of legislation or prescriptive rights, American courts have protected the earlier dam against upstream or downstream structures which threatened to impair the power potential.[13] Similar protections are accorded hydro-electric dams erected in accordance with state-granted permits or franchises.[14]

"Dams often disrupt the natural flow of the stream, especially in dry periods when water flowing down the stream is held behind the dam to maintain the head or power potential. Cases from mill dam and logging dam days willingly (and understandably) sustained as reasonable the complete retention of the full flow of the river for days at a time.[15] Economic needs dictated these blows at "natural flow" ideals. Far from protecting a bare technical right to the natural flow of the watercourse,[16] courts permitted complete disruption of the flow for sustained periods of time. Nor have the legislatures failed to react to similar pressures. A Wisconsin statute, for example, requires the hydro-dam proprietor to let by, not the entire natural flow, but as little as 25% of it.[17]"

BOLLINGER v. HENRY

Supreme Court of Missouri, 1964.
375 S.W.2d 161.

STOCKARD, COMMISSIONER. Defendant has appealed from the judgment of the trial court in plaintiffs' suit to quiet title and for an injunction to prohibit defendant from taking water from a millrace.
* * *

On September 2, 1936, E.S. Bollinger and his wife purchased from J.B. Dolle and others 2.40 acres of land on which was located a mill. At the same time and by the same deed they also purchased an irregular strip of land, described by metes and bounds, approximately one mile in length and varying in width (the width is not shown but from an exhibit it appears that the width would vary from approximately 20 feet to more than 100 feet) and extending from the 2.40 acre tract northwesterly to and including a portion of the Big Whitewater Creek,

12. See, for example, Wis.Rev.Stats. ch. 56, § 1 (1858).

13. Black's Pomeroy, The Law of Water Rights § 10 (1893) and cases cited. See also Bissell Chilled Plow Works v. Bend Mfg. Co., 64 Ind.App. 1, 111 N.E. 932 (1916).

14. See Wis.Stat.Ann. 31.06(3). In considering applications for dams the commission is to protect "property" which persumably includes prior dams—at least so the statute has been interpreted.

15. Coldwell v. Sanderson, 69 Wis. 52, 28 N.W. 232 (1886), affirmed on rehearing, 69 Wis. 57, 33 N.W. 591 (1887). Apfelbacher v. State, 167 Wis. 233, 167 N.W. 244 (1918) and cases cited.

16. In United States v. Gerlach, 339 U.S. 725 (1950), Mr. Justice Jackson said that such riparianism pressed to the limits to the limits of its logic enables one to play dog-in-the-manger.

17. Wis.Stats.Ann. 31.34.

a nonnavigable stream, where there was located a then deteriorated log dam. On this irregular strip of land was located a millrace which carried water from the pool caused by the dam to the mill and then through a tailrace back to Big Whitewater Creek. We shall hereafter refer to this irregular strip of land as the millrace strip.

The dam, millrace and mill were first built within a short time after 1800, and for approximately 75 years prior to 1936 had been owned by the Dolle family. After E.S. Bollinger bought the property he rebuilt the dam with concrete, and Terry Bollinger, his son, operated the mill under an oral lease or agreement and engaged in grinding flour, corn meal and livestock feed. In the "early forties" the grinding of feed by use of water power was discontinued and thereafter it was ground by use of a gasoline powered engine. In April 1958 the grinding of flour was completely discontinued, and there is nothing to indicate any intention to resume that operation. Since April 1958 the mill has been used only one day each week, Saturday, to grind corn meal by use of water power. * * *

For seven years previous to the trial appellant pumped water each year from the millrace for irrigation purposes during July and August, or the "dry part of the summer," except two years when irrigation was not needed. * * * Although appellant pumped water from the millrace for five out of the previous seven years, neither E.S. nor Terry Bollinger objected to him doing so prior to the filing of this suit. * * *

The rights of a riparian owner in the water of a stream, in jurisdictions wherein the doctrine of riparian rights obtain, include "the right to the flow of the stream in its natural course and in its natural condition in respect of both volume and purity, except as affected by reasonable use by other proprietors, * * *," 56 Am.Jur. Waters § 273, and a reasonable use by other proprietors includes the "limited right to use the water to irrigate his riparian lands," 94 C.J.S. Waters § 314(1), subject to the priority of riparian owners for the supply of "natural wants" which include drinking water for family and for livestock. Kinney on Irrigation and Water Rights, 2d Ed., §§ 500–504. See also Farnham on Waters and Water Rights, § 599. What constitutes a reasonable use is a question of fact depending on the circumstances of each particular case, including, among other things, the volume of water in the stream, the seasons and climatic conditions, and the needs of other riparian proprietors. 94 C.J.S. Waters § 314(2); 56 Am.Jur. Waters § 342; Kinney on Irrigation and Water Rights, 2d Ed., §§ 490 and 495; Gould on Waters 3rd Ed., § 208.

We have established that appellant is entitled to the use for irrigation purposes of some water from the millrace at the place where it crosses his land, and respondents admit that on approximately six days out of every seven the water in the millrace flows unused past the mill except to provide drinking water for a few hogs running on the millrace property. We necessarily conclude that the trial court erroneously enjoined appellant from taking any water at any time from the millrace for any purpose whatever.

Respondents make an impassioned plea in their brief for the "preservation of our heritage" as typified by the mill, and asserts that this suit "was brought primarily * * * to help preserve this portion of our heritage." The applicable common law doctrine of reasonable use of water by riparian owners affords an adequate basis to the trial court for the preservation of the mill if the litigants as reasonable men with the aid of enlightened counsel cannot amicably settle their differences. * * *

The judgment is reversed and the cause remanded for further proceedings according to the views expressed herein.

Notes

1. Many other cases which purport to balance the relative reasonableness of plaintiff's existing use and of defendant's new use and which are resolved in favor of the defendant seem in fact to be holdings that the harm to the plaintiff is not substantial in economic terms or is the type of inconvenience that is the inevitable result of progress and development. For example, in Gehlen v. Knorr, 101 Iowa 700, 70 N.W. 757 (1897), the plaintiff complained of defendant's new dam for an ice pond, yet it was filled in two days and neither removal of ice nor seepage and evaporation from the dam materially affected plaintiff's mill. *De minimus non curat lex* and *damnum absque injuria* are important principles in riparian law, although the courts have not always identified them as such or distinguished the two. See also Elliott v. Fitchburg Ry. Co., 10 Cush. 191 (Mass. 1852); Meyers v. Lafayette Club, 197 Minn. 241, 266 N.W. 861 (1936); Heise v. Schultz, 167 Kan. 34, 204 P.2d 706 (1949); Louisville v. Tway, 297 Ky. 565, 180 S.W.2d 278 (1944); Montelious v. Elsea, 110 Ohio 2d 57, 161 N.E.2d 675 (1959).

2. In Ripka v. Wansing, 589 S.W.2d 333 (Mo.App.1979), defendant pumped water from Sugar Creek two to three hours a day to irrigate corn and alfalfa when rain was insufficient. Plaintiff had cattle on land downstream. The pumping reduced the flow of the creek by 240 gallons per minute, which may or may not have had an appreciable effect on the size of the stream. At any rate, enough was left for the cows. An injunction was denied. The court noted that *Bollinger* had involved an artificial watercourse and that no Supreme Court case clearly adopted any riparian rule, and continued,

> If Missouri has not adopted the reasonable use theory, we believe it should. It appears to be more flexible and promotes the most beneficial use of water resources. The reasonable use theory is adopted by the Restatement. Restatement of Torts, Second, §§ 850–850A (1977). The elements to determine reasonable uses are set forth in § 850A of the Restatement of Torts, Second. * * *
>
> It is with these guidelines in mind that we consider the questions presented. Plaintiffs' first point claims that the trial court should not have allowed evidence that plaintiffs had no specific loss or damage to

their cattle business. Plaintiffs contend that the appropriate standard is whether defendants interfered with the riparian rights of plaintiffs by substantially reducing the flow of Sugar Creek. As earlier noted, this argument seems to be based upon the principles of the natural flow theory. We do not believe this argument has merit when we consider it in view of the reasonable use theory. Under the reasonable use theory, the court should consider "the needs of other riparian proprietors". Bollinger v. Henry, supra, 375 S.W.2d at 166. The court should also consider the extent and amount of harm the defendants' use causes. Restatement of Torts, Second, § 850A(e), p. 220 (1977). Point I is ruled against plaintiffs.

3. Restatement (Second) of Torts (1979): [18]

§ 850A. Reasonableness of the Use of Water

The determination of the reasonableness of a use of water depends upon a consideration of the interests of the riparian proprietor making the use, of any riparian proprietor harmed by it and of society as a whole. Factors that affect the determination include the following: * * *, (e) the extent and amount of the harm it causes, * * *.

HAZARD POWDER CO. v. SOMERSVILLE MANUFACTURING CO.

Supreme Court of Errors of Connecticut, 1905.
78 Conn. 171, 61 A. 519.

Torrance, C.J. The plaintiff is a corporation engaged in the manufacture of gunpowder in mills at Scitico and Hazardville, in this state, upon the Scantic river, while the defendant is a corporation engaged in the manufacture of woolen goods in a mill at Somersville, on said river, above the mills of the plaintiff; and the principal dispute between them in this case is whether the defendant, as an upper riparian proprietor, has made an unreasonable use of the water as against the plaintiff, a lower riparian proprietor. * * * Upon the facts stated in the finding, the court found the issues for the defendant, and rendered judgment in its favor.

The following is a somewhat condensed statement of the controlling facts found:

"The plaintiff and its predecessors in title have carried on the manufacture of powder at Hazardville and Scitico for more than 50 years. It employs about 90 work people at Hazardville and 10 at Scitico. In making powder the plaintiff uses five kinds of mills, called pulverizer, wheel, press, cracker, and glaze mills, respectively. The wheel mills are run by the plaintiff day and night, the glaze mills are sometimes run a portion of the night, and the other mills run only a few hours in the daytime. For its night work the plaintiff employs 2

18. Copyright 1979. Reprinted with the permission of the American Law Institute.

men at Scitico and 5 at Hazardville. These night operations of the plaintiff are carried on for the sole purpose of increasing the daily output of powder. The mill site of the defendant has been used and occupied as such for more than 100 years—at first by a saw mill and grist mills, to which was added later on a fulling mill, subsequently changed into a woolen mill. Since 1883 the defendant has carried on there the manufacture of woolen goods and it now employs more than 300 persons in its mills. The defendant and its predecessors in title have always operated the mills on said location during the usual working hours of the day only, closing the gates at night, and thus filling the pond for use next day; and such detention is necessary to the successful prosecution of the defendant's business. * * * The plaintiff's ponds at both of its plants are small; and grass and weeds are growing up in the center of the one at Scitico, and this latter one has become largely filled up, and also smaller in area, and has failed to store the water let down from the mills above it. It is not sufficient to retain for use during the night the 10¾ hours' flow of water let down to it by the upper riparian proprietors. * * * It is entirely feasible for the plaintiff, if it desires to run nights, to raise its Scitico dam, or erect a new dam at the site of the present dam at Scitico, so as to create a pond of sufficient capacity to retain and hold all the waters of the river let down by the upper mill owners during the usual working hours of the day; and such a pond would enable the plaintiff to operate its works nights, as well as days, to the extent of the entire flow of the waters in said stream. The raising of said dam 4¼ feet higher would overflow about 25 acres of land. The injury which the plaintiff alleges it suffered is imputable to the insufficiency of its present privilege at Scitico, and is not the result of detention of water by the defendant, as complained of by the plaintiff. The defendant has not diverted the water of said stream, and has never, by its use and detention of the waters thereof, had a purpose of injuring the plaintiff. It has not acted maliciously or wantonly, but has acted with the sole purpose of obtaining the beneficial use of the stream for its own mills; and I find that all the acts of the defendant in endeavoring to obtain such beneficial use have been, and are, reasonable."

Upon these facts the court held that the detention and discharge of the waters of Scantic river, made by the defendant in the manner and under the circumstances detailed in the finding, was a reasonable, and therefore a rightful, use of said waters as against the plaintiff; and whether the court erred in so holding is the principal question in the case. Upon the facts found the case involves, not the right of an upper riparian proprietor to divert or pollute the water to the prejudice of a lower proprietor, nor the right of such upper proprietor to wantonly or maliciously detain, discharge, or use the water, but merely his right to detain the water for a reasonable time, and to discharge it in a reasonable manner, for the purpose and in the process of utilizing it for power.

As against a lower, an upper, riparian proprietor has clearly the right to use the water for power, and this involves the right to detain it long enough, and to discharge it in such a manner as will make it useful; but he has no right to detain or to discharge the water in an unreasonable manner. In cases like the present, for determining the question whether the use of the water by the upper riparian proprietor was rightful, the only general rule which the law has laid down, or perhaps can lay down, is that the detention, discharge, and use must be reasonable under the circumstances of the particular case. Keeney & Wood Mfg. Co. v. Union Mfg. Co., 39 Conn. 576; Mason v. Hoyle, 56 Conn. 255, 14 A. 786. See, also, cases cited in note in 41 L.R.A. 738. The question in a given case whether the use proved is a reasonable one is essentially one of fact, in the sense that it is to be decided by the tribunal empowered to determine the facts—by the trial judge if the case is tried to the court, and by the jury if the case is tried to the jury. Keeney & Wood Mfg. Co. v. Union Mfg. Co., 39 Conn. 576; Mason v. Hoyle, 56 Conn. 255, 14 A. 786; Parker v. Hotchkiss, 25 Conn. 321. In this state, however, in cases like the present, where all the subordinate facts bearing upon the question of reasonable use are spread upon the record, the conclusion of the trial judge, upon the question of reasonable use may be reviewed by this court. Nolan v. New York, N.H. & H.R. Co., 70 Conn. 159, 39 A. 115, 43 L.R.A. 305. Assuming, then, that this court may do this, and that the finding as made is to stand, we are of opinion, upon a careful consideration of the facts found, that, within the principles laid down in our own cases upon this subject hereinbefore cited, the trial judge did not err in holding that the defendant's use of the water was such a reasonable use of the water as it was entitled to make. * * *

There is no error. In this opinion the other Judges concurred.

Notes

1. Restatement (Second) of Torts (1979): [19]

§ 850A. Reasonableness of the Use of Water

The determination of the reasonableness of a use of water depends upon a consideration of the interests of the riparian proprietor making the use, of any riparian proprietor harmed by it and of society as a whole. Factors that affect the determination include the following: * * *, (f) the practicality of avoiding the harm by adjusting the use or method of use of one proprietor or the other, * * *.

Comment

h. Avoiding harm by adjustment of uses. When one riparian's use of water causes harm to another's use the policy of accommodating as many beneficial uses as possible may call for some practical adjustment that will eliminate the harm and allow both uses to co-exist. The law requires reasonable efficiency in facilities for and methods of using water. Both

19. Copyright 1979. Reprinted with the permission of the American Law Institute.

uses must be subject to scrutiny in this regard and either the plaintiff or the defendant may have to make some improvement in his works or methods in order to qualify his use as a reasonable one. A defendant's use that causes harm because it is wasteful of water or inefficient in method, but that would cause no harm if the waste or inefficiency were eliminated, may be held unreasonable and subject him to liability. A plaintiff's wasteful or inefficient use may be held unreasonable and not worthy of protection if he could avoid the harm by changing his method of accomplishing his use.

Harm that can be avoided at trifling expense or inconvenience to the plaintiff is not significant harm and a court may ignore it and deny liability. Very often, however, the cost of improvement is substantial. In these cases the person whose use must be improved is not necessarily the person who must pay that cost. The question of where to place the burden may be a difficult one. If the defendant's use is the one that must be improved to avoid harm to the plaintiff, the defendant must normally bear the expense of eliminating the harm. When it is the plaintiff's use that must be improved, he, the person harmed, may sometimes be required to avoid the harm by installing a reasonably efficient method of diversion and use even though this puts him to more than negligible expense. Ordinarily a riparian must employ facilities and engage in practices that will allow full scope for development by other riparians. The suitability of the works and of the method of use may depend upon the state of development on the stream and the normal and customary methods of carrying out development in the area. This is not to say that what is customary or suitable when a use is initiated is the standard for all time. As development proceeds and demands on the water resource increase, the requirements of efficiency may change so that what was not wasteful may become wasteful. A water user who first initiated his project may have enjoyed the good fortune of cheap diversion and use for a time, but may have to pay costs common to others similarly situated when development approaches the maximum use of the resource and all uses must be of comparable efficiency.

On the other hand, it may be just to charge the expense to the person whose use has created the necessity of making the improvement. The choice of where to place the burden may depend upon the relative positions of the parties and their capacities to bear the burden. Later users with superior economic capacity should not be allowed to impose upon smaller water users costs that are beyond their economic reach or that will render their uses unprofitable.

If because of these considerations it would be unreasonable to place the burden of making the changes on the injured water user, the use that causes the harm is to this extent unreasonable and the user is subject to liability for the expense of the improvement. If an injunction is sought, considerations of relative hardship may require that the injunction be denied on the condition that the defendant pay the costs of making the improvement to the plaintiff's facilities. (See § 941).

2. Rancho Santa Margarita v. Vail, 11 Cal.2d 501, 81 P.2d 533 (1938), involved two huge ranches in southern California through which flowed a

river used on both for irrigation and stock water. "Another point that should be mentioned is that, in considering whether an injunction should be granted in such a case, it is the duty of the trial court to ascertain whether there is a physical solution of the problem that will avoid waste and which will not unreasonably or adversely affect the rights of the parties. No injunction should be granted if its effect will be to waste water than [sic] can be used. Article 14, section 3 of the Constitution provides that: ' * * * The right to water or to the use or flow of water in or from any natural stream or watercourse in this state is and shall be limited to such water as shall be reasonably required for the beneficial use to be served, and such right does not and shall not extend to the waste or unreasonable use or unreasonable method of use or unreasonable method of diversion of water.' Under this section it has been held that it is not only within the power, but it is the duty of the trial court, to work out, if possible, a physical solution, and if none is suggested by the parties to work out one independently of the parties. * * * It may be that there are storage and reservoir sites so located on appellants' ranch, that by the diversion and storage of winter waters that now go to waste, supplemented perhaps by a small portion of the summer flow, appellants can secure all the water they reasonably need. Perhaps by regulating the releases from such reservoirs in the summer months surface flow can be made available to respondent. On the other hand, there may also be reservoir and storage sites on respondent's property whereby, by the expenditure of reasonable sums of money, winter water can be conserved and released in the summer months. * * * It may also be possible to install pumping plants upstream from the reservoir so as to provide drinking places for respondent's cattle."

3. In Mason v. Hoyle, 56 Conn. 255, 14 A. 786 (1888), defendant had a large dam on a small stream. His mill could be run by either steam or water power, and for a time he used both simultaneously, then changed his operation and used them alternately. During low flows he stored all the water for five days, which gave him enough to run his mill for five hours. While the dam was refilling and he was running the mill with steam power, plaintiff's small downstream mill was deprived of water. Enlarging the plaintiff's small dam would involve "perhaps ruinous expenditure." The court said, "While the defendant has, of course, lost no rights to the water by the possession of steam power, yet the fact that he is using such power, and can, by using the water in connection with it, get a reasonably advantageous use of the latter, without injury to the owners below, making his present mode of using it unnecessary, is a matter proper to be considered in determining whether he should be restrained from such injurious use."

4. Is the problem, or the solution, any different from that in an appropriation state? Recall the materials on whether an appropriator's priority protects his means of diversion, supra pp. 103 to 114.

EVANS v. MERRIWEATHER

Supreme Court of Illinois, 1842.
3 Scam. (4 Ill.) 492.

LOCKWOOD, JUSTICE, delivered the opinion of the court:

This was an action on the case, brought in the Greene Circuit Court, by Merriweather against Evans, for obstructing and diverting a water course. The plaintiff obtained a verdict, and judgment was rendered thereon. On the trial the defendant excepted to the instructions asked for and given, at the instance of the plaintiff. The defendant also excepted, because instructions that were asked by him, were refused. After the cause was brought into this court, the parties agreed upon the following statement of facts, as having been proved on the trial, to wit: "It is agreed between the parties to this suit, that the following is the statement of facts proved at the trial in this case, and that the same shall be considered as part of the record by the court, in the adjudication of this cause. Smith and Baker, in 1834, bought of T. Carlin six acres of land, through which a branch ran, and erected a steam mill thereon. They depended upon a well and the branch for water in running their engine. About one or two years afterwards, John Evans bought of T. Carlin six acres of land, on the same branch, above and immediately adjoining the lot owned by Smith & Baker, and erected thereon a steam mill, depending upon a well and the branch for water in running his engine.

"Smith & Baker, after the erection of Evans' mill, in 1836 or 1837, sold the mill and appurtenances to Merriweather, for about $8,000. Evans' mill was supposed to be worth $12,000. Ordinarily there was an abundance of water for both mills; but in the fall of 1837, there being a drought, the branch failed, so far that it did not afford water sufficient to run the upper mill continually. Evans directed his hands not to stop, or divert the water, in the branch; but one of them employed about the mill did make a dam across the branch, just below Evans' mill, and thereby diverted all the water in the branch into Evans' well. Evans was at home, half a mile from the mill, and was frequently about his mill, and evidence was introduced conducing to prove that he might have known that the water of the branch was diverted into his well. After the diversion of the water into Evans' well, as aforesaid, the branch went dry below, and Merriweather's mill could not and did not run, in consequence of it, more than one day in a week, and was then supplied with water from his well. Merriweather then brought this suit, in three or four weeks after the putting of the dam across the branch for the diversion of the water, and obtained a verdict for $150. This suit, it is admitted, is the first between the parties litigating the right as to the use of the water. It is further agreed, that the branch afforded usually sufficient water for the supply of both mills, without materially affecting the size of the current, though the branch was not depended upon exclusively for that purpose. Furthermore, that at the time of the grievances complained of by the plaintiff below, the defendant had water hauled in part for the supply of his boilers. That the dam was made below the defendant's well, across the branch, which diverted as well the water hauled and poured out into the branch above the well, as the water of the branch, into the defendant's well."

Upon this state of facts, the question is presented, as to what extent riparian proprietors, upon a stream not navigable, can use the water of such stream? The branch mentioned in the agreed statement of facts, is a small natural stream of water, not furnishing, at all seasons of the year, a supply of water sufficient for both mills. There are no facts in the case showing that the water is wanted for any other than milling purposes, and for those purposes to be converted into steam, and thus entirely consumed. * * *

Each riparian proprietor is bound to make such a use of running water as to do as little injury to those below him as is consistent with a valuable benefit to himself. The use must be a reasonable one. Now the question fairly arises, is that a reasonable use of running water by the upper proprietor, by which the fluid itself is entirely consumed? * * * But where the water * * * is not sufficient for each proprietor living on the stream, to carry on his manufacturing purposes, how shall the water be divided? We have seen that, without a contract or grant, neither has a right to use all the water; all have a right to participate in its benefits. Where all have a right to participate in a common benefit, and none can have an exclusive enjoyment, no rule, from the very nature of the case, can be laid down, as to how much each may use without infringing upon the rights of others. In such cases, the question must be left to the judgment of the jury, whether the party complained of has used, under all the circumstances, more than his just proportion.

It appears, from the facts agreed on, that Evans obstructed the water by a dam, and diverted the whole into his well. This diversion, according to all the cases, both English and American, was clearly illegal. For this diversion, an action will lie. * * *

For these reasons I am of opinion that the judgment ought to be affirmed, with costs.

Notes

1. Restatement (Second) of Torts (1979): [20]

§ 850A. Reasonableness of the Use of Water

The determination of the reasonableness of a use of water depends upon a consideration of the interests of the riparian proprietor making the use, of any riparian proprietor harmed by it and of society as a whole. Factors that affect the determination include the

20. Copyright 1979. Reprinted with the permission of the American Law Institute.

following: * * *, (g) the practicality of adjusting the quantity of water used by each proprietor, * * *.

2. Sharing of shortages has an egalitarian appeal but entails a number of difficulties. If competing uses are incompatible in the sense that they cannot both exist in a reduced amount, an equal sharing of the supply might effectively destroy one or both uses. An irrigator of annual crops might reduce the acreage he waters so long as he will have water enough to mature the remainder of his crop, but if reducing his share means that he would be cut off completely in mid season, he may lose the entire crop. Cutting the supply of a fruit grower could result in loss of part of the orchard. The reduction of water power below a certain point may stop a mill completely. A reduced water supply may allow one enterprise to continue operation at reduced levels of production and profit, while it may put another out of business if profitability depends upon maintenance of a high level of production because of fixed costs. The irrigator who takes his share by lowering a lake level may spoil for a summer some recreational features on which a resort depends and may induce ecological changes which have an even more lasting effect on fishing.

3. When do the virtues of sharing become the evils of "common pool exploitation?" What is a shortage? Suppose a drought of the same severity in 1830 had reduced the branch to the 1837 flow. Was there then a shortage? Suppose another one, in 1835 after the Smith & Baker mill was erected but before Evans' was in operation? How many more mills will riparian law allow to be built on the branch?

4. What happens if a shortage becomes so acute or demand so large that the shares are sufficient for no one? The riparian vineyardists of the Napa Valley ward off frost damage by pumping water from the Napa River and spraying their vines with a fine mist. In a cold snap all spray together which threatens to dry up the river and thus creates a great hazard to all the wine growers. The State Water Resources Control Board sought to force construction of a storage reservoir on the river by obtaining a declaratory judgment that the simultaneous diversion of unstored water in this manner was an unreasonable use and method of use proscribed by the California Constitution. (See *Joslin,* infra p. 305). Held, the Board's complaint states a cause of action and the case should proceed to a determination of whether, under the facts and circumstances of the case, these simultaneous uses of unstored water were unreasonable. (Sec. 275, West's Ann.Cal.Water Code, gives the Board standing to bring actions to prevent unreasonable uses and method of uses.) People ex rel. State Water Resources Control Bd. v. Forni, 54 Cal.App.3d 743, 126 Cal.Rptr. 851 (1976).

5. Sharing of shortages by persons similarly situated is widely practiced in western irrigation districts, which take water wholesale and retail it to consumers. When stream flow or storage is insufficient to supply in full the district's appropriation, the shortage is shared *pro rata* by the irrigators. See infra p. 503.

HARRIS v. HARRISON

Supreme Court of California, 1892.
93 Cal. 676, 29 P. 325 (1892).

McFARLAND, J. This action was brought to quiet plaintiffs' title to the right to the use of certain water, alleged to flow naturally through a stream called "Harrison Canon." Judgment was rendered for plaintiffs, and defendants appeal.

Plaintiffs and defendants are the owners of adjoining land; defendants' land lying on Harrison canon, above and to the north of the land of plaintiffs. The real merits of the case, underlying incidental points of pleading and practice, rest upon the issue whether or not there is any water-course in Harrison canon. * * * The evidence was certainly very conflicting; and, without reviewing it here in detail, it is sufficient to say that its character is such that the finding of the lower court that there was a water-course, as claimed by plaintiffs, must be taken as final.

The most important question of law involved in the case, (although not much argued in the briefs,) arises out of the form of the judgment. The court found "that, in order that the water of said stream may be made available for the purposes of irrigation to advantage, it is necessary that the full flow of the stream be used at once;" and it was decreed in the judgment that plaintiffs are the owners of, and entitled to the full flow of, the water, every 3½ days out of every 7 days, and that defendants are entitled to such flow for 3½ days out of every 7, and plaintiffs' title to such flow is quieted. * * * But could the court apportion the use of the water between the parties, as was attempted to be done by the judgment?

According to the common-law doctrine of riparian ownership, as generally declared in England and in most of the American states, upon the facts in the case at bar, the plaintiffs would be entitled to have the waters of Harrison canon continue to flow to and upon their land as they were naturally accustomed to flow, without any substantial deterioration in quality or diminution in quantity. But in some of the western and southwestern states and territories, where the year is divided into one wet and one dry season, and irrigation is necessary to successful cultivation of the soil, the doctrine of riparian ownership has by judicial decision been modified, or rather enlarged, so as to include the reasonable use of natural water for irrigating the riparian land, although such use may appreciably diminish the flow down to the lower riparian proprietor; and this must be taken to be the established rule in California, at least where irrigation is thus necessary. Lux v. Haggin, 69 Cal. 394, 10 P. 674. Of course, there will be great difficulty in many cases to determine what is such reasonable use; and "what is such reasonable use is a question of fact, and depends upon the circumstances appearing in each particular case." Lux v. Haggin, supra. The larger the number of riparian proprietors whose rights are involved, the greater will be the difficulty of adjustment. In such a case, the length of the stream, the volume of water in it, the extent of each ownership along the banks, the character of the soil owned by each contestant, the area sought to be irrigated by each,—all these and many other considerations must enter into the solution of the problem; but one principle is surely established, namely, that no proprietor can absorb all the water of the stream, so as to allow none to flow down to his neighbor. In the case at bar only the rights of two riparian proprietors are to be considered. None other are involved. And the amount of water in the stream is so small that it is apparent that defendants could not use it for any useful irrigation without practically absorbing it all, and leaving none to flow down to plaintiffs' land. There was sufficient evidence to warrant the finding of the court that in order to irrigate, "it is necessary that the full flow of the stream be used at once." But defendants, as well as plaintiffs, were entitled to a reasonable use of the water for irrigation; and the rights of either could be declared or preserved by an attempted division of the flow of the water without reference to time. The only way, therefore, to preserve those rights, and to render them beneficial, was to decree to the parties the use of the full flow of the stream during alternate periods of time; and we do not see why the court could not decree a division of the use of the water according to that method, when there was no other method by which it could be done. And that the division was a just one, and not erroneously determined upon, seems clear. The evidence showed that the arable and irrigable land of each party was about equal in area; and there is no contention that the division was not equitable, provided that all the other facts were correctly found by the court.

We see no difficulty in the point that the pleadings do not support the judgment. We see no reason why a court of equity, in a case like this, could not decree such an adjustment of disputed water-rights as was decreed in this case upon the ordinary pleadings in an action to quiet title. Under such pleadings the rights of the parties to and in the property involved are at issue, and the court has jurisdiction to definitely and finally determine them. The pleadings in this case, however, set up the rights of the parties to irrigate their respective lands by the use of the water-right in litigation; and it is difficult to see what further pleadings were necessary. * * *

Judgment affirmed.

Notes

1. Hunter Land Co. v. Laugenour, 140 Wash. 558, 250 P. 41 (1926) involved three riparians who owned 133, 70 and 2 acres respectively, in a basin containing 1040 irrigable riparian acres. They were decreed rights to 133/1040ths, 70/1040ths and 2/1040ths of the water of the stream. In Tulare Irrigation Dist. v. Lindsay-Strathmore Irrigation Dist., 3 Cal.2d 489, 45 P.2d 972 (1935), a dispute between riparians and appropriators, the 1928

constitutional amendment (infra p. 306) was held to require a finding as to exactly what quantity is the reasonable need of each riparian.

2. "The right of a riparian owner to the use of the water is not, however, measured by the amount which he actually uses, and it is not to be assumed that the same amount of land will be cultivated in every succeeding year. The amount of irrigable land belonging to each party, rather than the amount of land already under cultivation, would be properly made a controlling element in adjusting their respective rights to the flow of the stream; otherwise a readjustment would be necessary whenever either party should cultivate a greater or less area." Wiggins v. Muscupiabe Land & Water Co., 113 Cal. 182, 45 P. 160, 163 (1896). In Southern California Investment Co. v. Wilshire, 144 Cal. 68, 77 P. 767 (1904), it was held error to divide the water solely on the basis of the proportion of the frontage of the owners' lands upon the stream.

3. "It will also be seen from the foregoing that the amount of water, in inches, to which a riparian owner may be entitled for irrigation as against other riparian owners, is absolutely impossible of estimation, as it must continually vary, not only from the varying volume of water flowing down the stream at different times of the year or during different years, but also from the amount of land that may have been settled upon; and the extent of the use of water for the so-called ordinary or natural purposes which in itself varies with the population of the riparian district and the number of domestic animals kept thereon." Lone Tree Ditch Co. v. Cyclone Ditch Co., 26 S.D. 307, 128 N.W. 596, 598 (1910).

4. Warren v. Westbrook Mfg. Co., 88 Me. 58, 33 A. 665 (1895): "To make water power of economic value, the rights to its use and the division of its use, according to those rights, should be determined in advance. This prior determination is evidently essential to the peaceful and profitable use by the different parties having rights in a common power. To leave them in their uncertainty,—to leave one to encroach upon the other, is to leave the whole subject matter to possible waste and destruction."

PRATHER v. HOBERG

Supreme Court of California, 1944.
24 Cal.2d 549, 150 P.2d 405.

[Plaintiff has for forty years operated a summer resort in the California mountains, on two adjoining tracts known as "Tract 1, or the Price Ranch" and "Tract 2." Through these runs Big Canyon Creek, whose source is Prather Spring. He has used the water for domestic purposes at the resort, and for irrigating a small garden and about 15 acres of the Price Ranch. Defendant operates a resort on "Lot 1" and "Parcel 2" above the plaintiff's land. Lot 1 is riparian to the stream; the status of Parcel 2 was not proved. He dug a tunnel that intercepted the water of the spring, and diverted water for use at his resort. The trial court found that defendant was using an unreasonably large portion of the water, and limited his diversions to 1/5 of the supply at the tunnel, fixed at 6000 gallons per day. Reversed.]

SHENK, JUSTICE. * * * [T]he judgment fails to make provision for seasonal fluctuation in the quantity of water available to both parties. By limiting defendant to 6,000 gallons a day it in effect allows plaintiffs all of the water over that amount irrespective of the available supply. As between riparian owners it is preferable, whenever possible, to have an apportionment decreed in terms of a percentage or proportional allotment. The reason is obvious. A riparian owner has no right to any mathematical or specific amount of the water of a stream as against other like owners. He has only a right in common with the owners to take a proportional share from the stream—a correlative right which he shares reciprocally with the other riparian owners. No mathematical rule has been formulated to determine such a right, for what is a reasonable amount varies not only with the circumstances of each case but also varies from year to year and season to season. * * * Although problems of measurement and pumping engendered by reason of the underground character of the flow may have impelled the specific allotment in this case, it may be possible upon the retrial to decree an apportionment in a proportional or some other more equitable form. The apportionment should be measured in the "manner best calculated to a reasonable result," and the court may adopt any standard of measurement "that is reasonable on the facts to secure equality." Wiel on Water Rights, 3d Ed., p. 820, § 751.

In another respect the findings and judgment are uncertain in specifying the basis of the apportionment. The trial judge expressed the view that in an apportionment between riparian owners a "natural" as distinguished from an "artificial" use was entitled to preference; that a use for resort purposes was an artificial commercial use contributing to the land owner's profit in a business enterprise, a use not within the purview of a "natural use" by a riparian owner arising out of the necessities of life on the riparian land, such as a household and drinking use and the watering of stock, and that here, so far as any purely domestic need or natural use is concerned, the issue may be eliminated as each party has a sufficient water supply for such purpose distinct from the supply in controversy.

In the findings, however, the court declared, apparently as the basis for the apportionment, that there is no substantial agricultural use for any of the water on defendant's Lot One of 17 acres; that "the plaintiffs have a much greater need for irrigation for agricultural purposes based upon acreage and considerations of past and possible future use than the said defendant; that the resort * * * of plaintiffs has for a long time been larger than defendant's, and from the standpoint of existing permanent improvements as well as area of riparian land to be capable of greater expansion and under a heavier necessity for the use of the said water supply from the said underground stream supplying the said Hoberg tunnel and Prather Spring, than defendant herein; that only recently has the number even of transient guests at defendant's resort approximated those at plaintiffs', and the more recent growth of the said defendant's resort has, to a material extent been made possible by the defendant's diversion of the water supply to his whole resort and not alone Lot One (1) to plaintiff's substantial injury."

The consideration of the element of a greater past commercial use by plaintiffs than by defendant would seem to be immaterial, for it is the present reasonable beneficial uses to which the water may properly be put by the riparian owners, consideration being given of course to preferential uses, that determines an apportionment.

So far as acreage is concerned, plaintiffs possess 200 acres in Tract Two, upon which their resort and former garden and dairy are located, and 160 acres in Tract One or the Price Ranch, only 15 acres of which were formerly cultivated, or 360 acres in all. Defendant's Lot One contains 17 acres, uncultivated, and Parcel Two contains 160 acres, or a total of 177 acres involved in this controversy. Assuming that in reaching a basis for computation of its apportionment the trial court compared the respective acreage which it considered to be entitled to preferential agricultural use, and then the water requirements of the respective competing resorts, which are now of about equal size, it would appear that the acreage was not properly considered as an element in the absence of a determination as to what part of defendant's acreage in Parcel Two is riparian, upon what part of it the water might rightly be used, what portion is under or susceptible of present cultivation, and what portion is devoted to resort purposes.

The question to what extent the use of water by paying guests residing on riparian land is a domestic use, sometimes called a natural use, as distinguished from a commercial use, often referred to as an artificial use, is one on which no authority directly in point is cited. * * *

Without question the authorities approve the use of water for domestic purposes as first entitled to preference. That use includes consumption for the sustenance of human beings, for household conveniences, and for the care of livestock. The fact that human beings are occupants of hotels, apartment houses, boarding houses, auto camps, or resorts such as those conducted by the parties to this action does not necessarily exclude them from the preferential class. * * * But it may well be that the commercial character of the proprietor's business in serving his guests may be so extensive that a lower riparian whose domestic use, whether or not commercialized, would be prejudiced by the business activities of the upper riparian and to such an extent as to require the interposition of a court of equity to safeguard his rights. This would especially be true where swimming pools, ornamental pools, boating, and the like are furnished as a part of the service to the guests (see Wiel, supra, pp. 803–807), which uses, in themselves, have been held to be not domestic. * * * The question is whether under all the circumstances of the case the use of water by the one is reasonable and consistent with the corresponding enjoyment of the right by the other. * * * What constitutes reasonable use is, in the first instance, a question for the trier of facts. * * *

The judgment is reversed.

Note

The preference for natural uses, under which an upper riparian may take the full flow of the stream even though such use would deprive a lower riparian of any use of the water whatever, had its origin in a dictum from Evans v. Merriweather, supra: "Now the question fairly arises, is that a reasonable use of running water by the upper proprietor, by which the fluid itself is entirely consumed? To answer this question satisfactorily, it is proper to consider the wants of man in regard to the element of water. These wants are either natural or artificial. Natural are such as are absolutely necessary to be supplied, in order to his existence. Artificial, such only, as by supplying them, his comfort and prosperity are increased. To quench thirst, and for household purposes, water is absolutely indispensable. In civilized life, water for cattle is also necessary. These wants must be supplied, or both man and beast will perish. The supply of man's artificial wants is not essential to his existence; it is not indispensable; he could live if water was not employed in irrigating lands, or in propelling his machinery. In countries differently situated from ours, with a hot and arid climate, water doubtless is absolutely indispensable to the cultivation of the soil, and in them, water for irrigation would be a natural want. Here it might increase the products of the soil, but it is by no means essential, and cannot therefore be considered a natural want of man. So of manufacturers, they promote the prosperity and comfort of mankind, but cannot be considered absolutely necessary to his existence; nor need the machinery which he employs be set in motion by steam."

The suggestion of a natural use preference for irrigation in areas where that practice is necessary for the successful cultivation of crops was rejected in Watkins Land Co. v. Clements, 98 Tex. 578, 86 S.W. 733 (1905) and Meng v. Coffey, 67 Neb. 500, 93 N.W. 713 (1903).

In City of Canton v. Shock, 66 Ohio St. 19, 63 N.E. 600 (1902), expressing the minority view that a city may be a riparian proprietor, it was held that the city's domestic use would be entitled to a preference over manufacturing uses. In U.S. v. Fallbrook Public Utility Dist., 108 F.Supp. 72 (S.D.Cal.1952), the use of water for domestic purposes by 50,000 soldiers in a military camp was held a proper and reasonable riparian use, on the authority of the Prather case. However, the court did not accord it a preferred status, and in a later phase of the case, 109 F.Supp. 28 (S.D.Cal. 1952), the court limited the use of water for the military purposes of the camp to the maximum amount allowable for agricultural use on the ranch which had been purchased for the camp.

HARRIS v. BROOKS

Supreme Court of Arkansas, 1955.
225 Ark. 436, 283 S.W.2d 129.

WARD, JUSTICE. The issues presented by this appeal relate to the relative rights of riparian landowners to the use of a privately owned nonnavigable lake and the water therein.

Appellant, Theo Mashburn, lessee of riparian landowners conducts a commercial boating and fishing enterprise. In this business he rents cabins, sells fishing bait and equipment, and rents boats to members of the general public who desire to use the lake for fishing and other recreational purposes. He and his lessors filed a complaint in chancery court on July 10, 1954 to enjoin appellees from pumping water from the lake to irrigate a rice crop, alleging that, as of that date, appellees had reduced the water level of the lake to such an extent as to make the lake unsuitable "for fishing, recreation, or other lawful purposes." After a lengthy hearing, the chancellor denied injunctive relief, and this appeal is prosecuted to reverse the chancellor's decision.

Factual Background. Horseshoe Lake, located about 3 miles south of Augusta, is approximately 3 miles long and 300 feet wide, and, as the name implies, resembles a horseshoe in shape. Appellees, John Brooks and John Brooks, Jr., are lessees of Ector Johnson who owns a large tract of land adjacent to the lake, including three-fourths of the lake bed.

For a number of years appellees have intermittently raised rice on Johnson's land and have each year, including 1954, irrigated the rice with water pumped from the lake. They pumped no more water in 1954 than they did in 1951 and 1952, no rice being raised in 1953. Approximately 190 acres were cultivated in rice in 1954.

The rest of the lake bed and the adjoining land is divided into four parts, each part owned by a different person or group of persons. One such part is owned by Ed Harris, Jesse Harris, Alice Lynch and Dora Balkin who are also appellants. In March 1954 Mashburn leased from the above named appellants a relatively small camp site on the bank of the lake and installed the business above mentioned at a cost of approximately $8,000, including boats, cabins, and fishing equipment. Mashburn began operating his business about the first of April, 1954, and fishing and boat rentals were satisfactory from that time until about July 1st or 4th when, he says, the fish quit biting and his income from that source and boat rentals was reduced to practically nothing.

Appellees began pumping water with an 8 inch intake on May 25, 1954 and continued pumping until this suit was filed on July 10, and then until about August 20th. They quit pumping at this time because it was discovered fish life was being endangered. The trial was had September 28, 1954, and the decree was rendered December 29, 1954.

The Testimony. Because of the disposition we hereafter make of this case, it would serve no useful purpose to set out the voluminous testimony in detail or attempt to evaluate all the conflicting portions thereof. The burden of appellants' testimony, given by residents who had observed the lake over a period of years and by those familiar with fish life and sea level calculations, was directed at establishing the *normal* or *medium* water level of the lake. The years 1952, 1953 and 1954 were unusually dry and the water levels in similar lakes in the same general area were unusually low in August and September of 1954. During August 1954 Horseshoe Lake was below "normal", but it is not entirely clear from the testimony that this was true on July 10 when the suit was filed. It also appears that during the stated period the water had receded from the bank where Mashburn's boats were usually docked, making it impossible for him to rent them to the public. There is strong testimony, disputed by appellees, that the *normal* level of the lake is 189.67 feet above sea level and that the water was below this level on July 10. Unquestionably the water was below normal when this suit was tried the latter part of September, 1954.

On the part of appellees it was attempted to show that; they had used the water for irrigation several years dating back to 1931 and Mashburn knew this when he rented the camp site; although they had been pumping regularly since May 25, 1954 the water did not begin to fall in the lake until July 1st or 4th; an agent of the Arkansas Game and Fish Commission examined the lake and the water about July 2nd and found no condition endangering fish life, and similar examinations after suit was filed showed the same condition and; they stopped pumping about August 20th when they first learned that fish life was being endangered.

Issues Clarified. In refusing to issue the injunction the chancellor made no finding of facts, and did not state the ground upon which his decision rested. Appellants strongly insist that the chancellor was forced by the testimony to conclude first that the normal level of the lake was 189.67 feet above sea level and second that the water in the lake was at or below this level when the suit was filed on July 10th. This being true, appellants say, it was error for the chancellor to refuse to enjoin appellees from pumping water out of the lake. If it be conceded that the testimony does show and the chancellor should have found that the water in Horseshoe Lake was at or below the normal level when this suit was filed on July 10th, then appellants would have been entitled to an injunction provided this case was decided strictly under the uniform flow theory mentioned hereafter. However as explained later we are not bound by this theory in this state. It appears to us there might have been some confusion as to the ground upon which appellants based their contention for relief. Under the pleadings it appears that they may be asking for relief on two separate grounds: (a) The right to fish and (b) The right to conduct a commercial boating enterprise. It was incumbent upon appellants to show that one or both rights were unreasonably interfered with when the water level sank below "normal". It is difficult to tell whether the testimony establishes this fact in either instance. (a) The only testimony in the first instance is that fish quit biting somewhere about the 4th of July but there was no conclusive evidence that this was caused by the lake being below "normal" level. It is common knowledge that fish quit biting some time for no apparent good reason. There was no testimony that fish life was endangered before July 10th but on the other hand there was positive testimony to the contrary. (b) Likewise there was no conclusive testimony showing that it was impractical to dock or run boats on the lake prior to July 10th. Moreover it would be pure conjecture to say that the same water level, whether normal or otherwise, controlled both fishing and boating. Certainly appellants made no attempt to make any distinction either in the pleadings or by the testimony between the two causes of action.

In view of the above situation it is urged by appellees that the case should therefore be affirmed, but we have concluded that the best interest of the parties hereto and the public in general will be served by concluding this case in the light of the announcements hereafter made and the conclusions hereafter reached. Before attempting such conclusion it appears proper to make some general observations relative to the law regulating the use of water in lakes and streams.

Two Basic Theories. Generally speaking two separate and distinct theories or doctrines regarding the right to use water are recognized. One is commonly called the "Appropriation Doctrine" and the other is the "Riparian Doctrine".

Appropriation Doctrine. Since it is unnecessary to do so we make no attempt to discuss the varied implications of this doctrine. Generally speaking, under this doctrine, some governmental agency, acting under constitutional or legislative authority, apportions water to contesting claimants. It has never been adopted in this state, but has been in about 17 western states. This doctrine is inconsistent with the common law relative to water rights in force in this and many other states. One principal distinction between this doctrine and the riparian doctrine is that under the former the use is not limited to riparian landowners.

Riparian Doctrine. This doctrine, long in force in this and many other states, is based on the old common law which gave to the owners of land bordering on streams the right to use the water therefrom for certain purposes, and this right was considered an incident to the ownership of land. Originally it apparently accorded the landowner the right to have the water maintained at its normal level, subject to use for strictly domestic purposes. Later it became evident that this strict limitation placed on the use of water was unreasonable and unutilitarian. Consequently it was not long before the demand for a greater use of water caused a relaxation of the strict limitations placed on its use and this doctrine came to be divided into (a) the natural flow theory and (b) the reasonable use theory.

(a) *Natural Flow Theory.* Generally speaking again, under the natural flow theory, a riparian owner can take water for domestic purposes only, such as water for the family, live stock, and gardening, and he is entitled to have the water in the stream or lake upon which he borders kept at the normal level. There are some expressions in the opinions of this court indicating that we have recognized this theory, at least to a certain extent.

Reasonable Use Theory. This theory appears to be based on the necessity and desirability of deriving greater benefits from the use of our abundant supply of water. It recognizes that there is no sound reason for maintaining our lakes and streams at a normal level when the water can be beneficially used without causing unreasonable damage to other riparian owners. The progress of civilization, particularly in regard to manufacturing, irrigation, and recreation, has forced the realization that a strict adherence to the uninterrupted flow doctrine placed an unwarranted limitation on the use of water, and consequently the court developed what we now call the reasonable use theory. This theory is of course subject to different interpretations and limitations. In 56 Am.Jur., page 728, it is stated that "The rights of riparian proprietors on both navigable and unnavigable streams are to a great extent mutual, common, or correlative. The use of the stream or water by each proprietor is therefore limited to what is reasonable, having due regard for the rights of others above, below, or on the opposite shore. In general, the special rights of a riparian owner are such as are necessary for the use and enjoyment of his abutting property and the business lawfully conducted thereon, qualified only by the correlative rights of other riparian owners, and by certain rights of the public, and they are to be so exercised as not to injure others in the enjoyment of their rights." It has been stated that each riparian owner has an equal right to make a reasonable use of waters subject to the equal rights of other owners to make the reasonable use, United States v. Willow River Power Co., 324 U.S. 499, 65 S.Ct. 761, 89 L.Ed. 1101. The purpose of the law is to secure to each riparian owner equality in the use of water as near as may be by requiring each to exercise his right reasonably and with due regard to the rights of others similarly situated. Meng v. Coffey, 67 Neb. 500, 93 N.W. 713, 60 L.R.A. 910.

This court has to some extent recognized the reasonable use theory. Thomas v. La Cotts, 222 Ark. 171, 257 S.W.2d 936; Harrell v. City of Conway, 224 Ark. 100, 271 S.W.2d 924, but we have also said in the City of Conway case that the uniform flow theory and the reasonable use theory are inconsistent and, further that we had not yet made a choice between them. It is not clear that we made a choice in that case. The nucleus of this opinion is, therefore, a definite acceptance of the reasonable use theory. We do not understand that the two theories will necessarily clash in every case, but where there is an inconsistency, and where vested rights may not prevent, it is our conclusion that the reasonable use theory should control.

In embracing the reasonable use theory we caution, however, that we are not necessarily adopting all the interpretations given it by the decisions of other states, and that our own interpretation will be developed in the future as occasions arise. Nor is it intended hereby that we will not in the future, under certain circumstances, possibly adhere to some phases of the uniform flow system. It is recognized that in some instances vested rights may have accrued to riparian landowners and we could not of course constitutionally negate those rights. * * *

The result of our examination of the decisions of this court and other authorities relative to the use by riparian proprietors of water in non-navigable lakes and streams justifies the enunciation of the following general rules and principles:

(a) The right to use water for strictly domestic purposes—such as for household use—is superior to many other uses of water—such as for fishing, recreation and irrigation.

(b) Other than the use mentioned above, all other lawful uses of water are equal. Some of the lawful uses of water recognized by this state are: fishing, swimming, recreation, and irrigation.

(c) When one lawful use of water is destroyed by another lawful use the latter must yield, or it may be enjoined.

(d) When one lawful use of water interferes with or detracts from another lawful use, then a question arises as to whether, under all the facts and circumstances of that particular case, the interfering use shall be declared unreasonable and as such enjoined, or whether a reasonable and equitable adjustment should be made, having due regard to the reasonable rights of each.

Application to This Case. Some of the questions, therefore, which must be considered are these:

(a) Had appellees on July 10, 1954, by the continued use of water from Horseshoe Lake, destroyed appellants' right to fish and conduct the boating enterprise? If so, the injunction should be granted.

(b) If it is found however that appellants' rights had only been impaired at the stated time, then it must be judged, under all the facts and circumstances as before mentioned, whether such impairment is unreasonable. If it is so found then the injunction should issue. If it is found that appellants' rights have not been unreasonably impaired, having due regard to all the facts and circumstances and the injury which may be caused appellees as weighed against the benefits accruing to appellants, then the injunction should be denied.

We do not minimize the difficulties attendant upon an application of the reasonable use rule to any given set of facts and circumstances and particularly those present in this instance. It is obvious that there are no definite guide posts provided and that necessarily much must be left to judgment and discretion. The breadth and boundaries of this area of discretion are well stated in Restatement of the Law, Torts, § 852c in these words: "The determination in a particular case of the unreasonableness of a particular use is not and should not be an unreasoned, intuitive conclusion on the part of the court or jury. It is rather an evaluating of the conflicting interests of each of the contestants before the court in accordance with the standards of society, and a weighing of those, one against the other. The law accords equal protection to the interests of all the riparian proprietors in the use of water, and seeks to promote the greatest beneficial use of the water, and seeks to promote the greatest beneficial use by each with a minimum of harm to others. But when one riparian proprietor's use of the water harmfully invades another's interest in its use, there is an incompatibility of interest between the two parties to a greater or lesser extent depending on the extent of the invasion, and there is immediately a question whether such a use is legally permissible. It is axiomatic in the law that individuals in society must put up with a reasonable amount of annoyance and inconvenience resulting from the otherwise lawful activities of their neighbors in the use of their land. Hence it is only when one riparian proprietor's use of the water is unreasonable that another who is harmed by it can complain, even though the harm is intentional. Substantial intentional harm to another cannot be justified as reasonable unless the legal merit or utility of the activity which produces it outweighs the legal seriousness or gravity of the harm."

In all our consideration of the reasonable use theory as we have attempted to explain it we have accepted the view that the benefits accruing to society in general from a maximum utilization of our water resources should not be denied merely because of the difficulties that may arise in its application. In the absence of legislative directives, it appears that this rule or theory is the best that the courts can devise.

Our Conclusion. After careful consideration, an application of the rules above announced to the complicated fact situation set forth in this record leads us to conclude that the Chancellor should have issued an order enjoining appellees from pumping water out of Horseshoe Lake when the water level reaches 189.67 feet above sea level for as long as the material facts and circumstances are substantially the same as they appear in this record. We make it clear that this conclusion is not based on the fact that 189.67 is the normal level and that appellees would have no right to reduce such level. Our conclusion is based on the fact that we think the evidence shows this level happens to be the level below which appellants would be unreasonably interferred with. * * *

We think the conclusion we have reached is not only logical but practical. Although appellees had quit using water from the lake when this case was tried yet they testified that they intended to use water therefrom in 1955. We might assume that they would want to also use water in subsequent years, so it would seem to be to the best interest of all parties concerned to have a definite level fixed at which pumping for irrigation must cease in order to avoid useless litigation.

Appellees make the point that the Chancellor should be sustained because they have acquired a prescriptive right to the unlimited use of the water in Horseshoe Lake, and, to the same effect, that appellants are estopped from asserting any rights to the contrary. We cannot sustain this contention. Although appellees, according to the record, have used this water for irrigation purposes on several occasions in previous years, dating back for more than seven years, yet it appears that appellants had not been disturbed in the exercise of their riparian rights previous to 1954. Prior to that year appellees had merely been exercising their lawful rights as riparian owners and their exercise of those rights was in no way adverse to the rights of any one. (56 Am. Jur. p. 730, § 343) In the City of Conway case, supra, where the same contention was made that appellees here make the contention was denied, the court saying [271 S.W.2d 927]: "We are unable to find any act or acts on the part of Conway of an adverse claim or nature, or such as would put appellants on notice of any adverse claim." The court then followed with citations which are applicable here.

Reversed with direction to the trial court to enter a decree in conformity with this opinion.

Notes

1. What is the basis of the decision in Harris v. Brooks? Is it another "sharing" case, in which the water is divided horizontally at the 189.67 ft. level? Is it another "accommodation case", in which Brooks can grow a crop using less water? If it is neither of these, and if Brooks had since 1931 annually lowered the water below the 189.67 ft. level and cannot now grow a rice crop with the water above the 189.67 ft. level, then the court has "reallocated" the water of the lake from Brooks to Harris's lessees, from rice irrigation to fishing resort operation.

"Under riparian law, * * * flexibility is achieved by permitting new riparian users of the water to compete on an equal footing with the old. The highest economic use of water may receive judicial recognition as the more reasonable, and at any time a court may reshuffle the water rights to exclude old uses as no longer reasonable and to permit new uses." Trelease, A Model State Water Code for River Basin Development, 22 Law and Contemporary Problems 302, 314 (1957). The learned author cites no authority for this statement. Perhaps it was his deduction from the Restatement, Torts (1939): [21]

21. Copyright 1939. Reprinted with the permission of the American Law Institute.

"§ 851. INTENTIONAL HARM BY ONE RIPARIAN PROPRIETOR TO ANOTHER

"Unless he has a special privilege, a riparian proprietor on a watercourse or lake who, in using the water therein, intentionally causes substantial harm to another riparian proprietor thereon through invasion of such other's interest in the use of water therein, is liable to the other in an action for damages if, but only if, the harmful use of water is unreasonable in respect to the other proprietor.

"§ 852. UNREASONABLENESS; GRAVITY OF HARM AND UTILITY OF USE

"A riparian proprietor's use of water is unreasonable, under the rule stated in § 851, unless the utility of the use outweighs the gravity of the harm."

2. Does the "sharing" rule produce a reallocation of water? Perhaps some of the western cases dividing irrigation water among all riparians in a valley resulted in the earlier irrigators having to cut back their originally irrigated acreage when the later irrigators began to take their share. If so, was this an application of the Restatement rule?

3. The various forms of the reasonable use rule (and the original 1939 Restatement rule) were applied both to water supply cases and to pollution cases. The utility-harm formula of § 852 is exactly the same as the formula applied to determine a nuisance under § 826. Is there value in using a flexible balancing process in water pollution cases so that while some water deterioration can be allowed under current conditions the door can be left open to future reassessment? The Restatement (Second) of Torts (1979) includes water pollution in the chapter on nuisances and restricts the operation of its chapter on riparian rights to acts affecting the physical volume of the water, such as a diversion, withdrawal, obstruction, storage, or consumption that interferes with a beneficial use of water. Chapter 41, Scope Note.

4. The Handy Horsecollar Company manufactures harness, using the waters of the small stream on its property to tan leather. Horse harness is of very little utility today, demand is low, and the company is barely getting along. General Motors acquires the land upstream and builds a $40,000,000 plant to manufacture emission control devices for its new compact cars. It takes all the water for drinking, sanitary and processing purposes in its plant, and pipes all its waste water to a metropolitan sewage treatment plant so that none of it returns to the stream. The Handy Company sues General Motors for damages. What result? The Handy Company sues for an injunction. What result?

FARRELL v. RICHARDS

New Jersey Court of Chancery, 1879.
30 N.J.Eq. 511.

THE CHANCELLOR. The bill is filed by the owners and lessee of the property in Atlantic county long known as the Pleasant Mills, but now, also, as the Nescochague Mills, against Augustus H. Richards, to restrain him from diverting, to the damage of the complainants, as owners and lessee of the mill property, a stream known as the Forge stream, by which one of the two ponds of the complainants, known as the Forge pond, is supplied with water. From that pond the other, called the Pleasant Mills pond, and on which their mills are, draws part of its supply; and the mills, which are driven by water-power, depend wholly on the ponds for their power. The two ponds are connected by a ditch or canal. This connection between the ponds, and the use of the water in both of them to drive the machinery of the mills, have existed for over fifty years, though there was an interval of about ten years from the time when the mills were burned to the time when they were rebuilt (which was in or about 1860) when the mill site was not used.

The defendant, by various conveyances to him from the year 1858, has become the owner of a large tract of land, of about two thousand five hundred acres, extending from the head of the Forge stream up and along that stream for about three miles and a half. This property, or a considerable part of it, is used by him for the production of cranberries. In 1876 (according to the evidence it was probably in the summer and fall), he dug a large ditch, extending from the upper part of that tract to the Forge pond. His object in digging the ditch was, to irrigate his land. He also, at the same time, for the purpose of diverting the water of the stream into the ditch, constructed, with stones, brickbats and pieces of fence-rails driven into the bottom of the stream by way of piling, a dam in the stream. He and his witnesses say that it extended only partially across the stream; but some of the complainants' witnesses testify that it is entirely across the main body of the stream.

In the summer of 1877, the complainants, William E. Farrell (he is the owner of two undivided thirds of the Pleasant Mills property) and Lucius H. Warren (lessee of the other third), were operating the mills as partners. They then, in the month of August, perceived a sudden and very considerable diminution of their water-power, which was found to be due to the decrease of the water in the Forge pond. The season being an unusually wet one, and they being unable to account for the diminution of the water, set on foot investigations which resulted in the discovery of the existence of the dam and ditch. The ditch was then found to be draining the water from the Forge stream in large quantities. In January, 1878, they filed their bill in this cause for relief, praying that the defendant may be restrained from interfering in any way with the natural and ancient flow of the water down the Forge stream, and from storing or retaining the water of the stream, and that the dam built by him, or so much of it as may be found to interfere with the natural, ancient flow of the water in the stream, may be decreed to be a nuisance. They show, by the bill, a case of irreparable injury. On the filing of the bill, an order to show cause why an injunction should not be issued was made, and under it numerous affidavits were taken on both sides, which have been read without objection.

* * * The proof is that, as soon as the ditch began to withdraw the water from the stream the effect was perceived at the mills, and in

August, 1877, the effect was so great that the operations of the mills were seriously affected. These facts are conclusive as to the amount withdrawn, and the consequent injury to the complainants. The defendant has no right to so use the water as to diminish its quantity to the prejudice of the complainants. While every riparian owner has a right to use the water flowing through his land for the proper irrigation of his land, his use for that purpose must be such as not essentially to interfere with the natural flow of the stream, or essentially and to the material injury of the proprietors below to diminish the quantity of water that goes to them. * * *

I do not deem it necessary to discuss the evidence. A careful consideration of it leads me to the conclusion that the defendant, by means of the dam and ditch, has withdrawn from the stream so much water as seriously to affect the complainants' water-power, and to do them irreparable injury. He still claims the right to divert the water, but insists that, in so doing, he does the complainants no injury, and causes no diminution whatever of the water in the pond. The evidence satisfies me that, by the withdrawal of the water, he not only causes diminution of the water in the pond, but diminishes it to such an extent as to cause very serious injury to the complainants. The complainants, when he began to divert the water, had enjoyed the unquestioned right of the water for over half a century. They are entitled to the protection of this court. * * *

The defendant should be restrained from diverting the water and maintaining the dam. There will be an injunction accordingly.

MACOMBER v. GODFREY

Supreme Judicial Court of Massachusetts, 1871.
108 Mass. 219.

Tort for the diversion of a watercourse by the defendant, whereby the water was prevented from flowing through the plaintiffs' land and irrigating their crops. Trial in the superior court, before Scudder, J., who made the following report thereof:

[A brickmaker, who owned and occupied a tract of land for his business, was accustomed to vary the course of a brook across it, from time to time, to suit the convenience of the business, but never varied it so as to prevent its traversing the whole tract. Upon his death, his two heirs, who knew of this custom, divided the tract between themselves by mutual deeds of quitclaim, after which the heir who took the upper portion of it diverted the brook from flowing through the lower portion.]

> "The defendant requested the judge to instruct the jury, that if they should find that the tract of land had always, so far back as the testimony goes, before the division between the heirs of John Godfrey, been used by him for making brick, and that the water running on to it had always been turned as suited the exigencies of the brick manufacture, and that at the time of the division this was known to the heirs, then the present owner and the other heirs took under the division

their several shares subject to the right of the heir to whom the special tract, so used, had been assigned, to turn the water as the exigencies of the brick business required.

"The judge refused to give this instruction, but instructed the jury that the plaintiffs must prove that there was in the year 1851, at the time of the conveyance to the plaintiffs, a natural watercourse running from the land at the same time conveyed to the defendant, over and through the land at the same time conveyed to the plaintiffs; and if so, that the plaintiffs became entitled to its enjoyment and continued flow through their land, and if the defendant thereafter diverted the stream on his own land, turning it in another direction so that it ceased to flow over and upon the land of the plaintiffs, thereby diminishing the value of their land and crops for want of the usual irrigation, the defendant would be liable. * * *"

CHAPMAN, C.J. The defendant admits the well established principle, that, where there is a natural watercourse, each successive riparian proprietor has a right of property in it, and may maintain an action against one who diverts it from coming down to his land. * * * The defendant's request for instructions was based on the idea that John Godfrey, the ancestor of the parties, might during his lifetime, by a particular use of the stream, create an easement upon his own land. But his ownership of the fee merged all inferior rights, and one part of his land could gain no rights adverse to any other part. Upon his death, the property descended to his heirs in fee and in common.

When the heirs made partition of the land by quitclaim deeds, if one of them desired to acquire any right to divert the stream from its natural channel, in which it then flowed, it would be necessary to have the right expressed in the deeds; otherwise, the party who took the lot upon which the channel of the stream was situated would take the stream as well as the soil. The use which the ancestor had been accustomed to make of the water would give the defendant no easement in the plaintiffs' lot. The defendant took no grant of such easement, and made no reservation of it, and therefore obtained no right to the water. However useful or necessary the water might be to his business of brickmaking, neither utility nor necessity would authorize him to take what belonged to the plaintiffs. The ruling and the refusal to rule were in conformity with the legal rights of the parties under their quitclaim deeds.

Exceptions overruled.

Notes

1. Are *Farrell* and *Macomber* merely "natural flow" decisions since overruled by "reasonable use" cases? *Macomber* came after Elliott v. The Fitchburg Ry. Co., 10 Cush. 151 (Mass.1952), which established the reasonable use rule for Massachusetts. Or do they bear out Professor Beuscher's dictum, "There is actually much more protection given to the prior user of water as against a subsequent water claimant than one would have any

reason to expect from a mere recitation of black-letter riparianisms," supra page 274?

The typical expression of the reasonable use rule omits any reference to priority of uses and there are some cases that expressly say it is immaterial, e.g., Tyler v. Wilkinson, 24 Fed.Cas. 472 (C.C.R.I.1827); McCarter v. Hudson Co. Water Co., 70 N.J.Eq. 695, 65 A. 489 (1906). Nevertheless, it is occasionally stated as a factor to be considered: "It is also material, sometimes, to ascertain which party first erected his works and began to appropriate the water." Strobel v. Kerr Salt Co., 164 N.Y. 303, 58 N.E. 142 (1900).

2. Where a new use by an upstream riparian is incompatible with an established use of a downstream proprietor, that is, the two uses cannot be reconciled by adjustment of one or the other as in *Hazard* and cannot coexist in normal times and share shortages as in *Evans,* a decision in favor of defendant would result in a reallocation of plaintiff's water supply to defendant. One would expect this to happen occasionally if the quotation from Trelease, supra page 318, were accurate. That author has since tried to substantiate his statement. But only if several doubts about Harris v. Brooks are resolved (Note 1 page 318, supra) or if the following case, *Joslin,* is thought to be derived from principles applicable to a suit between private riparians, is there any case in which such a reallocation has been made. In addition to *Farrell* and *Macomber,* there are a number of cases in which a riparian plaintiff is using water by diverting or impounding it for a reasonable beneficial use and a riparian defendant starts a new use upstream which takes the water supply of the plaintiff. All result in the defendants being enjoined or made to pay damages: Stratton v. Mt. Hermon Boys School, supra page 254, Higgins v. Flemington Water Co., 36 N.J.Eq. 538 (1883); Willis v. Perry, 92 Iowa 417, 60 N.W. 726 (1894); Harp v. Iowa Falls Electric Co., 196 Iowa 317, 191 N.W. 520 (1923); Weare v. Chase, 93 Me. 264, 44 A. 900 (1889); Pollitt v. Long, 5 Barb. 20 (New York, 1870); Miller v. Baker, 68 Wash. 19, 122 P. 604 (1912); Apfelbacher v. State, 167 Wis. 233, 167 N.W. 244 (1918); and Mason v. Hoyle, 56 Conn. 255, 14 A. 786 (1888).

It will be noted that in some of the above cases the court uses natural flow language, some speak of reasonable use and some of nonriparian use, but regardless of the form of statement, the downstream plaintiff with the priority receives protection.

In another group of cases, in which the riparian plaintiff has used a lake or stream for fishing and boating recreation and a riparian defendant initiates a use which lowers the water level or otherwise harms or destroys the plaintiff's use, the plaintiff's use has been protected and he is given damages or obtains an injunction: Taylor v. Tampa Coal Co., 46 So.2d 392 (Fla.1950); Hoover v. Crane, 362 Mich. 36, 106 N.W.2d 563 (1960); Bach v. Sarich, 74 Wash.2d 483, 445 P.2d 648 (1968); Scott v. Slaughter, 237 Ark. 394, 373 S.W.2d 577 (1964); Sturtevant v. Ford, 280 Mass. 303, 182 N.E. 560 (1932), cf. Thompson v. Enz (No. 2), supra p. 272.

Is this substantial unanimity merely a coincidence? In none of these cases does the court overtly balance utility and harm in the manner prescribed by Restatement, Torts, §§ 851 and 852 (1939) (supra page 299).

In *Macomber,* the court expressly refused to consider the utility of brickmaking, it was enough that the defendant took the plaintiff's irrigation water.

Could it be possible that the statement made by Trelease in 1957 was wrong?

3. Is Harris v. Brooks a priority case? The court's statement, "When one lawful use of water is destroyed by another lawful use, the latter must yield," sounds like a rule of priority. Brooks first irrigated rice in 1931, but the court finds he has no prescriptive right. The irrigation was of course intermittent, begun and ended each year at the beginning and end of the growing season. The plaintiff's fishing camp began operations in March and April, 1954, and on May 25 of that year Brooks began his pumping for the irrigation season. Does the court regard each year's resumption of irrigation as a new use, and the 1954 use as a new one which destroyed a preexisting use?

4. If the "reallocation" theory were law, there should be cases where an upstream riparian takes all or most of the water, and a downstream riparian proposes or installs a new use and sues the upstream user for a water supply. Are there such cases?

5. Are priority and sharing inconsistent or incompatible? Is there a difference between requiring several riparians whose needs can be satisfied in times of a normal or "dependable" flow to share in an occasional unusual shortage in the supply, and forcing them to share when a perpetual shortage is created by new uses that increase the demand until it exceeds the dependable supply? The leading cases requiring riparian irrigators to restrict their withdrawals to proportions of the flow were all triggered by drought or unusually low flows. Clark v. Allaman, 71 Kan. 206, 80 P. 571 (1905); Frizell v. Brindley, 144 Kan. 84, 58 P.2d 95 (1936); Meng v. Coffey, 67 Neb. 500, 93 N.W. 713 (1903); Half Moon Bay Co. v. Cowell, 173 Cal. 543, 160 P. 675 (1916); Nesalhous v. Walker, 45 Wash. 621, 88 P. 1032 (1907). When flows are above the normal level each riparian may take as much as he wants as long as he causes no harm. Half Moon Bay Co. v. Cowell, supra.

The concept of dependable flow as the normal flow for purposes of making an equitable apportionment between states was developed in Wyoming v. Colorado, 259 U.S. 419 (1922). Some indication that the courts will stop further development when the capacity of the stream has been reached is found in the following excerpts from Mason v. Hoyle, 56 Conn. 255, 14 A. 786 (1888): "Every owner improving a mill privilege has a right to consider the law as protecting him against any unfair use by any other owner who may establish a mill above him. * * * It is for the public interest that all our streams be improved as far as they can be. * * * These men of moderate capital, investing their means in mills upon our lesser streams should be protected against such a use of the streams by mills disproportioned to their capacities as would practically deprive them of water and ruin their privileges. * * * Now, may we not advance a step, and adopt the principle that if seasons of great scarcity occur so regularly, and continue so long, as to fix the character of the stream in that regard, the upper proprietor must adapt the running of his machinery to that condition?"

See also Thompson v. Enz (No. 2), supra p. 272.

6. Restatement (Second) of Torts (1979): [22]

§ 850A. REASONABLENESS OF THE USE OF WATER

The determination of the reasonableness of a use of water depends upon a consideration of the interests of the riparian proprietor making the use, of any riparian proprietor harmed by it and of society as a whole. Factors that affect the determination include the following: * * *, (h) the protection of existing values of water uses, land, investments and enterprises, * * *.

JOSLIN v. MARIN MUNICIPAL WATER DISTRICT

Supreme Court of California, 1967.
67 Cal.2d 132, 60 Cal.Rptr. 377, 429 P.2d 889.

SULLIVAN, JUSTICE. Plaintiffs, owners of lands riparian to Nicasio Creek in Marin County, appeal from a summary judgment for defendant entered in an action in inverse condemnation for damages resulting from defendant's construction of a dam across said creek at a point above plaintiffs' lands.

Plaintiffs' third amended complaint (complaint) alleges that since March 1955 plaintiffs have been, and now are, the owners of a parcel of five acres of land; that a stream (Nicasio Creek) runs through their property; that the normal flow of the waters of the stream carried in suspension rock, sand and gravel which were deposited on plaintiffs' lands; that plaintiffs operated on their property a rock and gravel business in the course of which they sold and used the deposits of rock and gravel; that defendant is a municipal water district organized and existing under the Municipal Water District Act of 1911; that prior to May 1962 defendant constructed a dam across Nicasio Creek; that as a result the normal flow of waters in said stream was obstructed to such an extent that "the normal and usual replenishment of rocks and gravel" upon plaintiffs' lands ceased; that the value of plaintiffs' lands was thereby diminished in the amount of $250,000, and that plaintiffs had been deprived of gravel and rock having an accrued value of $25,000 at the time of filing the complaint.

Defendant moved for summary judgment. The declaration of its general manager, filed in support of the motion, states that defendant duly filed its application with the State Water Rights Board (board) for a permit to appropriate and store unappropriated waters from Nicasio Creek for municipal water supply purposes (Wat.Code, §§ 1250–1266) * * *.

22. Copyright 1979. Reprinted with the permission of the American Law Institute.

The court granted defendant's motion for summary judgment "upon the ground there was no substantive right of plaintiffs violated by defendant."

With some variance in language the parties assert that the principal issue before us is whether defendant, an upstream appropriator of water, is liable in damages to plaintiffs, downstream riparian owners, by reason of having appropriated the waters of the creek under the above-mentioned circumstances. * * *

[The court discussed California water law at length, with emphasis on the difficulties caused by the rule that as against an appropriator a riparian had a right to the natural flow, and on the history behind the 1928 amendment to Cal.Const. Art. XIV § 3, which is now Cal.Const. Art. X § 2:

> "It is hereby declared that because of the conditions prevailing in this State the general welfare requires that the water resources of the State be put to beneficial use to the fullest extent of which they are capable, and that the waste or unreasonable use or unreasonable method of use of water be prevented, and that the conservation of such waters is to be exercised with a view to the reasonable and beneficial use thereof in the interest of the people and for the public welfare. The right to water or to the use or flow of water in or from any natural stream or water course in this State is and shall be limited to such water as shall be reasonably required for the beneficial use to be served, and such right does not and shall not extend to the waste or unreasonable use or unreasonable method of use or unreasonable method of diversion of water. Riparian rights in a stream or water course attach to, but to no more than so much of the flow thereof as may be required or used consistently with this section, for the purposes for which such lands are, or may be made adaptable, in view of such reasonable and beneficial uses; provided, however, that nothing herein contained shall be construed as depriving any riparian owner of the reasonable use of water of the stream to which his land is riparian under reasonable methods of diversion and use, or of depriving any appropriator of water to which he is lawfully entitled. This section shall be self-executing, and the Legislature may also enact laws in the furtherance of the policy in this section contained."]

It has been long and clearly settled in California that the effect of the passage of article XIV, section 3, "has been to modify the longstanding riparian doctrine * * * and to apply, by constitutional mandate the doctrine of reasonable use between riparian owners and appropriators, and between overlying owners and appropriators." * * * "The right to the waste of water is not now included in the riparian right." (Peabody v. City of Vallejo, supra, at p. 368, 40 P.2d at p. 492.) What is a reasonable use or method of use of water is a question of fact to be determined according to the circumstances in each particular case. (Gin S. Chow v. City of Santa Barbara, supra, at p. 706, 22 P.2d 5.) * * *

Although, as we have said, what is a reasonable use of water depends on the circumstances of each case, such an inquiry cannot be resolved *in vacuo* isolated from state-wide considerations of transcendent importance. Paramount among these we see the ever increasing need for the conservation of water in this state, an inescapable reality of life quite apart from its express recognition in the 1928 amendment. On the other hand, unlike the unanimous policy pronouncements relative to the use and conservation of natural waters, we are aware of none relative to the supply and availability of sand, gravel and rock in commercial quantities. Plaintiffs do not urge that the general welfare or public interest requires that particular or exceptional measures be employed to insure that such natural resources be made generally available and should therefore be carefully conserved.

Is it "reasonable" then, that the riches of our streams, which we are charged with conserving in the great public interest, are to be dissipated in the amassing of mere sand and gravel which for aught that appears subserves *no* public policy? We cannot deem such a use to be in accord with the constitutional mandate that our limited water resources be put only to those beneficial uses "to the fullest extent of which they are capable," that "waste or unreasonable use" be prevented, and that conservation be exercised "in the interest of the people and for the public welfare." [Cal.Const., art. X, § 2.] We are satisfied that in the instant case the use of such waters as an agent to expose or to carry and deposit sand, gravel and rock, is as a matter of law unreasonable within the meaning of the constitutional amendment. (See Peabody v. City of Vallejo, supra, 2 Cal.2d 351, 369, 40 P.2d 486.) * * *

While plaintiffs correctly argue that a property right cannot be taken or damaged without just compensation, they ignore the necessity of first establishing the legal existence of a compensable property interest. Such an interest consists in their right to the *reasonable* use of the flow of the water. Their riparian rights attach to no more of the flow of the stream than that which is required for such use. (Cal. Const., art. XIV, § 3; see fn. 5, ante.) As we said in Ivanhoe Irr. Dist. v. All Parties, supra, 47 Cal.2d 597, 623, 306 P.2d 824, 839: "*Within the scope of reasonable beneficial use,* vested rights of the riparian owner continued to attach to his land as a part and parcel of the land itself, and as such was necessarily protected from unlawful encroachment by both state and federal Constitutions. The result is that this vested right *as now defined* may not be destroyed or infringed upon without due process of law or without just compensation under either Constitution." (Emphasis added.) There is now no provision of law which authorizes an unreasonable use or endows such use with the quality of a legally protectible interest merely because it may be fortuitously beneficial to the lands involved. * * *

From the foregoing we arrive at the conclusion that since there was and is no property right in an unreasonable use, there has been no taking or damaging of property by the deprivation of such use and, accordingly, the deprivation is not compensable. * * *

Plaintiffs direct our attention to United States v. Gerlach Live Stock Co. (1950) 339 U.S. 725, 70 S.Ct. 955, 94 L.Ed. 1231, as compelling a different conclusion. In that case riparian owners sought compensation for the loss of irrigating waters which overflowed the banks of the San Joaquin River onto their lands when the river flooded each year. There was no question but that the use of water for irrigating riparian lands was a reasonable use, within the meaning of the constitutional amendment. The court concluded that the use in question was a property interest which survived the amendment and was compensable.

Gerlach, of course, is distinguishable from the instant case in that plaintiffs here are not making a use of the natural flow of waters which can be deemed reasonable, and it was on the determination of a reasonable use that *Gerlach* turned: "Any hazard to claimants' rights lurks in the following clause: 'and such right does not and shall not extend to the waste or unreasonable use or unreasonable method of use or unreasonable method of diversion of water.' Since riparian rights attach to, and only to, so much of the flow of the San Joaquin as may be put to beneficial use consistently with this clause, claimants can enforce no use of wasteful or unreasonable character." (339 U.S. at p. 752, 70 S.Ct. at p. 969.) Accordingly *Gerlach* affords no aid to plaintiffs. * * *

Our foregoing conclusion disposes of plaintiffs' contention that they have a right to recover damages under section 1245 of the Water Code. As we have explained, since there was and is no property right in the instant unreasonable use, there has been no taking or damaging of property. Since by constitutional fiat no property right exists, none is created by statutory provisions intended to provide compensation for the deprivation of protectible property interests. Thus plaintiffs' reliance upon section 1245 which imposes liability upon municipal entities for damage caused to any "property, business, trade, profession or occupation" by the municipality's entry into a watershed "for the purpose of acquiring or increasing a water supply" is misplaced for the reason that there is no damaging of any property interest to which plaintiffs have a lawful right. * * *

The judgment is affirmed.

TRAYNOR, C.J., and MCCOMB, PETERS, TOBRINER, MOSK and BURKE, JJ., concur.

Notes

1. Note that the court states, "There was no question but that the use of water for irrigating riparian lands was a reasonable use, within the meaning of the constitutional amendment." Suppose the dam had been built by an association of farmers to irrigate their riparian lands. Same result? Suppose these facts were to occur in a state in which "reasonable use" is a common law requirement rather than a constitutional one?

2. "The Pareto criterion says that a change that makes at least one individual better off and leaves no individual worse off represents an increase in welfare. This criterion is usually interpreted to mean that welfare is increased by a change rendering it 'possible' to make at least one individual better off and leave no individual worse off by compensating the losers. Most of the discussion in the new welfare economics deals with this compensation principle." Ciriacy-Wantrup, Concepts Used as Economic Criteria for a System of Water Rights, in The Law of Water Allocation in the Eastern United States (Haber and Bergen, eds.) 531, 546 (1958).

The compensation principle has respectable support in the law. The leading riparian rights case is Strobel v. Kerr Salt Co., 164 N.Y. 303, 58 N.E. 142 (1900): "[The defendant's acts] would amount to a virtual confiscation of the property of small owners in the interest of a strong combination of capital. * * * We have never adopted that rule [of destroying one water use by another which would produce greater wealth] in this state and no public necessity exists therefor, even if it would ever warrant the courts in relaxing rules for the protection of property of small value in the interests of some business required to develop the resources of the state and in which much capital had embarked, giving employment to a great number of people." A leading case protecting a riparian right against public impairment without compensation is United States v. Gerlach Live Stock Co., 339 U.S. 725 (1950). A California riparian's use of water was destroyed by the Friant Dam built by the United States Bureau of Reclamation as part of the great Central Valley Project. The United States Supreme Court held, "But the public welfare, which requires claimants to sacrifice their benefits to broader ones from a higher utilization, does not necessarily require that their loss be uncompensated any more than in other takings where private rights are surrendered in the public interest. * * * No reason appears why those who get the waters should be spared from making whole those from whom they are taken. Public interest requires appropriation: it does not require expropriation." The Court also emphasized the loss distribution factor and pointed out that the project beneficiaries could well afford to reimburse the riparian for his loss of irrigation.

A classic statement is that of Baron Bramwell in Bamford v. Turnley, 3 B. & S. 66, 84–85, 122 Eng.Rep. 25, 33 (Ex.Ch.1862); "The public consists of all the individuals of it, and a thing is only for the public benefit when it is productive of good to those individuals on the balance of loss and gain to all. So that if all the loss and all the gain were borne and received by one individual, he on the whole would be a gainer. But whenever this is the case—whenever a thing is for the public benefit, properly understood—the loss to the individuals of the public who lose will bear compensation out of the gains of those who gain. It is for the public benefit there should be railways, but it would not be unless the gain of having the railway was sufficient to compensate the loss by the use of the land required for its site; and accordingly, no one thinks it would be right to take an individual's land without compensation to make a railway. It is for the public benefit that trains should run but not unless they pay their expenses."

A recent reaffirmation of this principle is found in Furrer v. Talent Irrigation District, 466 P.2d 605 (Oregon, 1970): "In setting these general standards, the courts have established the principle that if the plaintiff's land is harmed by the conduct of the defendant, the latter cannot escape compensating the plaintiff for the harm simply by showing that the defendant's use had a greater social value than the plaintiff's. Thus, in the present case it is immaterial that defendant's conduct in the operation of the canals was of great social value in that it would substantially benefit the other farmers in the area and the public generally, far outweighing the harm done to plaintiff alone. A landowner does not have to contribute to others a part of the value of his land without compensation, even if it is for a public purpose. The requested instruction, in effect, would have told the jury that it could deny plaintiff recovery if it decided that the social value of operating the canal was sufficiently great. This would clearly have constituted reversible error."

3. Restatement (Second) of Torts (1979): [23]

§ 850A. Reasonableness of the Use of Water

The determination of the reasonableness of a use of water depends upon a consideration of the interests of the riparian proprietor making the use, of any riparian proprietor harmed by it and of society as a whole. Factors that affect the determination include the following: * * *, (i) the justice of requiring the user causing harm to bear the loss.

4. Consider the proposition urged in Farnham, The Improvement and Modernization of New York Water Law Within the Framework of the Riparian System, 3 Land & Water L.Rev. 378 (1968). New York has a "harmless use law" that eliminates uncertainties caused by some remnants of the natural flow doctrine. McKinney Consol. Laws of N.Y. (Environmental Control Act) § 15–0701.2. Professor Farnham prefers protection of investments in riparian land and values based on unused rights to protection of investments in water facilities and values of water using enterprises, on the theory that the water user's expectations are not frustrated since they are based on knowledge that the riparian rights of others are not lost by non-use. Yet there is sufficient doubt that this is the New York rule to cause him to urge the enactment of a "harmful use bill" providing that an alteration in the natural condition of a body of water would be lawful even though it causes substantial harm, if the alteration is reasonable under all the facts and circumstances. Such a law, he concludes, would be constitutional even if it were to diminish riparian interests without compensation. An example given by Professor Farnham is instructive:

"Thus, if *A* begins to irrigate, withdrawing *X* gallons daily for use on his riparian land; if *B*, higher up on the stream, thereafter begins to irrigate, withdrawing *Y* gallons daily for use on his riparian land; if *B's* withdrawals leave available for *A* only *X* minus *Y* gallons; if *X* minus *Y* equals one-half of *X* gallons; and if *A's* crop is substantially reduced

23. Copyright 1979. Reprinted with the permission of the American Law Institute.

because *A* can now obtain only half the water originally available to him, *B's* alteration of the stream by his withdrawal of *Y* gallons daily will clearly have caused *A* substantial harm, and would therefore appear to be unlawful under a rule that an alteration in the natural condition of a body of water which causes substantial harm to another riparian owner is wrongful.

"It is submitted that the result which would apparently follow in this hypothetical case under such a restrictive rule affords evidence of the undesirability of the rule. In the first place, such a result would be in conflict with several basic principles of the riparian doctrine: viz., that priority in time does not necessarily create priority in right; that riparian rights are not lost by non-use; and that the extent of riparian rights varies from time to time in response to changes in the situation—in the hypothetical case, the situation changed when *B* began to irrigate. In the second place, the result which would be arrived at in the hypothetical case under the restrictive rule would tend toward an undesirable rigidity in the pattern of water use, which would make it difficult to satisfy important new water needs as they arose from time to time."

The New York Legislature considered such a bill in 1968, but it failed of passage. See National Water Commission, Summary-Digest of State Water Laws (Dewsnup, Jensen and Swenson, eds.) 548 (1973).

5. It must be conceded that the restated rule adopted by the American Law Institute raises questions of how it can be reconciled with several assertions which have been stated with such frequency as to have the flavor of maxims: "Every riparian has the right to make a reasonable use of the water." "All riparian propriators have equal rights to the water." "Riparian rights do not depend on use and are not lost by non-use." Test the validity of these propositions against the results of the cases in this section. Apply them, and the Restatement (Second) rules, to similar cases in which the situation of the parties is reversed in time or in location on the stream.

NOTE ON LOUISIANA WATER LAW

Louisiana has a form of riparian rights that is based on her Civil Code rather than on the common law. Civil law traditions go back to Roman law, but most modern civil codes stem from the Code Napoleon, adopted in 1810. Louisiana's Civil Code is not a direct borrowing of the French law, however, it is a slightly modified Spanish version introduced during Spain's regime over the territory.

The theory of the Civil Code is that all the law relating to persons, property, contracts, etc., is written into a single set of precepts, and the solution to disputes must be found within the four corners of the Code. The Code is not an ordinary statute. An important difference is that each decision is made by direct reference to the governing article of the Code. *Stare decisis* is not the rule, "the jurisprudence," as prior decisions are called, is persuasive, but the judge is free to interpret the Code afresh in each new case before him. In practice the jurisprudence is very important and Louisiana lawyers cite and argue the applicability of cases much as do lawyers in other states. Precedents from common law jurisdictions are used freely where the Code and the common law are more or less to the same point.

In addition to the Civil Code, Louisiana has many statutes, which are treated much the same as statutes in common law states.

The Civil Code was revised in 1978, but most of the provisions regarding water remain unchanged. One amendment that may be significant took water out of the category of "common things * * * that may be freely used by anyone." The new Article 450 provides,

> Art. 450. Public Things.
>
> Public things are owned by the state or its political subdivisions in their capacity as public persons.
>
> Public things that belong to the state are such as running waters, the waters and bottoms of natural and navigable water bodies, the territorial sea, and the seashore.

The change is thought to insure that water resources are assets of society, not capable of private appropriation except under regulations that protect the general interests.

The relationship between landowners whose use of land or water is affected by or affect each other's land or use is regulated by the law of servitudes, which are similar but not identical to common law easements. There are several different kinds of servitudes, including natural servitudes that arise from the natural situation of estates (Art. 654). The relative rights of riparian owners are governed by three sections of the Code:

> Art. 657. Estate Bordering on Running Water.
>
> The owner of an estate bordering on running water may use it as it runs for the purpose of watering his estate or other purposes.
>
> Art. 658. Estate Through Which Water Runs.
>
> The owner of an estate through which water runs, whether it originates there or passes from lands above, may make use of it while it runs over his lands. He cannot stop it or give it another direction and is bound to return it to its ordinary channel where it leaves his estate.
>
> Art. 667. Limitations on Use of Property.
>
> Although a proprietor may do with his estate whatever he pleases, still he can not make any work on it, which may deprive his neighbor of the liberty of enjoying his own, or which may be the cause of any damage to him.

The basic nature of a riparian right—natural flow or reasonable use—is not made clear by the Code. Analysis of the exact language does not give a definite answer to the question of how the courts will ultimately view the riparian's right. There are two Louisiana precedents, however, which might be persuasive authority that the reasonable use rule is to be followed in the state. The first is Long v. Louisiana Creosoting Co., 137 La. 861, 69 So. 281 (1915), in which the court decided a pollution case by using common law principles of reasonable use. It cited no Civil Code article. The other is Jackson v. Walton, 2 La.App. 53 (1925), involving a bayou which the court treated as though it were not a running stream. The court reversed an injunction against a non-riparian defendant who was taking water under a contract entered into with the owner of the land between his property and the bayou. The plaintiff owned land on the opposite side of the bayou. The decision was not based on an analysis of Arts. 657 and 658, instead, the court rested its decision on the law of remedies and denied the injunction on the grounds that the plaintiff showed no actual or impending damage. Neither of these cases is decisive, but there are no contrary precedents indicating an absolute right to the full flow or natural state of the water.

Non-riparian withdrawals are common in Louisiana. Certainly the tenor of practical operations and the assumption of the legislature has been that surplus water may be taken from the streams for non-riparian uses. There is nothing specific in the Code forbidding it, and the Code has a number of provisions dealing with "servitudes of aqueduct," which would seem to indicate that some right to water may be purchased by a non-riparian. Cities, waterworks, waterworks corporations, irrigation companies and irrigation districts extensively use water for non-riparian purposes. Most of these have powers of "expropriation" that seem broad enough to permit the condemnation of riparian rights interfered with by their stream withdrawals, but no cases involving such expropriation have come before the courts.

In 1910 the legislature declared the waters of "bayous, lagoons, lakes, and bays, and the beds thereof, * * * to be the property of the state." La.Acts 1910, No. 258. In 1954 this was amended to include the waters of rivers and streams. La.Rev.Stat. 9:1101. In 1964 an act setting up the Water Resources Study Commission declared that "the public welfare requires that such [ground and surface] water be put to the highest beneficial use * * *. The ownership and control of development and use of ground and surface waters for all beneficial purposes are within the jurisdiction of the state." La.Acts 1964, No. 188. As far as water rights *per se* are concerned, this declaration has been implemented only once, by giving corporations formed for gravity irrigation "the right to utilize the waters of navigable streams and other waters of the state for irrigation purposes." La.Rev.Stat. 45:62.

Louisiana has a large number of water control districts, many of which operate dams for multiple purposes which include various types of water supply. Irrigation districts and private companies withdraw large quantities of water for rice irrigation. Municipal suppliers take substantial quantities from streams. If the needs of these in combination impose demands upon a stream in excess of the supply, there is nothing to indicate which of them has the better right or how the water will be shared.

SECTION 3. NONRIPARIAN USES; PRESCRIPTION AND GRANT

KENNEBUNK, KENNEBUNKPORT & WELLS WATER DISTRICT v. MAINE TURNPIKE AUTHORITY

Supreme Judicial Court of Maine, 1950.
145 Me. 35, 71 A.2d 520.

MERRILL, JUSTICE. On exceptions. This is an action on the case instituted by Kennebunk, Kennebunkport and Wells Water District, hereinafter called the District, against Maine Turnpike Authority, hereinafter called the Authority. The District is a body politic and corporate created by the Legislature of this State for the purpose of supplying water to towns and individuals within its territorial limits. Priv. & Sp.Laws 1921, Chap. 159. The Authority is a body politic and corporate created in like manner for the purpose of constructing and operating a turnpike from a point at or near Kittery to a point at or near Fort Kent. Priv. & Sp.Laws 1941, Chap. 69.

The District in this action seeks to recover damages for injury to its water supply, Branch Brook, which injury and damages it alleges were caused by the Authority by the construction of its turnpike across Branch Brook and its watershed. The injury claimed was the creation of a turbid condition of the water. To remedy this condition the District claims that it was compelled to construct a sedimentation plant which cost between $163,000.00 and $164,000.00.

The writ was dated April 16, A.D.1947, returnable to the Superior Court in York County at the May 1947 Term. In said court the case was referred to three referees with the right of exceptions as to matters of law reserved. After hearing, the referees filed their report, finding for the plaintiff and assessing damages in the sum of $70,000.00. * * *

As the case comes to this Court, although the record is very voluminous, the issues for our determination are contained within narrow compass. The plaintiff seeks to recover damages for injury to its claimed property right to take water from Branch Brook under legislative charter and to make use of said water for distribution to the public under the same. It claims that the defendant, although it was a governmental agency created by legislative charter, and although it was engaged in a governmental function, within the authorization of its charter, to wit, building a turnpike across Branch Brook and the watershed thereof, so constructed the same and used such methods of construction that the quality of the water of Branch Brook was rendered so impure, viz, so turbid, that it was unfit for distribution by the plaintiff to its customers. The sole injury claimed by the plaintiff was to the waters of Branch Brook as used by it for a source of public water supply, and the sole damages claimed were to its use by the plaintiff as such. * * *

It might be inferred from the evidence that the District owned land on the brook where its pumping station and intake were situate and also that it owned some riparian land on the brook above its pumping station and below the riparian land owned by the Authority. The only purpose for which the District's ownership of such riparian land can be considered, however, is whether or not such ownership conferred upon it the right to use the waters of Branch Brook as a source of supply for public distribution, this being the only right that the District claimed to have and the only right which it claimed was invaded by the Authority.

The defendant was an upper riparian proprietor, it had title to its right of way across Branch Brook and its watershed. As such riparian proprietor it asserted that it had a right to use its land for all reasonable purposes; that so far as the rights of the plaintiff are concerned, the building of the turnpike across the watershed of Branch Brook and Branch Brook, and all acts which it did in connection therewith were authorized by its charter and constituted only a reasonable use of its own land by it as an upper riparian proprietor; and that if in so acting it injuriously affected the quality of the water of Branch Brook, such injury was only the result of a reasonable use by it of its own land and was *damnum absque injuria* so far as the plaintiff was concerned. * * *

The case here presented to us is of novel impression in this State, and so far as we can discover, there is no precedent exactly in point. However, an application of general principles of law governing the rights and duties of land owners, one to another, and of the law respecting the correlative rights and duties of riparian proprietors upon the same stream will afford a solution.

The leading case in this State, and one which had been approved by many text writers and many courts of last resort, is Lockwood Co. v. Lawrence, 77 Me. 297, 52 Am.Rep. 763. In this case, 77 Me. on pages 316 and 317 we said:—

> "Every proprietor upon a natural stream is entitled to the reasonable use and enjoyment of such stream as it flows through or along his own land, taking into consideration a like reasonable use of such stream by all other proprietors above or below him. The rights of the owners are not absolute but qualified, and each party must exercise his own reasonable use with a just regard to the like reasonable use by all others who may be affected by his acts. Any diversion or obstruction which substantially and materially diminishes the quantity of water, so that it does not flow as it has been accustomed to, or which defiles and corrupts it so as to essentially impair its purity, thereby preventing the use of it for any of the reasonable and proper purposes to which it is usually applied, is an infringement of the rights of other owners of land through which the stream flows, and creates a nuisance for which

those thereby injured are entitled to a remedy. Merrifield v. Lombard, 13 Allen [Mass. 16] 17, 90 Am.Dec. 188." * * *

It is to be noted that in the rule as laid down in Lockwood Co. v. Lawrence, supra, it is stated:—"The rights of the owners are not absolute but qualified, and each party must exercise his own reasonable use with a just regard to the like *reasonable use by all others who may be affected by his acts.*" (Emphasis ours.) Therefore, in determining whether or not the use made by the Authority of its land and the stream was a reasonable one *as against the District* as a lower riparian proprietor, we must determine whether or not the use by the District of the stream, as its source of public water supply, and which is the only use that it claims was injuriously affected by the acts of the Authority, was itself a reasonable use thereof. * * *

The rights of the District, derived from its charter, to use the waters of Branch Brook are governed by the law as set forth in Hamor v. Bar Harbor Water Co., 78 Me. 127, 3 A. 40, * * *.

> "Neither can water be diverted from a private stream under authority granted by the legislature in the exercise of the right of eminent domain, for the purpose of supplying a town or village with pure water, without making compensation to the riparian proprietors whose rights are thereby injuriously affected."

In the Hamor case the Court further held that a mere use of the water did not constitute a taking, but that all of the required steps incident to the accomplishment of a legal taking by the exercise of the power of eminent domain must be followed.

The fact that the District may be a riparian proprietor does not confer upon it the right to abstract water from Branch Brook for distribution under its charter. The right of a riparian proprietor to draw water from the stream is only for a riparian use, viz, a reasonable use upon the riparian land. Abstraction for sale to others is not such reasonable use. As said in Restatement Torts, Vol. 4, Chap. 41, Sec. 855, page 374, "Non-riparian uses are those made neither on nor in connection with the use of the riparian land and include such uses as the diversion and sale of water from the stream for non-riparian consumption." Neither does the fact that the District is a quasi municipal corporation enlarge its rights as a riparian proprietor. The great weight of authority is that a municipal corporation cannot by virtue of the ownership of riparian lands abstract water from a brook on which they are located for public distribution. The authorities are collected in an extensive note in 141 A.L.R. 639. The majority rule is the necessary consequence of the principles enunciated by us in Hamor v. Bar Harbor Water Co., supra. To hold otherwise would allow a municipal corporation to take private property without the payment of just compensation.

The only use of the water of a stream which will restrict the rights of a lower riparian proprietor in its use of such water, or which will restrict the use which an upper riparian proprietor may make of his own land, is a use which the one exercising the same has the legal right to exercise. If the use exercised by a riparian proprietor be a riparian use, the right to exercise it was acquired as a usufructuary right growing out of and annexed to the ownership of the riparian land. If, however, as here it be a non-riparian use, the right to exercise the same must be acquired by purchase or grant from, or by the exercise of the right of eminent domain against those whose rights it is sought to restrict by the exercise of such use. Unless so acquired, the non-riparian use will not be a reasonable use against either upper or lower riparian proprietors, and its exercise will not be a factor entering into the determination of whether or not the use of his land by an upper riparian proprietor is a reasonable use thereof. The upper proprietor may make any use of his land not forbidden by law that he could make if such use by the lower proprietor was not being exercised.

There is no evidence in the record that the District had ever acquired, either by purchase, grant or the exercise of its right of eminent domain, any right to use water from Branch Brook as a source of public water supply.

We hold as a matter of law that as against such use of the water by the District, the use by the Authority of its own land was a reasonable use.

There is no evidence in the record that the District was making, ever had made, or even intended to make, any use of the water of Branch Brook for any purpose to which it was entitled to use the same as a riparian proprietor, nor did it claim damages for any injury to any such right of user. * * *

We sustain the action of the presiding Justice only upon the grounds set forth in this opinion, which grounds are within the objections specifically set forth in writing, and the exceptions are overruled. The case is remanded to the Superior Court.

Exceptions overruled.

Notes

1. On remand, the plaintiff was able to amend to state facts which would justify a recovery for damages because of injury to the brook as a source of public water supply. Kennebunk, Kennebunkport and Wells Water District v. Maine Turnpike Authority, 147 Me. 149, 84 A.2d 433 (1951).

2. Many cases state the preference for riparian uses over uses by nonriparians. Stockport Waterworks Co. v. Potter, 3 H. & C. 300, 159 Eng. Rep. 545 (1864); Bradford v. Cressey, 45 Me. 9 (1858); Hopkins v. Kent, 9 Ohio 14 (1839); Tulare Irrigation Dist. v. Lindsay-Strathmore Irrigation Dist., 3 Cal.2d 489, 45 P.2d 972 (1935); Brown v. Chase, 125 Wash. 542, 217 P. 23 (1923); Wasserburger v. Coffee, 180 Neb. 149, 141 N.W.2d 738 (1966).

The Restatement (Second) of Torts § 856, Comment *a* (1979)[24] nevertheless accords the nonriparian some rights:

"*a. Riparian preferences over nonriparian.* The basic principle of riparian law is that rights to the water of a watercourse or lake belong to the owners of riparian lands. A nonriparian may acquire a right to the water by grant from a riparian proprietor or permit or license from the state, as noted in Subsections (2) and (3) of this Section, and nonriparian members of the public may have certain rights in public waters as noted in Subsection (4); but otherwise a nonriparian has no interest or property in the water. Therefore no use he makes is entitled to protection from infringement by one who uses the water pursuant to a riparian right. Nevertheless, the interest of a riparian proprietor is the right to make a reasonable use of the water (see § 850, Comment *c*), and the reasonableness of the use would be tested, for the purposes of this Section, by the factors stated in §§ 850A(a)–850A(g) and discussed in Comments *a* through *i* of that Section. Any use of water by a riparian proprietor that is an exercise of his riparian rights and meets these tests of reasonableness is preferred over any use by the nonriparian and may be made without liability to him.

"Nevertheless it has been recognized that a nonriparian is privileged to make a beneficial use of the water as long as he does not cause substantial harm to the use of a riparian proprietor. Although this privilege of a nonriparian is subject to defeasance by the exercise of riparian rights and must yield to a reasonable use by riparian proprietor, it is to some extent a legally protected interest. A nonriparian who is making a reasonable and beneficial use of water that causes no harm to a riparian is entitled to protection from the wasteful features of an inefficient use of water by a riparian and to protection from intentional or unintentional conduct, other than the exercise of a riparian right, which may constitute a tort under the rules stated in other Chapters."

The matter is of considerable importance since it has been speculated that a great deal of nonriparian use occurs in the eastern and mid-western states but goes unquestioned, apparently because of the abundance of water in the streams. Such users have no prescriptive rights since they do no harm.

There seem to be no eastern cases on the question of what happens when one nonriparian interferes with another nonriparian's use. In the "California doctrine" states, nonriparian users are invariably appropriators who receive protection under the law of prior appropriation. What law would an eastern state draw on for an analogy in such a situation? The protection given the first occupant of vacant land? Or a riparian-type reasonable sharing? Cf. Hackensack Water Co. v. Nyack, 289 F.Supp. 671 (S.D.N.Y.1968).

3. In McCord v. Big Brothers Movement, 120 N.J.Eq. 446, 185 A. 480 (1936), the defendant was making a nonriparian use of the water. "Defendant contends that after it has extracted its requirements from the stream, there remains ample flow at all times for the operation of complainants'

24. Copyright 1979. Reprinted with the permission of the American Law Institute.

mill, and that because complainants' diverting dams are poorly constructed and are not kept in repair and water escapes through and over them and passes by complainants' mill pond, complainants fail to obtain the use of the full flow of the stream. I do not consider their contention a valid objection to granting the relief complainants seek. They are entitled to have the natural flow of the stream let down to them in its accustomed channel, undiminished by unreasonable use thereof by an upper riparian owner. Before defendant operated its pump, complainants were able to run their mill with so much of the flow as came to their millpond, except in occasional periods of dry weather. Complainants are entitled to receive such flow without the use of diverting dams. Certainly they cannot be required to incur the expense of constructing solid or substantial dams in the stream to meet a condition wrongfully created by defendant."

4. A nonriparian who uses water to the detriment of an existing riparian use is universally regarded as a tortfeasor. Apparently no nonriparian has ever challenged this rule and all of the law has been declared in cases in which some other claim of right was made but failed, such as an unsuccessful claim to a prescriptive right, a nonriparian use by a riparian where such privilege is not recognized, or a claim that a statutory right gave the power to injure without payment of compensation. Illustrative cases are Adams v. Greenwich Water Co., 138 Conn. 205, 83 A.2d 177 (1951); Hittinger Fruit Co. v. Cambridge, 218 Mass. 220, 105 N.E. 868 (1914); Stratton v. Mount Hermon Boys School, supra p. 254.

PABST v. FINMAND

Supreme Court of California, 1922.
190 Cal. 124, 211 P. 11.

LENNON, J. This action was instituted by the plaintiffs, Charlie Lee Pabst and the Priors, against H.H. Finmand and N.H. Finmand and the Cambrons, to quiet title to the waters of Eagle creek, in the county of Modoc, state of California. Eagle creek, rising in the Warner Mountains, west of the lands of both plaintiffs and defendants, flows in a single channel until just before it reaches the land of the plaintiffs, Priors, and the defendant, N.H. Finmand. There it forks and the north branch flows across the northwest corner of N.H. Finmand's lands and across the Prior lands. The south branch flows across the south portion of N.H. Finmand's lands and thence onto and across the lands of plaintiff Pabst.

The lands of the other defendant, H.H. Finmand, are not riparian to the creek. They lie to the west of the lands of the plaintiffs Priors and to the northwest of the lands of the plaintiff Pabst and the defendant N.H. Finmand, and are irrigated by means of two ditches, the "Gee" and the "Grider" ditches, which run from the main channel of Eagle creek before it forks, northerly to the lands of H.H. Finmand.

The trial court found that the lands of the defendant N.H. Finmand were riparian to Eagle creek, and that the defendant N.H. Finmand was entitled, as an appropriator, to a first right to 300 inches of the water of Eagle creek, measured under a 4-inch pressure, and that said defendant also had a prescriptive right to said quantity of water. The court found that the defendant H.H. Finmand was entitled to a first right of 200 inches of water from Eagle creek through what is known as the "Gee" ditch, and a first right to 200 inches of water through what is known as the "Grider" ditch, both under a right by prior appropriation and by prescription. Judgment was accordingly rendered and entered in favor of the defendant N.H. Finmand for 300 miner's inches of water under a 4-inch pressure, and in favor of H.H. Finmand for 400 miner's inches of water under a 4-inch pressure, for the irrigation of his lands through the Gee and Grider ditches. It is from this judgment that plaintiffs appeal.

The N.H. Finmand lands being riparian, whereas the H.H. Finmand lands are nonriparian, the rights arising from the use of water on these different tracts are necessarily based upon different principles, and for this reason these different tracts of lands will be considered separately.

As to the rights of the N.H. Finmand lands, it is conceded by counsel for defendants that the right to the amount of water awarded to the defendants by the judgment of the trial court must rest upon a prescriptive right alone. This is so for the reason that, as admitted by defendants, the right by appropriation is not supported by the evidence, and, while the trial court found that N.H. Finmand was a riparian owner, no judgment was given such defendant based upon his right as a riparian owner, and no attempt was made to apportion the waters among the plaintiffs and defendants as riparian owners.

The judgment for a prescriptive right was given in favor of the N.H. Finmand lands against both the Prior lands and the Pabst lands. The N.H. Finmand lands claimed this right, and it was adjudged to those lands upon the theory that said lands had gained it by adverse use of the water which was taken from the south fork of the creek. As to the Prior lands no right could be gained by prescription. This is so because the water used on the N.H. Finmand lands was taken from the south fork of the stream, which runs below and does not border the Prior lands, whereas the water diverted for use on the Prior lands is taken from the north fork of the creek, which runs by a small portion of the northwest corner of the N.H. Finmand lands and on to the Prior lands. The Prior lands, therefore, are riparian only to the north fork of the stream. A right can be gained by prescription only by acts which operate as an invasion of the rights of the person against whom the right is sought and which afford a ground of action by such party against such claimant, and it is a rule of law so well settled by decisions in this and other states as to scarcely need any citation to support it that a lower use, since it interferes in no way with the flow above, constitutes no invasion of the upper riparian owner's right, and cannot, therefore, afford any basis for a prescriptive right. * * *

As to the Pabst lands, the N.H. Finmand lands are the upper riparian lands, and the Pabst lands are lower riparian lands. It is the contention of defendants that the continuous use of a certain amount of water each year for the statutory period of time gave to them a prescriptive right to that certain quantity of water so used by them, and this in spite of the fact that the use of the water by the lower riparian owner was never in any manner interrupted or interfered with by such use, and in the absence of any indication or bringing of knowledge home to the lower riparian owner that the upper riparian owner was claiming such right, not as a riparian owner, but adversely to him. This contention cannot be maintained. In the absence of a showing that the upper owner is using the water under a claim of prescriptive right, the lower owner has the right to presume that such owner is only taking that to which he is entitled as a riparian owner by virtue of his riparian right. * * * Such use was not hostile unless there was an actual clash between the rights of the respective owners. While there was sufficient water flowing down the stream to supply the wants of all parties, its use by one was not an invasion of the rights of the other. * * *

A riparian owner is entitled to a reasonable amount of water for use on his riparian lands. What is a reasonable amount varies with the circumstances of each particular case and also varies from year to year, for the amount which might be reasonable in a season of plenty might be manifestly unreasonable in a season of drought. Nor is the question of reasonableness to be tested solely by the needs of the upper riparian proprietor. The rights of riparian proprietors are correlative, and the "reasonable" amount to which any one riparian owner is entitled is to be measured by comparison with the needs of the other riparian proprietors. The fact that there was always sufficient water coming down the creek for the Pabst lands with the exception of the two years prior to the trial is undisputed by any evidence offered by the defendants. And, so long as defendants left sufficient water in the stream for the use of the lower riparian proprietors, it cannot be said that they were using an unreasonable amount, and, so long as they were not using an "unreasonable" amount, the plaintiffs had no cause to complain, nor was any right of theirs invaded. * * *

The adverse use must be such as to raise a presumption of a grant of an easement as the only hypothesis on which to account for the other party's failure to complain thereof. * * * In the absence of any facts showing an actual knowledge by plaintiffs of the adverse nature of defendants' claim or of any facts sufficient to create a presumption of a knowledge of that claim, it cannot be said that a failure of plaintiffs to assert their rights by bringing an action against the defendants was such a submission as could be accounted for only on the hypothesis of a grant. Indeed, defendants have not shown such an unreasonable use of the water on their lands as to put plaintiffs on notice of their claim. We do not mean to hold that a right may not be gained by an upper riparian proprietor by prescription, but to do so it must be clearly shown either that actual notice of the adverse claim of such owner has been brought home to the other party, or that the circumstances are such, as, for instance, the use of all of the water of the creek, that such party must be presumed to have known of the adverse claim. In the instant case there was nothing to indicate to the lower riparian owners that the owners of the N.H. Finmand lands were exercising, or attempting to exercise, any more than their riparian rights, and, in the absence of such indication to plaintiffs that the owners of the N.H. Finmand lands were asserting a right hostile to the rights of the plaintiffs, no prescriptive title was acquired. Even if the upper riparian owner is using all the water of the stream, still, if the lower riparian owner is not then using any and has no desire to do so, such use by the upper riparian owner would not be adverse, and, and if continued five years, would not gain him a prescriptive right. * * *

It is the contention of plaintiffs that there was no invasion of plaintiffs' riparian rights by the nonriparian owners of the H.H. Finmand lands by the diversion by such nonriparian owners of water which the riparian owners did not need, and therefore no prescriptive right to the use of the water could be acquired in the absence of a showing of actual damage to the lands of the riparian owners caused by a deprivation of the water. As to a nonriparian owner the riparian owner is under no duty to share the waters of the creek, and the slightest use by such nonriparian owner diminishes to some extent the flow of the stream. Obviously, there is no question of reasonable use in the sense in which that term is applied to the rights of respective riparian owners, since a riparian owner, as against a nonriparian owner, is entitled to the full flow of the stream without the slightest diminution. The initial step in the diversion of the water by the nonriparian owner is therefore an invasion of the right of the lower riparian owner, and every subsequent diversion is a further invasion of that right. Against a person who seeks to divert water to nonriparian lands, the riparian owner is entitled to restrain any diversion, and he is not required to show any damage to his use. Although no damage to the present use of the riparian owner results from the diversion, yet damage to the future use may result, and an injunction will be granted to prevent the diversion from growing into a right by the lapse of the statutory period. * * * In the instant case the adverse use of the water on nonriparian lands was continued "openly and notoriously" for a period longer than five years, and, the slightest use by the owners of these lands being notice to all the lower riparian owners that a hostile right was being asserted, a prescriptive right was acquired by such adverse use on those lands. * * *

Judgment reversed.

Notes

1. If the reasonable use rule is given its full meaning, that the fundamental right of a riparian proprietor is to be free from unreasonable uses which cause harm to his own reasonable use of the water, it logically

follows that a non-riparian use that does not interfere with downstream riparian uses gives rise to no cause of action and does not ripen into a prescriptive right no matter how long continued. See Kennedy v. Niles Water Co., 173 Mich. 474, 139 N.W. 241 (1913). Cf. Pasadena v. Alhambra, 33 Cal.2d 908, 207 P.2d 17 (1949). This reasoning is not always strictly followed and a number of courts which clearly employ the reasonable use rule when the controversy is between riparians seem to recognize the possibility that a non-harmful non-riparian use will ripen into a prescriptive right if continued for the period of limitations. See Jones v. Conn, 39 Or. 30, 64 P. 855 (1901). It seems probable that a number of courts purporting to apply the natural flow theory in cases deciding that a riparian may complain of a nonriparian use which causes no actual harm are using this device to protect the future uses of the riparian plaintiff. See Harvey Realty Co. v. Wallingford, 111 Conn. 352, 150 A. 60 (1930); Exton v. Glen Gardner Water Co., 3 N.J.Eq. 613, 129 A. 255 (1925).

2. Since in most cases a downstream use causes no harm to an upstream riparian, a long-continued downstream nonriparian use does not create a prescriptive right that can receive protection against a new upstream use that causes harm to it. Kennebunk, Kennebunkport and Wells Water District v. Maine Turnpike Authority, 147 Me. 149, 84 A.2d 433 (1951). In the west this rule has become epitomized as "prescription does not run upstream." But see Dontanello v. Gust, 86 Wash. 268, 150 P. 420 (1915).

3. If a nonriparian use causes no present harm but is enjoined to prevent the acquisition of a prescriptive right, a "dog in the manger" situation results in which desirable use of water resources is inhibited. New York solved this problem by the enactment of the "harmless use law," McKinney Consol.Laws of N.Y. (Environmental Conservation law) § 15–0701:

"1. An alteration (whether or not it causes water to cover or permeate land previously dry) in the natural flow, quantity, quality or condition of a natural watercourse or lake situated in this state and either on or below the surface of the earth, effected by the use either on or off riparian land, withdrawal, impoundment, or obstruction of the water in such watercourse or lake, or by the addition of water thereto, or by changes in the banks, bed, course or other physical characteristics of such watercourse or lake, is reasonable and lawful as against any person, as defined in subdivision two of section 15–0107, having an interest in such watercourse or lake, unless such alteration is causing harm to him or it, or would cause him or it immediate harm if and when begun. No action for nominal damages or for an injunction shall be maintainable because of such an alteration against any person or corporation, whether a riparian owner or not, on the ground that such alteration is an infringement of the plaintiff's private rights and privileges in the waters of, or with respect to, such watercourse or lake unless such alteration is causing plaintiff harm, or would cause him or it immediate harm if and when begun. This subdivision shall apply to such an action regardless of whether the alteration sought to be made the basis of it was caused before or after the effective date of this section. * * *

"4. The cause of action essential to the initiation and creation of a prescriptive right or privilege against a private riparian owner to continue an alteration in the natural condition of such a watercourse or lake shall not be supplied by such an alteration until it shall have caused such riparian owner harm and then only if it is unreasonable."

The necessity for and constitutionality of this law is discussed in Farnham, The Improvement and Modernization of New York Water Law Within the Framework of the Riparian System, 3 Land and Water L.Rev. 377, 382–388 (1968).

4. Should the extent of a prescriptive right be fixed in terms of a specific quantity of water, or should it be measured by the proportion of the total flow of the stream that was diverted? In Mally v. Weidensteiner, 88 Wash. 398, 153 P. 342 (1915) the court put both limitations on an adverse claimant who had diverted and used 1½ c.f.s., but never more than one-third of the stream. However, in Akin v. Spencer, 21 Cal.App.2d 325, 69 P.2d 430 (1937), an adverse user of six inches of water was held to be absolutely entitled to this quantity as against downstream riparians, and could not be compelled to prorate very low flows with the riparians.

5. Can principles of prescription or estoppel create a right to the continuation of a long-existing use by another? In Kray v. Muggli, 84 Minn. 90, 86 N.W. 882 (1901) the court enjoined the removal of 40-year old mill dam.

> The dam in question, having been erected for the purpose of developing power to operate mill machinery, must be taken to be a permanent obstruction; and, it having existed and been maintained as such for so great a length of time, the artificial conditions created thereby must be deemed to have become the natural conditions. * * * The authorities all hold, as far as our examination has extended, that in such cases the conditions arising from the permanent obstruction, though artificial to begin with, become by long lapse of time the natural conditions, and interested parties are bound by the rules of law applicable to such conditions. [Citations omitted.] In the case at bar even nature herself became adapted to the new surroundings. A native growth of hard-wood timber sprang up along the shore of the lakes formed by the raise of the river, thus giving a natural effect and appearance to the conditions created by the dam. The government, in the survey of the lands in that vicinity, recognized the artificial as the natural state, and surveyed the public lands with reference to the lakes, meandering them precisely as other natural bodies of water are surveyed and meandered.

Contra, Kiwanis Club Foundation Inc. of Lincoln v. Yost, 179 Neb. 598, 139 N.W.2d 359 (1966).

Some states may require the owners of dams to maintain them against their will. See Minn.Stat.Ann. § 105.43; Wis.Stat.Ann. 31.185. How can these be enforced perpetually? In New Jersey, a dam 20 years old or older, upon which other landowners have made permanent improvements, may be ordered maintained, but if the expense would be an undue burden on the owner the landowners around the reservoir may be ordered to pay part or all of it. N.J.Stat.Ann. 58:4–10.

The water level in natural lakes, and often as well in man-made reservoirs, has important implications for residential, recreational and environmental values. The protection afforded by the common law has been noted in Section 2 of this chapter. Several states have imposed extensive controls on fluctuations and minimum levels.

Minnesota requires a permit to remove or abandon a reservoir or dam, Minn.Stat.Ann. § 105.43. Reservoir levels may be fixed in Minnesota, ibid., and Michigan (by county boards of supervisors), Mich.Comp.Laws Ann. § 281.63. Natural lake levels are the subject of regulation in Vermont and Indiana, Vt.Stat.Ann. T. 10 §§ 905, 1421–1426; Burns' Ind.Stat. Ann. § 13–2–13–1. See Bartke, Navigability in Michigan in Retrospect and Prospect, 16 Wayne L.Rev. 409, 440 (1970).

DUCKWORTH v. WATSONVILLE WATER & LIGHT CO.

Supreme Court of California, 1910.
158 Cal. 206, 110 P. 927.

[Plaintiff Duckworth is the owner of lands riparian to Pinto Lake, formerly owned by McKinley, who deeded to defendant company all the water rights pertaining to the land. Defendant is diverting water and selling it to persons who use it on nonriparian lands. Plaintiff is now irrigating his lands from the lake, and brings this action to quiet his title to the water. Held, defendant has a right superior to the plaintiff's, to take water from the lake in any quantity, for any purpose.]

SHAW, J. I concur. * * * Perhaps something more should be said regarding the effect of a conveyance, by the owner of riparian land, of his riparian right therein, to another for nonriparian use. The court below seems to have been of the opinion that the riparian right consisted of the ownership of a definite quantity of the water of the lake, a quantity equal only to the amount which could be beneficially used on the riparian land concerned, and that the conveyance merely transferred to the grantees that quantity from the lake, leaving the riparian grantor free to take thereafter an equal or greater quantity therefrom and use it on the identical land, provided only that he must leave enough to furnish to the grantees the definite quantity which, by this theory, was conveyed, or if the grantees were using less, then enough to provide for their actual use from time to time. This was not the legal effect of the conveyance. The riparian right exists solely because the land abuts upon the water. It is parcel of the land. It extends to all the water which may be reached from the land, and not to any specific particles or definite quantity or area of it. It is the right to make reasonable use and consumption of the water on the adjoining land and to a reasonable use of the water, in place, in connection with and for the benefit of the land. The water cannot be severed from the land and transferred to a third person so as to give him the title and right to remove it, as against other riparian owners. The grantor alone will be estopped by such a conveyance. The estoppel against him, with respect to the use and consumption of the water, or diversion from its natural position, must be as complete and extensive as was the right he conveyed. The McKinley deeds conveyed the entire right to use this water for irrigation on these lands to the defendant's predecessors, and it now belongs to the defendant, and not to Duckworth. A man may not eat his cake and have it. A man who sells a right to do a thing cannot thereafter exercise the right himself, except by permission of the buyer, and it is immaterial that the buyer may not be using or exercising it. If the water company had obtained similar deeds from the owners of all the lands abutting upon the lake and its tributaries, it would have obtained a complete estoppel against such landowners which would have prevented them from interfering with any use it saw fit to make of the water, and such estoppel would undoubtedly extend to all the water of the lake. If, having this right of estoppel, it chose to use only a part of the water, or none of it, this neglect to use it would not give any of the owners the right to take that which the company suffered to remain unused. A judgment which purported to give such owners the unqualified right to use the water on their respective tracts, as against the company, would operate to deprive the company of the property which it had bought and paid for and to return that property to the person who sold it and received payment of the price. The same principle must apply when the estoppel has been obtained as to one, only, of the riparian owners. He is absolutely estopped to use any part of the water on the land, except as specified in the deed by which he is bound. These propositions are fully established by the * * * authorities. * * *

Note

Other cases giving no effect, as against other riparians, to a grant from a riparian to a non-riparian are *Kennebunk,* supra, Hendrix v. Roberts Marble Co., 175 Ga. 389, 165 S.E. 223 (1932); Roberts v. Martin, 72 W.Va. 92, 77 S.E. 535 (1913) and Williams v. Wadsworth, 51 Conn. 277 (1883).

PYLE v. GILBERT

Supreme Court of Georgia, 1980.
245 Ga. 403, 265 S.E.2d 584.

HILL, JUSTICE.

This is a water rights case involving a non-navigable watercourse. It presents a confrontation between the past and the present. Plaintiffs are the owners of a 140-year-old water-powered gristmill. They emphasize the natural flow theory. Defendants are upper riparians using water to irrigate their farms. They emphasize the reasonable use theory of water rights.

The plaintiffs, Willie and Arlene Gilbert, own property commonly known as Howard's Mill located on Kirkland's Creek, a non-navigable stream in Early County which goes into the Chattahoochee River. They acquired a partial interest in the property in 1974. The other interest was acquired at the same time by their daughter and son-in-law. In 1977, they purchased the other interest and now own the fee. Until August 31, 1978, the Gilberts owned and operated a water-powered gristmill on their property. They also rented boats for profit and permitted fishing and swimming in the 40-acre pond. * * *

On July 7, 1978, the Gilberts filed a complaint against Sanford Hill, who is an owner of property that is upper riparian in relation to the Gilbert's property, alleging that since 1975 he has been diverting and using water from Kirkland's Creek for irrigation, * * *

The testimony at a hearing on July 18, 1978, revealed to plaintiffs that other upper riparian owners also had irrigated with water from the creek. The plaintiffs subsequently added four defendants: George Edgar Pyle, Jimmy Doster, Philip Buckhalter and Vinson Evans.[a] Following discovery, the trial court made an extensive examination of our water law and granted the plaintiffs' motions for summary judgment as to liability against all defendants, holding that the defendants' use of the water for irrigation constituted a diversion, a trespass, a nuisance and an unreasonable use as a matter of law, and enjoining any future use. The issue of damages was reserved for trial. The defendants appeal. * * *

We do not find that the record supports the conclusion that the uses complained of were unreasonable as a matter of law. Whether the use of water for irrigation is reasonable or unreasonable presents a triable question. White v. East Lake Land Co., supra, 96 Ga. at 417, 23 S.E. 393; Price v. High Shoals Mfg. Co., supra, 132 Ga. at 249, 64 S.E. 87. It was error to grant summary judgment to the plaintiffs.

In its detailed analysis of Georgia water law, the trial court had to apply Hendrix v. Roberts Marble Co., 175 Ga. 389, 394, 165 S.E. 223, 226 (1932), to the effect that "* * * riparian rights are appurtenant only to lands which actually touch on the watercourse, or through which it flows, and that a riparian owner or proprietor can not himself lawfully use or convey to another the right to use water flowing along or through his property * * *" Thus *Hendrix* held water could only be used on riparian lands. Yet four years later, in reversing the denial of an injunction against the use of water on non-riparian land, the court did not rely heavily on *Hendrix,* supra. Instead the court (Russell, C.J., writing the opinion in both cases) based its decision more on general riparian water law principles than on the non-riparian use. Robertson v. Arnold, 182 Ga. 664, 671, 186 S.E. 806 (1936). To the extent that Robertson v. Arnold might reflect ambivalence as to the rule announced in *Hendrix,* that concern is well-founded.

A major study of Georgia water law concluded that "Another disadvantage of this doctrine is that it permits the use of stream water

a. Vinson Evans owns non-riparian property which he admits having irrigated with the alleged permission of a riparian owner. The evidence does not show that he owns any riparian property. The second and fourth findings of fact by the trial court must be reversed to the extent that they imply he is an upper riparian landowner to the plaintiffs.

only in connection with riparian land." Institute of Law and Government, University of Georgia Law School, A Study of the Riparian and Prior Appropriation Doctrines of Water Law (1955), p. 104. Likewise, the American Law Institute now recommends allowing use of water by riparian owners on non-riparian land, Rest. Torts 2d § 855, as well as allowing non-riparian owners to acquire a right to use water from riparian owners. Id., § 856(2), (see also 7 Clark, Waters and Water Rights 71–72, § 614.1 (1976)). The Restatement relies on two principles: that riparian rights are property rights and as such could normally be transferred, and that water law should be utilitarian and allow the best use of the water. Id., Comment b. Also, the Institute considers the acquisition of water rights by condemnation a "grant of riparian right." Id., Comment c.

Georgia recognizes the power to condemn riparian rights; in fact, this court relied on that principle in affirming an injunction in City of Elberton v. Hobbs, 121 Ga. 749(2), 49 S.E. 779 (1905) (see also the second City of Elberton v. Hobbs, 121 Ga. 750, 49 S.E. 780 (1905)). City of Elberton, in turn, was relied on by the court in *Hendrix* for the proposition that water could not be used on non-riparian lands. In our view, City of Elberton is not good authority for that rule; rather, it established that the right to use water on non-riparian lands can be acquired by condemnation. We agree with the American Law Institute that the right to use water on non-riparian land should be permitted and if that right can be acquired by condemnation, it can also be acquired by grant. Thus we find that the right to the reasonable use of water in a non-navigable watercourse on non-riparian land can be acquired by grant from a riparian owner. The contrary conclusion in Hendrix v. Roberts Marble Co., supra, will not be followed.

In summary, the grant of summary judgment, and the permanent injunction based thereon, against each of the defendants must be reversed. On remand, the issues must be tried in accordance with the foregoing decision, looking always to see if, insofar as injunctive relief is concerned, all the uses of the creek and pond can be accommodated.

Judgment reversed.

Notes

1. Accord: Gillis v. Chase, 67 N.H. 161, 31 A. 18 (1892); Thurston v. Portsmouth, 205 Va. 909, 140 S.E.2d 678 (1965); Elliot v. Fitchburg Ry. Co., 10 Cush. 191 (Mass.1852); Concord Manufacturing Co. v. Robinson, 66 N.H. 1, 25 A. 718 (1890); Doremus v. Paterson, 63 N.J.Eq. 605, 52 A. 1107 (1902); St. Anthony Water Power Co. v. Minneapolis, 41 Minn. 270, 43 N.W. 56 (1889); Lawrie v. Silsby, 76 Vt. 240, 56 A. 1106 (1904).

2. In Smith v. Stanolind Oil & Gas Co., 197 Okl. 499, 172 P.2d 1002 (1946), the riparian owner leased water to the company for use in drilling operations on nonriparian lands. A lower riparian sought an injunction. Held, the company's right to use water was a derivative right to be measured by the extent of the rights of the riparian owner who granted it.

Since the use by a riparian owner on non-riparian lands would not be unreasonable per se, the nonriparian grantee could similarly use the water so long as the plaintiff's present uses for domestic and stock water were not substantially impaired.

STATE v. APFELBACHER

Supreme Court of Wisconsin, 1918.
167 Wis. 233, 167 N.W. 244.

Action by George Apfelbacher against the State of Wisconsin and others. Judgment for plaintiff, and defendants bring error. Affirmed.

The appeal in this case (no bill of exceptions being before us in the record), presents only the pleadings, findings, and judgment for review. From these findings it appears:

That the defendant Humphrey and his predecessors have for many years operated a gristmill at the outlet of Lake Nagawicka in Waukesha county. Lake Nagawicka has an area of 1.41 square miles, and its waters are held and maintained, to a certain extent, by a dam owned and controlled by defendant Humphrey at this outlet. The stream forming the inlet and outlet to this lake is Bark river. One mile below Lake Nagawicka and on Bark river plaintiff and his predecessors had for many years also maintained a dam and operated a similar mill. The millpond at this point was about 25 acres in extent and held only sufficient water supply to run plaintiff's mill for a few hours. The mill and water power of defendant Humphrey was the elder of the two.

In 1906 the State of Wisconsin established a fish hatchery just below Nagawicka Lake with ponds numbered 1, 2, and 3 just below the lake and on the north side of the Bark river, and ponds numbered 4, 5, and 6 south thereof. Ponds 1, 2, and 3 were supplied with water from a spillway on Lake Nagawicka; ponds 4, 5, and 6 by a 12-inch pipe running from the waters of Lake Nagawicka through or under ponds 1, 2, and 3 and the Bark river. The waters from these six ponds, save such as is lost by seepage or evaporation, ultimately find their way into Bark river above the plaintiff's dam. The total fall between the two dams is 10½ feet.

That for upwards of 20 years prior to 1906, as the two water powers were being operated by their respective owners, and with the natural flow of the Bark river between them, the upper mill had been operated practically every day continuously, and the plaintiff was thereby enabled to also operate his mill continuously.

By a written contract made in 1906 between the defendant Humphrey and the State of Wisconsin it was agreed that the state might place and maintain in Lake Nagawicka, for the purpose of drawing water for use in the fish hatchery, the 12-inch pipe connected with the ponds numbered 4, 5, and 6, and might use for the hatchery so much of the waters of Lake Nagawicka as could be drawn through such pipe, and that, if at any time such use by the state and by defendant

Humphrey in connection with his mill should lower the waters in the lake to a point 12 inches below a certain high-water mark, then the said Humphrey, his heirs and assigns, would absolutely desist and refrain from using any water from said lake for the running of the mill property, or for any other purpose, until the waters of said lake should again reach a point within 12 inches below such high-water mark.

That the defendant state by reason of such agreement claimed to have the right to, and did, exercise practical control over the waters at said dam, and did at several times subsequent to 1906 shut off the outflow of the waters in Lake Nagawicka so that for periods of one or two weeks each the plaintiff was practically deprived of the use of the waters of Bark river and forced thereby to shut down his mill. That the natural flow of water from Lake Nagawicka into Bark river and from thence on into Upper Nemahbin Lake is sufficient to operate the two mills in question, and that each of such mills is reasonably adapted to such water course and the ordinary operation of the fish hatchery maintained by the state of Wisconsin is also a reasonable use of the natural flow of Bark river. That it is not necessary for the maintenance of the fish hatchery and its efficient operation that the defendant state of Wisconsin should avail itself of the attempted grant of power under the agreement between itself and the defendant Humphrey, and that the exercise of such attempted grant of power on its part is to impair the power and destroy the use of the mill of plaintiff in dry or low water seasons. The operation of plaintiff's mill prior to the agreement between defendants in 1906 was of substantial value to him, but by the exercise by the state of such claim of right under the agreement there has been a substantial interference with, if not destruction of, the plaintiff's business. * * *

That the mill of the defendant Humphrey may be efficiently operated, although not to its full capacity, when the waters of Lake Nagawicka are down as low as a point 15 inches below such high-water mark. By lowering the water in Lake Nagawicka proportionally more and more water is needed to generate the same amount of power in Humphrey's mill, and that, therefore, as riparian owner, defendant Humphrey has the optional right, when the water in the millpond is as low as 12 inches below high-water mark, to either close his mill so that more water and power may be accumulated or to run his mill under low-water pressure.

As conclusions of law the court found that the defendant state of Wisconsin has made an unreasonable use of the waters of Lake Nagawicka and Bark river, and that both defendant state and the defendant Humphrey should be restrained from exercising or attempting to exercise, the power attempted to be given under the agreement between them so far as it affected the detaining of the water from Bark river in such manner as theretofore done under such claim of right and except only when such detention is a reasonable one having relation to the correlative rights and duties existing between the plaintiff and the defendant Humphrey as riparian owners. From such judgment the defendants appeal.

ESCHWEILER, J. (after stating the facts as above). * * *

In this state the owner of an upper dam has the right to withhold the waters of the stream at certain periods in order that there may be thereby created a sufficient storage of water to more properly and efficiently carry out the purpose to which he, as riparian owner, may put the waters of the stream. Mabie v. Matteson, 17 Wis. 1; Timm v. Bear, 29 Wis. 254; Coldwell v. Sanderson, 69 Wis. 52, 28 N.W. 232, 33 N.W. 591; Lawrence v. Am. W.P. Co., 144 Wis. 556, 563, 128 N.W. 440.

But the right to detain for a time, as well as every other right which a riparian owner acquires as such, to the waters of the stream flowing through or by his land is restricted always to that which is a reasonable detention or a reasonable use, and these terms are to be measured and determined by the extent and capacity of the stream, the uses to which it is and has been put, and the rights that other riparian owners on the same stream also have. There can be no absolute or fixed standard for the measure of such relative rights. The essential question to be determined by the court or jury trying the issues between the parties in each particular case is what is reasonable under the circumstances there presented. This was the view adopted by the trial court, and his finding, therefore, that the state's withholding at times the flow of water from Lake Nagawicka was not a reasonable or necessary use of the waters of Lake Nagawicka and the Bark river for the proper carrying on of the fish hatchery, is the controlling fact in this case. * * *

The right that defendant Humphrey has to hold back the waters of Lake Nagawicka for a time when below the high-water mark so that the supply of water may thereby be increased is one that is necessarily also within the limitation prescribed for all riparian rights of being kept within the boundaries of what is reasonable, and it cannot be severed from his entire rights as riparian owner so that this particular element of those rights that is, to withhold the natural flow of the Bark river, can be, in a measure, carved out therefrom and transferred to some one else, and by that person used in a manner that would be unreasonable if the use were by Humphrey himself. The conveyance by Humphrey to the state confers no greater right with reference to these flowing waters than Humphrey himself had. The condition of reasonable use attached to it before he conveyed it, and remained with it after such conveyance. The state stands in no better position with reference to its exercise than did or would the defendant Humphrey.

The judgment of the circuit court is affirmed.

Note

Compare Farmers Highline Canal and Reservoir Co. v. Golden, supra p. 197.

SECTION 4. MUNICIPAL SUPPLY

ADAMS v. GREENWICH WATER CO.

Supreme Court of Errors of Connecticut, 1951.
138 Conn. 205, 83 A.2d 177.

INGLIS, JUDGE. The plaintiffs, who are riparian owners along the Mianus River in Greenwich, instituted this action to enjoin the defendant from diverting, and from attempting to take by condemnation, any of the waters of that stream. The defendant filed a cross complaint claiming a declaratory judgment determining whether it has the right to condemn the water rights although part of the benefits may accrue to inhabitants of Port Chester, New York. * * *

The defendant is a corporation specially chartered by the Connecticut General Assembly in 1880. 8 Spec.Laws 406. By virtue of its charter and amendments thereof, it has the franchise to furnish water for public and domestic use in the town of Greenwich, in a small portion of the town of Stamford adjacent to the Mianus River, in the town of Rye, New York, including Port Chester, and in Westchester County, New York, whenever that use in Westchester County will not curtail the supply adequate for the inhabitants of Connecticut. In the summer of 1929 the defendant, in order to supplement its water supply, started to pump water from the Mianus River at Farms Road, which is upstream from the plaintiffs' properties. The riparian owners instituted suits, and as a result of their action the defendant entered into a contract in 1933 with the Stamford Water Company for a supplemental supply of water and ceased the taking of water from the Mianus.

A period of extreme drought occurred in the summer of 1949. The defendant's water supply diminished rapidly. By August 1 its reservoirs were only about 60 per cent full. Notice was received that the Stamford Water Company would have to reduce the amount of water to be furnished by it below the four million gallons daily called for by the contract. Thereupon, on August 9, 1949, the defendant began pumping water, at the rate of about a million gallons daily, from the Mianus River at Farms Road into a pipe line which led into one of its reservoirs. When this came to the attention of the plaintiff Altschul, inquiries were made of the defendant on her behalf and a series of conferences and letters between the parties ensued. The defendant acknowledged that it had no legal right to divert the water as it was doing without purchasing or condemning the water rights but took the position that conditions required it to do so. * * * On January 1, 1950, the defendant had less than forty days' supply of water on hand, and on February 4 the Stamford Water Company cut off its supply completely. This necessitated the installation of an additional pump and the pumping of a greater quantity of water from the Mianus. Between August 9, 1949, and June 1, 1950, the approximate date of the trial of this case, the defendant diverted from the river an average of

1.56 million gallons daily. During that same period the average flow of the river was 16.2 million gallons daily. At no time did the defendant cut off the flow in the river completely, although during the driest period of the diversion the defendant was taking more than half of the flow. During most of the period the flow of the river was in such quantity that the diversion resulted in no inconvenience or detriment to the plaintiffs. Even during the driest periods the plaintiffs suffered no actual or substantial damage.

The original charter of the defendant granted it the right to take by eminent domain any land or water in the town of Greenwich for its corporate purpose. 8 Spec.Laws 406. In 1927, after its franchise had been extended in 1925 to include the furnishing of water to Rye, 19 Spec.Laws 848, the General Assembly granted it authority, for the purpose of supplying water for public or private use, to take by eminent domain, purchase or otherwise all or any part of the waters of the Mianus River, to construct such reservoirs as it might deem necessary to impound such water, and to take by eminent domain, purchase or otherwise such property as it might deem necessary for the construction of reservoirs, the protection of its watershed or any other corporate purpose. This authority, however, was made subject to the right of the New York, New Haven and Hartford Railroad Company to take water from the Mianus River for its electric power generating plant at Cos Cob, up to, after 1941, five million gallons daily. 20 Spec.Laws, 429.

At the present time the defendant has as reservoirs Rockwood Lake, Putnam Lake and Brush Dam, with a total maximum storage capacity of 1,086 million gallons. As an additional source of supply, the defendant has the contract, referred to above, with the Stamford Water Company, whereby the latter is obligated, subject to acts of God, to furnish the defendant six million gallons daily for the first six months of each year and four million gallons daily for the balance of the year. This contract expires in 1953. For various reasons this contract can no longer be counted upon to provide a reliable source of supply. The water coming from the Stamford Water Company is pumped through a twenty-inch pipe line into Rockwood Lake. Rockwood Lake and Converse Lake empty into Putnam Lake. At the lower end of Putnam Lake is a filter system through which the water passes into one main which leads to Greenwich and another which leads to Rye. All of the water supplied to Rye is sold and delivered at the state line to the Port Chester Water Works, Inc., an affiliated company. The defendant does not now serve, or plan to serve in the future, any of Westchester County outside of Rye.

A water company in the situation of the defendant should plan for a supply of water to meet conditions as they will be at least ten and preferably fifteen or twenty years in the future. The safe yield of the defendant's present water supply system, not including the water it receives under its contract with the Stamford Water Company, based on experience during the dry year June 1, 1949—June 1, 1950, is only about four million gallons daily. In 1949 Greenwich consumed about five million gallons daily and Port Chester and Rye about four million. It is estimated that in 1960 there will be required for Greenwich 6.8 million gallons a day and for Port Chester and Rye 4.3 million, while in 1970 Greenwich will take 8.75 million gallons daily and Port Chester and Rye 4.65 million. Thus it appears that the safe yield of the defendant's own system without aid from the Stamford company was not adequate in 1948–49 to take care of the needs of the defendant's Connecticut customers alone, and as time goes on this yield will become less able to do so. To meet this condition, the defendant plans to construct a reservoir by damming the Mianus River above Farms Road. This will give the defendant additional storage capacity of approximately 2,200 million gallons. From this reservoir certain quantities of water will be conducted through the present pipe line into Rockwood Lake. The defendant will be bound to allow enough water to flow down the river to meet the needs of the New York, New Haven and Hartford Railroad Company, and its plan is to release sufficient water down the stream to equalize the flow over the entire year. A portion of the proposed reservoir and a major portion of its watershed will be in New York state, and the land for that portion will be acquired by the Port Chester Water Works, Inc. The defendant has no permanent source of water storage available to it other than the Mianus River.

On the foregoing facts the trial court concluded that, because the damage suffered by the plaintiffs from the diversion of the water of the river was far outweighed by the utility of the defendant's conduct and the interests of the public therein, no injunction should issue against future diversion. It also decided, with reference to the prayer for a declaratory judgment, that the defendant may exercise its right of eminent domain in respect to lands and water rights on the Mianus River, "including those of the plaintiffs," in order to increase its water supply storage, although a portion of such additional supply may be delivered to and used by those inhabitants of the state of New York to whom the defendant may supply water under existing legislative grants. It followed from this that the prayer for an injunction against such condemnation was denied.

We will first consider the question whether the defendant has the power to condemn the water rights of the plaintiffs for the purpose of constructing its proposed reservoir. Clearly, the General Assembly, by the amendment of the defendant's charter in 1927, purported to grant it that right. The taking of water by a water company chartered to supply water to the public is a taking for a public use. * * * When the legislature endows a public utility company with the power to take by eminent domain such property as is necessary to fulfill its corporate purposes without restriction, the determination of what is necessary to be taken lies in the discretion of the company. The courts will interfere with the exercise of that discretion only in cases of bad faith or unreasonable conduct. * * * On the question of the necessity of a taking, needs which will arise in the reasonably foreseeable future must be taken into consideration. * * * Upon the subordinate facts found, there can be no question that it is reasonably necessary for the defendant to acquire water rights for the construction of a reservoir in the Mianus River in order to continue to furnish an adequate supply of water to its customers in Connecticut, to say nothing of the users of its water in New York state. The court would not be warranted in concluding the contrary. * * *

We turn now to a consideration of the plaintiffs' prayer for an injunction restraining the defendant from further diverting the water of the Mianus by pumping. It is well established that a riparian owner is entitled to have the water of the stream upon which he borders continue to flow in its wonted manner. * * * Any infringement of that right entitles him to relief, at least by way of damages, even though the actual, provable damage is small. * * * It does not necessarily follow, however, that he is entitled to relief by way of injunction, for the granting of such relief lies in the sound discretion of the court. * * *

The trial court denied the injunction in this case because it concluded that to grant it would result in damage to the defendant disproportionate in amount to the damage refusal of the injunction would cause the plaintiffs and would be detrimental to the public interest. * * *

The limitations on the propriety of the denial of an injunction on the theory of comparative damage between the parties do not apply to the refusal of an injunction which, if issued, would seriously affect public interest. It is well within a court's discretion to deny an injunction against the infringement of riparian rights if to grant it would adversely affect the interest of the public. * * * The subordinate facts found amply supported the court's conclusion in the instant case that the issuance of the injunction prayed for would seriously and adversely affect the public interest at the time the case was tried. Except for one consideration, therefore, the denial of the plaintiffs' prayer for that injunction was correct.

That consideration is this: The plaintiffs do have property rights to the accustomed flow of the Mianus River. In the emergency of a drought the public interest may require the court to refuse to protect those rights by way of injunction. However, the riparian owners ought not to be deprived permanently of those rights without compensation. If the judgment of the trial court stands in its present form, there is nothing to prevent the defendant from continuing indefinitely to pump water from the river as the most economical way of getting its required supply. By doing this it might well be able to avoid the building of its proposed reservoir. The result would be that the plaintiffs would for many years continue to be deprived of their rights without any compensation except that which they might recover by a multiplicity of actions. It is obviously not doing equity to leave them in such a position. Under the circumstances of this case, equity demanded that the defendant be allowed a reasonable time within which to make adequate compensation to the plaintiffs for the permanent taking of their water rights if it intends to acquire them, and, if that compensation is not made within such reasonable time, the defendant should be enjoined from further diversion of the waters of the stream. * * * Although the granting or withholding of an injunction lies in the discretion of a trial court, when the only reasonable conclusion is that a plaintiff is, in equity, entitled to an injunction in a given form, it is competent for us to order such an injunction even though the trial court has refused it. * * * The trial court was in error in unconditionally denying the injunction against the diversion of the waters of the stream.

There is error in part, the judgment is set aside and the case is remanded with direction to hear the parties and determine what will be a reasonable time to be allowed to the defendant to acquire the water rights of the plaintiffs by condemnation or otherwise—that to be the sole issue of fact to be tried—and then to enter a judgment which shall (1) direct that unless compensation is made within that reasonable time the defendant shall be enjoined from further diversion of the waters of the stream as prayed, (2) deny the prayer for an injunction against condemning such water rights of the plaintiffs as will be taken for the construction of the proposed reservoir, and (3) deny the prayer of the cross complaint for a declaratory judgment.

In this opinion the other judges concurred.

Notes

1. What will the city acquire by condemning such water rights of the plaintiffs as will be taken for the construction of the proposed reservoir? We are told that in subsequent eminent domain proceedings no claims for compensation were pressed because the riparian owners felt they would collect only nominal damages. Leonard, An Economic Evaluation of Connecticut Water Law: Water Rights, Public Water Supply and Pollution Control, Report No. 11, Institute of Water Resources, University of Connecticut, 11 (1970).

2. In most states the procedure of "inverse condemnation" is available. Ferguson v. Hamburg, 272 N.Y. 234, 5 N.E.2d 801 (1936), was a suit for injunction brought by downstream riparians claiming injury from a diminution caused by a reservoir built and operated by defendant village. The lower court granted alternative relief in the form of an injunction which would go into effect unless the village commenced an action to acquire the rights. The Court of Appeals reversed, with orders to the lower court to ascertain the damages and issue an injunction unless within a reasonable time the defendant paid or tendered to the plaintiff the damages so fixed. A simpler form of inverse condemnation is the ordinary damage action brought against the city for injury to the plaintiff's riparian rights. See Pernell v. Henderson, 220 N.C. 79, 16 S.E.2d 449 (1941).

3. A New Jersey statute provides that riparian rights purchased by a city vest "in as full and ample a matter as the same were theretofore held and enjoyed by the person or persons owning the same." N.J.Stat.Ann. 40:69–4.3. Cases involving cities and water companies in that state are handled simply on a riparian basis. Mayor of Paterson v. East Jersey Water Co., 74 N.J.Eq. 49, 70 A. 472, aff'd 78 A. 1134 (1908).

4. Cities and public water supply companies were originally given powers to procure their supplies by special acts or by the charters incorporating them. See e.g., Acts and Resolves of Massachusetts, 1889, c. 244, p. 954; and see the statute recited in West Hartford v. Board of Water Commissioners, 68 Conn. 322, 36 A. 786 (1896). More commonly today, the power is given in general statutes applicable to all municipalities or water companies.

5. On some public waters (See Section 5, infra) cities have been held to partake of the superior rights of the public and to have power to take water without compensating injured riparians. Watuppa Reservoir Co. v. Fall River, 147 Mass. 548, 18 N.E. 465 (1888) (great ponds); Minneapolis Mill Co. v. St. Paul Water Commissioners, 56 Minn. 485, 58 N.W. 33 (1894) (navigable waters).

ROCKLAND COUNTY ANTI-RESERVOIR ASS'N v. DURYEA

Supreme Court of New York, Appellate Division, 1953.
282 App.Div. 457, 123 N.Y.S.2d 445.

HALPERN, JUSTICE. This is a proceeding under Article 78 of the Civil Practice Act to review a determination of the Water Power and Control Commission which approved an application by Spring Valley Water Works and Supply Company (hereinafter referred to as Spring Valley) for the construction of an impounding reservoir on the Hackensack River in Rockland County, New York.

Spring Valley supplies water to several communities in the southern part of Rockland County. It is a wholly owned subsidiary of Hackensack Water Company, which supplies water to communities in the northern part of New Jersey, and which obtains its water supply from the Hackensack River through reservoirs in New Jersey. * * *

The Commission found that Spring Valley was currently meeting its demands for service by overpumping its wells, which were its only source of supply. The Commission found that the communities served by Spring Valley had been steadily growing and the needs of its industrial customers had been expanding and that "the acquisition of additional sources of supply, to provide at least ten million gallons daily, is therefore necessary". The Commission recognized that this was in excess of Spring Valley's current water requirements but the Commission concluded, upon the basis of substantial evidence, that an additional source of supply of this magnitude was essential in order to assure Spring Valley an adequate supply for its present and future needs.

The Commission found that the construction of the proposed dam would impound waters sufficient to provide a dependable yield of twenty million gallons per day. About one-half of this yield, or ten million gallons per day, would have to be released in order to maintain the flow of the river in proper volume, in recognition of the legal rights of the down stream owners, both in New York State and in New Jersey. The Commission specifically directed that the remaining yield, about ten million gallons per day, should forever be reserved to supply the needs of the residents of Rockland County through the facilities of Spring Valley. The Commission recognized that the benefit to be derived by the Hackensack Water Company and other down stream owners from the regulated flow of the river would be substantial but it held that this benefit was a necessary and incidental effect of the project.

In their brief and argument in this court, the petitioners do not directly attack the factual basis of the Commission's determination nor do they attempt to demonstrate that the Commission's determination did not rest upon a substantial foundation in the evidence. The petitioners' principal attack is upon the legal sufficiency of the Commission's findings, it being their contention that the Commission failed to make findings upon essential issues. The evidence before the Commission is discussed by the petitioners only obliquely, as tending to show the importance of the alleged omissions in the Commission's findings.

We have concluded that the petitioners' objections to the sufficiency of the Commission's findings, and an additional constitutional point raised by them, are all without merit.

(1) The petitioners contend that the Commission failed to comply with section 523 of the Conservation Law, requiring it to make findings as to whether the plans "make fair and equitable provisions for the determination and payment of any and all legal damages to persons and property" affected by the project. We are satisfied that the Commission's findings upon this point are adequate and that they are based upon substantial evidence.

In addition to making the statutory finding, in the language of the statute, the Commission found that an intercompany plan had been agreed upon between Spring Valley and its parent, by which sufficient funds would be produced to pay all costs of the project, including, of course, the cost of acquisition of all necessary lands. * * *

(2) The Commission's findings upon the subject of the "public necessity" for the project were adequate. The Commission's findings with respect to Spring Valley's need for an additional source of supply have been referred to above. In addition, the Commission found what the total cost of the project would be and then found that the capital cost and the operating costs would be apportioned between Spring Valley and its parent under an intercompany plan, which it described as follows:

"Since the Hackensack Water Company, a downstream owner, will benefit from a regulated stream flow, as will all other downstream owners, including the Village of Nyack, the financing plan envisions an advance from the Hackensack Company to cover the cost of the project and an apportionment of the annual cost of operation, and of debt service on the project, between the two companies. As the water requirements on the applicant's system increase, its diversion from the proposed reservoir will become greater resulting in an increase in its portion of the annual costs, with a proportionate decrease in the charges to the Hackensack Company."

The petitioners' principal criticism is that the Commission failed to make findings as to the comparative cost of supplying the water from the proposed reservoir and supplying it from additional wells. The petitioners argue that the Commission should have made a finding upon this subject, as bearing upon the question of "public necessity" for the project. But the petitioners overlook the fact that the Commission found, upon the basis of substantial evidence, that the drilling of additional wells was not an acceptable method of supplying the water requirements of the company, because of the speculative character and unreliability of such a source and the detrimental effect which additional wells would have upon the existing wells of the company and upon the underground water table of the whole area. Although this conclusion was controverted by the petitioners' expert, the Commission had the right to reject his view and to accept that of the other witnesses. In view of the Commission's conclusion upon this underlying issue, no useful purpose would have been served by the Commission's making any findings upon the question of the comparative cost of wells and of the reservoir. No findings on that subject were necessary in order to enable the Commission to reach a fair determination upon the issue of the public necessity for the reservoir project. * * *

Determination by the Water Power and Control Commission confirmed, with Fifty dollars costs.

Notes

1. The New York Statute requiring approval of plans of public water supply projects is now McKinney Consol.Laws N.Y. Environmental Conservation Law, §§ 15–0501 to 15–1529. The requirement that the plans make fair and equitable provisions for the determination of payment of damages is not strictly construed to require advance details. "The public purse of the village, coupled with its taxing and borrowing powers, provide available, adequate and certain financial sources whereby petitioners may be indemnified for any invasion of their property rights occasioned by the diversion and the commission, in effect, so found." Spring Valley Water Works & Supply Co. v. Wilm, 14 A.D.2d 658, 218 N.Y.S.2d 800 (1961).

2. R.I.Gen.Laws 1980 Reenact. § 46–15–7: No municipal water department or agency, special water district or private water company engaged in the distribution of water for potable purposes shall have any power

(1) To acquire or take a water supply or an additional water supply from an existing approved source; or

(2) To take or condemn lands for any new or additional sources of water supply or for the utilization of such supplies; or

(3) To extend its supply or distribution mains into a municipality or special water district wherein it has not heretofore legally supplied water; or

(4) To construct any extension of its transmission mains; or

(5) To extend the boundaries of a special water district; or

(6) To supply water in or for use in any other municipality or civil division of the state which owns and operates a water supply system therein, or in any duly organized special water district supplied with water by another municipal water department or agency, special water district or private water company; until such municipal water department or agency, special water district or private water company has first submitted the maps and plans therefor to the board, as hereinafter provided, and until the board shall have approved the same, or approved the same with such modifications as it may determine to be necessary, provided, however, this subsection shall not apply to any area presently served by any municipal water department or agency, or special water district.

3. In 1939 Pennsylvania created a priority system among public water supply agencies, 32 Pa.Stat. §§ 631–641. Unused water rights of any such agency were declared null and void, § 632, and all other water rights had to be registered with and their validity determined by the Water and Power Review Board, §§ 633 and 634. Compliance with the Act was made the exclusive method of acquiring water rights, § 635. A permit to acquire (by purchase, eminent domain, payment of damages, etc.) designated water rights (of riparians) must be applied for, § 636. "However, if the board finds that the proposed new source or additional supply will not conflict with the rights to such water or to water rights held by any other public water supply agency which are reasonably necessary for its present purposes or future needs, and that the water or the water rights proposed to be acquired are reasonably necessary for the present purposes and future needs of the public water supply agency making application, that the taking of said water or the exercise of said water rights will not interfere with navigation, jeopardize public safety, or cause substantial injury to the Commonwealth, then, and in that case, the board shall approve the application and shall issue a permit therefor." § 637. If the rights are not acquired within one year or the water is not actually taken within four years, the permit may be revoked, but, "if the project required for the taking of water has been commended in good faith or if the commencement thereof has been prevented by events beyond the control of the permittee, the board shall have the power, upon application of the permittee, to grant such extensions of said period as the board deems to be necessary to enable the permittee to complete the project required for the taking of water." § 638.

4. There has been little litigation on the question of the relative rights of eastern cities that are competing for the same water, but in it the courts have given a rule for every taste.

In Massachusetts priority was the basis of the decision. The legislature in 1926 authorized the town of Somerset "to take by eminent domain * * * or acquire by purchase or otherwise * * * the waters of the Segreganset River." Prior to 1961 the only use of the river was to recharge the town's well field by flooding it in dry years. In that year a survey was undertaken for a diversion of water from the stream to an off-stream reservoir, money was appropriated to purchase land for the project, and bonds for construction funds were authorized. Meanwhile, the Dighton Water District had been established by legislative act in 1950 and authorized to acquire water from any stream within its service area "not already appropriated and used for the purpose of public water supply." Learning of Somerset's plans in 1962, the District hastily recorded an "order of taking" which purported to appropriate all the water of the Segreganset not already appropriated and used for public water supply. Held, the District's authority should be construed to mean that it could not take water "appropriated *or* used" for public supply, and that "appropriated" meant "permitted by legislative authority to be taken." Somerset v. Dighton Water Dist., 347 Mass. 738, 200 N.E.2d 237 (1964).

In New York, an "administrative allocation" was made. The City of Syracuse long ago was given legislative authority to take from Skaneateles Lake, through a 30 inch pipe, water not needed for the Erie Canal. In the twentieth century it almost doubled its withdrawals under authority of an order of the Water Power and Control Commission that contained the following clause, "The Commission reserves the right from time to time to authorize the amount of water found reasonably necessary for the supply of other parts of the state and the inhabitants thereof to be taken from Skaneateles Lake and applicant shall have no claim for compensation to the water so diverted unless it shall render a service in connection therewith * * *." In 1935 the Commission ordered the city to share its supply with the village of Jordan, which had no water works of its own. On appeal, affirmed. "The city accepted the determination and acted upon it, necessarily assumed and agreed to any burdens it imposed and is not now in any position to question the propriety of the limitations, conditions, or restrictions fixed or the power of the Commission to impose them." The order was held reasonable and fully sustained by the evidence. Syracuse v. Gibbs, 283 N.Y. 275, 28 N.E.2d 835 (1940).

An interstate case was decided on riparian sharing. The Hackensack River flows from New York into New Jersey. In New York it is used by defendant Village of Nyack and several neighboring villages. Once used, the water is not returned to the Hackensack but is released into the Hudson. In New Jersey the plaintiff Hackensack Water Company diverts most of the water to serve 800,000 people in several cities. The plaintiff has several dams, some built in New York under authority of the New York Water Resources Commission, some in New Jersey, approved by that state's Department of Commerce and Development, Division of Water Policy and Supply. When Nyack took steps to increase its supply, claiming the right to do so under the terms of the New York Commission's orders allowing the dams, the plaintiff claimed that as builder of the dams it was entitled to the undiminished flow of the regulated river, and brought this action to determine its right to compensation for the proposed "withdrawal without return." The case came up on a motion for a summary judgment. In the stated facts it appeared that the plaintiff company owned 90% of the riparian land in New Jersey, but the defendant Village's holdings, if any, were not mentioned, and the reason for treating both parties as riparian proprietors was not discussed. Nevertheless the court set out at some length the "respective rights of upstream and downstream riparian owners," and discussed riparian principles applicable to diversions without return to the stream, domestic consumption and reasonable use. "From the foregoing it is apparent that the right of the plaintiff to the undiminished flow of the Hackensack River cannot be established as a matter of law. On the other hand, it is by no means clear that as a matter of fact the defendant's use of water of the Hackensack River is reasonable." The court overruled the motion and set these issues of fact for trial. Hackensack Water Co. v. Nyack, 289 F.Supp. 671 (S.D.N.Y.1968).

SECTION 5. STATE REGULATION

MUENCH v. PUBLIC SERVICE COMMISSION

Supreme Court of Wisconsin, 1952.
261 Wis. 492, 53 N.W.2d 514.

On March 8, 1950, the Namekagon Hydro Company (hereinafter referred to as the "Company") filed an application with the Public Service Commission to construct, operate, and maintain a hydro-electric dam on the Namekagon River in Washburn county. The Conservation Commission entered its appearance and objected to construction of the dam on the ground that it was violative of public rights and in particular the right declared by sec. 31.06(3), Stats., to *"the enjoyment of natural scenic beauty".* The Conservation Commission was represented at the hearing by the attorney general acting on the express direction of the governor of the state. * * *

Under date of September 29, 1950, the commission issued its findings, conclusions, and certificate of permit to the Company. The effect of the Public Service Commission's findings was to determine that the statutory requirements entitling the Company to a permit to construct the dam existed, and that there were no public rights which required denial of the application.

After the permit was issued both the Conservation Commission and the petitioner Muench filed motions for rehearing before the Public Service Commission, which motions were denied by an order entered December 6, 1950. Muench, a private citizen who is also president of the state division of the Izaak Walton League, had appeared as a party at the original hearing before the Public Service Commission. * * *

CURRIE, JUSTICE. We are concerned in this case with the problem of the nature of public rights in the navigable streams of the state and the beds underlying the same, and the protection of such rights. A review of the historical background and a sketching of the development of the recognition of these public rights in the court decisions and statutes of this state should prove to be helpful in passing upon the specific issues presented by the appeals therein.

After the Revolutionary War, the original thirteen states were impoverished and were confronted with the problem of paying the debts created by the war. States without western lands demanded that Virginia and other states claiming such lands to the west should cede the same to the Confederation to be sold to pay such debts. In 1783 the Virginia legislature authorized the ceding of the Northwest Territory to the Confederation, and the actual deed of conveyance was executed March 1, 1784. This cession was made upon two conditions: (1) The new states to be admitted as members of the Federal Union were to have the same rights to sovereignty as the original states; and (2) The navigable waters flowing into the Mississippi and the St. Lawrence rivers, and the carrying places between them were to be forever free public highways. These conditions were incorporated into the Northwest Ordinance of 1787, which set up the machinery for the government of the Northwest Territory.

Art. IX, sec. 1, of the Wisconsin Constitution, adopted by the Territorial Convention on February 17, 1848, and approved by the act of Congress admitting Wisconsin into the Union, incorporated verbatim the wording of the Northwest Ordinance with respect to navigable waters, such section reading as follows:

> "The state shall have concurrent jurisdiction on all rivers and lakes bordering on this state so far as such rivers or lakes shall form a common boundary to the state and any other state or territory now or hereafter to be formed, and bounded by the same; and the river Mississippi and the navigable waters leading into the Mississippi and St. Lawrence, and the carrying places between the same, shall be common highways and forever free, as well to the inhabitants of the state as to the citizens of the United States, without any tax, impost or duty therefor." * * *

One of the early cases which established the "saw-log" test of navigability in the state is that of Olson v. Merrill, 1877, 42 Wis. 203, 212. * * *

It will thus be seen that Wisconsin, in adopting the saw-log test of navigability, based the same on commercial considerations. * * * In Diana Shooting Club v. Husting, 1914, 156 Wis. 261, 271, 145 N.W. 816, 820, * * * the defendant Paul O. Husting (later United States Senator from Wisconsin) entered his hunting boat floating upon the waters of Rock river, and with the aid of a pole and paddle propelled it down the river to the place of the alleged trespass for the purpose of shooting wild ducks * * *. This case is significant in that the navigability was established not through any commercial use, such as floating of logs, but through the use of shallow draft boats for purposes of recreation. * * *

In 1911 Wisconsin enacted the first Water Power Act, ch. 652, Laws of 1911, which contained a new definition of navigable streams and rivers which was very similar in wording to our present sec. 30.01(2), Stats., which reads:

> "All rivers and streams which have been meandered and returned as navigable by the surveyors employed by the government of the United States, and all rivers, streams, sloughs, bayous and marsh outlets, whether meandered or nonmeandered *which are navigable in fact for any purpose whatsoever* are hereby declared navigable to the extent that no dam, bridge, or other obstruction shall be made in or over the same without the permission of the legislature."

Therefore, since 1911 it is no longer necessary in determining navigability of streams to establish a past history of floating of logs, or other uses of commercial transportation, because any stream is *"navigable in fact"* which is capable of floating any boat, skiff or canoe, of the shallowest draft used for recreational purposes. * * *

Our present Water Power Law dates from 1915, ch. 380, Laws of 1915, and such act contained a provision, sec. 1596–7, Stats.1915, which required the Railroad Commission (predecessor to the Public Service Commission), in granting a permit to construct a dam upon a navigable stream, to find that "the proposed dam will not materially obstruct existing navigation *or violate other public rights* ". This same provision is now contained in sec. 31.06(3), Stats.

The nature of these *"other public rights"* referred to in sec. 31.06(3) Stats., is elucidated in the opinion of this court in Nekoosa-Edwards Paper Co. v. Railroad Comm., 1930, 201 Wis. 40, 46–47, 228 N.W. 144, 147, 229 N.W. 631. * * *

> "Many of the meandered lakes and streams of this state, navigable in law, have ceased to be navigable for pecuniary gain. They are still navigable in law; that is, subject to the use of the public for all the incidents of navigable waters. As population increases, these waters are used by the people for *sailing, rowing, canoeing, bathing, fishing, hunting, skating and other public purposes.* While the public right may have originated in the older use or capacity of the waters for navigation, such public right having once accrued, it is not lost by the failure of pecuniary profitable navigation, but resort may be had thereto for any other public purpose. Our state has for many years been extensively engaged in the propagation of fish and the stocking of the waters of the state with fish fry in order that the public may more fully enjoy the sport and recreation of fishing. By reason of the state's enterprise in behalf of the public, the small streams of the state are fishing streams to which the public have a right to resort so long as they do not trespass on the private property along the banks." * * *

The 1929 legislature enacted ch. 523, Laws of 1929, which amended sec. 31.06, Stats., so as to provide that *the enjoyment of scenic beauty is* *a public right* to be considered by the Public Service Commission in making findings as to whether a permit for a proposed dam shall be issued. Thus we have a further public right in navigable streams recognized by legislative enactment which is highly illustrative of the trend to extend and protect the rights of the public to the recreational enjoyment of the navigable waters of the state. * * *

The second question to be passed upon is whether the petitioner Muench is a person *"aggrieved"* and *"directly affected"*, under the provisions of sec. 227.16(1), Stats., by the decision of the Commission in this instance which is reviewable under sec. 227.15, Stats. The Company contends that Muench is not directly affected by the Commission's decision because he has no direct pecuniary interest which would be jeopardized by the issuance of a permit to erect the dam. The right of the citizens of the state to enjoy our navigable streams for recreational purposes, including the enjoyment of scenic beauty, is a legal right that is entitled to all the protection which is given financial rights. * * * Such rights would be severely limited, curtailed, or endangered if we did not hold that any citizen who has appeared at a hearing of the Public Service Commission, held under sec. 31.06 with respect to an application to erect a dam in a navigable stream is *"aggrieved"* and *"directly affected"* by a decision of the Commission finding that public rights will not be violated by erection of a proposed dam so as to entitle him to petition for review under sec. 227.15, Stats. We conclude that petitioner Muench was therefore entitled to petition the circuit court for review.

Our holding in this respect is in keeping with the trend manifested in the development of the law of navigable waters in this state to extend the rights of the general public to the recreational use of the waters of this state, and to protect the public in the enjoyment of such rights. * * *

The state contends that the Namekagon river, on which the proposed dam is to be erected, is famous throughout the eastern half of the United States because of its scenic beauty, desirability for float trips and canoeing, and for a type of fishing water which the Federal Fishing and Wildlife Service has described as rapidly disappearing from the state of Wisconsin. The Public Service Commission will be required to make findings as to whether public rights for the recreational enjoyment of this stream in its present natural condition outweigh the benefits to the public which would result in the construction of the dam.

Judgment reversed with directions to remand the cause to the Public Service Commission for further proceedings in accordance with this opinion.

Notes

1. Much of the movement for statutory regulation of water uses in the eastern states is directed at environmental protection. The State of Wis-

consin was a leader in this regard as its legislature and courts built on the "public rights" concept, and *Muench* (case and man) should not be forgotten when the environmental movement is characterized as "new" or "different."

2. Many early water regulation statutes and special acts authorized the construction of dams, operation of log booms and diversions to canals. For the most part these were limited, as is the statute in the principal case, to navigable waters over which the state as the embodiment of the public has clear powers. This was not a particularly limiting factor in Wisconsin, which has so broad a definition of navigability that it applied to quite small streams such as Buena Vista Creek, involved in the next case. As one official of the Wisconsin Conservation Commission said, "If a perch can swim in it—even on his side like a flounder—it's navigable, and we'll take charge."

Some of the earliest statutes, however, were directed at the use of private water. The mill dam statutes of New England gave the privilege of erecting dams across streams which were not navigable and gave the power to lawfully flood the lands of upper riparians. "From these provisions it is an inevitable implication, that, although the right is given indiscriminately to all riparian proprietors, he who first erects and establishes his mill does, by his priority of occupation, acquire to that extent a title to the use of the water in the stream prior and superior to that of any other person, and a right to maintain his dam against all proprietors of lands both above and below his own." Smith v. Agawam Canal Co., 2 Allen 355 (Mass.1861).

Today it is generally recognized that state powers over public waters are not the only source of water legislation and that the general police power is the basis for statutes affecting all types of waters.

3. Many eastern states have long had limited permit systems for certain uses, like Wisconsin's Water Power Law. Another Wisconsin statute requires a permit for the diversion of surplus water (not beneficially used by riparians) to maintain the normal level or natural flow of a lake or stream in a watershed. Non-surplus water may be diverted for irrigation use only with the consent of injured riparians. In essence, this means the irrigator must buy water from power companies with run-of-the-river low head hydroelectric power plants. See Nekoosa-Edwards Paper Co. v. Public Service Commission, 8 Wis.2d 582, 99 N.W.2d 821 (1959), and Ellis, Beuscher, Howard and DeBraal, Water Use Law and Administration in Wisconsin, 223–316 (1970).

Some permit statutes regulate, protect, and sometimes give special powers to certain types of favored water users. The western Great Lakes states give this preferential treatment to taconite (low-grade iron) mines. Wis.Stat.Ann. 144.855; Minn.Stat.Ann. § 105.64; Mich.Comp.Laws Ann. § 323.251. Illinois grants permits to persons or firms, not riparian owners, to use the water from any of the public bodies of water for industrial manufacturing or public utility purposes. Smith-Hurd Ill.Ann.Stat. ch. 19, § 65. See also the permits for municipal supply issued by the states of New York, Pennsylvania and Rhode Island discussed supra pp. 339 to 340.

The Indiana Flood Control and Water Resources Commission may grant any person, including a non-riparian owner, the right to divert flood waters from a watercourse for any useful purpose, provided such diversion does not cause injury to landowners in the watershed in which the watercourse is located and the diversion does not limit any existing right. Burns' Ind.Stat. § 13–2–1–6.

Many other eastern states have statutes regulating the construction of dams, e.g., Conn.Gen.Stat.Ann. §§ 22a–401 to 22a–410; Iowa Code Ann. §§ 469.1 to 469.31; W.Va.Code. § 20–5–1. Some are applicable only to navigable rivers, many deal only with safety licensing and inspection. For many years Wisconsin has not only licensed the initial construction of dams but engaged in extensive regulation of the relations between power companies, between power companies and riparians, and between power companies and the public. Wis.Stat.Ann. 31.01–31.38. The Arkansas Soil and Water Conservation Commission not only controls and regulates the building of dams, but also some relations between water users. A permit is required, but only surplus water may be impounded by virtue of it. "Surplus" is whatever remains in excess of a continuous discharge, fixed by the Commission in amount to protect lower riparian rights and fish and wildlife. The person constructing the dam under a permit has an exclusive right to the use of the water impounded. Ark.Stats. § 21–1301.

VILLAGE OF TEQUESTA v. JUPITER INLET CORPORATION

Supreme Court of Florida, 1979.
371 So.2d 663.

[The Jupiter Inlet Corporation owned property on which it planned to build a 120 unit condominium project, supplied with water from an underlying shallow aquifer. The property was less than a quarter of a mile from the well field that supplied the Village of Tequesta with water from seven wells which pumped more than one million gallons per day from a depth of 75 to 90 feet. This is the entire "safe yield" of the shallow aquifer, since greater withdrawals would induce the intrusion into the aquifer of salt water from the nearby Intercoastal Waterway, a canal connected to the Atlantic Ocean. The only other nearby source of fresh water is a deep artesian aquifer which can be tapped only by 1200 foot wells, at greatly increased drilling and pumping costs.

Florida's common law applicable to ground water gave the overlying landowner a right to reasonable use of the water, modified by the correlative rights of adjacent landowners to use the same water, if it could move freely through the land of one owner to the land of the other. Reasonableness of a landowner's particular use was determined in much the same way as the reasonableness of a riparian use of water in a water course. As explained in the opinion, the Florida Water Resources Act of 1972 applies to both stream water and ground water, requires a permit for all substantial new withdrawals and provides for regularizing existing common law withdrawals by issuing permits for them. Tequesta applied for and received permits for its wells. When Jupiter applied for a permit to take water from the shallow aquifer, its application was denied. Jupiter now sues Tequesta in inverse condemnation, claiming that Tequesta had deprived Jupiter of the beneficial use of its property rights and thereby effected a taking of the property. The legal problem is essentially identical to that which would exist if Jupiter's property were riparian to a small stream, upstream from a point where Tequesta took the entire flow for municipal supply.]

ADKINS, JUSTICE.

* * *

The State of Florida operates under an administrative system of water management pursuant to the terms of the Florida Water Resources Act. Ch. 373, Fla.Stat. (1972). The law prior to the Florida Water Resources Act did not allow ownership in the corpus of the water, but only in the use of it. Even then, the use was bounded by the perimeters of reasonable and beneficial use. Legislation limiting the right to the use of the water is in itself no more objectionable than legislation forbidding the use of property for certain purposes by zoning regulations. Village of Euclid v. Ambler Realty Co., 272 U.S. 365, 47 S.Ct. 114, 71 L.Ed. 303 (1926); 54 A.L.R. 1016 (1928).

The Florida Water Resources Act, in recognizing the need for conservation and control of the waters in the state (Section 373.016, Fla.Stat. (1973)) makes all waters in the state subject to regulation, unless otherwise specifically exempt. § 373.023(1) Fla.Stat. (1973). The Department of Environmental Regulation and the various water management districts are given the responsibility to accomplish the conservation, protection, management, and control of the waters of the state. § 373.016(3) Fla.Stat. (1973). In order to exercise such controls a permitting system is established which requires permits for consumptive use of water, exempting only "domestic consumption of water by individual users" from the requirements of a permit. § 373.219(1) Fla. Stat. (1973). Jupiter, in serving a 120-unit condominium, does not qualify as an individual user and thus must secure a permit in order to draw water from beneath its property. Without a permit Jupiter has no such property right to the use of water beneath its land for which, upon deprivation, it must be compensated through inverse condemnation.

The Water Resources Act of 1972 recognizes a right to use water under the common law as separate from the right to use water under a permit granted pursuant to the act. This is done by a provision concerning the termination of the common-law right and a transitional procedure. The holder of such a common-law water-use right was given two years to convert the common-law water right into a permit water right. § 373.226(3) Fla.Stat. (1973). In order to qualify for the initial permit under section 373.226(2) Florida Statutes (1973), the right must have been exercised prior to the implementation of the Florida Water Resources Act by a water management district with geographical jurisdiction in that area. Otherwise the right is abandoned and extinguished requiring a new application for a permit. Tequesta had acquired the permit and Jupiter was merely a proposed user. The

Florida Water Resources Act makes no provision for the continuation of an *unexercised* common-law right to use water. Jupiter had perfected no legal interest to the use of the water beneath its land which would support an action in inverse condemnation.

Section 373.1961 Florida Statutes (1975) provides additional powers and duties for the governing boards of the water management district. Subsection (7) provides that the governing board:

> May acquire title to such interest as is necessary in real property, by purchase, gift, devise, lease, eminent domain, or otherwise, *for water production and transmission* consistent with this section. However, the district shall not use any of the eminent domain powers herein granted to acquire water and water rights already devoted to reasonable and beneficial use or any water production or transmission facilities owned by any county, municipality, or regional water supply authority. [Emphasis supplied].

Condemnation of "water rights" is not granted in the first sentence of this subsection. The authority granted is specifically limited to the acquisition of land for the purpose of constructing and operating well fields and other withdrawal facilities and for the right-of-way necessary for the transmission of water to consumers. The second sentence prohibits the use of eminent domain to acquire such "water rights" which were *already* being put to a reasonable and beneficial use. The statutory prohibition of the use of eminent domain in one situation cannot be used as authority for its use by implication in another, as the statute must be strictly construed. Canal Authority v. Miller, 243 So. 2d 193 (Fla.1970). All that Section 373.1961(7) Florida Statutes (1975) accomplishes is to further protect presently existing legal uses of water. No implication can be drawn that this section intends to include any "water right" other than the permit that may be granted by a water management district. After all, if a use of water is both preexisting and also reasonable and beneficial, after two years, it must be either under permit or it is conclusively presumed to be abandoned. There was no necessity for the Water Resources Act to provide for the condemnation of an unexercised right to use water, as the owner became subject to the permit provisions of the law. There was no "taking" of this right.

Jupiter's remedy is only through proper application for a permit under the Florida Water Resources Act.

Notes

1. A full description, analysis and critique of eastern state permit systems is given in Ausness, Water Rights Legislation in the East: A Program for Reform, 24 William & Mary L.Rev. 547 (1983).

2. The Florida permit system has been a substantial success in two respects, in the registration and quantification of preexisting uses and in the control of the initiation of new withdrawals. The applicant for a permit must demonstrate that the proposed use will be "reasonable-benefi-

cial," that it will not interfere with any presently existing legal water use, and that it will be consistent with the public interest. Fla.Stat.Ann. § 373.223(1) (West 1974). The reasonable-beneficial standard limits water use to the quantity needed for the economic and the efficient utilization, for a purpose and in a manner which are both reasonable and in the public interest. § 373.019(4). The new use must comport with the state's water plan which may not only provide for development, protection and management of water resources but may also prohibit or restrict uses on designated streams that might impair public recreation or harm fish and wildlife. § 373.036(7). Further environmental protection is given by minimum flow requirements setting the limit at which further withdrawals would be significantly harmful to the water resources or ecology of the area. § 373.042.

In practice, the success of the permit granting process seems largely attributable to putting as much priority into the system as possible. The requirement of non-interference with existing uses is heavily stressed. Some permits have been conditioned to coordinate withdrawals, rotating the pumping of different users, scheduling withdrawals to avoid depletion of minimum flows or fluctuation of lake levels, and when visual effects are offensive by allowing pumping only at night. Some actual priority is practiced—some permits forbid withdrawals when they would interfere with the supply of an existing permit holder, and some permittees have been required to build retaining ponds to store water for use during times of peak demand. See § 373.229(1).

The permit statutes of other states similarly prohibit the water agency from issuing new permits that impair the rights of existing water users. Iowa Code Ann. § 455B.265; Indiana Code Ann. § 13–2–2–5; Ky.Rev.Stat. Ann. § 151.170(2).

Nearly all of the eastern statutes provide for registration and quantification of pre-existing uses. Some require the user to meet the requirements of new permitted uses. (Georgia Code Ann. § 12–5–31(g).)

None of the statutes specifically authorizes nonriparian uses, but none of them limits permits to riparian proprietors. A few early statutes were administered as if the permits were merely regulatory measures affecting the exercise of riparian rights. See Nekoosa-Edwards Paper Company v. Public Service Commission, 8 Wis.2d 582, 99 N.W.2d 821 (1959).

3. The Florida statute is taken almost verbatim from F. Maloney, R. Ausness and J. Morris, A Model Water Code (1972). A severely critical review of the book raised strong objections to administrative distribution of water among users in times of shortage. Trelease, The Model Water Code, The Wise Administrator and the Goddam Bureaucrat, 14 Nat. Resources J. 207 (1974):

> Reduction, restriction, changes in permits, suspension of permits, apportionment, rotation, limitation, prohibition—these are what the water user may expect. The Code's solution to the legal uncertainties of riparian rights is the substitution of these administrative uncertainties.

To what end? Protection of the public, the environment? No—that is all taken care of. To understand the choice between property rights and administrative distribution, it must be very clearly kept in mind that all we are talking about is water already allocated to private use, that the state and its administrators have issued permits for its use, that every use is reasonable-beneficial, that all the uses can be made in times of water plenty. It must be remembered that all minimum flow requirements are met, that all other environmental factors are protected, and that the state water plan is observed and even furthered. The 'public interest' stands neutral, and the only question is, which people get to use the water. The choice is between giving people, industries and cities water rights that entitle them to water under stated conditions, rights that they may use as they see fit and adjust among themselves as they may agree, or giving the regulatory official the power to determine in his discretion which water users get water in times of shortage, and to shift water between uses and users as time progresses.

Since that article was written the shortage plans of the decentralized water management districts have been devised and adopted and many of these terrible things have not occurred. Each district is required by § 373.244(1) to prepare a shortage plan. These extensive documents are essentially plans for droughts, for periods of subnormal precipitation that require temporary cutbacks when the supply drops below the level usually sufficient for all. The shortage plans all follow a pattern, although all are not identical. The Water Shortage Plan of the St. Johns River Water Management District is typical (Fl.Adm.Code, Ch. 40C–21, 1884). Uses are classified by source of water, type of use, and method of abstraction or diversion. Shortages are classified as moderate, severe, extreme and critical, or as emergencies. Target cutbacks are set at 15% through 30%, 45% and 60%. Voluntary reductions in use are primarily relied on in the early stages. As the shortage deepens strict provisions against waste and careless or profligate use are instituted, fountains are shut off, and irrigation of lawns, trees and golf courses is limited by day of the week, hour of use, and time of day. Car washing and street and sidewalk flushing are restricted. Overhead spray irrigation of agricultural crops is restricted by day, hour and length, flood irrigation to a few days a month, and frost protection to forecasts of severe freeze.

Essentially, these shortage plans set up mechanisms for sharing a temporary drought in a usually abundant supply. Sharing, of course, occurs among householders during droughts in cities of other states, and among irrigators in western irrigation districts when project supplies are below normal. Sharing among persons similarly situated is quite fair as long as the shares do not become too small for everyone. When not all uses are the same, however, less than a full supply may stop some processes. Perhaps for this reason the Florida shortage plans typically contain very specific rules for mines and processing plants.

Two areas of bureaucratic rule over the fortunes of water users may remain. The system of classification allows uses and users to be ranked according to official notions of which are least essential and can be cut off first. Farmers, however, are the most vulnerable. Irrigated agriculture is the largest water user and receives the brunt of the cutbacks. In an extreme shortage or emergency, an overall allocation is made to each class of water. The total agricultural irrigation allocation is set, but it is not necessarily shared equally. "The share available to each user will be based on any prioritization among crops, the District establishes based on economic loss and equity considerations and the acreage and quantity of withdrawals for which the user has been permitted. (Fla.Adm.Code § 40.C–21.621(2)(a)6)."

In other states administrators are given wide discretionary powers to determine who gets water and who does not, guided only by vague and general criteria such as "the best interest of the public" (Ky.Rev.Stat.Ann. § 151.200(1); giving priority to "(i) sustaining life, (ii) maintaining health, (iii) increasing wealth" (Ark.Stat.Ann. § 21–1308); and "to protect public health and safety [and prevent] serious harm to the water resources" (Georgia Code § 12–5–31(c)).

4. In the eastern states, a "shortage" seems to be conceived of as a one-sided phenomenon, a temporary subnormal supply of natural origin. There seems to be no recognition that demands upon normal supplies can exceed the available quantity and thus create a shortage. Although in the *Tequesta* case a new permit was refused because increased drafts on the supply would ruin the entire source for everyone, there are no statutes or cases which recognize that too many permits can produce a permanent shortage or that on a fluctuating source each new permit will cause the next "shortage" to cut deeper, and will bring the one after that sooner. There seems to be no recognition that as the permit-granting process continues the existing uses will be impaired by having their shares reduced during the next below-normal year. There are no statutory requirements that call for halting the issuance of permits when some limit of safe yield or dependable supply is reached. The Florida shortage plans mention no reduction in future use or restrictions on new permits, but seem to assume the resumption of business as usual with the return of the rains.

5. There is a subliminal recognition that limits of supply will be reached and that some method must be devised to accommodate new demands and uses and to reallocate water in use to different and more productive purposes. See Trelease, The Model Water Code, the Wise Administrator and the Goddam Bureaucrat, 14 Nat.Resources J. 207 (1974):

> Under the Model Code, the mechanism to accomplish these shifts is the issuance of new permits to newly-favored users upon the expiration of old and now-to-be-discarded uses. I see several difficulties with this process. First, to the extent that the 'normal' permit lasts twenty years, flexibility is surrendered during its life. If the application for the new use does not coincide with permit expirations, the new user may have to wait a fairly long time before water becomes available. Second, the investment may have been only partly amortized during the 20-year (or shorter) period. Third, the holder will in most cases lose an asset more valuable than his investment, that is, the going concern value of his enterprise, the continuing opportunity to make a profit, which is presumably a contribution to the economy. Fourth, if

it were my enterprise, I would suspect that some Bureaucrat might solve the first problem and aggravate the second and third by simply granting the permit and squeezing the water out of me and other less favored users under the shortage plans and emergency measures.

6. How transferable is a 20-year water right in its 17th year? Suppose an irrigation system of pumps and sprinklers, which initially cost $40,000, hopelessly breaks down in the 15th year. Will it be replaced?

A mid-western farmer with sandy soils can, under normal rainfall, grow small grain that brings him $50 per acre. With irrigation, he can grow vegetable crops that bring in $200 per acre. He obtains an irrigation permit, borrows $40,000 from the bank, and buys pumps, pipes and sprinklers. After ten years the mortgage is paid off. His permit is then cancelled, or expires and is not renewed. Has he suffered a loss? Suppose a western appropriator whose permit runs "in perpetuity" sells his land with appurtenant water right at $500 per acre when dry land in the neighborhood is selling at $100 per acre. Has he made a "windfall profit?" Suppose he sells an acre's worth of water right at $400?

Suppose an Iowa farmer has a permit to irrigate 160 acres, and that withdrawals under it often reduce the stream to its minimum flow. A downstream cannery needs a water supply, and could pay the farmer more than he realizes through irrigation. Iowa Code Ann. § 455B.273 provides, "A permittee may sell, transfer, or assign his permit by conveying, leasing, or otherwise transferring the ownership of the land described in the permit * * *." Will the water move to its "highest and most productive use?" (The answer is yes. As lawyer for the cannery, what arrangements would you make?)

SECTION 6. ABOLITION AND COMBINATION (INCLUDING THE "CALIFORNIA DOCTRINE")

COFFIN v. LEFT HAND DITCH CO.

Supreme Court of Colorado, 1882.
6 Colo. 443.

[See opinion, supra p. 75.]

Notes

1. The leading cases in other states that have extinguished riparian rights to the use of water and adopted the "Colorado doctrine" are Van Dyke v. Midnight Sun Mining & Ditch Co. (Alaska) 177 F. 85 (9th Cir.1910); Clough v. Wing, 2 Ariz. 371, 17 P. 453 (1888); Drake v. Earhart, 2 Idaho 716, 23 P. 541 (1890) (See also Hutchinson v. Watson Slough Ditch Co., 16 Idaho 484, 101 P. 1059 (1909); Mettler v. Ames Realty Co., 61 Mont. 152, 201 P. 702 (1921); Jones v. Adams, 19 Nev. 78, 6 P. 442 (1885); Albuquerque Land & Irrigation Co. v. Gutierrez, 10 N.Mex. 177, 61 P. 357 (1900), affirmed 188 U.S. 545, 23 S.Ct. 338, 47 L.Ed. 588 (1903); Stowell v. Johnson, 7 Utah 215, 26 P. 290 (1891); Moyer v. Preston, 6 Wyo. 308, 44 P. 845 (1896).

2. In Boquillas Land & Cattle Co. v. Curtis, 213 U.S. 339, 29 S.Ct. 493, 53 L.Ed. 822 (1909) a riparian, seeking to protect his unused right against an upstream appropriation, argued that the Arizona statute adopting the common law of England conferred upon him property rights not subject to legislative change. Mr. Justice Holmes disposed of this contention with one of his famous aphorisms, that this statute "* * * is far from meaning that patentees of a ranch on the San Pedro are to have the same rights as owners of an estate on the Thames."

3. The phrase "riparian rights" frequently describes rights to ownership of land, such as the bed of a stream or fast land created by accretion, rights to protect the bank from stream erosion, rights to fish in waters, and rights to access to waters. For the status of these rights in Colorado doctrine states, see Note, Riparian Rights in Appropriation States, 9 Wyo. L.J. 130 (1955).

LUX v. HAGGIN

Supreme Court of California, 1886.
69 Cal. 255, 10 P. 674.

[Henry Miller, the "Cattle King", head of the firm of Miller & Lux, owned land for 120 miles on both sides of the San Joaquin River and other streams of California's Central Valley. In the southern end of his domain vast areas of "grass lands" were naturally irrigated by annual spring floods of the Kern River, which split into numerous channels and sloughs. When the floods subsided, the water was spread over the land by dams thrown across the sloughs. Huge quantities of native hay were produced in this fashion. The lands had been purchased in 1872 from the State of California, which had acquired them from the federal government in 1850 under the terms of the Federal Swamp Land Act, granting overflowed lands to the states.

Haggin was the promoter of the Kern River Land & Canal Company, a large irrigation project. In 1875 he and the company acquired an appropriation of 74,000 inches of the Kern. His point of diversion was on federal public lands upstream from the land of Miller & Lux. Some of these facts, and more interesting background on the case, are found in Wiel, Fifty Years of Water Law, 50 Harv.L.Rev. 252, 256 (1937).

Miller & Lux brought suit against Haggin and the company to enjoin the proposed diversion on the ground that it would interfere with their riparian rights to the overflow. The trial court denied relief. The Supreme Court of California reversed by a four to three decision. The majority opinion on rehearing, by McKinstry, J., from which the following excerpts are taken, dealt very extensively with the development of water law in the West, and covered 200 pages in the California reports and 110 in the Pacific Reporter.]

A grant of public land of the United States carries with it the common-law rights to an innavigable stream thereon, unless the waters are expressly or impliedly reserved by the terms of the patent, or of the statute granting the land, or unless they are reserved by the congression-

al legislation authorizing the patent or other muniment of title. * * *

It has often been held by this court and its predecessors that a grant of a tract of land bounded by a river or creek not navigable, conveys the land to the thread of the stream; and from a very early day the courts of this state have considered the United States government as the owner of such running waters on the public lands of the United States, and of their beds. Recognizing the United States as the owner of the lands and waters, and as therefore authorized to permit the occupation or diversion of the waters as distinct from the lands, the state courts have treated the prior appropriator of water on the public lands of the United States as having a better right than a subsequent appropriator, on the theory that the appropriation was allowed or licensed by the United States. It has never been held that the right to appropriate waters on the public lands of the United States was derived directly from the state of California as the owner of innavigable streams and their beds; and, since the act of congress granting or recognizing a property in the waters actually diverted and usefully applied on the public lands of the United States, such rights have always been claimed to be deraigned by private persons under the act of congress, from the recognition accorded by the act, or from the acquiescence of the general government in previous appropriations made with its presumed sanction and approval. * * *

It has never been held by the supreme court of the United States, or by the supreme court of this state, that an appropriation of water on the public lands of the United States (made after the act of congress of July 26, 1866, or the amendatory act of 1870) gave to the appropriator the right to the water appropriated as against a grantee of riparian lands, under a grant made or issued prior to the act of 1866, except in a case where the water so subsequently appropriated was reserved by the terms of such grant.

Since, as before, September 28, 1850, the United States has been the owner of lands in California, with power to dispose of the same in such manner, and on such terms and conditions, (not interfering with vested rights derived from the United States,) as it deemed proper. But neither the legislation of congress with respect to the disposition of the public lands, nor its apparent acquiescence in the appropriation by individuals of waters thereon, *subsequent* to the act of September, 1850, granting the swamp lands to the state, can affect the title of the state to lands and waters granted by that act. Neither the supreme court of the United States, nor the supreme court of California, has ever held in opposition to this view. * * *

In Broder v. Water Co., 101 U.S. 274, it appeared: In the year 1853 the defendant completed a canal, through which it had continuously conducted waters and distributed them for mining, agricultural, and other uses; that a portion of the land through which the canal ran was included in the land granted to the Pacific Railroad (under whom plaintiff claimed) by the act of July 2, 1864; that the plaintiff also claimed as a pre-emptor, the inception of his claim as such being a declaratory statement filed August 6, 1866. The court held that the plaintiff was not entitled to have the canal running through his land abated as a nuisance by reason of his pre-emption right, because previous to the initiation of proceedings to secure pre-emption, on the twenty-sixth of July, 1866, (14 St. at Large, 251,) congress had enacted a statute, the ninth section of which contained the declaration "that wherever, by priority of possession, rights to the use of water for mining, agricultural, manufacturing, or other purposes have vested and accrued, and the same are recognized and acknowledged by the local customs, laws, and the decisions of courts, the possessors and owners of such vested rights shall be maintained and protected in the same; and the right of way for the construction of ditches and canals, for the purposes aforesaid, is hereby acknowledged and confirmed." The court also held that the plaintiff was not entitled to relief under his deraignment of title from the railroad company, because the grant to the company of July 2, 1864, contained the following reservation:

> "Any lands granted by this act, or the act to which this is an amendment, shall not defeat or impair any pre-emption, homestead, swamp-land, or other *lawful claim,* nor include any government reservation or mineral lands, or the improvements of any *bona fide* settler on any lands returned or denominated as mineral lands, and the timber necessary to support his said improvements as a miner or agriculturist."

In the opinion of the court the section of the act of 1866 above quoted "was rather a voluntary recognition of a pre-existing right of possession, constituting a valid claim to its continued use, than the establishment of a new one," and that the claim of the defendant to the right of way was such a "lawful claim" as was unaffected by the grant to the railroad company made before the act of 1866 was passed. * * *

In Broder v. Water Co. the claim of the appropriator was recognized in the grant to the railroad company, and prior to the initiation by the plaintiff of proceedings to secure a pre-emption. In the case at bar the grant of the lands to the state (containing no reservation of the waters of flowing streams, express or to be implied from its terms) was made nearly 30 years before the first appropriation of water by the defendant, which was *after* the act of congress of July, 1866, and the amendatory act of 1870. Copp, Min.Dec. 1873–74, 296.

In Osgood v. Water Co., 56 Cal. 571, it was held that where a person acquired a right, by appropriation, to water upon the public lands of the United States, *before* the issuance of a patent to another for lands through which the stream ran, the patentee's rights were, "by express statutory enactment, subject to the rights of the appropriator." The court cited the amendatory act of congress above referred to, the seventeenth section of which reads:

"That all patents granted, or pre-emptions or homesteads allowed, shall be subject to any vested and accrued water-rights, or rights to ditches and reservoirs used in connection with such water-rights, as may have been acquired under or recognized by the ninth section of the act of which this is amendatory." * * *

Both Broder v. Water Co. and Osgood v. Water Co. are (by strongest implication) authority for the statement that one who acquired a title to riparian lands from the United States prior to the act of July 26, 1866, could not (in the absence of reservation in his grant) be deprived of his common-law rights to the flow of the stream by one who appropriated its waters after the passage of that act.

Much stress is laid by counsel on the language used in Broder v. Water Co., supra, with reference to the clause in the act of 1866, that water-rights recognized or acknowledged by the local customs, etc., "shall be maintained and protected," "was rather a recognition of a pre-existing right of possession, constituting a valid claim to its continued use, than the establishment of a new one." But this language is to be interpreted in view of the context. The language cannot be construed as a recognition by the court of vested rights in appropriators of water, created by mere appropriation and independent of statute. The case proceeds on the assumption that neither the plaintiff nor the defendant had any rights except such as were granted or recognized by acts of congress. It holds that appropriators of water from streams on (or flowing to) the lands granted by the act of 1864 were "recognized" or admitted to have rights which were protected by that act, because the act by its terms reserved from the grant to the railroad company every "lawful claim;" that one who had been permitted to divert water from those lands had a claim which was not in itself unlawful; and that the reservation included "*every honest claim* evidenced by acts of possession." There is no statement in the opinion in Broder v. Water Co., that except for the reservation found in the act of 1864, and the provision in the act of 1866, the defendant would have any right to the water as against the grantees named in the act first named, or their successors in interest. The court holds that Broder acquired no right by virtue of his preemption, because his proceedings to secure it were begun after the act of 1866, which recognized the prior appropriation of the water as being a right in the appropriator, and that Broder acquired no right under the railroad grant, because the water previously appropriated was reserved in that grant. * * *

It may be suggested, however, that the rulings of the courts of California with reference to possessory rights on the public mineral lands enter into, and in some manner limit, the effect of grants of land by the government of the United States, made, as is assumed, under statutes enacted in view of the local law, and of the varying rules and regulations of mining districts. The statutes passed long afterwards cannot affect rights acquired by the state by virtue of a grant made in 1850, nor can the subsequent *policy* of the United States (which is supposed to be indicated by a failure, by express laws, to prohibit the occupation of portions of its lands for mining, etc., and by the omission of the executive officers to attempt to remove miners and other occupants by force) be held to affect the rights acquired by the state through the grant of 1850. * * *

[Reversed.]

Notes

1. This is the "California Doctrine" in its purest form, though the term is sometimes applied to any system recognizing both riparian and appropriative rights. Since the early appropriations had been from streams "on the public domain", the California courts later seized upon this phrase and gave it new significance, requiring that the actual diversion of the water must take place on public land. Thus the California rule came to be that where an appropriator diverted the water from the stream at a point where it touched private land, no rights were acquired that were superior to the later uses of upstream riparians who subsequently acquired their lands. San Joaquin and Kings River Canal & Irrigation Co. v. Worswick, 187 Cal. 674, 203 P. 999 (1922). See Thorne v. McKinley Bros., 5 Cal.2d 704, 56 P.2d 204 (1936); compare Brown v. Baker, 39 Or. 66, 65 P. 799 (1901) and Offield v. Ish, 21 Wash. 277, 57 P. 809 (1899).

2. Is an analysis of the federal land statutes necessary to a determination of whether a patentee of a parcel of land from the public domain acquires riparian rights? Or whether a state may authorize an appropriation of water? Or whether, as between holders of private rights, one type of right is superior to the other? See Connecticut v. Massachusetts, 282 U.S. 660, 51 S.Ct. 286, 75 L.Ed. 602 (1931). Compare Sturr v. Beck, 133 U.S. 541, 33 L.Ed. 761, 10 S.Ct. 350 (1890) with Boquillas Land & Cattle Co. v. Curtis, 213 U.S. 339, 29 S.Ct. 493, 53 L.Ed. 822 (1909), as to the effect of local law on the incidents of ownership of land acquired by patent. In neither case does the Court make a direct connection, but is it merely coincidence that in Dakota, where the Territory had codified riparian law, the patentee had riparian rights, while in Arizona, where neither the Territory nor the preceding Mexican State of Sonora recognized such rights, the patentee acquired none?

In California-Oregon Power Co. v. Beaver Portland Cement Co., 295 U.S. 142, 55 S.Ct. 725, 79 L.Ed. 1356 (1935), the Supreme Court gave some credence to the notion that the federal land laws control the question of whether a parcel of riparian land patented by the government had an appurtenant federally created riparian right, but concluded that those laws left to the states the "power * * * to legislate in respect of waters and water rights as they deemed wise in the public interest * * * with the right in each to determine for itself to what extent the rule of appropriation or the common law rule in respect to riparian rights should obtain. For since 'Congress cannot enforce either rule upon any state' State of Kansas v. Colorado, 206 U.S. 46, 94, 27 S.Ct. 655, 666, 51 L.Ed. 596, the full power of choice must remain with the state." See Chapter 2, § 1, p. 22 supra.

As to the extent to which the federal laws reserve to the national government a residuum of "title to unappropriated water" and of power to dispose of the water as a part of the public domain, see Chapter 8, infra.

3. Texas, by statute, established a cut-off date after which a person acquiring public land would not receive riparian rights. Vernon's Ann. Tex.Civ.St. art. 7619. Another important limitation in Texas is that Spanish and Mexican grants of land along the lower Rio Grande have no appurtenant riparian rights. State v. Valmont Plantations, 346 S.W.2d 853 (Tex.Civ.App.1961), affirmed 163 Tex. 381, 355 S.W.2d 502 (1962). This ruling was modified to some extent in State v. Hidalgo County Water Control and Improvement Dist. No. 18, 443 S.W.2d 728 (Tex.Civ.App.1969), the case from which *Valmont Plantations* was spun off. The court recognized "equitable" water rights of several types, including some held by owners of riparian tracts in Spanish land grants whose land had been irrigated under the claim to riparian rights rejected in *Valmont.* The decision was motivated by the "unprecedented situation" resulting from the fact that two large reservoirs (Falcon and Amistad) had been constructed on the Rio Grande by the federal government pursuant to a treaty with Mexico, which had made large quantities of water available for use in Texas at no expense to irrigators. On "water-short Cibolo Creek," however, an attempt by the owner of a riparian Spanish land grant tract to claim an "equitable right" was not successful. In re Water Rights of Cibolo Creek Watershed, 568 S.W.2d 155 (Tex.Civ.App.1978).

In 1895 Nebraska passed a comprehensive water code, which the court held prevented by implication the acquisition of any riparian rights in lands thereafter acquired. Crawford Co. v. Hathaway, 67 Neb. 325, 93 N.W. 781 (1903). Nevertheless, in Brummund v. Vogel, 184 Neb. 415, 168 N.W.2d 24 (1969), the owner of farm property which abutted on a creek claimed the right to use water from this stream for domestic purposes superior to an appropriator's right to build a dam upstream. The landowner was held to have this riparian right despite the fact that he neither pleaded nor proved that he or his predecessors had owned the land before the cutoff date of April 4, 1895.

4. Although riparians are generally regarded as having rights in navigable waters, the Supreme Court of Washington held that since that state's constitution declares that the state owns the bed and shores of all navigable waters up to the line of ordinary high water, an owner of the shore of a navigable lake cannot make a riparian claim to the waters of the lake for irrigation that is good against the state, or against one who appropriates water in pursuance of the laws of the State. State ex rel. Ham v. Superior Court, 70 Wash. 442, 126 P. 945 (1912).

A similar approach in Texas confined riparian rights to low-water flows, with the result that large quantities of the annual flow of variable streams were reserved for use by appropriators. In Motl v. Boyd, 116 Tex. 82, 286 S.W. 458 (1926), the court said that riparian rights could attach only to waters below the line of highest ordinary flow, which it defined as the highest line of flow which the stream reaches and maintains for a sufficient length of time to become characteristic when its waters are in their ordinary normal and usual condition, uninfluenced by recent rainfall or surface runoff. The Texas water officials, in an attempt to introduce a measure of certainty into the rule as a guide to determining the availability of water for appropriation, translated the court's definition of "highest ordinary flow" into "modal flow," that level of water most frequently occurring in daily measurements of the actual flow of the stream. Carter, Proceedings, Water Law Conferences, University of Texas School of Law, 194 (1954).

JOSLIN v. MARIN MUNICIPAL WATER DISTRICT

Supreme Court of California, 1967.
67 Cal.2d 132, 60 Cal.Rptr. 377, 429 P.2d 889.

[Facts, see case as reported supra, p. 305.]

With some variance in language the parties assert that the principal issue before us is whether defendant, an upstream appropriator of water, is liable in damages to plaintiffs, downstream riparian owners, by reason of having appropriated the waters of the creek under the above-mentioned circumstances.

To bring this appeal into focus, we must first briefly review the growth and development of California water law. In its first stage which began with the "gold rush," this law dealt mainly with those who diverted water from streams in the public domain for mining purposes and sought to adjudicate the competing claims of the parties using such water on the basis of a principle of prior appropriation. Subsequently with the increasing importance of agriculture over mining, the courts became more involved with riparian rights. This doctrine which had its genesis in the common law of England initially was made to rest in California on the basic principle "that the riparian proprietor is entitled to the full flow of the stream, reduced only by the proper riparian uses which may be made of the water by proprietors above him." (Miller & Lux v. Enterprise C. etc. Co. (1915) 169 Cal. 415, 443, 147 P. 567, 578; see Lux v. Haggin (1886) 69 Cal. 255, 390–394, 4 P. 919, 10 P. 674; Herminghaus v. Southern California Edison Co. (1926) 200 Cal. 81, 94–96, 252 P. 607.) Such riparian rights extended to "the entire flow of the waters of [a] river, considering the same with its seasonal accretions as the usual and ordinary flow of said stream during each and every year." (Herminghaus v. Southern California Edison Co., supra, at p. 91, 252 P. at p. 611.)

It was inevitable that the claims of appropriators and riparian owners would collide and that the legal principles upon which they were asserted would appear to be in conflict. Reconciling these principles, this court in the leading case of Lux v. Haggin, supra, 69 Cal. 255, 4 P. 919, 10 P. 674, declared " 'that the rights of the riparian owners to the use of the waters of the abutting stream were paramount to the rights of any other persons thereto; that such rights were parcel of the land and that any diminution of the stream against the will of the riparian owner by other persons was an actionable injury. The question was settled by that case and the riparian right has never since been disputed.' " As a result the principle emerged that an upstream appropriator could not deprive a downstream riparian owner of his right to the use of the full flow of a stream, even though only a small percentage of the flow was utilized to benefit the lands of the downstream riparian. (Herminghaus v. Southern California Edison Co., supra, 200 Cal. 81, 94–103, 252 P. 607; see also Tulare Irr. Dist. v. Lindsay-Strathmore Dist. (1935) 3 Cal.2d 489, 523–524, 45 P.2d 972.

Thereafter, and in apparent response to the *Herminghaus* decision (see Gin S. Chow v. City of Santa Barbara (1933) 217 Cal. 673, 699–700, 22 P.2d 5), the California Constitution was amended in 1928. (Art. XIV, § 3.)[a] [Now Art. X, § 2.] The amendment was generally construed as applying a rule of reasonable use "to all water rights enjoyed or asserted in this state, whether the same be grounded on the riparian right or the right, analogous to the riparian right, of the overlying land owner, or the percolating water right, or the appropriative right." (Peabody v. City of Vallejo (1935) 2 Cal.2d 351, 383, 40 P.2d 486, 499.) Thus the rule of reasonableness of use as a measure of the water right which had theretofore been applied as between other contesting claimants but had been denied application as between riparian owners and appropriators was finally extended to include the latter.

As epitomized in *Peabody,* the amendment is said to declare: "1. The right to the use of water is limited to such water as shall be reasonably required for the beneficial use to be served. 2. Such right does not extend to the waste of water. 3. Such right does not extend to unreasonable use or unreasonable method of use or unreasonable method of diversion of water. 4. Riparian rights attach to, but to no more than so much of the flow as may be required or used consistently with this section of the Constitution."

It has been long and clearly settled in California that the effect of the passage of article [X, § 2] "has been to modify the long-standing riparian doctrine * * * and to apply, by constitutional mandate the doctrine of reasonable use between riparian owners and appropriators,

a. The amendment has not since been modified, altered or changed, and provides: "It is hereby declared that because of the conditions prevailing in this State the general welfare requires that the water resources of the State be put to beneficial use to the fullest extent of which they are capable, and that the waste or unreasonable use or unreasonable method of use of water be prevented, and that the conservation of such waters is to be exercised with a view to the reasonable and beneficial use thereof in the interest of the people and for the public welfare. The right to water or to the use or flow of water in or from any natural stream or water course in this State is and shall be limited to such water as shall be reasonably required for the beneficial use to be served, and such right does not and shall not extend to the waste or unreasonable use or unreasonable method of use or unreasonable method of diversion of water. Riparian rights in a stream or water course attach to, but to no more than so much of the flow thereof as may be required or used consistently with this section, for the purposes for which such lands are, or may be made adaptable, in view of such reasonable and beneficial uses; provided, however, that nothing herein contained shall be construed as depriving any riparian owner of the reasonable use of water of the stream to which his land is riparian under reasonable methods of diversion and use, or of depriving any appropriator of water to which he is lawfully entitled. This section shall be self-executing, and the Legislature may also enact laws in the furtherance of the policy in this section contained."

and between overlying owners and appropriators." (Tulare Irr. Dist. v. Lindsay-Strathmore Dist., supra, 3 Cal.2d 489).

> "The right to the waste of water is not now included in the riparian right." (Peabody v. City of Vallejo, supra, at p. 368, 40 P.2d at p. 492.) What is a reasonable use or method of use of water is a question of fact to be determined according to the circumstances in each particular case.

In *Peabody,* several lower riparian owners sought to enjoin the City of Vallejo, as an appropriator, from storing the waters of a creek by the construction of a dam and thereafter diverting them to municipal uses. Peabody, one of the plaintiffs, asserted a right to have all the waters flow without interruption since by normally overflowing his land they not only deposited silt thereon but also washed out salt deposits on portions of the land. The court held that "[t]his asserted right does not inhere in the riparian right at common law, and as a natural right cannot be asserted as against the police power of the state in the conservation of its waters. This asserted right involves an unreasonable use or an unreasonable method of use or an unreasonable method of diversion of water as contemplated by the Constitution." (Peabody v. City of Vallejo, supra, 2 Cal.2d 351, 369, 40 P.2d 486, 492.)

Although, as we have said, what is a reasonable use of water depends on the circumstances of each case, such an inquiry cannot be resolved *in vacuo* isolated from state-wide considerations of transcendent importance. Paramount among these we see the ever increasing need for the conservation of water in this state, an inescapable reality of life quite apart from its express recognition in the 1928 amendment. On the other hand, unlike the unanimous policy pronouncements relative to the use and conservation of natural waters, we are aware of none relative to the supply and availability of sand, gravel and rock in commercial quantities. Plaintiffs do not urge that the general welfare or public interest requires that particular or exceptional measures be employed to insure that such natural resources be made generally available and should therefore be carefully conserved.

Is it "reasonable." then, that the riches of our streams, which we are charged with conserving in the great public interest, are to be dissipated in the amassing of mere sand and gravel which for aught that appears subserves *no* public policy? We cannot deem such a use to be in accord with the constitutional mandate that our limited water resources be put only to those beneficial uses "to the fullest extent of which they are capable," that "waste or unreasonable use" be prevented, and that conservation be exercised "in the interest of the people and for the public welfare." (Cal. Const., [Art. X, § 2.] XIV, § 3.) We are satisfied that in the instant case the use of such waters as an agent to expose or to carry and deposit sand, gravel and rock, is as a matter of law unreasonable within the meaning of the constitutional amendment.

* * *

While plaintiffs correctly argue that a property right cannot be taken or damaged without just compensation, they ignore the necessity of first establishing the legal existence of a compensable property interest. Such an interest consists in their right to the *reasonable* use of the flow of the water. Their riparian rights attach to no more of the flow of the stream than that which is required for such use. * * * There is now no provision of law which authorizes an unreasonable use or endows such use with the quality of a legally protectible interest merely because it may be fortuitously beneficial to the lands involved. * * *

From the foregoing we arrive at the conclusion that since there was and is no property right in an unreasonable use, there has been no taking or damaging of property by the deprivation of such use and, accordingly, the deprivation is not compensable. * * *

Notes

1. The most frequent application of the reasonable use rule to accommodate riparian rights and appropriations on the same stream is in the converse situation, where the defendant's appropriation that depletes the natural flow of the stream leaves sufficient water for the riparian plaintiff's reasonable use. Brown v. Chase, 125 Washington 452, 217 P. 23 (1923).

2. Under the original form of the "California Doctrine," water rights acquired by prior appropriation were regarded simply as non-riparian uses subject to defeasance by the subsequent exercise of theretofore unused riparian rights. This rule once had currency in all of the West Coast states and the tier of Great Plains states that stretches from North Dakota to Texas. Only California now retains it.

Nebraska was once thought to have abolished it. As the result of a series of cases decided shortly after the turn of the century, it was generally believed that the appropriation statutes authorized any appropriator to take water, that the only remedy of an injured riparian was to sue for damages, and that he was entitled only to nominal damages for loss of unused rights. See Trelease, Coordination of Riparian and Appropriative Rights to the Use of Water, 33 Tex.L.Rev. 24, 60–62 (1954). But in Wasserburger v. Coffee, 180 Neb. 149, 141 N.W.2d 738 (1966), the court said that the earlier cases had been misread, that only public irrigation organizations had this power, and ruled that a landowner had a riparian right for watering his cattle that required a private prior appropriator to release water used for irrigation. Instead of holding that the riparian had the superior right, however, the court said that the relative rights of appropriator and riparian were to be determined by relative reasonableness, applying between them the balance of utility v. harm that the Restatement, Torts, § 851 (1939) applied between riparians.

3. Shaw, The Development of the Law of Waters in the West, 10 Cal. L.Rev. 443, 455 (1922): "If the doctrine of the riparian right had been strictly enforced in all cases by the abutting land owners, it is obvious that it would have prevented all use of the waters of streams passing through

lands in private ownership, on any non-riparian land. The rightful use of such waters on non-riparian land would have been impossible, for such land owners could not lawfully take out the water without infringing upon the right of every riparian owner along the stream to have the water flow as it was accustomed to flow. * * *

"Notwithstanding the existence of these vested rights, there has been a very general use of water on non-riparian land. This has been made possible by several causes. The most important and effective cause of a legal nature is the common law rule, now expressed in section 1007 of the Civil Code, that a title by prescription, good against all owners of private property, may be acquired by adverse occupancy for the period of five years continuously. Other causes arise from natural conditions. Any person who does not own land on a stream may obtain access to the water thereof by purchasing the right to do so from the owner of any parcel of riparian land. Usually the banks of the larger streams are so high that the owner of a small tract cannot bring the water upon his land, except by a diversion on land above him, to which, of course, he must have the consent of the owner thereof. Such owners frequently made little use of the water for irrigation and were indifferent to their riparian rights therein. Hence they usually made no objection to a diversion therefrom until five years had elapsed. The large diversions, almost without exception, have been made near the point of emergence of the streams from the mountains, where land had little value for any purpose, and where the diversion would have little effect on the land near by and were so far from the land seriously affected thereby that they provoked no immediate opposition. In these ways and for these reasons, innumerable prescriptive rights to the use of the water of streams have been acquired from the riparian owners of private land, either without objection, or by successful litigation. As a net result the irrigated land in the state is almost all non-riparian, and the existence of the riparian right has not prevented the beneficial use of the greater part of the waters of the streams."

As pointed out in the principal case, the 1928 amendment to the California constitution eliminates the riparian's former right to insist on the natural flow of the stream as against the nonriparian, and gives the riparian no cause of action until an appropriator actually interferes with his reasonable uses. In City of Pasadena v. City of Alhambra, 33 Cal.2d 908, 207 P.2d 17 (1949), a ground water case in which the court relied on rules of stream water law as an analogy, the court said, "Prescriptive rights are not acquired by the taking of surplus or excess water, since no injunction may issue against the taking and the appropriator may take the surplus without giving compensation." Two dissenting judges argued that this dictum failed to recognize fundamental principles of adjusting California riparian and appropriative rights which the amendment was not intended to abrogate, and that it would overrule a long line of cases (it took a column of the Pacific Reporter to list them!).

Martin v. Burr, 111 Tex. 57, 228 S.W. 543 (1921) was an action to quiet the title of the riparian plaintiff against upper riparian owners who were allegedly using the waters of the stream in excess of their riparian rights. The trial court ruled out the defenses of either "limitation" or "prescription"; the Supreme Court held this was error. First the court pointed out that this action, not being an action to recover real estate, was governed by a general 4-year statute of limitations, which would bar the action within four years after the riparian suffered substantial injuries and acquired a right of action. The court then went on to say that in so far as the defendant's claim was based on an alleged paramount right acquired by prescription, it raised a distinct question from that of limitation. As to prescription, it said: "It is not an open question in Texas that an upper riparian proprietor may, by prescription, acquire the right to use the water of a running stream, in a special way and in excess of the right arising from ownership of his land, to the injury and detriment of lower riparian owners. And the time to perfect such a right by prescription is ten years".

IN RE WATERS OF LONG VALLEY CREEK STREAM SYSTEM

Supreme Court of California, 1979.
25 Cal.3d 339, 158 Cal.Rptr. 350, 599 P.2d 656.

MOSK, JUSTICE.

The significant problem in this case is the extent to which the State Water Resources Control Board (Board) has the power to define and otherwise limit prospective riparian rights when, pursuant to the statutory adjudication procedure set forth in Water Code section 2500 et seq., it determines all claimed rights to the use of water in a stream system. * * *

The action arises out of a statutory proceeding to adjudicate the rights of all claimants to the waters of the Long Valley Creek Stream System (stream system) in Lassen, Sierra and Plumas Counties. The stream system, which contains a 465-square-mile watershed, lies astride the California-Nevada border starting at its uppermost extremity about 8 miles northwest of Reno, Nevada, and extending northwesterly about 45 miles in length to the east end of Honey Lake near Herlong, California. Long Valley Creek and its main tributaries, Purdy Creek and Balls Creek, originate in the melting snow of the Sierra Nevada near Babbit Peak. From there they flow into a semi-arid and desert portion of California. In most years, there is a surplus of water early in the spring, with the flow receding rapidly when the snow has melted; this may occur as early as April or as late as June. After the snowmelt runoff is depleted, there is only enough water to irrigate a small portion of the total irrigable land.

Because of the limited water supply, there has been prolific litigation among the various water claimants in the area since at least 1883. In the interest of resolving the conflicts that have fostered such litigation, nine claimants filed a petition in 1966 with the Board for statutory adjudication of all water rights in the stream system. (Wat.Code, § 2525.) The staff of the Board conducted a preliminary investigation and recommended in favor of the petition, which the Board subsequently granted. Thereafter the Board prepared and published a notice of the proceedings (id., §§ 2526, 2527), and all persons claiming a right to the waters of the stream system notified the Board of their intention to file a claim. (Id., § 2528.) As required by Water Code section 2550, the Board then conducted an extensive investigation; it published a report containing the results of this investigation for the principal purpose of assisting water users in filing their claims of right.

After filing its report, the Board advised persons who notified it of their intention to file a claim that the claim and proof in support of it must be formally presented. It heard 234 claims and proofs, and 42 contests thereto, concerning the rights of the stream system. After consideration of these claims, proofs and contests, it "entered of record in its office an order determining and establishing the several rights to the water of the stream system." (Id., § 2700.)

Donald Ramelli (Ramelli), as a party aggrieved or dissatisfied with the order of determination, filed a notice of exceptions in the superior court pursuant to Water Code section 2757. Ramelli owns land upon which Balls Creek originates. For the past approximately 60 years he and his predecessors have irrigated 89 acres of this land, but before the Board he claimed prospective riparian rights in the creek for an additional 2,884 acres. The order of determination nevertheless awarded him various amounts of water for only the 89 acres as to which he was currently exercising his riparian rights; it extinguished entirely his claim as a riparian landowner to the future use of water with respect to the remaining 2,884 acres.[a]

The trial court denied Ramelli's exceptions and entered a decree consistent with the Board's order of determination. Ramelli appealed from the decree, and we reverse.

* * *

Ramelli's principal contention is that the trial court erroneously failed to recognize his riparian right to prospective use of the stream system. In support of this contention, he initially insists that California judicial decisions have without question recognized such a right.

* * *

Water Code section 2501 provides that "The board may determine, in the proceedings provided for in this chapter *all* rights to water of a stream system whether based upon appropriation, *riparian right,* or other basis of right." (Italics added.) * * * The above statutory language clearly discloses that the Legislature intended to grant the Board broad authority pursuant to the statutory adjudication procedure to define and otherwise limit the scope of a riparian's future right.

In this case the Board entirely extinguished Ramelli's riparian claim to the future use of water. Such extinction raises a substantial

a. Presently only an estimated 4,130 acres are irrigated in the entire Long Valley Creek watershed area. Moreover, Balls Creek contributes to Long Valley Creek the largest flow of any of its tributaries. Thus, the trial court found that under the circumstances "To allow dormant riparian owners to cast a shadow over uses of water by established developments would not only be unequitable but would create chaos."

constitutional issue as a result of our holding in Tulare Dist. v. Lindsay-Strathmore Dist. (1935) supra, 3 Cal.2d 489, 531, 45 P.2d 972, that section 11 of the Water Commission Act violated article X, section 2 (formerly art. XIV, § 3); the section, as stated above, provided in essence for the complete extinction of riparian rights that remained unused for 10 consecutive years. We consequently decline to construe the statutory adjudication procedure as authorizing the Board to extinguish altogether future riparian rights.

* * *

We next examine whether such a broad grant of authority to the Board is consistent with the constitutional holding of Tulare Dist. v. Lindsay-Strathmore Dist., supra, 3 Cal.2d 489, 45 P.2d 972. Ramelli argues that a riparian's prospective right cannot be defined or otherwise limited in a statutory proceeding because of our holding in *Tulare* that section 11 of the Water Commission Act—which declared that 10 years' nonuse, without an intervening use, constituted an abandonment of a riparian right—was "incongruous and in violation of the spirit of the constitutional provision * * *." Ramelli's expansive reading of the limits *Tulare* places on legislative authority is unsupportable in light of the amendment's grant of authority to the Legislature to enact laws in the furtherance of the constitutionally expressed state water policy. Moreover, *Tulare* is distinguishable from the issue before us in that the statute therein treated the right as automatically abandoned as a result of 10 years' nonuse, without consideration of other needs and uses of the water in the stream system. The statute therefore was inconsistent with the mandate of the amendment to promote the reasonable beneficial use of state waters. * * * In light of these considerations, it is clear that Ramelli's extravagant reading of our decision in *Tulare* to strike down section 11 of the Water Commission Act would unduly restrict the Legislature's authority to promote the reasonable and beneficial use of state waters and thereby would contravene article X, section 2.

This conclusion is supported by compelling policy considerations. The Legislature has enacted a comprehensive administrative scheme for the final determination of *all* rights in a stream system. (Wat.Code, § 2500 et seq.) The statutory adjudication procedure involves a complex balancing of both public and private interests, with the final decree assuring certainty to the existing economy and reasonable predictability to the uses of water in a stream system. In so doing, it falls within the amendment's specific grant of authority to the Legislature. (Cal.Const., art. X, § 2.) That the statutory adjudication procedure promotes the policies of the amendment is reflected in a recent report of the Governor's Commission to Review California Water Rights Law. (Final Rep. (Dec.1978).) This document identifies uncertainty as one of the major problems in contemporary California water rights law (id., at pp. 16–49), and it discloses that riparian rights are a principal source of this uncertainty. (Id., at pp. 18–21.)

Uncertainty concerning the rights of water users has pernicious effects. Initially, it inhibits long range planning and investment for the development and use of waters in a stream system. (Robie & Steinberg, Existing Water Laws and Industry Practices: Their Contribution to the Waste of Water (1977) 53 L.A.Bar J. 164, 171–172; Governor's Com. to Review Cal. Water Rights Law, Final Rep. (Dec. 1978) supra, at p. 16.) Thus with respect to dormant riparian rights, one authority has observed: "These rights constitute the main threat to nonriparian and out-of-watershed development, they are the principal cause of insecurity of existing riparian uses, and their presence adds greatly to the cost of obtaining firm water rights under a riparian system. They are unrecorded, their quantity is unknown, their administration in the courts provides very little opportunity for control in the public interest. To the extent that they may deter others from using the water for fear of their ultimate exercise, they are wasteful, in the sense of costing the economy the benefits lost from the deterred uses." (Trelease, A Model State Water Code for River Basin Development (1957) 22 Law & Contemp.Prob. 302, 318; see also Milliman, Water Law and Private Decisionmaking: A Critique (1959) 2 J. Law & Econ. 41, 47.)

Uncertainty also fosters recurrent, costly and piecemeal litigation. In the present case, for example, there has been incessant litigation between the claimants to the waters of the stream system since about 1883. And, as the Board engineer observed, the inconclusive fragmentary definition of water rights resulting from that litigation was "the prime reason for the proposed adjudication." The principal cause of this untoward effect appears to be that a private suit for determining title to water binds only those who are parties to the suit; such suits are inadequate, however, because shortages in supply or new appropriations or riparian uses have the potential for bringing all water users on the stream in conflict. (Governor's Com. To Review Cal. Water Rights Law, Final Rep. (Dec.1978) supra, at p. 22.)

Finally, uncertainty impairs the state's administration of water rights. "Lack of knowledge of water use by non-statutory right holders affects decisions to grant permits, because the availability of water for appropriation and the existence and extent of other beneficial uses of water are uncertain. It also affects the ability of the Board to set meaningful terms and conditions to provide effective enforcement and protection of statutory water rights." (Id., at p. 22.)

These pernicious effects of uncertainty provide strong support for the conclusions of the Governor's Commission to Review California Water Rights Law, that comprehensive determination of water rights has salutary results because it (1) provides "valuable information for water rights administration and for planning purposes," (2) "prevents recurrent litigation and gives the certainty of official recognition to private property rights," and (3) creates "the basis for the orderly control and management of water on a stream." (Id., at p. 28.) Thus, we find unpersuasive Ramelli's argument that *Tulare* should be read as prohibiting the Board from defining or otherwise limiting future riparian rights.

* * *

A more difficult question is whether the Board may constitutionally extinguish a riparian landowner's unexercised claim to the use of water. The Attorney General has not presented a persuasive argument for concluding that complete extinction of such rights is necessary to the promotion of the reasonable and beneficial use of a stream system, nor has he established in this case that the reasonable and beneficial use of the waters in the Long Valley Creek cannot be equally well promoted by placing limitations on Ramelli's future riparian right other than complete extinction. * * * It is true that *Tulare* is distinguishable from this case; in *Tulare* the Legislature had enacted a blanket extinction of unexercised riparian rights when there was no basis for concluding that such an extinction was consistent with the promotion of the reasonable and beneficial use of state waters. In light of *Tulare's* holding that section 11 of the Water Commission Act was unconstitutional, however, we are reluctant to conclude that the Board may altogether extinguish a riparian's future claim when it has not been established that the imposition of other less drastic limitations on the claim would be less effective in promoting the most reasonable and beneficial use of the stream system. Because no such showing has been made in this case, it is clear that the Board's decision to extinguish Ramelli's future riparian claim raises a serious constitutional issue. Thus, since the Legislature has not clearly expressed an intention that the statute should be construed otherwise, we interpret it as not authorizing the Board in these circumstances to extinguish altogether Ramelli's claim to the future use of waters in the Long Valley stream system.

For the future guidance of the Board, however, we undertake to identify the limitations on unexercised riparian claims that are constitutionally permissible and thus authorized by the statute in light of our analysis herein. As previously discussed, when the Board determines all rights to the use of the water in a stream system, an important interest of the state is the promotion of clarity and certainty in the definition of those rights; such clarity and certainty foster more beneficial and efficient uses of state waters as called for by the mandate of article X, section 2. Thus, the Board is authorized to decide that an unexercised riparian claim loses its priority with respect to all rights currently being exercised. Moreover, to the extent that an unexercised riparian right may also create uncertainty with respect to permits of appropriation that the Board may grant after the statutory adjudication procedure is final, and may thereby continue to conflict with the public interest in reasonable and beneficial use of state waters, the Board may also determine that the future riparian right shall have a lower priority than any uses of water it authorizes before the riparian in fact attempts to exercise his right. In other words, while we interpret the Water Code as not authorizing the Board to extinguish altogether a future riparian right, the Board may make determinations as to the scope, nature and priority of the right that it deems reasonably necessary to the promotion of the state's interest in fostering the most reasonable and beneficial use of its scarce water resources. * * *

The judgment is reversed for further proceedings consistent with this opinion.

BIRD, C.J., and TOBRINER and NEWMAN, JJ., concur.

RICHARDSON, JUSTICE, concurring and dissenting. * * *

Thus, *Tulare* stands for this one simple proposition: A riparian owner's unexercised right to future water use is *constitutionally* protected and cannot properly be limited, fixed, quantified or subordinated "until the need for such use arises." I emphasize the fact that our *Tulare* decision not merely protects the riparian owner's prospective rights against total extinguishment, but also protects against premature limitation, quantification or subordination. * * * Although a *presently exercised* riparian use must be "reasonable and beneficial" under the constitutional provision, no limitation or quantification of a reasonable *future* use is possible in light of the difficulty in predicting future needs. As quite properly observed by the recent *Soquel* court, "the possible future use of a riparian right cannot be anticipated, and obviously, to that extent, uncertainty exists as to what a court in the future may find to be reasonable and beneficial." (In re Waters of Soquel Creek Stream System, supra, 79 Cal.App.3d at p. 689, 145 Cal. Rptr. at p. 150.) * * *

I would reverse the trial court's judgment with directions to amend its decree in recognition of appellant's unexercised riparian rights and to retain its continuing jurisdiction in the event an exercise of those rights is eventually proposed.

CLARK, J., concurs.

MANUEL, JUSTICE, concurring and dissenting.

* * *

I share the majority's concern—and that of the Board—over the severe problems of uncertainty caused by "dormant" riparian rights. As pointed out by the Governor's commission in its recent final report, such uncertainty not only hampers the local and statewide management and supervision of water uses but has historically resulted in recurrent and costly litigation. (Governor's Com. to Review Cal. Water Rights Law, Final Rep. (Dec.1978) pp. 21–25.) Clearly one means of avoiding this uncertainty is through the unified statutory adjudication procedure contemplated by section 2500 et seq. of the Water Code, whereby the Board is empowered to "determine * * * all rights to water of a stream system whether based upon appropriation, *riparian right,* or other basis of right." (§ 2501; italics added.) Insofar as this procedure contemplates a present quantification of *all* such rights, I perceive no constitutional impediment to it. * * *

I conclude for the foregoing reasons that the Board, in the context of a statutory adjudication of rights to water within a given stream system, has the power to presently quantify all such rights—including the future aspect of riparian rights. The Constitution, as I read it, offers no obstacle to such a procedure, and the relevant statutes clearly contemplate it. What the Constitution does not permit, in my view, is the actual or virtual extinguishment of the future aspect of riparian rights—either through outright extinction or through the device, adopted by the majority, of consigning that aspect of the right to some lesser status, to be administered by the Board on the same basis as all other rights in the stream when the riparian proposes to use it. Under our Constitution the riparian right, in both its present and future aspects, is *primary* in priority. The majority, in allowing the future aspect of the right to be denigrated to a lower status, does so in the face of a clear constitutional command to the contrary.

Notes

1. One way to get rid of unused riparian rights is for the appropriators to buy them. In *Tulare* the court said, speaking of the powers of condemnation enjoyed by public districts, "as to prospective uses, however, it is obvious that when, as here, the appropriator takes the water and devotes the same to a public use, prior to the time such prospective needs arise, a public use has intervened as to the quantity required for such future uses. The appropriator may not desire to appropriate the water and to construct large and expensive works with the possibility constantly in the offing that the riparians, who have been protected by a declaration of their rights in the water for future purposes will increase their reasonable and beneficial use of the water, so that ultimately, perhaps, none is left for appropriation. The appropriator may and probably would desire to condemn the riparians' right to use of the water in the stream for these prospective purposes. No good reason suggests itself why the appropriator should not be permitted to do this in the injunction suit by means of an inverse condemnation. The same compelling reasons that exist for permitting such a procedure when the entire riparian right is sought to be condemned likewise exists where the appropriator simply desires to condemn the right of the riparian to whatever additional water he may later need for prospective reasonable beneficial purposes. In both cases, the all important fact must exist that a public use has attached, but once that is present, this procedure seems to use sensible and well calculated to prevent multiplicity of suits and interminable delays."

2. Some of California's riparian-appropriation controversies have been given the "California solution" under which water problems are solved by pouring water on them, i.e., by augmenting supply rather than regulating demand. The United States Bureau of Reclamation's Central Valley Project and the State Department of Water Resource's State Water Project annually release water from Shasta Dam and Oroville Dam to

supply 370,300 acre feet to Sacramento River riparians and 295,000 acre feet for use on land riparian to the Feather, Yuba and Bear Rivers, in addition to releases of appropriated water for delivery pursuant to contracts with districts serving non-riparian irrigated land. Anderson, Riparian Water Rights in California 6–8 (Staff Paper No. 4, Governor's Commission to Review California Water Rights Law, 1977).

IN THE MATTER OF DEADMAN CREEK DRAINAGE BASIN

Supreme Court of Washington, 1985.
103 Wn.2d 686, 694 P.2d 1071.

I

In the early 1900's, John Fuher began operating a sawmill on the banks of Deadman Creek on property now owned by Riddle, the respondent in this appeal. The sawmill diverted water from the creek for log washing. * * * In August 1911, after the sawmill was already operating, Fuher filed a notice of appropriation with the Spokane County Auditor declaring his intent to divert 4.0 cubic feet per second (c.f.s.) of water for irrigation and other beneficial uses.

Sixty years later, on September 24, 1971, J.C. Riddle filed water right claim 5924, claiming the right to divert and use 4.0 c.f.s. of the waters of Deadman Creek for irrigation of 200 acres. Although the water has been used for irrigation for at least the last 15 to 20 years, the referee in a 1982 adjudication denied Riddle's claim of a water right of that quantity acquired from Fuher and confirmed a water right of a much smaller amount. The referee indicated that Fuher irrigated only about 15 acres in either 1922 or 1923. Except for the sawmill, there was no evidence of continuous use between the early 1920's and the early 1950's. The trial court, relying on Riddle's status as a riparian, granted Riddle partial summary judgment and remanded to the referee. * * *

II

Riparian rights, where they exist, derive from the ownership of land contiguous to or traversed by a watercourse. Crook v. Hewitt, 4 Wash. 749, 749–50, 31 P. 28 (1892) ("the law is uniformly settled that every proprietor of lands on the bank of a river has naturally an equal right to the use of the water which flows in the stream adjacent to his lands, as it was wont to run, without diminution or alteration"). Riparian rights in Washington can be traced to an enactment of the territorial Legislature adopting the common law of England as the rule of decision in territorial courts. *See* Laws of 1862, p. 82, ch. 1; see also Benton v. Johncox, 17 Wash. 277, 280–81, 49 P. 495 (1897).

The Washington Constitution did not mention riparian rights. As to water rights, it provides in article 21, section 1 that the "use of the waters of this state for irrigation, mining and manufacturing purposes shall be deemed a public use." * * * The implementing statute passed in 1891 provided:

> The right to the use of water in any lake, pond or flowing spring in this state, or the right to the use of water flowing in any river, stream or ravine of this state for irrigation, mining or manufacturing purposes, or for supplying cities, towns or villages with water, or for water works, may be acquired by appropriation, and as between appropriations the first in time is the first in right.

Laws of 1891, ch. 142, § 1, p. 327. * * * The 1891 act also stated that "this act shall not be construed to interfere with vested rights." Laws of 1891, ch. 142, § 7, p. 328.

Appropriative rights, as provided for by statute, and riparian rights, derived from the common law, existed simultaneously. Conflict between riparian and appropriative rights was addressed as early as the first volume of Washington Reports. Geddis v. Parrish, 1 Wash. 587, 21 P. 314 (1889). The "California" or dual system, of riparian and appropriative rights was fully recognized in our state in Benton v. Johncox, supra. There, the court recognized riparian ownership as superior to subsequent appropriation. * * *

Erosion of riparian rights as the dominant force in Washington water law continued with the enactment of the water code of 1917. Until 1917, there existed two ways for a nonriparian owner to obtain an appropriative right to water: by taking water from the public domain and putting it to beneficial use, Thorpe v. Tenem Ditch Co., 1 Wash. 566, 20 P. 588 (1889), or by posting a statutory notice at the point of diversion and commencing construction of the works. Laws of 1891, ch. 142, § 2, p. 327. The 1917 code abrogated the acts of 1890 and 1891 and provided for a new system of application, permit and certification by the supervisor of hydraulics (now the supervisor of water resources).

The water code of 1917 declares that, subject to existing rights, "*all* waters within the state belong to the public, and any right thereto * * * shall be hereafter acquired * * * in the manner provided and not otherwise". (Italics ours.) RCW 90.03.010. "Any person * * * desiring to appropriate water for a beneficial use shall [apply] to the supervisor of water resources for a permit * * * and shall not use or divert such waters until he has received a permit". RCW 90.03.250. No exception is made for waters devoted to "ordinary", "natural" or domestic uses. There is no indication that rights which vested before the water code were to be excluded from general water rights adjudications or otherwise treated differently. For example, RCW 90.03.120 calls for service in an adjudication of "all known persons claiming the right to divert the water involved". No distinction is made as to the kind of use.

Nothing in the 1917 water code "shall be construed to lessen, enlarge, or modify the *existing* rights of any riparian owner, or any existing right acquired by appropriation, or otherwise." (Italics ours.)

RCW 90.03.010. The code also continued and enlarged condemnation rights by giving any person the power to condemn an inferior use for a superior beneficial use. RCW 90.03.040. Shortly after adoption of the code, the Supreme Court held that a riparian owner *intending* future use could not prevent condemnation by a nonriparian owner for an *immediate* use for power. State ex rel. South Fork Log Driving Co. v. Superior Court, 102 Wash. 460, 470, 173 P. 192 (1918) (the test for condemnation is "the extent and manner of the proposed use as compared with the present use"). Finally, the 1917 water code required that a change in use of all pre-Code vested rights must be approved by the supervisor of hydraulics. RCW 90.03.380.

The trial judge in this case, despite the shift away from the primacy of riparian rights by the courts and Legislature, concluded that the appropriative permit system embodied in the 1917 water code applied only to *surplus* waters in excess of those required for "ordinary" or "natural" domestic uses by riparians. * * *

We cannot agree with the trial court's conclusion. The trial judge relied on two decisions subsequent to the 1917 water code. * * * Brown v. Chase, 125 Wash. 542, 217 P. 23 (1923) and Proctor v. Sim, 134 Wash. 606, 236 P. 114 (1925), were both concerned with determining whether the clause in the 1917 code protecting the "existing rights" of riparian owners, *see* RCW 90.03.010, applied to unused rights.

Whether unused riparian rights survived adoption of the use-oriented 1917 water code has been much discussed. See Horowitz, Riparian and Appropriation Rights to the Use of Water in Washington, 7 Wash.L.Rev. 197 (1932); Morris, Washington Water Rights—A Sketch, 31 Wash.L.Rev. 243 (1956); Johnson, Riparian and Public Rights to Lakes and Streams, 35 Wash.L.Rev. 580 (1960); Corker & Roe, Washington's New Water Rights Law—Improvements Needed, 44 Wash.L.Rev. 85 (1968). The referee in this case determined that the "[e]xtent of the right is limited to the amount of water developed and used under diligent pursuance and completion of any project as originally contemplated and which was initiated within three years after the effective date of the 1917 Surface Water Code. (June 6, 1917)" Report of Referee, at 15.

Brown v. Chase, supra, presented a contest between riparians whose rights were unexercised and an applicant for an appropriation permit under the 1917 water code. The trial court overturned a permit on the grounds that a riparian owner is entitled to "the undiminished unpolluted flow of the stream past his land." In reversing the trial court, the Supreme Court adopted the approach taken in *Kettle Falls Power,* and stated:

> [I]n consonance with the general needs and welfare of the state, especially in the arid and semi-arid regions, and in harmony with the legislation upon the matter, we are now prepared to declare . . . that (1) waters of non-navigable streams in excess of the amount which can be beneficially used, either directly or prospectively, *within a reasona-*

> *ble time,* on, or in connection with riparian lands, are subject to appropriation for use on nonriparian lands.

(Italics ours.) 125 Wash. at 553, 217 P. at 26–27.

Proctor v. Sim, supra, involved a situation similar to that in Brown v. Chase, supra. On the other hand, Brown v. Chase, supra, and Proctor v. Sim, supra, both imply that the code did not extinguish unused water rights as of 1917 but as of a later date, adequate to allow riparian owners to learn about the code and take steps to protect their interests. Many commentators, and several courts, have determined that either the statute or the decisional law of this court has eliminated unused riparian rights. Disagreement, however, is widespread as to when that relinquishment occurred. *See* Corker & Roe, 44 Wash.L.Rev. at 114–18; *see also* 2 W. Hutchins, Water Rights Laws in the Nineteen Western States 14 (1974). The time when relinquishment occurred must be settled to decide today's case.

Six years after Proctor v. Sim, supra, was decided, four members of Department One of this court agreed that a claim to riparian rights which had not and would not be exercised "within a reasonable time" was properly rejected by a trial court reviewing an adjudication. In re Sinlahekin Creek, 162 Wash. 635, 299 P. 649 (1931). Because *Sinlahekin Creek* and the other cases applying the "reasonable time" standard are all forward looking, the Department of Ecology suggests 1932 as the date by which unused riparian rights must have been put to use or forfeited. Our cases support adoption of that year as the cutoff date for exercise of unused riparian rights; 15 years after enactment of the water code, we now hold, as a matter of law, constitutes adequate notice.

The referee's denial of Riddle's claim based on Fuher's riparian status was proper. No rights sought were exercised for irrigation purposes prior to 1917. Fuher lost his claim to these unexercised riparian rights by 1932 and therefore transferred only those exercised to Riddle. * * *

III

Riddle asserts that the forfeiture of riparian rights for nonuse effects an unconstitutional taking. In Washington, we have previously held that the permit requirement for bringing a water right into existence in the first instance is a reasonable exercise of the state's police power. Peterson v. Department of Ecology, 92 Wash.2d 306, 596 P.2d 285 (1979). In other states, it is well established that riparian rights may be extinguished or limited by statute. 2 W. Hutchins, at 290–97. That a state has the power to either modify or reject the doctrine of riparian rights because unsuited to the conditions in the state and to put into effect the doctrine of prior appropriation has long been settled. See, e.g., Baumann v. Smrha, 145 F.Supp. 617, 624 (D.Kan.), aff'd, 352 U.S. 863, 77 S.Ct. 96, 1 L.Ed.2d 73 (1956); In re Hood River, 114 Or. 112, 227 P. 1065 (1924). * * *

There has been no unconstitutional taking. The steady and gradual evolution toward prior appropriation by the court and the Legislature in the early days of statehood, culminating in the 1917 water code and the cases following from it, constituted sufficient notice and opportunity for exercise of unused riparian rights so that no compensable taking occurred by the reversion of unused riparian rights to the state.
* * *

The summary judgment of the trial court is reversed and remanded in light of the determinations above.

Notes

1. In Oregon, the Water Code of 1909 made all waters within the state appropriable for beneficial use, provided no "vested rights" were taken away or impaired. The vested rights of riparian proprietors were defined to include only the actual application of water to a beneficial use prior to the passage of the Act. Or.Laws 1909, c. 216, p. 319. The "Oregon plan" has been upheld as constitutional. In re Hood River, 114 Or. 112, 227 P. 1065 (1924); California-Oregon Power Co. v. Beaver Portland Cement Co., 73 F.2d 555 (9th Cir.1934), affirmed on other grounds 295 U.S. 142, 55 S.Ct. 725, 79 L.Ed. 1356 (1935). The statute made no provision for compensating the riparian owner for the loss of his unused rights.

2. The similar Kansas statute was upheld in State ex rel. Emery v. Knapp, 167 Kan. 546, 207 P.2d 440 (1949). It was also upheld by a three-judge federal court, in a decision affirmed without opinion by the United States Supreme Court. Baumann v. Smrha, 145 F.Supp. 617, (D.C.Kan. 1956), affirmed 352 U.S. 863, 77 S.Ct. 96, 1 L.Ed.2d 73 (1956). The trial court said, "The power of a state either to modify or reject the doctrine of riparian rights because unsuited to the conditions in the state and to put into force the doctrine of prior appropriation and application to beneficial use or of reasonable use has long been settled by the adjudicated cases. Of course, such a modification in the law of the state must recognize valid existing vested rights, but we do not regard a landowner as having a vested right in underground waters underlying his land which he has not appropriated and applied to beneficial use. We hold that the state could properly apply the doctrine of prior appropriation and application to beneficial use to unused and unappropriated waters so long as it recognized and afforded protection to rights which landowners had acquired at the time of the effective date of the Act to appropriate and use water."

3. In re Adjudication of Water Rights in the Upper Guadalupe River, 642 S.W.2d 438 (Tex.1982), upheld that part of the Texas Water Adjudication Act that limited riparian claimants to the quantity of water actually beneficially used during one of the five years between 1963 and 1967. The court held that after notice and upon reasonable terms, the statute's termination of the riparians' continuous nonuse of water is not a taking of their property. The court cited the Oregon and Kansas cases, and drew additional support from Texaco, Inc. v. Short, 454 U.S. 516, 102 S.Ct. 781, 70 L.Ed.2d 738 (1982) in which the Supreme Court said:

We have concluded that the State may treat a mineral interest that has not been used for 20 years and for which no statement of claim has been filed as abandoned; it follows that, after abandonment, the former owner retains no interest for which he may claim compensation. *It is the owner's failure to make any use of the property*—and not the action of the State—that causes the lapse of the property right; there is no "taking" that requires compensation. The requirement that an owner of a property interest that has not been used for 20 years must come forward and file a current statement of claim is not itself a "taking."

4. Unused riparian rights have been effectively abolished and the post-statute water user must go the appropriation route in all of the other "California Doctrine" states, with the possible exception of Nebraska. See Note 2 to *Joslin,* supra p. 363. The Oregon system was expressly adopted in South Dakota (except for domestic uses), So.Dak.Compiled Laws 46–1–9, and in Mississippi, Miss.Code 1972, § 51–3–7. The same result is reached by 82 Okl.Stat.Ann. § 105.2, and by No.Dak.Cent.Code 61–01–01.1, (since repealed) after a rather garbled legislative process described in 1 Hutchins, Water Rights Laws in the Nineteen Western States, 198, 213–215 (1971).

Under the South Dakota statute, S.D.C.L. §§ 46–1–9(2), 46–1–5(1), a riparian owner has vested rights to use stream water for irrigation purposes only to the extent of previous beneficial use, but he has the further right to take and use water for domestic use (irrigation of gardens, trees, shrubbery or orchids and stock watering), and such use takes precedence over all appropriative rights. Belle Fourche Irrigation Dist. v. Smiley, 87 S.D. 151, 204 N.W.2d 105 (S.D.1973).

In Alaska, usually classified as a Colorado doctrine state, some quasi-riparian rights attached to mining claims existed under a territorial statute. All of these in use were simply converted into appropriations when the state enacted a comprehensive water code. Alaska Stat. 46.15.060; Trelease, Alaska's New Water Use Act, 2 Land & Water L.Rev. 1 (1967).

ROBINSON v. ARIYOSHI

United States Court of Appeals Ninth Circuit, 1985.
753 F.2d 1468.

GOODWIN, CIRCUIT JUDGE.

The district court, in an action brought under 42 U.S.C. § 1983 challenging an alleged threat to divest plaintiffs' irrigation water rights, enjoined the named state officials from taking any action to enforce a recent decree of the state courts that appeared to be adverse to the property rights of the plaintiffs. The state officials appeal, raising a number of procedural and substantive issues. We will first set out the factual context in which this dispute has kept territorial, state, and federal courts intermittently busy for more than sixty years.

In 1889 the predecessors in title of the plaintiffs, Gay and Robinson, owned substantial land grants within the ahupuaa of Hanapepe, a local designation of land extending from the top of the central mountain mass of the Island of Kauai to the sea and roughly encompassing the drainage of the Hanapepe River. At the mauka, or upper part of the ahupuaa, the annual rainfall ranges from four to five hundred inches. At lower elevations rainfall averages as little as twenty-three inches and in many parts of the ahupuaa most types of agriculture are not possible without irrigation.

In the early days of the development of sugar cane fields on Kauai, the owners and lessees of the privately-owned lands built dams, flumes and ditches in order to distribute the abundant rainfall from the wettest portions of their lands to fertile but dry neighboring land areas. As the years went by and more lands were brought into production, the irrigation works became fairly elaborate. By 1922 Gay and Robinson had been to court at least once and had their title confirmed by the territorial courts to a substantial portion of the lands. The lands known as the Ili of Koula were drained by the Koula branch of the Hanapepe River, and from this drainage substantial volumes of irrigation water were diverted into a dry area that was outside the Hanapepe ahupuaa. Similar diversions of water to dry land were being made contemporaneously by Gay and Robinson from their nearby lands in the Ili of Manuahi, the other principal branch feeding the Hanapepe River. This state of affairs had evolved gradually over the years, beginning before 1891, and has been in effect more or less continually until the present time. * * *

In the 1920's the territorial government's increasing interest in water for the development of dry lands at lower elevations, some of which were owned or controlled by the Territory of Hawaii, produced litigation which in 1931 resulted in a decree of the Territorial Court. The Territorial Court held that Gay and Robinson were the owners of "normal surplus" water flowing from their Ilis of Koula and Manuahi into the Hanapepe River, and confirmed their right to divert that water for use outside the Hanapepe drainage. Territory v. Gay, 31 Hawaii 376, 387–88 (1930), aff'd, 52 F.2d 356 (9th Cir.) 284 U.S. 677, 52 S.Ct. 131, 76 L.Ed. 572 (1931) (*Territory I*).

In 1941 the Olokele Sugar Company succeeded to certain lands that were being supplied with irrigation water from the Gay and Robinson engineering efforts, and in 1949 the Gay and Robinson successors opened a new tunnel to supply water to their own and Olokele lands known locally as the Makaweli district.

The Hawaiian Statehood Act, Pub.L. No. 86–3, 73 Stat. 4, *reprinted in* 1959 U.S.Code Cong. & Ad.News 5, *inter alia,* confirmed existing statutory law of the territory and approved the new state's constitution. Gay and Robinson claim that the state constitution includes protection of their court-decreed and vested right to divert and use water from their mauka lands drained by the Koula and Manuahi branches of the Hanapepe. The state officials, however, argue as if the matter were open for a fresh decision, that the private use outside the ahupuaa of a large volume of Hanapepe water by Gay and Robinson and their associates is both undesirable and contrary to state law.

In 1959 the McBryde Sugar Company commenced in the new state court an action against a number of defendants, among whom Gay and Robinson were named. McBryde sued the state, Olokele, Gay and Robinson, and others referred to as the "small owners" to obtain a declaration of the rights of various parties along the Hanapepe upstream and downstream to various water rights, appurtenant, prescriptive, "ancient," or otherwise derived. The Hawaii state trial court in 1968 declared in a 65-page decision the rights of the parties including "other" small holders whose "ancient" and "appurtenant" rights were acknowledged by the principal parties in the controversy. McBryde Sugar Co. v. Robinson, S.P. No. 108 (5th Cir.Ct. of Hawaii, Dec. 10, 1968). Both the state and the larger owners appealed to the Supreme Court of Hawaii, challenging various portions of the trial court's decree. No party questioned existing Hawaii water law as announced in a number of earlier territorial cases.

The Supreme Court of Hawaii in 1973 *sua sponte* overruled all territorial cases to the contrary and adopted the English common law doctrine of riparian rights. McBryde Sugar Co. v. Robinson, et al., 54 Hawaii 174, 504 P.2d 1330, 1344 (1973). In this decision, which we will refer to as *McBryde I,* the court also held *sua sponte* that there was no such legal category as "normal daily surplus water" and declared that the state, as sovereign, owned and had the exclusive right to control the flow of the Hanapepe River. Id. 504 P.2d at 1345. *McBryde I* further announced that because the flow of the Hanapepe was the sovereign property of the State of Hawaii, McBryde's claim of a prescriptive right to divert water could not be sustained against the state. Id.

The parties adversely affected by the holding in *McBryde I* petitioned for rehearing and the state supreme court allowed a rehearing on the limited issue of the proper construction of Hawaii Rev.Stat. § 7–1 (a century-old territorial statute dealing largely with drinking water and rights of way on roads over private lands) and the meaning of the word "appurtenant". The parties attempted to enlarge the scope of the rehearing to include state and federal constitutional claims but their attempt was summarily rejected. See Robinson v. Ariyoshi, 441 F.Supp. 559, 564 (D.Hawaii 1977) (Robinson I). Rehearing was denied in McBryde Sugar Co. v. Robinson, 55 Hawaii 260, 517 P.2d 26 (1973) (McBryde II). In due course the Supreme Court of the United States denied review, McBryde Sugar Co. v. Hawaii, 417 U.S. 962, 94 S.Ct. 3164, 41 L.Ed.2d 1135 (1974) (McBryde III), and in 1974 this litigation began in the United States District Court for the District of Hawaii. The decision in the district court permanently enjoined the named state officials from enforcing against these plaintiffs any "new law" announced in *McBryde I* and *II. Robinson I,* 441 F.Supp. at 586. * * *

The state conceded at oral argument that the Fourteenth Amendment would require it to pay just compensation if it attempted to take vested property rights. The substantive question, therefore, is whether the state can declare, by court decision, that the water rights in this case have not vested. The short answer is no.

The district court's opinion in *Robinson I* makes clear that considerable property interests were at stake. 441 F.Supp. at 572–80. In summary form, the interests affected by *McBryde I* and *II* include:

(1) The water rights which as private property had been bought, sold and leased freely, and which had been the subject of state and local taxation as well as condemnation for ditch rights-of-way;

(2) The expenditures by G & R and Olokele of almost one million dollars in building an extensive water transportation system for irrigation of their sugar lands, lands now potentially destined to become pasture; and

(3) The interests of McBryde Sugar Company, which stands, if its rights are vested, in the same position as Gay and Robinson.

On April 28, 1930, the Supreme Court of the Territory of Hawaii, in litigation between substantially the same parties that are here today, except for the McBryde Sugar Company, held that the common law doctrine of riparian rights was not in force in Hawaii with reference to surplus waters of the normal flow of a stream. The same court further held that the owner (konohiki) of the land (ili) could use the water collected on his ili as he saw fit, subject to the rights of downstream owners to drinking water and other domestic uses that the parties in all this litigation have agreed have not been in controversy. Territory I, 31 Hawaii at 387–88, 395. When that case reached this court, we affirmed in an opinion which stated that the definition of property rights and water rights in light of the feudal history of land tenure in the islands was best left to the local courts. Territory of Hawaii v. Gay, 52 F.2d 356, 359 (9th Cir.1931) (*Territory II*). The water law, at least between the territorial government and the Gay and Robinson interests, thereafter remained settled until statehood.

Relying upon the decrees in *Territory I and II,* Gay and Robinson proceeded with further development of their plantations. By the time this litigation reached the district court, in *Robinson I,* improvements costing many millions of dollars had been constructed on the affected lands. By any reasonable interpretation of the word "vested," Gay and Robinson's rights to the continued use of their water and related engineering works had become vested.

* * *

The parties concede that the State of Hawaii has the sovereign power to change its laws from time to time as its legislature may see fit, and may, by changing its laws, radically change the definitions of property rights and the manner in which property rights can be controlled or transferred.

The state may also change its laws by judicial decision as well as by legislative action. Insofar as judicial changes in the law operate prospectively to affect property rights vesting after the law is changed, no specific federal question is presented by the state's choice of implement in changing state law.

We assume, therefore, for the purposes of this case, that the Supreme Court of Hawaii was acting well within its judicial power under the state constitution when it overruled earlier cases and declared for the first time, after more than a century of a different law, that the common law doctrine of riparian ownership was the law of Hawaii. This declaration of a change in the water law of Hawaii may be effective with respect to real property rights created in Hawaii after the *McBryde I* decision became final. New law, however, cannot divest rights that were vested before the court announced the new law.

There is no constitutional barrier to the state's exercise of its power of eminent domain to condemn and take vested property rights for public purposes. See Hawaii Housing Authority v. Midkiff, ___ U.S. ___, 104 S.Ct. 2321, 2330, 81 L.Ed.2d 186 (1984). ("Redistribution of fees simple [can be] a rational exercise of the eminent domain power.") The state has the power to take over the water works constructed by Gay and Robinson and their associates upon exercising the powers of eminent domain in a manner compatible with the Fourteenth Amendment. See Pennsylvania Coal Co. v. Mahon, 260 U.S. 393, 415, 43 S.Ct. 158, 160, 67 L.Ed. 322 (1922).

In light of the above authorities, the plaintiffs in this case, having acquired through judicial process a *de jure* vested right to divert water from their lands within the Hanapepe watershed to their own or related lands outside the watershed, *Territory I*, 31 Hawaii at 386, cannot now be divested of this right without just compensation. * * *

As noted, the district court entered a decree granting injunctive relief against named state officials. Because the state officers in these proceedings have taken no steps to interfere with plaintiffs' property, and have denied that they are presently planning to take such steps, the injunction may have been premature. * * * A declaration of the rights of the parties would appear to be sufficient to assure the owners of the rights confirmed in *Territory II.* The state must bring condemnation proceedings before it can interfere with vested water rights and the enjoyment of the improvements made in reliance thereon.

The judgment of the district court is affirmed in all respects insofar as it declares the rights of the parties. The injunctions against the named defendants are vacated without prejudice to the continuing jurisdiction of the district court to enjoin future state officeholders from conduct, if any, in violation of the rights of the plaintiffs should such a case arise.

Notes

1. The Hawaiian court had based its 1973 *McBryde I* ruling that there was no normal daily surplus water on a surprising interpretation of an 1850 royal statute preserved as Haw.Rev.Stat. § 7–1, that gave land owners "a right to drinking water and running water." This, it was said, incorporated ideas of English and Massachusetts common law riparian rights brought to the Islands by missionaries. Only natural flow cases were cited, and the riparian right was epitomized as "the right to use water flowing therein without prejudicing the riparian rights of others and the right to the natural flow of the stream without substantial diminution and in the size and shape given it by nature." McBryde Sugar Co. v. Robinson, 54 Haw. 174, 504 P.2d 1330 (1973).

In Robinson v. Ariyoshi, 65 Haw. 641, 66 Haw. 528, 658 P.2d 287 (1982) (*Robinson II*), the state court's reply to the questions referred to it by the Ninth Circuit, the court shifted its ground. The principal water law inquiry of the federal court had related to whether ownership of "surplus water" had been a settled question in Hawaiian law before *McBryde I.* The state court's answer was, in effect, that the territorial law had been too uncertain to form the basis for vested rights, that the law was in a state of flux, and that the meaning of "normal daily surplus water" had not been identified with certainty. The court also took the opportunity to stake a state claim to water resources and to declare a state power to control water uses. The territorial cases had said that the water "belonged to" the chiefs, and the court said that the real effect of *McBryde I* was to substitute the state for the chiefs as the owner of the water. The state ownership of the water was said not to be ownership in the corporeal sense that the state may do with the property as it pleases, but that the water was held subject to a public trust, a retention of authority and the imposition of duty to maintain the purity and flow of the waters for future generations and to assure that the waters are put to reasonable and beneficial uses for the common good. The court reasoned that reassertion of the public interest in the diversion and application of Hawaii's waters had become essential with the increasing scarcity of the resource and the recognition of the public's interest in utilization and flow of the waters, that while there are relative usufructuary rights among land owners using the waters, such rights can no longer be treated as though they were absolute and exclusive interests in the waters of the state, and that underlying every private diversion and application there has always been a superior public interest.

McBryde's delineation of riparian rights and appurtenant rights received further clarification in Reppun v. Board of Water Supply, 65 Hawaii 531, 656 P.2d 57 (1982), brought by six taro farmers to enjoin the board's diminution of the stream that watered their small plots. The land owned or leased by plaintiffs had been acquired in 1850 by its first fee owner in a grant of crown lands. In 1950 the current owner transferred all the water rights to one company and all the land to another, subject to the reservation of water. In 1955 the water rights were granted to the board. The plaintiffs subsequently acquired their lands subject to restrictions that limited the right to take water for taro to a very small amount. Plaintiffs allege that a much larger quantity is needed to protect the crops from a virulent fungus, and claim they still retained riparian and appurtenant rights to as much water as is needed.

The court held that under *McBryde,* the appurtenant rights could not be reserved or transferred, and that the deed attempting to reserve them instead extinguished them. Thus neither the board nor the plaintiffs had such rights at the time of suit. The riparian rights created by the 1850 royal statute (now Haw.Rev.Stat. § 7–1) was part of a law enacted to protect the common people by giving title to the lands they cultivated. Since their sole purpose was to provide water to make the tenants' land productive, no other incident of ownership attached. Therefore they were not subject to reservation by deed, they were not the grantor's to reserve. Although *McBryde* had characterized Hawaiian riparian rights as following the natural flow theory, that doctrine was subject to evolution with changing needs and conditions, and the modern law is the reasonable use rule. The plaintiffs' historical method of taro cultivation was held to be reasonable and the defendants diminution of the stream to the point that damage resulted was unreasonable.

2. The konohiki right of the chief of an ahupuaa or ili has been said to arise from an ancient Hawaiian rule that a land owner is entitled to water that falls on his land, although today the right is usually characterized as a right to the water of the stream into which the rainfall flows or seeps. See Hutchins, The Hawaiian System of Water Rights, 67, 77 (1946). The purchase by sugar planters of the mauka lands on the steep mountain sides, unarable and covered with worthless brush, is claimed to have included ownership of the water that drained from them into the stream. Not all of these konohiki rights have been exhausted by "kuleana rights" of villagers to water for domestic use and taro irrigation, by use on the plantations of the purchasers, or by sale to other planters or to municipalities.

After *McBryde, Robinson II* and *Reppun,* the unused water would appear to be subject to the law of riparian rights and to use by riparians, subject to state controls under the state ownership and public trust theories. Has the property of the mauka land owners been taken?

3. Suppose that since 1950 the Florida Sugar Company has irrigated its 1,000 acre cane field with 4,000 acre feet of water per year from the mythical Okatala River. In 1960 it replaced its ditches and furrows with a pump and sprinkler system financed by a bank loan. In 1972, pursuant to the Florida Water Resources Act, it applied for a "grandfather" permit to irrigate the land, and received from the Okatala Water Management District a permit which recited that it was issued for a term of 10 years, "subject to renewal according to law." In 1982 the company applied for a renewal of the permit. The application was denied in a letter in which the district explained (1) that the City of Okatala has applied for a permit to withdraw 4,000 acre feet per year from the Okatala River for municipal and domestic purposes, (2) that while West's Fla.Stat.Ann. §§ 373.239 and 373.233 provide that preference should be granted to renewal applications of equal merit with new applications, the district may award the permit to a more productive use, (3) that Okatala City is a fast-growing retirement

center, and its only other source of water would be very expensive wells to a 1,000 foot deep aquifer, (4) that withdrawal of more than 4,000 acre feet per year from the Okatala River would violate the minimum flow requirements set for the river, (5) that the company had fully amortized its water utilizing equipment, and (6) the Florida Water Plan and the public interest would be best served by granting the competing application of the city.

The Florida Sugar Company cannot economically procure its water from the deep aquifer or any other source. The only other economical use of its land is as cattle pasture. The difference between the value of the land as sugar cane fields and as pasture is $1,000,000. Has there been a taking of the company's property?

4. In the eastern states which adopted permit systems, most exercises of riparian rights initiated in the future (in the areas where the statutes apply) must be made by virtue of a permit, the issuance of which is to some degree discretionary. In none of them are permits specifically limited to riparians. 7 Del.C. §§ 6003, 6004; West's Fla.Stat.Ann. § 373.219; Iowa Code Ann. § 455B.264; Ky.Rev.Stat. 151.140; Md.Code Ann. § 8–802; N.J. Stat.Ann. 58:1A–5; N.C.Gen.Stat. § 143–215.15.

It is not clear in all of these states just what effect the statutes have on existing uses under riparian law. In some states it is specifically stated that the uses must be confirmed by a permit. Fla.Stat.Ann. § 373.226; Iowa Code Ann. § 455B.267; N.J.Stat.Ann. 58:1A–6. In Florida such a permit will be issued if the use is reasonable-beneficial, in Iowa unless some other riparian user is damaged. All of the other statutes are subject to the interpretation that a permit is required for continuation of an existing use, and all permits are subject to denial on various grounds of administrative discretion. All are issued for short terms and many are subject to discretionary cancellation. In many cases the quantity of water a riparian may withdraw and the arrangement for distribution of water among permit holders in times of shortage may be changed from what would have been allowable under common law.

These fairly extensive changes in the nature and attributes of riparian rights may be thought to raise constitutional questions. A great deal of discussion of constitutional issues has occurred, but no courts have decided the questions. Few commentators seem to have many qualms as to the validity of these acts. Fisher, Due Process and the Effect of Eastern Appropriation Proposals on Existing Rights, in Haber & Bergen, The Law of Water Allocation in the Eastern United States, 441 (1958); Lauer, The Riparian Right as Property, Water Resources and the Law 131 (1958); King, Regulation of Water Rights Under the Police Power, Water Resources and the Law 269 (1958); O'Connell, Iowa's New Water Statute—The Constitutionality of Regulating Existing Uses of Water, 47 Iowa L.Rev. 549 (1962); Hines, A Decade of Experience Under the Iowa Water Permit System—Part II, 8 Natural Resources J. 21 (1968); National Water Commission, Water Policies for the Future, 282–283 (1973).

Chapter 4

GROUNDWATER

SECTION 1. DOCTRINES

CROSBY, A LAYMAN'S GUIDE TO GROUNDWATER HYDROLOGY

Corker, Groundwater Law, Management and Administration, National Water Commission, Legal Study No. 6, Chapter II, 38–47, 72–75 (1971).

* * * We adopt the definition of groundwater employed by Professor William C. Walton (1970, p. 29) in Groundwater Resource Evaluation:

> "Water that exists in the interstices of rocks is called *subsurface water* * * *; that part of subsurface water in interstices completely saturated with water is called groundwater." [Emphasis in original.]

This definition is useful both for its simplicity and because it accurately identifies the bulk of the subsurface water about which managerial and legal decisions are made—most typically the decision either to withdraw or to permit withdrawal of water from the ground or to leave it in the ground available for later withdrawal or discharge.

Few technical subjects have been encumbered with the misinformation, misunderstandings, and mysticism that have plagued groundwater hydrology. Groundwater has been reputed to occur in underground rivers, in underground lakes, and in veins. It has been credited with moving in ways unknown and unknowable and has always been a favorite refuge for quacks and pseudoscientists. Countless thousands of dollars still migrate, annually, to the coffers of the practitioners of the willow branch or the brass welding rod.

1. Important Rock Properties

To understand the groundwater environment, one needs only to consider the void spaces, or *porosity,* of an accumulation of sand or gravel; or to view the fractures and crevices in the granites or limestones that form the walls of a road cut; or to note the open spaces that occur between the successive lava flows exposed in the walls of a valley. Picture, then, the environment that would exist if these unconsolidated or consolidated rock masses were partially submerged beneath water, perhaps by rising waters of a lake or reservoir. The air occupying the different types of openings would be displaced by water which, in the natural setting, would be called groundwater. The upper surface of the water-saturated zone, or the air-water interface, would be called the water table. Should impermeable materials be present at the normal position of the upper surface of the zone of saturation, no water table exists. Groundwater sometimes is confined under pressure between or under impermeable or semi-permeable rocks in much the same manner that water is pressurized in a pipeline network. Water in wells penetrating through impermeable material into the underlying permeable materials may rise above the top of the aquifer or water-bearing formation. Such groundwater is said to be under artesian pressure. The pressure is from gravity, just as is the water pressure on a dam impounding water in a surface reservoir.

Depending upon the type of rock material saturated, the voids or empty spaces can be expected to range from about one percent to more than 30 percent. At saturation, in other words, such rocks can contain between one and 30 or more percent of their total volume as water. Much of this water might be contained in voids so small that, even given the opportunity, it could never drain out; it would be retained as though the rock were a blotter. Such water would not flow into wells, and hence it could not be extracted from the ground by any normal means.

The capacity of a rock to transmit water through its interconnected pore spaces is called its *permeability*. The capacity of a porous material to store water need have no bearing on its capacity to transmit water. Thus, a clay usually has high porosity but low permeability. On the other hand, an unconsolidated gravel may have both high porosity and high permeability. * * *

The relatively small size of rock openings and the tortuous nature of the tunnel-like interconnected pore spaces present tremendous frictional resistance to the movement of groundwater. This factor is dominant in establishing the permeability of a porous material. Frictional limitations to flow, coupled with the typically low gradients (or slopes), contribute to the very low flow velocities prevalent in the groundwater environment. Normal flow velocities range from five feet per day to five feet per year. However, velocities as high as 100 feet per day have been reported.

The saturated, permeable earth materials from which significant quantities of water can be produced are called *aquifers*. This term, like permeability, is purely relative and must be considered within the framework of the local hydrogeology. Thus, a farmer drilling a domestic well in the basalts of eastern Washington might consider a well producing a gallon or two per minute a totally successful well. To his neighbor, who needs 500 gallons per minute for irrigation, any lesser quantity is for practical purposes a dry hole. * * *

A special class of hydrogeologic conditions are known as perched water bodies and have perched water tables. Perched waters form whenever the conditions of geologic structure and permeability restrict the free gravitational seepage of vadose waters, causing their build-up in local accumulations at elevations above the regional water table. An analogous condition would be presented by a porcelain saucer buried in a tank of sand through which waters are allowed to seep. Some of the downward moving water would be captured by the saucer and would form a suspended zone of saturation. * * *

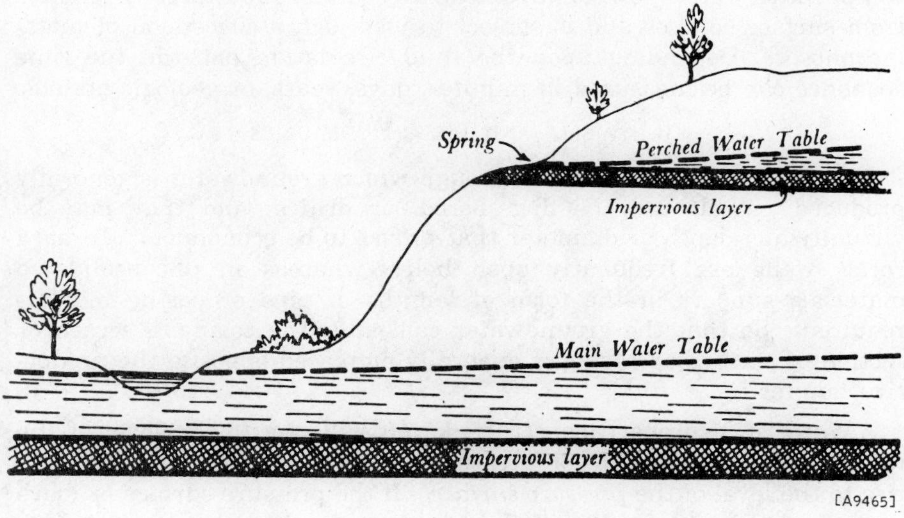

An unconfined aquifer may be viewed as an underground reservoir. As with a surface reservoir, one important characteristic of an aquifer is the quantity of withdrawable water which it contains. Still more pertinent is the amount of water that can be withdrawn from storage for each foot of water-level decline. Another characteristic is the capacity of the reservoir to contain water, regardless of whether at a given time it is full, partly full, or empty. In an unconfined groundwater reservoir capacity to store water is a function of the volume of the water-bearing materials, and the percentage of those materials which consist of voids or spaces capable of receiving water.

The water remaining in storage at a given time is a resultant of the extent to which portions of the water-bearing material have been dewatered. It can be estimated from driller's and geophysical well logs, from depths to groundwater in various portions of the aquifer, and from comparative quantities of inflow and outflow. Available storage capacity of an aquifer can change with time and further complicate storage calculations. As water-bearing sediments are dewatered, they tend to undergo compaction, which reduces pore volume. Recharge may or may not restore some or all of the lost storage capacity lost by compaction.

2. Solution Caverns

Does the definition of groundwater include water in underground caverns? * * *

Underground rivers flowing through caverns are rare, and therefore this problem of classification is not troublesome. However, moving water which is groundwater in one location, surface water in another location, and again groundwater is a very common phenomenon which complicates water "ownership." Nearly all groundwater originates from surface sources and is subject to just such a succession of metamorphoses. Depending upon the fluid circulation pattern, the time sequence can be measured in minutes, days, years, or geologic periods.

3. Wells and Well Hydraulics

Wells are the instruments through which groundwater is generally produced. Wells may be dug, bored, or drilled, and they may be virtually any depth or diameter that proves to be economical. In hard rocks, wells are frequently open holes, whereas in unconsolidated materials support in the form of lengths of pipe or casing may be required. So that the groundwater can enter the casing, a screen or section of perforated casing is generally emplaced opposite the productive aquifer.

Water in a properly-constructed well will rise to the level of the water table. If artesian, or pressure conditions exist, the water will rise to the level of the *pressure surface.* If the pressure surface is above ground surface, the well will flow freely unless capped.

The development of the deep well turbine pump provided the impetus for the great expansion in groundwater development and use, both in the United States and elsewhere. Ackerman and Lof (1959, p. 281) record that "About 1937 the vertical turbine pump was finally perfected and commercialized."

As pumping is commenced in a well, a quantity of water is discharged by the pump, lowering the water level in the well and nearby formation below the initial water surface in the formation. A gradient, therefore, is created between the nearby water table and the more distant water table. This gradient causes additional water to flow toward the well under the influence of gravity. The water table near the well takes the form of a hole or depression formed in the groundwater surface. Because it appears as an inverted cone around the pumping well, it is appropriately called the *cone of depression.* When the cones of depression of two or more wells overlap, interference results and decline of the water table is accelerated.

If the water-bearing formation has a high permeability, only a small gradient is required to produce a relatively large quantity of water. However, if the permeability is low, it may be found that the gradient required to produce a desired quantity of water exceeds the limit established by the depth at which the pump intake is set. The capacity of the well is exceeded and the pump soon starts sucking air. It is well to note that although the well is sucked dry in this situation, the pump can be turned off and after a period of recovery, the water in the well will return to nearly its original level. The groundwater has in no way been exhausted by the pumping. Rather, the well went dry temporarily and only because the formation was expected to release its stored water at a rate in excess of its physical capabilities.

Notes

1. National Water Commission, Water Policies for the Future 230 (1973):

How much water is this? The ground water supply in storage to a depth of one-half mile within the 48 contiguous States has been estimated at 180 billion acre-feet. In contrast, the larger lakes of North America contain about 27 billion acre-feet. Natural annual recharge may average more than 1 billion acre-feet. While this estimate of recharge may be liberal, it indicates the general magnitude of annual recharge compared to ground water in storage. On the basis of the above estimates, the volume of ground water in storage to a depth of one-half mile is roughly equivalent to the total of all recharge during the last 160 years.

The total amount of ground water in storage which is usable with present technology is said to approximate 10 years' annual precipitation or 35 years' annual surface runoff—some 46 billion acre-feet. Ground water supplies about 22 percent of the water withdrawn for use in the country, and this percentage is likely to increase because of increasing demands and the wide availability of ground water. Between one-third and one-half of the coterminous United States is underlain by ground water areas capable of yielding 50 gallons per minute or more to wells.

2. As the foregoing indicates, groundwater and surface water differ markedly in physical occurrence, which explains, at least in large part, why groundwater receives separate legal treatment. The differences are numerous. However, in considering the materials in this chapter the student should bear in mind three characteristics of groundwater which have most often affected the development of the law.

First, groundwater is hidden from sight. Thus, the characteristics of a given aquifer are not visible. Similarly, the effects of manmade alterations, such as pumping, cannot easily be seen. The science of hydrology has made great progress in understanding the principles which determine groundwater behavior. However, typically it will be necessary to monitor existing wells and drill and monitor additional wells over a broad geographic area for an extended period before these principles can be applied to a particular aquifer. Because this is expensive and time consuming, adequate data is often unavailable. Consequently, the uncertainties which exist in a particular situation are often substantial. This is reflected in the lawyers' dictum that in groundwater litigation the person with the burden of proof always loses.

Second, because groundwater is in the ground, wells must be drilled and pumps must usually be installed if it is to be used. Consequently, the expense associated with groundwater use varies directly with the depth at which it is available.

Third, the water available for use in most aquifers consists of both annual recharge and water in storage, in varying degrees. Thus, unlike surface water which is primarily a "flow" resource, groundwater consists of both a "flow" resource and a "stock" resource. The ability of an aquifer to store water and the existence of a stock of water which may be used only once present opportunities, create problems, and require policy choices not presented, created, or required in using surface water.

STATE v. MICHELS PIPELINE CONSTR., INC.

Supreme Court of Wisconsin, 1974.
63 Wis.2d 278, 217 N.W.2d 339.

WILKIE, JUSTICE.

This case involves the unrestrained use of percolating ground water to the alleged detriment of owners of neighboring land. In 1972 Michels Pipeline Construction, Inc., contracted with the Metropolitan Sewerage Commission of Milwaukee county to install a 60-inch-diameter sewer in the Root River Parkway, Greenfield, Wisconsin. * * * The complaint alleged that in September of 1972 the defendants began pumping water from wells in the city of Greenfield at a rate of 5,500 gallons per minute in order to dewater the soil to a depth sufficient to permit tunneling for the sewer, approximately 40 feet beneath the ground surface. The complaint alleged that numerous citizens were caused great hardship by the drying up of wells, decreasing capacity and water quality in others, and by the cracking of foundations, basement walls and driveways, due to subsidence of the soil. The State asked that the defendants be ordered to conduct construction of the sewer so as not to create a nuisance and to take action to eliminate or ameliorate the hardship and adverse effect imposed upon state citizens.

The defendants demurred to the complaint on the ground that it did not state facts sufficient to constitute a cause of action. * * *

The trial court granted the demurrer of the defendants-respondents on the basis that the case of Huber v. Merkel [a] established that there is no cause of action for interference with ground water. This is a correct statement of the holding of that case. In Huber v. Merkel an owner of real estate attempted to have another landowner in his vicinity enjoined from wasting and unreasonably using water from artesian wells on the person's property. The defendant allowed his wells to flow continuously, the excess simply spilling on the ground and this adversely affected the artesian pressure of all the wells which tapped the same aquifer. This court held that it was the almost universal concensus of judicial opinion that:

a. (1903), 117 Wis. 355, 94 N.W. 354.

> "* * * If the waters, simply percolate through the ground, without definite channel, they belong to the realty in which they are found, and the owner of the soil may divert, consume, or cut them off with impunity. If, on the other hand, the subterranean waters flow in a defined channel, the rules which govern the use of surface streams apply; but the presumption is that the waters are percolating waters until it is shown that they are supplied by a definite, flowing stream." * * *

What is the basis of the English or common-law rule? The basis for this rule of absolute ownership of percolating ground water was a feeling that the ways of underground water were too mysterious and unpredictable to allow the establishment of adequate and fair rules for regulation of competing rights to such water. So the English courts adopted the position that everyone was permitted to take and use all of which they could get possession.

In Acton v. Blundell [b] the English courts held the law of surface waters did not apply to percolating ground water because:

> "* * * no man can tell what changes these underground sources have undergone in the progress of time * * * therefore, * * * there can be no ground for implying any mutual consent or agreement, for ages past * * * which is one of the foundations on which the law as to running streams is supposed to be built * * *."

And the early American case of Roath v. Driscoll [c] said with regard to percolating water:

> "* * * The laws of its existence and progress * * * cannot be known or regulated. It rises to great heights, and moves collaterally, by influences beyond our apprehension. These influences are so secret, changeable and uncontrollable, we cannot subject them to the regulations of law, nor build upon them a system or rules, as has been done with streams upon the surface."

Even in 1903 when the Huber v. Merkel case was written, the awe of mysterious, unknowable forces beneath the earth was fast becoming an outmoded basis for a rule of law. The court in Huber v. Merkel discussed the subject of artesian water with a certain degree of sophistication. However, artesian water may have been better understood than other types of percolating ground water. However, today scientific knowledge in the field of hydrology has certainly advanced to the point where a cause and effect relationship can be established between a tapping of underground water and the level of the water table in the area so that liability can be fairly adjudicated consonant with due process. Our scientific knowledge also establishes the interdependence of all water systems.

> "* * * The hydrologic cycle traces all existing water from the oceans to the atmosphere, to the land and ultimately back to the oceans. In nature, there is an inseparable relationship between all

b. (Ex.1843), 12 Mees. & W. 324, 350, 351, 152 Reprint 1223.

c. (1850), 20 Conn. 533, 541.

water, whether in the atmosphere, on the earth's surface, or under the earth's surface."

It makes very little sense to make an arbitrary distinction between the rules to be applied to water on the basis of where it happens to be found. There is little justification for property rights in ground water to be considered absolute while rights in surface streams are subject to a doctrine of reasonable use. The Huber v. Merkel case certainly gives no explanation of why a property right in ground water should be an exception to the general maxim—*sic utere tuo ut alienum non laedas.*

Also, although at the time of the decision of Huber v. Merkel the English rule did probably prevail, it was not a common-law rule of venerable, entrenched and ancient origin. The first decisions which enunciated the doctrine were decided in the early 1840's only a short time before Wisconsin achieved statehood. * * *

For the reasons discussed above, we overrule our decision in Huber v. Merkel and for that reason we find it necessary to adopt a rule of law more in harmony with present scientific and legal principles.

What rule should this court now adopt as to the use of percolating ground water? There are three distinct doctrines applied in various American jurisdictions regarding rights in percolating water:

(a) The English or Common-Law Rule:

> "* * * the person who owns the surface may dig therein, and apply all that is there found to his own purposes at his free will and pleasure; and if, in the exercise of such right, he intercepts or drains off the water collected from underground springs in his neighbor's well, this inconvenience to his neighbor falls within the description of damnum absque injuria, which cannot become the ground of an action. * * *"

There is one limitation that the actions may not be motivated by malice and waste of water can be actionable. Although framed in property language this doctrine is really a rule of capture. The landowner may sell and grant his right to withdraw the water to others.

(b) Reasonable Use:

As stated in Corpus Juris Secundum:

> "In some states, the rule of the common law followed in early decisions has given way to the doctrine of reasonable use limiting the right of a landowner to percolating water in his land to such an amount of water as may be necessary for some useful or beneficial purpose in connection with the land from which it is taken, not restricting his right to use the water for any useful purpose on his own land, and not restricting his right to use it elsewhere in the absence of proof of injury to adjoining landowners. * * *"

(c) Correlative Rights:

Again Corpus Juris Secundum defines this doctrine as:

> "Under the rule of correlative rights, the rights of all landowners over a common basin, saturated strata, or underground reservoir are coequal or correlative, and one cannot extract more than his share of the water, even for use on his own land, where others' rights are injured thereby."

In many early cases the two doctrines of reasonable use and correlative rights seem to have been mixed together as the "American rule." However, as Corpus Juris Secundum makes clear, they are two distinct doctrines. According to the appellant's brief only three states adhere to the correlative rights doctrine. This doctrine applies the basic rules of the reasonable use doctrine, but calls for apportionment of underground water where there is not a sufficient supply for all reasonable uses. We are not shown here that water conditions in Wisconsin are so critical as to necessitate the adoption of this doctrine. Also the administrative difficulties of a court trying to make such an apportionment would militate against its adoption.

The "reasonable use" doctrine has been widely adopted in the United States. However, a close reading of the language of the doctrine shows that it is not a very radical departure from the common-law rule. It still contains quite a broad privilege to use ground water. The respondents in their brief seem to misunderstand the real scope of the "reasonable use" rule as it has been applied. On page 11 of their brief they state:

> "* * * In this case, the right being claimed by the plaintiff is the right to put down any type of well the owner wishes and be assured thereafter that no one else will use the aquifer in a manner that will affect that well's production. Such a property right does not and should not exist in Wisconsin."

This is not the impact of the reasonable use doctrine. This is because the term "reasonable" has a very special restricted meaning. A waste of water or a wasteful use of water is not unreasonable only if it causes harm, and a use of water that causes harm is nevertheless reasonable if it is made in connection with the overlying land. The withdrawal of water for use elsewhere for beneficial purposes such as municipal supply or domestic supply is not "reasonable" in this special sense, but such removal may be made without liability if no harm results.

Thus it can be seen that the scare story of the respondents is not true. One may sink a well for domestic use or other use on his land without liability to his neighbors for effects on their wells as long as he acts without malice and is not wasting water to their detriment.

The "reasonable use" rule basically only affords protection from cities withdrawing large quantities of water for municipal utilities. The rule forces cities to pay those affected by such excessive use damages or the cost of new wells and pumping equipment and is very much in accord with policies of loss distribution and requiring the beneficiaries of harmful activities to pay the costs thereof. However, under the rule there is no apportionment of water as between adjoining landowners. If water is withdrawn for a beneficial use on the land from which it is taken there is no liability for any harm to adjoining property owners. In effect, the rule gives partial protection to small wells against cities or water companies, but not protection from a large factory or apartment building on the neighboring land.

We choose not to adopt any of the three rules here discussed, but rather to adopt the rule set forth in Tentative Draft No. 17 of the Restatement of the Law Second, Torts, as proposed on April 26, 1971, for adoption by the American Law Institute. The revisors of this section indicated that they felt the rules set forth in the Restatement of the Law First, Torts, were a curious mixture of both the "reasonable use" and "correlative rights" doctrines, but without the idea that any beneficial use on the overlying land was reasonable. Also apportionment of water was on the basis of a balancing of utility against harm, rather than on the equality of right that underlies the correlative rights doctrine.

Sec. 858A significantly changes the rule of the Restatement of Law First, and broadens the protection of the "reasonable use" rule. As stated in the analysis section of the proposal:

> "*Analysis.* The rule adopted in this Topic can be described as the American rule with its protection broadened. It gives more or less unrestricted freedom to the possessor of overlying land to develop and use ground water and it permits the grant and sale of ground water to persons who need water but do not possess land overlying it. It does not attempt to apportion the water among users except to the extent that the special conditions of underground streams and interconnected ground and stream water permit it to be done on a rational basis. It gives the protection of the American rule to owners of small wells harmed by large withdrawals for use elsewhere, but extends that protection in proper cases to harm done by large withdrawals for operations on overlying lands."

The proposed section of the Restatement Second reads as follows:

> "Sec. 858A. NON-LIABILITY FOR USE OF GROUND WATER—EXCEPTIONS.
>
> "A possessor of land or his grantee who withdraws ground water from the land and uses it for a beneficial purpose is not subject to liability for interference with the use of water by another, unless
>
> "(a) The withdrawal of water causes unreasonable harm through lowering the water table or reducing artesian pressure, * * * "

Thus the rule preserves the basic expression of a rule of nonliability—a privilege if you will—to use ground water beneath the land. The formulation of the exception to this basic rule recognizes that there is usually enough water for all users so that apportionment is not necessary but that the problem is who shall bear the costs of deepening prior wells, installing pumps, paying increased pumping costs, etc., necessitated by a lowering of the water table by a large user. The common law placed the burden of making improvements on each user. The "reasonable use" rule gives protection to existing wells if the water withdrawal is taken off the land for use elsewhere but not if the water is used for beneficial purposes on the overlying land. The proposed rule of the Restatement Second would place the matter of cost on the same rational basis as the rule applicable to surface streams, the reasonableness of placing the burden upon one party or the other.

The comment on the meaning of "unreasonable harm" as used in the Restatement rule explains that as in other situations, reasonableness will vary with the circumstances. * * *

In adopting the rule proposed in the Restatement of Torts, we necessarily overrule the order of the trial court sustaining the demurrer here, and we remand for further proceedings in the trial court.

Notes

1. The "English rule" of absolute ownership of ground waters was first stated in cases in which the basic conflict was between competing land uses, and not between water users competing for the supply. The leading cases in England and America both involved defendants who were lowering the water table as a result of pumping water from mines so that mining operations could be carried on; in each case the plaintiff was deprived of well or spring water for use in manufacturing. Acton v. Blundell, 12 Mees. & W. 324, 152 Eng.Rep. 1223 (1843); Wheatley v. Baugh, 25 Pa.St.Rep. 528 (1855). In the leading case establishing the American rule of reasonable use, Forbell v. City of New York, 164 N.Y. 522, 58 N.E. 644 (1900), plaintiff and defendant were competing for the water, which plaintiff used for subirrigation of crops and defendant transported away from its land to the city for sale.

2. In Adams v. Grigsby, 152 So.2d 619 (La.App.1963, certiorari refused), the court held that under the Louisiana Civil Code neither of two overlying landowners owned the percolating water in a common sand under their lands, and that the water was unowned, like wild animals, "*ferae naturae*" over which ownership is acquired by capturing and reducing to possession. What is the difference in result between the common law "ownership" rule and the civil law "non-ownership" rule?

3. Texas has long adhered to the English rule of absolute ownership, at least to the extent that while the overlying landowner may not maliciously take water for the sole purpose of injuring his neighbor, he can use all the percolating water he can capture for beneficial purposes on or off the land, and can likewise sell it, as he can other property, for use off the land and outside the basin where produced. In City of Corpus Christi v. City of Pleasanton, 154 Tex. 289, 276 S.W.2d 798 (1955), the court permitted Corpus Christi to purchase land overlying an artesian basin, drill wells which flow 10,000,000 gallons of water per day, flow the water into a river in which 63% to 74% of the water is lost by evaporation and seepage, and take the remainder of the water into its municipal system 118 miles away, despite the existence of a statute prohibiting the waste of artesian water.

A recent case adds another restriction on the landowner. See Friendswood Development Co. v. Smith-Southwest Industries, infra p. 449.

An unusual side effect of the English rule occurred in Sun Oil Co. v. Whitaker, 483 S.W.2d 808 (Tex.1972). Whitaker purchased land subject to an oil and gas lease which included a grant of the use of water "for all operations hereunder." Sun Oil began the use of groundwater for "water flood secondary recovery" in which water is injected down abandoned oil wells into the oil sands so it will drive the oil to producing wells. Whitaker drilled wells into the same aquifer for irrigation of the land. The withdrawal of water for either purpose would materially interfere with its use for the other, and Sun Oil sued to enjoin Whitaker's use. Injunction granted by a divided court, the majority holding that whatever is appropriate to obtaining the minerals is included in the lessor's grant of the mineral estate. The minority felt that the water granted in the lease covered only ordinary uses in drilling and primary production, and noted a custom of purchasing water for secondary recovery.

4. Arizona, with statutory modifications to be noticed later, adhered to the American rule of reasonable use in Bristor v. Cheatham, 75 Ariz. 227, 255 P.2d 173 (1953): "This rule does not prevent the extraction of ground water subjacent to the soil so long as it is taken in connection with a beneficial enjoyment of the land from which it is taken. If it is diverted for the purpose of making reasonable use of the land from which it is taken, there is no liability incurred to an adjoining owner for a resulting damage."

5. Regardless of whether a common law state follows the rule of absolute ownership or the rule of reasonable use, the water, if found to be an "underground stream," will be apportioned between the overlying owners on the basis of the law applicable to surface streams, riparian or appropriative. An underground stream must have "bed, banks and a current of water," just like a surface stream, but this usually means only that the groundwater must be in a narrow confined aquifer, not that it must flow freely in a cavernous opening.

Underground streams are subject to the law of surface streams, riparian or appropriative. Verdugo Canyon Water Co. v. Verdugo, 152 Cal. 655, 93 P. 1021 (1908); Pima Farms Co. v. Proctor, 30 Ariz. 96, 245 P. 369 (1926). In Clinchfield Coal Corp. v. Compton, supra, the court required proof of the existence of an underground stream to be by reasonable inference from existing and observed facts on the natural surface of the ground, without recourse to abstruse speculation of scientific persons. But in Maricopa County Municipal Water Conservation Dist. No. 1 v. Southwest Cotton Co., 39 Ariz. 65, 4 P.2d 369 (1931), the court opened the way to engineering and geologic opinions and scientific data gathered from wells or borings and the effect of some wells on the flow of others, but still required reasonable certainty in the location of the bed and banks of the stream. However, a broad aquifer filling an entire valley floor has been called an underground lake. City of Los Angeles v. Hunter, 156 Cal. 603, 105 P. 755 (1909). One form of an underground stream is the subflow of a surface stream, percolating from the banks and supporting the stream, so that drawing off the subsurface water would appreciably and directly diminish the surface flow.

Montecito Valley Water Co. v. City of Santa Barbara, 144 Cal. 578, 77 P. 1113 (1904).

The use of the "underground stream" concept has been criticized as "an attempt to restate the physical universe," and it is said that although "hydrogeological fictions" may have some utility, they do more harm than good since the law cannot rationally develop when so divorced from actuality. Corker, Ground Water Law, Management and Administration, National Water Commission Legal Study No. 6, 147 (1971).

6. Most of the recent groundwater cases in the eastern states have fit the *Michels* pattern in which the plaintiff is a water user of one sort or another and the defendant is getting rid of the water in order to utilize the land or mine its contents. In Maerz v. United States Steel Corp., 116 Mich. App. 710, 323 N.W.2d 524 (1982), defendant's dewatering of a limestone quarry lowered the water table in neighboring lands and "caused the loss of" plaintiff's domestic well. The trial court ruled that disposal of percolating waters in order to use or enjoy the land from which they are taken is not actionable. The upper court reversed, quoting from the Restatement of Torts, 2d, § 858 and noting that in cases of lowering water tables § 858 refers to the riparian principles stated in §§ 850–857 for determining liability for unreasonable interference. "We * * * hold that the principles expressed in Restatement Torts, 2d § 858, are consistent with the Michigan adjudications on the subject and the general trend of decisions in other states, are less harsh and arbitrary and more fair and just than the English rule, and should be followed in Michigan."

Ohio fell in line with Wisconsin and Michigan in Cline v. American Aggregates Corporation, 15 Ohio St.3d 384, 474 N.E.2d 324 (1984). The trial court gave summary judgment in favor of the defendant, whose dewatering of its limestone quarry caused dewatering and pollution of the wells of nearby homeowners. The supreme court reversed, overruling its old "English rule of absolute ownership" cases, adopted the full text of Restatement of Torts, 2d., § 858 "as the common law of Ohio," and remanded the case for trial under those rules.

Indiana refused to follow this trend in Wiggins v. Brazil Coal and Clay Corporation, 452 N.E.2d 958 (Ind.1983). Wiggins was the developer of a subdivision called "Sugar Ridge Lake Estates," on land reclaimed from an old strip mine, containing a lake created by the abandoned open pit operation. No stream or springs fed the lake; the lake was filled at the level of the water table. Defendant, mining coal from 50-foot deep open pits on its nearby land, found its operations were hampered by groundwater. To remove the water, pumps were installed in old shafts to abandoned deep vein mines. As the water was lowered in the defendant's works, Sugar Ridge Lake dried up. The court reverted to the old rule that "groundwater is part of the land in which it is present and belongs to the owner of that land, [and] may be put to use to the fullest extent to further enjoyment of the land," and held that dewatering the mine was a beneficial use of the water in connection with the land. The dissent and the court of appeals, would have adopted Restatement of Torts, 2d, § 858 as the rule of decision, and urged that determining the reasonableness of defendant's lowering the water table and interfering with the lake should be tested by the principle that the cost of harm to an innocent party's property should be born by the business operation that caused the loss.

Are these water rights cases or land use cases? Henderson v. Wade Sand and Gravel Company, 388 So.2d 900 (Ala.1980) involved damage from subsidence, when dewatering a quarry leached the water from under plaintiffs' houses, leaving large cavities and sink holes through which rains carried away subsoil and surface soil. Old cases from the 1930's had applied the American rule of reasonable use as imposing no liability on a landowner who drained his property in order to conduct operations for which the land was adapted. The Restatement, 2d, rule was urged on the court as continuing this principle. The court overruled the earlier cases, but refused to accept the Restatement as the rule of decision. That rule was designed for competition between persons making use of groundwater to which both have access, said the court, while the dewatering cases are concerned with the proprietary use of land, in which the water is only incidentally affected. Where water use is interfered with not by competing use but by diversion to make use of adjoining land, said the court, rules of nuisance will apply.

Is the disposal of unwanted groundwater a "use" for a "beneficial purpose?" Is the harm it causes "unreasonable" under the tests of §§ 850A–857, incorporated into § 858? (See chapter 3, section 2) Is dewatering the neighboring tracts an invasion of the use and enjoyment of land under the rules of nuisance set out in Restatement of Torts, 2d, §§ 822–831? Is the result of the cases likely to change if one set of rules is used rather than the other?

7. One eastern case that does involve competing uses is Woodsum v. Township of Pemberton, 172 N.J.Super. 489, 412 A.2d 1064 (1980). Plaintiff's residence was supplied with groundwater from a well that reached a large aquifer. Defendant constructed a municipal plant and drilled two wells into the same source, at a total cost of $1,370,000. The water table was lowered below plaintiff's intake. If plaintiff had anticipated additional use of the aquifer and drilled to a reasonable depth, the added cost would have been $750; to deepen it now might cost as much as $1700. Plaintiff sued in inverse condemnation for a taking of his property.

The court wrote a small treatise on the English rule, the American rule, the correlative rights rule, the prior appropriation rule and the Restatement rule; reviewed the New Jersey cases and concluded that Meeker v. East Orange, 77 N.J.L. 623, 74 A. 379 (1909) had adopted for New Jersey the correlative rights rule. Although it doubted that *Meeker's* rule would adequately serve New Jersey's modern needs, the court felt bound by *stare decisis,* refused to adopt the Restatement rule, and applied Meeker. Nevertheless, *Meeker* had held that municipal suppliers taking water for use not connected with the overlying land were liable only for interference with the *reasonable* use of water on neighboring land, and the court found that plaintiff's use did not meet the reasonableness test. "The landowner who provides for his domestic supply of water through a shallow well, possibly because of a high subterranean water table, and who constructs that well at a time when no other users affect his water supply, does so with the knowledge that other users may appear who may lower the water table and diminish or eliminate his water supply. He is bound to share his water with such other users on a reasonable basis. Therefore, if his use is to be described as 'reasonable' he must dig his well to a depth which anticipates the lowering of the water table by virtue of other proper users."

What would the result have been under Restatement of Torts, 2d § 858?

KATZ v. WALKINSHAW

Supreme Court of California, 1903.
141 Cal. 116, 70 P. 663, 74 P. 766.

This appeal is taken from a judgment of nonsuit entered against plaintiffs on motion of defendant. The action was brought to enjoin defendant from drawing off and diverting water from an artesian belt which is in part on or under the premises of plaintiffs, and to the water of which they have sunk wells, thereby causing the water to rise and flow upon the premises of plaintiffs, and which they ever had constantly so flowed for 20 years before the wrong complained of was committed by defendant. The water is necessary for domestic purposes, and for irrigating the lands of plaintiffs, upon which there are growing trees, vines, shrubbery, and other plants, which are of great value to plaintiffs. All of said plants will perish, and plaintiffs will be greatly and irreparably injured, if the defendant is allowed to divert the water. These facts are admitted, and further that defendant is diverting the water for sale, to be used on lands of others distant from the saturated belt from which the artesian water is derived. * * *

The defense, conceding that the water held in the earth is percolating water, relies upon certain decisions which assert and apply literally the maxim, "Cujus est solum, ejus est usque ad inferos," and that water percolating in the ground, or held there in saturation, belongs to the landowner as completely as do the rocks, ground, and other material of which the land is composed, and therefore he may remove it and sell it, or do what he pleases with it. * * *

SHAW, J. * * *

We do not see how the doctrine contended for by defendant could ever become a rule of property of any value. Its distinctive feature is the proposition that no property rights exist in such waters except while they remain in the soil of the landowner; that he has no right either to have them continue to pass into his land as they would under natural conditions, or to prevent them from being drawn out of his land by an interference with natural conditions on neighboring land. Such right as he has is therefore one which he cannot protect or enforce by resort to legal means and one which he cannot depend on to continue permanently or for any definite period.

It is apparent that the parties who have asked for a reconsideration of this case, and other persons of the same class, if the rule for which they contend is the law, or no-law, of the land, will be constantly threatened with danger of utter destruction of the valuable enterprises and systems of waterworks which they control, and that all new enterprises of the same sort will be subject to the same peril. They will have absolutely no protection in law against others having stronger pumps, deeper wells, or a more favorable situation, who can thereby take from them unlimited quantities of the water, reaching to the entire supply, and without regard to the place of use. We cannot perceive how a doctrine offering so little protection to the investments in and product of such enterprises, and offering so much temptation to others to capture the water on which they depend, can tend to promote developments in the future or preserve those already made, and therefore we do not believe that public policy or a regard for the general welfare demands the doctrine. An ordinary difference in the conditions would scarcely justify the refusal to adopt a rule of the common law, or one which has been so generally supposed to exist; but where the differences are so radical as in this case, and would tend to cause so great a subversion of justice, a different rule is imperative.

The doctrine of reasonable use, on the other hand, affords some measure of protection to property now existing, and greater justification for the attempt to make new developments. It limits the right of others to such amount of water as may be necessary for some useful purpose in connection with the land from which it is taken. If, as is claimed in the argument, such water-bearing land is generally worthless except for the water which it contains, then the quantity that could be used on the land would be nominal, and injunctions could not be obtained, or substantial damages awarded, against those who carry it to distant lands. So far as the active interference of others is concerned, therefore, the danger to such undertakings is much less, and the incentive to development much greater, from the doctrine of reasonable use than from the contrary rule. No doubt there will be inconvenience from attacks on the title to waters appropriated for use on distant lands made by persons who claim the right to the reasonable use of such waters on their own lands. Similar difficulties have arisen and now exist with respect to rights in surface streams, and must always be expected to attend claims to rights in a substance so movable as water. But the courts can protect this particular species of property in water as effectually as water rights of any other description.

It may, indeed, become necessary to make new applications of old principles to the new conditions; and, in view of the novelty of the doctrine and the scope of argument, it is not out of place to indicate to some extent how it should be done, although otherwise it would not be necessary to the decision of the case. The controversies arising will naturally divide into classes. There will be disputes between persons or corporations claiming rights to take such waters from the same strata or source for use on distant lands. There is no statute on this subject, as there now is concerning appropriations of surface streams; but the case is not without precedent. * * * The principles which, before the adoption of the Civil Code, were applied to protect appropriations and possessory rights in visible streams, will, in general, be found applicable to such appropriations of percolating waters, either for public or private use, and will suffice for their protection as against other appropriators. Such rights are usufructuary only, and the first taker who with diligence puts the water in use will have the better right. And in ordinary cases of this character the law of prescriptive titles and rights and the statute of limitations will apply. In controversies between an appropriator for use on distant land and those who own land overlying the water-bearing strata, there may be two classes of such landowners—those who have used the water on their land before the attempt to appropriate, and those who have not previously used it, but who claim the right afterwards to do so. Under the decision in this case the rights of the first class of landowners are paramount to that of one who takes the water to distant land, but the landowner's right extends only to the quantity of water that is necessary for use on his land, and the appropriator may take the surplus. As to those landowners who begin the use after the appropriation, and who, in order to obtain the water, must restrict or restrain the diversion to distant lands or places, it is perhaps best not to state a positive rule. Such rights are limited at most to the quantity necessary for use, and the disputes will not be so serious as those between rival appropriators. Disputes between overlying landowners, concerning water for use on the land, to which they have an equal right, in cases where the supply is insufficient for all, are to be settled by giving to each a fair and just proportion. And here again we leave for future settlement the question as to the priority of rights between such owners who begin the use of the waters at different times. The parties interested in the question are not before us. * * *

The objection that this rule of correlative rights will throw upon the court a duty impossible of performance—that of apportioning an insufficient supply of water among a large number of users—is largely conjectural. No doubt cases can be imagined where the task would be extremely difficult, but, if the rule is the only just one—as we think has been shown—the difficulty in its application in extreme cases is not a sufficient reason for abandoning it and leaving property without any protection from the law. * * *

The judgment of the court below is reversed, and a new trial ordered.

Notes

1. Mr. Justice Shaw wrote two later opinions for cases which supplied the rankings missing from his *Katz* opinion. Burr v. Maclay Rancho Water Co., 154 Cal. 428, 98 P. 260 (1908), held that an overlying landowner who has not yet used the groundwater on his land can obtain a declaratory judgment to protect his paramount right to do so as against an appropriator who has previously put the water to use. Hudson v. Dailey, 156 Cal.

617, 105 P. 748 (1909), held that as between two overlying landowners their rights are equal and correlative, without mention of priority of use.

In San Bernardino v. Riverside, 186 Cal. 7, 198 P. 784 (1921), the court held that an overlying city's withdrawal from municipal supply was not a correlative right but an appropriation, and rejected the argument that the city had in some manner become substituted as administrator of the rights of its inhabitants owning overlying land.

2. The courts of several states have interjected notions that shortages should be shared under a rule of correlative rights into cases that did not require an apportionment: see Hanks & Hanks, The Law of Water in New Jersey: Groundwater, 24 Rutgers L.Rev. 621, 639 (1970); Meeker v. East Orange, 77 N.J.Law 623, 74 A. 379 (1909); Erickson v. Crookston Waterworks Power & Light Co., 105 Minn. 182, 117 N.W. 435 (1908); Jones v. Oz-Ark-Val Poultry Co., 228 Ark. 76, 306 S.W.2d 111 (1957); Higday v. Nickolaus, 469 S.W.2d 859 (Mo.App.1971).

In MacArtor v. Graylyn Crest III Swim Club, Inc., 41 Del.Ch. 26, 187 A.2d 417 (1963), the large well that supplied the club's swimming pool lowered the water table below a neighboring householder's "bricked well." The court applied the "doctrine of reasonable use" although the club well was apparently on its overlying land, and said that the club's abnormally large withdrawal (compared to domestic use) "was not unqualifiedly reasonable" and required it to share the cost of deepening plaintiff's well.

3. The American Law Institute rejected the notion expressed in *Michels Pipeline,* supra, that administrative difficulties of court apportionment of groundwater militate against the correlative rights doctrine. In its final form the Restatement (Second) of Torts states: [1]

§ 858. Liability for Use of Ground Water

(1) A proprietor of land or his grantee who withdraws ground water from the land and uses it for a beneficial purpose is not subject to liability for interference with the use of water by another, unless

(a) the withdrawal of ground water unreasonably causes harm to a proprietor of neighboring land through lowering the water table or reducing artesian pressure,

(b) the withdrawal of ground water exceeds the proprietor's reasonable share of the annual supply or total store of ground water, or

(c) the withdrawal of the ground water has a direct and substantial effect upon a watercourse or lake and unreasonably causes harm to a person entitled to the use of its water.

(2) The determination of liability under clauses (a), (b) and (c) of Subsection (1) is governed by the principles stated in §§ 850 to 857.

Comment on Clause (b):

g. Reasonable shares. The underground stream concept (see Introductory Note to this Topic) came into being in cases in which it seemed clear that a defendant had not merely deprived plaintiff of access to the remain-

1. Copyright 1979. Reprinted with the permission of the American Law Institute.

ing water in an aquifer by lowering the water table but that he had literally taken so much of the available supply that he had deprived plaintiff of water that he had previously put to use. The "correlative rights doctrine" (see Introductory Note) originated in the west in cases in which large withdrawals for irrigation made it apparent that the supply of ground water could not support unlimited withdrawals and that it was necessary to limit the claimants to overlying landowners and to make an equitable division of the resource in proportion to their holdings of overlying land. A number of eastern states have accepted the principle of correlative rights although they place more emphasis on "reasonableness" than on a rigid acreage formula.

Both the underground stream concept and the correlative rights doctrine resulted in the application of the law of surface streams to ground water bodies. This Section merges the concept and the doctrine into a single rule. The provisions of §§ 850A to 857 relating to riparian rights will be applicable to ground water whenever one user takes the supply of another or whenever the total withdrawals of all users threaten to reach a rate or amount that will endanger the availability, continuation or usefulness of the resource and the preservation of these values requires some restriction on the number of claimants or on the rate or quantity of each withdrawal.

4. The Nebraska rule, according to dicta in Olson v. City of Wahoo, 124 Neb. 802, 248 N.W. 304 (1933) was a combination of the American rule of reasonable use on the overlying land, "and if the natural underground supply is insufficient for all owners, each is entitled to a reasonable proportion of the whole." In Prather v. Eisenmann, 200 Neb. 1, 261 N.W.2d 766 (1978) this rule was said to be modified by § 46–613 Neb.Rev. Stat., "Preference in the use of underground water shall be given to those using the water for domestic purposes. They shall have preference over those claiming it for any other purpose. Those using the water for agricultural purposes shall have the preference over those using the same for manufacturing or industrial purposes." The case did not involve apportionment of the supply; there was sufficient water in the aquifer for all parties but an irrigator pumping 650 g.p.m. from his well lowered the water level below the depth of several small wells supplying neighboring residences. He was held liable for the costs of deepening the domestic wells and replacing a burnt out pump.

STATE v. DORITY

Supreme Court of New Mexico, 1950.
55 N.M. 12, 225 P.2d 1007.

BRICE, CHIEF JUSTICE. The State of New Mexico, upon relation of its State Engineer John H. Bliss, brought separate suits against Bert Troy Dority, Loman Wiley and S. A. Lanning, Jr., the purpose of which was to enjoin the respective defendants from unlawfully using for irrigating lands, waters drawn from what is known as the Roswell Artesian Basin, and the valley fill above it, which plaintiff asserts under Ch. 131, N.M.L.1931, 1941 Comp. § 77–1101 et seq., are subject to appropriation as provided therein. * * *

Defendants' lands are situated in Chaves County, New Mexico, and are located within the external boundaries of two underground water sources, one of which is an artesian basin lying between confining strata, the waters of which are commonly referred to as artesian water; and the other, plaintiff asserts, is an underground reservoir or lake in the valley fill overlying such artesian basin, the waters of which are commonly referred to as shallow ground water. About 45,000 acres are irrigated from shallow ground water and 55,000 acres from artesian water. * * * [T]he plaintiff asserts that the defendant Dority is irrigating 96.7 acres of land illegally, in that he has not been granted the right to so use the water; that the defendant Wiley was in like manner illegally using water to irrigate 48.7 acres of land; and the defendant Lanning was illegally using water to irrigate 120 acres. The defendants admit that they have been using, and will continue to use, the water without a permit unless enjoined from so doing. They deny that their use of it is in violation of law. The principal contention is that the New Mexico statutes providing for the appropriation of subsurface water is unconstitutional upon several grounds stated.

The statutes of New Mexico declaring that the artesian and shallow ground water from which defendants obtained the water to irrigate their land belongs to the public and providing for their appropriation for beneficial use, are as follows:

> "The waters of underground streams, channels, artesian basins, reservoirs, or lakes, having reasonably ascertainable boundaries, are hereby declared to be public waters and to belong to the public and to be subject to appropriation for beneficial use." Sec. 77–1101, N.M.Sts. 1941.

> "Beneficial use is the basis, the measure and the limit to the right to the use of the waters described in this act." Sec. 77–1102, N.M.Sts. 1941.

> "Any person, firm or corporation desiring to appropriate for irrigation or industrial uses any of the waters described in this act shall make application to the state engineer in a form to be prescribed by him in which said applicant shall designate the particular underground stream, channel, artesian basin, reservoir or lake from which water is proposed to be appropriated, the beneficial use to which it is proposed to apply such water, the location of the proposed well, the name of the owner of the land on which such well will be located, the amount of water applied for, the use for which it is desired and if the proposed use is irrigation, the description of the land to be irrigated and the name of the owner thereof. (Then follows a provision for the publication of notice of any objections to granting the permit, a provision that such application should be granted if there are any waters subject to appropriation, and the manner of hearing protests on such application, if any.)" Sec. 77–1103, N.M.Sts.1941.

> "Existing water rights based upon application to beneficial use are hereby recognized. Nothing herein contained is intended to impair the

same or to disturb the priorities thereof." Sec. 77–1104, N.M.Sts.1941.
* * *

"Any person using or appropriating water without a permit, contrary to the provisions of section 1 of chapter 70, of the New Mexico Session Laws of 1943, designated as section 77–1103 of the New Mexico Statutes, 1941, Annotated; or who changes the location of his well or use of the water except as provided and permitted by section 77–1107 of said New Mexico Statutes, 1941, Annotated; or who appropriates to his own use without a permit from the state engineer forfeited water or water rights under the provisions of section 77–1108 of said New Mexico Statutes, 1941, Annotated, shall be guilty of a misdemeanor and, on conviction thereof in any court of competent jurisdiction, shall be punished * * *." Laws 1943, Ch. 70, Sec. 2; Laws 1947, Ch. 21, Sec. 1, Sec. 77–1112, N.M.Sts.1941. * * *

The State Engineer has the jurisdiction and authority to determine the boundaries of any of the underground waters declared to be public waters, and no judicial determination is necessary to the jurisdiction given him by the laws in question.

No right to the use of water from such sources was obtained by its use by defendants in violation of law, nor can it be. The statutory manner of securing such rights is exclusive. Pecos Valley Artesian Cons. District v. Peters, 50 N.M. 165, 173 P.2d 490. We so held as to the irrigation law of 1907 in Harkey v. Smith, 31 N.M. 521, 247 P. 550. The same legal principles apply here.

The principal question raised is whether the Act of 1931, which we have quoted, that declared the ownership of the waters in question to be in the public, violates the 14th Amendment to the Constitution of the United States and Sec. 18 of Art. 2 of the Constitution of New Mexico, in that it authorizes the state to deprive its citizens and others of their property without due process of law, and denies them the equal protection of the laws; and violates Sec. 20 of Art. 2 of the Constitution of New Mexico in that it authorizes the taking of private property for public use without just compensation.

The whole argument is based on the assumption that the water described in Sec. 1 of the Act of 1931 belongs to the owners of the overlying land. Each of the defendants claims that the underground water under his land is his property acquired through mesne conveyances from the United States, beginning with the patent from the Government and that such patent and mesne conveyances transferred to him the water underlying the land conveyed. In other words, that the common law, or at least the law of correlative rights in such waters, is the law of this state. * * * The substance of the contention of each of the appellants is that he has a vested interest in the title to the water under his lands, to the center of the earth, of which he cannot be deprived by any legislative act.

This question was settled by this court in Yeo v. Tweedy, supra. It was held in that case that the title to the water described in Sec. 1 of the 1931 Act belonged to the public and was subject to appropriation for beneficial uses. We do not deem it necessary to go into this question extensively again, but because of decisions of this and other courts on the question since Yeo v. Tweedy, which was decided April 16, 1930, we will review them. * * *

We hold that under the Federal law and that of New Mexico the waters described in Sec. 1 of the Act of 1931 are subject to appropriation under that Act. * * *

There is another consideration which requires the affirmance of the trial court's decree. The decision of Yeo v. Tweedy, supra, has become a rule of property. In the nineteen years since that decision it may be assumed that many thousands of acres of the one hundred thousand irrigated with water from the Roswell Artesian basin and the valley fill have been sold to purchasers who relied on that decision as determining title to the right to use the water here involved, and the water rights to which would be injured or destroyed if Yeo v. Tweedy is overruled. Whether it stated the correct rule of law (and we are of the opinion that it did), it is now a rule of property that we will not disturb. * * *

* * * The patents to defendants' lands carried no right to the use of water, except as to that actually applied to the reclaiming of land * * * and not thereafter abandoned. All other water belonged to the State as trustee for the public. * * *

The decree of the district court is affirmed, and it is so ordered.

Notes

1. Knight v. Grimes, 80 S.D. 517, 127 N.W.2d 708 (1964), took a more direct approach to the constitutionality of superimposing a ground water appropriation statute upon the rule of absolute ownership of percolating waters. In view of a statute, in effect since territorial days, that "The owner of the land owns water standing thereon, or flowing over or under its surface, but not forming a definite stream," the court said that beyond doubt the statute is an invasion of a pre-existing right or interest, but that nevertheless the legislature was fully justified in finding that the public welfare requires the maximum protection and utilization of its water supply, and that the police power permitted the adoption of a statute imposing regulations that are not unreasonable or arbitrary.

See also Baumann v. Smrha, 145 F.Supp. 617 (D.C.Kan.1956), affirmed 352 U.S. 863, 77 S.Ct. 96, 1 L.Ed.2d 73 (1956), upholding the Kansas groundwater appropriation statute.

2. The following statutes are appropriation laws which are applicable to and apply approximately the same procedures to both surface streams and groundwaters: Alaska Stat. 46.15.010 to 46.15.270; Kan.Gen.Stat. 82a–701 to 82a–725; Mont.Code Ann. 1983 §§ 85–2–101 to 85–2–807; N.D.Cent. Code 61–01–01 to 61–04–31; Utah Code Ann. 1953, 73–3–1 to 73–3–28.

Other western states have separate groundwater codes: Colo.Rev.Stat. '73 37–90–101 to 37–90–141; Idaho Code §§ 42–226 to 42–237g; Nev.Rev.

Stat. 534.010 to 534.190; N.M.Stat.Ann. 1953, §§ 75–11–1 to 75–11–40; Or. Rev.Stat. 537.505 to 537.795; Wash.Rev.Code Ann. 90.44.010 to 90.44.250; Wyo.Stat. 1977 §§ 41–3–901 to 41–3–938.

3. Colorado has long distinguished "groundwater tributary to a stream" which is treated as part of the surface stream and subject to the court-administered prior appropriation law, Safranek v. Limon, 123 Colo. 330, 228 P.2d 975 (1951), from "nontributary groundwater" owned by the overlying landowner subject to the reasonable use rule, Whitten v. Coit, 153 Colo. 157, 385 P.2d 131 (1963).

Building on this dichotomy, the legislature enacted the Colorado Groundwater Management Act (Colo.Rev.Stat.1973, §§ 37–90–101 to 37–90–141), which applies a priority permit system to "designated groundwater" (nontributary), and the Water Right Determination and Administration Act (Colo.Rev.Stat.1973, §§ 37–92–101 to 37–92–602), which applies the surface water appropriation rules to tributary water. The latter act declares a state policy "to integrate the appropriation, use and administration of underground water tributary to a stream with the use of surface water, in such a way as to maximize the beneficial use of all of the waters of this state." Giving the Commission jurisdiction over some groundwater and the courts jurisdiction over other groundwater has led to expectable problems. See Larrick v. District Court, 177 Colo. 237, 493 P.2d 647 (1972); Hall v. Kuiper, 181 Colo. 130, 510 P.2d 329 (1973); Larrick v. North Kiowa-Bijou Management Dist., 181 Colo. 395, 510 P.2d 323 (1973); Kuiper v. Lundvall, 187 Colo. 40, 529 P.2d 1328 (1974); Sweetwater Development Corp. v. Schubert Ranches, Inc., 188 Colo. 379, 535 P.2d 215 (1975).

4. The common law groundwater rules of a number of states are superseded by permit systems: 7 Del.Code Ann. § 6003; West's Fla.Stat. Ann. § 373.023; Ga.Code § 17–1101; Hawaii Rev.Stat. § 177–1; Minn.Stat. Ann. § 105.37; S.C.Code 1976, § 49–5–10.

Permits are required for many groundwater uses or in some parts of several states: Reissue Neb.Rev.Stat.1943, § 46–637; N.J.Stat.Ann. 58:4A–5; McKinney Consol.Laws of N.Y. Environmental Conservation Law 15–1527; N.C.Gen.Stat. § 143–215.15; Wis.Stat.Ann. 144.025(2)(e); Va.Code §§ 62.1–44.83 to 62.1–44.107.

Several of these laws provide allocation schemes based on nonpriority factors: 7 Del.Code Ann. § 6101; Fla.Stat.Ann. § 373.016; Hawaii Rev. Stat. § 177–22; Minn.Stat.Ann. § 105.41.

5. Most states have statutes that require the capping, casing and controlling of artesian wells, and that control well specifications and license well drillers.

6. Geothermal energy is heat which occurs in the earth's interior. One method of utilizing geothermal energy is to extract naturally occurring geothermal fluids (steam or heated water) through a well. The legal relationship between the extraction of geothermal fluids and groundwater regulation is a developing one. In some states the geothermal developer must have a groundwater permit. In others, groundwater laws do not apply to geothermal development unless groundwater supplies are affected. Finally, some states have not addressed the matter at all. See Olpin and

Thompson, Water Law and the Development of Geothermal Resources, 14 Nat.Res.L. 635 (1981–82) for an examination of this problem and a summary of the approaches taken in various western states.

SECTION 2. PROBLEMS

THOMPSON v. COLORADO GROUND WATER COMM.

Supreme Court of Colorado, 1978.
194 Colo. 489, 575 P.2d 372.

ERICKSON, JUSTICE.

On February 13, 1974, Gordon L. Thompson (plaintiff) filed an application with the Colorado Ground Water Commission (commission) seeking a permit to construct a well and to appropriate designated ground water from the Northern High Plains Designated Ground Water Basin in Yuma County. The commission denied the application on the basis that the proposed appropriation would unreasonably impair existing water rights. * * *

The plaintiff thereafter appealed the commission's decision to the district court in and for Yuma County and a trial de novo was held pursuant to statute. Section 37–90–115, C.R.S.1973. Expert witnesses appeared on behalf of both the plaintiff and the commission. On April 14, 1976, the district court entered a judgment denying the application because unappropriated water was not available when the application was considered under the commission's guidelines. * * * This appeal was then perfected. * * *

In determining whether a proposed well will unreasonably injure the rights of existing appropriators the commission is required to consider the "quantity of existing claims." Section 37–90–107(5), C.R.S.1973. The plaintiff does not challenge the duty of the commission to protect valid senior rights, but does take issue with the manner in which the commission determines the "quantity of existing claims." He asserts that the "existing claims" protected by the commission are inflated and unenforceable under Colorado water law.

The "quantity of existing claims" which must be considered by the commission, is the sum of all water rights which have been appropriated and those water rights which are in the process of being appropriated under conditional permits. The legislative intent evidenced in the Colorado Ground Water Management Act is that the issuance of final permits, which requires proof and verification of the extent of beneficial use, would serve a function equivalent to the final surface water decree and establish senior rights. But to compute the "quantity of existing claims" only on the basis of rights represented by final permits would ignore the rights that holders of conditional permits have to perfect their appropriations to the full extent of their conditional permits. These rights in the process of being appropriated, therefore, must be considered by the commission in their calculations of the "quantity of existing claims." The plaintiff's arguments are directed, not at the procedure contemplated by the legislature, but rather at the commission's failure to issue final permits and its assumption that all conditional permits represent valid water rights to the full extent of the permit.

Leonard A. Mercer, the chief of the ground water section of the state engineer's office, testified before the commission that the usual claim for the irrigation of a standard 160-acre tract is exaggerated by 21% because most irrigators employ pivot-point sprinklers which operate in a circular manner, irrigating only 126 of the 160 acres claimed. He stated that, "This is a thing that is going on that I deeply wish the commission would change. It is a safety factor, but it is also a phoney appropriation right." A second factor which inflates the commission's appropriation figure is the commission's policy of allocating thirty inches (2½ acre feet) for each irrigated acre when, in fact, these acres normally consume only sixteen to eighteen inches.

The district court made the following findings of fact which are supported by the record:

> "The Court finds that the amount of acreage claimed in the application to construct a well and in the conditional permits heretofore granted is rarely the amount of acreage actually irrigated.
>
> "The Court further finds that as of the date of the trial of the issues in this case no independent investigation had been made by any regulatory agency as to the amount of water actually placed to a beneficial use under any of the conditional permits, and that as of that time no final permits had been issued.
>
> "The Court further finds that in all prior instances permit claimants had claimed at least the two and one half acre feet permitted by the Commission. The evidence further discloses that the average annual application in the area involved has been approximately eighteen inches per year."

The commission seeks to justify its present policy. It contends that it is required by statute to consider the quantity of existing claims under conditional permits, regardless of the actual extent of beneficial use, because they represent valid rights which can be exercised to their full extent. The commission's policy guidelines, therefore, require "the assumption that, for the purpose of this analysis, all rights to appropriate are being fully exercised."

If final permits had been issued, pursuant to section 37–90–108, C.R.S.1973 (1976 Supp.), no error would be found in the policy guideline directive. Final permits, however, have not been issued, and conditional permits do not permit their holders to sleep on water rights and later expand their use to the full extent of their permits.

Regardless of the quantity specified in a decree, the amount of water actually applied to beneficial use defines the full extent of the water right. Green v. Chaffee Ditch Company, 150 Colo. 91, 371 P.2d

775 (1962). Normally, the extent of beneficial use and the measure of the water right is fixed at the time a final decree is entered. The legislature also intended that the extent of beneficial use would limit the ground water appropriator by providing for the issuance of final permits based upon proof of beneficial use. Section 37–90–108, C.R.S.1973 (1976 Supp.).

The commission cannot rely upon conditional permits as though they are enforceable "existing claims" without implementing the legislative scheme which includes the issuance of final permits. Such a practice has two effects. First, it does afford protection as contemplated by the legislature to appropriators who are proceeding according to statutory directive to place the full amount of water under their conditional permits to beneficial use. But, secondly, it permits appropriators who have placed a lesser quantity of water to beneficial use, and who are not proceeding with due diligence to place the full quantity of water under their conditional permits to beneficial use, to sleep on water rights which are not validly appropriated under Colorado law. Green v. Chaffee Ditch Company, supra.

The final permit is essential to the legislative scheme for the administration of ground water rights. Once final permits are issued, the "quantity of existing claims" can be determined by combining the quantity of rights evidenced by final permits with the quantity of rights represented by conditional permits engaged in the statutory process that will result in the issuance of a final permit. Only then can the commission conclude with certainty whether unappropriated water exists. The commission's failure to follow the legislative directives contained within the Colorado Ground Water Management Act may have had the effect of denying the plaintiff his statutory right to divert unappropriated designated ground water.

This opinion is not intended to affect valid water rights which are presently represented by conditional permits. The commission's failure to proceed in accordance with the legislature's mandate will not be permitted to adversely affect existing appropriations. The commission and the state engineer are directed by statute to issue final permits by implementing the procedures provided in section 37–90–108, C.R.S.1973 (1976 Supp.). Final permits, when issued, will protect existing rights based upon the extent of beneficial use. Section 37–90–108, C.R.S.1973 (1976 Supp.).

Accordingly, the judgment is reversed, and the cause is remanded to the trial court with directions to enter findings of fact as directed in this opinion and for proceedings not inconsistent with this opinion.

Notes

1. Preventing overdevelopment of an aquifer involves an attempt to strike some sort of balance between withdrawals and supply. The principal case deals with legal problems encountered in determining withdrawals. However, determination of supply is more often the problem. See, Corker,

Groundwater Law, Management and Administration, National Water Commission, Legal Study No. 6, pp. 18–33 (1971). An accurate determination of supply requires detailed physical information about the aquifer, which is frequently not available. Moreover, as subsequent notes and cases indicate, the calculation of supply is not solely a matter of physical measurement, but involves economic and social considerations as well.

2. McGuinness, Water Law with Special Reference to Ground Water (Geol.Surv.Circ. 117) 11 (1951):

"Regulation of water use to prevent over-development of an aquifer, or a part of it, involves the determination of a safe or optimum rate of withdrawal and the holding of withdrawals to it. This is true whether the doctrine of prior appropriation or that of correlative rights is applied. Such a determination generally is much more difficult for a ground-water reservoir than for a surface stream or reservoir, for it inevitably involves the economic feasibility of a given means of withdrawal or a given pumping lift, not only in an aquifer as a whole but in different parts of it. Because of variations in the cost of withdrawal in relation to the use to which the water is put, it is impracticable or at least very difficult to define by statute the conditions determining optimum yield. For example, a pumping lift of 100 feet may be feasible for all users in a given area, whereas 200 feet may be feasible for some but not for others. Yet the perennial yield of the aquifer may be greatly different at the two pumping levels. Where should the regulating official set the limit of pumping? * * *

3. Bagley, Water Rights Law and Public Policies Relating to Ground Water "Mining" in the Southwestern States, 4 J.Law and Econ. 144, 166–7 (1961):

"In * * * other states, the official position is to prevent withdrawals in excess of the average recharge or of the 'safe yield,'[2] and in Nevada * * * protection of the prior appropriator appears to limit withdrawals to less than average recharge in certain cases. The Nevada law prohibits further withdrawals when 'safe yield' has been reached, when the water table has been lowered to the point where the pump lift approaches maximum economic limits, or when further diversions would adversely affect the economy of the area, whichever is reached first. The State Engineer may also order restrictions in withdrawals under existing rights to conform to priorities if 'average annual replenishment' is inadequate to supply all right holders. Apparently, therefore, there are several possible stopping points before 'safe yield' is reached. * * *"

4. Crosby, supra p. 385, at 75–76:

What is the "Yield" of a Groundwater Basin?

An often more important characteristic of a reservoir, surface or underground, is its capacity to produce water over a period of time. The

2. It should be noted that "safe yield" and average recharge are not necessarily interchangeable terms. Where compaction, subsidence, or bad water intrusion results from lowering the water level, "safe yield" may be less than average recharge. Also average recharge does not imply any particular average water level. When natural discharge is reduced as much as pumpage the level will stabilize. This may occur at many levels and the maximum may be near the original level or it may not be reached until the stored water is largely depleted. Moreover, lowering the level may bring increased recharge.

capacity calculation requires detailed information as to inflow and outflow with respect to time and the fixed capacity of the reservoir to furnish water from storage during cyclical dry periods of less than average inflow. The "safe yield" of a groundwater reservoir is a term sometimes used to indicate a reasonable rate of production from the reservoir. *Safe yield* has been variously defined. Todd (1959) states, "The safe yield of a groundwater basin is the amount of water which can be withdrawn from it annually without producing an undesired result." Banks *et al* (1961, p. 53) indicate that, "Safe yield might presently [1960] best be regarded as a sound concept based on the renewability of the hydrologic cycle, which has been useful in groundwater development, and which, with our increasing understanding of hydrology, deserve sharper definition." They continue by listing four alternative yield concepts:

"a. Maximum sustained yield is the maximum rate at which water can be withdrawn perennially from a particular source.

"b. Permissive sustained yield is the maximum rate at which water can economically and legally be withdrawn perennially from a particular source for beneficial purposes, without bringing about some undesired result.

"c. Maximum mining yield is the total volume of water in storage in a particular source that can be extracted and utilized.

"d. Permissive mining yield is the maximum volume of water in storage in a particular source that can economically and legally be extracted and utilized for beneficial purposes, without bringing about some undesired result."

Meinzer (1923b, p. 55) had earlier defined safe yield as, "the rate at which water can be withdrawn from an aquifer without depleting the supply to such an extent that withdrawal at this rate is harmful to the aquifer itself, or to the quality of the water, or is no longer economically feasible."

It is apparent that usage has not made the term specific and that it is inherently ambiguous because it may or may not invite subjective and/or economic judgments above the gravity of the risk from a water shortage. It has the additional disadvantage that decisions made in good faith may prove to be, in time, poorly considered. A regimen of totally "safe" operation which avoided all risks would utilize much less than the optimum usable storage capacity.

Definition of the groundwater basin characteristics which must be considered in any yield concept may be subject to considerable error. The hydrogeology of some basins is well enough known that predictions of performance are reasonably good but still subject to unforeseen dynamic changes or statistical variance. In other basins forecasts of water level declines in response to anticipated pumpage have been grossly in error. The storage capacity of some aquifer materials has been unusually difficult to establish by accepted techniques. However, as further technological advances are made, such difficulties may be largely overcome.

It is evident that the approach to basin yield should depend on explicit administrative intent and that concepts should be given definitions with explicit meanings to both hydroscientist and administrator. "Permissive mining yield" or "permissive sustained yield" could be useful terms if precisely defined.

5. A basin-wide determination may be made. The Oregon and Wyoming statutes provide procedures under which the state water officials may declare the existence of "critical areas" and close the areas to appropriation and refuse to grant further permits. Or.Rev.Stat. 537.730, 537.735; Wyo.Stat.1977, §§ 41–3–912, 41–3–915.

6. Control of over-development is possible under other rules. Arizona supplemented her "American rule of reasonable use" with a procedure for designating "critical ground water areas" in which new irrigation wells were prohibited. However, critical areas proved ineffective in resolving Arizona's groundwater problems and were abandoned in 1980 in favor of more complex management devices. See Town of Chino Valley v. City of Prescott, infra page 437.

7. In Texas, the English rule of ownership could be affected markedly by controls imposed by local districts. These were once admired from afar:

"Texas adopted a local control type statute in 1949 when it authorized creation of ground water conservation districts. These districts are designated by the Texas Water Commission at the state level, and must be an area having the same boundaries as an underground reservoir or subdivision thereof. 'Reservoir' is defined as a specific subsurface water-bearing reservoir which has ascertainable boundaries and contains underground water capable of being produced from a well at not less than 150,000 gallons per day. If the district lies in a single county, its creation depends on the county commissioners; if the land in the district is in two or more counties, then the question goes to the Water Commission. After creation, the qualified resident property-owning taxpaying voters determine whether or not to confirm the district. If a majority of those voting at the election favor confirmation, the district is ratified and may begin to incur indebtedness. Municipal corporations within the area are separate voting entities, and votes are counted separately in rural areas and in each municipality.

"Ground water districts may require that permits be obtained before landowners drill wells capable of producing over 100,000 gallons per day, may provide for the spacing of wells, and may regulate withdrawals from wells so as to minimize as far as practicable the drawdown of the water table or the reduction of artesian pressure. In addition, districts may formulate plans and carry out projects for recharging reservoirs.

"A district in Texas has no authority, however, to determine priorities between users or to prorate underground water in the event of shortage, and the statute expressly recognizes that landowners own the water under their lands. Therefore, conflicts between individual users must still be decided by the courts. The constitutionality of requiring well spacing and regulating pumping have not been tested; and although the Texas Supreme Court has adopted the absolute ownership rule, it does not necessarily follow that regulation by the underground water districts violates the due process clauses of the federal and Texas constitutions.

"In Texas, particularly in the high plains, * * * local districts operate on a large scale. For instance, the High Plains Underground Conservation District No. 1 in Texas consists of parts of thirteen counties and covers about five million acres." Harnsberger, Nebraska Ground Water Problems, 42 Neb.L.Rev. 721, 757–759 (1963).

In 1977, an on-the-spot observer noted that few districts had exercised their authority and that it is doubtful they ever will. "When the same persons who stand to receive the most economic gain from increased production are also the supposed regulators, one can hardly expect an effective regulatory system * * * this is especially true if the detrimental effects of wasteful pumping fall outside the district." Smith, The Valley Water Suit and Its Impact on Texas Water Policy, 8 Tex.Tech.L.Rev. 577, 634 (1977). Events seem to have borne out Smith's prediction. As reported in 1982, only three districts were then active and, although the most active district had regulated well spacing and attempted to prevent excessive use of water in irrigation, it had not undertaken the curtailment of withdrawals to extend the life of the aquifer. Johnson, Texas Groundwater Law: A Survey and Some Proposals, 22 Nat.Res.J. 1017, 1020 (1982).

8. After some experience with ineffective local districts, in 1975 Nebraska provided for control areas managed by its Natural Resources Districts, large organizations that exercise broad water and related land management powers over entire river basins and supplant a number of older districts with more limited areas and powers. The State Director of Water Resources designates the control areas and oversees the regulatory activities of the districts. New wells need permits, pumping may be limited and rotation may be imposed, presumably in furtherance of the "preferred correlative rights" doctrine of Prather v. Eisenmann, supra p. 403, Note 4. Cf. Southwest Engineering Co. v. Ernst, 79 Ariz. 403, 291 P.2d 764 (1955). See also Aiken & Supulla, Groundwater Mining and Western Water Rights Law: The Nebraska Experience, 24 S.Dak.L.Rev. 607 (1979).

FUNDINGSLAND v. COLORADO GROUND WATER COMMISSION

Supreme Court of Colorado, 1970.
171 Colo. 487, 468 P.2d 835.

PRINGLE, JUSTICE. On September 2, 1966, Mr. Fundingsland (hereinafter referred to as the plaintiff) filed an application with the Colorado Ground Water Commission (hereinafter referred to as the commission) for a permit to drill a well on certain property located in the Northern High Plains Designated Ground Water Basin in Kit Carson County. No objections to the application were filed. On February 27, 1967, the plaintiff's application was denied by the commission on the basis that there was over appropriation in the area where the well was to be drilled. The plaintiff objected to the ruling of the commission, and a hearing was held before the commission on December 12, 1967. As the result of the hearing the commission sustained its previous denial of the plaintiff's application. The commission's order was subsequently withdrawn on the basis that there was new information to be considered by the commission. This information was presented to the commission on March 19 and 20, 1968, and on May 15, 1968 the commission published an order denying the plaintiff's application.

The plaintiff appealed the decision of the commission to the district court, and a trial de novo was held with expert testimony being presented by both the plaintiff and the commission. The record of the testimony given before the commission during the December 12th hearing was made a part of the evidence, as specifically provided for by statute. The trial judge entered a judgment denying the plaintiff's application, and the plaintiff brings writ of error to this Court from that judgment. Plaintiff makes it very clear that he does not in any way contest the constitutionality of the Ground Water Act under which this proceeding was conducted. He alleges as grounds for reversal (1) that the denial of his application was not supported by the evidence and was arbitrary and capricious; (2) that denial of the application deprives the plaintiff of his constitutional right to appropriate; and (3) that the rule upon which the commission relied was adopted in violation of the provisions of the Administrative Code and cannot be enforced. This Court finds no error, and we affirm the judgment of the district court.

The court and the commission derive their authority to pass on the plaintiff's application from 1965 Perm.Supp., C.R.S.1963, 148–18–1 *et seq.* (formerly Senate Bill 367) which deals with captive ground water. Under 148–18–6 the commission is empowered to deny an application if it finds that the proposed appropriation will unreasonably impair existing water rights from the same source, or will create unreasonable waste. The act further provides in 148–18–6(5):

> "In ascertaining whether a proposed use will create unreasonable waste or unreasonably affect the rights of other appropriators, the commission shall take into consideration the area, and geologic conditions, the average annual yield and recharge rate of the appropriate water supply, the priority and quantity of existing claims of all persons to use the water, the proposed method of use, and all other matters appropriate to such questions. With regard to whether a proposed use will impair uses under existing water rights, impairment shall include the unreasonable lowering of the water level, or the unreasonable deterioration of water quality, beyond reasonable economic limits of withdrawal or use."

Upon trial de novo, as provided in the statute, the trial court made detailed findings of fact concerning the proper tests to be used in determining whether the proposed use of water by the plaintiff would unreasonably impair existing water rights from the same source or create unreasonable waste. And after making those findings, the court determined that they supported a denial of the plaintiff's application.

Among these findings, the trial court determined that a so-called three mile test provided a reasonable basis for assessing the effect of a proposed use on other users in the district. The three mile test was developed for use in the Northern High Plains. It is partly based on policy and partly based on fact and theory. Using that test, a circle with a three mile radius is drawn around the proposed well site. A rate of pumping is determined which would result in a 40% depletion of the available ground water in that area over a period of 25 years. If that rate of pumping is being exceeded by the existing wells within the circle, then the application for a permit to drill a new well may be denied.

The three mile test takes into account all of the considerations specified in the statute. The factors involved in the three mile test were explained to the court by Mr. Erker, senior engineer in the ground water section of the State Engineer's office. He testified that the three mile circle represents the area over which a well, located at the center, would have an effect if permitted to pump intermittently for 25 years. Intermittent pumping, he explained, meant approximately 100 days per year. Other factors which are considered are the saturated thickness of the aquifer within the three mile circle, the number of wells located within the circle, and the yield of those wells. Multiplying the number of wells within the circle times the yield of those wells gives the total, present appropriation within the three mile circle.

Mr. Romero, an assistant water resource engineer for the State of Colorado Division of Water Resources, testified that the modified Theiss equation was used in determining what the draw down effect on the water in the aquifer would be within the three mile circle. He further testified that in determining the balance of water in the aquifer, he considered the fact that there was only intermittent pumping, the amount of recharge to the aquifer due to precipitation and ground water inflow from outlying areas, recharge due to excess irrigation, and possibly recharge from some other source such as leakage from ditches or rivers.

There does not seem to be any contention that the 40% depletion figure is unreasonable or irrational. The assumption in the three mile test is that a 40% depletion of the aquifer within that area would constitute lowering of the water balance beyond reasonable economic limits of withdrawal or use for irrigation.

Likewise, the selection of 25 years as the period during which the 40% depletion is to be allowed is not contested. Mr. Leslie, a farm and ranch loan representative for Northwestern Mutual Life Insurance Company, testified that 25 years was a reasonable, average period in which a loan for the construction of well facilities would have to be repaid.

The testimony and other evidence in the record before the district court support the reasonableness of the three mile test and establish that the three mile test takes into account the factors specified by the statute. If the three mile test was a proper method for the court to use in determining the effect of plaintiff's proposed use on the ground water supply in the district, then the decision of the district court must be upheld.

* * * Finally, it was admitted on both sides that the commission is dealing in a complex area about which little is known. Experts testifying for the commission stated that the three mile test is the best tool they presently have to work with, and that it will be refined as they continue to learn more about the area.

The plaintiff's application did not present the court with a close question of whether the granting of a new permit would work unreasonable injury to existing wells. According to the three mile test, seventeen wells in the three mile circle pumping intermittently with a 1,000 gallon capacity per minute would deplete the water resource 40% in 25 years. There were 28 registered wells within the three mile circle encompassing the plaintiff's proposed well site. These 28 wells had a registered yield of 29,700 gallons per minute while the maximum yield allowable under the three mile test would be 17,000 gallons per minute.

Ground water existing in designated underground water basins is made subject to the doctrine of prior appropriation by 1965 Perm.Supp., C.R.S.1963, 148–18–1. The statute further provides:

> "* * * While the doctrine of prior appropriation is recognized, such doctrine should be modified to permit the full economic development of designated ground water resources. Prior appropriations of ground water should be protected and reasonable ground water pumping levels maintained, but not to include the maintenance of historical water levels. * * *"

Underground water basins require management that is different from the management of surface streams and underground waters tributary to such streams. In the case of the latter waters, seasonal regulation of diversion by junior appropriators can effectively protect the interests of more senior appropriators and no long range harm can come of over appropriations since the streams are subject to seasonal recharge. The underground water dealt with by 148–18–1 is not subject to the same ready replenishment enjoyed by surface streams and tributary ground water. It is possible for water to be withdrawn from the aquifer in a rate in excess of the annual recharge creating what is called a mining condition. Unless the rate of pumping is regulated, mining must ultimately result in lowering the water balance below a level from which water may be economically withdrawn. Due to the slow rate at which underground waters flow through and into the aquifer, it may be many years before a reasonable water level may be restored to a mined aquifer.

It is clear that the policies of protecting senior appropriators and maintaining reasonable ground water pumping levels set forth by the underground water act require management which takes into account the long range effects of intermittent pumping in the aquifer. In this case all of the experts testifying before the commission and the district court were in agreement that a mining condition exists in the Northern High Plains Designated Ground Water Basin. The commission has determined that proper use of the ground water resource requires that the mining be allowed to continue. However, the maximum allowable rate of depletion, at least when considering applications for permits to drill new wells, has been set at 40% depletion in 25 years. We have pointed out that the depletion rate in the area which would be affected by the plaintiff's proposed well is in excess of the rate allowed by the commission and approved by the district court.

If the plaintiff were permitted to proceed on his theory of "unappropriated water" and pump water from his proposed well until such time as it was no longer economically feasible to withdraw water from the aquifer, then no subsequent regulation of his pumping could protect senior appropriators, and all pumping from the basin within the area of influence of the plaintiff's well would have to cease until a reasonable pumping level was restored through the slow process of recharge. This is not the concept of appropriation contained in the statute, and not the one this Court will follow.

When, as in this case, water is being mined from the ground water basin, and a proposed appropriation would result in unreasonable harm to senior appropriators, then a determination that there is no water available for appropriation is justified. * * *

The judgment is affirmed.

Notes

1. Thompson v. Colorado Groundwater Commission, supra page 408, involved a modification of the three-mile test where the circle is bisected by the Nebraska state line. The Commission looked only at the portion of the circle in Colorado and the development in Colorado, and determined that the area around plaintiff's proposed well was over-appropriated. The Commission admitted that if the entire circle and the amount of Nebraska development were considered (or if the entire circle had been in Colorado) the area would not have been considered over-appropriated. The court upheld this "state line policy," saying, "Expert testimony supported the Commission's position that over-appropriation of the aquifer at the state line, with the intent to stabilize or reverse the aquifer flow to the benefit of Colorado, would seriously injure vested Colorado rights far west of the state line and could ignite a destructive aquifer depletion race with Nebraska, an adjoining state. Evidence that a portion of Colorado's groundwater naturally flows into adjoining states, when considered in the context of the Commission's overall groundwater policy, does not establish a breach of statutory duty by the Commission in its determination." See Burke and Muys, Interstate Allocation and Management of Nontributary Groundwater, Western "Governors" Association, (1985); Fisher, Management of Interstate Groundwater, 7 Natural Resources L. 521 (1974); Interstate Groundwater Rights: Protecting the Interests of the States, 20 So.Dak.L. Rev. 641 (1975).

2. The first case dealing explicitly with groundwater mining was Mathers v. Texaco, Inc., 77 N.M. 239, 421 P.2d 771 (1966). Texaco was given a permit to appropriate 350 acre feet per year from the Lea County underground water basin for the purpose of water flooding an oil field.

The fresh water in the basin is found in the Ogalalla formation which varies in thickness from a thin edge to over 200 feet. The water in the formation is replenished only by a very limited surface precipitation which is just about equaled by natural discharge from the basin so that for practical purposes no recharge takes place. The State Engineer calculated the amount of water that could be withdrawn from a township of overlying land and still leave one-third of the water in storage at the end of 40 years, at which point it would no longer be economically feasible to withdraw water for agricultural and most other purposes. Mathers and others, existing appropriators and withdrawers of water for agricultural purposes, protested the issuance of the permits. In upholding the permit, the court said:

"The administration of a non-rechargeable basin, if the waters therein are to be applied to a beneficial use, requires giving to the stock or supply of water a time dimension, or, to state it otherwise, requires the fixing of a rate of withdrawal which will result in a determination of the economic life of the basin at a selected time.

"The very nature of the finite stock of water in a non-rechargeable basin compels a modification of the traditional concept of appropriate supply under the appropriation doctrine. * * *

"The rights of the protestants to appropriate water from this basin are subject to this time limitation, just as are the rights of all other appropriators. A lowering of the water level in the wells of protestants, together with the resulting increase in pumping costs and the lowering of pumping yields, does not constitute an impairment of the rights of protestants as a matter of law. These are inevitable results of the beneficial use by the public of these waters."

An interesting sidelight to the case is supplied by Corker, Groundwater Law, Management and Administration, National Water Commission Legal Study No. 6,176 (1971):

"According to S.E. Reynolds, State Engineer, forty years was selected because it is two generations, and forty years corresponds to provisions in federal reclamation law for repayment by irrigator beneficiaries."

3. The National Water Commission concluded that groundwater mining is not inherently wrong, an assessment shared by many other commentators. See Water Policies for the Future, National Water Commission, pp. 238–243 (1973). However, groundwater mining presents a number of potential problems which must be considered in deciding whether to permit it in a particular situation.

One inevitable result of mining is a decline in the water table, resulting in increased costs of extraction. Other physical problems which may accompany a decline in the water table include compaction of the aquifer, resulting in loss of transmissivity and storage capacity, surface subsidence, and saltwater intrusion.

Economic problems associated with the "common pool" nature of groundwater may also result. If a groundwater pool is shared, as it usually is, there is little incentive for individual users to conserve the water in storage for future use because water not pumped now will be taken by someone else. This results in undervaluing and overusing water presently. In addition, the potential economic and social dislocations resulting from the eventual physical or economic depletion of the aquifer due to mining must be considered.

The National Water Commission suggested pump taxes, set at a rate equal to the predicted future value of the water discounted to present value, as a device for solving common pool problems. Transferable quotas were another alternative suggested by the commission. In either case the commission suggested that the life of the aquifer must be fixed, taking into account the relative benefits of present and future use.

Some of the problems of groundwater mining are taken up in subsequent materials. An excellent discussion of economic considerations involved in groundwater mining is found in Bagley, Water Rights Law & Public Policies Relating to Ground Water "Mining" in the Southwestern States, 4 J. Law & Econ 144 (1961).

4. What happens to the existing groundwater users within a given three mile circle in the Northern High Plains (*Fundingsland*) when uneconomic pumping depths are reached after 25 years? One possibility is that they will simply quit irrigating and return to dry land farming or allow the land to revert to prairie. This seems to be the premise on which the regulations in both Colorado and New Mexico were based, because the life of the aquifer was set to give the users an adequate opportunity to amortize the investment in their wells before economic exhaustion of the resource occurred.

Another solution is to supplement supplies by importing water. For example, much of the early growth of Los Angeles was based on groundwater drawn from overdrafted aquifers. This provided Los Angeles with cheap water on which to develop the economic strength to import water from the Owens Valley, some 300 miles away, in 1913.

Critics of groundwater mining argue that frequently it creates a crisis situation, leading to demands for a "rescue project" to supply supplemental water at subsidized prices. An example is the Central Arizona Project, which transports Colorado River water to central Arizona. Although not originally conceived as a "rescue project," when finally approved by Congress in 1968, its purpose was exactly that.

5. United States v. Shurbet, 347 F.2d 103 (5th Cir.1965), ruled that an irrigation user of ground water from the Southern High Plains is entitled to a cost depletion deduction in computing his federal income tax, under Int.Rev.Code of 1954, § 611(a), which allows a reasonable deduction in the case of mines, oil and gas wells "and other natural deposits." The court noted that under Texas law the taxpayer "owns the soil and the percolating water which is part of the soil." Are neighboring "water miners" in New Mexico entitled to a depletion allowance, though there the state is said to own the water? See Bagley, The Groundwater Depletion Allowance Under the Federal Income Tax, 12 Nat.Res.J. 445 (1972).

BAKER v. ORE–IDA FOODS, INC.

Supreme Court of Idaho, 1973.
95 Idaho 575, 513 P.2d 627.

SHEPARD, JUSTICE.

This is an appeal from a judgment for plaintiffs enjoining defendants from operating their irrigation wells. Defendants' wells pumped from a ground water aquifer underlying both plaintiffs' and defendants' land. This Court must for the first time, interpret our Ground Water Act (I.C. § 42–226 et seq.) as it relates to withdrawals of water from an underground aquifer in excess of the annual recharge rate. We are also called upon to construe our Ground Water Act's policies of promoting "full economic development" of ground water resources and maintaining "reasonable pumping levels."

This case focuses on approximately 20 irrigation wells developed during the late 1950's and early 1960's in the Cottonwood Creek-Buckhorn Creek area of Cassia County in southern Idaho. The parties to this suit were engaged in farming operations in that area. Underlying this area is a limestone aquifer of unknown depth. This aquifer is recharged primarily by means of precipitation. There is not enough annual recharge water to satisfy the needs of all the well owners during the summer irrigation season.

Plaintiffs-respondents Baker, et al., originally brought this action in July 1965 seeking to enjoin defendants-appellants Ore-Ida Foods, et al. from pumping irrigation water from their wells until such time as plaintiffs' wells resumed normal production. In February, 1969 the case was tried to the district court sitting without a jury. The trial was essentially a battle between three hydrology experts. The record in the case is voluminous including prolix water records extending back more than 20 years. The district court entered its amended decree October 5, 1971.

The district court found that the parties and their predecessors in interest had developed irrigation wells having a certain order of priority. The district court also found that all of the wells drew water from a common aquifer underlying the area. The aquifer was of unknown depth but was capable of a metes and bounds description. The court further found that the aquifer is recharged primarily by precipitation, at an average rate of 5,500 acre ft. per year. The court concluded that during the period 1961 through 1968 the parties had withdrawn water from the aquifer far in excess of the annual recharge rate causing a 20 ft. per year drop in the aquifer's water level. In other words the parties were apparently "mining" the aquifer, i.e., perennially withdrawing ground water at rates beyond the recharge rate. * * *

The court calculated that one cubic foot per second of water flowing for 24 hours would produce 1.983 acre ft. and held that the average annual natural recharge could be pumped entirely by the four senior wells. The court enjoined pumping from all other wells and assigned further administration of its decree to the Idaho Department of Water Administration (IDWA), [formerly the Department of Reclamation, *see* I.C. § 42–1801a]. The decree granted the IDWA full power to expand or limit the amounts of available water for pumping so long as the pumping never exceeded the annual rate of recharge. The amended decree also granted the IDWA the authority to modify its determination of the annual recharge rate. * * *

The instant case requires construction of the Ground Water Act against the backdrop of the uneven development of our common law concerning ground water. Idaho has vacillated on the question of the appropriability of ground water. * * *

In Hinton v. Little, 50 Idaho 371, 296 P. 582 (1931) the court eradicated the questionable historical distinction between underground streams and percolating waters and stated that *all* underground waters are percolating waters. *Hinton* rejected the absolute ownership doctrine and held that the litigants could appropriate a common body of artesian water under their land. * * *

In 1963 amendments to the Ground Water Act, I.C. § 42–229 (S.L. 1963, ch. 216, § 1, p. 624) [were enacted.] We construed that amendment in State ex rel. Tappan v. Smith, 92 Idaho 451, 456, 444 P.2d 412, 417 (1968) and held:

> "This section of the statute does not deny the right to appropriate ground water, but regulates the method and means by which one may perfect a right to the use of such water. The regulation is in accord with Article 15, Sections 1 and 3, of Idaho's Constitution, and with I.C. §§ 42–103 and 42–226. Thereby the legislature prescribed that from the effective date of the act which precedes the present action, the statutory method of appropriation would be the sole method of appropriating ground water. The trial court did not err in finding that our laws require an appropriator of ground water to follow the application, permit and license procedure of the Department of Reclamation."

The Idaho Ground Water Act, I.C. § 42–237a(g) provides in pertinent part:

> " * * * *Water in a well shall not be deemed available to fill a water right therein* if withdrawal therefrom of the amount called for by such right would affect, contrary to the declared policy of this act, the present or future use of any prior surface or ground water right or *result in withdrawing the ground water supply at a rate beyond the reasonably anticipated average rate of future natural recharge.*" (Emphasis supplied)

We now hold that Idaho's Ground Water Act forbids "mining" of an aquifer. The evidence herein clearly shows that the pumping by all parties was steadily drawing down the water in the aquifer at the rate of 20 ft. per year. Since our statute explicitly forbids such pumping, the district court did not err in enjoining pumping beyond the "reasonably anticipated average rate of future natural recharge." * * *

Idaho's Ground Water Act seeks to promote "full economic development" of our ground water resources. I.C. § 42–226. Other western states have enacted analogous ground water legislation enunciating the same policy. Sax, J.L. Water Law, Planning & Policy 469 (1968). We hold that the Ground Water Act is consistent with the constitutionally enunciated policy of promoting optimum development of water resources in the public interest. Idaho Const. art. 15, § 7. Full economic development of Idaho's ground water resources can and will benefit all of our citizens. Trelease, F.J., Policies for Water Law: Property Rights, Economic Forces, and Public Regulations, 5 Nat.Res.J. 1, (1965); Hutchins, W.A., Ground Water Legislation, 30 Rocky Mtn.L.Rev. 416 (1958).

Appellants contend that our Act's use of the phrase "reasonable pumping levels" means that senior appropriators are not necessarily entitled to maintenance of historic pumping levels. We agree with appellants in this regard. However, our agreement avails appellants nothing because the trial court found the aquifer's water supply inadequate to meet the needs of all appropriators. * * *

The judgment of the district court is affirmed. Costs to Respondents.

Notes

1. In further proceedings the Director of the Department of Water Resources made some interesting findings. He determined that the prior rights should be fixed at the historical amount of use rather than on the maximum amount that could have been pumped. Rather than assuming the water had been pumped at the licensed rate for 24 hours on 180 days a year, he examined the power company records for the pumps associated with each license in order to determine the hours or days that the pump was in operation each year. He found the length of the pumping season had been from 150–160 days per year, and fixed the annual water right at the highest five year average, expressed in acre feet per year. This reduced the water rights by 28% to 38% and allowed more appropriators to pump. Then, based on the premise that in a dry year good farming practice could require the use of more than the annual water right, while in a wet year an irrigator might not need his total right, the Director allowed the water users to pump any amount of water necessary in a given year so long as the water user did not pump over five times his annual water right in any consecutive five year period. The case was again appealed on a rather narrow point, Briggs v. Golden Valley Land and Cattle Co., 97 Idaho 427, 546 P.2d 382 (1976), where these findings are recited but not reviewed.

2. *Fundingsland* and *Mathers* permit "mining," whereas *Baker* does not. Are there physical differences in the aquifers involved which explain the difference in result? Consider the following comments from an omitted part of the opinion in *Baker:*

"We reiterate out holding that Idaho's Ground Water Act clearly prohibits the withdrawal of ground water beyond the average rate of future recharge. In this regard Idaho differs from those of other less fortunate states because we have not yet had to develop legislation regarding withdrawals from non-rechargeable aquifers."

3. What was the effect of priority in *Baker?* In *Fundingsland?* Is its effect in groundwater cases the same as its effect in cases involving surface streams?

4. McGuinness, Water Law with Special Reference to Ground Water 117 (Geological Survey Circular 47, 1951):

"Again, in most aquifers the distribution of wells affects the perennial yield significantly. With a given distribution of wells, an enforced reduction in pumping by cutting off the later appropriators (or, under correlative rights, by reducing the pumpage of all in proportion to the estimated perennial yield of the aquifer and to the amount of land owned by each user) may not prevent local overdevelopment. Reducing the pumpage in one part of an aquifer may not result in an equivalent addition to the supply for other wells, either for a long time or, if the reduction simply results in an increase in the natural discharge from the aquifer, possibly not at all."

5. Wyo.Stat.1977 § 41-3-915:

"[a] * * * If the state engineer shall find after the hearing, and after receiving the advice of the control area advisory board, that the underground water in that area is insufficient for all of the appropriators, he may by order adopt one or more of the following corrective controls: * * *

(ii) He may determine the permissible total withdrawal of underground water in the control area for each day, month or year, and, insofar as may be reasonably done, he shall apportion such permissible total withdrawal among the appropriators holding valid rights to the underground water in the control area in accordance with the relative dates of priority of such rights.

(iii) If he finds that withdrawals by junior appropriators have a material and adverse effect upon the supply available for and needed by senior appropriators, he may order such junior appropriators to cease or reduce withdrawals forthwith.

(iv) If he finds that cessation or reduction of withdrawals by junior appropriators will not result in proportionate benefits to senior appropriators, he may require and specify a system of rotation of use of underground water in the control area.

* * *

(c) Appropriators of underground water from a control area may agree to any method or scheme of control of withdrawals, apportionment, rotation or proration of the common supply of underground water. The state engineer shall encourage and promote such agreements and supply the parties with information and advice. When the state engineer, with the advice of the control area advisory board, shall find that any such agreement, executed in writing and filed in his office, is consistent with the intent, purposes and requirements of this act, and would not be detrimental to the public interest or to the rights of other persons not parties to the agreement, he shall approve the agreement, and thereafter such agreement shall control, until terminated as hereinafter provided, in lieu of any order issued pursuant to subsection (a) of this section."

PASADENA v. ALHAMBRA

Supreme Court of California, 1949.
33 Cal.2d 908, 207 P.2d 17.

[Numerous persons, municipalities and water companies have pumped water for many years from a 40 square mile aquifer known as the western unit of the Raymond Basin. The City of Pasadena brought this action to determine the rights to ground water in the basin and to enjoin an alleged overdraft. The case was referred to the Division of Water Resources of the California Department of Public Works. On the basis of its report, the trial court found that the safe yield of the basin was 18,000 acre feet per year, and that annual withdrawals totalled 24,000 acre feet. This condition had existed since about 1913 and the water table had been steadily lowered toward the point of unreasonable depletion and possible destruction of the source. Most of the parties entered into a stipulation based on the report, restricting total withdrawals to the annual yield, and the court entered a judgment substantially enforcing the stipulation against all parties, allocating to each about two-thirds of the amount previously pumped, and enjoining all pumping in excess of the rights decreed to each party. The California-Michigan Land and Water Company appealed.]

GIBSON, CHIEF JUSTICE. * * * The question of who shall bear the burden of curtailing the overdraft, and in what proportion, depends upon the legal nature and status of the particular water right held by each party. Rights in water in an underground basin, so far as pertinent here, are classified as overlying, appropriative, and prescriptive. Generally speaking, an overlying right, analogous to that of a riparian owner in a surface stream, is the right of the owner of the land to take water from the ground underneath for use on his land within the basin or watershed; the right is based on ownership of the land and is appurtenant thereto. * * * The right of an appropriator depends upon an actual taking of water. * * * Where a taking is wrongful, it may ripen into a prescriptive right. * * *

In the present case some of the parties, including owners of ranches, golf clubs, and cemeteries, have pumped water solely for use on their own land, and their rights at the outset were overlying. The principal takers of water, however, are public utility corporations and municipalities which have either exported water or have used it within the Western Unit for municipal purposes or for sale to the public, and their taking, when commenced, was entirely appropriative. * * *

It follows from the foregoing that, if no prescriptive rights had been acquired, the rights of the overlying owners would be paramount, and the rights of the appropriators would depend on priority of acquisition under the rule that the first appropriator in time is the first in right. The latest in time of the appropriations would then be the first to be curtailed in limiting total production of the area to the safe yield. If such were the case, the overdraft could be eliminated simply by enjoining a part of the latest appropriations, since the record shows that there is ample water to satisfy the needs of all the overlying users and most of the appropriators.

The principal dispute between appellant and respondents, however, concerns whether any water rights in the Western Unit have become prescriptive and, if so, to what extent. Respondents assert that the rights of all the parties, including both overlying users and appropriators, have become mutually prescriptive against all the other parties and, accordingly, that all rights are of equal standing, with none prior or paramount. * * *

The record shows that there has been an actual adverse user of water in the Western Unit. There was an invasion, to some extent at least, of the rights of both overlying owners and appropriators commencing in the year 1913–1914, when the overdraft first occurred. Each taking of water in excess of the safe yield, whether by subsequent appropriators or by increased use by prior appropriators, was wrongful and was in injury to the then existing owners of water rights, because the overdraft, from its very beginning, operated progressively to reduce the total available supply. Although no owner was immediately prevented from taking the water he needed, the report demonstrates that a continuation of the overdraft would eventually result in such a depletion of the supply stored in the underground basin that it would become inadequate. The injury thus did not involve an immediate disability to obtain water, but, rather, it consisted of the continual lowering of the level and gradual reducing of the total amount of stored water, the accumulated effect of which, after a period of years, would be to render the supply insufficient to meet the needs of the rightful owners. * * *

The lowering of the water table resulting from the overdraft was plainly observable in the wells of the parties. * * * This evidence is clearly sufficient to justify charging appellant with notice that there was a deficiency rather than a surplus and that the appropriations causing the overdraft were invasions of the rights of overlying owners and prior appropriators. The elements of prescription being present in the record, the statute of limitations ran against the original lawful holders of water rights to whatever extent their rights were invaded. * * *

Adoption of appellant's position that the water must be allocated, at least as between the municipalities and public utility companies, strictly on the basis of priority in time of appropriation, * * * would result in an unequal sharing of the burden of curtailing the overdraft in that all pumping conducted under authority of certain of the later appropriations would be completely eliminated, whereas no restriction in amount would be imposed upon pumping based on earlier appropriations. Such a result does not appear to be justified where all of the parties have been producing water from the underground basin for many years, and none of them have acted to protect the supply or prevent invasion of their rights until this proceeding was instituted. Moreover, it seems probable that the solution adopted by the trial court will promote the best interests of the public, because a pro tanto reduction of the amount of water devoted to each present use would normally be less disruptive than total elimination of some of the uses.

We hold, therefore, that prescriptive rights were established by appropriations made in the Western Unit subsequent to the commencement of the overdraft, that such rights were acquired against both overlying owners and prior appropriators, that the overlying owners and prior appropriators also obtained, or preserved, rights by reason of the water which they pumped, and that the trial court properly concluded that the production of water in the unit should be limited by a proportionate reduction in the amount which each party had taken throughout the statutory period. * * *

[Affirmed.]

Note

Tehachapi-Cummings County Water Dist. v. Armstrong, 49 Cal.App.3d 992, 122 Cal.Rptr. 918 (1975) held that where all parties in a groundwater basin adjudication are overlying owners using the water for overlying uses, the mutual prescription doctrine should not be applied. The rights of each overlying user must be calculated on the correlative rights doctrine, and if the quantity is insufficient, each is limited to his proportionate share of the total amount available based upon his reasonable need. This share "is predicated not on his past use over a specified period of time, nor on the time he commenced pumping, but solely on his current reasonable and beneficial need for water."

LOS ANGELES v. SAN FERNANDO

Supreme Court of California, 1975.
14 Cal.3d 199, 123 Cal.Rptr. 1, 537 P.2d 1250.

WRIGHT, CHIEF JUSTICE.

The City of Los Angeles filed this action on September 30, 1955, (1) to quiet its title and obtain a declaration of its prior rights to the water underlying the Upper Los Angeles River Area (hereafter referred to as "ULARA"), and (2) to enjoin the defendants from extracting such water other than in subordination to the plaintiff's prior rights. Numerous defendants were eliminated from the case before trial by dismissal, disclaimer, default, or stipulated judgment, and are not parties to this appeal. The remaining defendants now before us are the Cities of San Fernando, Glendale, and Burbank, the Crescenta Valley County Water District, and several private parties whose water claims are all smaller than those of the defendant cities and water district. After a nonjury trial between plaintiff and these defendants, judgment was entered on March 15, 1968, denying plaintiff's claims, awarding prescriptive rights to plaintiff and defendants, and imposing continuous restrictions on the parties' extractions of water commensurate with the available supply. Plaintiff appeals from this judgment and from a judgment entered the same date in favor of the State Water Resources Control Board for its expenses as referee.

The ULARA is the entire watershed of the Los Angeles River and its tributaries. The "valley fill" portion of the ULARA is divided into four subareas. By far the largest of these subareas, comprising 112,047 out of the 123,428 acres in the total valley fill, is the San Fernando subarea. The other three subareas of the valley fill are designated as Sylmar, Verdugo, and Eagle Rock. Sylmar is the area north of the city of San Fernando. Most of Sylmar is within the City of Los Angeles, but it also includes a small slice of San Fernando. * * *

[The court held that in the San Fernando basin all rights are based on the City of Los Angeles' pueblo rights to all sources of the Los Angeles River (see Note 5, supra p. 221) or on each city's right to recapture water imported by it and recharged into the aquifers. Los Angeles was held to have no rights in the Verdugo basin and no issues pertaining to the Eagle Rock area were presented on appeal.]

The trial court's judgment awarded "mutually prescriptive rights" and "restricted pumping" quotas to the parties purportedly pursuant to the decision in City of Pasadena v. City of Alhambra, supra, 33 Cal.2d 908, 207 P.2d 17. Determination of the propriety of this application of *Pasadena* to the present case raises a number of serious legal questions not resolved in *Pasadena.* These include * * * the claimed immunity of cities to prescriptive claims of public and private parties under the 1935 amendment to section 1007 of the Civil Code, the definition of "overdraft," and the requirements of notice of adverse use as they bear on the commencement of the prescriptive period.

In arguing that these and related questions should be resolved in a manner that will sustain the judgment below, defendants seek to reinforce their position by holding up the "mutual prescription doctrine" of the *Pasadena* case as a beneficent instrument for conservation and equitable apportionment of water in ground basins which are subjected to extractions in excess of the replenishment supply. * * * [However,] the allocation of water in accordance with prescriptive rights mechanically based on the amounts beneficially used by each party for a continuous five-year period after commencement of the prescriptive period and before the filing of the complaint, does not necessarily result in the most equitable apportionment of water according to need. A true equitable apportionment would take into account many more factors.[a]

a. The principles by which the United States Supreme Court equitably apportions water among states are illustrated in Nebraska v. Wyoming, 325 U.S. 589, 618, 65 S.Ct. 1332, 1351, 89 L.Ed. 1815 (1945). After observing that apportionment between states whose laws base water rights on priority of appropriation should primarily accord with that principle, the court said: "But if an allocation between appropriation States is to be just and equitable, strict adherence to the priority rule may not be possible. For example, the economy of a region may have been established on

* * *

All water from wells in the Sylmar subarea is drawn from confined aquifers, that is, bodies of ground water cut off from free hydraulic connection with overlying ground water except at the intake. These aquifers reach 12,000 feet in depth.

In the Sylmar basin, the court found that there was overdraft from 1936–1937 through 1941–1942, 1944–1945 through 1953–1954, and 1959–1960 through 1964–1965, and that in the intervening years there was surplus, i.e., the draft was less than the safe yield. Based on the commencement of this overdraft, the court fixed mutually prescriptive rights in the Sylmar basin. However, the court found that the Sylmar basin's safe yield for 1964–1965 exceeded the total of the mutually prescriptive rights, and provided for the "restricted pumping," to which each party is limited in the judgment, by *increasing* the mutually prescriptive rights proportionately so as to aggregate the 1964–1965 safe yield. The respective rights fixed by the court in Sylmar basin, in acre feet, were as follows:

	Mutually prescriptive right	Restricted pumping
Los Angeles	2,440	2,818
San Fernando	2,370	2,737
Two private defendants	567	655
	5,377	6,210

Defendants claim they have acquired rights by mutual prescription under the principles of City of Pasadena v. City of Alhambra (1949) 33 Cal.2d 908, 207 P.2d 17. * * *

Plaintiff contends that its water rights are not subject to prescription, mutual or otherwise, because of the express provisions of Civil Code section 1007. Between 1935 and 1968, this section stated that "no possession by any person, firm or corporation no matter how long continued of any land, *water, water right,* easement or other property whatsoever dedicated to or owned by any * * * city * * * shall ever ripen into any title, interest or right against such * * * city * * *." (Italics added.) * * *

Defendants argue that City of Pasadena v. City of Alhambra, supra, decided that the acquisition of water rights against cities by prescription was not barred by the 1935 amendment to Civil Code section 1007, which had been in effect for two years when the complaint in that

the basis of junior appropriations. So far as possible those established uses should be protected though strict application of the priority rule might jeopardize them. Apportionment calls for the exercise of an informed judgment on a consideration of many factors. Priority of appropriation is the guiding principle. But physical and climatic conditions, the consumptive use of water in the several sections of the river, the character and rate of return flows, the extent of established uses, the availability of storage water, the practical effect of wasteful uses on downstream areas, the damage to upstream areas as compared to the benefits to downstream areas if a limitation is imposed on the former—these are all relevant factors. They are merely an illustrative, not an exhaustive catalogue. They indicate the nature of the problem of apportionment and the delicate adjustment of interests which must be made."

action was filed. But this court did not reach the issue in that case.
* * *

Defendants argue that the limitations placed by Civil Code section 1007 on the acquisition of prescriptive rights apply only to "absolute" prescription and not to "mutual prescription" in which the prescriptive water right is proportionately limited by the continued pumping and use of the water by the owners of the prior rights. Yet defendants correctly acknowledge that this court arrived at its decision in the *Pasadena* case by applying traditional principles of prescription. Moreover, the wording of the statutory restriction is not directed merely at absolute prescriptive rights. The statute declares that "no possession by any person, firm or corporation no matter how long continued" of specified property "shall ever ripen into *any title, interest or right*" against specified public owners. (Italics added.) The restriction clearly encompasses the acquisition of any property interest based on continuous adverse possession or use.

Defendants contend that even if section 1007 immunizes the property of cities and other public entities from the acquisition of prescriptive rights by private parties, it does not interfere with the acquisition of prescriptive rights by public entities against each other. It is argued that the phrase "person, firm or corporation" by which the statute describes the class of parties whose possession is not permitted to ripen into prescriptive rights against specified publicly owned property refers only to *private* persons, firms, and corporations.

We are of the opinion that the 1935 amendment to section 1007 was intended to enlarge the classes of property exempt from prescription by *any* party rather than to immunize such enlarged classes of property from prescription by private parties only. * * *

The decisions forbidding acquisition of prescriptive title to property owned by the state or a local governmental body and devoted to a public use make no distinction based on the private or governmental nature of the party making the prescriptive claim. * * *

* * *

A ground basin is in the state of surplus when the amount of water being extracted from it is less than the maximum that could be withdrawn without adverse effects on the basin's long term supply. While this state of surplus exists, none of the extractions from the basin for beneficial use constitutes such an invasion of any water right as will entitle the owner of the right to injunctive, as distinct from declaratory, relief. Overdraft commences whenever extractions increase, or the withdrawable maximum decreases, or both, to the point where the surplus ends. Thus on the commencement of overdraft there is no surplus available for the acquisition or enlargement of appropriative rights. Instead, appropriations of water in excess of surplus then invade senior basin rights, creating the element of adversity against those rights prerequisite to their owners' becoming entitled to an injunction and thus to the running of any prescriptive period against them.

The trial court defined "surplus" and "overdraft" in terms of "safe yield." The findings state that "[s]urplus is that condition which exists when the draft on the ground water supply is less than the safe yield," and that overdraft exists when such draft "exceeds the safe yield." "Safe yield" is defined as "the maximum quantity of water which can be withdrawn annually from a ground water supply under a given set of conditions without causing an undesirable result." The phrase "undesirable result" is understood to refer to a gradual lowering of the ground water levels resulting eventually in depletion of the supply.

Although the parties differ sharply over the correct meanings of "surplus" and "overdraft" under the present facts, they are in accord over the concept of "safe yield" and the essential correctness of the method by which the referee and the expert witnesses computed the safe yield of the ULARA and its component basins for particular years. Basically, safe yield was deemed equivalent to an adjusted figure for net ground water recharge, consisting of (A) recharge from (1) native precipitation and associated runoff, (2) return flow from delivered imported water, and (3) return flow from delivered ground water less (B) losses incurred through natural ground water depletions consisting of (1) subsurface outflow, (2) excessive evaporative losses in high ground water areas and through vegetation along streams, (3) ground water infiltration into sewers, and (4) rising water outflow, or water emerging from the ground and flowing past Gauging Station No. F57 down the river channel to the sea. The component figures for the particular safe yield year being determined were adjusted to eliminate the effect of fluctuations extraneous to the long range calculation. The adjustment of chief importance here was the use of a 29-year base period, consisting of the water years 1928–1929 through 1956–1957, for the computation of all items dependent upon precipitation. This 29-year period was selected as one for which (1) adequate hydrological data was available and (2) precipitation figures were representative, in both average level and fluctuations, of the 85 years for which weather records were relatively complete.

Plaintiff contends that the trial court's definition of overdraft as a condition in which draft exceeds safe yield, although consistent with the *Pasadena* decision, is insufficient for the facts of the present case. According to plaintiff, overdraft commenced in the ULARA only when (1) total extractions exceeded safe yield and (2) the available water storage capacity of the basin was sufficient to permit cycling of the safe yield throughout the 29-year base period of wet and dry years without causing a waste of water in the wet years. The referee's report as well as other evidence showed that when ground basin levels were relatively high, and storage space correspondingly diminished, waste occurred. Ground basin levels tended to vary in accordance with wide fluctuations in precipitation. Thus if a rising level of extractions were halted at the point of the safe yield based on the 29-year average, ensuing heightening of ground water levels during years of higher-than-average precipitation would cause waste. Since this waste would constitute a loss of basin water in addition to the safe yield extractions, it would eventually create enough additional storage space to stop further similar waste, but the wasted water itself would be lost to any beneficial use. On the other hand, a withdrawal of water from the basin over and above its safe yield in the amount necessary to create the storage space sufficient to prevent the waste would result in a net addition to the beneficially used supply.

We agree with plaintiff that if a ground basin's lack of storage space will cause a limitation of extractions to safe yield to result in a probable waste of water, the amount of water which if withdrawn would create the storage space necessary to avoid the waste and not adversely affect the basin's safe yield is a temporary surplus available for appropriation to beneficial use. Accordingly, overdraft occurs only if extractions from the basin exceed its safe yield plus any such temporary surplus.

On remand questions may arise as to the acquisition of prescriptive rights by plaintiff or defendant City of San Fernando, or both, against the overlying or appropriative rights of private defendants in the Sylmar basin. * * * The findings declare that each party's taking and use of water from each basin "has at all times been open [and] notorious" and for a period of over five years prior to the filing of the complaint has been "continuous" and "continuously and uninterruptedly asserted by [such party] to be and was adverse to any and all claims of each and all of the other parties taking * * * and using water from [the same] basin." * * *

The fact that one party's taking of water from a basin is open, notorious, and under claim of right does not invade any other party's water rights in the basin so as to entitle the other party to injunctive relief or start the running of any prescriptive period against the other party's rights so long as the taking is only from a surplus of basin water, that is, so long as there is not an overdraft on the basin supply. The commencement of overdraft provides the element of adversity which makes the first party's taking an invasion constituting a basis for injunctive relief to the other party. But if the other party is not on *notice* that the overdraft exists, such adverse taking does not cause the commencement of the prescriptive period.

Thus in the present case the trial court erred in basing an award of prescriptive rights on the running of a prescriptive period whose commencement coincided with the commencement of overdraft without making any determination of the time at which the owners of the rights being lost by such prescription were first chargeable with notice of the overdraft. The findings that the takings from the basin were open and notorious and were continuously *asserted* to be adverse does not establish that the owners were on notice of adversity *in fact* caused by the actual commencement of overdraft. Nor have the parties called to our attention any evidence in the record from which the trial court could have fixed any time at which the owners of Sylmar basin rights should reasonably be deemed to have received notice of the commencement of overdraft in the basin. Accordingly, the parties should be permitted to introduce evidence on this issue on remand insofar as necessary to determine prescriptive claims in Sylmar basin consistently with this opinion.

In the Sylmar basin, the trial court found that prior to the filing of the complaint at the end of the water year 1954–1955, overdraft existed continuously from 1936–1937 through 1941–1942 and from 1944–1945 through 1953–1954 but that conversely surplus existed in 1942–1943, 1943–1944 and 1954–1955. Prescriptive rights in the basin were awarded to plaintiff, defendant City of San Fernando and two private defendants based on the "highest continuous annual production of water for beneficial use in any five (5) year period *subsequent to the commencement of overdraft and prior to the filing of the complaint* by each of the parties from the Sylmar basin as to which there has been no cessation of use by it during any subsequent continuous five (5) year period." (Italics added.) From this formula it appears that the award of prescriptive rights may have been based on extractions of water during a continuous five-year period which included years of surplus.

Years of surplus should not be included in the prescriptive period because the taking of surplus water cannot invade the basin water rights of others. Moreover, since adverse taking is impossible during surplus years their occurrence breaks the continuity required for the running of a prescriptive period. Accordingly, the prescriptive period for ground basin water rights must consist of five consecutive years of overdraft.

Under the judgment each party that was awarded a prescriptive right in the Sylmar basin was also assigned a "restricted pumping" quota which was approximately 15 percent greater than such party's prescriptive right. These quotas were arrived at by dividing the 1964–1965 safe yield, found to be 6,210 acre feet, among the parties in proportion to their prescriptive rights. The quotas were not based on any finding that the parties had actually appropriated those amounts.

It was improper to limit total pumping to safe yield by allocating quotas based simply upon a computation of proportionate *increases* in each party's prescriptive right. It was not a foregone conclusion that each party's need for water would increase in exact proportion to its prescriptive right or that other entities would not be desirous and able to apply the increment in supply to other beneficial uses. * * * The trial court lacked authority, however, to allocate unappropriated quantities of water for future taking. (City of San Bernardino v. City of Riverside, supra, 186 Cal. 7, 25, 30–31, 198 P. 784.)

SUMMARY OF RIGHTS AND APPROPRIATE RELIEF

The parties claiming ground water rights in the Sylmar basin are plaintiff, defendant City of San Fernando, and two private defendants, Moordigian and the Wellesley Company. Plaintiff has a prior right to the return flow derived from its deliveries of water it imports into the Sylmar basin from outside the ULARA, similar to its right to such flow in the San Fernando basin. * * * The trial court's award of mutually prescriptive rights in the Sylmar basin's entire safe yield cannot be sustained even as a basis for determining rights in the *native* waters of the basin derived from precipitation within the ULARA because as previously discussed such award disregarded the exemption of cities' water rights from prescription under the 1935 amendment to Civil Code section 1007 and in addition applied incorrect principles in computing the commencement and running of the prescriptive period. Hence, the parties' rights to the native waters of the basin depend on factual issues which the trial court did not consider and which the parties will have an opportunity to litigate after remand.

The record before us indicates that the parties may be able to prove the following kinds of rights in the ground waters of the Sylmar basin:

1. In addition to plaintiff's rights in the return flow attributable to its delivered imports, plaintiff may be able to establish appropriative rights to native ground water, based on its appropriations in excess of such return flow during periods of basin surplus.

2. Defendant San Fernando may show appropriative rights based on its takings during periods of basin surplus of (1) native ground water and (2) any portion of the return flow attributable to plaintiff's delivered imports not recaptured by plaintiff (hereafter referred to as "unrecaptured return flow").

3. The private defendants may show overlying rights to native ground water for reasonable beneficial uses on their overlying land, subject to any prescriptive rights of another party.[b]

4. The private defendants may show appropriative rights to native ground water and unrecaptured return flow based on takings for nonoverlying beneficial uses during periods of basin surplus, subject to any prescriptive rights of another party.

5. Any of the parties may be able to show that the circumstances under which such party extracted water during a period of overdraft

b. Overlying rights take priority over appropriative rights in that if the amounts of water devoted to overlying uses were to consume all the basin's native supply, the overlying rights would supersede any appropriative claims by any party to the basin's native ground water (Corona Foothill Lemon Co. v. Lillibridge (1937) 8 Cal.2d 522, 530–531, 66 P.2d 443) except insofar as the appropriative claims ripened into prescriptive rights (City of Pasadena v. City of Alhambra, supra, 33 Cal.2d at pp. 926–927, 207 P.2d 17). Such prescriptive rights would not necessarily impair the private defendants' rights to ground water for *new* overlying uses for which the need had not yet come into existence during the prescriptive period. (Tulare Irr. Dist. v. Lindsay-Strathmore Irr. Dist., supra, 3 Cal.2d 489, 525–526, 45 P.2d 972.)

before commencement of the present action gave it a prescriptive right against the water rights concurrently held by a private defendant. The effect of the prescriptive right would be to give to the party acquiring it and take away from the private defendant against whom it was acquired either (1) enough water to make the ratio of the prescriptive right to the remaining rights of the private defendant as favorable to the former in time of subsequent shortage as it was throughout the prescriptive period (City of Pasadena v. City of Alhambra, supra, 33 Cal.2d at pp. 931–933, 207 P.2d 17) or (2) the amount of the prescriptive taking, whichever is less (id., at p. 937, 207 P.2d 17).[c]

Principles hereinbefore set forth will govern the trial court's determination on remand of (1) the existence of basin surplus or overdraft in relation to the parties' claims of appropriative rights and (2) the commencement and running of prescriptive periods affecting the parties' claims of prescriptive rights. The court should determine whether the total amount of water covered by all of the rights of the parties exceeds the available supply consisting of the basin's safe yield and any temporary surplus, less possible rights of nonparties.[d] If an insufficiency in the available supply is found to exist, such supply should be allocated as follows: (1) Plaintiff should be allocated the ground water it requires for reasonable beneficial use from the part of the supply shown to constitute return flow attributable to plaintiff's delivered imports. (2) Private defendants should be awarded the full amount of their overlying rights, less any amounts of such rights lost by prescription, from the part of the supply shown to constitute native ground water. (3) The rest of the available supply should be allocated among the holders of appropriative and prescriptive rights in accordance with the principle that "the one first in time is the first in right" (Civ.Code, § 1414). (City of Pasadena v. City of Alhambra, supra, 33 Cal.2d at p. 926, 207 P.2d 17; City of San Bernardino v. City of Riverside, supra, 186 Cal.2d 7, 28, 198 P. 784 (priority principle applies to prescriptive as well as appropriative rights).) * * *

The principal judgment is reversed and the cause is remanded for further proceedings consistent with this opinion.

Notes

1. Case Note: Water Law—A Postscript to the Mutual Prescription Doctrine, XI Land and Water L.Rev. 131 (1976):

c. Even though cities cannot *lose* their water rights by prescription, their *acquisition* of prescriptive ground water rights is subject to the limitations stemming from the lawful owner's self help set forth in City of Pasadena v. City of Alhambra, supra, 33 Cal.2d at pp. 931–933, 207 P.2d 17.

d. The trial court found that no water was being pumped from the San Fernando, Sylmar or Verdugo basins by persons or entities not parties to the action in 1964–1965. Jurisdiction was retained to consider the effect of any subsequent pumping by nonparties on the amounts of pumped water allowed each party under the judgment.

"As a result of *Pasadena,* California cities began to pump as much water as possible in basins other than the Raymond Basin. They had little to lose, since by increasing their extractions, cities could (1) increase their share of an adjusted safe yield prescriptively, (2) retain their share of an adjusted safe yield by increasing their extractions in proportion to other users or (3) at least minimize their loss of the adjusted safe yield by decreasing the proportion available to other users.

"* * *

"By the *Los Angeles* decision, the court lessened the likelihood of overdevelopment of groundwater basins, and encouraged long-range water planning by cities. As cities and other public entities representing the class of groundwater appropriators will be recognized as statutorily protected from prescription, the need to insure their prior rights by 'racing to the pump' will be eliminated. Due to the statutory exemption of cities and other public users, the total water to which one can acquire a prescriptive right has been substantially reduced, thus decreasing the utility of any attempt to acquire prescriptive rights. In addition, the court has placed a barrier to gaining prescription even against statutorily unprotected basin users due to the difficulty of showing notice of adversity which would comply with the requirement for notice set forth in *Los Angeles.*

"The court's utilization of an alternative allocation formula to that found in *Pasadena* was also aimed at alleviating the overdevelopment of groundwater basins by substantially lessening the advantages to be obtained in seeking prescriptive rights. A party pumping after the overdraft has begun may receive nothing, as any prescriptive right gained might be later in time and thus judicially unrecognized.

"* * *

"Coupling the procedural difficulty of acquiring prescriptive rights with the limited amount of water to which prescriptive title may be gained, the *Los Angeles* decision has made the speculative acquisition of prescriptive rights less attractive than other possibilities, though it has not completely eliminated the possibility of an exempted party taking groundwater from an unprotected user without compensation. To the extent that the acquisition of prescriptive rights is deterred by the *Los Angeles* decision, the resources of large producers and distributors should now be turned to development of secured sources of water, with the concomitant rewards for planning of water needs."

2. Could the rule of Los Angeles v. San Fernando be more succinctly stated as follows: "Groundwater rights may be lost by prescription as in *Pasadena,* and the prescribers will take the lost amount in order of priority?"

Can paragraph 5, p. 434, be translated into an algebraic formula? If X equals the total amount of water gained and lost by prescription, then:

$$\frac{\text{Takers' } \textit{Katz} \text{ rights} + X}{\text{Losers' } \textit{Katz} \text{ rights} - X} = \frac{\text{Takers' pumping}}{\text{Losers' pumping}}$$

3. Footnote b of the principal case indicates that unexercised overlying rights may not be subject to prescription. Nevertheless, the trial court in Wright v. Goleta Water District, 174 Cal.App.3d 74, 219 Cal.Rptr. 740 (1985), held that such rights may be subordinated to appropriative and

overlying rights which are being exercised. Noting that an overlying owner's right to groundwater is analogous to a riparian owner's right to a surface stream, the trial court extended *Long Valley*, supra page 365, to groundwater disputes. Consequently, the trial court awarded unexercised overlying rights a lower priority than rights actually being exercised. The Court of Appeals reversed. Finding that *Long Valley* is based on a statutory procedure for the comprehensive determination of all water rights in a stream system by the Water Resources Control Board, it reasoned that the principles of that case were not applicable to groundwater because there exists no similar scheme for the comprehensive determination of groundwater rights.

TOWN OF CHINO VALLEY v. CITY OF PRESCOTT

Supreme Court of Arizona, 1981.
131 Ariz. 78, 638 P.2d 1324.

STRUCKMEYER, CHIEF JUSTICE.

This appeal is from an order of the Superior Court of Yavapai County dismissing the Town of Chino Valley's complaint to enjoin the City of Prescott from withdrawing groundwater from the Granite Creek Critical Groundwater Area. Order of the Superior Court affirmed.

The Town of Chino Valley lies approximately fifteen miles north of the City of Prescott in Yavapai County, Arizona. Prescott owns 164 acres of land in the Chino Valley. In 1948, it drilled wells on some of its Chino Valley property and began transporting groundwater through a seventeen-mile pipeline to its municipal customers. In 1962, pursuant to a petition by Chino Valley residents and A.R.S. § 45–301 et seq., the State Land Department established the Granite Creek Critical Groundwater Area. On September 20, 1970, the Town was incorporated. It was within the Granite Creek Critical Groundwater Area and it owned lands and was withdrawing groundwater from the same underground basin as Prescott. Prescott, itself, was not within the Granite Creek Critical Groundwater Area.

This action was filed on August 21, 1972, seeking to enjoin the pumping of groundwater by Prescott. It did not seek damages for the unlawful pumping or transportation of groundwaters. The lawsuit proceeded at a desultory pace until the order of dismissal on November 3, 1980. Meanwhile, in 1977 the Legislature amended the Arizona Groundwater Code. The Town in 1978 brought an original action in this Court which challenged the constitutionality of the prohibitions against injunctive relief contained in the 1977 amendments. That challenge was rejected. Town of Chino Valley v. State Land Department, 119 Ariz. 243, 580 P.2d 740 (1978).

Thereafter, in June of 1980, the Legislature enacted the Groundwater Management Act, herein called the Act or the 1980 Act.* It

* The 1980 Act provided for the establishment of Active Management Areas which are geographical areas where groundwater supplies are imperiled. A.R.S. §§ 45–411 to –637. Active Management Areas encompass a whole ground-

repealed the 1977 amendments and abolished critical groundwater areas, substituting geographic units of groundwater management called Active Management Areas and Irrigation Non-Expansion Areas. Certain areas which had been declared critical groundwater areas under former laws were included in the Active Management Areas. By A.R.S. § 45–411(A)(3), the Prescott Active Management Area was established. It includes the Little Chino and Upper Agua Fria Sub-basins. Both the Town of Chino Valley and Prescott are within the Little Chino Sub-basin of the Prescott Active Management Area.

By A.R.S. § 45–541(A) of the 1980 Act, transportation of groundwater is allowed within a sub-basin of an Active Management Area. Prescott, being within the Little Chino Sub-basin from which it was drawing water, moved for dismissal of the Town's complaint for injunctive relief. The Superior Court granted Prescott's motion, but ordered that the Town have twenty days in which to file an amended complaint specifying any damages. The Town's appeal from that portion of the trial court's order dismissing appellants' claim for injunctive relief is based upon the asserted unconstitutionality of the Act of 1980 since the Act, by permitting the transportation of groundwater, legitimatizes the prospective withdrawal of groundwater from the Little Chino Sub-basin by Prescott. Appellants' principal attack is that the Act takes property without due process of law and without just compensation. * * *

water basin or basins. A.R.S. § 45–412(B). Groundwater basins are areas designated as enclosing a relatively hydrologically distinct body or related bodies of groundwater. A.R.S. § 45–402(10). Groundwater sub-basins are areas designated so to enclose a smaller hydrologically distinct body of groundwater found within a groundwater basin. A.R.S. § 45–402(25).

The 1980 Act provides limitations on use of groundwater in Active Management Areas. In general the Act restricts new uses of water drawn from Active Management Areas. The Act sets up a system of determining grandfathered rights to use groundwater in Active Management Areas, A.R.S. §§ 45–461 to –482, defining certain usages of groundwater previously being made and allowing these usages to continue. A.R.S. § 45–462. The Act also establishes the rights of cities, towns, private water companies and irrigation districts in Active Management Areas to withdraw as much groundwater as is needed from within their service areas to serve their customers although restrictions are provided on extensions of service areas and the types of service that may be provided by these entities. A.R.S. § 45–491. The Act also specifies a few other new uses of groundwater that may be made in Active Management Areas. It allows limited new withdrawals for domestic purposes. A.R.S. § 45–454. It also sets up a system for obtaining permits to withdraw new amounts of water for certain specific purposes. A.R.S. §§ 45–511 to –528.

Provided withdrawal is permitted under any of the provisions of the Act, transportation of groundwater within the same sub-basin may be made without payment of damages. A.R.S. § 45–541. Transportation of groundwater between sub-basins or away from Active Management Areas is also authorized if the groundwater is allowed to be withdrawn under the Act's provisions, but damages must be paid for any injury caused. A.R.S. §§ 45–542, –543. Rules for determining damage are set out in A.R.S. § 45–545. The transportation rules apply whether in or outside of Active Management Areas, A.R.S. § 45–544, although the restrictions on new uses of groundwater do not apply outside of Active Management Areas. A.R.S. § 45–453.

The Act provides for conservation for all uses of groundwater in Active Management Areas. A.R.S. §§ 45–561 to –579. The Act ends with provisions governing the drilling and registering of wells for withdrawing groundwater, A.R.S. §§ 45–591 to –604, and financial and enforcement provisions to carry out the legislation, A.R.S. §§ 45–611 to –615, –631 to –637.

By the Constitution of Arizona, art. 17, § 1, effective at statehood in 1912, it was provided that the common law doctrine of riparian water rights "shall not obtain or be of any force or effect in the State." See Brasher v. Gibson, 101 Ariz. 326, 330, 419 P.2d 505, 509 (1966). Thereafter, in 1919, the Arizona Legislature provided that the water of all sources falling in streams, canyons, ravines, natural channels or definite underground channels belonged to the public and were subject to appropriation for beneficial use. Waters percolating beneath the soil were not included among those subject to appropriation. Appellants rely on the cases of Howard v. Perrin, 8 Ariz. 347, 76 P. 460 (1904), and Maricopa County Water Conservation District No. 1 v. Southwest Cotton Co., 39 Ariz. 65, 4 P.2d 369 (1931), for their basic proposition that they own the water percolating beneath their lands under the doctrine of reasonable use.

* * *

Appellants urge that the 1980 Act denies them due process of law and just compensation. The question therefore is, what are a landowner's rights in the water percolating under his lands?

In our recent case of Town of Chino Valley v. State Land Dept., 119 Ariz. 243, 580 P.2d 704 (1978) we said:

> "Under the doctrine of reasonable use property owners have the right to capture and use the underground water beneath their land for a beneficial purpose on that land * * *."

This statement we think is supported by the better reasoned decisions in this country. In the absolute sense, there can be no ownership in seeping and percolating waters until they are reduced to actual possession and control by the person claiming them because of their migratory character. Like wild animals free to roam as they please, they are the property of no one. * * *

* * *

We therefore hold that there is no right of ownership of groundwater in Arizona prior to its capture and withdrawal from the common supply and that the right of the owner of the overlying land is simply to the usufruct of the water.

This brings us to conclude that appellants' position that the 1980 Act violates the Fifth and Fourteenth Amendments to the Constitution of the United States and art. 2, § 17 of the Constitution of the State of Arizona as a taking of private property without due process of law and just compensation cannot be sustained.

The Legislature, in Ch. 2 of the 1980 Act, A.R.S. § 45–401, declared:

> "A. The legislature finds that the people of Arizona are dependent in whole or in part upon groundwater basins for their water supply and that in many basins and sub-basins withdrawal of groundwater is greatly in excess of the safe annual yield and that this is threatening to destroy the economy of certain areas of this state and is threatening to do substantial injury to the general economy and

welfare of this state and its citizens. The legislature further finds that it is in the best interest of the general economy and welfare of this state and its citizens that the legislature evoke its police power to prescribe which uses of groundwater are most beneficial and economically effective.

B. It is therefore declared to be the public policy of this state that in the interest of protecting and stabilizing the general economy and welfare of this state and its citizens it is necessary to conserve, protect and allocate the use of groundwater resources of the state and to provide a framework for the comprehensive management and regulation of the withdrawal, transportation, use, conservation and conveyance of rights to use the groundwater in this state."

We do not doubt but that the overdraft of groundwater in this state is a serious problem which has no chance of correcting itself, and that it is necessary for comprehensive legislation to both limit groundwater use and allocate its use among competing interests.

More than twenty-five years ago, this Court decided that the Legislature might choose between competing interests where the supply of groundwater was limited. In Southwest Engineering Co. v. Ernst, 79 Ariz. 403, 291 P.2d 764 (1955), we said in holding constitutional the groundwater act of 1948:

"The legislative finding that the exhaustion of ground water by excessive withdrawals threatens to destroy one of the principal economic resources of the state to the consequential serious injury of all is not disputed. Such a conclusion is obviously justified because unrestrained use must inevitably result either in complete exhaustion of the state's ground water so that in the end the lands dependent thereon will revert to their desert state or in the lowering of water tables so that the increased cost of pumping will reduce these lands to a marginal or submarginal condition." Id. at 408–09, 291 P.2d at 768 (footnote omitted).

We held that there was a preponderant public interest in the preservation of lands then in cultivation as against lands potentially reclaimable "and that where as here the choice is unavoidable because a supply of water is not available for both, we cannot say that the exercise of such choice, controlled by considerations of social policy which are not unreasonable, involves a denial of due process." Id. at 410, 291 P.2d at 769. The Legislature in the Act of 1980 again recognized that the supply of groundwater is limited and again exercised a choice for the preservation and use of groundwater.

Legislation which denies or restricts rights to use property necessarily results in a diminution of that property's value. Yet the United States Supreme Court has on numerous occasions upheld under the state's police power regulations of land use which have virtually destroyed private interests. * * * In the present case, appellants may make such use of their property as they choose, except that their lands may not be irrigated if they were not legally irrigated in the last five years. The 1980 Act furthers legitimate state interests.

Legislatures of various states have from time to time abolished the prevailing uses of groundwater and substituted other plans for its use. State courts have uniformly rejected the idea that groundwater percolating through the soil may not be limited and regulated and must be acquired by eminent domain. Village of Tequesta v. Jupiter Inlet Corp., 371 So.2d 663 (Fla.), cert. denied, 444 U.S. 965, 100 S.Ct. 453, 62 L.Ed.2d 377 (1979); Williams v. Wichita, 190 Kan. 317, 340–41, 374 P.2d 578, 595–96 (1962), cert. denied, 375 U.S. 7, 84 S.Ct. 46, 11 L.Ed.2d 38 (1963); Crookston Cattle Co. v. Minnesota Department of Natural Resources, 300 N.W.2d 769, 774 (Minn.1980); Baeth v. Hoisveen, 157 N.W.2d 728, 733 (N.D.1968); Knight v. Grimes, 80 S.D. 517, 523–27, 127 N.W.2d 708, 711–14 (1964).

> "Like zoning legislation, legislation which limits or regulates the right to use underlying water is permissible. * * * Where regulation operates to arbitrate between competing public and private land uses, however, as does the water priority statute in this case, such legislation is upheld even where the value of the property declines significantly as a result." Crookston Cattle Co. v. Minnesota Department of Natural Resources, 300 N.W.2d at 774 (citation omitted).

We hold that the Act of 1980 does not deny appellants due process of law and does not require that they be paid compensation for any possible diminution of their rights which they may have had under the doctrine of reasonable use.

* * *

Many and varied interests are affected by the 1980 Act. These interests are apparent in the briefs which amici curiae have filed. We express our appreciation for their excellence and the assistance which they have given the Court. Some matters have been raised and argued which were not addressed by the parties. As to these, it is the rule that amici curiae are not permitted to create, extend, or enlarge issues beyond those raised and argued by the parties. City of Tempe v. Prudential Insurance Company of America, 109 Ariz. 429, 510 P.2d 745 (1973). And see the second *Bristor* opinion, 75 Ariz. 227, 230, 255 P.2d 173, 175 (1953), where the Court commented:

> "It was never alleged in the complaint nor contended by the plaintiffs in assignment of error or briefs that they had appropriated percolating water. This issue was apparently introduced into the case by amici curiae who have no right to create, extend or enlarge the issues."

This Court will only decide issues raised and argued by the parties.

The order of the court below is affirmed.

Notes

1. The court in *Chino Valley* glosses over the long and tortuous path of Arizona groundwater law from ownership to reasonable use, through critical areas and prohibitions against transportation. The ancient history

is well told in Mann, The Politics of Water in Arizona (University of Arizona 1963); the struggle to free the water from the overlying land can be found in Jarvis v. State Land Department (I), 104 Ariz. 527, 456 P.2d 385 (1969); (II), 106 Ariz. 506, 479 P.2d 169 (1970); (III), 113 Ariz. 350, 550 P.2d 227 (1976); and Farmers Investment Co. v. Bettwy, 113 Ariz. 520, 558 P.2d 14 (1976). The Arizona Groundwater Management Act is largely a reaction to the last case. The "legislative history" of this "most comprehensive groundwater code in the nation" was short: a special session passed the act in a single day and the Governor signed it into law the following day. The truly amazing story of the Groundwater Study Commission that prepared the first draft and the negotiations, concessions and compromises of the cities, farmers and mining companies whose "hired guns" hammered out the final bill in a "rump session" is told in Connall, A History of the Arizona Groundwater Management Act, 1982 Arizona State L.J. 313.

The act can only be described as enormous, and enormously complicated. The court's summary in the footnote is a thumbnail sketch; another attempt, with different emphasis, was made in Trelease, Conjunctive Use of Groundwater and Surface Water, 27A Rocky Mt.Min.L.Inst. 1853 (1982):

"The 1980 Arizona Groundwater Management Act is the culmination of a long struggle to bring some order out of the chaos resulting from the disastrous judicial adherence to the so-called "reasonable use rule" that allowed every landowner unrestricted pumping for use on his land, but severely limited the transportation of water to places where it was needed for municipal and industrial use. The rate of overdraft was checked by the legislative restriction of new irrigation wells in critical areas, but cities, mining companies, and farmers hacked away at Arizona's very slowly recharging aquifers until overdraft of groundwater reached 2.2 million acre-feet per year. The Act is an enormously complex piece of regulation, carefully designed to impose strict controls on previously unregulated groundwater withdrawals with the least possible disruption. All existing uses of groundwater are converted into 'grandfathered rights' and adjusted in quantity to meet new standards of conservation. The law's main design is to reduce overdraft, so it requires maximum use of surface water before groundwater is used. 'Surface water' will include a very large block of Colorado River water imported under the Central Arizona Project (CAP) now nearing completion. CAP importations will begin at 1.6 million acre-feet per year, but this will reduce to 1.1 million acre-feet as upper basin states use up their entitlement under the Colorado River Compact.

"The Arizona scheme will be more than merely adding CAP water to existing uses. By 1990, each of the four major water-short areas must have a program for augmentation that must include incentives for artificial recharge. The State Director of Water Resources also has general management powers that will enable him to make substitute water supplies available for users who can or must take them in place of groundwater.

"The largest type of conjunctive use will be the joint use by irrigation districts of groundwater and imported and stored surface waters. Where these are commingled prior to being delivered to users, the irrigation district must manage them in a way that will best promote conservation of both surface and groundwater supplies and minimize the pumping of groundwater. For ease of delivery and other reasons, some users in conjunctive use areas will receive less surface water than their rights call for, and the balance will be made up from groundwater. Other users will receive predominantly surface water. The district will keep accounts which will treat all recipients as having received the maximum amount of surface water to which they were entitled and an amount of groundwater sufficient to make up the total received, even though in particular instances all groundwater or all surface water may have been received. An important reason for this is that groundwater uses are subject to 'irrigation water duties,' strict controls on the quantity used. While groundwater duties cannot be used to diminish surface water deliveries under appropriative rights, if a farm is irrigated by both surface and groundwater, the total is subject to the groundwater duty.

"Of particular interest to this audience are the provisions relating to mining and power generation. If new and expanded uses will require water in addition to grandfathered rights, a company can get a permit to pump new groundwater, but only after almost every other possible source has been exhausted. A permit may be issued only if the amount of groundwater available from dewatering the mine is insufficient, and if uncommitted municipal and industrial CAP water is not available at current industrial delivery rates. Furthermore, before a mining or industrial use permit can be granted, water of adequate quality available from other sources, such as saline water or treated sewage effluent, must be used even though the cost may exceed by up to 25% what the permittee would otherwise pay to pump groundwater. The permit will be issued for fifty years, subject to renewal, and if at any time during the permit period CAP water or surface water or effluent can be substituted for groundwater, the Director may require the permittee to use such water."

Additional institutional and economic measures are summarized in Note at the end of this chapter, page ——, infra.

2. The doctrine of reasonable use threatened to strangle Arizona's growth and economy by restricting the use of water to lands overlying aquifers. At the same time, the doctrine proved ineffective in preventing ruinous overdevelopment of Arizona's groundwaters. What premise central to the reasonable use doctrine was missing in Arizona? See, Restatement of Torts, 2d, § 858, comments b and e.

3. The English rule, of course, permits the person seeking a supply of groundwater for non-overlying uses to purchase the land on which the wells are to be located or to buy the landowner's right to abstract the subjacent water. See Fire District No. 1 v. Graniteville Spring Water Co., 103 Vt. 89, 152 A. 42 (1930); Texas Co. v. Burkett, 117 Tex. 16, 296 S.W. 273 (1927).

The American rule in and of itself does not prohibit the use of groundwater off the overlying land. The water is still regarded as the overlying landowner's "property," to make use of where he pleases or to sell if he chooses, as long as he does not harm his neighbor. Schenck v. Ann Arbor, 196 Mich. 75, 163 N.W. 109 (1917).

The great majority of cases adopting the "American rule" are styled "______ v. City of ______." Why?

In Canada v. City of Shawnee, 179 Okl. 53, 64 P.2d 694 (1936), the city bought a 73 acre tract of rural land, installed 12 wells with powerful pumps and lowered the water table below a neighboring farmer's domestic well. He sought and obtained an injunction, but on rehearing, the court remanded the cause with directions for the trial court to set a reasonable time within which the defendant city might tender the issue of eminent domain and proceed to determine the damages in the manner provided by statute for that purpose, and to issue the injunction only if this procedure was not followed or damages were not paid.

What would a city condemn from an overlying landowner? How would it be valued under the English rule? Under the American rule? In an "American rule" jurisdiction, what would it condemn from neighboring landowners?

3. Under the Oklahoma Groundwater Act the Water Resources Board is to make a hydrologic survey of each fresh water groundwater basin or sub-basin, determine its maximum annual yield based on a minimum life for the basin of 20 years and, after hearing, allocate this to each acre of land overlying the basin or subbasin. Permits are issued only to applicants owning the land on which a well is to be located or holding a valid lease from such owner. 82 Okl.Stat.Ann. §§ 1020.4–1020.6, 1020.11. As yet, however, this apparent attempt to make the absolute ownership concept come true seems to be considerably modified in its administration. By 1985, determinations of annual yield and proportionate shares had been completed in only a few basins. In the remaining areas of the state the Water Resources Board has been quite restrained in doling out to overlying owners only "temporary permits" to "appropriate" limited amounts of groundwater based not on allocations under the statute but on specific needs for beneficial, non-wasteful uses. See Lowrey v. Hodges, 555 P.2d 1016 (Okla.1976); Texas County Irrigation & Water Resources Ass'n, Inc. v. Cities Service Oil Co., 570 P.2d 49 (Okla.1977); Hodges v. Oklahoma Water Resources Bd., 580 P.2d 980 (Okla.1978). Oklahoma Water Resources Bd. v. Texas County Irrigation and Water Resources Ass'n., 711 P.2d 38 (Okla. 1985). The last case confirmed that the groundwater act permits groundwater to be taken off the lands from which it is produced. However, the case also introduced concepts of "waste by depletion" and "waste by pollution," which seem contrary to the intent of the act and seem certain to complicate implementation of the act even further.

STOKES v. MORGAN

Supreme Court of New Mexico, 1984.
101 N.W. 195, 680 P.2d 335.

FEDERICI, CHIEF JUSTICE.

This is an action involving two applications for change in point of diversion and place of use of groundwater rights in the Portales Underground Water Basin (Basin). The State Engineer approved the changes and the protestants appealed the decisions to the District Court of Roosevelt County. By agreement of the parties, the actions were combined for trial. In a trial de novo the court ruled in favor of the protestants and denied the transfers. Both applicants appealed the district court decision. We reverse.

On December 1, 1981, the Federal Land Bank of Wichita and David Sanders (Sanders) filed three applications to change the point of diversion and place of use of irrigation rights within the eastern administrative area of the Basin. Calvin Blevins and Robert Stokes (protestants) protested the move pursuant to NMSA 1978, Section 72–12–7, claiming that the move would impair their existing water rights. After an administrative hearing, the State Engineer found that the proposed move would not impair existing water rights and granted the permit to move the point of diversion.

On January 4, 1982, Robert Morgan (Morgan) filed an application for a permit to change the point of diversion of certain wells in the Basin. Protestants objected to this move for the same reasons that they challenged the Sanders application. The State Engineer concluded that the move would not impair existing water rights and granted the permit to move the point of diversion.

In both cases the parties agreed that the quantitative change in the water supply would be insignificant. The real issue in each case was whether termination of pumping at the move-from wells and commencement of pumping at the move-to wells would cause an increase in salinity in neighboring wells which would result in a decrease in crop yields. The Morgan and Sanders applications have three things in common: (1) all of the move-from and move-to locations are located in the eastern administrative area of the Basin; (2) Calvin Blevins and Robert Stokes protested each application; and (3) the important issue in each case is whether the moves would cause an increase in salinity which would constitute impairment of neighboring water rights. Because of these similarities the two cases were consolidated for appeal in the district court. On December 9, 1982, the district court judge rendered a single decision reversing the two orders of the State Engineer. In the appeal to this Court, Morgan and Sanders (applicants) claim that the district court erred in finding impairment, and also erred in the issuance of a single judgment to dispose of two factually distinct applications.

The move-from and move-to locations in these cases are located in the Portales Valley, a broad, shallow depression in the eastern plains area of New Mexico. Surface water in the valley is scarce and consists primarily of relatively small, saline lakes. The Basin is geologically an abandoned river valley filled with alluvial material derived from the Rocky Mountains. Saturated thickness of the aquifer in the area in question varies from 40 to 140 feet. The aquifer is being mined heavily, primarily for irrigation purposes. Water in the southern part of the aquifer is of a lower quality than that to the north. The water quality interface runs generally from the southeast to northwest, from the north of Section 29, Township 2 S., Range 36 E. to the southern half of Section 10, Township 2 S., Range 35 E. * * * The interface appears to coincide with a depression or trough in the water table. The move-from locations of Sanders' wells are south of this interface and the move-to locations and protestants' wells are north of the interface. The Morgan move-from and move-to locations both appear to be north of the interface, although its configuration is not well defined in this area. In the time period from 1962 to 1982 the interface has migrated some distance to the north. Protestants argue that water to the south of the interface is not suitable for irrigation and that granting the Morgan and Sanders applications will accelerate the rate of intrusion of salt water into the aquifer underlying their wells. Protestants claim that this acceleration will shorten the effective lives of their wells and that this reduction in life expectancy constitutes impairment of their rights.

In a case such as this there are two separate bases upon which a showing of no impairment may be founded. The first is that the proposed increase in pumping will not significantly accelerate the rate of intrusion of poor quality water. The second is that the quality of the intruding water is still good enough to be used for existing purposes.

The rate of movement of water within an aquifer has been studied and a simple relationship between the hydrostatic gradient and water velocity has been found. This relationship generally follows Darcy's Law.

The rate of intrusion is important because, as this Court has previously recognized, "the beneficial use by the public of the waters in a closed or non-rechargeable basin requires giving to the use of such waters a time limitation." Mathers v. Texaco, Inc., 77 N.M. 239, 245, 421 P.2d 771, 776 (1966). The supply of water available from the shallow nonrecharging aquifer system of the Basin is primarily limited to stored water that has accumulated in the aquifer system over a period of several thousand years. At the present time water is being mined from the aquifer at a rate which is significantly higher than the recharge rate. Therefore, the aquifer has a finite life expectancy.

The State Engineer has developed a system of administration for the Basin which is intended to provide a reasonable measure of protection to existing water rights without unduly restricting the full economic utilization of existing water supplies in the Basin. S. Galloway and J. Wright, Administration of Water Rights, Portales Valley Underground Water Basin, New Mexico 17 (Office of the State Engineer, 1968) (introduced as State's Exhibit No. 5). For purposes of administration, townships within the Basin were divided into nine square units of four sections each. Life expectancies for each block were calculated by dividing the average effective saturated thickness of the aquifer by the average annual historical water level change beneath the block. Decisions as to whether to allow additional appropriations are based on the life expectancy of the administrative block and immediately surrounding blocks. If the life expectancy is calculated to be less than 40 years from 1956, the block is considered to be fully appropriated. Id. at 24. Although this system obviously does not take into account water quality problems, it nonetheless indicates a time frame which should be considered in a determination of whether an increased rate of intrusion constitutes impairment.

The second important consideration in salinity impairment cases is the quantification of acceptable levels of degradation in water quality. Applicants contend that impairment, in the context of agricultural water use, should be defined as a decrease in crop yield. Applicants argue that any increase in salinity in protestants' wells which does not result in decreased productivity does not constitute impairment. This appears to be the standard that was followed in City of Roswell v. Reynolds, 86 N.M. 249, 522 P.2d 796 (1974). Protestants contend, on the other hand, that lower salinity water is always preferable to higher salinity water for agricultural purposes and that any measurable increase in salinity necessarily constitutes impairment. The actual determination of whether an increase in salinity constitutes impairment is more complex than either party suggests.

An argument presented by applicants is that an increase in salinity is analogous to a lowering of the level of the water table (or a decrease in pressure in an artesian aquifer). This Court has held that a lowering of the water table does not necessarily constitute impairment of the water rights of adjoining appropriators. Mathers v. Texaco, Inc., 77 N.M. 239, 421 P.2d 771 (1966); Application of Brown, 65 N.M. 74, 332 P.2d 475 (1958). It is not clear that this analogy is a good one. A lowering of the water table may require existing wells to be deepened or pumping lift increased. Although this places an increased economic burden on owners of existing wells, it does not normally destroy the usefulness of the well. Generally, wells which must be retired from agricultural use because of insufficient quantities of water for irrigation may still produce enough water for domestic use. Increased salinity, however, has been recognized as a more serious, long-lasting problem in the underground water supply.

* * *

Regardless of the classification system used, in this case it appears that water south of the trough is of significantly lower quality than that north of the trough. Therefore, a situation exists in which intrusion of poor quality water could result in impairment of existing rights. Although it is clear that all factors must be considered on a case-by-case basis, City of Roswell v. Berry, 80 N.M. 110, 452 P.2d 179 (1969), a change in water quality from Dregne and Maker class 1 to class 2 (or from class 2 to class 3) that would result from the granting of a permit creates a strong inference of impairment. In this case there is at least a one-class difference between water north of the interface and that to the south. However, in order to find impairment, there must also be evidence that the grant of a permit would result in a reasonable scientific probability of a significant increase in the rate of intrusion of lower quality water into the fresh water aquifer. There must also be evidence of a causal connection between the drilling of the well in question and the increased movement of the water quality interface. In this case there is a lack of evidence in the record to support the impairment claimed due to an increased rate of intrusion.

Protestants argue that NMSA 1978, Section 72–12–7 imposes the burden of proof on the applicant to show no impairment will result from the relocation of the well. "No impairment" does not necessarily mean "no change in conditions." This Court has previously held that the lowering of a water table does not necessarily constitute impairment, even though there may be some negative economic impact on adjacent water users. Mathers v. Texaco, Inc., 77 N.M. 239, 421 P.2d 771 (1966); Application of Brown, 65 N.M. 74, 332 P.2d 475 (1958). This result is necessary if the water is to be put to beneficial use, and if the use is to be made available to more than the initial appropriator. 77 N.M. at 245, 421 P.2d at 777. The same common-sense approach should be applied in salinity cases. New withdrawals which cause a minimal acceleration in the rate of saltwater intrusion or a minimal increase in salinity do not constitute impairment as a matter of law. Because of the number of variables involved it is impossible to set strict guidelines as to what constitutes a reasonable scientific probability of a significant increase in the rate of intrusion. The determination of whether there is impairment must be made on a case-by-case basis.

In applying this standard to the case before us we find that both applicants met their burden of proof. Testimony that the State Engineer has made a finding of no impairment pursuant to a valid hearing is considered strong evidence of no impairment. Spencer v. Bliss, 60 N.M. 16, 287 P.2d 221 (1955). The special knowledge and experience of state agencies should be accorded deference.

The State Engineer found, and there was expert testimony at the trial, that the small amount of water being pumped would have a minimal effect on the movement of the poor quality water in the vicinity of the move-to wells.

In opposition to the applicants' case, protestants presented expert testimony that increased pumping to the north would accelerate movement of the poor quality water in that direction. Protestants, however, failed to present evidence on the magnitude of this acceleration claiming that any increase, no matter how small, constitutes impairment. Protestants' expert, Mr. Kelly, admitted on cross-examination that the amount and rate of movement of the saline water was not a part of his study. Mr. Kelly also testified that it is clear that the quality of water in this area has degraded in the last twenty years. This degradation is undoubtedly an unfortunate condition but protestants have not shown that the proposed move will cause a significant change in the rate of deterioration.

* * *

The district court is reversed in both cases. The cause is remanded for entry of judgment granting permits to both applicants. Appellants shall recover their costs on appeal.

Notes

1. In Colorado, transfers of rights to groundwaters tributary to a stream are within the jurisdiction of the water judge of the appropriate water division. Colo.Rev.Stat.1973 § 37–92–203. For the division of authority over transfers of rights in designated groundwater basins between the Colorado Ground Water Commission and Ground Water Management Districts, see Cherokee Water Dist. v. State, 196, Colo. 192, 585 P.2d 586 (1978).

2. Unappropriated water in quantities usable by a city underlie A's irrigable lands, and the City of B desires to drill a well on the land and build a pipeline across it. In an appropriation state, what would the city buy or condemn from A? Suppose (a) that the city's withdrawals will not prevent A from obtaining a permit for a well to irrigate his land, or (b) that because of well-spacing requirements and "safe yield" restrictions on withdrawals B's well will prevent A from obtaining an appropriation for irrigating his land. See the dictum in Fairfield Irrigation Co. v. Carson, 122 Utah 225, 247 P.2d 1004 (1952): "Under our concept of the law of artesian basins prior to 1935, no one could by appropriation and beneficial use acquire a right to such waters as against the owner of the land on which the basin was located * * *. Under the new concept, the only difference is that such waters are subject to appropriation in accordance with the law even as against the landowner where the basin is located."

Suppose the C Co. seeks the water under A's land for industrial use. Most of the statutes allowing private eminent domain for obtaining rights-of-way for ditches and pipelines (supra pp. 114 to 121) do not expressly include wells. Can A demand a "lease" from C similar to an oil and gas lease, requiring payment of a royalty to him? Can A base the consideration charged for a grant of a right-of-way on the quantity of water withdrawn? Does it make any difference whether A will or will not be able to make a subsequent appropriation for irrigation? Does it make any difference whether the appropriation statute is based on the theory of *Dority,* supra p. 403, or *Knight,* p. 406, Note 1?

FRIENDSWOOD DEVELOPMENT CO. v. SMITH–SOUTHWEST INDUSTRIES, INC.

Supreme Court of Texas, 1978.
576 S.W.2d 21.

DANIEL, JUSTICE.

The question in this case is whether landowners who withdrew percolating ground waters from wells located on their own land are liable for subsidence which resulted on lands of others in the same general area.

Smith-Southwest Industries and other landowners located in the Seabrook and Clear Lake area of Harris County brought this class action in 1973 against Friendswood Development Company and its corporate parent, Exxon Corporation, alleging that severe subsidence of their lands was caused by the defendants' past and continuing withdrawals of vast quantities of underground water from wells on defendants' nearby lands. Friendswood, alleged to be the operator of the wells, joined as third party defendants numerous parties alleged to be withdrawing ground water in the same general area. Friendswood and Exxon moved for a summary judgment against the plaintiffs, and it was granted by the trial court along with denial of relief in the third party actions. The Court of Civil Appeals reversed and remanded, holding that plaintiffs' petition stated a cause of action in nuisance and negligence and that the summary judgment record raises genuine issues of material fact with regard thereto. * * *

Reports in the record and publications of official agencies reflect that land subsidence in Harris County is not peculiar to or confined within the Galveston Bay and Clear Creek areas described in plaintiffs' petition. Rather it is a problem which has existed for many years in Harris and Galveston Counties. Harris County alone had 2,635 ground water wells in the inventory compiled by the U.S. Geological Survey in cooperation with the Texas Water Development Board in 1972. The Chicot and Evangeline aquifers underlie the Houston-Galveston region, which includes all of Harris and Galveston Counties and parts of adjacent counties. These two aquifers furnish all of the ground water pumped in the Houston-Galveston region, according to the U.S. Geological Report prepared by R.K. Gabrysch and C.W. Bonnet in 1974. This report states that water level declines of as much as 200 feet have resulted in wells completed in the Chicot aquifer and as much as 325 feet in the Evangeline aquifer during 1943–73, and "the declines in artesian pressures have resulted in a pronounced regional subsidence of the land surface." It states that the area in which there has been subsidence of one foot or more has increased from 350 square miles in 1954 to about 2,500 square miles in 1973. The contour lines of this area encompass practically all of Harris and Galveston Counties and include all of the principal areas of ground water withdrawals. Maps in the report indicate that the land and wells involved in this suit are in or near the "Johnson Space Center Area," where the land surface subsided about 2.12 feet between 1964 and 1973. * * *

Plaintiffs have alleged an action in tort based upon the general rule that a landowner has a duty not to use his property so as to injure others—*sic utere tuo ut alienum non laedas.* Storey v. Central Hide & Rendering Co., 148 Tex. 509, 226 S.W.2d 615 (1950); Turner v. Big Lake Oil Co., 128 Tex. 155, 96 S.W.2d 221 (1936); Gulf, C. & S.F. Ry. Co. v. Oakes, 94 Tex. 155, 58 S.W. 999 (1900). The Court of Civil Appeals cited the above cases and this general rule of tort law in holding that plaintiffs were entitled to a trial on the allegations of nuisance and negligence. The problem is that those cases, none of which related to ground water withdrawals, involved liability for the *unreasonable use* of correlative property rights or the balancing of legal and equitable rights between property owners. This is a concept which was deliberately rejected with respect to withdrawals of underground water when this Court adopted the common law rule that such rights are not correlative, but are absolute, and thus are not subject to the conflicting "reasonable use" rule. Houston & T.C. Ry. Co. v. East, 98 Tex. 146, 81 S.W. 279 (1904). * * *

In holding that the owner may withdraw water from beneath his land without liability for lowering the water table and thus damaging his neighbor's well and land, the Court mentioned only waste and malice as possible limitations to the rule. Absent these, the Court clearly embraced the doctrine stated in Acton v. Blundell, supra, that this type of damage "falls within the description *damnum absque injuria,* which cannot become the ground of action." * * *

In 1975 the Legislature undertook to retard further subsidence in Harris and Galveston Counties by creating a subsidence district with power to prevent future well spacing and excessive pumping of the nature alleged to have occurred in this case. Previously, in 1949 the Legislature provided for the creation of districts for the purpose of "conservation, preservation, protection, recharging, and prevention of waste of underground water * * *." In 1973, the Legislature added to such purposes the authority "to control subsidence caused by withdrawal of water * * *."

It is of some importance to note that in the laws authorizing these regulatory Underground Water Districts and the Harris-Galveston Coastal Subsidence District, the Legislature specifically confirmed private ownership of underground water. It provided: "The ownership and rights of the owner of land and his lessees and assigns in underground water are hereby recognized, and nothing in this Act shall be construed as depriving or divesting the owner or his lessees and assigns of the ownership or rights * * *," subject only to the regulatory rules to be promulgated by the districts. See Vernon's Tex.Water Code Ann. § 52.002 and Sec. 29, Ch. 284, Acts 64 Leg. 1975.

Although the *East, Corpus Christi,* and *Williams* cases involved damages to wells and lands of the plaintiffs because the water tables beneath their lands were lowered by ground water withdrawals of the defendants, none of these nor any other Texas case has dealt specifically with land subsidence resulting from such pumping of underground waters. In other jurisdictions adhering to the English ground water rule, liability for neighboring land subsidence has been denied. Langbrook Properties, Ltd. v. Surrey County Council, [1969] 3 ALL E.R. 1424 (Ch.1969); New York Continental Jewell Filtration Co. v. Jones, 37 App.D.C. 511 (D.C.Cir.1911); English v. Metropolitan Water Board, 1 K.B. 588 (1907); Elster v. City of Springfield, 30 N.E. 274 (Ohio 1892); Popplewell v. Hodgkinson, [1861–73] ALL E.R. 996 (Ex.1869). * * *

We agree that some aspects of the English or common law rule as to underground waters are harsh and outmoded, and the rule has been severely criticized since its reaffirmation by this Court in 1955. Most of the critics, however, recognize that it has become an established rule of property law in this State, under which many citizens own land and water rights. The rule has been relied upon by thousands of farmers, industries, and municipalities in purchasing and developing vast tracts of land overlying aquifers of underground water. Approximately 50,000 wells are used to irrigate 2,800,000 acres in the thirteen county High Plains area of West Texas. As shown in the official reports cited earlier in this opinion, over 2,600 water wells have been drilled in Harris County alone while this rule of immunity from liability was in effect. The very wells which brought about this action were drilled after the English rule had been reaffirmed by this Court in 1955.

As heretofore mentioned, the Legislature has entered the field of regulation of ground water withdrawals and subsidence. This occurred after geologists, hydrologists, and engineers had developed more accurate knowledge concerning the location, source, and measurement of percolating underground waters, and after legislators became aware of the potential conflicts inherent in the unregulated use of ground water under the English rule of ownership. With a rule that recognizes ownership of underground water by each individual under his own land, but with no limitation on the manner and amount which another individual landowner might produce (absent willful waste and malicious malice), legislative action was essential in order to provide for conservation and protection of public interests.

The legislative policy contained in Chapter 52 of the Texas Water Code is designed to limit the exercise of that portion of the English rule which has been interpreted as giving each landowner the right to take all the water he pleases without regard to the effect on other lands in the same area. * * * Providing policy and regulatory procedures in this field is a legislative function. It is well that the Legislature has assumed its proper role, because our courts are not equipped to regulate ground water uses and subsidence on a suit-by-suit basis.

This case, however, gives the Court its first opportunity to recognize, and to encourage compliance with, the policy set forth by the Legislature and its regulatory agencies in an effort to curb excessive underground water withdrawals and resulting land subsidence. It also affords us the opportunity to discard an objectionable aspect of the court-made English rule as it relates to subsidence by stating a rule for the future which is more in harmony with expressed legislative policy. We refer to the past immunity from negligence which heretofore has been afforded ground water producers solely because of their "absolute" ownership of the water.

As far as we can determine, there is no other use of private real property which enjoys such an immunity from liability under the law of negligence. This ownership of underground water comes with ownership of the surface; it is part of the soil. Yet, the use of one's ground-level surface and other elements of the soil is without such insulation from tort liability. Our consideration of this case convinces us that there is no valid reason to continue this special immunity insofar as it relates to future subsidence proximately caused by negligence in the manner which wells are drilled or produced in the future. It appears that the ownership and rights of all landowners will be better protected against subsidence if each has the duty to produce water from his land in a manner that will not negligently damage or destroy the lands of others.

Therefore, if the landowner's manner of withdrawing ground water from his land is negligent, willfully wasteful, or for the purpose of malicious injury, and such conduct is a proximate cause of the subsidence of the land of others, he will be liable for the consequences of his conduct. The addition of negligence as a ground of recovery shall apply only to future subsidence proximately caused by future withdrawals of ground water from wells which are either produced or drilled in a negligent manner after the date this opinion becomes final.

While this addition of negligence as a ground of recovery in subsidence cases applies to future negligence in producing water from existing wells and those drilled or produced in a negligent manner in the future, it has been suggested that this new ground of recovery should be applied in the present cause of action. This is often done when a court writes or adds a new rule applicable to personal injury cases, but seldom when rules of property law are involved. Klocke v. Klocke, 276 Mo. 572, 208 S.W. 825 (1919); 10 A.L.R.3d 1371, 1388; Currier, *Time and Change in Judge-Made Law: Prospective Overruling,* 51 Va.L.Rev. 201, 242–43 (1965). This is because precedent is necessarily a highly important factor when problems regarding land or contracts are concerned. In deeds, property transactions, and land developments, the parties should be able to rely on the law which existed at the time of their actions.

Accordingly, the judgment of the Court of Civil Appeals is reversed and the judgment of the trial court is affirmed.

POPE, JUSTICE, dissenting.

I respectfully dissent. The court has decided this cause upon the mistaken belief that the case is governed by the ownership of ground water. Plaintiffs assert no ownerships to the percolating waters pumped and extracted from the ground by defendants. They make no complaint that their own wells have been or will be pumped dry. They seek no damages for the defendants' sale of the water. Plaintiffs' action calls for no change in nor even a review of the English rule of "absolute ownership" of ground water, the American rule of "reasonable use" of ground water, nor the Texas rule of "nonwasteful" use of ground water. They claim no correlative rights in the water. The Texas law of percolating waters is not put in issue by this suit, and there is no occasion to overrule that law either now or prospectively.
* * *

Plaintiffs' complaint is that defendants are causing subsidence of their land. They assert an absolute right to keep the surface of their land at its natural horizon. The landowners' right to the subjacent support for their land is the only right in suit, and this is a case of original impression. * * *

The error of the majority is its narrow focus upon the right of the defendants to pump ground water. We should enlarge our vision so we can see what this lawsuit is about. I do not believe it is sound law that the right to pump water is the power to destroy the surface of surrounding landowners. If defendants argue that they have an absolute right to pump groundwater, plaintiffs reply that they too have an absolute right to the support of their natural surface. According to some of the summary judgment proofs, the defendants with knowledge have destroyed and are destroying the natural surface estate of the plaintiffs. The summary judgment proofs include showings that the plaintiffs own lands that were originally seven feet above sea level; today their land is flooded or subject to periodic flooding and the situation is getting worse. The natural shoreline banks which once protected lands from Galveston Bay and Clear Lake have now fallen below sea level. Lands are innundated. More lands will be innundated in the future. Lands that were once above sea level are now under salt water. * * *

I would hold that an owner of land may assert an action against one who destroys the lateral or subjacent support to his land in its natural state when: (1) he engages in conduct knowing that it will cause damages to another's land by loss or destruction of the subjacent support, Paris Purity Coal Co. v. Pendergrass, 193 Ark. 1031, 104 S.W. 2d 455 (1937); or (2) the plaintiff proves negligence, or (3) the plaintiff proves a nuisance, and here a balancing will be a factor. * * * The balancing of lawful but competing property rights has been the rule previously approved by our Texas courts. * * *

Notes

1. "The United States Water Resources Council has estimated that annual damage from land subsidence in the Houston-Galveston area is approximately $32 million. 2 U.S. Water Resources Council, The Nations Water Resources 1975–2000: Water Quantity, Quality, and Related Land Considerations, pt. 2, at 16 (Dec. 1978) [hereinafter cited as U.S. Water Resources-2]. In one small area of the San Joaquin Valley, California, there have been land surface drops of as much as twenty-eight feet. Governor's Commission to Review Calif. Water Rights Law, Final Report 141 (Dec. 1978) [hereinafter cited as Cal. Gov's Comm'n Final Report]. See also National Water Commission, Water Policies for the Future 232 (1973). One of the best documented examples of land subsidence is a seven and one-half foot drop which occurred in Pinal County, Arizona, between 1948 and 1967. Earth fissures as long as eight miles have also occurred in this area. Inventory of Resources and Uses: Phase I Arizona State Water Plan 148 (July 1975) [hereinafter cited as Inventory of Resource and Uses]; U.S. Water Resources-2, supra, note 3, pt. 2, at 15." Johnson, The 1980 Arizona Groundwater Management Act and Trends in Western States Groundwater Administration and Management: A Minerals Industry Perspective, 26 Rocky Mtn.Min.L.Inst. 1031, 1032, n. 3 (1980).

2. In Alameda County Water Dist. v. Niles Sand & Gravel Co., 37 Cal. App.3d 924, 112 Cal.Rptr. 846 (1974), the Company operated commercial sand and gravel pits in the area overlying the Niles Groundwater Basin. The District was engaged in a continuous program of groundwater replenishment, diverting and storing the water of Alameda Creek and placing it in recharge pits so it would percolate down into the basin to provide storage of fresh water for future consumption and to prevent salt water intrusion into the basin from nearby San Francisco Bay. Surface elevation at the Company's pits was 60 feet and the natural elevation of the water table was 20 feet above sea level. At the time of the trial some of the pits had been dug to 120 feet below the surface elevation, 80 feet below the water table. The water in the pits was a hindrance to mining and the Company installed pumps and at the time of trial was emptying water from the pits and pumping it into Alameda Creek and thence into San Francisco Bay at the rate of 5 million gallons per day, enough fresh water to meet the daily needs of a city of 30,000.

In interrelated actions the trial court enjoined the Company from wasting water into the Bay and denied damages on its claim for inverse condemnation. The Court of Appeal affirmed.

Although the court mentioned some aspects of the correlative rights doctrine and the prohibition against waste contained in Cal.Const. Art. X, § 2, the court focused on the statutory powers of the District "to take any action necessary" to prevent interference with the water, to store water underground "for the common benefit of the district," and to commence or intervene in actions begun to prevent interference with, diminution, pollution, or unlawful exportation of any water in the district. These, it was held, imposed a public servitude "limiting the use of lands lying in a particular geographical area, where an overriding public interest requires it." As an alternative ground for denying compensation, the court found that the District's absolute control of water within the basin was a proper exercise of the state's police power, rather than a taking of the Company's property.

The decision has drawn praise for its protection of underground storage and groundwater replenishment rights, Gleason, Water Projects Go Underground, 5 Ecol.L.Q. 625 (1976). What other grounds of decision could have been used to reach this result and secure these advantages? What are the Company's rights, what are the limitations on those rights? What advantages might there be to this approach, rather than presupposing a property right, as the court did, then subjecting it to the servitude or the police power? See Note, Land Use and Rights in Groundwater, X Land & Water L.Rev. 489 (1975).

3. Mineral deposits frequently lie in or below the water table, making it necessary to pump out groundwater if mining is to be conducted. This process, which is sometimes referred to as mine dewatering, can create the usual conflicts and problems associated with groundwater removal. Acton v. Blundell, 12 Mees. & W. 324, 152 Eng.Rep. 1223 (1843), the first groundwater case, involved such a situation and resulted in the rule of absolute ownership. The contemporary reaction of eastern courts to this situation is discussed in note 6 and 7, pp. 397–399.

Some appropriation states have held that mine dewatering requires a groundwater permit; however, others have reached an opposite conclusion. New Mexico provides an example of the latter. Until 1980, dewatering did not require a permit, unless the miner wanted to use the water after pumping it out of the mine. This result was based on the premise that dewatering itself was not a beneficial use of water and, thus, no permit was required.

In 1980, New Mexico enacted a mine dewatering act to strike a balance between the needs of miners and the protection of other groundwater users. N.Mex.Comp.L. §§ 72–12A–1 to 72–12A–13. The act requires a permit for mine dewatering and requires a miner to provide replacement water to groundwater users whose rights are impaired by dewatering. A dewatering permit does not confer water rights. Arizona has adopted similar legislation. Ariz.Rev.Stat. § 45–513. The New Mexico situation and the law in other western states are discussed in Stephson and Utton, The Challenge of Mine Dewatering to Western Water Law and the New Mexico Response, 15 Land and Water Law Review 445 (1980). See also Novak, The Legal Dilemma in Dewatering Mines, 17 Rocky Mt.Min.L.Inst. 657 (1972).

CROSBY, A LAYMAN'S GUIDE TO GROUNDWATER HYDROLOGY

Corker, Groundwater Law, Management and Administration, National Water Commission Legal Study No. 6, Chapter II, 66, 69–70, 78–79 (1971).

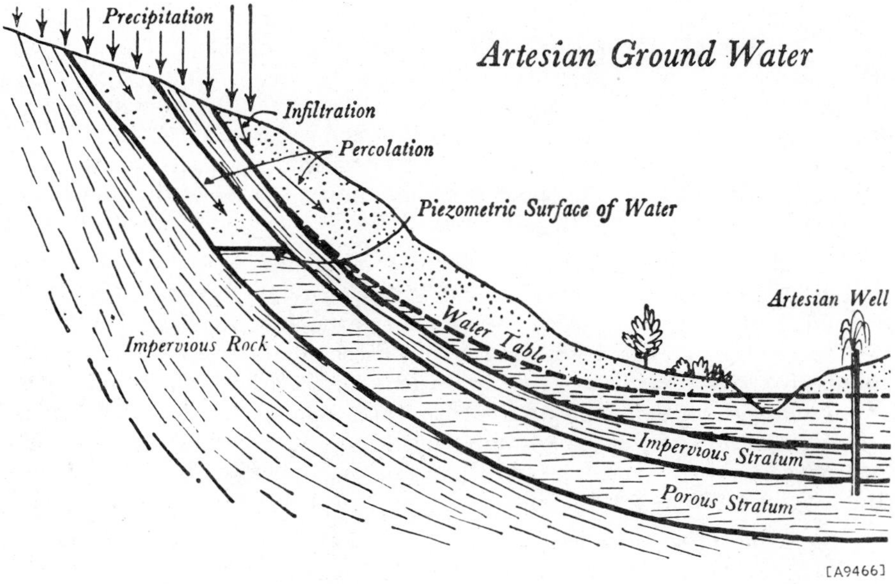

Wells which penetrate a geologically confined aquifer may produce water at the surface, sometimes in large quantities, under artesian or hydrostatic pressure. Artesian pressure may be insufficient, either initially or after water has been withdrawn for a period of time, to deliver water to the surface. Where confining pressures are insufficient or absent (as in the case of a water table aquifer where the water surface is at atmospheric, or zero gauge, pressure), water must be pumped. * * *

WHAT IS THE NATURE OF GROUNDWATER STORAGE?

Before this question can be appropriately answered, we must distinguish still further between unconfined (water table) aquifers and confined (artesian) aquifers. The water level in wells penetrating water table aquifers will stand at the level of the water table where the pressure is that of the atmosphere. On the contrary, the water level in an artesian well will stand at the elevation of an imaginary pressure surface, some distance above the aquifer.

When water table wells are pumped, stored waters are removed by physically dewatering the pore spaces, first those in the immediate cone of depression. Should there be no recharge or natural discharge, the amount of water pumped would represent the volume of pore space which is dewatered. This is not true for confined conditions. When an artesian well flows or is pumped, a cone of depression is created in the pressure surface but no physical dewatering of aquifer pore volume occurs. The pores remain at full saturation as long as confinement exists, and throughout the confined portion of the aquifer. Waters released from storage are derived entirely from elastic rebound of the aquifer, from expansion of the aquifer skeleton and from expansion of the water. Each of these, in turn, is attributable to the relief of pressure. Because neither rock material nor water is notably compressible it is obvious that the quantities of stored waters made available by their expansion will be small. The amount of water released from storage for each foot of water level decline in the artesian case is much less than for the comparable water table case.

The astute layman will immediately wonder about the circumstance in which the pressure surface of an artesian aquifer drops below the bottom of the confining stratum. Will not physical dewatering of the aquifer then occur? Obviously, yes. When the confining pressure is dissipated, the system reverts to the water table condition and removal of waters from the interstices follows. Associated with this change, the quantity of water available from storage per foot of water level decline increases greatly. However, the pumping lifts also increase to the extent that the pressure head or water level has been reduced.

WHAT IS A "REASONABLE" PUMP LIFT?

The groundwater statutes of certain states prescribe protection of a prior appropriator to a "reasonable pump lift" or terms of similar import. Herein lies one of the single greatest obstacles to groundwater management in states recognizing appropriative doctrines.

What is a reasonable pump lift? Is it based upon economic or social criteria? What may be reasonable to an irrigator may be totally unacceptable to a farmer dependent upon groundwater for his domestic supply and yet these people must share the fruits of the same resource. All too frequently the development of deep, highly productive irrigation wells has had a detrimental effect upon shallower domestic wells, occasionally causing them to go completely dry. Proper management, however, might provide adequate protection for the shallow production or replacement by supplemental sources.

CURRENT CREEK IRRIGATION CO. v. ANDREWS

Supreme Court of Utah, 1959.
9 Utah 2d 324, 344 P.2d 528.

WADE, JUSTICE. Three cases are consolidated involving claims to water rights in various wells and springs in an underground water basin near Mona, Juab County, Utah. It is unnecessary at this point to detail the claims and counterclaims, appeals and cross-appeals. The position of the parties on the issues involved will be apparent. We group them according to their interests, and refer to them as Andrews (Orville Andrews, et al.), Fowkes (Gerald Fowkes, et al.), Current Creek Co. (Current Creek Irrigation Co.), and the State Engineer.

The central problem is whether prior appropriators of water from an underground basin, who receive it by means of flowing wells and springs, have a vested right to continue receiving water by artesian pressure; and whether subsequent appropriators, whose withdrawals of water lower the water table and reduce the flow of prior wells, must restore the pressure or bear the expense of replacing the water of prior appropriators.

All of the wells and springs belonging to the parties are in a single broad alluvial fan, which slopes westward from the Wasatch Mountains, in north Juab Valley. * * *

The alluvial fan on the east side of the valley is built of sands and gravels which have been carried from the mountains by streams and water drainage over many thousand of years; and similar materials deposited there by the currents of Lake Bonneville, which covered the valley at one time. These relatively loose materials become saturated as moisture seeps into the ground from the heavy snow and rainfall in the mountains, and readily carry the moisture beneath the surface downward toward the water basin in the center of the valley. These strata and the basin itself are the sources of the waters with which we are concerned.

Fowkes are owners of 11 artesian wells and one spring which are located well up eastward on the alluvial fan and toward its northern part: the use is for domestic purposes and for irrigation of approximately 115 acres of land. * * *

Andrews are the owners of a spring and five flowing wells located roughly one-half mile southeast of the Fowkes wells and therefore higher on the fan, which are used to irrigate about 150 acres of land. They date to 1915 or before but are later in priority than the Fowkes wells. Andrews also own the right to use water from a number of seeps and springs which irrigate meadow land and which also have been so used since before 1903. They have further initiated a claim as of March 14, 1950, for a pump well which produces six second feet of water. This was by application to the State Engineer and use is permitted only during the irrigation season.

Current Creek Company's main water source is known as Mona Reservoir, which lies at the center of the valley near its north end. The water is transported about 12 miles to the south for irrigation. The company has also initiated a claim to appropriate 18 second feet of underground water to be pumped from three wells near the reservoir to augment its supply. * * * The priority date of application for these wells is 1951, although they were not drilled until 1954. They flow by natural pressure about 2.74 second feet of water and are allowed to flow during the entire year for storage in the Mona Reservoir.

This basin upon which all of the wells are situated is classified as a sensitive "cone of influence," because the wells readily affect each other. That is, when the Andrews' pump well is started, the water level drops and the pressure ceases in Andrews' other wells, and in the wells owned by Fowkes; when the pump well is turned off the level pressure rises in the others. Opening and closing the Current Creek Company's wells has the same, although somewhat less, effect. The evidence indicates that the hydrostatic pressure in the Fowkes' and Andrews' flowing wells decreased from about 11 feet above ground in the beginning of 1953 to about 8.5 feet below ground in October, 1956. During the summer of 1956, studies by the State Engineer and the U.S. Geological Survey showed that operation of the Current Creek Company's wells diminished the flow of other wells in the area. * * *

The trial court found that the relative time priorities of the parties to the water in the basin were: (1) springs owned by Andrews and Fowkes, (2) the flowing wells of Andrews and Fowkes, (3) the Andrews' pump well, and (4) the Current Creek Company wells. * * * The court found that there is unappropriated water within the basin. * * *

The court further found that the pump wells of both Andrews and Current Creek interfered with the flow of the flowing wells of Andrews and Fowkes. As to Andrews, it refused to find that the interference in their flow well was caused by the Current Creek wells, as distinguished from the effect caused by their own pump well, and therefore refused to allow them any redress. The decree required Andrews and Current Creek Company to replace for Fowkes 1.775 second feet of water during the irrigation season and 27.11 gallons of water per minute during the nonirrigation season to be supplied by furnishing and installing pumps and sources of power, the cost to be shared equally between them. It further prohibited Andrews and Current Creek from using their pump wells and required them to desist from pumping water until and unless they replaced the water to Fowkes as just stated. * * *

Prior appropriators of this underground water who have beneficially used it through the natural flow of springs or artesian wells are entitled to have the subsequent appropriators restrained from drawing the water out of and lowering the static head pressure of this underground basin unless they replace the quantity and quality of the water by pumping or other means to the prior appropriators at the sole cost of the subsequent appropriators. The same rule should apply to all junior appropriators present and future. They can appropriate water to a beneficial use from the underground basin if it is available but they must replace the flow of the wells and springs at the prior appropriator's place of diversion solely at their own cost. * * *

There can be no doubt that the above is a correct statement of the rules governing this situation. Section 73–3–23, U.C.A.1953, expressly grants the right of replacement to any junior appropriator whose appropriation diminishes the quantity or quality of previously appropriated underground water at the sole cost or expense of the junior appropriator. The wording of this statute is clear, unambiguous and positive. This court has the highest duty to enforce it and not repeal it by judicial legislation. This section was added by the 1935 Legislature with other sections in order to adapt the law to the new concepts that underground waters are subject to appropriation in accordance with the then very recent decisions of Wrathall v. Johnson and Justesen v. Olsen. There can be no doubt that the legislature and this court intended to protect the rights of the prior appropriators, and that both those decisions and this legislation were arrived at and enacted for that purpose.

The doctrine that underground basins of water could be appropriated through artificial flowing wells was first recognized in the Wrathall and Justesen decisions in 1935. * * * Prior to 1935 we held that percolating waters are a part of the soil and not subject to appropriation, and that underground artesian basins are percolating waters. Still all of our decisions have protected the rights to have the static head pressure maintained. We have consistently enjoined the lowering of the static head pressure which had the effect of preventing a prior user from continuing a beneficial use of underground waters. This was just as true in Horne v. Utah Oil Refining Co. and Glover v. Utah Oil Refining Co., wherein we applied the correlative rights doctrine, as in the Wrathall and Justesen cases, where we applied the right to appropriate theory. It was also equally true in the cases where the water escaped from the underground basin by springs, seepage or other natural means. Obviously the correlative rights doctrine was made use of to protect prior rights to pressure while giving lip service to the theory that percolating waters are a part of the soil. So in all of these cases, including Hanson v. Salt Lake City, 1949, we recognized the right to static head pressure. We have found no case in this state involving this question where the court has failed to approve the doctrine that the static head pressure of a prior appropriator should be protected. This seems to have been universally recognized in other states. * * *

The facts of our present case do not indicate that less water will be beneficially used if we continue to follow the right to static head pressure theory. Before the static head pressure was lowered Fowkes received their water without pumping. Now Current Creek gets more water than Fowkes claims from a lower elevation without pumping. There is no reason to believe that the cost of replacement to Current Creek will be prohibitive but that the cost of pumping to Fowkes will be otherwise. So far as this case is concerned, we have the choice between protecting a junior or senior appropriator with nothing whatever to indicate that more water will be beneficially used one way or the other. It would be a mistake to change an age-old system merely in the hope that in some future case more water may be used beneficially under a different system. This court should not completely change the law and ignore an express statute without a showing that such change would cause more water to be beneficially used. * * *

Judgment affirmed. Costs to respondents.

CROCKETT, CHIEF JUSTICE (dissenting). * * * It seems to me that it is always an illusion to regard any right as absolute. A right may be so assertable under some circumstances, but not under others. All rights in property, and personal liberties, or even the right to life itself are subject to limitations, or to forfeiture under certain conditions. * * *

I doubt the wisdom of seeking solutions to problems such as the instant ones in such a generality as a rule that a prior user has the absolute right not only to the water, but to have preserved to him the pressure and the means of diversion under all circumstances. Such a rule may seem easy for the court to apply to rid itself of immediate problems, but it is far from easy in practical operation. More important, it does not serve the fundamental purpose of our water law of providing for the fullest conservation and the highest development of water by making it available to all users in the most convenient and economical way.

The difficulty with preserving to the prior user the absolute right to water and also to the pressure and means of diversion is that projecting its application to basins where there are a great number of users reveals that it does not work to serve the necessary purpose of maximum development and use of water. The evidence indicates and it is a well-known and observable fact, that when the water table of an underground basin is maintained at a high enough level to sustain pressure in flowing wells in the higher areas, there will be water above and near the surface in the lower areas forming ponds, marshes and swamps. This results in wasteful losses from surface evaporation and from consumption by water-loving plants, tules, reeds and rushes, indigenous to such areas, which are of little or no value. There is often further wastage from drainage of the basin by streams or by leakage and seepage out of it.

Under a rule of absolute right to water and pressure, there are other difficulties to be encountered in allocating all the usable water to users. * * * The administrative problems relating to the determination of costs of maintaining pressure for prior users, and allocation against later users, would be insuperable. In addition thereto the cost imposed upon the initiator of a new well might be prohibitive, so that even where there was unused water in the basin it would not be put to use. The various difficulties just discussed make it apparent that it is quite impractical to insure to prior appropriators not only the amount of water they claim, but also the right to have the same pressure maintained as when they made the original appropriation.

In fairness I must concede that the language of Sec. 73–3–23, U.C.A.1953: "* * * In all cases replacement shall be at the sole cost and expense of the applicant" may reasonably be given the meaning espoused by the majority opinion. But that is only half of the sentence; it continues, "* * * and subject to such rules and regulations as the state engineer may prescribe." However, the preceding language, which provides the foundation for "replacement" states, that "the right of replacement is hereby *granted* to any junior appropriator whose appropriation may diminish the quantity or injuriously affect the quality of [prior] appropriated underground water. * * *" (Emphasis added.) Thus *granting* the junior appropriator the *right* of replacement does not necessarily make it mandatory that he maintain pressure and means of diversion under all circumstances. I do not regard the case of Hanson v. Salt Lake City referred to in the main opinion as so holding. The court was much concerned about the difficulties involved in giving Hanson, a senior appropriator, absolute right to water and pressure, and he was refused redress against the city for interference with the flow of his well. I agree that this was based partly on the fact that he had not established the right to as much water and pressure as he claimed and that he was actually getting adequate water by means of a pump. A reservation was expressed as to whether a prior appropriator could use waters inefficiently and deprive others of them. My interpretation of that case is that the prior appropriator gets the right to use the water and to such means of diversion as is reasonably efficient and does not cause undue waste of water.

It is of vital significance, insofar as the authority of the Hanson case is concerned, that Justices Wolfe and Latimer in concurring opinions pointed out that prior appropriators of underground water should not be deemed to get an absolute right to pressure, but only to the water; and that the means of diversion must be reasonable and consistent with the state of development of water in the area and not inimical to the overall purpose of putting all of the usable water in the basin to use. * * *

Notes

1. As can be gleaned from Crosby, a "safe yield" with a "reasonable pumping lift" requires some lessening of artesian pressure or lowering of the water table. Suppose a condition of equilibrium with recharge is reached and maintained after A, B, C and D each have drilled a well, each one month later than the last. B imposes added pumping costs on A, C on A and B, and D on A, B, and C. Does B "cause harm to A," C to B and A, etc.? Suppose this is in a "mining" situation and each junior well shortens the life of the seniors and accelerates the decline in the water table. Does B cause harm to A, etc.? What rule is implicit in *Fundingsland* and *Mather,* supra, pp. 414 to 420?

Review Coase, The Problem of Social Cost, supra, p. 111. Given Coase's "costless market," which rule, "junior pays senior's added costs" or "each pays his own costs" will produce the optimum *social* welfare, the amount and value of product from the water that just equals the cost of producing the water? Is there any other criterion which tells which rule is "best?"

2. Colorado Springs v. Bender, 148 Colo. 458, 366 P.2d 552 (1961):

"At his own point of diversion on a natural water course, each diverter must establish some reasonable means of effectuating his diversion. He is not entitled to command the whole or a substantial flow of the stream merely to facilitate his taking the fraction of the whole flow to which he is entitled. Schodde v. Twin Falls Land & Water Co., 224 U.S. 107, 119, 32 S.Ct. 470, 56 L.Ed. 686. This principle applied to diversion of underflow or underground water means that priority of appropriation does not give a right to an inefficient means of diversion, such as a well which reaches to such a shallow depth into the available water supply that a shortage would occur to such senior even though diversion by others did not deplete the stream below where there would be an adequate supply for the senior's lawful demand. * * *

"In determining [the elevation of water in the aquifer at which each junior appropriator must cease to divert water in order to meet the demands of a senior appropriator must be fixed,] the conditions surrounding the diversion by the senior appropriator must be examined as to whether he has created a means of diversion from the aquifer which is reasonably adequate for the use to which he has historically put the water of his appropriation. If adequate means for reaching a sufficient supply can be made available to the senior, whose present facilities for diversion fail when water table is lowered by acts of the junior appropriators, provision for such adequate means should be decreed at the expense of the junior appropriators, it being unreasonable to require the senior to supply such means out of his own financial resources. This reasonable provision of the law recognizes that the nature of underground aquifers is such that they sometimes have very great depth. In such circumstances an economical and productive diversion might be made by a junior appropriator of a very high value use with which a senior could not compete; and while the junior might well afford the expense of a deep withdrawal, and even leave an adequate volume of water available for a senior, yet the expense of bringing it to the surface would be beyond the reasonable economic reach of the latter. Such situations do not ordinarily develop with regard to surface stream developments.

"A determination of these questions is necessary. The court must determine what, if anything, the plaintiffs should be required to do to make more efficient the facilities at their point of diversion, due regard being given to the purposes for which the appropriation had been made, and the 'economic reach' of plaintiffs. The plaintiffs cannot reasonably 'command the whole' source of supply merely to facilitate the taking by them of the fraction of the entire flow to which their senior appropriation entitles them. On the other hand, plaintiffs cannot be required to improve their extraction facilities beyond their economic reach, upon a consideration of all the factors involved."

3. In a later Utah case, Wayman v. Murray City Corp., 23 Utah 2d 97, 458 P.2d 861 (1969), five householders within the city had small artesian wells which diminished in flow when the city changed its diversion from seven old wells with rights aggregating 750 g.p.m. to a new large well with a capacity of flowing 1100 g.p.m., although it was restricted to 750 g.p.m. The artesian basin had a natural outflow of 34,000 acre feet per year, so it was obvious there was enough water for all. The lower court directed the state engineer to include in his order approving the change in well location the requirement that the city must at its sole cost replace to the plaintiffs' water in amount and quality equal to their former use. The Supreme Court reversed. *Current Creek* was said not to be applicable because the old city wells had a priority earlier than that of the householders, and that priority was transferred to the new well. The court remanded the case, directing the district court to apply a "rule of reasonableness," analyzing the total situation and balancing individual rights in relationship to each other in a reasonable way which would best serve the overall objective of seeing that all available water is put to beneficial use. The rights of the individual must be compared to the rights of the group, (the state), said the court, and it is both logical and necessary that the rights of each individual should be to some degree subordinate to and correlated with reasonable conditions and limitations established by law for the general good. All users should therefore be required, where necessary, to employ reasonable and efficient means in taking their own waters in relation to the others.

In Erickson v. Crookston Water Works Power & Light Co., 105 Minn. 182, 117 N.W. 435 (1908), the court applied the rule of correlative rights to a dispute between a householder who procured domestic water from a small artesian well and the water company which pumped from large deep wells. Yet it said, "If it [the company] is employing the most approved and economical method to secure [the water], and as an incident to such method the head of respondent's [householder's] well is reduced so that it becomes necessary to put in a power pump, then it follows that respondent, and others similarly situated, may reasonably be required to assume that burden."

In Bishop v. Casper, 420 P.2d 446 (Wyo.1966), a householder in an area served by the city had a 24 foot well into an alluvial aquifer which was dried up when the city drilled three large wells into the same aquifer and lowered the water table by its pumping. Wyo.Stat.1957, § 41–128 then provided, "Whenever a well withdrawing water for beneficial purposes other than for domestic or stock use exempted from regulation by section 2 of this act shall interfere unreasonably with an adequate well developed solely for such exempted uses, whether in a critical area or not, the state engineer, may, on complaint of the operator of the exempted well, order the interfering appropriator to cease or reduce withdrawals of underground water, unless such appropriator shall furnish at his own expense, sufficient water at the former place of use to meet the need for domestic or stock use." In a suit to enjoin the city from withdrawing water or in lieu thereof to furnish water to the householder without charge, the court, in a decision reminiscent of medieval cases on common law pleading, threw out the case on the basis that the plaintiff had failed to allege that his well was "adequate."

Would the decisions in *Wayman, Erickson* and *Bishop* appeal to you as "just," "right," or "equitable" if the domestic users had been farmers living at a distance from the city? In Pima Farms Co. v. Proctor, 30 Ariz. 96, 245 P. 369 (1926) the early appropriator (from an underground stream to which the Arizona court applied the rule of appropriation) used his shallow well for irrigation of his small farm, and the junior company drilled several very large wells which supplied many farmers. The court said, "* * * to permit a junior appropriator, who, perhaps, obtains his knowledge of such body of water by the pioneering explorations and sacrifices of the first appropriator, to lower the water level and thereby destroy or greatly impair the latter's means of diversion, including his pumps and water containers, does not comport with justice and equity, nor is it in conformity with the spirit of the rules adopted by the courts for the adjustment of disputes over water and its use in the arid regions of the West. We think in such a case the first appropriator should be protected. * * *" But the court denied an injunction if the junior would furnish water to the plaintiff: "His right may be protected and at the same time the defendant be permitted to appropriate for beneficial use the unappropriated waters of the underground stream by requiring the latter to provide plaintiff from its water system the amount of his appropriation. This arrangement will effectually carry out the policy of the state of not permitting any one to so exercise his water right as to restrict or limit the use of the public waters of the state. Since it appears the defendant is a public service corporation, already actually engaged in the delivery of water to the larger part of the 8,000 acres of land now under cultivation, it seems improbable that to require it to deliver water to the plaintiff, upon the same or equal terms that it is delivering water to its other customers, will work any severe hardship."

Is this result consistent with the rule announced by the Arizona court? Does it give a hint as to the proper solution in the *Wayman, Erickson* and *Bishop* cases? In the hypothetical variation on those cases where the domestic user and the city's large wells are both far outside the city limits?

4. Bagley, Water Rights Law and Public Policies Relating to Ground Water "Mining" in the Southwestern States, 4 J.Law and Econ. 144, 161 (1961): "Interesting economic questions are raised by doctrines which protect the original appropriator's means of diversion, quite apart from

effects on policy relating to depletion of stocks of water. In some cases the value of the water to a junior appropriator would be great enough to warrant his compensating or supplying the senior appropriator. This might be true if there are not many senior appropriators and if the supply available to the junior appropriator is large. But if there are many hundreds or thousands of prior appropriators who must be compensated for falling water levels additional appropriations may be effectively blocked. Under these conditions unappropriated parts of the perennial yield might go to waste. Considerations of economic effects as well as equity dictate, however, recognition of the fact that falling water levels create burdens on water users. The mere fact that water may be wasted unless junior appropriators are allowed to take supplies without compensating senior appropriators as long as perennial yield is not exceeded or economic pumping limits not yet reached does not imply that allowing such appropriations will enlarge net economic benefits. The higher pumping cost to prior appropriators is a real cost—and there is a question whether cheap methods of obtaining the water with some waste are more economical than more expensive methods which utilize supplies more completely. On the other hand, there may also be a difficult, if not impossible, administrative task which entails expensive costs in measuring the amount of damage additional withdrawals will inflict on prior appropriators. The best policy from an economic standpoint will depend on the facts of the case and would not necessarily always be one way or the other."

5. Compare the following statutes with the Utah statute in the principal case, the Wyoming statute in Note 3, supra, and with each other:

Nev.Rev.Stat. 534.110: "It shall be an express condition of each appropriation of ground water acquired under NRS 534.010 to 534.190, inclusive, that the right of the appropriator shall relate to a specific quantity of water and that such right must allow for a reasonable lowering of the static water level at the appropriator's point of diversion. In determining such reasonable lowering of the static water level in a particular area, the state engineer shall consider the economics of pumping water for the general type of crops growing and may also consider the effect of water use on the economy of the area in general. * * *

"In any basin or portion thereof in the state designated by the state engineer, the state engineer may restrict drilling of wells in any portion thereof if he determines that additional wells would cause an undue interference with existing wells. * * *"

Wash.Rev.Code Ann. 90.44.070: "No permit shall be granted for the development or withdrawal of public ground waters beyond the capacity of the underground bed or formation in the given basin, district, or locality to yield such water within a reasonable or feasible pumping lift in case of pumping developments, or within a reasonable or feasible reduction of pressure in the case of artesian developments. The supervisor of water resources shall have the power to determine whether the granting of any such permit will injure or damage any vested or existing right or rights under prior permits and may in addition to the records of his office, require further evidence, proof, and testimony before granting or denying any such permits."

Wyo.Stat.1977, § 41–3–933: "It is an express condition of each underground water permit that the right of the appropriator does not include the right to have the water level or artesian pressure at the appropriator's point of diversion maintained at any level or pressure higher than that required for maximum beneficial use of the water in the source of supply. The state engineer may issue any permits subject to such conditions as he may find to be in the public interest."

Kan.Stat.Ann.1977, § 82a–711a: "It shall be an express condition of each appropriation of surface or ground water that the right of the appropriator shall relate to a specific quantity of water and that such right must allow for a reasonable raising or lowering of the static water level and for the reasonable increase or decrease of the streamflow at the appropriator's point of diversion: *Provided,* That in determining such reasonable raising or lowering of the static water level in a particular area, the chief engineer shall consider the economics of diverting or pumping water for the water uses involved; and nothing herein shall be construed to prevent the granting of permits to applicants later in time on the ground that the diversions under such proposed later appropriations may cause the water level to be raised or lowered at the point of diversion of a prior appropriator, so long as the rights of holders of existing water rights can be satisfied under such express conditions."

Grant, Reasonable Groundwater Pumping Levels Under the Appropriation Doctrine: Underlying Social Goals, 23 Nat.Res.J. 53, 74 (1983).

"The earlier article opened by quoting the following statement about the reasonable pumping level concept from a National Water Commission study: 'No definitive guidelines exist as to what the measure of reasonableness is or how it will be applied.' Although the reasonable pumping level statutes incompletely enumerate factors that should bear on the measure of reasonableness, the root cause of the uncertainty lies deeper. Additional factors can be ascertained from study of appropriation doctrine laws and traditions, albeit with varying degrees of clarity. Definitive guidelines in the sense of rules that will yield mechanical answers, however, are impossible or at least unwise. Unless one is willing to accept a simplistic, tunnel vision approach, the need is inevitable to weigh potentially competing concerns about economic efficiency, wealth and merit good distribution, and (perhaps) other social goals.

"The task then is to develop procedures to achieve knowledgeable and responsible weighing of such concerns. The essence of the problem is captured by the following commentary upon water management under the Alaska water code. That code allows new appropriations only for uses that will be in the public interest, and it enumerates a number of factors bearing on the public interest. Despite the enumeration Frank Trelease, the code's principal draftsman, has commented:

> Making decisions such as these will be very difficult. No law can make them. They must be made by people. No economic formula can solve these problems by push button techniques. * * * It is believed that the real strength of the Code lies in its procedures, which will enable all viewpoints to be brought together and all factors considered, so that choices will be made, not by action of an appropriator or

> polluter, and not to further the policy of a single purpose agency, but on an informed basis by officials responsible to the State for 'maximum use consistent with the public interest' for the 'maximum benefit of (all) its people.

"Similarly, the strongest approach to the pumping level problem seems to be to use procedures which will enable all viewpoints to be brought together and all factors considered, so that choices will be made on an informed basis by officials responsible to the state for the maximum benefit of all its people. The reasonable pumping level statutes are readily adaptable to that approach."

The earlier article referred to is Grant, Reasonable Groundwater Pumping Levels Under the Appropriation Doctrine: The Law and Underlying Economic Goals, 21 Nat.Res.J. 1 (1981). These two articles contain a thorough discussion of the economic and social considerations involved in establishing pumping levels.

6. The Nebraska statute giving preference in the use of underground water to domestic users over all others and to agricultural purposes over manufacturing or industrial purposes, Rev.Stat.Neb. § 46–613, was held to apply to maintenance of water level and pressure in Prather v. Eisenmann, 200 Neb. 1, 261 N.W.2d 766 (1978), where an irrigation well withdrawing 650 gallons per minute reduced the artesian head and water level in nearby residential wells.

So.Dak.Compiled Laws 46–6–6.1: "In addition to powers otherwise provided the water rights commission is authorized to adopt rules and regulations controlling the location and capacity of irrigation, industrial, municipal, and other large capacity wells for the purpose of ensuring or protecting water for reasonable domestic use, without the necessity of requiring maintenance of artesian head pressure in a domestic use well. In addition to other criteria the commission deems relevant to comply with these provisions the rules and regulations shall provide:

(1) For regulation of the use of large capacity wells in the degree necessary to maintain an adequate depth of water for reasonable domestic needs and for a prior appropriator at his point of diversion, in wells which meet minimum well construction standards;

(2) For minimum construction standards for all wells in South Dakota which standards shall be based upon the ability of a well to produce water independent of artesian pressure;

* * *

(4) Standard which will provide for lowering of a water lift mechanism to a depth near the bottom of the ground water supply or, in artesian water to a substantial depth below the geological formation confining the ground water;

(5) For regulation which will provide for a reasonable life of all wells."

CROSBY, A LAYMAN'S GUIDE TO GROUNDWATER HYDROLOGY

Corker, Groundwater Law, Management and Administration, National Water Commission Legal Study No. 6, Chapter II, 56–54 (1971)

C. WHERE DOES GROUNDWATER COME FROM?

For all practical purposes, the origin of groundwater can be regarded as meteoric, meaning that it comes from the atmosphere. There is also water derived from sources deep within the earth which is not associated with the hydrologic cycle but which may accrue thereto from geologic processes. This is called *magmatic, primary,* or *juvenile* water. While the subject has not been without controversy, the consensus of professional opinion is that such water is not added in useful quantity and quality. The important sources of groundwater are:

1. Precipitation

This is indirectly the source of all fresh groundwater, except for the water just mentioned, and directly the source of much groundwater. Much of the precipitation falling on the earth's surface infiltrates the soil zone where it is utilized by plants and satisfies the capillary requirements (soil moisture deficiency) of the soil. Infiltrating precipitation in excess of these requirements tends to move downward through the zone of aeration under the influence of gravity until it reaches the water table. Some of the excess precipitation moves directly or indirectly by flow over the land surface to streams, from which it may, in part, move into a groundwater body.

2. Stream Flow

Surface streams are sometimes classified as gaining streams or losing streams (or, in the language of the technologist, effluent streams or influent streams, respectively). That is, they acquire water from or lose water to the groundwater body, depending on whether the stream is incised below or elevated above the water table. Inflow of a stream to a valley, less outflow from the valley, less evaporation, less consumption by native and cultivated vegetation, and less other artificial consumptive uses and water exports, again permit calculation of a surface stream's contribution to groundwater.

3. Return Flow to Groundwater

Most diversions of groundwater for use are not totally consumed and may return, in part, to some groundwater aquifer. Because irrigation is the major consumptive use of groundwater, it warrants special attention. Depending upon the physical setting and the quantity of groundwater pumped for irrigation, as much as half the diversion may return to the groundwater source. Other types of diversions, including

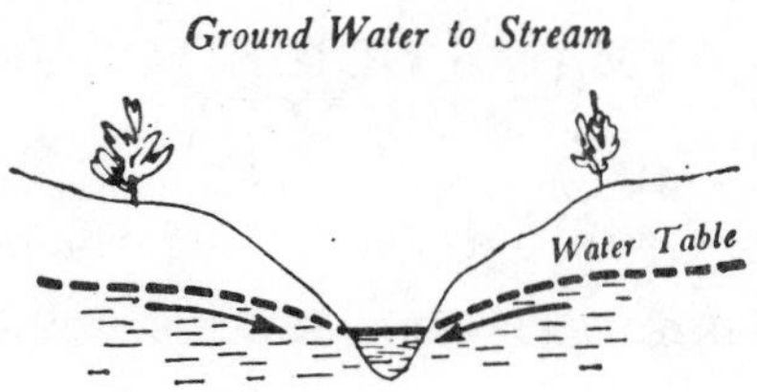

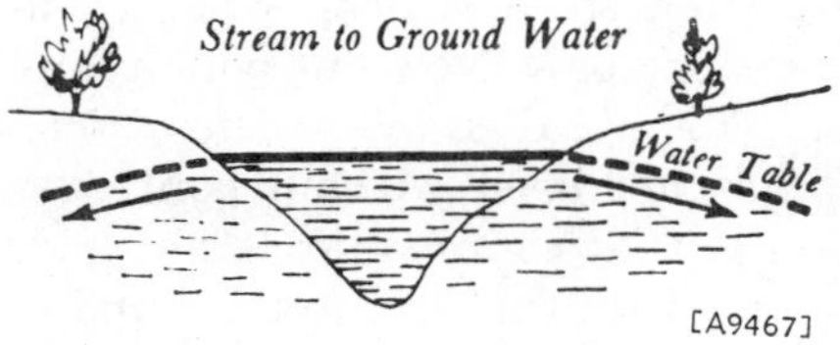

[A9467]

that of local surface waters, may also contribute return flow to the groundwater resource. Surface waters often are imported in tremendous quantities for irrigation and substantial percentages ultimately accrue to groundwater. The large available quantities of return flow of sewage in urban areas have prompted their ever increasing use, after treatment, in artificial groundwater recharge. In these operations soil mechanisms are called upon to further upgrade partially treated sewage. Any, or all, of these return flows can be important sources of recharge to a given groundwater basin. In some cases there can be so much recharge associated with irrigation operations utilizing imported waters that lakes and swamps are created in the lowlands and expensive drainage works must be engineered and constructed to alleviate the problem.

4. *Artificial Recharge*

Water may be imported to a drainage basin or existing basin waters may be allocated for the express purpose of storage underground. Or this storage may be an incidental and, ordinarily, welcomed circumstance, even when not undertaken for the specific purpose. Groundwater recharge may be induced or facilitated by spreading over areas of high infiltration capacity or by injection into deep wells under pressure. * * *

D. How is Groundwater Discharged?

Groundwater does not cease its movement after reaching an underground reservoir or aquifer. However, in rare instances groundwater may reach a closed basin from which no outflow other than evapotranspiration is possible. Such basins must be lower than all possible avenues of outflow or isolated by impermeable geologic barriers. Otherwise, groundwater is eventually discharged to the surface. The rate of movement varies widely, depending on the permeability of the underground material and the slope of the water table or hydraulic gradient. Discharge can occur by natural or artificial means or a combination of both.

1. Natural Discharge

Outflow of groundwater by seepage to lakes, streams, and oceans has already been described. Outflow visibly concentrated in a single location is a spring. Groundwater near enough to the surface to be penetrated by roots of plants is consumed by natural processes of evaporation and transpiration and loss to the atmosphere. * * * Such use of groundwater by vegetation has been called subirrigation. However, some usage of the term "irrigation" is limited to the artificial or purposeful application of water, as distinguished from natural processes.

Springs, like surface streams, flow under the influence of gravity. A spring is formed at a point of natural groundwater discharge from an aquifer. Such discharges occur where the land surface intersects a perched or general water table, usually in a valley wall or a hillside slope. More rarely springs are formed where fractures or similar openings in the earth intersect and release confined, or artesian, waters.

2. Interconnecting Aquifers

Within any groundwater basin some natural communication between the individual aquifers can be expected under undisturbed conditions. Transfer of water between aquifers can be increased when wells are drilled which penetrate two or more water-bearing zones. Such transfers can be controlled by casing requirements for each well. Failure to provide such controls usually results in dewatering of the upper aquifers and the "drying up" of shallow water supplies.

Notes

1. The Colorado State Engineer denied applications for permits to construct two wells that would have withdrawn 240 acre feet per year, at a rate of 1,000 g.p.m., from the shallow aquifer (20 feet to water) connected to the Cache La Poudre River thirteen miles away. The water in the aquifer moves toward the river at the rate of .3 of a mile per year. The river is over appropriated. No particular surface water right could be shown to be injured, but in the aggregate the adjudicated surface water rights in the river would be deprived of a material portion of the water. In Hall v. Kuiper, 181 Colo. 130, 510 P.2d 329 (1973), the court affirmed the denial on the grounds that there was no unappropriated water available and that the vested rights of others would be materially injured.

2. City of Albuquerque v. Reynolds, 71 N.M. 428, 379 P.2d 73 (1963) involved applications by the city for permits to appropriate, by means of wells, water from the Rio Grande Underground Water Basin. The evidence showed that the underground waters constitute a part of the "base

flow" of the Rio Grande, and that all of the waters flowing in that river have been fully appropriated. The court said,

"Having found legislative authority in the state engineer to deny the city's applications on the ground that their granting would result in impairment of the rights of Rio Grande River appropriators, we next consider the argument that the state engineer exceeded his power and jurisdiction by establishing and promulgating rules and regulations requiring the retirement of surface water rights as a condition to new appropriations of underground water from the Rio Grande Underground Water Basin. * * * If we assume, as we must, from the findings made by the state engineer and also by the district court that the underground waters in question cannot be taken without impairment to the rights of the river appropriators, even though there are unappropriated underground waters in the basin, then it would seem to follow that some method should be devised, if possible, whereby the available unappropriated water can be put to beneficial use. Because of the interrelationship between the two waters, as discussed in the findings of the state engineer from which we have extracted quotations supra, it would seem that a method has been devised to serve this purpose * * * Furthermore, no quarrel is made here with the physical fact stated by the state engineer, that:

> The relationships derived from Darcy's law show that the effects of ground-water withdrawals on a nearby stream arise gradually and that if the well is some distance from the stream many years elapse before the effects of the withdrawal are fully reflected in the stream-flows. The relationships show, however, that ultimately the annual stream-flow is reduced by an amount equal to the annual ground-water appropriation. The relationships also show that once a ground-water appropriation is made, and continued for a period of time, the effects on surface water flows are not terminated at the time that the ground-water appropriation is terminated but continue, gradually diminishing, for many years after the ground-water appropriation is ended.

"The conditions imposed by the state engineer provide for measuring the pumped water and the return flow to the stream, and take into account the accretion to the stream flow which would result therefrom and, in his decision, the state engineer referred to calculations and charts, introduced as exhibits in the hearing before him, showing that under the applications of the city and with a return flow of 40% from the city's works, as at present, the water taken from the basin would, over a 75-year period, be extracted about one-half from underground storage and one-half from surface flows.

"We feel constrained to hold that the state engineer adopted the only known plan to avoid impairment to existing rights and that his requirement, that surface rights be retired to the extent necessary to protect prior stream appropriators as a condition of the granting of an application to appropriate from the basin, is within the lawful power and authority of the state engineer."

3. Wyo.Stat.1957 § 41–3–916:

"Where underground waters in different acquifers are so interconnected as to constitute in fact one source of supply, or where underground waters and the waters of surface streams are so interconnected as to constitute in fact one source of supply, priorities of rights to the use of all such interconnected waters shall be correlated and such single schedule of priorities shall relate to the whole common water supply. The state engineer may by order adopt any of the corrective controls specified in section 17 of this act [§ 41–132]."

4. Compare the Texas approach, epitomized in Pecos County Water Control & Improvement Dist. v. Williams, 271 S.W.2d 503 (Tex.Civ.App. 1954):

"The controversy arose by virtue of the fact that plaintiff claims and alleges that the properties serviced by it have used and enjoyed the waters of Comanche Springs for some ninety years, and that prior to the institution of this lawsuit about 1951 the defendants, owners of land south and west of said springs, drilled various water wells and began pumping them with mechanical pumps, and that as a result Comanche Springs ceased flowing and plaintiffs were unable to use the waters therefrom for irrigation, as they had done for many years. * * *

"We deal first with the laws of Texas insofar as they relate to percolating waters. It seems clear to us that percolating or diffused and percolating waters belong to the landowner, and may be used by him at his will. There has been no allegation in this case that the defendants have been wasting any of the water. * * *

"With reference to plaintiffs' claim of appropriation it is clear on the authority of the Texas cases cited above that its appropriation, if any, could extend only to the waters of Comanche Springs at and after their emergence from the ground, and the same is true of riparian rights."

5. Many eastern cases on the common law rights of landowners to groundwaters have involved a diminution of springs and surface streams by groundwater pumping. Typical is *Meeker,* supra, p. 402, n. 2. Many involve the reverse situation of a reservoir which raises the water table to the surface of surrounding land and saturates it to the point where it is unfit for use. A surprising number of the cases have gone on doctrines other than water law. An exhaustive study of these problems, with comparisons to western solutions, is found in Davis, Wells and Streams: Relationship at Law, 37 Mo.L.Rev. 189 (1972).

See Restatement of the Law of Torts, 2d, § 858, quoted supra, p. 402, Note 3.

TEMPLETON v. PECOS VALLEY ARTESIAN CONSERVANCY DISTRICT

Supreme Court of New Mexico, 1958.
65 N.M. 59, 332 P.2d 465.

H. VEARLE PAYNE, DISTRICT JUDGE. This is an appeal from a judgment of the District Court of Chaves County. The appellees filed with the State Engineer their applications to drill wells in the Roswell Shallow Water Basin. Although these were on the usual forms for applications to appropriate underground waters, it was agreed by all of the parties that in effect these applications constituted applications for the changing of the point of diversion of waters from points in the Rio Felix to points in the Valley Fill of the Roswell Shallow Water Basin. The applications were denied by the State Engineer, and an appeal was perfected to the District Court of Chaves County. Upon hearing before the District Court, judgment was entered in favor of the applicants from which the Pecos Valley Artesian Conservancy District and S.E. Reynolds, State Engineer of the State of New Mexico, have appealed.

* * *

The ownership of the land, the description thereof, water rights appurtenant thereto, and other related matters are not in controversy. The water rights of the appellees were to irrigate certain land out of the Rio Felix. The amount of water in the Rio Felix has decreased in recent years for the reasons hereinafter mentioned, so that the water in the river is insufficient to irrigate the land of the appellees and they have applied for permits to drill wells to supplement this water to the extent necessary to produce the amount of water originally appropriated.

It is the contention of the appellants that this constitutes a new appropriation of water, and that it will impair existing rights, which contentions are denied by the appellees. In order to understand the contentions, it will be necessary to set forth certain facts and background concerning the waters and water rights involved.

The Rio Felix is a small water course which crosses Chaves County from the west toward the east, and empties into the Pecos River. There are two underground bodies of water in this area. The deepest one is known as the Roswell Artesian Basin, and the upper body of water is known as the Roswell Shallow Water Basin. These two bodies of water are separated by impervious red shale and gypsum, known as the Pecos Red Beds. Below the Pecos Red Beds is the body of artesian water and above the Pecos Red Beds is the Roswell Shallow Water Basin. Above the Pecos Red Beds and spreading over the basin is what is known as the Valley Fill which consists of topsoil, sand, gravel, shale, clay, and boulders which have been washed in and deposited through the centuries. The Shallow Water Basin is held in this Valley Fill and varies in thickness from nothing on the west to two hundred and fifteen feet or more on the east.

The Rio Felix channel passes across this Valley Fill and at places is as deep as twenty-five feet or more into the Valley Fill. The water flow of this river, except for flood waters, rises into the channel from the Valley Fill wherever the waters of the Shallow Basin are higher than the bed of the river.

The Rio Felix is a stream that heads in the foothills of the Sacramento Mountains and runs down to the Pecos River. It is not a continuous stream except in flood times. The waters that fall on the headwaters of the stream run for a distance and then they lose themselves in the ground. In other words, the headwaters of the Rio

Felix sink and become a part of the Valley Fill except for the times when the stream is in flood stage. * * *

Until the year 1952, the flow of the Rio Felix supplied enough water for the irrigation of the lands involved, but about that time the water table began to lower materially, and thus decreased the amount of water which, except for floods, flowed into the Rio Felix, so that the appellees have been unable to secure sufficient waters from the river to properly irrigate their lands. This decrease in the water table was due to the pumping of water from irrigation wells which have been drilled into the Shallow Water Basin in later years, aggravated by several years of drouth. * * *

Witness Brown is an Engineer with many years of experience. He testified as follows:

> "Q. Is there any difference in the water that is produced by the shallow wells, or wells in the shallow basin, from the Felix water? A. No, and I would like to explain that this way. In a natural state, the shallow ground water is discharged into the Felix, as described by prior witnesses, because the Felix is cut down below the ground water table. When the first shallow wells were drilled and pumped, the effect of withdrawal of water from the shallow wells was to intercept the ground water that was migrating toward the Felix, so that it reduced the discharge into the Felix, but as the wells were pumped, and the levels of the ground water was lowered, the water level in the wells got down to where they were below the bed of the Felix, and when water is withdrawn under that condition, instead of intercepting water which is going to the Felix, it actually diverts water from the Felix, just as certainly as if it was pumped out of the river, or as if a person had built a dam and taken it off through a canal. Likewise, these appellants, when their wells are put down and water is pumped from them, they will be withdrawing water from the Felix to some extent, the same as these shallow waters in the surrounding area are now doing."
>
> * * *

The Court concluded that the water of appellees appropriated from the natural flow of the Rio Felix included the waters in the Valley Fill that would have naturally reached the river, except for the acts of subsequent appropriators. The Court further concluded that the restoration to the appellees of the quantity of water originally appropriated by means of wells sunk into the Valley Fill at the locations designated by the appellees, cannot and does not impair any other water right. * * *

The next contention of the appellants is that the proposed change of point of diversion amounts to a new appropriation in an underground basin that is fully appropriated. This proposition is based on the assumption that there is no connection between the surface flow of the Rio Felix and the underground water basin. The findings of the lower court do not support this assumption. The lower court found that the headwaters of the Rio Felix sank into the ground and became a part of the Valley Fill and then rose again into the river and that the appropriations made by the appellees amounted to appropriations out of the Valley Fill.

In 93 C.J.S. Waters § 170, p. 909, is found the following:

> "An appropriation when made follows the water to its original source, whether through surface or subterranean streams or through percolations."

In the case of Richlands Irrigation Company v. Westview Irrigation Company, 96 Utah 403, 80 P.2d 458, 465, the Supreme Court of Utah had the following to say:

> "The entire watershed to its uttermost confines, covering thousands of square miles, out to the crest of the divides which separate it from the adjacent watersheds, is the generating source from which the water of a river comes or accumulates in its channel. Rains and snows falling on this entire vast area sink into the soil and find their way by surface or underground flow or percolation through the sloping strata down to the central channel. This entire sheet of water, or water table, constitutes the river and it never ceases to be such in its centripetal motion towards the channel. Any appropriator of water from the central channel is entitled to rely and depend upon all the sources which feed the main stream above his own diversion point, clear back to the farthest limits of the watershed."

In the later case of Little Cottonwood Water Company v. Sandy City, 123 Utah 242, 258 P.2d 440, 443, the Supreme Court of Utah stated:

> "Also, no one can interfere with the source of supply of this stream, regardless of how far it may be from the place of use, and whether it flows on the surface or underground, in such a manner as will diminish the quantity or injuriously affect the quality of the water of these established rights." * * *

Applying the foregoing principles to this case would lead to the conclusion that the appellees were entitled to the waters of the Valley Fill that flowed into the Rio Felix at the time of their appropriation. It seems that there is nothing in the law that would prevent them from following this water through an application for a change of point of diversion, provided that it does not impair any other existing rights. In other words, their applications do not amount to a request for a new appropriation in the underground water basin, but merely a request to follow the source of their original appropriation. * * *

The appellants argue that this amounts to a change from a river or surface water right to an underground water right. If the river and the underground waters had two separate sources of supply and if there were no connection between them, this argument might be sound, but under the facts set forth above, the Valley Fill was the source of the flow of the river.

The next contention of the appellants, was that the change of point of diversion would impair existing rights. * * * Apparently this is based on the assumption that the appellees are seeking a new appropriation. As pointed out above, they are not seeking a new appropriation but merely seeking a change in the point of diversion. Previously the water flowed from the Valley Fill into the Rio Felix and was then lifted on to the land by means of dams or pumping plants. The appellees now intend to lift the water directly out of the Valley Fill, due to the fact that the water table has been lowered. This does not mean that it is a new appropriation at all, but merely a change in the method of extracting the water from the Valley Fill. * * *

[Affirmed.]

Note

In Kelley v. Carlsbad Irrigation District, 76 N.M. 446, 415 P.2d 849 (1966), the applicant claimed ownership rights in diffused surface water and sought to recapture it by a well tapping the groundwater basin into which it seeped. The water had never been sufficient to irrigate his lands. The Supreme Court held that the application should be denied, resting its decision on the basis that when the water reached the underground basin it lost its identity as applicant's water and became subject to appropriation.

Durand v. Reynolds, 75 N.M. 497, 406 P.2d 817 (1965), concerned an application similar to that in Templeton, which was denied when applicant failed to prove that the water to be taken from the wells was the water which had supplied the surface right. "Thus it is not merely a case of change in point of diversion and impairing existing rights in the 'valley fill' alone; it is an attempt to obtain a new appropriation to water in a fully appropriated basin."

In Langenegger v. Carlsbad Irrigation District, however, 82 N.M. 416, 483 P.2d 297 (1971), the court extended the rule of *Templeton* one step further back in the hydrologic cycle. The Pecos River is much like the Felix, in that the water in its valley fill originally supported the river. Two factors were different: pumping had exhausted the shallow acquifier, and the river was not the only source of the natural water in the fill. The "Red Beds" that supported the shallow acquifier and confined the underlying artesian Roswell Underground Basin in this area leaked water upwards from the basin into the fill. The court held that an appropriator from the Pecos who could no longer get his water from the river might drill through the valley fill and the Red Beds and tap the artesian water. *Durand,* the court said, should not be construed to require a showing that the water taken from the new diversion point was identical to that taken from the old. The appropriator could rely on all the sources which feed the waters to which he is entitled and could "pursue to their sources the waters from which the appropriations were made." He therefore might change his diversion to any source from which he could obtain his water without injury to other water users.

Existing wells can be used as an alternative diversion point for a surface water right. State of New Mexico v. Molybdenum Corp. of America, 570 F.2d 1364 (10th Cir.1978).

ALAMOSA–LA JARA WATER USERS PROTECTIVE ASSOCIATION v. GOULD

Supreme Court of Colorado, 1983.
674 P.2d 914.

DUBOFSKY, J. This is an appeal from a judgment of the district court for Water Division 3 regarding rules promulgated by the Colorado State Engineer limiting the use of surface and underground water in the San Luis Valley. Curtailment of water use in the valley is required by the terms of an interstate stipulation under which Colorado must meet its Rio Grande Compact obligation to deliver scheduled amounts of Rio Grande water at the Colorado-New Mexico border on an annual basis. The dispute over the proposed rules concerns the distribution of that curtailment * * * between well owners and surface diverters. The water court * * * disapproved rules which phased out all wells in the San Luis Valley unless each well owner could demonstrate a lack of material injury to senior surface water users or provide a plan of augmentation to replace the water taken by a well. * * * We * * * affirm the water court's underground water ruling.

I.

* * *

The upper 6000 feet of fill below the valley surface consists of unconsolidated clay, silt, sand, and gravel, and interbedded lava flows, containing an estimated two billion acre-feet of underground water. Some of the underground water is in an unconfined acquifer system at shallow depths. Beneath the unconfined aquifer are relatively impermeable beds of clay and basalt and beneath these confining layers are substantial quantities of water which comprise the confined aquifer. The confining clay layer generally does not exist around the valley's perimeter, and the confined aquifer system is recharged from surface flow to the underground water system at the edges of the valley. Because the recharge areas are higher in elevation than the floor of the valley, the confined aquifer is under artesian pressure, resulting in the free flow of water from some artesian wells and springs at natural breaks in the confining layer. In some places, where the confining layer is less thick and more transmissive, water from the confined aquifer will leak upward through the confining clay layers into the unconfined aquifer. The unconfined aquifer is directly connected with the surface streams is some places. To varying degrees, the surface streams, the unconfined aquifer, and the confined aquifer are hydraulically connected.

The first appropriations from streams in the valley began in the 1850s on the Conejos River. The first appropriation on the Rio Grande mainstem was in 1866, and the most extensive development for irrigation purposes on both rivers was between 1880 and 1890. By 1900, the natural flow of all surface streams in the valley was over-appropriated. High spring runoff and low summer flows in valley streams, coupled with years of severe drought, resulted in undependable water supplies for irrigation; thus, farmers turned to wells and reservoirs to supplement and regulate their water supply.

Well construction in the valley began as early as 1850. Between 1880 and 1891, about 2,000 artesian wells were drilled. Withdrawals from the confined aquifer by wells remained relatively constant until the early 1950s when a number of large capacity wells were constructed. In 1972, the state engineer ceased issuing permits for wells to be drilled into the confined aquifer after determining that both aquifers were tributary to the surface streams in the valley, based on studies by the United States Geologic Survey and state water agencies. There are more wells on land irrigated by surface water from the Rio Grande mainstem than on land in the Conejos River Basin because many of the Conejos farms are too small to use sprinklers connected to wells and wells in the Conejos River basin west of Antonito must be drilled to such depths that pumping them is uneconomical.

Since before the turn of the century, valley water users have had to contend with out-of-state demands for Rio Grande water. * * * To avoid litigation, Colorado, New Mexico, and Texas began in 1923 to make efforts towards a negotiated apportionment of Rio Grande water. Negotiators from the three states signed a permanent compact in 1938. The compact subsequently was ratified by the legislature of each state and approved by the United States Congress in 1939. 53 Stat. 785 (1939). Codified at section 37–66–101, C.R.S., the compact obligates Colorado to deliver water in the Rio Grande at the New Mexico border based upon two schedules tying delivery obligations to levels of inflow, as measured at upstream gauges on the Rio Grande mainstem and the Conejos River * * *. The amount of required discharge varies according to natural supply. In low water years, small deliveries are required; in high water years, large deliveries are required.

Governed by the stipulation, the state engineer is required to administer the Conejos River and Rio Grande mainstem on the basis of projected annual runoff. Since 1968, when the state engineer began enforcing the stipulation, water users on both the Conejos and Rio Grande have experienced substantial curtailments of their diversions. Between 1969 and 1975, the state engineer developed annual operating criteria to deliver water to the state line.

In 1975, the state engineer promulgated the proposed rules, publishing them in all counties of Water Division No. 3, which is generally coterminous with the San Luis Valley. The proposed rules fall into three categories. * * * Third, the underground water rules provide for phasing out of underground water diversions unless the underground water user submits proof to the division engineer that the user's well is operating under a decreed plan of augmentation or has a decree as an alternate point of diversion, or that the underground water appropriation can occur without impairing the right of a senior appropriator. Numerous protests to the proposed rules were filed, requiring a hearing before a water judge under section 37–92–501(2)(h), C.R.S. * * *.

* * *

At trial, the proposed rules' proponents and the protestants submitted documents detailing the legislative history of the compact and testimony from administrators about operative interpretations of the compact. All parties agreed that historical hydrologic patterns in the valley have changed dramatically, particularly since 1950, because of a combination of natural and man-made causes, resulting in an overall reduction in surface water supplies. The state and the Conejos District asserted that the primary cause of the reduction is increased well pumping, but there was also evidence that decreased snowpack runoff and more efficient irrigation are responsible causes. The theories were supported by studies, which contrasted stream system inflow and outflow, and computer modelling, which estimated overall stream depletions from well withdrawals. Farmers testified to the effect of loss of surface water on their ability to grow crops and the need for supplemental well water when surface supplies are undependable. Finally, evidence was presented that the natural consumptive use of water by evapotranspiration from native grasses and phreatophytes, such as cottonwood, greasewood and rabbitwood, accounts for a large portion of the annual loss of water in the valley. Expert testimony indicated, and the water court found, that when wells are pumped, lowering the water table below phreatophyte root zones, the result is a substantial salvage of water, perhaps as much as one million acre-feet a year, that would otherwise be lost through evapotranspiration.

* * *

The water court disapproved the underground water rules, suggesting that section 37–92–502, C.R.S. requires that the state engineer must determine that each well causes material injury to a senior appropriator before that well may be curtailed and holding the rules to be inconsistent with the statutory and judicial policy of maximum utilization of water. The court held, relying on section 37–92–102, C.R.S. and Fellhauer v. People, 167 Colo. 320, 447 P.2d 986 (1968), that in some instances senior appropriators may be required to drill new wells to augment or replace their surface water diversions before curtailment of junior rights can be required. * * * The state and the Conejos District appeal the water court's disapproval of the underground water rules.

III.

The proposed underground water rules tie tributary underground water administration in the valley to regulation for compact requirements by integrating tributary underground water diversions into the priority system for surface streams. The rules are intended over a five-year period to curtail well diversions unless individual well owners prove that their wells do not cause injury to senior water rights or remedy such injury through plans for augmentation.

In support of the underground water rules, the state engineer introduced voluminous exhibits which showed that well pumping decreases artesian pressure, resulting in increased recharge to the confined aquifer from the streams in the recharge areas and decreased flow into surface streams from springs fed from the confined aquifer, and ultimately, in streamflow depletion. The state engineer estimated that well diversions from both aquifers annually deplete the Rio Grande mainstem by 17,700 acre-feet and the Conejos River by 16,400 acre-feet. He concluded that junior well diversions were causing material injury to senior water rights throughout the valley.

The water court found that the underground water was tributary to the surface streams; that surface decrees were experiencing increasing curtailment; and that underground water withdrawals had accelerated in recent years, affecting surface flows. The court also found that the effect of underground water withdrawals had not been specifically quantified and had not been attributed to individual wells. None of the parties take issue with the water court's general factual findings. Instead the rules' proponents challenge the legal bases of the water court's disapproval of the underground water rules.

* * *

The water court disapproved the well regulations because they did not contain a requirement that stream appropriators tap the enormous supply of water underlying the surface of the valley. Relying upon the reasonable-means-of-diversion requirement adopted in Colorado Springs v. Bender, 148 Colo. 458, 366 P.2d 552 (1961) and codified in section 37–92–102(2)(b), C.R.S.; the policy of "maximum utilization" of the State's water as recognized in Fellhauer v. People, 167 Colo. 320, 447 P.2d 986 (1968); and the requirement under section 37–92–102(1), C.R.S., of integration of administration of underground water tributary to a stream with the use of surface water, the water court held that, under certain circumstances, surface stream appropriators have a duty to withdraw underground water tributary to the stream in order to satisfy their surface appropriations. The court observed that this may take the form of requiring senior appropriators to drill new wells to augment or replace their surface water diversions before they can require curtailment of junior rights, and that *Bender* provides that the sole limitation on seniors' duty to effectuate reasonable means of diversion is that senior appropriators cannot be required to improve their extraction facilities beyond their economic reach.

The state engineer asserts that the proposed rules properly place the burden of remedying the injury caused to senior appropriators on junior water users and that the water court's ruling is a misapplication of law. The state engineer relies upon the principle, codified in section 37–92–102, C.R.S., that the priority system governs water allocation and that junior water rights from whatever source are not entitled to divert water that otherwise would be available for use by senior water rights. See also sections 37–92–301(3) and 37–92–501, C.R.S. Under the prior appropriation doctrine, it is argued, the burden of integrating surface and groundwater rights falls upon junior water users, primarily through plans for augmentation under section 37–92–103(9), C.R.S. See Hillhouse, supra, at 710. The state engineer also relies upon Kuiper v. Well Owners Conservation Association, 176 Colo. 119, 490 P.2d 268 (1971), in which this court held: "[I]t is not the present state of the law that the State Engineer is required to compel a person with a senior surface priority to use his ground water to apply on that priority before he makes a call." Id. at 283.

* * *

Here, several witnesses testified that the water in storage in the valley's aquifers provides the support for the water above it to move to the streams. The well owners and the communities argue that it is not unreasonable to require surface diverters to deepen their headgates if the water from the stream is beneath their feet. The argument continues that the surface owners have lost nothing except a gravity flow source of supply which is cheaper and easier to divert, and that the loss only occurs at times when the surface stream is inadequate to fill the surface diverters' priorities. A reasonable means of diversion in this case, it is argued, is one that eliminates the need for supporting the surface stream, thereby freeing the underground water for maximum beneficial use.

The Conejos District recognizes the development of the maximum utilization of water under *Fellhauer* and the 1969 Act. However, Conejos argues that augmentation is one of the means provided to achieve maximum utilization under the 1969 Act, and that because the proposed rules require junior wells to augment, the rules are consistent with the policy of maximum utilization. Evaluation of different means of achieving maximum utilization, however, is a matter of policy, and therefore a task to be performed by the state engineer after full consideration of the available alternatives. In proposing the instant rules, the state engineer, relying upon the narrow construction of the 1969 Act in *Well Owners,* excluded consideration of the reasonableness of surface diversions, concluding that the prior appropriation doctrine prevented any means of maximizing utilization of the waters of the San Luis Valley other than what could be accomplished by augmentation plans developed by junior well owners.

We believe that *Well Owners* construed the 1969 Act too narrowly. The prior appropriation doctrine is not a legal barrier to the concurrent consideration by the state engineer of the various methods of implementing the state policy of maximum utilization set out in the 1969 Act. See Baker v. Ore-Ida Foods, Inc., 95 Idaho 575, 513 P.2d 627 (1973); Trelease, Conjunctive Use of Ground Water and Surface Water, 27 Rocky Mtn.Min.L.Inst. 1853 (1982); Hillhouse, *supra;* Harrison & Sandstrom, The Ground Water Surface Water Conflict and Recent Colorado Water Legislation, 43 U.Colo.L.Rev. 1 (1971). Therefore, to the degree *Well Owners* precludes consideration of a reasonable-means-of-diversion requirement as a method of maximizing utilization of integrated underground and surface waters, we overrule *Well Owners.*

The water court held that, under certain circumstances, surface stream appropriators may be required to withdraw underground water tributary to the stream in order to satisfy their surface appropriations. We affirm this legal conclusion and return the proposed well rules to the state engineer for consideration of whether the reasonable-means-of-diversion doctrine provides, in this case, a method of achieving maximum utilization of water—a consideration which the state engineer erroneously believed was foreclosed. We note that the policy of maximum utilization does not require a single-minded endeavor to squeeze every drop of water from the valley's aquifers. Section 37–92–501(e) makes clear that the objective of "maximum use" administration is "optimum use." Optimum use can only be achieved with proper regard for all significant factors, including environmental and economic concerns. See section 37–92–102(3), C.R.S. (recognizing the need to correlate the activities of mankind with reasonable preservation of the natural environment); Harrison & Sandstrom, supra, at 14–15 (An increase of well diversions at the expense of maintenance of a surface flow would increase the efficiency of irrigation at the expense of other environmental and economic values.). See also Trelease, supra, at 1866–1872 (Determination of what constitutes a reasonable means of diversion may be more a question of the proper allocation of the costs of more efficient diversion than of the quantity of water ultimately diverted.). The water court observed that the state engineer's reconsideration might take the form of requiring senior appropriators to drill new wells before requiring curtailment of junior rights and listed a number of suggestions for increasing utilization. Similarly, the state engineer's reconsideration might result in assessment to junior appropriators of the cost of making those improvements to seniors' diversions which are necessitated by junior withdrawals. Selection among these and other possibilities, including retention of the scheme of the proposed rules, is a policy decision to be made by the state engineer, after consideration of all relevant factors.

We remand the rules to the water court for return to the state engineer. * * * For the reasons set forth in Part III, supra, we affirm the water court's disapproval of the underground water rules. Although we approve the water court's findings of fact on this issue, * * * we remand the rules for the state engineer's consideration of the policy of maximum utilization and the reasonable-means-of-diversion doctrine.

Judgment affirmed in part and reversed in part.

Notes

1. Harrison and Sandstrom, The Groundwater-Surface Water Conflict and Recent Colorado Water Legislation, 43 U. of Colo.L.Rev. 1, 17–18 (1971):

"The relationship between pumping and streamflow has been under intensive study in recent years. The United States Geological Service (USGS) has developed a concept called the 'stream depletion factor.' This is a parameter describing the time-effect that pumping has on the stream. The analysis is defined in terms of the number of days required for a certain well to have taken some certain per cent of its total pumped volume from the stream or from water that would have reached the stream. As an example, if a pump were to draw 100 acre-feet of water in a 10 day period and 28 acre-feet of the amount would have reached the stream if no pumping occurred, then that well has a 10 day 28 per cent 'stream depletion factor.' The farther from the stream the well is located, or the less permeable the material, the greater the 'stream depletion factor' will be. At any rate, in a determinable number of days of pumping well can affect the stream flow.

"The Colorado State Engineer's Office, using unpublished USGS data, has calculated a similar parameter intended for use in regulation of well pumping in river valleys. This 'stream depletion factor' is based on a five per cent volume interception rate. Thus, a five per cent 'stream depletion factor' of 20 days means that a well will begin taking water destined for the stream at the rate of five per cent of the stream's total flow in 20 days. It is meaningful to speak of stream depletion factor for any location within the aquifer, not just for developed wells. By interpreting hydrologic information, a line connecting points of equal stream depletion factor can be drawn, resulting in a map of 'contours' showing the effects in terms of days. As with any contour map, sacrifices for detail may be made in order to get a simultaneous overview of the total system, but basically such maps offer a regulatory solution to extremely complex hydrologic situations where an actual detailed water budget cannot be kept. On the Arkansas and South Platte Rivers, computer models have been developed to solve simultaneously many hydrologic problems, including the calculation of stream depletion factors and the generation of stream depletion contour maps.

"It is worthwhile to emphasize the time dimension of this problem. The basic parameter of the stream depletion factor is a time unit. The overall result of this hydrologic method is the development of a concept of hydrologic time-space. When a user or water official discovers that a senior right is being damaged by a well far away in terms of stream depletion factor, it may be too late to cure the situation. The well pumping can be shut down immediately but it may be days before the effect of the shutdown is felt. For the irrigator the water must be delivered at a crucial time; a delay may mean crop destruction. In the past, the Colorado water rights scheme depended entirely on the occurrence of present damage. A senior could 'call' only when he could not get his water from his diversion works, not simply on the basis of fear of future shortage. The legislature, in its most recent attempt to modernize water law, has given ironic recognition to this problem through the definition of a concept commonly called 'futile call.' A senior cannot shut down an injuring junior if it will not have the effect of delivering water at the time and place of need. Generally, if a well is located at a stream depletion contour of, for example, 30 days, and it is within a month of the end of the irrigation season, no user on the stream can cause the well to be shut down. In fact, a large number of wells are located so far from the stream that they may, practically speaking never be subject to regulation by the present system."

2. In Matter of Arkansas River, 195 Colo. 557, 581 P.2d 293 (1978), the court gave an indication of the complexities involved in conjunctive use:

"The purpose of the State Engineer in adopting the Amendment was to protect decreed rights to surface water against encroachment by wells. This is not, however, a case in which surface appropriators generally are pitted against well owners. A substantial part of the farm ground water users also have surface water rights and they use the surface water and ground water conjunctively for irrigation.

"One study admitted in evidence states that there are annually a total of 4,200,000 acre-feet of *surface* water *rights* in the basin with only an average annual surface *supply* of 700,000 acre-feet. As mentioned, there is in evidence that in 1972 there were withdrawals of over 200,000 acre-feet from wells. The court made a finding that an estimated 2,000,000 acre-feet of water is generally held in transient storage within the alluvial material in the basin.

"When water in the aquifer is brought to the surface by a well and there is a consumptive use of that water by evaporation and evapotranspiration of phreatophytes, generally the surface supply is depleted by the amount of such consumptive use. The evidence and findings in this case demonstrate, however, that the restriction of wells does not necessarily result in a comparable increase in the supply of surface water. There are countereffects which offset or modify the depletive use of well water. Some of these are: variations in the amount of river flow; more winter irrigation; reduction in evaporation and phreatophyte losses as a result of lowering of water tables; changes in ground water storage; extent of alluvium recharge occurring during wet cycles or as a result of widespread winter irrigation practices; and increased irrigation efficiencies. Other factors which may also be involved are increased ground water storage, stock ponds, municipal sewage lagoons, potholes, changes in side channel inflows, and cyclical fluctuations through wet and dry periods."

WATER POLICIES FOR THE FUTURE

National Water Commission, 1973.
Pp. 234–236.

The Commission recommends that States in which ground water is an important source of supply commence conjunctive management of surface water (including imported water) and ground water through public management agencies. * * *

Different management tools can be used in different circumstances. Where a basin has already undergone adjudication and many private rights have been decreed, management may amount to little more than administration of the decreed rights and regulation of new withdrawals. On the other hand, the management agency might use economic tools in lieu of, or in addition to, regulatory ones. A water management agency having the power to impose pump charges would be able to introduce incentives to affect decisions of water users in the interest of the best use and conservation of the resource. Through taxing or pricing mechanisms a management agency may, in effect, efficiently ration ground and surface water.

An illustration is provided by the management scheme employed by the Orange County Water District in Southern California. The District can buy imported water from the Metropolitan Water District of Southern California. Ground water is also available, but sole reliance on it would cause an overdraft, as it has in the past. Each year the Orange County Water District determines how much of the water demand shall be supplied from ground water and how much from imported water. The determination of the amount of ground water withdrawal is based in part on the quantity in storage in the aquifer and the anticipated recharge, including artificial recharge.

Suppose in a given year that the District decides to meet demand with 60 percent ground water and 40 percent surface water; these percentages establish each user's "fair share" of basin supply. Then the District establishes the cost differential between pumped water and imported water. Suppose imported water costs $14 per acre-foot more than pumped water. If a water user takes a total of 100 acre-feet of water during the year, pumping 60 percent and taking imported water for the other 40 percent, he pays no special charge, although he has, of course, paid a premium of $14 per acre-foot for the imported water. If the user takes the full 100 acre-feet in ground water, he must pay a Basin Equity Assessment of $14 per acre-foot on 40 of the 100 acre-feet that he pumped. If another user takes his 100 acre-feet all in imported water (paying the $14 per acre-foot premium on the total imported), the District will credit him with $14 per acre-foot for the 60 acre-feet he could have pumped from the aquifer. As a consequence, all water users in the District pay approximately the same price per acre-foot for water no matter what the source, and all water users pay part of the costs for importing water even though some may use no part of it. Even in the absence of a supply of imported water, a similar pricing system can be used to apportion withdrawals between indigenous surface supply and ground water supply.

Notes

1. A very full discussion of physical management techniques is found in Harrison and Sandstrom, The Groundwater-Surfacewater Conflict and Recent Colorado Water Legislation, 43 U. of Colo.L.Rev. 1 (1971). These include storage of high stream flows in aquifer-reservoirs for later withdrawals by wells during low flow seasons or drought years, "by-pass pumping" by which a fraction of pumped water is released to the stream to replace natural flow, artificial recharge, exchange of water stored in a surface reservoir to replace stream flow decreased by pumping a larger amount. The authors state that these are available under existing Colora-

do law if proper arrangements are made, and could be expanded basinwide by formation of a sufficiently large conservancy district, also available under existing law, to which appropriators might assign control over their rights in return for a guarantee of water.

2. One class of claims propounded in State v. Southeastern Colorado Water & Conservancy District, 671 P.2d 1294 (Colo.1983) involved an interesting variation of conjunctive use:

"The class I claimant requests decrees for underground water storage where a naturally occurring glacial terminal moraine creates an underground dam. Each storage area lies directly under a surface flowing river or stream. The claimant proposes to withdraw the water presently held in these underground reservoirs, release it into the overlying streams, and obtain storage decrees permitting it to refill these reservoirs from the surface streams to the capacity created by the initial pumping. The special water judge dismissed all applications within class I on two grounds. First, the judge stated that the methods proposed by the claimant were infeasible and would necessarily affect the surface stream flow and existing decreed appropriations. Second, the judge found that the representative application requests vast quantities of water for beneficial uses stated in the broadest terms and that, therefore, the claims were merely speculative and made for the purpose of profit.

"In ruling on the class I claims, the special water judge considered only the representative application, oral argument, legal briefs and exhibits, and treated the proceeding as one in the nature of a motion to dismiss or for summary judgment. The trial court declined to consider 'Hypothetical Fact Situations and/or Offers of Proof' filed by the class I applicant when members of the trial committee challenged that document with a motion to strike. The court did not hold an evidentiary hearing on the class I representative claim or the other applications in that class to determine whether the method for implementing the proposed storage right was feasible and to determine with more specificity the exact uses for the water. We believe that the approach taken by the trial court was incorrect and unfairly places a burden on the applicant not contemplated by the statutory scheme for adjudication of rights to tributary ground water.

"Section 37–92–302 of the 1969 Act sets forth the procedure for applying for a determination of rights to tributary water and requires the inclusion of certain information in standard application forms. Subsection (2) of section 37–92–302 states that the application shall contain 'a legal description of the diversion or proposed diversion, a description of the source of the water, the date of the initiation of the appropriation or proposed appropriation, the amount of water claimed, and the use or proposed use of the water.' Our review of the class I representative application shows that it contains all the basic information required by statute. Dismissal of the class I claims based on the general information contained in the representative application and oral argument by the claimant penalizes it for following statutory application procedures. The record before us does not contain sufficient information to support the trial court's ruling that the class I claims are infeasible and speculative. We reverse the trial court's dismissal of these claims and remand them to the appropriate water divisions for further proceedings."

3. Schneider, Groundwater Rights in California 37–53 (Staff Paper No. 2, Governor's Commission to Review California Water Rights Law, 1977):

"Water producers and users in a number of basins have created water organizations or have had water district acts of existing districts amended in self-help efforts to manage groundwater. Immediate problems of salt-water intrusion, critically-lowered water tables, subsidence, and ground-water quality degradation have moved these groundwater basin users to provide local districts with sufficient power and financial capability to respond to such problems.

"Water districts appear to be the most frequently used type of water management organization chosen in California to manage groundwater basins. Water districts are formed either under general district acts or special district acts. A general district act is an enabling statute which can be used to set up a local district; it does not actually create a specific local district. A special district act is a statute that does create a specific local district.

"Three general district acts, the Water Replenishment District Act, the Water Conservation District Act of 1931, and the Municipal Water District Law of 1911, specifically authorize replenishment programs and pump taxes. Replenishment and pump tax powers have been added to several special district acts. * * *

"Water management organizations have also been used as a tool for redistributing available water to ease the burden which the mutual prescription doctrine's 'race to the pumphouse' effect placed on groundwater production. For example, the Metropolitan Water District of Southern California (Metropolitan) provides imported water to supplement ground-water supplies. To obtain the imported water, communities must form water organizations that can distribute and finance the imported supply. Many water organizations in Southern California are members of Metropolitan and pay taxes to Metropolitan for the right to purchase imported water. Following the *Pasadena* decision, many users within Metropolitan's member organizations preferred to maximize pumping rather than to use the imported supply. Metropolitan's favorable pricing policy for replenishment water and the in-lieu statutes countered the incentive to overdraft to some extent. * * *

"The interrelationship of districts and adjudications in the West and Central Basins of Southern California illustrates another type of district-based management solution that has been developed. In 1945, an adjudication of the West Basin was begun. The basin was overdrafted and threatened by permanent damage from salt water intrusion. The trial court referred the matter to the predecessor of the State Water Resources Control Board for a determination of the facts. In 1961, the court issued a judgment based on agreement and stipulation by owners of more than 80 percent of pumping rights. The judgment allocated the groundwater, set up an exchange pool, reserved jurisdiction, and continued court supervision through a watermaster, the Department of Water Resources.

"The court's order was upheld on appeal. The Court of Appeal expressly affirmed the lower court's determination:

> [T]here was no necessity for distinguishing between the overlying users and appropriators. The object of the judgment was to relieve the overdraft and prevent salt water intrusion.

Supplemental surface water was available to make the court's physical solution, the watermaster-run exchange pool, workable, since the West Basin Municipal Water District had joined the Metropolitan Water District of Southern California in 1948. * * *

"Under the exchange pool system, member pumpers with access to alternate surface water supplies reduce pumping below the amount of their 'adjudicated right' so that other pumpers without surface water connections may pump more than their adjudicated right. Pumpers who pump more than their adjudicated right pay the watermaster for the exchange pool water they receive, and he in turn pays the parties who 'released' water to the exchange pool. * * *

"The West Basin is downstream from the Central Basin. Overdraft in the Central Basin aggravated the West Basin's problems. The Central Basin Municipal Water District was formed in 1952, and was annexed to the Metropolitan Water District of Southern California in 1954. The availability of supplemental surface water did not ease the Central Basin overdraft.

"In an effort to control Central Basin pumping, the Central and West Basin Water Replenishment District (CWBWRD) was formed in 1959, under the general act. The CWBWRD has replenishment and pump tax powers and the CWBWRD boundaries conform to the boundaries of the two basins.

"In 1961, the CWBWRD began an adjudication of the Central Basin in order to control pumping there to the same extent as in the West Basin. Based on agreement and stipulation by owners of 'over 75 percent of the Assumed Relative Rights within the Basin', the court issued an interim order in 1961, which controlled basin pumping and appointed the Department of Water Resources as watermaster. The court entered a final judgment in 1965, again pursuant to an agreement and stipulation by the parties, and after only one week of trial.

"In the West and Central Basins, the court-appointed watermasters cooperate closely with the CWBWRD. While the watermaster administers the exchange pools in the two basins based on data it collects cooperatively with CWBWRD, CWBWRD carries on several replenishment and salt water intrusion barrier programs.

"One program is an 'in-lieu replenishment' program in which CWBWRD contracts with pumpers who have access to supplemental water to use that water instead of pumping groundwater. CWBWRD can use this program to:

Alter pumping patterns within a ground water basin; replenish areas of low transmissibility where conventional recharge techniques are ineffective; heighten the effect of injecting water to form a sea-water barrier by reducing extractions in the vicinity; reduce the amount of replenishment water purchased by CWBWRD; and reduce the annual ground water extraction from a ground water basin.

"Pumping is not limited to safe yield in either the West or Central Basins. The CWBWRD Act provides:

> [F]ollowing a final adjudication of all or substantially all of the rights to extract ground water and a determination of the natural safe yield of the ground water supplies within the district, and a determination of the amount or extent to which the rights to extract ground water so adjudicated may be exercised without exceeding the natural safe yield of such ground water supplies, the board of such district shall recognize such judicial determination by exempting from replenishment assessments the amount of water pumped by each person whose rights have been so adjudicated which does not exceed his proportionate share of the natural safe yield. * * *

"Since safe yield figures have not been set for the basins, the pump tax is a gross pump tax that is applied to all pumping. Use of a gross pump tax lessens the economic advantage of adjudicated rights within the safe yield."

The institutional and legal complexities caused by the number and variety of water districts and their relationship to state and federal water agencies is mind-boggling in some geographic areas of California. An in-depth look at one such situation is given in Andrews and Fairfax, Groundwater and Intergovernmental Relations In the Southern San Joaquin Valley of California: What Are All These Cooks Doing to the Broth?, 55 Colo.L.Rev. 145 (1984).

3. Trelease, Conjunctive Use of Groundwater and Surface Water, 27A Rocky Mt.Min.L.Inst. 1853 (1981):

"In Arizona, the management institution will be very different. The Active Management Areas (AMA's) are not autonomous local agencies governed by locally-elected boards, as in California. They are areas, not districts, and operations within them will be governed by a powerful state official, the Director of the new Department of Water Resources. The four AMA's in existence were established by legislative fiat, not by vote of the affected people or water users. Three cover the largest population centers, the other a major agricultural region. Additional areas may be created by the director if he determines they are necessary to preserve existing groundwater supplies for future needs, to prevent land subsidence, or to prevent groundwater quality degradation. AMA's may also be created upon petition and vote of the electorate.

"The organizations are different because their functions are different. The California district's purpose is to supply water, the AMA's is to cut down water use. In the two California districts, the only limit on total water use is price. Up to now, at least, the Colorado River Aqueduct and the State Water (Feather River) Project have been regarded as bottomless barrels that can never be emptied; so as more water is needed, more is taken. In Arizona, the Central Arizona Project can never import enough water to make up the overdraft in full. The added water cannot supply new uses; it can only reduce the amount that must be cut back to enable Arizona to live within its means. So while the California district is primarily a wholesaler, providing the physical and financial mechanisms for bringing in and paying for whatever amount of water is desired, the Arizona director must be a strictly regulatory officer, enforcing, restricting, and reducing the number and quantity of groundwater rights until demands are trimmed to match supply.

"Inside the AMA's, some of these measures will be drastic. The 'grandfathered rights' fixed by past use are adjusted downward in quantity. Irrigation rights will be cut to 'water duties' fixed by the director. Residential uses will be subjected to increasingly stringent conservation measures. Industrial users must employ the latest commercially available technology consistent with economic return. New rights to pump will be strictly limited to permits for mineral extraction and processing, industrial use and electrical generation, and to such increased pumping as cities, towns, and water companies may undertake within their service areas. Subdivided land cannot be sold unless the subdivision, water company, city, or town has an assured water supply, either a 100-year supply or an arrangement to buy CAP water. A series of mandatory plans will be formulated by the director, each requiring additional conservation measures and aimed at achieving by the year 2025 a 'safe yield,' defined as a long-term balance between the amount of groundwater withdrawn and the amount of natural and artificial recharge.

"Some economic controls, incentives, and cost-sharing methods will be included. Administration of the Act will be financed by a pump tax ("groundwater withdrawal fee") of up to $1.00 per acre-foot. By 1990, each management area will be required to have a water augmentation plan, financed by a $2.00 per acre-foot addition to the pump tax, which may be used in part to reduce the cost of alternative water supplies so they can be offered to persons who can use them on acceptable terms. To this extent, the costs will be shared by other users in the basin, since all will benefit from the corresponding reduction in pumping. The ultimate solution is expected to come from the purchase of irrigated farmland and the transfer of grandfathered irrigation rights to accommodate new needs and growth. Irrigation now accounts for 89% of total water depletions in the state. If these economic pressures fail to produce the needed change, a third increment of $2.00 per acre-foot to the pump tax can be added to provide a fund for the purchase and retirement of farmland by the state."

4. Storage of water underground is regulated by statute in several states. West's Ann.Calif. Water Code § 1242 makes storage of water underground a beneficial use for which an appropriation of streamwater can be made. If the operation is performed by a Water Replenishment District, no person can acquire any property or right in the waters,

§ 60351, and the district may charge rates, § 60245, tax real property, § 60252, or levy assessments payable by persons benefited, § 60325.

An appropriation for storage in an underground basin can be made in Utah, if the point of intake, the location of the basin and the points of collection therefrom are identified. Utah Code Ann.1953, 73–3–2. "Artifically stored groundwater" is defined and preserved from appropriation by Wash.Rev.Code Ann. 90–44.035, 90.44.040. Where a groundwater regulatory area is established, the person who has been so storing water must claim and identify it, Section 94.44.130.

Chapter 5

WATER DISTRIBUTION ORGANIZATIONS

SECTION 1. PRIVATE CORPORATIONS

JACOBUCCI v. DISTRICT COURT

Supreme Court of Colorado, 1975.
___ Colo. ___, 541 P.2d 667.

ERICKSON, JUSTICE.

On November 14, 1973, the City cf Thornton instituted an action in eminent domain in the Jefferson County District Court against Farmers Reservoir and Irrigation Company, the City of Westminster, a shareholder in Farmers, the Treasurer of Jefferson County, the Treasurer of Boulder County, and other unknown persons claiming any interest in the proceeding. Farmers Reservoir and Irrigation Company (Farmers) is a mutual ditch company, organized pursuant to section 7–42–102 et seq., C.R.S.1973, as a Colorado corporation.

The petitioners here are Victor L. Jacobucci, Dorothy Jacobucci, Paul Jacobucci, Mary J. Jacobucci, Jean J. Jacobucci, Albert Sack, Anne Sack, Casper Sack, Katherine Sack, and Yoxall Farms, Inc. The petitioners, all shareholders in Farmers, filed a cross-petition, pursuant to section 38–1–109, C.R.S.1973, in order to intervene as defendants in the condemnation proceedings. This motion was denied by the District Court on February 11, 1975, after the court concluded that the shareholders of Farmers were not indispensable parties to the proceeding. Thereafter, this court was petitioned, pursuant to its original jurisdiction under C.A.R. 21, to grant the petitioners relief. The petition requested an order permitting the shareholders to intervene and compelling their joinder as parties in the condemnation proceeding. We issued a rule to show cause why the relief requested should not be granted.

The issue we address in this original proceeding, which renders the other issues moot, is whether the individual shareholders of a mutual ditch company are indispensable parties in an action to condemn the shareholders' decreed water priorities. We hold that they are.

Farmers, a mutual ditch company, administers an extensive water distribution system divided into four divisions. The Standley Lake Division includes a storage reservoir known as Standley Lake located in Jefferson County. The decreed water rights of this reservoir are used to irrigate approximately 15,000 acres of land situated in Jefferson, Adams, and Weld Counties. Property rights administered by the Standley Lake Division are the subject of the condemnation action which created the issues in this proceeding.

At the time of the institution of the condemnation proceeding, Farmers represented a total of 1,105 shareholders, 271 of whom owned shares allocated to the Standley Lake Division of Farmers. * * * The record title to the physical properties of the ditches, reservoir, lands, and rights-of-way stands in the name of Farmers.

In order to determine whether the shareholders of Farmers are indispensable parties to the condemnation proceedings, we must define the nature of their relationship to the mutual ditch company and to the rights and properties administered by the corporation. The history behind the growth and purposes of mutual ditch companies is necessary to an analysis of the issue which is before us.

The rapid development and expansion of agriculture in the arid regions of the west led to the increased importance of irrigation. Irrigation itself, however, proved to be a great obstacle to farmers in need of irrigation water. The construction and maintenance of canals and ditches required the outlay of large sums of money. The average farmer did not have sufficient means to construct, own, or operate an irrigation ditch to convey water to his land. The most economical solution was to convey the water over a great distance through a single large main and laterals and then distribute it to consumers by means of smaller laterals. Golden Canal Co. v. Bright, 8 Colo. 144, 6 P. 142 (1884).

In response to the enormous task of supplying water to the parched farmlands, farmers banded together and formed mutual ditch companies for the express purpose of storing and conducting water for irrigation purposes. Farmer who may have previously owned ditches as tenants-in-common would transfer their ownership rights to mutual ditch companies and in return receive stock representing their water rights. This made possible the distribution of water over large areas of land, often remote from the source of supply, and increased the availability of irrigated farmland at reasonable costs. Not only was the management of the ditches and reservoirs made more efficient, but capital was made more available through the operation of these companies. See J. Long, Law of Irrigation (1st ed. 1901).

Mutual ditch companies in Colorado have been recognized as quasi-public carriers. Farmers Independent Ditch Co. v. Agricultural Ditch

Co., 22 Colo. 513, 45 P. 444 (1896). Farmers is not organized for profit or hire and exists primarily for the benefit of its shareholders. Farmers is engaged in the business of storing and transporting water to shareholders who own the right to use the water. Farmers Independent Ditch Co. v. Agricultural Ditch Co., supra; cf. White v. Farmers' Highline Canal and Reservoir Co., 22 Colo. 191, 43 P. 1028 (1896); Wyatt v. Larimer and Weld Irrigation Co., 18 Colo. 298, 33 P. 144 (1893); Wheeler v. Northern Colorado Irrigation Co., 10 Colo. 582, 17 P. 487 (1887).

Mutual ditch companies like Farmers were formed expressly for the purpose of furnishing water to shareholders, not for profit or hire. See Combs v. Agricultural Ditch Co., 17 Colo. 146, 28 P. 966 (1892); C. Kinney, Irrigation & Water Rights § 1482 (2d ed. 1912). Delivery of water to the consumers is conditioned upon the payment of an annual assessment levied by the company to meet operating expenses and, if they exist, debt installments. Section 7–42–104, C.R.S.1973. These companies are not organized under the general Colorado corporation statutes, but under special legislation for ditch and reservoir companies. Section 7–42–101 et seq., C.R.S.1973, According to Colo. Const. Art. X, Sec. 3, "[d]itches, canals and flumes owned and used by individuals or corporations for irrigating land owned by such individuals or corporations, or the individual members thereof, shall not be separately taxed so long as they shall be owned and used exclusively for such purposes." "Ditches, canals and flumes" have been defined so as to include headgates, dams, reservoirs, reservoir beds, the earth upon which the dam stands, and the lands surrounding the reservoirs with the improvements thereon that are an integral part of the irrigation system as a whole and necessary for its proper maintenance and operation. Cf. Logan Irrigation District v. Holt, 110 Colo. 253, 133 P.2d 530 (1943); see Shaw v. Bond, 64 Colo. 366, 171 P. 1142 (1918).

The relationship between the mutual ditch corporation and its shareholders arises out of contract, implied in a subscription for stock and construed by the provisions of a charter or articles of incorporation. Supply Ditch Co. v. Elliot, 10 Colo. 327, 15 P. 691 (1887); C. Kinney, Irrigation & Water Rights § 1482 (2d ed. 1912).

The articles of incorporation or charter of a mutual ditch company sets forth the express purposes which the corporation undertakes to carry out. The corporation is not only obligated to furnish a proper proportion of water to each of its shareholders, but it is liable in damages for the failure to do so. Rocky Ford Canal Co. v. Simpson, 5 Colo.App. 30, 36 P. 638 (1894). The corporation must protect and preserve the interests of the shareholders by keeping the ditches, canals, reservoir, and other works in good repair (Supply Ditch Co. v. Elliot, supra), the expense of which is paid from the special assessment. Sections 7–42–104, 7–42–107, 7–42–108, C.R.S.1973.

The shares of stock in a mutual ditch corporation represent the " 'consumer's interest in the reservoir, canal and water rights.' " Beaty

v. Board of County Comm'rs. of Otero County, 101 Colo. 346, 73 P.2d 982 (1937); Comstock v. Olney Springs Drainage District, 97 Colo. 416, 50 P.2d 531 (1935); Kendrick v. Twin Lakes Reservoir Co., 58 Colo. 281, 144 P. 884 (1914). The benefit derived from the ownership of such stock is the right to the exclusive use of the water it represents, the water being divided pro-rata according to the number of shares of stock held by each shareholder. Kendrick v. Twin Lakes Reservoir Co., supra; Billings Ditch Co. v. Industrial Comm'n., 127 Colo. 69, 253 P.2d 1058 (1953). The shareholders have the right to change the place of the use of the water if other users are not injured thereby. See Wadsworth Ditch Co. v. Brown, 39 Colo. 57, 88 P. 1060 (1907); Cache La Poudre Irr. Co. v. Larimer & Weld Reservoir Co., 25 Colo. 144, 53 P. 318 (1898).

As a mutual ditch company, Farmers is "merely the vehicle by which its owners operate and manage its affairs." Billings Ditch Co. v. Industrial Comm'n., supra. The corporation, like other mutual ditch companies, was organized solely for the convenience of its members in the management of the irrigation and reservoir systems. Billings Ditch Co. v. Industrial Comm'n., supra. The ownership of the shares of stock is merely incidental to the ownership of the water rights by the shareholders. Comstock v. Olney Springs Drainage District, supra; Billings Ditch Co. v. Industrial Comm'n, supra. We wish to emphasize that the shares of stock owned by Farmers' shareholders represent a definite and specific water right, as well as a corresponding interest in the ditch, canal, reservoir, and other works by which the water right is utilized.

The City of Thornton seeks to analogize the position of the shareholders in Farmers to that of the shareholders in any other corporation. On this basis, they argue that the shareholders in Farmers are not necessary parties to this litigation, because the corporation, under principles of corporation law, is bound to protect their interests. We have held that a mutual ditch corporation is responsible for maintaining actions in the corporate name to secure or protect the consumers' water rights or other property and to represent the shareholders in civil actions. Montrose Canal Co. v. Loutsenhizer Ditch Co., 23 Colo. 233, 48 P. 532 (1896); see also Farmers' Independent Ditch Co. v. Agricultural Ditch Co., 22 Colo. 513, 45 P. 444 (1896); Supply Ditch Co. v. Elliot, supra. Inasmuch as Farmers holds legal title to the physical properties sought to be condemned, Thornton argues that Farmers is the real party in interest, not the shareholders. See In re Babcock, 26 F.2d 153 (7th Cir.1928).

In the first place, as petitioners rightly point out, a mutual ditch corporation is not organized under the general corporation laws, but under a separate and independent statutory provision. Section 7–42–101 et seq., C.R.S.1973. We find that the unique character of these corporations mandates different treatment which is not fully in accord with the principles applicable to corporations in general. As noted above, the shares of stock held by the consumers in a mutual ditch corporation represent a specific property interest in a water right. The interest of these shareholders cannot be "defeated or altered by any action of the ditch company or its other shareholders." United States v. 508.88 Acres of Land, U.S. District Ct. (D.Colo. May 8, 1973, Unpublished); Bent v. Second Extension Water Co., 51 Cal.App. 648, 197 P. 657 (1921). While the "naked title" may stand in the name of Farmers, the ditch, reservoir and water rights are actually owned by the farmers who are served thereby. Billings Ditch Co. v. Industrial Comm'n., supra; accord Beaty v. Board of County Comm'rs. of Otero County, supra; Comstock v. Olney Springs Drainage District, supra. The shareholders are the real parties in interest in the condemnation action, not the corporation. See Stuart v. Jefferson County, 25 Colo.App. 568, 139 P. 577 (1914).

In our view, shareholders are indispensable parties. C.R.C.P. 19. * * * The shareholders of Farmers are so situated that their ability to protect their interest in the beneficial application of the water to their land is, as a practical matter, impaired. * * * The condemnation action here in issue has the potential of seriously disrupting the shareholders' property interests. See Potts v. Gordon, Colo.App., 525 P.2d 500 (1974). That the water rights owned by Farmers' shareholders are property rights is well established by Colorado law. Billings Ditch Co. v. Industrial Comm'n., supra; Brighton Co. v. Englewood, 124 Colo. 366, 237 P.2d 116 (1951); Beaty v. Board of County Comm'rs. of Otero County, supra; Comstock v. Olney Springs Drainage District, supra; Kendrick v. Twin Lakes Reservoir Co., supra.

At least 271 shareholders, as of the date of the petition in condemnation, are faced with the prospect of having their farmlands denied a substantial source of water. The productivity and value of their lands, as well as the assurance of their livelihoods, is in many cases entirely dependent upon the continuing flow of water from Standley Reservoir. No court can ignore the magnitude of disruption which would result in a successful condemnation action by the City of Thornton. Moreover, each shareholder stands in a different position from the others and is likely to be affected differently by the condemnation action. Their ability to protect those individualized interests would surely be impaired if this action were allowed to proceed in their absence.

The evidence in the present case does not suggest that joinder would be infeasible. All shareholders of Farmers similarly situated to the petitioners herein are subject to service of process. * * * Therefore, pursuant to C.R.C.P. 19, and this court's power under C.A.R. 21, the District Court should join as parties to the condemnation action those shareholders in the Standley Lake Division of Farmers whose water rights would be affected by the condemnation action of Thornton as of the date of the initiation of the condemnation action and all parties in interest.

Accordingly, the rule to show cause is made absolute, and we remand to the District Court for further proceedings consonant with the views expressed in this opinion.

Notes

1. There are many variations on the theme of the mutual water company, arising from the physical nature of the project, the purpose of the incorporators, the powers granted to the corporation by statute and charter, and the arrangement between the corporation and its stockholders. Sometimes much of the land irrigable by the corporation's works was already irrigated under existing water rights, and the corporate ditch was a substitute method of diversion, carrying to the consumer the water to which he was entitled under his old appropriation. In some such cases the consumers conveyed their old rights to the company in exchange for shares and thereafter took a share in the company's rights. Sometimes the company existed prior to settlement by the farmers. Many mutual corporations were created as subsidiaries of land promotion corporations. A "land company" or "land and water company", financed as a commercial venture with private capital (often from eastern states, England and Europe) purchased or obtained control of a large area of land and constructed irrigation works, subdivided the land and sold settlers farms and shares in a subsidiary "water company" or "ditch company". Many other mutual water companies were originally formed as commercial enterprises to profit from the sale of water. The failure of such ventures, and their abandonment by their managers, forced the consumers to take over the system on a cooperative basis, either by purchase in bankruptcy or by more informal methods. Thus the grandiose "Humboldt-Lovelock Irrigation, Light & Power Company" degenerated into a mutual nonprofit irrigation company whose shares are mere muniments of title to water rights and interests in the works. Pacific Savings & Loan Corp. v. Schmitt, 103 F.2d 1002 (9th Cir. 1939).

A few "Carey Act corporations" are still in existence. To encourage the reclamation of arid western lands, Congress enacted the Carey Act, 28 Stat. 372 (1894), as amended, 43 U.S.C.A. § 641 (1964). It provided that 1,000,000 acres of arid lands of the public domain would be donated to each of the western "public land states", if those states would see to its reclamation and settlement. Most of these states carried out the obligation of the Act by contracting with private corporations to build and operate the reclamation works necessary to bring the water to the lands. The state sold the lands to settlers who bought their water rights from the construction company in the form of stock in a mutual water company formed to operate the works. The water company stock was usually bought under contract secured by a mortgage on the land in favor of the construction company. Many of the projects were not carefully planned and were economically infeasible so that the settlers were in trouble from the start, and many Carey Act corporations have been reorganized into irrigation districts.

Another specialized form of mutual water company is the "water users' association", a corporation formed to contract with the Secretary of the Interior for the repayment to the government of the reimbursable costs of a Reclamation project. Formed under the corporation law of the state in which located, the association issued stock in proportion to the irrigable acreage of the settlers. It levied assessments against the landowners, secured by liens on both stock and land, thus collecting on behalf of the United States the charges of construction, operation and maintenance of the project. Today the Bureau of Reclamation prefers to deal with irrigation districts, and many of these associations have changed their form, though they are still used to a considerable extent in Arizona and Utah.

Mutual water companies are organized under the general incorporation laws of the state in which they are formed, but most of the western states have additional provisions supplementing these laws, placing restrictions on their formation and regulating their relations with their stockholders. The state "Blue Sky" laws, and in some instances the federal securities laws, regulate the issuance of securities by mutual companies. Few mutual water companies that require financing from sources other than the water users are formed today. Some have issued bonds secured by a mortgage on the works, or on the stockholder's lands.

Mutual water companies are discussed and contrasted with other forms of organization in Irrigation-Enterprise Organizations, United States Department of Agriculture Circular No. 934 (1953); Russell, Mutual Water Companies in California, 12 So.Calif.L.Rev. 155 (1939); Moses, Irrigation Corporations, 32 Rocky Mt.L.Rev. 527 (1960).

2. The most common apportionment of stock among the shareholders is to issue one share of stock for each acre of land to be irrigated. The irrigator is entitled to such proportion of the water available to the company as his land (or stock) bears to the total. However, in some instances, shares of stock entitle the holder to a specific quantity of water, or to a specific fraction of the water available to the company, regardless of the acreage irrigated. In the former case, the stock is usually made appurtenant to the land, and the land is specifically described in the stock certificate. The stock may be made inseverably appurtenant by provision in the articles or by-laws that it shall be transferred only with the land and shall pass with a conveyance thereof. It may be severable from the land, despite its appurtenancy, so that while it would pass with a conveyance of the land if not mentioned, it can be sold separately or retained on a sale of the land. The transferability of the stock, as a method of transferring a water right from land to land, may be affected by statutes imposing restrictions on such changes of water rights. Even where a transfer of water right is permitted, a transfer of the stock to different land may be subject to reasonable regulations of the company, and the by-laws or the stock certificate may require the consent of the corporation to such a transfer. Riverside Land Co. v. Jarvis, 174 Cal. 316, 163 P. 54 (1917). In California, it is held that a company issuing non-appurtenant shares may prevent a shareholder from transferring the water represented by the shares to the intake of another ditch. Consolidated Peoples Ditch Co. v. Foothill Ditch Co., 205 Cal. 54, 269 P. 915 (1928). On the other hand, the Colorado court in Wadsworth Ditch Co. v. Brown, 39 Colo. 57, 88 P. 1060 (1907), permitted a shareholder in a mutual company to transfer water to lands beyond the service area of the ditch and apply it through other ditches, so long as he continued to bear his proportionate share of the cost of maintaining the mutual ditch.

A Utah statute provides that water rights shall be transferred by deed, except when they are represented by stock in a corporation, in which case water shall not be deemed to be appurtenant to the land. In Brimm v. Cache Valley Banking Co., 2 Utah 2d 93, 269 P.2d 859 (1954), this statute was construed as follows: "We think the effect of the 1943 amendment to section 100–1–10, U.C.A.1943 (now 73–1–10, U.C.A.1953) which added the phrase, 'in which case water shall not be deemed to be appurtenant to the land' was to establish a rebuttable presumption that a water right represented by shares of stock in a corporation did not pass to the grantee as an appurtenance to the land upon which the water right was used, but that the grantee could overcome such presumption if he could show by clear and convincing evidence that said water right was in fact appurtenant and that the grantor intended to transfer the water right with the land, even though no express mention of any water right was made in the deed. * * * In other words, the 1943 amendment merely obviated the necessity for a grantor, who owned a water right represented by shares of stock in a corporation but who did not desire to transfer that water right to the grantee of the land upon which the water was being used, to make an express reservation of that water right in the deed. But the amendment does not foreclose the water right from passing if the grantee can show such was the intention of the grantor. * * *"

3. Section 1 of the Uniform Stock Transfer Act provides: "Title to a certificate and to the shares represented thereby can be transferred only, (a) By delivery of the certificate indorsed either in blank or to a specified person by the person appearing by the certificate to be the owner of the shares represented thereby, or (b) By delivery of the certificate and a separate document containing a written assignment of the certificate or a power of attorney. * * *" What effect would this statute have upon these rules? See Russell, supra n. 1, at pages 161–163.

4. Payment of the annual assessment for operation and maintenance, and for other proper charges such as for improvements or for paying off bonds or other indebtedness, is enforced in the first instance by the simple process of denying water to the non-paying stockholder. He has no right to damages or for affirmative relief if he has not fulfilled his part of the bargain. Henderson v. Kirby Ditch Co., 373 P.2d 591 (Wyo.1962). Typically the articles, by-laws or stock certificates provide that an unpaid assessment shall be a lien upon the stock, which may be forfeited to the company for nonpayment, or sold to other water users. By agreement, the assessments may be made a lien upon the water user's land or a personal obligation. However, if the statutes provide for stock liens as the exclusive method of enforcing the payment of assessments, the imposition of other liens or personal liability is beyond the corporate powers and ultra vires. Thirty Mile Canal Co. v. Carskadon, 160 Neb. 496, 70 N.W.2d 432 (1955).

5. Ditches shared by several people under simpler and more informal arrangements are variously called joint, common and partnership ditches. The relationships between the owners, their shares in the water and their responsibilities for maintenance costs are generally governed by the law of property, contract or partnership. E.g., Moss v. Rose, 27 Or. 595, 41 P. 666 (1895). In some states these matters are elaborately regulated by statute.

E.g., Wyo.Stat.1977 §§ 41–5–102, 41–5–103, 41–6–303 to 41–6–308. In Wyoming the water commissioner may divide the water in the ditch among the partners or co-tenants, Wyo.Stat.1977, §§ 41–3–604, 41–6–301, while in other states his authority ends at the headgate in the river bank, Colo.Rev. Stat. '63, 148–15–3, Cache La Poudre Irrigation Ditch Co. v. Hawley, 43 Colo. 32, 95 P. 317 (1908).

6. Acequias, or community ditches, are a unique feature of New Mexico law. Derived from a mixture of Indian customs and Moorish-Spanish institutions brought by the first colonists, early Mormon settlers added some features of the mutual ditch company.

"Although the community ditch has both public and private components which are recognized in law, it is usually operated as a private enterprise. * * *

"The statutes continue to speak ambiguously of 'private or common acequias,' 'all acequias, public or private,' 'community or other ditches,' and 'public involuntary quasi corporations,' i.e., community acequias. This imprecision in language is the product of unclear understanding of private and public functions and above all the historical background of both terms. It appears that the community acequia was primarily public while serving a pueblo or municipality and that it developed stronger private aspects as the institution was applied and ditches were constructed beyond the municipality. * * *

"This old legislation apparently allows three gradations of control over acequias, or makes possible here the use of analogies based on these distinctions: (1) community, municipality or public control, where the analogy is to the public or municipal corporation and to its status as a political subdivision of the state; (2) private control by joint owners, mainly in non-municipal areas and where the similarity is to the private incorporated mutual company; and (3) the private corporation that is publicly regulated in the manner of a public utility.

"The statutes provide for the election of community ditch officers—three commissioners and one mayordomo or superintendent. Each must own an interest in the ditch or a water right. Qualifications for voters in the ditch election include ownership of ditch or water rights and payment of assessments. The powers of the officers include the right to make 'true, just and equitable apportionment and distribution of the water for their respective ditches,' where two or more ditches are served by one source, 'in accordance with the rights of each ditch, and in proportion to the lands irrigated by each ditch,' except in the case of 'ditches constructed from and conveying waters from the Rio Grande.' The law is also inapplicable to specific counties of the state. A 1963 amendment provides that persons, who after written notice of delinquent assessments failed to pay or do the work required under the statute, shall not be entitled to water during the period of their default.

"Despite the lack of clarity, which has existed for decades in some sections of the law, the community acequia as an institution remains important in several areas of the state." Clark, New Mexico Water Resources Law 47–52 (1964).

ROBINSON v. BOOTH-ORCHARD GROVE DITCH CO.

Supreme Court of Colorado, 1934.
94 Colo. 515, 31 P.2d 487.

BURKE, JUSTICE. * * * Defendant company owns and operates an irrigation ditch, and its stock is divided into three classes based upon the dates of priority. It amended its articles of incorporation to permit each class of stock to be assessed for ditch maintenance on the basis of benefits, and its officers proceeded accordingly. Plaintiff, an owner of class A stock, which bore the heaviest assessment, brought this suit to have the amendment nullified and the defendant officials enjoined from further action under it. Defendants demurred for want of facts. The demurrer was sustained, and plaintiff elected to stand. Thereupon the cause was dismissed at plaintiff's costs, and to review that judgment he prosecutes this writ.

Section 2356, C.L.1921, as amended by chapter 80, p. 263, Laws 1927, provides that: "Any corporation owning any ditch or canal for conveying * * * water for irrigation purposes, and when it is deemed necessary to raise funds to keep its ditch, * * * in good repair, * * * shall have power to make an assessment on the capital stock thereof, to be levied pro rata on the shares of stock. * * *"

Plaintiff says the amendment to the articles violates this section and defendants that it does not. * * *

The 1,600 shares of defendant company are divided and assessed as follows: 900 class A shares, having priorities up to 1881, assessed $4 per share; 105 class B shares, having priorities from 1881 to 1888, assessed $2 per share; 595 class C shares, having priorities later than 1888, assessed $2 per share.

Since each class of stock should bear its equitable portion of upkeep, and since earlier appropriators presumably use the ditch when there is no water for later, the earlier should bear the greater burden. Since presumptions favor the action of defendant officials, we must assume, in the absence of contrary allegations, that they have done their duty. Let us suppose there was also a class D stock whose priorities were limited to flood waters appearing only in small quantities and at limited times at intervals of a year, or several years. The injustice of forcing upon such stock an equal burden with class A for daily maintenance is apparent.

Where stock, as here, is divided into different classes, each entitled to a different use, and varying, therefore, in benefits from maintenance, the pro rata mandate requires only that cost shall be equitably apportioned between the classes and that the assessment on each share in a given class be the same.

The judgment is affirmed.

Notes

1. Idaho Code § 42–904, specifically provides for dividing the rights of landowners into classes where the distributing agency has more than one right or priority. Brose v. Nampa and Meridian Irrigation Dist., 20 Idaho 281, 118 P. 504 (1911), 24 Idaho 116, 132 P. 799 (1913), holds that under this statute a canal company cannot adjudicate the rights of users between themselves, since a classification by the company is not a permanent adjustment, so that any water user who deems himself aggrieved may take the matter of his relative priority vis-à-vis others into court.

2. The rule of no priority between shareholders with a proportionate interest in the same water right applies even where the water is insufficient for all. Sanderson v. Salmon River Canal Co., 34 Idaho 303, 200 P. 341 (1921). The Supreme Court of Wyoming rather callously stated, in Anderson v. Wyoming Development Co., 60 Wyo. 417, 154 P.2d 318 (1944), that the company is under no duty to establish a dependable supply or to limit sales of water rights to the amount of land that can be irrigated with its supply. But in Laramie Rivers Co. v. Watson, 69 Wyo. 333, 241 P.2d 1080 (1952), the court said "It would be unjust to the present water-right holders in the Pioneer Canal Company to dilute their rights by the selling of any more shares of stock when the water actually available is barely sufficient for the present holders of water rights."

3. In a dispute between shareholders of a mutual water company, Great Western Sugar Co. v. Jackson Lake Reservoir and Irrigation Co., 681 P.2d 484 (Colo.1984), the court applied the rule that a water user may not make a change in the nature of his water right that will injure another user. The shareholder's plan to delay the use of reservoir water until after the irrigation season would deprive other shareholders of winter carryover of surplus water that minimized seepage and evaporation. Permission to make the change was denied, unless additional terms to prevent the injury were proposed.

4. Priorities can exist between users who draw their water from a mutual ditch if the users formed the company and constructed the ditch to replace their individual works. Under some arrangements a private company distributing water to customers may be regarded as providing a service to water right owners rather than as selling its water to them. See Denver v. Brown, 56 Colo. 216, 138 P. 44 (1914).

5. The "carrier ditch" concept reached its high point in Arizona. Its nature was clearly brought out in Slosser v. Salt River Valley Canal Co., 7 Ariz. 376, 65 P. 332 (1901). The Arizona court analogized the ditch to a public road, and the facts of that case bring out the validity of this comparison. Slosser first drew his water from the "Chivari Ditch," when that was washed out by a flood, he switched to the "Farmers' Ditch," and when the great Salt River Valley Canal was built above the small ditches, encircling and capable of serving all the land, he drew his water from it, paying an annual charge to the company that built it. Nothing could be more clear than that he was the owner of his own water right and that these canals carried his water, much as a railroad might carry his goods.

6. Private contract water companies are rare today. Many of the early ones made contracts for permanent service at fixed rates, and rising costs forced most of them into bankruptcy and reorganization as mutual corporations or irrigation districts. A number still exist in Texas, distributing water under annual or short term contracts. For some of the Texas problems, see Edinburg Irrigation Co. v. Ledbetter, 285 S.W. 185 (Tex.Com. App.1926); Willis v. Neches Canal Co., 16 S.W.2d 266 (Tex.Com.App.1929); Roberts, Problems Connected with the Distribution of Irrigation Water in Texas, Proceedings, Water Law Conferences 79 (Univ. of Tex. 1952, 1954).

7. Whether the distributing agency or the consumer "owns" the water right often presents perplexing problems of semantics. Doctrines of ownership in the consumer seem to have arisen from the necessity of protecting the water user by giving him a permanent right to the water, instead of leaving him to the mercy of the commercial company. The water laws of the state, the history of the project, the legislation authorizing the formation of the organization, and the form and powers eventually adopted, combine to permit a wide variety of arrangements.

Whether the form of organization was a mutual water company, carrier ditch, community ditch or commercial company, three types of cases could be expected to arise: the customers might squabble among themselves, a customer might find himself at odds with the distributor, and the organization might dispute with other appropriators over priorities and shares of the stream. Yet in result, a surprisingly uniform pattern has arisen.

Between the water users, the result is the protection of one against an attempt by another to increase the latter's share at the expense of the former. Between the distributor and the water user, the most frequent problem arose when the company tried to stop delivery of the water to the customer, and courts throughout the west were quick to find some sort of enforceable right in the customer to have the service continued, since the customer's livelihood was at stake. Against the outside world in the shape of other appropriators from the stream, the usual solution was to leave the defense of the water right to the diverter-distributor as the representative of all its consumers.

The rule that the consumer is the owner of the water right is applied in community acequia and carrier ditch cases. Slosser v. Salt River Valley Canal Co., 7 Ariz. 376, 65 P. 332 (1901); Snow v. Abalos, 18 N.M. 681, 140 P. 1044 (1914), Holmberg v. Bradford, 56 N.M. 401, 244 P.2d 785 (1952). In *Holmberg* the rule of ownership protected one consumer against another, in *Slosser,* a consumer against the distributor, in *Snow* the right of a consumer against the claims of other appropriators.

As noted above, many irrigators from mutual ditches retained their own water rights when a common ditch was constructed, which of course gave them protection from other users seeking to take more than their share from the ditch. Where the company owns the water rights, the water is usually distributed in proportion to shareholdings, as in *Holmberg,* supra, and these property rights or corporation laws and bylaws prevent one consumer from encroaching on the other. See Robinson v. Booth-Orchard Grove Ditch Co., supra p. 502. In true mutual water companies, organized, owned and controlled by farmers for their mutual benefit, difficulties between consumer and distributor would of course be rare, and indeed there seem to be no such cases. But if the company's charter expires, the shareholders who have used the water for years retain the water right. St. George City v. Kirkland, 17 Utah 2d 292, 409 P.2d 970 (1966). Yet when the interests of consumers of water carried by one company conflict with the interests of consumers under another ditch, the ditch company is regarded as the representative of its consumers, and a decree awarding the appropriation to it is binding not only on the company but also on the consumers of water under its ditch. Combs v. Farmers Highline Canal & Reservoir Co., 38 Colo. 420, 88 P. 396 (1907). For these purposes, therefore, the distributing company is the "owner."

Companies seeking to make money by selling water as a commodity might naturally be expected to come in conflict with their customers, and these commercial companies raise the problem in the form it most frequently takes. Denver v. Brown, supra note 4, is illustrative on this point. First the court holds that the farmers are appropriators permanently entitled to water supply, but since this seemed to run counter to *Combs* the cases are reconciled by saying that the company is "*in effect* * * * the proprietor of the appropriation." Again we see that in external relations between the project and other claimants to the water the distributing agency is the "owner" but internally, between the distributor and its customers, the consumer has property rights that the court will protect by arbitrary action by the distributor.

Other solutions to the problem of giving protection to the irrigator have been found in other places, without declaring the consumer to be the owner of the appropriation. Constitutional and statutory rights perform this function in some states instead of property rights. Idaho avoided the "ownership" bog in Hard v. Boise City Irrigation and Land Co., 9 Idaho 589, 76 P. 331 (1904), by citing Idaho Constitution Art. 15, § 4, which makes a sale, rental or distribution of water for agricultural purposes an exclusive dedication to such use and gives the irrigator protection against being deprived of the annual use of water as long as he pays for it and complies with terms prescribed by law. A Texas court held that the carrier is in fact the owner of the appropriation, Willis v. Neches Canal Co., 16 S.W.2d 266, 269 (Tex.Com. of Appeals, 1929), but a Texas consumer holding an "annual contract" is protected by a statute which gives a right of renewal at the same terms provided in the contract, or in case no contract has been entered into, at just and reasonable rates without discrimination. Vernon's Tex.Code Ann. § 11.040. See also 4 Clark, Waters and Water Rights 408 (1970).

In several states the ownership of the right to water stored in a reservoir is vested in the landowner by a device known as a "secondary permit". The organization receives a "primary permit" to construct the dam and store the water; the consumer applies for a "secondary permit" to apply the stored water to beneficial use upon the land, and the water right is eventually adjudicated to him. Ariz.Rev.Stat. § 45–151; Nev.Rev.Stat. 533.440; Or.Rev.Stat. 537.300; Wash.Rev.Code Ann. 90.03.370; Wyo.Stat. 1977, §§ 41–3–301, 41–3–302.

YUCAIPA WATER CO. NO. 1 v. PUBLIC UTILITIES COMMISSION

Supreme Court of California, 1960.
54 Cal.2d 823, 357 P.2d 295.

TRAYNOR, JUSTICE. In this proceeding Yucaipa Water Company No. 1 attacks an order of the Public Utilities Commission determining that it is a public utility water corporation subject to the jurisdiction of the commission and directing it to file a financial report and cease and desist from increasing its rates to the Yucaipa Domestic Water Company pending further commission action.

No. 1 is organized as a nonpublic utility mutual water company and has not heretofore been regulated by the commission. Domestic is a regulated public utility water corporation. It secures all of its water from No. 1 and owns approximately 5 percent of No. 1's stock. In 1959 a dispute arose between the two companies over a substantial increase in the rate No. 1 proposed to charge Domestic and extensions of service by Domestic into areas served by No. 1. Each company filed a complaint against the other with the commission, and thereafter the commission instituted an investigation on its own motion into the operations of No. 1. The parties stipulated that the commission should first determine whether or not No. 1 is a public utility subject to its jurisdiction, and its determination of that issue is the only question before us for review. The commission found that No. 1 is a public utility that has dedicated its property to public use (see, Pub.Util.Code, §§ 216, 240, 241, 2701, 2702) and that it is not exempt from regulation under section 2705 of the Public Utilities Code. No. 1 attacks both of these findings.

No. 1 operates in an area of about 3,500 acres including Yucaipa township. It was organized in 1910 and initially supplied water primarily for irrigation purposes. At the present time, however, about 74 percent of its sales are to domestic users. It also provides service to the Yucaipa Domestic Water Company, poultry farms, trailer parks, scheduled water users, and special users at specified rates. Special users include hospitals, schools, churches, parks, and other large users. With the exception of one domestic user, it supplies water only to its shareholders and lessees of shares from its shareholders. Its shares are freely transferable and are not appurtenant to the land, and users may obtain water in addition to the per-share entitlement by paying special rates. In 1959 No. 1 had about 2,000 domestic users and supplied water to over 100 lessees of shares. It maintained a list of shareholders who were willing to lease shares and referred nonshareholder applicants for service to them. It billed lessees of shares directly, but held the shareholder liable for any unpaid bill. In each of the years 1956, 1957, and 1958 it added 80 to 100 new domestic users to its system, and to increase the number of permissible service connections, it split its stock to permit a connection for each half share instead of each share.

No. 1 contends that since it is organized as a nonpublic utility mutual water corporation that supplies water only to its shareholders, lessees of shares from its shareholders, and one other person, it has not held itself out as willing to supply water to the public or any portion thereof and that it has not therefore dedicated its property to public use. See, Richfield Oil Corp. v. Public Utilities Commission, 54 Cal.2d 419, 6 Cal.Rptr. 548, 354 P.2d 4, and cases cited. No. 1's organization as a mutual and its formal limitations on its services do not preclude a finding of dedication, however, if it has held itself out as willing to supply water to the public or any portion thereof. * * *

The evidence supports the commission's finding of dedication in this case. It is true that No. 1 did not expressly offer service to everyone in its service area on condition that prospective consumers purchase shares of stock from it. Had it done so, its holding itself out to serve the public would be patent, and the attaching of a condition that any member of the public could meet would not affect its offer. Dedication may also be shown by implication, however, and in the present case, it may clearly be inferred. Thus, No. 1 steadily increased the number of its service connections; it split its shares to double the permissable number of such connections; it supplied water to a substantial number of lessees of shares; and it expedited the leasing of shares to those who wished water service. There is no evidence that anyone in its service area who wished water service could not obtain it by purchasing or leasing half a share or more. Under these circumstances, the commission could reasonably infer that No. 1 supplied its shareholders and lessees of its shares not merely for the reason "peculiar and particular to them" that they were such, but primarily for the reason that they were members of the public in No. 1's service area who accepted its offer of service by becoming shareholders or lessees of shares.

No. 1 contends that even if it has dedicated its property to public use, it is exempted from public utility regulation by section 2705 of the Public Utilities Code. That section provides:

> "Any corporation or association which is organized for the purpose solely of delivering water to its stockholders or members at cost, and which delivers water to no one except its stockholders or members, or to the State or any agency or department thereof, or to any school district, or to any other mutual water company, at cost, is not a public utility, and is not subject to the jurisdiction, control or regulation of the commission." * * *

The exemption created by section 2705 indicates a legislative determination that when a mutual water corporation is substantially customer-controlled and delivers water at cost, the usual judicial contract remedies available to those who deal with it are an adequate substitute for public utility regulation. That determination applies when the customers include a public utility as much as when they do not. * * *

The commission contends, however, that a utility is at the mercy of a mutual when, as in this case, the mutual is the utility's sole source of supply and that commission regulation of the mutual is therefore essential. The utility is no more at the mercy of the mutual than any individual customer who has no other source of water, and as to individual customers, the Legislature has clearly determined that public utility regulation is not essential. Moreover, neither an individual shareholder nor a utility shareholder is at the mercy of a mutual because the mutual is the only source of water. They not only have a voice in the management of the mutual, but they may invoke the jurisdiction of the commission if the mutual has stepped outside of the exemption provided by section 2705, and they may enforce their water rights in court if it has not. It is true that the public utility's customers have no voice in the management of the mutual, but they are protected vis-à-vis the utility by commission regulation, and the utility's securing water from the mutual poses no greater indirect threat to its customers' interests than its securing water from any other unregulated source.

In the present case, however, the evidence supports the commission's finding that No. 1 delivered water to others than stockholders; it delivered water to over 100 lessees of shares of stock and one other person. Even if it is assumed that the latter delivery was *de minimis,* the deliveries to lessees were not. Lessees of shares are not stockholders, and to interpret the word "stockholders" in section 2705 to mean "stockholders or lessees of stock" would not only require reading into the statute words that are not there but violate the basic principle of customer control on which the exemption is based. * * * No. 1 was not obligated to deliver water to lessees of shares, for it could have insisted, in accord with its declared corporate purpose, on delivering water only to shareholders. Instead, however, it actively expedited the leasing of shares to those who wished water service, and such activity coupled with its other activities set forth above clearly supported the commission's finding that it had dedicated its property to public use. * * *

The order is affirmed.

Notes

1. In a companion case, Corona City Water Co. v. P.U.C., 54 Cal.2d 834, 357 P.2d 301 (1960), the Temescal Water Company, organized as a non-public mutual water company, completely dominated Corona, a public utility company, through stock ownership and interlocking boards of directors and officers. Temescal "supplied" Corona with water stock and water to meet the full requirements of the latter company. Held, Temescal was a public utility. Justice Traynor said that the exemption of Section 2705 did not apply where a "captive" stockholder has no voice in the management of the mutual and is in no position to enforce its rights as a shareholder. "[T]he intercorporate relationship is fraught with hazards to Corona and its customers. Thus, the largely agricultural independent stockholders of

Temescal are in a position to subsidize their water service at the expense of Corona and to prevent Corona's objecting by their control of it."

In the following session of the legislature, Section 2705 was amended to permit a mutual to keep its non-public status even though it delivers water at cost to a lessee of its stock, or to land leased by a stockholder to another, or in an emergency to nonstockholders within or adjacent to its service area, or pursuant to a pre-existing contract in settlement of litigation involving disputed water rights or in consideration of the conveyance of a well or water right.

For a discussion of other intricacies of the problem, and of earlier cases, see Russell, Mutual Water Companies in California, 12 So.Cal.L.Rev. 155, 182–192 (1939).

2. Public utility status subjects many of the financial and operational aspects of the company to public regulation. In many states, a water utility must procure a certificate of convenience and necessity, i.e. a license, to enter the business. West's Ann.Calif.Pub.Util.Code, § 1001. It can be compelled to render service to consumers within its service area, Olsen v. Union Canal & Irrigation Co., 58 Ariz. 306, 119 P.2d 569 (1941), within the limits of its water supply, Butte County Water Users' Ass'n v. Railroad Commission, 185 Cal. 218, 196 P. 265 (1921). It cannot discriminate between its customers by giving preferred services or rates to some. Butte County Water Users' Ass'n v. Railroad Commission, supra; Live Oak Water Users' Ass'n v. Railroad Commission, 192 Cal. 132, 219 P. 65 (1923), error dismissed, 269 U.S. 354, 46 S.Ct. 149, 70 L.Ed. 305. Its transactions with other companies and its acquisitions or dispositions of property are subject to scrutiny by the regulatory commission for their conformity with the public interest. Corona City Water Co. v. P.U.C., supra n. 1. It cannot discontinue its services, even by going out of business, without the permission of the commission. Van Hoosear v. Railroad Commission, 184 Cal. 553, 194 P. 1003 (1920).

3. Most important, the rates charged for services are subject to regulation. Rates are fixed to cover operating expenses, including depreciation on its properties, and a fair return on the value of the property devoted to public use. A battle has long raged over whether the rate base should be valued on the amount prudently invested in the business or on the cost of reproduction of the facilities.

A utility may not add a royalty for the use of its water right, over and above reasonable charges for water rent, since the water is the property of the state, not of the utility. Wheeler v. Northern Colorado Irrigation Co., 10 Colo. 582, 17 P. 487 (1888). Where the water right is not the property of the company, but belongs to the consumers, the company cannot include a value for the water right in its rate base, but in figuring a fair return on the base the priority of the water rights may be considered, since this will reflect on the value of the securities of the utility as investments. Board of County Commissioners v. Rocky Mountain Water Co., 102 Colo. 351, 79 P.2d 373 (1938); 106 Colo. 276, 103 P.2d 686 (1940). In California, no holder of a permit or license to appropriate may assign or claim any value in excess of the actual amount paid to the state for the water right in proceedings for the regulation of the price of the services. West's Ann.Cal. Water Code, §§ 1392, 1629.

In most states, rates are fixed by public utility commissions. In Colorado, the constitution gives the Boards of County Commissioners the power to establish reasonable maximum rates to be charged for the use of water, whether furnished by individuals or corporations. See Farmers Water Development Co. v. Barrett, 151 Colo. 133, 376 P.2d 693 (1962). In Texas, the power is given to the Texas Water Commission. Vernon's Tex. Codes Ann. Water § 12.013(a).

What is the effect of a statute such as Wyo.Stat.1977, § 41–3–325: "The owner or owners of a reservoir impounding a greater quantity of water than the owner or owners thereof necessarily use for irrigation and other beneficial purposes in connection with their own lands shall, when application is made to them for that purpose, furnish such surplus water at reasonable rates to the owners of lands lying under and capable of being irrigated from such reservoir for the purpose of irrigating and rendering the same productive, and maintaining their productiveness, and in case of refusal so to do, the owner or owners of such reservoir may be compelled by proper proceedings to furnish such water on such reasonable terms as to the court may seem meet and proper. The water user who may have used any water from such reservoir for any particular year shall have the preference as to the use of the same water for the next ensuing year. The state engineer, the water commissioner of the particular district and the water superintendent having jurisdiction over the region of any reservoir, shall together constitute a board of special commissioners, and shall have power, when application is made to them by either party interested, to establish reasonable maximum rates to be charged for the use of water from any reservoir, whether furnished by individuals or a corporation. The establishment of such rate shall be made only after notice given and public hearing had, at which hearing the applicants may produce witnesses and evidence, and such witnesses must be sworn and may be cross-examined. No commissioner shall sit upon such board and determine such rate who is employed by one of the applicants or if the relationship of debtor or creditor exists between him and one of the applicants. Nothing contained in this section shall be construed to deny the right to store water for use for more than one year." Consider Hissem v. Guran, 112 Ohio St. 59, 146 N.E. 808 (1925), and Wyo.Const. art. 8, § 1.

4. Unless made so by statute, a water company supplying a municipality is not necessarily a public utility. Junction Water Co. v. Riddle, 108 N.J.Eq. 523, 155 A. 887 (1931). However, most are so designated in the statutes establishing public service commissions.

A water company's contract with a city may give the city powers to require service and to this extent supersede the powers of the state public service commission. Portsmouth, Berkley and Suffolk Water Co. v. Portsmouth, 112 Va. 158, 70 S.E. 529 (1911). A city charter may empower a city to impose regulations in lieu of the public service commission. New York v. New York Water Service Corp., 274 N.Y. 100, 8 N.E.2d 294 (1937).

5. The inhabitants of a city who consume water which is diverted, stored and distributed by a public utility company do not own appropria-

tions of water or water rights of any kind, but have instead rights to service arising under public utility law.

SECTION 2. PUBLIC AGENCIES

SULLIVAN v. BLAKESLEY

Supreme Court of Wyoming, 1926.
35 Wyo. 73, 246 P. 918.

Plaintiff, E.J. Sullivan, brings this action, on behalf of himself and others similarly situated, against Lou Blakesley, county treasurer of Big Horn county, and the commissioners of the Greybull Valley irrigation district. The petition alleges the due organization of said irrigation district under the laws of this state; that an assessment against the lands in said district was made in 1925 to meet the expenses of the district for the current year; that plaintiff is the owner of lands affected by such assessment, and that the county treasurer of said county threatens to sell such land for the nonpayment of such assessment; that the commissioners of said irrigation district threaten to issue and sell the bonds of said district, said bonds to be paid by assessments levied against the property of plaintiff and others similarly situated; that the irrigation district law of this state is unconstitutional for various specified reasons, and plaintiff accordingly seeks an injunction against the collection of said tax and the issuance of the bonds aforesaid. The case comes to this court upon reserved constitutional questions, and we are asked to answer whether or not the irrigation district law of this state is in conflict with * * * the Constitution of this state. * * *

The irrigation district law referred to is contained in chapter 75, W.C.S.1920, being sections 951 to 956, inclusive, first passed by the Legislature of this state in 1920. * * * For the purposes of this case, it will be sufficient to state the following provisions of the law: A certain number of owners or holders of land in the district may sign and present to the district court a petition, stating therein the name of the proposed district, the necessity of the proposed work, the object and purpose thereof, a general description of the lands proposed to be included in the district, the names of the freeholders owning lands therein, and a prayer for the organization of the district. A preliminary engineering report of the feasibility of the project must accompany the petition. Section 951, W.C.S.1920. The court or the judge thereof must cause notice to be given of the presentation of the petition, fixing the date for the hearing thereon. Sections 953 to 955. Upon the hearing, the district court may approve and confirm the petition, define the boundaries of the district, and establish it as a corporation by the name proposed with powers to sue and be sued, adopt a corporate seal, have perpetual succession, exercise the power of the eminent domain and generally carry out the purposes of the organization. Section 960, as amended by chapter 53, § 1, Sess.L.1925. Commissioners are appointed by the court, who are required to organize, who constitute the corporate authority of the district, who are declared to be public officers, and for whom successors are provided by election. Sections 987 and 960, 963, 992, as amended. Other lands may subsequently be included in the district, and lands originally embraced therein may be excluded therefrom. Section 964, as amended (Laws 1923, c. 90), and section 966. Immediately after the organization of the district, the commissioners thereof are required to cause surveys, a map, plans, and specifications to be made of the proposed work, and determine, as near as may be, the cost of said work. They must assess against the lands embraced within the district the total amounts of benefits, such benefits to constitute the basis of all assessments; apportion and assess the cost of construction with certain exceptions which need not be noted here, against the several benefited tracts in the irrigation district, in proportion to the benefits which have been assessed against the same, and apportion the water right, expected to be acquired by the proposed work, to each tract of land assessed. A report of such action must be made to the court. Section 964, as amended. Notice of the hearing thereon must be given to all parties interested. Upon such hearing, the court may confirm the report of the commissioners and the assessments made as aforesaid, which assessments may be made payable in installments, as fixed by the court. Sections 967, 970, and section 973, as amended. Additional assessments may be made subsequently, to be confirmed by the court upon due notice given to the interested parties. Section 979, as amended by chapter 14, Sess.L.1923. The assessments become a lien upon the various tracts assessed, and may be enforced in the same manner as a judgment, or may be assessed and collected as taxes. Sections 977, 985, and section 975, as amended, and section 976, as amended. The commissioners may borrow money and issue the bonds of the district therefor and such bonds are declared to be a lien upon the assessments for the repayment of the principal and interest thereof. Section 981, as amended by chapter 14, Sess.L.1923. More specific provisions as to some of these matters will be set forth in the opinion.

BLUME, J. (after stating the facts as above). 1. An irrigation district, reclaiming, as it does, desert lands in the state, and accordingly, conferring a benefit, not alone upon the private individuals within the district, but also upon the people of the state as a whole, is a public rather than a private, corporation. * * * Such districts have at times been designated as municipal corporations, and they might be such within the meaning of laws or constitutional provisions not now under consideration, but it is clear that they are not municipal corporations as generally understood. They are merely special state organizations for state purposes with limited powers, created to perform certain work which the policy of the state requires or permits to be done, and to which the state has given a certain degree of discretion in reclaiming desert lands. * * *

There is no special constitutional limitation that we know of limiting the mode or method of the establishment of such districts provided that it is done under a general law. It may be left to a board or commission, or the court. The Legislature has seen fit to cause such districts to be created upon petition of a certain number of people owning or holding lands therein, and upon a hearing, after due notice, upon such petition by the district court. The method of thus establishing the districts is, we think, constitutional.

The functions of the districts are, under the law, performed by the properly constituted authorities thereof. The power to make improvements or to levy taxes therein is not in any way delegated, but is exercised by the districts themselves, through their own proper officials, except only that the proper counties and proper county treasurers perform ministerial duties in aid of the levy and collection of taxes and assessments. * * * The exactions authorized to be made by such districts may, in a broad sense, be termed taxes, but they are distinguishable therefrom, for they are levied for local benefits to be spread on the property in the districts in proportion to the peculiar advantages accruing to each parcel therein from the improvement made. Whether in the form of special assessments or in the form of taxes, they are essentially assessments for local benefits, and not levied for general governmental purposes. * * *

2. We come, then, to the consideration as to whether or not the legislation in question is in violation of section 13, art. 15, of the Constitution, which provides that no tax shall be levied except in pursuance of law, and that each law imposing a tax shall state distinctly the object of the same, to which only it shall be applied. * * * The argument is far afield. * * * We might accordingly very well pass this subject without anything further; but inasmuch as we are also asked whether the irrigation district law is in violation of section 33, article 1, that "private property shall not be taken or damaged for public or private use without just compensation," and inasmuch as a complete answer perhaps involves the subject-matter referred to by counsel, we shall discuss it somewhat at length. * * * It has been held in Norris v. Montezuma Valley Irrigation District, 248 F. 369, 160 C.C.A. 379; American Falls Reservoir District v. Thrall, 39 Idaho 105, 228 P. 236; State ex rel. Clancy v. Irrigation District, 121 Wash. 86, 208 P. 27; and Noble v. Yancey (Or.) 241 P. 335, that bonds issued by an irrigation district constitute a general lien obligation of the district. The contrary has been held in the case of Interstate Trust Co. v. Montezuma, 66 Colo. 219, 181 P. 123, and Nelson v. Board, 62 Utah 218, 218 P. 952. And the Supreme Court of Colorado in the case just cited holds that to consider such bonds as general lien obligations of the district would be violative of both state and federal Constitutions, presumably because of taking property without due process of law or taking property without just compensation. A like view is expressed in the minority opinion in Norris v. Montezuma Valley Irrigation District,

supra. The difference in opinion as to the character of such bonds may, to some extent at least, be accounted for by the difference in the laws of the several states, and, in order to arrive at the proper conclusion herein, it will be necessary to consider the laws of this state that bear upon the point in question. * * *

We do not think, as contended by counsel, that these provisions leave in doubt the character or extent of the lien of the various assessments. The bonds provided for by the statute constitute a lien upon the assessments, and are in that respect somewhat dissimilar from the bonds discussed in the Washington, Oregon, and Idaho cases heretofore cited. The provisions made for the assessments, however, make such bonds, in a limited sense, similar in character to those discussed in these cases. The Legislature evidently intended to make the assessments a general lien against all of the assessed property in the district, within the limitation heretofore and hereafter mentioned, since it has provided for the levy in each year of an amount sufficient to meet the principal and interest that may fall due during that year, to be apportioned to all the lands to which benefits are assessed, just as payments of principal and interest are met on general municipal bonds. But there is a limitation. The assessments cannot be in excess of the benefits assessed against the several parcels of land in the district. The objection accordingly urged by the Colorado Supreme Court in the case of Interstate Trust Company v. Montezuma Valley Irrigation District, supra, does not, we think, hold good under the laws of this state even if it were true that the principle there stated would apply in the absence of such limiting provisions of the statute. Made as the assessments are, because and on the theory that they equal the amount of the benefits, they do not constitute a taking of property without due process of law or without just compensation, in the case of irrigation districts any more than under a like situation in the case of municipal improvements generally, and it is well settled that in the latter case there is no violation of constitutional provisions in that regard. 28 Cyc. 1104. It was held in Re Drainage District, 24 Wyo. 143, 161, 156 P. 610, that assessments made for the purpose of constructing drains are not in violation of section 33, article 1, of our Constitution. Assessments made in drainage districts are similar in kind to assessments in irrigation districts. They are all based upon the same underlying principle. Fallbrook Irrigation District v. Bradley, supra; Board of Directors v. Tregea, 88 Cal. 334, 26 P. 237. It may, possibly, happen, as suggested that the benefits assessed to all or part of the lands within the irrigation district by reason of the construction of improvements, may become exhausted before the full amount of the cost of such improvement is paid. But it is not shown that such contingency will arise, and we are not called upon to anticipate it any more than we are called upon to anticipate that the total cost of making the improvements might happen to be greater than the total amount of the benefits. Butters v. City of Oakland, 263 U.S. 162, 44 S.Ct. 62, 68 L.Ed. 228; Martin v. District of Columbia, 205 U.S. 135, 27 S.Ct. 440, 51 L.Ed.

743; Louisville & Nashville R.R. Co. v. Barber, 197 U.S. 430, 25 S.Ct. 466, 49 L.Ed. 819. We answer, accordingly, that the irrigation district law of this state is not in conflict with either of the two constitutional provisions last herein discussed.

Notes

1. All of the 17 western states have irrigation district laws, though some are called water conservation, water improvement or reclamation districts. Historically, they all stem from California's Wright Act, Cal.Stat. 1887, c. 34. Details of the method of organization differ widely. There are variations from state to state in the persons who vote (electors, landowners, owners of a majority of lands) and in the majorities required. Commonly, the Board of County Commissioners approve the formation of the district, rather than the courts as in the principal case. In some states approval of the state irrigation officials is required for the project or of the engineering aspects of it.

Irrigation-Enterprise Organizations, U.S.Dept.Ag.Cir. No. 934 (1953) contains a parallel treatment of mutual companies, commercial companies, and irrigation districts, contrasting their organizations, powers, revenues, water services, management and public regulation.

2. The cumulative assessment that makes each parcel of land security for all the bonds has been called "widow's law," protecting investors from partial default. Conversely, the individual assessment that makes each landholding subject only to its proportionate share of the debt is "farmer's law," saving the whole project from complete failure.

"The Oregon case of Yancey v. Noble is representative of the majority view respecting this sort of cumulative assessments. Provision for such assessments, strengthening the position of bond holders and facilitating financing of irrigation undertakings, has been referred to as the 'last honest acre doctrine,' and as the 'inexhaustable taxing power.' But it may be noted that an inexhaustable taxing power is not always the equivalent of an inexhaustable tax-collecting power." 3 Report of the President's Water Resources Policy Commission, Water Resources Law 173 (1950). Compare: "The courts held that bond holders could resort only to the delinquent lands for recovery on their security, and that cumulative assessments were void. Thus any landowner who paid his tax was secure, regardless of the failure of his neighbor to pay." Moses, Irrigation Corporations, 32 Rocky Mountain Law Review, 527, 530 (1960).

3. As noted in the principal case, the commissioners of a Wyoming district may proceed to issue bonds after formation of the district has been approved. More commonly, statutes provide for submitting proposed bond issues to the electors at a special election. Also common are statutory proceedings initiated by the governing officers of the district, in which all questions relating to the organization of the district and the proceedings of the board with respect to the issue and sale of the bonds may be judicially approved and confirmed. These proceedings are in rem and are conclusive as to the validity of the bonds, but not, of course, as to subsequent negotiation or transfer of the bonds.

"The depression of the 1930's led to defaults by many irrigation districts, including a number that previously had paid all their obligations as due. During the middle 1930's the chief characteristic of district financing was the refinancing of defaulted issues by the Reconstruction Finance Corporation." Irrigation-Enterprise Organizations 24, supra n. 1.

In Padlock Ranch, Inc. v. Washakie Needles Irrigation Dist., 50 Wyo. 253, 60 P.2d 819, 61 P.2d 410 (1936), the court indicated that the feasibility report required in the formation of a district should consider the cost of the project, and the court should go into the matters of the ability of the landowner to meet the assessments and the amount of the burden on the landowners as compared with the benefits to be received. A Nebraska court refused to validate bonds on the ground that a feasible plan of irrigation was not presented, when it appeared that the water rights of the district had been abandoned. In re Gothenburg South Side Irrigation Dist., 113 Neb. 99, 202 N.W. 452 (1925).

The California Districts Securities Commission law, West's Ann.Calif. Water Code, § 20000 et seq. provides an elaborate mechanism for districts desiring their bonds to be certified as legal investments for trust, insurance, bank and school funds. The Commission must report upon the feasibility and economic soundness of the project, and supervises the expenditures of the funds raised by the bond issue.

4. The principal case gives the rule that the assessments levied against the property must be apportioned among the property holders in accordance with the actual benefits received by the property. Where this is the rule, it is illegal to treat all land as equal and levy an equal assessment against each acre. Wheatland Irrigation Dist. v. Short, 80 Wyo. 136, 339 P.2d 403 (1959). It is permissible to divide land into classes according to size, topography, soil classification, etc., fix a value for each class, and apply the formula to all acres in the district. Kansas-Bostwick Irrigation Dist. No. 2 v. Mizer, 176 Kan. 354, 270 P.2d 261 (1954).

In other states, e.g., California, an assessment on an ad valorem basis is permitted, levied at a standard rate against property valued at market or cash value. See Reed v. Oroville-Wyandotte Irrigation Dist., 147 Cal.App. 2d 16, 304 P.2d 731 (1956).

A third method, permissible in some states, is assessment according to area, imposing an equal charge against each irrigable acre.

Still another source of revenue is a direct charge for water delivered. "The statutes of various States authorize the obtaining of revenue through tolls or charges for use of water. These tolls or charges are fixed by the board of directors, either in addition to the levying of assessments or in lieu thereof. They are collected by the district secretary or district treasurer. Some statutes provide that tolls may be made payable in advance of the delivery of water. * * * Tolls are used by many California districts, usually in addition to assessments. They are used to a lesser extent in some of the other Western States. * * * One irrigation district in California relied entirely upon toll charges for the use of water to cover expenses for operation and maintenance and for bond service as well. As rice was the only major crop grown in the district, this method was preferred because of the large area of rice land idle each year. But the power to assess the land is available in case the toll system proves inadequate to meet the district's financial requirements."

"Irrigation districts in various Western States have statutory authority to rent or lease water to lands outside their boundaries. This authorization generally applies only to water not needed by district landowners. In some cases, it is further limited to short-term services and by the provision that no vested right to such service may be acquired thereby." Irrigation-Enterprise Organizations 39, 40, supra n. 1.

5. Many irrigation districts were organized primarily as fiscal agents for the United States Bureau of Reclamation. The construction costs of Reclamation projects are "reimbursable" and must be repaid to the United States by the settlers and landowners on the project. Reclamation projects are built with federal financing, and such a district has no need to issue bonds for construction funds. Instead, it enters into a "repayment contract" with the Secretary of the Interior, in which it agrees to collect from the water users assessments to cover the operation and maintenance costs and the construction charges. Since, under Reclamation law, not all of the costs of construction are reimbursable, and since even the construction costs attributable to irrigation but beyond the water user's ability to pay may be assigned for reimbursement out of the power revenues of a multi-purpose project, the standard of economic feasibility is considerably relaxed in approving the organization of such districts. Gies v. Boehm, 78 Wyo. 449, 329 P.2d 807 (1958).

6. There is usually no controversy over whether an irrigation district or other public agency that distributes water "owns" the water rights as against the consumer, since the relations and duties of the district to its consumers are fixed by the statutes under which they are created, and those statutes without exception clearly give the district the power to appropriate or purchase water rights. One state has invented a special property right to protect the consumer, but it is not a water right. In California an irrigation district is said to own the water right but the courts have construed this ownership to be a trusteeship for the beneficial owners, the water users. Lindsay-Strathmore Irrigation District v. Wutchumna Water Co., 11 Cal.App. 688, 296 P. 933 (1931).

The Washington statutes governing adjudications for the determination of water rights generally require personal service of process or publication of notice to claimants of the right to divert water to appear in the proceeding or be subject to loss of their water rights. Specifically, Rev. Code Wash. § 90.03.120 provides that any person claiming the right to the use of water by virtue of a contract with a claimant of the right to divert the water shall not be a necessary party. The Yakima River Adjudication covered 6062 square miles, 475,000 irrigated acres and 40,000 people. Most are served by irrigation districts, canal companies, ditch companies, cities, and towns. In State Department of Ecology v. Acquavella, 100 W.2d 651, 674 P.2d 160 (1983), the court held that while property owners receiving water from distribution entities have a vested interest in the water right to the extent that the water is beneficially used on the land, there is an identity of interest between the distributor and user, and the distributor is fully empowered to represent the water users in this type of proceeding.

Individual landowners do not have rights appurtenant to their land which they can assert as their own. Thus where landowners opt out of a district and vote to form their own district they do not take with them a share of the original district's water right. Madera Irrigation Dist. v. All Persons, 47 Cal.2d 681, 306 P.2d 886 (1957).

8. What powers do districts have to allocate their water among the water users within their service areas? Many state laws are silent as to how the water must be distributed, and it seems to be generally assumed that all land owners are to be treated equally. Some statutes, however, may give a district some degree of discretion by granting general powers to establish rules and regulations for the distribution and use of water, e.g., Ore.Rev.Stats. 545.064. Utah Code Ann. § 73–7–27 provides that in case of shortage district officials may distribute the water "upon certain or alternate days to different localities as they may in their judgment think best for the interest of all parties concerned," and Ariz.Code § 45–1589 has this same language but adds, "so that the available water is distributed in as nearly equal proportions as possible to all land within the district."

Where annual arrangements are made to meet variable requirements, as in many California districts, greater flexibility may exist. The principal distributors of irrigation water in California are "irrigation districts" and "California water districts," and the basic statute for each provides, "all water distributed by districts for irrigation purposes shall except when otherwise provided in this article be apportioned rateably to each land owner upon the basis of the ratio which the last assessment against his land for district purposes bears to the whole sum assessed to the district for district purposes." West's Ann.Calif.Water Code §§ 22250, 35420.

In 1947 an element of priority was added by § 22252.1 and § 35453, which require applications for water (either for all crops or only for annual crops and new plantings) to be filed by a date specified by the district board. In case of shortage, the board may "give preference to or serve only the land for which application was filed prior to the date set and the land for which no application was required." A cash deposit was required, subject to forfeiture if the water was not used when the district had it available. Each statute ended, "Nothing in this section shall prohibit apportionment of available water to land given preference under this section or otherwise restrict or limit existing powers of the board to control and provide for the distribution of water."

In 1977, during an extreme drought, the legislature provided, "In districts where meters or other volumetric measuring instruments or facilities are not available or are inadequate to measure substantially all agricultural water deliveries, the district may establish annual water requirements in the district for growing each type of crop grown in the district, accept such applications for water based on proposed crops to be grown and acreage of each proposed crop, and determine the quantity of water apportioned under [the above statutes] expressed in terms of acreage of each type of proposed crop to be served. In such a district, the district may refuse to deliver water to, or assess penalties on, the landowner who uses such water on a greater acreage of such crops than such landowner's share of the estimated available water will bring to maturity based on the requirements established for growing such crops in the district.

"In establishing annual water requirements for growing particular types of crops, as authorized in this section, the district, with respect to those crops which ordinarily require periodic irrigation, may designate the number of irrigation runs and the amount of water to be allocated to each run with respect to each crop and, may give the water user water credits measured by the designated irrigation runs with respect to each such crop as to which the water user has notified the district he intends to underirrigate.

"This section provides a means of measuring the allocation of water to land based on the type of crop grown and does not authorize a district to designate, the crops to be grown on such land." §§ 22252.3, 35454.5.

Although sponsors of this statute insist that it is "a measurement statute" and not an "allocation statute," it seems inescapable that the effect of the law is to establish a comprehensive allocation scheme for providing water according to crop as well as according to acreage. The practice seems to have been to give a preference to needs of perennial plants (orchards, vineyards) as against annual crops. Apparently if a district has accurate metering devices, a ratable allocation would be made unless the district and the water users cooperated in some form of "water banking." See Note 4, supra p. 224.

The California "county water district" may have still broader powers: "to restrict the use of district water during any emergency caused by drought or other threatened or existing water shortage and to prohibit the waste of district water during such periods, for any purpose other than household uses or such other restricted uses as may be determined to be necessary by the district, and may prohibit the use of such water during such period which the district may * * * find to be nonessential." § 31026.

9. The 1982 California legislature authorized interdistrict transfers. West's Ann.Cal.Water Code § 380 now declares that since the water needs of the state differ widely among the various regions of the state and regional differences affect decisions regarding water allocation, many water management decisions regarding the maximization of efficient water use can be best made at the local or regional level. Section 382 gives local or regional public water agencies the authority to sell, lease, exchange or otherwise transfer water that is surplus to the needs of the water users of the agency for use outside the agency. Section 383 defines "surplus" as water appropriated by the agency which the agency finds will be in excess of the needs of the water users within the agency for the duration of the transfer, water appropriated by the agency which the water user agrees with the agency on mutually satisfactory terms to forego the use of for the duration of the transfer, or water appropriated by a water user within the agency where the water user and the agency agree that the water user will forego use for the period of the transfer and that the agency shall act as agent to effect the transfer. Section 385 forbids the transfer of water for use within the boundaries of another agency that furnishes the same water service, without the consent of the latter agency. Section 386 requires

compliance with all general laws of the state relating to the transfer of water or water rights, and § 387 limits the duration of these transfers to seven years.

IN RE RENO PRESS BRICK CO.

Supreme Court of Nevada, 1937.
58 Nev. 164, 73 P.2d 503.

TABER, JUSTICE. Respondent corporation is the owner of 33 acres of land included within the boundaries of appellant irrigation district. Acting under the provisions of section 44 of the Irrigation District (section 8059, N.C.L.1929), as amended, Statutes of Nevada 1933, pp. 278, 279, c. 186, § 8, respondent, on April 30, 1936, applied in writing to appellant's board of directors for the exclusion from the district of said piece of land. After considering the application, the board of directors of the irrigation district, on July 9, 1936, rejected respondent's application in whole. Thereafter, respondent petitioned the district court to set aside said order of appellant's board of directors, and to direct that said land be excluded from the district. The matter was later tried, and, in December, 1936, the district court granted respondent's application, and adjudged that said land be excluded from the irrigation district. This appeal is taken from said judgment, and from an order of said district court denying a motion for a new trial.

The portion of said section 44 of the Irrigation District Act with which we are primarily concerned, reads as follows: "The board of directors of any district now or hereafter formed under the provisions of this act, either upon its own initiative or upon the application in writing of any holder of title or of evidence of title to land in the district, may, by a majority vote, exclude from the district any land or lands theretofore included in the district, and change the boundary lines of the district so as to exclude or leave out certain tracts or portions of tracts when the proposed system or systems of irrigation cannot practically include land or lands, or when such land or lands would not be benefited by the district or by any improvement it might make." Respondent's application for exclusion of its land was and is based upon the contention that said land would not be benefited by certain improvements contemplated by the district.

The tract of land sought to be excluded from the irrigation district adjoins the city of Reno on the north. No part of it is within the city limits, but its southern boundary line is identical along its whole length with a portion of the northern boundary line of the city of Reno. The land has been irrigated for the past twenty or twenty-one years. For the first five or six years, two crops of alfalfa were grown upon it annually. After that, it was allowed to go to pasture. With an ample supply of water, it will produce good pasturage crops. * * *

During the three or four years that Parker Brick Company owned this property, it was used for the manufacture of brick, and to that extent the statement heretofore made, that this land has been irrigated for some twenty or twenty-one years, must be qualified. The buildings and machinery which had been used by Parker Brick Company in the manufacture of brick on said premises were of small value at the time the property was purchased by respondent. The premises have not been used for brick making at any time since respondent has owned them. * * *

Without water the land in controversy would be valueless for agricultural purposes. With an adequate water right it would be worth from $125 to $150 per acre for agricultural purposes. With the exception of about three and one-half acres, the land is susceptible of irrigation by gravity. * * * It is estimated that this property would be worth about $400 an acre if subdivided for residential purposes. * * *

There is no substantial conflict in the testimony in this case. The question we have to determine is the interpretation to be put on the word "benefited" as applied to the undisputed facts disclosed by the testimony. Upon respondent rests the burden of proving by a fair preponderance of evidence that the Truckee river upstream storage project will not benefit its 33-acre tract of land.

Appellant contends that this court should follow the decisions of courts of other states in holding that the benefit to the land, as contemplated by said amended section 44 of the Irrigation District Act, may be indirect as well as direct. * * *

Respondent takes the position that, in Nevada, land within an irrigation district should be excluded therefrom on application of the owner when such land will not be directly benefited by the district or by any improvement it might make. * * *

We find it unnecessary to decide whether, in Nevada, an indirect benefit to land, within the meaning of amended section 44 of the Irrigation District Act, may be sufficient to justify a refusal to exclude such land from an irrigation district, because the uncontradicted evidence satisfies us that respondent has not met the burden imposed upon it by the statute to show that its said land will not be directly benefited by the Truckee river upstream storage project. We shall proceed to set forth some of the reasons which have influenced us in reaching this conclusion.

The land is not now being used for the manufacture of clay products, and will probably not be so used for at least ten or twelve years, because the supply of superior clay where respondent company is now manufacturing its products will, it is estimated, last that long, and respondent has other clay deposits superior in quality to that in its said 33-acre tract. * * *

It will not be necessary for respondent to go to any considerable expense in irrigating this land, because a neighboring farmer has offered to allow respondent to carry water through his ditch for a very small consideration. * * *

If the land were not susceptible of any use for agriculture, as was alleged to be the case in Northern Pac. Ry. Co. v. Walla Walla County, 116 Wash. 684, 200 P. 585; if, as appeared in the case of In re Central Pac. Ry. Co., 144 Or. 527, 25 P.2d 927, irrigation would constitute a detriment to the clay content of the land; or if the land were now being used for the manufacture of clay products, or definite plans were now being made to use it for that purpose within a reasonably short time, we might well have decided to affirm the judgment of the district court.

It does not result from the refusal to allow respondent's 33-acre tract to be excluded from the district that respondent must irrigate the land. It need not exercise that right unless it so chooses, and, so far as the court can see, respondent may rent or otherwise dispose of it. * * *

The court is not to be understood as holding that respondent may not at some future time be entitled to have this land excluded from the district; but viewing the situation, as we must, as it existed at the time of the filing of respondent's application and at the time of the trial in the district court, it is the court's opinion that, under the law, respondent is not entitled at this time to have said tract excluded from appellant conservation district. We find nothing in the law which would prevent respondent's filing another application for exclusion of this land from the district at a time when conditions may be different from those shown by the evidence to exist in this case.

The judgment and order appealed from are reversed.

Notes

1. Ordinarily, the fact that land is irrigated from another source is a ground for exclusion of the land from the district, unless the district facilities are used to transport the water to the land, or unless the district furnishes supplemental water to the land. However, where a district is formed to protect future as well as present underground water resources, or one of its purposes is to replenish ground waters, any overlying land may be considered benefited by the district. Atchison, Topeka & Santa Fe Ry. Co. v. Kings County Water Dist., 47 Cal.2d 140, 302 P.2d 1 (1956); Hobe v. Madera Irrigation Dist., 128 Cal.App.2d 9, 274 P.2d 874 (1954).

2. Can the district include land that is physically irrigable, but which cannot legally be irrigated by the landowner? Under Reclamation law, no water right from a federal project can accrue to more than 960 acres of land held by an individual, or to 640 acres owned by a corporation. What if one person or corporation owns more than these limits within the district? See pp. 695–697, infra.

3. In Foster v. Sunnyside Irrigation District, 102 W.2d 395, 687 P.2d 841 (1984), a landowner within an irrigation district subdivided his farm into residential plots without providing for irrigation water rights of way or pipes. Foster purchased a homesite upon which the district levied an assessment for maintenance and operation costs. He petitioned to be excluded from the district on the ground that the statute requires assessed

land to be "irrigable." Held, that even though land ceases to be irrigable, it will not be excluded on the basis of frustration of purpose when the landowner himself (or his predecessor) caused the change in condition.

MILLIS v. BOARD OF COUNTY COMMISSIONERS OF LARIMER COUNTY

Supreme Court of Colorado, 1981.
626 P.2d 652.

LOHR, JUSTICE.

The appellants are nonresidents of Colorado who own vacation property in the High Drive Water District (District) near Estes Park. On August 13, 1975, the Larimer County Board of County Commissioners (Board) adopted a formal resolution approving the modified service plan submitted by the District to provide domestic water for district residents. The appellants filed suit against the Board and the District, seeking relief under C.R.C.P. 106(a)(4) on the basis that the Board's approval exceeded its jurisdiction and was an abuse of discretion. The appellants suffered an adverse judgment in the trial court and brought this appeal. We affirm that judgment.

* * * The District consists of approximately 120 to 130 residences or parcels eligible for service, only 9 of which are owned by persons who utilize their property year-around. The majority of the parcels are owned by persons who, like the appellants, live out of state. Pursuant to sections 32–4–104 to 107, C.R.S.1973, the District was organized in 1974. The petition for organization carried by a vote of 27 to 21. * * *

The District's board of directors proposed to issue general obligation bonds in the amount of $350,000 to finance the construction and installation of a water system. Pursuant to section 32–4–124, C.R.S. 1973, the question of issuing the bonds was submitted to the qualified voters of the District, and the measure passed.

As part of the procedure for formation of the District, a service plan projecting the sale of bonds totaling $350,000 and bearing interest at 7% per annum had been submitted to and approved by the Board. Subsequent to the organization of the District, bond market rates rose. It appeared that the bonds could not be sold at a 7% interest rate and, upon recommendation of the underwriter of the proposed bond issue, the District's board of directors proposed a modified service plan raising the authorized interest on the bonds to 9%. Pursuant to section 32–1–209(3), C.R.S.1973, the District submitted the modified service plan to the Board for approval. A public hearing was held on that plan, after which the Board approved it.

The appellants then filed a complaint in the Larimer County district court, claiming principally that the modified service plan was economically unfeasible. * * * The appellants also challenged the Board's approval of the modified service plan as a taking of property without due process of law. They apparently claim that the ad valorem tax burden necessary to finance the proposed water system is confiscatory and will not benefit the appellants, for they use their property only in the summer months. We do not agree with this analysis.

A water district is organized not for the improvement of land or to benefit only landowners. Such a district is created to "promote the health, safety, prosperity, security and general welfare" of its inhabitants. Section 32–4–101, C.R.S.1973; see Ruberoid Co. v. North Pecos Water and Sanitation District, supra. The statute with respect to creation and operation of water districts is to be liberally construed to effect its purposes. Section 32–4–130, C.R.S.1973. The District's board of directors therefore has the power to levy general ad valorem taxes upon property within the District without according a benefit in proportion to the tax burden imposed. Section 32–4–114, C.R.S.1973; see Ruberoid Co. v. North Pecos Water and Sanitation District, supra; People ex rel. Rogers v. Letford, 102 Colo. 284, 79 P.2d 274 (1938); see generally B. Novak, Legal Classifications of Special District Corporate Forms in Colorado, 45 Denver L.J. 347 (1968). The fact that the appellants' property may be taxed according to its value regardless of whether the appellants choose to participate in the proposed water system, therefore, does not have any constitutional significance. The United States Supreme Court has held that the Fourteenth Amendment does not "prohibit unwise taxes, merely because they are unwise, or unfair or burdensome taxes, merely because they are unfair or burdensome." International Harvester Co. v. Wisconsin Department of Taxation, 322 U.S. 435, 444, 64 S.Ct. 1060, 1065, 88 L.Ed. 1373, 1381 (1944). * * *

Although the due process guarantee may not impose a significant limitation on the District's power to levy ad valorem taxes in order to finance the proposed water system, section 32–1–205, C.R.S.1973, does require that the service plan for the District reflect an ability to provide economical and sufficient service to the area and that the area included within the District have sufficient financial ability to discharge any proposed indebtedness on a reasonable basis. The Board was charged with assessing these criteria when it approved the modified service plan. It is to the validity of that approval which we now turn.

A water district may not provide domestic water to its inhabitants except pursuant to a service plan which has been approved by the Board and, with respect to an original service plan, by the district court. Sections 32–1–202 to 209, C.R.S.1973. * * *

Section 32–1–205, C.R.S.1973, sets forth the reasons for which a service plan or modification thereof may be disapproved. For purposes of this challenge subsections (d) and (e) are relevant. Respectively, these allow disapproval of the modified plan if:

> "(d) The proposed special district is incapable of providing economical and sufficient service to the area within its proposed boundaries; or

(e) The area to be included in the proposed district does not have, or will not have, the financial ability to discharge the proposed indebtedness on a reasonable basis;"

The primary dispute over the modified plan concerned projections as to how many persons would "tap in" to the proposed water system. It was conceded that a decrease in the income from tap fees and water charges caused by a smaller number of persons utilizing the system would have to be made up by increases in the ad valorem tax burden on all District property, increases in tap fees and water charges to those who were on the system, or a combination of such increases. Witnesses for the District, nevertheless, testified that such a decrease would not render the plan economically unfeasible. Although there was testimony at the hearing that some District landowners would not tap in, there was no proof that a substantial number would not do so.

The district court may not substitute its judgment for that of the Board, nor may we. * * * Upon review of the record we conclude that the district court's finding that competent evidence exists to support the Board's decision is correct.

The judgment of the district court is affirmed.

Note

Practically all states authorize the creation of a wide variety of districts, with various names, for the purpose of supplying water for domestic and household purposes outside of incorporated areas. For the most part these depend on fees and charges for water delivered to obtain money for operation and maintenance and for bond retirement, although some have general taxing powers. See for example, Smith-Hurd Ill.Ann. Stat. ch. 111⅔, §§ 188–212.16, Public Water Districts; §§ 213–22.1, Water Service Districts; §§ 223–250, Water Authorities.

FULGHUM v. SELMA

Supreme Court of North Carolina, 1953.
238 N.C. 100, 76 S.E.2d 368.

[Selma Mill Village is a small unincorporated community just outside the town of Selma, North Carolina. In 1946 the town entered into a contract to sell water to plaintiff Fulghum for distribution to the inhabitants of the village through Fulghum's pipes. The water was delivered at a meter just inside the town limits, at the same rate charged to residents of the town. Fulghum charged somewhat higher rates to the inhabitants of the village.

The contract had no fixed duration. In 1952 the town passed an ordinance amending its water rates, charging $1 per 1,000 gallons for water supplied for consumption outside the town limits and $.20 per 1,000 gallons for water consumed within the town. Fulghum brought suit to have the ordinance declared void and to enjoin the city from shutting off his water supply. The trial court dismissed the action.]

ERVIN, JUSTICE. There may be more than a modicum of truth in the assertion of the plaintiffs that the defendant enacted the ordinance and its amendment for the coercive purpose of inducing Fulghum to abandon his water service to the inhabitants of Selma Mill Village and transfer his pipe lines to the defendant at less than their value. Be this as it may, we must remember that hard cases are the quicksands of the law and confine ourselves to our appointed task of declaring the legal rights of the parties.

The crucial question raised by the appeal is this: Does the evidence of the plaintiffs suffice to show that Fulghum has the legal right to compel the Town of Selma to supply water to him at the rates charged consumers within its corporate limits for resale beyond its boundaries?

The plaintiffs insist initially that this question must be answered in the affirmative on the ground that the contract made by Fulghum with the Town of Selma in 1946 gives Fulghum this legal right.

* * * Where the parties to a contract calling for a continuing performance fix no time for its duration and none can be implied from the nature of the contract or from the surrounding circumstances, the contract is terminable at will by either party on reasonable notice to the other. * * *

The plaintiffs maintain secondarily that their evidence is sufficient to establish a legal right in Fulghum to the relief sought irrespective of the matter of contract right. They argue in this connection that when the Town of Selma established its waterworks and undertook to distribute water for compensation, it became the legal duty of the Town of Selma to supply Fulghum water for any purpose at the same rates as those charged consumers residing within its corporate limits. * * *

A municipality which operates its own waterworks is under no duty in the first instance to furnish water to persons outside its limits. It has the discretionary power, however, to engage in this undertaking. G.S. § 160–255. When a municipality exercises this discretionary power, it does not assume the obligations of a public service corporation toward nonresident consumers. G.S. § 62–30(3); 67 C.J., Waters, section 739. It retains the authority to specify the terms upon which nonresidents may obtain its water. Atlantic Construction Co. v. City of Raleigh, 230 N.C. 365, 53 S.E.2d 165. In exerting this authority, it "may fix a different rate from that charged within the corporate limits". G.S. § 160–256.

The rates fixed by the ordinance and the amendment for water supplied by the Town of Selma for consumption outside its corporate limits are not discriminatory in a legal sense. They apply alike to all nonresidents who purchase town water. The Town of Selma was empowered by law to make these rates different from those charged within its corporate limits. Since a nonresident must pay the uniform rates fixed by the Town of Selma for other nonresidents in order to obtain town water, it is immaterial that he deems such rates to be exorbitant or unreasonable. Atlantic Construction Co. v. City of Raleigh, supra; Childs v. City of Columbia, supra. * * *

When a municipality engages in supplying water to its inhabitants, it owes the duty of equal service in furnishing water only to consumers within its corporate limits. It is under no legal obligation to supply water to a resident for resale to others either within or without its municipal limits. Brand v. Board of Water Commissioners of Town of Billerica, 242 Mass. 223, 136 N.E. 389.

Fulghum does not seek to have the water in controversy furnished to him as a consumer residing within the boundaries of the Town of Selma. His sole purpose is to resell the water to persons living outside its corporate limits. This being true, he cannot complain of the refusal of the Town of Selma to furnish him the water in controversy at the same rate charged resident consumers of the same quantity of water. * * *

[Affirmed.]

Note

Generally, the rule is that a municipal corporation has express or implied authority to supply water to consumers outside its corporate limits. Richards v. Portland, 121 Or. 340, 255 P. 326 (1927). This is especially clear when the contracts are limited to surplus water. Crandall v. Safford, 47 Ariz. 402, 56 P.2d 660 (1936).

The question of whether a municipality or a public service company formed to serve the municipality has a duty to serve outsiders is more complex. Usually the suburban residents have no enforceable right to service from the city. Colorado Springs v. Kitty Hawk Development Co., 154 Colo. 535, 392 P.2d 467 (1964). If a city undertakes to serve some outsiders, however, others similarly situated may be entitled to claim discrimination if they are not served. Milwaukee v. Public Service Commission, 268 Wis. 116, 68 N.W.2d 716 (1954). But incidental service to nonresidents may not be converted into an obligation to render additional nonresident service that tends to jeopardize service within the municipality. Mongrello v. Hightstown, 17 N.J. 611, 112 A.2d 241 (1955). The matter is governed by statutes in a relatively few instances, e.g., Mich.Comp.Laws Ann. §§ 123.141–123.144.

Rates present another difficult question. The traditional view is that since the city is under no duty to supply the water, the city is free to set its own terms in making contractual arrangements. Hobbs v. Sonora, 142 Cal. 2d 457, 298 P.2d 578 (1956); Childs v. Columbia, 87 S.C. 566, 70 S.E. 296 (1910). A few courts have moved to a new view of this matter and rule that a city which serves outsiders is like a public utility and must provide service on reasonable and nondiscriminatory terms. Texarkana v. Wiggins, 151 Tex. 100, 246 S.W.2d 622 (1952); Barr v. First Taxing District of Norwalk, 151 Conn. 53, 192 A.2d 872 (1963).

Sometimes cities, trading on their monopoly position, exact terms not germane to water supply or distribution, such as requirements that the residents of the area accept other city services or agree to annexation. See Colorado Springs v. Kitty Hawk Development Company supra, Hicks v. Monroe, 237 La. 848, 112 So.2d 635 (1959); Carvalho v. Levesque, 96 R.I. 291, 191 A.2d 165 (1963).

Sax, Municipal Water Supply for Non-residents: Recent Developments and a Suggestion for the Future, 5 Natural Resources J. 54 (1965), finds a trend toward "a rule of reason," but says that it works poorly in practice and suggests some procedural remedies.

As to whether a municipal corporation that sells outside its limits becomes subject to public utility commission regulation, see Englewood v. Denver, 123 Colo. 290, 229 P.2d 667 (1951); Barr v. First Taxing District of Norwalk, supra; Knier, State Supervision Over Municipally Owned Utilities, 49 Columbia L.Rev. 180 (1949).

PEOPLE EX REL. ROGERS v. LETFORD

Supreme Court of Colorado, 1938.
102 Colo. 284, 79 P.2d 274.

KNOUS, JUSTICE. This is an original proceeding in quo warranto upon information of the Attorney General to try the right of respondents to occupy the office and exercise the duties of directors of Northern Colorado Water Conservancy District, organized under the provisions of the Water Conservancy Act of Colorado, chapter 266, p. 1309, Sess.Laws 1937, by the findings and decree of the district court of the Eighth judicial district sitting in and for Weld county. * * *

The Colorado act was passed by the Thirty-First General Assembly and became effective on May 13, 1937. It was intended to make possible the organization of what is designated as "Water Conservancy Districts." Section 1 of the act (C.S.A.'37 Supp. c. 173A, § 15), states the purpose of the Legislature in passing the law in the following words:

> "It is hereby declared that to provide for the conservation of the water resources of the State of Colorado and for the greatest beneficial use of water within this state, the organization of water conservancy districts and the construction of works as herein defined by such districts are a public use and will:
>
> "a. Be essentially for the public benefit and advantage of the people of the state of Colorado.
>
> "b. Indirectly benefit all industries of the state.
>
> "c. Indirectly benefit the State of Colorado in the increase of its taxable property valuation.
>
> "d. Directly benefit municipalities by providing adequate supplies of water for domestic use.
>
> "e. Directly benefit lands to be irrigated from works to be constructed.

"f. Directly benefit lands now under irrigation by stabilizing the flow of water in streams and by increasing flow and return flow of water to such streams.

"g. Promote the comfort, safety and welfare of the people of the State of Colorado, and it is therefore declared to be the policy of the State of Colorado:

"1. To control, make use of and apply to beneficial use all unappropriated waters originating in this state to a direct and supplemental use of such waters for domestic, manufacturing, irrigation, power and other beneficial uses.

"2. To obtain from water originating in Colorado the highest duty for domestic uses and irrigation of lands in Colorado within the terms of interstate compacts.

"3. To cooperate with the United States under the Federal Reclamation laws now or hereinafter enacted and other agencies of the United States Government for the construction and financing of works in the State of Colorado as herein defined and for the operation and maintenance thereof.

"4. To promote the greater prosperity and general welfare of the people of the State of Colorado by encouraging the organization of water conservancy districts as provided in this article [Act]."

The act is general in its nature, and upon compliance with its terms a water conservancy district can be formed at any place within the State of Colorado. * * *

Pursuant to this act, and admittedly in strict accordance with its procedural provisions, the district court of Weld county, on September 20, 1937, entered its findings and decree organizing the Northern Colorado Water Conservancy District, which includes generally the lands in the agricultural areas in the vicinity of the St. Vrain, Big Thompson, Cache la Poudre rivers, and of the Platte river from Platteville to the eastern line of Colorado. The approximate present total valuation of these farm lands and improvements thereon within the district is alleged to be $40,000,000, in addition to which it is said there has been an economic development within the district of approximately $100,000,000, making a total assessed valuation of all property within the district, both real and personal, of approximately $140,000,000. This economic development has resulted from the building of the cities of Greeley, Eaton, Boulder, Fort Collins, Longmount, Loveland, Fort Morgan, Brush, Sterling and Julesburg, and numerous other towns and hamlets of various size. In this economic development is also embraced a number of sugar factories, extensive public carrier and utility developments, and other large and prosperous businesses, all of which is due principally to the agricultural development which has been made in the district by application of water for the irrigation of the lands therein. The projected further development of this section by the construction of what is commonly known as the "Colorado-Big Thompson Project" allegedly is the motivating cause for the formation of the Northern

Colorado Water Conservancy District. The Colorado-Big Thompson Project contemplates the construction of a number of large reservoirs on the western slope of the Continental Divide on the Colorado river and its tributaries, and the diversion of the waters of that river through the Continental Divide by means of canals and tunnels to the Big Thompson river on the eastern slope of the Continental Divide, from whence, through a series of reservoirs, canals, and other facilities, the water ultimately is destined for delivery to the municipalities and lands in the district. As an integral part of the project, the construction of a reservoir on the Blue river on the western slope for the purpose of replacement of water diverted to the eastern slope and to compensate and stabilize the flow of the Colorado river is included. After a detailed survey made under its auspices, with funds provided by the United States, the Bureau of Reclamation has approved the feasibility of the project. * * *

Preliminary to the consideration of the various constitutional questions involved and as decisive of many of these points, it is necessary to determine the legal nature and character of the corporation intended to be created under the Water Conservancy Act. The act itself, in section 7, declares that: "The district shall be a political subdivision of the State of Colorado and a body corporate with all the powers of a public or municipal corporation." While a legislative declaration of this nature is not conclusive upon a court, it must be seriously regarded in the construction of an act. In this connection also must be considered the purpose of the law, not only as disclosed by its words, but also in the light of the physical conditions of the state, its needs, and the character and extent of the projected benefits. * * *

These circumstances demonstrate, and we conclude, as the language of the act states, that its objects are of sufficient public benefit and advantage to the people of Colorado as a whole to constitute a public purpose and that the water conservancy districts authorized thereby are state agencies and public corporations. * * *

Our Legislature did not confer the ordinary functions of local governments enjoyed by towns and cities on the Water Conservancy Districts contemplated, but did vest in them powers which have come to be associated with true municipal corporations, including the power of taxation to further its purpose. * * *

Section 15 of our Conservancy Act is as follows:

"Section 15. *Classification of Taxes and Assessments—Powers.*

"In addition to the other means of providing revenue for such districts as herein provided, the Board shall have power and authority to levy and collect taxes and special assessments for maintaining and operating such works and paying the obligations and indebtedness of the district by any one or more of the methods or combinations thereof, classified as follows:

"Class A. To levy and collect taxes upon all property within the district as hereinafter provided.

"Class B. To levy and collect assessments for special benefits accruing to property within municipalities for which use of water is allotted as hereinafter provided.

"Class C. To levy and collect assessments for special benefits accruing to lands within irrigation districts for which use of water is allotted as hereinafter provided.

"Class D. To levy and collect assessments for special benefits accruing to lands for which use of water is allotted as hereinafter provided."

Under class A the Legislature has authorized districts to levy and collect general taxes on all property, real and personal, within the district, and in classes B, C, and D to levy and collect assessments for special benefits.

The express authorization for power to levy taxes conferred by the Legislature upon the district here involved is found in article 10, § 7, of the Colorado Constitution, which reads as follows: "*Municipal taxation.*—The general assembly shall not impose taxes for the purposes of any county, city, town or other municipal corporation, but may by law, vest in the corporate authorities thereof respectively, the power to assess and collect taxes for all purposes of such corporation."

In this grant of power lies the distinction between a water conservancy district under this act and the irrigation districts authorized by the Colorado Irrigation District Act of 1905, as amended, supra, '35 C.S.A. c. 90, § 377 et seq. The public character of the water conservancy district is the occasion for this difference. * * *

The relator contends that the due process clauses of the Federal Constitution, the Fourteenth Amendment, and the Colorado Constitution, art. 2, § 25, are contravened by numerous provisions of the Water Conservancy Act.

Under this head it is said the act is fatally defective because no appraisal of benefits or hearing thereon is provided either as to the general mill levy or special assessments.

Our determination that the general tax authorized is for a public purpose and is not a special assessment in effect disposes of the specially urged contention, based generally upon the objection last discussed as to lack of benefits, that the order of court creating the district and the act itself violate the due process clauses as to the owners of: (1) Real property within the limits of incorporated cities and towns lying within the district; (2) lands not susceptible of irrigation; (3) lands already having an adequate water supply; and (4) personal property. All of these owners are subject to the general ad valorem tax by reason of the situs of their property in the same manner as property owners in ordinary political subdivisions are liable for taxation to support the diversified activities of such subdivisions, which liability is not contingent upon direct benefits, and, as to such tax, as we have indicated, the due process clauses have no application. Under the terms of the act, personal property under no circumstances can be directly liable for the special assessments therein contemplated. The liability of landowners under classes 2 and 3 for special assessments can arise only by a contractual relation initiated by them, and those in class 1 can be affected solely when the town or city in which they reside assumes the special assessments by agreement, in which event the urban landowner, in common with his fellow residents, is subject only to a corporate tax imposed by the authorities of said city or town to pay the special assessment for the domestic water supply contracted for, and for which a general liability would exist if domestic water was secured. To this situation, * * * the due process clauses have no application.

We now refer to the power conferred by the Water Conservancy Act to levy special assessments. As a general proposition, special assessments are permitted by authorized governmental agencies upon the theory that the property against which they are levied derives some peculiar benefit by reason of the projected improvement different from that enjoyed by other property in the community in which the improvement is to be made. Santa Fe Land Imp. Co. v. Denver, 89 Colo. 309, 2 P.2d 238. The so-called assessments for special benefits provided for in classes B, C, and D of section 15 of the act are unique in character and are not directly analogous to special assessments as they generally are known in ordinary local improvement districts. This difference lies in the fact that under the act the liability for these assessments can arise only by the voluntary act of the individuals and corporations affected, whereas in ordinary cases the special assessments are imposed upon the property owners involuntarily on the basis of the benefit fixed by some public board or authority. In effect, the individuals, cities, towns, irrigation districts, and mutual ditch companies who become liable for such special assessments through agreement with the water conservancy district themselves ascertain the amount of the benefit and the extent of their liability in applying for the water which they deem necessary for their purposes. These contracts are the basis for the lien created by the act against the property of the applicant for water. The terms of an act authorizing such assessments cannot be held violative of due process of law, as each individual landowner and designated corporation agrees to process before he or it becomes subject to any special assessment. * * *

We have refrained from discussing the policy of the act or the wisdom of its provisions, since within the lawful limits of its discretion these are matters of legislative concern over which we have no control. Neither must our holding that the act itself is constitutional be taken as a conclusive determination that the district may not transgress through the manner in which it may exercise some of the powers conferred.

The demurrer of relator is overruled and the writ discharged.

Notes

1. Other cases sustaining districts with ad valorem taxing powers, against attacks on state constitutional grounds, are Santa Barbara County Water Agency v. All Persons, 47 Cal.2d 699, 306 P.2d 875 (1957); Nebraska Mid-State Reclamation Dist. v. Hall County, 152 Neb. 410, 41 N.W.2d 397 (1950); In re Arch Hurley Conservancy Dist., 52 N.M. 34, 191 P.2d 338 (1948); Patterick v. Carbon Water Conservancy Dist., 106 Utah 55, 145 P.2d 503 (1944).

2. The Colorado River Storage Project for the comprehensive development of the water resources of the Upper Colorado River Basin requires that "* * * prior to construction of irrigation distribution facilities, repayment contracts shall be made with an 'organization' * * * which has the capacity to levy assessments upon all taxable real property located within its boundaries to assist in making repayments * * *." 43 U.S.C.A. § 620c.

3. The conservancy district was invented in Ohio. See Craine, The Muskingum Watershed Conservancy District: A Study of Local Control, 22 Law and Contemporary Problems 378 (1957). A more recent discussion of their financial powers appears in Dorrian v. Scioto Conservancy District, 27 Ohio St.2d 102, 271 N.E.2d 834 (1971).

4. Many states provide for multi-purpose districts controlling water not only for irrigation purposes but also for such things as flood control, production of hydro-electric power, municipal water supply, drainage, control of ground water withdrawals, and ground water replenishment. When the production of hydro-electric power is a feature, a common financial device is the issue of revenue bonds secured by a pledge of income from the sale of electric energy.

In some states general statutes provide for many types of special purpose and multi-purpose districts having water as their central object. These give the careful legal shopper quite a choice of organizations, powers and financial arrangements. In some states, notably Texas and California, the legislatures have created many districts by special acts tailored to meet particular situations.

"The [Texas] Legislature has made statutory provision for the creation of the following types of water districts:

1. Water control and improvement district (Chapter 3A of Title 128);
2. Water improvement district (Chapter 2 of Title 128);
3. Water control and preservation district (Chapter 3 of Title 128);
4. Fresh water supply district (Chapter 4 of Title 128);
5. Levee improvement district (Chapter 6 of Title 128);
6. Drainage district (Chapter 7 of Title 128);
7. Irrigation district (Chapter 9 of Title 128);
8. Water conservation and reclamation district (Chapter 8 of Title 128).

"In addition to the above water districts are the closely related soil conservation districts and municipalities whose plans and programs directly affect the water resources of the State. Also, there have been many special districts created by the Legislature with such high-sounding names as river authorities, valley authorities, municipal water supply districts, water recreational districts, water supply districts, flood control districts, conservation districts, canal and conservancy districts, water supply and control districts, sanitation authorities, water and soil conservation districts, sanitation authorities, water and soil conservation authorities, navigation and port districts, and water, sewer and improvement districts. Add to these the underground water conservation districts authorized to be created by the Legislature in 1949 (Article 7880–3c), and you come up with such an array of districts that it is small wonder that even legislators and attorneys become confused when the subject of water districts arise." Carter, Overlapping of Powers and Functions of Water Districts and River Authorities, Proceedings, Water Law Conference 104 (Univ. of Tex.1956). For the comparable California picture see Henley, The Evolution of Forms of Water Users Organizations in California, 45 Cal.L.Rev. 665 (1957), which gives a useful summary of factors influencing the choice of organization.

5. National Water Commission, Water Policies for the Future, 442–449 (1973):

The primary objectives of water management for metropolitan areas must be (1) to provide the three basic water services—water supply, wastewater collection and treatment, and storm water management—efficiently and effectively, (2) to make efficient use of scarce water resources, and (3) to lessen the disruptive and degrading effect of urban growth and development on the urban environment and water quality. In pursuing these objectives, metropolitan water planners and managers encounter numerous obstacles and problems which vary widely from area to area depending on the size of the population served, the geographic area involved, the source of water supply, topography, climate, natural drainage, political boundaries, and a host of other factors. The problems of most frequent occurrence are these:

1. Inadequate or unnecessarily costly service because too many different water agencies are operating within the same metropolitan area.

2. Poor integration of water supply, wastewater treatment and drainage services with each other and with planning for the use and occupancy of land.

3. Insufficient attention to the nonutility aspects of providing metropolitan water services—including neglect of recreational, esthetic, and environmental values.

4. Inadequate data, particularly on current water management practices in metropolitan areas.

5. Inability to finance future water needs of metropolitan areas.

6. Inadequate institutions for managing metropolitan water services and for determining and representing metropolitan viewpoints in Federal, State, regional, and multistate water resource management.

7. Water pollution, a substantial portion of which comes from nonpoint-sources outside current pollution control programs, particularly in growing communities.

8. The encroachment of urbanization upon watersheds and the resulting deterioration of the quality of water supplies. * * *

Within a typical large metropolitan area there may be hundreds of local jurisdictions—cities, towns, counties, and special districts—that divide responsibility for management of the basic water services of the area among them. * * *

The National Water Commission cannot invent or prescribe precise institutional arrangements for planning and managing water resources that would be appropriate for every one of the Nation's metropolitan areas. Metropolitan areas are too diverse in size, topography, climate, hydrology, political setting, and social characteristics to be analyzed and treated in a manner leading to prescription of uniform institutional arrangements. Arrangements prescribed for the Philadelphia-New Jersey-New York complex would necessarily differ from arrangements designed for Phoenix or for Portland-Vancouver. Each metropolitan area must fashion particular organizational arrangements suited to its own situation.

SALYER LAND CO. v. TULARE LAKE BASIN WATER STORAGE DISTRICT

Supreme Court of the United States, 1973.
410 U.S. 719, 93 S.Ct. 1224, 35 L.Ed.2d 659.

MR. JUSTICE REHNQUIST delivered the opinion of the Court.

This is another in the line of cases in which the Court has had occasion to consider the limits imposed by the Equal Protection Clause of the Fourteenth Amendment on legislation apportioning representation in state and local governing bodies and establishing qualifications for voters in the election of such representatives. Reynolds v. Sims, 377 U.S. 533, 84 S.Ct. 1362, 12 L.Ed.2d 506 (1964), enunciated the constitutional standard for apportionment of state legislatures. Later cases such as Avery v. Midland County, 390 U.S. 474, 88 S.Ct. 1114, 20 L.Ed. 2d 45 (1968) and Hadley v. Junior College District, 397 U.S. 50, 90 S.Ct. 791, 25 L.Ed.2d 45 (1970), extended the Reynolds rule to the governing bodies of a county and of a junior college district, respectively. We are here presented with the issue expressly reserved in *Avery,* supra:

> "Were the [county's governing body] a special-purpose unit of government assigned the performance of functions affecting definable groups of constituents more than other constituents, we would have to confront the question whether such a body may be apportioned in ways which give greater influence to the citizens most affected by the organization's functions." 390 U.S., at 483–484, 88 S.Ct., at 1120.

The particular type of local government unit whose organization is challenged on constitutional grounds in this case is a water storage district, organized pursuant to the California Water Storage District Act, Calif.Water Code, § 39000 et seq. * * *

Some history of the experience of California and the other Western States with the problems of water distribution is contained in Fallbrook Irrigation District v. Bradley, 164 U.S. 112, 151–154, 17 S.Ct. 56, 60–61, 41 L.Ed. 369 (1896), in which the constitutionality of California's Wright Act was sustained against claims of denial of due process under the Fourteenth Amendment to the United States Constitution. While the irrigation district was apparently the first local governmental unit authorized to deal with water distribution, it is by no means the only one. General legislation in California authorizes the creation not only of irrigation districts, but of water conservation districts, water storage and conservation districts, flood control districts, and water storage districts such as appellee.

Appellee district consists of 193,000 acres of intensively cultivated, highly fertile farm land located in the Tulare Lake Basin. Its population consists of 77 persons, including 18 children, most of whom are employees of one or another of the four corporations that farm 85% of the land in the district.

Such districts are authorized to plan projects and execute approved projects "for the acquisition, appropriation, diversion, storage, conservation, and distribution of water * * *." Calif.Water Code § 42200 et seq. Incidental to this general power, districts may "acquire, improve, and operate" any necessary works for the storage and distribution of water as well as any drainage or reclamation works connected therewith, and the generation and distribution of hydroelectric power may be provided for. Id., §§ 43000, 43025. They may fix tolls and charges for the use of water and collect them from all persons receiving the benefit of the water or other services in proportion to the services rendered. Id. § 43006. The costs of the projects are assessed against district land in accordance with the benefits accruing to each tract held in separate ownership. Id. §§ 46175, 46176. And land that is not benefited may be withdrawn from the district on petition. Id. § 48029. * * *

Governance of the districts is undertaken by a board of directors. Id. § 40658. Each director is elected from one of the divisions within the district, id. § 39929, and each must take an official oath and execute a bond. Id. § 40301. General elections for the directors are to be held in odd-numbered years. Id. §§ 39027, 41300 et seq.

It is the voter qualification for such elections that appellants claim invidiously discriminate against them and persons similarly situated. Appellants are landowners, a landowner-lessee, and residents within the area included in the appellee's water storage district. They brought this action under 42 U.S.C. § 1983, seeking declaratory and injunctive relief in an effort to prevent appellee from giving effect to certain provisions of the California Water Code. They allege that §§ 41000 and 41001 unconstitutionally deny to them the equal protection of the laws guaranteed by the Fourteenth Amendment, in that only landowners are permitted to vote in water storage district general elections, and votes in those elections are apportioned according to the assessed valuation of the land. * * *

We conclude that the appellee water storage district, by reason of its special limited purpose and of the disproportionate effect of its activities on landowners as a group, is the sort of exception to the rule laid down in *Reynolds* which the quoted language from *Hadley,* supra, and the decision in *Avery,* supra, contemplated.

The appellee district in this case, although vested with some typical governmental powers, has relatively limited authority. Its primary purpose, indeed the reason for its existence, is to provide for the acquisition, storage, and distribution of water for farming in the Tulare Lake Basin. It provides no other general public services such as schools, housing, transportation, utilities, roads or anything else of the type ordinarily financed by a municipal body. App. p. 86. There are no towns, shops, hospitals or other facilities designed to improve the quality of life within the district boundaries and it does not have a fire department, police, buses, or trains. Ibid.

Not only does the district not exercise what might be thought of as "normal governmental" authority, but its actions disproportionately affect landowners. All of the costs of district projects are assessed against land by assessors in proportion to the benefits received. Likewise, charges for services rendered are collectible from persons receiving their benefit in proportion to the services. When such persons are delinquent in payment, just as in the case of delinquency in payments of assessments, such charges become a lien on the land. Calif.Water Code §§ 47183, 46280. In short, there is no way that the economic burdens of district operations can fall on residents *qua* residents, and the operations of the districts primarily affect the land within their boundaries.

Under these circumstances it is quite understandable that the statutory framework for election of directors of the appellee focuses on the land benefited, rather than on people as such. California has not opened the franchise to all residents, as Missouri had in *Hadley,* supra, nor to all residents with some exceptions, as New York had in *Kramer.* The franchise is extended to landowners, whether they reside in the district or out of it, and indeed whether or not they are natural persons who would be entitled to vote in a more traditional political election. Appellants do not challenge the enfranchisement of nonresident landowners or of corporate landowners for purposes of election of the directors of appellee. Thus to sustain their contention that all residents of the district must be accorded a vote would not result merely in the striking down of an exclusion from what was otherwise a delineated class, but would instead engraft onto the statutory scheme a wholly new class of voters in addition to those enfranchised by the statute.

We hold, therefore, that the popular election requirements enunciated by *Reynolds,* supra, and succeeding cases are inapplicable to elections such as the general election of appellee Water Storage District. * * *

The last claim by appellants is that § 41001, which weights the vote according to assessed valuation of the land, is unconstitutional. They point to the fact that several of the smaller landowners only have one vote per person whereas the J.G. Boswell Company has 37,825 votes, and they place reliance on the various decisions of this Court holding that wealth has no relation to resident-voter qualifications and that equality of voting power may not be evaded. See, e.g., Gray v. Sanders, 372 U.S. 368, 83 S.Ct. 801, 9 L.Ed.2d 821 (1963); Harper v. Virginia State Board of Elections, 383 U.S. 663, 86 S.Ct. 1079, 16 L.Ed. 2d 169 (1966).

Appellants' argument ignores the realities of water storage district operation. Since its formation in 1926, appellee district has put into operation four multi-million-dollar projects. The last project involved the construction of two laterals from the Basin to the California State Aqueduct at a capital cost of about $2,500,000. Three small landowners having land aggregating somewhat under four acres with an assessed valuation of under $100 were given one vote each in the special election held for the approval of the project. The J.G. Boswell Company, which owns 61,665.54 acres with an assessed valuation of $3,782,220 was entitled to cast 37.825 votes in the election. By the same token, however, the assessment commissioners determined that the benefits of the project would be uniform as to all of the acres affected, and assessed the project equally as to all acreage. Each acre has to bear $13.26 of cost and the three small landowners, therefore, must pay a total of $46, whereas the Company must pay $817,685 for its part. Thus, as the District Court found, "the benefits and burdens to each landowner in the District are in proportion to the assessed value of the land." We cannot say that the California legislative decision to permit voting in the same proportion is not rationally based.

Accordingly, we affirm the judgment of the three-judge District Court and hold that the voter qualification statutes for California water storage district elections are rationally based, and therefore do not violate the Equal Protection Clause.

Affirmed.

MR. JUSTICE DOUGLAS, with whom MR. JUSTICE BRENNAN and MR. JUSTICE MARSHALL concur, dissenting.

The vices of this case are four-fold.

First. Lessees of farmlands, though residents of the district, are not given the franchise.

Second. Residents who own no agricultural lands but live in the district and face all the perils of flood which the district is supposed to control are disfranchised.

Third. Only agricultural landowners are entitled to vote and their vote is weighted, one vote for each one hundred dollars of assessed valuation as provided in § 41001 of the California Water Code.

Fourth. The corporate voter is put in the saddle.

There are 189 landowners who own up to 80 acres each. These 189 represent 2.34% of the agricultural acreage of the district. There are 193,000 acres in the district. Petitioner Salyer Land Company is one large operator, West Lake Farms and South Lake Farms are also large operators. The largest is J.G. Boswell Co. These four farm almost 85% of all the land in the district. Of these J.G. Boswell Co. commands the greatest number of votes, 37,825, which are enough to give it a majority of the board of directors. As a result it is permanently in the saddle. Almost all of the 77 residents of the district are disfranchised. The hold of J.G. Boswell Co. is so strong that there has been no election since 1947, making little point of the provision in § 41300 of the California Water Code for an election every other year.

The result has been calamitous to some, who though landless have even more to fear from floods than the ephemeral corporation. * * * Ellison, one of the petitioners who lives in the district is not an agricultural landowner. But his residence was 15½ feet below the water level of the crest of the flood in 1969.

The respondent district has large levees; and if they are broken, damages to houses and losses of lives are imminent.

Landowners—large or small—resident or nonresident, lessees or landlords, sharecroppers or owners—all should have a say. But irrigation, water storage, the building of levees, flood control, implicate the entire community. All residents of the district must be granted the franchise. * * * One corporation can outvote 77 individuals in this district. Four corporations can exercise these governmental powers as they choose, leaving every individual inhabitant with a weak ineffective voice. The result is a corporate political kingdom undreamed of by those who wrote our Constitution.

Notes

1. A companion case to *Salyer* was Associated Enterprises, Inc. v. Toltec Watershed Improvement District, 410 U.S. 743, 93 S.Ct. 1237, 35 L.Ed.2d 675 (1973), involving a Wyoming watershed district, which like the California water storage district is a governmental unit of special or limited purpose whose activities have a disproportionate effect on landowners within the district, since the district's operations are conducted through projects, the land is assessed for any benefits received and the assessment remains a lien on the land until paid. The Court held that the state could rationally conclude that landowners are primarily burdened and benefited by the establishment and operation of a watershed district and that it might limit the vote to establish them to landowners and weight the vote according to acreage. Again Justices Douglas, Brennan, and Marshall dissented:

"It is also inconceivable that a body with the power to destroy a river by damming it and so deprive a watershed of one of its salient environmental assets does not have 'sufficient impact' on the interests of people generally to invoke the principles of *Avery* and *Hadley*. * * * Dams may be vital or they may be disastrous. The sedimentation rate in some areas is so fast as to reduce the life of dams to a few decades. Dams may destroy valued fish runs. Dams substitute a reservoir for a river and wipe out the varied life of a river course, including its wildlife, canoe waters, camping and picnic grounds, and nesting areas of birds. This reshaping of the face of the Nation may be disastrous, no matter who casts the ballots. The enormity of the violation of our environmental ethics, represented by state and federal laws, is only increased when the ballot is restricted to or heavily weighted on behalf of the few who are important only because they are wealthy."

2. The right to serve on the governing board of a water district was said to depend upon much the same considerations in Choudry v. Free, 17 Cal.3d 660, 131 Cal.Rptr. 654, 552 P.2d 438 (1976). Section 21100 of West's Ann.Cal.W.Code makes only "freeholders" eligible to be directors of a California irrigation district, which is more like the Colorado conservancy district involved in *Letford,* supra p. 528, than the Wyoming irrigation district analyzed in *Sullivan,* supra p. 511. The Imperial Irrigation District serves 500,000 acres and 100,000 residents with irrigation and domestic water, electric power, drainage, flood control, sewage disposal and recreation facilities. Only half its residents own their own homes.

The California court held that Choudry, who resided and voted but owned no property in the district, was denied the equal protection of the laws when he was kept off the ballot in a district election. *Salyer* was distinguished:

"[T]he limitation involved in the present case has an appreciable impact upon the equality and fairness of the electoral process. The freeholder requirement has the effect of denying nonlandowner voters the right to elect candidates who do not own real property. The voters' choice is thus confined to those whose predilections may favor the special concerns of landowners over the general welfare of all residents. Since the directors of the district decide such issues as rate increases for water and power the distribution of water between agricultural and nonagricultural uses, and other matters which could vitally affect the economic welfare of the residents as well as the environment in which they live, the bar of section 21100 imposes a substantial burden upon the right of franchise. Manifestly it also imposes a serious barrier to a candidate's ability to run for office.

* * *

"Although many of the powers of a water storage district referred to in *Salyer* are also exercised by irrigation districts, there are significant differences between the operations of the two entities. The basic function of a water storage district is to acquire, store and distribute water for farming. In connection with this primary purpose, the district may acquire and operate works for drainage, reclamation and the generation of hydroelectric power as well as for the distribution of water, and engage in flood control activities. An irrigation district, by contrast, may produce or purchase electric power and operate flood control facilities without regard to whether such functions are ancillary to irrigation and, in addition, it may operate sewage disposal works, if authorized by the electorate, and recreational facilities in connection with property under its control.

"Moreover, in the present case, unlike *Salyer,* assessments against land are not the sole means by which the district's expenses are paid. The district may collect charges for the sale of domestic water, electric power, sewage disposal and other services in lieu of assessments, and such charges are paid by both landowners and those who do not own land. And it is authorized to pay its bonds from revenues other than assessments."

3. Ball v. James, 451 U.S. 355, 101 S.Ct. 1811, 68 L.Ed.2d 150 (1981), followed *Salyer* in holding that voting could be restricted to landowners and weighted according to acreage, although the Salt River Project Agricultural Improvement & Power District was more like the Imperial Irrigation District than the Tulare Water District.

> The public entity at issue here is the Salt River Project Agricultural Improvement and Power District, which stores and delivers untreated water to the owners of land comprising 236,000 acres in central Arizona. The District, formed as a governmental entity in 1937, subsidizes its water operations by selling electricity, and has become the supplier of electric power for hundreds of thousands of people in an area including a large part of metropolitan Phoenix. Nevertheless, the history of the District began in the efforts of Arizona farmers in the 19th century to irrigate the arid lands of the Salt River Valley, and, as the parties have stipulated, the primary purposes of the District have always been the storage, delivery, and conservation of water.
>
> As noted by the Court of Appeals, the services currently provided by the Salt River District are more diverse and affect far more people than those of the Tulare Lake Basin District. Whereas the Tulare District included an area entirely devoted to agriculture and populated by only 77 persons, the Salt River District includes almost half the population of the State, including large parts of Phoenix and other cities. Moreover, the Salt River District, unlike the Tulare District, has exercised its statutory power to generate and sell electric power, and has become one of the largest suppliers of such power in the State. Further, whereas all the water delivered by the Tulare Lake Basin District went for agriculture, roughly 40% of the water delivered by the Salt River District goes to urban areas or is used for nonagricultural purposes in farming areas. Finally whereas all operating costs of the Tulare District were borne by the voting landowners through assessments apportioned according to land value, most of the capital and operating costs of the Salt River District have been met through the revenues generated by the selling of electric power. Nevertheless, a careful examination of the Salt River District reveals that, under the principles of the *Avery, Hadley,* and *Salyer* cases, these distinctions do not amount to a constitutional difference.
>
> First, the District simply does not exercise the sort of governmental powers that invoke the strict demands of *Reynolds.* The District cannot impose ad valorem property taxes or sales taxes. It cannot

enact any laws governing the conduct of citizens, nor does it administer such normal functions of government as the maintenance of streets, the operation of schools, or sanitation, health, or welfare services.

Second, * * * even the District's water functions, which constitute the primary and originating purpose of the District, are relatively narrow. The District and Association do not own, sell, or buy water, nor do they control the use of any water they have delivered. The District simply stores water behind its dams, conserves it from loss, and delivers it through project canals. It is true, as the Court of Appeals noted, that as much as 40% of the water delivered by the District goes for nonagricultural purposes. But the distinction between agricultural and urban land is of no special constitutional significance in this context. The constitutionally relevant fact is that all water delivered by the Salt River District, like the water delivered by the Tulare Lake Basin District, is distributed according to land ownership, and the District does not and cannot control the use to which the landowners who are entitled to the water choose to put it.

Finally, neither the existence nor size of the District's power business affects the legality of its property-based voting scheme. As this Court has noted in a different context, the provision of electricity is not a traditional element of governmental sovereignty, Jackson v. Metropolitan Edison Co., 419 U.S. 345, 353, 95 S.Ct. 449, 454, 42 L.Ed. 2d 477, and so is not in itself the sort of general or important governmental function that would make the government provider subject to the doctrine of the *Reynolds* case.

Justice White, with whom were Justices Brennan, Marshall and Blackmun, dissented:

In terms of the relative impact of the Salt River District's operations on the favored landowner voters and those who may not vote for the officers of this municipal corporation, the contrast with the Water District in *Salyer* is even more pronounced. A bird's-eye view of the District's operations will be helpful. Historically, the Salt River District was concerned only with storing water and delivering it for agricultural uses within the District. This was a crucial service, but it proved too expensive for a wholly private concern to maintain. It needed public help, which it received. It became a municipal corporation, a transformation which rendered its bonds and property tax exempt. It also needed a public subsidy, which was provided by authorizing it to engage in the generation and sale of electricity. It was also authorized to supply water for municipal and other nonagricultural uses.

The area within the District, once primarily rural, now encompasses eight municipalities and a major part of the city of Phoenix. Its original purpose, the supply of irrigation water, now provides only a tiny fraction of its gross income. * * * It must also be noted that at the present time, 40% of the water delivered by the District is used for nonagricultural purposes—25% for municipal purposes and 15% to schools, playgrounds, parks, and the like.

> With these facts in mind, it is indeed curious that the Court would attempt to characterize the District's electrical operations as "incidental" to its water operations, or would consider the power operations to be irrelevant to the legality of the voting scheme. The facts are that in *Salyer* the burdens of the Water District fell entirely on the landowners who were served by the District. Here the landowners could not themselves afford to finance their own project and turned to a public agency to help them. That agency now subsidizes the storage and delivery of irrigation water for agricultural purposes by selling electricity to the public at prices that neither the voters nor any representative public agency has any right to control. Unlike the situation in *Salyer,* the financial burden of supplying irrigation water has been shifted from the landowners to the consumers of electricity. * * *

4. Millis v. Larimer County, supra p. 523, involved the converse problem. Millis, the nonresident owner of a mountain cabin in Colorado, served by the High Drive Water District, was denied the right to vote in elections for the formation of the district and approval of its plans. The district furnished domestic water, financed by general obligation bonds, payable out of general ad valorem taxes levied by the district board on property within the district. Only "taxpaying electors," persons qualified to vote in general elections who reside in or own property in the district, may vote in district elections.

In a parallel federal case, the United States Supreme Court affirmed without opinion a federal district court's holding that Millis' Fourteenth Amendment rights were not violated. Millis v. High Drive Water District, 439 U.S. 802, 99 S.Ct. 58, 58 L.Ed.2d 95 (1978).

The Colorado Supreme Court refused to declare that Millis had greater rights under the state constitution:

> With respect to restrictions on the franchise, classifications based upon residency, citizenship or age have never been considered suspect.
>
> The appellants contend that there is no rational reason for granting district voting rights to Colorado residents who own land but do not reside within the district, while denying electoral participation to district landowners who live out of state. The federal district court found that Colorado residents are more likely to share a common concern regarding urban development, and its effect on this state's natural environment, than are residents of other states. Because the formation and operation of a water district affects this concern the federal court concluded that a rational basis exists for excluding nonresidents from direct political participation in water district matters. Similarly, the creation of adequate water supply and distribution systems and the provision of adequate sewage collection and disposal facilities implicate important public health considerations. These too are concerns which the legislature rationally might have considered to affect Colorado residents more directly than nonresidents. We can also conceive that the legislature wishes to decrease the change that nonresidents would control the formation and operation of water districts to the detriment of those who are full-time district residents. (Citations omitted.)

4. A symposium of five articles on the changing form and evolving functions of the western water district contains the following articles: Leshy, Irrigation Districts in a Changing West—An Overview, 1982 Ariz.St. L.J. 345; Benson, Desert Survival: The Evolving Western Irrigation District, 1982 Ariz.St.L.J. 377; Young, Governing Special Districts: The Conflict Between Voting Rights and Property Privileges, 1982 Ariz.St.L.J. 419; and McDowell and Ugone, The Effect of Institutional Setting on Behavior in Public Enterprises: Irrigation Districts in the Western States, 1982 Ariz. St.L.J. 453.

Another symposium, focusing primarily on the social and political aspects, is found in Special Water Districts: Challenge for the Future, (J. Corbridge, Ed., 1983).

STATE PROJECTS

The State of California has engaged in the largest state program of water control and supply projects. The California State Water Project develops surplus northern California water and distributes it to areas of need in northern California, the San Francisco Bay area, the San Joaquin Valley and Southern California. Water in the Feather River watershed is stored behind Oroville Dam in Butte County, then flows through natural channels to the Sacramento-San Joaquin Delta, where it is pumped into the California Aqueduct. The North Bay Aqueduct supplies water to Napa County and eventually will supply Solano County as well. The South Bay Aqueduct supplies water to Alameda and Santa Clara counties.

The California Aqueduct runs south into the San Joaquin valley, supplying water for agriculture and cities there. The remaining water is pumped over the Tehachapi Mountains to flow into Southern California, with a west branch serving Los Angeles and other coastal cities and an east branch serving the Antelope Valley and San Bernardino, Riverside, Orange and San Diego Counties.

At ultimate capacity, the Project will deliver 4.23 million acre feet to 31 contracting agencies. The Project operates 25 dams and reservoirs, 684 miles of canals, pipelines and tunnels, 8 power plants and 22 pumping plants. The Project is a net consumer of power.

Three general types of financing have been used for the Project. Funds derived from the sale of California Water Resources Development Bonds and a portion of the state's tideland oil and gas revenues are deposited in the California Water Fund as authorized by the Burns-Porter Act, West's Ann.Cal. Water Code §§ 12930–12944, approved by the electorate in 1960. Revenue bond financing was authorized by the Central Valley Project Act, West's Ann.Cal.Water Code §§ 11100–11925. Authority to issue revenue bonds was confirmed by the Supreme Court of California in Warne v. Harkness, 60 Cal.2d 579, 35 Cal. Rptr. 601, 387 P.2d 377 (1963). The fund also receives miscellaneous receipts derived from payments and appropriations authorized by a variety of legislative actions and special contracts and cost-sharing agreements.

A summary of state laws providing for state water development and supply projects, state financing of local district project, and state financial participation in federal projects is found in Western States Water Council, State/Federal Financing and Western Water Development (1984 Update) 16–86.

Chapter 6

PUBLIC RIGHTS

DIANA SHOOTING CLUB v. HUSTING

Supreme Court of Wisconsin, 1914.
156 Wis. 261, 145 N.W. 816.

Action of trespass. The complaint alleges the incorporation of the plaintiff, that on the 24th day of September, 1911, it was lawfully in possession of section 19 in the town of Williamstown, Dodge county, Wis., and was the owner of the exclusive right and title to the hunting and shooting privileges upon said section. It then charges that the defendant unlawfully broke and entered upon the same, trod down and injured the grass, rushes, wild rice, and herbage growing thereon, and disturbed the plaintiff in the use and occupation of its land, and interfered with its exclusive right to hunt and shoot thereon, to its damage in the sum of $50. * * *

The trial court found these facts: The defendant, at the time of the alleged trespass, was a resident and citizen of this state in possession of a valid hunting license. On September 24, 1911, without trespassing upon the lands of the plaintiff, he entered his hunting boat floating upon the waters of Rock river, and, with the aid of pole and paddle, propelled it down the river to the place of the alleged trespass, and there, for the purpose of shooting wild ducks flying over the place, he pushed it into a growth of vegetation known as "flag," which grew from the bottom of the water to a height of from four to five feet above the surface. The place of the alleged trespass was within the area of what is known as Malzahn's Bay, which is a widening of the river, and is about one-half mile wide and about five-eighths of a mile long. * * * During the period ending in June of each year the place of the alleged trespass is covered with water in common with the remaining area of Malzahn's Bay, and during all of the time within the last 35 years has been navigable and navigated the same as, and as a part of, said Malzahn's Bay, and during such period said place has not been distinguishable in appearance from any other part of the bay. After the month of June in each year vegetation, consisting of wild rice, bulrushes, water lilies and flag, take root below the surface of the water in the soft muck of the bottom and grow above the surface to a height of from four to five feet, forming blinds or cover in which hunters conceal themselves from view of the ducks flying over. The flag extended west and north from where the trespass is alleged to have occurred for a distance of about ten to twelve rods to what is known as the old river bed, which is between two to three rods in width, and during the periods of each year ending in June is navigable in fact, and has always been in fact navigated with the remaining area of Malzahn's Bay. Later in the year, in times of low water, the water recedes, sometimes leaving the bottom of the old river bed exposed, and sometimes leaving it with a shallow covering of water. At such times the river bed is dotted with sparsely growing aquatic vegetation, such as rushes, rice, and flag. Up to and including the month of June each year the place of the alleged trespass is separated from the hard bog or shore by such strip of water. To the west and north of said old river bed again occurs a growth of flag and rushes, which continues to the west and north of the hard bog or shore of the bay. At the time and place in question the water below the boat of the defendant was about twelve inches deep, and his boat was floating upon the water. At the time of the alleged trespass the plaintiff had a valid subsisting lease of certain land abutting on Rock river, and the bed of the river, including Malzahn's Bay at the point of the alleged trespass, was embraced within the descriptions of premises covered by said lease, which, in its terms, purported to give to the plaintiff exclusive hunting privileges upon the premises owned by the lessors and covered by the lease. * * *

VINJE, J. (after stating the facts as above). The ordinance of 1787 establishing the government of the Northwest territory, of which Wisconsin formed a part, provided that "the navigable waters leading into the Mississippi and St. Lawrence, and the carrying places between the same, shall be common highways, and forever free, as well to the inhabitants of the said territory, as to the citizens of the United States, and those of any other states that may be admitted into the confederacy, without any tax, impost or duty therefor." The act of April 20, 1836, establishing the territorial government of Wisconsin, provided in section 12 thereof that the inhabitants of the territory should be subject to all the conditions, and restrictions, and prohibitions contained in the ordinance of 1787. The act of August 6, 1846, enabling the people of Wisconsin territory to form a state, declared that "the said state of Wisconsin shall have concurrent jurisdiction on the Mississippi and all other rivers and waters bordering on the said state of Wisconsin, so far as the same shall form a common boundary to said state and any other state or states now or hereafter to be formed or bounded by the same; and said river and waters, and the navigable waters leading into the same, shall be common highways and forever free, as well to the inhabitants of said state as to all other citizens of the United States, without any tax, duty, impost or toll therefor." Section 1, art. 9, of our Constitution provides that "the river Mississippi and the navigable waters leading into the Mississippi and St. Lawrence, and the carrying places between the same, shall be common highways and forever free, as well to the inhabitants of the state as to the citizens of the United States, without any tax, impost or duty therefor."

It will thus be seen that ever since the organization of the Northwest territory in 1787 to the time of the adoption of our Constitution the right to the free use of the navigable waters of the state has been jealously reserved, not only to citizens of the territory and state, but to all citizens of the United States alike. All that part of Rock river as far north as the northern boundary of Dodge county is by section 1607, Stats.1913, declared navigable, and the court found it, as well as the locus in quo, to be so in fact, at the time the alleged trespass was committed. The case, therefore, presents the question whether the right to hunt on navigable waters of the state is reserved to the residents thereof, where the title to the land covered by such waters is in private parties. At common law the rights of hunting and of fishing were held to be incident to the right of navigation. In England, however, only waters on which the tide ebbed and flowed were held navigable. Such limitation upon navigable waters has never obtained in the United States. Navigability in fact for products of the forest, field, or commerce for regularly recurrent annual periods has, in our state, been held sufficient to constitute a stream navigable. Olson v. Merrill, 42 Wis. 203 * * *.

In some of the states embraced within the Northwest territory the title to the bed of navigable streams remained in the state. In Wisconsin it is held to be in the riparian owners. So far as the right of navigation, and the rights incident thereto, are concerned, it is entirely immaterial who holds the title, the state or the riparian owners. Such title is equally subject to the rights mentioned. It is beyond the power of the state to alienate it freed from such rights. * * * As was pointed out in Willow River Club v. Wade, 100 Wis. 86, 76 N.W. 273, 42 L.R.A. 305, riparian owners on navigable streams have only a qualified title to the beds thereof, which title is entirely subordinated to, and not inconsistent with, the rights of the state to secure and preserve to the people the full enjoyment of navigation and the rights incident thereto.

The same case also clearly establishes the right of the public to fish in all the navigable waters of the state, holding as it does that the right of navigation carries with it the right of fishing, which is incident to the right to navigate. The same process of reasoning applies to the right to hunt on navigable waters as an incident to the right of navigation. No difference in principle is perceived. Indeed, if there is any force at all in assuming that there is no relation between the title to the bed of a navigable stream and the fish in the waters above it, there would seem to be less relation between game and the title to such bed. However, neither the right to fish nor to hunt need be grounded on the absence or presence of such a relation. It is perfectly logical and consistent to extend to our navigable waters such rights as were by the common law of England extended to waters declared navigable by it, even though we enlarge the field of navigability. * * *

The wisdom of the policy which, in the organic laws of our state, steadfastly and carefully preserved to the people the full and free use of public waters cannot be questioned. Nor should it be limited or curtailed by narrow constructions. It should be interpreted in the broad and beneficent spirit that gave rise to it in order that the people may fully enjoy the intended benefits. Navigable waters are public waters, and as such they should enure to the benefit of the public. They should be free to all for commerce, for travel, for recreation, and also for hunting and fishing, which are now mainly certain forms of recreation. Only by so construing the provisions of our organic laws can the people reap the full benefit of the grant secured to them therein. This grant was made to them before the state had any title to convey to private parties, and it became a trustee of the people charged with the faithful execution of the trust created for their benefit. Riparian owners, therefore, took title to lands under navigable waters with notice of such trust, and subject to the burdens created by it. It was intended that navigable waters should be public navigable waters, and only by giving members of the public equal rights thereon so far as navigation and its incidents are concerned can they be said to be truly public.

Hunting on navigable waters is lawful when it is confined strictly to such waters while they are in a navigable stage, and between the boundaries of ordinary high-water marks. When so confined it is immaterial what the character of the stream or water is. It may be deep or shallow, clear or covered with aquatic vegetation. By ordinary high-water mark is meant the point on the bank or shore up to which the presence and action of the water is so continuous as to leave a distinct mark either by erosion, destruction of terrestrial vegetation, or other easily recognized characteristic. Lawrence v. American W.P. Co., 144 Wis. 556, 562, 128 N.W. 440. And where the bank or shore at any particular place is of such a character that it is impossible or difficult to ascertain where the point of ordinary high-water mark is, recourse may be had to other places on the bank or shore of the same stream or lake to determine whether a given stage of water is above or below ordinary high-water mark. * * *

Judgment affirmed.

Notes

1. In some states the existence of public rights depends on whether the public or the riparian proprietor owns the bed underlying the water. If the water is "navigable," title to the bed of the stream or lake passed to the state when it achieved statehood. But for the purpose of determining title, the question of navigability is a federal question, to be determined by the "federal test" of whether the water in its natural and ordinary condition was usable by the customary modes of trade or travel on water when the

state was admitted to the Union. See Brewer-Elliott Oil and Gas Co. v. United States, 260 U.S. 77, 43 S.Ct. 60, 67 L.Ed. 140 (1922); United States v. Holt State Bank, 270 U.S. 49, 46 S.Ct. 197, 70 L.Ed. 465 (1926); and United States v. Utah, 283 U.S. 64, 51 S.Ct. 438, 75 L.Ed. 844 (1931). For an analysis of these cases and their effect, see Johnson and Austin, Recreational Rights and Titles to Beds on Western Lakes and Streams, 7 Natural Resources J. 1 (1967). A shorter and more general treatment is Leighty, The Source and Scope of Public and Private Rights in Navigable Waters, 5 Land & Water L.Rev. 391 (1970). The more recent cases are reviewed in Frank, Forever Free: Navigability, Inland Waterways, and the Expanding Public Interest, 16 U.C. Davis L.Rev. 570 (1983).

Title to the beds of non-navigable waters ordinarily passes to the riparian landowner with the acquisition of title to the fast land. State v. Bollenbach, 241 Minn. 103, 63 N.W.2d 278 (1954); Hartman v. Tresise, 36 Colo. 146, 84 P. 685 (1905); Day v. Armstrong, 262 P.2d 137 (Wyo.1961). There are some variations on these rules, left over from the days before the Supreme Court clarified this question, when state tests of navigability were sometimes used for title determination purposes. In Wisconsin the beds of lakes navigable under the state but not the federal test remain in state ownership, the beds of streams navigable only by state law are held by the riparian owner subject to public rights. Illinois Steel Company v. Bilot, 109 Wis. 418, 84 N.W. 855 (1901); Ne-pee-nauk Club v. Wilson, 96 Wis. 290, 71 N.W. 661 (1897); Baker v. Voss, 217 Wis. 550, 259 N.W. 412 (1935). In Iowa and possibly some other states mapped under the public land surveys the title to beds of non-navigable waters "meandered" (marked and identified by the survey) is in the state. Shortell v. Des Moines Electric Company, 186 Iowa 469, 172 N.W. 649 (1919). For other variations see Johnson and Austin, supra.

Bed ownership can be important for reasons other than the existence of public rights. If the bed is exposed by natural or man-made causes, it may have value for surface uses. More commonly, bed ownership is important for purposes of determining title to minerals lying under the bed. A recent example is provided by United States v. Louisiana, ___ U.S. ___, 105 S.Ct. 1074, 84 L.Ed.2d 73 (1985), which concerned a dispute between the United States on the one hand and the states of Mississippi and Alabama on the other hand over the ownership of the seabed, minerals, and other natural resources underlying Mississippi Sound. An extensive discussion of these problems in inland bodies of water is found in Wilson, Ownership of Mineral Interests Underlying Inland Bodies of Water and the Effects of Accretion and Erosion, 30 Rocky.Mtn.Min.L.Inst. 14–1 (1984).

Somewhat similar questions arise when waterbodies form the boundaries between parcels of land. The common law rule for non-navigable bodies puts the boundary in the center of the stream. If the location of a body shifts or recedes slowly ("accretion", "reliction", or "erosion") there is general agreement that the boundary shifts with it. Similarly, it is generally agreed that the boundary does not shift if the body of water shifts location rapidly ("avulsion"). However, there is no uniform treatment of what qualifies as a rapid or slow shift. These matters and related complications are discussed in Wilson, supra.

2. A number of states hold that public rights exist only in waters navigable under the federal title test, Adams v. Pease, 2 Conn. 481 (1818); State v. Bollenbach, 241 Minn. 103, 63 N.W.2d 278 (1954). Many, however, have a more liberal "state test" of navigability for the purpose of establishing public rights in waters overlying private land. During Wisconsin's timber boom, that state started with the "sawlog test," Olson v. Merrill, 42 Wis. 203 (1877), and in its present posture as a vacation land ends up declaring navigable all waters sufficient to float the lightest skiff or canoe. Muench v. Public Service Commission, 261 Wis. 492, 53 N.W.2d 514 (1952). For other variations, see Johnson and Austin, supra; Leighty, Public Rights in Navigable State Waters—Some Statutory Approaches, 6 Land & Water L.Rev. 459 (1971). The Wisconsin approach, sometimes called the "pleasure boat" test, has received increasing acceptance in recent years. See e.g., People ex rel Baker v. Mack, 19 Cal.App.3d 1040, 97 Cal.Rptr. 448 (1971); Brown v. Newport Concrete Co., 44 Ohio App.2d 121, 336 N.E.2d 453 (1975).

3. As for the Northwest Ordinance as a source of public rights, see Waite, Public Rights to Use and Have Access to Navigable Waters, 1958 Wis.L.Rev. 335; Waite, The Dilemma of Water Recreation and a Suggested Solution, 1958 Wis.L.Rev. 542.

4. As the foregoing indicates, "navigability" is important in determining the ownership of beds of bodies of water and in determining public rights in water. In addition, navigability is an important source of authority for federal powers and programs relating to the use of water. These powers and programs are discussed in Chapter 8, section 1.

ILLINOIS CENTRAL RAILROAD v. ILLINOIS

Supreme Court of the United States, 1892.
146 U.S. 387, 13 S.Ct. 110, 36 L.Ed. 1018.

MR. JUSTICE FIELD delivered the opinion of the court.

This suit was commenced on the 1st of March, 1883, in a circuit court of Illinois, by an information or bill in equity filed by the attorney general of the state, in the name of its people, against the Illinois Central Railroad Company, a corporation created under its laws, and against the city of Chicago. * * *

The object of the suit is to obtain a judicial determination of the title of certain lands on the east or lake front of the city of Chicago, situated between the Chicago river and Sixteenth street, which have been reclaimed from the waters of the lake, and are occupied by the tracks, depots, warehouses, piers, and other structures used by the railroad company in its business, and also of the title claimed by the company to the submerged lands, constituting the bed of the lake, lying east of its tracks, within the corporate limits of the city, for the distance of a mile, and between the south line of the south pier near Chicago river, extended eastwardly, and a line extended in the same direction from the south line of lot 21 near the company's roundhouse and machine shops. The determination of the title of the company will involve a consideration of its right to construct, for its own business, as well as for public convenience, wharves, piers, and docks in the harbor. * * *

We proceed to consider the claim of the railroad company to the ownership of submerged lands in the harbor, and the right to construct such wharves, piers, docks, and other works therein as it may deem proper for its interest and business. The claim is founded upon the third section of the act of the legislature of the state passed on the 16th of April, 1869, the material part of which is as follows:

> "Sec. 3. The right of the Illinois Central Railroad Company under the grant from the state in its charter, which said grant constitutes a part of the consideration for which the said company pays to the state at least seven per cent. of its gross earnings, and under and by virtue of its appropriation, occupancy, use, and control, and the riparian ownership incident to such grant, appropriation, occupancy, use, and control, in and to the lands submerged or otherwise lying east of the said line running parallel with and 400 feet east of the west line of Michigan avenue, in fractional sections ten and fifteen, township and range as aforesaid, is hereby confirmed; and all the right and title of the state of Illinois in and to the submerged lands constituting the bed of Lake Michigan, and lying east of the tracks and breakwater of the Illinois Central Railroad Company, for a distance of one mile, and between the south line of the south pier extended eastwardly and a line extended eastward from the south line of lot twenty-one, south of and near to the roundhouse and machine shops of said company, in the south division of the said city of Chicago, are hereby granted in fee to the said Illinois Central Railroad Company, its successors and assigns: provided, however, that the fee to said lands shall be held by said company in perpetuity, and that the aid company shall not have power to grant, sell, or convey the fee to the same, * * *."

The act of which this section is a part was accepted by a resolution of the board of directors of the company at its office in the city of New York, July 6, 1870, but the acceptance was not communicated to the state until the 18th of November, 1870. A copy of the resolution was on that day forwarded to the secretary of state, and filed and recorded by him in the records of his office. On the 15th of April, 1873, the legislature of Illinois repealed the act. The questions presented relate to the validity of the section cited, of the act, and the effect of the repeal upon its operation. * * *

The act, if valid and operative to the extent claimed, placed under the control of the railroad company nearly the whole of the submerged lands of the harbor, subject only to the limitations that it should not authorize obstructions to the harbor, or impair the public right of navigation, or exclude the legislature from regulating the rates of wharfage or dockage to be charged. With these limitations, the act put it in the power of the company to delay indefinitely the improvement of the harbor, or to construct as many docks, piers, and wharves and other works as it might choose, and at such positions in the harbor as might suit its purposes, and permit any kind of business to be conducted thereon, and to lease them out on its own terms for indefinite periods. The inhibition against the technical transfer of the fee of any portion of the submerged lands was of little consequence when it could make a lease for any period, and renew it at its pleasure; and the inhibitions against authorizing obstructions to the harbor and impairing the public right of navigation placed no impediments upon the action of the railroad company which did not previously exist. A corporation created for one purpose, the construction and operation of a railroad between designated points, is by the act converted into a corporation to manage and practically control the harbor of Chicago, not simply for its own purpose as a railroad corporation, but for its own profit generally. * * *

The question, therefore, to be considered, is whether the legislature was competent to thus deprive the state of its ownership of the submerged lands in the harbor of Chicago, and of the consequent control of its waters; or, in other words, whether the railroad corporation can hold the lands and control the waters by the grant, against any future exercise of power over them by the state.

That the state holds the title to the lands under the navigable waters of Lake Michigan, within its limits, in the same manner that the state holds title to soils under tide water, by the common law, we have already shown; and that title necessarily carries with it control over the waters above them, whenever the lands are subjected to use. But it is a title different in character from that which the state holds in lands intended for sale. It is different from the title which the United States hold in the public lands which are open to pre-emption and sale. It is a title held in trust for the people of the state, that they may enjoy the navigation of the waters, carry on commerce over them, and have liberty of fishing therein, freed from the obstruction or interference of private parties. The interest of the people in the navigation of the waters and in commerce over them may be improved in many instances by the erection of wharves, docks, and piers therein, for which purpose the state may grant parcels of the submerged lands; and, so long as their disposition is made for such purpose, no valid objections can be made to the grants. It is grants of parcels of lands under navigable waters that may afford foundation for wharves, piers, docks, and other structures in aid of commerce, and grants of parcels which, being occupied, do not substantially impair the public interest in the lands and waters remaining, that are chiefly considered and sustained in the adjudged cases as a valid exercise of legislative power consistently with the trust to the public upon which such lands are held by the state. But that is a very different doctrine from the one which would sanction the abdication of the general control of the state over lands under the navigable waters of an entire harbor or bay, or of a sea or lake. Such abdication is not consistent with the exercise of that trust which requires the government of the state to preserve such waters for the use of the public. The trust devolving upon the state for the public, and which can only be discharged by the management and control of property in which the public has an interest, cannot be relinquished by a transfer of the property. The control of the state for the purposes of the trust can never be lost, except as to such parcels as are used in promoting the interests of the public therein, or can be disposed of without any substantial impairment of the public interest in the lands and waters remaining. It is only by observing the distinction between a grant of such parcels for the improvement of the public interest, or which when occupied do not substantially impair the public interest in the lands and waters remaining, and a grant of the whole property in which the public is interested, that the language of the adjudged cases can be reconciled. General language sometimes found in opinions of the courts, expressive of absolute ownership and control by the state of lands under navigable waters, irrespective of any trust as to their use and disposition, must be read and construed with reference to the special facts of the particular cases. A grant of all the lands under the navigable waters of a state has never been adjudged to be within the legislative power; and any attempted grant of the kind would be held, if not absolutely void on its face, as subject to revocation. The state can no more abdicate its trust over property in which the whole people are interested, like navigable waters and soils under them, so as to leave them entirely under the use and control of private parties, except in the instance of parcels mentioned for the improvement of the navigation and use of the waters, or when parcels can be disposed of without impairment of the public interest in what remains, than it can abdicate its police powers in the administration of government and the preservation of the peace. In the administration of government the use of such powers may for a limited period be delegated to a municipality or other body, but there always remains with the state the right to revoke those powers and exercise them in a more direct manner, and one more conformable to its wishes. So with trusts connected with public property, or property of a special character, like lands under navigable waters; they cannot be placed entirely beyond the direction and control of the state.

The harbor of Chicago is of immense value to the people of the state of Illinois, in the facilities it affords to its vast and constantly increasing commerce; and the idea that its legislature can deprive the state of control over its bed and waters, and place the same in the hands of a private corporation, created for a different purpose,—one limited to transportation of passengers and freight between distant points and the city,—is a proposition that cannot be defended.

The area of the submerged lands proposed to be ceded by the act in question to the railroad company embraces something more than 1,000 acres, being, as stated by counsel, more than three times the area of the outer harbor, and not only including all of that harbor, but embracing adjoining submerged lands, which will, in all probability, be hereafter included in the harbor. It is as large as that embraced by all the merchandise docks along the Thames at London; is much larger than that included in the famous docks and basins at Liverpool; is twice that of the port of Marseilles, and nearly, if not quite, equal to the pier area along the water front of the city of New York. And the arrivals and clearings of vessels at the port exceed in number those of New York, and are equal to those of New York and Boston combined. Chicago has nearly 25 per cent. of the lake carrying trade, as compared with the arrivals and clearings of all the leading ports of our great inland seas. In the year ending June 30, 1886, the joint arrivals and clearances of vessels at that port amounted to 22,096, with a tonnage of over 7,000,000; and in 1890 the tonnage of the vessels reached nearly 9,000,000. As stated by counsel, since the passage of the lake front act, in 1869, the population of the city has increased nearly 1,000,000 souls, and the increase of commerce has kept pace with it. It is hardly conceivable that the legislature can divest the state of the control and management of this harbor, and vest it absolutely in a private corporation. Surely an act of the legislature transferring the title to its submerged lands and the power claimed by the railroad company to a foreign state or nation would be repudiated, without hesitation, as a gross perversion of the trust over the property under which it is held. So would a similar transfer to a corporation of another state. It would not be listened to that the control and management of the harbor of that great city—a subject of concern to the whole people of the state—should thus be placed elsewhere than in the state itself. All the objections which can be urged to such attempted transfer may be urged to a transfer to a private corporation like the railroad company in this case.

Any grant of the kind is necessarily revocable, and the exercise of the trust by which the property was held by the state can be resumed at any time. Undoubtedly there may be expenses incurred in improvements made under such a grant, which the state ought to pay; but, be that as it may, the power to resume the trust whenever the state judges best is, we think, incontrovertible. The position advanced by the railroad company in support of its claim to the ownership of the submerged lands, and the right to the erection of wharves, piers, and docks at its pleasure, or for its business in the harbor of Chicago, would place every harbor in the country at the mercy of a majority of the legislature of the state in which the harbor is situated.

We cannot, it is true, cite any authority where a grant of this kind has been held invalid, for we believe that no instance exists where the harbor of a great city and its commerce have been allowed to pass into the control of any private corporation. But the decisions are numerous which declare that such property is held by the state, by virtue of its sovereignty, in trust for the public. The ownership of the navigable waters of the harbor, and of the lands under them, is a subject of public concern to the whole people of the state. The trust with which they are held, therefore, is governmental, and cannot be alienated, except in those instances mentioned, of parcels used in the improvement of the interest thus held, or when parcels can be disposed of without detriment to the public interest in the lands and waters remaining.

This follows necessarily from the public character of the property, being held by the whole people for purposes in which the whole people are interested. * * *

[Affirmed.]

Note

Wisconsin, although it places great emphasis in its decisions and statutes on "public rights in water" and on the "trust doctrine," takes a more limited view of the restraints these concepts place on public action affecting public waters. In practice, the use of the public rights concept seems a method of stating the idea that the public interest in recreation is one of the most important of the state's interests to be fostered by water law, and the public trust is a method chosen by the courts to indicate that this public interest will be entitled to maximum protection in the courts. It looks very much like "protection of the public interest," with its balancing of costs and benefits. For example, the right of the public to fish in a lake did not prevent a city from filling part of the lake for a park. State v. Public Service Commission, 275 Wis. 112, 81 N.W.2d 71 (1957). The disappointment of fishermen was held to be negligible when compared to the greater convenience of the public resulting from the use of the park. A grant by the state of a substantial area of harbor, "held in trust," to a steel company for docks and loading facilities was approved when the court balanced the "trifling" interference with navigation against the increase in welfare of the city and of the entire state. Milwaukee v. State, 193 Wis. 423, 214 N.W. 820 (1927). In Madison v. State, 1 Wis.2d 252, 83 N.W.2d 674 (1957), a similar lake fill to build an auditorium and civic center was approved, on much the same grounds, although the court added that the use was not "unrelated to the use and enjoyment of the lake" in that the view from the lake would be improved and a vantage point would be provided from which to enjoy the beauties of the lake. In State v. Village of Lake Delton, 93 Wis.2d 78, 286 N.W.2d 622 (App.1979) the court held that a municipal ordinance giving a licensee the exclusive right to use a section of a navigable lake for water ski exhibitions on designated dates and hours was not a violation of the public trust. Noting that presence of the public as viewers of the exhibition was the foundation of the ordinance, the court stated that no single public interest in the use of navigable waters is absolute, that some uses must yield if others are to exist at all, and that the uses must be balanced and accommodated on a case-by-case basis.

For a somewhat different analysis of some of these decisions, see Sax, infra, pp. 568, n. 3.

Still a third attitude toward the public trust is illustrated by the Florida experience. The state started with a strong policy of *encouraging* land fills, to the extent of giving a riparian title to submerged lands which he filled. This progressed through a requirement that the riparian purchase the lands, to a position in which land fills are strictly regulated, with much emphasis on environmental consequences and the setting by local authorities of bulkhead lines limiting fills. See Maloney, Plager, and Baldwin, Water Law and Administration: The Florida Experience, 346–405 (1968).

NATIONAL AUDUBON SOCIETY v. SUPERIOR COURT OF ALPINE COUNTY

Supreme Court of California, 1983.
33 Cal.3d 419, 189 Cal.Rptr. 346, 658 P.2d 709.

BROUSSARD, JUSTICE.

Mono Lake, the second largest lake in California, sits at the base of the Sierra Nevada escarpment near the eastern entrance to Yosemite National Park. The lake is saline; it contains no fish but supports a large population of brine shrimp which feed vast numbers of nesting and migratory birds. Islands in the lake protect a large breeding colony of California gulls, and the lake itself serves as a haven on the migration route for thousands of Northern Phalarope, Wilson's Phalarope, and Eared Grebe. Towers and spires of tufa on the north and south shores are matters of geological interest and a tourist attraction.

Although Mono Lake receives some water from rain and snow on the lake surface, historically most of its supply came from snowmelt in the Sierra Nevada. Five freshwater streams—Mill, Lee Vining, Walker, Parker and Rush Creeks—arise near the crest of the range and carry the annual runoff to the west shore of the lake. In 1940, however, the Division of Water Resources, the predecessor to the present California Water Resources Board, granted the Department of Water and Power of the City of Los Angeles (hereafter DWP) a permit to appropriate virtually the entire flow of four of the five streams flowing into the lake. DWP promptly constructed facilities to divert about half the flow of these streams into DWP's Owens Valley aqueduct. In 1970 DWP completed a second diversion tunnel, and since that time has taken virtually the entire flow of these streams.

As a result of these diversions, the level of the lake has dropped; the surface area has diminished by one-third; one of the two principal islands in the lake has become a peninsula, exposing the gull rookery there to coyotes and other predators and causing the gulls to abandon the former island. The ultimate effect of continued diversions is a matter of intense dispute, but there seems little doubt that both the scenic beauty and the ecological values of Mono Lake are imperiled.

Plaintiffs filed suit in superior court to enjoin the DWP diversions on the theory that the shores, bed and waters of Mono Lake are protected by a public trust. Plaintiffs' suit was transferred to the federal district court, which requested that the state courts determine the relationship between the public trust doctrine and the water rights system, and decide whether plaintiffs must exhaust administrative remedies before the Water Board prior to filing suit. The superior court then entered summary judgments against plaintiffs on both matters, ruling that the public trust doctrine offered no independent basis for challenging the DWP diversions, and that plaintiffs had failed to exhaust administrative remedies. Plaintiffs petitioned us directly for writ of mandate to review that decision; in view of the importance of the issues presented, we issued an alternative writ.

This case brings together for the first time two systems of legal thought: the appropriative water rights system which since the days of the gold rush has dominated California water law, and the public trust doctrine which, after evolving as a shield for the protection of tidelands, now extends its protective scope to navigable lakes. Ever since we first recognized that the public trust protects environmental and recreational values (Marks v. Whitney (1971) 6 Cal.3d 251, 98 Cal.Rptr. 790, 491 P.2d 374), the two systems of legal thought have been on a collision course. (Johnson, Public Trust Protection for Stream Flows and Lake Levels (1980) 14 U.C.Davis L.Rev. 233.) They meet in a unique and dramatic setting which highlights the clash of values. Mono Lake is a scenic and ecological treasure of national significance, imperiled by continued diversions of water; yet, the need of Los Angeles for water is apparent, its reliance on rights granted by the board evident, the cost of curtailing diversions substantial.

* * *

1. Background and history of the Mono Lake litigation

DWP supplies water to the City of Los Angeles. * * *

After purchasing the riparian rights incident to Lee Vining, Walker, Parker and Rush Creeks, as well as the riparian rights pertaining to Mono Lake,[a] the city applied to the Water Board in 1940 for permits to appropriate the waters of the four tributaries. At hearings before the board, various interested individuals protested that the city's proposed appropriations would lower the surface level of Mono Lake and thereby impair its commercial, recreational and scenic uses.

The board's primary authority to reject that application lay in a 1921 amendment to the Water Commission Act of 1913, which authorized the board to reject an application "when in its judgment the proposed appropriation would not best conserve the public interest." (Stats.1921, ch. 329, § 1, p. 443, now codified as Wat.Code, § 1255.) The 1921 enactment, however, also "declared to be the established policy of this state that the use of water for domestic purposes is the highest use of water" (id., now codified as Wat.Code, § 1254), and directed the Water Board to be guided by this declaration of policy. Since DWP sought water for domestic use, the board concluded that it had to grant

a. Between 1920 and 1934, the city purchased lands riparian to creeks feeding Mono Lake and riparian rights incident to such lands. In 1934, the city brought an eminent domain proceeding for condemnation of the rights of Mono Lake landowners. (City of Los Angeles v. Aitken, (1935) 10 Cal.App.2d 460, 52 P.2d 585.)

the application notwithstanding the harm to public trust uses of Mono Lake.[b]

The board's decision states that "[i]t is indeed unfortunate that the City's proposed development will result in decreasing the aesthetic advantages of Mono Basin but *there is apparently nothing that this office can do to prevent it.* The use to which the City proposes to put the water under its Applications * * * is defined by the Water Commission Act as the highest to which water may be applied and to make available unappropriated water for this use the City has, by the condemnation proceedings described above, acquired the littoral and riparian rights on Mono Lake and its tributaries south of Mill Creek. This office therefore has *no alternative but to dismiss all protests based upon the possible lowering of the water level in Mono Lake and the effect that the diversion of water from these streams may have upon the aesthetic and recreational value of the Basin.*"

* * *

2. The Public Trust Doctrine in California

* * *

(a) The purpose of the public trust

The objective of the public trust has evolved in tandem with the changing public perception of the values and uses of waterways. As we observed in Marks v. Whitney, supra, 6 Cal.3d 251, 98 Cal.Rptr. 790, 491 P.2d 374, "[p]ublic trust easements [were] traditionally defined in terms of navigation, commerce and fisheries. They have been held to include the right to fish, hunt, bathe, swim, to use for boating and general recreation purposes the navigable waters of the state, and to use the bottom of the navigable waters for anchoring, standing, or other purposes." We went on, however, to hold that the traditional triad of uses—navigation, commerce and fishing—did not limit the public interest in the trust res. In language of special importance to the present setting, we stated that "[t]he public uses to which tidelands are subject are sufficiently flexible to encompass changing public needs. In administering the trust the state is not burdened with an outmoded

b. DWP calls our attention to a 1940 decision of the Water Board involving Rock Creek, a tributary of the Owens River, in which the board stated that "the Water Commission Act requires it to protect streams in recreational areas by guarding against depletion below some minimum amount consonant with the general recreational conditions and the character of the stream." (Div.Wat.Resources Dec. 3850 (Apr. 11, 1940), at p. 24.) The decision concluded that the board had insufficient information to decide what conditions, if any, to place upon DWP's application to divert water from Rock Creek for hydroelectric generation.

We do not know why the board was seemingly more willing to limit diversions to protect recreational values for Rock Creek than for the creeks flowing into Mono Lake. (Neither do we know the eventual outcome of the Rock Creek application.) The language of the board's opinions suggests that the crucial distinction was that the application for the Mono Lake streams was for domestic use, the highest use under the Water Code, while the Rock Creek application was for power generation.

classification favoring one mode of utilization over another. There is a growing public recognition that one of the most important public uses of the tidelands—a use encompassed within the tidelands trust—is the preservation of those lands in their natural state, so that they may serve as ecological units for scientific study, as open space, and as environments which provide food and habitat for birds and marine life, and which favorably affect the scenery and climate of the area."

Mono Lake is a navigable waterway. (City of Los Angeles v. Aitken, supra, 10 Cal.App.2d 460, 466, 52 P.2d 585.) It supports a small local industry which harvests brine shrimp for sale as fish food, which endeavor probably qualifies the lake as a "fishery" under the traditional public trust cases. The principal values plaintiffs seek to protect, however, are recreational and ecological—the scenic views of the lake and its shore, the purity of the air, and the use of the lake for nesting and feeding by birds. Under Marks v. Whitney, supra, 6 Cal.3d 251, 98 Cal.Rptr. 790, 491 P.2d 374, it is clear that protection of these values is among the purposes of the public trust.

(b) The scope of the public trust

Early English decisions generally assumed the public trust was limited to tidal waters and the lands exposed and covered by the daily tides (see Stevens, op. cit. supra, 14 U.C.Davis L.Rev. 195, 201 and authorities there cited); many American decisions, including the leading California cases, also concern tidelands. (See, e.g., City of Berkeley v. Superior Court (1980) 26 Cal.3d 515, 162 Cal.Rptr. 327, 606 P.2d 362; Marks v. Whitney, supra, 6 Cal.3d 251, 98 Cal.Rptr. 790, 491 P.2d 374; People v. California Fish Co. (1913) 166 Cal. 576, 138 P. 79.) It is, however, well settled in the United States generally and in California that the public trust is not limited by the reach of the tides, but encompasses all navigable lakes and streams. * * *

Mono Lake is, as we have said, a navigable waterway. The beds, shores and waters of the lake are without question protected by the public trust. The streams diverted by DWP, however, are not themselves navigable. Accordingly, we must address in this case a question not discussed in any recent public trust case—whether the public trust limits conduct affecting nonnavigable tributaries to navigable waterways.

* * *

We conclude that the public trust doctrine, as recognized and developed in California decisions, protects navigable waters from harm caused by diversion of nonnavigable tributaries.[c]

c. In view of the conclusion stated in the text, we need not consider the question whether the public trust extends for some purposes—such as protection of fishing, environmental values, and recreation interests—to nonnavigable streams. For discussion of this subject, see Walston, The Public Trust Doctrine in the Water Rights Context: The Wrong Environmental Remedy (1982) 22 Santa Clara L.Rev. 63, 85.

(c) Duties and powers of the state as trustee.

In the following review of the authority and obligations of the state as administrator of the public trust, the dominant theme is the state's sovereign power and duty to exercise continued supervision over the trust. One consequence, of importance to this and many other cases, is that parties acquiring rights in trust property generally hold those rights subject to the trust, and can assert no vested right to use those rights in a manner harmful to the trust.

In summary, the foregoing cases amply demonstrate the continuing power of the state as administrator of the public trust, a power which extends to the revocation of previously granted rights or to the enforcement of the trust against lands long thought free of the trust (see City of Berkeley v. Superior Court, supra, 26 Cal.3d 515, 162 Cal.Rptr. 327, 606 P.2d 362). Except for those rare instances in which a grantee may acquire a right to use former trust property free of trust restrictions, the grantee holds subject to the trust, and while he may assert a vested right to the servient estate (the right of use subject to the trust) and to any improvements he erects, he can claim no vested right to bar recognition of the trust or state action to carry out its purposes.

Since the public trust doctrine does not prevent the state from choosing between trust uses (Colberg, Inc. v. State of California, supra, 67 Cal.2d 408, 419, 62 Cal.Rptr. 401, 432 P.2d 3; County of Orange v. Heim (1973) 30 Cal.App.3d 694, 707, 106 Cal.Rptr. 825), the Attorney General of California, seeking to maximize state power under the trust, argues for a broad concept of trust uses. In his view, "trust uses" encompass all public uses, so that in practical effect the doctrine would impose no restrictions on the state's ability to allocate trust property. We know of no authority which supports this view of the public trust, except perhaps the dissenting opinion in Illinois Central R. Co. v. Illinois, supra, 146 U.S. 387, 13 S.Ct. 110, 36 L.Ed. 1018. Most decisions and commentators assume that "trust uses" relate to uses and activities in the vicinity of the lake, stream, or tidal reach at issue (see, e.g., City of Los Angeles v. Aitken, supra, 10 Cal.App.2d 460, 468–469; State of Cal. ex rel. State Lands Com. v. County of Orange, supra, 134 Cal.App. 3d 20, 184 Cal.Rptr. 423; Sax, op. cit. supra, 68 Mich.L.Rev. 471, 542.) The tideland cases make this point clear; after City of Berkeley v. Superior Court, supra, 26 Cal.3d 515, 162 Cal.Rptr. 327, 606 P.2d 362, no one could contend that the state could grant tidelands free of the trust merely because the grant served some public purpose, such as increasing tax revenues, or because the grantee might put the property to a commercial use.

Thus, the public trust is more than an affirmation of state power to use public property for public purposes. It is an affirmation of the duty of the state to protect the people's common heritage of streams, lakes, marshlands and tidelands, surrendering that right of protection only in rare cases when the abandonment of that right is consistent with the purposes of the trust.

3. THE CALIFORNIA WATER RIGHTS SYSTEM

"It is laid down by our law writers, that the right of property in water is usufructuary, and consists not so much of the fluid itself as the advantage of its use." (Eddy v. Simpson (1853) 3 Cal. 249, 252.) Hence, the cases do not speak of the ownership of water, but only of the right to its use. (Rancho Santa Margarita v. Vail (1938) 11 Cal.2d 501, 554–555, 81 P.2d 533; see generally Hutchins, The Cal.Law of Water Rights (1956) pp. 36–38; 1 Rogers & Nichols, Water for Cal. (1967) p. 191.) Accordingly, Water Code section 102 provides that "[a]ll water within the State is the property of the people of the State, but the right to the use of water may be acquired by appropriation in the manner provided by law."

* * *

"[In 1913 the state enacted] the Water Commission Act, which created a Water Commission and provided a procedure for the appropriation of water for useful and beneficial purposes. The main purpose of the act was 'to provide an orderly method for the appropriation of [unappropriated] waters.' (Temescal Water Co. v. Dept. Public Works (1955) 44 Cal.2d 90, 95 [280 P.2d 1]; Bloss v. Rahilly (1940) 16 Cal.2d 70, 75 [104 P.2d 1049].) By amendment in 1923, the statutory procedure became the exclusive means of acquiring appropriative rights. (§ 1225, Stats.1923, ch. 87.) The provisions of the Water Commission Act, as amended from time to time, have been codified in Water Code, divisions 1 and 2. (Stats.1943, ch. 368.)"

According to the courts, the function of the Water Board was restricted to determining if unappropriated water was available; if it was, and no competing appropriator submitted a claim, the grant of an appropriation was a ministerial act. (Tulare Water Co. v. State Water Com. (1921) 187 Cal. 533, 202 P. 874.)

In 1926, however, a decision of this court led to a constitutional amendment which radically altered water law in California and led to an expansion of the powers of the board. In Herminghaus v. South California Edison Co. (1926) 200 Cal. 81, 252 P. 607, we held not only that riparian rights took priority over appropriations authorized by the Water Board, a point which had always been clear, but that as between the riparian and the appropriator, the former's use of water was not limited by the doctrine of reasonable use. That decision led to a constitutional amendment which abolished the right of a riparian to devote water to unreasonable uses, and established the doctrine of reasonable use as an overriding feature of California water law.

* * *

Article X, section 2 (enacted in 1928 as art. XIV, § 3) reads in pertinent part as follows: "It is hereby declared that because of the conditions prevailing in this State the general welfare requires that the water resources of the State be put to beneficial use to the fullest extent of which they are capable, and that the waste or unreasonable use or unreasonable method of use of water be prevented, and that the conservation of such waters is to be exercised with a view to the reasonable and beneficial use thereof in the interest of the people and for the public welfare. The right to water or to the use or flow of water in or from any natural stream or water course in this State is and shall be limited to such water as shall be reasonably required for the beneficial use to be served, and such right does not and shall not extend to the waste or unreasonable use or unreasonable method of use or unreasonable method of diversion of water * * *. This section shall be self-executing, and the Legislature may also enact laws in the furtherance of the policy in this section contained."

This amendment does more than merely overturn *Herminghaus*—it establishes state water policy. All uses of water, including public trust uses, must now conform to the standard of reasonable use.

* * *

The 1928 amendment itself did not expand the authority of the Water Board. The board remained, under controlling judicial decisions, a ministerial body with the limited task of determining priorities between claimants seeking to appropriate unclaimed water. More recent statutory and judicial developments, however, have greatly enhanced the power of the Water Board to oversee the reasonable use of water and, in the process, made clear its authority to weigh and protect public trust values.

* * *

[T]he function of the Water Board has steadily evolved from the narrow role of deciding priorities between competing appropriators to the charge of comprehensive planning and allocation of waters. This change necessarily affects the board's responsibility with respect to the public trust. The board of limited powers of 1913 had neither the power nor duty to consider interests protected by the public trust; the present board, in undertaking planning and allocation of water resources, is required by statute to take those interests into account.

4. THE RELATIONSHIP BETWEEN THE PUBLIC TRUST DOCTRINE AND THE CALIFORNIA WATER RIGHTS SYSTEM

As we have seen, the public trust doctrine and the appropriative water rights system administered by the Water Board developed independently of each other. Each developed comprehensive rules and principles which, if applied to the full extent of their scope, would occupy the field of allocation of stream waters to the exclusion of any competing system of legal thought. Plaintiffs, for example, argue that the public trust is antecedent to and thus limits all appropriative water rights, an argument which implies that most appropriative water rights in California were acquired and are presently being used unlawfully. Defendant DWP, on the other hand, argues that the public trust doctrine as to stream waters has been "subsumed" into the appropriative water rights system and, absorbed by that body of law, quietly disappeared; according to DWP, the recipient of a board license enjoys a vested right in perpetuity to take water without concern for the consequences to the trust.

We are unable to accept either position. In our opinion, both the public trust doctrine and the water rights system embody important precepts which make the law more responsive to the diverse needs and interests involved in the planning and allocation of water resources. To embrace one system of thought and reject the other would lead to an unbalanced structure, one which would either decry as a breach of trust appropriations essential to the economic development of this state, or deny any duty to protect or even consider the values promoted by the public trust. Therefore, seeking an accommodation which will make use of the pertinent principles of both the public trust doctrine and the appropriative water rights system, and drawing upon the history of the public trust and the water rights system, the body of judicial precedent, and the views of expert commentators, we reach the following conclusions:

a. The state as sovereign retains continuing supervisory control over its navigable waters and the lands beneath those waters. This principle, fundamental to the concept of the public trust, applies to rights in flowing waters as well as to rights in tidelands and lakeshores; it prevents any party from acquiring a vested right to appropriate water in a manner harmful to the interests protected by the public trust.

b. As a matter of current and historical necessity, the Legislature, acting directly or through an authorized agency such as the Water Board, has the power to grant usufructuary licenses that will permit an appropriator to take water from flowing streams and use that water in a distant part of the state, even though this taking does not promote, and may unavoidably harm, the trust uses at the source stream. The population and economy of this state depend upon the appropriation of vast quantities of water for uses unrelated to in-stream trust values. California's Constitution (see art. X, § 2), its statutes (see Wat.Code, §§ 100, 104), decisions (see, e.g., Waterford I. Dist. v. Turlock I. Dist. (1920) 50 Cal.App. 213, 220, 194 P. 757), and commentators (e.g., Hutchins, the Cal.Law of Water Rights, op, cit. supra, p. 11) all emphasize the need to make efficient use of California's limited water resources: all recognize, at least implicitly, that efficient use requires diverting water from in-stream uses. Now that the economy and population centers of this state have developed in reliance upon appropriated water, it would be disingenuous to hold that such appropriations are and have always been improper to the extent that they harm public trust uses, and can be justified only upon theories of reliance or estoppel.

c. The state has an affirmative duty to take the public trust into account in the planning and allocation of water resources, and to protect public trust uses whenever feasible.[d] Just as the history of this state shows that appropriation may be necessary for efficient use of water despite unavoidable harm to public trust values, it demonstrates that an appropriative water rights system administered without consideration of the public trust may cause unnecessary and unjustified harm to trust interests. (See Johnson, op. cit. supra, 14 U.C.Davis L.Rev. 233, 256–257; Robie, Some Reflections on Environmental Considerations in Water Rights Administration (1972), 2 Ecology L.Q. 695, 710–711; Comment, op. cit. supra, 33 Hastings L.J. 653, 654.) As a matter of practical necessity the state may have to approve appropriations despite foreseeable harm to public trust uses. In so doing, however, the state must bear in mind its duty as trustee to consider the effect of the taking on the public trust (see United Plainsmen v. N.D. State Water Con. Commission (N.D.1976) 247 N.W.2d 457, 462–463), and to preserve, so far as consistent with the public interest, the uses protected by the trust.

Once the state has approved an appropriation, the public trust imposes a duty of continuing supervision over the taking and use of the appropriated water. In exercising its sovereign power to allocate water resources in the public interest, the state is not confined by past allocation decisions which may be incorrect in light of current knowledge or inconsistent with current needs.

The state accordingly has the power to reconsider allocation decisions even though those decisions were made after due consideration of their effect on the public trust.[e] The case for reconsidering a particular decision, however, is even stronger when that decision failed to weigh and consider public trust uses. In the case before us, the salient fact is that no responsible body has ever determined the impact of diverting the entire flow of the Mono Lake tributaries into the Los Angeles Acqueduct. This is not a case in which the Legislature, the Water Board, or any judicial body has determined that the needs of Los Angeles outweigh the needs of the Mono Basin, that the benefit gained

d. Amendments to the Water Code enacted in 1955 and subsequent years codify in part the duty of the Water Board to consider public trust uses of stream water. (See, ante, p. 363 of 189 Cal.Rptr., p. 726 of 658 P.2d). The requirements of the California Environmental Quality Act (Pub.Resources Code, § 21000 et seq.) impose a similar obligation. (See Robie, op. cit. supra, 2 Ecology L.Q. 695.)

These enactments do not render the judicially fashioned public trust doctrine superfluous. Aside from the possibility that statutory protections can be repealed, the noncodified public trust doctrine remains important both to confirm the state's sovereign supervision and to require consideration of public trust uses in cases filed directly in the courts without prior proceedings before the board.

e. The state Attorney General asserts that the Water Board could also reconsider the DWP water rights under the doctrine of unreasonable use under article X, section 2. DWP maintains, however, that its use of the water for domestic consumption is prima facie reasonable. The dispute centers on the test of unreasonable use—does it refer only to inordinate and wasteful use of water, as in Peabody v. City of Vallejo, supra, 2 Cal.2d 351, 40 P.2d 486, or to any use less than the optimum allocation of water? (On this question, see generally Joslin v. Marin Mun. Water Dist., supra, 67 Cal.2d 132, 138–141, 60 Cal.Rptr. 377, 429 P.2d 889.) In view of our reliance on the public trust doctrine as a basis for reconsideration of DWP's usufructuary rights, we need not resolve that controversy.

is worth the price. Neither has any responsible body determined whether some lesser taking would better balance the diverse interests. Instead, DWP acquired rights to the entire flow in 1940 from a water board which believed it lacked both the power and the duty to protect the Mono Lake environment, and continues to exercise those rights in apparent disregard for the resulting damage to the scenery, ecology, and human uses of Mono Lake.

It is clear that some responsible body ought to reconsider the allocation of the waters of the Mono Basin. No vested rights bar such reconsideration. We recognize the substantial concerns voiced by Los Angeles—the city's need for water, its reliance upon the 1940 board decision, the cost both in terms of money and environmental impact of obtaining water elsewhere. Such concerns must enter into any allocation decision. We hold only that they do not preclude a reconsideration and reallocation which also takes into account the impact of water diversion on the Mono Lake environment. * * *

This opinion is but one step in the eventual resolution of the Mono Lake controversy. We do not dictate any particular allocation of water. Our objective is to resolve a legal conundrum in which two competing systems of thought—the public trust doctrine and the appropriative water rights system—existed independently of each other, espousing principles which seemingly suggested opposite results. We hope by integrating these two doctrines to clear away the legal barriers which have so far prevented either the Water Board or the courts from taking a new and objective look at the water resources of the Mono Basin. The human and environmental uses of Mono Lake—uses protected by the public trust doctrine—deserve to be taken into account. Such uses should not be destroyed because the state mistakenly thought itself powerless to protect them.

Let a peremptory writ of mandate issue commanding the Superior Court of Alpine County to vacate its judgment in this action and to enter a new judgment consistent with the views stated in this opinion.

Notes

1. The first case to apply the public trust doctrine to consumptive water rights was United Plainsmen Ass'n v. North Dakota State Water Conservation Com'n, supra page 159. However, that case involved the creation of new rights, not existing rights, and it seems that the result could have been reached on other grounds.

2. In Summa Corp. v. California ex rel. State Lands Com'n, 466 U.S. 198, 104 S.Ct. 1751, 80 L.Ed.2d 237 (1984), the Supreme Court reversed a decision of the California Supreme Court which had held that Los Angeles could dredge a privately owned lagoon and make improvements in it without exercising its power of eminent domain. Summa Corporation owned fee title to Ballona Lagoon, a narrow body of water connected to Marina del Rey in Los Angeles. The lagoon had originally been part of a

Mexican land grant, known as Rancho Ballona, made in 1832 and confirmed by the United States in 1873.

California did not claim title to the lagoon. Rather it asserted that it had been impressed by Mexican law with a public servitude in favor of the Mexican government to which California succeeded upon admission to the Union. The Court held that even if it was assumed that the lagoon was a tidelands and was subject to a servitude by Mexican law, the state's claim to the servitude did not survive the issuance of the fee patent by the federal government under the Act of March 3, 1851. The Court noted that patents issued under the 1851 Act, which Congress had passed to implement international obligations of the United States under the Treaty of Guadalupe Hidalgo, were confirmatory patents and did not expand the title of the Mexican grantees. However, after stating that California had the right to participate in the confirmation proceedings and after noting that the expansive nature of the public trust servitude under California law leaves a landowner with little more than the "naked fee," the court held that:

"California cannot at this late date assert its public trust easement over petitioner's property, when petitioner's predecessors-in-interest had their interest confirmed without any mention of such an easement in proceedings taken pursuant to the Act of 1851. The interest claimed by California is one of such substantial magnitude that regardless of the fact that the claim is asserted by the State in its sovereign capacity, this interest * * * must have been presented in the patent proceedings or be barred." Id. at page 1758.

A similar attitude was expressed by the Florida Supreme Court in Odom v. Deltona Corporation, 341 So.2d 977 (Fla.1976). In that case certain state agencies attempted to regulate drainage, dredging, and other developmental activities by Deltona Corporation in lakes and ponds within the boundaries of lands owned by Deltona. The authority of the state agencies to regulate these activities turned on the question of ownership of the beds of the lakes. Deltona traced its title to various federal patents and to deeds from the state of lands acquired by the state under the Swamp and Overflow Lands Grant Act of September 28, 1850. The agencies claimed that the lakes involved were navigable, and thus were vested in the state as "sovereignty lands" in trust for the people. In holding for Deltona the court said:

"An examination of the Constitution and statutes indicates that both the people and the Legislature strongly feel that valid federal and state grants of title to real property without any reservation of public rights in and to waters thereon should not be upset because of new standards of value relating to ecology and other matters created by population growth, recreational needs and other issues of current importance to Florida. In fact, the Commission's assertion of regulatory authority does not comport with existing state law; this Court has delineated rather forcefully the absence of public rights, including fishing, in privately owned lakes. It seems logical to this Court that, when the Legislature enacts a Marketable Title Act, as found at Chapter 712, Florida Statutes, clearing any title having been in existence thirty years or more, the state should conform to the same standard as it requires of its citizens; the claims of the Trustees to beds underlying navigable waters previously conveyed are extinguished by the Act. Stability of titles expressly requires that, when lawfully executed land conveyances are made by public officials to private citizens without reservation of public rights in and to the waters located thereon, a change of personnel among elected state officials should not authorize the government to take from the grantee the rights which have been conveyed previously without appropriate justification and compensation. If the state has conveyed property rights which it now needs, these can be reacquired through eminent domain; otherwise, legal estoppel is applicable and bars the Trustees' claim of ownership, subject to rights specifically reserved in such conveyances.

"It appears that public officials operating under a color of law have acquiesced in the development of the land surrounding the chain of inland lakes over which this litigation arose, indicating willingness for residential development contiguous to the waters, including necessary modification of lake bottoms. Many private persons have contracted with Appellee relying upon this development, and we feel it highly inequitable and inappropriate for the state at this late date to renounce its earlier action taken under the direction of prior officials. We feel that equitable estoppel is properly invoked in this particular set of circumstances.

* * *

"It should be reiterated that * * * ancient conveyances of sovereign lands in existence for more than thirty years, when the State has made no effort of record to reclaim same, clearly vest marketable title in the grantees, their successors or assigns and the land may be recovered only by direct purchase or through eminent domain proceedings."

In 1978 the Florida legislature amended the Marketable Title Act to exclude state title to lands beneath navigable waters acquired by virtue of sovereignty. West's Fla.Stat.Ann. § 712.03(7). However, in Coastal Petroleum Co. v. American Cyanamid, 454 So.2d 6 (App.1984) the court again ruled in favor of a private land owner on the basis of estoppel and on the basis that the state's claims had been extinguished by the Marketable Title Act as it existed prior to the 1978 amendment.

The Ninth Circuit also expressed similar views in Robinson v. Ariyoshi, supra, page 377.

3. The seminal article is Sax, The Public Trust Doctrine in Natural Resource Law: Effective Judicial Intervention, 68 Mich.L.Rev. 471 (1970), which urged wider application of the doctrine by courts reviewing legislative and administrative action alleged to be detrimental to the environment. In this article Sax saw the public trust doctrine largely as a procedural device used by the courts to correct insufficiencies in the democratic process. As Sax explained it, sometimes democratic institutions (legislatures and administrative bodies) ignore broadly based public interests because a well-organized minority is able to gain advantage over a diffuse, disorganized majority. Thus, Sax asserted, the courts use the public trust doctrine as an instrument for democratizing decision-making in these situations. Frequently, Sax said, courts accomplish this by moving a decision from one constituency to another. For example, a court may find

that an agency cannot divert trust property to a use which lessens public use without specific legislative authority, thereby moving the decision from the agency, with its narrow constituency, to the legislature, with its broad constituency. Despite the procedural emphasis of this article, later Sax gave the doctrine greater substantive content, stating that its function is to protect public expectations against destabilizing changes. Sax, Liberating the Public Trust Doctrine, 14 U.C.Davis L.Rev. 185, 188 (1980). Sax's urgings were enthusiastically received by writers and courts, and the period since the publication of the first article has seen a great expansion in the doctrine, both as to the scope of resources subjected to it and the interests protected by it.

Not everyone views the public trust doctrine so positively. Consider the following:

"Most simply put, the historic function of the public trust doctrine has been to provide a public property basis for resisting the exercise of private property rights in natural resources deemed contrary to the public interest. In recent decades, however especially during the last ten years, modern trends in natural resources law have increasingly eroded traditional concepts of private property rights in natural resources and substituted new notions of sovereign power over those resources. These trends, reflected in a wide variety of legal contexts, ranging from federal environmental protection statutes, new state resource allocation laws, to evolving common law principles of tort law, are currently weaving a new fabric for natural resources law that is more responsive to current social values and the physical characteristics of the resources. By continuing to resist a legal system that is otherwise being abandoned, the public trust doctrine obscures analysis and renders more difficult the important process of reworking natural resources law. Of even broader concern, the doctrine threatens to fuel a developing clash in liberal ideology between furthering individual rights of security and dignity, bound up in notions of private property protection, and supporting environmental protection and resource preservation goals, inevitably dependent on intrusive governmental programs designed to achieve longer-term collectivist goals.

"* * *

"Assessment of the public trust doctrine on this basis [on the basis that the doctrine is a legal fiction] leads to the conclusion that the day of "final reckoning" for the doctrine is here, or soon will be, and reliance upon it is no longer in order. As shown in the following sections, the law of standing, tort law, property law, administrative law, and the police power have all evolved in response to increased societal concern and awareness of environmental and natural resources problems and are weaving a new and unified fabric for natural resources problems. Whether these developments are viewed as totally independent of the doctrine or, alternatively as somehow having subsumed the doctrine's principles is no matter. The conclusion is the same viewed from either perspective: Much of what the public trust doctrine offered in the past is now, at best, superfluous and, at worst, distracting and theoretically inconsistent with new notions of property and sovereignty developing in the current reworking of natural resources law.

"* * *

"In sum, the apparent litigation achievements of the public trust doctrine dim considerably, if not diminish altogether, when studied in light of independent developments in more generally applicable areas of the law, such as standing, nuisance, the police power, and administrative law. The doctrine's successes in various cases amount to little more than isolated reflections of these more fundamental trends, but with a public trust label prominently attached. In addition, the basic force of the public trust doctrine rests on legal theories fundamentally inconsistent with current notions of property and sovereignty in natural resources. The doctrine's only independent role remains much where it began in this country, with the narrow concern of access to beaches and beds of navigable waters."

Lazarus, Changing Conceptions of Property and Sovereignty in Natural Resources: Questioning the Public Trust Doctrine, 71 Iowa L.Rev. — Copyright 1986 University of Iowa.

STATE v. BLECK

Supreme Court of Wisconsin, 1983.
114 Wis.2d 454, 338 N.W.2d 492.

WILLIAM A. BABLITCH, JUSTICE.

This is a review of an unpublished decision of the court of appeals, 109 Wis.2d 694, 326 N.W.2d 783 (1983), affirming judgments of the circuit court for Dane county, Honorable Moria Krueger, Judge. Martin Bleck, Bryan Keleny and William Prince (petitioners) were convicted of violating sec. 30.15(1)(d), Stats., which provides that anyone who constructs or places any structure or deposits any material in navigable waters in violation of secs. 30.12 or 30.13, is subject to a forfeiture not to exceed $50.

* * *

In the spring of 1980, the petitioners placed a water ski jump on Bass Lake, which is located in Dane county. The ski jump measured twenty-two feet by fourteen feet by six feet, and either rested on the lake bed or was secured to the lake bottom by ropes connected to four sixteen-gallon drums filled with concrete.

In May, 1980, the petitioners, who are not riparian owners, applied to the department of natural resources (DNR) for a permit to place the ski jump on Bass Lake, pursuant to sec. 30.12, Stats. * * *

DNR rejected the application because it was not made by a riparian owner, as required by sec. 30.12, Stats. The petitioners left the ski jump on Bass Lake during the summer of 1980, even though DNR had not issued a permit. On September 17, 1980, a warden from DNR observed the ski jump still on the lake. He issued citations to the petitioners pursuant to sec. 30.15(1)(d) for violation of sec. 30.12.

After a trial to the circuit court, the court found the petitioners guilty of violating sec. 30.15(1)(d), Stats., and imposed a forfeiture of $50 on each. The court found that Bass Lake is a navigable lake within the meaning of sec. 30.10(1). The court also determined that sec. 30.12 is applicable to the petitioner's ski jump, and it concluded that sec. 30.12

did not violate the public trust doctrine or the equal protection guarantees of the Wisconsin and United States Constitutions.

* * *

The petitioners contend that the application of sec. 30.12, Stats., to their placement of the ski jump is contrary to the public trust doctrine because the result is that only riparian owners may seasonally moor recreational water facilities on the beds of navigable waters. The petitioners base this conclusion on the fact that only riparians may obtain permits under sec. 30.12. The petitioners argue that this result contravenes the public trust doctrine, which they contend is designed to protect the recreational use of navigable waters by all citizens.

* * *

Although the public trust doctrine safeguards interests of all members of the public in navigable waters, Wisconsin has also recognized the existence of certain common law rights that are incidents of riparian ownership of property adjacent to a body of water. See, e.g., Mayer, 29 Wis.2d at 174, 138 N.W.2d at 22; Note, Riparian Water Law—Lakeshore Developments, 1966 Wis.L.Rev. 172, 173. Such riparian rights include the use of the shoreline of the riparian owner's property, the reasonable use of the water, and the privilege to use a lake for bathing, swimming and boating. Bino v. Hurley, 273 Wis. 10, 16, 76 N.W.2d 571 (1956). A riparian who owns property abutting navigable lakes has been held to have a right of access to and from the lake upon his land, a right to build wharves and piers in aid of navigation, and a right to have water flow to his land without artificial obstruction. See Boorman v. Sunnuchs, 42 Wis. 233, 242 (1877); Delaplaine v. C. & N.W. Ry. Co., 42 Wis. 214, 215 (1877). The traditional distinction between riparian owners and nonriparians was noted in The Attorney General ex rel. Askew v. Smith, 109 Wis. 532, 85 N.W. 512 (1901), in which this court indicated that a riparian owner could construct a pier in a lake in aid of navigation if not prohibited by state law. The construction of a pier by a nonriparian, however, was considered to be an unauthorized invasion of the public's rights because the right to place a pier is merely an incident of riparian ownership. 109 Wis. at 540, 85 N.W. 512.

The common law distinction between riparians and nonriparians is also reflected throughout ch. 30, Stats., which governs navigable waters, harbors, and navigation, and of which sec. 30.12 is a part. Section 30.11(4), provides that riparian proprietors may place solid structures or fill up to a bulkhead line established under sec. 30.11(1). Section 30.13(1), permits riparian proprietors to construct a wharf or pier in a navigable water without a sec. 30.12 permit if certain conditions are satisfied. Neither provision grants the same right to non-riparians.

We conclude that the application of sec. 30.12, Stats., to the petitioners' placement of a ski jump does not violate the public trust doctrine. The fact that sec. 30.12 allows only riparians to apply for permits is simply an acknowledgment by the legislature of certain common law riparian rights that are incidents of their ownership of property abutting the water. Such rights, however, are still subject to the public's paramount right and interest in navigable waters. Under sec. 30.12(2), DNR may grant a permit to a riparian to place a structure only if that structure does not materially obstruct navigation, or reduce the effective flood flow capacity of a stream, or if it is not detrimental to the public interest. There is, therefore, no guarantee that a riparian owner who applies for a permit would obtain a permit under sec. 30.12 to place the type of ski jump the petitioners installed.

* * *

The decision of the court of appeals is affirmed.

Notes

1. A recurring problem where riparians own the shores of navigable waters is the question of how the public can get access to them. A Wisconsin statute provides that the county board may condemn a right of way for any public highway to any navigable stream or lake. In Branch v. Oconto County, 13 Wis.2d 595, 109 N.W.2d 105 (1961), Branch had purchased a 100-foot strip completely around a 390-acre lake which was two to four feet deep and while not suitable for fishing or swimming was excellent for duck hunting. The county condemned a road to the lake. Held, Branch was not entitled to the diminution of the value of his property due to loss of exclusive use.

In State v. Bollenbach, 241 Minn. 103, 63 N.W.2d 278 (1954), the court held that a similar statute, permitting condemnation of access to "public waters * * * upon which the public has a right to hunt and fish" had no application to private non-navigable waters. The lake involved was considerably bigger than the lake in *Oconto County,* but the Minnesota court limited public waters to those navigable by the federal test.

2. For the right of the riparian to "wharf out" into navigable waters, see Plager, Interference with the Public Right of Navigation and the Riparian Owners' Claim of Privilege, 33 Mo.L.Rev. 608 (1968).

3. Wilbour v. Gallagher, 77 Wash.2d 306, 462 P.2d 232 (1969), dealt with Lake Chelan, a long scenic navigable lake that had been converted into a hydroelectric power reservoir by a dam at its mouth. Gallagher's land, "Blocks Two and Three, Plat of Lake Park," abutted the original shoreline and a part of it was annually submerged as 21 feet of water was stored behind the dam in the spring and released during the fall and winter. Gallagher filled the land to 5 feet above the artificial highwater mark so that he might use it. Wilbour, whose land adjoined Gallagher's on the upland side, brought suit, complaining of loss of ability to use the water. Held, the fill must be removed as an obstruction to navigation. While the defendant can prevent trespass on his land between high and low water marks when it is not submerged, when it is covered by the navigable water the public has rights of fishing, boating, swimming, water skiing and other recreational activities in that water.

Wilbour was received with mixed reactions. In Corker, Thou Shalt Not Fill Public Waters without Public Permission—Washington's Lake

Chelan Decision, 45 Wash.L.Rev. 65 (1970), it was hailed as a significant victory for the public, applicable to all waters of the state, with broad implications for all privately owned shore lands and tide lands. On the other hand, in Rauscher, The Lake Chelan Case—Another View, 45 Wash. L.Rev. 523 (1970), it was urged that *Wilbour* is narrowly restricted to its facts, as an unusual case in which the customary fee title to intermittently overflowed land was not acquired by the overflower, hence not applicable to property overflowed by naturally fluctuating water and not affecting the property rights of the owners of such lands or their rights to fill.

DAY v. ARMSTRONG

Supreme Court of Wyoming, 1961.
362 P.2d 137.

MR. JUSTICE HARNSBERGER delivered the opinion of the court.

Plaintiff in March, 1958, sought judgment declaring his rights and those of the public, under applicable provisions of the Federal Constitution, the State Constitution, the laws of Wyoming, and judicial decisions, to go upon the channel, between its high water marks, and to float upon the waters of the North Platte River where it flows upon and across defendants' lands. * * *

The State of Wyoming by its Attorney General was allowed to appear as amicus curiae.

Other parties permitted to intervene likewise asked for declaratory judgment, but claimed for the public only the right to float upon or within the waters of the river as it flowed upon and across the lands of the defendants. * * *

The admitted facts as exhibited by the complaint are: Defendants own land through which the North Platte River flows; at intermittent periods the river can float canoes, rowboats, outboard motors and other floating craft capable of carrying as many as six people; in the month of August and until spring runoff, craft carrying people and drawing more than one foot of water cannot be floated, with minor exceptions, i.e., short stretches or reservoirs; craft drawing less than one foot of water can be floated carrying people until about the middle of October when freezing occurs; from early days until 1940, the river was used commercially for floating logs, ties and timber; plaintiff can enter the river by boat from lands of a national forest, by boat or wading, or from a point where the county road right of way crosses the channel, or by boat or wading from lands of other private owners, and the channel may sometimes be entered between high water marks by walking. * * *

The "Brief Amicus Curiae of Wyoming Wool Growers Association and Wyoming Stock Growers Association" advises the court that the members of those organizations have always contended the owner of lands through which flows a stream nonnavigable in the Federal sense may deny fishermen, hunters, wanderers, and campers the right to use his property, and although the Constitution declares all water is the property of the State, that provision is limited to right of appropriation for irrigation and other beneficial uses; that while the Legislature has provided for appropriation for water for those purposes, it has not declared streams stocked with fish to be "public ways" nor regulated that type of use. * * *

It is our understanding that a fair summary of the respective position of the parties is as follows: The plaintiff insists the river is navigable because it will float craft, and, therefore, the bed of the river is public property and can be used by the public between its high water marks for any purpose of which it is susceptible. The Attorney General denies the river is navigable, but asserts it may be used for floating of certain craft and for fishing and other lawful purposes. Defendants contend no one except themselves has any rights in the river as it passes through their properties. The intervenors claim for themselves and the public only the right to float upon and fish within the river. The wool growers and stock growers maintain no one has a right on streams which pass through properties in private ownership except the proprietors of the land. * * *

Nothing is found in either our State Constitution, the Act of Congress admitting the State to the Union, or any subsequent act of Congress, which limits the kind or type of use the State may make of its waters.

We understand that "navigability in the Federal sense" means the capability or susceptibility of waters, in their natural condition, of being used for navigation in interstate or international commerce, and navigability in any other sense may mean any one of a variety of definitions given navigability by either of the several states of the Union.

There is an element of paramount control by the Federal government with respect to navigable waters, but that superior right exists only where navigable waters may be used in either interstate or international commerce. * * *

However, except when so used or available for use in interstate or international commerce, the exclusive control of waters is vested in the state, whether the waters are deemed navigable in the Federal sense or in any other sense. * * * It follows the state may lay down and follow such criteria for cataloging waters as navigable or nonnavigable, as it sees fit, and the state may also decide the ownership of submerged lands, irrespective of the navigable or nonnavigable character of waters above them. * * *

The basic reason for using navigability as a classification was to designate certain waters as public and others as private, and to give to public authority, not only ownership and control of navigable waters, but also ownership and control of their beds and channels while leaving in private ownership and control the beds and channels of nonnavigable waters. In the instant case, however, this test is rendered unnecessary to establish the ownership of the waters, because by our Constitution and its Congressional approval, the title of all waters of the State is placed in public ownership. * * *

Streams in their natural state, such as that described by the factual matter appearing in the record before us, although capable of intermittent floating of craft for recreational use and for small commercial use in the floating of ties, logs, and timber, are nevertheless unsuited for navigation in interstate or international commerce and are not of such economic value for transportation as justifies their being classified as navigable waters, thereby taking from riparian proprietors the title and ownership of the bed and channel of the river where it flows by, through, over, across, or upon their lands. So we must hold the portion of the river here in question is nonnavigable and that its bed and channel are the property of the riparian owner. * * *

Article 8, § 1, of our Wyoming Constitution declares the waters of all natural streams, springs, lakes, or other collections of still water, within the boundaries of the State, are the property of the State. * * * This court has interpreted the State's title to the waters to be one of trust for the benefit of the people. * * * Additionally, Ch. 89, Laws of Wyoming, 1901, and Ch. 16, S.L. of Wyoming, 1903, now § 41–224, W.S.1957, regulated the driving or floating of logs, timber or lumber down or upon any stream in the State, without reference to its being navigable or nonnavigable. These statutes indicate the Legislature was aware that, without regard to their being navigable or nonnavigable in the Federal sense or any other concept of navigability, its waters were usable for purposes other than irrigation, consumption, power or mining, and the waters might be used for transportation by flotation. So it would seem that subject to whatever statutory limitations may be imposed by the State on such use, or by the Federal government when interstate or international rights are involved, the actual usability of the waters is alone the limit of the public's right to so employ them. * * *

All parties seem to recognize that if a river is nonnavigable the bed and channel of the stream belong to the riparian owner. No one seriously disputes that the waters themselves belong to the State and are held in trust by it for the benefit of the public. So if the river is nonnavigable we would have a clear case of divided ownership of the river as an entity, because title to the bed and channel would be in the riparian owner and title to the waters is in the State. * * *

The title to waters within this State being in the State, in concomitance, it follows that there must be an easement in behalf of the State for a right of way through their natural channels for such waters upon and over lands submerged by them or across the bed and channels of streams or other collections of waters. * * * The waters not being in trespass upon or over the lands where they naturally appear, they are available for such uses by the public of which they are capable. When waters are able to float craft, they may be so used. When so floating craft, as a necessary incident to that use, the bed or channel of the waters may be unavoidably scraped or touched by the grounding of craft. Even a right to disembark and pull, push or carry over shoals, riffles and rapids accompanies this right of flotation as a necessary incident to the full enjoyment of the public's easement. * * * See * * * Elder v. Delcour, * * * 364 Mo. 835, 269 S.W.2d 17, 47 A.L.R.2d 370. * * * On the other hand, where the use of the bed or channel is more than incidental to the right of floating use of the waters, and the primary use is of the bed or channel rather than the floating use of the waters, such wading or walking is a trespass upon lands belonging to a riparian owner and is unlawful. Such trespass cannot be made lawful either by legislative or judicial action. Thus the use of waters for the floating of which they are capable and uses incidental thereto, as distinguished from unlicensed use of the land beneath them, is within the public's right unless made unlawful by statute. Except as herein specified, to use the bed or channel of the river to wade or walk the stream remains an unlawful trespass. This disagrees somewhat with * * * Elder v. Delcour, supra; and perhaps with some other authorities.

Notwithstanding that the Elder-Delcour case was decided with reference to what was said to be its own peculiar facts, those facts are so closely paralleled in the matter before us as to make them quite helpful here. There the river in question was held to be nonnavigable, notwithstanding it could be floated by canoes, rowboats and other small craft and in the past had been used for floating and transporting logs and timber. The stream was well stocked with fish and was heavily fished by sportsmen, both by wading and floating and from the banks. Also access to the river could be gained from a public road and at points where it crossed privately owned lands. It was claimed the public had the right not only to float by craft upon the waters of the river and to leave the river and carry or drag around obstructions, but also the right to wade the river and use its banks for camping and recreation.

Under our conception of the law, if we hold the river in question here is nonnavigable, then title to the bed or channel of the stream will be in the riparian owner. By Constitutional edict, title to all waters is in the State. Under such circumstances the use of waters for floating, with incidental use of their beds and channels, cannot be interfered with or obstructed by the riparian owner. However, in using the State's waters for floating, the public is not privileged, except as incidental to such use, to violate other property rights of riparian owners. * * * We are not inclined to go as far as the Missouri court when it permitted wading or walking upon the bed or channel of the river or use of its banks for recreation. Perhaps the reason for our difference with the Missouri court is seated in the fact that our conclusions are based solely upon Wyoming's Constitutional declaration that all waters within its boundaries belong to the State, while the court in Missouri, which state does not have such an express constitutional declaration as ours, may have been largely influenced by other considerations.

In conclusion, * * * we hold: That the portion of the river in dispute is nonnavigable; that its riparian owners have title to the bed and channel of the river, but that this title is subject to an easement for a right of way of the river's waters in their natural channel through, over and across defendants' lands; that the waters of the river are the property of the State and are held by it in trust for the equal use and benefit of the public; that the waters of the river may be used by the public for floating usable craft therein or thereon and for transporting in such usable craft persons or property; that as an incident to the full enjoyment and use of the State's easement for its waters over and across the lands held in private ownership, persons so floating in usable craft may, when necessary, disembark and walk, or wade upon submerged lands in order to pull, push, or carry craft over or across shallows, riffles, rapids or obstructions; that while so floating in usable craft, the public may fish or hunt or do any and all other things which are not otherwise made unlawful, * * * that the waters of the river, if capable thereof, may also be used for transporting logs, ties, timber and other material when permitted by State law; that riparian owners of lands bordering upon or through which the river flows may not in any manner obstruct the flow of the river's waters so as to interfere with or prevent the free passage of any craft used commercially or for recreation or for floating ties, logs, or timber; * * * and that the judgment appealed from must be reversed insofar as it permits unrestricted walking or wading in or upon the bed or channel of the river and that the judgment of the lower court be vacated in this respect. * * *

Reversed in part and remanded with directions.

Notes

1. Two recent Montana opinions Montana Coalition for Stream Access, Inc. v. Curran, 682 P.2d 163 (Mont.1984) and Montana Coalition for Stream Access v. Hildreth, 684 P.2d 1088 (Mont.1984) utilized a similar approach. In these opinions the court cited both the public trust doctrine and the 1972 Montana Constitution, which provides that all waters are the property of the state, as the basis for its holding that the only possible limitation on the use of waters by the public is the characteristics of the waters themselves. However, the Montana Supreme Court gave the public greater rights than did the Wyoming Supreme Court, holding that the public has the right to use the bed and banks of streams up to the ordinary high water mark. After these decisions, the Montana legislature enacted legislation regulating public access to streams. H.B. 265, 49th Legislature, 1985. The legislation divides the states waters into two classes. Class I waters are waters navigable for title purposes or capable of supporting commercial activities. Class II waters are all waters except class I waters. The public is given somewhat greater rights to make use of the beds of class I waters than of class II waters.

In People v. Emmert, 198 Colo. 137, 597 P.2d 1025 (1979) the Colorado Supreme Court upheld the conviction of the defendants for criminal trespass in floating and fishing on a non-navigable stream without the consent of the landowner. Although the Colorado Constitution declares that the waters of the state to be the property of the public, the court expressly declined to follow the rationale of Day v. Armstrong. In addition, the court rejected various other rationales, including the public trust doctrine. The decision of the court followed an earlier Colorado decision, Hartman v. Tresise, 36 Colo. 146, 84 P. 685 (1905), which had held unconstitutional a state statute which gave the public the right to fish on all streams stocked at public expense.

The definitive work on the problem is Johnson and Austin, Recreational Rights and Titles to Beds on Western Lakes and Streams, 7 Nat.Res.J. 1 (1967).

2. Another form of non-navigable public water goes back to the very origins of American history. The Massachusetts Bay Colony Ordinance of 1641–1647 provides, "And for great ponds lying in common, though within the bounds of some town, it shall be free for any men to fish or foul there, and may pass and repass on foot through any man's property for that end, so they trespass not upon any man's corn or meadow." Today this concept is broadened to include most fields of water recreation, and is still applicable to most fresh water lakes in Maine, Massachusetts and New Hampshire. See Leighty, Public Rights in Navigable State Waters—Some Statutory Approaches, 6 Land & Water L.Rev. 459, 471–472 (1971).

3. Other states have made certain waters public by the *ipse dixit* of the legislature. Minnesota has declared all water capable of substantial public use to be public, regardless of who owns the bed or whether the waters are navigable. Minn.Stat.Ann. § 105.37(14)(i). Indiana has claimed control of all lakes "used by the public with the acquiescence of any or all riparian owners," for use by all its citizens for fishing, boating, swimming and the storage of water to maintain water levels. Burns' Ind.Ann.Stat. §§ 13–2–14–1, 13–2–14–2. Iowa Code Ann. § 107.24 provides for the condemnation or access to all water suitable for hunting, fishing and trapping, without distinguishing between navigable and non-navigable waters. The Iowa Supreme Court has indicated that the state may use this authority to condemn access ways to any waters overlying private beds entirely surrounded by private property. See Peck v. Olsen Constr. Co., 216 Iowa 519, 245 N.W. 131 (1932).

4. California adds to public waters in two ways. Article I, § 25 of the California Constitution provides: "The people have the right to fish upon and from the public lands of the state and in the waters thereof, excepting upon lands set aside for fish hatcheries, and no land owned by the state shall ever be sold or transferred without reserving to the people the absolute right to fish thereupon; * * *." West's Ann.Cal.Fish and Game Code § 5943 provides: "The owner of a dam shall accord to the public for the purpose of fishing, the right of access to the waters impounded by the dam during the open season for the taking of fish in such stream or river, subject to the regulations of the commission." Both provisions were

involved in State v. San Luis Obispo Sportman's Ass'n., 22 Cal.3d 440, 149 Cal.Rptr. 482, 584 P.2d 1088 (1978).

5. The "wild river" is a new concept that has substantial effects on both public and private rights to use waters. In 1966 Maine established the Allagash Wilderness Waterway, Maine Rev.Stat.Ann. § 12–661 et seq.; in 1965 and 1969 Wisconsin designated the Pine and Popple Rivers as "wild rivers," Wis.Stat.Ann. 30.26; and in 1970 Michigan empowered the Department of Natural Resources to designate rivers or portions thereof as "natural river areas." Mich.Comp.Laws Ann. § 281.761 et seq. For the most part, the waters affected would be considered public waters before such designation and the methods of preservation consist largely of land use planning and zoning of the banks. Nevertheless, the expressed purpose of these statutes is to preserve the designated rivers in their free-flowing condition and to protect them from development, and the implementation of this policy will tremendously enlarge restrictions on riparian uses to the end of greater public use.

Chapter 7

INTERSTATE ALLOCATION

SECTION 1. EQUITABLE APPORTIONMENT

KANSAS v. COLORADO

Supreme Court of the United States, 1907.
206 U.S. 46, 27 S.Ct. 655, 51 L.Ed. 956.

On May 20, 1901, pursuant to a resolution passed by the legislature of Kansas (Kan.Laws 1901, chap. 425), and upon leave obtained, the state of Kansas filed its bill in equity in this court against the state of Colorado. To this bill the defendant demurred. * * * In delivering the opinion of the court [185 U.S. 125, 22 S.Ct. 552, 46 L.Ed. 838] the Chief Justice disclosed in the following words the general character of the controversy, and the conclusions arrived at (p. 145, S.Ct. p. 559, L.Ed. p. 846):

> "The gravamen of the bill is that the state of Colorado, acting directly herself as well as through private persons thereto licensed, is depriving and threatening to deprive the state of Kansas and its inhabitants of all the water heretofore accustomed to flow in the Arkansas river through its channel on the surface, and through a subterranean course across the state of Kansas; that this is threatened not only by the impounding and the use of the water at the river's source, but as it flows after reaching the river. Injury, it is averred, is being, and would be, thereby inflicted on the state of Kansas as an individual owner, and on all the inhabitants of the state, and especially on the inhabitants of that part of the state lying in the Arkansas valley. The injury is asserted to be threatened, and as being wrought, in respect of lands located on the banks of the river; lands lying on the line of a subterranean flow; and lands lying some distance from the river, either above or below ground, but dependent on the river for a supply of water. And it is insisted that Colorado, in doing this, is violating the fundamental principle that one must use his own so as not to destroy the legal rights of another.
>
> "The state of Kansas appeals to the rule of the common law that owners of lands on the banks of a river are entitled to the continual

flow of the stream; and while she concedes that this rule has been modified in the Western states so that flowing water may be appropriated to mining purposes and for the reclamation of arid lands, and the doctrine of prior appropriation obtains, yet she says that that modification has not gone so far as to justify the destruction of the rights of other states and their inhabitants altogether; and that the acts of Congress of 1866 and subsequently, while recognizing the prior appropriation of water as in contravention of the common-law rule as to a continuous flow, have not attempted to recognize it as rightful to that extent. In other words, Kansas contends that Colorado cannot absolutely destroy her rights, and seeks some mode of accommodation as between them, while she further insists that she occupies, for reasons given, the position of a prior appropriator herself, if put to that contention as between her and Colorado.

"Sitting, as it were, as an international as well as a domestic tribunal, we apply Federal law, state law, and international law, as the exigencies of the particular case may demand, and we are unwilling, in this case, to proceed on the mere technical admissions made by the demurrer. * * *" The issue between these several parties having been perfected by replications, a commission was appointed to take evidence, and, after that had been taken and abstracts prepared, counsel for the respective parties were heard in argument, and upon the pleadings and testimony the case was submitted. * * *

MR. JUSTICE BREWER delivered the opinion of the court: * * *

One cardinal rule, underlying all the relations of the states to each other, is that of equality of right. Each state stands on the same level with all the rest. It can impose its own legislation on no one of the others, and is bound to yield its own views to none. Yet, whenever * * * the action of one state reaches through the agency of natural laws, into the territory of another state, the question of the extent and the limitations of the rights of the two states becomes a matter of justiciable dispute between them, and this court is called upon to settle that dispute in such a way as will recognize the equal rights of both and at the same time establish justice between them. In other words, through these successive disputes and decisions this court is practically building up what may not improperly be called interstate common law. This very case presents a significant illustration. Before either Kansas or Colorado was settled the Arkansas river was a stream running through the territory which now composes these two states. Arid lands abound in Colorado. Reclamation is possible only by the application of water, and the extreme contention of Colorado is that it has a right to appropriate all the waters of this stream for the purposes of irrigating its soil and making more valuable its own territory. But the appropriation of the entire flow of the river would naturally tend to make the lands along the stream in Kansas less arable. It would be taking from the adjacent territory that which had been the customary natural means of preserving its arable character. On the other hand, the possible contention of Kansas, that the flowing water in the Arkansas must, in accordance with the extreme doctrine of the common law of England, be left to flow as it was wont to flow, no portion of it being appropriated in Colorado for the purposes of irrigation, would have the effect to perpetuate a desert condition in portions of Colorado beyond the power of reclamation. Surely here is a dispute of a justiciable nature which might and ought to be tried and determined. If the two states were absolutely independent nations it would be settled by treaty or by force. Neither of these ways being practicable, it must be settled by decision of this court. * * *

In deciding this case on demurrer we said:

> "As will be perceived * * * the mere fact that a state had no pecuniary interest in the controversy would not defeat the original jurisdiction of this court, which might be invoked by the state as *parens patriae,* trustee, guardian, or representative of all or a considerable portion of its citizens; and that the threatened pollution of the waters of a river flowing between states, under the authority of one of them, thereby putting the health and comfort of the citizens of the other in jeopardy, presented a cause of action justiciable under the Constitution.
>
> "In the case before us, the state of Kansas files her bill as representing and on behalf of her citizens, as well as in vindication of her alleged rights as an individual owner, and seeks relief in respect of being deprived of the waters of the river accustomed to flow through and across the state, and the consequent destruction of the property of herself and of her citizens and injury to their health and comfort. The action complained of is state action, and not the action of state officers in abuse or excess of their powers."

It is the state of Kansas which invokes the action of this court, charging that, through the action of Colorado, a large portion of its territory is threatened with disaster. In this respect it is in no manner evading the provisions of the 11th Amendment to the Federal Constitution. It is not acting directly and solely for the benefit of any individual citizen to protect his riparian rights. Beyond its property rights it has an interest as a state in this large tract of land bordering on the Arkansas river. Its prosperity affects the general welfare of the state. The controversy rises, therefore, above a mere question of local private right and involves a matter of state interest, and must be considered from that standpoint. Georgia v. Tennessee Copper Co., 206 U.S. 230, 51 L.Ed. 1038, 27 S.Ct. 618.

This changes in some respects the scope of our inquiry. It is not limited to the simple matter of whether any portion of the waters of the Arkansas is withheld by Colorado. We must consider the effect of what has been done upon the conditions in the respective states, and so adjust the dispute upon the basis of equality of rights as to secure as far as possible to Colorado the benefits of irrigation without depriving Kansas of the like beneficial effects of a flowing stream. * * *

It cannot be denied, in view of all the testimony * * * that the diminution of the flow of water in the river by the irrigation of

Colorado has worked some detriment to the southwestern part of Kansas, and yet, when we compare the amount of this detriment with the great benefit which has obviously resulted to the counties in Colorado, it would seem that equality of right and equity between the two states forbids any interference with the present withdrawal of water in Colorado for purposes of irrigation.

Summing up our conclusions, we are of that opinion that * * * the appropriation of the waters of the Arkansas by Colorado, for purposes of irrigation, has diminished the flow of water into the state of Kansas; that the result of that appropriation has been the reclamation of large areas in Colorado, transforming thousands of acres into fertile fields, and rendering possible their occupation and cultivation when otherwise they would have continued barren and unoccupied; that while the influence of such diminution has been of perceptible injury to portions of the Arkansas valley in Kansas, particularly those portions closest to the Colorado line, yet, to the great body of the valley it has worked little, if any, detriment, and regarding the interests of both states, and the right of each to receive benefit through irrigation and in any other manner from the waters of this stream, we are not satisfied that Kansas has made out a case entitling it to a decree. At the same time it is obvious that if the depletion of the waters of the river by Colorado continues to increase there will come a time when Kansas may justly say that there is no longer an equitable division of benefits, and may rightfully call for relief against the action of Colorado, its corporations and citizens, in appropriating the waters of the Arkansas for irrigation purposes.

The decree which, therefore, will be entered, * * * will also dismiss the bill of the state of Kansas as against all the defendants, without prejudice to the right of the plaintiff to institute new proceedings whenever it shall appear that, through a material increase in the depletion of the waters of the Arkansas by Colorado, its corporations or citizens, the substantial interests of Kansas are being injured to the extent of destroying the equitable apportionment of benefits between the two states resulting from the flow of the river. Each party will pay its own costs.

Notes

1. This controversy came again to the Supreme Court in Colorado v. Kansas, 320 U.S. 383, 64 S.Ct. 176, 88 L.Ed. 116 (1943), in which Colorado took the initiative, asking for an injunction against litigation by citizens of Kansas being carried on in lower courts, involving claims inconsistent with the principal case. Kansas alleged that Colorado users had increased their diversions to the detriment of Kansas, and prayed for an apportionment of the river. The Court held that again Kansas had failed to show a serious detriment to her substantial interests and refused any relief other than dismissal of the litigation complained of by Colorado.

2. Although the court indicated that international law was applicable, it made no use of its principles. Conversely, the rule of this and other American interstate cases has been suggested as the solution to some problems arising out of conflicting claims to international rivers. See Garretson, Hayton and Olmstead, The Law of International Drainage Basins (1967); International Law Association, Helsinki Rules on the Uses of the Waters of International Waters (1966). See also, for management and apportionment of United States international rivers, Meyers and Noble, The Colorado River: The Treaty with Mexico, 19 Stanford L.Rev. 367 (1967); Krutilla, The Columbia River Treaty: The Economics of an International River Basin Development (1967); Bloomfield and Fitzgerald, Boundary Waters Problems: Canada and the United States (1958); Utton, International Streams and Lakes, in 2 Water and Water Rights (Clark, ed.) 401 (1967).

WYOMING v. COLORADO

Supreme Court of the United States, 1922.
259 U.S. 419, 42 S.Ct. 552, 66 L.Ed. 999.

MR. JUSTICE VAN DEVANTER delivered the opinion of the Court.

This is an original suit in this court by the state of Wyoming against the state of Colorado and two Colorado corporations to prevent a proposed diversion in Colorado of part of the waters of the Laramie river, an interstate stream. * * *

The Laramie is an unnavigable river which has its source in the mountains of Northern Colorado, flows northerly 27 miles in that state, crosses into Wyoming, and there flows northerly and northeasterly 150 miles to the North Platte river, of which it is a tributary. Both Colorado and Wyoming are in the arid region, where flowing waters are, and long have been, commonly diverted from their natural channels and used in irrigating the soil and making it productive. For many years some of the waters of the Laramie river have been subjected to such diversion and use, part in Colorado and part in Wyoming.

When this suit was brought, the two corporate defendants, acting under the authority and permission of Colorado, were proceeding to divert in that state a considerable portion of the waters of the river and to conduct the same into another watershed, lying wholly in Colorado, for use in irrigating lands more than 50 miles distant from the point of diversion. The topography and natural drainage are such that none of the water can return to the stream or ever reach Wyoming.

By the bill Wyoming seeks to prevent this diversion on two grounds: One that, without her sanction, the waters of this interstate stream cannot rightfully be taken from its watershed and carried into another, where she never can receive any benefit from them; and the other that through many appropriations made at great cost, which are prior in time and superior in right to the proposed Colorado diversion, Wyoming and her citizens have become and are entitled to use a large portion of the waters of the river in the irrigation of lands in that state and that the proposed Colorado diversion will not leave in the stream sufficient water to satisfy these prior and superior appropriations, and so will work irreparable prejudice to Wyoming and her citizens. * * *

Both Colorado and Wyoming are along the apex of the Continental Divide, and include high mountain ranges where heavy snows fall in winter and melt in late spring and early summer; this being the chief source of water supply. Small streams in the mountains gather the water from the melting snow and conduct it to larger streams below, which ultimately pass into surrounding states. The flow in all streams varies greatly in the course of the year, being highest in May, June, and July, and relatively very low in other months. There is also a pronounced variation from year to year. * * *

The decision in Kansas v. Colorado, 206 U.S. 46, 27 S.Ct. 655, 51 L.Ed. 956, was a pioneer in its field. * * * Like that case, the one now before us presents a controversy over the waters of an interstate stream. But here the controversy is between states in both of which the doctrine of appropriation has prevailed from the time of the first settlements, always has been applied in the same way, and has been recognized and sanctioned by the United States, the owner of the public lands. Here the complaining state is not seeking to impose a policy of her choosing on the other state, but to have the common policy which each enforces within her limits applied in determining their relative rights in the interstate stream. * * * And here the complaining state is not seeking to interfere with a diversion which has long been practiced and under which much reclamation has been effected, but to prevent a proposed diversion for the benefit of lands as yet unreclaimed. * * *

The objection of Wyoming to the proposed diversion on the ground that it is to another watershed, from which she can receive no benefit, is also untenable. The fact that the diversion is to such a watershed has a bearing in another connection, but does not in itself constitute a ground for condemning it. In neither state does the right of appropriation depend on the place of use being within the same watershed. Diversions from one watershed to another are commonly made in both states and the practice is recognized by the decisions of their courts. * * *

We are thus brought to the question of the basis on which the relative rights of these states in the waters of this interstate stream should be determined. Should the doctrine of appropriation, which each recognizes and enforces within her borders, be applied? Or is there another basis which is more consonant with right and equity? * * *

In neither state was the right to appropriate water from this interstate stream denied. On the contrary, it was permitted and recognized in both. The rule was the same on both sides of the line. Some of the appropriations were made as much as 50 years ago, and many as much as 25. In the circumstances we have stated, why should not appropriations from this stream be respected, as between the two states, according to their several priorities, as would be done if the stream lay wholly within either state? By what principle of right or equity may either state proceed in disregard of prior appropriations in the other?

Colorado answers that this is not a suit between private appropriators. This is true, but it does not follow that their situation and what has been accomplished by them for their respective states can be ignored. As respects Wyoming, the welfare, prosperity, and happiness of the people of the larger part of the Laramie valley, as also a large portion of the taxable resources of two counties, are dependent on the appropriations in that state. Thus the interests of the state are indissolubly linked with the rights of the appropriators. To the extent of the appropriation and use of the water in Colorado a like situation exists there.

Colorado further answers that she can accomplish more with the water than Wyoming does or can; that she proposes to use it on lands in the Cache la Poudre valley; and that they with less water will produce more than the lands in the portion of the Laramie valley known as the Laramie Plains. It is true that irrigation in the Poudre valley has been carried to a higher state of development than elsewhere in the Rocky Mountain region, and that the lands of that valley lie at a lower altitude than do those in the Laramie Plains, and generally are better adapted to agriculture. In some parts they also require less water. It may be assumed that the lands intended to be reclaimed and irrigated in the Poudre valley conform to the general standard, although this is left uncertain. But for combined farming and stock-raising those of the Laramie Plains offer opportunities and advantages which are well recognized. It is to this use that they chiefly are devoted. It is a recognized and profitable industry, has been carried on there for many years, and is of general economic value. Many of the original ranchmen still are engaged in it—some on the tracts where they first settled. With the aid of irrigation, native hay of a high quality, alfalfa, oats, and other forage are grown for winter feeding; the live stock being grazed most of the year on unirrigated areas and in the neighboring hills and mountains. In this way, not only are the irrigated tracts made productive, but the utility and value of the grazing areas are greatly enhanced. The same industry is carried on in the same way in sections of Colorado. In both states this is a purpose for which the right to appropriate water may be exercised, and no discrimination is made between it and other farming. Even in this suit Colorado is asserting appropriations of this class for 4,250 acres in the portion of the Laramie valley in that state, and is claiming under them an amount of water in excess of what she asserts will irrigate a like acreage in the Poudre valley. * * *

We conclude that Colorado's objections to the doctrine of appropriation as a basis of decision are not well taken, and that it furnishes the only basis which is consonant with the principles of right and equity applicable to such a controversy as this is. The cardinal rule of the doctrine is that priority of appropriation gives superiority of right. Each of these states applies and enforces this rule in her own territory, and it is the one to which intending appropriators naturally would turn for guidance. The principle on which it proceeds is not less applicable to interstate streams and controversies than to others. Both states pronounce the rule just and reasonable as applied to the natural conditions in that region, and to prevent any departure from it the people of both incorporated it into their Constitutions. It originated in the customs and usages of the people before either state came into existence, and the courts of both hold that their constitutional provisions are to be taken as recognizing the prior usage rather than as creating a new rule. These considerations persuade us that its application to such a controversy as is here presented cannot be other than eminently just and equitable to all concerned.

In suits between appropriators from the same stream, but in different states recognizing the doctrine of appropriation, the question whether rights under such appropriations should be judged by the rule of priority has been considered by several courts, state and federal, and has been uniformly answered in the affirmative. * * *

The question first in order, and the one most difficult of solution, relates to the flow of the Laramie river, the common source of supply. The difficulty arises chiefly out of the fact that the flow varies greatly in the course of the year, and also from year to year. * * *

[The court did not directly enforce priorities. Instead, it found that the river had a "dependable flow" of 312,250 acre feet per year, and that the priorities were as follows: first, 20,000 acre feet to existing Colorado diversions out of the basin, second, 4,250 acre feet for use on the Colorado meadow lands in the basin adjacent to the river, third, 272,500 acre feet for Wyoming rights. This left 15,500 for the new Laramie-Poudre Tunnel, and the Court's decree was in form an injunction against diverting more than this amount through the tunnel. In practical operation, this amounted to an apportionment of 39,750 acre feet to Colorado and the balance of the river to Wyoming.]

Notes

1. In subsequent enforcement proceedings it was determined that individual water users, not parties to the action, were represented by their respective states and were bound by the decree, 286 U.S. 494, 52 S.Ct. 621, 76 L.Ed. 1245 (1932); that Colorado might permit diversions by any of the recognized transmountain ditches in excess of the amount credited to it in the opinion, so long as the total diversions under all did not exceed the aggregate of the quantities accredited to them severally, since no injury to Wyoming would result from such changes in the point of diversion, 298 U.S. 573, 56 S.Ct. 912, 80 L.Ed. 1339 (1936); and that the distribution, in accordance with Colorado law, of more than 4,250 acre-feet per year to the meadow land appropriators was not a violation of the decree so long as the

total of 39,750 acre-feet was not exceeded, 309 U.S. 572, 60 S.Ct. 765, 84 L.Ed. 954 (1940). The allocation of 4,250 acre-feet had been an obvious mistake, a substitution of consumptive use for diversions, which had been in fact much larger. The Colorado irrigators later agreed to split the 39,750 acre-feet evenly, 19,875 to the out-of-basin diverters and 19,875 to the meadow land users in the basin. This resulted in large return flows to Wyoming. When the meadow land users threatened to sell their rights to the out-of-basin users, Wyoming irrigators agreed to permit even greater in-basin diversions if this plan were abandoned. The two states consented to an amended decree enjoining Colorado from diverting more than 19,875 acre-feet from the basin, and permitting the use of 29,500 acre-feet on the meadow land during a specified irrigating season. 353 U.S. 953, 77 S.Ct. 865, 1 L.Ed.2d 906 (1957).

3. Priorities of individual claims to interstate streams have been adjudicated in a number of cases. Bean v. Morris, 221 U.S. 485, 31 S.Ct. 703, 55 L.Ed. 821 (1911); Albion-Idaho Land Co. v. Naf Irrigation Co., 97 F.2d 439 (10th Cir.1938); U.S. v. Walker River Irrigation Dist., 11 F.Supp. 58 (D.Nev.1935); Willey v. Decker, 11 Wyo. 496, 73 P. 210 (1903). The water right situated outside the territorial jurisdiction of the court cannot be directly affected by in rem action, but an in personam decree can be rendered coercing action respecting it, Vineyard Land & Stock Co. v. Twin Falls Salmon River Land & Water Co., 245 F. 9 (9th Cir.1917) and the decree will be enforced by contempt proceedings, Brooks v. U.S., 119 F.2d 636 (9th Cir.1941). The question of the equitable apportionment of the water between the states cannot be raised in such a suit between individual water users. Vineyard Co. v. Twin Falls Co., supra.

NEW JERSEY v. NEW YORK

Supreme Court of the United States, 1931.
283 U.S. 336, 51 S.Ct. 478, 75 L.Ed. 1104. Entered, 283 U.S. 805, 51 S.Ct. 645, 75 L.Ed. 1425.

MR. JUSTICE HOLMES delivered the opinion of the Court.

This is a bill in equity by which the State of New Jersey seeks to enjoin the State of New York and the City of New York from diverting any waters from the Delaware River or its tributaries, and particularly from the Neversink River, Willowemoc River, Beaver Kill, East Branch of the Delaware River and Little Delaware River, or from any part of any one of them. The other rivers named are among the headwaters of the Delaware and flow into it where it forms a boundary between New York and Pennsylvania. The Delaware continues its course as such boundary to Tristate Rock, near Port Jervis in New York, at which point Pennsylvania and New York are met by New Jersey. From there the river marks the boundary between Pennsylvania and New Jersey until Pennsylvania stops at the Delaware state line, and from then on the river divides Delaware from New Jersey until it reaches the Atlantic between Cape Henlopen and Cape May.

New York proposes to divert a large amount of water from the above-named tributaries of the Delaware and from the watershed of that river to the watershed of the Hudson River in order to increase the water supply of the City of New York. New Jersey insists on a strict application of the rules of the common law governing private riparian proprietors subject to the same sovereign power. Pennsylvania intervenes to protect its interests as against anything that might be done to prejudice its future needs.

We are met at the outset by the question what rule is to be applied. It is established that a more liberal answer may be given than in a controversy between neighbors members of a single State. Connecticut v. Massachusetts, 282 U.S. 660, 51 S.Ct. 286, 75 L.Ed. 602, February 24, 1931 (see, also, Id., 283 U.S. 789, 51 S.Ct. 356, 75 L.Ed. 1416). Different considerations come in when we are dealing with independent sovereigns having to regard the welfare of the whole population and when the alternative to settlement is war. In a less degree, perhaps, the same is true of the quasi-sovereignties bound together in the Union. A river is more than an amenity, it is a treasure. It offers a necessity of life that must be rationed among those who have power over it. New York has the physical power to cut off all the water within its jurisdiction. But clearly the exercise of such a power to the destruction of the interest of lower States could not be tolerated. And on the other hand equally little could New Jersey be permitted to require New York to give up its power altogether in order that the river might come down to it undiminished. Both States have real and substantial interests in the River that must be reconciled as best they may. The different traditions and practices in different parts of the country may lead to varying results but the effort always is to secure an equitable apportionment without quibbling over formulas. See Missouri v. Illinois, 200 U.S. 496, 520, 26 S.Ct. 268, 50 L.Ed. 572; Kansas v. Colorado, 206 U.S. 46, 98, 117, 27 S.Ct. 655, 51 L.Ed. 956; Georgia v. Tennessee Copper Co., 206 U.S. 230, 237, 27 S.Ct. 618, 51 L.Ed. 1038, 11 Ann.Cas. 488; Wyoming v. Colorado, 259 U.S. 419, 465, 470, 42 S.Ct. 552, 66 L.Ed. 999; Connecticut v. Massachusetts, February 24, 1931.

This case was referred to a Master and a great mass of evidence was taken. In a most competent and excellent report the Master adopted the principle of equitable division which clearly results from the decisions of the last quarter of a century. Where that principle is established there is not much left to discuss. The removal of water to a different watershed obviously must be allowed at times unless States are to be deprived of the most beneficial use on formal grounds. In fact it has been allowed repeatedly and has been practiced by the States concerned. Missouri v. Illinois, 200 U.S. 496, 526, 26 S.Ct. 268, 50 L.Ed. 572; Wyoming v. Colorado, 259 U.S. 419, 466, 42 S.Ct. 552, 66 L.Ed. 999; Connecticut v. Massachusetts, February 24, 1931.

New Jersey alleges that the proposed diversion will transgress its rights in many respects. That it will interfere with the navigability of the Delaware without the authority of Congress or the Secretary of War. That it will deprive the State and its citizens who are riparian owners of the undiminished flow of the stream to which they are entitled by the common law as adopted by both States. That it will injuriously affect water power and the ability to develop it. That it will injuriously affect the sanitary conditions of the River. That it will do the same to the industrial use of it. That it will increase the salinity of the lower part of the River and of Delaware Bay to the injury of the oyster industry there. That it will injure the shad fisheries. That it will do the same to the municipal water supply of the New Jersey towns and cities on the River. That by lowering the level of the water it will injure the cultivation of adjoining lands; and finally, that it will injuriously affect the River for recreational purposes. The bill also complains of the change of watershed, already disposed of; denies the necessity of the diversion; charges extravagant use of present supplies, and alleges that the plan will violate the Federal Water Power Act, 16 U.S.C.A. §§ 791–823 (but see U.S.Code, tit. 16, § 821 [16 U.S.C.A. § 821]), interfere with interstate commerce, prefer the ports of New York to those of New Jersey and will take the property of New Jersey and its citizens without due process of law.

The Master finds that the above-named tributaries of the Delaware are not navigable waters of the United States at and above the places where the City of New York proposes to erect dams. * * *

With regard to water power the Master concludes that any future plan of New Jersey for constructing dams would need the consent of Congress and of the States of New York and Pennsylvania and though possible as a matter of engineering probably would not pay. He adds that there is no such showing of a present interest as to entitle New Jersey to relief. New York v. Illinois, 274 U.S. 488, 490, 47 S.Ct. 661, 71 L.Ed. 1164; New Jersey v. Sargent, 269 U.S. 328, 46 S.Ct. 122, 70 L.Ed. 289. We have spoken at the outset of the more general qualifications of New Jersey's rights as against another State. The Master finds that the taking of 600 millions of gallons daily from the tributaries will not materially affect the River or its sanitary condition, or as a source of municipal water supply, or for industrial uses, or for agriculture, or for the fisheries for shad. The effect or the use for recreation and upon its reputation in that regard will be somewhat more serious as will be the effect of increased salinity of the River upon the oyster fisheries. The total is found to be greater than New Jersey ought to bear, but the damage can be removed by reducing the draft of New York to 440 million gallons daily; constructing an efficient plant for the treatment of sewage entering the Delaware or Neversink (the main source of present pollution) thereby reducing the organic impurities 85%, and treating the effluent with a germicide so as to reduce the Bacillus Coli originally present in the sewage by 90%; and finally, subject to the qualifications in the decree, when the stage of the Delaware falls below 50 c.s.m. at Port Jervis, New York, or Trenton, New Jersey, by releasing water from the impounding reservoirs of New York, sufficient to restore the flow at those points to .50 c.s.m. We are of opinion that the

Master's report should be confirmed and that a decree should be entered to the following effect, subject to such modifications as may be ordered by the Court hereafter.

1. The injunction prayed for by New Jersey so far as it would restrain the State of New York or City of New York from diverting from the Delaware River or its tributaries to the New York City water supply the equivalent of 440 million gallons of water daily is denied, but is granted to restrain the said State and City from diverting water in excess of that amount. The denial of the injunction as above is subject to the following conditions.

(a) Before any diversion shall be made an efficient plant for the treatment of sewage at Port Jervis, New York, shall be constructed and the sewage of Port Jervis entering the Delaware or Neversink Rivers shall be treated to such an extent as to effect a reduction of 85% in the organic impurities. And the effluent from such plant shall be treated with a chemical germicide, or otherwise, so that the B. coli originally present in the sewage shall be reduced by 90%.

Untreated industrial waste from plants in said town of Port Jervis shall not be allowed to enter the Delaware or Neversink Rivers, and the treatment of such industrial wastes shall be such as to render the effluent practically free from suspended matter and non-putrescent; and said treatment of sewage and industrial waste shall be maintained so long as any diversion is made from the Delaware River or its tributaries.

(b) At any time the stage of the Delaware River falls below .50 c.s.m. at Port Jervis, New York, or Trenton, New Jersey, or both (.50 c.s.m. being equivalent to a flow of 1535 c.f.s. at Port Jervis and 3400 c.f.s. at Trenton), water shall be released from one or more of the impounding reservoirs of New York City in sufficient volume to restore the flow at Port Jervis and Trenton to .50 c.s.m., provided, however, that there is not required to be released at any time water in excess of 30% of the diversion area yield, and the diversion area yield having been ascertained to be 2.2 c.s.m., the maximum release required shall be 30% of that amount, or .66 cubic feet per second per square mile of the areas from which water is diverted.

In determining the quantity of water to be released so as to add to the flow of the Delaware River, the Neversink River shall be treated as if it flowed into the Delaware River above Port Jervis, and the number of second feet of water released from the impounding reservoir on the Neversink River shall be added to the number of second feet of water released from other reservoirs, so as to determine whether the quantity of water, required by this decree to be released, has been released.

2. The diversion herein allowed shall not constitute a prior appropriation and shall not give the State of New York and City of New York any superiority of right over the State of New Jersey and Common-

wealth of Pennsylvania in the enjoyment and use of the Delaware River and its tributaries.

3. The prayer of the intervenor, Commonwealth of Pennsylvania, for the present allocation to it of the equivalent of 750 million gallons of water daily from the Delaware River or its Pennsylvania tributaries is denied without prejudice. * * *

6. Any of the parties hereto, complainant, defendants or intervenor, may apply at the foot of this decree for other or further action or relief and this Court retains jurisdiction of the suit for the purpose of any order or direction or modification of this decree, or any supplemental decree that it may deem at any time to be proper in relation to the subject matter in controversy.

Notes

1. Was this an apportionment of the river? Of the "benefits resulting from the flow of the river?"

In 1954 the decree was amended to permit New York to construct a new reservoir and made an additional diversion of 800 m.g.p. subject to a guarantee of delivery of a minimum flow to New Jersey of 1,750 c.f.s., 347 U.S. 995, 74 S.Ct. 867, 98 L.Ed. 1127.

2. Recall Hackensack Water Company v. Nyack, 289 F.Supp. 671 (S.D. N.Y.1968), supra, p. 369, in which two water companies on opposite sides of the state line were treated as riparians for purposes of dividing the water of the Hackensack River between them. It was argued that the doctrine of equitable apportionment should be applied, not riparian law.

"The present lawsuit, however, does not involve either the State of New York or the State of New Jersey. Neither state has demonstrated an interest in this controversy, and the power of the upper riparian state, New York, to cut off the water supply of the lower riparian owner and New Jersey has not been exercised. The present record is not sufficient to determine whether this suit involves the same considerations as a suit between two riparian owners in the same state, or whether defendant is entitled to greater or lesser rights by virtue of its location near the New York-New Jersey border, across that border from the plaintiff."

3. In Idaho v. Oregon, 462 U.S. 1017, 103 S.Ct. 2817, 77 L.Ed.2d 387 (1983), Idaho sought an equitable apportionment of the anadromous fish (chinook salmon and steelhead trout) that migrate from the Pacific up the Columbia and Snake Rivers to their spawning grounds in Idaho. The Court held the rule of equitable apportionment was applicable to interstate disputes over fish as well as to disputes over water, and added a new thought to its doctrinal foundation:

> The doctrine of equitable apportionment is neither dependent on nor bound by existing legal rights to the resource being apportioned. The fact that no State has a pre-existing legal right of ownership in the fish, Hughes v. Oklahoma, 441 U.S. 322, 329–336, 99 S.Ct. 1727, 1732–1736, 60 L.Ed.2d 250 (1979), does not prevent an equitable apportionment. Conversely, although existing legal entitlements are important

factors in formulating an equitable decree, such legal rights must give way in some circumstances to broader equitable considerations. * * *

At the root of the doctrine is the same principle that animates many of the Court's Commerce Clause cases: a State may not preserve solely for its own inhabitants natural resources located within its borders. Consistent with this principle, States have an affirmative duty under the doctrine of equitable apportionment to take reasonable steps to conserve and even to augment the natural resources within their borders for the benefit of other States. Colorado v. New Mexico, 459 U.S., at 185, 103 S.Ct., at 546; Wyoming v. Colorado, 259 U.S. 419, 484, 42 S.Ct. 552, 564, 66 L.Ed. 999 (1922). Even though Idaho has no legal right to the anadromous fish hatched in its waters, it has an equitable right to a fair distribution of this important resource.

While the Court found that Washington and Oregon had in the past permitted some overfishing of the Columbia, the Court agreed with the Special Master that Idaho had not carried its burden of demonstrating a substantial likelihood of future injury. The action was dismissed without prejudice to new proceedings if it should later appear that Idaho is being deprived of its equitable share of the fish.

NEBRASKA v. WYOMING

Supreme Court of the United States, 1945.
325 U.S. 589, 65 S.Ct. 1332, 89 L.Ed. 1815.

MR. JUSTICE DOUGLAS delivered the opinion of the Court.

Nebraska brought this suit in 1934 against Wyoming, invoking our original jurisdiction under Article III, Section 2 of the Constitution. 293 U.S. 523, 55 S.Ct. 115, 79 L.Ed. 635. Colorado was impleaded as a defendant. 296 U.S. 553, 56 S.Ct. 369, 80 L.Ed. 390. The United States was granted leave to intervene. 304 U.S. 545, 58 S.Ct. 1035, 82 L.Ed. 1519. Issues were joined. A Special Master, Honorable Michael J. Doherty, was appointed and hearings were held before him. The matter is before us on exceptions to his report.

The controversy pertains to the use for irrigation purposes of the water of the North Platte River, a non-navigable stream. * * *

The North Platte River rises in Northern Colorado in the mountainous region known as North Park. It proceeds in a northerly direction on the east side of the Continental Divide, enters Wyoming west of Cheyenne, and continues in a northerly direction to the vicinity of Casper. There it turns east across the Great Plains and proceeds easterly and southerly into and across Nebraska. About 40 miles west of the Nebraska line it is joined by the Laramie River. At North Platte, Nebraska, it is joined by the South Platte, forming the Platte River. It empties into the Missouri River at Plattsmouth, near the western border of Iowa. In North Park it is a rapid mountain stream. In eastern Wyoming it gradually broadens out, losing velocity. In western and central Nebraska its channel ranges from 3000 to 6000 feet; it frequently divides into small channels; and in times of low water is lost in the deep sands of its bed. Here it is sometimes characterized as a river "two miles wide and one inch deep." * * *

[The earliest developments on the river took place downstream, near the Nebraska-Wyoming line. Some of the first canals were in Wyoming, but five large Nebraska canals with early priorities take out a mile east of the line at the Tri-State Dam. These are known as the State Line Canals. The French Canal originates in Wyoming but crosses the line and irrigates land in both states.

In 1904 the United States Bureau of Reclamation started the North Platte Project with the construction of Pathfinder Reservoir, just above Casper, Wyoming. It has a capacity of 1,000,000 acre feet. A small auxiliary reservoir, Guernsey, below Casper, has a priority of 1923. Water from these is released into the river and then diverted at Whalen Dam, in eastern Wyoming, into the Interstate Canal and the Fort Laramie Canal. These extend far into Nebraska, and irrigate some land in Wyoming, and a very large acreage in Nebraska. In the area below Whalen Dam, the principal crops are alfalfa, sugar beets, potatoes and grain.

Above Pathfinder, Wyoming ranchers irrigate about 168,000 acres of hay lands, mostly from tributaries. In North Park, Colorado, 131,000 acres of hay lands are irrigated. Most of these water rights are junior to the State Line Canals, and about half of them are junior to Pathfinder.

In 1931 the Bureau of Reclamation started the Kendrick Project, consisting of Seminoe Reservoir above Pathfinder, and the Casper Canal to take the water to 35,000 acres of Wyoming land. Alcova Reservoir, just below Pathfinder, was added to this project in 1934. These two reservoirs have a total capacity of over 1,200,000 acre feet.]

The combined storage capacity of the reservoirs of these two federal projects—Kendrick and North Platte—is 2,313,270 acre feet which, as the Special Master found, is 175 per cent of the long-time average annual run-off of the river at Pathfinder. * * *

Prior to the time when the North Platte project went into operation there was a serious shortage of water for irrigation in western Nebraska and to some extent in eastern Wyoming. Many irrigation enterprises were closed. After the North Platte Project had been in operation for a while most of the projects which had been abandoned were reopened. From then until 1931 the supply was reasonably adequate for most of the canals. But the year 1931 started the driest cycle or swing in the North Platte and Platte River valleys of which there is any record. The annual flow at Pathfinder had always fluctuated widely. The average flow for the 37 years commencing in 1904 was 1,315,900 acre feet, the maximum was 2,399,400 in 1917, the minimum was 382,200 in 1934. But a critical condition arose in 1931 with the advent of the dry cycle. The flow for each of the years between 1931 and 1940 as compared with the mean of the flow for the 37 year period ending in 1940 was as follows:

1931	55 per cent	1936	81 per cent
1932	116 per cent	1937	87 per cent
1933	89 per cent	1938	103 per cent
1934	30 per cent	1939	54 per cent
1935	54 per cent	1940	44 per cent

Since 1930 only one year equalled the mean of the 1904 to 1930 period. Previous droughts had not exceeded two or three years. The present cycle has persisted for 13 years.

The commencement of this dry cycle plus the initiation of the Kendrick project precipitated the present controversy. Nebraska rests her case essentially on evidence of shortage and of misappropriation of water by the upper States since 1930 and of threats of more serious shortage and diversions in the future. * * *

Colorado moves to dismiss the proceeding. She asserts that the pleadings and evidence both indicate that she has not injured nor presently threatens to injure any downstream water user. * * * And she emphasizes that during the drought there was a divertible flow passing Tri-State Dam during the irrigation season. The argument is that the case is not of such serious magnitude and the damage is not so fully and clearly proved as to warrant the intervention of this Court under our established practice. State of Missouri v. Illinois, 200 U.S. 496, 521, 26 S.Ct. 268, 269, 50 L.Ed. 572; State of Colorado v. Kansas, 320 U.S. 383, 393, 394, 64 S.Ct. 176, 180, 181, 88 L.Ed. 116. The argument is that the potential threat of injury, representing as it does only a possibility for the indefinite future, is no basis for a decree in an interstate suit since we cannot issue declaratory decrees. State of Arizona v. California, 283 U.S. 423, 462–464, 51 S.Ct. 522, 528, 529, 75 L.Ed. 1154, and cases cited.

We fully recognize those principles. But they do not stand in the way of an entry of a decree in this case.

The evidence supports the finding of the Special Master that the dependable natural flow of the river during the irrigation season has long been over-appropriated. A genuine controversy exists. The States have not been able to settle their differences by compact. * * *

What we have then is a situation where three States assert against a river, whose dependable natural flow during the irrigation season has long been over appropriated, claims based not only on present uses but on projected additional uses as well. * * *

Colorado's motion to dismiss is accordingly denied. * * *

The equitable apportionment which Nebraska seeks is based on the principle of priority of appropriation applied interstate. Colorado and Wyoming have the rule of priority of appropriation as distinguished from the rule of riparian rights. * * * The rights asserted by Nebraska in this suit are based wholly on appropriations which have been obtained and recognized under Nebraska law. The appropriation system is dominant in the regions of Nebraska which are involved in the present litigation. Hence we, like the Special Master, treat the case as one involving appropriation rights not only in Colorado and Wyoming but in Nebraska as well. * * *

We recognize the difficulties of the problem. The matter is a delicate one and extremely complex. The Special Master recommended a decree based on that principle. That was indeed the principle adopted by the Court in State of Wyoming v. Colorado, supra, where an apportionment of the waters of an interstate stream was made between two States, each of which had the rule of appropriation. * * * Since Colorado, Wyoming, and Nebraska are appropriation States, that principle would seem to be equally applicable here.

That does not mean that there must be a literal application of the priority rule. We stated in State of Colorado v. Kansas, supra, that in determining whether one State is "using, or threatening to use, more than its equitable share of the benefits of a stream, all of the factors which create equities in favor of one state or the other must be weighed as of the date when the controversy is mooted." 320 U.S. page 394, 64 S.Ct. 181, 88 L.Ed. 116. That case did not involve a controversy between two appropriation States. But if an allocation between appropriation States is to be just and equitable, strict adherence to the priority rule may not be possible. For example, the economy of a region may have been established on the basis of junior appropriations. So far as possible those established uses should be protected though strict application of the priority rule might jeopardize them. Apportionment calls for the exercise of an informed judgment on a consideration of many factors. Priority of appropriation is the guiding principle. But physical and climatic conditions, the consumptive use of water in the several sections of the river, the character and rate of return flows, the extent of established uses, the availability of storage water, the practical effect of wasteful uses on downstream areas, the damage to upstream areas as compared to the benefits to downstream areas if a limitation is imposed on the former—these are all relevant factors. They are merely an illustrative not an exhaustive catalogue. They indicate the nature of the problem of apportionment and the delicate adjustment of interests which must be made.

Practical considerations of this order underlie Nebraska's concession that the priority rule should not be strictly applied to appropriations in Colorado, though some are junior to the priorities of appropriators in Wyoming and Nebraska. As the Special Master points out the flowage time of water from North Park to Bridgeport, Nebraska is between two and three weeks. If a canal in North Park were closed to relieve the shortage of a senior appropriator in Nebraska, it would be highly speculative whether the water would reach the Nebraska appropriator in time or whether the closing of the Colorado canal would work more hardship there than it would bestow benefits in Nebraska. Moreover, there is loss of water in transit from the upper to the downstream sections, increasing with the distance. The lower appropriator thus receives less than the upper appropriator loses. And there is evidence that a river-wide priority system would disturb and disrupt long established uses. * * *

We are satisfied that a reduction in present Colorado uses is not warranted. The fact that the same amount of water might produce more in lower sections of the river is immaterial. State of Wyoming v. Colorado, supra, page 468, 42 S.Ct. page 558, 66 L.Ed. 999. The established economy in Colorado's section of the river basin based on existing use of the water should be protected. Cf. State of Colorado v. Kansas, supra, 320 U.S. page 394, 64 S.Ct. page 181, 88 L.Ed. 116. Appropriators in Colorado junior to Pathfinder have made out-of-priority diversions of substantial amounts. Strict application of the priority rule might well result in placing a limitation on Colorado's present use for the benefit of Pathfinder. But as we have said, priority of appropriation, while the guiding principle for an apportionment, is not a hard and fast rule. Colorado's countervailing equities indicate it should not be strictly adhered to in this situation. * * *

The Special Master recommends that Wyoming be enjoined from diverting water from the main river above Guernsey and from its tributaries above Pathfinder for the irrigation of more than 168,000 acres. * * * As we have noted, most of the land under irrigation in the section above Pathfinder is irrigated from tributaries. The rights are small but very numerous. The total acreage under irrigation is 153,000 acres, allowing for a margin of error. Below Pathfinder and above Guernsey the Special Master dealt only with diversions from the main river. He concluded that the run-off of the tributaries becomes so far exhausted before any shortage of water occurs in the main river that any regulation of the tributary diversions would be of no material benefit. The tributary inflow is greater than the depletion of the river. There is some out-of-priority diversion as we have noted. But possibilities for future developments are largely nonexistent. The Special Master concluded that if Wyoming were limited to the irrigation of 15,000 acres (which is the extent of present irrigation with a margin of error) natural conditions would militate against this section getting more than its equitable share of the water.

We think that is a practical and fair adjustment. So far as the tributaries above Pathfinder are concerned, practical difficulties of applying restrictions which would reduce the amount of water used by the hundreds of small irrigators would seem to outweigh any slight benefit which senior appropriators might obtain. This does not seem to be denied. * * *

The priority of Pathfinder is December 6, 1904 and of Guernsey April 20, 1923. Between Pathfinder and the Nebraska state line there are 32 canals on the main river which have priorities senior to Pathfinder. The State Line Canals in Nebraska also are senior to Pathfinder. And Guernsey is junior to all canals below it down to the Nebraska line. * * * Under Wyoming law reservoirs in storing water must observe the priority of all senior, Wyoming canals below them on the main river. * * * Seminoe Reservoir has a priority of December 1, 1931; Casper Canal, July 27, 1934 (natural flow); Alcova Reservoir, April 25, 1936. Apart from minor exceptions Seminoe is junior to every appropriator from Alcova to the Tri-State Dam. The project is expected to operate chiefly on storage water. In its early stages its water requirements will be heavier than they will be later, due to ground absorption and storage. When the project has been in operation a while, the depletion during the irrigation season will be about 122,000 acre feet, except as water stored in non-irrigation season is used. The Special Master found, however, that without violating the Pathfinder priority, the Kendrick project could have stored no water since 1930 and can store none in the future if present conditions continue. He also found that under the average conditions which prevailed from 1895 to 1939 water could be conserved by Seminoe and Alcova without violation of the priorities between Pathfinder and Tri-State Dam and in sufficient quantities to supply Kendrick and to leave considerable return flow to the river in the irrigation season. * * * The Special Master recommends that Wyoming be enjoined from the storage of water in these four reservoirs and from the diversion of natural flow water through the Casper Canal for the Kendrick Project, between and including May 1 and September 30 of each year, otherwise than in accordance with the rule of priority in relation to the appropriations of the Nebraska lands supplied by the French Canal and by the State Line Canals; that all those Nebraska appropriations for that purpose be adjudged senior to those four reservoirs and to Casper Canal. * * *

We have noted the priorities of Pathfinder and Guernsey, as well as those of the Kendrick Project. We have noted that their priorities make them junior to many downstream appropriators including the State Line Canals. While the four reservoirs in question are Wyoming appropriators, Pathfinder and Guernsey were designed more for the benefit of Nebraska than of Wyoming lands. Recognition of the priorities interstate makes obvious the propriety of an interstate apportionment. * * *

The Special Master recommends that Wyoming be enjoined to respect the rule of priority of these reservoirs in respect to each other and that the order of seniority as between them be defined as follows: (1) Pathfinder, (2) Guernsey, (3) Seminoe, and (4) Alcova. * * *

Whalen to Tri-State Dam. This is the pivotal section of the river around which the central problems of this case turn. Apart from the Kendrick project, the demand for water is as great in this short section of the river as in the entire preceding 415 miles from North Park to Whalen. The lands irrigated from the river in this section total 326,000 acres as compared with 339,200 acres in the upper valley—

main river and tributaries. The consumptive use on this 326,000 acres far exceeds that of the upper sections combined. * * *

As respects priority, the canals * * * fall into thirteen groups, seven in Wyoming and six in Nebraska. The earliest in priority are some canals in Wyoming, then some in Nebraska, then others in Wyoming and so on. * * *

As we have said, this is the critical section of the river. The main controversy centers around it and around the Special Master's proposal for dealing with it. He proposes that the natural flow water in this section between May 1 and September 30 each year be apportioned on the basis of 25 per cent to Wyoming and 75 per cent to Nebraska. He recommends that Nebraska be given the right to designate from time to time the portion of its share which shall be delivered to the Interstate, Ft. Laramie, French and Mitchell Canals for use on Nebraska lands served by them and that Wyoming be enjoined from diversions contrary to this apportionment.

None of the parties agrees to this apportionment. * * *

Wyoming argues for a mass allocation, e.g. 705,000 acre feet to be allocated to Nebraska for diversion in this section during the irrigation season for Nebraska lands. The Special Master rejected that method. He concluded that it was based on an assumption of dependability of flow which would be bound to result in injustice to one or other of the States * * *. We repeat that the inadequacy of the supply is too clear to permit adoption of Wyoming's formula. * * *

Our problem is not to determine what allocation would be equitable among the canals in Nebraska or among those in Wyoming. That is a problem of internal administration for each of the States. Our problem involves only an appraisal of the equities between the claimants whom Wyoming represents on the one hand and those represented by Nebraska on the other. We conclude that the early Wyoming uses, the return flows, and the greater storage water rights which Nebraska appropriators have in this section as compared with those of Wyoming appropriators tip the scales in favor of the flat percentage system recommended by the Special Master. It should be noted, moreover, that that method of apportionment, though not strictly adhering to the principle of priority, gives it great weight and does not cause as great a distortion as might appear to be the case. * * *

If a division of flow were made according to total acreage, total requirements, or acreage or requirements of senior and junior appropriators, it would be as follows:

	Wyoming	Nebraska
Total Acreage	27%	73%
Total Requirement in Acre feet	23%	77%
Total Senior Acreage	24%	76%
Total Junior Acreage	28%	72%
Total Acre feet Requirement, Senior Acreage	22%	78%
Total Acre feet Requirement, Junior Acreage	23%	77%

Accordingly, we conclude that the flat percentage method recommended by the Special Master is the most equitable method of apportionment. * * *

Decree in accordance with opinion.

MR. JUSTICE JACKSON took no part in the consideration or decision of this case.

MR. JUSTICE ROBERTS. I am unable to agree with the court's disposition of this case. I think the decision constitutes a departure from principles long established and observed by the court in litigations between the states of the Union, and adopts a course diametrically opposed to our most recent adjudication in the field of interstate waters. Without proof of actual damage in the past, or of any threat of substantial damage in the near future, the court now undertakes to assume jurisdiction over three quasi-sovereign states and to supervise, for all time, their respective uses of an interstate stream on the basis of past use, including, over a ten year term, the greatest drought in the history of the region, admitting, in effect, that its allocation of privileges to the respective states will have to be revised and modified when that drought ceases and more water becomes available for beneficial use. I doubt if, in such interstate controversies, any state is ever entitled to a declaratory judgment from this court. I am sure that, on the showing in the present record, none of the states is entitled to a declaration of rights. * * *

The bill should be dismissed.

MR. JUSTICE FRANKFURTER and MR. JUSTICE RUTLEDGE join in this opinion.

Notes

1. The Court has refused apportionment of interstate waters in a number of cases. The denial of relief has been predicated on a wide variety of factors, most of which bear on the general principle expressed in New York v. New Jersey, 256 U.S. 296, 309, 41 S.Ct. 492, 496, 65 L.Ed. 937 (1921): "Before this court can be moved to exercise its extraordinary power under the Constitution to control the conduct of one state at the suit of another, the threatened invasion of rights must be of serious magnitude and it must be established by clear and convincing evidence."

In Washington v. Oregon, 297 U.S. 517, 56 S.Ct. 540, 80 L.Ed. 837 (1936), it appeared that little water would arrive at the headgates of the Washington prior appropriators if the junior Oregon diversions were shut off, and that one of the large irrigators in Washington was guilty of laches or abandonment so that as to Oregon water users its early priority need not be recognized. "The case comes down to this: the court is asked upon uncertain evidence of prior right and still more uncertain evidence of damage to destroy possessory interests enjoyed without challenge for over half a century. In such circumstances an injunction would not issue if the contest were between private parties, at odds about a boundary. Still less will it issue herein a contest between states, a contest to be dealt with in the large and ample way that alone becomes the dignity of the litigants concerned."

Kansas made a second bid for an apportionment of the Arkansas River in Colorado v. Kansas, 320 U.S. 383, 64 S.Ct. 176, 88 L.Ed. 116 (1943). The evidence showed that Colorado had authorized the diversion of more than the dependable flow of the river. Nevertheless, the useable flow passing the state line had increased, due to return flows from Colorado irrigation, and while irrigation in Colorado had increased since the Court first denied relief, Kansas had been able to increase her own irrigated acreage in greater proportion, though in smaller amount. The Court refused to speculate how much more might have been accomplished by Kansas under more favorable conditions. Equities in favor of Colorado were that she had provided extensive storage for flood and winter flows, while Kansas had not, and that further Kansas irrigation could be developed from available ground water, while cutting back Colorado appropriators would probably result in abandonment of improvements and migration from farms. Relief was again denied.

An injunction against diverting the headwaters of the Connecticut River for use in metropolitan Boston was sought in Connecticut v. Massachusetts, 282 U.S. 660, 51 S.Ct. 286, 75 L.Ed. 602 (1931). Relief was denied, the Court refusing to apply strict riparian principles:

"Connecticut suggests that, under the common law in force in both States, each riparian owner has a vested right in the use of the flowing waters and is entitled to have them to flow as they were wont, unimpaired as to quantity and uncontaminated as to quality. It maintains that the taking of waters from the Ware and Swift infringes vested property rights in that State which cannot be taken without its consent against the will of the owners. And it insists that this Court, following the law enforced by each of the States within its own boundaries, should grant injunction against any diversion from the watersheds of these rivers.

"But the laws in respect of riparian rights that happen to be effective for the time being in both States do not necessarily constitute a dependable guide or just basis for the decision of controversies such as that here presented. The rules of the common law on that subject do not obtain in all the States of the Union, and there are variations in their application. The doctrine of appropriation prevails in some States. And every State is free to change its laws governing riparian ownership and to permit the appropriation of flowing waters for such purposes as it may deem wise."

No detrimental effect on navigation, agriculture, fish life or purity was shown, and a possible future power dam was not allowed to stand in the way of Boston's use of the water.

2. An important limitation on the interstate lawsuit may arise if the United States has such an interest in the river as to make its presence in the suit essential. Since sovereign immunity prevents the United States from being sued without its consent, the complaining state may be unable to obtain any judicial relief.

In Arizona v. California, 298 U.S. 558, 56 S.Ct. 848, 80 L.Ed. 1331 (1936) a suit was brought against all the other states in the Colorado River basin, seeking apportionment of the unappropriated water. This was dismissed on the ground that the United States, having a paramount power to control the unappropriated waters for the purpose of improving navigation, was an indispensable party in whose absence the water could not be apportioned. The Court said:

"Arizona, by her proposed bill of complaint, asserts no right arising from her own appropriation of the waters of the Colorado river. No infringement of her rights acquired by appropriation is alleged, and no relief for their protection is prayed. While it is alleged that definite plans have been made for the irrigation of 1,000,000 acres of unirrigated land in Arizona, and a right to share in the water for that purpose is asserted, it does not appear that any initial step toward appropriation of water for such a project has been taken * * *

"The allegations and prayer of the bill are of significance only if Arizona, in advance of any act of appropriation, and independently of any rights which she may have acquired under the Boulder Canyon Project Act, may demand a judicial decree exempting the available water of the river, or some of it, from appropriation by other states until the indefinite time in the future when she or her inhabitants may see fit to appropriate it. A justiciable controversy is presented only if Arizona, as a sovereign state, or her citizens, whom she represents, have present rights in the unappropriated water of the river, or if the privilege to appropriate the water is capable of division and when partitioned may be judicially protected from appropriations by others pending its exercise * * *.

"We leave undecided the question whether an equitable division of the unappropriated water of the river can be decreed in a suit in which the United States and the interested states are parties."

In an early stage of the North Platte litigation, Wyoming moved to dismiss the action on the ground that the Secretary of the Interior was an indispensable party. "The bill alleges, and we know as matter of law, that the Secretary and his agents, acting by authority of the Reclamation Act and supplementary legislation, must obtain permits and priorities for the use of water from the State of Wyoming in the same manner as a private appropriator or an irrigation district formed under the state law. His rights can rise no higher than those of Wyoming, and an adjudication of the defendant's rights will necessarily bind him. Wyoming will stand in judgment for him as for any other appropriator in that state. He is not a necessary party." Nebraska v. Wyoming, 295 U.S. 40, 55 S.Ct. 568, 79 L.Ed. 1289 (1935).

Although its presence in the suit cannot be compelled, the United States may voluntarily enter the litigation. It did intervene in the principal case, asking for an allocation of the North Platte to it to enable it to manage its Reclamation projects free from state control. The court denied the apportionment, but inferentially recognized it as a proper party to urge protection of its claims to stored water and to efficient management of the projects.

In the latest case styled "Arizona v. California," the United States chose to intervene. 344 U.S. 919, 73 S.Ct. 385, 97 L.Ed. 708 (1953). But Texas v. New Mexico, 352 U.S. 991, 77 S.Ct. 552, 1 L.Ed.2d 540 (1957), was dismissed because of the absence of the United States as an indispensable party, after six years of litigation, including two references to a master. The interest of the United States arose from its obligations to Indian tribes. "The Attorney General has only his own conscience to guide him in the exercise of his discretion." Corker, Water Rights and Federalism, 45 Cal. L.R. 604, 631 (1957).

Consent has been granted to the joinder of the United States, as a defendant or otherwise, in a suit by any state of the Colorado River Basin to enforce compliance by the Secretary of the Interior with certain compacts and laws in the storage and release of water from reservoirs in the basin. Colorado River Storage Project Act, § 14, 70 Stat. 110 (1956), 43 U.S.C.A. § 620m (1964).

COLORADO v. NEW MEXICO

Supreme Court of the United States, 1982.
459 U.S. 176, 103 S.Ct. 539, 74 L.Ed.2d 348.

JUSTICE MARSHALL delivered the opinion of the Court.

* * *

The Vermejo River is a small, nonnavigable river that originates in the snow-belt of the Rocky Mountains in southern Colorado and flows southeasterly into New Mexico for a distance of roughly 55 miles before it joins the Canadian River. The major portion of the river is located in New Mexico. The Colorado portion consists of three main tributaries that combine to form the Vermejo River proper approximately one mile below the Colorado-New Mexico border. At present there are no uses of the water of the Vermejo River in Colorado, and no use or diversion has ever been made in Colorado. In New Mexico, by contrast, farmers and industrial users have diverted water from the Vermejo for many years. In 1941 a New Mexico state court issued a decree apportioning the water of the Vermejo River among the various New Mexico users.

In 1975, a Colorado corporation, Colorado Fuel and Iron Steel Corporation ("C.F. & I."), obtained in Colorado state court a conditional right to divert 75 cubic feet per second from the headwaters of the Vermejo River. C.F. & I. proposed a transmountain diversion of the water to a tributary of the Purgatoire River in Colorado to be used for industrial development and other purposes. * * *

In June 1978 Colorado moved for leave to file an original complaint in this Court. New Mexico opposed the motion. On April 16, 1979, we granted Colorado's motion and appointed the Honorable Ewing T. Kerr, Senior Judge of the United States District Court for the District of Wyoming, as Special Master in this case. * * *

The Special Master found that most of the water of the Vermejo River is consumed by the New Mexico users and that very little, if any, reaches the confluence with the Canadian River. He thus recognized that strict application of the rule of priority would not permit Colorado any diversion since the entire available supply is needed to satisfy the demands of appropriators in New Mexico with senior rights. Nevertheless, applying the principle of equitable apportionment established in our prior cases, he recommended permitting Colorado a transmountain diversion of 4,000 acre-feet of water per year from the headwaters of the Vermejo River. He stated:

> "It is the opinion of the Master that a transmountain diversion would not materially affect the appropriations granted by New Mexico for users downstream. A thorough examination of the existing economies in New Mexico convinces the Master that the injury to New Mexico, if any, will be more than offset by the benefit to Colorado."

Explaining his conclusion, the Special Master noted that any injury to New Mexico would be restricted to the Conservancy District, the user in New Mexico furthest downstream, since there was sufficient water in the Vermejo River for the three other principal New Mexico water users. Vermejo Park, Kaiser Steel, and Phelps Dodge. He further found that the "Vermejo Conservancy District has never been an economically feasible operation."

* * *

Equitable apportionment is the doctrine of federal common law that governs disputes between states concerning their rights to use the water of an interstate stream. Kansas v. Colorado, 206 U.S. 46, 98, 27 S.Ct. 655, 667–668, 51 L.Ed. 956 (1907); Connecticut v. Massachusetts, 282 U.S. 660, 670–671, 51 S.Ct. 286, 289–290, 75 L.Ed. 602 (1931). It is a flexible doctrine which calls for "the exercise of an informed judgment on a consideration of many factors" to secure a "just and equitable" allocation. Nebraska v. Wyoming, 325 U.S. 589, 618, 65 S.Ct. 1332, 1350–1351, 89 L.Ed. 1815 (1945). * * *

In reaching his recommendation the Special Master did not focus exclusively on the rule of priority, but considered other factors such as the efficiency of current uses in New Mexico and the balance of benefits to Colorado and harm to New Mexico. New Mexico contends that it is improper to consider these other factors. It maintains that this Court has strictly applied the rule of priority when apportioning water between states adhering to the prior appropriation doctrine, and has departed from that rule only to protect an existing economy built upon junior appropriations. Since there is no existing economy in Colorado dependent upon the use of water from the Vermejo River, New Mexico contends that the rule of priority is controlling. We disagree with this inflexible interpretation of the doctrine of equitable apportionment.

Our prior cases clearly establish that equitable apportionment will protect only those rights to water that are "reasonably acquired and applied." Wyoming v. Colorado, 259 U.S. 419, 484, 42 S.Ct. 552, 564, 66 L.Ed. 999 (1922). Especially in those Western states where water is scarce, "[t]here must be no waste * * * of the 'treasure' of a river * * *. Only diligence and good faith will keep the privilege alive." Washington v. Oregon, 297 U.S. 517, 527, 56 S.Ct. 540, 544–545, 80 L.Ed. 837 (1936). Thus, wasteful or inefficient uses will not be protected. See ibid.; Nebraska v. Wyoming, supra, 325 U.S., at 618, 65 S.Ct., at 1350–1351. Similarly, concededly senior water rights will be deemed forfeited or substantially diminished where the rights have not been exercised or asserted with reasonable diligence. Washington v. Oregon, 297 U.S., at 527–528, 56 S.Ct., at 544–545 (1936); Colorado v. Kansas, 320 U.S. 383, 394, 64 S.Ct. 176, 181, 88 L.Ed. 116 (1943).

We have invoked equitable apportionment not only to require the reasonably efficient use of water, but also to impose on states an affirmative duty to take reasonable steps to conserve and augment the water supply of an interstate stream. In Wyoming v. Colorado, Wyoming brought suit to prevent a *proposed* diversion by Colorado from the Laramie River. This Court calculated the dependable supply available to both states, subtracted the senior Wyoming uses, and permitted Colorado to divert an amount not exceeding the balance. In calculating the dependable supply we placed on each state the duty to employ "financially and physically feasible" measures "adapted to *conserving and equalizing* the natural flow." 259 U.S., at 484, 42 S.Ct., at 564 (emphasis added). Adopting a position similar to New Mexico's in this case, Wyoming objected to a requirement that it employ conservation measures to facilitate Colorado's proposed uses. The answer we gave is especially relevant to this case:

> "The question here is not what one state should do for the other, but how each should exercise her relative rights in the waters of this interstate stream * * *. Both states recognize that conservation within practicable limits is essential in order that needless waste may be prevented and the largest feasible use may be secured. This comports with the all-pervading spirit of the doctrine of appropriation and takes appropriate heed of the natural necessities out of which it arose. We think that doctrine lays on each of these states a duty to exercise her right reasonably and in a manner calculated to conserve the common supply." Ibid.

We conclude that it is entirely appropriate to consider the extent to which reasonable conservation measures by New Mexico might offset the proposed Colorado diversion and thereby minimize any injury to New Mexico users. Similarly, it is appropriate to consider whether Colorado has undertaken reasonable steps to minimize the amount of diversion that will be required.

In addition, we have held that in an equitable apportionment of interstate waters it is proper to weigh the harms and benefits to competing states. In Kansas v. Colorado, supra, where we first announced the doctrine of equitable apportionment, we found that users in Kansas were injured by Colorado's upstream diversions from the Arkansas River. 206 U.S., at 113–114, 117, 27 S.Ct., at 674, 675–676. Yet we declined to grant any relief to Kansas on the ground that the great benefit to Colorado outweighed the detriment to Kansas. Id., at 100–101, 113–114, 117, 27 S.Ct., at 668–669, 674, 675–676. Similarly, in Nebraska v. Wyoming, supra, we held that water rights in Wyoming and Nebraska, which under state law were senior, had to yield to the "countervailing equities" of an established economy in Colorado even though it was based on junior appropriations. 325 U.S., at 622, 65 S.Ct., at 1352. We noted that the rule of priority should not be strictly applied where it "would work more hardship" on the junior user "than it would bestow benefits" on the senior user. Id., at 619, 65 S.Ct., at 1351. * * *

We recognize that the equities supporting the protection of existing economies will usually be compelling. The harm that may result from disrupting established uses is typically certain and immediate, whereas the potential benefits from a proposed diversion may be speculative and remote. Under some circumstances, however, the countervailing equities supporting a diversion for future use in one state may justify the detriment to existing users in another state. This may be the case, for example, where the state seeking a diversion demonstrates by clear and convincing evidence that the benefits of the diversion substantially outweigh the harm that might result. In the determination of whether the state proposing the diversion has carried this burden, an important consideration is whether the existing users could offset the diversion by reasonable conservation measures to prevent waste. This approach comports with our emphasis on flexibility in equitable apportionment and also accords sufficient protection to existing uses.

We conclude, therefore, that in the determination of an equitable apportionment of the water of the Vermejo River the rule of priority is not the sole criterion. While the equities supporting the protection of established, senior uses are substantial, it is also appropriate to consider additional factors relevant to a just apportionment, such as the conservation measures available to both states and the balance of harm and benefit that might result from the diversion sought by Colorado.

Applying the doctrine of equitable apportionment, the Special Master recommended that Colorado be permitted to divert 4,000 acre-feet of water per year from the headwaters of the Vermejo River. Because all of the water of the Vermejo River is currently consumed by New Mexico appropriators, the recommended diversion would necessarily reduce the amount of water available to New Mexico.

In explaining the basis for his recommendation, the Special Master stated that the diversion would not "materially affect" existing New Mexico appropriations. This conclusion appears to reflect certain assumptions about the ability of New Mexico users to implement water conservation measures. See supra, at 544, and n. 7. The Special Master also concluded that any injury to New Mexico would be "more than offset" by the benefits to Colorado. Report of Special Master, p. 23. Both the availability of conservation measures and a weighing of the harm and benefits that would result from the diversion are factors relevant to the determination of a just and equitable apportionment. However, the Special Master did not clearly state the factual findings supporting his reliance on these factors. * * *

The flexible doctrine of equitable apportionment clearly extends to a state's claim to divert water for future uses. Whether such a diversion should be permitted will turn on an examination of all factors relevant to a just apportionment. It is proper, therefore, to consider factors such as the extent to which reasonable conservation measures by existing users can offset the reduction in supply due to diversion, and whether the benefits to the state seeking the diversion substantially outweigh the harm to existing uses in another state. We remand for specific factual findings relevant to determining a just and equitable apportionment of the water of the Vermejo River between Colorado and New Mexico.

It is so ordered.

CHIEF JUSTICE BURGER, with whom JUSTICE STEVENS joins, concurring in the opinion and the judgment.

* * *

I emphasize that under our prior holdings these two states come to the Court on equal footing. See Kansas v. Colorado, 206 U.S. 46, 27 S.Ct. 655, 51 L.Ed. 956 (1907). Neither is entitled to any special priority over the other with respect to use of the water. Colorado cannot divert all of the water it may need or can use simply because the river's headwaters lie within its borders, Wyoming v. Colorado, 259 U.S. 419, 466, 42 S.Ct. 552, 558, 66 L.Ed. 999 (1922). Nor is New Mexico entitled to any particular priority of allocation or undiminished flow simply because of first use: See, e.g., Colorado v. Kansas, 320 U.S. 383, 393, 64 S.Ct. 176, 180, 88 L.Ed. 116 (1943). Each state through which rivers pass has a right to the benefit of the water but it is for the Court, as a matter of discretion, to measure their relative rights and obligations and to apportion the available water equitably. As the Court's opinion states, in the process of apportioning the water, prior dependence and inefficient uses may be considered in balancing the equities. But no state has any priority over any other state. It is on this understanding of the Court's holding that I join the opinion and the judgment.

JUSTICE O'CONNOR, with whom JUSTICE POWELL joins, concurring in the judgment.

The doctrine of prior appropriation includes the requirement that the appropriator's use of water be beneficial and reasonable. What is reasonable, of course, does not admit of ready definition, being dependent upon the particular facts and circumstances of each case. In this case, the Special Master has cast an accusatory finger at the Vermejo Conservancy District, concluding that "[t]he system of canals used to transport the water to the fields is inefficient." Report of the Special Master, p. 8.

Undoubtedly, there is evidence in the record indicating that large losses of water occur through seepage and evaporation in transporting waters of the Vermejo through open ditches for irrigation and stock watering. Tr. 1315. It is a leap, however, from observing that large losses occur to concluding, as Colorado would have the Court do, that the practices of the Conservancy District are wasteful or unreasonable. As the Court observes, ante, at 546, 547, the extent of the duty to conserve that may be placed upon the user is limited to measures that are "financially and physically feasible," Wyoming v. Colorado, 259 U.S. 419, 484, 42 S.Ct. 552, 564, 66 L.Ed. 999 (1922), and "within practicable limits." Ibid.[a]

Nevertheless, in concluding that the Conservancy District's distribution system is "inefficient," the Special Master made no factual finding that improved economy in that system is within the practicable means available to the District.

Colorado would have the Court assess the Conservancy District's "waste" and "inefficiency" by a new yardstick—i.e., not by comparing the economic gains to the District with the costs of achieving greater efficiency, but by comparing the "inefficiency" of New Mexico's uses with the relative benefits to Colorado of a new use. The Special Master has succumbed to this suggestion. His recommendation that Colorado be permitted a diversion embodies the judgment that, because Colorado can, in some *unidentified* sense, make "better" use of the waters of the Vermejo, New Mexico may be forced to change her present uses.

Today the Court has also gone dangerously far toward accepting that suggestion. The Court holds, ante, at 547, that it is appropriate in equitable apportionment litigation to weigh the harms and benefits to the competing States. It does so notwithstanding its recognition, ante, at 547, that the potential benefits from a *proposed* diversion are likely to be speculative and remote, and therefore difficult to balance against any threatened harms, and its concession, ibid., that the equities supporting protection of an existing economy will usually be compelling.

This case therefore highlights the restraint with which the Court should proceed in apportioning interstate waters between a State seeking a *future* use and a State with an existing economy dependent upon the waters to be apportioned. The Court can only invite litigation within its original jurisdiction if it permits one State to obtain a diversion for a new use upon that State's allegation that the second State is engaging in "wasteful" practices or that she can make "better" use of the waters, even if the second State's uses are entirely reasonable. * * *

The Court's remand reflects its judgment that the paucity of the factual findings before us furnishes an inadequate basis upon which to make "the delicate adjustment of interests" at stake, Nebraska v. Wyoming, 325 U.S. 589, 618, 65 S.Ct. 1332, 1350–1351, 89 L.Ed. 1815

a. It is significant to note that in Wyoming v. Colorado, 259 U.S. 419, 42 S.Ct. 552, 66 L.Ed. 999 (1922), upon which the Court relies for the proposition that an affirmative duty to conserve may be imposed on the States, ante, at 546, the Wyoming appropriators *already* had storage facilities in place for equalizing the river's natural flow. * * *

(1945). I concur in that disposition insofar as the Special Master's findings and conclusions do not provide a basis for determining whether Colorado has demonstrated by clear and convincing evidence that the Conservancy District has engaged in unreasonably wasteful practices.

COLORADO v. NEW MEXICO

Supreme Court of the United States, 1984.
467 U.S. 310, 104 S.Ct. 2433, 81 L.Ed.2d 247.

JUSTICE O'CONNOR delivered the opinion of the Court.

Last Term, because our initial inquiry turned on the factors relevant to determining a just apportionment, the Court explained in detail the law of equitable apportionment. This Term, because our inquiry turns on the evidentiary material Colorado has offered in support of its complaint, we find it necessary to explain the standard by which we judge proof in actions for equitable apportionment. * * *

Last Term, the Court made clear that Colorado's proof would be judged by a clear-and-convincing-evidence standard. * * * Requiring Colorado to present clear and convincing evidence in support of its proposed diversion is necessary to appropriately balance the unique interests involved in water rights disputes between sovereigns. The standard reflects this Court's long-held view that a proposed diverter should bear most, though not all, of the risks of erroneous decision: "The harm that may result from disrupting established uses is typically certain and immediate, whereas the potential benefits from a proposed diversion may be speculative and remote." Colorado v. New Mexico, 459 U.S., at 187, 103 S.Ct., at 547; see also id., at 182, n. 9, 103 S.Ct., at 544, n. 9. In addition, the clear-and-convincing-evidence standard accommodates society's competing interests in increasing the stability of property rights and in putting resources to their most efficient uses: "[T]he rule of priority [will] not be strictly applied where it 'would work more hardship' on the junior user 'than it would bestow benefits' on the senior use[r, * * * though] the equities supporting the protection of existing economies will usually be compelling." Id., at 186, 103 S.Ct., at 547 (quoting Nebraska v. Wyoming, 325 U.S. 589, 619, 65 S.Ct. 1332, 1351, 89 L.Ed. 1815 (1945)). In short, Colorado's diversion should and will be allowed only if actual inefficiencies in present uses or future benefits from other uses are highly probable. * * * Upon our independent review of the record, we find that Colorado has failed to meet its burden.

To establish whether Colorado's proposed diversion could be offset by eliminating New Mexico's nonuse or inefficiency, we asked the Master to make specific findings concerning existing uses, supplies of water, and reasonable conservation measures available to the two States. After assessing the evidence both States offered about existing uses and available supplies, the Master concluded that "current levels of use primarily reflect failure on the part of existing users to fully develop and put to work available water." Moreover, with respect to reasonable conservation measures available, the Master indicated his belief that more careful water administration in New Mexico would alleviate shortages from unregulated stockponds, fishponds, and water detention structures, prevent waste from blockage and clogging in canals, and ensure that users fully devote themselves to development of available resources. He further concluded that "the heart of New Mexico's water problem is the Vermejo Conservancy District," id., at 20, which he considered a failed "reclamation project [that had] never lived up to its expectations or even proved to be a successful project, * * * and [that] quite possibly should never have been built." Though the District was quite arguably in the "middle range in reclamation project efficiencies," the Master was of the opinion "that [the District's] inefficient water use should not be charged to Colorado." Furthermore, though Colorado had not submitted evidence or testimony of any conservation measures that C.F. & I. would take, the Master concluded that "it is not for the Master or for New Mexico to say that reasonable attempts to conserve water will not be implemented by Colorado."

We share the Master's concern that New Mexico may be overstating the amount of harm its users would suffer from a diversion. Water use by appropriators along the Vermejo River has remained relatively stable for the past 30 years, and this historic use falls substantially below the decreed rights of those users. Unreliable supplies satisfactorily explain some of this difference, but New Mexico's attempt to excuse three decades of nonuse in this way is, at the very least, suspect. Nevertheless, whatever the merit of New Mexico's explanation, we cannot agree that Colorado has met its burden of identifying, by clear and convincing evidence, conservation efforts that would preserve any of the Vermejo River water supply.

For example, though Colorado alleged that New Mexico could improve its administration of stockponds, fishponds, and water detention structures, it did not actually point to specific measures New Mexico could take to conserve water. Thus, ultimately all the Master could conclude was that some unspecified "[r]eduction and/or regulation * * * could not help but be an effort, however small, to conserve the water supply * * *." * * *

Colorado's attack on current water use in the Vermejo Conservancy District is inadequate for much the same reason. Our cases require only conservation measures that are "financially and physically feasible" and "within practicable limits." See, e.g., Colorado v. New Mexico, supra, 459 U.S., at 192, 103 S.Ct., at 550; Wyoming v. Colorado, 259 U.S. 419, 484, 42 S.Ct. 552, 564, 66 L.Ed. 999 (1922). New Mexico submitted substantial evidence that the District is in the middle of reclamation project efficiencies and that the District has taken considerable independent steps—including, the construction, at its own expense and on its own initiative, of a closed stockwater delivery system—to improve the efficiency of its future water use. * * * Colorado has not identified any "financially and physically feasible" means by which the District can further eliminate or reduce inefficiency and, contrary to the Master's suggestion, we believe that the burden is on Colorado to do so. A State can carry its burden of proof in an equitable apportionment action only with specific evidence about how existing uses might be improved, or with clear evidence that a project is far less efficient than most other projects. Mere assertions about the relative efficiencies of competing projects will not do.

Finally, there is no evidence in the record that "Colorado has undertaken reasonable steps to minimize the amount of the diversion that will be required." Colorado v. New Mexico, supra, 459 U.S., at 186, 103 S.Ct., at 547. Nine years have past since C.F. & I. first proposed diverting water from the Vermejo River. Yet Colorado has presented no evidence concerning C.F. & I.'s inability to relieve its needs through substitute sources. Furthermore, there is no evidence that C.F. & I. has settled on a definite or even tentative construction design or plan, or that it has prepared an economic analysis of its proposed diversion. * * *

Society's interest in minimizing erroneous decisions in equitable apportionment cases requires that hard facts, not suppositions or opinions, be the basis for interstate diversions. In contrast to Justice STEVENS, we do not believe Colorado has produced sufficient facts to show, by clear and convincing evidence, that reasonable conservation efforts will mitigate sufficiently the injury that New Mexico successfully established last Term that it would suffer were a diversion allowed. No State can use its lax administration to establish its claim to water. But once a State successfully proves that a diversion will cause it injury, the burden shifts to the diverter to show reasonable conservation measures exist. Colorado has not carried this burden.

* * *

We also asked the Master to help us balance the benefits and harms that might result from the proposed diversion. The Master found that Colorado's proposed interim use is agricultural in nature and that more permanent applications might include use in coal mines, timbering, power generation, domestic needs, and other industrial operations. The Master admitted that "[t]his area of fact finding [was] one of the most difficult [both] because of the necessarily speculative nature of [the] benefits * * * " and because of Colorado's "natural reluctance to spend large amounts of time and money developing plans, operations, and cost schemes * * *." Nevertheless, because the diverted water would, at a minimum, alleviate existing water shortages in Colorado, the Master concluded that the evidence showed considerable benefits would accrue from the diversion. * * *

Again, we find ourselves without adequate evidence to approve Colorado's proposed diversion. Colorado has not committed itself to any long-term use for which future benefits can be studied and predicted. Nor has Colorado specified how long the interim agricultural use might or might not last. All Colorado has established is that a steel corporation wants to take water for some unidentified use in the future.

By contrast, New Mexico has attempted to identify the harms that would result from the proposed diversion. New Mexico commissioned some independent economists to study the economic effects, direct and indirect, that the diversion would have on persons in New Mexico. The study these economists produced was submitted at the original hearing, conducted prior to the remand, as evidence of the injury that would result from the reduction in water supplies. No doubt, this economic analysis involved prediction and forecast. But the analysis is surely no more speculative than the generalizations Colorado has offered as "evidence." New Mexico, at the very least, has taken concrete steps toward addressing the query this Court posed last Term. Colorado has made no similar effort.

Colorado objects that speculation about the benefits of future uses is inevitable and that water will not be put to its best use if the expenditures necessary to development and operation must be made without assurance of future supplies. We agree, of course, that asking for absolute precision in forecasts about the benefits and harms of a diversion would be unrealistic. But we have not asked for such precision. We have only required that a State proposing a diversion conceive and implement some type of long-range planning and analysis of the diversion it proposes. Long-range planning and analysis will, we believe, reduce the uncertainties with which equitable apportionment judgments are made. If New Mexico can develop evidence to prove that its existing economy is efficiently using water, we see no reason why Colorado cannot take similar steps to prove that its future economy could do better.

In the nine years that have passed since C.F. & I. first requested a diversion, neither it nor Colorado has decided upon a permanent use for the diverted water. It therefore is no surprise that Colorado cannot conduct studies or make predictions about the benefits and harms of its proposed diversion. Under the clear-and-convincing-evidence standard, it is Colorado, and not New Mexico, that must bear the risk of error from the inadequacy of the information available.

As a final consideration, the Master pointed out that approximately three-fourths of the water in the Vermejo River system is produced in Colorado. He concluded, therefore, that "the equities are with Colorado, which requests only a portion of the water which it produces." Last Term, the Court rejected the notion that the mere fact that the Vermejo River originates in Colorado automatically entitles Colorado to a share of the river's waters. Both Colorado and New Mexico recognize the doctrine of prior appropriation, and appropriative, as opposed to riparian, rights depend on actual use, not land ownership. It follows, therefore, that the equitable apportionment of appropriated rights should turn on the benefits, harms, and efficiencies of competing uses, and that the source of the Vermejo River's waters should be essentially irrelevant to the adjudication of these sovereigns' competing claims. To the extent the Master continued to think the contrary, he was in error.

We continue to believe that the flexible doctrine of equitable apportionment extends to a State's claim to divert previously appropriated water for future uses. But the State seeking such a diversion bears the burden of proving, by clear and convincing evidence, the existence of certain relevant factors. The complainant must show, for example, the extent to which reasonable conservation measures can adequately compensate for the reduction in supply due to the diversion, and the extent to which the benefits from the diversion will outweigh the harms to existing users. This evidentiary burden cannot be met with generalizations about unidentified conservation measures and unstudied speculation about future uses. The Special Master struggled, as best he could, to balance the evidentiary requirement against the inherent limitations of proving a beneficial future use. However, we do not find enough evidence to sustain his findings. Until Colorado can generate sufficient evidence to show that circumstances have changed and that a diversion is appropriate, the equities compel the continued protection of the existing users of the Vermejo River's waters.

Accordingly, we sustain the State of New Mexico's exceptions to the Special Master's Report and Additional Factual Findings, and dismiss the case.

It is so ordered.

JUSTICE STEVENS, dissenting.

* * *

The Special Master's task was not to draw up blueprints for New Mexico to eliminate its waste. The Master, based on all the evidence, concluded that reasonable conservation efforts in New Mexico would offset the effects of the Colorado diversion. * * * My examination of the testimony persuades me that that conclusion is supported by the record.

Accordingly, I respectfully dissent.

Notes

1. The two opinions in Colorado v. New Mexico are analyzed against the historical development of the doctrine of equitable apportionment, and the future path of the doctrine is predicted, in Tarlock, The Law of Equitable Apportionment Revisited, Updated and Restated, 56 U.Colo.L. Rev. 501 (1985).

2. A new type of interstate conflict seems to be developing over the waters of the Missouri River, which straddles the 98th meridian, the line between east and west, between the humid and arid zones. In the western basin the present use and future need is to take water from the river for use on farms, in cities and industries, and for development of energy. In the east, the primary use of the water is within its banks, to transport

freight by barge and tugboat. In the Flood Control Act of 1944 Congress authorized the "Pick-Sloan Plan," the Sloan Plan to supply water for irrigation, municipal and other uses from Bureau of Reclamation projects in the upper basin, the Pick Plan to provide flood control, hydroelectric power and navigation to downstream cities and states by Corps of Engineers dams. As of 1985, only about 40 percent of the Sloan Plan had been consummated, while the Pick Plan, with four great reservoirs on the main stem of the river, was practically complete. Section 6 of the Flood Control Act authorized the Corps to furnish surplus water for domestic and industrial use, and Section 9(c) authorized the Secretary of the Interior to proceed under the Reclamation law, which has been construed to allow the Bureau of Reclamation to furnish industrial water pursuant to repayment contracts for reimbursement of a share of project costs.

In 1982 the State of South Dakota issued a permit to the South Dakota Conservancy District to appropriate water from the Missouri River at Oahe Dam, constructed on the Missouri River in South Dakota by the Corps for multiple purposes that included navigation, flood control and a Reclamation project. The district contracted to furnish water to a coal slurry pipeline for the transportation of coal to midwest power plants. The Secretary of the Interior, claiming jurisdiction over that part of the water reserved for the Reclamation project, issued a water service contract for the delivery of 20,000 to 50,000 acre feet per year to the pipeline.

The States of Missouri, Iowa and Nebraska brought suit against the federal officials, alleging that the water service contract was illegally issued and that South Dakota's allocation of the water to the pipeline company was unlawful. (Missouri v. Andrews, 586 F.Supp. 1268 (D.Neb. 1984). The State of South Dakota was not made a defendant, and was denied permission to intervene.

The district court granted an injunction against performance of the contract on the ground that since the dam was constructed and operated by the Corps of Engineers, the Corps, not the Bureau of Reclamation, had the contracting power.

While an appeal was pending, the pipeline company terminated its contract with the district. The plaintiff states moved to dismiss the case as moot. The federal defendants urge its continuance in order to get a definitive ruling on the issue of which agency has the power to issue the water supply contract. An affirmance of the district court's rule would place completion of the Sloan Plan in jeopardy.

This conflict between upstream consumptive uses and downstream instream flows threatens to grow to serious magnitude. The plaintiff states claim prospective harm to their citizens from the loss of water needed to supply municipal and agricultural purposes, to generate inexpensive electric energy, to provide barge transportation for heavy commodities, and to avoid environmental damage from loss of ox bow lakes and lowering of the river levels. The 50,000 acre feet maximum of the water service contract has been stated to amount to 16,000,000,000 gallons per year. Looked at from another perspective, this is two-tenths of one percent of the average annual virgin flow of the Missouri River at Sioux Falls, South Dakota. Obviously the downstream states are frightened by the "camel's nose under the tent" presented by the pipeline contract, while the upper basin states fear loss of future irrigation and energy development if further consumption is curtailed.

Guhin, The Law of the Missouri, 30 So.Dak.L.Rev. 347 (1985) contains a full discussion of the Flood Control Act of 1944, its legislative history and supporting documents, and a critical review of *Missouri v. Andrews.*

3. The threatened loss of the benefits of navigation has spawned another form of interstate water controversy that may have some relevance for the Missouri River. The "Great Lakes Cases" involved a controversy that arose between Illinois and the "downstream" states on the Lakes when the Sanitary District of Chicago dredged a canal to the Mississippi River, reversed the flow of the Chicago River, sent Chicago's sewage down the Mississippi in a large quantity of Lake Michigan water, lowered the level of the Lakes, and incidentally opened a navigable waterway between the Great Lakes and the Gulf of Mexico. The opening gun was not an interstate lawsuit but does have a bearing on the right of a state to the maintenance of artificially improved navigation. The first withdrawals were made pursuant to an order of the Secretary of War under an act of Congress. When he issued a new order for a reduction in the amount of diversion, the Sanitary District refused to comply. The first case in the litigation, Sanitary District of Chicago v. U.S., 266 U.S. 405, 45 S.Ct. 176, 71 L.Ed. 164 (1925), was an action by the United States to enforce the reduction, and the Court issued the requested injunction. Several states bordering on the Mississippi River were allowed to file briefs in favor of the diversion, and in the Supreme Court they objected that their interests were not considered by the Secretary when he issued the order reducing the flow. Mr. Justice Holmes said, for a unanimous Court,

> The interest that the river states have in increasing the artificial flow from Lake Michigan is not a right, but merely a consideration they may address to Congress, if they see fit to induce a modification of the law that now forbids that increase. * * * The Secretary, by his action, took no rights of any kind.

In an early stage of the litigation, New York v. Illinois, 274 U.S. 488, 47 S.Ct. 661, 71 L.Ed. 1164 (1927), an injunction was sought to enjoin the continuation of the diversion of Lake Michigan water through the sanitary canal. A major argument was that the diversion might interfere with or prevent the use of the Niagara and St. Lawrence Rivers for the development of power. This phase of the case was held to present no ground for relief:

> But [New York] does not show that there is any present use of the waters for such purposes which is being or will be disturbed; nor that there is any definite projection for so using them which is being or will be affected. The waters are international and their use for developing power may require the assent of the Dominion of Canada and the United States. No consent of either is shown. The suit is one for an injunction, a form of relief which must rest on an actual or presently threatened interference with the rights of another. Plainly, no basis for such relief is disclosed in what is said about water power development. At best, the [claim] does no more than present abstract ques-

tions respecting the right of the plaintiff state and their citizens to use the waters for purposes in the indefinite future. We are not at liberty to consider abstract questions.

In the final stage the Court ruled indirectly that an illegal and unauthorized diversion of navigable waters did give a state a cause of action. The Great Lakes litigation was renewed by the six Lake states in Wisconsin v. Illinois, 278 U.S. 367, 49 S.Ct. 163, 73 L.Ed. 426 (1929). The Secretary of War had issued a new permit that allowed Chicago to divert a much larger amount to carry its sewage down the Mississippi. This caused a six inch drop in the lake levels and the loss of 3,346,000 tons of freight by reducing the draft of cargo vessels using the connecting locks and canals. The only issue in the case, however, was the legality of the Secretary's orders; there was no discussion of the nature of the plaintiffs' rights. Since the Secretary was not empowered to permit withdrawals of navigable waters for purposes of sanitation and power production, the order was held illegal and an injunction was issued, to take effect as soon as Chicago could construct adequate treatment plants. Today, the master's finding in Wisconsin v. Illinois that "damage due to the diversion at Chicago relates to * * * the convenience of summer resorts, to hunting and fishing and grounds, to public parks * * * and to riparian property," would be characterized as indicating a state's right to complain of environmental harms caused by upstream diversion.

SECTION 2. INTERSTATE COMPACTS

HINDERLIDER v. LA PLATA RIVER & CHERRY CREEK DITCH CO.

Supreme Court of the United States, 1938.
304 U.S. 92, 58 S.Ct. 803, 82 L.Ed. 1202.

MR. JUSTICE BRANDEIS delivered the opinion of the Court.

The La Plata River & Cherry Creek Ditch Company, a Colorado corporation, owns a ditch by which it diverts from that river in Colorado water for irrigation. On July 5, 1928, it brought in the district court for La Plata county a suit which charged that since June 24, 1928, the defendants, Hinderlider, State Engineer of Colorado, and his subordinates, have so administered the water of the river as to deprive the plaintiff of water which it claims the right to divert. A mandatory injunction was sought.

The defendants admit that in administering the water of the stream during the period named they shut the headgate of the Ditch Company so as to deprive it of water for purposes of irrigation; but assert that they did so pursuant to the requirements of the La Plata River Compact entered into by the States of Colorado and New Mexico with the consent of the Congress of the United States.

The Compact provides that each State shall receive a definite share of water under the varying conditions which obtain during the year, and, among other things: * * *

"3. Whenever the flow of the river is so low that in the judgment of the State engineers of the States the greatest beneficial use of its waters may be secured by distributing all of its water successively to the lands in each State in alternating periods, in lieu of delivery of water as provided in the second paragraph of this article, the use of the waters may be so rotated between the two States in such manner, for such periods, and to continue for such time as the State Engineers may jointly determine." * * * During the ten days commencing June 24, 1928, all the water of the river (except small amounts diverted in Colorado for domestic and stock requirements) was thus allowed to pass to New Mexico; and during the succeeding ten-day period all the water in the stream was similarly allowed to be diverted in Colorado. The defendant water officials contend that in so rotating the water of the stream they administered it as required by the Compact and wisely. * * *

The relative rights of all claimants to divert in Colorado water from the La Plata River were adjudicated in a proceeding under the Colorado statutes. By decree therein of January 12, 1898 (and later amended), the Ditch Company was declared entitled to divert 39¼ cubic feet of water per second, subject to five senior priorities aggregating 19 second feet. On June 24, 1928, there was in the stream, at the recognized Colorado gauging station, 57 second feet of water. The Ditch Company claimed that by reason of the 1898 decree it was entitled to all the water in the stream except that required to satisfy the Colorado priorities. If it had been permitted to draw all that water, none would have been available to the New Mexico water claimants, who, under similar laws, had made appropriations. Some of them were earlier in date that the Ditch Company's. * * *

[The Colorado courts held that the compact was not a defense, and ordered the defendants to permit the plaintiff to divert water whenever there was water in the stream not subject to prior Colorado appropriations.]

First. As the La Plata River flows from Colorado into New Mexico and in each State the water is used beneficially, it must be equitably apportioned between the two. * * *

It may be assumed that the right adjudicated by the decree of January 12, 1898 to the Ditch Company is a property right, indefeasible so far as concerns the State of Colorado, its citizens, and any other person claiming water rights there. But the Colorado decree could not confer upon the Ditch Company rights in excess of Colorado's share of the water of the stream; and its share was only an equitable portion thereof. * * *

Second. The declared purpose of the Compact was, as the preamble recites, equitable apportionment. * * *

The extent of the existing equitable right of Colorado and of New Mexico in the La Plata River could obviously have been determined by a suit in this Court, as was done in Kansas v. Colorado, supra, in respect to rights in the Arkansas River and in Wyoming v. Colorado, supra, in respect to the Laramie. But resort to the judicial remedy is never essential to the adjustment of interstate controversies, unless the States are unable to agree upon the terms of a compact, or Congress refuses its consent. The difficulties incident to litigation have led States to resort, with frequency, to adjustment of their controversies by compact, even where the matter in dispute was the relatively simple one of a boundary. In two such cases this Court suggested "that the parties endeavor with consent of Congress to adjust their boundaries." State of Minnesota v. Wisconsin, 252 U.S. 273, 283, 40 S.Ct. 313, 319, 64 L.Ed. 558; State of Washington v. Oregon, 214 U.S. 205, 217, 218, 29 S.Ct. 631, 53 L.Ed. 969. In New York v. New Jersey, 256 U.S. 296, 313, 41 S.Ct. 492, 497, 65 L.Ed. 937, which involved a more intricate problem of rights in interstate waters, the recommendation that treaty-making be resorted to was more specific; and compacts for the apportionment of the water of interstate streams have been common.

Third. Whether the apportionment of the water of an interstate stream be made by compact between the upper and lower States with the consent of Congress or by a decree of this Court, the apportionment is binding upon the citizens of each State and all water claimants, even where the State had granted the water rights before it entered into the compact. That the private rights of grantees of a State are determined by the adjustment by compact of a disputed boundary was settled a century ago in Poole v. Fleeger, 11 Pet. 185, 209, 9 L.Ed. 680. * * *

Fourth. As the States had power to bind by compact their respective appropriators by division of the flow of the stream, they had power to reach that end either by providing for a continuous equal division of the water from time to time in the stream, or by providing for alternate periods of flow to the one State and to the other of all the water in the stream. To secure "the greatest beneficial use of" the water in the stream, the Compact provided that the water may be "rotated between the two States, in such manner for such periods, and to continue for such time as the State Engineers may jointly determine." That such alternate rotating flow was then a more efficient use of the stream than if the flow had been steadily divided equally between the Colorado and the New Mexico appropriators was conclusively established by the evidence. That is, the rotating supply which the Compact authorized, and the two State Engineers agreed upon, was clearly more beneficial to the Ditch Company than to have given to it and other Colorado appropriators steadily one-half of the water in the river. The delegation to the State Engineers of the authority to determine when the waters should be so rotated was a matter of detail clearly within the constitutional power. There is no claim that the authority conferred was abused.

Fifth. As Colorado possessed the right only to an equitable share of the water in the stream, the decree of January 12, 1898, in the

Colorado water proceeding did not award to the Ditch Company any right greater than the equitable share. Hence the apportionment made by the Compact can not have taken from the Ditch Company any vested right, unless there was in the proceedings leading up to the Compact or in its application, some vitiating infirmity. No such infirmity or illegality has been shown. * * *

It has been suggested that this Court lacks jurisdiction to determine the validity and effect of the Compact because Colorado and New Mexico, the parties to it, are not parties to this suit and cannot be made so. The contention is unsound. The cases are many where title to land dependent upon the boundary between States has been passed upon by this Court upon review of judgments of federal and of State courts in suits between private litigants.

Reversed.

Notes

1. The definitive work on interstate compacts is Frankfurter & Landis, The Compact Clause of the Constitution—a Study in Interstate Adjustments, 34 Yale L.J. 685 (1925). More recent reviews of the procedures of compact negotiation, Congressional consent, and state legislative ratification are found in Zimmermann & Wendell, The Interstate Compact since 1925 (Council of State Governments 1951); King, Interstate Water Compacts, in Water Resources and the Law, 355 (University of Michigan 1958). Witmer, Documents on the Use and Control of the Waters of Interstate and International Streams (H.R.Doc. No. 319, 90th Cong.2d Sess.1968) sets out the full text of all water compacts effective at that date, and of some negotiated but unratified or lacking Congressional consent. A list, and comparison of features, is found in King, supra.

A comprehensive treatment is found in Muys, Interstate Water Contracts: The Interstate Compact and Federal-Interstate Compact, National Water Commission Legal Study No. 14 (1971).

2. Texas v. New Mexico, 462 U.S. 554, 103 S.Ct. 2558, 77 L.Ed.2d 1 (1983), was a suit to require New Mexico to deliver water to Texas in accordance with the Pecos River Compact. The Pecos is an intermittent, highly variable stream, and the Compact bound New Mexico to "not deplete by man's activities the flow * * * below an amount which will give to Texas a quantity of water equivalent to that available to Texas under the 1947 condition," calculated pursuant to a specified formula. The Compact set up a commission with a representative from each state and a non-voting federal member, and empowered it to adopt any other "more feasible method." The commission was also authorized to determine any shortfall in the promised flow. The formula turned out to be badly flawed and flows at the state line were below expected levels even when not influenced by man's activities, but the two states' commissioners became deadlocked, unable to agree on the amount of shortfall or an improved method of calculating it.

The Supreme Court refused to rewrite the Compact to provide a tie-breaking mechanism the parties had not agreed to. And, since "congressional consent transforms an interstate compact * * * into a law of the United States, * * * no court may order relief inconsistent with its expressed terms. * * * Nevertheless, * * * the mere existence of a compact does not foreclose the possibility that we will be required to resolve a dispute between the compacting States." Such a dispute was found to be present. The commission was held not to be the exclusive forum for all disputes. "It is difficult to conceive that Texas would trade away its right to seek an equitable apportionment of the river in return for a promise that New Mexico could, for all practical purposes, avoid at will. In the absence of an explicit provision or other clear indication that a bargain to that effect was made, we shall not construe a compact to preclude a state from seeking judicial relief when the compact does not provide an equivalent method of vindicating the state's rights."

The case was remanded to the Special Master to make an independent determination of the factors that produced the 1947 condition, and to find, first, the difference between the quantity of water Texas could have expected to receive in each year and the quantity it actually received, and second, to what extent the shortfalls were due to man's activities in New Mexico. The Court closed its opinion with the observation that it is difficult to believe that the *bona fide* differences in the two states' views would justify the expense and time necessary to obtain a judicial resolution of the controversy, and the suggestion that the dispute could more wisely and easily be solved by cooperative study and mutual consent on the part of states.

3. In Intake Water Company v. Yellowstone River Compact Commission, 769 F.2d 568 (9th Cir.1985), the company had plans for a transdivide diversion from the Yellowstone River, for use in Montana and North Dakota. Article X of the Yellowstone River Compact provides, "No waters shall be diverted from the Yellowstone River Basin without unanimous consent of all the signatory states." The Compact had been adopted by the legislatures of all three states and ratified by Congress (63 Stat. 663 (1951)). Intake challenged the validity of this restriction as state action that places an unreasonable burden on interstate commerce, but the court held that Congress had converted the Compact into federal law, and hence immunized it from constitutional attack on interstate commerce grounds.

4. The federal-interstate compact is a device much preferred, by the states concerned, to the complete federalization of the basin program and unification of all federal functions in an agency such as the Tennessee Valley Authority, which is a federal corporation enjoying substantial independence from other federal agencies and reporting directly to the President and the Congress. See Martin, The Tennessee Valley Authority: A Study of Federal Control, 22 Law and Contemporary Problems 351 (1957); Swidler and Marquis, TVA in Court: A Study of TVA's Constitutional Litigation, 32 Iowa L.Rev. 296 (1947). The TVA has been much copied in foreign countries as the most suitable institutional form for river basin development, but it seems unlikely that it will be again used in the United States.

5. The first suggestion for a federal-interstate compact came from Zimmerman and Wendell, supra Note 1. The first concrete proposal was

presented in 1953 by the three dissenting members of the Missouri Basin Survey Commission, a temporary agency appointed by President Truman composed of Congressional and public members. Several were admirers of the Tennessee Valley Authority and originally favored a similar organization for the Missouri Basin. Eventually, the Commission's majority recommended a new form of coordinating agency to plan and direct within the basin the activities of the traditional federal agencies for land and water development. It was to be much more than a river basin interagency consulting commission but much less than a valley authority with corporate form that would itself perform the major functions of project construction and operation. The proposed organization would have been a five-man independent agency, its members appointed by the President, with broad powers over the Corps of Engineers, the Department of the Interior, the Department of Agriculture, and others. This body was to have combined the agencies' plans into a master plan, reviewed requests for authorizations before transmission to Congress, prepared a basin-wide multi-agency budget for Congress, and provided central control of river operations. The dissenting Commissioners believed that the coordinating agency should be established by a federal-interstate compact rather than by Congress, and that it should be composed of one member from each state and one from the federal government. (Missouri: Land and Water, Report of the Missouri Basin Survey Commission, 1953, pp. 8–14). A tentative draft of a compact to be signed by the states and the nation was prepared by representatives of several basin states, and the legal ramifications were explored. (See Trelease, A Federal-State Compact for Missouri Basin Development, 7 Wyoming L.J. 161, 1953.)

The idea was renewed in the later 1950's by the eastern states of the Delaware River Basin. Those states already had INCODEL, the Interstate Commission on the Delaware River Basin, created not by compact but by the enactment of identical and reciprocal legislation by Pennsylvania, New Jersey, and New York. INCODEL's primary emphasis was on water quality control, but it had some authority for general planning of water development. Experience showed the desirability of this cooperative approach and the need for its expansion, and the Delaware River Basin Compact was negotiated and ratified by the states, and Congress both consented to and joined in the compact in 1961. (75 Stat. 688, 1961.)

The compact set up the Delaware River Basin Commission, consisting of the Governors of New York, Pennsylvania, New Jersey and Delaware, or their alternates, and one federal commissioner. Its major function is to prepare a comprehensive plan for development of the basin, including all public and private projects and facilities, followed up by an ongoing six-year program of implementation, annually revised. The Commission licenses each project to be undertaken, and can itself construct and operate projects. It even has the "* * * power from time to time as need appears, in accordance with the doctrine of equitable apportionment, to allocate the waters of the basin to and among the states signatory to this compact and to and among their respective political subdivisions, and to impose conditions, obligations and release requirements related thereto." (Sec. 3.3.) The Commission can also regulate withdrawals of surface and ground waters in areas of shortage and cases of emergency. (Secs. 10.4,

10.5.) It exercised these powers during an extended drought that reached the emergency stage in 1965, curtailing New York City's withdrawals and Philadelphia's water intakes. (*Muys,* supra Note 1, pp. 117–192, gives a full case history of the negotiations for and operations under the Delaware River Basin Compact.)

There are few legal problems connected with the federal-interstate compact. The power of the United States to enter into permanent agreements with the states, ceding to them federal works and powers, was first recognized in Seawright v. Stokes, 3 How.U.S. 149 (1845). The major problem on the Delaware was the relationship of the Commission's comprehensive plan to the federal government's programs. Conflicts with the national power over navigation were seen as difficult, and were avoided by leaving that subject outside the scope of the Commission's activities. The compact provides that as to all projects, including federal projects, no expenditures or construction shall be made if the project is not included in the plan. The federal government has only one vote on the five-member Commission, so that as the compact is written, the Commission could veto a federal project by a vote of the states. This was unacceptable to the federal government, so in the consent legislation a reservation recites that while nothing in the compact shall impair the constitutional authority of the United States or any of its rights or authority under existing or future legislation, the exercise of those federal powers shall not substantially conflict with a Commission plan concurred in by the federal member. The President may also suspend any provision of the plan in the national interest. (See *Muys,* 206a–225).

SECTION 3. CONGRESSIONAL APPORTIONMENT

ARIZONA v. CALIFORNIA

Supreme Court of the United States, 1963.
373 U.S. 546, 83 S.Ct. 1468, 10 L.Ed.2d 572.

MR. JUSTICE BLACK delivered the opinion of the Court.

In 1952 the State of Arizona invoked the original jurisdiction of this Court by filing a complaint against the State of California and seven of its public agencies. Later, Nevada, New Mexico, Utah, and the United States were added as parties either voluntarily or on motion. The basic controversy in the case is over how much water each State has a legal right to use out of the waters of the Colorado River and its tributaries. After preliminary pleadings, we referred the case to George I. Haight, Esquire, and upon his death in 1955 to Simon H. Rifkind, Esquire, as Special Master to take evidence, find facts, state conclusions of law, and recommend a decree, all "subject to consideration, revision, or approval by the Court." The Master conducted a trial lasting from June 14, 1956, to August 28, 1958, during which 340 witnesses were heard orally or by deposition, thousands of exhibits were received, and 25,000 pages of transcript were filled. Following many motions, arguments, and briefs, the Master in a 433-page volume reported his findings, conclusions, and recommended decree, received by the Court on January 16, 1961. The case has been extensively briefed here and orally argued twice, the first time about 16 hours, the second, over six. As we see this case, the question of each State's share of the waters of the Colorado and its tributaries turns on the meaning and the scope of the Boulder Canyon Project Act passed by Congress in 1928.[a] That meaning and scope can be better understood when the Act is set against its background—the gravity of the Southwest's water problems; the inability of local groups or individual States to deal with these enormous problems; the continued failure of the States to agree on how to conserve and divide the waters; and the ultimate action by Congress at the request of the States creating a great system of dams and public works nationally built, controlled, and operated for the purpose of conserving and distributing the water.

The Colorado River itself rises in the mountains of Colorado and flows generally in a southwesterly direction for about 1,300 miles through Colorado, Utah, and Arizona and along the Arizona-Nevada and Arizona-California boundaries, after which it passes into Mexico and empties into the Mexican waters of the Gulf of California. On its way to the sea it receives tributary waters from Wyoming, Colorado, Utah, Nevada, New Mexico, and Arizona. The river and its tributaries flow in a natural basin almost surrounded by large mountain ranges and drain 242,000 square miles, an area about 900 miles long from north to south and 300 to 500 miles wide from east to west—practically one-twelfth the area of the continental United States excluding Alaska. Much of this large basin is so arid that it is, as it always has been, largely dependent upon managed use of the waters of the Colorado River System to make it productive and inhabitable. The Master refers to archaeological evidence that as long as 2,000 years ago the ancient Hohokam tribe built and maintained irrigation canals near what is now Phoenix, Arizona, and that American Indians were practicing irrigation in that region at the time white men first explored it. In the second half of the nineteenth century a group of people interested in California's Imperial Valley conceived plans to divert water from the mainstream of the Colorado to give life and growth to the parched and barren soil of that valley. As the most feasible route was through Mexico, a Mexican corporation was formed and a canal dug partly in Mexico and partly in the United States. Difficulties which arose because the canal was subject to the sovereignty of both countries generated hopes in this country that some day there would be a canal wholly within the United States, an all-American canal.

During the latter part of the nineteenth and the first part of the twentieth centuries, people in the Southwest continued to seek new ways to satisfy their water needs, which by that time were increasing rapidly as new settlers moved into this fast-developing region. But

a. Boulder Canyon Project Act, 45 Stat. 1057 (1928), 43 U.S.C.A. §§ 617–617t.

none of the more or less primitive diversions made from the mainstream of the Colorado conserved enough water to meet the growing needs of the basin. The natural flow of the Colorado was too erratic, the river at many places in canyons too deep, and the engineering and economic hurdles too great for small farmers, larger groups, or even States to build storage dams, construct canals, and install the expensive works necessary for a dependable year-round water supply. Nor were droughts the basin's only problem; spring floods due to melting snows and seasonal storms were a recurring menace, especially disastrous in California's Imperial Valley where, even after the Mexican canal provided a more dependable water supply, the threat of flood remained at least as serious as before. Another troublesome problem was the erosion of land and the deposit of silt which fouled waters, choked irrigation works, and damaged good farmland and crops.

It is not surprising that the pressing necessity to transform the erratic and often destructive flow of the Colorado River into a controlled and dependable water supply desperately needed in so many States began to be talked about and recognized as far more than a purely local problem which could be solved on a farmer-by-farmer, group-by-group, or even state-by-state basis, desirable as this kind of solution might have been. * * *

The prospect that the United States would undertake to build as a national project the necessary works to control floods and store river waters for irrigation was apparently a welcome one for the basin States. But it brought to life strong fears in the northern basin States that additional waters made available by the storage and canal projects might be gobbled up in perpetuity by faster growing lower basin areas, particularly California, before the upper States could appropriate what they believed to be their fair share. These fears were not without foundation, since the law of prior appropriation prevailed in most of the Western States. Under that law the one who first appropriates water and puts it to beneficial use thereby acquires a vested right to continue to divert and use that quantity of water against all claimants junior to him in point of time. "First in time, first in right" is the short hand expression of this legal principle. * * * In view of California's phenomenal growth, the Upper Basin had particular reason to fear that California, by appropriating and using Colorado River water before the upper States, would, under the interstate application of the prior appropriation doctrine, be "first in time" and therefore "first in right." Nor were such fears limited to the northernmost States. Nevada, Utah, and especially Arizona were all apprehensive that California's rapid declaration of appropriative claims would deprive them of their just share of basin water available after construction of the proposed United States project. It seemed for a time that these fears would keep the States from agreeing on any kind of division of the river waters. Hoping to prevent "conflicts" and "expensive litigation" which would hold up or prevent the tremendous benefits expected from extensive federal development of the river, the basin States requested and Congress passed an Act on August 19, 1921, giving the States consent to negotiate and enter into a compact for the "equitable division and apportionment * * * of the water supply of the Colorado River."

Pursuant to this congressional authority, the seven States appointed Commissioners who, after negotiating for the better part of a year, reached an agreement at Santa Fe, New Mexico, on November 24, 1922. The agreement, known as the Colorado River Compact,[b] failed to fulfill the hope of Congress that the States would themselves agree on each State's share of the water. The most the Commissioners were able to accomplish in the Compact was to adopt a compromise suggestion of Secretary of Commerce Herbert Hoover, specially designated as United States representative. This compromise divides the entire basin into two parts, the Upper Basin and the Lower Basin, separated at a point on the river in northern Arizona known as Lee Ferry. Article III(a) of the Compact apportions to each basin in perpetuity 7,500,000 acre-feet of water a year from the Colorado River System, defined in Article II(a) as "the Colorado River and its tributaries within the United States of America." In addition, Article III(b) gives the Lower Basin "the right to increase its beneficial consumptive use of such waters by one million acre-feet per annum." Article III(c) provides that future Mexican water rights recognized by the United States shall be supplied first out of surplus over and above the aggregate of the quantities specified in (a) and (b), and if this surplus is not enough the deficiency shall be borne equally by the two basins. Article III(d) requires the Upper Basin not to deplete the Lee Ferry flow below an aggregate of 75,000,000 acre-feet for any 10 consecutive years. Article III(f) and (g) provide a way for further apportionment by a compact of "Colorado River System" waters at any time after October 1, 1963. While these allocations quieted rivalries between the Upper and Lower Basins, major differences between the States in the Lower Basin continued. Failure of the Compact to determine each State's share of the water left Nevada and Arizona with their fears that the law of prior appropriation would be not a protection but a menace because California could use that law to get for herself the lion's share of the waters allotted to the Lower Basin. Moreover, Arizona, because of her particularly strong interest in the Gila, intensely resented the Compact's inclusion of the Colorado River tributaries in its allocation scheme and was bitterly hostile to having Arizona tributaries, again particularly the Gila, forced to contribute to the Mexican burden. Largely for these reasons, Arizona alone, of all the States in both basins, refused to ratify the Compact.

Seeking means which would permit ratification by all seven basin States, the Governors of those States met at Denver in 1925 and again in 1927. As a result of these meetings the Governors of the upper States suggested, as a fair apportionment of water among the Lower

b. The Compact can be found at 70 Cong.Rec. 324 (1928), and U.S. Dept. of the Interior, Documents on the Use and Control of the Waters of Interstate and International Streams 39 (1956).

Basin States, that out of the average annual delivery of water at Lee Ferry required by the Compact—7,500,000 acre-feet—Nevada be given 300,000 acre-feet, Arizona 3,000,000, and California 4,200,000, and that unapportioned waters, subject to reapportionment after 1963, be shared equally by Arizona and California. * * * This proposal foundered because California held out for 4,600,000 acre-feet instead of 4,200,000 and because Arizona held out for complete exemption of its tributaries from any part of the Mexican burden.

Between 1922 and 1927 Congressman Philip Swing and Senator Hiram Johnson, both of California, made three attempts to have Swing-Johnson bills enacted, authorizing construction of a dam in the canyon section of the Colorado River and an all-American canal. * * *

Finally, the fourth Swing-Johnson bill passed both Houses and became the Boulder Canyon Project Act of December 21, 1928, 45 Stat. 1057. The Act authorized the Secretary of the Interior to construct, operate and maintain a dam and other works in order to control floods, improve navigation, regulate the river's flow, store and distribute waters for reclamation and other beneficial uses, and generate electrical power. The projects authorized by the Act were the same as those provided for in the prior defeated measures, but in other significant respects the Act was strikingly different. The earlier bills had offered no method whatever of apportioning the waters among the States of the Lower Basin. The Act as finally passed did provide such a method, and, as we view it, the method chosen was a complete statutory apportionment intended to put an end to the long-standing dispute over Colorado River waters. To protect the Upper Basin against California should Arizona still refuse to ratify the Compact, § 4(a) of the Act as finally passed provided that, if fewer than seven States ratified within six months, the Act should not take effect unless six States including California ratified and unless California, by its legislature, agreed "irrevocably and unconditionally * * * as an express covenant" to a limit on its annual consumption of Colorado River water of "four million four hundred thousand acre-feet of the waters apportioned to the lower basin States by paragraph (a) of Article III of the Colorado River compact, plus not more than one-half of any excess or surplus waters unapportioned by said compact." Congress in the same section showed its continuing desire to have California, Arizona, and Nevada settle their own differences by authorizing them to make an agreement apportioning to Nevada 300,000 acre-feet, and to Arizona 2,800,000 acre-feet plus half of any surplus waters unapportioned by the Compact. The permitted agreement also was to allow Arizona exclusive use of the Gila River, wholly free from any Mexican obligation, a position Arizona had taken from the beginning. Sections 5 and 8(b) of the Project Act made provisions for the sale of the stored waters. The Secretary of the Interior was authorized by § 5 "under such general regulations as he may prescribe, to contract for the storage of water in said reservoir and for the delivery thereof at such points on the river and on said canal as may be agreed upon, for irrigation and domestic uses * * *." Section 5 required these contracts to be "for permanent service" and further provided, "No person shall have or be entitled to have the use for any purpose of the water stored as aforesaid except by contract made as herein stated." Section 8(b) provided that the Secretary's contracts would be subject to any compact dividing the benefits of the water between Arizona, California, and Nevada, or any two of them, approved by Congress on or before January 1, 1929, but that any such compact approved after that date should be "subject to all contracts, if any, made by the Secretary of the Interior under section 5 hereof prior to the date of such approval and consent by Congress."

The Project Act became effective on June 25, 1929, by Presidential Proclamation, after six States, including California, had ratified the Colorado River Compact and the California legislature had accepted the limitation of 4,400,000 acre-feet as required by the Act. Neither the three States nor any two of them ever entered into any apportionment compact as authorized by §§ 4(a) and 8(b). After the construction of Boulder Dam the Secretary of the Interior, purporting to act under the authority of the Project Act, made contracts with various water users in California for 5,362,000 acre-feet, with Nevada for 300,000 acre-feet, and with Arizona for 2,800,000 acre-feet of water from that stored at Lake Mead.

The Special Master appointed by this Court found that the Colorado River Compact, the law of prior appropriation, and the doctrine of equitable apportionment—by which doctrine this Court in the absence of statute resolves interstate claims according to the equities—do not control the issues in this case. The Master concluded that, since the Lower Basin States had failed to make a compact to allocate the waters among themselves as authorized by §§ 4(a) and 8(b), the Secretary's contracts with the States had within the statutory scheme of §§ 4(a), 5, and 8(b) effected an apportionment of the waters of the mainstream which, according to the Master, were the only waters to be apportioned under the Act. The Master further held that, in the event of a shortage of water making it impossible for the Secretary to supply all the water due California, Arizona, and Nevada under their contracts, the burden of the shortage must be borne by each State in proportion to her share of the first 7,500,000 acre-feet allocated to the Lower Basin, that is, $\frac{4.4}{7.5}$ by California, $\frac{2.8}{7.5}$ by Arizona, and $\frac{.3}{7.5}$ by Nevada, without regard to the law of prior appropriation.

Arizona, Nevada, and the United States support with few exceptions the analysis, conclusions, and recommendations of the Special Master's report. * * *

California is in basic disagreement with almost all of the Master's Report. * * *

I.

ALLOCATION OF WATER AMONG THE STATES AND DISTRIBUTION TO USERS

We have concluded, for reasons to be stated, that Congress in passing the Project Act intended to and did create its own comprehensive scheme for the apportionment among California, Arizona, and Nevada of the Lower Basin's share of the mainstream waters of the Colorado River, leaving each State its tributaries. Congress decided that a fair division of the first 7,500,000 acre-feet of such mainstream waters would give 4,400,000 acre-feet to California, 2,800,000 to Arizona, and 300,000 to Nevada; Arizona and California would each get one-half of any surplus. Prior approval was therefore given in the Act for a tri-state compact to incorporate these terms. The States, subject to subsequent congressional approval, were also permitted to agree on a compact with different terms. Division of the water did not, however, depend on the States' agreeing to a compact, for Congress gave the Secretary of the Interior adequate authority to accomplish the division. Congress did this by giving the Secretary power to make contracts for the delivery of water and by providing that no person could have water without a contract.

A. *Relevancy of Judicial Apportionment and Colorado River Compact.*—We agree with the Master that apportionment of the Lower Basin waters of the Colorado River is not controlled by the doctrine of equitable apportionment or by the Colorado River Compact. It is true that the Court has used the doctrine of equitable apportionment to decide river controversies between States. But in those cases Congress had not made any statutory apportionment. In this case, we have decided that Congress has provided its own method for allocating among the Lower Basin States the mainstream water to which they are entitled under the Compact. Where Congress has so exercised its constitutional power over waters courts have no power to substitute their own notions of an "equitable apportionment" for the apportionment chosen by Congress. Nor does the Colorado River Compact control this case. Nothing in that Compact purports to divide water among the Lower Basin States nor in any way to affect or control any future apportionment among those States or any distribution of water within a State. * * *

B. *Mainstream Apportionment.*—The congressional scheme of apportionment cannot be understood without knowing what water Congress wanted apportioned. Under California's view, which we reject, the first 7,500,000 acre-feet of Lower Basin water, of which California has agreed to use only 4,400,000, is made up of both mainstream and tributary water, not just mainstream water. Under the view of Arizona, Nevada, and the United States, with which we agree, the tributaries are not included in the waters to be divided but remain for the exclusive use of each State. Assuming 7,500,000 acre-feet or more in the mainstream and 2,000,000 in the tributaries, California would get

1,000,000 acre-feet more if the tributaries are included and Arizona 1,000,000 less. * * *

C. *The Project Act's Apportionment and Distribution Scheme.*— The legislative history, the language of the Act, and the scheme established by the Act, for the storage and delivery of water convince us also that Congress intended to provide its own method for a complete apportionment of the mainstream water among Arizona, California, and Nevada. * * *

In the first section of the Act, the Secretary was authorized to "construct, operate, and maintain a dam and incidental works * * * adequate to create a storage reservoir of a capacity of not less than twenty million acre-feet of water * * *" for the stated purpose of "controlling the floods, improving navigation and regulating the flow of the Colorado River, providing for storage and for the delivery of the stored waters thereof for reclamation of public lands and other beneficial uses * * *," and generating electrical power. The whole point of the Act was to replace the erratic, undependable, often destructive natural flow of the Colorado with the regular, dependable release of waters conserved and stored by the project. Having undertaken this beneficial project, Congress, in several provisions of the Act, made it clear that no one should use mainstream waters save in strict compliance with the scheme set up by the Act. Section 5 authorized the Secretary "under such general regulations as he may prescribe, to contract for the storage of water in said reservoir and for the delivery thereof at such points on the river * * * as may be agreed upon, for irrigation and domestic uses * * *." To emphasize that water could be obtained from the Secretary alone, § 5 further declared, "No person shall have or be entitled to have the use for any purpose of the water stored as aforesaid except by contract made as herein stated." The supremacy given the Secretary's contracts was made clear in § 8(b) of the Act, which provided that, while the Lower Basin States were free to negotiate a compact dividing the waters, such a compact if made and approved after January 1, 1929, was to be "subject to all contracts, if any, made by the Secretary of the Interior under section 5" before Congress approved the compact.

These several provisions, even without legislative history, are persuasive that Congress intended the Secretary of the Interior, through his § 5 contracts, both to carry out the allocation of the waters of the main Colorado River among the Lower Basin States and to decide which users within each State would get water. The general authority to make contracts normally includes the power to choose with whom and upon what terms the contracts will be made. When Congress in an Act grants authority to contract, that authority is no less than the general authority, unless Congress has placed some limit on it. * * *

III.

APPORTIONMENT AND CONTRACTS IN TIME OF SHORTAGE

We have agreed with the Master that the Secretary's contracts with Arizona for 2,800,000 acre-feet of water and with Nevada for 300,000, together with the limitation of California to 4,400,000 acre-feet, effect a valid apportionment of the first 7,500,000 acre-feet of mainstream water in the Lower Basin. There remains the question of what shall be done in time of shortage. The Master, while declining to make any findings as to what future supply might be expected, nevertheless decided that the Project Act and the Secretary's contracts require the Secretary in case of shortage to divide the burden among the three States in this Proportion: California $\frac{4.4}{7.5}$; Arizona $\frac{2.8}{7.5}$; Nevada $\frac{.3}{7.5}$ While pro rata sharing of water shortages seems equitable on its face, more considered judgment may demonstrate quite the contrary. Certainly we should not bind the Secretary to this formula. We have held that the Secretary is vested with considerable control over the apportionment of Colorado River waters. And neither the Project Act nor the water contracts require the use of any particular formula for apportioning shortages. While the Secretary must follow the standards set out in the Act, he nevertheless is free to choose among the recognized methods of apportionment or to devise reasonable methods of his own. This choice, as we see it, is primarily his, not the Master's or even ours. And the Secretary may or may not conclude that a pro rata division is the best solution.

It must be remembered that the Secretary's decision may have an effect not only on irrigation uses but also on other important functions for which Congress brought this great project into being—flood control, improvement of navigation, regulation of flow, and generation and distribution of electric power. Requiring the Secretary to prorate shortages would strip him of the very power of choice which we think Congress, for reasons satisfactory to it, vested in him and which we should not impair or take away from him. For the same reasons we cannot accept California's contention that in case of shortage each State's share of water should be determined by the judicial doctrine of equitable apportionment or by the law of prior appropriation. These principles, while they may provide some guidance, are not binding upon the Secretary where, as here, Congress, with full power to do so, has provided that the waters of a navigable stream shall be harnessed, conserved, stored, and distributed through a government agency under a statutory scheme.

None of this is to say that in case of shortage, the Secretary cannot adopt a method of proration or that he may not lay stress upon priority for use, local laws and customs, or any other factors that might be helpful in reaching an informed judgment in harmony with the Act, the best interests of the Basin States, and the welfare of the Nation. It will be time enough for the courts to intervene when and if the Secretary, in making apportionments or contracts, deviates from the standards Congress has set for him to follow, including his obligation to respect "present perfected rights" as of the date the Act was passed. At this time the Secretary has made no decision at all based on an actual or anticipated shortage of water, and so there is no action of his in this respect for us to review. Finally, as the Master pointed out, Congress still has broad powers over this navigable international stream. Congress can undoubtedly reduce or enlarge the Secretary's power if it wishes. Unless and until it does, we leave in the hands of the Secretary, where Congress placed it, full power to control, manage, and operate the Government's Colorado River works and to make contracts for the sale and delivery of water on such terms as are not prohibited by the Project Act. * * *

THE CHIEF JUSTICE took no part in the consideration or decision of this case.

MR. JUSTICE HARLAN, whom MR. JUSTICE DOUGLAS and MR. JUSTICE STEWART join, dissenting in part.

I dissent from so much of the Court's opinion as holds that the Secretary of the Interior has been given authority by Congress to apportion, among and within the States of California, Arizona, and Nevada, the waters of the mainstream of the Colorado River below Lee Ferry. * * *

(In * * * other respects MR. JUSTICE STEWART and I—but not MR. JUSTICE DOUGLAS—agree with and join in the Court's opinion. * * *

In my view, it is the equitable principles established by the Court in interstate water-rights cases, as modified by the Colorado River Compact and the California limitation, that were intended by Congress to govern the apportionment of mainstream waters among the Lower Basin States, whether in surplus or in shortage. * * *

The Court's conclusions respecting the Secretary's apportionment powers, particularly those in times of shortage, result in a single appointed federal official being vested with absolute control, unrestrained by adequate standards, over the fate of a substantial segment of the life and economy of three States. Such restraint upon his actions as may follow from judicial review are, as will be shown, at best illusory. Today's result, I venture to say, would have dumbfounded those responsible for the legislation the Court construes, for nothing could have been farther from their minds or more inconsistent with their deeply felt convictions.

The Court professes to find this extraordinary delegation of power principally in § 5 of the Project Act, the provision authorizing the Secretary to enter into contracts for the storage and delivery of water. But § 5, as is more fully shown below, 83 S.Ct. pp. 1505–1508, infra, had no design resembling that which the Court now extracts from it.

Rather it was intended principally as a revenue measure, and the clause *requiring* a contract as a condition of delivery was inserted at the insistence not of the Lower but of the Upper Basin States in an effort to insure that nothing would disturb that basin's rights under the Colorado River Compact. There was no thought that § 5 would give authority to apportion water among the Lower Basin States. * * *

It is manifest that § 4(a), on which the Court so heavily relies, neither apportions the waters of the river nor vests power in any official to make such an apportionment. The first paragraph does not *grant* any water to anyone; it merely conditions the Act's effectiveness on seven-state ratification of the Compact or on six-state ratification, plus California's agreement to a limitation, *i.e.,* a *ceiling,* on her appropriations. The source of authority to make such appropriations must be found elsewhere. And the second paragraph of § 4(a), suggesting a particular interstate agreement, similarly makes no apportionment of water among the States and delegates no power to any official to make such an apportionment. * * *

MR. JUSTICE DOUGLAS, dissenting.

This case, I think, has been haunted by several irrelevancies. * * *

Third, is a mood about the controversy that suggests that here, as in the cases involving multipurpose federal dams, federal control of navigable streams controls this litigation. The right of the Federal Government to the flow of the stream is not an issue here. * * *

At issue on the other main phase of the case is the meaning of the California limitation contained in § 4(a) of the Project Act. The Court, however, does not use the present litigation as an occasion to determine Arizona's and California's rights under the Act, but as a vehicle for making a wholly new apportionment of the waters in the Lower Basin and turning over all unresolved problems to the Secretary of the Interior. The Court accomplishes this by distorting both the history and language of the Project Act.

The Court relies heavily on the terms and history of a proposed tri-state compact, authorized by § 4(a) *but never adopted by the States concerned, viz., Arizona, California and Nevada.* The proposed tri-state compact provided for a division of tributary waters identical to that made by the Court, insofar as the Gila is awarded to Arizona. The Court in reality enforces its interpretation of the proposed tri-state compact and imposes its terms upon California. * * *

Notes

1. Congress had previously made a different sort of "equitable apportionment of benefits resulting from the flow of the river." (Kansas v. Colorado, supra p. 580.) The Colorado River Storage Act, 70 Stat. 105 (1956), 43 U.S.C.A. § 620, provides for four great storage dams and hydroelectric power plants in the upper basin, and "participating projects" for

irrigation, part of the costs of which will be repaid from power revenues from the storage dams. The Act apportions this benefit by assigning these funds for use in the states of the upper basin in proportion to the amount of the flow of the river arising in each state.

2. For discussions of this phase of the case, See Trelease, Arizona v. California: Allocation of Water Resources to People, States and Nation, 1963 Supreme Court Rev. 158, 166–183; Clyde, The Colorado River Decision—1963, 8 Utah L.Rev. 299, 308–312 (1964); Wilmer, Arizona v. California, a Statutory Construction Case, 6 Ariz.L.Rev. 40, 54–64 (1964).

3. As a means of settling interstate controversies over the allocation of water, judicial apportionment is criticized and congressional apportionment is praised in Meyers, The Colorado River, 19 Stanford L.Rev. 1 (1966). Dean Meyers also sees advantages of Congressional action over negotiated interstate compacts.

4. Except for the Boulder Canyon Project Act, as construed in Arizona v. California, Congress has never simply divided a river among the states through which it flows. It is probable that a partial allocation of water to a state accompanies any federal project on an interstate river. This was not always recognized as true. The original Colorado River Compact of 1922 allocated 7.5 million acre feet per year to the states of the upper basin, subject to an obligation to deliver a like amount to the lower basin. At the close of World War II the Bureau of Reclamation announced a plan for the development of the upper basin, listing a number of possible projects in each state. However, the Secretary of the Interior announced that he would not push for congressional authorization of the projects until the upper basin states had reached agreement on their respective shares of the water allocated to that basin. House Doc. No. 419, 80th Cong. 1st Sess., 1947. The Bureau had no wish to construct a project within a state and later find that that state did not have a legal claim to sufficient water for it. Since Arizona v. California, this fear can be seen as unfounded. The water needed by each could be said to have been allocated by the authorizing legislation, and thus placed beyond the power of Court or states to reassign. A basin-wide federal project with structures and operations in several states would have the same effect.

5. An interstate case pending in the United States Supreme Court asserts that Congress made an apportionment of the Missouri River in the Flood Control Act of 1944. Recall Missouri v. Andrews, supra, p. 614, brought by the downstream states against the federal officers who share control of the Pick-Sloan Plan, which includes Oahe Dam in South Dakota, built by the Corps of Engineers for navigation, power and irrigation purposes. The United States District Court for the District of Nebraska ruled that the Bureau of Reclamation had no authority to issue a water service contract to supply a coal slurry pipeline with water for industrial purposes, that it was the Corps of Engineers that had jurisdiction to contract for the sale of surplus water from the dam.

The State of South Dakota was excluded from that suit. South Dakota counter-attacked with a suit in the original jurisdiction of the Supreme Court, South Dakota v. Nebraska, Iowa and Missouri, No. ——, Original, October Term 1985. South Dakota contends that the claims of the downstream states and the decree in *Andrews* cast a cloud on her sovereign powers, that diversions of her share of the Missouri's waters can lawfully be made only pursuant to a permit from South Dakota, and that in operating the dams and reservoirs within the state's boundaries, the Bureau and the Corps provide water storage only, they do not provide water or grant water rights.

South Dakota argues that the Flood Control Act provides a congressional apportionment of a portion of the waters of the Missouri River to the State of South Dakota, with certain rights and duties delegated to the Secretary of the Army, and with other rights and duties, including the right to contract for the storage of the waters, delegated to the Secretary of the Interior, both of whom must conform to applicable state water laws in exercising their functions. Particular reliance is placed on the O'Mahoney-Millikin Amendment to the Act,' which provides,

> The use for navigation * * * shall be only such use as does not conflict with any beneficial consumptive use, present or future, [in the upstream states] of such waters for domestic, municipal, stock water, irrigation, mining, or industrial purposes.

The legislative history of this preference of upstream consumptive uses over downstream navigation is said to be to confirm and protect "the historic and traditional rights of the people of the west to use the water rising in the west in the manner which has been recognized by law, and by court decision for almost 100 years."

The state does not seek a literal allocation of a specified portion of the water to it. The prayer of the complaint is that the court should adjudicate and declare, in the nature of a quiet title action, the right, power and authority of South Dakota to use or allocate the waters of the Missouri River stored for reclamation and irrigation purposes behind mainstream dams within its territorial boundaries, in accord with the provisions, intent and history of the Flood Control Act of 1944 and the Reclamation laws.

The Flood Control Act and its history are exhaustively analyzed in Guhin, The Law of the Missouri, 30 So.Dak.L.Rev. 347 (1985). Wright Water Engineers and F. Trelease, A Water Protection Strategy for Montana (Montana Department of Natural Resources and Conservation 1982) assesses existing and potential interstate conflicts in the Missouri basin, their economic impact, and the legal aspects of solutions by equitable apportionment, interstate compact, and congressional action.

6. Modern water problems increase in size and spread across state lines. Compacts and decrees have been criticized as inflexible, as time has demonstrated that needs develop in ways different from those envisioned when the pact was negotiated or the judgment handed down. Needs arise in one state that call for the importation in interstate commerce of supplies of *intrastate* sources in a neighboring state. See Sporhase v. Nebraska, infra p. 671. These barriers to practical solutions of regional problems, and their possible judicial and legislative solutions (including the *reallocation* of compacted and decreed water), are discussed in Simms, Water Transfers Across States Systems, 31 Rocky Mtn. Mineral L. Institute —— (1985).

Chapter 8

FEDERAL WATER LAW

SECTION 1. NATIONAL POWERS AND PROGRAMS

UNITED STATES v. APPALACHIAN ELECTRIC POWER CO.

Supreme Court of the United States, 1940.
311 U.S. 377, 61 S.Ct. 291, 85 L.Ed. 243.

MR. JUSTICE REED delivered the opinion of the Court.

This case involves the scope of the federal commerce power in relation to conditions in licenses, required by the Federal Power Commission, for the construction of hydroelectric dams in navigable rivers of the United States. To reach this issue requires, preliminarily, a decision as to the navigability of the New River, a watercourse flowing through Virginia and West Virginia. The district court and the circuit court of appeals have both held that the New River is not navigable, and that the United States cannot enjoin the respondent from constructing and putting into operation a hydroelectric dam situated in the river just above Radford, Virginia.

Sections 9 and 10 of the Rivers and Harbors Act of 1899 make it unlawful to construct a dam in any navigable water of the United States without the consent of Congress. By the Federal Water Power Act of 1920, however, Congress created a Federal Power Commission with authority to license the construction of such dams upon specified conditions. Section 23 of that Act provided that persons intending to construct a dam in a nonnavigable stream may file a declaration of intention with the Commission. If after investigation the Commission finds that the interests of interstate or foreign commerce will not be affected, permission shall be granted for the construction. Otherwise construction cannot go forward without a license.

The Radford Dam project was initiated by respondent's predecessor, the New River Development Company, which filed its declaration of intention with the Federal Power Commission on June 25, 1925. * * *

On July 1, 1927, the Commission tendered to respondent a standard form license which the respondent refused in April, 1928, principally on the ground that the conditions—especially those concerning rates, accounts and eventual acquisition—were unrelated to navigation. * * *

The respondent began construction work on the dam about June 1, 1934. On May 6, 1935, the United States filed this bill for an injunction against the construction or maintenance of the proposed dam otherwise than under a license from the Federal Power Commission, and in the alternative a mandatory order of removal. * * *

After trial, in an opinion reinforced by formal findings of fact and law, the district court decided that the New River is not a navigable water of the United States. * * * The district court's finding that the New River was not navigable was concurred in by the circuit court of appeals after a careful appraisal of the evidence in the record. * * *

The power of the United States over its waters which are capable of use as interstate highways arises from the commerce clause of the Constitution, art. 1, § 8, cl. 3. "The Congress shall have Power * * * To regulate Commerce * * * among the several States." It was held early in our history that the power to regulate commerce necessarily included power over navigation.[a] To make its control effective the Congress may keep the "navigable waters of the United States" open and free and provide by sanctions against any interference with the country's water assets.[b] It may legislate to forbid or license dams in the waters;[c] its power over improvements for navigation in rivers is "absolute."[d] * * *

The navigability of the New River is, of course, a factual question but to call it a fact cannot obscure the diverse elements that enter into the application of the legal tests as to navigability. We are dealing here with the sovereign powers of the Union, the Nation's right that its waterways be utilized for the interests of the commerce of the whole country. It is obvious that the uses to which the streams may be put vary from the carriage of ocean liners to the floating out of logs; that the density of traffic varies equally widely from the busy harbors of the seacoast to the sparsely settled regions of the Western mountains. The tests as to navigability must take these variations into consideration.

a. Gibbons v. Ogden, 9 Wheat. 1, 189, 6 L.Ed. 23; Leovy v. United States, 177 U.S. 621, 632, 20 S.Ct. 797, 801, 44 L.Ed. 914.

b. Gilman v. Philadelphia, 3 Wall. 713, 724, 725, 18 L.Ed. 96; United States v. Coombs, 12 Pet. 72, 78, 9 L.Ed. 1004.

c. Willson v. Black Bird Creek Marsh Co., 2 Pet. 245, 250, 7 L.Ed. 412; United States v. Rio Grande Irrigation Co., 174 U.S. 690, 703, 19 S.Ct. 770, 775, 43 L.Ed. 1136.

d. United States v. River Rouge Co., 269 U.S. 411, 419, 46 S.Ct. 144, 147, 70 L.Ed. 339.

Both lower courts based their investigation primarily upon the generally accepted definition of The Daniel Ball.[e] In so doing they were in accord with the rulings of this Court on the basic concept of navigability. Each application of this test, however, is apt to uncover variations and refinements which require further elaboration.

In the lower courts and here, the Government urges that the phrase "susceptible of being used, in their ordinary condition," in the Daniel Ball definition, should not be construed as eliminating the possibility of determining navigability in the light of the effect of reasonable improvements. * * *

To appraise the evidence of navigability on the natural condition only of the waterway is erroneous. Its availability for navigation must also be considered. "Natural or ordinary conditions" refers to volume of water, the gradients and the regularity of the flow. A waterway, otherwise suitable for navigation, is not barred from that classification merely because artificial aids must make the highway suitable for use before commercial navigation may be undertaken. Congress has recognized this in section 3 of the Water Power Act by defining "navigable waters" as those "which either in their natural or improved condition" are used or suitable for use. * * *

Although navigability to fix ownership of the river bed or riparian rights is determined as of the formation of the Union in the original states or the admission to statehood of those formed later, navigability, for the purpose of the regulation of commerce, may later arise. An analogy is found in admiralty jurisdiction, which may be extended over places formerly nonnavigable. * * *

New River may be said to assume its character as such at the mouth of Wilson Creek near the North Carolina-Virginia line. From that point it flows first in a northeast and then in a northwest direction something over 250 miles to Kanawha Falls, West Virginia. It passes through Allisonia and Radford, Virginia, and then Hinton, West Virginia. It is joined by many tributaries, the largest of which is the Gauley. At Kanawha Falls, it changes its name to the Kanawha, a navigable river of commercial importance which joins the Ohio 97 miles below. The whole territory traversed by the New is broken and mountainous. Between Hinton and Kanawha Falls, the river is swift and the gorge precipitous. Above Hinton the river flows more slowly,

e. 10 Wall. 557, 563, 19 L.Ed. 999:

"* * * Those rivers must be regarded as public navigable rivers in law which are navigable in fact. And they are navigable in fact when they are used, or are susceptible of being used, in their ordinary condition, as highways for commerce, over which trade and travel are or may be conducted in the customary modes of trade and travel on water. And they constitute navigable waters of the United States within the meaning of the acts of Congress, in contradistinction from the navigable waters of the States, when they form in their ordinary condition by themselves, or by uniting with other waters, a continued highway over which commerce is or may be carried on with other States or foreign countries in the customary modes in which such commerce is conducted by water."

through a broader valley and between less rugged mountains. The same may be said of the area above Radford. Throughout the river there is an abundance of water, and the respondent hardly denies that the flowage suffices if other conditions make the New available for navigation. * * *

[The evidence showed fairly extensive commercial navigation in the 1870's and 80's by flatbottomed keelboats, carrying 10 to 12 tons of lumber, tobacco, iron and transhipped rail freight, in the 24 and 28 miles stretches above Radford and Hinton. The "crucial" 59 mile intermediate stretch varied from "good water" with a fall of 4 feet or less to the mile, to rapids and small falls with grades of 8, 9, and even 11½ feet to the mile. It had been traversed in both directions by various types of boats, but only sporadically and with difficulty. In 1872 the Corps of Engineers reported this stretch could be improved for the typical light commercial traffic of the time. Improvements costing $109,000 were made between 1877 and 1891 in the reaches above Radford and Hinton. Plans for improving the intermediate stretch were abandoned when the region's need for river transportation declined, and in 1912 the Corps referred to the cost of further improvements as "prohibitive."]

From the use of the Radford-Wiley's Falls stretch and the evidence as to its ready improvability at a low cost for easier keelboat use, we conclude that this section of the New River is navigable. It follows from this, together with the undisputed commercial use of the two stretches above Radford and Hinton, that the New River from Allisonia, Virginia, to Hinton, West Virginia, is a navigable water of the United States. * * * But even accepting the navigability of the New River, the respondent urges that certain provisions of the license, which seek to control affairs of the licensee, are unconnected with navigation and are beyond the power of the Commission, indeed beyond the constitutional power of Congress to authorize. * * *

There is no contention that the provisions of the license are not authorized by the statute. In the note below [f] the chief statutory conditions for a license are epitomized. The license offered the respon-

f. § 4(a) of the Act allows the Commission to regulate the licensee's accounts.

§ 6 limits licenses to 50 years.

§ 8 requires Commission approval for voluntary transfers of licenses or rights granted thereunder.

§ 10(a), as amended in 1935, requires that the project be best adapted to a comprehensive plan for improving or developing the waterway for the use or benefit of interstate or foreign commerce, for the improvement and utilization of water-power development, and for other beneficial public uses, including recreational purposes. Under § 10(c) the licensee must maintain the project adequately for navigation and for efficient power operation, must maintain depreciation reserves adequate for renewals and replacements, and must conform to the Commission's regulations for the protection of life, health and property; (d) out of surplus earned after the first 20 years above a specified reasonable rate of return, the licensee must maintain amortization reserves to be applied in reduction of net investment; (e) the licensee must pay the United States reasonable annual charges for administering the Act, and during the first 20 years the United States is to expropriate excessive profits until the state prevents such profits; (f) the licensee may be ordered to reimburse those by whose construction work it is benefited.

dent on May 5, 1931, embodied these statutory requirements and we assume it to be in conformity with the existing administration of the Power Act. We shall pass upon the validity of only those provisions of the license called to our attention by the respondent as being unrelated to the purposes of navigation. These are the conditions derived from sections 10(a), 10(c), 10(d), 10(e) and 14. * * *

The respondent is a riparian owner with a valid state license to use the natural resources of the state for its enterprise. Consequently it has as complete a right to the use of the riparian lands, the water, and the river bed as can be obtained under state law. The state and respondent, alike, however, hold the waters and the lands under them subject to the power of Congress to control the waters for the purpose of commerce. The power flows from the grant to regulate, i.e., to "prescribe the rule by which commerce is to be governed." This includes the protection of navigable waters in capacity as well as use. This power of Congress to regulate commerce is so unfettered that its judgment as to whether a structure is or is not a hindrance is conclusive. Its determination is legislative in character. The Federal Government has domination over the water power inherent in the flowing stream. It is liable to no one for its use or non-use. The flow of a navigable stream is in no sense private property; "that the running water in a great navigable stream is capable of private ownership is inconceivable." Exclusion of riparian owners from its benefits without compensation is entirely within the Government's discretion.

Possessing this plenary power to exclude structures from navigable waters and dominion over flowage and its product, energy, the United States may make the erection or maintenance of a structure in a navigable water dependent upon a license. * * *

In our view, it cannot properly be said that the constitutional power of the United States over its waters is limited to control for navigation. By navigation respondent means no more than operation of boats and improvement of the waterway itself. In truth the authority of the United States is the regulation of commerce on its waters. Navigability, in the sense just stated, is but a part of this whole. Flood protection, watershed development, recovery of the cost of improvements through utilization of power are likewise parts of commerce control. As respondent soundly argues, the United States cannot by calling a project of its own "a multiple purpose dam" give to itself additional powers, but equally truly the respondent cannot, by seeking to use a navigable waterway for power generation alone, avoid the

By § 11, for projects in navigable waters of the United States the Commission may require the licensee to construct locks, etc., and to furnish the United States free of cost (a) lands and rights-of-way to improve navigation facilities, and (b) power for operating such facilities.

§ 14 gives the United States the right, upon expiration of a license, to take over and operate the project by paying the licensee's "net investment" as defined, not to exceed fair value of the property taken. However, the right of the United States or any state or municipality to condemn the project at any time is expressly reserved.

§ 19 allows state regulation of service and rates; if none exists, the Commission may exercise such jurisdiction.

authority of the Government over the stream. That authority is as broad as the needs of commerce. Water power development from dams in navigable streams is from the public's standpoint a by-product of the general use of the rivers for commerce. To this general power, the respondent must submit its single purpose of electrical production. The fact that the Commission is willing to give a license for a power dam only is of no significance in appraising the type of conditions allowable. It may well be that this portion of the river is not needed for navigation at this time. Or that the dam proposed may function satisfactory with others, contemplated or intended. It may fit in as a part of the river development. The point is that navigable waters are subject to national planning and control in the broad regulation of commerce granted the Federal Government. The license conditions to which objection is made have an obvious relationship to the exercise of the commerce power. Even if there were no such relationship the plenary power of Congress over navigable waters would empower it to deny the privilege of constructing an obstruction in those waters. It may likewise grant the privilege on terms. * * *

The respondent urges that as riparian owner with state approval of its plans, it is entitled to freedom in the development of its property and particularly cannot be compelled to submit to the acquisition clause with a price fixed at less than a fair value, in the eminent domain sense, at the time of taking. Such a taking, it is contended, would violate the Fifth Amendment. It is now a question whether the Government in taking over the property may do so at less than a fair value. It has been shown, note 77, supra, that there is no private property in the flow of the stream. This has no assessable value to the riparian owner. If the Government were now to build the dam, it would have to pay the fair value, judicially determined, for the fast land; nothing for the water power. We assume without deciding that by compulsion of the method of acquisition provided in section 14 of the Power Act and the tendered license, these riparian rights may pass to the United States for less than their value. In our view this "is the price which [respondents] must pay to secure the right to maintain their dam." * * *

Reversed and remanded to the District Court with instructions to enter an order enjoining the construction, maintenance or operation of the Radford project otherwise than under a license, accepted by the respondent within a reasonable time, substantially in the form tendered respondent by the Federal Power Commission. * * *

Notes

1. In 1890, Congress prohibited the creation of obstructions to the navigable capacity of any waters in respect of which the United States has jurisdiction. (26 Stat. 426, 454). This was held to apply to an irrigation project in the nonnavigable upper reaches of the Rio Grande in New Mexico in United States v. Rio Grande Dam and Irrigation Co., 174 U.S.

690, 19 S.Ct. 770, 43 L.Ed. 1136 (1899). "It is not a prohibition of any obstruction to the navigation, but any obstruction to the navigable capacity, and anything, wherever done or however done, within the limits of the jurisdiction of the United States which tends to destroy the navigable capacity of one of the navigable waters of the United States, is within the terms of the prohibition. [The power of the state to authorize the appropriation of water] is limited by the superior power of the General Government to secure the uninterrupted navigability of all navigable streams within the limits of the United States."

2. If the United States has the power to prevent obstruction of navigable waters, it may choose to exercise that power selectively, as in the licensing program of the Federal Power Act.

Section 23(b) of that act permits the Commission to require a license for a project on non-navigable waters "if the interests of interstate or foreign commerce" will be affected, and in practice the Commission has chosen to insist on licenses for practically all projects that have material effects upon stream flow. In Federal Power Commission v. Union Electric Co., 381 U.S. 90, 85 S.Ct. 1253, 14 L.Ed.2d 239 (1965), the Commission sought to compel a license for a "pumped storage" project which utilized the headwaters of a navigable river over and over but which did not affect their downstream flow. Pumped storage facilities are used in conjunction with steam power plants, which have a relatively inflexible output. Water from a high reservoir is released through turbines to generate high-priced power during periods of peak demand. It is caught in a lower reservoir, and during periods of low demand is pumped back uphill to the high reservoir, using the cheap stand-by power generated by the steam plant. Although there was no depletion of the flow of the downstream navigable waters by the Union Electric plant, the Court held that the fact that the power generated was transmitted across state lines gave the Commission jurisdiction. The Court said, "The language of the Act, in our view, plainly requires a license in the circumstances of this case. Section 23(b) prohibits construction of nonlicensed hydroelectric projects on navigable streams, regardless of any effect, detrimental or beneficial, on navigation or commerce by water and requires those proposing a project on a nonnavigable stream to file a declaration of intention and to come before the Commission for a determination of whether the 'interests of interstate or foreign commerce would be affected,' a determination which obviously does not speak in terms of the interests of navigation or water commerce. Plainly the provision does not require a license only where 'the interests of interstate or foreign commerce *on navigable waters* would be affected.' Although transportation on interstate waterways is interstate commerce, the phrase 'affect the interests of commerce' on its face hardly supports any claim that Congress sought to regulate only such transportation. Rather, it strongly implies that Congress drew upon its full authority under the Commerce Clause, including but not limited to its power over water commerce." Three justices dissented, on the ground that the legislative history revealed an express Congressional intent to limit the application of the licensing provisions to projects affecting navigable waters, as shown in part by the fact that the act exempts steam power plants even though they transmit their energy across state lines. Licenses have since been retroactively required of projects previously exempted from licensing because they did not affect navigability, see Nantahala Power & Light Co. v. F.P.C., 384 F.2d 200 (4th Cir.1967), certiorari denied 390 U.S. 945, 88 S.Ct. 1030, 19 L.Ed.2d 1134 (1968).

In Chemehuevi Tribe of Indians v. FPC, 420 U.S. 395, 95 S.Ct. 1066, 43 L.Ed.2d 279 (1974), certain Indian tribes and environmental groups filed a complaint with the Federal Power Commission asking it to assert jurisdiction over a group of electric utilities constructing six steam-electric generating plants in the Colorado River basin. Complainants contended that licenses were required for such plants on the ground that all were "project works" within the meaning of section 4(e) of the Act and two plants would utilize "surplus water" from Federal dams on the Colorado. The Commission dismissed the complaint, finding the complainants' contentions were refuted by the Act's legislative history, the Commission's long-standing administrative construction of the Act, and the Supreme Court's decision in FPC v. Union Electric Co.

The Court of Appeals for the District of Columbia Circuit affirmed the Commission's decision that the plants were not "project works" within the meaning of the Act, but reversed the Commission's interpretation of its "surplus water" jurisdiction, which it found had a broader purpose than the "project works" clause. It therefore remanded the case to the FPC for a determination as to whether any of the plants were in fact using such "surplus waters" for cooling purposes. The Supreme Court reversed in an 8–0 decision, affirming the FPC's reading of the Act, its legislative history, and the Court's *Union Electric* decision. Recognizing the broader sweep of Congressional power, the Court held that the 1920 Federal Water Power Act was nevertheless intended to regulate only the development of *water power* through the use of hydroelectric generating facilities.

All functions of the Federal Power Commission, including hydroelectric licensing, were transferred to the Federal Energy Regulatory Commission within the Department of Energy by the Energy Reorganization Act of 1977, 91 Stat. 565, 42 U.S.C.A. §§ 7171, 7172(a)(1)(A).

3. The United States also uses its powers over navigable waters affirmatively as the basis for an extensive program of river and harbor improvement projects. The federal program of navigation improvement had its start in 1824, when Congress first used the officers of the Corps of Engineers of the United States Army to remove a few snags and sandbars that were interfering with navigation on the Mississippi and Ohio Rivers. In many Rivers and Harbors bills Congress has authorized and appropriated funds for dredging, protective works, locks and dams to store water for release during low flows. The National Water Commission reported that the United States now has more than 25,000 miles of commercially navigable waterways, more than 15,000 have depths of nine feet or more, almost 9,000 with a depth of twelve feet or more. Of special note is the system in the Mississippi River Basin, which has 9,000 miles of federally improved waterways extending from the Gulf of Mexico to the upper reaches of the Mississippi and Ohio Rivers and to established ports well up on the Arkansas, Tennessee, Cumberland, and Missouri Rivers, connecting with Lake Michigan through the Illinois River. The Gulf Intra-Coastal Water-

way is another heavily used component. Commercial traffic on the inland waterway system totaled about 204 billion ton-miles in 1970, about 10% of the nation's inter-city traffic. Over 1800 transportation companies operate on the waterways, using 24,000 vessels and barges.

No tolls are charged for the use of federal navigation facilities, except on the St. Lawrence Seaway, although Congress has occasionally required certain local interests especially benefited to contribute cash, lands, or work for the construction of the project. See the comments of the National Water Commission, Water Policies for the Future 111–118 (1973):

"The Federal program to make the inland waterways navigable had its beginnings in an era when the young Nation had practically no transportation system for bringing the products of the border regions to its cities, or to its coastal harbors for export. Navigable waterways were essential if those regions were to be settled, become productive, and thus make the Nation stronger and its people more prosperous. There being but few settlers in the undeveloped hinterlands, it was obvious that if the waterways were to be built the Nation as a whole would have to bear the cost. Today, the regions served are highly developed and the beneficiaries of new waterways are in a position to help pay for them. Moreover, the Nation has a nationwide transportation system providing alternatives to waterway transportation. The problem is no longer one of developing the only practicable means of transporting goods, but of developing the most efficient combination of transportation modes. When a region to be served by a waterway had few people living in it, there was no way for local beneficiaries to assume any part of the cost of improvements and it was in the national interest for the Federal Government to bear these costs. As time passed, other means of transportation were developed, and the regions served by waterways increased in population and affluence. The national purpose of pushing back the frontier and developing underdeveloped regions was achieved. Eventually, railways, highways, and pipelines were developed, and improving technology made the waterways a highly efficient and competitive mode of transport, the costs of which can easily be paid by the direct beneficiaries. However, the policy of Federal assumption of practically all costs which had been established during the formative period of the Nation's economic growth has never been adjusted to take into account the present competitive situation in the Nation's transportation system. New waterway projects serving highly developed regions are still being installed entirely at Federal expense, paid for from the general revenues. Commercial users of inland waterways pay no Federal fuel tax, nor any lockage fees or other form of remuneration for the cost of providing and maintaining the waterways. A change in the policy governing the division of the cost of waterway projects between the public Treasury and those who directly benefit from the low-cost transportation facilities is long overdue. The lack of an equitable cost-sharing policy is a major weakness of the present waterway program. * * *

"As indicated previously, there is no longer any rational justification for assumption by the Federal Treasury of the entire cost of constructing, operating, and maintaining navigable waterways. Once this is accepted, the problem becomes one of deciding what share of the cost should be borne by non-Federal interests, and what is the best way to collect that share. Many who have advocated cost-sharing have proposed that the carriers operating on Federal waterways be required to pay tolls, or user charges. Others have suggested a fuel tax. Another means, less frequently proposed, would be to require the carriers to maintain a record of their use of Federal waterways, probably in terms of ton-miles, and periodically to submit a report somewhat like an income tax return, along with a payment of whatever tax might be due for the number of units of use reported."

4. Flood control activities of the federal government are based on the theory that the work protects the navigable waters and navigation facilities from harm as well as on the power to obstruct navigable waters. The Corps of Engineers is also in charge of the main stem portion of this program. Flood control projects were for a long time confined principally to the Mississippi Valley, but in 1936 Congress adopted a national policy and a continuing program for controlling this menace to national welfare. 33 U.S.C.A. § 701a. Projects are authorized and funded periodically in flood control bills.

In Oklahoma v. Guy F. Atkinson Co., 313 U.S. 508, 61 S.Ct. 1050, 85 L.Ed. 1487 (1941), the court sustained flood control works on nonnavigable tributaries of navigable waters, and the addition of power generating facilities to a flood control dam. "For just as control over the nonnavigable parts of the river may be essential or desirable in the interests of the navigable portions, so may the key to flood control on a navigable stream be found in whole or in part in flood control on its tributaries. * * * There is no constitutional reason why Congress cannot, under the commerce power, treat the watersheds as a key to flood control on navigable streams and their tributaries."

The Department of Agriculture has been given important flood control duties. The 1936 Flood Control Act provided that the Department should investigate watersheds and measures for run-off and water flow retardation and soil erosion prevention. 33 U.S.C.A. § 701b–1. The Soil Conservation Service conducts surveys, investigations, and administers an extensive program of water conservation, including measures to prevent run-off, the building of check dams and ponds, and facilities for applying water to the land, channeling financial and technical assistance to the land owners through soil conservation districts created under state law. (16 U.S.C.A. § 590(a)–(h)).

In 1954 the Hope-Aitken Small Watersheds Act, or "Public Law 566" (16 U.S.C.A. §§ 1001–1008) was enacted to fill the gap between these programs, which emphasized land treatment and very small individual structures, and the program of the Corps of Engineers, with its emphasis on large dams on the main stems. As supplemented by the 1956 Poague Amendment (16 U.S.C.A. § 1005) this act provides for financial and technical assistance to state and local agencies in the construction of multipurpose projects for flood control and the conservation, development, utilization and disposal of water in watersheds up to 250,000 acres. The federal government assumes up to $1,000,000 of the cost of flood prevention features and loans the local agency the balance, up to $5,000,000. Dams may be constructed that will impound 25,000 acre feet, including 12,500 acre feet of floodwater detention, and even larger projects are possible with the approval of Congress and other interested agencies.

No assessment is made against lands for benefits received from flood control works. On some small projects for local protective works, local agencies have been required to provide necessary lands, easements, and rights-of-way, to promise to indemnify the United States from damages due to the work, and to maintain and operate the works. 33 U.S.C.A. § 701c. These conditions are not applicable to most large projects that include flood control dams. 33 U.S.C.A. § 701c–1.

Recently the Corps of Engineers' flood control activity has become more and more concerned with increasing the number of acres in the nation's agricultural land base and increasing the productivity of agricultural land now farmed. Protection of much agricultural land is more or less incidental to protection of urban and suburban developed areas, but reclamation of large areas of low-lying lands has been the principal purpose of a number of recent Corps of Engineers flood control and major drainage projects, particularly in the lower Mississippi Valley and in Florida. See National Water Commission, Water Policies for the Future, 122–125.

The stream channelization program of the Department of Agriculture, undertaken as part of the Small Watersheds Act and also aimed at increasing farmland, has come under heavy fire for its adverse effects and environmental consequences caused by downstream flooding, sedimentation, lowering of groundwater levels and loss of fish and wildlife habitat and esthetic values. See Stream Channelization, Hearings before the Conservation and Natural Resources Subcommittee of the Committee on Government Operations, H.R., 92d Cong., 1st Sess. (1971); Arthur D. Little, Inc., Channel Modifications—An Environmental, Economic and Financial Assessment, Prepared for the Council on Environmental Quality (1972); National Water Commission, Water Policies for the Future, Ch. 2 (1973).

"Some conception of the magnitude of the Department of Agriculture programs is revealed by gross expenditures and other operational data. The Agricultural Conservation Program of ASCS and predecessor agencies in the 35 years of operation between 1935 and 1970 disbursed $6.7 billion on land and water conservation measures, improving the drainage on more than 52 million acres and assisting construction of some 80,000 small irrigation reservoirs and over 2 million ponds and pits providing water for agricultural use.

"The small watershed program of the SCS under Public Law 566 has led to authorization for the installation of more than 1,000 projects (as of June 30, 1971) at a cost of about $2.3 billion. These projects deal with watersheds totaling roughly 66 million acres, but no estimate of the agricultural land benefited or the crops which will be produced on those lands is available in a form useful for making policy recommendations. Stream channeling for drainage and flood protection is part of the small watershed program, and estimates indicate that more than 20,000 miles of streams will be altered. Some 6,000 miles of channel alterations have already been completed at a cost of $166.5 million. In January 1972, slightly under 3,000 applications for grants under the program were pending for a like number of small watersheds embracing 227 million acres." National Water Commission, supra, p. 122.

National Water Commission, Water Policies for the Future, 159 (1973):

"The United States has made heroic efforts to protect the lives and property of those who live on flood plain lands, and to maintain the flow of wealth that results from the use of these lands. Citizens in all parts of the Nation have been content to see billions of dollars spent to help fellow citizens subject to loss of life or fortune. But, throughout the many years that this benevolent effort has been under way, other individuals have been busily developing other flood plain areas in such ways that the initial goal of rescuing those unfortunate enough to be endangered by floods has become less and less attainable. Obviously, there must be a drastic change in the Nation's attitudes and programs."

The Commission, while recommending that flood plain lands should be treated as an important resource and managed so as to make the maximum net contribution to national welfare, reminds the Congress that the material wealth of the nation is not enhanced by development of lands subject to flood overflow unless the net value of the resulting production exceeds the costs of development plus the flood losses, or the cost of preventing such losses, and that non-material values sacrificed through the development must be counted as costs. The Commission emphasized that fuller consideration should be given to alternative measures such as flood plain management plans and zoning, development of other lands not subject to flooding, and use of flood plains for open space, recreational and park purposes, and recommended that costs of projects should be recouped through local units of government or districts that have power to levy assessments on benefited lands. Pp. 160–161.

5. "Navigable waters of the United States" is a term of art that identifies the area of operation of the federal programs for river and harbor improvements, flood control and hydroelectric power dams, and defines the reach of the federal courts' admiralty jurisdiction. It does not, however, exhaust national powers over water. The Clean Water Act governs pollution control activities in "the Nation's waters," "navigable waters," and "waters of the United States," using all these terms to include all waterways capable of carrying pollutants. See Sec. 2 of this Chapter, infra pp. 739–741.

6. Several other constitutional powers have been called upon to justify federal water development and control. One of these is the property clause, Art. IV, § 3: "The Congress shall have power to dispose of and make all needful Rules and Regulations respecting the Territory or other Property belonging to the United States." Power and control over water arising out of the ownership of the public domain are considered in connection with Reclamation projects, infra p. 731, and in Oregon v. Federal Power Commission, infra, p. 808. The property clause also finds employment as the connecting link between the authority of the United States under the commerce clause and the production of hydro-electric power at federal dams. "The power of falling water was an inevitable incident of the construction of the dam. That water power came into the exclusive control of the Federal Government. The mechanical energy was

convertible into electrical energy, and the water power, the right to convert it into electric energy, and the electric energy thus produced, constitute property belonging to the United States. * * * The Government could lease or sell and fix the terms." Ashwander v. Tennessee Valley Authority, 297 U.S. 288, 56 S.Ct. 466, 80 L.Ed. 688 (1936).

Article 1, §§ 8 and 9 of the Constitution give to Congress the power to declare war and to levy taxes and appropriate money to provide for the common defense of the United States. Under the 1916 National Defense Act, Congress authorized the President to investigate means for the production of nitrates and other products for munitions of war, and to designate sites on rivers and public land suitable for generation of power for the production of nitrates and other useful products. The Wilson Dam at Muscle Shoals on the Tennessee River was constructed under this authority, and later incorporated into the system of the T.V.A. Its hydro-electric energy was sold in peacetime for distribution in the Tennessee Valley area. In Ashwander v. T.V.A., supra, the court concluded that the dam and power plant were "adapted to the purposes of national defense" and that the maintenance of these properties in operating condition, and the resulting assurance of an abundance of electric energy in the event of war, were national defense assets which the government might constitutionally construct and acquire.

Treaties, made by the president by and with the advice and consent of the Senate (U.S. Constitution, Art. II, § 2), are, together with the federal constitution and laws, "the supreme Law of Land." (U.S. Constitution, Art. VI.) The text of treaties and conventions between the United States and Canada and Mexico is given in Witmer, Documents on the Use and Control of the Waters of Interstate and International Streams (U.S.Dept.Int.1956). These impose obvious limitations on state action affecting boundary waters and other waters flowing across the boundary or into the boundary waters. "The interests of the nation are more important than those of any state," and the federal government may act to prevent a state from interfering with a national treaty obligation. Sanitary District of Chicago v. United States, 266 U.S. 405, 45 S.Ct. 176, 69 L.Ed. 352 (1925). Treaty obligations of the United States give the nation an additional basis for authorizing works of improvements on international waterways. Arizona v. California, 283 U.S. 423, 51 S.Ct. 522, 75 L.Ed. 1154 (1931).

The State Department may seem an unusual place to find water resources management programs, but the International Boundary and Water Commission has constructed and operated Falcon and Amistad Dams on the Rio Grande for these and other purposes, in connection with the treaty dividing the water between the United States and Mexico.

Although the Constitution gives Congress the power to levy taxes and to appropriate funds to provide for the general welfare of the United States, (U.S. Constitution Art. I, §§ 8 and 9) it was not until 1936 that it was thought that this clause delegated a separate power to the national government. In that year United States v. Butler, 297 U.S. 1, 56 S.Ct. 312, 80 L.Ed. 477 (1936), held that the general welfare clause was not restricted by the specific powers enumerated in the constitution, such as the power to regulate commerce. The necessity for "highly fictional" extensions of the commerce clause disappeared with the Butler case, and in United States v. Gerlach Livestock Co., 339 U.S. 725, 70 S.Ct. 955, 94 L.Ed. 1231 (1950), the Court said that one of the largest federal basin-wide development projects—The Central Valley Project in California—could be sustained under this power. "Congress has a substantive power to tax and appropriate for the general welfare, limited only by the requirement that it shall be exercised for the common benefit as distinguished from some mere local purpose. * * * Thus the power of Congress to promote the general welfare through large-scale projects for reclamation, irrigation, and other internal improvement, is now as clear and ample as its power to accomplish the same results indirectly through resort to strained interpretation of the power over navigation."

7. Government projects and programs undertaken under the General Welfare power or as incidental to the exercise of specific powers take many forms. Flood control is handled not only by the Corps of Engineers and the Department of Agriculture. In the West the Bureau of Reclamation includes flood control and water storage for navigation releases in its larger projects. The TVA has completely taken over these functions in the territory it serves.

The Corps has no single purpose irrigation projects, but supplies water from many of its western dams to the Bureau of Reclamation for distribution to irrigators under the Flood Control Act of 1944, 43 U.S.C.A. § 390b. In the East, the Corps provides very large amounts of irrigation water in central and southern Florida.

The production of hydroelectric power has been an incidental feature of federal water projects since 1906, when the Bureau of Reclamation was authorized to include generating facilities in a project to run pumps to raise the water to the ditches, and to sell the surplus power. Since then almost every federal dam project has included power features and today over one-half the hydroelectric power in the country is produced at federal dams constructed by the Bureau of Reclamation, the Corps of Engineers, The Tennessee Valley Authority, the International Boundary and Water Commission and the St. Lawrence Seaway Corporation.

Water supply for municipalities and industry is now included in nearly every multi-purpose federal dam. The storage of water to provide firm supplies for these purposes is an important feature of Bureau of Reclamation dams in the West and of Corps of Engineer dams throughout the country.

In 1958 the Fish and Wildlife Coordination Act, 16 U.S.C.A. § 661 et seq., required that fish and wildlife receive "equal consideration" with other project purposes in planning any water project construction licensed or funded by the federal government. The act provides for enhancing these values where possible, and authorizes compensatory wildlife features such as fish hatcheries where some damage is inevitable.

Outdoor recreation has experienced a phenomenal boom in the past two decades as a result of a general increase in leisure time for the average American, improved mobility, and a generally prosperous economy. Since about half of all outdoor recreation is water-oriented, the national government's water-related activities have taken an important shift in the direction of enhancement of recreational opportunities, beginning with the act creating the Bureau of Outdoor Recreation, 16 U.S.C.A. §§ 460*l* to 460*l*–3, which established a national policy, set up a staff to give technical assistance to the private sector, and provided for coordination of all federal recreational activities. The Land and Water Conservation Fund Act of 1964, 16 U.S.C.A. §§ 460*l*–4 to 460*l*–11, provides grants-in-aid to state and local governments for outdoor recreation land acquisition and development. The Federal Water Project Recreation Act, 16 U.S.C.A. §§ 460*l*–12 to 460*l*–22, deals with recreation at federal multi-purpose water resource projects, and declares: "* * * it is the policy of the Congress * * * that * * * in investigating and planning any federal navigation, flood control, reclamation, hydroelectric, or multi-purpose water resource project, full consideration shall be given to opportunities, if any, which the project affords for outdoor recreation."

In addition to building its own projects, the United States has long had programs that encourage and assist water development and use by the private sector and by local governments and public agencies. The Department of Agriculture's Soil Conservation Service has supplied technical assistance and machinery for the control and prevention of erosion and for many improved land use measures and practices, channeled to individual farmers through Soil Conservation Districts. The Agricultural Conservation Program adds cost-sharing assistance to individuals and community groups for many types of soil improvement and water utilization, which may include installation of individual irrigation systems and farm and stockwater ponds. The Farmer's Home Administration provides credit, grants and technical assistance to rural groups for developing community water supply and waste disposal systems. The Bureau of Outdoor Recreation coordinates and develops programs under the Land and Water Conservation Fund Act of 1965, administering a program of grants to states for planning, acquiring, and developing outdoor recreation facilities. Water-based recreation sites are an important part of this program, and are usually made in connection with Small Watershed and Small Reclamation projects. The Department of Housing and Urban Development contains the Community Resources Development Administration, which gives planning, technical and financial assistance, in the form of loans and grants, for the construction of new water and sewer facilities basic to orderly community growth and development. The Department of Commerce, through the Economic Development Administration, provides financial assistance to governmental and non-governmental applicants for projects which will stimulate employment and increase income in depressed areas. Water and related land resources projects such as water supply, sewers, recreation and port facilities make up a large portion of these projects.

The description presented above does not exhaust the total of federal-water related activities, and does not include the government's numerous data gathering, research, planning and service functions, or its various administrative, financial and management agencies. A useful compendium of statutes, regulations and programs is found in National Water Commission, A Summary-Digest of the Federal Water Laws and Programs (DeWeerdt and Glick, eds.) (1973).

UNITED STATES v. RANDS

Supreme Court of the United States, 1967.
389 U.S. 121, 88 S.Ct. 265, 19 L.Ed.2d 329.

MR. JUSTICE WHITE delivered the opinion of the Court.

In this case the Court is asked to decide whether the compensation which the United States is constitutionally required to pay when it condemns riparian land includes the land's value as a port site. Respondents owned land along the Columbia River in the State of Oregon. They leased the land to the State with an option to purchase, it apparently being contemplated that the State would use the land as an industrial park, part of which would function as a port. The option was never exercised, for the land was taken by the United States in connection with the John Day Lock and Dam Project, authorized by Congress as part of a comprehensive plan for the development of the Columbia River. Pursuant to statute the United States then conveyed the land to the State of Oregon at a price considerably less than the option price at which respondents had hoped to sell. In the condemnation action, the trial judge determined that the compensable value of the land taken was limited to its value for sand, gravel, and agricultural purposes and that its special value as a port site could not be considered. The ultimate award was about one-fifth the claimed value of the land if used as a port. The Court of Appeals for the Ninth Circuit reversed, apparently holding that the Government had taken from respondents a compensable right of access to navigable waters and concluding that "port site value should be compensable under the Fifth Amendment." 367 F.2d 186, 191 (1966). We granted certiorari, 386 U.S. 989, 87 S.Ct. 1308, 18 L.Ed.2d 334, because of a seeming conflict between the decision below and United States v. Twin City Power Co., 350 U.S. 222, 76 S.Ct. 259, 100 L.Ed. 240 (1956). We reverse the judgment of the Court of Appeals because the principles underlying *Twin City* govern this case and the Court of Appeals erred in failing to follow them.

The Commerce Clause confers a unique position upon the Government in connection with navigable waters. "The power to regulate commerce comprehends the control for that purpose, and to the extent necessary, of all the navigable waters of the United States * * *. For this purpose they are the public property of the nation, and subject to all the requisite legislation by Congress." Gilman v. City of Philadelphia, 3 Wall. 713, 724–725, 18 L.Ed. 96 (1866). This power to regulate navigation confers upon the United States a "dominant servitude," FPC v. Niagara Mohawk Power Corp., 347 U.S. 239, 249, 74 S.Ct. 487, 493, 98 L.Ed. 686 (1954), which extends to the entire stream and the stream bed below ordinary high-water mark. The proper exercise of this power is not an invasion of any private property rights in the stream or the lands underlying it, for the damage sustained does not result from taking property from riparian owners within the meaning of the Fifth

Amendment but from the lawful exercise of a power to which the interests of riparian owners have always been subject. United States v. Chicago, M., St. P. & P.R. Co., 312 U.S. 592, 596–597, 61 S.Ct. 772, 775, 85 L.Ed. 1064 (1941); Gibson v. United States, 166 U.S. 269, 275–276, 17 S.Ct. 578, 580, 41 L.Ed. 996 (1897). Thus, without being constitutionally obligated to pay compensation, the United States may change the course of a navigable stream. State of South Carolina v. State of Georgia, 93 U.S. 4, 23 L.Ed. 782 (1876), or otherwise impair or destroy a riparian owner's access to navigable waters, Gibson v. United States, 166 U.S. 269, 17 S.Ct. 578 (1897); Scranton v. Wheeler, 179 U.S. 141, 21 S.Ct. 48, 45 L.Ed. 126 (1900); United States v. Commodore Park, Inc., 324 U.S. 386, 65 S.Ct. 803, 89 L.Ed. 1017 (1945), even though the market value of the riparian owner's land is substantially diminished.

The navigational servitude of the United States does not extend beyond the high-water mark. Consequently, when fast lands are taken by the Government, just compensation must be paid. But "just as the navigational privilege permits the Government to reduce the value of riparian lands by denying the riparian owner access to the stream without compensation for his loss, * * * it also permits the Government to disregard the value arising from this same fact of riparian location in compensating the owner when fast lands are appropriated." United States v. Virginia Elec. & Power Co., 365 U.S. 624, 629, 81 S.Ct. 784, 788, 5 L.Ed.2d 838 (1961). Specifically, the Court has held that the Government is not required to give compensation for "water power" when it takes the riparian lands of a private power company using the stream to generate power. United States v. Chandler-Dunbar Water Power Co., 229 U.S. 53, 73–74, 33 S.Ct. 667, 676, 57 L.Ed. 1063 (1913). Nor must it compensate the company for the value of its uplands as a power plant site. Id., at 76, 33 S.Ct. at 677. Such value does not "inhere in these parcels as upland," but depends on use of the water to which the company has no right as against the United States: "The government had dominion over the water power of the rapids and falls, and cannot be required to pay any hypothetical additional value to a riparian owner who had no right to appropriate the current to his own commercial use." Ibid.

All this was made unmistakably clear in United States v. Twin City Power Co., 350 U.S. 222, 76 S.Ct. 259, 100 L.Ed. 240 (1956). The United States condemned a promising site for a hydroelectric power plant and was held to be under no obligation to pay for any special value which the fast lands had for power generating purposes. The value of the land attributable to its location on the stream was "due to the flow of the stream; and if the United States were required to pay the judgments below, it would be compensating the landowner for the increment of value added to the fast lands if the flow of the stream were taken into account." 350 U.S., at 226, 76 S.Ct., at 261.

We are asked to distinguish between the value of land as a power site and its value as a port site. In the power cases, the stream is used as a source of power to generate electricity. In this case, for the property to have value as a port, vessels must be able to arrive and depart by water, meanwhile using the waterside facilities of the port. In both cases, special value arises from access to, and use of, navigable waters. With regard to the constitutional duty to compensate a riparian owner, no distinction can be drawn. It is irrelevant that the licensing authority presently being exercised over hydroelectric projects may be different from, or even more stringent than, the licensing of port sites. We are dealing with the constitutional power of Congress completely to regulate navigable streams to the total exclusion of private power companies or port owners. As was true in *Twin City,* if the owner of the fast lands can demand port site value as part of his compensation, "he gets the value of a right that the Government in the exercise of its dominant servitude can grant or withhold as it chooses. * * * To require the United States to pay for this * * * value would be to create private claims in the public domain." 350 U.S., at 228, 76 S.Ct., at 263. * * *

For the foregoing reasons, the judgment of the Court of Appeals is reversed and the case remanded with direction to reinstate the judgment of the District Court.

Notes

1. As its name indicates, the navigation servitude was originally a right of way for the public to use a stream for travel despite private ownership of the bed or bank of the river. The doctrine has been used in this sense to permit the government to remove an obstacle to navigation, such as unauthorized bridge, without compensating the person who obstructed the river. Union Bridge Co. v. United States, 204 U.S. 364, 27 S.Ct. 367, 51 L.Ed. 523 (1907). Does *Rands* turn it into a property right to the water, owned by the federal government? See Bartke, Navigation Servitude and Just Compensation—Struggle for a Doctrine, 48 Or.L.Rev. 1 (1968), Munro, The Navigation Servitude and the Severance Doctrine, 6 Land & Water L.Rev. 491 (1971). Compare the following quotation from *Twin City,* relied on in *Rands:*

"It is no answer to say that these private owners had interests in the water that were recognized by state law. We deal here with the federal domain, an area which Congress can completely preempt, leaving no vested private claims that constitute "private property" within the meaning of the Fifth Amendment. Location of the lands might under some circumstances give them special value, as our cases have illustrated. But to attach a value of water power of the Savannah River due to location and to enforce that value against the United States would go contra to the teaching of Chandler-Dunbar—'that the running water in a great navigable stream is capable of private ownership is inconceivable.' 229 U.S., at page 69, 33 S.Ct. at page 674."

Professor Eva Hanks of Yeshiva University traced the development of the identification of the navigation servitude with the national power over navigable waters in Morreale, Federal Power in Western Waters: The

Navigation Power and the Rule of No Compensation, 3 Natural Resources J. 1 (1963). An ancient common law principle made the obstruction or destruction of the right of passage, even by the exercise of an otherwise lawful right, an abatable nuisance. No compensation was owed, of course, to the tortfeasor compelled to remove the obstruction. When the United States Constitution gave the nation the power to protect and promote navigation in aid of commerce, the exercise of the power by restoring or improving passage on a waterway would often coincide with enforcement of the servitude and could result in the uncompensated destruction of a private dam or bridge. As the power over waterways was expanded for purposes not concerned with transportation, the no compensation rule was applied to loss of or damage to private interests that did not interfere with navigation but did depend upon use of or access to the water. As the Court expanded the navigation power, matching the needs of the United States for river development, it simultaneously expanded the range of noncompensable losses. Professor Hanks argued that this result was not constitutionally necessary and was not economically desirable. As applied to western waters, she said,

"It should be noted that none of the previously discussed cases, whether denying or granting compensation, concerned a consumptive water right or, more narrowly, an irrigation water right. Congress, of course, has often been solicitous of state-created Western water rights. * * * But while there is no case subjecting irrigation water rights to the rule of no compensation nothing on the other hand suggests their compensability. * * *

"Finally, brief consideration shall be given to a fear that has repeatedly been voiced, namely that the full application of navigation power and servitude principles will lead to the evaluation of desert uplands as *dry* land rather than as *irrigated* land when taken in connection with a navigation power project. As was shown earlier, the evaluation of uplands excludes any consideration of their adaptability as dam sites. That was so because the value thus added to the land derived 'in the end' from the stream itself. It was, in other words, dependent on a right to the water which the United States could destroy without compensation. Similarly, of course, it could be said that such value as is added to desert land by irrigation is dependent on the consumptive use of water, a use which can be destroyed without compensation by the exercise of the navigation power. The noncompensable destruction of that which gave the land its additional value would thus lead to the noncompensable destruction of that additional value itself. On purely logical terms, therefore, the fears regarding the evaluation of irrigated desert land are justified."

2. United States v. Cress, 243 U.S. 316, 37 S.Ct. 380, 61 L.Ed. 746 (1917), involved a federal dam on a navigable stream that raised the level of water in a nonnavigable tributary, destroying the effectiveness of a mill site by reducing the head of water. Held, a property right granted by state law had been taken and compensation must be paid.

In United States v. Grand River Dam Authority, 363 U.S. 229, 80 S.Ct. 1134, 4 L.Ed.2d 1186 (1960), the Authority, an agency of the state created to develop hydro-electric power on a nonnavigable stream, claimed a

$10,000,000 compensable loss when the United States, as a part of a comprehensive plan for navigation, flood control, and electric power, constructed a dam at a site on which the Authority had planned to build. The Court found it unnecessary to rule on the government's contention that the navigation servitude of the United States extends also to nonnavigable waters, preempting state-created property rights in such waters. But it did say, relying on Oklahoma v. Atkinson, infra p. 669, "When the United States appropriates the flow either of a navigable or a nonnavigable stream pursuant to its superior power under the Commerce Clause, it is exercising established prerogatives and is beholden to no one." As for the Authority's claim to water rights by virtue of its state charter, it was said that while the Federal Power Act requires a licensee to compensate the holder of such rights, no such requirement obtains when the United States builds a dam on its own account. "The United States did not appropriate any business, contract, land, or property of respondent. It had the superior right by reason of the Commerce Clause to build the Fort Gibson Project itself or to license another to do it. The frustration of respondent's plans and expectations which resulted when the United States chose to undertake the project on its own account did not take property from respondent in the sense of the Fifth Amendment."

Did *Cress* survive *Grand River*?

3. Enough criticism was leveled at *Rands* to cause Congress to reverse it with § 111 of the Rivers and Harbors and Flood Control Act of 1970: "In all cases where real property shall be taken by the United States for the public use in connection with any improvement of rivers, harbors, canals, or waterways of the United States, and in all condemnation proceedings by the United States to acquire lands or easements for such improvements, the compensation to be paid for real property taken by the United States above the normal high water mark of navigable waters of the United States shall be the fair market value of such real property based upon all uses to which such real property may reasonably be put, including its highest and best use, any of which uses may be dependent upon access to or utilization of such navigable waters. In cases of partial takings of real property, no depreciation in the value of any remaining real property shall be recognized and no compensation shall be paid for any damages to such remaining real property which result from loss of or reduction of access from such remaining real property to such navigable waters because of the taking of real property or the purposes for which such real property is taken. The compensation defined herein shall apply to all acquisitions of real property after December 31, 1970, and to the determination of just compensation in any condemnation suit pending on December 31, 1970." 33 U.S.C.A. § 595a.

Clearly § 111 reverses *Rands.* It seems fairly clear that it would also reverse *Twin City.* That case involved a "condemnation proceeding by the United States to acquire lands," and § 111 says that "the compensation to be paid for real property taken by the United States above the normal high water mark * * * shall be the fair market value * * * based on all uses to which such real property may reasonably be put * * * any of which uses may be dependent upon access to or utilization of such navigable waters." This seems to exactly describe the Twin City Company's rocky hillsides, suitable for dam building. Furthermore, *Rands* was so directly based on *Twin City* that any shot aimed at it must hit *Twin City*. What of *Chandler-Dunbar* on which *Twin City* was in turn directly based? There the value was ascribed to the "raw water," an unusual concept. Commonly the values attributable to a stream are incorporated into the value of the riparian land. If a case arose today with identical facts to those of *Chandler-Dunbar,* could the riparian's claim be phrased as one to recover for the value of the upland parcels when used for a power plant?

Does § 111 put an end to the fears expressed by Professor Hanks, supra Note 1?

4. There are other instances of Congressional waiver of the servitude and election to pay compensation. U.S. v. Gerlach Live Stock Co., 339 U.S. 725, 70 S.Ct. 955, 94 L.Ed. 1231 (1950) involved the Central Valley Project, a gigantic undertaking to rearrange California water resources. Major features of the project were Friant Dam on the San Joaquin River and two great canals that would divert and distribute almost the entire flow of the river. The plaintiffs in the Court of Claims were owners of "uncontrolled grass lands" that had been naturally irrigated by spring high water before these works were built. The project had started out as a state enterprise but was taken over by the United States during the depression as a public works project. The authorizing legislation spoke of "improvement of navigation and flood control," but also provided that the work would be undertaken by the Bureau of Reclamation and that the provisions of Reclamation Law would govern. Under Reclamation Law the Secretary must condemn water rights needed for projects. The Court held that Congress had elected to treat the project as a Reclamation project and that compensation was due. The opinion contains the famous quotation: "* * * we need not ponder whether by virtue of a highly fictional navigational purpose, the Government could destroy the flow of a navigable stream and carry away its waters for sale to private interests without compensation to those deprived of them. We have never held that or anything like it * * *. But the public welfare, which requires claimants to sacrifice their benefits to broader ones from a higher utilization, does not necessarily require that their loss be uncompensated any more than in other takings where private rights are surrendered in the public interest. The waters of which claimants are deprived are taken for resale largely to other private landowners not riparian to the river and to some located in a different watershed. Thereby private lands will be made more fruitful, more valuable, and their operation more profitable. The reclamation laws contemplate that those who share these advantages shall, through water charges, reimburse the government for its outlay. * * * No reason appears why those who get the waters should be spared from making whole those from whom they are taken. Public interest requires appropriation; it does not require expropriation."

Congress has given western water users assurance that the navigation servitude will not be used to take irrigation waters without compensation in certain specific instances. See the O'Mahoney-Milliken Amendment to the Flood Control Act of 1944, 58 Stat. 887, 889, 33 U.S.C.A. § 701–1(b):

"The use for navigation, in connection with the operation and maintenance of such works herein authorized for construction, of waters arising in States lying wholly or partly west of the ninety-eighth meridian shall be only such use as does not conflict with any beneficial consumptive use, present or future, in States lying wholly or partly west of the ninety-eighth meridian, of such waters for domestic, municipal, stock water, irrigation, mining, or industrial purposes."

In several aspects of the Federal Power Act, Congress has elected not to exercise the navigation servitude. The United States itself may build a dam on a navigable stream and back up water against an upstream dam, thus partially destroying its value. United States v. Willow River Power Co., 324 U.S. 499, 65 S.Ct. 761, 89 L.Ed. 1101 (1945). But when it licenses the construction of a power dam which will have a similar effect, the licensee must compensate the owner of the upstream dam. Henry Ford & Son, Inc. v. Little Falls Fiber Co., 280 U.S. 369, 50 S.Ct. 140, 74 L.Ed. 483 (1930). And although, as in United States v. Appalachian Power Co., supra, p. 704, the United States might in the first instance take or prevent the exercise of riparian power rights, if it grants a license under the Power Act, and then under Sec. 14 of that Act elects to "recapture" the plant, it will pay an amount that includes the unamortized investment of the licensee in state water rights. F.P.C. v. Niagara Mohawk Power Co., 347 U.S. 239, 74 S.Ct. 487, 98 L.Ed. 666 (1954).

5. When the navigation servitude is not involved, the United States may condemn and pay for water rights needed for a congressionally authorized project. What if the project interferes with a right that has not been condemned? Until 1976, the doctrine of sovereign immunity prevented the injured person from obtaining an injunction, or even a declaratory judgment, against the government, a cabinet officer, or the officials in charge of the project. The only remedy was a suit for damages in the Court of Claims. Dugan v. Rank, 372 U.S. 609, 83 S.Ct. 999, 10 L.Ed.2d 15 (1963). An amendment to the Administrative Procedure Act, "APA", 5 U.S.C.A. Section 702, now allows a person suffering a legal wrong or adversely affected by agency action to obtain judicial review by suing the United States, stating a claim that an agency or an officer or employee thereof acted or failed to act in an official capacity or under color of legal authority, and specifying the responsible federal officer or officers.

In South Delta Water Agency v. U.S., 767 F.2d 531 (9th Cir.1985), the court refused to dismiss a suit by irrigators receiving water from a project of the Bureau of Reclamation who claimed injury from the Bureau's failure to comply with applicable federal and state law. The court held that the case was a proper one for court review under the APA and that under this section the federal government had waived its sovereign immunity.

KAISER AETNA v. UNITED STATES

Supreme Court of the United States, 1979.
444 U.S. 164, 100 S.Ct. 383, 62 L.Ed.2d 332.

MR. JUSTICE REHNQUIST delivered the opinion of the Court.

[Kuapa Pond on the island of Oahu was originally a lagoon separated from Manualua Bay on the Pacific Ocean by a barrier beach. The early Hawaiians cut an opening to the sea, installed sluice gates to control tidal flow, and used the pond to raise fish. In 1848 the pond and the surrounding land passed into private ownership, and in 1961 were acquired by Kaiser Aetna for "Hawaii Kai," a suburb of Honolulu. With the permission of the Corps of Engineers, the developer deepened the channel and the pond, which was then used as a yacht basin by the occupants of 1500 "marina waterfront" lots as well as by a number of residents of back lots and nonresident boat owners who paid fees for maintenance, privacy and security. The United States brought suit to declare that as a result of the improvements, the pond had become "navigable waters of the United States," open to the public. Kaiser Aetna argued that although the pond was "navigable water" for purposes of regulating construction and excavation and setting rules of the road for boat traffic, the water was not subject to the navigation servitude. Kaiser Aetna claimed that under Hawaii law the pond was private property in which it had invested millions of dollars and that to convert it to a public aquatic park would be a taking of its property.]

* * *

The Government contends that petitioners may not exclude members of the public from the Hawaii Kai Marina because "[t]he public enjoys a federally protected right of navigation over the navigable waters of the United States." * * * The position advanced by the Government, and adopted by the Court of Appeals below, presumes that the concept of "navigable waters of the United States" has a fixed meaning that remains unchanged in whatever context it is being applied. While we do not fully agree with the reasoning of the District Court, we do agree with its conclusion that all of this Court's cases dealing with the authority of Congress to regulate navigation and the so-called "navigational servitude" cannot simply be lumped into one basket. * * *

It is true that Kuapa Pond may fit within definitions of "navigability" articulated in past decisions of this Court. But it must be recognized that the concept of navigability in these decisions was used for purposes other than to delimit the boundaries of the navigational servitude: for example, to define the scope of Congress' regulatory authority under the Interstate Commerce Clause, see, e.g., United States v. Appalachian Power Co., 311 U.S. 377, 61 S.Ct. 291, 85 L.Ed. 243 (1940); * * * to determine the extent of the authority of the Corps of Engineers under the Rivers and Harbors Appropriation Act of 1899, and to establish the limits of the jurisdiction of federal courts conferred by Art. III, § 2, of the United States Constitution over admiralty and maritime cases. Although the Government is clearly correct in maintaining that the now dredged Kuapa Pond falls within the definition of "navigable waters" as this Court has used that term in delimiting the boundaries of Congress' regulatory authority under the Commerce Clause, * * * this Court has never held that the navigational servitude creates a blanket exception to the Takings Clause whenever Congress exercises its Commerce Clause authority to promote navigation. Thus, while Kuapa Pond may be subject to regulation by the Corps of Engineers, acting under the authority delegated it by Congress in the Rivers and Harbors Appropriation Act, it does not follow that the pond is also subject to a public right of access.

Reference to the navigability of a waterway adds little if anything to the breadth of Congress' regulatory power over interstate commerce. It has long been settled that Congress has extensive authority over this Nation's waters under the Commerce Clause. Early in our history this Court held that the power to regulate commerce necessarily includes power over navigation. * * * [But], a wide spectrum of economic activities "affect" interstate commerce and thus are susceptible of congressional regulation under the Commerce Clause irrespective of whether navigation, or, indeed, water, is involved. The cases that discuss Congress' paramount authority to regulate waters used in interstate commerce are consequently best understood when viewed in terms of more traditional Commerce Clause analysis than by reference to whether the stream in fact is capable of supporting navigation or may be characterized as "navigable water of the United States." With respect to the Hawaii Kai Marina, for example, there is no doubt that Congress may prescribe the rules of the road, define the conditions under which running lights shall be displayed, require the removal of obstructions to navigation, and exercise its authority for such other reason as may seem to it in the interest of furthering navigation or commerce.

In light of its expansive authority under the Commerce Clause, there is no question but that Congress could assure the public a free right of access to the Hawaii Kai Marina if it so chose. Whether a statute or regulation that went so far amounted to a "taking," however, is an entirely separate question. Pennsylvania Coal Co. v. Mahon, 260 U.S. 393, 415, 43 S.Ct. 158, 160, 67 L.Ed. 322 (1922). As was recently pointed out in Penn Central Transportation Co. v. New York City, 438 U.S. 104, 98 S.Ct. 2646, 57 L.Ed.2d 631 (1978), this Court has generally "been unable to develop any 'set formula' for determining when 'justice and fairness' require that economic injuries caused by public action be compensated by the government, rather than remain disproportionately concentrated on a few persons." Id., at 124, 98 S.Ct., at 2659. Rather, it has examined the "taking" question by engaging in essentially ad hoc, factual inquiries that have identified several factors—such as the economic impact of the regulation, its interference with reasonable investment backed expectations, and the character of the governmental action—that have particular significance. Ibid. When the "taking" question has involved the exercise of the public right of navigation over interstate waters that constitute highways for commerce, however, this Court has held in many cases that compensation may not be required as a result of the federal navigational servitude. See, e.g., United States v. Chandler-Dunbar Co., 229 U.S. 53, 33 S.Ct. 667, 57 L.Ed. 1063 (1913).

The navigational servitude is an expression of the notion that the determination whether a taking has occurred must take into consideration the important public interest in the flow of interstate waters that in their natural condition are in fact capable of supporting public navigation. See United States v. Cress, 243 U.S. 316, 37 S.Ct. 380, 61 L.Ed. 746 (1917). Thus, in United States v. Chandler-Dunbar Co., supra, 229 U.S., at 69, 33 S.Ct., at 674, this Court stated that "the running water in a great navigable stream is [incapable] of private ownership * * *." And, in holding that a riparian landowner was not entitled to compensation when the construction of a pier cut off his access to navigable water, this Court observed:

> "The primary use of the waters and the lands under them is for purposes of navigation, and the erection of piers in them to improve navigation for the public is entirely consistent with such use, and infringes no right of the riparian owner. Whatever the nature of the interest of a riparian owner in the submerged lands in front of his upland bordering on a public navigable water, his title is not as full and complete as his title to fast land which has no direct connection with the navigation of such water. It is a qualified title, a bare technical title, not at his absolute disposal, as is his upland, but to be held at all times subordinate to such use of the submerged lands and of the waters flowing over them as may be consistent with or demanded by the public right of navigation." Scranton v. Wheeler, 179 U.S. 141, 163, 21 S.Ct. 48, 57, 45 L.Ed. 126 (1900).

For over a century, a long line of cases decided by this Court involving Government condemnation of "fast lands" delineated the elements of compensable damages that the Government was required to pay because the lands were riparian to navigable streams. The Court was often deeply divided, and the results frequently turned on what could fairly be described as quite narrow distinctions. * * *

There is no denying that the strict logic of the more recent cases limiting the Government's liability to pay damages for riparian access, if carried to its ultimate conclusion, might completely swallow up any private claim for "just compensation" under the Fifth Amendment even in a situation as different from the riparian condemnation cases as this one. But, as Mr. Justice Holmes observed in a very different context, the life of the law has not been logic, it has been experience. The navigational servitude, which exists by virtue of the Commerce Clause in navigable streams, gives rise to an authority in the Government to assure that such streams retain their capacity to serve as continuous highways for the purpose of navigation in interstate commerce. Thus, when the Government acquires fast lands to improve navigation, it is not required under the Eminent Domain Clause to compensate landowners for certain elements of damage attributable to riparian location, such as the land's value as a hydroelectric site or a port site. But none of these cases ever doubted that when the Government wished to acquire fast lands, it was required by the Eminent Domain Clause of the Fifth Amendment to condemn and pay fair value for that interest. * * *

Here, the Government's attempt to create a public right of access to the improved pond goes so far beyond ordinary regulation or improvement for navigation as to amount to a taking under the logic of Pennsylvania Coal Co. v. Mahon, 260 U.S. 393, 43 S.Ct. 158, 67 L.Ed. 322 (1922). * * *

We have not the slightest doubt that the Government could have refused to allow such dredging on the ground that it would have impaired navigation in the bay, or could have conditioned its approval of the dredging on petitioners' agreement to comply with various measures that it deemed appropriate for the promotion of navigation. * * *

In this case, we hold that the "right to exclude," so universally held to be a fundamental element of the property right, falls within this category of interests that the Government cannot take without compensation. This is not a case in which the Government is exercising its regulatory power in a manner that will cause an insubstantial devaluation of petitioners' private property; rather, the imposition of the navigational servitude in this context will result in an actual physical invasion of the privately owned marina. * * * And even if the Government physically invades only an easement in property, it must nonetheless pay just compensation. * * * Thus, if the Government wishes to make what was formerly Kuapa Pond into a public aquatic park after petitioners have proceeded as far as they have here, it may not, without invoking its eminent domain power and paying just compensation, require them to allow free access to the dredged pond while petitioners' agreement with their customers call for an annual $72 regular fee.

Accordingly the judgment of the Court of Appeals is reversed.

MR. JUSTICE BLACKMUN, with whom MR. JUSTICE BRENNAN and MR. JUSTICE MARSHALL join, dissenting.

* * *

[The] cases establish a key principle that points the way for decision in the present context. In most of them, the noncompensable loss was related, either directly or indirectly, to the riparian owner's "access to, and use of, navigable waters." United States v. Rands, 389 U.S., at 124–125, 88 S.Ct., at 268. However that access or use may have been turned to account for personal gain, and no matter how much the riparian owner had invested to enhance the value, the Court held that these rights were shared with the public at large. Actions taken to improve their value for the many caused no reimbursable damage to the few who, by the accident of owning contiguous "fast land," previously enjoyed the blessings of the common right in greater measure.

Application of this principle to the present case should lead to the conclusion that the developers of Kuapa Pond have acted at their own risk and are not entitled to compensation for the public access the Government now asserts. See Union Bridge Co. v. United States, 204 U.S., at 400, 27 S.Ct., at 380. The chief value of the pond in its present state obviously is a value of access to navigable water. Development was undertaken to improve and enhance this value, not to improve the value of the pond as some aquatic species of "fast land." Petitioners do not question the Federal Government's plenary control over the waters of the Bay, and they have no vested right in access to its open water. Since the value of the pond and the motive for improving it lie in access to a highway of commerce, I am drawn to the conclusion that the petitioners' interest in the improved waters of the pond is not subject to compensation. Whatever expectancy petitioners may have had in control over the pond for use as a fishery was surrendered in exchange for the advantages of access when they cut a channel into the Bay.

In contrast, the Government's interest in vindicating a public right of access to the pond is substantial. It is the very interest in maintaining "common highways, * * * forever free." After today's decision, it is open to any developer to claim that private improvements to a waterway navigable in interstate commerce have transformed "navigable water of the United States" into private property, at least to the extent that he may charge for access to the portion improved. Such appropriation of navigable waters for private use directly injures the freedom of commerce that the navigational servitude is intended to safeguard. * * *

Notes

1. What is the difference between a port and a marina? Suppose that as mere acreage for homesites with a view of a shallow pond, Kaiser Aetna's land was worth $1,000,000, but its proximity to the sea and suitability for an exclusive suburb centered on a yacht club raised its raw land value to $3,000,000. Suppose that prior to any development the United States had planned to make the beach at Manualua Bay a National Seashore, with park headquarters and a public marina on dredged out Kuapa Pond, and had condemned the land for that purpose. How much would the award be under the *Rands* theory? Section 111? Justice Rehnquist's *Kaiser Aetna* approach?

Compare United States v. Fuller, 409 U.S. 488, 93 S.Ct. 801, 35 L.Ed.2d 16 (1973). Under the Taylor Grazing Act, a rancher owning "base property" may obtain a permit to graze cattle on nearby federal public lands in lieu of the old privilege to use the open range. The permit is transferable with a sale of the home ranch and adds considerably to its sales price, but is revocable. Fuller's ranch was condemned by the United States, and he sought the full market value he could have obtained for land and permit at a private sale. The Court, however, in an opinion by Justice Rehnquist, held that since the government could have first revoked the permit and then condemned the land, the value of the permit should be excluded in computing the award.

2. Suppose that the condemnation for the National Seashore came after Kaiser Aetna had dredged the pond and constructed the facilities. The improvements cost $5,000,000, and the total value of the site became $8,000,000. Opening the marina to the public would diminish the market value to $7,000,000. What compensation would be awarded?

3. Does *Kaiser Aetna* signal a major shift in the attitude of the Court to the no compensation feature of the navigation servitude, or is it only a narrow exception to the rule? Justice Rehnquist considers a number of factors in his opinion. Are any of the following controlling, or essential, to the decision?

(1) The pond was not navigable in its natural condition.

(2) The nonnavigable pond was private property under state law, "strikingly similar * * * to fast land."

(3) The owner of the underlying land had created the reach of navigable water.

(4) The imposition of the servitude would result in actual physical invasion of the property.

(5) Although the proximity of the navigable bay and ocean gave some values to the land, opening the water to the public would also destroy other values created by the owner.

4. Suppose that after all improvements have been constructed it is found that onshore winds make the long breakwater protecting the entrance to the channel a hazard to navigation on Manualua Bay. The Corps of Engineers orders it removed. Without the breakwater yachts cannot make a safe entry into the pond, and the marina becomes unusable. The value of the site drops from $8,000,000 to $1,000,000. Has Kaiser Aetna's property been taken?

5. Professor Hanks, in Federal Power in Western Waters: The Navigation Power and the Rule of No Compensation, supra, note 1, page 652, argued that the Supreme Court has never given a satisfactory explanation of the reason for merging the no compensation rule with the nation's power over navigable waters. She pointed out that the Court could have expanded the commerce power and left the navigation servitude to its historical role as a right of way. She argued that in the taking cases, the United States should pay compensation whenever payment would be due if Congress had exercised some other regulatory power.

How close to Professor Hanks' position does Justice Rehnquist come in the *Kaiser Aetna* opinion, where he says, "Reference to the navigability of a water way adds little, if anything, to the breadth of Congress' regulatory power over interstate commerce. * * * The navigational servitude is an expression of the notion that the determination whether a taking has occurred must take into consideration the important public interests in the flow of interstate waters that in their natural condition are, in fact, capable of supporting public navigation." Did the dictum of *United States v. Grand River Dam Authority* (supra, note 2, p. 658) survive *Kaiser Aetna*?

FIRST IOWA HYDRO-ELECTRIC COOPERATIVE v. FEDERAL POWER COMMISSION

Supreme Court of the United States, 1946.
328 U.S. 152, 66 S.Ct. 906, 90 L.Ed. 1143.

MR. JUSTICE BURTON delivered the opinion of the Court.

This case illustrates the integration of federal and state jurisdictions in licensing water power projects under the Federal Power Act. The petitioner is the First Iowa Hydro-Electric Cooperative, a cooperative association organized under the laws of Iowa with power to generate, distribute and sell electric energy. On January 29, 1940, pursuant to § 23(b) of the Federal Power Act, it filed with the Federal Power Commission a declaration of intention to construct and operate a dam, reservoir and hydro-electric power plant on the Cedar River, near Moscow, Iowa.

On April 2, 1941, it also filed with the Commission an application for a license, under the Federal Power Act, to construct an enlarged project essentially like the one it now wishes to build. The cost of the enlarged project is estimated at $14,600,000. It calls for an 8,300 foot earthen dam on the Cedar River near Moscow, an 11,000 acre reservoir at that point and an eight mile diversion canal to a power plant to be built near Muscatine on the Mississippi. The canal will create two other reservoirs totaling 2,000 acres. It is alleged that the three reservoirs incidentally will provide needed recreational facilities. The power plant will have four turbo-generating units with a total capacity of 50,000 kw., operating with an average head of 101 feet of water provided by the fall from the canal to the Mississippi. Water will be pumped from the Mississippi up to the head bays of the power intake dam at the plant to meet possible shortages in supply. The tailrace will extend for a mile along the shore of the Mississippi to a point below Dam 16 on that River. Transmission lines will connect the project with a source of steam standby electric current at Davenport, Iowa, 24 miles up the Mississippi. The plant is expected to produce 200,000,000 kwh. of marketable power per year, of which 151,000,000 kwh. will be firm energy in an average year. Interchange of energy is proposed with the Moline-Rock Island Manufacturing Company near Davenport and the project is suggested as an alternative to the addition of a 50,000 kw. unit to the plant of that company. The power will be available especially to non-profit rural electrification cooperative associations and to cities and towns in 35 or more nearby counties.

The Cedar River rises in Minnesota and flows 270 miles southeasterly through Iowa to Moscow which is 10 miles west of the Mississippi. From there it flows southwesterly 29 miles to Columbus Junction where it joins the Iowa River and returns southeasterly 28 miles to the Mississippi. The proposed diversion will take all but about 25 c.f.s. of water from the Cedar River at Moscow. This will correspondingly reduce the flow in the Iowa River while the diverted water will enter the Mississippi at Muscatine, about 20 miles above its present point of entry at the mouth of the Iowa River. There are no cities or towns on the Cedar River between Moscow and Columbus Junction and the record indicates that the petitioner has options upon 98% of the riparian rights on the Cedar River in that area. At petitioner's request, this application was treated as a supplement to its then pending declaration of intention to construct the smaller project.

On June 3, 1941, the Commission made the following findings:

> "(1) That the Cedar and Iowa Rivers are navigable waters of the United States; * * *
>
> "(6) That a license for the construction proposed above is required under the provisions of the Federal Power Act." 2 Fed.Power Comm. Rep. 958.

On August 11, 1941, the petitioner, pursuant to that finding, filed with the Commission an application for a license to construct the project above described. On November 4, 1941, the Commission granted the State of Iowa's petition to intervene and, since then, the State has opposed actively the granting of the federal license.

On January 29, 1944, after extended hearings, the Commission rendered an opinion including the following statements: * * *

> "The applicant has not presented satisfactory evidence, pursuant to § 9(b) [a] of the Federal Power Act, of compliance with the requirements of applicable laws of the state of Iowa requiring a permit from the State Executive Council to effect the purposes of a license under the Federal Power Act, and the pending application, as supplemented, should be dismissed without prejudice." * * *

The laws of Iowa which that State contends are applicable and require a permit from its Executive Council to effect the purposes of the federal license are all in Iowa Code Ann. §§ 7767–7796.1, constituting Chapter 363, entitled "Mill Dams and Races." Section 7767 of that chapter is alleged to require the issuance of a permit by the Executive Council of the State and is the one on which the Commission's order must depend. It provides:

> "7767 Prohibition—permit. No dam shall be constructed, maintained, or operated in this state in any navigable or meandered stream

a. "Sec. 9. That each applicant for a license hereunder shall submit to the commission—

. . .

"(b) Satisfactory evidence that the applicant has complied with the requirements of the laws of the State or States within which the proposed project is to be located with respect to bed and banks and to the appropriation, diversion, and use of water for power purposes and with respect to the right to engage in the business of developing, transmitting, and distributing power, and in any other business necessary to effect the purposes of a license under this Act." 41 Stat. 1068, 16 U.S.C. § 802(b), 16 U.S.C.A. § 802(b).

for any purpose, or in any other stream for manufacturing or power purposes, nor shall any water be taken from such streams for industrial purposes, unless a permit has been granted by the executive council to the person, firm, corporation, or municipality constructing, maintaining, or operating the same."

To require the petitioner to secure the actual grant to it of a State permit under § 7767 as a condition precedent to securing a federal license for the same project under the Federal Power Act would vest in the Executive Council of Iowa a veto power over the federal project. Such a veto power easily could destroy the effectiveness of the federal act. It would subordinate to the control of the State the "comprehensive" planning which the Act provides shall depend upon the judgment of the Federal Power Commission or other representatives of the Federal Government. * * * For example, § 7776 of the State Code requires that "the method of construction, operation, maintenance, and equipment of any and all dams in such waters shall be subject to the approval of the executive council." This would subject to State control the very requirements of the project that Congress has placed in the discretion of the Federal Power Commission. A still greater difficulty is illustrated by § 7771. This states the requirements for a State permit as follows:

"7771 When permit granted. If it shall appear to the council that the construction, operation, or maintenance of the dam will not materially obstruct existing navigation, or materially affect other public rights, will not endanger life or public health, and *any water taken from the stream in connection with the project is returned thereto at the nearest practicable place* without being materially diminished in quantity or polluted or rendered deleterious to fish life, it shall grant the permit, upon such terms and conditions as it may prescribe." (Italics supplied.)

This strikes at the heart of the present project. The feature of the project which especially commended it to the Federal Power Commission was its diversion of substantially all of the waters of the Cedar River near Moscow, to the Mississippi River near Muscatine. * * * It is this diversion that makes possible the increase in the head of water for power development from a maximum of 35 feet to an average of 101 feet, the increase in the capacity of the plant from 15,000 kw. to 50,000 kw. and its output from 47,000,000 kwh. to 200,000,000 kwh. per year. * * *

Compliance with State requirements that are in conflict with federal requirements may well block the federal license. For example, compliance with the State requirement that the water of the Cedar River all be returned to it at the nearest practicable place would reduce the project to the small one which is classified by the Federal Power Commission as "neither desirable nor adequate." Similarly, compliance with the engineering requirements of the State Executive Council, if additional to or different from the federal requirements, may well result in duplications of expenditures that would handicap the financial success of the project. * * * On the other hand, there is ample opportunity for the Federal Power Commission, under the authority expressly given to it by Congress, to require by regulation the presentation of evidence satisfactory to it of the petitioner's compliance with any of the requirements for a State permit on the state waters of Iowa that the Commission considers appropriate to effect the purposes of a federal license on the navigable waters of the United States. This evidence can be required of the petitioner upon the remanding of this application to the Commission.

In the Federal Power Act there is a separation of those subjects which remain under the jurisdiction of the states from those subjects which the Constitution delegates to the United States and over which Congress vests the Federal Power Commission with authority to act. To the extent of this separation, the Act establishes a dual system of control. The duality of control consists merely of the division of the common enterprise between two cooperating agencies of Government, each with final authority in its own jurisdiction. The duality does not require two agencies to share in the final decision of the same issue. Where the Federal Government supersedes the state government there is no suggestion that the two agencies both shall have final authority. In fact a contrary policy is indicated in §§ 4(e), 10(a)(b) and (c), and 23(b). In those sections the Act places the responsibility squarely upon federal officials and usually upon the Federal Power Commission. A dual final authority, with a duplicate system of state permits and federal licenses required for each project, would be unworkable. "Compliance with the requirements" of such a duplicated system of licensing would be nearly as bad. Conformity to both standards would be impossible in some cases and probably difficult in most of them. * * *

The securing of an Iowa state permit is not in any sense a condition precedent or an administrative procedure that must be exhausted before securing a federal license. It is a procedure required by the State of Iowa in dealing with its local streams and also with the waters of the United States within that State in the absence of an assumption of jurisdiction by the United States over the navigability of its waters. Now that the Federal Government has taken jurisdiction of such waters under the Federal Power Act, it has not by statute or regulation added the state requirements to its federal requirements. * * *

The Act leaves to the states their traditional jurisdiction subject to the admittedly superior right of the Federal Government, through Congress, to regulate interstate and foreign commerce, administer the public lands and reservations of the United States and, in certain cases, exercise authority under the treaties of the United States. * * *

The resulting integration of the respective jurisdictions of the state and Federal Governments, is illustrated by the careful preservation of the separate interests of the states throughout the Act, without setting up a divided authority over any one subject.[b]

Sections 27 and 9 are especially significant in this regard. Section 27 expressly "saves" certain state laws relating to property rights as to the use of water, so that these are not superseded by the terms of the Federal Power Act. It provides:

> "Sec. 27. That nothing herein contained shall be construed as affecting or intending to affect or in any way to interfere with the laws of the respective States relating to the control, appropriation, use, or distribution of water used in irrigation or for municipal or other uses, or any vested right acquired therein." 16 U.S.C.A. § 821. * * *

The effect of § 27, in protecting state laws from supersedure, is limited to laws as to the control, appropriation, use or distribution of water in irrigation or for municipal or other uses of the same nature. It therefore has primary, if not exclusive reference to such proprietary rights. The phrase "any vested right acquired therein" further emphasizes the application of the section to property rights. * * *

Section 9(b) does not resemble § 27. It must be read with § 9(a) and (c). The entire section is devoted to securing adequate information for the Commission as to pending applications for licenses. Where § 9(a) calls for engineering and financial information, § 9(b) calls for legal information. * * * It does not itself require compliance with any state laws. Its reference to state laws is by way of suggestion to the Federal Power Commission of subjects as to which the Commission may wish some proof submitted to it of the applicant's progress. The evidence required is described merely as that which shall be "satisfactory" to the Commission. The need for compliance with applicable state laws, if any, arises not from this federal statute but from the effectiveness of the state statutes themselves. When this application has been remanded to the Commission, that Commission will not act as a substitute for the local authorities having jurisdiction over such questions as the sufficiency of the legal title of the applicant to its riparian rights, or as to the validity of its local franchises, if any, relating to proposed intrastate public utility service. Section 9(b) says that the Commission may wish to have "satisfactory evidence" of the progress made by the applicant toward meeting local requirements but it does not say that the Commission is to assume responsibility for the legal sufficiency of the steps taken. The references made in § 9(b) to beds

b. Instances of such provisions are the following: § 4(a) and (c), cooperation of the Commission with the executive departments and other agencies of the State and National Governments is required in the investigation of such subjects as the utilization of water resources, water-power industry, location, capacity, development costs and the relation to markets of power sites, and the fair value of power. § 4(f), notice of application for a preliminary permit is to go to any State or municipality likely to be interested. § 7(a), in issuing permits and licenses preference is to be given to States and municipalities. § 10(e), licenses to States and municipalities under certain circumstances shall be issued and enjoyed without charge. § 14, a right is reserved not only to the United States but to any State or municipality to take over any licensed project at any time by condemnation and payment of just compensation. §§ 19 and 20, regulation of service and rates is preserved to the states.

and banks of streams, to proprietary rights to divert or use water, or to legal rights to engage locally in the business of developing, transmitting and distributing power neither add anything to nor detract anything from the force of the local laws, if any, on those subjects. In so far as those laws have not been superseded by the Federal Power Act, they remain as applicable and effective as they were before its passage. The State of Iowa, however, has sought to sustain the applicability and validity of Chapter 363 of the Code of Iowa in this connection, on the ground that the Federal Power Act, by the implications of § 9(b), has recognized this chapter of Iowa law as part of a system of dual control of power project permits, cumbersome and complicated though it be. * * *

The inappropriateness of such an interpretation is apparent in the light of the circumstances which culminated in the passage of the Federal Water Power Act in 1920. The purposes of the Act were then so generally known as to have made such a restrictive interpretation impossible and a denial of it unnecessary. It was the outgrowth of a widely supported effort of the conservationists to secure enactment of a complete scheme of national regulation which would promote the comprehensive development of the water resources of the Nation, in so far as it was within the reach of the federal power to do so, instead of the piecemeal, restrictive, negative approach of the River and Harbor Acts and other federal laws previously enacted.

It was a major undertaking involving a major change of national policy. That it was the intention of Congress to secure a comprehensive development of national resources and not merely to prevent obstructions to navigation is apparent from the provisions of the Act, the statutory scheme of which has been several times reviewed and approved by the courts. * * *

The detailed provisions of the Act providing for the federal plan of regulation leave no room or need for conflicting state controls. * * * It is the Federal Power Commission rather than the Iowa Executive Council that under our constitutional Government must pass upon these issues on behalf of the people of Iowa as well as on behalf of all others.

We accordingly reverse the judgment of the court below with directions to remand the case to the Federal Power Commission for further proceedings in conformity with this opinion.

Notes

1. Requirements of state law that a permit or license be obtained from state authorities before beginning construction of water control structures have no application to the United States when it constructs works on navigable streams. The first "Arizona v. California", 283 U.S. 423, 51 S.Ct. 522, 75 L.Ed. 1154 (1931), was a suit brought to enjoin Ray Lyman Wilbur, Secretary of the Interior, from constructing Hoover Dam under authority of

the Boulder Canyon Project Act, 43 U.S.C.A. § 617. California and other states were in the suit only as necessary parties.

"The wrongs against which redress is sought are, first, the threatened invasion of the quasi sovereignty of Arizona by Wilbur in building the dam and reservoir without first securing the approval of the State Engineer as prescribed by its laws; and, second, the threatened invasion of Arizona's quasi sovereign right to prohibit or to permit appropriation, under its own laws, of the unappropriated water of the Colorado River flowing within the state. The latter invasion, it is alleged, will consist in the exercise, under the Act and the compact, of a claimed superior right to store, divert, and use such water.

"*First.* The claim that quasi sovereign rights of Arizona will be invaded by the mere construction of the dam and reservoir rests upon the fact that both structures will be located partly within the State. At Black Canyon, the site of the dam, the middle channel of the river is the boundary between Nevada and Arizona. The latter's statutes prohibit the construction of any dam whatsoever until written approval of plans and specifications shall have been obtained from the State Engineer; and the statutes declare in terms that this provision applies to dams to be erected by the United States. * * * The United States has not secured such approval; nor has any application been made by Wilbur, who is proceeding to construct said dam in complete disregard of this law of Arizona.

"The United States may perform its functions without conforming to the police regulations of a State. * * * If Congress has power to authorize the construction of the dam and reservoir, Wilbur is under no obligation to submit the plans and specifications to the State Engineer for approval. And the Federal Government has the power to create this obstruction in the river for the purpose of improving navigation if the Colorado River is navigable. * * *"

2. In Oklahoma ex rel. Phillips v. Guy F. Atkinson Co., 313 U.S. 508, 61 S.Ct. 1050, 85 L.Ed. 1487 (1941), the state sought to enjoin the construction by agencies of the United States of a dam and reservoir on the Red River for joint purposes of flood control and power production. The project would inundate 100,000 acres of Oklahoma land, 3,800 of which were owned by the state, it would displace 8,000 persons, destroy productive farm land, stop the production and further development of oil resources, and seriously injure the state and local taxing units by causing the loss of taxable values and going concern values of the destroyed industry. The benefits of the project did not compensate Oklahoma for these losses; it was alleged that most of the power produced would be marketed in Texas, and the major flood control and navigation benefits would occur far downstream in Arkansas, and below the mouth of the Red in the lower Mississippi basin. The United States Supreme Court did not dwell on the congressional function, in authorizing the project, of balancing interests within the entire region, and the obvious unsuitability of state governments to make such a regional decision. It simply concentrated on the aspects of federal power to undertake the project, and closed its opinion denying the injunction with, "Since the construction of this dam and reservoir is a valid exercise by Congress of its commerce power, there is no interference with

the sovereignty of the state. * * * And the suggestion that this project interferes with the state's own program for water development and conservation is likewise of no avail. That program must bow before the 'superior power' of Congress."

3. In response to the "energy crisis" of the 1970's, Congress enacted a number of measures designed to stimulate hydroelectric power production. Under the Small Hydroelectric Power Projects Act, 16 U.S.C.A. §§ 2701 et seq., loans up to 75% of costs were made available for projects adding power generation facilities of under 30 megawatts to existing dams or utilizing natural water features without the need for any dam or impoundment, if all licenses and other required federal state and local approvals necessary for construction of the project have been issued, if the project will have no significant adverse environmental effects on fish and wildlife, recreational use of water and stream flow, and if the project will not have a significant adverse effect on any other use of the water used by the project. FERC was directed to establish a simple and expeditious licensing procedure under the Federal Power Act, and in the Energy Security Act of 1980, 16 U.S.C.A. § 2705(d), FERC was empowered to exempt plants of no more than 5 megawatts from the licensing and other requirements of the Federal Power Act. The Public Utility Regulatory Act, 16 U.S.C.A. § 824a–3, added another exemption for small conduit hydroelectric facilities, located on private lands, having installed generating capacity of 15 megawatts or less and utilizing the waters of tunnels, canals and flumes operated for agricultural, municipal or industrial water use. Projects utilizing natural features without new dams or other impoundments can be exempted under 16 U.S.C.A. § 2708(b), but this applies only to use of waterfalls or perched lakes, etc., and projects that require a diversion dam or an impoundment as small as two acre feet must be licensed. Tulalip Tribes of Washington v. FERC, 732 F.2d 1451 (9th Cir.1984).

PURPA also provided the principal financial incentive. Under FERC rules, electric utilities are required to purchase electric energy from such facilities at rates that are just and reasonable to the electricity consumers, non-discriminatory, and do not exceed the incremental cost to the utility of alternative electric energy, rather than rates based on the old public utility rule of cost of service. In American Paper Institute v. American Electric Power Service Corp., 461 U.S. 402, 103 S.Ct. 1921, 76 L.Ed.2d 22 (1983), the Court upheld rules that required the utilities to interconnect with such small power producers and that set the rate at "full avoided cost" in order to provide the maximum incentive, rather than at a percentage in order to share the avoided costs with the utility customers. Energy tax credits, 26 U.S.C.A. § 46(a)(2)(C), § 48(1)(13), add additional attractions.

These measures spurred a large number of small projects in the western states, and the *First Iowa* doctrine has raised a number of state-federal problems and conflicts. FERC has taken the position that even an applicant for an exemption is entitled to take advantage of the preemptive effect of the Federal Power Act and need not comply with state law. These matters are discussed in detail in Wolfe, Hydropower: FERC Licensing and Emerging State-Federal Water Rights Conflicts, 29 Rocky Mountain Mineral Law Institute 851 (1983). New FERC regulations for licenses, preliminary permits, exemptions from licensing, competing applications and contests are found in Tit. 18 CFR Part 4, as amended March 25, 1985, 50 Fed.Reg. 11676–11689.

During the energy crisis of the 1970's and 1980's, the State of California placed great emphasis on the development of renewable sources of energy. The 1982 legislature declared a state policy of supporting and encouraging environmentally compatible small hydroelectric projects that do not result in surface distances in sensitive areas such as wild and scenic rivers, wilderness areas and the "Critical Condor Habitat." State agencies were forbidden to approve projects within these areas, and were directed to identify significant adverse impacts associated with other projects. West's Ann.Cal.Water Code § 106.7.

SPORHASE v. NEBRASKA ex rel. DOUGLAS

Supreme Court of the United States, 1982.
458 U.S. 941, 102 S.Ct. 3456, 73 L.Ed.2d 1254.

JUSTICE STEVENS delivered the opinion of the Court.

Appellants challenge the constitutionality of a Nebraska statutory restriction on the withdrawal of ground water from any well within Nebraska intended for use in an adjoining State. * * *

Appellants jointly own contiguous tracts of land in Chase County, Nebraska, and Phillips County, Colorado. A well physically located on the Nebraska tract pumps ground water for irrigation of both the Nebraska tract and the Colorado tract. Previous owners of the land registered the well with the State of Nebraska in 1971, but neither they nor the present owners applied for the permit required by § 46–613.01 of the Nebraska Revised Statutes. That section provides:

> "Any person, firm, city, village, municipal corporation or any other entity intending to withdraw ground water from any well or pit located in the State of Nebraska and transport it for use in an adjoining state shall apply to the Department of Water Resources for a permit to do so. If the Director of Water Resources finds that the withdrawal of the ground water requested is reasonable, is not contrary to the conservation and use of ground water, and is not otherwise detrimental to the public welfare, he shall grant the permit if the state in which the water is to be used grants reciprocal rights to withdraw and transport ground water from that state for use in the State of Nebraska."

Appellee brought this action to enjoin appellants from transferring the water across the border without a permit. The trial court rejected the defense that the statute imposed an undue burden on interstate commerce and granted the injunction. The Nebraska Supreme Court affirmed. 208 Neb. 703, 305 N.W.2d 614 (1981). It held that, under Nebraska law, ground water is not "a marketable item freely transferable for value among private parties, and therefore [is] not an article of commerce." * * *

I

In holding that ground water is not an article of commerce, the Nebraska Supreme Court and appellee cite as controlling precedent Hudson County Water Co. v. McCarter, 209 U.S. 349, 28 S.Ct. 529, 52 L.Ed. 828 (1908). In that case a New Jersey statute prohibited the interstate transfer of any surface water located within the State. The Hudson County Water Company nevertheless contracted with New York City to supply one of its boroughs with water from the Passaic River in New Jersey. The state attorney general sought from the New Jersey courts an injunction against fulfillment of the contract. Over the water company's objections that the statute impaired the obligation of contract, took property without just compensation, interfered with interstate commerce, denied New York citizens the privileges afforded New Jersey citizens, and denied New York citizens the equal protection of the laws, the injunction was granted. This Court, in an opinion by Justice Holmes, affirmed.

Most of the Court's opinion addresses the just compensation claim. Justice Holmes refused to ground the Court's holding, as did the New Jersey state courts, on "the more or less attenuated residuum of title that the State may be said to possess." Id., at 355, 28 S.Ct., at 530. For the statute was justified as a regulatory measure that, on balance, did not amount to a taking of property that required just compensation. Putting aside the "problems of irrigation," the State's interest in preserving its waters was well within its police powers.[a] * * * That interest was not dependent on any demonstration that the State's water resources were inadequate for present or future use. * * * The State "finds itself in possession of what all admit to be a great public good, and what it has it may keep and give no one a reason for its will." Id., at 357, 28 S.Ct., at 531.

Having disposed of the just compensation claim, Justice Holmes turned very briefly to the other constitutional challenges. In one paragraph, he rejected the Contract Clause claim. In the remaining paragraph of the opinion, he rejected all the other defenses. His treatment of the Commerce Clause challenge consists of three sentences: "A man cannot acquire a right to property by his desire to use it in commerce among the States. Neither can he enlarge his otherwise limited and qualified right to the same end. The case is covered in this respect by Geer v. Connecticut, 161 U.S. 519 [, 16 S.Ct. 600, 40 L.Ed. 793] [(1896)]." 209 U.S., at 357, 28 S.Ct., at 531.

While appellee relies upon *Hudson County,* appellants rest on our summary affirmance of a three-judge district court judgment in City of Altus v. Carr, 255 F.Supp. 828 (W.D.Tex.), aff'd mem., 385 U.S. 35, 87

a. "The problems of irrigation have no place here. Leaving them on one side, it appears to us that few public interests are more obvious, indisputable and independent of particular theory than the interest of the public of a State to maintain the rivers that are wholly within it substantially undiminished, except by such drafts upon them as the guardian of the public welfare may permit for the purpose of turning them to a more perfect use." Id., at 356, 28 S.Ct., at 531.

S.Ct. 240, 17 L.Ed.2d 34 (1966). The City of Altus is located near the southern border of Oklahoma. Large population increases rendered inadequate its source of municipal water. It consequently obtained from the owners of land in an adjoining Texas county the contractual right to pump the ground water underlying that land and to transport it across the border. The Texas legislature thereafter enacted a statute that forbade the interstate exportation of ground water without the approval of that body. The City filed suit in federal district court, claiming that the statute violated the Commerce Clause.

* * * Second, the State argued that the statute regulated ground water and that ground water is not an article of commerce, citing Geer v. Connecticut, supra, and *Hudson County,* supra. The court rejected this argument since the statute directly regulated the interstate transportation of water that had been pumped from the ground, and under Texas law such water was an article of commerce. The court then had little difficulty in concluding that the statute imposed an impermissible burden on interstate commerce.

City of Altus, however, is inconsistent with *Hudson County.* For in the latter case the Court found Geer v. Connecticut, supra, to be controlling on the Commerce Clause issue. *Geer,* which sustained a Connecticut ban on the interstate transportation of game birds captured in that State, was premised on the theory that the State owned its wild animals and therefore was free to qualify any ownership interest it might recognize in the persons who capture them. One such restriction is a prohibition against interstate transfer of the captured animals. This theory of the public ownership was advanced as a defense in *City of Altus.* The State argued that it owned all subterranean water and therefore could recognize ownership in the surface owner who withdraws the water, but restrict that ownership to use of the water within the State. That theory, upon which the Commerce Clause issue in *Hudson County* was decided, was rejected by the district court in *City of Altus.* In expressly overruling *Geer* three years ago, this Court traced the demise of the public ownership theory and definitively recast it as " 'but a fiction expressive in legal shorthand of the importance to its people that a State have power to preserve and regulate the exploitation of an important resource.' " Hughes v. Oklahoma, 441 U.S. 322, 334, 99 S.Ct. 1727, 1735, 60 L.Ed.2d 250 (1979). * * * In *Hughes* the Court found the State's interests insufficient to sustain a ban on the interstate transfer of natural minnows seined from waters within the State.

Appellee insists, however, that Nebraska water is distinguishable from other natural resources. The surface owner who withdraws Nebraska ground water enjoys a lesser ownership interest in the water than the captor of game birds in Connecticut or minnows in Oklahoma or ground water in Texas, for in *Geer, Hughes,* and *City of Altus* the States permitted intrastate trade in the natural resources once they were captured. Although appellee's greater ownership interest may not be irrelevant to Commerce Clause analysis, it does not absolutely remove Nebraska ground water from such scrutiny. For appellee's argument is still based on the legal fiction of state ownership. The fiction is illustrated by municipal water supply arrangements pursuant to which ground water is withdrawn from rural areas and transferred to urban areas. * * *

The Western States' interests, and their asserted superior competence, in conserving and preserving scarce water resources are not irrelevant in the Commerce Clause inquiry. Nor is appellee's claim to public ownership without significance. Like Congress' deference to state water law, * * * these factors inform the determination whether the burdens on commerce imposed by state ground water regulation are reasonable or unreasonable. But appellee's claim that Nebraska ground water is not an article of commerce goes too far: it would not only exempt Nebraska ground water regulation from burden-on-commerce analysis, it also would curtail the affirmative power of Congress to implement its own policies concerning such regulation. See Philadelphia v. New Jersey, 437 U.S. 617, 621–623, 98 S.Ct. 2531, 2534–2535, 57 L.Ed.2d 475 (1978). If Congress chooses to legislate in this area under its commerce power, its regulation need not be more limited in Nebraska than in Texas and States with similar property laws. Ground water overdraft is a national problem and Congress has the power to deal with it on that scale.

II

Our conclusion that water is an article of commerce raises, but does not answer, the question whether the Nebraska statute is unconstitutional. For the existence of unexercised federal regulatory power does not foreclose state regulation of its water resources, of the uses of water within the State, or indeed, of interstate commerce in water. * * * Determining the validity of state statutes affecting interstate commerce requires a more careful inquiry:

> "Where the statute regulates evenhandedly to effectuate a legitimate local public interest, and its effects on interstate commerce are only incidental, it will be upheld unless the burden imposed on such commerce is clearly excessive in relation to the putative local benefits. If a legitimate local purpose is found, then the question becomes one of degree. And the extent of the burden that will be tolerated will of course depend on the nature of the local interest involved, and on whether it could be promoted as well with a lesser impact on interstate activities." Pike v. Bruce Church, Inc., 397 U.S. 137, 142, 90 S.Ct. 844, 847, 25 L.Ed.2d 174 (1970) (citation omitted).

The only purpose that appellee advances for § 46–613.01 is to conserve and preserve diminishing sources of ground water. The purpose is unquestionably legitimate and highly important, and the other aspects of Nebraska's ground water regulation demonstrate that it is genuine. Appellants' land in Nebraska is located within the boundaries of the Upper Republican Ground Water Control Area, which was designated as such by the Director of the Nebraska Department of Water Resources based upon a determination "that there is an inadequate ground water supply to meet present or reasonably foreseeable needs for beneficial use of such water supply." Neb.Rev.Stat. § 46–658(1); see App. 56–60. Pursuant to § 46–666(1), the Upper Republican Natural Resources District has promulgated special rules and regulations governing ground water withdrawal and use. See App. 61–82. The rules and regulations define as "critical" those townships in the control area in which the annual decline of the ground water table exceeds a fixed percentage; appellants' Nebraska tract is located within a critical township. The rules and regulations require the installation of flow meters on every well within the control area, specify the amount of water per acre that may be used for irrigation, and set the spacing that is required between wells. They also strictly limit the intrastate transfer of ground water: transfers are only permitted between lands controlled by the same ground water user, and all transfers must be approved by the district board of directors. Id., at 68–69.

The State's interest in conservation and preservation of ground water is advanced by the first three conditions in § 46–613.01 for the withdrawal of water for an interstate transfer. Those requirements are "that the withdrawal of the ground water requested is reasonable, is not contrary to the conservation and use of ground water, and is not otherwise detrimental to the public welfare." Although Commerce Clause concerns are implicated by the fact that § 46–613.01 applies to interstate transfers but not to intrastate transfers, there are legitimate reasons for the special treatment accorded requests to transport ground water across state lines. Obviously, a State that imposes severe withdrawal and use restrictions on its own citizens is not discriminating against interstate commerce when it seeks to prevent the uncontrolled transfer of water out of the State. An exemption for interstate transfers would be inconsistent with the ideal of evenhandedness in regulation. At least in the area in which appellants' Nebraska tract is located, the first three standards of § 46–613.01 may well be no more strict in application than the limitations upon intrastate transfers imposed by the Upper Republican Natural Resources District.

Moreover, in the absence of a contrary view expressed by Congress, we are reluctant to condemn as unreasonable measures taken by a State to conserve and preserve for its own citizens this vital resource in times of severe shortage. Our reluctance stems from the "confluence of [several] realities." Hicklin v. Orbeck, 437 U.S. 518, 534, 98 S.Ct. 2482, 2491, 57 L.Ed.2d 397 (1978). First, a State's power to regulate the use of water in times and places of shortage for the purpose of protecting the health of its citizens—and not simply the health of its economy—is at the core of its police power. For Commerce Clause purposes, we have long recognized a difference between economic protectionism, on the one hand, and health and safety regulation, on the other. See H.P. Hood & Sons v. Du Mond, 336 U.S. 525, 533, 69 S.Ct. 657, 662, 93 L.Ed.

865 (1949). Second, the legal expectation that under certain circumstances each State may restrict water within its borders has been fostered over the years not only by our equitable apportionment decrees, see, e.g., Wyoming v. Colorado, 353 U.S. 953, 77 S.Ct. 865, 1 L.Ed. 2d 906 (1957), but also by the negotiation and enforcement of interstate compacts. Our law therefore has recognized the relevance of state boundaries in the allocation of scarce water resources. Third, although appellee's claim to public ownership of Nebraska ground water cannot justify a total denial of federal regulatory power, it may support a limited preference for its own citizens in the utilization of the resource. See Hicklin v. Orbeck, supra, 437 U.S., at 533–534, 98 S.Ct., at 2491. In this regard, it is relevant that appellee's claim is logically more substantial than claims to public ownership of other natural resources. See supra, at 3461–3462. Finally, given appellee's conservation efforts, the continuing availability of ground water in Nebraska is not simply happenstance; the natural resource has some indicia of a good publicly produced and owned in which a State may favor its own citizens in times of shortage. See Reeves, Inc. v. Stake, 447 U.S. 429, 100 S.Ct. 2271, 65 L.Ed.2d 244 (1980); cf. Philadelphia v. New Jersey, supra, 437 U.S., at 627–628, 98 S.Ct., at 2537 and n. 6; Baldwin v. Fish and Game Comm'n, supra. A facial examination of the first three conditions set forth in § 46–613.01 does not, therefore, indicate that they impermissibly burden interstate commerce. Appellants, indeed, seem to concede their reasonableness.

Appellants, however, do challenge the requirement that "the state in which the water is to be used grants reciprocal rights to withdraw and transport ground water from that state for use in the State of Nebraska"—the reciprocity provision that troubled the Chief Justice of the Nebraska Supreme Court. Because Colorado forbids the exportation of its ground water,[b] * * * the reciprocity provision operates as an explicit barrier to commerce between the two States. The State therefore bears the initial burden of demonstrating a close fit between the reciprocity requirement and its asserted local purpose. Hughes v. Oklahoma, supra, 441 U.S., at 336, 99 S.Ct., at 1736; Dean Milk Co. v. City of Madison, 340 U.S. 349, 354, 71 S.Ct. 295, 297, 95 L.Ed. 329 (1951).

The reciprocity requirement fails to clear this initial hurdle. For there is no evidence that this restriction is narrowly tailored to the conservation and preservation rationale. Even though the supply of water in a particular well may be abundant, or perhaps even excessive,

b. Colo.Rev.Stat. § 37–90–136 provides as follows:

> "For the purpose of aiding and preserving unto the state of Colorado and all its citizens the use of all ground waters of this state, whether tributary or nontributary to a natural stream, which waters are necessary for the health and prosperity of all the citizens of the state of Colorado, and for the growth, maintenance, and general welfare of the state, it is unlawful for any person to divert, carry, or transport by ditches, canals, pipelines, conduits, or any other manner any of the ground waters of this state, as said waters are in this section defined, into any other state for use therein."

and even though the most beneficial use of that water might be in another State, such water may not be shipped into a neighboring State that does not permit its water to be used in Nebraska. If it could be shown that the State as a whole suffers a water shortage, that the intrastate transportation of water from areas of abundance to areas of shortage is feasible regardless of distance, and that the importation of water from adjoining States would roughly compensate for any exportation to those States, then the conservation and preservation purpose might be credibly advanced for the reciprocity provision. A demonstrably arid state conceivably might be able to marshall evidence to establish a close means-end relationship between even a total ban on the exportation of water and a purpose to conserve and preserve water. Appellee, however, does not claim that such evidence exists. We therefore are not persuaded that the reciprocity requirement—when superimposed on the first three restrictions in the statute—significantly advances the State's legitimate conservation and preservation interest; it surely is not narrowly tailored to serve that purpose. The reciprocity requirement does not survive the "strictest scrutiny" reserved for facially discriminatory legislation. Hughes v. Oklahoma, supra, 441 U.S., at 337, 99 S.Ct., at 1736.[c]

* * *

The reciprocity requirement of Neb.Rev.Stat. § 46–613.01 violates the Commerce Clause. We leave to the state courts the question whether the invalid portion is severable. The judgment of the Nebraska Supreme Court is reversed and the case is remanded for proceedings not inconsistent with this opinion.

It is so ordered.

JUSTICE REHNQUIST, with whom JUSTICE O'CONNOR joins, dissenting.

The issue presented by this case, and the only issue, is whether the existence of the Commerce Clause of the United States Constitution by itself, in the absence of any action by Congress, invalidates some or all of § 46–613.01 of the Nebraska Revised Statutes, which relates to groundwater. But instead of confining its opinion to this question, the Court first quite gratuitously undertakes to answer the question of whether the authority of Congress to regulate interstate commerce, conferred by the same provision of the Constitution, would enable it to legislate with respect to groundwater overdraft in some or all of the States.

That these two questions are quite distinct leaves no room for doubt. Congress may regulate not only the stream of commerce itself, but activities which affect interstate commerce, including wholly intrastate activities. * * * The question actually involved in this case is whether Neb.Rev.Stat. § 46–613.01 runs afoul of the unexercised authority of Congress to regulate interstate commerce. * * *

c. The reciprocity requirement cannot, of course, be justified as a response to another State's unreasonable burden on commerce. A & P Tea Co. v. Cottrell, 424 U.S. 366, 379–381, 96 S.Ct. 923, 931–932, 47 L.Ed.2d 55 (1976).

In my view, these cases appropriately recognize the traditional authority of a State over resources within its boundaries which are essential not only to the well-being, but often to the very lives of its citizens. In the exercise of this authority, a State may so regulate a natural resource so as to preclude that resource from attaining the status of an "article of commerce" for the purposes of the negative impact of the Commerce Clause. It is difficult, if not impossible, to conclude that "commerce" exists in an item that cannot be reduced to possession under state law and in which the State recognizes only a usufructuary right. "Commerce" cannot exist in a natural resource that cannot be sold, rented, traded, or transferred, but only *used.*

Of course, a State may not discriminate against interstate commerce when it regulates even such a resource. If the State allows indiscriminate interstate commercial dealings in a particular resource, it may have a difficult task proving that an outright prohibition on interstate commercial dealings is not such a discrimination. * * * By contrast, Nebraska so regulates groundwater that it cannot be said that the State permits any "commerce," intrastate or interstate, to exist in this natural resource. * * *

Since Nebraska recognizes only a limited right to use groundwater on land owned by the appropriator, it cannot be said that "commerce" in groundwater exists as far as Nebraska is concerned. Therefore, it cannot be said that Neb.Rev.Stat. § 46–613.01 either discriminates against, or "burdens," interstate commerce. Section 46–613.01 is simply a regulation of the landowner's *right to use* groundwater extracted from lands he owns within Nebraska. * * *

Notes

1. By the use of the "negative" or "dormant" Commerce Clause (contrasted to the Constitution's positive or express grant of power to Congress in Art. I, Sec. 8) the Supreme Court may strike down state laws found to be inconsistent with national interests even though Congress has not legislated on the subject. Congress may, of course, exercise its power by expressly permitting the states to impose restrictions on interstate commerce that would be otherwise impermissible, by clearly expanding the limits of state power or by legislatively overruling decisions of the Supreme Court. See New England Power Co. v. New Hampshire, 455 U.S. 331, 102 S.Ct. 1096, 71 L.Ed.2d 188 (1982). An omitted portion of the *Sporhase* opinion found no such grant of power to burden commerce in federal laws that have approved the use of state water laws for federal projects and programs or have consented to interstate water compacts.

2. El Paso, Texas, sits below New Mexico's southern border. To support its growing population and stimulate economic growth, the city filed with the New Mexico State Engineer 326 applications for permits to appropriate 296,000 acre-feet of water per year from wells in New Mexico. All applications were denied on the basis of a New Mexico statute (since repealed) that expressly barred the transportation of New Mexico ground water for such purpose. In City of El Paso v. Reynolds, 563 F.Supp. 379

(D.N.M., 1983), the State Engineer was enjoined from enforcing the statute. The court did not attempt to test the statute against the requirement of reasonableness or to fit it into any of the *Sporhase* exceptions, but ruled that under *Sporhase,* a state may discriminate in favor of its citizens only to the extent that water is essential to human survival. "Outside of fulfilling human survival needs, water is an economic resource."

Pending appeal of this decision, the New Mexico legislature repealed the statute and substituted a requirement for a permit to withdraw water from any surface or underground water source in New Mexico for transportation for use outside the state. In order to approve an application, the State Engineer must find that the proposed use would not impair existing water rights, and would not be contrary to the conservation of water or otherwise detrimental to the public welfare, after balancing statewide and local supply of and demand for New Mexico water against the sources available and the demand at the out-of-state place of use. The case was remanded for fresh consideration in the light of the new law. In *El Paso II,* 597 F.Supp. 694 (D.N.M., 1984), the district court rejected a challenge to the new requirements for permits to appropriate water. Requiring the exporter to meet conservation and public welfare criteria is not on its face discriminatory, said the court, since much the same requirements are applied to appropriations for local use. Comparing water supply and demand in New Mexico with that in the importing state was said to be a necessary step in applying the balancing test prescribed by *Sporhase.* "Simple economic protectionism" is still forbidden, said the court, but some burdens on commerce may be valid if outweighed by "non-economic local benefits."

The New Mexico statute requires the same export permit in the case of a sale by New Mexico appropriater of water or the water right to an out-of-state user. The El Paso litigation embraced the possible transfer to Texas of water from four existing wells in New Mexico. Since New Mexico's laws allow instate water transfers if no injury is done to other appropriaters and the conservation and public welfare tests are not required for transfers between points within the state, the *El Paso II* Court held that the statute is facially unconstitutional for imposing this extra burden on exports. (The Legislature promptly added the conservation and welfare requirements to domestic transfers, N.M.Stat.Ann. § 72–5–23, Supp.1985.)

3. Are the appropriation and transfer situations the same? In Trelease, State Water and State Lines: Commerce in Water Resources, 56 U.Colo.L.Rev. 347 (1985), it is argued, "that *Sporhase* does not apply to the initial allocation of unappropriated water by the state to a person who seeks to put the water to future use; *Sporhase* deals instead with the commerce that occurs when a person who owns a right to use water on land in one state transfers the water across the state line for use on land in a different state. When a state is doling out unappropriated water, it may place restraints upon itself; it may limit its grants of rights to develop its natural resources in such a way as to insure that at least the primary benefits of the first use are realized within the state. But further economic activity by the water user in the processing, sale, or transportation of goods or crops, or in the sale or transportation of water itself as a product, may

not be regulated to keep the benefits of that activity within the state. * * * Oil and gas captured and brought to the surface, netted shrimp, seined minnows, felled trees from state public land—all these things and creatures—were once 'natural resources,' free-roaming or at least unpossessed, subject to no private claim of ownership. All are now property in the hands of those who reduced them to possession or have acquired a property right to take them. The state has received the economic benefit from the activity that transferred them out of the public domain and into private hands, but it may not burden or prevent interstate commerce carried on by the owners of the appropriated things. *Sporhase* correctly adds water to this list."

Literature regarding the principal case has been diverse. Tarlock, So It's Not "Ours"—Why Can't We Still Keep It? A First Look at Sporhase v. Nebraska, 18 Land and Water L.Rev. 1 (1983) criticizes the case as too restrictive on the powers of the states. Barnett, Mixing Water and the Commerce Clause: The Problems of Practice, Precedent, and Policy in Sporhase v. Nebraska, 24 Natural Resources J. 161 (1984), although approving some embargoes on economic grounds, views *Sporhase* as allowing too much state control over interstate commerce. Corker, Sporhase v. Nebraska: Does the Dormant Commerce Clause *Really* Limit the Power of the State to Forbid (1) The Export of Water and (2) The Creation of a Water Right for Use in Another State?, 54 U.Colo.L.Rev. 393 (1983) demonstrates how *Sporhase* may impede state administration of water rights and water resources, but suggests remedies for the existing vacuum in which Congress has not acted and state cannot act. Simms, Water Transfers across State Systems, 31 Rocky Mtn.Min.L.Inst. —— (1985), sees a tension between interstate apportionment rules that magnify state lines and interstate commerce rules that seem to erase them. Allocations such as those in *Colorado v. New Mexico* (supra, p. 609) and some compacts tend to Balkanize water resources while cases like *Sporhase* and *El Paso II* seem to create free trade areas for unapportioned waters. Simms sees congressional action as the ultimate solution, including the possibility of reinterpretation and reallocation of present arrangements.

4. The *Sporhase* Court seems to limit exceptions to its ban on protectionism to "times of severe shortage," or "times of shortage" or to "demonstrably arid states," and to presume the existence of an active state regulatory process that alters the allocation or distribution of water to meet current climatological conditions. How could a western State Engineer administer a typical system of prior appropriation permits to allow exports of water from a variable stream in years of high water and forbid them in years of drought? Suppose the source was an aquifer with a stabilized annual recharge, or with a finite supply of non-recharging water? What is an arid state? The arid zone is scientifically defined as a place where potential evapo-transpiration exceeds the average annual precipitation. Except for vagaries of storms, no water would flow off the land. Every western state has enclaves of humid climate in its mountains, where rainfall and snowmelt produce streams that flow to and through the dry plains.

CALIFORNIA v. UNITED STATES

Supreme Court of the United States, 1978.
438 U.S. 645, 98 S.Ct. 2985, 57 L.Ed.2d 1018.

MR. JUSTICE REHNQUIST delivered the opinion of the Court.

Respondent seeks to impound 2.4 million acre-feet of water from California's Stanislaus River as part of its Central Valley Project. The California State Water Resources Control Board ruled that the water could not be allocated to respondent under state law unless it agreed to and complied with various conditions dealing with the water's use. Respondent then sought a declaratory judgment in the District Court for the Eastern District of California to the effect that the United States can impound whatever unappropriated water is necessary for a federal reclamation project without complying with state law. The District Court held that, as a matter of comity, the United States must apply to the State for an appropriation permit, but that the State must issue the permit without condition if there is sufficient unappropriated water. United States v. California, 403 F.Supp. 874 (1976). The Court of Appeals for the Ninth Circuit affirmed, but held that § 8 of the Reclamation Act of 1902, 32 Stat. 388, 390, as amended, 43 U.S.C.A. §§ 372, 383, rather than comity, requires the United States to apply for the permit. 558 F.2d 1347 (1977). We granted certiorari to review the decision of the Court of Appeals insofar as it holds that California cannot condition its allocation of water to a federal reclamation project. We now reverse.

In order to correctly ascertain the meaning of the Reclamation Act of 1902, we must recognize the obvious truth that the history of irrigation and reclamation before that date was much fresher in the minds of those then in Congress than it is to us today. * * * The final expansion of our Nation in the 19th century into the arid lands beyond the hundredth meridian of longitude, which had been shown on early maps as the "Great American Desert," brought the participants in that expansion face to face with the necessity for irrigation in a way that no previous territorial expansion had. * * *

The arid lands were not all susceptible of the same sort of reclamation. The climate and topography of the lands that constituted the "Great American Desert" were quite different than the climate and topography of the Pacific Coast States. As noted in both Gerlach Livestock Co. v. United States, 339 U.S. 725, 70 S.Ct. 955, 94 L.Ed. 1231 (1950) and Ivanhoe Irrigation District v. United States, 357 U.S. 275, 78 S.Ct. 1174, 2 L.Ed.2d 1313 (1958), the latter States not only had a more pronounced seasonal variation and precipitation than the intermountain States, but the interior portions of California had climatic advantages which many of the intermountain States did not. * * *

If the term "cooperative federalism" had been in vogue in 1902, the Reclamation Act of that year would surely have qualified as a leading example of it. In that Act, Congress set forth on a massive program to construct and operate dams, reservoirs, and canals for the reclamation of the arid lands in 17 western States. Reflective of the "cooperative federalism" which the Act embodied is § 8, whose exact meaning and scope are the critical inquiries in this case:

> "[*N*]*othing in this Act shall be construed as affecting or intended to affect or to in any way interfere with the laws of any States or Territory relating to the control, appropriation, use or distribution of water used in irrigation,* or any vested rights acquired thereunder, *and the Secretary of the Interior, in carrying out the provisions of this Act, shall proceed in conformity with such laws,* and nothing herein shall in any way affect any right of any State or of the Federal Government or of any landowner, appropriator, or user of water in, to or from any interstate stream or the waters thereof: Provided, That the right to use of water acquired under the provisions of this Act shall be appurtenant to the land irrigated, and beneficial use shall be the basis, the measure, and the limit of the right." 43 U.S.C.A. § 383 (emphasis added).

The New Melones Dam, which this litigation concerns, is part of the California Central Valley Project, the largest reclamation project yet authorized under the 1902 Act. The Dam, which will impound 2.4 million acre-feet of water of California's Stanislaus River, has the multiple purposes of flood control, irrigation, municipal use, industrial use, power, recreation, water quality control and the protection of fish and wildlife. The waters of the Stanislaus River that will be impounded behind the New Melones Dam arise and flow solely in California.

The United States Bureau of Reclamation, as it has with every other federal reclamation project, applied for a permit from the appropriate state agency, here the California State Water Resources Control Board, to appropriate the water that would be impounded by the Dam and later used for reclamation. After lengthy hearings, the State Board found that unappropriated water was available for the New Melones Project during certain times of the year. Although it therefore approved the Bureau's applications, the State Board attached 25 conditions to the permits. California State Water Resources Control Board, Decision 1422 (April 15, 1973). The most important conditions prohibit full impoundment until the Bureau is able to show firm commitments, or at least a specific plan, for the use of the water.[a] The

a. Other conditions prohibit collection of water during periods of the year when unappropriated water is unavailable; require that a preference be given to water users in the water basin in which the New Melones Project is located; require storage releases to be made so as to maintain maximum and minimum chemical concentrations in the San Joaquin River and protect fish and wildlife; require the United States to provide means for the release of excess waters and to clear vegetation and structures from the reservoir sites; require the filing of additional reports and studies; and provide for access to the project site by the State Board and the public. Still other conditions reserve jurisdiction to the Board to impose further conditions on the appropriations if necessary to protect the "beneficial use" of the water involved. Respondent did not challenge any of the conditions under state law, but instead filed the federal declaratory action that is now before us.

State Board concluded that without such a specific plan of beneficial use the Bureau had failed to meet the California statutory requirements for appropriation. * * *

The history of the relationship between the Federal Government and the States in the reclamation of the arid lands of the western States is both long and involved, but through it runs the consistent thread of purposeful and continued deference to state water law by Congress. The rivers, streams and lakes of California were acquired by the United States under the 1848 Treaty of Guadalupe Hidalgo, 9 Stat. 922. Within a year of that treaty, the California gold rush began, and the settlers in this new land quickly realized that the riparian doctrine of water rights that had served well in the humid regions of the East would not work in the arid lands of the West. Other settlers coming into the intermountain area, the vast basin and range country which lies between the Rocky Mountains on the east and the Sierra Nevada and Cascade Ranges on the west, were forced to the same conclusion. In its place, the doctrine of prior appropriation, linked to beneficial use of the water, arose through local customs, laws, and judicial decisions. Even in this early stage of the development of western water law, before many of the western States had been admitted to the Union, Congress deferred to the growing local law.

In 1850, California was admitted as a State to the Union "on an equal footing with the original States in all respects whatever." 9 Stat. 452. While § 3 of the Act admitting California to the Union specifically reserved to the United States all "public lands" within the limits of California, ibid., no provision was made for the unappropriated waters in California's streams and rivers. One school of legal commentators held the view that, under the equal footing doctrine, the western States, upon their admission to the Union, acquired exclusive sovereignty over the unappropriated waters in their streams. In 1903, for example, one leading expert on reclamation and water law observed that "[i]t has heretofore been assumed that the authority of each State in the disposal of the water-supply within its borders was unquestioned and supreme and two of the States have constitutional provisions asserting absolute ownership of all water-supplies within their bounds." Mead, Irrigation Institutions 372 (1903). * * *

As noted earlier, reclamation of the arid lands began almost immediately upon the arrival of pioneers to the western States. Huge sums of private money were invested in systems to transport water vast distances for mining, agriculture, and ordinary consumption. Because a very high percentage of land in the West belonged to the Federal Government, the canals and ditches that carried this water frequently crossed federal land. In 1862, Congress opened the public domain to homesteading. Homestead Act of 1862, 12 Stat. 392. And in 1866, Congress for the first time expressly opened the mineral lands of the public domain to exploration and occupation by miners. Mining Act of 1866, 14 Stat. 251. Because of the fear that these Acts might in some way interfere with the water rights and systems that had grown up under state and local law, Congress explicitly recognized and acknowledged the local law:

> "[W]henever, by priority of possession, rights to the use of water for mining, agricultural, manufacturing, or other purposes, have vested and accrued, and the same are recognized and acknowledged by the local customs, laws, and the decisions of the courts, the possessors and owners of such vested rights shall be maintained and protected in the same." Mining Act of 1866, § 9, 14 Stat. 251, 253.

The Mining Act of 1866 was not itself a grant of water rights pursuant to federal law. Instead, as this Court observed, the Act was "a voluntary recognition of a preexisting right of possession, constituting a valid claim to its continued use." United States v. Rio Grande Dam & Irrig. Co., 174 U.S. 690, 705, 19 S.Ct. 770, 776, 43 L.Ed. 1136 (1899). Congress intended "to recognize as valid the customary law with respect to the use of water which had grown up among the occupants of the public land under the peculiar necessities of their condition." Basey v. Gallagher, 87 U.S. 670, 20 Wall. 670, 684, 22 L.Ed. 452 (1874). See Broder v. Natomic Water & Min. Co., 101 U.S. 274, 276, 25 L.Ed. 790 (1880); Jennison v. Kirk, 98 U.S. 453, 459–461, 25 L.Ed. 240 (1878).

In 1877, Congress took its first step towards encouraging the reclamation and settlement of the public desert lands in the West and made it clear that such reclamation would generally follow state water law. In the 1877 Desert Lands Act, 19 Stat. 377, Congress provided for the homesteading of arid public lands in larger tracts

> "by conducting water upon the same, within the period of three years [after filing a declaration to do so], *Provided however* that the right to the use of water by the person so conducting the same * * * shall not exceed the amount of water actually appropriated, and necessarily used for the purpose of irrigation and reclamation: *and all surplus water over and above such actual appropriation and use, together with the water of all lakes, rivers and other sources of water supply upon the public lands and not navigable, shall remain and be held free for the appropriation and use of the public for irrigation, mining and manufacturing purposes subject to existing rights.*" 19 Stat. 377 (emphasis added).

This Court has had an opportunity to construe the 1877 Desert Lands Act before. In California Oregon Power Co. v. Beaver Portland Cement Co., 295 U.S. 142, 55 S.Ct. 725, 79 L.Ed. 1356 (1935), Justice Sutherland explained that, through this language, "[Congress] effected a severance of all waters upon the public domain, not theretofore appropriated, from the land itself." Id., at 158, 55 S.Ct. at 729. The nonnavigable waters thereby severed were "reserved for the use of the public under the laws of the states and territories." Ibid. Congress' purpose was not to federalize the prior appropriation doctrine already evolving under local law. Quite the opposite:

> "What we hold is that following the act of 1877, if not before, all non-navigable waters then a part of the public domain became *publici juris,* subject to the plenary control of the designated states, including those since created out of the territories named, with the right in each to determine for itself to what extent the rule of appropriation or the common-law rule in respect of riparian rights should obtain. For since 'Congress cannot enforce either rule upon any state,' Kansas v. Colorado, 206 U.S. 46, 94, 27 S.Ct. 655, 666, 51 L.Ed. 956, the full power of choice must remain with the state. The Desert Land Act does not bind or purport to bind the states to any policy. It simply recognizes and gives sanction, in so far as the United States and its future grantees are concerned, to the state and local doctrine of appropriation, and seeks to remove what otherwise might be an impediment to its full and successful operation. See Wyoming v. Colorado, 259 U.S. 419, 465, 42 S.Ct. 552, 557, 66 L.Ed. 999." Id., at 163, 55 S.Ct. at 731.

It is against this background that Congress passed the Reclamation Act of 1902. * * * Private and state reclamation projects had gone far towards reclaiming the arid lands, but massive projects were now needed to complete the goal and these were beyond the means of private companies and the States. * * *

As a result of the public demand for federal reclamation funding, a bill was introduced into the 57th Congress to use the money from the sale of public lands in the western States to build reclamation projects in those same States. * * *

From the legislative history of the Reclamation Act of 1902, it is clear that state law was expected to control in two important respects. First, and of controlling importance to this case, the Secretary would have to appropriate, purchase, or condemn necessary water rights in strict conformity with state law. According to Representative Mondell, the principal sponsor of the reclamation bill in the House, once the Secretary determined that a reclamation project was feasible and that there was an adequate supply of water for the project, "the Secretary of the Interior would proceed to make the appropriation of the necessary water *by giving the notice and complying with the forms of law of the State or Territory in which the waters were located.*" 35 Cong.Rec. 6678 (1902) (emphasis added). The Secretary of the Interior could not take any action in appropriating the waters of the state streams "which could not be undertaken by an individual or corporation if it were in the position of the Government as regards the ownership of its lands." H.R.Rep. No. 794, 57th Cong., 1st Sess., at 7–8. Thus, in response to the statement of an opponent to the bill that the Secretary would be allowed to condemn water even if in violation of state law, Representative Mondell briskly responded

> "Whereabouts does the gentleman find any such provision as he is arguing? Whereabouts in the bill is there anything that attempts to give the Federal Government any right to condemn or to take any water right or do anything which an individual could not do? Will the

gentleman point out any place or any provision for the Federal Government to do anything that I could not do if I owned the public land?

"MR. RAY of New York. Do you say there is nothing in this bill that provides for condemnation?

"MR. MONDELL. *The bill provides explicitly that even an appropriation of water can not be made except under State law.*" 35 Cong.Rec. 6687 (1902) (emphasis added).

Second, once the waters were released from the dam, their distribution to individual landowners would again be controlled by state law. As explained by Senator Clark of Wyoming, one of the principal supporters of the reclamation bill in the Senate, "the control of the water after leaving the reservoirs shall be vested in the State and Territories through which such waters flow." Id., at 2222. * * * As Representative Sutherland, later to be a Justice of this Court, succinctly put it, "if the appropriation and use were not under the provisions of the State law the utmost confusion would prevail." Id., at 6770. Different water rights in the same State would be governed by different laws and would frequently conflict.[b]

For almost half a century, this congressionally mandated division between federal and state authority worked smoothly. No project was constructed without the approval of the Secretary of the Interior, and the United States through this official preserved its authority to determine how federal funds should be expended. But state laws relating to water rights were observed in accordance with the congressional directive contained in § 8 of the Act of 1902. In 1958, however, the first of

b. Congress did not intend to relinquish total control of the actual distribution of the reclamation water to the States. Congress provided in § 8 itself that the water right must be appurtenant to the land irrigated and governed by beneficial use, and in § 5 Congress forbade the sale of reclamation water to tracts of land of more than 160 acres. It is conceivable, of course, that Congress may not have intended to actually override state law when inconsistent with these other provisions but instead only intended to exercise a veto power over any reclamation project that, because of state law, could not be operated in compliance with these provisions. A project simply would not be built by the Federal Government if such a conflict existed. * * *

In previous cases interpreting § 8 of the 1902 Reclamation Act, however, this Court has held that state water law does not control in the distribution of reclamation water *if* inconsistent with other congressional directives to the Secretary. See Ivanhoe Irrigation District v. McCracken, 357 U.S. 275, 78 S.Ct. 1174, 2 L.Ed.2d 1313 (1958); City of Fresno v. California, 372 U.S. 627, 83 S.Ct. 996, 10 L.Ed.2d 28 (1963). We believe that this reading of the Act is also consistent with the legislative history and indeed is the preferable reading of the Act. See infra, n. 11. Whatever the intent of Congress with respect to state control over the distribution of water, however, Congress in the 1902 Act intended to follow state law as to appropriation of water and condemnation of water rights. Under the 1902 Act, the Secretary of the Interior was authorized in his discretion to 'locate and construct' reclamation projects. As the legislative history of the 1902 Act convincingly demonstrates, however, if state law did not allow for the appropriation or condemnation of the necessary water, Congress did not intend the Secretary of the Interior to initiate the project. Subsequent legislation authorizing a specific project may by its terms signify congressional intent that the Secretary condemn or be permitted to appropriate the necessary water rights for the project in question, but no such legislation was considered by the Court of Appeals in its opinion in this case. That court will be free to consider arguments by the Government to this effect on remand.

two cases was decided by this Court in which private land owners or municipal corporations contended that state water law had the effect of overriding specific congressional directives to the Secretary of the Interior as to the operation of federal reclamation projects. In Ivanhoe Irrigation District v. McCracken, 357 U.S. 275, 78 S.Ct. 1174, 2 L.Ed.2d 1313 (1958), the Supreme Court of California decided that California law forbade the 160-acre limitation on irrigation water deliveries expressly written into § 5 of the Reclamation Act of 1902, and that therefore, under § 8 of the Reclamation Act, the Secretary was required to deliver reclamation water without regard to the acreage limitation. Both the State of California and the United States appealed from this judgment, and this Court reversed it, saying:

> "Section 5 is a specific and mandatory prerequisite laid down by the Congress as binding in the operation of reclamation projects, providing that '[no] right to the use of water * * * shall be sold for a tract exceeding one hundred and sixty acres to any one landowner. * * *' * * * Without passing generally on the coverage of § 8 in the delicate area of federal-state relations in the irrigation field, we do not believe that the Congress intended § 8 to override the repeatedly reaffirmed national policy of § 5." Id., at 291–292, 78 S.Ct., at 1184.

Five years later, in City of Fresno v. California, 372 U.S. 627, 83 S.Ct. 996, 10 L.Ed.2d 28 (1963), this Court affirmed a decision of the United States Court of Appeals for the Ninth Circuit holding that § 8 did not require the Secretary of the Interior to ignore explicit congressional provisions preferring irrigation use over domestic and municipal use.[c]

Petitioner does not ask us to overrule these holdings, nor are we presently inclined to do so. Petitioner instead asks us to hold that a State may impose any condition on the "control, appropriation, use or distribution of water" through a federal reclamation project that is not inconsistent with clear congressional directives respecting the project. Petitioner concedes, and the government relies upon, dictum in our

c. "Section 9(c) of the Reclamation Project Act of 1939 * * * provides: 'No contract relating to municipal water supply or miscellaneous purposes * * * shall be made unless, in the judgment of the Secretary [of the Interior], it will not impair the efficiency of the project for irrigation purposes.' * * * It therefore appears clear that Fresno has no preferential rights to contract for project water, but may receive it only if, in the Secretary's judgment, irrigation will not be adversely affected." 372 U.S., at 630–631, 83 S.Ct., at 998.

The Court also concluded in a separate portion of its opinion that "§ 8 does not mean that state law may operate to prevent the United States from exercising the power of eminent domain to acquire the water rights of others. * * * Rather, the effect of § 8 in such a case is to leave to state law the definition of the property interests, if any, for which compensation must be made." 372 U.S., at 630, 83 S.Ct., at 998. Because no provision of California law was actually inconsistent with the exercise by the United States of its power of eminent domain, this statement was dictum. It also might have been apparent from examination of the congressional authorization of the Central Valley Project that Congress intended the Secretary to have the power to condemn any necessary water rights. We disavow this dictum, however, to the extent that it implies that state law does not control even where not inconsistent with such expressions of congressional intent.

cases that may point to a contrary conclusion. Thus, in *Ivanhoe,* the Court went beyond the actual facts of that case and stated:

> "As we read § 8, it merely requires the United States to comply with state law when, in the construction and operation of a reclamation project, it becomes necessary for it to acquire water rights or vested interests therein. * * * We read nothing in § 8 that compels the United States to deliver water on conditions imposed by the State." 357 U.S. 275, at 291–292, 78 S.Ct., at 1184.

Like dictum was repeated in City of Fresno, 372 U.S., at 630, 83 S.Ct., at 998, and in this Court's opinion in Arizona v. California, 373 U.S. 546, 83 S.Ct. 1468, 10 L.Ed.2d 542 (1963), where the Court also said:

> "The argument that § 8 of the Reclamation Act requires the United States in the delivery of water to follow priorities laid down by state law has already been disposed of by this Court in Ivanhoe Irr. Dist. v. McCracken, * * * and reaffirmed in City of Fresno v. California * * *. Since § 8 of the Reclamation Act did not subject the Secretary to state law in disposing of water in [*Ivanhoe*], we cannot, consistently with *Ivanhoe,* hold that the Secretary must be bound by state law in disposing of water under the Project Act." Id., at 586–587, 83 S.Ct., at 1491.

While we are not convinced that the above language is diametrically inconsistent with the position of petitioner, or that it squarely supports respondent, it undoubtedly goes further than was necessary to decide the cases presented to the Court. *Ivanhoe* and *City of Fresno* involved conflicts between § 8, requiring the Secretary to follow state law as to water rights, and other provisions of reclamation acts that placed specific limitations on how the water was to be distributed. Here respondent contends that it may ignore state law even if no explicit congressional directive conflicts with the conditions imposed by the California State Water Control Board.

But because there is at least tension between the above quoted dictum and what we conceive to be the correct reading of § 8 of the Reclamation Act of 1902, we disavow the dictum to the extent that it would prevent petitioner from imposing conditions on the permits granted to the United States which are not inconsistent with congressional provisions authorizing the project in question. Section 8 cannot be read to require the Secretary to comply with state law only when it becomes necessary to purchase or condemn vested water rights. That section does, of course provide for the protection of vested water rights, but it also requires the Secretary to comply with state law in the "control, appropriation, use, or distribution of water." Nor, as the United States contends, does § 8 merely require the Secretary of the Interior to file a notice with the State of its intent to appropriate but to thereafter ignore the substantive provisions of state law. The legislative history of the Reclamation Act of 1902 makes it abundantly clear that Congress intended to defer to the substance, as well as the form, of state water law. The Government's interpretation would trivialize the broad language and purpose of § 8. * * *

Indeed, until the unnecessarily broad language of the Court's opinion in *Ivanhoe,* both the uniform practice of the Bureau of Reclamation and the opinions of the Court clearly supported petitioner's argument that it may impose any condition not inconsistent with congressional directive. * * *

The United States suggests that, even if the Congress of 1902 intended the Secretary of the Interior to comply with state law, more recent legislative enactments have subjected reclamation projects "to a variety of federal policies that leave no room for state controls on the operation of a project or on the choice of uses it will serve." Brief for the United States, at 86. While later Congresses have indeed issued new directives to the Secretary, they have consistently reaffirmed that the Secretary should follow state law in all respects not directly inconsistent with these directives. The Flood Control Act of 1944, for example, which first authorized the New Melones Project, provides that it is the "policy of Congress to recognize the interest and rights of the States in determining the development of watersheds within their borders and likewise their interests and rights in water utilization and control." * * *

Because the District Court and the Court of Appeals both held that California could not impose any conditions whatever on the United States' appropriation permits, those courts did not reach the United States' alternative contention that the conditions actually imposed are inconsistent with congressional directives as to the New Melones Project. Nor did they reach California's contention that the United States is barred by principles of collateral estoppel from challenging the consistency of the permit conditions. Assuming, *arguendo,* that the United States is still free to challenge the consistency of the conditions, resolution of their consistency may well require additional fact-finding. We therefore reverse the judgment of the Court of Appeals and remand for further proceedings consistent with this opinion.

Reversed.

MR. JUSTICE WHITE, with whom MR. JUSTICE BRENNAN and MR. JUSTICE MARSHALL join, dissenting.

Early in its opinion, the majority identifies the critical issues in this case as to the "meaning and scope" of § 8 of the Reclamation Act of 1902. In quest of suitable answers, the majority launches on an extensive survey of 19th-and 20th-century statutory and judicial precedents that partially delineate the relationship between federal and state law with respect to the conservation and use of the water resources of the western States. At the end of this Odyssean journey, the conclusion seems to be that under the relevant federal statutes containing the reclamation policy of the United States, the intention of the Congress has been to recognize local and state law as controlling both the "appropriation and distribution" of the water resources that are the object of federal reclamation projects.

Straightaway, however, and with obvious reluctance, it is conceded in a footnote that § 8 does not really go so far and that Congress, after all, "did not intend to relinquish total control of the actual distribution of the reclamation water to the States." Ante, at n. 10. Where following state law would be inconsistent with other provisions of the Reclamation Act or with congressional directives to the Secretary contained in other statutes, § 8 and local law must give way. Otherwise, however, it is insisted that by virtue of § 8, state policy must govern federal projects. The next section of the majority opinion is devoted to defending this conclusion and to explaining why it refuses to follow our prior cases construing § 8 much more narrowly than the present temporal majority finds acceptable.

Meanwhile, the opinion has also concluded that because of § 8, the United States may not acquire water rights by appropriation or condemnation except in accordance with state law. If, for example, particular water rights are not subject to condemnation under state law by private interests, neither may they be taken by the United States. This issue, going to the acquisition by the United States of water rights by eminent domain, is not among the questions presented in this case, and the views expressed in this respect are no sounder and no less inconsistent with our prior cases than is the majority's view that the distribution of water developed by federal reclamation projects is to be governed by state law.

Four of the five major cases bearing on the construction of § 8 have arisen out of the Central Valley Reclamation Project, a massively expensive reclamation undertaking which aimed at redistributing the water in California's Central Valley, which the State was unable to finance and which the Federal Government eventually undertook. * * * United States v. Gerlach Live Stock Co., 339 U.S. 725, 70 S.Ct. 955, 94 L.Ed. 1231 (1950); Ivanhoe Irrigation District v. McCracken, 357 U.S. 275, 78 S.Ct. 1174, 2 L.Ed.2d 1313 (1958); Dugan v. Rank, 372 U.S. 609, 83 S.Ct. 999, 10 L.Ed.2d 15 (1963), and City of Fresno v. California, 372 U.S. 627, 83 S.Ct. 996, 10 L.Ed.2d 28 (1963). * * *

In *Gerlach,* supra, the Court of Claims had made compensation awards to the owners of certain riparian grasslands that had been watered by the seasonal overflow of the river. This overflow would no longer take place. * * * Since the closing of the dam would terminate the annual inundation of the lands involved, the inquiry became whether there had been a taking of any water rights defined and recognized by state law. After an extensive inquiry, the Court determined that the Court of Claims had properly understood state law, and the compensation awards were affirmed.

The next case before this Court involving the Central Valley Project was *Ivanhoe,* supra. That case arose out of proceedings in the state courts, required by federal statute, to confirm contracts for the use of water entered into between state irrigation districts and a state water agency, on the one hand, and the United States on the other. The contracts contained provisions against the use of project water on tracts in excess of 160 acres, a provision specified by § 5 of the Reclamation Act of 1902 and substantially re-enacted in the Omnibus Adjustment Act of 1926, 44 Stat. 649, as amended, 70 Stat. 524, 43 U.S. C.A. § 423e. * * * The Court rejected the argument that § 8 required the Secretary to follow state law that was inconsistent with § 5. As the Court understood § 8, "[I]t merely requires the United States to comply with state law when, in the construction and operation of a reclamation project, it becomes necessary for it to *acquire* water rights or vested interests therein." (emphasis added). The United States would be obliged to pay for any water rights which were vested under state law and which it took, "[b]ut the *acquisition* of water rights must not be confused with the *operation* of federal projects." (emphasis added). * * *

Like *Gerlach,* the *Dugan* and *Fresno* cases involved the consequences of the Friant Dam on those dependent on the first 60 miles of the San Joaquin downstream from the project. * * * Plaintiffs contended, among other things, that Congress had not conferred any right to condemn water rights along this stretch of the river and that in any event plaintiffs had rights under California's county-of-origin and county-of-watershed statutes that were not subject to condemnation under state law and hence, pursuant to § 8, were not seizable by the United States. * * * This Court in *Dugan,* however, unanimously agreed with the Court of Appeals that the United States had ample statutory authority to take the asserted rights. "The question was specifically settled in Ivanhoe Irrigation District v. McCracken * * *, where we said that such rights could be acquired by the payment of compensation 'either through condemnation or, if already taken, through action of the owners in the courts.'" Dugan, 372 U.S. 609, 619, 83 S.Ct. 999, 1006, 10 L.Ed.2d 15 (1963). * * *

The Court also granted the petition for certiorari filed by the city of Fresno and dealt separately with the city's case. 372 U.S. 627, 83 S.Ct. 996, 10 L.Ed.2d 28 (1963). * * * Among other things, the city claimed that the water necessary to satisfy its rights was being diverted to areas beyond the limits permitted by the county-of-origin and watershed-of-origin statutes of the State of California; under these statutes the city's rights were preferred and were not subject to condemnation under § 8 and state law. * * *

The Court rejected each of these claims. The United States had authority, despite § 8 and state law, to acquire Fresno's riparian rights, and had done so. To that extent, the city's recourse was in the Court of Claims, as in *Dugan.* Section 8 "does not mean that state law may operate to prevent the United States from exercising the power of eminent domain to acquire the water rights of others. This was settled in Ivanhoe Irrigation District v. McCracken * * *." 372 U.S., at 630,

83 S.Ct., at 998. Nor did § 8 require "compliance with California statutes relating to preferential rights of counties and watersheds of origin and to the priority of domestic over irrigation uses." Id., at 629–630, 83 S.Ct., at 998. The more limited role of § 8 "is to leave to state law the definition of the property interests, if any, for which compensation must be made." * * *

Our cases that the Court now discards are relatively recent decisions dealing with an issue of a statutory construction and with a subject matter that is under constant audit by Congress. * * * Only the revisionary zeal of the present majority can explain its misreading of our cases and its evident willingness to disregard them. Congress has not disturbed these cases, and until it does, I would respect them. * * *

Although I do not join the Court in reconstruing the controlling statutes as it does, the Court's work today is a precedent for "setting things right" in the area of statutory water law so as to satisfy the views of a current Court majority. And surely the dicta with which the Court's opinion is placed today deserve no more or no less respect than what it has chosen to label as dicta in past Court decisions. Of course, the matter is purely statutory and Congress could easily put an end to our feuding if it chose to make it clear that local authorities are to control the spending of federal funds for reclamation projects and to control the priorities for the use of water developed by federal projects.

Notes

1. Trelease, Reclamation Water Rights, 32 Rocky Mt.L.Rev. 464, 465 (1960):

"When the United States, by the passage of the Reclamation Act of 1902, entered the field of building large scale irrigation projects, its new policy of water development carried forward a much older policy of recognizing the law of the states and territories as the source of water rights. The government had from the beginning of western settlement permitted the miners and settlers to take the waters found on the public domain to work their mines and irrigate their lands. * * *

"The Carey Act of 1894 was the first attempt of the national government to assume an active role in the development of western irrigation. It placed a million acres at the disposal of each participating state that would build (or cause to be built by private capital) large irrigation works and would sell the lands to settlers in tracts of 160 acres. However, the Carey Act was substantially a failure. Few projects were built and on most of them the settlers found themselves in severe financial difficulties resulting from the heavy mortgages placed upon the lands to secure repayment of the cost of construction of the irrigation works.

"The Reclamation Act marked a departure from this pattern of private development. Since the need for large dams and canals was not being fully met by private capital, the act introduced federal financing of projects. A revolving fund was established with moneys received from the sale of public lands, and the Secretary of the Interior was directed to survey the west and locate and construct irrigation projects, opening up the improved public lands to settlement under the homestead laws. Where private lands were included within the area irrigable by project works, water rights might be sold to the landowners for the irrigation of tracts not exceeding 160 acres. Construction costs were to be repaid into the fund by the settlers and landowners in ten annual installments without interest.

"This basic statute has been amended, supplemented, and superseded by a long series of acts, some general in nature, some relating to specific projects. A compilation of all laws pertaining to Reclamation now fills two substantial volumes. Nowadays the Bureau of Reclamation builds multi-purpose projects which include features for production of hydroelectric power, control of floods, navigation improvement, municipal and industrial water supplies, recreation, and fish and wildlife preservation, as well as for irrigation. Projects now encompass the comprehensive development of entire river basins. The revolving fund was long ago exhausted and today's projects are built with general funds. Repayment periods have been stretched out. However, the fundamental concepts of the 1902 Act remain."

2. Kelley, Staging a Comeback—Section 8 of the Reclamation Act, 18 U.C. Davis L.Rev. 97 (1984), provides an exhaustive and perceptive review of California v. U.S., its predecessor cases, its subsequent history, and its progeny. Professor Kelley leads the way through seven phases of the procedural fencing and substantive conflicts of the New Melones case. She urges that federal and state administrators and judges should approach the problems raised by Section 8 with sensitive appreciation of the complexities of their task. One who follows the professor's guide through the thickets of conformity, deference, pre-emption and supremacy cannot fail to get at least that appreciation.

3. The "severance" concept utilized by the Supreme Court in California Oregon Power Co. v. Beaver Portland Cement Co. as a basis for state jurisdiction over water rights results from the premise that the federal government initially "owned" all waters in the western states. Is the concept of "ownership" a useful one in analyzing and resolving federal-state conflicts involving water? Consider the following:

"Better results [than those based on spinning theories of 'ownership'] can be reached by sticking to what the Supreme Court has said—that the government had power to dispose of the water. It had that power in 1802, when Ohio became the first state created out of the public domain, but it did not exercise it. Congress might have adopted a federal water law for disposing of water rights as it enacted laws to dispose of the lands, but it did not do so. As the western public lands states were born, they took over the function of establishing water rights by common law and statutes, as had been done in the original thirteen states in which there was no public domain. * * * They did what all states had always done, exercised what the Supreme Court has called their 'traditional jurisdiction' over water. There is no evidence that the legislators or courts of any state from Ohio to California had any thought that they were dealing with water that belonged to the federal government until California's 1886 mistake [in deciding Lux v. Haggin]. The states filled the vacuum left by federal inaction, and the United States gave its sanction by its 'silent acquiescense,' which means that Congress gave the matter no thought either.

"The holding of the case [of California Oregon Power Co. v. Beaver Portland Cement Co.] gave the western states the rule they had always hoped was law, that each could decide the form of its own water law. Nevertheless, the grounds on which the decision was rested left uneasy doubts as to its universal application. The Court's use of the Desert Land Act in its reasoning creates several difficulties. The act did not cover all the appropriation law states, for it had no force in Kansas, Nebraska and Oklahoma, and it was not applied to Colorado until amended in 1891. The proviso excepts from its operation navigable waters, but surely this could not mean that landowners along the Missouri River in Montana have federal riparian rights. That state recognizes no such rights and inconceivable choas would result if such rights were held to exist by virtue of federal law. The Act was passed in 1877 and if it in that year severed the water from the federal lands and patents, this could be taken as an indication that patents granted before its enactment did carry riparian rights. Such a ruling would raise havoc with the water law systems of all of the Colorado doctrine states. The Court did leave a way out of this construction by saying that the severance occurred in 1877 'if not before,' and it is commonly supposed that the reference is to the Act of 1866. This is only a less unsatisfactory solution, because much land had been patented in the Colorado doctrine states before that date. Only if 'if not before' refers back to the beginning of state and territorial governments and if each state or territory had from the beginning the right to determine for itself the law of water rights, can the *Beaver* holding be sustained on the reasoning of a severance. And if that is done, we are back to the original proposition here proposed, that the state laws have validity not because of an act of Congress but because of the 'silent acquiescence' of the federal government. Water law was the subject of concurrent federal and state jurisdiction. The states could exercise their traditional jurisdiction unless their laws were superseded by a federal law disposing of the water. Since the federal government never enacted such a law, the state law stood." (Trelease, Federal-State Relations in Water Law, National Water Commission Legal Study No. 5, 113–224, 147b–147h (1971).)

Major J.W. Powell, famous explorer of the West and Director of the U.S. Geological Survey, recommended to Congress a system of federal grants of water rights coupled into a reformed system of federal disposal of the land in the public domain. Report on the Lands of the Arid Regions of the United States (1879). His proposals were never enacted.

Meanwhile the western states laid claim to the "ownership" of the waters within their borders and made the argument that the United States is or should be subject to state control whenever it engaged in water resources development activities, under Reclamation law or otherwise. Merrill v. Bishop, 74 Wyo. 298, 287 P.2d 620 (1955); Preservation of Integrity of State Water Laws, Committee of the National Reclamation Association (1942). Some logical and historical fallacies of this position were explored in Trelease, Government Ownership and Trusteeship of

Water, 45 Calif.L.Rev. 638 (1957), and Note, Federal-State Conflicts Over the Control of Western Waters, 60 Colum.L.Rev. 967 (1960), and it seems to have been completely demolished by Goldberg, Interposition—Wild West Water Style, 17 Stan.L.Rev. 1 (1964), and by Morreale, Federal-State Conflicts over Western Waters—A Decade of Attempted "Clarifying Legislation," 20 Rutgers L.Rev. 423 (1966).

4. President Theodore Roosevelt conceived of the Reclamation Act as reopening the American frontier and giving a new wave of settlers the opportunity to "go west," settle on family-sized farms and continue the "agrarian myth" that America's strength lay in her rural population. Section 5 of the Act provided that no right to the use of water would be sold for land in excess of 160 acres in one ownership. When public lands were improved by early reclamation projects, the "160-acre limitation" on the the size of the homestead granted to each settler received no criticism. Most projects, however, were capable of irrigating land in private ownership as well as public lands. When dry lands in private hands were watered by some projects, the owners were often glad to sell excess sagebrush lands in order to obtain a fertile irrigated farm. The owner of a 640-acre grazing homestead was usually pleased to trade off 480 acres worth $2 an acre in order to receive water that made the remaining 160 acres of his land worth $40 an acre. A married couple could retain 320 acres.

The "Omnibus Adjustment Act of 1926" ended contracts with individual settlers and water users' associations and required the United States to enter into contracts with irrigation districts, quasi-governmental agencies that would distribute water to eligible landowners, collect charges for water, operation and maintenance, and reimburse the United States for the allocated costs of construction of the project. The districts were required by the contracts to withhold project water from private land in excess of 160 acres in one ownership unless the owner executed a recordable contract with the Secretary of the Interior obligating the owner to sell excess land at a price excluding incremental value attributable to availability of water from the project. Much excess land was on large farms settled long before the project, irrigated with junior water rights that furnished only a partial or part-time supply. On some projects the contracts postponed the sale of the land for a period of 10 years and allowed delivery of project water to all the excess land in the meantime. The landowner had the choice of keeping all his land, with its pre-project supply, if any, or using all the land for the next 10 years with a full supply of water, then selling the excess.

The voluntary nature of the landowner's decision to retain or sell his excess lands is considerably reduced where irrigation districts assess all land irrigable from the project as improved, but deny water to excess lands. The landowner cannot afford to pay the assessments and hold the land as dry land. By this device, projects that need full participation and require assessment of all lands to make repayment feasible cannot be blocked by a few large landowners. Wyoming districts originally followed this practice, but it was held illegal in In re Owl Creek Irrigation Dist., 71 Wyo. 30, 253 P.2d 867 (1953). The irrigation district statute requires district boundaries to be fixed in such a manner as to be just, and it was held not just to include all of the land and force an owner to sell part of it whether he wishes to do so or not, at prices he may disapprove of and in the fixing of which he has had nothing to say. Quaere: Could the United States condemn the land for the purpose of dividing it into family-sized farms and resettling it? Compare Berman v. Parker, 348 U.S. 26, 75 S.Ct. 98, 99 L.Ed. 63 (1954).

On some projects water users in financial straits received dispensations and extensions that left irrigated excess lands in their hands for long periods. On some projects with poor quality land larger farm units were allowed, e.g., 480 acres on Kendrick Project, Wyoming; some allow larger amounts of poor land up to the "equivalent" of 160 acres of Class I land, e.g., Seedskadee Project, Wyoming; some allow excess lands if interest is paid on reimbursement, e.g., Washoe Project, California-Nevada. Some projects where all land receives only supplemental water were completely exempted from the operation of the excess land laws and private landowners could receive project water for their total holdings, e.g., Colorado-Big Thompson Project, Colorado. For a complete list of laws and projects, see 42 Fed.Reg. 43045–6 (1977).

In some areas, notably the Central Valley of California, large corporate farms and "agribusinesses" challenged the "family farm" as an economic unit for the production of food and other agricultural products. After many years of debate and trial balloons, Congress finally passed the Reclamation Reform Act, Title II of P.L. 97–293, 96 Stat. 1263 (1982), 43 U.S.C.A. §§ 390aa–390zz, which made major changes in Reclamation law, primarily in regard to acreage limitations. The basic rule is now that a "qualified recipient" (an individual citizen or resident alien, or a corporation benefiting twenty-five persons or less) may not receive project water at subsidized reclamation prices for more than 960 acres, and a "limited recipient" (a corporation benefiting more than twenty-five persons) may not receive water for more than 640 acres. (§ 399dd). Of the 640 acres, only the first 320 acres may receive subsidized water and only if water was being delivered to the land prior to October 1, 1981; "full cost" must be paid for the remainder. However, the holder of excess lands may receive water for those lands under one of two conditions: at subsidized rates if the owner executes a recordable contract to sell the excess acreage within a reasonable time, not to exceed ten years (§ 390ii), or at full cost for the water delivered on the excess land (§ 390ee). "Full cost" is a price fixed to recover actual construction, operation and maintenance costs and interest at market rates, at least 7% (§ 390bb(3) A, B, C). The subsidized cost of water to non-excess lands continues to be based on the ability of the project farmer to pay. The acreage limitations are based on the very best "Class I" lands; larger acreages of less productive lands may be allowed to give the farmer the equivalent of Class I land.

A number of other changes are significant. The recipient may lease other lands, land leased is included in "ownership," and if excess it can receive water at full cost. Ordinarily, leases must not exceed ten years, but leases for perennial crops (orchards, vineyards) may run up to twenty-five years (§ 390yy). The acreage limitations do not apply to a project built by the Corps of Engineers unless Congress clearly made it a Reclamation

Project or the Bureau has provided project works for control or conveyance of water (§ 390*ll*).

A transitional provision permits districts with existing contracts to agree to amendments that give them the benefits of the new law, but districts that elect not to amend (some have long term contracts at much more favorable rates than "full cost") were made subject to the prior law. Unless the contract is amended by April 1987, any water delivered to land in excess of 160 acres will be charged at full cost (§ 390cc). If a district does not amend its contract, however, an individual water recipient may qualify for the benefits of the act by executing a separate recordable contract to sell his or its excess lands.

5. Under the usual type of repayment contract, authorized by § 9(d) of the Reclamation Project Act of 1939, the individual irrigator's share of project costs is amortized over a forty year period, after a ten year development period, and is assessed to the lands by the district and collected along with annual operation and maintenance charges.

Under such a contract, the irrigator becomes the owner of a permanent water right, Ickes v. Fox, 300 U.S. 82, 57 S.Ct. 412, 81 L.Ed. 525 (1937), and under procedures current in some states, the water right is adjudicated to him under state law, Nebraska v. Wyoming, supra, p. 598. § 9(e) authorizes the Secretary of the Interior to enter into contracts under which the United States furnishes water, for periods up to forty years, at rates fixed so as to cover operating costs and only such share of construction costs as the Secretary deems proper. These were designed for situations where total repayment in forty years would be beyond the ability of the water users to pay, and have been likened to the arrangement made by a public utility furnishing water to consumers. They have been widely used in the Central Valley Project. In another phase of the *Ivanhoe case* the validity of this type of contract was questioned. The California Supreme Court indicated that constitutional principles would be violated by a contract which imposed on the landowners "a burden under which they may suffer the loss of water rights at the discretion of the United States," but avoided so holding by construing § 8 of the Reclamation Act as requiring the United States to comply with California's law regulating public utilities. The United States Supreme Court reversed, on the ground that in the operation of federal projects the government is not bound to deliver water on conditions imposed by the state. The Court was not impressed by the supposed insecurity of the irrigator. "It would be a physical impossibility to withdraw the facilities. As for the possibility of discrimination in the administration of those facilities, it seems farfetched to foresee the Federal Government 'turning its back upon a people who had been benefited by it' and allowing their lands to revert to desert. The prospect is too improbable to figure in our decision." 357 U.S. 275, 299, 78 S.Ct. 1174, 1188.

Actually, as pointed out by the Court, most of the objections to the contract had been eliminated by a 1956 act which requires the Secretary to include in 9(e) contracts provisions for renewal, and for continued rights to a share of project waters during the term of the contract or any renewal, and a permanent right upon complete repayment of construction costs. 43 U.S.C.A. § 485h–1. Eventually, then, all water users on reclamation projects will have the same type of right, whether they started with 9(d) or 9(e) contracts.

A less permanent water right may be obtained by non-project landowners under the Warren Act, 43 U.S.C.A. §§ 523, 524 (1911). The Secretary may agree to provide water users outside the project with water from the project works when their capacity exceeds the project's needs. The contracts may provide for temporary deliveries pending full development of the project or for the "rental" of water on terms providing such use is secondary and inferior to the right to use the water on the project.

6. In Chapter 2 the transfer of water rights as a method of shifting water uses to new demands, particularly from agriculture to municipal and industrial water, was discussed from the point of view of state law. Since over 25% of the irrigated land in the western states is supplied with water by the Bureau of Reclamation, the transferability of project water is a matter of some importance. The practice of the Bureau has not been uniform. In general, there is no express restriction in federal law against transfers, and although water rights are made appurtenant to land and one landowner may not by purchase or otherwise irrigate more than 160 acres, these provisions do not seem to add up to a prohibition of sales. Practically all Bureau of Reclamation repayment contracts, however, require the consent of the Bureau to any transfer of water rights. Officials of the Bureau have generally had a strong policy against transfer of project water by owners of irrigated land. Their reluctance is based in part on the theory of preventing windfall profits that would accrue to the farmer who reaps the irrigation subsidy in such case, in part on the fear of jeopardizing repayment. See Sax, Selling Reclamation Water Rights: A Case Study in Federal Subsidy Policy, 64 Mich.L.Rev. 13 (1965). Since no firm policy has been established at the national level, in most areas transfers are discouraged, but in others, as in the Northern Colorado Conservancy District, there is an active market in project water. See Anderson, Windfall Gains from Transfers of Water Allotments Within the Colorado-Big Thompson Project, 40 Land Econ. 265 (1967). A penetrating study is Meyers and Posner, Market Transfers of Water Rights: Toward an Improved Market in Water Resources, National Water Commission, Legal Study No. 4 (1971).

7. The Reclamation Project Act of 1939, 43 U.S.C.A. § 485, authorizes the allocation of costs of multipurpose projects to the various purposes undertaken. Costs allocated to navigation and flood control are nonreimbursable. (Costs allocated to the preservation and propagation of fish and wildlife are made nonreimbursable by a later act, 16 U.S.C.A. § 661). Irrigation, power and municipal supply costs are to be returned to the United States by the water users and from net power revenues. In practice, costs allocated to irrigation but beyond the water user's ability to pay are assigned for return from revenues received for power and municipal supply.

In the 1944 Flood Control Act, the Bureau of Reclamation's program in the entire Missouri Basin was treated as a single project, 33 U.S.C.A. § 701–1(b), and basin-wide allocations were made.

"In a study of how Basin projects, including all the main stem dams, would pay out, published in 1951, the Bureau [of Reclamation] showed the allocation of costs to various purposes as follows:

	Allocations	Scheduled Repayments
"Irrigation	$2,577,113,000	$ 905,367,400
Power	687,038,000	2,333,550,400
Municipal water	19,695,000	49,235,200
Fish and wildlife	660,000	———
Recreation	3,647,000	———
Reserve (power system)	59,330,000	59,330,000
	3,347,483,000	3,347,483,000

"The repayment of reimbursable costs was computed on a schedule that would return the Federal investment, without interest, to the Treasury in 86 years. * * *

"Thus, a basin account is a concept of pooling the costs and revenues of those reimbursable portions of the program that are to be included in the account. * * * The account is nonexistent in the sense that the funds are held and expended for purposes of constructing future projects. Rather, it is a concept under which the Federal Government gets back the same number of dollars that it had put into the reimbursable features. * * *" Missouri: Land and Water, Report of the Missouri Basin Survey Commission, 107–108 (1953).

The Colorado River Storage Act, 70 Stat. 105, 43 U.S.C.A. § 620, provides for three major dams and a number of "participating projects" in upper basin states. The large dams are for storage to meet the requirements of delivery of water to lower basin states under the Colorado River Compact, and for the production of power; the participating projects are primarily for irrigation and municipal supply. A basin fund is created which in effect permits the use of power revenues in excess of the return of costs allocated to power to be used for reimbursement of the costs of the participating projects. These funds are assigned for use in the states of the upper basin in proportion to the amount of flow of the river arising in each state.

The National Water Commission did not accept the theory that irrigation reciprocally subsidizes electric power because the cost of power production facilities is limited to features added onto the irrigation project and no part of dam costs are assigned to it, although the Bureau of Reclamation claims that sales of power are increased by the cheap rates made possible by this method of allocating joint costs.

"A primary weakness of the Federal water resources development projects is that they have been heavily subsidized by the Federal Government; that is, by all the taxpayers of the Nation, to provide benefits for a few. The water users on some modern Federal Reclamation projects, for example, repay no more than 10 percent of the construction costs attributable to irrigation, the remaining cost being borne by the Federal Government in three ways: by not requiring the water users to reimburse the Treasury for the interest on the capital advanced for project construction, by permitting power revenues and sometimes other nonirrigation revenues to be credited toward irrigation reimbursement, and by allocating an unduly large part of the costs to nonreimbursable purposes. Water Policies for the Future 128 (1973)."

During the administrations of Presidents Carter and Reagan, federal investment in water resources program was severely curtailed, in large part due to deficits in the federal budget. "New starts" on authorized projects of the Bureau of Reclamation, the Corps of Engineers and the Soil Conservation Service came almost to a standstill, and progress and current construction was slowed in ongoing projects. Many suggestions have been made for "cost sharing," contributions from the states toward financing water projects. For a discussion of the proper roles of the federal and state governments and the desirable shares of water development project costs that should be borne by beneficiaries, state and local governments, and the federal government, see Western States Water Council, State/Federal Financing and Western Water Resource Development (1984 update).

ARIZONA v. CALIFORNIA

Supreme Court of the United States, 1963.
373 U.S. 546, 83 S.Ct. 1468, 10 L.Ed.2d 542.

[In that part of Arizona v. California reported in Chapter 7, supra, the Supreme Court decided that Congress had apportioned 7,500,000 acre feet annually to the three states of the lower basin, 4.4 million to California, 2.8 to Arizona and .3 to Nevada. Shortages in the available supply are to be divided among the states by the Secretary of the Interior, giving preference to "present perfected rights" but otherwise unhampered by any formula or binding guidelines. The Court then turned to the distribution within the states of the shares allocated to each state.

Section 14 of the Boulder Canyon Project Act of 1928, 43 U.S.C.A. § 617m provided: "This subchapter shall be deemed a supplement to the reclamation law, which said reclamation law shall govern the construction, operation and management of the works herein authorized, except as otherwise herein provided." * * * Section 18 of the Act also stated, "Nothing herein shall be construed as interfering with such rights as the states now have either to the waters within their borders or to adopt such policies and enact such laws as they may deem necessary with respect to the appropriation, control, and use of waters within their borders * * *." Section 5 authorized the Secretary of the Interior " * * * under such general regulations as he may prescribe, to contract for the storage of water in said reservoir and for the delivery thereof at such points on the river * * * as may be agreed upon, for irrigation and domestic uses * * *." Reading the legislative history of the Act, the Court concluded, " * * * it is the Act and the Secretary's contracts, not the law of prior appropriation, that control the apportionment of water among the states. Moreover, * * * we hold that the Secretary in choosing between users within each state and in settling the terms of the contracts is not bound by these sections to follow state law." After discussing *Ivanhoe,* the Court concluded:]

Since § 8 of the Reclamation Act did not subject the Secretary to state law in disposing of water in that case, we cannot, consistently with Ivanhoe, hold that the Secretary must be bound by state law in disposing of water under the Project Act.

Nor does § 18 of the Project Act require the Secretary to contract according to state law. That Act was passed in the exercise of congressional power to control navigable water for purposes of flood control, navigation, power generation, and other objects, and is equally sustained by the power of Congress to promote the general welfare through projects for reclamation, irrigation, or other internal improvements. Section 18 merely preserves such rights as the States "now" have, that is, such rights as they had at the time the Act was passed. While the States were generally free to exercise some jurisdiction over these waters before the Act was passed, this right was subject to the Federal Government's right to regulate and develop the river. Where the Government, as here, has exercised this power and undertaken a comprehensive project for the improvement of a great river and for the orderly and beneficial distribution of water, there is no room for inconsistent state laws.

In undertaking this ambitious and expensive project for the welfare of the people of the Lower Basin States and of the Nation, the United States assumed the responsibility for the construction, operation, and supervision of Boulder Dam and a great complex of other dams and works. * * * All this vast, interlocking machinery—a dozen major works delivering water according to congressionally fixed priorities for home, agricultural, and industrial uses to people spread over thousands of square miles—could function efficiently only under unitary management, able to formulate and supervise a coordinated plan that could take account of the diverse, often conflicting interests of the people and communities of the Lower Basin States. Recognizing this, Congress put the Secretary of the Interior in charge of these works and entrusted him with sufficient power, principally the § 5 contract power, to direct, manage, and coordinate their operation. Subjecting the Secretary to the varying, possibly inconsistent, commands of the different state legislatures could frustrate efficient operation of the project and thwart full realization of the benefits Congress intended this national project to bestow. We are satisfied that the Secretary's power must be construed to permit him, within the boundaries set down in the Act, to allocate and distribute the waters of the mainstream of the Colorado River. * * *

THE CHIEF JUSTICE took no part in the consideration or decision of this case.

MR. JUSTICE HARLAN, whom MR. JUSTICE DOUGLAS and MR. JUSTICE STEWART join, dissenting in part.

* * * I also dissent from the holding that in times of shortage the Secretary has discretion to select or devise any "reasonable method" he wishes for determining which users within these States are to bear the burden of that shortage. * * * State law was intended to control apportionment among users within a single State. * * *

Still another, and profoundly significant, factor in understanding the effect of the Project Act on the law of appropriation and judicial apportionment is the pervasive hostility that many westerners had to any form of federal control of water rights.

Congress' entire approach to the problems of prior appropriation was governed by this deep-seated hostility to federal dictation of water rights. * * * The law of appropriation, basic to western water law, was greatly respected * * *.

It is inconceivable that such a Congress intended that the sweeping federal power which it declined to exercise—a power even the most avid partisans of national authority might hesitate to grant to a single administrator—be exercised at the unbridled discretion of an administrative officer, especially in the light of complaints registered about "bureaucratic" and "oppressive" interference of the Department which that very officer headed. * * *

MR. JUSTICE DOUGLAS, dissenting. * * *

Much is written these days about judicial lawmaking; and every scholar knows that judges who construe statutes must of necessity legislate interstitially, to paraphrase Mr. Justice Cardozo. Selected Writings (1947 Hall ed.), p. 160. The present case is different. It will, I think, be marked as the baldest attempt by judges in modern times to spin their own philosophy into the fabric of the law, in derogation of the will of the legislature. The present decision, as MR. JUSTICE HARLAN shows, grants the federal bureaucracy a power and command over water rights in the 17 Western States that it never has had, that it always wanted, that it could never persuade Congress to grant, and that this Court up to now has consistently refused to recognize. * * *

The principle that water priorities are governed by state law is deep-seated in western reclamation law. In spite of the express command of § 14 of the Project Act, which makes the system of appropriation under state law determine who has the priorities, the Secretary of the Interior is given the right to determine the priorities by administrative *fiat*. Now one can receive his priority because he is the most worthy Democrat or Republican, as the case may be.

The decision today, resulting in the confusion between the problem of priority of water rights and the public power problem, has made the dream of the federal bureaucracy come true by granting it, for the first time, the life-and-death power of dispensation of water rights long administered according to state law. * * *

Notes

1. A definitive article putting Arizona v. California in its setting is Meyers, The Colorado River, 19 Stanford L.Rev. 1 (1966). This extremely important decision received its proper share of comment. Critical reviews, at least disapproving of the Court's finding that the Boulder Canyon Project Act intended to give such broad powers to the Secretary of the Interior, are found in Clyde, The Colorado River Decision—1963, 8 Utah L.Rev. 299 (1964), and Trelease, Arizona v. California: Allocation of Water Resources to People, States and Nation, 1963 Supreme Court Rev. 158. The decision is justified, in the light of the need for a national policy and for the management of integrated basin-wide programs, in Sax, Problems of Federalism in Reclamation Law, 37 U. of Colo.L.Rev. 49 (1964) and Haber, Arizona v. California—A Brief Review, 4 Natural Resources J. 17 (1964).

2. The Colorado River Basin Project Act, 43 U.S.C.A. § 1521, provided for the long-awaited final development of the lower river, for which Arizona v. California had cleared the way. Section 301(a) authorized the Central Arizona Project that finally brought Colorado River water to the Phoenix-Tucson area, where the streams had long been over-appropriated and groundwater levels were declining.

The decree in Arizona v. California, Art. II(B)(3), directed the Secretary, when the flow available to the lower basin fell below 7.5 million acre feet per year, to first satisfy present perfected rights without regard to state lines and to apportion the remainder "in such manner as is consistent with the Boulder Canyon Project Act as interpreted by the opinion of this Court herein, and with other applicable federal statutes, but in no event shall more than 4,400,000 acre feet be apportioned for use in California including all present perfected rights." As to this, the 1968 Project Act continued:

"(b) Article II(B)(3) of the decree of the Supreme Court of the United States in Arizona against California (376 U.S. 340) shall be so administered that in any year in which, as determined by the Secretary, there is insufficient main stream Colorado River water available for release to satisfy annual consumptive use of seven million five hundred thousand acre-feet in Arizona, California, and Nevada, diversions from the main stream for the Central Arizona Project shall be so limited as to assure the availability of water in quantities sufficient to provide for the aggregate annual consumptive use by holders of present perfected rights, by other users in the State of California served under existing contracts with the United States by diversion works heretofore constructed, and by other existing Federal reservations in that State, of four million four hundred thousand acre-feet of mainstream water, and by users of the same character in Arizona and Nevada. Water users in the State of Nevada shall not be required to bear shortages in any proportion greater than would have been imposed in the absence of this subsection. This subsection shall not affect the relative priorities, among themselves, of water users in Arizona, Nevada, and California which are senior to diversions for the Central Arizona Project, or amend any provisions of said decree."

3. The "present perfected rights" of private appropriators, given first priority in the Colorado River Compact and the Project Act, were settled by supplemental decree, 439 U.S. 419, 99 S.Ct. 995, 58 L.Ed.2d 627 (1979).

4. Practically all of the land in the Imperial Valley of California was settled and all was irrigated by the predecessors of the Imperial Irrigation District before the Boulder Canyon Project Act of 1928 was enacted, the Imperial Dam was constructed and the All American Canal replaced the flood-prone Alamo Canal through Mexico. Section 14 of the Project Act makes Reclamation law applicable to the construction, operation and management of the works. In 1933 Secretary of the Interior Ray Lyman Wilbur wrote the district a letter, apparently for use in a pending case, in which he stated that § 5 of the 1902 Reclamation Act, which prohibits the sale of water to one landowner for a tract exceeding 160 acres, had no application because project water was not "sold" to the landowners but only "delivered" in return for reimbursement of canal costs. The letter did not refer to § 46 of the 1926 Act, which does prohibit delivery of water prior to the signing of recordable contracts. Doubts as to the legal validity of the Wilbur letter were voiced by various Solicitors and Secretaries of the Department of the Interior in 1944, 1945, 1948, 1961 and 1964, but the Bureau of Reclamation did not enforce the 160 acre limitation in the Imperial Valley.

In 1967 the United States brought suit against the district seeking a declaratory judgment that the land limitation provisions of § 46 of the Omnibus Adjustment Act (43 USCA § 423e) applied to private lands receiving water from the canal. In U.S. v. Imperial Irrigation Dist., 559 F.2d 509 (9th Cir.1977), the court held that § 46 applies to the Imperial Valley. Furthermore, said the court, the Wilbur letter and the inaction of the Department of the Interior did not constitute a consistent and long standing administrative interpretation to which the court felt it should defer.

The Supreme Court reversed, sub nom. Bryant v. Yellen, 447 U.S. 352, 100 S.Ct. 2232, 65 L.Ed.2d 184 (1980). The district's Alamo Canal water rights were "present perfected rights," said the Court, recognized by the Project Act as superior to the water rights of the project. They were obtained under state law, protected from impairment by Section 18 of the Act, and state law made the landowners who received the water the beneficial owners of the water right and placed no restriction on the district's delivery to individual farms. The Court found nothing to indicate that Congress had the intent to effect so serious a change in the nature of the water rights as to do away with the district's privilege and duty to service farms regardless of their size. The Secretary's 1933 letter was given weight as a contemporary construction of Project Act that the acreage limitation did not apply to lands with the district then being irrigated.

SECTION 2. ENVIRONMENTAL PROTECTION

INTRODUCTORY NOTE

Environmental law covers many facets of the relation of man to nature—land, air, water, plants and creatures. Environmental law is a much broader subject than water law, but the two touch at many points. We have seen state laws that regulate or prevent the use of water in order to enhance or preserve values of recreation, scenic enjoyment, and fish and wildlife habitat. This section presents federal environmental law in two aspects: first, as controlling the United States and its officials in constructing projects and carrying out programs, and second, as limiting or modifying the operation of state water laws or state-created water rights.

Federal environmental law, as a constraint on federal projects and activities, got its start with "cost-benefit analysis." Since 1936 it has been national policy that all navigation improvements and flood control projects should be authorized only " * * * if the benefits to whomsoever they may accrue are in excess of the estimated costs." 33 U.S.C.A. § 701A. Bureau of Reclamation projects were in theory authorized on a showing of "financial feasibility," whether the project would pay out under reimbursement policies, but benefit-cost analysis was still necessary for non-reimbursable features such as navigation and flood control and improvement of fish and wildlife habitat. The Office of Management and Budget, however, subjects Reclamation projects to much the same benefit-cost requirements that governs the others.

Recognition that adverse effects on the environment should be counted as costs began with Namekagon Hydro Co. v. Federal Power Commission, 216 F.2d 509 (7th Cir.1954), where the company sought a license for a 1500 kilowatt power plant. The low dam would create a narrow reservoir with six and one-half miles of slack water in the middle of a twenty-two mile free-flowing stretch of beautiful stream. The court held the license was properly denied, comparing the relatively small water power development against the unique and special recreational values that would be destroyed—canoe float trips by many groups of Boy Scouts, Girl Scouts and others, and the national reputation of the stream for bass fishing:

> But perhaps the uniqueness of the river is more apparent to those who take a float trip. Many of such persons are from urban centers and to see wild life in a natural setting is a thrill indeed. Such a float trip is exciting as well as peaceful. Passing by heavily wooded banks on either side, with no noise or sound to be heard from highways or railroads, the canoeist has the illusion of being in a forest primeval, far from civilization. Each bend of the river is watched with anticipation for a deer may be seen on the bank, or, occasionally, a black bear scurrying for the timber. There are very few, if any, comparable stretches of river left in Wisconsin. A

canoe trip on the Namekagon often calls for a repeat performance, one witness testifying that he had made 90 canoe trips thereon.

A decade later Scenic Hudson Preservation Conference v. Federal Power Commission, 354 F.2d 608 (2d Cir.1965), cert. denied 384 U.S. 941, 86 S.Ct. 1462, 16 L.Ed.2d 540 (1966), held that a simple balancing was not enough. The Commission granted a license for a very large pumped storage plant on Storm King Mountain. The court reversed:

> The Storm King project is to be located in an area of unique beauty and major historical significance. The highlands and gorge of the Hudson offer one of the finest pieces of river scenery in the world. The great German traveler Baedeker called it "finer than the Rhine." Petitioners' contention that the Commission must take these factors into consideration in evaluating the Storm King project is justified by the history of the Federal Power Act. * * *
>
> The Federal Power Act seeks to protect non-economic as well as economic interests. Indeed, the Commission recognized this in framing the issue in this very case:
>
> "The project is to be physically located in a general area of our nation steeped in the history of the American Revolution and of the colonial period. It is also a general area of great scenic beauty. The principal issue which must be decided is whether the project's effect on the scenic, historical and recreational values of the area are such that we should deny the application." * * *
>
> Especially in a case of this type, where public interest and concern is so great, the Commission's refusal to receive the * * * testimony [on gas turbines], as well as proffered information on fish protection devices and underground transmission facilities, exhibits a disregard of the statute and of judicial mandates instructing the Commission to probe all feasible alternatives. * * *
>
> The Federal Power Commission argues that having intervened "petitioners cannot impose an affirmative burden on the Commission." But, as we have pointed out, Congress gave the Federal Power Commission a specific planning responsibility. See Federal Power Act § 10(a), 16 U.S.C. § 803(a). The totality of a project's immediate and long-range effects, and not merely the engineering and navigation aspects, are to be considered in a licensing proceeding.
>
> In this case, as in many others, the Commission has claimed to be the representative of the public interest. This role does not permit it to act as an umpire blandly calling balls and strikes for adversaries appearing before it; the right of the public must receive active and affirmative protection at the hands of the Commission.

In 1973 the United States Water Resources Council published, and the President approved, Water and Related Land Resources: Establishment of Principles and Standards for Planning, 38 Fed.Reg. 24778 (1973). These were designed to systematically relate all aspects of water and related land resources planning to economic, environmental, regional and social well-being criteria.

The Principles and Standards were found to be too complicated and detailed, unnecessarily burdensome, and inflexibly binding, and on February 3, 1983, they were replaced by new Economic and Environmental Principles and Guidelines for Water and Related Land Resources Implementation Studies. The Principles are stated in two pages. Excerpts follow:

1. Purpose and Scope

These principles are intended to ensure proper and consistent planning by Federal agencies in the formulation and evaluation of water and related land resources implementation studies.

Implementation studies of the following agency activities are covered by these principles:

(a) Corps of Engineers (Civil Works) water resources project plans;

(b) Bureau of Reclamation water resources project plans;

(c) Tennessee Valley Authority water resources project plans;

(d) Soil Conservation Service water resources project plans.

Implementation studies are pre- or post-authorization project formulation or evaluation studies undertaken by Federal agencies.

2. Federal Objective

The Federal objective of water and related land resources project planning is to contribute to national economic development consistent with protecting the Nation's environment, pursuant to national environmental statutes, applicable executive orders, and other Federal planning requirements.

(a) Water and related land resources project plans shall be formulated to alleviate problems and take advantage of opportunities in ways that contribute to this objective.

(b) Contributions to national economic development (NED) are increases in the net value of the national output of goods and services, expressed in monetary units. Contributions to NED are the direct net benefits that accrue in the planning area and the rest of the Nation. Contributions to NED include increases in the net value of those goods and services that are marketed, and also of those that may not be marketed.

* * *

5. Alternative Plans

Various alternative plans are to be formulated in a systematic manner to ensure that all reasonable alternatives are evaluated.

(a) A plan that reasonably maximizes net national economic development benefits, consistent with the Federal objective, is to be formulated. This plan is to be identified as the NED plan.

(b) Other plans which reduce net NED benefits in order to further address other Federal, State, local, and international concerns not fully addressed by the NED plan should also be formulated.

(c) Plans may be formulated which require changes in existing statutes, administrative regulations, and established common law; such required changes are to be identified.

(d) Each alternative plan is to be formulated in consideration of four criteria: completeness, effectiveness, efficiency, and acceptability. Appropriate mitigation of adverse effects is to be an integral part of each alternative plan.

(e) Existing water and related land resources plans, such as State water resources plans, are to be considered as alternative plans if within the scope of the planning effort.

6. Plan Selection

A plan recommending Federal action is to be the alternative plan with the greatest net economic benefit consistent with protecting the Nation's environment (the NED plan), unless the Secretary of a department or head of an independent agency grants an exception to this rule. Exceptions may be made when there are overriding reasons for recommending another plan, based on other Federal, State, local and international concerns.

7. Accounts

Four accounts are established to facilitate evaluation and display of effects of alternative plans. The national economic development account is required. Other information that is required by law or that will have a material bearing on the decision-making process should be included in the other accounts, or in some other appropriate format used to organize information on effects.

(a) The national economic development (NED) account displays changes in the economic value of the national output of goods and services.

(b) The environmental quality (EQ) account displays nonmonetary effects on significant natural and cultural resources.

(c) The regional economic development (RED) account registers changes in the distribution of regional economic activity that result from each alternative plan. Evaluations of regional effects are to be carried out using nationally consistent projections of income, employment, output, and population.

(d) The other social effects (OSE) account registers plan effects from perspectives that are relevant to the planning process, but are not reflected in the other three accounts.

* * *

10. Risk and Uncertainty

Planners shall identify areas of risk and uncertainty in their analysis and describe them clearly, so that decisions can be made with knowledge of the degree of reliability of the estimated benefits and costs and of the effectiveness of alternative plans.

* * *

The planning Guidelines fill 137 pages with explanations, examples and procedures for agency calculation of costs and benefits and evaluation of projects. In the environmental section, primary emphasis is placed on coordinating the water resources planning process with NEPA requirements and other statutory provisions relating to environmental quality. The procedures for evaluation of environmental quality still encompass elaborate directions for identification and evaluation of ecological, cultural and aesthetic factors that cannot be measured in monetary terms (those that can be so measured are included in the NED account). The guidelines are not regulations and do not have the force of law; unlike the requirements of NEPA and procedures mandated by such laws as the Endangered Species Act (16 U.S.C.A. §§ 1531 et seq.) and the Coastal Zone Management Act (16 U.S.C.A. §§ 1451 et seq.), these do not create any substantive or procedural rights in private parties or organizations.

Valuable additions to the economic literature on cost-benefit analysis are E.J. Michan, Cost-Benefit Analysis (1976); Wildavsky, the Political Economy of Efficiency: Cost-Benefit Analysis, Systems Analysis and Program Budgeting, in Political Science and Public Policy 57 (Ranney, ed. 1968); and Rodgers, Benefits, Costs and Risks: Oversight of Health and Environmental Decision Making, 4 Harv.Env.L.Rev. 191 (1980).

NATIONAL ENVIRONMENTAL POLICY ACT OF 1969

Public Law 91–190, 42 U.S.C.A. §§ 4331–4335.

PURPOSE

Sec. 2. [42 U.S.C.A. § 4321] The purposes of this Act are: To declare a national policy which will encourage productive and enjoyable harmony between man and his environment; to promote efforts which will prevent or eliminate damage to the environment and biosphere and stimulate the health and welfare of man; to enrich the understanding of the ecological systems and natural resources important to the Nation; and to establish a Council on Environmental Quality.

Title I

Declaration of National Environmental Policy

Sec. 101. [42 U.S.C.A. § 4331] (a) The Congress, recognizing the profound impact of man's activity on the interrelations of all components of the natural environment, particularly the profound influences of population growth, high-density urbanization, industrial expansion, resource exploitation, and new and expanding technological advances and recognizing further the critical importance of restoring and maintaining environmental quality to the overall welfare and development of man, declares that it is the continuing policy of the Federal Government, in cooperation with State and local governments, and other concerned public and private organizations, to use all practicable means and measures, including financial and technical assistance, in a manner calculated to foster and promote the general welfare, to create and maintain conditions under which man and nature can exist in productive harmony, and fulfill the social, economic, and other requirements of present and future generations of Americans.

(b) In order to carry out the policy set forth in this Act, it is the continuing responsibility of the Federal Government to use all practicable means, consistent with other essential considerations of national policy, to improve and coordinate Federal plans, functions, programs, and resources to the end that the Nation may—

(1) fulfill the responsibilities of each generation as trustee of the environment for succeeding generations;

(2) assure for all Americans safe, healthful, productive, and esthetically and culturally pleasing surroundings;

(3) attain the widest range of beneficial uses of the environment without degradation, risk to health or safety, or other undesirable and unintended consequences;

(4) preserve important historic, cultural, and natural aspects of our national heritage, and maintain, wherever possible, an environment which supports diversity and variety of individual choice;

(5) achieve a balance between population and resource use which will permit high standards of living and a wide sharing of life's amenities; and

(6) enhance the quality of renewable resources and approach the maximum attainable recycling of depletable resources.

(c) The Congress recognizes that each person should enjoy a healthful environment and that each person has a responsibility to contribute to the preservation and enhancement of the environment.

Sec. 102. [42 U.S.C.A. § 4332] The Congress authorizes and directs that, to the fullest extent possible: (1) the policies, regulations, and public laws of the United States shall be interpreted and administered in accordance with the policies set forth in this Act, and (2) all agencies of the Federal Government shall—

(A) utilize a systematic, interdisciplinary approach which will insure the integrated use of the natural and social sciences and the environmental design arts in planning and in decisionmaking which may have an impact on man's environment;

(B) identify and develop methods and procedures, in consultation with the Council on Environmental Quality established by title II of this Act, which will insure that presently unquantified environmental amenities and values may be given appropriate consideration in decisionmaking along with economic and technical considerations;

(C) include in every recommendation or report on proposals for legislation and other major Federal actions significantly affecting the quality of the human environment, a detailed statement by the responsible official on—

(i) the environmental impact of the proposed action,

(ii) any adverse environmental effects which cannot be avoided should the proposal be implemented,

(iii) alternatives to the proposed action,

(iv) the relationship between local short-term uses of man's environment and the maintenance and enhancement of long-term productivity, and

(v) any irreversible and irretrievable commitments of resources which would be involved in the proposed action should it be implemented.

Prior to making any detailed statement, the responsible Federal official shall consult with and obtain the comments of any Federal agency which has jurisdiction by law or special expertise with respect to any environmental impact involved. Copies of such statement and the comments and views of the appropriate Federal, State, and local agencies, which are authorized to develop and enforce environmental standards, shall be made available to the President, the Council on Environmental Quality and to the public as provided by section 552 of title 5, United States Code, and shall accompany the proposal through the existing agency review processes;

(D) study, develop, and describe appropriate alternatives to recommended courses of action in any proposal which involves unresolved conflicts concerning alternative uses of available resources;

(E) recognize the worldwide and long-range character of environmental problems and, where consistent with the foreign policy of the United States, lend appropriate support to initiatives, resolutions, and programs designed to maximize international cooperation in anticipating and preventing a decline in the quality of mankind's world environment;

(F) make available to States, counties, municipalities, institutions, and individuals, advice and information useful in restoring, maintaining, and enhancing the quality of the environment;

(G) initiate and utilize ecological information in the planning and development of resource-oriented projects; and

(H) assist the Council on Environmental Quality established by title II of this Act. * * *

Sec. 104. [42 U.S.C.A. § 4334] Nothing in Section 102 or 103 shall in any way affect the specific statutory obligations of any Federal agency (1) to comply with criteria or standards of environmental quality, (2) to coordinate or consult with any other Federal or State agency, or (3) to act, or refrain from acting contingent upon the recommendations or certification of any other Federal or State agency.

Sec. 105. [42 U.S.C.A. § 4335] The policies and goals set forth in this Act are supplementary to those set forth in existing authorizations of Federal agencies.

CALVERT CLIFFS' COORDINATING COMMITTEES, INC. v. UNITED STATES ATOMIC ENERGY COMMISSION

United States Court of Appeals, District of Columbia Circuit, 1971.
146 U.S.App.D.C. 33, 449 F.2d 1109.

[The AEC adopted rules for incorporating NEPA requirements into its procedures for licensing atomic power plants that limited the scope and time of considering environmental impacts, relied on the parties and intervenors to raise environmental issues and supply information, and relied on determinations and standards supplied by other agencies. In disapproving these, Circuit Judge J. Skelly Wright issued a directive to all federal agencies:]

In these cases, we must for the first time interpret the broadest and perhaps most important of the recent statutes: the National Environmental Policy Act of 1969 (NEPA). We must assess claims that one of the agencies charged with its administration has failed to live up to the congressional mandate. Our duty, in short, is to see that important legislative purposes, heralded in the halls of Congress, are not lost or misdirected in the vast hallways of the federal bureaucracy.

NEPA, like so much other reform legislation of the last 40 years, is cast in terms of a general mandate and broad delegation of authority to new and old administrative agencies. It takes the major step of requiring all federal agencies to consider values of environmental preservation in their spheres of activity, and it prescribes certain procedural measures to ensure that those values are in fact fully respected. * * * Section 101 sets forth the Act's basic substantive policy: that the federal government 'use all practicable means and measures' to protect environmental values. Congress did not establish environmental protection as an exclusive goal; rather, it desired a reordering of priorities, so that environmental costs and benefits will assume their proper place along with other considerations. In Section 101(b), imposing an explicit duty on federal officials, the Act provides that "it is the continuing responsibility of the Federal Government to use all practicable means, consistent with other essential considerations of national policy," to avoid environmental degradation, preserve "historic, cultural, and natural" resources, and promote "the widest range of beneficial uses of the environment without * * * undesirable and unintended consequences."

Thus the general substantive policy of the Act is a flexible one. It leaves room for a responsible exercise of discretion and may not require particular substantive results in particular problematic instances. However, the Act also contains very important "procedural" provisions—provisions which are designed to see that all federal agencies do in fact exercise the substantive discretion given them. These provisions are not highly flexible. Indeed, they establish a strict standard of compliance.

NEPA, first of all, makes environmental protection a part of the mandate of every federal agency and department. * * * Perhaps the greatest importance of NEPA is to require the Atomic Energy Commission and other agencies to *consider* environmental issues just as they consider other matters within their mandates. * * *

The sort of consideration of environmental values which NEPA compels is clarified in Section 102(2)(A) and (B). In general, all agencies must use a "systematic, interdisciplinary approach" to environmental planning and evaluation "in decisionmaking which may have an impact on man's environment." In order to include all possible environmental factors in the decisional equation, agencies must "identify and develop methods and procedures * * * which will insure that presently unquantified environmental amenities and values may be given appropriate consideration in decisionmaking along with economic and technical considerations." "Environmental amenities" will often be in conflict with "economic and technical considerations." To "consider" the former "along with" the latter must involve a balancing process. In some instances environmental costs may outweigh economic and technical benefits and in other instances they may not. But NEPA mandates a rather finely tuned and "systematic" balancing analysis in each instance.

To ensure that the balancing analysis is carried out and given full effect, Section 102(2)(C) requires that responsible officials of all agencies prepare a "detailed statement" covering the impact of particular actions on the environment, the environmental costs which might be avoided, and alternative measures which might alter the cost-benefit equation. The apparent purpose of the "detailed statement" is to aid in the agencies' own decision making process and to advise other interested agencies and the public of the environmental consequences of planned federal action. Beyond the "detailed statement," Section 102(2)(D) requires all agencies specifically to "study, develop, and describe appropriate alternatives to recommended courses of action in any proposal which involves unresolved conflicts concerning alternative uses of available resources." This requirement, like the "detailed statement" requirement, seeks to ensure that each agency decision maker has before him and takes into proper account all possible approaches to a particular project (including total abandonment of the project) which would alter the environmental impact and the cost-benefit balance. Only in that fashion is it likely that the most intelligent, optimally beneficial decision will ultimately be made. Moreover, by compelling a formal "detailed statement" and a description of alternatives, NEPA provides evidence that the mandated decision making process has in fact taken place and, most importantly, allows those removed from the initial process to evaluate and balance the factors on their own. * * *

Unlike the substantive duties of Section 101(b), which requires agencies to "use all practicable means consistent with other essential considerations," the procedural duties of Section 102 must be fulfilled to the "fullest extent possible." * * * Thus the Section 102 duties are not inherently flexible. They must be complied with to the fullest extent, unless there is a clear conflict of *statutory* authority. Considerations of administrative difficulty, delay or economic cost will not suffice to strip the section of its fundamental importance.

We conclude, then, that Section 102 of NEPA mandates a particular sort of careful and informed decisionmaking process and creates judicially enforceable duties. The reviewing courts probably cannot reverse a substantive decision on its merits, under Section 101, unless it be shown that the actual balance of costs and benefits that was struck was arbitrary or clearly gave insufficient weight to environmental values. But if the decision was reached procedurally without individualized consideration and balancing of environmental factors—conducted fully and in good faith—it is the responsibility of the courts to reverse. * * * Compliance to the "*fullest*" possible extent would seem to demand that environmental issues be considered at every important stage in the decision making process concerning a particular action—at every stage where an overall balancing of environmental and nonenvironmental factors is appropriate and where alterations might be made in the proposed action to minimize environmental costs. * * *

NEPA establishes environmental protection as an integral part of the Atomic Energy Commission's basic mandate. The primary responsibility for fulfilling that mandate lies with the Commission. Its responsibility is not simply to sit back, like an umpire, and resolve adversary contentions at the hearing stage. Rather, it must itself take the initiative of considering environmental values at every distinctive and comprehensive stage of the process beyond the staff's evaluation and recommendation. * * *

NEPA mandates a case-by-case balancing judgment on the part of federal agencies. In each individual case, the particular economic and technical benefits of planned action must be assessed and then weighed against the environmental costs; alternatives must be considered which would affect the balance of values. The magnitude of possible benefits and possible costs may lie anywhere on a broad spectrum. Much will depend on the particular magnitudes involved in particular cases. In some cases, the benefits will be great enough to justify a certain quantum of environmental costs; in other cases, they will not be so great and the proposed action may have to be abandoned or significantly altered so as to bring the benefits and costs into a proper balance. The point of the individualized balancing analysis is to ensure that, with possible alterations, the optimally beneficial action is finally taken.

Certification by another agency that its own environmental standards are satisfied involves an entirely different kind of judgment. Such agencies, without overall responsibility for the particular federal action in question, attend only to one aspect of the problem: the magnitude of certain environmental costs. They simply determine whether those costs exceed an allowable amount. Certifying agencies do not attempt to weigh that damage against the opposing benefits. Thus the balancing analysis remains to be done. It may be that the environmental costs, though passing prescribed standards, are nonetheless great enough to outweigh the particular economic and technical benefits involved in the planned action. The only agency in a position to make such a judgment is the agency with overall responsibility for the proposed federal action—the agency to which NEPA is specifically directed.

Notes

1. On the problems of choosing the "lead agency" when several are involved, deference by one agency to the standards and findings of others, and cooperation between agencies in preparation of the environmental impact statement, see Sierra Club v. Froehlke, 359 F.Supp. 1289, 1348 (S.D. Tex.1973), rev'd. sub nom. Sierra Club v. Callaway, 499 F.2d 982 (5th Cir. 1974), and 40 C.F.R. 1501.5.

2. NEPA requires an EIS in all cases of "major federal action significantly affecting the quality of the human environment." What is major? Federal? Action? What significantly affects the environment? These difficult questions have given rise to much litigation that has resulted in a few rules of thumb and a good deal of crystalized agency practice. In the water field, see, e.g., County of Trinity v. Andrus, 438 F.Supp. 1368 (E.D. Cal.1977) (continued operation of a project within the range originally contemplated by the authorizing statute does not require preparation of an EIS). See Rodgers, Environmental Law 751 (1977).

In making a "negative determination" that no EIS is needed, many agencies have used "ministatements," "environmental impact reports," or "environmental analyses." The new regulations standardize these into the "environmental assessment," described as

"A concise public document for which a Federal agency is responsible that serves to:

"(1) Briefly provide sufficient evidence and analysis for determining whether to prepare an environmental impact statement or a finding of no significant impact.

"(2) Aid an agency's compliance with the Act when no environmental impact statement is necessary.

"(3) Facilitate preparation of a statement when one is necessary.

"(b) Shall include brief discussions of the need for the proposal, of alternatives as required by sec. 102(2)(E), of the environmental impacts of the proposed action and alternatives, and a listing of agencies and persons consulted." (40 CFR 1508.9.)

MONTGOMERY v. ELLIS

United States District Court, Northern District of Alabama, 1973.
364 F.Supp. 517.

GUIN, DISTRICT JUDGE. This action is brought to enjoin implementation or construction of a stream channelization project of the Soil Conservation Service of the U.S. Department of Agriculture ("SCS") on Blue-Eye Creek, a tributary of the Coosa River, in Talladega County, Alabama. The case is before the Court upon reconsideration of the cross motions for summary judgment filed by plaintiff and by the defendant SCS officials. Plaintiff has alleged that the SCS has failed to file an adequate "detailed statement" as required under the National Environmental Policy Act of 1969 (42 U.S.C.A. § 4321 et seq.) ("NEPA"), that the SCS has been arbitrary in the environmental impact statement it did file ("the EIS") in failing adequately to consider or describe all reasonable available alternatives to the project and in employing an unrealistic interest rate and project life in computing benefits and costs of the project, and finally that the SCS officials have failed to follow the pertinent applicable regulations of the Department of Agriculture. In response, the SCS claimed that it did not have to file an environmental impact statement and, even if it did, the one that it did file was sufficient and that its departmental regulations had been complied with.

The Court has heard argument on these points in chambers with attorneys for all parties present and has reviewed the briefs filed by plaintiff and the defendant SCS officials on the need for and adequacy of the environmental impact statement for this project. It is the Court's opinion that an environmental impact statement is required for the project in question; that the one filed by the SCS is inadequate both in failure adequately to set forth the available alternatives and other matters required by NEPA and in failure to employ a realistic interest rate and project life in computing the benefits and costs of this project; and that the SCS has failed to comply with applicable law in the other respects set forth below. Accordingly, an injunction will issue in the form specifically set forth at the end of this opinion, against any construction, installation, or further authorization or financing of the stream channelization of Blue-Eye Creek pursuant to the Blue-Eye Creek Watershed Project. Discussion of the issues before the Court is as follows:

I. Need for Environmental Impact Statement

The measures proposed to be installed on Blue-Eye Creek pursuant to the work plan prepared by SCS for the Blue-Eye Creek Watershed Project consist of two water retention structures, completed in 1968 and 1969, respectively, and a stream channelization project of the creek below the two dams that has not yet been installed. Since the water retention structures have been completed, have been in operation for several years and, according to the EIS and a report of the SCS (excerpts from which have been set forth in one of the affidavits filed in behalf of plaintiff), have been operating properly, it appears to the Court that the stream channelization, not yet installed, is a separate project or, at the very least, is a major part of an on-going project.

Accordingly, pursuant to the great weight of authority under NEPA, the Court finds that an environmental impact statement is required and that authorization prior to the effective date of NEPA on January 1, 1970, is no defense. * * *

It, thus, seems clear to the Court that an environmental impact statement is required for this channelization project; and this much may, in effect, have been recognized by SCS since it prepared the environmental impact statement approved on August 30, 1971, by Mr. William B. Lingle, SCS State Conservationist for Alabama, who is one of the defendants in this case.

II. Failure to File Adequate "Detailed Statement" Under NEPA

Section 102(2)(C) of NEPA requires, among other subjects to be covered, "*a detailed statement* by the responsible official on the environmental impact of the proposed action, any adverse environmental effects which cannot be avoided should the proposal be implemented," and "alternatives to the proposed action." (Emphasis supplied.) "Copies of such statement and the comments and views of the appropriate Federal, State, and local agencies, which are authorized to develop and enforce environmental standards, shall be made available to the President, the Council on Environmental Quality and to the public * * *". As stated in the leading case of *Calvert Cliffs',* supra, 449 F.2d at 1114,

> "* * * By compelling a formal 'detailed statement' and a description of alternatives, NEPA provides evidence that the mandated decision making process had in fact taken place and, most importantly, allows

> those removed from the initial process to evaluate and balance the factors on their own."

The court in *Gillham Dam* stressed this requirement, stating, "*at the very least, NEPA is an environmental full disclosure law.*" (Emphasis supplied.) 325 F.Supp. at 759.

Notwithstanding the fact as stated that the SCS filed an environmental impact statement covering the Blue-Eye Creek Project, the Court finds that the EIS, which is attached to both motions for summary judgment, is on its face insufficient in a number of material respects:

(1) *Failure to set forth physical characteristics of project.* Perhaps the most obvious deficiency in the EIS is failure adequately to describe the proposed channel project. All that is set forth is that a certain number of miles of stream will be channelized, and plaintiff states all that he really knows is that the easement sought to be condemned across his land is to be 150 feet from the centerline of the creek. It would seem elemental for an environmental impact statement to describe adequately the project in question so that those removed from the initial decisionmaking process may be able to appraise what type of project is being considered. The Court feels that, at the very least, the EIS should set forth the width and depth proposed for the stream channel—such as at its source and mouth—and its general direction so that the property owners whose lands are being affected, as well as governmental officials removed from the decisionmaking process, can have some idea of what the SCS is proposing and whether or not the channel is to follow the natural stream bed. Without such basic information, the EIS must be deemed insufficient on its face.

(2) *Failure to set forth benefit and cost factors.* As to the matter of benefits and costs from the project, the EIS merely sets forth (on page 2),

> "Average annual benefits accruing from the project *are estimated to be $21,650.* Average annual costs which were updated to a 1971 price base *are estimated to be $20,584.* The cost is based on a *100-year evaluation period with* a 3⅛% interest rate for measures installed and a *3¼% interest rate* for measures to be installed. * * * It is further estimated that *for each dollar of cost approximately $1.05 in benefits* will be realized." (Emphasis supplied.)

It is readily apparent from the above minimal information that persons removed from making the initial decision, such as the President, the Council on Environmental Quality ("CEQ") and the public, can have no way of ascertaining, as contemplated by NEPA, the justification for or desirability of this project, since what costs are allocated to what items and what amounts of benefits are claimed from others are not in the EIS. The information may be somewhere in the files of the SCS, but this cannot satisfy the requirement of NEPA that it be made available to public officials removed from the initial decision-making process and to the public in general. As stated in *Calvert Cliffs',* supra, the "detailed statement" is to cover "the environmental costs which might be avoided", 449 F.2d at 1114, and,

> "In each individual case, the particular *economic and technical benefits* of planned action *must be assessed and then weighed against the environmental costs*; alternatives must be considered which will affect the balance of values * * * In some cases, the benefits will be great enough to justify a certain quantum of environmental costs; in other cases, they will not be so great and the proposed action may have to be abandoned or significantly altered so as to bring the benefits and costs into a proper balance. The point of the individualized *balancing analysis is to ensure* that, with possible alterations, *the optimally beneficial action is finally taken.*" (Emphasis supplied.) 449 F.2d at 1123. * * *

Those entitled to receive information about a project under the mandate of NEPA are entitled to know the facts on which the decision to proceed was based, such as to which items were included and which were not and what evaluations were given them. It is obvious, however, that those facts are not adequately covered by the minimal information from the EIS quoted above. Such is not the full disclosure required by NEPA and the above decisions. Consequently, the EIS must be regarded as deficient on its face in this respect. * * *

(4) *Failure adequately to consider or describe available alternatives to project.* NEPA requires under Section 102(2)(C) "a detailed statement by the responsible official on * * * (iii) alternatives to the proposed action", and Section 102(2)(D) requires all agencies of the Federal Government to:

> "study, develop, and describe appropriate alternatives to recommended courses of action in any proposal which involves unresolved conflicts concerning alternative uses of available resources * * *"

Certain alternatives not discussed in the EIS may be readily apparent; but, for some guidelines as to what alternatives should be considered and discussed, we may look to the recent decision of the Eighth Circuit in Environmental Defense Fund v. Froehlke, 473 F.2d 346 (8th Cir.1972), involving channelization of the Cache River by the Corps of Engineers. Among the alternatives required to be discussed in detail, for which insufficiency the impact statement was ruled inadequate, were "flood plain zoning", "crop insurance" and "plans consisting of various combinations of diversions, floodways, reservoirs, interceptor ditches and levees". While one of such alternatives, i.e. levees, is discussed in the EIS on Blue-Eye Creek, virtually nothing is said of the others. In addition, while the Eighth Circuit observed that some of such alternatives were mentioned in the impact statement, it held that none were discussed in sufficient detail to comply with NEPA and the guidelines of the CEQ promulgated thereunder, which state:

> "A rigorous explanation and objective evaluation of *alternative actions that might avoid some or all of the adverse environmental effects is essential.* Sufficient analysis of such alternatives and *their*

> *costs and impact on the environment* should accompany the proposed action through the agency review process in order not to foreclose prematurely options which might have less detrimental effects." (Emphasis supplied.) CEQ Guidelines, Para. 6(a)(iii), 36 Fed.Reg. 7724, April 23, 1971.

The court continued:

> "To fulfill these mandates, the impact study should not just list the alternatives to the proposed project but it should also include the results of the Corps' own investigation and evaluation of alternatives so that the reasons for the choice of a course of action are clear. * * * The complete impact study must contain more than a catalog of environmental facts, however. The agency must also 'explicate fully its course of inquiry, its analysis and its reasoning.' Ely v. Velde, 451 F.2d 1130, 1139 (4th Cir.1971)." 473 F.2d at 350–351. * * *

The EIS for Blue-Eye Creek shows on its face that it is inadequate in discussing at least the following alternatives:

(a) *Elimination of channelization.* While the EIS refers to loss of some claimed benefits if the channelization of Blue-Eye Creek were not installed, that comment is described only as an estimate and no background details are given. On the other hand, SCS has apparently not considered the combined benefits—or at least the EIS does not discuss this alternative—from the water retention structures already constructed and from leaving the rest of Blue-Eye Creek alone so as to avoid the adverse effects of the channelization, some of which are listed in the EIS (on page 7).

Under the above decisions, not carrying out a project is always an alternative to be considered in an impact statement; and this should especially be true here where, as set forth in the EIS, the channelization of the entire creek will only reduce flood damages an estimated 77%.

(b) *Water retarding structures or other methods of controlling run-off on tributary creeks.* A map of the area, filed as an exhibit by the SCS defendants (see footnote 3, supra), shows that there are tributaries to Blue-Eye Creek that would contribute to any flooding problem and one of which the SCS proposes to channelize by a lateral channel. In addition, the map referred to shows there are at least five water retention structures on small tributary streams but none yet on two of the three major tributaries. However, the EIS fails to discuss the alternative of water retention structures, land treatment measures or other methods of controlling water run-off in those tributaries as an alternative to channelization and the accompanying environmental damage to the watershed of Blue-Eye Creek. These facts of record show that this is an alternative that should and could have been explored and may well be the solution to the entire problem. Such an alternative is one of those required to be considered under *Cache River,* supra; however, it is not appraised or even discussed in the EIS. * * *

(d) *Flood insurance.* The necessity to consider this alternative is specifically mentioned in both *Cache River* and *Gillham Dam,* supra. It is noteworthy that a complete solution to the alleged flooding problem is not offered by the Blue-Eye Creek Project; in fact, it is not contended that it would eliminate more than 77% of the alleged flooding even if none of the above alternatives were employed and even if the channelization project were carried out. Thus, it is obviously not a solution to the entire problem. Consequently, flood insurance to cover those floods that might occur in the future is clearly an alternative that should be considered. * * *

(5) *Erroneous inclusion of recreational benefits.* Recreational benefits from lakes behind the dams have apparently been included in the benefits justifying this project as they appear listed as a favorable environmental effect in the EIS (page 7). Plaintiff, however, has pointed out in his affidavit that the impoundments are not open to the general public and, consequently, since those benefits are not available, they should not be considered "because the lakes are on private property from which the general public has been barred." In response, the SCS has attempted to defend its position by claiming that "recreational use *will* be made of the 25 surface acres of water. The evaluation of these incidental recreational benefits was in keeping with Soil Conservation Service procedures." The court notes, however, that this affidavit by Mr. Ernest V. Todd, Assistant State Conservationist for SCS in Alabama, does not directly controvert that of plaintiff. It does not state that recreational use is available to the public but only that it "will be" made.

In addition, apparently feeling that the public might not be permitted to use the areas, SCS has in its brief advanced the position (which, however, is not set forth in the EIS) that use by the landowner or his neighbors or friends, even though the lakes might not be available to the general public, should be counted as a benefit. No authority is cited for that proposition, and the Court knows of none. On the other hand, the Court feels that logic dictates that if an impoundment constructed with public funds is not available to the general public, recreational benefits should not be claimed. In the interest of flood control it may be very desirable to construct the impoundment; but if it is not available for public recreation, the recreational benefits should not be claimed. Further, regardless of disposition of this issue, it should be covered in the EIS so that those removed from the initial decisionmaking process will know the true circumstances of the claimed recreational benefits and will not be misled into thinking a public recreational lake has been created. * * *

(6) *In General.* In its brief, the SCS has cited certain statements by courts that not every detail must be set forth in impact statements. However, the Court feels that the above omissions are no mere details but, instead, are significant factors that need to be brought to the

attention of those removed from the decisionmaking process as required by the express provisions of NEPA.

While the Court certainly agrees that length is no guarantee of an adequate "detailed statement" as required by NEPA, it is noted that in *Gillham Dam,* supra, one of the cases principally relied on by SCS, the initial environmental impact statement was held inadequate in Environmental Defense Fund v. Corps of Engineers, 325 F.Supp. 728, 749 (E.D.Ark.1970–71). When a new impact statement was prepared and was held sufficient in 342 F.Supp. 1211 (E.D.Ark.1972), it is noted that it was prepared after two hearings, the adverse comments in which were included in the new statement, and that it consisted of 200 pages with six appendices (aggregating about 1500 pages). The district court even then said that it was not "as fair and impartial and objective as if it had been compiled by a disinterested third person", but felt that all necessary factors could be found somewhere within its bounds. Such a presentation is in considerable contrast to the existing statement on Blue-Eye Creek, which consists actually of only nine pages plus five pages under "consultation" summarizing certain comments by other agencies.

This last factor also indicates clearly that the EIS in this case is merely a reworking of some basic data compiled long ago; and, in fact, this seems to be admitted in the SCS's brief. It is also indicated by the fact, discussed in Part IV of this opinion, that the SCS officials have not re-evaluated the project as required by SCS regulations. * * *

The Court understands plaintiff contends that a stream channelization project such as this will have the adverse effects of increased downstream flooding, increased erosion and, as a result, increased downstream sedimentation, and perhaps lowering of the water level that would result in draining the springs on his property and impairing the water resources for his pastures. On the other hand, the position of SCS as indicated in the EIS and in its brief is that such effects should be insignificant and, as to erosion and downstream siltation, are expected to be limited in duration. The Court, however, in rendering its judgment is not basing its decision on any such matters that may, at this juncture, be considered disputed matters of fact. Instead, it is passing only upon those insufficiencies that appear on the face of the EIS or as to which there appear to be no genuine issue of material fact to be resolved. Under such circumstances, summary judgment under Rule 56 is the appropriate remedy.

Now, therefore, summary judgment is hereby granted in favor of the plaintiff and it is hereby ordered, adjudged and decreed that the defendants in this action, William B. Lingle, Claude W. Friday, C.W. Munroe and John R. Ellis (including those persons in their official capacities) and all officers, agents, servants and employees and those persons in active concert or participation with them who receive actual notice hereof, as prescribed in Rule 65, Fed.R.Civ.Proc., be, and they hereby are, enjoined and restrained from constructing, installing, or further authorizing or financing any stream modification or channelization of said Blue-Eye Creek pursuant to the so-called Blue-Eye Creek Watershed Project, its work plan or otherwise, until:

(1) An adequate environmental impact statement is prepared, circulated under NEPA as required by law, and presented to and found sufficient by this Court;

(2) In preparing such a statement, the substantive requirements of NEPA as outlined above, are complied with; * * *.

The Court retains jurisdiction to assure compliance with this opinion and order.

Notes

1. The Council on Environmental Quality published a new set of guidelines for "streamlining the EIS process" on November 29, 1978, 43 Fed.Reg. 55978–56007, 40 CFR 1500.1–1508.28. The accompanying information spoke of: "* * * an evolution of inconsistent agency practices and interpretations of the law. The lack of a uniform, government-wide approach implementing NEPA has impeded federal coordination and made it more difficult for those outside government to understand and participate in the environmental review process. It has also caused unnecessary duplication, delay and paper work. * * * The environmental impact statement has tended to become an end in itself, rather than a means to making better decisions. Environmental impact statements have often failed to establish the link between what is learned through the NEPA process and how the information can contribute to decisions which further national environmental policies and goals. * * *" The CEQ's regulations are binding on all federal agencies, replace some 70 different sets of agency regulations, and provide uniform standards applicable throughout the federal government for conducting environmental reviews. The regulations also establish formal guidance from the Council on the requirements of NEPA for use by the courts in interpreting this law.

The new regulations are addressed to reduced paper work, the emphasis on real alternatives, a new "scoping" process for determining real issues, the use of plain language, a uniform format, simplified procedures and measures for reducing delay and promoting interagency cooperation.

2. The CEQ guidelines consolidate and restate all phases of agency procedures required by § 101(2) of NEPA including integrating the NEPA process into early planning to insure appropriate consideration of NEPA policies and to eliminate delay, an early and open process (called "scoping"), for determining the scope of issues to be addressed and identifying the significant issues related to a proposed action, requirements of the EIS itself, comments, public involvement, and referring to CEQ federal interagency disagreements concerning actions that may cause unsatisfactory environmental effects.

3. A troublesome problem concerns the question whether an agency with on-going responsibilities should file a programmatic, area-wide or regional EIS, or file individual statements for individual actions or component projects. See Kleppe v. Sierra Club, 427 U.S. 390, 96 S.Ct. 2718, 49

L.Ed.2d 576 (1976). For Bureau of Reclamation problems, see Environmental Defense Fund, Inc. v. Armstrong, 487 F.2d 814 (9th Cir.1973) (Central Valley Project or New Melones Dam?); Environmental Defense Fund, Inc. v. Morton, 420 F.Supp. 1037 (D.C.Mont.1976) (marketing plan and option contracts for industrial water from project, or final contracts after routes, sites, and quantities are known?).

The CEQ guidelines require "tiering" to avoid paper work, incorporating in the site-specific statement the general issues and discussion in the broader statement. 40 CFR 1508.28.

On judicial review of cost-benefit analysis, see Rodgers, Environmental Law 745 (1977), Environmental Defense Fund v. Corps of Engineers, 348 F.Supp. 916 (D.C.Miss.1972) ("Not a judicial question.")

The new CEQ guidelines provide, "If a cost-benefit analysis relevant to the choice among environmentally different alternatives is being considered for the proposed action, it shall be incorporated by reference or appended to the statement as an aid in evaluating the environmental consequences. * * * For purposes of complying with the act, the weighing of the merits and drawbacks of the various alternatives need not be displayed in a monetary cost-benefit analysis and should not be where there are important qualitative considerations. In any event, an environmental impact statement should at least indicate those considerations, including factors not relating to environmental quality, which are likely to be relevant and important to the decision."

STRYCKER'S BAY NEIGHBORHOOD COUNCIL v. KARLEN

Supreme Court of the United States, 1980.
444 U.S. 223, 100 S.Ct. 497, 62 L.Ed.2d 433.

[In 1962 the New York City Planning Commission and the United States Department of Housing and Urban Development began formulating a plan for the West Side Urban Renewal Area. Originally the plan called for a mix of 70% middle-income and 30% low-income housing. In 1969, when plans were substantially complete, local agencies urged the need for more low-income units and in 1972 HUD approved an amendment that would add a 160 unit highrise apartment building. Neighborhood groups attacked this decision in the United States District Court, which in 1974 found compliance with NEPA. In 1975 the Second Circuit reversed on the ground that consideration by HUD of alternatives to placing low income housing on the site was either highly limited or nonexistent. A lengthy report was prepared in 1977, which evaluated nine alternatives and rejected all of them on the ground that any relocation of the units would entail an unacceptable delay of two years or more. The district court again upheld the agency.]

PER CURIAM:

* * *

On appeal, the Second Circuit vacated and remanded again. Karlen v. Harris, 590 F.2d 39 (1978). The appellate court focused upon that part of HUD's report where the agency considered and rejected alternative sites, and in particular upon HUD's reliance on the delay such a relocation would entail. The Court of Appeals purported to recognize that its role in reviewing HUD's decision was defined by the Administrative Procedure Act (APA), 5 U.S.C. § 706(2)(A), which provides that agency actions should be set aside if found to be "arbitrary, capricious, an abuse of discretion, or otherwise not in accordance with law * * *." Additionally, however, the Court of Appeals looked to "[t]he provisions of NEPA" for "the substantive standards necessary to review the merits of agency decisions * * *." 590 F.2d, at 43. The Court of Appeals conceded that HUD had "given 'consideration' to alternatives" to redesignating the site. Id., at 44. Nevertheless, the court believed that " 'consideration' is not an end in itself." Ibid. Concentrating on HUD's finding that development of an alternative location would entail an unacceptable delay, the appellate court held that such delay could not be "an overriding factor" in HUD's decision to proceed with the development. Ibid. According to the court, when HUD considers such projects, "environmental factors, such as crowding low-income housing into a concentrated area, should be given determinative weight." Ibid. The Court of Appeals therefore remanded the case to the District Court, instructing HUD to attack the shortage of low-income housing in a manner that would avoid the "concentration" of such housing on Site 30. Id., at 45.

In Vermont Yankee Nuclear Power Corp. v. NRDC, 435 U.S. 519, 558, 98 S.Ct. 1197, 1219, 55 L.Ed.2d 460 (1978), we stated that NEPA, while establishing "significant substantive goals for the Nation," imposes upon agencies duties that are "essentially procedural." As we stressed in that case, NEPA was designed "to insure a fully informed and well-considered decision," but not necessarily "a decision the judges of the Court of Appeals or of this Court would have reached had they been members of the decisionmaking unit of the agency." Ibid. *Vermont Yankee* cuts sharply against the Court of Appeals' conclusion that an agency, in selecting a course of action, must elevate environmental concerns over other appropriate considerations. On the contrary, once an agency has made a decision subject to NEPA's procedural requirements, the only role for a court is to insure that the agency has considered the environmental consequences; it cannot "interject itself within the area of discretion of the executive as to the choice of the action to be taken.' " Kleppe v. Sierra Club, 427 U.S. 390, 410, n. 21, 96 S.Ct. 2718, 2730, n. 21, 49 L.Ed.2d 576 (1976). See also FPC v. Transcontinental Gas Pipe Line Corp., 423 U.S. 326, 96 S.Ct. 579, 46 L.Ed.2d 533 (1976).[a]

a. If we could agree with the dissent that the Court of Appeals held that HUD had acted "arbitrarily" in redesignating the site for low-income housing, we might also agree that plenary review is warranted. But the District Court expressly concluded that HUD had not acted arbitrarily or capriciously and our reading of

In the present litigation there is no doubt that HUD considered the environmental consequences of its decision to redesignate the proposed site for low-income housing. NEPA requires no more. The petitions for certiorari are granted, and the judgment of the Court of Appeals is therefore reversed.

MR. JUSTICE MARSHALL, dissenting.

* * *

The issue before the Court of Appeals, therefore, was whether HUD was free under NEPA to reject an alternative acknowledged to be environmentally preferable solely on the ground that any change in sites would cause delay. This was hardly a "peripheral issue" in the case. Whether NEPA, which sets forth "significant substantive goals," Vermont Yankee Nuclear Power Corp. v. NRDC, supra, 435 U.S., at 558, 98 S.Ct., at 1219, permits a projected two-year time difference to be controlling over environmental superiority is by no means clear. Resolution of the issue, however, is certainly within the normal scope of review of agency action to determine if it is arbitrary, capricious, or an abuse of discretion. The question whether HUD can make delay the paramount concern over environmental superiority is essentially a restatement of the question whether HUD in considering the environmental consequences of its proposed action gave those consequences a "hard look," which is exactly the proper question for the reviewing court to ask. Kleppe v. Sierra Club, supra, 427 U.S., at 410, n. 21, 96 S.Ct., at 2730, n. 21. * * *

Notes

1. *Vermont Yankee* dealt with the EIS for a nuclear reactor. In the licensing process, conducted in 1973, the AEC had not considered whether "energy conservation" could affect the ruling that there was a public need for the power to be produced, and the Court of Appeals had reversed for a consideration of this issue. A unanimous Supreme Court reversed, Justice Rehnquist stating:

"There is little doubt that under the Atomic Energy Act of 1954 state public utility commissions or similar bodies are empowered to make the initial decision regarding the need for power. The Commission's prime area of concern * * * is public health and safety. * * *

"NEPA, of course, has altered slightly the statutory balance, requiring 'a detailed statement by the responsible official on * * * alternatives to the proposed action.' But as should be obvious even upon a moment's reflection, the term "alternatives" is not self-defining. To make an impact statement something more than an exercise in frivolous boilerplate the concept of alternatives must be bounded by some notion of feasibility. * * * Common sense also teaches us that the 'detailed statement of alternatives' cannot be found wanting simply because the agency failed to

the opinion of the Court of Appeals satisfies us that it did not overturn that finding. Instead, the appellate court required HUD to elevate environmental concerns over other, admittedly legitimate, considerations. Neither NEPA nor the APA provides any support for such a reordering of priorities by a reviewing court.

include every alternative device and thought conceivable by the mind of man. Time and resources are simply too limited to hold that an impact statement fails because the agency failed to ferret out every possible alternative, regardless of how uncommon or unknown that alternative may have been at the time the project was approved.

"With these principles in mind we now turn to the notion of 'energy conservation,' an alternative the omission of which was thought by the Court of Appeals to have been 'forcefully pointed out by Saginaw in its comments on the draft EIS'. 178 U.S.App.D.C., at 328, 547 F.2d, at 625. Again, as the Commission pointed out, 'the phrase "energy conservation" has a deceptively simple ring in this context. Taken literally, the phrase suggests a virtually limitless range of possible actions and developments that might, in one way or another, ultimately reduce projected demands for electricity from a particular proposed plant.' Moreover, as a practical matter, it is hard to dispute the observation that it is largely the events of recent years that have emphasized not only the need but also a large variety of alternatives for energy conservation. Prior to the drastic oil shortages imposed upon the United States in 1973, there was little serious thought in most government circles of energy conservation alternatives. * * *

"We think these facts amply demonstrate that the concept of 'alternatives' is an evolving one, requiring the agency to explore more or fewer alternatives as they become better known and understood. This was well understood by the Commission, which, unlike the Court of Appeals, recognized that the Licensing Board's decision had to be judged by the information then available to it. And judged in that light we have little doubt the Board's actions were well within the proper bounds of its statutory authority. Not only did the record before the agency give every indication that the project was actually needed, but there was nothing before the Board to indicate to the contrary."

For comment on *Vermont Yankee,* see Symposium by Professors Stewart, Byse, and Breyer in 91 Harvard Law Review 1804 (1978); and Rodgers, "A Hard Look at Vermont Yankee: Environmental Law Under Close Scrutiny," 67 Geo.L.J. 699 (1979).

2. Balancing costs and benefits project by project, even with careful consideration of environmental factors, may keep a river in constant jeopardy and subject to small incursions that may add up to ruin. Congress opted for absolutes in the Wild and Scenic Rivers Act of 1968, 16 U.S.C.A. § 1271, which declared a policy that certain selected rivers, and their immediate environments, which possess outstandingly remarkable scenic, recreational, geologic, fish and wildlife, historic, cultural or similar values, should be preserved in free-flowing condition and their environment protected for the benefit and enjoyment of present and future generations. Congress declared that the established national policy of dam and other construction on rivers needed to be complemented by a policy that will preserve other selected rivers or sections thereof. Section 3 of the Act identified three types of eligible streams: (1) wild rivers, free of impoundments and generally inaccessible except by trail, "vestiges of primitive America," (2) scenic rivers, free of impoundments with shoreline or water-

sheds largely primitive and undeveloped, but accessible in places by roads, and (3) recreational rivers, already accessible by road or railroad, that have some developments and impoundments upon them. 16 U.S.C.A. § 1273. The Act designated eight rivers as the National Wild and Scenic River System, and named more for further study. Others may be studied by the Secretary of the Interior (or the Secretary of Agriculture if they flow through national forest) and, if the Secretaries so recommend, may be included in the system by Congress. States may nominate still others, which will be recommended to the Congress if approved by the Secretary of the Interior. By 1983, 50 rivers were included and 88 were under study.

The principal effect of designation as a component of the National Wild and Scenic River System is the institution of a land use planning and management system for the banks and environs of the river. In addition, the Act prohibits the Federal Energy Regulatory Commission from licensing the construction of any dam, powerhouse, or transmission line on or directly affecting the rivers in the system or designated for study, and no other federal department may assist by loan, grant, license or otherwise in the construction of any water resources project that would have a direct and adverse effect on the values for which the river was established, except with the express permission of the Secretary of the Interior or Secretary of Agriculture, whichever is in charge of administering the particular river. The Act provides interim protection for rivers under study by the Secretaries. As to whether temporary protection is extended to rivers recommended by the states see North Carolina v. Federal Power Commission, 533 F.2d 702 (D.C.Cir.1976), cert. granted, vacated and remanded 429 U.S. 891, 97 S.Ct. 250, 50 L.Ed.2d 174 (1976).

Note on Pollution Control

1. *Relation to Water Law.* Water quality control is an important part of the course in environmental law, but presents only a peripheral aspect of water law. As traditionally defined, water law is concerned primarily with beneficial use, not abuse, with quantity, not quality. A person who gets rid of a noxious or offensive substance by discharging it into water receives a benefit of a sort, and his action may make the water as unavailable to another as if it had been consumed. On the other hand, a person who reduces the flow of a stream that dilutes a downstream influx of foreign matter may increase the concentration of the substance to intolerable limits. Nevertheless, there is little interplay between water law and pollution control law. The discharger was seldom treated as a water user, and while the diverter might be restrained, it would be by water law, not pollution law.

By the 1960's and 1970's, most states had well-staffed agencies and active programs for administering water quality control. Despite all their efforts, many of the nation's larger rivers and lakes became badly polluted by municipal, industrial, and agricultural sources of biological, chemical and physical wastes. As population and industry increased, sewage plants became outmoded and overwhelmed even as they were built. New plants and factories, though polluting less, increased total discharges faster than old sources could be cleaned up. Demands for food, timber and paper led to increased plowed fields and deforested hills, and increased loads of sediments and silt. Heated water from power plants and heavy industry caused drastic changes in many waters. Sometimes a riparian proprietor was said to have the right to freedom from harmful water pollution, Sandusky Portland Cement Company v. Dixon Pure Ice Co., 221 F. 200 (7th Cir.1915), sometimes an upper riparian's use of a stream for waste disposal was said to be an unreasonable exercise of his riparian rights, and sometimes a polluter has defended his fouling the stream as a privileged exercise of his riparian rights, Hazeltine v. Case, 46 Wis. 391, 1 N.W. 66 (1879). In many cases, however, these property theories had no application. In some the polluter was not a riparian, in some the plaintiff had no status as a riparian although he suffered serious harm. See Kennebunk Dist., supra p. 314, Thomas v. Clear Lake, 270 Wis. 630, 72 N.W.2d 541 (1955).

In the western states similar problems are raised by attempts to apply appropriation law to pollution problems. An appropriator may complain of pollution of his water supply, Game and Fish Commission v. Farmer's Irrigation Co., 162 Colo. 301, 426 P.2d 562 (1967), but can a riparian who is not an appropriator complain of water pollution in an appropriation state? See Conley v. Amalgamated Sugar Co., 74 Idaho 416, 263 P.2d 705 (1953). Does an appropriator obtain a prior right to water quality that cannot be impaired by later upstream users of the stream? See Dripps v. Allison's Mines Co., 45 Cal.App. 95, 187 P. 448 (1919). Does an appropriator whose use deteriorates the quality of water returned to the stream obtain a prior right to continue this "use" although it prevents beneficial use by subsequent downstream appropriators? Compare State v. California Packing Corp., 105 Utah 182, 141 P.2d 386 (1943) with Suffolk Gold Mining & Milling Co. v. San Miguel Consolidated Mining & Milling Co., 9 Colo.App. 407, 48 P. 828 (1896).

Riparian and appropriation law did not produce very satisfactory or predictable results in pollution cases. The emphasis on property doctrines tended to obscure the real factors of decision. Better results were obtained when the courts applied nuisance theories, as in Middlestadt v. Waupaca Starch and Potato Co., 93 Wis. 1, 66 N.W. 713 (1896); American Cyanamid Co. v. Sparto, 267 F.2d 425 (5th Cir.1959). In western states which gave no recognition to riparian rights, the concept of nuisance was often used to determine cases of water pollution. See North Point Consolidated Irrigation Co. v. Utah & Salt Lake Canal Co., 16 Utah 246, 52 P. 168 (1898); Wilmore v. Chain O'Mines, Inc., 96 Colo. 319, 44 P.2d 1024 (1934). The American Law Institute has now taken the firm position that, "The pollution of water by a riparian proprietor that creates a nuisance by causing harm to another proprietor's interest in land or water is not the exercise of a riparian right." Restatement (Second) of Torts, § 849(2) (1979).

2. *Civil Remedies.* Pollution of surface and groundwaters was a fertile field for litigation, and there were many suits for redress of wrongs and injunctions against permanent damage. These cases built up a substantial body of doctrine. Nuisance law has its intricacies—balancing utility against harm, public nuisance, and coming to the nuisance. There

are questions of standing, of proper parties, of joinder of parties, of class actions, problems of irreparable harm, balancing the equities, discretionary jurisdiction and conditional injunctions. None of this litigation had much effect upon the overall quality of water, and all these questions of torts, remedies and procedure lie outside the field of water law as such.

3. *State Controls.* Prior to 1948 pollution control was almost entirely a state effort. Water pollution control legislation started by giving State Health Departments the authority to preserve public health. In the early days the administrative approach was largely negative, abating as public nuisances those discharges that threatened the health of the people. Many specific activities, such as throwing slaughterhouse offal into streams, were made crimes. The desirability of maintaining water quality instead of correcting abuses led to much broader authority and a variety of preventive techniques. "Permits" to build and operate disposal plants and to discharge allowable wastes or amounts of waste were a favorite regulatory tool. "Effluent limitations" were set by law or tailored to individual plants by permits. They might take the form of "specification standards" which required particular treatment, facilities or processes, but more usually were stated as "performance standards" which required a particular result and left the means of achieving it to the permittee. "Variances" were often granted, allowing less stringent practices in cases of little harm or extreme hardship. The technique of "classification" of waters was a type of zoning that recognized that some waters were hopelessly lost while some could still be saved or used for different purposes. This led to the setting of receiving water standards which set limits on salinity, taste, odor, color, turbidity, amount of dissolved oxygen, bacteria count, etc., and required discharges to be adjusted until water of the desired quality was achieved or preserved. Some states attempted a unified planning process which established water quality objectives based on the present and probable future beneficial uses of water, the quality of water needed for those uses and a program to achieve or maintain that quality.

4. *Federal Laws.* The first Water Pollution Control Act, 62 Stat. 1155 (1948), offered the state agencies a comprehensive program of investigations, research and funds for operations and treatment works. It set up a complex enforcement system of notices, conferences, hearings and legal proceedings to abate pollution of interstate waters, but this was so chary of state responsibilities and sensibilities as to be completely ineffective. As amended in 1961, the Act was extended to all navigable waters, and in 1965 more amendments required the states to establish water quality standards for interstate streams. To simplify enforcement, federal abatement proceedings could be brought against persons who violated the standards even though no harm or threat to health was shown. Where numbers of polluters were involved, however, problems of proof were difficult, and practical and economic difficulties were excuses for non-compliance and variances.

The sleeping beauty of federal water pollution control turned out to be § 13 of the Rivers and Harbors Act of 1899, 33 U.S.C.A. § 407, which made it unlawful to throw, discharge or deposit any refuse of any kind or description, other than that flowing from streets and sewers in a liquid state, into navigable waters without a permit from the Secretary of the Army. For years this provision was applied only to discharges that threatened to impede navigation. Dusted off in 1970, rechristened the "Refuse Act," applied to all industrial discharges, administered by the Corps of Engineers under guidelines and standards issued by the Environmental Protection Agency, the Act became the basis of the first effective federal regulation of water pollution. The model of efficient, enforceable permits specifically regulating each discharger, coupled with a rising tide of pollution that in some places reached almost crisis proportions, led to the comprehensive Federal Water Pollution Control Act Amendments of 1972. The "amendments" rewrote the old Act completely and replaced the Refuse Act, and have since been renamed the Clean Water Act.

The principal focus of the Clean Water Act is on the pollutants, not on the harm done or the water itself. "Effluent limitations," based on technologically achievable treatment, are imposed on all operators of "point sources" of discharges into all surface waters. A system of permits transforms the general effluent limitations into specific treatment and clean-up requirements for each discharger. "Nonpoint sources," activities on land that cause polluting runoff (agriculture, forestry, road building, etc.), are to be controlled by land use plans.

NATIONAL WILDLIFE FEDERATION v. GORSUCH

United States Court of Appeals, District of Columbia Circuit, 1982.
693 F.2d 156.

WALD, CIRCUIT JUDGE.

The National Wildlife Federation petitioned the district court for a declaration that the Administrator of the Environmental Protection Agency (EPA) has a nondiscretionary duty to require dam operators to apply for pollutant discharge permits under § 402(a) of the Clean Water Act, 33 U.S.C. § 1342(a), and for an order directing her to perform that duty. The district court issued the requested declaration and order, 530 F.Supp. 1291 (D.D.C.1982), from which EPA and the numerous defendant-intervenors (principally electric utilities and water agencies) now appeal. The sole issue is whether certain dam-induced water quality changes constitute the "discharge of a pollutant" as that term is defined in § 502(12) of the Act, 33 U.S.C. § 1362(12). * * * Because we believe that EPA's interpretation is entitled to great deference and that its view of the statute is reasonable, we reverse.

I. BACKGROUND

A. Dam-Induced Water Quality Changes

Dams cause a variety of interrelated water quality problems, both in reservoirs and in river water downstream from a dam. The Wildlife Federation claims that five of these problems—low dissolved oxygen, dissolved minerals and nutrients, water temperature changes, sediment release, and supersaturation—require EPA to regulate dams under the § 402 permit program. * * *

1. Low Dissolved Oxygen

Water released from a reservoir through a dam into downstream water may be low in dissolved oxygen. The river below the dam will remain oxygen-depleted for some distance, although the river will gradually become reaerated through wind mixing as it flows downstream. If the oxygen level is too low, fish cannot survive. Also, a river low in oxygen has limited ability to break down pollutants and other organic matter. Because dissolved oxygen is important both for fish and for breakdown of organic matter, it is an important measure of water quality.

Only large storage dams have low dissolved oxygen problems, and then only during warmer months and only when water is released from the lower part of the reservoir. During warm months, deep reservoirs, like deep natural lakes, stratify into a cold, dense lower layer and a warmer, lighter upper layer. The upper layer, called the "epilimnion," is aerated by wind mixing; oxygen is also produced by photosynthesis. Thus, water quality in the upper layer is good. The lower level, called the "hypolimnion," is too deep to be aerated by wind action and light levels are too low to support photosynthesis. Organic decomposition, which consumes oxygen, leads to a continual net depletion of dissolved oxygen. Depletion continues until "fall turnover," when the two layers break up and the reservoir returns to full aeration. * * *

Several techniques can be used to prevent release of oxygen-depleted water. First, for many dams, water can be released from the epilimnion (which occurs automatically for natural lakes). Older dams were built with reservoir outlets at one level only, usually deep in the dam so that the outlet would remain below the surface of the reservoir even in dry years when the reservoir was low. Many newer dams, however, have outlets at several levels, permitting the dam operator to release high-quality epilimnion water. In single-outlet dams, one can aerate the reservoir (by pumping compressed air down to the hypolimnion) or destratify it (by pumping cold water from the hypolimnion to the surface). Alternatively, one can aerate the hypolimnion water as it is released from the reservoir, either by injecting air or by creating turbulence.

The record does not indicate the number of dams for which discharge of low-oxygen water is a significant problem, nor the cost of the various methods of mechanical aeration. But the problem is serious for at least some dams, and the cure is apparently expensive.

2. Dissolved Minerals and Nutrients

If dissolved oxygen is totally depleted from the hypolimnion, a further problem develops. A number of minerals and plant nutrients, insoluble under normal "aerobic" conditions, are soluble in zero-oxygen "anaerobic" water. These compounds—including iron, manganese and phosphates—therefore tend to be leached from bottom muds into the reservoir. High concentrations of these minerals and nutrients, released into the downstream river, can harm fish, make the water unpalatable for drinking, and foster undesirable plant growth.

* * *

Control of mineral leaching primarily involves destratifying or mechanically aerating the reservoir to prevent the hypolimnion from becoming totally depleted, or else discharging water from the epilimnion. When building a new dam, site preparation (e.g., removing organic soils) can reduce future leaching. Once again, the record reveals neither the number of dams for which mineral leaching is a significant problem nor the cost of cure.

3. *Temperature Changes*

In a thermally stratified reservoir, the lower hypolimnion layer will generally be colder than the upstream river, while the upper epilimnion layer will be warmer. Some species of fish can survive only in warm water; others can survive only in cold water. Thus, cold hypolimnion water, even if fully oxygenated, will harm or kill warm water fish but benefit cold water fish; conversely, warm epilimnion water will harm or kill cold water fish and benefit warm water fish. In some cases, cold water discharges may be desirable—to create a trout fishery, for example. Also, colder water has higher capacity to assimilate wastes, both because decomposition is slower and because oxygen is more soluble in cold water. In short, dams cause *changes* in the temperature of downstream water, and some of the time, but not all of the time, those changes are undesirable.

Changes in the temperature of downstream water can be prevented in dams with multiple outlet levels by release of an appropriate mix of epilimnion and hypolimnion water. For some dams without multiple outlet levels, destratifying the reservoir may be feasible. However, the goal of maintaining downstream water temperature, because it requires a mix of warm and cold water, may conflict with the goal of maintaining downstream oxygen levels, which calls for release of warm epilimnion water.

4. *Sediment*

Generally, large reservoirs act as sediment traps; the water velocity decreases (compared to the upstream river) and sediment settles to the bottom of the reservoir. Thus, water released from the dam will contain less sediment than upstream water. This is generally viewed as an improvement in water quality. However, the river will "tend to restore its equilibrium [sediment] loading by scouring the downstream channel." Also, the reservoir will tend to fill with sediment, which in some cases can require periodic dredging or sluicing. Dredging may temporarily increase sediment load in the reservoir (and hence in the downstream water); sluicing is a deliberate attempt to have the river carry accumulated sediment downstream.

Sediment release can be reduced by careful dredging or by filtering. There is no evidence in the record to suggest that increased sediment is a major problem.

5. *Supersaturation*

When water plunges at high velocity from the reservoir into the downstream river, it becomes mixed with air. Depending on the velocity and turbulence of the falling water and the depth of the receiving basin, this can cause downstream water to become "supersatured"—aerated in excess of normal concentration. Supersaturated water does not harm people and is suitable for most uses, but can be fatal to fish; documented fish kills have occurred at a number of dams.

Supersaturation can be prevented or reduced to non-fatal levels by reducing the turbulence of the falling water (water released from a spillway at the top of a dam is more turbulent than water released through a pipe in the dam), increasing reservoir capacity to reduce the need for spillway releases during flood periods, using a shallow receiving basin below the dam, or constructing spillway deflectors. Supersaturation does not appear at present to be a major problem. The most recent fish kills discussed in the record occurred at Truman Dam in Missouri in 1978 and 1979 while the dam was under construction, and subsequent installation of a spillway deflector has reduced supersaturation to non-fatal levels.

6. *Other Water Quality Changes*

Dams also cause numerous other changes in the nation's waters, not directly at issue in this litigation. On the positive side, dams can prevent floods, store drinking and irrigation water, provide a clean source of electric power (thus reducing other sources of pollution), moderate stream flow, and provide recreation opportunities. On the negative side, they can indirectly affect ground water quality and reduce stream flow and hence waste-assimilative capacity. In short, dams affect environmental quality in a large number of ways, both good and bad.

B. *Legal Issue Presented*

The issue in this case is one of statutory construction—which if any of the water quality changes caused by dams must be regulated under the National Pollutant Discharge Elimination System (NPDES) established by § 402 of the Clean Water Act, 33 U.S.C. § 1342. Under § 402(a), "the Administrator may, after opportunity for public hearing, issue a permit for the discharge of any pollutant." Unless the Administrator issues an NPDES permit, "the discharge of any pollutant by any person [is] unlawful." Id. § 301(a), 33 U.S.C. § 1311(a). Section 502(12), 33 U.S.C. § 1362(12), defines the key phrase "discharge of a pollutant" as "any addition of any pollutant to navigable waters from any point source." Thus, for dams to require NPDES permits, five elements must be present: (1) a *pollutant* must be (2) *added* (3) *to navigable waters* (4) *from* (5) *a point source.*

The parties agree that a dam can, in some circumstances, be a "point source," and that both the reservoir and the downstream river are "navigable waters" within the statutory meaning whether or not they are navigable in fact. They dispute whether low dissolved oxygen, cold, and supersaturation are "pollutants" and whether any of the disputed water quality problems constitute the "addition" of a pollutant "from" a point source.

The Wildlife Federation argues that any adverse changes in the quality of reservoir water from its natural state involves a "pollutant" and that release of polluted water through the dam into the downstream river constitutes the "addition" of a pollutant to navigable waters "from" a point source. If this is correct, the Administrator has a nondiscretionary duty to regulate dams under § 402.

EPA argues, on the other hand, that for addition of a pollutant from a point source to occur, the point source must *introduce* the pollutant into navigable water from the outside world; dam-caused pollution, in contrast, merely passes through the dam from one body of navigable water (the reservoir) into another (the downstream river). Also, while conceding that all adverse water quality changes are "pollution"—broadly defined in § 502(19), 33 U.S.C. § 1362(19), as "the man-made or man-induced alteration of the chemical, physical, biological, and radiological integrity of water"—EPA argues that low dissolved oxygen, cold, and supersaturation are not included in the narrower statutory term "pollutant," defined in § 502(6), 33 U.S.C. § 1362(6) as:

> dredged spoil, solid waste, incinerator residue, sewage, garbage, sewage sludge, munitions, chemical wastes, biological materials, radioactive materials, heat, wrecked or discarded equipment, rock, sand, cellar dirt and industrial, municipal, and agricultural waste discharged into water.

In EPA's view, the Act divides the causes and control of water pollution into two categories, *point sources of pollutants* (regulated through the § 402 permit program) and *nonpoint sources of pollution* (regulated by the states through "areawide waste treatment management plans" under § 208, 33 U.S.C. § 1288). The latter category is defined by exclusion and includes all water quality problems not subject to § 402.

The district court acknowledged that nothing in the Act or its legislative history suggests that Congress thought about the precise issue before us: whether dam-caused pollution should be regulated under the NPDES permit program. 530 F.Supp. at 1303. The court concluded, however, that had Congress considered the matter it would have included dams in the permit program. * * * As for the distinction between "pollutant" and "pollution," the court believed that the statutory list of pollutants was not exclusive. While declining to

wholly equate "pollutant" and "pollution," it believed that low dissolved oxygen, cold, and supersaturation were all similar enough to listed pollutants to be among "the kinds of pollution [Congress] intended to control through the NPDES program." Id. at 1311. The district court thus ruled in favor of the Wildlife Federation on the meaning of both "addition" and "pollutant." Recognizing that the large number of dams in the country made issuing individual permits impractical, it ordered EPA to establish "effluent limitations or other performance standards for dams on a categorical, as opposed to a case-by-case basis."
* * *

In this appeal, EPA and the Wildlife Federation largely repeat the statutory arguments they made below. In addition, EPA argues that the district court failed to give sufficient deference to EPA's interpretation of the Act. * * *

III. THE REASONABLENESS OF EPA'S INTERPRETATION

* * *

A. Specific Substantive Provisions

To briefly restate the issue before us, dams can release water into the downstream river which is low in dissolved oxygen, contains dissolved minerals and nutrients, is warm or cold, contains excess sediment, or is supersaturated. The statutory question is whether any or all of these conditions constitute the "addition of any pollutant to navigable waters from any point source" so as to require EPA to issue NPDES permits for dams under § 402.

1. "Pollutant"

Low dissolved oxygen, cold, and supersaturation do not plainly fall within the statutory list of pollutants in § 502(6), 33 U.S.C. § 1362(6)—"dredged spoil, solid waste, incinerator residue, sewage, garbage, sewage sludge, munitions, chemical wastes, biological materials, radioactive materials, heat, wrecked or discarded equipment, rock, sand, cellar dirt and industrial, municipal, and agricultural waste discharged into water." These dam-induced changes are water *conditions,* not substances added to water. Section 502(6), however, primarily lists substances; "heat" is the only listed water condition. Moreover, the wording of § 506(6) makes us cautious in adding new terms to the definition. Congress used restrictive phrasing—"[t]he term 'pollutant' *means* dredged spoil, [etc.]"—rather than the looser phrase "includes," used elsewhere in the Act. As a general rule, " '[a] definition which declares what a term "means" * * * excludes any meaning that is not stated.' " * * *

2. "Addition" of a Pollutant "from" a Point Source

The Act does not define what constitutes the "addition" of a pollutant. The parties agree that water quality problems that occur within a reservoir (e.g., dissolved minerals) are nonpoint pollution, for lack of a point source. The Wildlife Federation argues, however, that the statutorily necessary "addition * * * from a point source" occurs when (1) a dam causes pollutants to enter the reservoir and (2) the polluted water subsequently passes through the dam—the point source—into the formerly unpolluted river below. EPA responds that addition from a point source occurs only if the point source itself physically introduces a pollutant into water from the outside world. In its view, the point or nonpoint character of pollution is established when the pollutant first enters navigable water, and does not change when the polluted water later passes through the dam from one body of navigable water (the reservoir) to another (the downstream river). As for supersaturation, which does not exist in the reservoir, EPA argues that it occurs downstream, *after* the water is released from the dam.

In our view, the language of the statute permits either construction. The legislative history does not provide much help either. * * *

B. The Purposes of the Act

We conclude, then, on the basis of the text and history of the Act, that EPA's construction of relevant substantive provisions is reasonable. We consider next the Wildlife Federation's argument, accepted by the district court, that EPA's construction nonetheless will plainly frustrate the general congressional purposes underlying the Act. We find that it does not.

1. The Text of the "Purposes" Section

The district court, in giving "pollutant" and "addition" a broad reading, relied heavily on the "purposes" section of the Act, § 101(a), 33 U.S.C. § 1251(a). That section declares (emphasis added):

> The objective of this [Act] is to restore and maintain the chemical, physical, and biological integrity of the Nation's waters. In order to achieve this objective it is hereby declared that, consistent with the provisions of this [Act]—
>
> (1) it is the national goal that the discharge of pollutants into the navigable waters be eliminated by 1985;
>
> (2) it is the national goal that wherever attainable, an interim goal of [fishable and swimmable] water be achieved by July 1, 1983;
>
> (3) it is the national policy that the discharge of toxic pollutants in toxic amounts be prohibited * * *.

Undeniably, Congress' strong statement of its objective must color EPA's and our interpretation of specific provisions of the Act. But, as any student of the legislative process soon learns, it is one thing for Congress to announce a grand goal, and quite another for it to mandate full implementation of that goal. Read as a whole, the Clean Water Act shows not only Congress' determined effort to clean up our polluted lakes and rivers, but also its practical recognition of the economic, technological, and political limits on total elimination of all pollution from all sources. * * *

Moreover, even if we accept the purposes section at face value, it is only suggestive, not dispositive of whether EPA must issue NPDES permits for dams. Caution is always advisable in relying on a general declaration of purpose to alter the apparent meaning of a specific provision. Here, Congress' expressed goal to eliminate "the discharge of pollutants" does not necessarily require that we expansively construe the term "pollutant," which Congress itself specifically defined. As for the interim goal of fishable and swimmable water, the purposes section does not tell us how that goal is to be achieved. And Congress, although recognizing the weaknesses of past state water pollution efforts, explicitly chose not to completely federalize water pollution control, but instead directed the states to establish their own pollution control programs under EPA oversight. Had it considered the matter, Congress might well have decided that dam-caused pollution was a problem best addressed through state programs. * * *

3. *Policy Considerations*

Finally, as a policy matter (and recognizing our limited role in reviewing agency policy decisions) we are not convinced that EPA's decision to leave dam regulation to the states was so misguided as to frustrate congressional policy. EPA contends that requiring permits for 2,000,000 dams would be an impossible task. Yet, so far as the record shows, most, if not all of the dams that cause water quality problems are large hydroelectric dams. Thus, the number of dams that would require permits is probably no more than the 50,000 "large" dams in the country, and quite possibly only the 3,000 or so dams that are large enough to generate significant amounts of hydroelectric power. That is a manageable number even if it turns out to be impractical to issue categorical permits. Nor are we persuaded by EPA's argument that because the NPDES program requires discharge of pollutants to be eliminated to the extent technologically feasible, it will preclude beneficial dam-caused water changes, such as cold water discharges to support a trout fishery. It should be feasible for EPA to define "pollutant" to exclude beneficial water quality changes.

On the other hand, dam-caused pollution is unique because its severity depends partly on whether other sources have polluted the upstream river. The NPDES program, however, requires EPA to issue nationally uniform standards, and thus would not allow the agency to take full account of the interrelationship between dam-caused pollution and other pollution sources. Moreover, dams are a major component of state water management, providing irrigation, drinking water, flood protection, etc. In light of these complexities, which the NPDES program was not designed to handle, it may well be that state areawide water quality plans are the better regulatory tool.

Also, the severity of dam-caused pollution is highly site-specific. Common forms of NPDES limits (x% reduction in biochemical oxygen demand (BOD) or y pounds of BOD per ton of industrial output) would entail major costs at one dam, and only minor costs at another. Thus, it would be difficult at best for EPA to determine what level of reduction is obtainable by using the "best available technology *economically achieveable*" for each "category or class" of polluter. Clean Water Act § 301(b)(2)(A), 33 U.S.C. § 1311(b)(2)(A) (emphasis added). Control that is economically feasible at one site may be infeasible at another. Conversely, major expenditures might be required for dams where, say, dissolved oxygen levels are slightly reduced immediately below the dam, but not enough to harm fish, and the river is fully reaerated within a few miles.

Finally, we cannot say, on the record before us, that federal intervention is needed because the states have abdicated their § 208 responsibility over a truly pressing national problem. The record does not show how vigorous state enforcement has been, but at least some efforts have been made to remedy dam-caused pollution. Supersaturation and sediment releases appear to be minor problems. As discussed earlier, temperature changes are not always harmful, are not easily controllable at single-outlet dams, and can apparently be readily controlled at multiple-outlet dams. Low dissolved oxygen and dissolved minerals and nutrients are the most serious problems, but EPA has the authority, when it reviews state water pollution control plans, to insist if need be on stronger efforts in the future. Also, new dams cannot be built unless they comply with state water quality requirements; thus the problem is largely limited to existing dams.

Moreover, if dam-caused pollution was truly of major proportions, someone, be it EPA, the Wildlife Federation, or other environmental groups, would most likely have brought it to Congress' attention, either in 1972 or in 1977. And of course, the Wildlife Federation, if unhappy with our attempt to divine what Congress would have done about dam-caused pollution had it thought about it, is still free to seek a legislative solution. Unless and until Congress addresses the matter, we cannot say that the Act requires EPA to adopt the strictest possible regulatory solution.

V. Conclusion

In closing, we emphasize the narrowness of our decision. It is not our function to decide whether EPA's interpretation of the term "discharge of a pollutant" is the best one or even whether it is more reasonable than the Wildlife Federation's interpretation. We hold merely that EPA's interpretation is reasonable, not inconsistent with congressional intent, and entitled to great deference; therefore, it must be upheld. The judgment of the district court is reversed.

Notes

1. The key sections of the CWA make it unlawful to discharge any pollutant into "navigable waters." The waters protected are variously

referred to as "the Nation's water," "the navigable waters" and "the waters of the United States." These are *all* water courses in the United States, not merely the "navigable waters of the United States" as defined in U.S. v. Appalachian Power Co., supra p. 635. One general charge to the Administrator of EPA is to develop programs for "preventing, reducing or eliminating the pollution of the navigable waters and ground waters and improving the sanitary condition of surface and underground waters."

In fact there may be no water. In U.S. v. Phelps Dodge Corp., 391 F.Supp. 1181 (D.C.Ariz.1975), it was said,

"For the purposes of this Act to be effectively carried into realistic achievement, the scope of its control must extend to all pollutants which are discharged into *any waterway,* including normally dry arroyos, where any water which might flow therein could reasonably end up in any body of water, to which or in which there is some public interest, including underground waters.

"The intention of Congress was to eliminate or to reduce as much as possible *all water pollution* throughout the United States both surface and underground. * * *

"Thus a legal definition of 'navigable waters' or 'waters of the United States' within the scope of the Act includes any waterway within the United States also including normally dry arroyos through which water may flow, where such water will ultimately end up in public waters such as a river or stream, tributary to a river or stream, lake, reservoir, bay, gulf, sea or ocean either within or adjacent to the United States."

It may be possible to walk upon the water. One program of the CWA requires a "§ 404 permit" from the Corps of Engineers to discharge dredge and fill material into navigable water (33 U.S.C.A. §§ 1311, 1362 and 1444). For this purpose, the Corps has defined navigable waters to include "freshwater wetlands," in turn defined as "* * * those areas that are inundated or saturated by surface or ground water at a frequency and duration sufficient to support, and that under normal circumstances do support, a prevalence of vegetation typically adapted for life in saturated soil conditions. Wetlands generally include swamps, marshes, bogs and similar areas." An earlier version had required the land to be subject to periodic inundation. The owner of 80 acres of low lying marshy land desired to fill it to make it suitable for a housing development. The land was adjacent to a lake, but the source of the saturation was ground water, not the lake. The lower court held that frequent flooding by adjacent navigable water was still essential to regulation by the Corps. In United States v. Riverside Bayview Homes, Inc., 106 S.Ct. 455, ___ U.S. ___, 88 L.Ed.2d 419 (1985), the Supreme Court reversed.

> On a purely linguistic level, it may appear unreasonable to classify "lands," wet or otherwise, as "waters." Such a simplistic response, however, does justice neither to the problem faced by the Corps in defining the scope of its authority under § 404(a) nor to the realities of the problem of water pollution that the Clean Water Act was intended to combat. In determining the limits of its power to regulate discharges under the Act, the Corps must necessarily choose some point at which water ends and land begins. Our common experience tells us

that this is often no easy task: the transition from water to solid ground is not necessarily or even typically an abrupt one. Rather, between open waters and dry land may lie shallows, marshes, mudflats, swamps, bogs—in short, a huge array of areas that are not wholly aquatic but nevertheless fall far short of being dry land. Where on this continuum to find the limit of "waters" is far from obvious.
* * *

Ground waters as such are not navigable, with the possible exception of the River Styx. In Exxon Corp. v. Train, 554 F.2d 1310 (5th Cir.1977) waste water from natural gas production operations was discharged in part into pits, which concededly needed a permit, and in part into a 5,000 foot abandoned oil well, where it joined groundwater. It was not contended, however, that it would migrate to any surface water. The Administrator disclaimed authority to regulate subsurface waste disposal directly, but argued that he might place conditions in the permit required for the surface discharge that would limit or prohibit the subsurface disposal. The court ruled that the legislative history conclusively demonstrated that the CWA does not empower the Administrator to control deep well disposal of wastes, but rather left this to the states, most of which, said the court, had some type of control. Section 402(b) (33 U.S.C.A. § 1342(b)) does provide that the Administrator, in approving a state program for the NPDES, must determine that the state has adequate authority to issue permits which control the disposal of pollutants into wells. Reaching the same result was United States v. GAF Corporation, 389 F.Supp. 1379 (S.D. Texas 1975).

Regulations drafted pursuant to the Safe Drinking Water Act of 1974, 88 Stat. 1660, P.L. 93–523, 42 U.S.C.A. § 300h, include requirements for state programs to control underground injections in order to protect public water systems from contamination. See Friedman, Environmental Problems Relating to Uranium Mining and Milling, XI Natural Resources Lawyer 277 (1978). The Act places emphasis on protection of recharge zones of aquifers and on permits to control waste injection wells that might damage drinking water supplies. See Getches, Controlling Groundwater Use and Quality: A Fragmented System, 17 Natural Resources Lawyer 623, 631 (1985).

2. The effluent limitations required by the 1972 Amendments were fixed in terms of the "best practicable control technology currently available" (BPT) and the "best available technology economically achievable (BAT). Existing plants were to reach BPT by 1977, and to achieve BAT by 1983. BPT was based on average performance in the best existing plants. BAT was the best in operation or demonstrated by research. For instance, the meat packing industry was studied thoroughly and one of its effluents, BOD ("biological oxygen demand," pollutants such as blood and liquid offal that decompose and deplete oxygen) was set at a discharge of .12 lb. per 1000 lbs. of live weight killed, achieved in three midwestern plants. BAT was set at one-fourth this amount, shown to be achievable by new techniques or by combinations of processes in use. See American Meat Institute v. Environmental Protection Agency, 526 F.2d 442 (7th Cir.1975). When the NPDES permit is issued for a particular plant, it specifies the maximum daily average load that may be discharged under various condi-

tions. If the limitations are not currently met, the permit includes a schedule for achieving these goals. The plant must operate such settling ponds, chemical processes, bacteriological treatment and aerating lagoons as are necessary to comply with the permit.

The Clean Water Act of 1977 made some changes in the system, subdividing industrial wastes in a different fashion and adding a new timetable. It had been impossible for many dischargers to meet BPT (best practical control technology) by July 1, 1977, so the Act amended the 1972 Amendments by authorizing extensions to April 1, 1979, and in some cases to July 1, 1983. Toxic wastes were made the subject of a separate strategy and the general deadline for achieving BAT (best available control technology) for these discharges was postponed from July 1, 1983 to July 1, 1984. The Act created a new class of "conventional pollutants" (BOD, suspended solids, coliform bacteria and acidity) and dischargers of these may never be required to achieve BAT. The Act now requires BCT (best conventional pollutant control technology) by July 1, 1984. In setting BCT the Administrator may consider a number of more lenient factors—the relationship between the costs and the effluent reduction benefits derived, comparison of the costs and the level of reduction of pollutants, the age of equipment and facilities, various control techniques and processes and non-water quality environmental impacts such as energy requirements.

This leaves a class of pollutants that are neither toxic nor conventional (e.g. oil, grease, salts, nitrates and dyes) for which BAT will be required within three years after limitations for them are established, in no case later than July 1, 1987.

3. Some technology-based effluent limitations are set in terms of maximum pollutant discharges per unit of time (e.g., five pound daily average), others at maximum concentration of pollutants, e.g., 10 mg. per liter of discharge). Could the discharger's water rights for use of water be affected by a limitation on the total discharge of pollutants and carrying water? Cf. FMC Corp. v. Train, 539 F.2d 973 (4th Cir.1976). Could a discharger meet a limitation on concentration by "flow augmentation" that reduces the level of contaminants but does not reduce the total waste load? Cf. Ford Motor Co. v. EPA, 567 F.2d 661 (6th Cir.1977).

The best technology for a particular discharger may affect the quantity of water available to other water users. Reuse and recirculation of industrial and cooling water may increase consumption. Settling ponds and lagoons increase evaporation, and in arid areas where the rate of evaporation exceeds the input, small municipalities may meet best technology requirements and the "no discharge" goal of CWA by employing large lagoons or "land treatment," i.e., irrigation of crops not destined for human consumption, with primary treated sewage. What of downstream appropriators dependent upon "return flows" from municipal use? Cf. Thayer v. Rawlins, supra, p. 233, and cases cited.

See White, The Emerging Relationship between Environmental Regulations and Colorado Water Law, 53 U.Colo.L.Rev. 597 (1982).

4. United States ex rel. TVA v. Tennessee Water Quality Control Board, 717 F.2d 992 (6th Cir.1983) illustrates the administration of the

NPDES program. EPA sets the standards and requirements for permits and prescribes the conditions of permits. Upon approval of a state program by EPA, a state may issue its own permits for discharges into "navigable waters" within its jurisdiction. State permits and programs are reviewed by EPA, which may substitute federal action if it finds the state permits, program or enforcement to be inadequate. Section 510 of CWA allows the states to adopt or enforce effluent limitations, standards and prohibitions which are more stringent than the requirements of EPA under the federal Act. Section 313 of CWA requires federal officers and agencies to comply with all federal, state and local requirements, unless exempted by the president in the paramount national interest.

When TVA was founded, it took over Ocoee River Dam No. 2, a rock-filled timber crib diversion structure that stores no water but turns most of the river into a flume to a power plant. A small amount seeps through. In 1976 TVA ceased diversions and the river provided a popular rafting and canoeing water. TVA proposed to resume diversions after Congress refused to appropriate funds to compensate it for loss of power revenues. The state agency sought to regulate the flow by issuing an NPDES permit, claiming that the seepage through the dam was "polluted" by the reduction in flow. The court disagreed:

"The 'pollution' which the Commissioner of the Tennessee Department of Health identified is not subject to control or abatement by use of the discharge permit system. The right of the State to require discharge permits is derived solely from section 402. EPA has consistently treated dams as nonpoint sources of pollution which are not subject to the discharge permit requirements of section 402. We agree with the District of Columbia Circuit that this interpretation of the Act by the agency charged with its administration and enforcement is entitled to deference. Since EPA does not require discharge permits from dam operators under section 402(A), the states may not do so under section 402(B). Accordingly, we affirm the judgment of the district court in its holding that Tennessee could not require TVA to obtain a permit for the reconstruction and operation of Ocoee No. 2."

5. Prior to 1972, the principal effort of pollution control was directed at the protection of water by maintaining federally required, state-promulgated "receiving water standards." The shift to the technique of effluent limitations enforced by permits was designed to achieve a national goal "that the discharge of pollutants into the national water be *eliminated*." CWA § 101(a)(1). This was primarily a change in emphasis, and both the 1972 and 1977 laws retained an "interim goal of water quality which provides for the protection and propagation of fish, shellfish and wildlife and provides for recreation in and on the water," usually translated to "fishable/swimmable" (§ 101(a)(1)), and required each state to set water quality standards for all streams (§ 303). Regulations adopted by EPA in 1983 restate the rules and policies to be followed. States must designate the existing and attainable uses of each body of water and establish water quality criteria to protect those uses. An antidegradation policy is required; where actual quality exceeds the fishable/swimmable goal, that quality must be maintained "except to accommodate economic or social

development in the locality." Water quality of "outstanding natural resources" must be maintained and protected.

Waste transport and waste assimilation are not permissible designated uses, so apparently withdrawals upstream from correctible pollutant discharges are not affected. But since water quality is the relation between a measure of foreign matter and the quantity of carrying water, withdrawals of clear water could increase the concentration that naturally occurs as a stream continues on its downward course. Could there be a "water law" objection that a withdrawal from the headwaters of a western stream which produced this effect in downstream reaches would not be "beneficial" or "in the public interest"? See Chapter 2, supra.

STAFF DRAFT REPORT, NATIONAL COMMISSION ON WATER QUALITY

November, 1975, pp. 153–156, II168–II177.

3. IRRIGATION RETURN FLOWS

a. Introduction

About 25 percent of all farm sales in the United States are produced on the roughly 10 percent of cropland that is irrigated. Much of this land could not be farmed at all without irrigation. On the rest, irrigation is used to increase production, to produce different crops than could be grown without irrigation, or to assure the production of a crop each year.

Irrigated agriculture impacts water quality and quantity in at least six different ways: (1) it concentrates salts dissolved in water, primarily by the evapotranspiration of water; (2) it may weather naturally occurring minerals from irrigated soils; (3) it may add sediment to, or remove it from, receiving water; (4) it may add nitrogen and phosphorus to a receiving water; (5) it may add pesticides to a receiving water; and (6) it will alter the quantity and temporal distribution of downstream flows if it is derived from, or returned to, surface waters.

The volume of irrigation return flow produced by a farm is the difference between the volume diverted from the water supply and the volume consumed by evapotranspiration. The proportion of the total water infiltrated into the soil that is in excess of the consumptive requirements of the crop (for both evaporation and transpiration) is called the "leaching fraction." The leaching fraction returns to surface or groundwaters as an irrigation return flow.

The leaching water percolates through the soil where a portion of it may be intercepted by artificial drains, collected and discharged to a receiving water as a point source. Percolating water not intercepted in drainage systems joins the local groundwater. It may return quickly to a surface stream, or it may remain in the ground for an extended period. Certain irrigation waters, once diverted, do not enter the soil but are returned directly to a receiving stream. Most operators of flood irrigation systems or ditch and furrow types do not completely control water application. Excess waters that are diverted and pass over the surface rather than through the soil are called "tailwater." They are also frequently discharged as point source irrigation return flows.

(1) Salinity

The concentrations of total dissolved solids in subsurface irrigation return flows are higher, typically, than those in the water delivered to the field. The applied water contains some concentration of salts. Growing plants consume pure water, leaving the salts behind in a smaller remaining volume of water in the root zone. Leaching water serves to carry the salts away, maintaining the productivity of the soil. Increasing irrigation efficiency—reducing the leaching fraction—reduces the mass of salt diverted with the water. The volume of return flow in which the diverted salts are dissolved is reduced by a greater proportion, and the concentration of salts in the return flow is increased. The total mass of salt discharged is reduced, but the salts not diverted remain in the water supply.

In addition to the salts contained in the applied water, irrigation return flows may carry salts which are added to the leaching water as it passes through the subsoil. It may also leave some of the applied salts in the soil as precipitates, so that the relative concentrations of dissolved salts in applied water and return flows are different. The importance of this increment of salinity depends on the solubility and composition of the subsoil material, and on the size of the leaching fraction. In some regions it is of major importance, while elsewhere it is insignificant.

In most cases, regardless of the type of irrigation system used, and regardless of the efficiency of the irrigation system, most of the salt in irrigation return flow will be salt that was contained in the water applied to the land. Efficiency of irrigation has little effect on the quantity of water consumed by evapotranspiration. Any particular crop has a certain evapotranspiration requirement to produce a specified yield. Any water supplied in excess of this requirement will appear as return flow, and if a lesser quantity is applied, it will have an adverse effect on the yield and may cause a buildup of salts in the soil. Therefore, if the irrigation water is withdrawn from a stream, and the return flow is delivered back to the same stream, the efficiency of irrigation will not affect the total quantity of either water or salt transported by the stream in the long run, unless the soil being irrigated still contains native soluble salts.

(2) Suspended Sediment

Irrigation water which passes through the soil is essentially free of suspended sediment, but tailwater may contain sediments. Whether tailwater has a higher or lower concentration of suspended material than the initial supply depends upon local factors. The amount of sediment discharged with tailwater can be reduced by passing the return flow through a sedimentation basin or, under certain circumstances, the tailwater can be recovered and reapplied without any intervening discharge to a receiving water body.

In areas where the natural sediment burdens in streams are very large, the practice or irrigated agriculture can result in a net removal of suspended material. Sediments originally carried by a stream may be deposited in diversion channels or on irrigated lands.

The concentration of suspended material in watercourses is determined by stream velocity. At points where the velocity is low, sediments will be deposited; where the velocity is high, erosion will occur. Excepting areas where a stream bed is incised in bedrock, the burden of suspended material carried by a stream cannot be controlled by changing the discharge of sediment to it. * * *

b. Location and Distribution of Point Source Irrigation Return Flows

About 39 million acres of farm land were irrigated in the United States in 1969. About 97 percent of this land is located in the 17 western states, Arkansas, Louisiana, and Florida. About 257,000 farms in the United States were reported to be irrigated in 1969, and about 223,000 of them were in these twenty states. About 57 percent of all irrigated land is in California, Texas, Nebraska, Colorado, and Idaho, and 36 percent is in California and Texas alone. No state other than these five has as much as five percent of the total irrigated acreage.

All irrigated farms are potential point source dischargers, at least of tailwater, but only those that are artificially drained are potential point source dischargers of drainage water. Artificial drainage systems have been installed on only about 4.6 million acres (12 percent) of irrigated land. Artificial drainage systems have also been installed on about 55 million acres of non-irrigated land, but the cost and effectiveness of controls for this land were not determined. * * *

c. The Colorado River—A Special Case

The overriding water quality problem in the Colorado River is salinity. The salt loads in the river stem mainly from the weathering of the basin's saline soils. Man's affect on the salt concentrations arises from activities which both change the total amount of salt and decrease the river's flow. Under present conditions the net increment to the salt load from irrigated agriculture or other uses is probably less than half that from natural sources. However, consumptive use or out-of-basin transfers decrease dilution and further increase salt concentrations. The increment in salinity concentration attributable to reduced flow is at least as large as that from the increased salt load. Future water depletions have a greater potential for degrading water quality than new sources of salt.

Increased salt concentrations in the Colorado River tend to be more harmful to man than they are to the natural environment. The biological communities of the lower Colorado are tolerant of salt concentrations historically associated with low flow conditions. In contrast, man's use of the river, including irrigated agriculture and municipal and industrial use, are affected by the present salt concentrations. Some varieties of crops cannot be grown. Salt tolerant crops require increased quantities of irrigation water if salinity concentrations are high. Municipal or industrial users of water from the lower Colorado must meet costs for water softening or for controlling salt deposits.

The apportionment of the water resources of the Colorado River is governed by a complex set of treaties, compacts, Federal and state laws and court decisions. The present upper basin use amounts to about 3.7 million acre-feet each year. Consumptive use will increase in the future as the upstream states commit to use the quantities to which they are entitled. The Bureau of Reclamation has estimated that this demand could grow to be 5.9 million acre feet per year by the year 2000. When development occurs remedial actions to control downstream salinity concentrations will be required. Without such actions salinity at Imperial Dam could increase from the present 850 mg/1 to as much as 1,250 mg/1.

The program to control salinity in the Colorado may include a variety of measures. Title II of P.L. 93–320, the Colorado River Basin Salinity Control Act, authorizes the Secretary of the Interior, acting through the Bureau of Reclamation, to construct three projects to isolate and remove highly saline inflows and undertake improvements to decrease the seepage of irrigation water from the delivery and drainage canals in the Grand Valley area of Colorado. P.L. 93–320 also directs the Secretary of the Interior to complete planning reports on 12 additional salinity control projects. Of these projects, four would control salt loads from irrigation sources, three from natural springs, and five from natural diffuse sources.

The initial four projects are to be funded on a cost-sharing basis. 75 percent of the cost is Federal and 25 percent is derived from the Upper and Lower Colorado River Basin Development Funds. Over $125 million was authorized, but there have been no appropriations to date.

The seven basin states have developed and are in the process of adopting salinity standards, including both numerical criteria for salt concentrations and measures to assure their achievement and maintenance. The core of the program is the 16 Federal projects of P.L. 93–320. In addition, the implementation plan includes a "no salt return" policy for industrial uses and a reformulation of certain future agriculture development projects to minimize their salt discharges.

The Commission's findings confirm the *potential* for reducing the salt load in the river by increasing the efficiency of irrigation practices. Based upon general assumptions, a program to increase irrigation efficiency throughout the basin could potentially reduce the salt load in the river by 2.0 million tons per year from the current 9.0 million tons per year. Projects designed to decrease salinity through increased irrigation efficiency, however, should never be initiated without careful evaluation on a site-by-site basis. * * *

d. Cost and Effectiveness of Control Options

The cost and effectiveness of three levels of control of irrigation return flow were investigated: "Low", "Medium", and "High". The three levels are more descriptive of the cost of controls than, necessarily, of their relative effectiveness in the control of pollution.

Four primary methods are used for applying water to land. About 54 percent of the land is irrigated by furrows or ditches, 30 percent by flooding, 15 percent by sprinklers, and one percent by subirrigation, which is important in only a few regions of the country.

Sprinklers are generally the most efficient method of applying irrigation water because they allow excellent control of the amount applied and they provide uniform distribution of the applied water. There are many areas, however, where sprinklers cannot be used because of very low soil infiltration rates. * * *

The low level of control would reduce the mass emission of pollutants in return flow by increasing the efficiency of water use through irrigation management servicing (IMS), or by tailwater recovery, as applicable. In most cases, increasing efficiency reduces mass emission of dissolved salts simply by reducing the mass of salt applied to the land. This technique (IMS) has been developed in recent years and is presently applied to about 1 percent of irrigated land. Detailed accounts of soil moisture, soil moisture holding capacity, daily evapotranspiration requirements, and other pertinent data are kept on a field by field basis, usually on a computer. Proper manipulation of these data provides the farmer with accurate information regarding the optimum date and amount of his next irrigation.

This level of control was assumed to be applicable to all irrigated land with artificial subsurface drainage facilities. Its application to land that is irrigated by sprinklers and that is not artificially drained cannot be charged to abatement of pollution, because such lands do not normally have any point source return flows. Properly operated sprinkler systems do not produce tailwater, because they apply water at a rate equal to or less than the infiltration rate of the soil, and no surface runoff occurs. * * *

The medium level of control would improve irrigation efficiency to the maximum extent feasible by initiating IMS, lining unlined laterals and canals, and installing sprinkler systems on all land that is now surface irrigated. The above controls would apply only to surface irrigated land that has no installed drain. The medium level of control for land that is not artificially drained and that is surface irrigated would be either sedimentation basins to treat tailwater or recovery and reuse to eliminate the discharge of tailwater. Again, land that is without installed drains that is sprinkler irrigated would require no treatment. * * *

The high level of control investigated would add desalting of return flows from artificially drained lands to the medium level of control, and would prohibit the discharge of tailwater by requiring the installation of tailwater recovery systems, which are systems for capturing and returning to the delivery system any water that runs off the lower end of the field.

Where conditions are favorable, Irrigation Management Service can improve irrigation efficiency by approximately 20%, while increasing crop yields by about 15%. The use of the service can reduce the discharge of pesticides, phosphorus, sediment and organic matter by 20 or 40%. * * * The cost, where major structural improvements in delivery systems are not required, averages about $5 per acre per year.

Increasing irrigation efficiency by 20% would reduce irrigation water diversion by about 20% and reduce return flow volume from 40 to 50% but would increase the dissolved salt concentration in the return flow by 30 to 60%. It would generally have no effect on consumptive use of water by plants. It would decrease the mass emission of salt in the return flow by about 20%, and would alter the return flow by about 20%, and would alter the temporal distribution of downstream flow. The water quality impacts of these alterations may be beneficial or detrimental, depending on local conditions.

Major structural changes in water conveyance, distribution and application systems to improve efficiency are much more expensive, and have about the same average degree of effectiveness in reducing water use and return flow as IMS. The effectiveness of such structural changes in improving efficiency is highly dependent upon local soil types, being very effective in coarse grained soils and only marginally effective in soils with high clay content. Costs range upward to $78 per acre per year, depending upon local circumstances. * * *

Desalting all the drainage water from one acre of irrigated land costs up to $130 per year, * * *.

Notes

1. The 1972 Amendments dealt only obliquely with the problem of agricultural pollution. It was identified as a subject for study and research (§ 104(p)), and pollution from agriculturally related nonpoint sources was named as an item for consideration in areawide plans (§ 208(b)(2)(F)).

The EPA approached the regulation of irrigated agriculture very gingerly. It first excluded from the operation of the Act irrigated return flows drained from less than 3000 acres and thus put controls principally on the drains of irrigation and drainage districts. This was set aside in NRDC v. Train, 396 F.Supp. 1393 (D.D.C.1975), which held that the Agency had no power to ignore the Act and exempt point sources from the NPDES program. EPA then formulated plans for "general permits" on an area-wide basis, authorizing discharges from "conveyances carrying surface irrigation return flow as a result of the controlled application of water by any person to land used primarily for crops," (41 Fed.Reg. 24, 493 (1976)), instead of requiring individual farmers and districts to apply for permits. Before this program got under way, the Clean Water Act of 1977 was passed.

The Act reflected the concern of western irrigators and members of Congress. The "Wallop Amendment," § 101(g), added to the basic statute a disclaimer:

> "It is the policy of Congress that the authority of each State to allocate quantities of water within its jurisdiction shall not be superseded, abrogated or otherwise impaired by this Act. It is the further policy of Congress that nothing in this Act shall be construed to supersede or abrogate rights to quantities of water which have been established by any State. Federal agencies shall cooperate with State and local agencies to develop comprehensive solutions to prevent, reduce and eliminate pollution in concert with programs for managing water resources."

Section 102(g) sent the problem back to EPA for further study and a report to Congress that is to analyze "the relationship between programs under this Act and the programs by which State and Federal agencies allocate quantities of water." It went on to amend the definition of "point source" subject to regulation by adding, "This term does not include return flows from irrigated agriculture" (§ 502.14), and the NPDES provisions by adding, "The Administrator shall not require a permit under this section for discharges composed entirely of return flows from irrigated agriculture, nor shall the Administrator directly or indirectly require any State to require such a permit." (§ 402(1)). Finally, the Act handed to local "areawide waste treatment management planning agencies" the job of identifying nonpoint sources of "return flows from irrigated agriculture, and their cumulative effects." (§ 208(b)(2)(F)).

2. Much water pollution originates from nonpoint sources such as storm sewers, city streets, construction sites, road building, logging operations, cleared lands, open cut strip mines, mine dumps, hillside quarries, pastures, feed lots, overgrazed land, plowed land, junkyards, dumps, sanitary landfills, and sludge and pollutant disposal sites. It has been estimated that sediments from nonpoint sources are 360 times the quantity discharged from point sources, and BOD loadings from nonpoint sources are estimated at five times those from point sources. Council on Environmental Quality, 9th Annual Report, 119 (1978). "§ 208 planning" is a process designed to fit together all elements of water pollution control and cleanup into an effective working operation, locally designed and implemented. The area planning agency designated by the governor of the state may be an existing institution, a new state agency, or a committee of representatives of local governments. It must set in operation a "continuing areawide waste treatment management process" and develop a treatment plan "applicable to all wastes generated within the area involved." The agency

must identify significant non-point sources of pollution and develop plans to control them through "best management practices" (BMP's). Many sources must be regulated by land use control statutes or ordinances and by conditions imposed by permits and licenses needed to carry on the operations. Cities and counties may adopt ordinances, and the local agency itself may have sufficient powers to adopt regulations with the force of law. Some parts of the plan may be no more than recommendations to other agencies for action, or to the legislature for needed laws.

Establishment of minimum stream flows has been suggested as one method for preventing downstream runoff from being injuriously concentrated in depleted streams. Regulation of NonPoint Sources of Water Pollution in Oregon under Section 208 of the Federal Water Pollution Control Act, 60 Ore.L.Rev., 184, 189 (1981).

3. The Clean Water Act of 1977 contains one program that may take part of the sting out of restricting irrigation return flows bearing salts and silts. As noted, the costs of improving works, lining canals and installing sprinkler systems can be large. The Act establishes a new program in the Department of Agriculture, to be approved by EPA, that will give financial assistance to farmers and other owners and operators of rural land who install and maintain measures for improving water quality by reducing agricultural runoff in accordance with best management practices developed by the 208 agency and approved by PA. Generally, the Secretary of Agriculture, acting through the Soil Conservation Service, will pay up to 50% of the costs and will furnish technical assistance. While large sums were authorized (33 U.S.C.A. 1288j), appropriations have been limited to $70,000,000 to finance 21 experimental or pilot projects (93 Stat. 835 (1970); 94 Stat. 311 (1980)).

4. Another form of BMP is mandated by the Clean Water Act. Section 304(e) gives the EPA authority to require best management practices supplemental to effluent limitations for toxic and hazardous pollutants. These might include methods for control of plant site runoff, spillage or leaks, sludge or waste disposal, and drainage from raw material storage when these might contribute significant amounts of pollutants to waters.

In the struggle to protect the people against harm from toxic substances, the emphasis has shifted away from protection of waters to management and control of the substances themselves. The Toxic Substances Control Act, 15 U.S.C.A. §§ 2601 et seq., regulates the testing, manufacture and distribution of chemicals that present a risk of injury to health and the environment. The Resources Conservation and Recovery Act, 42 U.S.C.A. §§ 6921 et seq., regulates the current and future handling, storage, treatment, transportation and disposal of hazardous wastes. United States v. Vertac Chemical Corp., 489 F.Supp. 870 (E.D.Ark.1980) and United States v. Price, 688 F.2d 205 (3d Cir.1982) are examples of enforcement proceedings. The Comprehensive Environmental Response, Compensation, and Liability Act, 42 U.S.C.A. §§ 9601–9615, 9631–9657, establishes four measures directed toward cleanup of existing uncontrolled dump sites. It requires owners of hazardous sites to notify EPA of their existence and nature, it gives EPA authority to clean up the dump if the owner cannot be found or does not act, it establishes the "superfund" of $1.6 billion for cleanup, replenished by a tax on petrochemical plants and crude oil importers, and it creates liability for cleanup and restitution costs.

The Safe Drinking Water Act, 42 U.S.C.A. § 300f–j, may attack in still another direction, by preventing the use of contaminated supplies. Most water destined for domestic use is treated to some degree before being delivered to consumers. The Act empowers EPA to set maximum levels for contaminants in delivered water and to establish standards for monitoring, delegating enforcement to states with approved programs. All water delivered from public water supply (serving more than 25 persons or having 15 service connections) must meet the national standards. If standard treatment techniques cannot produce the required level, a variance or exception may be granted unless it will result in an unreasonable risk to health. The standard may include requirements as to the minimum quality of the raw water taken into the system. In case of emergency, in which a contaminant in or likely to enter a public water system may present an imminent and substantial endangerment to the health of persons, the appropriate state or federal authorities may take steps necessary to protect health, which may include an order to cease withdrawals from the source of raw water.

RIVERSIDE IRRIGATION DISTRICT v. ANDREWS

United States District Court, District of Colorado, 1983.
568 F.Supp. 583.

KANE, DISTRICT JUDGE.

This case involves the plaintiffs' construction of an earth-fill dam on Wildcat Creek in Colorado. Wildcat Creek is a tributary of the South Platte River, which is a tributary of the Missouri River, a navigable water of the United States. Because the construction of the dam involves the placement of fill material into a tributary of navigable waters of the United States, § 404 of the Clean Water Act, 33 U.S.C. § 1344, applies.

An interlocutory appeal was taken from my decision denying the government's motion to dismiss for lack of jurisdiction. These proceedings challenge the decision of the Army Corps' Engineer that the dam developers are not entitled to a nationwide temporary permit to discharge sand and gravel during the course of dam construction on a tributary of the South Platte River in Morgan County, Colorado. The Court of Appeals held that the decision of the Army Corps of Engineers that the dam developers were not entitled to the nationwide permit to discharge sand and gravel during the course of construction under nationwide permit regulations was reviewable. A nationwide permit is one covering a category of activities occurring throughout the country which involve discharges of dredged or fill material which will cause only minimal adverse effects on the environment when performed separately and which will have only minimal cumulative effects. Such a permit is automatic in that if one qualifies, no application is needed nor must notice be given before beginning the discharge activity.

As the Court of Appeals stated:

> The basic consideration is Section 404 of the Clean Water Act (33 U.S.C. § 1344) and the regulations issued under its authority. The regulations concerned, 33 C.F.R. § 323.4–2, relate to work on the site during the course of construction of the dam, and more particularly to the placement of fill material (discharge of fill material) during construction. As indicated above, the regulations provide for automatic authority to place fill material if certain conditions are met. The regulations do not expressly provide that the Engineer is the one to decide whether the conditions are met and that automatic (nationwide) authority thereby exists. In any event, the Engineer did make such a determination. He decided and advised the plaintiffs that they did not qualify for an automatic permit. He reached a decision and officially advised the plaintiffs. His letter to the parties was as follows:
>
> "Dear Mr. Douglas:
>
> "Reference is made to our previous meetings and discussions regarding the Nationwide Section 404 permit for the Wildcat Creek Dam project.
>
> "Since operation of the proposed reservoir could have an adverse impact on an endangered species (whooping crane), by letter dated 15 September 1978 my predecessor, Colonel James W. Ray, entered into consultation with the US Fish and Wildlife Service.
>
> "Inclosed is a copy of the biological opinion for the project which indicates that the operation of the reservoir is likely to jeopardize continued existence of the whooping crane and adversely modify a 53-mile reach of the Platte River which is critical habitat for the crane. Accordingly, construction of the proposed dam does not qualify for 'Nationwide' authorization within the meaning of 33 C.F.R. 323.4–2(a)(1) unless you exercise one of the two alternatives outlined in the biological opinion.
>
> "Should you elect to proceed with construction of the dam, an individual permit processed through the full public interest review will be required." Riverside Irrigation District v. Stipo, 658 F.2d 762 at 765–66.

It is thus clear that the Engineer did not base his decision on the issue of whether the placement of fill material during the construction of the dam would have an adverse effect on the environment but rather on whether the *operation* of the dam and the altered water flow would have an adverse impact on an endangered species whose critical habitat exists some 250 to 300 miles downstream. Both the Court of Appeals and the parties before me have assumed without contest that no problems would arise during construction. Virtually no one asserts that the construction work itself will in any way effect the crane habitat. Thus, the issue is whether the Engineer has exceeded his statutory authority. The Court of Appeals remanded the case to me

"* * * for a determination whether the Engineer acted within his authority and to resolve whatever issues may remain."

A new twist has been added to this case since the opinion of the Court of Appeals. The Corps of Engineers, through Colonel Andrews who is Colonel Stipo's successor in office and in this litigation, has now attempted to require plaintiffs to apply for an individual permit pursuant to 33 C.F.R. § 323.4–4. A new and more detailed biological opinion was received in April 1982. Relying on that opinion and this other regulation, Colonel Andrews sent a letter in June 1982 ordering the plaintiffs to file for the individual permit. * * *

The plaintiffs argue that the issue was, and still is, whether defendant has exceeded his authority under § 404 of the Clean Water Act by considering the downstream effects of the reduced flow on the whooping crane habitat in Nebraska. The case still boils down, they say, to a question of whether the defendant can consider quantity or just quality of the water and, consequently, whether the investigation can include the effects of continuing operation within the ambit of the statutory mandate to consider the construction itself. * * * The plaintiffs attempt to characterize the defendant's actions as an attempt to create a third class of federal water rights, superseding Colorado water law.

Rather than characterize the defendant's actions as the creation of a new class of federal water rights, a better approach is to determine whether his actions were a proper exercise of a federal police power.

Because the plaintiffs do not dispute that the Clean Water Act was a proper exercise of congress's constitutional authority, the only question in this case is whether the defendant's actions were proper under the Clean Water Act. Analysis should therefore focus on the scope of the defendant's authority under the Clean Water Act, rather than on an emotional flummery of states' rights. Although the defendant's actions may have a substantial effect on state water rights, such is the case with many federal laws which particularly preempt state water laws. For example, a congressional designation of a river as wild or scenic under the Wild and Scenic Rivers Act, 16 U.S.C. §§ 1271–1287, will bar most dams and other diversion works from being constructed on the designated section, often limiting the exercise of state water rights. Yet this act has not been successfully challenged as an improper intrusion on state water rights.

1. *Scope of defendant's authority and obligations under § 404*

Section 7(a)(2) of the Endangered Species Act, 16 U.S.C. § 1536(a)(2), provides, in relevant part:

> Each Federal agency shall, in consultation with and with the assistance of the Secretary [of the Interior], insure that any action authorized, * * * by such agency * * * is not likely to jeopardize the continued existence of any endangered species * * * or result in the destruction or adverse modification of habitat of such

species which is determined by the Secretary, * * *, to be critical.

In TVA v. Hill, 437 U.S. 153, 173, 98 S.Ct. 2279, 2291, 57 L.Ed.2d 117 (1978), the court stated:

> One would be hard pressed to find a statutory provision whose terms were any plainer than those in § 7 of the Endangered Species Act. Its very words affirmatively command all federal agencies 'to *insure* that actions *authorized, funded, or carried out* by them do not *jeopardize* the continued existence of an endangered species * * *' * * * [Emphasis added.] This language admits of no exception.[a]

While the Endangered Species Act does not expand the scope of federal agencies' authority, its clear language "shall insure" directs them to exercise their authority under other statutes to the fullest extent possible to carry out its aims. The question in this case is therefore whether the defendant's actions here, denial of plaintiffs' use of the nationwide permit because of potential deleterious downstream effects, was permissible under the Clean Water Act. If defendant's action was permissible under the Clean Water Act, then it was required under the Endangered Species Act.

Both parties spend considerable effort trying to distinguish between "direct" and "indirect" and between "primary" and "secondary" effects caused by the plaintiffs' project. Obviously it is usually not possible to draw a definite line between these different types of efforts. The case law, however, is clear that federal agencies are to consider many potential effects from a project on an endangered species. For example, in TVA v. Hill, 437 U.S. 153, 98 S.Ct. 2279, 57 L.Ed.2d 117 (1978), the court held that the defendant federal agency had to consider the effects caused by water that would back up from its dam, not just the direct physical impacts of the dam. In NWF v. Coleman, 529 F.2d 359, 373 (5th Cir.1976), rehearing denied, 532 F.2d 1375, cert. denied under Boteler v. NWF, 429 U.S. 979, 97 S.Ct. 489, 50 L.Ed.2d 587 (1976), the court reversed a trial court dismissal of an environmental group's complaint that a proposed highway would damage an endangered specie's habitat:

> Although it is clear that the crane can survive the direct loss of 300 acres of habitat, the evidence, * * * shows that it is questionable whether the crane can survive the additional loss of habitat caused by the indirect effects of the highway, coupled with the excavation of and drainage caused by borrow pits.

a. Since this opinion congress amended § 7(a)(2), changing "does not jeopardize" to "is not likely to jeopardize." While this amendment might change a federal agency's (and this court's) factual review standards, it does not change the inquiry in this case because no facts are in dispute. If there is actually a dispute on the actual effect that the dam will cause on the whooper habitat, that will have to be resolved through the individual permit process under § 404(a); the nationwide permit does not provide for such a factual inquiry.

> Principal among the indirect effects of the highway on the crane is the residential and commercial development that can be expected to result from the construction of the highway.

This is consistent with North Slope Borough v. Andrus, 642 F.2d 589, 608 (D.C.Cir.1980), where the appellate court adopted the district court's holding that, under the Endangered Species Act, caution can only be exercised if the agency takes a look at all the possible ramifications of the agency action. To the extent authorized by the Clean Water Act, the defendant therefore is required to consider indirect effects of the dams on the whoopers and their habitat.

Several courts have held that the Clean Water Act should be construed broadly to encompass deleterious environmental effects of projects. For example, in Minnehaha Creek Watershed Dist. v. Hoffman, 597 F.2d 617, 625–26 (8th Cir.1979), the court held that § 404 extended beyond adverse water-quality effects of projects to include potential physical effects on navigable waters caused by the discharge of chemically benign fill material.

Two district courts have held that the depletion of water, off of the project's site, is an effect that must be considered in determining whether to allow the project under § 404 of the Clean Water Act. In United States v. Fleming Plantations, 12 ERC 1705, 1709 (E.D.La.1978), the court granted the plaintiff's application for an injunction barring the defendants' construction of a levee that would have caused a tract of wetlands to dry up. In Nebraska v. REA, 12 ERC 1156, 1171–73 (D.Neb.1978), the court held that a federal agency sponsoring a dam in Wyoming and the Army Corps of Engineers were both obligated to insure that the dam's construction would not jeopardize the whoopers' habitat downstream in Nebraska. The court invalidated an individual § 404 permit for the dam because these agencies had not made the necessary assurances.

Because the Clean Water Act allows federal agencies to consider deleterious downstream environmental effects from a project and because the Endangered Species Act requires federal agencies to take whatever measures are necessary, within their authority, to protect an endangered species and its habitat, the defendant in the present case was required to halt the plaintiffs from proceeding under the nationwide permit when their project had the potential of adversely affecting the whoopers and their habitat downstream from the project.

2. *Effect of § 101(g) of the Clean Water Act*

Section 101(g) of the Clean Water Act, 33 U.S.C. § 1251(g), provides:

> It is the policy of Congress that the authority of each State to allocate quantities of water within its jurisdiction shall not be superseded, abrogated, or otherwise impaired by this chapter. It is the further policy of Congress that nothing in this chapter shall be construed to supersede or abrogate rights to quantities of water

> which have been established by any State. Federal agencies shall cooperate with State and local agencies to develop comprehensive solutions to prevent, reduce and eliminate pollution in concert with programs from managing water resources.

The plaintiffs argue that this section demonstrates that congress intended not to interfere with state water rights and interstate water compacts in enacting the Clean Water Act. While this argument is appealing, especially in light of the strong language of § 101(g), it should be rejected. First, congressional policy statements "cannot nullify a clear and specific grant of jurisdiction, even if the particular grant seems inconsistent with the broadly stated purpose." Connecticut Light & Power Co. v. Federal Power Commission, 324 U.S. 515, 527, 65 S.Ct. 749, 754, 89 L.Ed. 1150 (1945). Here § 510(2) of the Act, 33 U.S.C. § 1370(2), which is not a policy statement, provides,

> *Except as expressly provided in this chapter,* nothing shall * * * be construed as impairing or in any manner affecting any right of jurisdiction of the States with respect to the waters * * * of such States. [Emphasis added.]

Because both the statements of § 101(g)'s sponsor and the relevant committee report state that § 101(g) was not intended to change existing law, including § 510(2), congress did not intend to limit § 404's scope where it might affect state water rights law when it enacted § 101(g).

The plaintiffs' argument is further diminished because the defendant's actions did not abrogate or supersede any state water rights. As discussed above, the defendant only placed conditions on the construction of the dam that might affect the plaintiffs' water rights. While the defendant is barring the plaintiffs from exercising their water rights in a manner inconsistent with federal law, he is not taking away the rights. They may still be utilized, so long as in a manner consistent with federal law.

Conclusion

Resolution of this case depends largely on its characterization. If the case is characterized as an attempt by the defendant to condemn the plaintiffs' Colorado water rights, then the plaintiffs' should obviously prevail. On the other hand, if the case is characterized as an attempt by the defendant to exercise federal police power in a manner required by federal police power in a manner required by federal statutes, then the defendant should prevail, even if his actions affect the plaintiffs' exercise of their water rights. For the reasons set out above, I believe that the latter characterization is preferable, and that the defendant's actions were a proper exercise of federal police power, even though they will clearly affect the plaintiffs' exercise of their water rights. I must limit my decision to the propriety of the exercise of such power. Whether it is prudent to vest such power is a political question which must be addressed to congress not the courts.

In accordance with the mandate of the Court of Appeals, I hold that the Engineer acted within his authority.

IT IS ORDERED that plaintiffs complaint is hereby dismissed.

Notes

1. The Endangered Species Act protects animals, fish, most insects, and plants that are listed by the Secretary of the Interior as "endangered," subject to extinction throughout all of a significant part of their range, or as "threatened," likely to become endangered in the foreseeable future. The principal protective measure is preservation of the critical habitat of the listed species. The Act operates as a limit on the projects and activities of the federal government and its licensees; they may not jeopardize the continued existence of a listed species or destroy or adversely modify its critical habitat. A "biological assessment" must be obtained from the Fish and Wildlife Service before the action can proceed or the license be obtained. The agency or applicant must consult with the Secretary, who within 90 days must issue "jeopardy conclusions," which may bar the project, give it a green light, or suggest protective measures as alternatives.

The Act prohibits the "taking" of listed species by any person. This is construed to include killing or harassing the species, and most importantly, destruction of its critical habitat. The Secretary may grant a permit for a taking if (1) the harm is incidental to the project, (2) is minimized or mitigated to the maximum extent possible, and (3) will not appreciably reduce the likelihood of the survival and recovery of the species in the wild.

2. As can be gleaned from the principal case, the phrase "discharge of dredged and fill materials" covers much more than operations in the channel and filling of wetlands. Like "navigable waters," the term is carried over from earlier law but its meaning is considerably broadened. The Regulations of the Corps of Engineers defines it as including, "placement of fill that is necessary to the construction of any structure in a water of the United States; the building of any structure or impoundment requiring rock, sand, dirt, or other material for its construction; site-development fills for recreational, industrial, commercial, residential, and other uses; causeways or road fills; dams and dikes; artificial islands; property protection and/or reclamation devices such as riprap, groins, seawalls, breakwaters, revetments; beach nourishment; levees; fill for structures such as sewage treatment facilities, intake and outfall pipes associated with power plants and subaqueous utility lines; and artificial reefs. The term does not include plowing, cultivating, seeding and harvesting for the production of food, fiber, and forest products."

The § 404 permit system is administered by the Corps of Engineers pursuant to guidelines developed by the Administrator of EPA and regulations adopted by the Corps. Permits are issued by the Secretary of the Army, acting through the Chief of Engineers, and are subject to veto by the EPA.

The EPA guidelines require consideration of and findings on many environmental factors prior to issuance of a permit, and the Corps of Engineers regulations call for a "public interest review" in which, "the decision whether to issue a permit will be based on an evaluation of the probable impacts, including cumulative impacts, of the proposed activity and its intended use on the public interest. Evaluation of the probable impacts which the proposed activity may have on the public interest requires a careful weighing of all those factors which become relevant in each particular case. The benefits which reasonably may be expected to accrue from the proposal must be balanced against its reasonably foreseeable detriments. The decision whether to authorize a proposal, and if so the conditions under which it will be allowed to occur, are therefore determined by the outcome of the general balancing process. That decision should reflect the national concern for both protection and utilization of important resources. All factors which may be relevant to the proposal must be considered including the cumulative effects thereof. Among those are conservation, economics, aesthetics, general environmental concerns, wetlands, cultural values, fish and wildlife values, flood hazards, floodplain values, landuse, navigation, shore erosion and accretion, recreation, water supply and conservation, water quality, energy needs, safety, food and fiber production, mineral needs, considerations or property ownership, and, in general, the needs and welfare of the people." 33 CFR § 320.4(a)(1).

Although actions taken by the Administrator are exempt from the requirement of NEPA, § 404 permits issued by the Corps may be major federal actions significantly affecting the quality of the environment. The public interest review is thus not limited to direct effects of the placement of the material or structure in the stream nor to effects on water quality alone. Zabel v. Tabb, 430 F.2d 199 (5th Cir.1970), (holding NEPA applicable to the Refuse Act permits superseded by § 404). The environmental assessment and environmental impact statement processes will trigger consideration of not only the Endangered Species Act (16 U.S.C.A. §§ 1531–1534), but also the Fish and Wildlife Coordination Act (16 U.S.C.A. § 662), the Wild and Scenic Rivers Act (16 U.S.C.A. § 1271–1276), the Antiquities Act (16 U.S.C.A. § 433), and the Coastal Zone Management Act (16 U.S.C.A. §§ 1451–1464).

3. What if the dam on Wildcat Creek would have no effect on water quality and would involve none of these federal acts, but would adversely affect trout habitat and recreational features of the creek and the South Platte River? Assume that the Colorado Water Conservation Board has not appropriated a minimum stream flow in the creek or the river under Colo.Rev.Stat. § 37–92–102(3) (1973), and the Riverside District has a conditional decree for the appropriation and storage of the water for irrigation, municipal and industrial purposes under Colorado water law, although water is expected to be available only during fall and winter flows. May the § 404 permit be conditioned to preserve the fish and the fishing, if the minimum flow release would make it impossible to store enough water to make the project feasible? What is the effect of § 101(g), discussed in *Riverside* and *Gorsuch?* What does it add to the still extant § 510 of the 1972 Act, declaring that the Act was not to be construed "as impairing or in any manner affecting any right or jurisdiction of the state with respect to the waters (including boundary waters) of such states?" White, The Emerging Relationship Between Environmental Regulations and Colorado Water Law, 53 U.Colo.L.Rev. 597 (1982), asserts that under these disclaim-

ers state water allocation laws are controlling except where overruled to meet the specific requirements of federal legislation. Tarlock, The Endangered Species Act and Western Water Rights, 20 Land and Water L.Rev. 1 (1985) states that, "The net effect of present congressional responses to western concerns that state-created water rights will be displaced is to shift the task of striking an accommodation between state and federal interests to the courts and to give water rights holders a new but slim statutory basis to argue that a federal agency has abused its discretion," and that § 101(g) "reflects the principle that integration should take place by the least intrusive means available to the federal agency." (pages 19, 29.)

Current practice of the Corps of Engineers seems to assert the Tarlock approach but carry it almost to the White extreme. A "Regulatory Guidance Letter" (No. 82–5, Permit Conditioning for Minimum Stream Flows, DAEN–CWO–N, April 20, 1982) to District Commanders states, "(1) The primary responsibility for allocating water quantities rests with the states. (2) The public interest review criteria require district commanders to normally issue Corps permits where all local and state permits have been issued unless there are overriding factors of national concern. (3) When a conflict arises between state water quantity allocation and minimum instream flows for the purposes of maintaining viable aquatic habitat, district commanders will consider that the public interest is primarily represented by state water allocation rights and that any project alternative which supersedes, abrogates or otherwise impairs those quantities is not a practicable alternative from the federal regulatory perspective." Furthermore, the letter adds, even where minimum instream flows are required by federal statute or substantial national interest such as endangered species or navigation, a conflict with state water quantity allocation will be forwarded to Washington and settled at the Secretarial level.

Perhaps the ultimate solution might be for the state to take over administration of the § 404 permits by incorporating it into their state water rights granting and regulating activities and procedures, as allowed by § 404(g)–(t), upon a showing that the laws of the state provide adequate authority to carry out the program. The Administrator of EPA would retain authority to veto a permit and turn the application over to the Secretary in case of state refusal to modify it to meet federal objectives.

4. Two exceptions materially reduce the impact of § 404 on state water law and water rights. The Act itself exempts from the permit requirements activities undertaken "for the purpose of construction or maintenance of farm or stock ponds or irrigation ditches or the maintenance of drainage ditches." (§ 404(f)(1)(C).) The Regulations clarify the scope of the exemption by adding, "Discharges associated with siphons, pumps, headgates, wingwalls, weirs, diversion structures and such other facilities as are pertinent and functionally related to irrigation are included in this exemption." 33 CFR § 323.4(a)(3). Note that intake structures for municipal and industrial uses are not exempted.

Suppose that the Wildcat Creek Dam was a diversion structure and that irrigation was the sole beneficial use to be made of the water. Is there a "Catch 22" in § 404(f)(2): "Any discharge of dredged or fill material into the navigable waters incidental to any activity having as its purpose bringing an area of the navigable waters into a use to which it was not previously subject, where the flow or circulation of navigable waters may be impaired or the reach of such waters be reduced, shall be required to have a permit under this section." The regulations give two examples: "The conversion of a cypress swamp to some other use or the conversion of a wetland from silvicultural to agricultural use when there is a discharge of dredged or filled material into waters of the United States in conjunction with the construction of dikes, drainage ditches or other works or structures used to effect such construction. A discharge which elevates the bottom of waters of the United States without converting it to dry land does not thereby reduce the reach of, but may alter the flow or circulation of, waters of the United States." 33 CFR § 323.4(c), fn. 4. In a discussion of amendments to the regulations, EPA stated that there was no need for "a size limitation to prevent serious fish and wildlife losses from damming of a stream to take all its water for irrigation under this exemption," with the explanation, "EPA does not believe that such a size limitation is necessary in light of the safeguards provided by section 404(f)(2)." 49 F.R. 39479, October 5, 1984.

The second exception is found in a "nationwide permit" that allows all "dredge and fill" activities in the "headwaters," streams with less than five cubic feet per second average flow, provided that the activity does not threaten public water supply, destroy or modify critical habitat of endangered or threatened species or occur in a component of the National Wild and Scenic River System.

5. Rights of way for the construction of diversion works and transmission facilities on and over national forest lands and federal lands controlled by the Bureau of Land Management are governed by the Forest Service Organic Act (16 U.S.C.A. §§ 579) and the Federal Land Policy and Management Act (43 U.S.C.A. §§ 1751 ff). The granting of a use permit or right of way may be a major federal action calling for compliance with NEPA. Denial might be a way of enforcing compliance with the Endangered Species Act, the Antiquities Act, etc., consistent with the major land use planned for the area. Could the Supervisor of the Gila National Forest condition a grant of a right of way to the holder of a New Mexico permit to appropriate the waters of the Mimbres River on the release of a minimum flow, not to prevent frustration of purpose of a federal statute but simply to preserve trout habitat and recreational values? See, White, supra, Note 2, 53 U.Colo.L.Rev., at page 611, and cf. United States v. New Mexico, infra, page 797.

SECTION 3. INDIAN AND RESERVED RIGHTS

WINTERS v. UNITED STATES

Supreme Court of the United States, 1908.
207 U.S. 564, 28 S.Ct. 207, 52 L.Ed. 340.

[In 1874 Congress set apart and reserved for the occupation of the Gros Ventre, Peigan, Blood, Blackfeet and River Crow Indians a very large area of land in Montana. On May 1, 1888, the Indians by agreement "ceded, sold, transferred, and conveyed" to the United States all of the land except the present Ft. Belknap Indian reservation. The middle of the channel of the Milk River was made the northern boundary of the reservation. Most of the reservation was suitable for grazing, some of it for irrigated agriculture. The ceded land was opened to settlement and portions of it upstream from the reservation came into the hands of defendants, several individuals and a cattle company. Some time prior to 1898, the defendants appropriated under the laws of Montana 5000 inches (120 c.f.s.) of water from the Milk River for the irrigation of hay and grain. In 1898 an Indian project was constructed that required 5000 inches from the Milk for the irrigation of hay, grass, and vegetables. The United States alleged that it "has been enabled by means thereof to train, encourage, and accustom large numbers of Indians residing upon the said reservation to habits of industry and to promote their civilization and improvement." Withdrawals by defendants, however, left insufficient water for the Indian project.

The lower court granted an order enjoining the defendants from interfering in any manner with use on the reservation of 5000 inches of water.]

MR. JUSTICE MCKENNA delivered the opinion of the court: * * *

The case, as we view it, turns on the agreement of May, 1888, resulting in the creation of Fort Belknap Reservation. In the construction of this agreement there are certain elements to be considered that are prominent and significant. The reservation was a part of a very much larger tract which the Indians had the right to occupy and use, and which was adequate for the habits and wants of a nomadic and uncivilized people. It was the policy of the government, it was the desire of the Indians, to change those habits and to become a pastoral and civilized people. If they should become such, the original tract was too extensive; but a smaller tract would be inadequate without a change of conditions. The lands were arid, and, without irrigation, were practically valueless. And yet, it is contended, the means of irrigation were deliberately given up by the Indians and deliberately accepted by the government. The lands ceded were, it is true, also arid; and some argument may be urged, and is urged, that with their cession there was the cession of the waters, without which they would be valueless, and "civilized communities could not be established thereon." And this, it is further contended, the Indians knew, and yet made no reservation of the waters. We realize that there is a conflict of implications, but that which makes for the retention of the waters is of greater force than that which makes for their cession. The Indians had command of the lands and the waters,—command of all their beneficial use, whether kept for hunting, "and grazing roving herds of stock," or turned to agriculture and the arts of civilization. Did they give up all this? Did they reduce the area of their occupation and give up the waters which made it valuable or adequate? And, even regarding the allegation of the answer as true, that there are springs and streams on the reservation flowing about 2,900 inches of water, the inquiries are pertinent. If it were possible to believe affirmative answers, we might also believe that the Indians were awed by the power of the government or deceived by its negotiators. Neither view is possible. The government is asserting the rights of the Indians. But extremes need not be taken into account. By a rule of interpretation of agreements and treaties with the Indians, ambiguities occurring will be resolved from the standpoint of the Indians. And the rule should certainly be applied to determine between two inferences, one of which would support the purpose of the agreement and the other impair or defeat it. On account of their relations to the government, it cannot be supposed that the Indians were alert to exclude by formal words every inference which might militate against or defeat the declared purpose of themselves and the government, even if it could be supposed that they had the intelligence to foresee the "double sense" which might some time be urged against them.

Another contention of appellants is that if it be conceded that there was a reservation of the waters of Milk river by the agreement of 1888, yet the reservation was repealed by the admission of Montana into the Union, February 22, 1889, "upon an equal footing with the original states." The language of counsel is that "any reservation in the agreement with the Indians, expressed or implied, whereby the waters of Milk river were not to be subject of appropriation by the citizens and inhabitants of said state, was repealed by the act of admission." But to establish the repeal counsel rely substantially upon the same argument that they advance against the intention of the agreement to reserve the waters. The power of the government to reserve the waters and exempt them from appropriation under the state laws is not denied, and could not be. United States v. Rio Grande Dam & Irrig. Co., 174 U.S. 702, 43 L.Ed. 1141, 19 S.Ct. 770; United States v. Winans, 198 U.S. 371, 49 L.Ed. 1089, 25 S.Ct. 662. That the government did reserve them we have decided, and for a use which would be necessarily continued through years. This was done May 1, 1888, and it would be extreme to believe that within a year Congress destroyed the reservation and took from the Indians the consideration of their grant, leaving them a barren waste,—took from them the means of continuing their old habits, yet did not leave them the power to change to new ones. * * *

Decree affirmed.

Notes

1. Compare United States v. Winans, 198 U.S. 371, 25 S.Ct. 662, 49 L.Ed. 1089 (1905). The suit involved an 1859 treaty with the Yakima Nation in which the Indians ceded certain lands to the United States, and which contained the following article: "The exclusive right of taking fish in

all streams where running through or bordering said reservation is further secured to said Confederated Tribes and Bands of Indians, as also the right of taking fish at all usual and accustomed places, in common with citizens of the territory, and of erecting temporary buildings for curing them." White settlers who obtained title to lands bordering the river sought to exclude the Indians from placing their "fish wheels" (salmon traps) in their accustomed places, now on private lands. The Court said, "The right to resort to the fishing places in controversy was a part of larger rights possessed by the Indians, upon the exercise of which there was not a shadow of impediment, and which were not much less necessary to the existence of the Indians than the atmosphere they breathed * * *. The treaty was not a grant of rights to the Indians, but a grant of rights from them,—a reservation of those not granted." In *Winters,* did the Indians reserve the water from the cession of their ancestral lands? Does their priority date from 1874, 1888 or somewhere back in pre-history?

Some interesting light is shed on this and other aspects of the case by Hundley, The "Winters" Decision and Indian Water Rights: A Mystery Reexamined, 13 Western Historical Quarterly 20 (1982), which goes beyond the appellate opinions to contemporary historical materials.

Could such "aboriginal," "paramount and immemorial" rights be claimed by Indians occupying lands on reservations established by executive order rather than by treaty? By a tribe confined to a reservation far from their ancestral lands? See Veeder, Indian Prior and Paramount Rights to the Use of Water, 16 Rocky Mt. Mineral L.Inst. 631 (1971).

2. Arizona v. California, 373 U.S. 546, 83 S.Ct. 1468, 10 L.Ed.2d 542 (1963) was the next Supreme Court case directly involving Indian rights. The Master identified five Indian claims to be supplied out of the allocations of the states in which they were located. As to these, the Court said:

"The Government, on behalf of five Indian Reservations in Arizona, California, and Nevada, asserted rights to water in the mainstream of the Colorado River. The Colorado River Reservation, located partly in Arizona and partly in California, is the largest. It was originally created by an Act of Congress in 1865, but its area was later increased by Executive Order. Other reservations were created by Executive Orders and amendments to them, ranging in dates from 1870 to 1907. The Master found both as a matter of fact and law that when the United States created these reservations or added to them, it reserved not only land but also the use of enough water from the Colorado to irrigate the irrigable portions of the reserved lands. The aggregate quantity of water which the Master held was reserved for all the reservations is about 1,000,000 acre-feet, to be used on around 135,000 irrigable acres of land. * * *

"The Court in Winters concluded that the Government, when it created that Indian Reservation, intended to deal fairly with the Indians by reserving for them the waters without which their lands would have been useless. Winters has been followed by this Court as recently as 1939 in United States v. Powers, 305 U.S. 527, 59 S.Ct. 344, 83 L.Ed. 330. We follow it now and agree that the United States did reserve the water rights for the Indians effective as of the time the Indian Reservations were created. This means, as the Master held, that these water rights, having vested before the Act became effective on June 25, 1929, are 'present perfected rights' and as such are entitled to priority under the Act.

"We also agree with the Master's conclusion as to the quantity of water intended to be reserved. He found that the water was intended to satisfy the future as well as the present needs of the Indian Reservations and ruled that enough water was reserved to irrigate all the practicably irrigable acreage on the reservations. Arizona, on the other hand, contends that the quantity of water reserved should be measured by the Indians' 'reasonably foreseeable needs,' which, in fact, means by the number of Indians. How many Indians there will be and what their future needs will be can only be guessed. We have concluded, as did the Master, that the only feasible and fair way by which reserved water for the reservations can be measured is irrigable acreage."

On January 9, 1979, the Court entered a supplemental decree in the case fixing the "present perfected rights" in each state according to an agreement by all parties. The final quantification of the Indian claims totals 761,562 acre feet of annual diversions in Arizona, 131,400 in California and 12,534 in Nevada, for a new total of 905,496 acre feet per year.

The Indian tribes had been represented by the United States in this and earlier proceedings. They were now allowed to intervene. In what may be hoped is the last opinion styled "Arizona v. California," 460 U.S. 605, 103 S.Ct. 1382, 75 L.Ed.2d 318 (1983), they sought to reopen the question of the amount of irrigable acreage on the reservations, claiming (1) increased amounts of water for "omitted lands" within the reservations, which the United States had failed to inventory in the earlier proceedings, and (2) water for "boundary lands," which lie outside the boundaries used in the 1964 decree but are actually within the reservations. The Court refused to consider the claims for "omitted lands." That issue was fully and fairly litigated in 1963, said the Court. While the 1964 decree was left open to allow for amendment or further relief, principles akin to res judicata precluded reopening the issue.

> Certainty of rights is particularly important with respect to water rights in the Western United States. The development of that area of the United States would not have been possible without adequate water supplies in an otherwise water-scarce part of the country. Colorado River Water Cons. District v. United States, 424 U.S. 800, 804, 96 S.Ct. 1236, 1239, 47 L.Ed.2d 483 (1976). The doctrine of prior appropriation, the prevailing law in the western states, is itself largely a product of the compelling need for certainty in the holding and use of water rights.
>
> Recalculating the amount of practicably irrigable acreage runs directly counter to the strong interest in finality in this case. A major purpose of this litigation, from its inception to the present day, has been to provide the necessary assurance to states of the Southwest and to various private interests, of the amount of water they can anticipate to receive from the Colorado River system. "In the arid parts of the West * * * claims to water for use on federal reservations inescapably vie with other public and private claims for the limited quantities to be found in the rivers and streams." United States v. New Mexico,

> 438 U.S. 696, 699, 98 S.Ct. 3012, 3013, 57 L.Ed.2d 1052 (1978). If there is no surplus of water in the Colorado River, an increase in federal reserved water rights will require a "gallon-for-gallon reduction in the amount of water available for water-needy state and private appropriators." As Special Master Tuttle recognized, "not a great deal of evidence is really needed to convince anyone that western states would rely upon water adjudications." Tuttle Report at 46. Not only did the Metropolitan Water District in California and the Central Arizona Project predicate their plans on the basis of the 1964 allocations, but, due to the high priority of Indian water claims, an enlargement of the Tribes' allocation cannot help but exacerbate potential water shortage problems for these projects and their States.

Absence of the Indian tribes as formal parties to the prior proceedings did not call for relitigation of their rights.

> We find no merit in the Tribes' contention that the United States' representation of their interests was inadequate whether because of a claimed conflict of interests arising from the government's interest in securing water rights for other federal property, or otherwise. The United States often represents varied interests in litigation involving water rights, particularly given the large extent and variety of federal land holdings in the West. Indeed, the substantial water allocations awarded the Tribes reflect the competency of the United States' representation. We believe the issue of practicably irrigable acreage was fully and fairly litigated in 1963.

The "boundary lands" question, although it had been specifically left open for later determination, was not directly addressed. The original decree, said the Court, contemplated that the boundary disputes would be settled in other forums. Some quiet title suits, to which the states were not parties, were nevertheless held binding as a practical matter where they held the lands to be reservation lands. Several extensions of reservation boundaries by the Secretary of the Interior, however, were held not to be "final determinations," and the Court suggested that the United States District Court for the Southern District of California, in which California had already challenged the Secretary's orders, was an appropriate forum for final settlement of the reservation limits.

The lands of the Pueblo Indians were involved in New Mexico v. Aamodt, 537 F.2d 1102 (10th Cir.1976) cert. den. 429 U.S. 1121, 97 S.Ct. 1157, 51 L.Ed.2d 572 (1977). When the Spaniards came in 1541 they found established Indian communities along the Rio Grande and its tributaries. Titles to four square leagues of land surrounding the Pueblos were recognized by the Spanish and Mexican governments and were confirmed by Congress in the Treaty of Guadalupe Hidalgo, 11 Stat. 374 (1858). In this adjudication of the Nambe-Pojoaque river system the state asserted, and the district court found, that the Indians' water rights had been incorporated into the prior appropriation system. The Indians claimed that they had a reserved right or aboriginal right to as much water as needed for the irrigation of all lands of each Pueblo. (The so-called "pueblo rights" doctrine applicable to Spanish agricultural settlements in California, see supra Note 5, p. 221, has no application to the rights of Pueblo Indian

Tribes.) The Court of Appeals stated that the Pueblos held fee simple titles to their lands, which are not reservations, so that decisions like *Winters* are not technically applicable. The Pueblo Lands Acts of 1924 and 1933 provided for awards to compensate Indians for loss of lands to non-Indians who had encroached on the Pueblo lands during a period when it was thought they were open to sale, but the legislation added,

"Nothing herein contained shall in any manner be construed to deprive any of the Pueblo Indians of a prior right to the use of water from streams running through or bordering on their respective pueblos for domestic, stockwater, and irrigation purposes for the lands remaining in Indian ownership, and such water rights shall not be subject to loss by nonuse or abandonment thereof as long as title to said lands shall remain in the Indians."

The Court of Appeals reversed, holding that the district court must determine what rights the Indian held prior to 1858 under the pertinent laws of Spain and Mexico, and the effect on those rights of adverse user by non-Indians at various periods of time. But the court added,

"The answer depends on the meaning of 'prior right' as used in § 9. That term may not apply to a reserved right because the United States gave the Pueblos a quit claim deed to lands which were recognized by the Treaty of Guadalupe Hidalgo to be in their ownership. The United States had nothing to reserve. United States v. Sandoval, 231 U.S. 28, 34 S.Ct. 1, 58 L.Ed. 107, says, that the Pueblos 'have been regarded and treated by the United States as requiring special consideration and protection, like other Indian communities.' United States v. Candelaria, 271 U.S. 432, 46 S.Ct. 561, 70 L.Ed. 1023, reaffirms *Sandoval* and says that the lands of the Pueblos 'like the tribal lands of other Indians owned in fee under patents from the United States are "subject to the legislation of Congress enacted in the exercise of the Government's guardianship" over Indian tribes and their property.'

"When the 1924 and 1933 Acts were before Congress much discussion revolved around the reserved water doctrine approved in *Winters*. By using the phrase 'prior rights' in § 9 Congress may well have intended to recognize the *Winters* decision. Such an intent is consonant with both *Sandoval* and *Candelaria*. A recognition of any priority date for the Indians later than, or equal to, a priority date for a non-Indian violates the mandate of Congress that nothing in the 1933 Act shall deprive the Pueblos to a prior right to the use of water."

On remand, the district court found that the Spanish and Mexican governments had recognized that the Indians had property rights to the four square leagues of common lands, not subject to loss by adverse possession, and that for these lands the Pueblos had rights of *primacia*, first use, measured by the principle of *necesario para su sustento,* the amount customarily used to grow crops for basic life support. The court also found the aboriginal rights of the Indians included the right to irrigate other lands in response to need, so that acreage brought under irrigation between the 1858 Treaty and the 1924 Act had appurtenant aboriginal water rights. The 1924 Act, which gave non-Indians title to lands they had settled within the four square leagues of common land, did not transfer aboriginal rights to them; their rights date from the beginning of use. Except for a tract of former public land set aside for one Pueblo by executive order in 1902, the Indians were held to have no *Winters* rights. These principles were announced as the general standards for quantifying the rights in the pending adjudication. State ex rel. Reynolds v. Aamodt, 618 F.Supp. 993 (D.N.M.1985, appeal pending).

The complex of Spanish, Mexican, state and federal laws relating to the water rights of these communities is thoroughly explored in DuMars, O'Leary and Utton, Pueblo Indian Water Rights (U. of Ariz. Press 1984).

4. "Rancherias" are small plots of land in California, purchased to provide homes for Indians whose reservations did not contain sufficient land suitable for cultivation, and for homeless and wandering Indians. 34 Stat. 325, 333 (1906); 36 Stat. 70, 76 (1908). The Secretary of the Interior was authorized to construct any necessary irrigation ditches, flumes and reservoirs. Eighty-six such "reservations" were established, ranging in size from 640 acres to one or two acres, and any Indians, whether or not members of an organized tribe, were entitled to settle on them. Most were informally broken up into unsurveyed homesites. Many remained unoccupied. In 1958 the value of the program was questioned and the Secretary was instructed to distribute the lands and water rights on 41 rancherias to the residents or to sell the land for their benefit, with their approval. 72 Stat. 619 (1958). The Secretary was directed to install or rehabilitate such irrigation or domestic water systems as needed. When the lands were distributed, the many of the plots were sold to non-Indians.

The Robinson Rancheria in Lake County, California, was terminated under this act without provisions for sanitary or domestic water systems, and the United States was held liable for breach of trust to the individual transferees of the land. Duncan v. U.S., 667 F.2d 36, 229 Ct.Cl. 120 (1981).

The rancheria lands were purchased, not reserved or withdrawn from public lands. Section 4 of the Termination Act nevertheless provided, "Nothing in this act shall abrogate any water right that exists by virtue of the laws of the United States. To the extent that the laws of the State of California are not now applicable to any water right appurtenant to any lands involved herein they shall continue to be inapplicable while the water right is in Indian ownership for a period not to exceed 15 years after the conveyance pursuant to this act of an unrestricted title thereto, and thereafter the applicability of such laws shall be without prejudice to the priority of any such right not theretofore based on state law. During the time such state law is not applicable the Attorney General shall represent the Indian owner in all legal proceedings, including proceedings before administrative bodies, involving such water right, and any necessary affirmative action to prevent adverse appropriation of water which would encroach upon the Indian water right."

5. Interstate compacts commonly contain a savings clause that nothing in the compact shall be construed as affecting the obligation of the United States to Indians, or water rights owned by Indians, and a provision that water used to satisfy these obligations and rights shall be charged against the allocation to the state in which the use is made. Snake River

Compact, 64 Stat. 29 (1950); Upper Colorado River Compact, 63 Stat. 31 (1949), 43 U.S.C.A. § 617*l*.

COLVILLE CONFEDERATED TRIBES v. WALTON

United States Court of Appeals, Ninth Circuit, 1981.
647 F.2d 42, cert. denied 454 U.S. 1092, 102 S.Ct. 657, 70 L.Ed.2d 630.

* * *

In 1871 the predecessors of the Colville Confederated Tribes had no treaty with the United States and no reservation. These Indians were contemporaneously described as "good farmers, [who] raise extensive crops, make good improvements, and own stocks of cattle and horses." [1871] Report of the Commissioner of Indian Affairs, 277. After the Civil War, settlers had begun to encroach on Indian lands. The Farmer in charge of Fort Colville reported that violence was likely unless a reservation was established to protect Indian interests. Id. In response to a request from the Commissioner of Indian Affairs, President Grant created the Colville Reservation. * * * In 1906, Congress ratified an agreement with the Colvilles that provided for distribution of reservation lands to the Indians pursuant to the General Allotment Act of 1887, 24 Stat. 388, and for disposition of the remainder by entry and settlement. * * *

In 1917, a row of seven allotments was created in the No Name Creek watershed. Walton, a non-Indian, now owns the middle three, numbers 525, 2371 and 894. He bought them in 1948 from an Indian, not a member of the Tribe, who had begun to irrigate the land by diverting water for 32 acres from No Name Creek. Walton immediately procured a permit from the state to irrigate 65 acres by diverting up to 1 cubic foot per second "subject to existing rights." He now irrigates 104 acres and uses additional water for domestic and stock water purposes. The United States holds the remaining allotments in trust for the Colville Indians. * * *

The No Name Creek is a spring-fed creek flowing south into Omak Lake, which has no outlet and is saline. * * * Salmon and trout were traditional foods for the Colville Indians, but the salmon runs have been destroyed by dams on the Columbia River. In 1968, the Tribe, with the help of the Department of the Interior, introduced Lahonton cutthroat trout into Omak Lake. The species thrives in the lake's saline water, but needs fresh water to spawn. The Indians cultivated No Name Creek's lower reach to establish spawning grounds but irrigation use depleted the water flow during spawning season. The federal government has given the Indians fingerlings to maintain the stock of trout.

* * *

The trial court found that 1,000 acre feet per year of water were available in No Name Creek Basin in an average year. It calculated the quantity of the Colvilles' reserved water rights on the basis of irrigable acreage. * * * The trial court determined the Indians had a reserved right to 666.4 acre feet per year of water from the No Name Creek Basin. It held that Walton was not entitled to share in the Colvilles' reserved water rights. The trial court found, however, that the Colvilles were irrigating only a portion of the irrigable acres included in its calculation.

Under the district court's findings, in an average year there are 333.6 acre feet per year of water not subject to the Indians' reserved right. There are an additional 237.6 acre feet per year of water to which the Indians have a reserved right, but which they are not currently using. This water is available for appropriation by non-Indians, subject to the Indians' superior right. The court held that Walton had a right to irrigate the 32 acres under irrigation at the time he acquired his land, with a priority date of the actual appropriation of water for that use.

The court also held that the Indians were potentially entitled to use water to propagate trout, but refused to award water for that purpose. It concluded that spawning was unnecessary because fingerlings were provided free by the federal government. * * *

THE TRIBE'S WATER RIGHTS

* * * We hold that water was reserved when the Colville Reservation was created. The more difficult question concerns the amount of water reserved. * * * We conclude that, when the Colville reservation was created, sufficient appurtenant water was reserved to permit irrigation of all practicably irrigable acreage on the reservation. Providing for a land-based agrarian society, however, was not the only purpose for creating the reservation. The Colvilles traditionally fished for both salmon and trout. Like other Pacific Northwest Indians, fishing was of economic and religious importance to them. The Tribe's principal historic fishing grounds on the Columbia River have been destroyed by dams. The Indians have established replacement fishing grounds in Omak Lake by planting a non-indigenous trout.

We agree with the district court that preservation of the tribe's access to fishing grounds was one purpose for the creation of the Colville Reservation. Under the circumstances, we find an implied reservation of water from No Name Creek for the development and maintenance of replacement fishing grounds. * * * We affirm the district court's holding that the Colvilles have a reserved right to the quantity of water necessary to maintain the Omak Lake Fishery.

The district court held that water for spawning could not be awarded at this time because the federal government provides the necessary fingerlings. We reverse this holding. The right to water to establish and maintain the Omak Lake Fishery includes the right to sufficient water to permit natural spawning of the trout. When the Tribe has a vested property right in reserved water, it may use it in any lawful manner. As a result, subsequent acts making the historically intended use of the water unnecessary do not divest the Tribe of the right to the water. * * * Finally, we note that permitting the Indians to determine how to use reserved water is consistent with the general purpose for the creation of an Indian reservation—providing a homeland for the survival and growth of the Indians and their way of life.

THE GENERAL ALLOTMENT ACT OF 1887

We next consider Walton's rights as the fee owner of allotted land, and reverse the district court's judgment that he has no right to reserved water.

* * *

The General Allotment Act provided that land on reservations could be allotted for the exclusive use of individual Indians. Remaining land was to be made available for homesteading by non-Indians. After holding allotted lands in trust for individual Indians for a 25-year period, the federal government could convey the land to the allottee in fee, "discharged of said trust and free of all charge or incumbrance whatsoever." 25 U.S.C. § 348.

Because the use of reserved water is not limited to fulfilling the original purposes of the reservation, Congress had the power to allot reserved water rights to individual Indians, and to allow for the transfer of such rights to non-Indians. Whether it did so is a question of congressional intent.

The General Allotment Act represented the shift in federal objectives from segregation of Indians on reservations to assimilation of them in non-Indian culture and society. Its primary sponsor, Senator Dawes, explained that "the quicker [the Indian] is mingled with the whites in every particular the better it will be."

The Act was designed to encourage Indians to become self-supporting citizens by making them landowners. See generally D. Otis, The Dawes Act and the Allotment of the Indian Lands 8–32 (1978). Allotted lands were held in trust for a 25 year period because of

> the desire to protect the Indian against sharp practices leading to Indian landlessness, the desire to safeguard the certainty of titles, and the urge to continue an important basis of governmental activity [on the Indians' behalf].

F. Cohen, Handbook of Federal Indian Law 221 (1940); U.S. Department of Interior, Federal Indian Law 788–89 (1958).

The only reference to water rights in the Act is found in section 7:

> In cases where the use of water for irrigation is necessary to render the lands within any Indian reservation available for agricultural purposes, the Secretary of the Interior is authorized to prescribe such rules and regulations as he may deem necessary to secure a just and equal distribution thereof among the Indians residing upon any such reservation; and no other appropriation or grant of

> water by any riparian proprietor shall be authorized or permitted to the damage of any other riparian proprietor.

25 U.S.C. § 381.

The Act was passed over 20 years before the Supreme Court announced the implied-reservation doctrine in *Winters.* There is nothing to suggest Congress gave any consideration to the transferability of reserved water rights. To resolve this issue, we must determine what Congress would have intended had it considered it.

It is settled that Indian allottees have a right to use reserved water. United States v. Powers, 305 U.S. 527, 59 S.Ct. 344, 83 L.Ed. 330 (1939). "[W]hen allotments were made for exclusive use and thereafter conveyed in fee, the right to use some portion of tribal waters essential for cultivation passed to the owners." Id. at 532, 59 S.Ct. at 346. We must determine whether non-Indian purchasers of allotted lands also obtain a right to some portion of reserved waters.

The general rule is that termination or diminution of Indian rights requires express legislation or a clear inference of Congressional intent gleaned from the surrounding circumstances and legislative history. Upon careful consideration, we conclude this principle supports the proposition that an Indian allottee may sell his right to reserved water.

The district court's holding that an Indian allottee may convey only a right to the water he or she has actually appropriated with a priority date of actual appropriation reduces the value of the allottee's right to reserved water. We think this type of restriction on transferability is a "diminution of Indian rights" that must be supported by a clear inference of Congressional intent.

By placing allotted lands in trust for 25 years, Congress evinced an intent to protect Indians by preventing transfer of those lands. But there is no basis for an inference that some restrictions survived beyond the trust period. Congress provided for extensions of the trust period, but directed that fee title be conveyed to the allottee when the period expired. We think the fee included the appurtenant right to share in reserved waters, and see no basis for limiting the transferability of that right.

This conclusion is supported by our decision in United States v. Ahtanum Irrigation District, 236 F.2d 321, 342 (9th Cir.1956), cert. denied, 352 U.S. 988, 77 S.Ct. 386, 1 L.Ed.2d 367 (1957). *Ahtanum* held that non-Indian purchasers of allotted lands are entitled to "participate ratably" with Indian allottees in the use of reserved water. See United States v. Adair, 478 F.Supp. 336 (D.Or.1979); United States v. Hibner, 27 F.2d 909 (D.Idaho 1928).

In determining the nature of the right acquired by non-Indian purchasers, we consider three aspects of an allottee's right to use reserved waters. First, the extent of an Indian allottee's right is based on the number of irrigable acres he owns. If the allottee owns 10% of the irrigable acreage in the watershed, he is entitled to 10% of the water reserved for irrigation (i.e., a "ratable share"). This follows from the provision for an equal and just distribution of water needed for irrigation. A non-Indian purchaser cannot acquire more extensive rights to reserved water than were held by the Indian seller. Thus, the purchaser's right is similarly limited by the number of irrigable acres he owns.

Second, the Indian allottee's right has a priority as of the date the reservation was created. This is the principal aspect of the right that renders it more valuable than the rights of competing water users, and therefore applies to the right acquired by a non-Indian purchaser. In the event there is insufficient water to satisfy all valid claims to reserved water, the amount available to each claimant should be reduced proportionately.

Third, the Indian allottee does not lose by non-use the right to a share of reserved water. This characteristic is not applicable to the right acquired by a non-Indian purchaser. The non-Indian successor acquires a right to water being appropriated by the Indian allottee at the time title passes. The non-Indian also acquires a right, with a date-of-reservation priority date, to water that he or she appropriates with reasonable diligence after the passage of title. If the full measure of the Indian's reserved water right is not acquired by this means and maintained by continued use, it is lost to the non-Indian successor.

The full quantity of water available to the Indian allottee thus may be conveyed to the non-Indian purchaser. There is no diminution in the right the Indian may convey. We think Congress would have intended, however, that the non-Indian purchaser, under no competitive disability vis-a-vis other water users, may not retain the right to that quantity of water despite non-use. See United States v. Adair, 478 F.Supp. at 348–49; United States v. Hibner, 27 F.2d at 912.

The district court's holding that Walton has no right to share in water reserved when the Colville reservation was created is reversed. On remand, it will need to determine the number of irrigable acres Walton owns, and the amount of water he appropriated with reasonable diligence in order to determine the extent of his right to share in reserved water.

* * *

Reversed in part, affirmed in part, and remanded for proceedings in conformance with this opinion.

Notes

1. After remand, retrial and a second appeal, Walton was awarded only 120 acre-feet per year, four acre feet for each of the 30 acres first irrigated by his predecessor in title who initially purchased the land from the tribal allottee, 20 years before the sale to Walton. Walton's increase of irrigation to 104 acres, begun when he acquired the land, was held not to satisfy the requirement of reasonable diligence after the trust ended. The Tribe was awarded 666.4 acre feet per year, the full amount needed by the

total 166.6 acres of irrigable lands on the allotments remaining in Indian hands, although only 107.2 acres were being irrigated, and an additional 350 acre-feet per year needed to permit natural instream spawning of the Omak Lake trout. These awards total 1136.4 acre feet per year although the trial court had found that only 1000 acre feet was available. "Since all parties have a priority date as of the creation of the Reservation, each should bear a proportionate share of any adjustment required by shortages of water." Colville Confederated Tribes v. Walton, 752 F.2d 397 (9th Cir. 1985).

For somewhat differing analyses of Indian water rights and their transferability, see Getches, Water Rights on Indian Allotments, 26 So.Dak. L.Rev. 405 (1981); Collins, Indian Allotment Water Rights, 20 Land and Water L.Rev. 421 (1985).

2. The supplemental decree in Arizona v. California, 440 U.S. 59, 99 S.Ct. 995, 59 L.Ed.2d 144 (1979) (entered pursuant to joint motion of the states of Arizona, California and Nevada and the California cities and districts made defendants) contains the following provisions:

"The foregoing reference to a quantity of water necessary to supply consumptive use required for irrigation, and as that provision is included within paragraphs (1) through (5) of Art. II(D) of said Decree, shall constitute the means of determining quantity of adjudicated water rights but shall not constitute a restriction of the usage of them to irrigation or other agricultural application. If all or part of the adjudicated water rights of any of the five Indian Reservations is used other than for irrigation or other agricultural application, the total consumptive use, as that term is defined in Art. I(A) of said Decree, for said Reservation shall not exceed the consumptive use that would have resulted if the diversions listed in subparagraph (i) of paragraphs (1) through (5) of Art. II(D) of said Decree and the equivalent portions of any supplement thereto had been used for irrigation of the number of acres specified for that Reservation in said paragraphs and supplement and for the satisfaction of related uses."

3. United States v. Adair, 478 F.Supp. 336 (D.Or.1979) involved water on the terminated Klamath Indian Reservation. Much of the land had been allotted and was owned and farmed by individual Indians or had been sold to non-Indians. Upon termination, the United States acquired all the lands held in common by the tribes. Some was added to a national forest, and the 15,000 acre Klamath Marsh was made into a National Wildlife Refuge. The Indians had for more than a thousand years lived near the Marsh and depended upon it for a source of food—wildfowl, game and edible plants. The treaty creating the reservation was made in 1864, the act terminating the reservation was passed in 1954. The treaty reserved to the Indians the exclusive right to continue their activities in the Marsh, and in other litigation their hunting and fishing rights were held to have survived the termination act.

The court held that the tribe, though it no longer owns land, retains its treaty rights to hunt and fish, and still retains water rights essential to protect those rights. "If the preservation of these rights requires that the Marsh be maintained as wetlands and that the forest be maintained on a sustained-yield basis, then the Indians are entitled to whatever water is necessary to achieve those results."

Indian owners of allotments were held to have rights to irrigate their lands whenever the need arises, with an 1864 priority. Non-Indian owners of allotted lands were decreed an appurtenant right for the actual acreage under irrigation when title was obtained from an Indian, with an 1864 priority, and for such additional water as might have been placed under irrigation reasonable diligence.

Adair is also interesting because it dealt with a possible conflict between Indian rights. The treaty provided for the continued self-sufficiency of the Klamath in two ways, to maintain their traditional way of life, primarily hunting and fishing, and to encourage the Indians to adopt agriculture. The court held that the need to maintain the Marsh took precedence over irrigation of allotted lands because in 1864 hunting and fishing was more important to the Indians than agriculture, and ruled that the priority of the hunting and fishing rights dates from time immemorial, of the irrigation rights from 1864.

4. United States v. Anderson, 6 Indian L.Rep. F–129 (1979), dealt with Chamokane Creek, which flows from an upper valley over a falls and forms the eastern boundary of the Spokane Indian Reservation. The eastern boundary of the reservation is the eastern bank of the creek, so the creek itself is wholly within the reservation. The court found that the Spokane have used the creek as a food source since time immemorial, and ruled that the tribes had a reserved right for the preservation of the fishing. The trout in the creek cannot survive in water warmer than 68° and this temperature rather than the quantity of flow is the crucial factor. If the flow over the falls is reduced below 20 cfs the temperature will rise above 68°, and the court therefore fixed the reserved right at sufficient water to maintain the water temperature at 68°, at no time less than 20 cfs.

The court tabulated the water rights of all non-reservation appropriations above the falls, and determined the effect the exercise of each right would have in reducing the flow over the falls. The court appointed a water master to measure and record the temperature below the falls and regulate the uses of water by the upstream appropriators.

5. About 8% of the land within the external boundaries of the Yakima Indian Reservation is owned by non-Indians. The Yakima Nation adopted a water code that claimed "full equitable title" to all water arising on, bordering, traversing or underlying the reservation, although part of the water is used both within and outside the reservation by non-Indians and the amount needed for present or ultimate Indian use has never been adjudicated or otherwise quantified. All persons using or claiming the right to divert the water were required to file an application for a permit to use the water. Priorities among uses were established in the following order: (a) tribal or public use dedicated by the Tribal Council, (b) use for tribal enterprises, (c) farming use on Yakima allotments, (d) non-farm use on Yakima allotments, (e) use on allotments held by nonresident Yakimas, (f) use on lands held by non-Yakima Indians, and (g) use on formerly alloted lands now in non-Indian ownership. Within each class individual users were to receive a just and equitable distribution. A water resources

council was empowered to issue ten year permits. Any user who failed to apply for a permit waived all right to the water, and no use could be made without a permit.

The State of Washington, several non-Indian landowners and two small cities within the reservation, holding permits and certificates of appropriation from the state, filed suit against tribal officials to enjoin enforcement of the code. The trial court granted summary judgment in favor of plaintiffs. Citing the second *Walton* case, supra Note 1, the court ruled that the Nation's reserved rights extended only to water needed for the primary purposes of the reservation, found that excess water existed over and above that needed to satisfy the Nation's *Winters* rights, and held that the Yakima Nation does not have power to regulate the use of excess water by non-members on their fee land within or without the reservation. Holly v. Confederated Tribes and Bands of the Yakima Indian Nation, No. C–78–002–JLQ (E.D.Wash.1985, appeal pending).

6. The Court of Claims, in Gila River Pima-Maricopa Indian Community v. United States, 684 F.2d 852 (Ct.Cl.1982), was less than generous to the Indians. The tribes sued the United States for failure to protect their Winters rights from encroachment. The friendly Pimas and Maricopas were "a self-sufficient, pastoral people with entrepreneurial abilities," and the court held that the 1859 Gila River Reservation was intended to preserve their favorable status by rendering them secure in the possession of their villages and irrigated farms, free from incursions by settlers. Upstream settlers, however, took most of the river. The United States recognized the need to preserve or restore the water supply, but dawdled, and the lack of a dependable water supply caused the loss of the tribes' self-sufficiency. They claimed damages for the loss of 1,007,076 acre feet per year, enough to irrigate all the practicably irrigable land in the reservation, and approximately the total flow of the river. The court gave them considerably less:

> We do not decide whether the Pimas and Maricopas fall under the full *Winters* doctrine; their reservation may have been established to preserve what they had, not to change their habits from nomadic to pastoral, and this distinction could conceivably make a legal difference. But even if *Winters* applies fully to plaintiffs, we hold that, for monetary compensation on account of pre-August 1946 injuries under the Indian Claims Commission Act, these Indians are not entitled to damages for the failure of the defendant to supply them with all the water necessary to irrigate all the practicably irrigable acres of their reservation. The reason is that, as we have found, (a) the Indians were not in fact using more than 7,000 to 8,000 acres even when they had the full natural flow of the Gila River, and (b) they did not have the ability (i.e. capital) to build the facilities necessary for greater irrigation or to control the Gila River flow—in other words, they were unable to use more water than enough to cultivate 7,000–8,000 acres. The Indian Claims Commission Act, the aim of which was to grant monetary compensation for past (pre-August 1946) wrongs actually inflicted by the United States, does not call for damages based on theoretical maximum "rights" that the Indians were wholly unable to

utilize and to implement at the time, especially where the Government was under no moral or legal obligation to construct new facilities so that the Indians could then use the greater amount of water they now claim.

7. Section 4(e) of the Federal Power Act (16 U.S.C.A. § 797(e)) authorizes FERC to license hydroelectric power projects on the public lands and reservations of the United States, subject to such conditions as the Secretary in charge of the land deems necessary for the preservation and use of the reservation. Escondido Mutual Water Co. v. La Jolla, Rincon, San Pasqual, Pauma, and Pala Bands of Mission Indians, 466 U.S. 765, 104 S.Ct. 2105, 80 L.Ed.2d 753 (1984), involved an application for a small power facility in a diversion canal from the San Luis Rey River. The canal crossed the small reservations of three of the Bands, and the others had reservations within the watershed. All claimed rights to water in the canal and from other sources that could be affected by the project. The Commission refused to include in the license certain conditions prescribed by the Secretary of the Interior that would prohibit the licensee from interfering with the Bands' use of specific quantities of water from the canal and would protect a nearby source of groundwater. The Supreme Court reversed in part, holding that the Commission must accept without modification the Secretary's conditions as to the three reservations crossed by the canal, but that the other Bands must look to their legal rights under water law. The Court noted, however, that while the Commission is expressly forbidden to adjudicate water rights (16 U.S.C.A. § 821), it can condition a license to protect overriding beneficial public uses and can shape a license so the project will be best adapted for the improvement of water power development and other beneficial purposes (16 U.S.C.A. § 803(a)). Under these powers, the Commission might even require the licensee to surrender some of its water rights to protect the reservations if the Commission determined that such action would be in the public interest.

8. Congress has undertaken legislative resolution of several conflicts between Indian and state-created claims. The Yakima River Basin Water Enhancement Act, P.L.96–162, 93 Stat. 1241 (1979) calls for a feasibility study of enlarging the existing storage and distribution works of the Yakima Reclamation Project so as to improve the supply to both Indians and non-Indians and to increase the irrigated acreage on the Yakima Indian Reservation. In Arizona, where overpumping has dropped the water tables and forthcoming Central Arizona Project water is already overcommitted, solving the overlapping claims by increasing the size of the pie to be sliced may not be feasible. Indians faced with falling groundwater levels have threatened and in some cases begun suits against surrounding pumpers to enforce Winters rights, and against the United States for failure to protect tribal water resources and violation of trust obligations to make water available to the tribes. In the Ak-Chin settlement legislation, P.L.95–328, 92 Stat. 409 (1978), Congress committed $43 million to build well fields on and bring groundwater from nearby federal lands, and the Secretary of the Interior has contracted to supply 85,000 acre feet per year to the Ak-Chin reservation. In return, the Indian community has agreed to waive all of its past and present claims to both surface and

groundwater against the United States, the State of Arizona and any other person, corporation or municipal corporation, and to waive all of its future claims to both surface and groundwater against everybody except the United States. This arrangement looks like an augmentation of the supply similar to the purposed Yakima solution, but the feasibility and permanence of the solution has been questioned on the basis that the "new" water merely increases the withdrawal of groundwater in an already seriously overdrafted basin, and that the withdrawals from the public lands may run into serious legal problems with private interests and other Indians in the area. Shrago, Emerging Indian Water Rights: An Analysis of Recent Judicial and Legislative Developments, 29 Rocky Mtn.Min.L.Inst. 1105 (1980).

The Southern Arizona Water Rights Settlement Act of 1982, Title III, P.L.97–293, 96 Stat. 1274, obligates the Secretary to deliver to the Papago tribe 27,000 acre feet per year on the San Xavier reservation and 10,800 acre feet per year on the eastern Schuk Toak division, to construct and improve irrigation works in these areas, or to supply substitute water purchased from off-reservation irrigators or reclaimed by the first user. In addition, the Secretary is required, within the next ten years, to deliver to San Xavier and Schuk Toak 28,200 acre feet of water suitable for agricultural use. The settlement was made conditional on the City of Tucson's agreement to supply reclaimed water, treated to secondary standards, without costs. The Indians gave in return the same releases as in the Ak-Chin settlement.

In the Ak-Chin settlement the additional water supply is to be obtained at federal expense. President Reagan vetoed the first Southern Arizona Settlement Act on the ground that since the settlement would free off-reservation users from Indian claims, they should bear a part of the cost. The final act required substantial contributions from the state, the City of Tucson, several mining companies and a large corporate farming enterprise.

CAPPAERT v. UNITED STATES

Supreme Court of the United States, 1976.
426 U.S. 128, 96 S.Ct. 2062, 48 L.Ed.2d 523.

MR. CHIEF JUSTICE BURGER delivered the opinion of the Court.

The question presented in this litigation is whether the reservation of Devil's Hole as a national monument reserved federal water rights in unappropriated water.

Devil's Hole is a deep limestone cavern in Nevada. Approximately 50 feet below the opening of the cavern is a pool 65 feet long, 10 feet wide, and at least 200 feet deep, although its actual depth is unknown. The pool is a remnant of the prehistoric Death Valley Lake System and is situated on land owned by the United States since the Treaty of Guadalupe Hidalgo in 1848, 9 Stat. 922. By the Proclamation of January 17, 1952, President Truman withdrew from the public domain a 40-acre tract of land surrounding Devil's Hole, making it a detached component of the Death Valley National Monument. Proclamation No.

2961, 3 CFR 147 (1949–1953 Comp.). The Proclamation was issued under the American Antiquities Preservation Act, 34 Stat. 225, 16 U.S.C.A. § 431, which authorizes the President to declare as national monuments "objects of historic or scientific interest that are situated upon the lands owned or controlled by the Government of the United States * * *."

The 1952 Proclamation notes that Death Valley was set aside as a national monument "for the preservation of the unusual features of scenic, scientific, and educational interest therein contained." The Proclamation also notes that Devil's Hole is near Death Valley and contains a "remarkable underground pool." Additional preambulary statements in the Proclamation explain why Devil's Hole was being added to the Death Valley National Monument:

> "WHEREAS the said pool is a unique subsurface remnant of the prehistoric chain of lakes which in Pleistocene times formed the Death Valley Lake System, and is unusual among caverns in that it is a solution area in distinctly striated limestone, while also owing its formation in part to fault action; and
>
> "WHEREAS the geologic evidence that this subterranean pool is an integral part of the hydrographic history of the Death Valley region is further confirmed by the presence in this pool of a peculiar race of desert fish, and zoologists have demonstrated that this race of fish, which is found nowhere else in the world, evolved only after the gradual drying up of the Death Valley Lake System isolated this fish population from the original ancestral stock that in Pleistocene times was common to the entire region; and
>
> "WHEREAS the said pool is of such outstanding scientific importance that it should be given special protection, and such protection can be best afforded by making the said forty-acre tract containing the pool a part of the said monument * * *."

The Cappaert petitioners own a 12,000-acre ranch near Devil's Hole, 4,000 acres of which are used for growing Bermuda grass, alfalfa, wheat, and barley; 1,700 to 1,800 head of cattle are grazed. The ranch represents an investment of more than $7 million; it employs more than 80 people with an annual payroll of more than $340,000.

In 1968 the Cappaerts began pumping groundwater on their ranch on land 2½ miles from Devil's Hole; they were the first to appropriate groundwater. The groundwater comes from an underground basin or aquifer which is also the source of the water in Devil's Hole. After the Cappaerts began pumping from the wells near Devil's Hole, which they do from March to October, the summer water level of the pool in Devil's Hole began to decrease. Since 1962 the level of water in Devil's Hole has been measured with reference to a copper washer installed on one of the walls of the hole by the United States Geological Survey. Until 1968, the water level, with seasonable variations, had been stable at 1.2 feet below the copper marker. In 1969 the water level in Devil's Hole was 2.3 feet below the copper washer; in 1970, 3.17 feet; in 1971, 3.48 feet; and, in 1972, 3.93 feet.

When the water is at the lowest levels, a large portion of a rock shelf in Devil's Hole is above water. However, when the water level is at 3.0 feet below the marker or higher, most of the rock shelf is below water, enabling algae to grow on it. This in turn enables the desert fish (*cyprinodon diabolis,* commonly known as Devil's Hole pupfish), referred to in President Truman's Proclamation, to spawn in the spring. As the rock shelf becomes exposed, the spawning area is decreased, reducing the ability of the fish to spawn in sufficient quantities to prevent extinction.

In August 1971 the United States, invoking 28 U.S.C.A. § 1345, sought an injunction in the United States District Court for the District of Nevada to limit, except for domestic purposes, the Cappaerts' pumping from six specific wells and from specific locations near Devil's Hole. * * * The District Court found that if the injunction did not issue "there is grave danger that the Devil's Hole pupfish may be destroyed, resulting in irreparable injury to the United States." 375 F.Supp. 456, 460 (1974).

On April 9, 1974, the District Court entered its findings of fact and conclusions of law substantially unchanged in a final decree permanently enjoining pumping that lowers the level of the water below the 3.0-foot level. 375 F.Supp. 456 (1974).

The Court of Appeals for the Ninth Circuit affirmed, 508 F.2d 313 (1974).

We granted certiorari to consider the scope of the implied-reservation-of-water-rights doctrine.

This Court has long held that when the Federal Government withdraws its land from the public domain and reserves it for a federal purpose, the Government, by implication, reserves appurtenant water then unappropriated to the extent needed to accomplish the purpose of the reservation. In so doing the United States acquires a reserved right in unappropriated water which vests on the date of the reservation and is superior to the rights of future appropriators. Reservation of water rights is empowered by the Commerce Clause, Art. I, § 8, which permits federal regulation of navigable streams, and the Property Clause, Art. IV, § 3, which permits federal regulation of federal lands. The doctrine applies to Indian reservations and other federal enclaves, encompassing water rights in navigable and non-navigable streams. Colorado River Water Cons. Dist. v. United States, 424 U.S. 800, 805, 96 S.Ct. 1236, 1240, 47 L.Ed.2d 483 (1976); United States v. District Court for Eagle County, 401 U.S. 520, 522–523, 91 S.Ct. 998, 1000–1001, 28 L.Ed.2d 278, 280–281 (1971); Arizona v. California, 373 U.S. 546, 601, 83 S.Ct. 1468, 1498, 10 L.Ed.2d 542, 578 (1963); FPC v. Oregon, 349 U.S. 435, 75 S.Ct. 832, 99 L.Ed. 1215 (1955); United States

v. Powers, 305 U.S. 527, 59 S.Ct. 344, 83 L.Ed. 330 (1939); Winters v. United States, 207 U.S. 564, 28 S.Ct. 207, 52 L.Ed. 340 (1908). * * *

In determining whether there is a federally reserved water right implicit in a federal reservation of public land, the issue is whether the Government intended to reserve unappropriated and thus available water. Intent is inferred if the previously unappropriated waters are necessary to accomplish the purposes for which the reservation was created. See, e.g., Arizona v. California, supra, 373 U.S., at 599–601, 83 S.Ct., at 1497–1498, 10 L.Ed.2d, at 577–578; Winters v. United States, supra, 207 U.S., at 576, 28 S.Ct., at 211, 52 L.Ed., at 346. Both the District Court and the Court of Appeals held that the 1952 Proclamation expressed an intention to reserve unappropriated water, and we agree. The Proclamation discussed the pool in Devil's Hole in four of the five preambles and recited that the "pool * * * should be given special protection." Since a pool is a body of water, the protection contemplated is meaningful only if the water remains; the water right reserved by the 1952 Proclamation was thus explicit, not implied. * * *

The implied-reservation-of-water-rights doctrine, however, reserves only that amount of water necessary to fulfill the purpose of the reservation, no more. Arizona v. California, supra, 373 U.S., at 600–601, 83 S.Ct., at 1497–1498, 10 L.Ed.2d, at 578–579. Here the purpose of reserving Devil's Hole Monument is preservation of the pool. Devil's Hole was reserved "for the preservation of the unusual features of scenic, scientific, and educational interest." The Proclamation notes that the pool contains "a peculiar race of desert fish * * * which is found nowhere else in the world" and that the "pool is of * * * outstanding scientific importance * * *." The pool need only be preserved, consistent with the intention expressed in the Proclamation, to the extent necessary to preserve its scientific interest. The fish are one of the features of scientific interest. The preamble noting the scientific interest of the pool follows the preamble describing the fish as unique; the Proclamation must be read in its entirety. Thus, as the District Court has correctly determined, the level of the pool may be permitted to drop to the extent that the drop does not impair the scientific value of the pool as the natural habitat of the species sought to be preserved. The District Court thus tailored its injunction, very appropriately, to minimal need, curtailing pumping only to the extent necessary to preserve an adequate water level at Devil's Hole, thus implementing the stated objectives of the Proclamation. * * *

No cases of this Court have applied the doctrine of implied reservation of water rights to groundwater. Nevada argues that the implied-reservation doctrine is limited to surface water. Here, however, the water in the pool is surface water. The federal water rights were being depleted because, as the evidence showed, the "[g]roundwater and surface water are physically interrelated as integral parts of the hydrologic cycle." C. Corker, Groundwater Law, Management and Administration, National Water Commission Legal Study No. 6, p. xxiv (1971). Here the Cappaerts are causing the water level in Devil's Hole to drop by their heavy pumping. See Corker, supra; see also Water Policies for the Future—Final Report to the President and to the Congress of the United States by the National Water Commission 233 (1973). It appears that Nevada itself may recognize the potential interrelationship between surface and groundwater since Nevada applies the law of prior appropriation to both. Nev.Rev.Stat. §§ 533.010 et seq., 534.020, 534.080, 534.090 (1973). See generally F. Trelease, Water Law—Resource Use and Environmental Protection 457–552 (2d ed. 1974); C. Meyers & A. Tarlock, Water Resource Management 553–634 (1971). Thus, since the implied-reservation-of-water-rights doctrine is based on the necessity of water for the purpose of the federal reservation, we hold that the United States can protect its water from subsequent diversion, whether the diversion is of surface or groundwater. * * *

Petitioners argue that the Federal Government must perfect its implied water rights according to state law. They contend that the Desert Land Act of 1877, 19 Stat. 377, 43 U.S.C.A. § 321, and its predecessors severed nonnavigable water from public land, subjecting it to state law. That Act, however, provides that patentees of public land acquire only title to land through the patent and must acquire water rights in nonnavigable water in accordance with state law. California Oregon Power Co. v. Beaver Portland Cement Co., 295 U.S. 142, 162, 55 S.Ct. 725, 730, 79 L.Ed. 1356, 1363 (1935); see Morreale, Federal-State Conflicts Over Western Waters—A Decade of Attempted "Clarifying Legislation," 20 Rutgers L.Rev. 423, 432 (1966). This Court held in FPC v. Oregon, 349 U.S. 435, 448, 75 S.Ct. 832, 840, 99 L.Ed. 1215, 1226 (1955), that the Desert Land Act does not apply to water rights on federally reserved land. * * * The Desert Land Act still provides that the water rights of those who received their land from federal patents are to be governed by state law. That there may be no more federal land available for homesteading does not mean the Desert Land Act now applies to all federal land. Since the Act is inapplicable, determination of reserved water rights is not governed by state law but derives from the federal purpose of the reservation; the fact that the water rights here reserved apply to nonnavigable rather than navigable waters is thus irrelevant.

Since FPC v. Oregon, supra, was decided, several bills have been introduced in Congress to subject at least some federal water uses to state appropriation doctrines, but none has been enacted into law. The most recent bill, S. 28, 92d Cong., 1st Sess., was introduced on January 25, 1971, and reintroduced under the same number in the 93d Cong., 1st Sess., on January 4, 1973. See Morreale, supra. * * *

We hold, therefore, that as of 1952 when the United States reserved Devil's Hole, it acquired by reservation water rights in unappropriated appurtenant water sufficient to maintain the level of the pool to preserve its scientific value and thereby implement Proclamation No. 2961. Accordingly, the judgment of the Court of Appeals is

Affirmed.

Notes

1. For a better acquaintance with the Devil's Hole pupfish, see Trusso, Big Trouble for a Tiny Fish, 3 Smithsonian No. 4, 48 (July, 1972).

2. Trelease, Federal Reserved Water Rights since PLLRC, 54 Denver L.J. 473 (1977):

"Although it is now fashionable to say that the first precedents for the reserved doctrine were the dicta contained in the 1899 United States v. Rio Grande Irrigation Co.[1] case and the 1908 Winters v. United States Indian case, I can testify that no one regarded these as such prior to Federal Power Commission v. Oregon (Pelton Dam) in 1955.

"I was there. I took a course in water law in 1938 and got an A in it. I then went to work for L. Ward Bannister, one of the negotiators of the Colorado River Compact and lecturer in water law at Denver University and Harvard University. I helped to bring his notes up to date. I listened in on discourses he had with Ralph Carr, Jean Breitenstein, John Reed, and other 'irrigation lawyers' of the old school. I started to teach water law in 1946, and I was General Counsel for the Missouri River Basin Survey Commission in 1952. At no time prior to 1955 did I ever hear a suggestion that the reserved rights doctrine was anything but a special quirk of Indian water law.

"True, there was a notion lurking in the background that since the United States originally 'owned' the water in the West, as it owned the land of the public domain, it might still be the 'owner' of unappropriated water.[2] This theory was advanced by Attorneys General for the United States in a couple of interstate cases, but it was seemingly rejected in Kansas v. Colorado and was held inapplicable in Nebraska v. Wyoming. In the latter case the waters of the North Platte were being divided between the states and the Government asked, on the strength of this theory, that a separate allocation of water be made to the United States for its irrigation projects. That argument the Supreme Court put aside, on the basis that under the Reclamation Act the Government acquired its water rights through the state and the states therefore stood in judgment for the United States. Earlier, in California Oregon Power Co. v. Beaver Portland Cement Co., a suit between private parties, the Supreme Court, on what now seems to be a spurious reading of the Desert Land Act,[3] held that the Act

1. 174 U.S. 690 (1899). "[A] state cannot by its legislation destroy the right of the United States, as the owner of lands bordering on a stream, to the continued flow of its waters, so far at least as may be necessary for the beneficial uses of the government property." Id. at 703.

2. See Bannister, The Question of Federal Disposition of State Waters in the Priority States, 28 Harv.L.Rev. 270 (1915); Carpenter, Conflict of Jurisdiction Respecting Control of Waters in Western States, 2 Rocky Mtn.L.Rev. 162 (1929).

3. 43 U.S.C.A. §§ 321–399 (1970). See F. Trelease, Federal-State Relations in Water Law, National Water Commission Legal Study No. 5, at 147a–m (1971).

> effected a severance of all water on the public domain, not theretofore appropriated, from the land itself. * * * Congress intended to establish the rule that for the future the land should be patented separately; and that all nonnavigable waters thereon should be reserved for the use of the public under the laws of the states and territories * * *.

"So the western water lawyer, though he may have had some nagging fear in the back of his mind that the United States might have constitutional power to use water without complying with state law, or even power to regulate its use, nevertheless felt quite safe behind the twin shields of the Reclamation Act and the Desert Land Act.

"The safety thought provided by the Acts was weakened by the Supreme Court's *Pelton Dam* decision in 1955. The *Pelton Dam* case did not involve water rights as such. All it held was that a license from the United States to build a dam on reserved lands could not be thwarted by lack of state permission. But the language of both the majority and the dissent is susceptible of being construed as saying that the Desert Land Act's severance of the water from the public lands did not apply to reserved lands, which, therefore, still have water attached to them. It is generally assumed that the power company is now exercising, by some implied assignment, the right of the United States to use the water which it reserved from the jurisdiction of the State of Oregon when it reserved the power site. This was even worse than 'ownership of unappropriated water;' it was ownership of *appropriated* water, if the appropriation had been made subsequent to the reservation.

"This case was a real bombshell, and it certainly lit a fire under western water lawyers."

3. The first actual allocation of water for non-Indian lands and purposes under the reserved rights theory was made in 1963, in Arizona v. California. The Court said: "The Master ruled that the principle underlying the reservation of water rights for Indian Reservations was equally applicable to other federal establishments such as National Recreation Areas and National Forests. We agree with the conclusions of the Master that the United States intended to reserve water sufficient for the future requirements of the Lake Mead National Recreation Area, the Havasu Lake National Wildlife Refuge, the Imperial National Wildlife Refuge and the Gila National Forest." 373 U.S. at 601, 83 S.Ct. at 1498, 10 L.Ed. at 578.

COLORADO RIVER WATER CONSERVATION DIST. v. UNITED STATES

Supreme Court of the United States, 1976.
424 U.S. 800, 96 S.Ct. 1236, 47 L.Ed.2d 483.

MR. JUSTICE BRENNAN delivered the opinion of the Court.

The McCarran Amendment, 66 Stat. 560, 43 U.S.C.A. § 666, provides that "consent is hereby given to join the United States as a defendant in any suit (1) for the adjudication of rights to the use of water of a river system or other source, or (2) for the administration of such rights, where it appears that the United States is the owner of or is in the process of acquiring water rights by appropriation under State law, by purchase, by exchange, or otherwise, and the United States is a necessary party to such suit." The questions presented by this case concern the effect of the McCarran Amendment upon the jurisdiction of the federal district courts under 28 U.S.C.A. § 1345 over suits for determination of water rights brought by the United States as trustee for certain Indian tribes and as owner of various non-Indian Government claims.

It is probable that no problem of the Southwest section of the Nation is more critical than that of scarcity of water. As southwestern populations have grown, conflicting claims to this scarce resource have increased. To meet these claims, several Southwestern States have established elaborate procedures for allocation of water and adjudication of conflicting claims to that resource. In 1969, Colorado enacted its Water Rights Determination and Administration Act in an effort to revamp its legal procedures for determining claims to water within the State.

Under the Colorado Act, the State is divided into seven Water Divisions, each Division encompassing one or more entire drainage basins for the larger rivers in Colorado. Adjudication of water claims within each Division occurs on a continuous basis. Each month, Water Referees in each Division rule on applications for water rights filed within the preceding five months or refer those applications to the Water Judge of their Division. Every six months, the Water Judge passes on referred applications and contested decisions by Referees. A State Engineer and engineers for each Division are responsible for the administration and distribution of the waters of the State according to the determinations in each Division. * * *

The reserved rights of the United States extend to Indian reservations, Winters v. United States, 207 U.S. 564, 28 S.Ct. 207, 52 L.Ed. 340 (1908), and other federal lands, such as national parks and forests, Arizona v. California, 373 U.S. 546, 83 S.Ct. 1468, 10 L.Ed.2d 542 (1963). The reserved rights claimed by the United States in this case affect waters within Colorado Water Division No. 7. On November 14, 1972, the Government instituted this suit in the United States District Court for the District of Colorado, invoking the court's jurisdiction under 28 U.S.C.A. § 1345. The District Court is located in Denver, some 300 miles from Division 7. The suit, against some 1,000 water users, sought declaration of the Government's rights to waters in certain rivers and their tributaries located in Division 7. In the suit, the Government asserted reserved rights on its own behalf and on behalf of certain Indian tribes, as well as rights based on state law. It sought appointment of a water master to administer any waters decreed to the United States.

Prior to institution of this suit, the Government had pursued adjudication of non-Indian reserved rights and other water claims based on state law in Water Divisions 4, 5, and 6, and the Government continues to participate fully in those Divisions.

Shortly after the federal suit was commenced, one of the defendants in that suit filed an application in the state court for Division 7, seeking an order directing service of process on the United States in order to make it a party to proceedings in Division 7 for the purpose of adjudicating all of the Government's claims, both state and federal. On January 3, 1973, the United States was served pursuant to authority of the McCarran Amendment. Several defendants and intervenors in the federal proceeding then filed a motion in the District Court to dismiss on the ground that under the Amendment, the court was without jurisdiction to determine federal water rights. Without deciding the jurisdictional question, the District Court, on June 21, 1973, granted the motion in an unreported oral opinion stating that the doctrine of abstention required deference to the proceedings in Division 7. On appeal, the Court of Appeals for the Tenth Circuit reversed, United States v. Akin, 504 F.2d 115 (1974), holding that the suit of the United States was within district-court jurisdiction under 28 U.S.C.A. § 1345, and that abstention was inappropriate. We granted certiorari. * * *

We first consider the question of district-court jurisdiction under 28 U.S.C.A. § 1345. That section provides that the district courts shall have original jurisdiction over all civil actions brought by the Federal Government "[e]xcept as otherwise provided by Act of Congress." It is thus necessary to examine whether the McCarran Amendment is such an Act of Congress excepting jurisdiction under § 1345.

The McCarran Amendment does not by its terms, at least, indicate any repeal of jurisdiction under § 1345. * * *

Beyond its terms, the legislative history of the Amendment evidences no clear purpose to terminate any portion of § 1345 jurisdiction. Indeed, three bills, proposed at approximately the same time as the Amendment, which expressly would have had the effect of precluding suits by the United States in district court for the determination of water rights, failed of passage. * * * Accordingly, we hold that the McCarran Amendment in no way diminished federal-district-court jurisdiction under § 1345 and that the District Court had jurisdiction to hear this case.

We turn next to the question whether this suit nevertheless was properly dismissed in view of the concurrent state proceedings in Division 7.

First, we consider whether the McCarran Amendment provided consent to determine federal reserved rights held on behalf of Indians in state court. This is a question not previously squarely addressed by this Court, and given the claims for Indian water rights in this case, dismissal clearly would have been inappropriate if the state court had no jurisdiction to decide those claims. We conclude that the state court had jurisdiction over Indian water rights under the Amendment.

United States v. District Court for Eagle County, 401 U.S. 520, 91 S.Ct. 998, 28 L.Ed.2d 278 (1971), and United States v. District Court for Water Div. 5, 401 U.S. 527, 91 S.Ct. 1003, 28 L.Ed.2d 284 (1971), held that the provisions of the McCarran Amendment, whereby "consent is * * * given to join the United States as a defendant in any suit (1) for the adjudication * * * or (2) for the administration of [water] rights, where it appears that the United States is the owner * * * by appropriation under State law, by purchase, by exchange, or otherwise. * * *," subject federal reserved rights to general adjudication in state proceedings for the determination of water rights. More specifically, the Court held that reserved rights were included in those rights where the United States was "otherwise" the owner. United States v. District Court for Eagle County, supra, 401 U.S. at 524, 91 S.Ct. at 1002, 28 L.Ed.2d at 281. Though *Eagle County* and *Water Div. 5* did not involve reserved rights on Indian reservations, reviewing the Government's trusteeship of Indian rights as ownership, the logic of those cases clearly extends to such rights. Indeed, *Eagle County* spoke of non-Indian rights and Indian rights without any suggestion that there was a distinction between them for purposes of the Amendment. 401 U.S., at 523, 91 S.Ct., at 1001, 28 L.Ed.2d, at 281.

Not only the Amendment's language, but also its underlying policy, dictates a construction including Indian rights in its provisions. *Eagle County* rejected the conclusion that federal reserved rights in general were not reached by the Amendment for the reason that the Amendment "[deals] with an all-inclusive statute concerning 'the adjudication of rights to the use of water of a river system.'" Id., at 524, 91 S.Ct., at 1002, 28 L.Ed.2d, at 282. This consideration applies as well to federal water rights reserved for Indian reservations. * * * Thus, bearing in mind the ubiquitous nature of Indian water rights in the Southwest, it is clear that a construction of the Amendment excluding those rights from its coverage would enervate the Amendment's objective. * * *

The Government argues that because of its fiduciary responsibility to protect Indian rights, any state-court jurisdiction over Indian property should not be recognized unless expressly conferred by Congress. It has been recognized, however, that an action for the destruction of personal property may be brought against an Indian tribe where "[a]uthority to sue * * * is implied." Turner v. United States, 248 U.S. 354, 358, 39 S.Ct. 109, 110, 63 L.Ed. 291, 294 (1919). Moreover, the Government's argument rests on the incorrect assumption that consent to state jurisdiction for the purpose of determining water rights imperils those rights or in some way breaches the special obligation of the Federal Government to protect Indians. Mere subjection of Indian rights to legal challenge in state court, however, would no more imperil those rights than would a suit brought by the Government in district court for their declaration, a suit which, absent the consent of the

Amendment, would eventually be necessitated to resolve conflicting claims to a scarce resource. The government has not abdicated any responsibility fully to defend Indian rights in state court, and Indian interest may be satisfactorily protected under regimes of state law. * * * The Amendment in no way abridges any substantive claim on behalf of Indians under the doctrine of reserved rights. Moreover, as *Eagle County* said, "questions [arising from the collision of private rights and reserved rights of the United States], including the volume and scope of particular reserved rights, are federal questions which, if preserved, can be reviewed [by the Supreme Court] after final judgment by the Colorado court." 401 U.S., at 526, 91 S.Ct., at 1003, 28 L.Ed.2d, at 283.

Next, we consider whether the District Court's dismissal was appropriate under the doctrine of abstention. We hold that the dismissal cannot be supported under that doctrine in any of its forms. * * *

(a) Abstention is appropriate "in cases presenting a federal constitutional issue which might be mooted or presented in a different posture by a state court determination of pertinent state law." * * *

(b) Abstention is also appropriate where there have been presented difficult questions of state law bearing on policy problems of substantial public import whose importance transcends the result in the case then at bar. * * *

Although this case falls within none of the abstention categories, there are principles unrelated to considerations of proper constitutional adjudication and regard for federal-state relations which govern in situations involving the contemporaneous exercise of concurrent jurisdictions, either by federal courts or by state and federal courts. * * * It has been held, for example, that the court first assuming jurisdiction over property may exercise that jurisdiction to the exclusion of other courts. * * *

Turning to the present case, a number of factors clearly counsel against concurrent federal proceedings. The most important of these is the McCarran Amendment itself. * * * Beyond the congressional policy expressed by the McCarran Amendment and consistent with furtherance of that policy, we also find significant (a) the apparent absence of any proceedings in the District Court, other than the filing of the complaint, prior to the motion to dismiss, (b) the extensive involvement of state water rights occasioned by this suit naming 1,000 defendants, (c) the 300-mile distance between the District Court in Denver and the court in Division 7, and (d) the existing participation by the Government in Division 4, 5, and 6 proceedings. We emphasize, however, that we do not overlook the heavy obligation to exercise jurisdiction. * * * But the opposing factors here, particularly the policy underlying the McCarran Amendment, justify the District Court's dismissal in this particular case.

The judgment of the Court of Appeals is reversed and the judgment of the District Court dismissing the complaint is affirmed for the reasons here stated.

MR. JUSTICE STEWART, with whom MR. JUSTICE BLACKMUN and MR. JUSTICE STEVENS concur, dissenting. * * *

The Court's principal reason for deciding to close the doors of the federal courthouse to the United States in this case seems to stem from the view that its decision will avoid piecemeal adjudication of water rights. * * *

The Colorado courts are currently engaged in two types of proceedings under the State's water-rights law. First, they are processing new claims to water based on recent appropriations. Second, they are integrating these new awards of water rights with all past decisions awarding such rights into one all-inclusive tabulation for each water source. The claims of the United States that are involved in this case have not been adjudicated in the past. Yet they do not involve recent appropriations of water. In fact, these claims are wholly dissimilar to normal state water claims, because they are not based on actual beneficial use of water but rather on an intention formed at the time the federal land use was established to reserve a certain amount of water to support the federal reservations. The state court will, therefore, have to conduct separate proceedings to determine these claims. * * * Whether the virtually identical separate proceedings take place in a federal court or a state court, the adjudication of the claims will be neither more nor less "piecemeal." Essentially the same process will be followed in each instance. * * *

Second, some of the federal claims in this lawsuit relate to water reserved for Indian reservations. It is not necessary to determine that there is no state-court jurisdiction of these claims to support the proposition that a federal court is a more appropriate forum than a state court for determination of questions of life-and-death importance to Indians. This Court has long recognized that " '[t]he policy of leaving Indians free from state jurisdiction and control is deeply rooted in the Nation's history.' " McClanahan v. Arizona State Tax Comm'n, 411 U.S. 164, 168, 93 S.Ct. 1257, 1260, 36 L.Ed.2d 129, 133. * * *

I would affirm the judgment of the Court of Appeals.

Note

The McCarran Amendment's grant of jurisdiction over the United States in suits "for the adjudication of rights to the use of water of a river system or other source" applies only to "general adjudications" involving all the rights of various owners of a stream. It does not waive sovereign immunity in suits initiated by individuals, brought against the United States or its officials by water users who claim injury from Federal actions or projects, or who seek to determine their relative priority as against the United States. Dugan v. Rank, 372 U.S. 609, 83 S.Ct. 999, 10 L.Ed.2d 15 (1963).

ARIZONA v. SAN CARLOS APACHE TRIBE OF ARIZONA

Supreme Court of the United States, 1983.
463 U.S. 545, 103 S.Ct. 3201, 77 L.Ed.2d 837.

JUSTICE BRENNAN delivered the opinion of the Court.

These consolidated cases form a sequel to our decision in Colorado River Conservation District v. United States, 424 U.S. 800, 96 S.Ct. 1236, 47 L.Ed.2d 483 (1976).

The two petitions considered here arise out of three separate consolidated appeals that were decided within three days of each other by the same panel of the Court of Appeals for the Ninth Circuit. In each of the underlying cases, either the United States as trustee or certain Indian tribes on their own behalf, or both, asserted the right to have certain Indian water rights in Arizona or Montana adjudicated in federal court.

THE MONTANA CASES

In January 1975, the Northern Cheyenne Tribe brought an action in the United States District Court for the District of Montana seeking an adjudication of its rights in certain streams in that State. Shortly thereafter, the United States brought two suits in the same Court, seeking a determination of water rights both on its own behalf and on behalf of a number of Indian Tribes, including the Northern Cheyenne, in the same streams. Each of the federal actions was a general adjudication which sought to determine the rights *inter sese* of *all* users of the stream, and not merely the rights of the plaintiffs. On motion of the Northern Cheyenne, its action was consolidated with one of the Government actions. The other concerned Tribes intervened as appropriate.

At about the time that all this activity was taking place in federal court, the State of Montana was preparing to begin a process of comprehensive water adjudication under a recently passed state statute. In July 1975, the Montana Department of Natural Resources and Conservation filed petitions in state court commencing comprehensive proceedings to adjudicate water rights in the same streams at issue in the federal cases. * * *

In April 1979, the United States brought four more suits in federal court, seeking to adjudicate its rights and the rights of various Indian tribes in other Montana streams. One month later, the Montana legislature amended its water adjudication procedures "to expedite and facilitate the adjudication of existing water rights." Act to Adjudicate Claims of Existing Water Rights in Montana, § 1(1), 1979 Mont.Laws 1901. * * *

In November 1979, the two judges for the District of Montana jointly considered the motions to dismiss in each of the federal actions, and granted each of them. 484 F.Supp. 31 (D.C.1979). The court relied strongly on the new Montana legislation. * * *

On appeal, a divided Court of Appeals reversed. Northern Cheyenne Tribe v. Adsit, 668 F.2d 1080 (CA 9 1982). * * *

The second, and dispositive, ground of decision in the Court of Appeals, however, was its conclusion that "* * * [t]he limited factual circumstances of [*Colorado River*] prevent its application to the Montana litigation. 668 F.2d, at 1087. In reaching this conclusion, the court relied in part on the infancy of both the federal and state proceedings in the Montana litigation, the possible inadequacy of the state proceedings (which it did not discuss in great detail), and the fact that the Indians (who could not be joined involuntarily in the state proceedings) might not be adequately represented by the United States in state court in light of conflicts of interest between the Federal Government's responsibilities as trustee and its own claims to water.

THE ARIZONA CASES

In the mid-1970s, various water rights claimants in Arizona filed petitions in state court to initiate general adjudications to determine conflicting rights in a number of river systems. In early 1979, process was served in one of the proceedings on approximately 12,000 known potential water claimants, including the United States. In July 1981, process was served in another proceeding on approximately 58,000 known water claimants, again including the United States. In each case, the United States was joined both in its independent capacity and as trustee for various Indian tribes.

In March and April of 1979, a number of Indian tribes whose rights were implicated by the state water proceedings filed a series of suits in the United States District Court for the District of Arizona, asking variously for removal of the state adjudications to federal court, declaratory and injunctive relief preventing any further adjudication of their rights in state court, and independent federal determinations of their water rights. A number of defendants in the federal proceedings filed motions seeking remand or dismissal. The District Court, relying on *Colorado River,* remanded the removed actions, and dismissed most of the independent federal actions without prejudice. 484 F.Supp. 778 (D.C.1980). It stayed one of the remaining actions pending the completion of state proceedings. App. to Pet. for Cert. in No. 81–2147, p. D–1.

The Tribes appealed from these decisions, with the exception of the remand orders. The Court of Appeals reversed, * * *.

We granted certiorari, 459 U.S. 821, 103 S.Ct. 50, 74 L.Ed.2d 56 (1982), in order to resolve a conflict among the circuits regarding the role of federal and state courts in adjudicating Indian water rights.[a]

a. In Jicarilla Apache Tribe v. United States, 601 F.2d 1116 (CA 10 1979), the Court of Appeals for the Tenth Circuit held that the [State of] New Mexico * * * [had] jurisdiction over Indian water rights, and upheld the district court's dismissal of a general water adjudication brought in federal court by the Jicarilla Apache Tribe.

We now reverse.

* * *

The * * * crucial issue in these cases is whether our analysis in *Colorado River* applies with full force to federal suits brought by Indian tribes, rather than by the United States, and seeking adjudication only of Indian water rights. * * *

The United States and the various Indian respondents raise a series of arguments why dismissal or stay of the federal suit is not appropriate when it is brought by an Indian tribe and only seeks to adjudicate Indian rights. (1) Indian rights have traditionally been left free of interference from the States. (2) State courts may be inhospitable to Indian rights. (3) The McCarran Amendment, although it waived United States sovereign immunity in state comprehensive water adjudications, did not waive *Indian* sovereign immunity. It is therefore unfair to force Indian claimants to choose between waiving their sovereign immunity by intervening in the state proceedings and relying on the United States to represent their interests in state court, particularly in light of the frequent conflict of interest between Indian claims and other federal interests and the right of the Indians under 28 U.S.C. § 1362 to bring suit on their own behalf in federal court. (4) Indian water rights claims are generally based on federal rather than state law. (5) Because Indian water claims are based on the doctrine of "reserved rights," and take priority over most water rights created by state law, they need not as a practical matter be adjudicated *inter sese* with other water rights, and could simply be incorporated into the comprehensive state decree at the conclusion of the state proceedings.

Each of these arguments has a good deal of force. We note, though, that very similar arguments were raised and rejected in *Eagle County* and *Colorado River.* More important, all of these arguments founder on one crucial fact: If the state proceedings have jurisdiction over the Indian water rights at issue here, as appears to be the case, then concurrent federal proceedings are likely to be duplicative and wasteful, generating "additional litigation through permitting inconsistent dispositions of property." Colorado River, 424 U.S., at 819, 96 S.Ct., at 1247. Moreover, since a judgment by either court would ordinarily be res judicata in the other, the existence of such concurrent proceedings creates the serious potential for spawning an unseemly and destructive race to see which forum can resolve the same issues first—a race contrary to the entire spirit of the McCarran Amendment and prejudicial, to say the least, to the possibility of reasoned decisionmaking by either forum. * * *

* * *

The McCarran Amendment, as interpreted in *Colorado River,* allows and encourages state courts to undertake the task of quantifying Indian water rights in the course of comprehensive water adjudications. Although adjudication of those rights in federal court instead might in the abstract be practical, and even wise, it will be neither practical nor wise as long as it creates the possibility of duplicative litigation, tension and controversy between the federal and state forums, hurried and pressured decisionmaking, and confusion over the disposition of property rights.

Colorado River, of course, does not require that a federal water suit must always be dismissed or stayed in deference to a concurrent and adequate comprehensive state adjudication. Certainly, the federal courts need not defer to the state proceedings if the state courts expressly agree to stay their own consideration of the issues raised in the federal action pending disposition of that action. Moreover, it may be in a particular case that, at the time a motion to dismiss is filed, the federal suit at issue is well enough along that its dismissal would itself constitute a waste of judicial resources and an invitation to duplicative effort. See Colorado River, 424 U.S., at 820, 96 S.Ct., at 1248; Moses H. Cone Hospital, 460 U.S., at ——, 103 S.Ct., at 937. Finally, we do not deny that, in a case in which the arguments for and against deference to the state adjudication were otherwise closely matched, the fact that a federal suit was brought by Indians on their own behalf and sought only to adjudicate Indian rights should be figured into the balance. But the most important consideration in *Colorado River,* and the most important consideration in any federal water suit concurrent to a comprehensive state proceeding, must be the "policy underlying the McCarran Amendment," 424 U.S., at 820, 96 S.Ct., at 1248; see Moses H. Cone Hospital, supra, 460 U.S., at ——, 103 S.Ct., at 937, and, despite the strong arguments raised by the respondents, we cannot conclude that water rights suits brought by Indians and seeking adjudication only of Indian rights should be excepted from the application of that policy or from the general principles set out in *Colorado River.* In the cases before us, assuming that the state adjudications are adequate to quantify the rights at issue in the federal suits, and taking into account the McCarran Amendment policies we have just discussed, the expertise and administrative machinery available to the state courts, the infancy of the federal suits, the general judicial bias against piecemeal litigation, and the convenience to the parties, we must conclude that the District Courts were correct in deferring to the state proceedings.

We also emphasize, as we did in *Colorado River,* that our decision in no way changes the substantive law by which Indian rights in state water adjudications must be judged. State courts, as much as federal courts, have a solemn obligation to follow federal law. Moreover, any state court decision alleged to abridge Indian water rights protected by federal law can expect to receive, if brought for review before this Court, a particularized and exacting scrutiny commensurate with the powerful federal interest in safeguarding those rights from state encroachment.

The judgments of the Court of Appeals in each of these cases is reversed and the cases are remanded for further proceedings consistent with this opinion.

So ordered.

JUSTICE MARSHALL, dissenting.

* * *

Unlike the federal suit in *Colorado River,* the suits here are brought by Indian tribes on their own behalf. These cases thus implicate the strong congressional policy, embodied in 28 U.S.C. § 1362 of affording Indian tribes a federal forum. * * *

JUSTICE STEVENS, with whom JUSTICE BLACKMUN joins, dissenting. * * *

Unlike state-law claims based on prior appropriation, Indian reserved water rights are not based on actual beneficial use and are not forfeited if they are not used. Vested no later than the date each reservation was created, these Indian rights are superior in right to all subsequent appropriations under state law. Not all of the issues arising from the application of the *Winters* doctrine have been resolved, because in the past the scope of Indian reserved rights has infrequently been adjudicated. The important task of elaborating and clarifying these federal law issues in the cases now before the Court, and in future cases, should be performed by federal rather than state courts whenever possible. * * *

Although in some respects Indian tribes' water claims are similar to other reserved federal water rights, different treatment is justified. States and their citizens may well be more antagonistic toward Indian reserved rights than other federal reserved rights, both because the former are potentially greater in quantity and because they provide few direct or indirect benefits to non-Indian residents. Indians have historically enjoyed a unique relationship with the federal government, reflecting the tribes' traditional sovereign status, their treaty-based right to federal protection, and their special economic problems. Recently the Court reaffirmed " 'the distinctive obligation of trust incumbent upon the Government in its dealings with these dependent and sometimes exploited people.' " * * *

One important aspect of the special relationship is 28 U.S.C. § 1362, which embodies a federal promise that Indian tribes will be able to invoke the jurisdiction of federal courts to resolve matters in controversy arising under federal law.[b] Congress thereby assured Indians a neutral federal forum—a guarantee whose importance should not be underestimated. The Senate report noted,

> "There is great hesitancy on the part of tribes to use State courts. This reluctance is founded partially on the traditional fear that tribes have had of the States in which their reservations are situated.

b. The statute provides:

> "The district courts shall have original jurisdiction of all civil actions, brought by any Indian tribe or band with a governing body duly recognized by the Secretary of the Interior, wherein the matter in controversy arises under the Constitution, laws, or treaties of the United States."

Enacted in 1966, § 1362 was designed to remove the $10,000 jurisdictional amount limitation with respect to these claims.

> Additionally, the Federal courts have more expertise in deciding questions involving treaties with the Federal Government, as well as interpreting the relevant body of Federal law that has developed over the years." S.Rep. No. 1507, 89th Cong., 2d Sess. 2 (1966).

Section 1362 also assured the tribes that they need not rely on the federal government to protect their interests, an important safeguard in light of the undeniable potential for conflicts of interest between Indian claims and other federal Government claims. * * *

Notes

1. In *San Carlos,* the Supreme Court left to the state courts the effect of Arizona Constitution, Art. 20, § 4, in which the people of the state "forever disclaim all right and title to the public lands * * * and all lands * * * owned or held by any Indian or Indian tribe * * * and the same shall be, and remain, subject to the disposition and under the absolute jurisdiction and control of the Congress of the United States." In U.S. v. District Court for Maricopa County, 114 Ariz. 265, 697 P.2d 658 (1985), the court held that while this provision was intended to insure supremacy of federal policy and law with regard to Indian land, that policy, as asserted in the McCarran Amendment, is that the United States is to represent the Indian tribes in state water adjudications. Although an adjudication will affect title to Indian lands, it is not a state claim to that land, and the court will apply federal law to measure the water claims.

2. In Arizona v. California, supra Note 2, p. 622, the State of Arizona argued that the doctrine of equitable apportionment should be used to divide the water allocated to Arizona between the Indian and the other people of Arizona. The Court said,

"The last argument is easily answered. The doctrine of equitable apportionment is a method of resolving water disputes between States. It was created by this Court in the exercise of its original jurisdiction over controversies in which States are parties. An Indian Reservation is not a State. And while Congress has sometimes left Indian Reservations considerable power to manage their own affairs, we are not convinced by Arizona's argument that each reservation is so much like a State that its rights to water should be determined by the doctrine of equitable apportionment. Moreover, even were we to treat an Indian Reservation like a State, equitable apportionment would still not control since, under our view, the Indian claims here are governed by the statutes and Executive Orders creating the reservations."

Nevertheless, the State of Montana created a Reserved Water Rights Compact Commission that negotiated a compact with the Assiniboine and Sioux Tribes of the Fort Peck Indian Reservation, designed to settle the Indians' claims in several pending lawsuits and a water right adjudication. The compact states that the Tribes have the right to the lesser of the diversion or instream use of 1,050,472 acre feet per year or the consumptive use of 525,236 acre feet per year from the Missouri River, its tributaries and the groundwater beneath the reservation. The Tribes and the United States as trustee relinquish all other claims derived from any aboriginal use of land or water, treaty, act of Congress or executive act. The water may be used by all members of the Tribes, non-Indian successors to allottees and all persons receiving water from the Fort Peck irrigation project, for use on the reservation for any purpose authorized by the Tribes and for use off the reservation for any beneficial use as defined by state law, including instream water uses which will have a priority date of May 1, 1888. Transfers (not to exceed 50 years) of the tribal water right are regulated and sharing between the Tribes and the state of their benefits is authorized. The compact contemplates a tribal water code for administration and enforcement of the tribal water right, and creates a three-man board consisting of representatives of the Tribes and the state and a third person selected by the first two. The compact is to take effect on approval by the legislature, the Department of the Interior and the Department of Justice. Congressional approval is not contemplated.

Is this "compact" effective? Is it a compact?

2. Nevada v. United States, 463 U.S. 110, 103 S.Ct. 2906, 77 L.Ed.2d 509 (1983), involved a pre-McCarran Act adjudication of Indian rights. The Truckee River flows from the Sierra Nevada, through Lake Tahoe, to Pyramid Lake, "the most beautiful desert lake in North America," home of the Lahotan cutthroat trout and the unique cui-ui sucker. Surrounding the lake is the 1859 reservation of the Paiute Indians, who have always looked to the lake fish as an important source of food. A large portion of the Truckee's waters have been diverted by the United States Bureau of Reclamation to serve an irrigation project now managed by the Truckee-Carson Irrigation District, and a number of private landowners have water rights to the Truckee. In 1913 the United States, in order to assert and protect its water rights for the reservation and the project, instituted what came to be called the Orr Ditch Litigation in the United States District Court. In 1924 a master's report awarded the reservation an 1859 right for 58.7 cfs and 12,000 acre feet to irrigate 3,130 acres, and the project a 1902 priority for 1500 cfs. In 1926 the district court entered a temporary restraining order that put this award in force for an experimental period. In 1934 settlement negotiations, the United States demanded an increase in the Indian rights to allow for irrigation of an additional 2,745 acres of reservation land. This was accepted and a decree adopting the settlement was signed in 1935.

In the meantime the level of Pyramid Lake dropped, its surface acreage decreased, and the river formed a delta that prevented the trout from leaving the lake to spawn upstream. In 1973 the United States instituted a new suit against all users of Truckee water, asserting that the former decree determined only the reservation Indians' rights to irrigation water, and claiming an additional reserved right for water to maintain and preserve Pyramid Lake and maintain the lower Truckee as a natural spawning ground. The Court held that *res judicata* barred the United States from asserting this claim. Although the government had represented the project landowners as well as the Indian tribe, reallocating project water to the reservation would not be merely an internal shift by the United States of its own water, since the beneficial interest in the governments' water right for the reclamation project resided in the owners of the land irrigated by the project. And while the government owed a fiduciary duty to the tribe, it also had obligations to those who held beneficial ownership of the project water.

"Today, * * * it may well appear that Congress was requiring the Secretary of the Interior to carry water on at least two shoulders when it delegated to him both the responsibility for the supervision of the Indian tribes and the commencement of reclamation projects in areas adjacent to reservation lands. But Congress chose to do this, and it is simply unrealistic to suggest that the Government may not perform its obligation to represent Indian tribes in litigation when Congress has obliged it to represent other interests as well. In this regard, the Government cannot follow the fastidious standards of a private fiduciary, who would breach his duties to his single beneficiary solely by representing potentially conflicting interests without the beneficiary's consent. The Government does not 'compromise' its obligation to one interest that Congress obliges it to represent by the mere fact that it simultaneously performs another task for another interest that Congress has obligated it by statute to do."

The Court held that the same cause of action was litigated in both proceedings, and that all of the parties in the second suit were bound by the original Orr Ditch decree—the United States, the tribe, the water users in the Truckee-Carson Irrigation District, and the District. Even those private water users who have appropriated water from the Truckee since the Orr Decree can rely on that decree and hold the parties to the claims made in that case.

Brennan, J., concurred, but added that the Pyramid Lake Paiute Tribe should have a remedy against the United States for its breach of duty in the Orr Ditch case. "In the final analysis, our decision today is that hundreds of small farmers in northwestern Nevada can rely on specific promises made to their forebears two and three generations ago, and solemnized in a judicial decree, despite strong claims on the part of the Pyramid Lake Paiutes. * * * Yet the law can and should fix responsibility for loss and destruction that should have been avoided, and it can and should require that those whose rights are appropriated for the benefit of others receive appropriate compensation." On this point, the Court footnoted the majority opinion with the lower court's observation that Pyramid Lake has been stabilized for several years and a restocking program and a fishway bypassing the delta appear to justify optimism for eventual success in restoring the fishery.

UNITED STATES v. NEW MEXICO

Supreme Court of the United States, 1978.
438 U.S. 696, 98 S.Ct. 3012, 57 L.Ed.2d 1052.

MR. JUSTICE REHNQUIST delivered the opinion of the Court.

The Rio Mimbres rises in the southwestern highlands of New Mexico and flows generally southward, finally disappearing in a desert sink just north of the Mexican border. The river originates in the upper reaches of the Gila National Forest, but during its course it winds more than 50 miles past privately owned lands and provides substantial water for both irrigation and mining. In 1970, a stream adjudication was begun by the State of New Mexico to determine the exact rights of each user to water from the Mimbres. In this adjudication the United States claimed reserved water rights for use in the Gila National Forest. The State District Court held that the United States, in setting the Gila National Forest aside from other public lands, reserved the use of such water "as may be necessary for the purposes for which [the land was] withdrawn," but that these purposes did not include recreation, aesthetics, wildlife-preservation, or cattle grazing. The United States appealed unsuccessfully to the Supreme Court of New Mexico. Mimbres Valley Irrigation Co. v. Salopek, 90 N.M. 410, 564 P.2d 615 (1977). We granted certiorari to consider whether the Supreme Court of New Mexico had applied the correct principles of federal law in determining petitioner's reserved rights in the Mimbres. We now affirm.

The question posed in this case—what quantity of water, if any, the United States reserved out of the Mimbres River when it set aside the Gila National Forest in 1899—is a question of implied intent and not power. * * *

Recognition of Congress' power to reserve water for land which is itself set apart from the public domain, however, does not answer the question of the amount of water which has been reserved or the purposes for which the water may be used. Substantial portions of the public domain *have* been withdrawn and reserved by the United States for use as Indian reservations, forest reserves, national parks, and national monuments. And water is frequently necessary to achieve the purposes for which these reservations are made. But Congress has seldom expressly reserved water for use on these withdrawn lands. If water were abundant, Congress' silence would pose no problem. In the arid parts of the West, however, claims to water for use on federal reservations inescapably vie with other public and private claims for the limited quantities to be found in the rivers and streams. This competition is compounded by the sheer quantity of reserved lands in the western States, which lands form brightly colored swaths across the maps of these States.[a]

While many of the contours of what has come to be called the "implied-reservation-of-water doctrine" remain unspecified, the Court has repeatedly emphasized that Congress reserved "only that amount of water necessary to fulfill the purpose of the reservation, no more." Cappaert, 426 U.S., at 141, 96 S.Ct., at 2071. See Arizona v. California, 373 U.S., at 600–601, 83 S.Ct., at 1497–1498; District Court for Eagle County, 401 U.S., at 523, 91 S.Ct., at 1001. Each time this Court has

a. The percentage of federally owned land (*excluding* Indian reservations and other trust properties) in the western States ranges from 29.5% of the land in the State of Washington to 86.5% of the land in the State of Nevada, an average of about 46%. 33.6% of the land in the State of New Mexico is federally owned. General Services Administration, Inventory Report on Real Property Owned by the United States Throughout the World as of June 30, 1974, at 17, 34, and App. I, table 4.

applied the "implied-reservation-of-water doctrine," it has carefully examined both the asserted water right and the specific purposes for which the land was reserved, and concluded that without the water the purposes of the reservation would be entirely defeated.

This careful examination is required both because the reservation is implied, rather than expressed, and because of the history of congressional intent in the field of federal-state jurisdiction with respect to allocation of water. Where Congress has expressly addressed the question of whether federal entities must abide by state water law, it has almost invariably deferred to the state law. See California v. United States, 438 U.S., at 656, 670, 677, 98 S.Ct., at 2990, 2998, 3002, 57 L.Ed.2d 1018. Where water is necessary to fulfill the very purposes for which a federal reservation was created, it is reasonable to conclude, even in the face of Congress' express deference to state water law in other areas, that the United States intended to reserve the necessary water. Where water is only valuable for a secondary use of the reservation, however, there arises the contrary inference that Congress intended, consistent with its other views, that the United States would acquire water in the same manner as any other public or private appropriator.

Congress indeed has appropriated funds for the acquisition under state law of water to be used on federal reservations. Thus, in the National Parks Act of August 7, 1946, 60 Stat. 885, 16 U.S.C.A. § 17j–2, Congress authorized appropriations for the "[i]nvestigation and establishment of water rights *in accordance with local custom, law, and decisions of courts,* including the acquisition of water rights or of lands or interests in lands or rights-of-way for use and protection of water rights necessary or beneficial in the administration and public use of the national parks and monuments." The agencies responsible for administering the federal reservations have also recognized Congress' intent to acquire under state law any water not essential to the specific purposes of the reservation.[b]

The State District Court referred the issues in this case to a Special Master, who found that the United States was diverting 6.9 acre-feet per annum of water for domestic-residential use, 6.5 acre-feet for road

b. Before the Court's decisions in Federal Power Commission v. Oregon, 349 U.S. 435, 75 S.Ct. 832, 99 L.Ed. 1215 (1935) and Arizona v. California, recognizing reserved rights outside of Indian reservations, the Forest Service apparently believed that all of its water must be obtained under state law. "Rights to the use of water for National Forest purposes will be obtained in accordance with State law." Forest Service Manual (1936). While the Forest Service has apparently modified its policy since those decisions, their Service Manual still indicates a policy of deferring to state water law wherever possible. "The right of the States to appropriate and otherwise control the use of water is recognized, and the policy of the Forest Service is to abide by applicable State laws and regulations relating to water use. When water is needed by the Forest Service either for development of programs, improvements, or other uses, actions will be taken promptly to acquire necessary water rights. * * * The rights to use water for national forest purposes will be obtained in accordance with State law. This policy is based on the Act of June 4, 1897 (16 U.S.C. 481)." Forest Service Manual §§ 2514, 2514.1–2, and 2514.5 (Oct. 1965).

water use, 3.23 acre-feet for domestic-recreational use, and .10 acre-feet for "wildlife" purposes. The Special Master also found that specified amounts of water were being used in the Gila National Forest for stock watering and that an "instream flow" of six cubic-feet per second was being "used" for the purposes of fish preservation. The Special Master apparently believed that all of these uses fell within the reservation doctrine, and also concluded that the United States might have reserved rights for future water needs, ordering it to submit a report on future requirements within one year of his decision.

The District Court of Luna County disagreed with many of the Special Master's legal conclusions, but agreed with the Special Master that the Government should prepare within one year a report covering any future water requirements that might support a claim of reserved right in the waters of the Mimbres. The District Court concluded that the United States had not established a reserved right to a minimum instream flow for any of the purposes for which the Gila National Forest was established, and that any water rights arising from cattle grazing by permittees on the forest should be adjudicated "to the permittee under the law of prior appropriation and not to the United States."

The United States appealed this decision to the Supreme Court of the State of New Mexico. The United States contended that it was entitled to a minimum instream flow for "aesthetic, environmental, recreational and 'fish' purposes." 564 P.2d, at 617. The Supreme Court for the State of New Mexico concluded that, at least before the Multiple-Use Sustained-Yield Act of 1960, 74 Stat. 215, 16 U.S.C.A. § 528 et seq., national forests could only be created "to insure favorable conditions of water flow and to furnish a continuous supply of timber" and not for the purposes upon which the United States was now basing its asserted reserved rights in a minimum instream flow. 564 P.2d, at 617–619. The United States also argued that it was entitled to a reserved right for stockwatering purposes. The State Supreme Court again disagreed, holding that stockwatering was not a purpose for which the national forests were created. Id., at 619.

The quantification of reserved water rights for the national forests is of critical importance to the West, where, as noted earlier, water is scarce and where more than 50% of the available water either originates in or flows through national forests. When, as in the case of the Rio Mimbres, a river is fully appropriated, federal reserved water rights will frequently require a gallon-for-gallon reduction in the amount of water available for water-needy state and private appropriators. This reality has not escaped the attention of Congress and must be weighed in determining what, if any, water Congress reserved for use on the national forests.

Petitioner contends that Congress intended to reserve minimum instream flows for aesthetic, recreational, and fish-preservation purposes. An examination of the limited purposes for which Congress authorized the creation of national forests, however, provides no support for this claim. In the mid- and late-1800's, many of the forests on the public domain were ravaged and the fear arose that the forest lands might soon disappear, leaving the United States with a shortage both of timber and of watersheds with which to encourage stream flows while preventing floods. It was in answer to these fears that in 1891 Congress authorized the President to "set apart and reserve, in any State or Territory having public lands bearing forests, any part of the public lands wholly or in part covered with timber or undergrowth, whether of commercial value or not, as public reservations." Creative Act of March 3, 1891, 26 Stat. 1095, 1103, 16 U.S.C.A. § 471.

The Creative Act of 1891 unfortunately did not solve the forest problems of the expanding Nation. To the dismay of the conservationists, the new national forests were not adequately attended and regulated; fires and indiscriminate timber-cutting continued their toll. To the anguish of Western settlers, reservations were frequently made indiscriminately. President Cleveland, in particular, responded to pleas of conservationists for greater protective measures by reserving some 21 million acres of "generally settled" forest land on February 22, 1897. President Cleveland's action drew immediate and strong protest from Western Congressmen who felt that the "hasty and ill considered" reservation might prove disastrous to the settlers living on or near these lands.

Congress' answer to these continuing problems was three-fold. It suspended the President's Executive order of February 22, 1897; it carefully defined the purposes for which national forests could in the future be reserved; and it provided a charter for forest management and economic uses within the forests. Organic Administration Act of June 4, 1897, 30 Stat. 11, 16 U.S.C.A. § 473 et seq. In particular, Congress provided

> "*No national forest shall be established, except to improve and protect the forest within the boundaries, or for the purpose of securing favorable conditions of water flows, and to furnish a continuous supply of timber for the use and necessities of citizens of the United States*; but it is not the purpose or intent of these provisions, or of [the Creative Act of 1891], to authorize the inclusion therein of lands more valuable for the mineral therein, or for agricultural purposes, than for forest purposes." 30 Stat. 35, as amended, 16 U.S.C.A. § 475.

The legislative debates surrounding the Organic Administration Act of 1897 and its predecessor bills demonstrate that Congress intended national forests to be reserved for only two purposes—"[t]o conserve the water flows and to furnish a continuous supply of timber for the people." 30 Cong.Rec. 967 (1897) (Cong. McRae). See United States v. Grimaud, 220 U.S. 506, 515, 31 S.Ct. 480, 482, 551 L.Ed.2d 563 (1911). National forests were not to be reserved for aesthetic, environmental, recreational, or wildlife-preservation purposes. "The objects for which the forest reservation should be made are the protection of the forest growth against destruction by fire and axe and preservation of forest conditions upon which water conditions and water flow are dependent. The purpose, therefore, of this bill is to maintain favorable forest conditions, without excluding the use of these reservations for other purposes. They are not parks set aside for nonuse, but have been established for economic reasons." 30 Cong.Rec. 966 (1897) (Cong McRae). Administrative regulations at the turn of the century confirmed that national forests were to be reserved for only these two limited purposes.

Any doubt as to the relatively narrow purposes for which national forests were to be reserved is removed by comparing the broader language Congress used to authorize the establishment of national parks. In 1916, Congress created the National Park Service and provided that the

> "fundamental purpose of said parks, monuments, and reservations * * * is to conserve the scenery and the natural and historic objects and the wild life therein and to provide for the enjoyment of the same * * * unimpaired for the enjoyment of future generations." National Park Service Act of 1916, 39 Stat. 535, 16 U.S.C.A. § 1 et seq.

When it was Congress' intent to maintain minimum instream flows within the confines of a national forest, it expressly so directed, as it did in the case of the Lake Superior National Forest:

> "In order to preserve the shore lines, rapids, waterfalls, beaches and other natural features of the region in an unmodified state of nature, no further alteration of the natural water level of any lake or stream * * * shall be authorized." 16 U.S.C.A. § 577b. * * *

In 1960, Congress passed the Multiple-Use Sustained-Yield Act of June 12, 1960, 74 Stat. 215, 16 U.S.C.A. § 528 et seq., which provides

> "That it is the policy of Congress that the national forests are established and shall be administered for outdoor recreation, range, timber, watershed, and wildlife and fish purposes. The purposes of this Act are declared to be supplemental to, but not in derogation of, the purposes for which the national forests were established as set forth in the [Organic Administration Act of 1897.]"

The Supreme Court of the State of New Mexico concluded that this Act did not give rise to any reserved rights not previously authorized in the Organic Administration Act of 1897. * * * While we conclude that the Multiple-Use Sustained-Yield Act of 1960 was intended to broaden the purposes for which national forests had previously been administered, we agree that Congress did not intend to thereby expand the reserved rights of the United States.

The Multiple-Use Sustained-Yield Act of 1960 establishes the purposes for which the national forests "*are* established and *shall* be administered." The Act directs the Secretary of the Agriculture to administer all forests, including those previously established, on a multiple use and sustained yield basis. H.Rep. No. 10572, 86th Cong., 2d Sess., 1 (1960). In the administration of the national forests, therefore, Congress intended the Multiple-Use Sustained-Yield Act of 1960 to broaden the benefits accruing from all reserved national forests.

The House Report accompanying the 1960 legislation, however, indicates that recreation, range, and "fish" purposes are "to be supplemental to, but not in derogation of, the purposes for which the national forests were established" in the Organic Administration Act of 1897.

As discussed earlier, the "reserved rights doctrine" is a doctrine built on implication and is an exception to Congress' explicit deference to state water law in other areas. Without legislative history to the contrary, we are led to conclude that Congress did not intend in enacting the Multiple-Use Sustained-Yield Act of 1960 to reserve water for the *secondary* purposes there established.

What we have said also answers petitioner's contention that Congress intended to reserve water from the Rio Mimbres for stockwatering purposes. Petitioner issues permits to private cattle-owners to graze their stock on the Gila National Forest and provides for stockwatering at various locations along the Rio Mimbres. Petitioner contends that, since Congress clearly foresaw stockwatering on national forests, reserved rights must be recognized for this purpose. The New Mexico courts disagreed and held that any stockwatering rights must be allocated under state law to individual stockwaterers. We agree.

While Congress intended the national forests to be put to a variety of uses, including stockwatering, not inconsistent with the two principal purposes of the forests, stockwatering was not itself a direct purpose of reserving the land. If stockwatering could not take place on the Gila National Forest, Congress' purposes in reserving the land would not be defeated. Congress, of course, did intend to secure favorable water flows, and one of the uses to which the enhanced water supply was intended to be placed was probably stockwatering. But Congress intended the water supply from the Rio Mimbres to be allocated amongst private appropriators under state law. 16 U.S.C.A. § 481. There is no indication in the legislative histories of any of the forest acts that Congress foresaw any need for the Forest Service to allocate water for stockwatering purposes, a task to which state law was well suited. * * *

Affirmed.

MR. JUSTICE POWELL, with whom MR. JUSTICE BRENNAN, MR. JUSTICE WHITE, and MR. JUSTICE MARSHALL join, dissenting in part.

I agree with the Court that the implied-reservation doctrine should be applied with sensitivity to its impact upon those who have obtained water rights under state law and to Congress' general policy of deference to state water law. See ante, at 3013–3014, 3015, 3016–3017. I also agree that the Organic Administration Act of 1897, 30 Stat. 11, cannot fairly be read as evidencing an intent to reserve water for recreational or stockwatering purposes in the national forests.

I do not agree, however, that the forests which Congress intended to "improve and protect" are the still, silent, lifeless places envisioned by the Court. In my view, the forests consist of the birds, animals, and fish—the wildlife—that inhabit them, as well as the trees, flowers, shrubs, and grasses. I therefore would hold that the United States is entitled to so much water as is necessary to sustain the wildlife of the forests, as well as the plants. * * *

Notes

1. Trelease, Federal Reserved Water Rights since PLLRC, 54 Denver L.J. 473 (1977):

"A few years ago the big threat was thought to be that Mineral King, a huge proposed Walt Disney Inc. ski resort on the Inyo National Forest in the Sierras, would claim the forest's recreational prerogatives. But the Forest Service has abstained from assigning its recreation right to concessionaires there and in New Mexico, and I know of no current threats of this nature. It is possible, of course, that other types of reservations may take substantial quantities of water. The federal reserved water rights quantified for the National Wildlife refuges in Arizona v. California sound big—annual diversions of 41,838 and 28,000 acre-feet producing consumption of 37,339 and 23,000 acre-feet. But these are drops in the lower Colorado bucket, at most three-fourths of one percent of withdrawals, although they admittedly might loom large elsewhere. Furthermore, a second look at the facts in the Report of the Special Master shows that these waters are needed for artificial marshes and irrigated feeding grounds to be substituted for natural areas destroyed by channelizing the river; and it is a fair guess that this water is no more than that which was formerly soaked up by, and evaporated from, the original natural river bottom areas. At one time the Fish and Wildlife Service claimed the full flow of one of the Oregon streams feeding the Malheur Refuge and demanded that fifty-year-old irrigation ditches be closed, but that demand has been dropped.

"I am coming to believe that 'the Feds' were right all along. In 1964, at the height of the debates over the 'Western Water Rights Settlements Act,' it was pointed out that 'not a single case of harm has been reported,' [7] that 'for all of the outcry * * * not one state, not one county, not one municipality, not one irrigation district, not one corporation, not one individual has come forward to plead and prove that the United States * * * has destroyed any private right.' [8] Twenty-two years after *Pelton Dam* this is still true.

"The actual measurement of National Forest uses in Colorado shows how small they are, and the quantification of future forest uses shows that most fears from this source are groundless. Federal officials have refrained from pressing large claims or assigning them to private enterprises carrying out federal functions. Minimum flows are located for the most

7. Hearings on S. 1275 Before the Subcomm. on Irrigation and Reclamation of the Senate Comm. on Interior and Insular Affairs, 88th Cong. 2nd Sess. 39 (1964) (statement of Senator Clifford P. Anderson).

8. Id. (statement of Nicolas B. Katzenbach, Deputy Attorney General).

part where they can do the least harm, and the courts are unlikely to order, and the federal agencies are likely to abstain from enforcing, large instream flows that would force a rollback of longstanding uses that have done no harm. * * *

"So I no longer jump when the old tattered-sheet specter is thrust at me, and I am tired of leaping into action at every call of 'Wolf!' In the future, I intend to devote my waning energies to real problems like why the Cappaerts and the United States do not act like ordinary water users with a protection of diversion problem, and work out a physical and legal solution that will allow irrigation, yet preserve the water level and, thus, permit the Cappaerts and the pupfish each to do their thing."

2. All of the non-Indian federal water rights in western Colorado were at issue in United States v. Denver, 656 P.2d 1 (Colo.1982), an appeal from an adjudication of all federal claims in the three western water divisions of the state. The case involved thousands of claims for state-law appropriative rights, most of them on the public domain administered by the Bureau of Land Management, in addition to numerous claims of reserved rights for a national park, three national monuments, seven national forests, fifteen hundred water holes and springs, and two mineral hot springs. Decrees were awarded for minimum flows and lake levels in Rocky Mountain National Park for conservation of scenic, natural and historic objects and for recreational and esthetic purposes, but instream flows in the monuments were limited to those needed for the specific purposes for which the monument was formed and to preserve fish habitats of endangered species of historic and scientific interests. In particular, the court denied a very large claim of a reserved right for recreational purposes (river rafting) within Dinosaur National Monument, a claim that would have had a serious impact on junior appropriators from the Yampa River above the monument. Numerous diversions and offstream uses in the park, monuments and forests were confirmed, and amounts for future diversions and impoundments were allowed. Despite United States v. New Mexico, the United States again pressed claims for instream recreational, scenic and wildlife flows in the national forests, but these got short shrift. No claims for instream flows for watershed and timber protection were filed, but *appropriative* rights for instream use of water for fire protection, wildlife and livestock watering and recreation were held valid and entitled to recognition notwithstanding the absence of a permanent manmade diversion structure. The government had argued that the entire yield of public water holes and springs was reserved by withdrawals authorized by the Stock Raising Homestead Act of 1916, 43 U.S.C. §§ 300 et seq., but the court held that water was reserved for human and animal consumption only, in amounts necessary to prevent monopolization of the sources. The court finally held that the Geothermal Steam Act of 1970, 30 U.S.C.A. § 1001, which provided for leasing lands for power production, did not reserve water from hot springs on federal land.

3. In Sierra Club v. Watt, 659 F.2d 203 (D.C.Cir.1981), the plaintiff asked the court to declare the extent of federal reserved rights in four streams in Utah and Arizona, and to require the Secretary of the Interior to protect those rights against threatened encroachment by energy develop-

ment projects. The rights were alleged to arise under the Federal Land Policy and Management Act of 1976, 43 U.S.C.A. § 1701 et seq. (FLPMA). That act directed the Bureau of Land Management to undertake a comprehensive program of planning and management of 448 million acres of lands, not set aside for parks, monuments, forests, etc., for a multiplicity of purposes. One of the many policies to be furthered was the management of the public lands in a manner "that will protect the quality of scientific, scenic, historical, ecological, environmental, air and atmospheric, water resource, and archaeological values; that, where appropriate, will preserve and protect certain public lands in their natural condition; that will provide food and habitat for fish and wildlife and domestic animals; and that will provide for outdoor recreation and human occupancy and use." The action was dismissed. The Congress did not by this act "withdraw land from the public domain," these lands were the public domain itself; the act reserved no lands and reserved no water. In addition, the act carried a disclaimer that it should not be construed as expanding or diminishing federal or state jurisdiction or rights in water resources, which, said the court, can only mean that no federal water rights were reserved.

4. In the enabling acts creating new states out of the public domain of the United States, each state was granted at least two sections out of each township for the support of the public schools. Some states got more, and the later ones got still more for agricultural colleges, state universities and other purposes. The lands were to be sold for the creation of a permanent school fund or were to be leased, and only the interest or rent can be expended.

In Department of State Lands v. Pettibone, 702 P.2d 948 (Mont.1985), an adjudication proceeding, the water court awarded title to water rights appropriated by the lessees of several school sections to the lessees. The state appealed, urging *inter alia* that the state as trustee of the school lands succeeded to federally reserved water rights appurtenant to the lands. Holding in favor of the state on other grounds, the court stated that it deemed it best to keep the reserved rights doctrine confined to situations where it was most appropriate, to accommodations of federal and state interests.

5. If the United States has no reserved rights for its unreserved public domain, is there a "federal non-reserved right" that would give the government a claim to recreational and habitat flows of streams on public lands where state laws do not permit appropriation of instream flows? Brief mention should be made of the birth, short life and demise of this creature, created, modified and repudiated by three successive solicitors of the Department of the Interior. As originally conceived, the United States, by virtue of its "ownership of unappropriated water" (see Note 3 to California v. U.S., supra p. 681) was said to have powers under the Property Clause of the Constitution to use such water as it saw fit, with a priority as of the date of use, without regard to state law, although the government might appropriate it under state law as matter of comity. An alternative basis was found in the Supremacy Clause: if a constitutional act of Congress authorized a federal use of water, the United States must have power to so use it regardless of state law. Solicitor Krulitz made very broad claims to

such rights, ignoring the "dictum" of United States v. New Mexico that where the United States has not reserved water, "there arises the * * * inference that Congress intended * * * that the United States would acquire water in the same manner as any other public or private appropriator." Federal Water Rights of the National Park Service, Fish and Wildlife Service, Bureau of Reclamation, and Bureau of Land Management, 88 Interior Dec. 553 (1979). Solicitor Martz thought that such rights could exist when expressly or impliedly mandated by Congress, but that while FLPMA authorized the appropriation of water for land management use, it did not provide independent authority for water uses that are inconsistent with substantive state law. Memorandum of the Solicitor of the Department of the Interior, 88 Interior Dec. 253 (1981). Solicitor Coldrion came out flatly against it. "There is no 'federal non-reserved water right.'" Non-Reserved Water Rights—United States Compliance with State Law, 88 Interior Dec. 1055 (1981). Other agencies of the United States, particularly the Forest Service and the Department of Defense, would have interests in such rights if they exist, and the question was reviewed by the Department of Justice. Assistant Attorney General Olson of the Office of Legal Counsel concluded that ownership of unappropriated water, "if ownership is understood to mean a proprietary interest in the water" was an anomaly, and that, "Claims of ownership of natural resources by the states or by the federal government are best understood as claims of regulatory jurisdiction over these resources, either under the states' police powers or under the federal government's constitutional powers." While no purely federal water rights were identified, their possible existence was not ruled out. The Supremacy Clause, coupled with the Commerce Clause, the Property Clause and other federal powers, was said to give ample authority to supersede state laws, of course, but in the light of California v. United States and United States v. New Mexico (supra, pages 681 and 797), "the federal constitutional authority to preempt state water law must be clearly and specifically exercised, * * * otherwise the presumption is that western states retain control over the allocation of unappropriated water within their borders. * * * The exercise of such power must be explicit or clearly implied, however, and federal rights to water will not be found simply by virtue of the ownership, occupation, or use of federal land, without more." Legal Memorandum, Federal "Non-Reserved" Water Rights (1982). See also Trelease, Uneasy Federalism—State Water Laws and National Water Uses, 55 Wash.L.Rev. 751 (1980).

6. Federal agencies, particularly the Forest Service, had over the years made many small diversions on reserved lands, in reliance either on the theory that reserved rights were being exercised or on something like the federal non-reserved right. The State of California came to the rescue in 1983, but not to the extent of injuring any vested private rights. The priorities of noncomplying secondary uses were saved at least from future claims. West's Ann.Cal.Water Code § 1227.1 applies only to uses initiated prior to July 3, 1978, the date of the *New Mexico* decision. It allows the agency to file a statement with the State Water Resources Control Board, identifying the source, point of diversion, place of use and purpose of use, and giving a general description of the area of use, the year the diversion

was commenced and information as to the quantity used. The full scope and conditions of use are left for future determination.

Section 1227.2(a) gives each such claimed use a priority as of the initial date of use, over any water rights with a priority after July 1, 1984. Thus a secondary use so claimed, initiated prior to *New Mexico,* would take priority only over July 2, 1984 and later rights. A secondary use initiated after July 3, 1978 would have priority only as of the date of application to the Board for a permit.

7. Professor Tarlock, in The Endangered Species Act and Western Water Rights, 20 Land and Water L.Rev. 1. (1985), suggests a new class of "regulatory property rights" created by certain federal statutes that control private action or by conditions in permits issued under their authority. Does conceptualizing the result of regulating as the creation of a right facilitate the integration of or accommodation between state water law and state-created private water rights and federal powers and programs? When would an unquantified "right to habitat water for endangered fish" or a "right to a 10 cfs instream flow below the dam to protect the Colorado squawfish" produce a different result from the exercise by Congress or agency of federal powers? Compare *Riverside,* supra, p. 752, where the court refused to adopt this analysis. Would the choice of concept make a difference if the affected private water right were (a) created prior to enactment of the statute, (b) created after the statute, or (c) prevented by the federal statute or regulatory action from coming into existence?

Index

References are to Pages

References are to Pages

References are to Pages

References are to Pages

†